America Votes 35

Sara Miller McCune founded SAGE Publishing in 1965 to support the dissemination of usable knowledge and educate a global community. SAGE publishes more than 1000 journals and over 800 new books each year, spanning a wide range of subject areas. Our growing selection of library products includes archives, data, case studies and video. SAGE remains majority owned by our founder and after her lifetime will become owned by a charitable trust that secures the company's continued independence.

Los Angeles | London | New Delhi | Singapore | Washington DC | Melbourne

America Votes 35

ELECTION RETURNS BY STATE

J. MILES COLEMAN

2021–2022

Los Angeles | London | New Delhi
Singapore | Washington DC | Melbourne

FOR INFORMATION:

2455 Teller Road
Thousand Oaks, California 91320
E-mail: order@sagepub.com

1 Oliver's Yard
55 City Road
London, EC1Y 1SP
United Kingdom

Unit No. 323-333, Third Floor, F-Block
International Trade Tower
Nehru Place, New Delhi–110 019
India

18 Cross Street #10-10/11/12
China Square Central
Singapore 048423

Acquisitions Editor: Kaitlin Ciarmiello
Associate Editor: Elizabeth Hernandez
Researchers: Shashank Chamoli, Bhavna Chaudhary
Database Lead: Nora Varbedian
Database Team: Andre Messier
Production Editor: Astha Jaiswal
Typesetter: Hurix Digital
Proofreader: Laura Webb
Cover Designer: Candice Harman
Marketing Manager: Gabrielle Perretta

Copyright © 2023 by CQ Press, an imprint of Sage. CQ Press is a registered trademark of Congressional Quarterly Inc.

All rights reserved. Except as permitted by U.S. copyright law, no part of this work may be reproduced or distributed in any form or by any means, or stored in a database or retrieval system, without permission in writing from the publisher.

All third party trademarks referenced or depicted herein are included solely for the purpose of illustration and are the property of their respective owners. Reference to these trademarks in no way indicates any relationship with, or endorsement by, the trademark owner.

ACKNOWLEDGMENT: Richard M. Scammon
The publishers of *America Votes* wish to recognize the creator and long-time editor of *America Votes*, the late Richard M. Scammon. He brought his keen perceptions of the American electorate and his in-depth knowledge of U.S. voting patterns to his more than 40 years of work on the *America Votes* series. Scammon founded and directed the nonprofit Elections Research Center and was widely considered the most prominent American elections expert during his long career as a government official, advisor to presidents, and analyst of voting trends and developments. His love of elections was rooted in his lifelong commitment to democracy and his belief that the voice of one is always bested by the voice of the many.

Printed in the United States of America.

ISBN: 9781071894873

23 24 25 26 27 10 9 8 7 6 5 4 3 2 1

Contents

List of Maps	vi	Kansas	164
Introduction	vii	Kentucky	174
Errata	xiii	Louisiana	183
		Maine	191
Summary Tables		Maryland	198
Voter Turnout 2022	1	Massachusetts	207
Gubernatorial Elections 2021 and 2022	2	Michigan	215
Senate Elections 2021 and 2022	3	Minnesota	226
House of Representatives Elections 2022	4	Mississippi	236
		Missouri	242
Summary of House and Senate Special Elections 2021–2022	5	Montana	251
		Nebraska	256
Special Elections and Postelection Changes to the 116th Congress	5	Nevada	264
		New Hampshire	272
Changes Following the 2022 Election	8	New Jersey	280
		New Mexico	289
U.S. Presidential Elections		New York	296
Popular Vote for President 1920 to 2020	9	North Carolina	310
Electoral College Vote 1920 to 2020	9	North Dakota	321
		Ohio	329
County and District Results by State		Oklahoma	342
Alabama	10	Oregon	353
Alaska	20	Pennsylvania	362
Arizona	28	Rhode Island	373
Arkansas	37	South Carolina	380
California	44	South Dakota	389
Colorado	62	Tennessee	398
Connecticut	72	Texas	407
Delaware	79	Utah	430
Florida	85	Vermont	437
Georgia	100	Virginia	444
Hawaii	117	Washington	454
Idaho	123	West Virginia	464
Illinois	131	Wisconsin	470
Indiana	145	Wyoming	480
Iowa	154	District of Columbia	487

List of Maps

Alabama	11
Alaska	21
Arizona	29
Greater Phoenix Area	30
Arkansas	38
California	45
Greater Los Angeles, San Diego Areas	46
Greater San Francisco Bay Area	47
Colorado	63
Greater Denver Area	64
Connecticut	73
Delaware	80
Florida	86
Greater Miami, Fort Lauderdale, West Palm Beach Areas	87
Georgia	101
Greater Atlanta Area	102
Hawaii	118
Idaho	124
Illinois	132
Greater Chicago Area	133
Indiana	146
Iowa	155
Kansas	165
Kentucky	175
Louisiana	184
Maine	192
Maryland	199
Massachusetts	208
Greater Boston Area	209
Michigan	216
Greater Detroit Area	217
Minnesota	227
Minneapolis–St. Paul Area	228
Mississippi	237
Missouri	243
Montana	252
Nebraska	257
Nevada	265
New Hampshire	273
New Jersey	281
Northern New Jersey Gateway Area	282
New Mexico	290
New York	297
New York City Area	298
North Carolina	311
North Dakota	322
Ohio	330
Greater Cleveland Area	331
Oklahoma	343
Oregon	354
Pennsylvania	363
Rhode Island	374
South Carolina	381
South Dakota	390
Tennessee	399
Texas	408
Greater Dallas–Forth Worth Area	409
Greater Houston Area	410
Greater San Antonio and Austin Areas	411
Utah	431
Vermont	438
Virginia	445
Washington	455
Greater Seattle Area	456
West Virginia	465
Wisconsin	471
Wyoming	481
District of Columbia	487

Introduction

On January 20, 2021, Joe Biden, who had been chasing the presidency for much of his lengthy time in public life, finally achieved his goal. The new president entered office with what *Sabato's Crystal Ball* Managing Editor Kyle Kondik called "Democrats' 51% Trifecta": As Biden ousted Republican Donald Trump with 51% of the popular vote in the 2020 election, his Democratic Party won slim majorities in both chambers of Congress.

Unlike virtually all his modern predecessors, Biden did not have the benefit of an orderly transition. Two weeks before he took the oath of office, protesters at the Capitol complex, who were inspired by outgoing President Trump's frequent and baseless claims that the election was usurped from him, unsuccessfully attempted an insurrection on January 6. Once in office, though, Biden put his "51% Trifecta" to good use: He signed into law several pieces of landmark legislation – some big-ticket items even passed on a bipartisan basis, as was the case with a late-2021 infrastructure bill.

Biden would get the benefit of the doubt from voters for the first several months of his tenure, with the August 2021 United States withdrawal from Afghanistan marking the end of his "honeymoon" period. Though most Americans agreed the conflict had dragged on for too long, their television screens were inundated with chaotic images of the evacuation as the U.S.-backed government fell to the Taliban. According to FiveThirtyEight's polling aggregator, on August 16, the share of voters who approved of Biden's performance dipped below 50% for the first time. By the end of the month, his approval spread was in negative territory. Biden's numbers continued to slide as voters increasingly registered their closer-to-home complaints to pollsters. In late 2021, a sense of pre-pandemic "normalcy" had not totally returned, and Americans were constantly hit with rising gas and grocery prices.

In November 2021, gubernatorial elections in New Jersey and Virginia, which each gave Biden double-digit margins in 2020, did not paint an especially rosy picture for Democrats' midterm prospects. In the former, Gov. Phil Murphy became the first Democratic governor to win reelection in New Jersey since 1977 but did so by just a three-point margin. In Virginia, which got more attention, Republican businessman Glenn Youngkin prevailed by two points. During Barack Obama's presidency, Democrats often chalked their defeats in non-presidential year elections up to low turnout. But the Virginia result was not as easy to dismiss. Democrats' nominee, former governor Terry McAuliffe, earned more raw votes than any previous Democrat in the commonwealth's history – but Youngkin got more. Clearly, Republicans were energized.

As the 2022 election cycle began in earnest, Biden's situation prompted political observers to go on "wave watch." In the 2006, 2010, 2014, and 2018 midterm elections, voters opted to weaken the president's party – often in a dramatic fashion. With history on their side, Congressional Republicans vowed that a "red wave" would materialize in November. Meanwhile, in state-level races across the nation, Youngkin's campaign gave Republicans a ready-made playbook.

But while Biden's political standing was not enviable, Republicans did not have everything working in their favor. Trump, a showman who enjoys the limelight, remained involved in Republican primaries. Most of Trump's endorsed candidates parroted his dubious claims that Biden's election was illegitimate, and such candidates became popularly known as "election deniers." Speaking charitably, election deniers – who were defined, at least to some degree, by their loyalty to an unpopular former president – did not make for compelling general election candidates.

One of the defining events of the 2022 midterm year came in late June. In issuing its ruling in the *Dobbs v. Jackson Women's Health Organization* case, the U.S. Supreme Court overturned the nearly 50-year-old precedent that the *Roe v. Wade* case set. In the 1973 Roe case, the court found that the U.S. Constitution protects a woman's right to an abortion – with the Dobbs ruling, abortion became a state-by-state issue. Though most public opinion polling showed that inflation remained the top concern on voters' minds, backlash to Dobbs helped Democrats close the enthusiasm gap.

Immediately after the Dobbs decision was handed down, Democrats began overperforming in special elections. Days after the Supreme Court's decision came out, Republican Mike Flood held Nebraska's 1st District for his party, but his five-point margin was half of what

Trump would have carried the seat by in 2020. In August, Republicans held Minnesota's 1st District by an even narrower margin. A week later, Democrat Mary Peltola, who was, in retrospect, one of the party's best recruits of the cycle, defeated former GOP Vice Presidential nominee Sarah Palin to flip Alaska's At-Large seat – although it is worth noting that Peltola was likely aided by the state's newly adopted ranked choice voting system. Finally, as August was winding down, two Upstate New York seats held special elections. Democrats held an open seat in the Hudson Valley and came close to flipping a Republican-held Southern Tier seat. In the former, Pat Ryan, the Democratic nominee, made abortion rights a centerpiece of his campaign while Marc Molinaro, the Republican, stressed inflation.

The special elections previewed a dynamic that would define the coming general election. While Biden was not popular – by the time Election Day rolled around, his approval spread was a dozen points under water on FiveThirtyEight's aggregator – voters were not sold on his opposition.

The results: Not a clear-cut election

While the 2022 election did not bring the type of "red wave" that history suggested Republican candidates were poised to ride, House Republicans managed to reverse the 222–213 advantage that Democrats claimed after the 2020 elections. Still, Democrats defied expectations by expanding their majority in the Senate and gaining governor's mansions.

Table 1: Partisan control of seats before and after the 2022 elections

	Preelection			Postelection		
	Rep.	Dem.	Oth.	Rep.	Dem.	Oth.
Governors	28	22	0	26	24	0
Senate	50	48	2	49	49	2
House	213	222	0	222	213	0

Note: Independent Sens. Angus King of Maine and Bernie Sanders of Vermont caucus with Democrats. In December 2022, Arizona's Kyrsten Sinema, who was serving as a Democrat, became a third Democratic-caucusing independent. Sinema's change was not a direct result of the 2022 election, so it is not reflected on Table 1.

At the time, Donald Trump's sole midterm, 2018, was unique because it was the first in the direct election era where the president's party gained in the Senate while losing control of the House. Four years later, the same basic pattern unfolded, though there were a few slight differences. First, the overall turnover rate was lower in 2022 than in 2018. Second, Democrats' performance in the 2022 Senate races was more impressive than that of their Republican counterparts four years earlier. In 2018, Senate Republicans netted seats by ousting four incumbents in states that were otherwise generally red, while losing two of their own seats in more competitive states (Arizona and Nevada). In 2022, Senate Democrats essentially ran the table: They held all their seats and picked up an open GOP-held seat in Biden's native state, the very marginal Keystone State.

One pattern that did hold in 2022 was that the Senate and House continued to move in opposite directions. Table 2 considers the net seat changes in the two chambers of Congress over the last two decades.

Table 2: Parties that netted seats in each chamber of Congress since 2002

	2002	2004	2006	2008	2010	2012	2014	2016	2018	2020	2022
Senate	R	R	D	D	R	D	R	D	R	D	D
House	R	R	D	D	R	D	R	D	D	R	R

From 2002 to 2016, both the Senate and House moved in tandem each year. Then, in 2018, Republicans netted two Senate seats but lost 41 in the House. Two years later, in the shadow of a presidential election, Democrats gained three Senate seats, going from 47 to 50 – this was enough to give them control of the chamber, thanks to newly elected Vice President Kamala Harris's tiebreaking vote. But in 2020's House elections, Republicans beat expectations by netting about a dozen seats, though it was not enough to flip the chamber – in a very straight-party cycle, most of their gains came in seats that Trump carried. Then, in 2022, Republicans continued to gain in the House, limping to just a slight majority, while losing ground in the Senate.

Governors

In contrast to 2020, a year that was dominated by a national contest that featured minimal partisan ticket-splitting between races, 2022 was very much a state-by-state election. This dynamic was perhaps most evident in 2022's gubernatorial races.

My contention thus far has been that 2022 was, in a broad sense, not a "red wave" election. Though I stand by my claim, it was not entirely true everywhere. In the nation's two largest blue states, localized red waves formed as Democratic incumbents ran lackluster campaigns. California's Gavin Newsom, at times, seemed more concerned with cultivating his national image than tending to his home front, while New York's Kathy Hochul was caught flat footed against a lively challenge from GOP Rep. Lee Zeldin. Though both Democrats were reelected, they underperformed Biden's margins in their respective states by double-digits. Importantly, Newsom and Hochul's tepid showings did not boost Democrats in races further down the ballot. Meanwhile, in the four most populous Republican-held states – Texas, Florida, Ohio, and Georgia – GOP incumbents notched solid victories, although, of that quartet, only Florida saw an overwhelming red current.

In swing states where Republicans did not field strong candidates, though, the rest of their ticket suffered. Two of the most clear-cut examples of this were Michigan and Pennsylvania. In the former, Gov. Gretchen Whitmer beat a controversial Republican by more than ten points. On Election Day, Michigan voters also weighed in on an abortion referendum, and the pro-abortion rights side won out. The referendum likely helped Michigan Democrats because, during the campaign, it kept front-and-center an issue where they were on the prevailing side of public opinion. In Pennsylvania's open-seat race, state Attorney General Josh Shapiro defeated far-right state Sen. Doug Mastriano by nearly 15 points. Shapiro took his role as the leader of his party's ticket seriously, and his strength helped Democrats retain all their marginal House seats in the state.

All told, 28 of the 36 states that hosted gubernatorial contests featured incumbents running for reelection. Most of the governors seeking reelection were first elected in 2018 and were tasked with steering their states through the COVID-19 pandemic. Still, despite the myriad of state-level challenges that the pandemic brought, 2022 was an exceptional cycle to be an incumbent governor: It was the first midterm since 2002 where every incumbent who ran in a primary secured renomination. In the general election, the incumbent success rate was nearly perfect. Steve Sisolak, a Nevada Democrat, was the sole governor that got the boot from voters – and it may be worth noting that he only narrowly lost against a strong Republican, Joe Lombardo.

Despite their loss in Nevada, Democrats came out with a net gain of two governorships. Next door in Arizona, Republicans nominated Kari Lake, a pro-Trump election denier who, in so many words, told old school "McCain" Republicans not to vote for her. Lake got her wish: as she bombed in the suburbs where the late "maverick" always ran well, she lost to Democrat Katie Hobbs. On the East Coast, Democrats picked up Maryland and Massachusetts – in both cases, Republicans ran conservatives who could not replicate the crossover support that the retiring incumbents enjoyed.

The Senate

In 2014, the last pre-2022 midterm cycle that featured a Democratic president, Democrats lost control of the upper chamber. Something that most contributed to their losses (aside from Obama's subpar approval rating at the time) was the terrain of the map itself. Of the nine seats they lost that cycle, six came in states that Republican Mitt Romney would have carried by double-digits in the presidential race two years earlier – a seventh, North Carolina, gave Romney a smaller majority. In the cycles since then, partisan sorting and declining rates of split-ticket voting had influenced the Senate landscape. For Senate Democrats, the upside of that trend was that they'd enter the 2022 cycle only having to defend seats in states that Biden carried, although Trump came very close in several. So, at least for Democrats, their fight to defend the Senate would not be one fought on hostile turf.

In late 2021, Democrats caught a break when New Hampshire Republican Gov. Chris Sununu, who was reelected with 65% a year earlier as Biden carried the state by seven points, announced he would not challenge first-term Democratic Sen. Maggie Hassan. As Sununu opted to run for reelection, Granite State Republicans eventually nominated Don Bolduc, a pro-Trump veteran, for Senate. Hassan won a second term by nearly ten points. In other key states, Trump's endorsed candidates were outraised and outmaneuvered by battle-tested Democrats. This was the case in Arizona, Georgia, and Nevada – although in Nevada, Trump's choice, former state Attorney General Adam Laxalt, was something of a consensus pick among national Republicans. Though it was a Republican-held open seat, Pennsylvania essentially fit this pattern. Trump endorsed television doctor Mehmet Oz, who won a crowded primary. As Oz had weak connections to the state and proved an awkward general election candidate, Democrats were united behind Lt.

Gov. John Fetterman, who won by five points despite suffering a stroke right before the primary.

This is not to say that all of Trump's candidates lost. In Ohio, Trump backed venture capitalist and author J. D. Vance, who won a hotly contested primary. Though Vance was accused of running a lazy general election effort, he ultimately beat a serious Democratic opponent 53%–47%. In North Carolina, Trump took a bit of a gamble in endorsing Republican Rep. Ted Budd. But Republicans have won every Tar Heel State Senate race since 2010, usually by single-digit margins, and Budd was able to keep that pattern going.

In Wisconsin, Republican Ron Johnson, a strident conservative, was reelected by just one point, underperforming his polls. But given the Senate's broader, straight-ticket trend, Johnson was fortunate: in 2022, he was the only Senate candidate to win in a state that voted for the other party's presidential nominee in 2020 (Biden carried Wisconsin by less than one point).

The House

While the House attrition rate in November's general election was smaller than what most observers expected, the turnover in the primary stage of the campaign was notable. Indeed, 2022 was a rare cycle where more incumbents lost in the primary (15) than in the general election (nine). Although each race had unique dynamics, many of the primary losses could be chalked up to one of the two major factors that shaped the cycle: Donald Trump and redistricting.

On the "Trump" factor: As the then-president was on his way out of office, ten House Republicans joined a unanimous Democratic caucus in voting to impeach him over the attempted insurrection on January 6th. Though their votes were no doubt courageous, their stances would be hard to sell to a GOP primary electorate – and Trump would make sure Republican voters remembered their apostasies. Four of the ten retired, including Michigan's long-serving Fred Upton and Illinois's Adam Kinzinger, who was one of two Republicans that served on a select committee investigating the insurrection. Four more lost their primary elections, including Wyoming's Liz Cheney, who served as vice chair of the select committee and was Trump's most visible intraparty critic. To Democrats' delight, though, Republican voters opted to replace Michigan's Peter Meijer and Washington state's Jaime Herrera Beutler with candidates who had a hard time pivoting to the general election. Democrats easily won Meijer's Grand Rapids-area seat and, in a major upset, flipped Herrera Beutler's light red district in southwestern Washington. The only pro-impeachment Republicans that made it to the next Congress were California's David Valadao, who held a Biden-won seat in the Central Valley, and Washington state's Dan Newhouse, representing a deep red district east of the Cascades. Both victorious Republicans won in states that use open primary systems, although as Herrera Beutler's case showed, open primaries didn't totally insulate incumbents from defeat.

As with previous election years ending in "-2", the House's lines were redrawn for the 2022 elections – in each year ending in "-0," the census is taken, and seats are reapportioned accordingly. Though each state handles the redistricting process differently, Republicans ended up drawing considerably more districts than Democrats did, although a majority of the new districts were drafted either by state supreme courts or independent commissions.

Altogether, six Democrats lost primaries to fellow members as a direct result of redistricting while two Republicans did. The impact of redistricting was not confined to the primary stage of the campaign. In the general election, all three Republicans who lost their seats would have been better-positioned, if not outright favorites, in their old districts. Six Democratic incumbents lost to GOP challengers – redistricting made life harder for many, but not all, of those Democrats. Table 3 lists the defeated incumbents.

Table 3: Defeated House members in 2022

Defeated in primary		Defeated in general election	
Member	Terms served	Member	Terms served
J. Herrera Beutler (R, WA-3)^	6	Cindy Axne (D, IA-3)	2
Carolyn Bourdeaux (D, GA-7)*	1	Steve Chabot (R, OH-1)	13
Madison Cawthorn (R, NC-11)	1	Mayra Flores (R, TX-34)	<1
Liz Cheney (R, WY-AL)^	3	Yvette Herrell (R, NM-2)	1
Rodney Davis (R, IL-15)*	5	Al Lawson (D, FL-2)*	3
Mondaire Jones (D, NY-10)	1	Elaine Luria (D, VA-2)	2
Andy Levin (D, MI-11)*	2	Tom Malinowski (D, NJ-7)	2
Carolyn Maloney (D, NY-12)*	15	S. P. Maloney (D, NY-17)	5
David McKinley (R, WV-2)*	6	Tom O'Halleran (D, AZ-2)	3
Peter Meijer (R, MI-3)^	1		
Marie Newman (D, IL-6)*	1		
Steven Palazzo (R, MS-4)	6		
Tom Rice (R, SC-7)^	5		
Kurt Scrhrader (D, OR-5)	8		
Van Taylor (R, TX-3)	2		

Notes: * *indicates a member defeated by another member;* ^ *indicates a pro-impeachment Republican; Van Taylor placed first in his primary but withdrew after being forced into a runoff.*

Finally, one could argue that there was something of a Republican wave in the House – it was just a bizarrely inefficient one. Adding all the votes up, Republicans won the House popular vote by three percentage points after losing it by a similar margin in 2020. But Democrats suffered a net loss of just nine seats. As with the gubernatorial contests, part of this dynamic goes back to the state-by-state nature of the election. Between California and New York, Republicans won 11 districts that Biden would have carried in 2020, more than accounting for their national net gain. According to Daily Kos Election's tracking data, David Valadao's CA-22 was the district that saw the most spending by major outside groups (though Valadao was a pro-impeachment Republican, Democrats did not give him a pass). Though Valadao won by just three points, Trump lost the district by 13 points in 2020. At the same time, the second and third most expensive races were Michigan's 7th and Maine's 2nd districts – the former is a prime marginal seat while the latter is one of the reddest seats held by a Democrat. Both their Democratic incumbents, Elissa Slotkin and Jared Golden, won by more than five percentage points.

Table 4 shows the races that fell within five percentage points either way. Overall, the 19-17 Republican split of the group mirrored the GOP's slight national advantage.

Of the 19 Republican-won seats on Table 4, 13 came in crossover districts (seats that Biden would have carried in 2020), while only two Democrats on Table 4 hold Trump-won seats. Going forward, Democrats will surely target the Biden-district Republicans, and House Republicans also have some pickup opportunities of their own – so 2024 could be another very competitive cycle in the House.

Methodology and Acknowledgments

The 35th edition of America Votes follows the same basic format as the last several volumes. After this introductory section, each state has a dedicated chapter which contains election data. The focus of this edition is the 2022 midterm elections, although it includes some 2021 statewide elections in New Jersey and Virginia. Each state chapter includes county-by-county general election results for senator and governor, as well as the topline totals for statewide and House primaries. The election data in each chapter come from the individual secretaries of state, or the equivalent offices that provide direct election returns from each state. Maps of the 2022 Congressional Districts are also included, as is supplemental population data, provided from the Census Bureau.

One change for this edition is that, in addition to the data component of the book, trend analysis is provided for each state. My hope is that the data in this volume will be useful – but data, by itself, can often be cold and abstract. The new state-level trend narratives are meant to add some color to the series. My mentality, when writing them out, was, "As a political analyst, what trends or data points caught my attention?"

In most states, trend narratives are divided into "statewide" and "House" race sections – although the two categories are lumped together for states that are represented on an At-Large basis in the House. Redistricting, which was done leading up to the 2022 elections on a state-by-state basis, is covered in the "House" race portions of the narratives.

Of course, the most obvious change for the 35th installment of America Votes is the author. I'm thankful to Kaitlin Ciarmiello and Laura McEwan, both from Sage Publishing, for reaching out to me to replace Rhodes Cook. Rhodes, in addition to being one of my fellow contributors to *Sabato's Crystal Ball*, has been at the helm of the America Votes series since the 22nd edition, which covered the 1996 elections. Rhodes has ably chronicled American elections over the past several decades, and I

Table 4: Close House races

Democrats (17)	Percentage Margin	Republicans (19)	Percentage Margin
Yadira Caraveo, CO-8	0.7%	Lauren Boebert, CO-3*	0.2%
Gabe Vasquez, NM-2	0.7%	John Duarte, CA-13+	0.4%
Jahana Hayes, CT-5*	0.8%	John James, MI-10	0.5%
M. Gluesenkamp Perez, WA-3+	0.8%	Mike Lawler, NY-17+	0.6%
Pat Ryan, NY-18*	1.3%	Zach Nunn, IA-3	0.7%
Susan Wild, PA-7*	2.0%	David Schweikert, AZ-1*+	0.9%
Matt Cartwright, PA-8*+	2.4%	Brandon Williams, NY-22+	1.0%
Andrea Salinas, OR-6	2.5%	Juan Ciscomani, AZ-6+	1.5%
Wiley Nickel, NC-13	3.2%	Marc Molinaro, NY-19+	1.6%
Katie Porter, CA-47*	3.4%	L. Chavez-DeRemer, OR-5+	2.1%
Seth Magaziner, RI-2	3.7%	Don Bacon, NE-2*+	2.7%
Susie Lee, NV-3*	4.0%	Tom Kean, NJ-7+	2.8%
Eric Sorensen, IL-17	4.0%	David Valadao, CA-22*+	3.0%
Abigail Spanberger, VA-7*	4.7%	Ryan Zinke, MT-1	3.2%
Don Davis, NC-1	4.7%	Jen Kiggans, VA-2+	3.4%
Jared Moskowitz, FL-23	4.8%	Anthony D'Esposito, NY-4+	3.6%
Steven Horsford, NV-4*	4.8%	Derrick Van Orden, WI-3	3.7%
		Ken Calvert, CA-41*	4.7%
		Michelle Steel, CA-45*+	4.8%

*Notes: * indicates an incumbent; + indicates a crossover member*

have done my best to try to fill his shoes as author of this edition. When it came to collecting data and editing drafts, my primary contact at Sage was Liz Hernandez, who was a valuable partner. As in past editions, the maps throughout this volume usefully supplement the data – they were provided by Clark Benson of POLIDATA.

In 2019, Larry Sabato, Director of the Center for Politics at the University of Virginia, hired me to write full-time for his *Crystal Ball* newsletter – without him, I would probably not be working professionally in politics. I'm grateful to both Larry and Ken Stroupe, the Center's Associate Director, for allowing me to work on America Votes. My *Crystal Ball* associate, Kyle Kondik, provided useful guidance throughout the editorial process. Jackson Hamilton, one of my summer interns at the Center, also made some appreciated edits when combing through the narrative drafts.

Finally, I would like to dedicate this volume to my parents, John and Kathleen Coleman, who have long supported my interest in politics. In some ways, it's fitting that I'd begin as author of the America Votes series with the 35th edition. The first election I was ever involved in was Ray Nagin's campaign for Mayor of New Orleans, in 2002 – my father was a supporter, and, as a nine-year-old, I'd tag along with him to volunteer. In Louisiana, candidates are assigned a number on the ballot, and this number is often incorporated into their messaging. That year, Nagin, with "#35" visible on his advertising, cast himself as a reformer and won the election. Though Nagin eventually went to federal prison on public corruption charges – in a state known for producing less-than ethically pristine leaders, he was the first New Orleans mayor to wind up in the big house – I'm grateful to my father for introducing me to the political process.

J. Miles Coleman
July 2023

Errata

America Votes 34

The following corrections should be noted for the previous edition, *America Votes 34*, covering the 2019-2020 election.

Page v. On the Contents pages, the "Errata" line should be deleted since no errors from *America Votes 33* were noted.

Page 1. In the United States Voter Turnout 2020 table, there is no line for the District of Columbia.

Page 2. In the Gubernatorial Elections 2019 and 2020 table, the Total Vote percentages in Utah should be changed to read: "Republican Spencer J. Cox, 63.0%; Democrat Christopher Peterson, 30.3%."

Page 4. In the House of Representatives Elections 2020 table, the number of seats won Democrats in Alabama should be "1."

Page 10. In the United States President 2020 table, the Rep.-Dem. Plurality in North Dakota should read "120,709 R." The Other vote in the District of Columbia should be "8,447."

Page 11. In United States President 2020 Minor Parties table, the Other vote in North Dakota should read "11,231," with 9,371 Libertarian and 1,860 Write-In votes.

Page 12. In United States Popular Vote for President 1920 to 2020 table, the 2020 line should be rewritten as follows. These votes should be listed wherever the presidential vote is referenced, especially in tables on pages 1, 9, 11, and 12.

   Total Vote - 158,407,383

   Republican Vote - 74,223,509

   Democratic Vote - 81,282,965

   Other Vote - 2,900,909

   Plurality - 7,059,456 D

   Total Vote Rep. Percentage - 46.9%

   Total Vote Dem. Percentage - 51.3%

   Major Vote Rep. Percentage - 47.7%

   Major Vote Dem. Percentage - 52.3%

Page 233. In Louisiana Representatives list, the names of the 2nd and 5th District representatives are reversed. It should read: 2. Troy Carter (D); 5. Julia Letlow (R).

Page 487. The Utah President 2020 table is mislabeled. The results in that table are actually for the Utah Governor 2020 election. There is no correct table here for the 2020 Utah presidential vote.

Page 530. In the Wisconsin Postwar Vote for President table, all of the percentages in the Democratic Total Vote column from 1948 through 2016 are incorrect.

Page 545. In the District of Columbia 2020 General Elections: Other Votes section, the first two lines through "Independent (Brock Pierce)" are votes cast in the presidential election. The votes in the last three lines starting with "Libertarian (Patrick Hynes)" should be in a new entry labelled "Delegate."

UNITED STATES
VOTER TURNOUT 2022

STATE	2022 Est. Registration General Election	House (H)	Senate (S)	Governor (G)	High Race	High Race Vote	High Race Vote as Percentage of 2022 Registration General Election
Alabama	3,687,753	1,343,710	1,414,238	1,415,283	G	1,415,283	38.4%
Alaska	602,408	263,610	261,705	263,752	G	263,752	43.8%
Arizona	4,143,929	2,360,078	2,572,294	2,559,485	S	2,572,294	62.1%
Arkansas	1,765,681	895,102	901,306	907,037	G	907,037	51.4%
California	21,940,274	10,656,368	10,843,641	10,933,009	G	10,933,009	49.8%
Colorado	4,424,211	2,472,144	2,500,130	2,508,770	G	2,508,770	56.7%
Connecticut	2,474,398	1,261,351	1,259,887	1,268,898	G	1,268,898	51.3%
Delaware	764,765	321,649	—	—	H	321,649	42.1%
Florida	14,536,811	7,332,304	7,758,014	7,771,399	G	7,771,399	53.5%
Georgia	7,004,034	3,907,972	3,935,924	3,953,408	G	3,953,408	56.4%
Hawaii	853,874	401,174	408,517	413,262	G	413,262	48.4%
Idaho	1,006,180	583,628	590,890	592,624	G	592,624	58.9%
Illinois	9,648,000	4,049,405	4,100,739	4,104,774	G	4,104,774	42.5%
Indiana	4,760,880	1,856,849	1,860,154	—	S	1,860,154	39.1%
Iowa	2,234,696	1,211,700	1,216,646	1,221,864	G	1,221,864	54.7%
Kansas	1,975,535	1,001,817	1,004,956	1,008,998	G	1,008,998	51.1%
Kentucky	3,594,231	1,463,418	1,477,830	—	S	1,477,830	41.1%
Louisiana	3,016,626	1,133,124	1,383,290	—	S	1,383,290	45.9%
Maine	929,017	665,558	—	676,819	G	676,819	72.9%
Maryland	4,124,156	1,995,728	2,002,336	2,005,223	G	2,005,223	48.6%
Massachusetts	4,884,076	2,357,997	—	2,485,796	G	2,485,796	50.9%
Michigan	8,203,071	4,375,537	—	4,461,772	G	4,461,772	54.4%
Minnesota	3,562,500	2,495,832	—	2,510,661	G	2,510,661	70.5%
Mississippi	1,933,229	709,100	—	—	H	709,100	36.7%
Missouri	4,286,342	2,060,089	2,069,130	—	S	2,069,130	48.3%
Montana	762,959	463,632	—	—	H	463,632	60.8%
Nebraska	1,243,241	663,187	—	672,593	G	672,593	54.1%
Nevada	2,248,598	1,009,503	1,020,850	1,019,071	S	1,020,850	45.4%
New Hampshire	1,143,000	617,546	620,975	619,135	S	620,975	54.3%
New Jersey	6,505,751	2,609,716	—	2,614,886	G	2,614,886	40.2%
New Mexico	1,369,242	704,126	—	712,256	G	712,256	52.0%
New York	13,129,900	5,762,257	5,852,707	5,912,286	G	5,912,286	45.0%
North Carolina	7,413,909	3,760,753	3,773,924	—	S	3,773,924	50.9%
North Dakota*	564,935	238,586	240,140	—	S	240,140	42.5%
Ohio	8,029,950	4,109,711	4,133,342	4,134,877	G	4,134,877	51.5%
Oklahoma	2,295,906	1,146,311	1,150,732	1,153,284	G	1,153,284	50.2%
Oregon	3,003,625	1,906,940	1,927,949	1,952,883	G	1,952,883	65.0%
Pennsylvania	8,873,144	5,152,001	5,368,021	5,366,179	S	5,368,021	60.5%
Rhode Island	720,169	357,823	—	357,670	H	357,823	49.7%
South Carolina	3,355,321	1,602,341	1,695,702	1,703,192	G	1,703,192	50.8%
South Dakota	597,069	327,841	348,020	350,166	G	350,166	58.6%
Tennessee	4,212,431	1,710,425	—	1,739,882	G	1,739,882	41.3%
Texas	17,119,632	7,082,919	—	8,102,908	G	8,102,908	47.3%
Utah	1,910,239	1,063,255	1,076,061	—	S	1,076,061	56.3%
Vermont	503,129	282,026	287,100	284,801	S	287,100	57.1%
Virginia	6,092,214	3,047,729	—	3,288,318	G	3,288,318	54.0%
Washington	4,819,046	3,026,173	3,047,900	—	S	3,047,900	63.2%
West Virginia	1,146,071	471,967	—	—	H	471,967	41.2%
Wisconsin	3,534,794	2,531,324	2,652,477	2,656,490	G	2,656,490	75.2%
Wyoming	297,639	193,902	—	194,000	G	194,000	65.2%
District of Columbia	508,165	201,330	—	—	H	201,330	39.6%

Notes: Does not include special elections or elections for non-voting delegates. The gubernatorial vote includes 2021 elections in New Jersey and Virginia.
* North Dakota does not require voter registration.

GUBERNATORIAL ELECTIONS 2021 AND 2022

State	Total Vote	Republican Vote	Republican Candidate	Democratic Vote	Democratic Candidate	Other Vote	Rep.-Dem. Plurality	Total Vote Rep.	Total Vote Dem.	Major Vote Rep.	Major Vote Dem.
Alabama	1,415,283	946,932	Ivey, Kay*	412,961	Flowers, Yolanda Rochelle	9,432	533,971 R	66.9%	29.2%	69.6%	30.4%
Alaska	263,752	132,632	Dunleavy, Mike J.*	63,851	Gara, Les	784	68,781 R	50.3%	24.2%	67.5%	32.5%
Arizona	2,559,485	1,270,774	Lake, Kari	1,287,891	Hobbs, Katie	467	17,117 D	49.6%	50.3%	49.7%	50.3%
Arkansas	907,037	571,105	Huckabee Sanders, Sarah	319,242	Jones, Chris		251,863 R	63.0%	35.2%	64.1%	35.9%
California	10,933,009	4,462,910	Dahle, Brian	6,470,099	Newsom, Gavin*		2,007,189 D	40.8%	59.2%	40.8%	59.2%
Colorado	2,508,770	983,040	Ganahl, Heidi	1,468,481	Polis, Jared*	28,310	485,441 D	39.2%	58.5%	40.1%	59.9%
Connecticut	1,268,898	546,209	Stefanowski, Bob	710,191	Lamont, Ned*	98	163,982 D	43.0%	56.0%	43.5%	56.5%
Florida	7,771,399	4,614,210	DeSantis, Ron*	3,106,313	Crist, Charlie	19,299	1,507,897 R	59.4%	40.0%	59.8%	40.2%
Georgia	3,953,408	2,111,572	Kemp, Brian*	1,813,673	Abrams, Stacey		297,899 R	53.4%	45.9%	53.8%	46.2%
Hawaii	413,262	152,237	Aiona, Duke	261,025	Green, Josh		108,788 D	36.8%	63.2%	36.8%	63.2%
Idaho	592,624	358,598	Little, Brad*	120,160	Heidt, Stephen	12,031	238,438 R	60.5%	20.3%	74.9%	25.1%
Illinois	4,104,774	1,739,095	Bailey, Darren	2,253,748	Pritzker, Jay*	81	514,653 D	42.4%	54.9%	43.6%	56.4%
Iowa	1,221,864	709,198	Reynolds, Kim*	482,950	DeJear, Deidre	718	226,248 R	58.0%	39.5%	59.5%	40.5%
Kansas	1,008,998	477,591	Schmidt, Derek	499,849	Kelly, Laura*	11,106	22,258 D	47.3%	49.5%	48.9%	51.1%
Maine	676,819	287,304	LePage, Paul R.	376,934	Mills, Janet T.*		89,630 D	42.4%	55.7%	43.3%	56.7%
Maryland	2,005,223	644,000	Cox, Dan	1,293,944	Moore, Wes	37,178	649,944 D	32.1%	64.5%	33.2%	66.8%
Massachusetts	2,485,796	859,343	Diehl, Geoff	1,584,403	Healey, Maura	2,806	725,060 D	34.6%	63.7%	35.2%	64.8%
Michigan	4,461,772	1,960,635	Dixon, Tudor	2,430,305	Whitmer, Gretchen*	32,032	469,670 D	43.9%	54.5%	44.7%	55.3%
Minnesota	2,510,661	1,119,941	Jensen, Scott	1,312,349	Walz, Timothy J.*	49,025	192,408 D	44.6%	52.3%	46.0%	54.0%
Nebraska	672,593	398,334	Pillen, Jim	242,006	Blood, Carol	5,798	156,328 R	59.2%	36.0%	62.2%	37.8%
Nevada	1,019,071	497,377	Lombardo, Joe	481,991	Sisolak, Steve*	24,784	15,386 R	48.8%	47.3%	50.8%	49.2%
New Hampshire	619,135	352,813	Sununu, Chris*	256,766	Sherman, Tom	4,485	96,047 R	57.0%	41.5%	57.9%	42.1%
New Jersey (2021)	2,614,886	1,255,185	Ciattarelli, Jack	1,339,471	Murphy, Philip*	11,780	84,286 D	48.0%	51.2%	48.4%	51.6%
New Mexico	712,256	324,701	Ronchetti, Mark V.	370,168	Grisham, Michelle Lujan*		45,467 D	45.6%	52.0%	46.7%	53.3%
New York	5,912,286	2,762,581	Zeldin, Lee M.	3,140,415	Hochul, Kathy Courtney*		377,834 D	46.7%	53.1%	46.8%	53.2%
Ohio	4,134,877	2,580,424	DeWine, Michael*	1,545,489	Whaley, Nan	882	1,034,935 R	62.4%	37.4%	62.5%	37.5%
Oklahoma	1,153,284	639,484	Stitt, Kevin*	481,904	Hofmeister, Joy	15,653	157,580 R	55.4%	41.8%	57.0%	43.0%
Oregon	1,952,883	850,347	Drazan, Christine	917,074	Kotek, Tina	17,031	66,727 D	43.5%	47.0%	48.1%	51.9%
Pennsylvania	5,366,179	2,238,477	Mastriano, Douglas	3,031,137	Shapiro, Joshua	44,954	792,660 D	41.7%	56.5%	42.5%	57.5%
Rhode Island	357,670	139,001	Kalus, Ashley Marie	207,166	McKee, Daniel*	6,991	68,165 D	38.9%	57.9%	40.2%	59.8%
South Carolina	1,703,192	988,501	McMaster, Henry D.*	692,691	Cunningham, Joe	1,174	295,810 R	58.0%	40.7%	58.8%	41.2%
South Dakota	350,166	217,035	Noem, Kristi*	123,148	Smith, Jamie		93,887 R	62.0%	35.2%	63.8%	36.2%
Tennessee	1,739,882	1,129,390	Lee, Bill*	572,681	Martin, Jason Brantley	22,279	556,572 R	64.9%	32.9%	66.3%	33.7%
Texas	8,102,908	4,437,099	Abbott, Greg*	3,553,656	O'Rourke, Beto	30,221	883,443 R	54.8%	43.9%	55.5%	44.5%
Vermont	284,801	202,147	Scott, Phil*	68,248	Siegel, Brenda	8,384	133,899 R	71.0%	24.0%	74.8%	25.2%
Virginia (2021)	3,288,318	1,663,158	Youngkin, Glenn Allen	1,599,470	McAuliffe, Terry R.	2,583	63,688 R	50.6%	48.6%	51.0%	49.0%
Wisconsin	2,656,490	1,268,535	Michels, Tim	1,358,774	Evers, Tony*	1,983	90,239 D	47.8%	51.1%	48.3%	51.7%
Wyoming	194,000	143,696	Gordon, Mark*	30,686	Livingston, Theresa	8,157	113,010 R	74.1%	15.8%	82.4%	17.6%
Total	93,897,711	46,035,611		46,281,447		410,506	6,246,458 D	49.0%	49.3%	49.9%	50.1%

SENATE ELECTIONS 2021 AND 2022

State	Total Vote	Republican Vote	Republican Candidate	Democratic Vote	Democratic Candidate	Other Vote	Rep.-Dem. Plurality	Plurality Total Vote Rep.	Total Vote Dem.	Major Vote Rep.	Major Vote Dem.
Alabama	1,414,238	942,154	Britt, Katie	436,746	Boyd, Will	2,459	505,408 R	66.6%	30.9%	68.3%	31.7%
Alaska*	261,705	113,495	Murkowski, Lisa A.	27,145	Chesbro, Patricia		2,015 R	43.4%	10.4%	80.7%	19.3%
Arizona	2,572,294	1,196,308	Masters, Blake	1,322,027	Kelly, Mark	197	125,719 D	46.5%	51.4%	47.5%	52.5%
Arkansas	901,306	592,437	Boozman, John	280,187	James, Natalie		312,250 R	65.7%	31.1%	67.9%	32.1%
California	10,843,641	4,222,025	Meuser, Mark P.	6,621,616	Padilla, Alex		2,399,591 D	38.9%	61.1%	38.9%	61.1%
Colorado	2,500,130	1,031,693	O'Dea, Joe	1,397,170	Bennet, Michael F.	27,733	365,477 D	41.3%	55.9%	42.5%	57.5%
Connecticut	1,259,887	535,943	Levy, Leora R.	723,864	Blumenthal, Richard		187,921 D	42.5%	57.5%	42.5%	57.5%
Florida	7,758,014	4,474,847	Rubio, Marco	3,201,522	Demings, Val B.	49,468	1,273,325 R	57.7%	41.3%	58.3%	41.7%
Georgia	3,541,877	1,721,244	Walker, Herschel	1,820,633	Warnock, Raphael		99,389 D	48.6%	51.4%	48.6%	51.4%
Georgia (2021)**	4,484,902	2,214,979	Perdue, David A.	2,269,923	Ossoff, Jon		54,944 D	49.4%	50.6%	49.4%	50.6%
Hawaii	408,517	106,358	McDermott, Bob	290,894	Schatz, Brian	6,350	184,536 D	26.0%	71.2%	26.8%	73.2%
Idaho	590,890	358,539	Crapo, Michael D.	169,808	Roth, David	12,626	188,731 R	60.7%	28.7%	67.9%	32.1%
Illinois	4,100,739	1,701,055	Salvi, Kathy	2,329,136	Duckworth, Tammy	1,877	628,081 D	41.5%	56.8%	42.2%	57.8%
Indiana	1,860,154	1,090,390	Young, Todd	704,480	McDermott, Thomas M. Jr.	1,461	385,910 R	58.6%	37.9%	60.8%	39.2%
Iowa	1,216,646	681,501	Grassley, Charles E.	533,330	Franken, Michael		148,171 R	56.0%	43.8%	56.1%	43.9%
Kansas	1,004,956	602,976	Moran, Jerry	372,214	Holland, Mark R.		230,762 R	60.0%	37.0%	61.8%	38.2%
Kentucky	1,477,830	913,326	Paul, Rand	564,311	Booker, Charles	48	349,015 R	61.8%	38.2%	61.8%	38.2%
Louisiana	1,383,290	851,568	Kennedy, John Neely	246,933	Chambers, Gary	35,616	604,635 R	61.6%	17.9%	77.5%	22.5%
Maryland	2,002,336	682,293	Chaffee, Chris	1,316,897	Van Hollen, Chris Jr.		634,604 D	34.1%	65.8%	34.1%	65.9%
Missouri	2,069,130	1,146,966	Schmitt, Eric	872,694	Busch Valentine, Trudy	14,649	274,272 R	55.4%	42.2%	56.8%	43.2%
Nevada	1,020,850	490,388	Laxalt, Adam	498,316	Masto, Catherine Cortez	19,705	7,928 D	48.0%	48.8%	49.6%	50.4%
New Hampshire	620,975	275,928	Bolduc, Donald C.	332,193	Hassan, Maggie	464	56,265 D	44.4%	53.5%	45.4%	54.6%
New York	5,852,707	2,501,151	Pinion, Joe	3,320,561	Schumer, Charles E.	4,151	819,410 D	42.7%	56.7%	43.0%	57.0%
North Carolina	3,773,924	1,905,786	Budd, Ted	1,784,049	Beasley, Cheri	32,449	121,737 R	50.5%	47.3%	51.6%	48.4%
North Dakota	240,140	135,474	Hoeven, John	59,995	Christiansen, Katrina	265	75,479 R	56.4%	25.0%	69.3%	30.7%
Ohio	4,133,342	2,192,114	Vance, James David	1,939,489	Ryan, Tim	1,037	252,625 R	53.0%	46.9%	53.1%	46.9%
Oklahoma	1,150,732	739,960	Lankford, James	369,370	Horn, Madison	20,495	370,590 R	64.3%	32.1%	66.7%	33.3%
Oregon	1,927,949	788,991	Perkins, Jo Rae	1,076,424	Wyden, Ron	25,651	287,433 D	40.9%	55.8%	42.3%	57.7%
Pennsylvania	5,368,021	2,487,260	Oz, Mehmet	2,751,012	Fetterman, John K.	56,862	263,752 D	46.3%	51.2%	47.5%	52.5%
South Carolina	1,695,702	1,066,274	Scott, Tim	627,616	Matthews, Krystle		438,658 R	62.9%	37.0%	62.9%	37.1%
South Dakota	348,020	242,316	Thune, John	91,007	Bengs, Brian L.		151,309 R	69.6%	26.1%	72.7%	27.3%
Utah	1,076,061	571,974	Lee, Mike			44,129	112,016 R	53.2%	0.0%	0.0%	0.0%
Vermont	287,100	80,468	Malloy, Gerald	196,575	Welch, Peter	7,305	116,107 D	28.0%	68.5%	29.0%	71.0%
Washington	3,047,900	1,299,322	Smiley, Tiffany	1,741,827	Murray, Patty		442,505 D	42.6%	57.1%	42.7%	57.3%
Wisconsin	2,652,477	1,337,185	Johnson, Ron	1,310,467	Barnes, Mandela		26,718 R	50.4%	49.4%	50.5%	49.5%
Total	84,848,382	41,294,688		41,600,431		364,997	3,05,743 D	48.7%	49.0%	49.8%	50.2%

*As no candidate took a majority in the initial round, the contest went to ranked-choice balloting. Murkowski won, taking 136,330 votes (53.7%) to Tshibaka's 117,534 (46.3%).
** The Georgia race was a runoff held on January 5, 2021.

HOUSE OF REPRESENTATIVES ELECTIONS 2022

State	Seats Won Republican	Seats Won Democratic	Total Vote	Republican	Democratic	Other	Rep.-Dem. Plurality	Percentage Total Vote Rep.	Dem.	Percentage Major Vote Rep.	Dem.
Alabama	6	1	1,343,710	942,393	318,540	82,777	623,853 R	70.1%	23.7%	74.7%	25.3%
Alaska*	0	1	263,610	129,379	128,553	5,678	826 R	49.1%	48.8%	50.2%	49.8%
Arizona	6	3	2,360,078	1,324,961	1,004,462	30,655	320,499 R	56.1%	42.6%	56.9%	43.1%
Arkansas	4	0	895,102	598,000	271,771	25,331	326,229 R	66.8%	30.4%	68.8%	31.2%
California*	12	40	10,656,368	3,859,666	6,743,737	52,965	2,884,071 D	36.2%	63.3%	36.4%	63.6%
Colorado	3	5	2,472,144	1,050,960	1,365,427	55,757	314,467 D	42.5%	55.2%	43.5%	56.5%
Connecticut	0	5	1,261,351	526,372	721,526	13,453	195,154 D	41.7%	57.2%	42.2%	57.8%
Delaware	0	1	321,649	138,201	178,416	5,032	40,215 D	43.0%	55.5%	43.6%	56.4%
Florida	20	8	7,332,304	4,271,196	2,905,702	155,406	1,365,494 R	58.3%	39.6%	59.5%	40.5%
Georgia	9	5	3,907,972	2,044,102	1,863,870		180,232 R	52.3%	47.7%	52.3%	47.7%
Hawaii	0	2	401,174	124,091	271,953	5,130	147,862 D	30.9%	67.8%	31.3%	68.7%
Idaho	2	0	583,628	395,351	180,997	7,280	214,354 R	67.7%	31.0%	68.6%	31.4%
Illinois	3	14	4,049,405	1,768,865	2,271,361	9,179	502,496 D	43.7%	56.1%	43.8%	56.2%
Indiana	7	2	1,856,849	1,108,575	716,412	31,862	392,163 R	59.7%	38.6%	60.7%	39.3%
Iowa	4	0	1,211,700	677,857	526,460	7,383	151,397 R	55.9%	43.4%	56.3%	43.7%
Kansas	3	1	1,001,817	569,567	425,322	6,928	144,245 R	56.9%	42.5%	57.2%	42.8%
Kentucky	5	1	1,463,418	953,296	490,921	19,201	462,375 R	65.1%	33.5%	66.0%	34.0%
Louisiana*	5	1	1,133,124	773,701	318,932	40,491	454,769 R	68.3%	28.1%	70.8%	29.2%
Maine*	0	1	311,278	146,142	165,136		18,994 D	46.9%	53.1%	46.9%	53.1%
Maryland	1	7	1,995,728	690,463	1,291,446	13,819	600,983 D	34.6%	64.7%	34.8%	65.2%
Massachusetts	0	9	2,357,997	706,790	1,636,400	14,807	929,610 D	30.0%	69.4%	30.2%	69.8%
Michigan	6	7	4,375,537	2,083,361	2,184,504	107,672	101,143 D	47.6%	49.9%	48.8%	51.2%
Minnesota	4	4	2,495,832	1,200,855	1,250,518	44,459	49,663 D	48.1%	50.1%	49.0%	51.0%
Mississippi	3	1	709,100	509,132	196,399	3,569	312,733 R	71.8%	27.7%	72.2%	27.8%
Missouri	6	2	2,060,089	1,223,617	794,978	41,494	428,639 R	59.4%	38.6%	60.6%	39.4%
Montana	2	0	463,632	245,081	158,745	59,806	86,336 R	52.9%	34.2%	60.7%	39.3%
Nebraska	3	0	663,187	414,599	235,572	13,016	179,027 R	62.5%	35.5%	63.8%	36.2%
Nevada	1	3	1,009,503	515,535	480,774	13,194	34,761 R	51.1%	47.6%	51.7%	48.3%
New Hampshire	0	2	617,546	277,808	339,027	711	61,219 D	45.0%	54.9%	45.0%	55.0%
New Jersey	3	8	2,336,052	1,050,308	1,254,986	30,758	204,678 D	45.0%	53.7%	45.6%	54.4%
New Mexico	0	3	704,126	316,352	387,665	109	71,313 D	44.9%	55.1%	44.9%	55.1%
New York	11	15	5,762,257	2,525,335	3,199,496	37,426	674,161 D	43.8%	55.5%	44.1%	55.9%
North Carolina	7	7	3,760,753	1,956,906	1,795,170	8,677	161,736 R	52.0%	47.7%	52.2%	47.8%
North Dakota	1	0	238,586	148,399		90,187	58,755 R	62.2%	0.0%	100.0%	0.0%
Ohio	10	5	4,109,711	2,318,993	1,790,614	104	528,379 R	56.4%	43.6%	56.4%	43.6%
Oklahoma	5	0	1,146,311	760,639	356,988	28,684	403,651 R	66.4%	31.1%	68.1%	31.9%
Oregon	2	4	1,906,940	851,991	1,012,725	42,224	160,734 D	44.7%	53.1%	45.7%	54.3%
Pennsylvania	8	9	5,152,001	2,702,262	2,436,919	12,820	265,343 R	52.5%	47.3%	52.6%	47.4%
Rhode Island	1	1	357,823	194,287	157,487	6,049	36,800 R	54.3%	44.0%	55.2%	44.8%
South Carolina	5	2	1,602,341	866,107	707,100	29,134	159,007 R	54.1%	44.1%	55.1%	44.9%
South Dakota	1	0	327,841	253,821		74,020	179,801 R	77.4%	0.0%	100.0%	0.0%
Tennessee	8	1	1,710,425	1,101,928	581,902	26,595	520,026 R	64.4%	34.0%	65.4%	34.6%
Texas	25	13	7,082,919	3,890,438	2,999,053	193,428	891,385 R	54.9%	42.3%	56.5%	43.5%
Utah	4	0	1,063,255	670,924	342,078	50,253	328,846 R	63.1%	32.2%	66.2%	33.8%
Vermont	0	1	282,026	78,397	176,494	27,135	98,097 D	27.8%	62.6%	30.8%	69.2%
Virginia	5	6	3,047,729	1,462,049	1,572,296	13,384	110,247 D	48.0%	51.6%	48.2%	51.8%
Washington*	2	8	3,026,173	1,261,961	1,751,582	12,630	489,621 D	41.7%	57.9%	41.9%	58.1%
West Virginia	2	0	471,967	312,004	149,706	10,257	162,298 R	66.1%	31.7%	67.6%	32.4%
Wisconsin	6	2	2,531,324	1,403,080	1,012,955	115,289	390,125 R	55.4%	40.0%	58.1%	41.9%
Wyoming	1	0	193,902	132,206	47,250	14,446	84,956 R	68.2%	24.4%	73.7%	26.3%
TOTAL	222	213	107,012,134	53,767,518	51,551,516	1,693,100	2,216,002 D	50.2%	48.2%	51.1%	48.9%

Note: Does not include special elections. The following states allow cross-endorsement, that is, where third parties could endorse candidates of the major parties, and all such votes are credited to the major party with which the candidates identified: Connecticut, Delaware, Idaho, Mississippi, New York, Oregon, South Carolina, and Vermont.

*California and Washington hold jungle primaries, and the top two vote recipients, regardless of party, advance to the November general election where two candidates of the same party ran against each other, the vote totals for all Republicans and Democrats are included in the state total for each party. Louisiana holds first-round voting concurrent with the general election. If a candidate does not receive a majority of the vote, the top two vote getters advance to a runoff. Maine's ranked-choice voting system requires winning candidates to receive a majority vote. Candidates with the fewest ranked votes are eliminated, and their votes are transferred to the candidates ranked second on each voter's ballot. This process continues until a candidate receives a majority. Starting in 2022, Alaska began using a ranked-choice non-partisan primary system. In the initial round, all candidates, regardless of party, run on the same ballot. The top 4 finishers advance to a second round, where voters rank their preferences.

UNITED STATES

SUMMARY OF HOUSE AND SENATE SPECIAL ELECTIONS, 2021–2022

REPRESENTATIVES

District	Former Member	New Member	Date Elected	Winning Percentage	Total Vote
Louisiana 5th	Luke Letlow (R)	Julia Letlow (R)	March 20, 2021	64.5%	103,616
Louisiana 2nd	Cedric Richmond (D)	Troy Carter (D)	April 24, 2021	55.2%	87,810
New Mexico 1st	Debra Haaland's (D)	Melanie Ann Stansbury (D)	June 1, 2021	60.4%	132,263
Texas 6th*	Ronald Wright (R)	Jake Ellzey (R)	July 27, 2021	53.3%	39,166
Ohio 11th	Marcia Fudge (D)	Shontel Brown (D)	November 2, 2021	78.9%	105,111
Ohio 15th	Steve Stivers (R)	Mike Carey (R)	November 2, 2021	58.3%	162,089
Florida 20th	Alcee Hastings (D)	Sheila Cherfilus-McCormick (D)	January 11, 2022	79.0%	56,617
California 22nd	Devin Nunes (R)	Connie Conway (R)	June 7, 2022	62.1%	115,421
Texas 34th	Filemon Vela (D)	Mayra Flores (R)	June 14, 2022	50.9%	29,069
Nebraska 1st	Jeffrey Fortenberry (R)	Mike Flood (R)	June 28, 2022	52.7%	115,800
Minnesota 1st	Jim Hagedorn (R)	Brad Finstad (R)	August 9, 2022	50.7%	117,879
Alaska At Large	Sarah Palin (R)	Mary Peltola (D)	August 16, 2022	51.5%	188,666
New York 19th	Antonio Delgado (D)	Pat Ryan (D)	August 23, 2022	51.4%	132,246
New York 23rd	Tom Reed (R)	Joe Sempolinski (R)	August 23, 2022	52.6%	74,424
Indiana 2nd	Jackie Walorski (R)	Rudy Yakym (R)	November 8, 2022	63.3%	188,045

SENATORS

State	Former Member	New Member	Date Elected	Winning Percentage	Total Vote
California	Kamala Harris (D)	Alex Padilla (D)	November 8, 2022	60.9%	10,771,848
Oklahoma	Jim Inhofe (R)	Markwayne Mullin (R)	November 8, 2022	61.8%	1,150,481

Note: The Texas 6th District House race results presented here are for the runoff, since no candidate received a majority vote in the special election held May 1, 2021.

SPECIAL ELECTIONS AND POSTELECTION CHANGES TO THE 116TH CONGRESS

From the beginning of 2021 through the end of 2022, 15 special elections were held in the House to fill unexpired terms in the 117th Congress. There were two special elections in the Senate in this timeframe, and there was one party switch.

REPRESENTATIVES

LOUISIANA 5TH CD

Luke Letlow (R) was scheduled to take office on January 3, 2021, but died from COVID-19 complications on December 29, 2020. Julia Letlow (R) won the special primary election on March 2021.

March 20, 2021, Special Nonpartisan Primary Election

67,203 Julia Letlow (R); 28,255 Sandra Christophe (D); 5,497 Chad Conerly (R); 929 Robert Lansden (R); 464 Allen Guillory (R); 402 Jim Davis (No Party Affiliation); 334 Sancha Smith (R); 236 M.V. Mendoza (Independent); 131 Jaycee Magnuson (R); 67 Richard Pannell (R); 62 Horace Melton (R); 36 Errol Victor (R).

LOUISIANA 2ND CD

Cedric Richmond (D) resigned from the House on January 15, 2021, to serve in President Joe Biden's administration as a senior adviser to the president and director of the White House Office of Public Engagement. The nonpartisan primary was held on March 20, 2021. The primary's top two vote recipients advanced to the general election on April 24, 2021. Troy Carter (D) was elected to fill the remainder of the term of the 117th Congress.

March 20, 2021, Special Nonpartisan Primary

34,402 Troy Carter (D); 21,673 Karen Peterson (D); 20,163 Gary Chambers (D); 9,237 Claston Bernard (R); 3,218 Chelsea Ardoin (R); 2,349 Greg Lirette (R); 754 Sheldon Vincent Sr. (R); 699 Desiree Ontiveros (D); 598 Belden Batiste (Independent); 403 Harold John (D); 323 Mindy McConnell (L); 288 J. Christopher Johnson (D); 244 Jenette Porter (D); 122 Lloyd Kelly (D); 94 Brandon Jolicoeur (Independent).

April 24, 2021, Special General Election

48,513 Troy Carter (D); 39,297 Karen Peterson (D).

NEW MEXICO 1ST CD

Incumbent, Debra Haaland (D), was confirmed as secretary of the interior for Joe Biden's administration on March 15, 2021. The special general election to fill the vacancy was held on June 1, 2021. Melanie Ann Stansbury (D) was elected to fill the remainder of the term of the 117th Congress.

June 1, 2021, Special General Election

79,838 Melanie Ann Stansbury (D); 47,111 Mark Moores (R); 3,534 Aubrey Dunn (Independent); 1,734 Christopher Manning (L); 40 Laura Olivas (Independent); 6 Robert Ornelas (Independent).

TEXAS 6TH CD

Incumbent, Ronald Wright (R), died from COVID-19 related complications on February 7, 2021. The special election was held May 1, 2021, and the special runoff election was held July 27, 2021. Jake Ellzey (R) was elected to fill the remainder of the term of the 117th Congress.

May 1, 2021, Special General Election

15,077 Susan Wright (R); 10,865 Jake Ellzey (R); 10,518 Jana Sanchez (D); 8,485 Brian Harrison (R); 6,973 Shawn Lassiter (D); 4,321 John Castro (R); 4,240 Tammy Allison (D), 2,923 Lydia Bean (D); 2,509 Michael Wood (R); 2,225 Michael Ballantine (R); 2,088 Daniel Rodimer (R); 1,654 Daryl Eddings (D); 1,544 Michael Egan (R); 1,189 Patrick Moses (D); 1,120 Manuel Salazar (D); 889 Sery Kim (R); 460 Travis Rodermund (R); 351 Adrian Mizher (Independent) ; 271 Brian Stephenson (D); 265 Phil Gray (L); 252 Matt Hinterlong (D); 150 Jenny Garcia Sharon (R); 102 Christopher Suprun (D).

July 27, 2021, Special Runoff Election

20,873 Jake Ellzey (R); 18,293 Susan Wright (R).

OHIO 11TH CD

Marcia Fudge (D) was confirmed as secretary of housing and urban development for Joe Biden's administration on March 10, 2021. The special Democratic and Republican primary elections were held August 3, 2021. The special general election was held November 2, 2021. Shontel Brown (D) was elected to fill the remainder of the term of the 117th Congress.

August 3, 2021, Special Republican Primary

4,009 Laverne Gore; 1,405 Felicia Ross.

August 3, 2021, Special Democratic Primary

38,505 Shontel Brown; 34,239 Nina Turner; 1,388 Jeffrey Johnson; 801 John E. Barnes Jr.; 599 Shirley Smith; 493 Seth Corey; 184 Pamela Pinkney; 182 Will Knight; 134 Tariq Shabazz; 105 Martin Alexander; 101 James Jerome Bell; 61 Lateek Shabazz; 52 Isaac Powell.

November 2, 2021, Special General Election

82,913 Shontel Brown (D); 22,198 Laverne Gore (R).

OHIO 15TH CD

Steve Stivers (R) resigned May 16, 2021, to become President and CEO of the Ohio Chamber of Commerce. The special Democratic and Republican primary elections were held August 3, 2021. The special general election was held November 2, 2021. Mike Carey (R) was elected to fill the remainder of the term of the 117th Congress.

August 3, 2021, Special Republican Primary

18,805 Mike Carey; 6,776 Jeff LaRe; 6,676 Ron Hood; 6,407 Bob Peterson; 5,090 Ruth Edmonds; 2,499 Thomas Hwang; 2,363 Stephanie Kunze; 1,076 Thad Cooperrider; 907 Omar Tarazi; 173 John Adams; 83 Eric M. Clark

August 3, 2021, Special Democratic Primary

13,704 Allison Russo; 2,576 Greg Betts.

November 2, 2021, Special General Election

94,501 Mike Carey (R); 67,588 Allison Russo (D).

FLORIDA 20TH CD

Alcee Hastings (D) passed away April 6, 2021, from pancreatic cancer. The special general election was held January 11, 2022. Sheila Cherfilus-McCormick (D) was elected to fill the remainder of the term of the 117th Congress.

January 11, 2022, Special General Election

44,707 Sheila Cherfilus-McCormick (D); 10,966 Jason Mariner (R); 395 Mike Ter Maat (Libertarian); 265 Jim Flynn (No Party Affiliation); 262 Leonard Serratore (No Party Affiliation); 22 Shelley Fain (Write-In).

CALIFORNIA 22ND CD

Devin Nunes (R), resigned on December 31, 2021, to become CEO of former President Donald Trump's (R) media company, Trump Media & Technology Group. The special nonpartisan primary was held April 5, 2022. The special general election was held June 7, 2022. Connie Conway (R) was elected to fill the remainder of the term of the 117th Congress.

April 5, 2022, Special Nonpartisan Primary

30,559 Connie Conway (R); 16,905 Lourin Hubbard (D); 14,075 Matt Stoll (R); 12,556 Eric Garcia (D); 7,619 Michael Maher (R); 5,391 Elizabeth Heng (R).

June 7 11, 2022, Special General Election

71,720 Connie Conway (R); 43,701 Lourin Hubbard (D).

TEXAS 34TH CD

Incumbent, Filemon Vela (D), resigned on March 31, 2022, to accept a position with a lobbying firm in Washington DC. The special general election was held June 14, 2022. Mayra Flores (R) was elected to fill the remainder of the term of the 117th Congress.

June 14, 2022, Special General Election

14,799 Mayra Flores (R); 12,606 Dan Sanchez (D); 1,210 Rene Coronado (D); 454 Juana Cantu-Cabrera (R).

NEBRASKA 1ST CD

Jeffrey Fortenberry (R) resigned on March 31, 2022, after being convicted with three felony counts, including one count of scheming to falsify and conceal material facts and two counts of making false statements to federal investigators. The Democratic and Republican parties nominated candidates instead of having primaries. The special general election was held on June 28, 2022. Mike Flood (R) was elected to fill the remainder of the term of the 117th Congress.

June 28, 2022, Special General Election

61,017 Mike Flood (R); 54,783 Patty Pansing Brooks (D).

MINNESOTA 1ST CD

Jim Hagedorn (R) passed away on February 17, 2022. The special general election was held August 9, 2022. Brad Finstad (R) was elected to fill the remainder of the term of the 117th Congress.

August 9, 2022, Special General Election

59,788 Brad Finstad (R); 55,155 Jeff Ettinger (D); 1,536 Richard Reisdorf (Legal Marijuana Now); 865 Haroun McClellan (Grassroots-Legalize Cannabis Party); 548 Scattered Write-Ins.

ALASKA AT LARGE

Incumbent, Don Young (R) passed away on March 18, 2022. Starting in 2022, Alaska began using a ranked-choice non-partisan primary system. In the initial round, all candidates, regardless of party, run on the same ballot. The top four finishers advance to a second round, where voters rank their preferences. Mary Peltola (D) was elected to fill the remainder of the term of the 117th Congress.

August 16, 2022, Special General Primary

74,817 Mary Peltola (D); 58,339 Sarah Palin (R); 52,536 Nick Begich (R).

NEW YORK 19TH CD

Incumbent, Antonio Delgado (D), resigned from Congress on May 3, 2022, after New York Governor Kathy Hochul (D) selected him as lieutenant governor. Patrick Ryan (D) was elected to fill the remainder of the term of the 117th Congress.

August 23, 2022, Special General Election

67,996 Patrick Ryan (D); 9,987 Robert Franklin (D); 64,159 Marcus Molinaro (R); 91 Scattered Write-Ins.

NEW YORK 23RD CD

Tom Reed (R), resigned on May 10, 2022. Joseph Sempolinski (R) was elected to fill the remainder of the term of the 117th Congress.

August 23, 2022, Special General Election

39,128 Joseph Sempolinski (R); 35,075 Max Della Pia (D); 221 Scattered Write-Ins.

INDIANA 2ND CD

Jackie Walorski (R), died in a car accident on August 3, 2022. The general election was held November 8, 2022. Rudy Yakym (R) was elected to fill the remainder of the term of the 117th Congress.

November 8, 2022, Special General Election

118,997 Rudy Yakym (R); 62,792 Paul Steury (D); 6,113 William Henry (Libertarian); 143 Marla Godette (Independent).

SENATORS

CALIFORNIA

Kamala Harris (D) resigned January 18, 2021, to become Vice President of the United States. Alex Padilla (D) was appointed by Governor Gavin Newsom on January 20, 2021. A special nonpartisan primary to fill the rest of Kamala Harris' six-year term was held June 7, 2022. The special general election was held November 8, 2022, concurrent with the general election. Alex Padilla (D) was elected to fill the remainder of the term.

June 7, 2022, Special Nonpartisan Primary

3,740,582 Alex Padilla (D); 1,503,480 Mark Meuser (R); 472,052 James P. Bradley (R); 403,722 Jonathan Elist (R); 226,447 Timothy Ursich Jr. (D); 191,531 Dan O'Dowd (D); 143,038 Myron Hall (R); 112,191 Daphne Bradford (Independent); 9,951 John Thompson Parker (Peace and Freedom Party); 12 Irene Ratliff (Write-In).

November 8, 2022, Special General Election

6,559,308 Alex Padilla (D); 4,212,540 Mark Meuser (R).

OKLAHOMA

Jim Inhofe (R) resigned on January 3, 2023, to spend time with his family. A special election to fill the remainder of the term was scheduled for November 8, 2020, concurrent with the general election. Markwayne Mullin (R) was elected to fill the remainder of the term.

November 8, 2020, Special General Election

710,643 Markwayne Mullin (R); 405,389 Kendra Horn (D); 17,386 Robert Murphy (L); 17,063 Ray Woods (Independent).

CHANGES FOLLOWING THE 2022 ELECTION

Following the 2022 general election, and through August 25, 2023, the following changes took place in the membership of the 118th Congress.

REPRESENTATIVES

Virginia 4th District— Donald McEachin (D) died of colorectal cancer on November 28, 2022. The special general election was held February 21, 2023. Jennifer McClellan (D) was elected to complete the term. She was sworn in on March 7, 2023.

Rhode Island 1st District— David Cicilline (D) resigned May 31, 2023, to run the Rhode Island Foundation. A special primary will be held September 5. 2023. A special general election will be held November 7, 2023.

Utah 2nd District— Chris Stewart (R) announced plans to resign on September 15, 2023, due to his wife's illness. The special general election will be held November 21, 2023.

SENATOR

Nebraska—Ben Sasse (R) resigned January 8, 2023, to become president of the University of Florida. On January 12, 2023, Governor Jim Pillen appointed Pete Ricketts (R) to fill the vacancy. A special election is scheduled for November 5, 2024.

117TH CONGRESS PARTY SWITCHES

SENATORS

Arizona—Kyrsten Sinema switched from the Democratic Party to Independent on December 9, 2022.

UNITED STATES

POPULAR VOTE FOR PRESIDENT 1920 TO 2020

Year	Total Vote	Republican Vote	Republican Candidate	Democratic Vote	Democratic Candidate	Other Vote	Rep.-Dem. Plurality	Total Vote Rep.	Total Vote Dem.	Major Vote Rep.	Major Vote Dem.
2020	158,062,688	74,204,767	Trump, Donald J.	80,965,502	Joseph R. Biden Jr.	2,840,954	6,760,735 D	46.9%	51.2%	47.8%	52.2%
2016**	136,562,629	62,984,804	Trump, Donald J.	65,853,508	Clinton, Hillary	7,724,317	2,868,704 D	46.1%	48.2%	48.9%	51.1%
2012	129,085,474	60,933,500	Romney, W. Mitt	65,915,796	Obama, Barack	2,236,178	4,982,296 D	47.2%	51.1%	48.0%	52.0%
2008	131,313,820	59,948,323	McCain, John S. III	69,498,516	Obama, Barack	1,866,981	9,550,193 D	45.7%	52.9%	46.3%	53.7%
2004	122,295,345	62,040,610	Bush, George W.	59,028,439	Kerry, John	1,226,296	3,012,171 R	50.7%	48.3%	51.2%	48.8%
2000**	105,396,627	50,455,156	Bush, George W.	50,992,335	Gore, Albert Jr.	3,949,136	537,179 D	47.9%	48.4%	49.7%	50.3%
1996**	96,277,872	39,198,755	Dole, Bob	47,402,357	Clinton, Bill	9,676,760	8,203,602 D	40.7%	49.2%	45.3%	54.7%
1992**	104,425,014	39,103,882	Bush, George H.	44,909,326	Clinton, Bill	20,411,806	5,805,444 D	37.4%	43.0%	46.5%	53.5%
1988	91,597,809	48,886,097	Bush, George H.	41,812,075	Dukakis, Michael S.	899,637	7,074,022 R	53.4%	45.6%	53.9%	46.1%
1984	92,652,842	54,455,075	Reagan, Ronald	37,577,185	Mondale, Walter F.	620,582	16,877,890 R	58.8%	40.6%	59.2%	40.8%
1980**	86,515,221	43,904,153	Reagan, Ronald	35,483,883	Carter, Jimmy	7,127,185	8,420,270 R	50.7%	41.0%	55.3%	44.7%
1976	81,554,989	39,141,091	Ford, Gerald R.	40,829,763	Carter, Jimmy	1,584,135	1,688,672 D	48.0%	50.1%	48.9%	51.1%
1972	77,718,554	47,169,911	Nixon, Richard M.	29,170,383	McGovern, George S.	1,378,260	17,999,528 R	60.7%	37.5%	61.8%	38.2%
1968**	73,211,875	31,785,480	Nixon, Richard M.	31,275,166	Humphrey, Hubert H.	10,151,229	510,314 R	43.4%	42.7%	50.4%	49.6%
1964	70,644,592	27,178,188	Goldwater, Barry M.	43,129,566	Johnson, Lyndon B.	336,838	15,951,378 D	38.5%	61.1%	38.7%	61.3%
1960	68,838,219	34,108,157	Nixon, Richard M.	34,226,731	Kennedy, John F.	503,331	118,574 D	49.5%	49.7%	49.9%	50.1%
1956	62,026,908	35,590,472	Eisenhower, Dwight D.	26,022,752	Stevenson, Adlai E.	413,684	9,567,720 R	57.4%	42.0%	57.8%	42.2%
1952	61,550,918	33,936,234	Eisenhower, Dwight D.	27,314,992	Stevenson, Adlai E.	299,692	6,621,242 R	55.1%	44.4%	55.4%	44.6%
1948**	48,793,826	21,991,291	Dewey, Thomas E.	24,179,345	Truman, Harry S.	2,623,190	2,188,054 D	45.1%	49.6%	47.6%	52.4%
1944	47,976,670	22,017,617	Dewey, Thomas E.	25,612,610	Roosevelt, Franklin D.	346,443	3,594,993 D	45.9%	53.4%	46.2%	53.8%
1940	49,900,774	22,348,836	Willkie, Wendell	27,313,041	Roosevelt, Franklin D.	238,897	4,964,205 D	44.8%	54.7%	45.0%	55.0%
1936	45,654,763	16,684,231	Landon, Alfred M.	27,757,333	Roosevelt, Franklin D.	1,213,199	11,073,102 D	36.5%	60.8%	37.5%	62.5%
1932	39,761,034	15,760,684	Hoover, Herbert C.	22,829,501	Roosevelt, Franklin D.	1,170,849	7,068,817 D	39.6%	57.4%	40.8%	59.2%
1928	36,805,951	21,437,277	Hoover, Herbert C.	15,007,698	Smith, Alfred E.	360,976	6,429,579 R	58.2%	40.8%	58.8%	41.2%
1924**	29,095,023	15,719,921	Coolidge, Calvin	8,386,704	Davis, John W.	4,988,398	7,333,217 R	54.0%	28.8%	65.2%	34.8%
1920	26,768,150	16,153,115	Harding, Warren G.	9,133,092	Cox, James M.	1,481,943	7,020,023 R	60.3%	34.1%	63.9%	36.1%

Republican Donald J. Trump lost the popular vote in 2016, but won the electoral vote and was elected president. Republican George W. Bush lost the popular vote in 2000, but won the electoral vote and was elected president. **In past elections, the other vote included: 2016 - 4,489,325 Libertarian (Gary Johnson); 2000 - 2,882,738 Green (Ralph Nader); 1996 - 8,085,402 Reform (Ross Perot); 1992 - 19,741,657 Independent (Ross Perot); 1980 - 5,720,060 Independent (John Anderson); 1968 - 9,906,473 American Independent (George Wallace); 1948-1,176,125 States' Rights (Strom Thurmond); 1948-1,157,326 Progressive (Henry Wallace); 1924-4,832,532 Progressive (Robert LaFollette).

ELECTORAL COLLEGE VOTE 1920 TO 2020

Year	Total	Republican	Democratic	Other	Other Candidate	Other Party
2020	538	232	306			
2016	538	304	227	7	See Note*	See Note
2012	538	206	332	0		
2008	538	173	365	0		
2004	538	286	251	1	John Edwards*	Democrat
2000	538	271	266	1	Abstained*	
1996	538	159	379	0		
1992	538	168	370	0		
1988	538	426	111	1	Lloyd Bentsen*	Democrat
1984	538	525	13	0		
1980	538	489	49	0		
1976	538	240	297	1	Ronald Reagan*	Republican
1972	538	520	17	1	John Hospers*	Libertarian
1968	538	301	191	46	George Wallace	American Independent
1964	538	52	486	0		
1960	537	219	303	15	Harry Byrd	Democrat
1956	531	457	73	1	Walter Jones*	Democrat
1952	531	442	89	0		
1948	531	189	303	39	Strom Thurmond	States' Rights
1944	531	99	432	0		
1940	531	82	449	0		
1936	531	8	523	0		
1932	531	59	472	0		
1928	531	444	87	0		
1924	531	382	136	13	Robert M. La Follette	Progressive
1920	531	404	127	0		

Note: An asterisk (*) indicates "faithless" electors who did not vote for the presidential candidates to which they were pledged. One of the electoral votes for Strom Thurmond in 1948, Harry Byrd in 1960, and George Wallace in 1968 was cast by a faithless elector. The rest of Byrd's support in 1960 came from unpledged electors. Due to faithless electors in the 2016 election, the following individuals received electoral votes: Bernie Sanders (1), Ron Paul (1), John Kasich (1), Colin Powell (3), and Faith Spotted Eagle (1).

ALABAMA

Statewide elections

In deep red Alabama, most of the action in 2022 was not in the general election, but in the Republican primary. At age 78 on Election Day, Republican Gov. Kay Ivey was the oldest sitting governor in the nation. Ivey has been involved in politics for generations: In her younger days, she was a friend of the state's only other woman governor, Lurleen Wallace, who served in the 1960s (she was preceded in office by her more famous husband, George). In the primary, Ivey garnered several challengers, some of who tried to position themselves to her right. But Ivey's incumbency, coupled with her grandmotherly personality, was a formidable combination – she carried all 67 counties.

Alabama's other major statewide race was for Senate. Sen. Richard Shelby, who was originally elected to the chamber as a conservative Democrat in 1986 before switching parties in 1994, announced that, at age 88, he would not run for a seventh term. Initially, Donald Trump endorsed Rep. Mo Brooks, of the Huntsville-area 5th District. But as Brooks ran a sluggish campaign, Katie Britt, a longtime Shelby staffer, gained steam. Ahead of the May GOP primary, in a rare move, Trump rescinded his endorsement. On primary day, while Britt fell under the 50%+1 threshold needed to win outright, she took 45% to Brooks' 29%, with free-spending business executive Michael Durant placing a reasonably strong third. Brooks pressed on to the runoff, though his prospects appeared grim, especially considering Britt narrowly carried his district. In a final blow to the Brooks campaign, Trump endorsed Britt. She won 63% to 37%.

In the general election, both Britt and Ivey won by over 35 points. As was the case across the South, Black turnout appeared weak. Typically, other than Birmingham's Jefferson County, Democrats carry a string of about a dozen mostly rural counties that run horizontally across the state. This stretch makes up Alabama's portion of the "Black Belt," a term referring to the soil of the area, though it is also heavily Black by composition. The Republicans carried Marengo and Russell counties, two marginal Biden-won Black Belt counties. The Democratic lag was not limited to the rural counties: both Republican nominees came within 5 points in Jefferson County and within 20 in Montgomery County – Joe Biden carried them by 13 and 31 points in 2020, respectively.

House elections

None of Alabama's seven districts were competitive. The only Democratic-held seat is the Black-majority 7th District, held by Rep. Terri Sewell. Though 2022 marked the first election cycle since 2012 where the GOP fielded a challenger against Sewell, she won easily, with 64%.

Redistricting brought minimal changes to Alabama's House map, at least for the 2022 cycle. In June 2023, the U.S. Supreme Court ruled in the *Allen v. Milligan* case that Alabama must redraw its map to include another Black-majority seat. Such a seat would likely originate in Mobile and run through the Black Belt to reach Montgomery, and Democrats would be favored to win it in 2024.

ALABAMA

Congressional districts first established for elections held in 2022

7 members

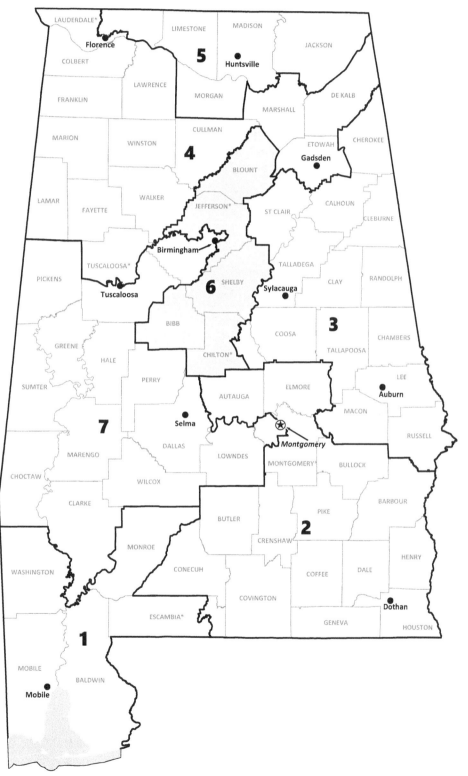

* Asterisk indicates a county whose boundaries include parts of two or more congressional districts.
CD 6 is highlighted for visibility.

ALABAMA

GOVERNOR
Kay Ivey (R). Reelected 2022 to a four-year term. Previously elected 2018. Assumed office April 10, 2017, to complete the remainder of the term vacated by the resignation of Robert Bentley (R).

SENATORS (2 Republicans)
Katie Britt (R). Elected 2022 to a six-year term.

Tommy Tuberville (R). Elected 2020 to a six-year term.

REPRESENTATIVES (6 Republicans, 1 Democrat)
1. Jerry Carl (R)
2. Barry Moore (R)
3. Mike Rogers (R)
4. Robert B. Aderholt (R)
5. Dale Strong (R)
6. Gary J. Palmer (R)
7. Terri A. Sewell (D)

POSTWAR VOTE FOR PRESIDENT

Year	Total Vote	Republican Vote	Republican Candidate	Democratic Vote	Democratic Candidate	Other Vote	Rep.-Dem. Plurality	Total Vote Rep.	Total Vote Dem.	Major Vote Rep.	Major Vote Dem.
2020	2,323,282	1,441,170	Trump, Donald J.*	849,624	Biden, Joseph R. Jr.	32,488	591,546 R	62.0%	36.6%	62.9%	37.1%
2016**	2,123,372	1,318,255	Trump, Donald J.	729,547	Clinton, Hillary Rodham	75,570	588,708 R	62.1%	34.4%	64.4%	35.6%
2012	2,074,338	1,255,925	Romney, W. Mitt	795,696	Obama, Barack H.*	22,717	460,229 R	60.5%	38.4%	61.2%	38.8%
2008	2,099,819	1,266,546	McCain, John S. III	813,479	Obama, Barack H.	19,794	453,067 R	60.3%	38.7%	60.9%	39.1%
2004	1,883,449	1,176,394	Bush, George W.*	693,933	Kerry, John F.	13,122	482,461 R	62.5%	36.8%	62.9%	37.1%
2000**	1,666,272	941,173	Bush, George W.	692,611	Gore, Albert Jr.	32,488	248,562 R	56.5%	41.6%	57.6%	42.4%
1996**	1,534,349	769,044	Dole, Robert "Bob"	662,165	Clinton, Bill*	103,140	106,879 R	50.1%	43.2%	53.7%	46.3%
1992**	1,688,060	804,283	Bush, George H.*	690,080	Clinton, Bill	193,697	114,203 R	47.6%	40.9%	53.8%	46.2%
1988	1,378,476	815,576	Bush, George H.	549,506	Dukakis, Michael S.	13,394	266,070 R	59.2%	39.9%	59.7%	40.3%
1984	1,441,713	872,849	Reagan, Ronald*	551,899	Mondale, Walter F.	16,965	320,950 R	60.5%	38.3%	61.3%	38.7%
1980**	1,341,929	654,192	Reagan, Ronald	636,730	Carter, Jimmy*	51,007	17,462 R	48.8%	47.4%	50.7%	49.3%
1976	1,182,850	504,070	Ford, Gerald R.*	659,170	Carter, Jimmy	19,610	155,100 D	42.6%	55.7%	43.3%	56.7%
1972	1,006,111	728,701	Nixon, Richard M.*	256,923	McGovern, George S.	20,487	471,778 R	72.4%	25.5%	73.9%	26.1%
1968**	1,049,922	146,923	Nixon, Richard M.	196,579	Humphrey, Hubert Horatio Jr.	706,420	49,656 D#	14.0%	18.7%	42.8%	57.2%
1964**	689,818	479,085	Goldwater, Barry M. Sr.		Johnson, Lyndon B.*	210,733	479,085 R	69.5%		100.0%	
1960	570,225	237,981	Nixon, Richard M.	324,050	Kennedy, John F.	8,194	86,069 D	41.7%	56.8%	42.3%	57.7%
1956	496,861	195,694	Eisenhower, Dwight D.*	280,844	Stevenson, Adlai E. II	20,323	85,150 D	39.4%	56.5%	41.1%	58.9%
1952	426,120	149,231	Eisenhower, Dwight D.	275,075	Stevenson, Adlai E. II	1,814	125,844 D	35.0%	64.6%	35.2%	64.8%
1948**	214,980	40,930	Dewey, Thomas E.		Truman, Harry S.*	174,050	40,930 R#	19.0%		100.0%	

Note: An asterisk (*) denotes incumbent. A pound sign (#) in the plurality column indicates that the winner in 1948 and 1968 did not run under the banner of either major party. **In past elections, the other vote included: 2016 - 44,467 Libertarian (Gary Johnson); 2000 - 18,323 Green (Ralph Nader); 1996 - 92,149 Reform (Ross Perot); 1992 - 183,109 Independent (Perot); 1980 -16,481 Independent (John Anderson); 1968 - 691,425 American Independent (George Wallace); 1964 - 210,732 Unpledged Democratic; 1948 -171,443 States' Rights (Strom Thurmond). In 1964 and 1948, the Democratic presidential candidates were not listed on the ballot. Wallace carried Alabama in 1968 with 65.9% of the total vote. Thurmond won the state in 1948 with 79.7%.

ALABAMA

POSTWAR VOTE FOR GOVERNOR

Year	Total Vote	Republican Vote	Republican Candidate	Democratic Vote	Democratic Candidate	Other Vote	Rep.-Dem. Plurality	Total Vote Rep.	Total Vote Dem.	Major Vote Rep.	Major Vote Dem.
2022	1,415,283	946,932	Ivey, Kay*	412,961	Flowers, Yolanda	9,432	533,971 R	66.9%	29.2%	69.6%	30.4%
2018	1,719,589	1,022,457	Ivey, Kay*	694,495	Maddox, Walter	2,637	327,962 R	59.5%	40.4%	59.6%	40.4%
2014	1,180,413	750,231	Bentley, Robert*	427,787	Griffith, Parker	2,395	322,444 R	63.6%	36.2%	63.7%	36.3%
2010	1,494,273	860,472	Bentley, Robert	625,710	Sparks, Ron	8,091	234,762 R	57.6%	41.9%	57.9%	42.1%
2006	1,250,401	718,327	Riley, Robert*	519,827	Baxley, Lucy	12,247	198,500 R	57.4%	41.6%	58.0%	42.0%
2002	1,367,053	672,225	Riley, Robert	669,105	Siegelman, Don*	25,723	3,120 R	49.2%	48.9%	50.1%	49.9%
1998	1,317,842	554,746	James, Forrest H. "Fob" Jr.*	760,155	Siegelman, Don	2,941	205,409 D	42.1%	57.7%	42.2%	57.8%
1994	1,201,969	604,926	James, Forrest H. "Fob" Jr.	594,169	Folsom, James E. Jr.*	2,874	10,757 R	50.3%	49.4%	50.4%	49.6%
1990	1,216,250	633,519	Hunt, Guy*	582,106	Hubbert, Paul R.	625	51,413 R	52.1%	47.9%	52.1%	47.9%
1986	1,236,230	696,203	Hunt, Guy	537,163	Baxley, Bill	2,864	159,040 R	56.3%	43.5%	56.4%	43.6%
1982	1,128,725	440,815	Folmar, Emory	650,538	Wallace, George C.	37,372	209,723 D	39.1%	57.6%	40.4%	59.6%
1978	760,474	196,963	Hunt, Guy	551,886	James, Forrest H. "Fob" Jr.	11,625	354,923 D	25.9%	72.6%	26.3%	73.7%
1974	598,305	88,381	McCary, Elvin	497,574	Wallace, George C.*	12,350	409,193 D	14.8%	83.2%	15.1%	84.9%
1970**	854,952			637,046	Wallace, George C.	217,906	637,046 D		74.5%		100.0%
1966	848,101	262,943	Martin, James D.	537,505	Wallace, Lurleen B.	47,653	274,562 D	31.0%	63.4%	32.8%	67.2%
1962	315,776			303,987	Wallace, George C.	11,789	303,987 D		96.3%		100.0%
1958	270,952	30,415	Longshore, William L. Jr.	239,633	Patterson, John	904	209,218 D	11.2%	88.4%	11.3%	88.7%
1954	333,090	88,688	Abernethy, Tom	244,401	Folsom, James E.	1	155,713 D	26.6%	73.4%	26.6%	73.4%
1950	170,591	15,177	Crowder, John S.	155,414	Persons, Gordon		140,237 D	8.9%	91.1%	8.9%	91.1%
1946	197,321	22,362	Ward, Lyman	174,959	Folsom, James E.		152,597 D	11.3%	88.7%	11.3%	88.7%

Note: An asterisk (*) denotes incumbent. **In past elections, the other vote included: 1970 - 125,491 National Democratic Party of Alabama (John Logan Cashin), who finished second. The Republican Party did not run a candidate in the 1962 and 1970 gubernatorial elections.

POSTWAR VOTE FOR SENATOR

Year	Total Vote	Republican Vote	Republican Candidate	Democratic Vote	Democratic Candidate	Other Vote	Rep.-Dem. Plurality	Total Vote Rep.	Total Vote Dem.	Major Vote Rep.	Major Vote Dem.
2022	1,414,238	942,154	Britt, Katie	436,746	Boyd, Will	35,338	505,408 R	66.6%	30.9%	68.3%	31.7%
2020	2,316,445	1,392,076	Tuberville, Thomas	920,478	Jones, Doug*	3,891	471,598 R	60.1%	39.7%	60.2%	39.8%
2017S**	1,348,720	651,972	Moore, Roy	673,896	Jones, Doug	22,852	21,924 D	48.3%	50.0%	49.2%	50.8%
2016	2,087,444	1,335,104	Shelby, Richard C.*	748,709	Crumpton, Ron	3,631	586,395 R	64.0%	35.9%	64.1%	35.9%
2014	818,090	795,606	Sessions, Jeff*			22,484	795,606 R	97.3%		100.0%	
2010	1,485,499	968,181	Shelby, Richard C.*	515,619	Barnes, William G.	1,699	452,562 R	65.2%	34.7%	65.3%	34.7%
2008	2,060,191	1,305,383	Sessions, Jeff*	752,391	Figures, Vivian Davis	2,417	552,992 R	63.4%	36.5%	63.4%	36.6%
2004	1,839,066	1,242,200	Shelby, Richard C.*	595,018	Sowell, Wayne	1,848	647,182 R	67.5%	32.4%	67.6%	32.4%
2002	1,353,023	792,561	Sessions, Jeff*	538,878	Parker, Susan	21,584	253,683 R	58.6%	39.8%	59.5%	40.5%
1998	1,293,405	817,973	Shelby, Richard C.*	474,568	Suddith, Clayton	864	343,405 R	63.2%	36.7%	63.3%	36.7%
1996	1,499,393	786,436	Sessions, Jeff	681,651	Bedford, Roger	31,306	104,785 R	52.5%	45.5%	53.6%	46.4%
1992	1,577,899	522,015	Sellers, Richard	1,022,698	Shelby, Richard C.	33,186	500,683 D	33.1%	64.8%	33.8%	66.2%
1990	1,185,563	467,190	Cabaniss, Bill	717,814	Heflin, Howell*	559	250,624 D	39.4%	60.5%	39.4%	60.6%
1986	1,211,953	602,537	Denton, Jeremiah*	609,360	Shelby, Richard C.	56	6,823 D	49.7%	50.3%	49.7%	50.3%
1984	1,371,238	498,508	Smith, Albert Lee Jr.	860,535	Heflin, Howell*	12,195	362,027 D	36.4%	62.8%	36.7%	63.3%
1980	1,296,757	650,362	Denton, Jeremiah	610,175	Folsom, James E. Jr.	36,220	40,187 R	50.2%	47.1%	51.6%	48.4%
1978	582,025			547,054	Heflin, Howell	34,971	547,054 D		94.0%		100.0%
1978S**	731,610	316,170	Martin, James D.	401,852	Stewart, Donald W.	13,588	85,682 D	43.2%	54.9%	44.0%	56.0%
1974	523,290			501,541	Allen, James B.*	21,749	501,541 D		95.8%		100.0%
1972	1,051,099	347,523	Blount, Winton M.	654,491	Sparkman, Richard D.*	49,085	306,968 D	33.1%	62.3%	34.7%	65.3%
1968	912,708	201,227	Hooper, Perry	638,774	Allen, James B.	72,707	437,547 D	22.0%	70.0%	24.0%	76.0%
1966	802,608	313,018	Grenier, John	482,138	Sparkman, John J.*	7,452	169,120 D	39.0%	60.1%	39.4%	60.6%
1962	397,079	195,134	Martin, James D.	201,937	Hill, Lister*	8	6,803 D	49.1%	50.9%	49.1%	50.9%
1960	554,081	164,868	Elgin, Julian	389,196	Sparkman, John J.*	17	224,328 D	29.8%	70.2%	29.8%	70.2%
1956	330,191			330,182	Hill, Lister*	9	330,182 D		100.0%		100.0%
1954	314,459	55,110	Guin, J. Foy Jr.	259,348	Sparkman, John J.*	1	204,238 D	17.5%	82.5%	17.5%	82.5%
1950	164,011			125,534	Hill, Lister*	38,477	125,534 D		76.5%		100.0%
1948	220,875	35,341	Parsons, Paul G.	185,534	Sparkman, John J.		150,193 D	16.0%	84.0%	16.0%	84.0%
1946S**	163,217			163,217	Sparkman, John J.*		163,217 D		100.0%		100.0%

Note: An asterisk (*) denotes incumbent. **The 1946 election, one of the 1978 elections, and the 2017 election were for short terms to fill vacancies. The Republican Party did not run a candidate in Senate elections in 1946, 1950, 1956, 1974, and 1978.

ALABAMA
GOVERNOR 2022

2020 Census Population	County	Total Vote	Republican (Ivey)	Democratic (Flowers)	Other	Rep.-Dem. Plurality	Total Vote Rep.	Total Vote Dem.	Major Vote Rep.	Major Vote Dem.
56,059	AUTAUGA	17,744	13,387	3,515	842	9,872 R	75.4%	19.8%	79.2%	20.8%
225,463	BALDWIN	73,187	58,823	10,296	4,068	48,527 R	80.4%	14.1%	85.1%	14.9%
24,575	BARBOUR	6,548	3,888	2,549	111	1,339 R	59.4%	38.9%	60.4%	39.6%
22,427	BIBB	5,884	4,681	930	273	3,751 R	79.6%	15.8%	83.4%	16.6%
57,997	BLOUNT	16,605	14,895	930	780	13,965 R	89.7%	5.6%	94.1%	5.9%
10,096	BULLOCK	2,653	802	1,806	45	1,004 D	30.2%	68.1%	30.8%	69.2%
19,424	BUTLER	5,932	3,856	1,937	139	1,919 R	65.0%	32.7%	66.6%	33.4%
113,714	CALHOUN	30,122	22,158	6,912	1,052	15,246 R	73.6%	22.9%	76.2%	23.8%
33,275	CHAMBERS	9,150	5,961	2,890	299	3,071 R	65.1%	31.6%	67.3%	32.7%
26,346	CHEROKEE	7,838	6,971	653	214	6,318 R	88.9%	8.3%	91.4%	8.6%
44,525	CHILTON	12,217	10,541	1,268	408	9,273 R	86.3%	10.4%	89.3%	10.7%
12,574	CHOCTAW	5,245	3,300	1,841	104	1,459 R	62.9%	35.1%	64.2%	35.8%
23,592	CLARKE	9,047	5,359	3,556	132	1,803 R	59.2%	39.3%	60.1%	39.9%
13,250	CLAY	4,245	3,638	480	127	3,158 R	85.7%	11.3%	88.3%	11.7%
14,941	CLEBURNE	4,617	4,200	276	141	3,924 R	91.0%	6.0%	93.8%	6.2%
52,521	COFFEE	14,004	11,267	2,221	516	9,046 R	80.5%	15.9%	83.5%	16.5%
55,354	COLBERT	17,274	13,001	3,739	534	9,262 R	75.3%	21.6%	77.7%	22.3%
12,050	CONECUH	4,477	2,618	1,782	77	836 R	58.5%	39.8%	59.5%	40.5%
10,687	COOSA	3,829	2,685	1,001	143	1,684 R	70.1%	26.1%	72.8%	27.2%
37,134	COVINGTON	11,274	9,735	1,193	346	8,542 R	86.3%	10.6%	89.1%	10.9%
13,798	CRENSHAW	4,591	3,622	851	118	2,771 R	78.9%	18.5%	81.0%	19.0%
84,084	CULLMAN	26,174	23,277	1,662	1,235	21,615 R	88.9%	6.3%	93.3%	6.7%
49,102	DALE	12,006	9,363	2,222	421	7,141 R	78.0%	18.5%	80.8%	19.2%
36,960	DALLAS	11,351	4,060	7,165	126	3,105 D	35.8%	63.1%	36.2%	63.8%
71,651	DEKALB	17,133	15,227	1,471	435	13,756 R	88.9%	8.6%	91.2%	8.8%
81,661	ELMORE	25,773	20,189	4,508	1,076	15,681 R	78.3%	17.5%	81.7%	18.3%
36,768	ESCAMBIA	9,682	7,286	2,167	229	5,119 R	75.3%	22.4%	77.1%	22.9%
102,381	ETOWAH	26,118	20,685	4,593	840	16,092 R	79.2%	17.6%	81.8%	18.2%
16,311	FAYETTE	5,513	4,708	628	177	4,080 R	85.4%	11.4%	88.2%	11.8%
31,353	FRANKLIN	7,452	6,592	646	214	5,946 R	88.5%	8.7%	91.1%	8.9%
26,333	GENEVA	7,978	7,049	700	229	6,349 R	88.4%	8.8%	91.0%	9.0%
8,096	GREENE	2,992	608	2,339	45	1,731 D	20.3%	78.2%	20.6%	79.4%
14,647	HALE	5,206	2,288	2,818	100	530 D	43.9%	54.1%	44.8%	55.2%
17,283	HENRY	6,751	5,102	1,490	159	3,612 R	75.6%	22.1%	77.4%	22.6%
106,174	HOUSTON	27,625	21,139	5,634	852	15,505 R	76.5%	20.4%	79.0%	21.0%
51,745	JACKSON	13,383	11,630	1,386	367	10,244 R	86.9%	10.4%	89.4%	10.6%
658,926	JEFFERSON	197,567	92,583	96,175	8,809	3,592 D	46.9%	48.7%	49.0%	51.0%
13,811	LAMAR	4,377	3,831	415	131	3,416 R	87.5%	9.5%	90.2%	9.8%
92,926	LAUDERDALE	25,901	20,235	4,761	905	15,474 R	78.1%	18.4%	81.0%	19.0%
32,984	LAWRENCE	10,798	8,629	1,707	462	6,922 R	79.9%	15.8%	83.5%	16.5%
165,375	LEE	40,593	27,242	11,803	1,548	15,439 R	67.1%	29.1%	69.8%	30.2%
99,825	LIMESTONE	31,372	23,770	6,289	1,313	17,481 R	75.8%	20.0%	79.1%	20.9%
9,686	LOWNDES	4,086	1,309	2,706	71	1,397 D	32.0%	66.2%	32.6%	67.4%
18,031	MACON	5,369	1,244	3,994	131	2,750 D	23.2%	74.4%	23.7%	76.3%
374,983	MADISON	120,378	72,059	42,176	6,143	29,883 R	59.9%	35.0%	63.1%	36.9%
18,832	MARENGO	7,293	3,851	3,317	125	534 R	52.8%	45.5%	53.7%	46.3%
29,782	MARION	8,409	7,625	528	256	7,097 R	90.7%	6.3%	93.5%	6.5%
96,982	MARSHALL	24,240	21,345	2,077	818	19,268 R	88.1%	8.6%	91.1%	8.9%
413,330	MOBILE	107,135	63,593	38,910	4,632	24,683 R	59.4%	36.3%	62.0%	38.0%
20,697	MONROE	7,044	4,313	2,609	122	1,704 R	61.2%	37.0%	62.3%	37.7%
225,904	MONTGOMERY	57,712	23,565	32,511	1,636	8,946 D	40.8%	56.3%	42.0%	58.0%
119,864	MORGAN	32,135	25,484	5,362	1,289	20,122 R	79.3%	16.7%	82.6%	17.4%
8,905	PERRY	3,185	942	2,187	56	1,245 D	29.6%	68.7%	30.1%	69.9%
19,928	PICKENS	6,609	4,212	2,249	148	1,963 R	63.7%	34.0%	65.2%	34.8%
33,118	PIKE	8,146	5,375	2,568	203	2,807 R	66.0%	31.5%	67.7%	32.3%
22,779	RANDOLPH	6,587	5,462	925	200	4,537 R	82.9%	14.0%	85.5%	14.5%
58,095	RUSSELL	11,569	6,144	5,146	279	998 R	53.1%	44.5%	54.4%	45.6%
218,514	SHELBY	69,939	51,196	14,913	3,830	36,283 R	73.2%	21.3%	77.4%	22.6%
90,004	ST. CLAIR	27,923	23,055	3,606	1,262	19,449 R	82.6%	12.9%	86.5%	13.5%
12,396	SUMTER	3,884	1,176	2,656	52	1,480 D	30.3%	68.4%	30.7%	69.3%

ALABAMA
GOVERNOR 2022

2020 Census Population	County	Total Vote	Republican (Ivey)	Democratic (Flowers)	Other	Rep.-Dem. Plurality	Total Vote Rep.	Total Vote Dem.	Major Vote Rep.	Major Vote Dem.
80,019	TALLADEGA	21,644	14,313	6,684	647	7,629 R	66.1%	30.9%	68.2%	31.8%
40,416	TALLAPOOSA	13,573	10,444	2,751	378	7,693 R	76.9%	20.3%	79.2%	20.8%
210,089	TUSCALOOSA	51,599	31,841	17,937	1,821	13,904 R	61.7%	34.8%	64.0%	36.0%
63,655	WALKER	17,836	15,217	1,905	714	13,312 R	85.3%	10.7%	88.9%	11.1%
16,314	WASHINGTON	5,929	4,584	1,206	139	3,378 R	77.3%	20.3%	79.2%	20.8%
10,364	WILCOX	3,903	1,371	2,489	43	1,118 D	35.1%	63.8%	35.5%	64.5%
23,651	WINSTON	6,928	6,331	344	253	5,987 R	91.4%	5.0%	94.8%	5.2%
4,914,536	TOTAL	1,415,283	946,932	412,961	55,390	533,971 R	66.9%	29.2%	69.6%	30.4%

ALABAMA
SENATOR 2022

2020 Census Population	County	Total Vote	Republican (Britt)	Democratic (Boyd)	Other	Rep.-Dem. Plurality	Total Vote Rep.	Total Vote Dem.	Major Vote Rep.	Major Vote Dem.
56,059	AUTAUGA	17,740	13,359	3,814	567	9,545 R	75.3%	21.5%	77.8%	22.2%
225,463	BALDWIN	73,197	59,501	11,478	2,218	48,023 R	81.3%	15.7%	83.8%	16.2%
24,575	BARBOUR	6,543	3,861	2,620	62	1,241 R	59.0%	40.0%	59.6%	40.4%
22,427	BIBB	5,869	4,694	971	204	3,723 R	80.0%	16.5%	82.9%	17.1%
57,997	BLOUNT	16,586	14,904	1,130	552	13,774 R	89.9%	6.8%	93.0%	7.0%
10,096	BULLOCK	2,644	785	1,827	32	1,042 D	29.7%	69.1%	30.1%	69.9%
19,424	BUTLER	5,909	3,789	2,039	81	1,750 R	64.1%	34.5%	65.0%	35.0%
113,714	CALHOUN	30,081	22,008	7,365	708	14,643 R	73.2%	24.5%	74.9%	25.1%
33,275	CHAMBERS	9,099	5,917	2,997	185	2,920 R	65.0%	32.9%	66.4%	33.6%
26,346	CHEROKEE	7,835	6,947	761	127	6,186 R	88.7%	9.7%	90.1%	9.9%
44,525	CHILTON	12,164	10,386	1,407	371	8,979 R	85.4%	11.6%	88.1%	11.9%
12,574	CHOCTAW	5,154	3,198	1,899	57	1,299 R	62.0%	36.8%	62.7%	37.3%
23,592	CLARKE	9,019	5,348	3,613	58	1,735 R	59.3%	40.1%	59.7%	40.3%
13,250	CLAY	4,233	3,628	505	100	3,123 R	85.7%	11.9%	87.8%	12.2%
14,941	CLEBURNE	4,604	4,212	308	84	3,904 R	91.5%	6.7%	93.2%	6.8%
52,521	COFFEE	13,998	11,411	2,298	289	9,113 R	81.5%	16.4%	83.2%	16.8%
55,354	COLBERT	17,256	12,748	4,181	327	8,567 R	73.9%	24.2%	75.3%	24.7%
12,050	CONECUH	4,435	2,564	1,830	41	734 R	57.8%	41.3%	58.4%	41.6%
10,687	COOSA	3,816	2,662	1,042	112	1,620 R	69.8%	27.3%	71.9%	28.1%
37,134	COVINGTON	11,272	9,852	1,289	131	8,563 R	87.4%	11.4%	88.4%	11.6%
13,798	CRENSHAW	4,562	3,607	895	60	2,712 R	79.1%	19.6%	80.1%	19.9%
84,084	CULLMAN	26,123	23,228	1,951	944	21,277 R	88.9%	7.5%	92.3%	7.7%
49,102	DALE	11,999	9,458	2,326	215	7,132 R	78.8%	19.4%	80.3%	19.7%
36,960	DALLAS	11,311	3,888	7,312	111	3,424 D	34.4%	64.6%	34.7%	65.3%
71,651	DEKALB	17,134	15,200	1,679	255	13,521 R	88.7%	9.8%	90.1%	9.9%
81,661	ELMORE	25,739	20,167	4,866	706	15,301 R	78.4%	18.9%	80.6%	19.4%
36,768	ESCAMBIA	9,652	7,284	2,247	121	5,037 R	75.5%	23.3%	76.4%	23.6%
102,381	ETOWAH	26,092	20,599	4,925	568	15,674 R	78.9%	18.9%	80.7%	19.3%
16,311	FAYETTE	5,501	4,697	690	114	4,007 R	85.4%	12.5%	87.2%	12.8%
31,353	FRANKLIN	7,438	6,547	770	121	5,777 R	88.0%	10.4%	89.5%	10.5%
26,333	GENEVA	7,978	7,113	763	102	6,350 R	89.2%	9.6%	90.3%	9.7%
8,096	GREENE	2,966	597	2,337	32	1,740 D	20.1%	78.8%	20.3%	79.7%
14,647	HALE	5,173	2,298	2,790	85	492 D	44.4%	53.9%	45.2%	54.8%
17,283	HENRY	6,732	5,085	1,560	87	3,525 R	75.5%	23.2%	76.5%	23.5%
106,174	HOUSTON	27,608	21,246	5,854	508	15,392 R	77.0%	21.2%	78.4%	21.6%
51,745	JACKSON	13,372	11,617	1,518	237	10,099 R	86.9%	11.4%	88.4%	11.6%
658,926	JEFFERSON	197,832	91,802	100,792	5,238	8,990 D	46.4%	50.9%	47.7%	52.3%
13,811	LAMAR	4,376	3,869	447	60	3,422 R	88.4%	10.2%	89.6%	10.4%
92,926	LAUDERDALE	25,888	19,893	5,453	542	14,440 R	76.8%	21.1%	78.5%	21.5%
32,984	LAWRENCE	10,728	8,573	1,916	239	6,657 R	79.9%	17.9%	81.7%	18.3%

ALABAMA
SENATOR 2022

2020 Census Population	County	Total Vote	Republican (Britt)	Democratic (Boyd)	Other	Rep.-Dem. Plurality	Total Vote Rep.	Total Vote Dem.	Major Vote Rep.	Major Vote Dem.
165,375	LEE	40,582	26,966	12,458	1,158	14,508 R	66.4%	30.7%	68.4%	31.6%
99,825	LIMESTONE	31,340	23,422	7,037	881	16,385 R	74.7%	22.5%	76.9%	23.1%
9,686	LOWNDES	4,071	1,277	2,734	60	1,457 D	31.4%	67.2%	31.8%	68.2%
18,031	MACON	5,371	1,153	4,131	87	2,978 D	21.5%	76.9%	21.8%	78.2%
374,983	MADISON	120,500	70,577	45,976	3,947	24,601 R	58.6%	38.2%	60.6%	39.4%
18,832	MARENGO	7,264	3,807	3,375	82	432 R	52.4%	46.5%	53.0%	47.0%
29,782	MARION	8,387	7,636	591	160	7,045 R	91.0%	7.0%	92.8%	7.2%
96,982	MARSHALL	24,227	21,211	2,461	555	18,750 R	87.6%	10.2%	89.6%	10.4%
413,330	MOBILE	107,100	64,378	40,266	2,456	24,112 R	60.1%	37.6%	61.5%	38.5%
20,697	MONROE	7,026	4,270	2,678	78	1,592 R	60.8%	38.1%	61.5%	38.5%
225,904	MONTGOMERY	57,705	22,741	33,685	1,279	10,944 D	39.4%	58.4%	40.3%	59.7%
119,864	MORGAN	32,105	25,310	5,879	916	19,431 R	78.8%	18.3%	81.2%	18.8%
8,905	PERRY	3,176	898	2,224	54	1,326 D	28.3%	70.0%	28.8%	71.2%
19,928	PICKENS	6,571	4,225	2,248	98	1,977 R	64.3%	34.2%	65.3%	34.7%
33,118	PIKE	8,135	5,359	2,661	115	2,698 R	65.9%	32.7%	66.8%	33.2%
22,779	RANDOLPH	6,577	5,471	991	115	4,480 R	83.2%	15.1%	84.7%	15.3%
58,095	RUSSELL	11,545	5,967	5,398	180	569 R	51.7%	46.8%	52.5%	47.5%
218,514	SHELBY	69,874	50,762	16,276	2,836	34,486 R	72.6%	23.3%	75.7%	24.3%
90,004	ST. CLAIR	27,920	23,049	3,933	938	19,116 R	82.6%	14.1%	85.4%	14.6%
12,396	SUMTER	3,876	1,163	2,684	29	1,521 D	30.0%	69.2%	30.2%	69.8%
80,019	TALLADEGA	21,620	14,269	6,891	460	7,378 R	66.0%	31.9%	67.4%	32.6%
40,416	TALLAPOOSA	13,568	10,421	2,914	233	7,507 R	76.8%	21.5%	78.1%	21.9%
210,089	TUSCALOOSA	51,626	31,879	18,591	1,156	13,288 R	61.7%	36.0%	63.2%	36.8%
63,655	WALKER	17,821	15,206	2,083	532	13,123 R	85.3%	11.7%	88.0%	12.0%
16,314	WASHINGTON	5,878	4,557	1,267	54	3,290 R	77.5%	21.6%	78.2%	21.8%
10,364	WILCOX	3,812	1,329	2,446	37	1,117 D	34.9%	64.2%	35.2%	64.8%
23,651	WINSTON	6,903	6,309	403	191	5,906 R	91.4%	5.8%	94.0%	6.0%
4,914,536	TOTAL	1,414,238	942,154	436,746	35,338	505,408 R	66.6%	30.9%	68.3%	31.7%

ALABAMA
HOUSE OF REPRESENTATIVES

CD	Year	Total Vote	Republican Vote	Republican Candidate	Democratic Vote	Democratic Candidate	Other Vote	Plurality	Total Vote Rep.	Total Vote Dem.	Major Vote Rep.	Major Vote Dem.
1	2022	168,150	140,592	CARL, JERRY*			27,558	140,592 R	83.6%		100.0%	
1	2020	329,075	211,825	CARL, JERRY	116,949	AVERHART, JAMES	301	94,876 R	64.4%	35.5%	64.4%	35.6%
1	2018	242,617	153,228	BYRNE, BRADLEY*	89,226	KENNEDY, ROBERT JR.	163	64,002 R	63.2%	36.8%	63.2%	36.8%
1	2016	215,893	208,083	BYRNE, BRADLEY*			7,810	208,083 R	96.4%		100.0%	
1	2014	152,234	103,758	BYRNE, BRADLEY*	48,278	LEFLORE, BURTON R.	198	55,480 R	68.2%	31.7%	68.2%	31.8%
1	2012	200,676	196,374	BONNER, JOSIAH ROBBINS "JO" JR.*			4,302	196,374 R	97.9%		100.0%	
2	2022	198,961	137,460	MOORE, BARRY*	58,014	HARVEY-HALL, PHYLLIS	3,487	79,446 R	69.1%	29.2%	70.3%	29.7%
2	2020	303,569	197,996	MOORE, BARRY	105,286	HARVEY-HALL, PHYLLIS	287	92,710 R	65.2%	34.7%	65.3%	34.7%
2	2018	226,230	138,879	ROBY, MARTHA*	86,931	ISNER, TABITHA	420	51,948 R	61.4%	38.4%	61.5%	38.5%
2	2016	276,584	134,886	ROBY, MARTHA*	112,089	MATHIS, NATHAN	29,609	22,797 R	48.8%	40.5%	54.6%	45.4%
2	2014	167,952	113,103	ROBY, MARTHA*	54,692	WRIGHT, ERICK	157	58,411 R	67.3%	32.6%	67.4%	32.6%
2	2012	283,953	180,591	ROBY, MARTHA*	103,092	FORD, THERESE	270	77,499 R	63.6%	36.3%	63.7%	36.3%
3	2022	190,406	135,602	ROGERS, MIKE D.*	47,859	VEASEY, LIN	6,945	87,743 R	71.2%	25.1%	73.9%	26.1%
3	2020	322,234	217,384	ROGERS, MIKE D.*	104,595	WINFREY, ADIA MCCLELLAN	255	112,789 R	67.5%	32.5%	67.5%	32.5%
3	2018	231,915	147,770	ROGERS, MIKE D.*	83,996	HAGAN, MALLORY	149	63,774 R	63.7%	36.2%	63.8%	36.2%
3	2016	287,104	192,164	ROGERS, MIKE D.*	94,549	SMITH, JESSE TREMAIN	391	97,615 R	66.9%	32.9%	67.0%	33.0%
3	2014	156,620	103,558	ROGERS, MIKE D.*	52,816	SMITH, JESSE TREMAIN	246	50,742 R	66.1%	33.7%	66.2%	33.8%
3	2012	273,930	175,306	ROGERS, MIKE D.*	98,141	HARRIS, JOHN ANDREW	483	77,165 R	64.0%	35.8%	64.1%	35.9%

ALABAMA

HOUSE OF REPRESENTATIVES

			Republican		Democratic		Other		Total Vote		Major Vote	
CD	Year	Total Vote	Vote	Candidate	Vote	Candidate	Vote	Plurality	Rep.	Dem.	Rep.	Dem.
4	2022	195,733	164,655	ADERHOLT, ROBERT*	26,694	NEIGHBORS, RICK	4,384	137,961 R	84.1%	13.6%	86.0%	14.0%
4	2020	318,083	261,553	ADERHOLT, ROBERT*	56,237	NEIGHBORS, RICK	293	205,316 R	82.2%	17.7%	82.3%	17.7%
4	2018	230,969	184,255	ADERHOLT, ROBERT*	46,492	AUMAN, LEE	222	137,763 R	79.8%	20.1%	79.9%	20.1%
4	2016	239,444	235,925	ADERHOLT, ROBERT*			3,519	235,925 R	98.5%		100.0%	
4	2014	134,752	132,831	ADERHOLT, ROBERT*			1,921	132,831 R	98.6%		100.0%	
4	2012	269,118	199,071	ADERHOLT, ROBERT*	69,706	BOMAN, DANIEL H.	341	129,365 R	74.0%	25.9%	74.1%	25.9%
5	2022	212,317	142,435	STRONG, DALE	62,740	WARNER-STANTON, KATHY	7,142	79,695 R	67.1%	29.6%	69.4%	30.6%
5	2020	264,160	253,094	BROOKS, MO*			11,066	253,094 R	95.8%		100.0%	
5	2018	260,673	159,063	BROOKS, MO*	101,388	JOFFRION, PETER	222	57,675 R	61.0%	38.9%	61.1%	38.9%
5	2016	308,326	205,647	BROOKS, MO*	102,234	BOYD, WILL	445	103,413 R	66.7%	33.2%	66.8%	33.2%
5	2014	154,974	115,338	BROOKS, MO*			39,636	115,338 R	74.4%		100.0%	
5	2012	291,293	189,185	BROOKS, MO*	101,772	HOLLEY, CHARLIE L.	336	87,413 R	64.9%	34.9%	65.0%	35.0%
6	2022	184,203	154,233	PALMER, GARY*			29,970	154,233 R	83.7%		100.0%	
6	2020	282,261	274,160	PALMER, GARY*			8,101	274,160 R	97.1%		100.0%	
6	2018	278,328	192,542	PALMER, GARY*	85,644	KLINE, DANNER	142	106,898 R	69.2%	30.8%	69.2%	30.8%
6	2016	329,306	245,313	PALMER, GARY*	83,709	PUTMAN, DAVID	284	161,604 R	74.5%	25.4%	74.6%	25.4%
6	2014	178,449	135,945	PALMER, GARY	42,291	LESTER, MARK	213	93,654 R	76.2%	23.7%	76.3%	23.7%
6	2012	308,102	219,262	BACHUS, SPENCER*	88,267	BAILEY, PENNY "COLONEL"	573	130,995 R	71.2%	28.6%	71.3%	28.7%
7	2022	193,940	67,416	NICHOLS, BEATRICE	123,233	SEWELL, TERRI A.*	3,291	55,817 D	34.8%	63.5%	35.4%	64.6%
7	2020	232,331			225,742	SEWELL, TERRI A.*	6,589	225,742 D		97.2%		100.0%
7	2018	189,163			185,010	SEWELL, TERRI A.*	4,153	185,010 D		97.8%		100.0%
7	2016	233,028			229,330	SEWELL, TERRI A.*	3,698	229,330 D		98.4%		100.0%
7	2014	135,899			133,687	SEWELL, TERRI A.*	2,212	133,687 D		98.4%		100.0%
7	2012	306,558	73,835	CHAMBERLAIN, DON	232,520	SEWELL, TERRI A.*	203	158,685 D	24.1%	75.8%	24.1%	75.9%
TOTAL	2022	1,343,710	942,393		318,540		82,777	623,853 R	70.1%	23.7%	74.7%	25.3%
TOTAL	2020	2,051,713	1,416,012		608,809		26,892	807,203 R	69.0%	29.7%	69.9%	30.1%
TOTAL	2018	1,659,895	975,737		678,687		5,471	297,050 R	58.8%	40.9%	59.0%	41.0%
TOTAL	2016	1,889,685	1,222,018		621,911		45,756	600,107 R	64.7%	32.9%	66.3%	33.7%
TOTAL	2014	1,080,880	704,533		331,764		44,583	372,769 R	65.2%	30.7%	68.0%	32.0%
TOTAL	2012	1,933,630	1,233,624		693,498		6,508	540,126 R	63.8%	35.9%	64.0%	36.0%

Note: An asterisk (*) denotes incumbent.

ALABAMA

GENERAL AND PRIMARY ELECTIONS

GENERAL ELECTIONS: OTHER VOTE

Governor Other vote was 45,958 Libertarian (Jimmy Blake), 9,432 Write-In (Scattered Write-In)

Senate Other vote was 32,879 Libertarian (John Sophocleus), 2,459 Write-In (Scattered Write-Ins)

House Other vote was:

CD 1 26,369 Libertarian (Alexander Remrey), 1,189 Write-In (Scattered Write-In)
CD 2 3,396 Libertarian (Jonathan Realz), 91 Write-In (Scattered Write-In)
CD 3 3,831 Independent (Douglas Bell), 3,034 Libertarian (Thomas Casson), 80 Write-In (Scattered Write-In)
CD 4 4,303 Libertarian (Johnny Cochran), 81 Write-In (Scattered Write-In)
CD 5 6,773 Libertarian (Phillip Greer), 369 Write-In (Scattered Write-In)
CD 6 27,833 Libertarian (Andria Chieffo), 2,137 Write-In (Scattered Write-In)
CD 7 3,212 Libertarian (Gavin Goodman), 79 Write-In (Scattered Write-In)

ALABAMA

GENERAL AND PRIMARY ELECTIONS

2022 PRIMARY ELECTIONS: SUPPLEMENTARY INFORMATION

Primary	May 24, 2022	Registration (as of May 24, 2022, and includes 444,310 inactive registrants)	3,638,986	No Party Registration
Primary Runoff	June 21, 2022			
Primary Type	Open—Any registered voter could vote in either the Democratic or the Republican primary. Democratic primary voters could participate in a Republican runoff. However, Republican primary voters could not cast a ballot in a Democratic runoff.			

	REPUBLICAN PRIMARIES			DEMOCRATIC PRIMARIES		
President						
Senator	Britt, Katie	289,425	44.8%	Boyd, Will	107,588	63.7%
	Brooks, Mo	188,539	29.2%	Dean, Brandaun	32,863	19.5%
	Durant, Michael "Mike"	150,817	23.3%	Jackson, Lanny	28,402	16.8%
	Schafer, Jake	7,371	1.1%			
	Dupriest, Karla	5,739	0.9%			
	Boddie, Lillie	4,849	0.7%			
	TOTAL	646,740		TOTAL	168,853	
	PRIMARY RUNOFF					
	Britt, Katie	253,251	63.0%			
	Brooks, Mo	148,636	37.0%			
	TOTAL	401,887				
Governor	Ivey, Kay	357,069	54.5%	Flowers, Yolanda Rochelle	56,991	33.9%
	Blanchard, Lindy	126,202	19.2%	Sanders-Fortier, Malika	54,699	32.5%
	James, Tim	106,181	16.2%	Jamieson, Patricia Salter	19,691	11.7%
	Burdette, Lew	42,924	6.5%	Kennedy, Arthur	15,630	9.3%
	Odle, Dean	11,767	1.8%	Smith, Doug "New Blue"	11,861	7.1%
	Jones, Donald Trent	3,821	0.6%	Martin, Chad "Chig"	9,352	5.6%
	Thomas, Dave	2,886	0.4%			
	George, Stacy Lee	2,546	0.4%			
	Young, Dean	2,356	0.4%			
	TOTAL	655,752		TOTAL	168,224	
				PRIMARY RUNOFF		
				Flowers, Yolanda Rochelle	32,529	55.1%
				Sanders-Fortier, Malika	26,469	44.9%
				TOTAL	58,998	
Congressional District 1						
Congressional District 2				Harvey-Hall, Phyllis	16,884	66.9%
				Patel, Vimal	8,347	33.1%
				TOTAL	25,231	
Congressional District 3	Rogers, Mike D.*	70,843	81.9%			
	Joiner, Michael T.	15,618	18.1%			
	TOTAL	86,461				
Congressional District 4				Neighbors, Rick	4,500	54.1%
				Gore, Rhonda	3,823	45.9%
				TOTAL	8,323	

ALABAMA
GENERAL AND PRIMARY ELECTIONS

Congressional District 5	Strong, Dale	45,319	44.7%	Warner-Stanton, Kathy	9,010	57.2%
	Wardynski, Casey	23,340	23.0%	Thompson, Charles Charlie	6,739	42.8%
	Roberts, John	13,979	13.8%			
	Sanford, Paul	11,573	11.4%			
	Blalock, Andy	5,608	5.5%			
	Wright, Harrison	1,509	1.5%			
	TOTAL	101,328		TOTAL	15,749	
	PRIMARY RUNOFF					
	Strong, Dale	48,138	63.4%			
	Wardynski, Casey	27,794	36.6%			
	TOTAL	75,932				
Congressional District 6						
Congressional District 7						

Note: An asterisk (*) denotes incumbent.

ALASKA

Statewide and House Races:

The 2022 elections in Alaska were shaped by two events. First, in 2020, Alaska voters narrowly approved Measure 2, which scrapped the state's partisan primary system and established a hybrid ranked-choice system. Under the new format, all candidates run on the same primary ballot and the top four finishers advance to a ranked-choice general election. The second key event came in March 2022. On a flight back home, Rep. Don Young (R), the curmudgeonly Dean of the House who had just reached 49 years in office, died unexpectedly. Though Young was 88, he could have easily passed for 68, and he kept a busy schedule – so his death came as a surprise. Importantly, this prompted a special election which gave the new ranked-choice system an early "test run."

But before the special election to replace Young had taken shape, the state's 2022 Senate contest was already underway. With Young's death, Republican Sen. Lisa Murkowski, who could be described as a political maverick, became the most senior member of the state's federal delegation. In 2010, she lost a GOP primary to a more right-wing challenger but made history in the general election as the first write-in candidate to win a Senate race since 1954 – she was heavily dependent on Native Americans and other usually Democratic constituencies. Her 2016 race flew under the radar, but she later earned Trump's ire by voting to convict him after the January 6 insurrection. Kelly Tshibaka, an environmental lawyer, got into the race in 2021 and quickly garnered Trump's support. Though Murkowski again courted Democratic votes, she got some financial cover from *Senate Leadership Fund*, a super PAC tied to Senate Republican Leader Mitch McConnell.

The special primary to replace Young drew roughly 50 candidates. The first-place finisher had left office a dozen years earlier but was well-known to state and national political observers: former Gov. Sarah Palin, who was also the GOP's 2008 vice presidential nominee. The second-place finisher was Nick Begich III, a Republican from a prominent Democratic political family who was running even before Young died. The last candidate to advance was Democrat Mary Peltola, an Alaska Native who served in the legislature (one of the top four candidates withdrew, so only three candidates advanced). Running on a memorable slogan – "Fish. Family. Freedom." – Peltola upset Palin by 3 points in the August special election.

The general election, a few months later, was a victory for what could be called the moderate "Don Young ticket." Despite their different parties, Peltola, as the incumbent, campaigned as a member who would carry on Young's work. She defeated Palin in a rematch by a comfortable 55%–45% margin. Meanwhile, Murkowski, who had a decades-long working relationship with Young that went back to her days as an intern for him, dispatched Tshibaka by a slightly lesser margin – her support overlapped with Peltola's.

Compared to the federal races, Alaska's gubernatorial contest seemed bland. First elected in 2018, Republican Gov. Mike Dunleavy had kept middling to decent approval ratings throughout most of his term. In the four-candidate second round that included his predecessor, Dunleavy took a small majority (taking 50.3 percent of the vote), precluding any additional ranked-choice balloting.

ALASKA

One member At Large

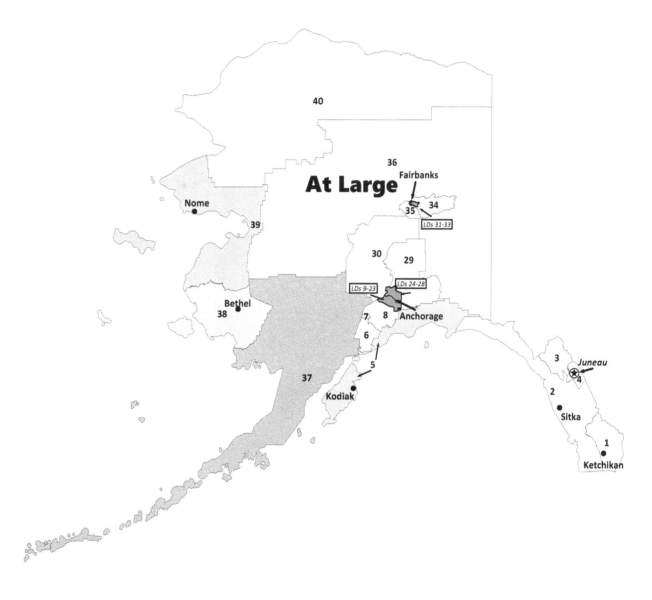

*Alaska reports election results by legislative district. The districts indicated were first effective for the 2022 elections on an interim basis.

*Legislative districts were established as an interim plan in May 2022 by the Alaska Redistricting Board.

Alaska includes more islands to the west of those that are illustrated on this map; they are in LD 37.

ALASKA

GOVERNOR
Mike Dunleavy (R). Reelected 2022 to a four-year term. Previously elected 2018.

SENATORS (2 Republicans)
Lisa Murkowski (R). Reelected 2022 to a six-year term. Previously elected 2004, 2010 as a write-in candidate, and 2016 as a Republican. Had been appointed December 20, 2002, to fill the vacancy created by the resignation of her father, Frank H. Murkowski (R), to become governor of Alaska.

Daniel Sullivan (R). Reelected 2020 to a six-year term. Previously elected 2014.

REPRESENTATIVE (1 Democrat)
At Large. Mary Sattler Peltola (D)

POSTWAR VOTE FOR PRESIDENT

		Republican		Democratic		Other Vote	Rep.-Dem. Plurality	Total Vote		Major Vote	
Year	Total Vote	Vote	Candidate	Vote	Candidate			Rep.	Dem.	Rep.	Dem.
2020	359,530	189,951	Trump, Donald J.*	153,778	Biden, Joseph R. Jr.	15,801	36,173 R	52.8%	42.8%	55.3%	44.7%
2016**	318,608	163,387	Trump, Donald J.	116,454	Clinton, Hillary Rodham	38,767	46,933 R	51.3%	36.6%	58.4%	41.6%
2012	300,495	164,676	Romney, W. Mitt	122,640	Obama, Barack H.*	13,179	42,036 R	54.8%	40.8%	57.3%	42.7%
2008	326,197	193,841	McCain, John S. III	123,594	Obama, Barack H.	8,762	70,247 R	59.4%	37.9%	61.1%	38.9%
2004	312,598	190,889	Bush, George W.*	111,025	Kerry, John F.	10,684	79,864 R	61.1%	35.5%	63.2%	36.8%
2000**	285,560	167,398	Bush, George W.	79,004	Gore, Albert Jr.	39,158	88,394 R	58.6%	27.7%	67.9%	32.1%
1996**	241,620	122,746	Dole, Robert "Bob"	80,380	Clinton, Bill*	38,494	42,366 R	50.8%	33.3%	60.4%	39.6%
1992**	258,506	102,000	Bush, George H.*	78,294	Clinton, Bill	78,212	23,706 R	39.5%	30.3%	56.6%	43.4%
1988	200,116	119,251	Bush, George H.	72,584	Dukakis, Michael S.	8,281	46,667 R	59.6%	36.3%	62.2%	37.8%
1984	207,605	138,377	Reagan, Ronald*	62,007	Mondale, Walter F.	7,221	76,370 R	66.7%	29.9%	69.1%	30.9%
1980**	158,445	86,112	Reagan, Ronald	41,842	Carter, Jimmy*	30,491	44,270 R	54.3%	26.4%	67.3%	32.7%
1976	123,574	71,555	Ford, Gerald R.*	44,058	Carter, Jimmy	7,961	27,497 R	57.9%	35.7%	61.9%	38.1%
1972	95,219	55,349	Nixon, Richard M.*	32,967	McGovern, George S.	6,903	22,382 R	58.1%	34.6%	62.7%	37.3%
1968**	83,035	37,600	Nixon, Richard M.	35,411	Humphrey, Hubert Horatio Jr.	10,024	2,189 R	45.3%	42.6%	51.5%	48.5%
1964	67,259	22,930	Goldwater, Barry M. Sr.	44,329	Johnson, Lyndon B.*		21,399 D	34.1%	65.9%	34.1%	65.9%
1960	60,762	30,953	Nixon, Richard M.	29,809	Kennedy, John F.		1,144 R	50.9%	49.1%	50.9%	49.1%

Note: An asterisk (*) denotes incumbent. **In past elections, the other vote included: 2016 - 18,725 Libertarian (Gary Johnson); 2000 - 28,747 Green (Ralph Nader); 1996 - 26,333 Reform (Ross Perot); 1992 - 73,481 Independent (Perot); 1980 - 18,479 Libertarian (Ed Clark) and 11,155 Independent (John Anderson); 1968 - 10,024 American Independent (George Wallace). Alaska was formally admitted as a state in January 1959.

ALASKA

POSTWAR VOTE FOR GOVERNOR

Year	Total Vote	Republican Vote	Republican Candidate	Democratic Vote	Democratic Candidate	Other Vote	Rep.-Dem. Plurality	Total Vote Rep.	Total Vote Dem.	Major Vote Rep.	Major Vote Dem.
2022	263,752	132,632	Dunleavy, Mike J.*	63,851	Gara, Les	67,269	68,781 R	54.8%	24.2%	69.3%	30.7%
2018	283,134	145,631	Dunleavy, Mike J.	125,739	Begich, Mark	11,764	19,892 R	51.4%	44.4%	53.7%	46.3%
2014**	279,958	128,435	Parnell, Sean R.*			151,523	128,435 R#	45.9%		100.0%	
2010	256,192	151,318	Parnell, Sean R.*	96,519	Berkowitz, Ethan A.	8,355	54,799 R	59.1%	37.7%	61.1%	38.9%
2006	237,322	114,697	Palin, Sarah H.	97,238	Knowles, Tony	25,387	17,459 R	48.3%	41.0%	54.1%	45.9%
2002	231,484	129,279	Murkowski, Frank H.	94,216	Ulmer, Fran	7,989	35,063 R	55.8%	40.7%	57.8%	42.2%
1998**	220,177	39,331	Lindauer, John	112,879	Knowles, Tony*	67,967	73,548 D	17.9%	51.3%	25.8%	74.2%
1994**	213,435	87,157	Campbell, James O.	87,693	Knowles, Tony*	38,585	536 D	40.8%	41.1%	49.8%	50.2%
1990**	194,750	50,991	Sturgulewski, Arliss	60,201	Knowles, Tony	83,558	9,210 D#	26.2%	30.9%	45.9%	54.1%
1986	179,555	76,515	Sturgulewski, Arliss	84,943	Cowper, Steve	18,097	8,428 D	42.6%	47.3%	47.4%	52.6%
1982**	194,885	72,291	Fink, Tom	89,918	Sheffield, Bill	32,676	17,627 D	37.1%	46.1%	44.6%	55.4%
1978**	126,910	49,580	Hammond, Jay S.*	25,656	Croft, Chancy	51,674	23,924 R	39.1%	20.2%	65.9%	34.1%
1974	96,163	45,840	Hammond, Jay S.	45,553	Egan, William A.*	4,770	287 R	47.7%	47.4%	50.2%	49.8%
1970	80,779	37,264	Miller, Keith	42,309	Egan, William A.	1,206	5,045 D	46.1%	52.4%	46.8%	53.2%
1966	66,294	33,145	Hickel, Walter J.	32,065	Egan, William A.*	1,084	1,080 R	50.0%	48.4%	50.8%	49.2%
1962	56,681	27,054	Stepovich, Mike	29,627	Egan, William A.*		2,573 D	47.7%	52.3%	47.7%	52.3%
1958	48,968	19,299	Butrovich, John Jr.	29,189	Egan, William A.	480	9,890 D	39.4%	59.6%	39.8%	60.2%

Note: An asterisk (*) denotes incumbent. A pound sign (#) in the plurality column indicates that the winners in 1990 and 2014 were independents. **In past elections, the other vote included: 2014 -134,658 Independent (Bill Walker); 1998 - 40,209 write-in (Robin Taylor), who finished second; 1994 - 27,838 Alaskan Independence (John B. "Jack" Coghill); 1990 - 75,721 Alaskan Independence (Walter J. Hickel); 1982 - 29,067 Libertarian (Richard L. Randolph); 1978 - 33,555 write-in (Hickel) and 15,656 Alaskans for Kelly (Tom Kelly). Walker won the 2014 election with 48.1 percent of the total vote and a plurality over the runner-up of 6,223 votes. Hickel won the 1990 election with 38.9 percent of the total vote and a plurality of 15,520 votes over the runner-up.

POSTWAR VOTE FOR SENATOR

Year	Total Vote	Republican Vote	Republican Candidate	Democratic Vote	Democratic Candidate	Other Vote	Rep.-Dem. Plurality	Total Vote Rep.	Total Vote Dem.	Major Vote Rep.	Major Vote Dem.
2022	261,705	113,495	Murkowski, Lisa A.*	27,145	Chesbro, Patricia	121,065	2,015 R	88.9%	10.4%	89.5%	10.5%
2020	354,587	191,112	Sullivan, Dan S.*	146,068	Gross, Al	17,407	45,044 R	53.9%	41.2%	56.7%	43.3%
2016**	311,441	138,149	Murkowski, Lisa A.*	36,200	Metcalfe, Ray	137,092	101,949 R	44.4%	11.6%	79.2%	20.8%
2014	282,400	135,445	Sullivan, Dan S.	129,431	Begich, Mark*	17,524	6,014 R	48.0%	45.8%	51.1%	48.9%
2010**	255,474	90,839	Miller, Joe	60,045	McAdams, Scott T.	104,590	30,794 R#	35.6%	23.5%	60.2%	39.8%
2008	317,723	147,814	Stevens, Ted*	151,767	Begich, Mark	18,142	3,953 D	46.5%	47.8%	49.3%	50.7%
2004	308,315	149,773	Murkowski, Lisa A.*	140,424	Knowles, Tony	18,118	9,349 R	48.6%	45.5%	51.6%	48.4%
2002	229,548	179,438	Stevens, Ted*	24,133	Vondersaar, Frank	25,977	155,305 R	78.2%	10.5%	88.1%	11.9%
1998	221,807	165,227	Murkowski, Frank H.*	43,743	Sonneman, Joseph	12,837	121,484 R	74.5%	19.7%	79.1%	20.9%
1996**	231,916	177,893	Stevens, Ted*	23,977	Obermeyer, Theresa N.	30,046	153,916 R	76.7%	10.3%	88.1%	11.9%
1992	239,714	127,163	Murkowski, Frank H.*	92,065	Smith, Tony	20,486	35,098 R	53.0%	38.4%	58.0%	42.0%
1990	189,957	125,806	Stevens, Ted*	61,152	Beasley, Michael	2,999	64,654 R	66.2%	32.2%	67.3%	32.7%
1986	180,801	97,674	Murkowski, Frank H.*	79,727	Olds, Glenn	3,400	17,947 R	54.0%	44.1%	55.1%	44.9%
1984	206,438	146,919	Stevens, Ted*	58,804	Havelock, John E.	715	88,115 R	71.2%	28.5%	71.4%	28.6%
1980	156,762	84,159	Murkowski, Frank H.	72,007	Gruening, Clark S.	596	12,152 R	53.7%	45.9%	53.9%	46.1%
1978	122,741	92,783	Stevens, Ted*	29,574	Hobbs, Donald W.	384	63,209 R	75.6%	24.1%	75.8%	24.2%
1974	93,275	38,914	Lewis, C. R.	54,361	Gravel, Mike*		15,447 D	41.7%	58.3%	41.7%	58.3%
1972	96,007	74,216	Stevens, Ted*	21,791	Guess, Gene		52,425 R	77.3%	22.7%	77.3%	22.7%
1970S**	80,364	47,908	Stevens, Ted*	32,456	Kay, Wendell P.		15,452 R	59.6%	40.4%	59.6%	40.4%
1968	80,931	30,286	Rasmuson, Elmer	36,527	Gravel, Mike	14,118	6,241 D	37.4%	45.1%	45.3%	54.7%
1966	65,250	15,961	McKinley, Lee L.	49,289	Bartlett, E. L.*		33,328 D	24.5%	75.5%	24.5%	75.5%
1962	58,181	24,354	Stevens, Ted	33,827	Gruening, Ernest*		9,473 D	41.9%	58.1%	41.9%	58.1%
1960	59,978	21,937	McKinley, Lee L.	38,041	Bartlett, E. L.*		16,104 D	36.6%	63.4%	36.6%	63.4%
1958**	48,837	7,299	Robertson, R. E.	40,939	Bartlett, E. L.	599	33,640 D	14.9%	83.8%	15.1%	84.9%
1958**	49,525	23,462	Stepovich, Mike	26,063	Gruening, Ernest		2,601 D	47.4%	52.6%	47.4%	52.6%

Note: An asterisk (*) denotes incumbent. A pound sign (#) in the plurality column indicates that the winner in 2010 was Republican Senator Lisa A. Murkowski, who ran as a write-in candidate. **In past elections, the other vote included: 2016 - 90,825 Libertarian (Joe Miller), who finished second, 47,324 votes behind Murkowski, 41,194 Non-Affiliated (Margaret Stock), who finished third; 2010 - 101,091 Republican write-in (Lisa Murkowski), who won re-election with 39.6 percent of the total vote and a plurality of 10,252 votes over the runner-up; 1996 - 29,037 Green (Jed Whittaker), who finished second. The 1970 election was for a short term to fill a vacancy. The two 1958 elections were held to indeterminate terms and the Senate later determined by lot that Senator Gruening would serve four years, Senator Bartlett two. The plurality for 2010 shows the difference between the official Republican and Democratic candidates.

ALASKA
GUBERNATORIAL GENERAL 2022

2020 Census Population	County	Total Vote	(*) (W) Mike Dunleavy Republican	Charlie Pierce Republican	Les Gara Democrat	Write-In Write-in	Bill Walker Non-partisan	RepDem. Plurality		Percentage Total Vote		Major Vote	
										Rep.	Dem.	Rep.	Dem.
17,921	Election District 1	6,777	3,504	340	1,169	25	1,739	2,675	R	56.7%	17.2%	76.7%	23.3%
18,048	Election District 2	7,439	2,785	336	1,715	25	2,578	1,406	R	42.0%	23.1%	64.5%	35.5%
18,195	Election District 3	8,706	2,954	261	2,196	50	3,245	1,019	NNP	36.9%	25.2%	59.4%	40.6%
18,122	Election District 4	7,638	1,858	144	2,131	7	3,498	129	NNP	26.2%	27.9%	48.4%	51.6%
18,707	Election District 5	5,895	2,590	276	1,295	18	1,716	1,571	R	48.6%	22.0%	68.9%	31.1%
18,434	Election District 6	9,707	4,405	912	2,831	30	1,529	2,486	R	54.8%	29.2%	65.3%	34.7%
18,465	Election District 7	7,372	4,540	744	1,106	31	951	4,178	R	71.7%	15.0%	82.7%	17.3%
18,471	Election District 8	8,713	5,597	877	1,291	23	925	5,183	R	74.3%	14.8%	83.4%	16.6%
18,284	Election District 9	10,225	4,765	253	2,927	24	2,256	2,091	R	49.1%	28.6%	63.2%	36.8%
18,205	Election District 10	7,050	3,476	232	1,966	22	1,354	1,742	R	52.6%	27.9%	65.4%	34.6%
18,103	Election District 11	8,129	4,075	276	2,109	25	1,644	2,242	R	53.5%	25.9%	67.4%	32.6%
18,217	Election District 12	6,728	3,110	180	2,090	5	1,343	1,200	R	48.9%	31.1%	61.2%	38.8%
18,523	Election District 13	5,744	2,688	171	1,895	13	977	964	R	49.8%	33.0%	60.1%	39.9%
18,185	Election District 14	6,067	2,099	187	2,426	23	1,332	140	D	37.7%	40.0%	48.5%	51.5%
18,168	Election District 15	7,636	3,639	277	2,088	30	1,602	1,828	R	51.3%	27.3%	65.2%	34.8%
18,182	Election District 16	8,007	3,055	175	2,698	14	2,065	532	R	40.3%	33.7%	54.5%	45.5%
18,213	Election District 17	6,380	1,815	125	2,789	13	1,638	849	D	30.4%	43.7%	41.0%	59.0%
18,239	Election District 18	2,261	977	109	796	11	368	290	R	48.0%	35.2%	57.7%	42.3%
18,203	Election District 19	3,649	1,307	145	1,457	23	717	5	D	39.8%	39.9%	49.9%	50.1%
18,243	Election District 20	5,425	2,159	148	2,001	5	1,112	306	R	42.5%	36.9%	53.6%	46.4%
18,414	Election District 21	7,238	3,230	227	2,560	12	1,209	897	R	47.8%	35.4%	57.5%	42.5%
18,285	Election District 22	3,926	1,792	178	1,433	16	507	537	R	50.2%	36.5%	57.9%	42.1%
18,023	Election District 23	8,252	4,684	352	1,953	27	1,236	3,083	R	61.0%	23.7%	72.1%	27.9%
18,032	Election District 24	7,947	4,924	337	1,516	18	1,152	3,745	R	66.2%	19.1%	77.6%	22.4%
18,822	Election District 25	8,304	5,297	363	1,565	24	1,055	4,095	R	68.2%	18.8%	78.3%	21.7%
18,007	Election District 26	7,114	5,195	382	931	34	572	4,646	R	78.4%	13.1%	85.7%	14.3%
18,799	Election District 27	6,604	4,720	436	906	30	512	4,250	R	78.1%	13.7%	85.1%	14.9%
18,793	Election District 28	7,048	4,962	360	1,082	22	622	4,240	R	75.5%	15.4%	83.1%	16.9%
18,780	Election District 29	8,154	5,339	355	1,238	21	1,201	4,456	R	69.8%	15.2%	82.1%	17.9%
18,736	Election District 30	8,004	5,214	455	1,395	42	898	4,274	R	70.8%	17.4%	80.3%	19.7%
18,294	Election District 31	5,257	2,366	216	1,201	19	1,455	1,381	R	49.1%	22.8%	68.3%	31.7%
18,522	Election District 32	3,382	1,924	162	569	7	720	1,517	R	61.7%	16.8%	78.6%	21.4%
18,500	Election District 33	6,211	4,310	382	706	3	810	3,986	R	75.5%	11.4%	86.9%	13.1%
18,382	Election District 34	7,611	3,915	288	1,349	23	2,036	2,854	R	55.2%	17.7%	75.7%	24.3%
18,367	Election District 35	7,809	3,044	261	1,889	24	2,591	1,416	R	42.3%	24.2%	63.6%	36.4%
18,351	Election District 36	7,859	4,396	341	1,251	15	1,856	3,486	R	60.3%	15.9%	79.1%	20.9%
18,226	Election District 37	3,557	1,574	151	889	7	936	836	R	48.5%	25.0%	66.0%	34.0%
17,853	Election District 38	3,588	1,470	126	1,080	9	903	516	R	44.5%	30.1%	59.6%	40.4%
17,453	Election District 39	3,691	1,616	165	845	8	1,057	936	R	48.3%	22.9%	67.8%	32.2%
18,824	Election District 40	2,648	1,262	112	517	6	751	857	R	51.9%	19.5%	72.7%	27.3%
3,184,793	TOTAL	263,752	132,632	11,817	63,851	784	54,668	68,781	R	54.8%	24.2%	69.3%	30.7%

ALASKA
SENATE 2022

2020 Census Population	County	Total Vote	(*) (W) Lisa Murkowski Republican	Kelly Tshibaka Republican	Buzz Kelley Republican	Patricia Chesbro Democrat	Write-In Write-in	Rep.-Dem. Plurality	Percentage Total Vote		Major Vote	
									Rep.	Dem.	Rep.	Dem.
	FEDERAL ABSENTEE	104	40	7	1	56	0	8 D	46.2%	53.8%	46.2%	53.8%
17,921	Election District 1	6,633	3,020	2,626	304	601	82	5,349 R	89.7%	9.1%	90.8%	9.2%
18,048	Election District 2	7,467	3,829	2,439	338	828	33	5,778 R	88.5%	11.1%	88.9%	11.1%
18,195	Election District 3	8,743	4,751	2,589	179	1,213	11	6,306 R	86.0%	13.9%	86.1%	13.9%
18,122	Election District 4	7,409	4,280	1,494	131	1,322	182	4,583 R	79.7%	17.8%	81.7%	18.3%
18,707	Election District 5	5,847	2,978	2,016	210	590	53	4,614 R	89.0%	10.1%	89.8%	10.2%
18,434	Election District 6	9,733	3,836	4,593	312	949	43	7,792 R	89.8%	9.8%	90.2%	9.8%
18,465	Election District 7	7,397	2,255	4,436	237	449	20	6,479 R	93.7%	6.1%	93.9%	6.1%
18,471	Election District 8	8,636	2,086	5,785	246	439	80	7,678 R	94.0%	5.1%	94.9%	5.1%
18,284	Election District 9	10,119	5,214	3,747	140	936	82	8,165 R	89.9%	9.2%	90.7%	9.3%
18,205	Election District 10	7,083	3,397	2,835	144	672	35	5,704 R	90.0%	9.5%	90.5%	9.5%
18,103	Election District 11	8,167	3,933	3,386	112	725	11	6,706 R	91.0%	8.9%	91.1%	8.9%
18,217	Election District 12	6,583	3,074	2,469	104	821	115	4,826 R	85.8%	12.5%	87.3%	12.7%
18,523	Election District 13	5,594	2,620	1,922	148	856	48	3,834 R	83.8%	15.3%	84.6%	15.4%
18,185	Election District 14	6,087	3,336	1,614	153	948	36	4,155 R	83.8%	15.6%	84.3%	15.7%
18,168	Election District 15	7,666	3,811	2,999	128	717	11	6,221 R	90.5%	9.4%	90.6%	9.4%
18,182	Election District 16	7,825	4,175	2,482	93	949	126	5,801 R	86.3%	12.1%	87.7%	12.3%
18,213	Election District 17	6,339	3,740	1,299	86	1,159	55	3,966 R	80.8%	18.3%	81.6%	18.4%
18,239	Election District 18	2,265	961	791	89	412	12	1,429 R	81.3%	18.2%	81.7%	18.3%
18,203	Election District 19	3,693	2,075	910	98	603	7	2,480 R	83.5%	16.3%	83.6%	16.4%
18,243	Election District 20	5,283	2,490	1,740	91	870	92	3,451 R	81.8%	16.5%	83.2%	16.8%
18,414	Election District 21	7,106	3,434	2,413	176	1,028	55	4,995 R	84.8%	14.5%	85.4%	14.6%
18,285	Election District 22	3,906	1,758	1,395	144	586	23	2,711 R	84.4%	15.0%	84.9%	15.1%
18,023	Election District 23	8,300	3,428	4,026	171	660	15	6,965 R	91.9%	8.0%	92.0%	8.0%
18,032	Election District 24	7,814	2,612	4,398	180	540	84	6,650 R	92.0%	6.9%	93.0%	7.0%
18,822	Election District 25	8,018	2,505	4,316	276	804	117	6,293 R	88.5%	10.0%	89.8%	10.2%
18,007	Election District 26	7,150	1,627	4,773	292	428	30	6,264 R	93.6%	6.0%	94.0%	6.0%
18,799	Election District 27	6,612	1,449	4,520	231	391	21	5,809 R	93.8%	5.9%	94.1%	5.9%
18,793	Election District 28	6,955	1,674	4,473	265	473	70	5,939 R	92.2%	6.8%	93.1%	6.9%
18,780	Election District 29	7,859	2,296	4,568	304	584	107	6,584 R	91.2%	7.4%	92.5%	7.5%
18,736	Election District 30	8,058	2,281	4,830	325	589	33	6,847 R	92.3%	7.3%	92.7%	7.3%
18,294	Election District 31	5,288	2,470	1,940	184	676	18	3,918 R	86.9%	12.8%	87.2%	12.8%
18,522	Election District 32	3,329	1,139	1,684	139	339	28	2,623 R	89.0%	10.2%	89.7%	10.3%
18,500	Election District 33	5,990	1,537	3,621	369	413	50	5,114 R	92.3%	6.9%	93.0%	7.0%
18,382	Election District 34	7,626	3,088	3,490	298	720	30	6,156 R	90.2%	9.4%	90.5%	9.5%
18,367	Election District 35	7,852	3,893	2,688	171	1,076	24	5,676 R	86.0%	13.7%	86.3%	13.7%
18,351	Election District 36	7,706	2,984	3,708	251	665	98	6,278 R	90.1%	8.6%	91.3%	8.7%
18,226	Election District 37	3,528	2,248	841	122	283	34	2,928 R	91.0%	8.0%	91.9%	8.1%
17,853	Election District 38	3,642	2,742	494	121	266	19	3,091 R	92.2%	7.3%	92.7%	7.3%
17,453	Election District 39	3,760	2,833	553	106	261	7	3,231 R	92.9%	6.9%	93.0%	7.0%
18,824	Election District 40	2,533	1,596	570	88	248	31	2,006 R	89.0%	9.8%	90.1%	9.9%
3,184,793	TOTAL	261,705	113,495	111,480	7,557	27,145	2,028	2,015 R	88.9%	10.4%	89.5%	10.5%

ALASKA

HOUSE OF REPRESENTATIVES

| | | | Republican | | Democratic | | Other | | Percentage Total Vote | | Percentage Major Vote | |
| | | | Vote | Candidate | Vote | Candidate | Vote | Plurality | Rep. | Dem. | Rep. | Dem. |
CD	Year	Total Vote	Vote	Candidate	Vote	Candidate	Vote	Plurality	Rep.	Dem.	Rep.	Dem.
At Large	2022	263,610	67,866	PALIN, SARAH H.	128,553	PELTOLA, MARY S.*	67,191	60,687 D	25.7%	48.8%	34.6%	65.4%
At Large	2020	353,165	192,126	YOUNG, DON*	159,856	GALVIN, ALYSE S.	1,183	32,270 R	54.4%	45.3%	54.6%	45.4%
At Large	2018	282,166	149,779	YOUNG, DON*	131,199	GALVIN, ALYSE S.	1,188	18,580 R	53.1%	46.5%	53.3%	46.7%
At Large	2016	308,198	155,088	YOUNG, DON*	111,019	LINDBECK, STEVE	42,091	44,069 R	50.3%	36.0%	58.3%	41.7%
At Large	2014	279,741	142,572	YOUNG, DON*	114,602	DUNBAR, FORREST	22,567	27,970 R	51.0%	41.0%	55.4%	44.6%
At Large	2012	289,804	185,296	YOUNG, DON*	82,927	CISSNA, SHARON M.	21,581	102,369 R	63.9%	28.6%	69.1%	30.9%
At Large	2010	254,335	175,384	YOUNG, DON*	77,606	CRAWFORD, HARRY T.	1,345	97,778 R	69.0%	30.5%	69.3%	30.7%
At Large	2008	316,978	158,939	YOUNG, DON*	142,560	BERKOWITZ, ETHAN A.	15,479	16,379 R	50.1%	45.0%	52.7%	47.3%
At Large	2006	234,645	132,743	YOUNG, DON*	93,879	BENSON, DIANE E.	8,023	38,864 R	56.6%	40.0%	58.6%	41.4%
At Large	2004	299,996	213,216	YOUNG, DON*	67,074	HIGGINS, THOMAS M.	19,706	146,142 R	71.1%	22.4%	76.1%	23.9%
At Large	2002	227,725	169,685	YOUNG, DON*	39,357	GREENE, CLIFFORD	18,683	130,328 R	74.5%	17.3%	81.2%	18.8%
At Large	2000	274,393	190,862	YOUNG, DON*	45,372	GREENE, CLIFFORD	38,159	145,490 R	69.6%	16.5%	80.8%	19.2%
At Large	1998	223,300	139,676	YOUNG, DON*	77,232	DUNCAN, JIM	6,392	62,444 R	62.6%	34.6%	64.4%	35.6%
At Large	1996	233,700	138,834	YOUNG, DON*	85,114	LINCOLN, GEORGIANNA	9,752	53,720 R	59.4%	36.4%	62.0%	38.0%
At Large	1994	208,240	118,537	YOUNG, DON*	68,172	SMITH, TONY	21,531	50,365 R	56.9%	32.7%	63.5%	36.5%
At Large	1992	239,116	111,849	YOUNG, DON*	102,378	DEVENS, JOHN S.	24,889	9,471 R	46.8%	42.8%	52.2%	47.8%
At Large	1990	191,647	99,003	YOUNG, DON*	91,677	DEVENS, JOHN S.	967	7,326 R	51.7%	47.8%	51.9%	48.1%
At Large	1988	192,955	120,595	YOUNG, DON*	71,881	GRUENSTEIN, PETER	479	48,714 R	62.5%	37.3%	62.7%	37.3%
At Large	1986	180,277	101,799	YOUNG, DON*	74,053	BEGICH, PEGGE	4,425	27,746 R	56.5%	41.1%	57.9%	42.1%
At Large	1984	206,437	113,582	YOUNG, DON*	86,052	BEGICH, PEGGE	6,803	27,530 R	55.0%	41.7%	56.9%	43.1%
At Large	1982	181,084	128,274	YOUNG, DON*	52,011	CARLSON, DAVE	799	76,263 R	70.8%	28.7%	71.2%	28.8%
At Large	1980	154,618	114,089	YOUNG, DON*	39,922	PARNELL, KEVIN	607	74,167 R	73.8%	25.8%	74.1%	25.9%
At Large	1978	124,187	68,811	YOUNG, DON*	55,176	RODEY, PATRICK	200	13,635 R	55.4%	44.4%	55.5%	44.5%
At Large	1976	118,208	83,722	YOUNG, DON*	34,194	HOPSON, EBEN	292	49,528 R	70.8%	28.9%	71.0%	29.0%
At Large	1974	95,921	51,641	YOUNG, DON*	44,280	HENSLEY, WILLIAM L.		7,361 R	53.8%	46.2%	53.8%	46.2%
At Large	1972	95,401	41,750	YOUNG, DON	53,651	BEGICH, NICHOLAS J.*		11,901 D	43.8%	56.2%	43.8%	56.2%
At Large	1970	80,084	35,947	MURKOWSKI, FRANK H.	44,137	BEGICH, NICHOLAS J.		8,190 D	44.9%	55.1%	44.9%	55.1%
At Large	1968	80,362	43,577	POLLOCK, HOWARD W.*	36,785	BEGICH, NICHOLAS J.		6,792 R	54.2%	45.8%	54.2%	45.8%
At Large	1966	65,907	34,040	POLLOCK, HOWARD W.	31,867	RIVERS, RALPH J.*		2,173 R	51.6%	48.4%	51.6%	48.4%
At Large	1964	67,156	32,566	THOMAS, LOWELL	34,590	RIVERS, RALPH J.*		2,024 D	48.5%	51.5%	48.5%	51.5%
At Large	1962	58,591	26,638	THOMAS, LOWELL	31,953	RIVERS, RALPH J.*		5,315 D	45.5%	54.5%	45.5%	54.5%
At Large	1960	59,063	25,517	RETTIG, R. L.	33,546	RIVERS, RALPH J.*		8,029 D	43.2%	56.8%	43.2%	56.8%
At Large	1958	48,644	20,699	BENSON, HENRY A.	27,945	RIVERS, RALPH J.		7,246 D	42.6%	57.4%	42.6%	57.4%

Note: An asterisk (*) denotes incumbent.

ALASKA

GENERAL AND PRIMARY ELECTIONS

GENERAL ELECTIONS: OTHER VOTE

Senate   Other vote was 111,480 Republican (Kelly Tshibaka), 7,557 Republican (Buzz Kelley), 2,028 Write-in (Write-In)

House   Other vote was:

  At Large   1,108 Write-in (Write-In)

ALASKA
GENERAL AND PRIMARY ELECTIONS

2022 PRIMARY ELECTIONS: SUPPLEMENTARY INFORMATION

Primary	August 16, 2022	**Registration** (as of June 3, 2022)	595,387	Republican	142,565
				Democratic	77,096
				Alaskan Independence	18,820
				Libertarian	6,873
				Green	1,503
				Veterans	1,390
				Constitution	721
				Moderate	301
				UCES' Clown	144
				Progressive	195
				Patriot's	189
				Owl	63
				Alliance	34
				Freedom Reform	2
				Nonpartisan	81,428
				Undeclared	264,063

Primary Type   Open—The top four vote-getters advance to the general election regardless of party.

ARIZONA

Statewide Races

If Arizona voters are feeling some electoral fatigue, it would be hard to blame them: since 2016, the state has held a Senate election every two years – and there is another on tap for 2024. In 2022, the state also saw the closest gubernatorial result (by percentage margin) in the nation.

In 2020, former astronaut Mark Kelly was among national Democrats' top Senate recruits. Aside from his impressive resume, he was married to former Rep. Gabrielle Giffords, a beloved figure in the state who survived a 2011 mass shooting. As Joe Biden carried the state by less than half a percentage point, Kelly ousted then-incumbent Republican Sen. Martha McSally in a special election to serve out the remainder of the late John McCain's term. In 2022, Kelly would have to run for a full six-year term.

In Arizona, the close margin of the presidential races in the state – Biden carried the state by about 10,000 votes out of 3.3 million cast – played into Donald Trump's theories that the election was stolen from him. Despite a 2021 audit of the state's largest county, Maricopa (Phoenix), that found no evidence of widespread voter fraud, some state Republicans took cues from Trump. One of them was a first-time candidate, Kari Lake. A prominent local news anchor for two decades, Lake left her broadcasting job to pursue the governorship – she made "election denialism" a centerpiece of her campaign.

In the early August primary, Lake defeated her main opponent, former state Board of Regents member Karrin Taylor Robson, by a 48%–43% margin. Meanwhile, another first-time, Trump-aligned candidate won the primary for Senate. Blake Masters, a venture capitalist in his mid-30s, received financial backing from billionaire Peter Thiel. Kelly won his primary unopposed and Democratic Secretary of State Katie Hobbs had light opposition in the gubernatorial primary.

But the Arizona Republican Party's ticket seemed too extreme for the state's voters, at least in the races at the top of the ballot. Kelly won by just over five points, the best showing for a Democrat in an Arizona Senate contest since 1988. In 2020, Kelly carried Maricopa County by 80,193 votes while losing the rest of the state by 1,387 votes. Two years later, he upped his raw vote margin in Maricopa County to 99,082 and still carried the balance of the state by almost 27,000 votes.

Kelly's showing helped lift Hobbs, who beat Lake by 17,117 votes, or about seven-tenths of a percentage point. Hobbs carried the same five counties that Kelly did, though by lesser margins. For months after the election, Lake complained the election was stolen – but Hobbs was sworn into office.

House Races

The post-2020 redistricting cycle was the third that featured Arizona's redistricting commission. After the 2010 census, the commission produced what seemed like a pro-Democratic map. After the 2020 census, though, Republicans were happier: with new lines for 2022, the Arizona delegation went from 5-4 Democratic to 6-3 Republican.

In northern Arizona, Democratic Rep. Tom O'Halleran's seat was redrawn to include deeply red Yavapai County, an electoral anchor that sunk his reelection prospects. Republicans also prevailed in the 1st and 6th districts, a pair of marginal Biden-won seats – the latter was a hold and the former was a gain, though both could again see close contests in 2024.

ARIZONA

Congressional districts first established for elections held in 2022

9 members

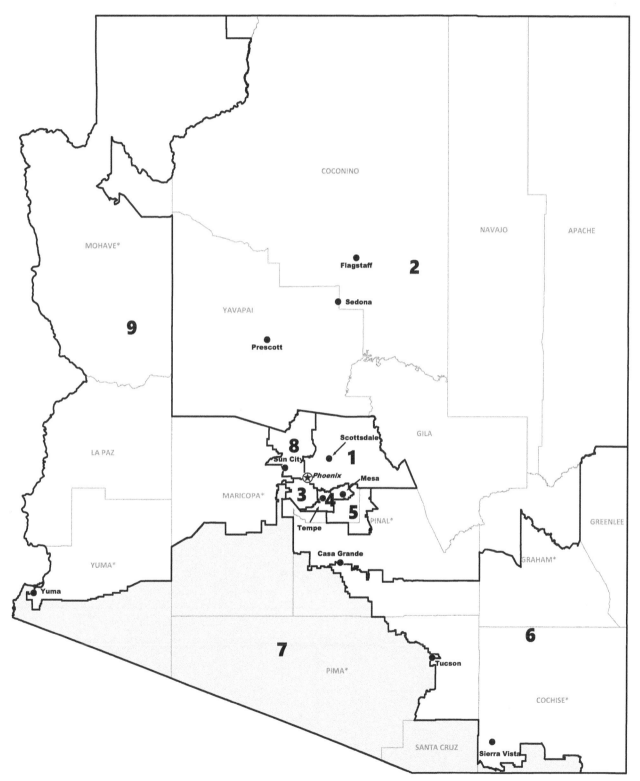

*Asterisk indicates a county whose boundaries include parts of two or more congressional districts.
CD 7 is highlighted for visibility. See Inset for Phoenix area.

ARIZONA
Greater Phoenix Area

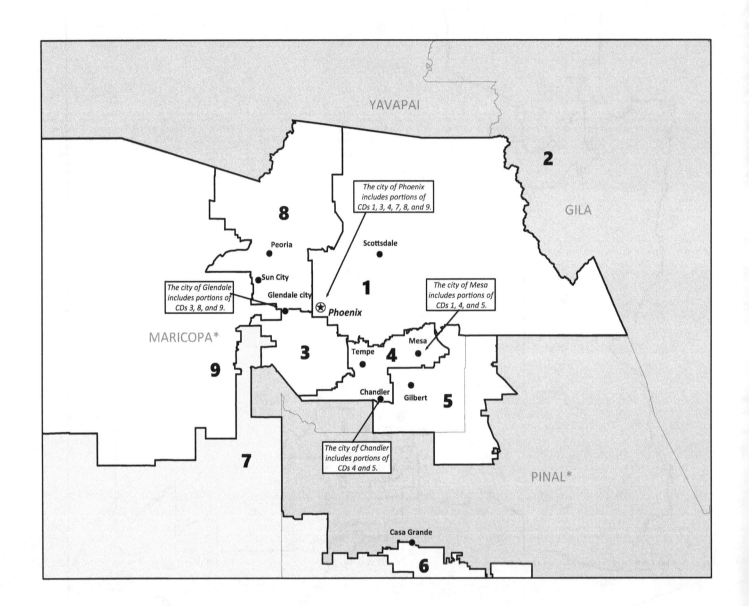

* Asterisk indicates a county whose boundaries include parts of two or more congressional districts.
CDs 2 and 7 are highlighted for visibility.

ARIZONA

GOVERNOR
Katie Hobbs (D). Elected 2022 to a four-year term.

SENATORS (1 Democrat, 1 Independent)
Kyrsten Sinema (I). Elected 2018 to a six-year term. Originally elected as a Democrat, and changed party to independent on December 9, 2022.

Mark Kelly (D). Reelected 2022 to a six-year term. Previously elected in a special election on November 3, 2020, to complete the term of John Kyl (R), who resigned December 12, 2018. Kyl was appointed by the governor on September 4, 2018, following the death of John McCain (R). Following Kyl's resignation, the governor appointed Martha McSally (R) to the seat, triggering a special election.

REPRESENTATIVES (6 Republicans, 3 Democrats)
1. David Schweikert (R)
2. Elijah Crane (R)
3. Ruben Gallego (D)
4. Greg Stanton (D)
5. Andy Biggs (R)
6. Juan Ciscomani (R)
7. Raúl M. Grijalva (D)
8. Debbie Lesko (R)
9. Paul A. Gosar (R)

POSTWAR VOTE FOR PRESIDENT

Year	Total Vote	Republican Vote	Republican Candidate	Democratic Vote	Democratic Candidate	Other Vote	Rep.-Dem. Plurality	Total Vote Rep.	Total Vote Dem.	Major Vote Rep.	Major Vote Dem.
2020	3,387,326	1,661,686	Trump, Donald J.*	1,672,143	Biden, Joseph R. Jr.	53,497	10,457 D	49.1%	49.4%	49.8%	50.2%
2016**	2,573,165	1,252,401	Trump, Donald J.	1,161,167	Clinton, Hillary Rodham	159,597	91,234 R	48.7%	45.1%	51.9%	48.1%
2012	2,299,254	1,233,654	Romney, W. Mitt	1,025,232	Obama, Barack H.*	40,368	208,422 R	53.7%	44.6%	54.6%	45.4%
2008	2,293,475	1,230,111	McCain, John S. III	1,034,707	Obama, Barack H.	28,657	195,404 R	53.6%	45.1%	54.3%	45.7%
2004	2,012,585	1,104,294	Bush, George W.*	893,524	Kerry, John F.	14,767	210,770 R	54.9%	44.4%	55.3%	44.7%
2000**	1,532,016	781,652	Bush, George W.	685,341	Gore, Albert Jr.	65,023	96,311 R	51.0%	44.7%	53.3%	46.7%
1996**	1,404,405	622,073	Dole, Robert "Bob"	653,288	Clinton, Bill*	129,044	31,215 D	44.3%	46.5%	48.8%	51.2%
1992**	1,486,975	572,086	Bush, George H.*	543,050	Clinton, Bill	371,839	29,036 R	38.5%	36.5%	51.3%	48.7%
1988	1,171,873	702,541	Bush, George H.	454,029	Dukakis, Michael S.	15,303	248,512 R	60.0%	38.7%	60.7%	39.3%
1984	1,025,897	681,416	Reagan, Ronald*	333,854	Mondale, Walter F.	10,627	347,562 R	66.4%	32.5%	67.1%	32.9%
1980**	873,945	529,688	Reagan, Ronald	246,843	Carter, Jimmy*	97,414	282,845 R	60.6%	28.2%	68.2%	31.8%
1976	742,719	418,642	Ford, Gerald R.*	295,602	Carter, Jimmy	28,475	123,040 R	56.4%	39.8%	58.6%	41.4%
1972	622,926	402,812	Nixon, Richard M.*	198,540	McGovern, George S.	21,574	204,272 R	64.7%	31.9%	67.0%	33.0%
1968**	486,936	266,721	Nixon, Richard M.	170,514	Humphrey, Hubert Horatio Jr.	49,701	96,207 R	54.8%	35.0%	61.0%	39.0%
1964	480,770	242,535	Goldwater, Barry M. Sr.	237,753	Johnson, Lyndon B.*	482	4,782 R	50.4%	49.5%	50.5%	49.5%
1960	398,491	221,241	Nixon, Richard M.	176,781	Kennedy, John F.	469	44,460 R	55.5%	44.4%	55.6%	44.4%
1956	290,173	176,990	Eisenhower, Dwight D.*	112,880	Stevenson, Adlai E. II	303	64,110 R	61.0%	38.9%	61.1%	38.9%
1952	260,570	152,042	Eisenhower, Dwight D.	108,528	Stevenson, Adlai E. II		43,514 R	58.3%	41.7%	58.3%	41.7%
1948	177,065	77,597	Dewey, Thomas E.	95,251	Truman, Harry S.*	4,217	17,654 D	43.8%	53.8%	44.9%	55.1%

Note: An asterisk (*) denotes incumbent. **In past elections, the other vote included: 2016 - Libertarian 106,327 (Gary Johnson); 2000 - 45,645 Green (Ralph Nader); 1996 - 112,072 Reform (Ross Perot); 1992 - 353,741 Independent (Perot); 1980 - 76,952 Independent (John Anderson); 1968 - 46,573 American Independent (George Wallace).

ARIZONA

POSTWAR VOTE FOR GOVERNOR

Year	Total Vote	Republican Vote	Republican Candidate	Democratic Vote	Democratic Candidate	Other Vote	Rep.-Dem Plurality	Total Vote Rep.	Total Vote Dem.	Major Vote Rep.	Major Vote Dem.
2022	2,559,485	1,270,774	Lake, Kari	1,287,891	Hobbs, Katie	820	17,117 D	49.6%	50.3%	49.7%	50.3%
2018	2,376,441	1,330,863	Ducey, Doug*	994,341	Garcia, David	51,237	336,522 R	56.0%	41.8%	57.2%	42.8%
2014	1,506,416	805,062	Ducey, Doug	626,921	Duval, Fred	74,433	178,141 R	53.4%	41.6%	56.2%	43.8%
2010	1,728,081	938,934	Brewer, Jan*	733,935	Goddard, Terry	55,212	204,999 R	54.3%	42.5%	56.1%	43.9%
2006	1,533,645	543,528	Munsil, Len	959,830	Napolitano, Janet*	30,287	416,302 D	35.4%	62.6%	36.2%	63.8%
2002	1,226,111	554,465	Salmon, Matt	566,284	Napolitano, Janet	105,362	11,819 D	45.2%	46.2%	49.5%	50.5%
1998	1,017,616	620,188	Hull, Jane Dee*	361,552	Johnson, Paul	35,876	258,636 R	60.9%	35.5%	63.2%	36.8%
1994	1,129,607	593,492	Symington, Fife*	500,702	Basha, Eddie	35,413	92,790 R	52.5%	44.3%	54.2%	45.8%
1991S**	940,737	492,569	Symington, Fife	448,168	Goddard, Terry		44,401 R	52.4%	47.6%	52.4%	47.6%
1986**	866,984	343,913	Mecham, Evan	298,986	Warner, Carolyn	224,085	44,927 R	39.7%	34.5%	53.5%	46.5%
1982	726,364	235,877	Corbet, Leo	453,795	Babbitt, Bruce*	36,692	217,918 D	32.5%	62.5%	34.2%	65.8%
1978	538,556	241,093	Mecham, Evan	282,605	Babbitt, Bruce*	14,858	41,512 D	44.8%	52.5%	46.0%	54.0%
1974	552,202	273,674	Williams, Jack R.*	278,375	Castro, Raul H.	153	4,701 D	49.6%	50.4%	49.6%	50.4%
1970**	411,409	209,522	Williams, Jack R.*	201,887	Castro, Raul H.		7,635 R	50.9%	49.1%	50.9%	49.1%
1968	483,998	279,923	Williams, Jack R.*	204,075	Goddard, Sam		75,848 R	57.8%	42.2%	57.8%	42.2%
1966	378,342	203,438	Williams, Jack R.	174,904	Goddard, Sam*		28,534 R	53.8%	46.2%	53.8%	46.2%
1964	473,502	221,404	Kleindienst, Richard	252,098	Goddard, Sam		30,694 D	46.8%	53.2%	46.8%	53.2%
1962	365,841	200,578	Fannin, Paul*	165,263	Goddard, Sam		35,315 R	54.8%	45.2%	54.8%	45.2%
1960	397,107	235,502	Fannin, Paul*	161,605	Ackerman, Lee		73,897 R	59.3%	40.7%	59.3%	40.7%
1958	290,465	160,136	Fannin, Paul	130,329	Morrison, Robert		29,807 R	55.1%	44.9%	55.1%	44.9%
1956	288,592	116,744	Griffen, Horace B.	171,848	McFarland, Ernest W.*		55,104 D	40.5%	59.5%	40.5%	59.5%
1954	243,970	115,866	Pyle, Howard*	128,104	McFarland, Ernest W.		12,238 D	47.5%	52.5%	47.5%	52.5%
1952	260,285	156,592	Pyle, Howard*	103,693	Haldiman, Joe C.		52,899 R	60.2%	39.8%	60.2%	39.8%
1950	195,227	99,109	Pyle, Howard	96,118	Frohmiller, Ana		2,991 R	50.8%	49.2%	50.8%	49.2%
1948	175,767	70,419	Brockett, Bruce D.	104,008	Garvey, Dan E.	1,340	33,589 D	40.1%	59.2%	40.4%	59.6%
1946	122,462	48,867	Brockett, Bruce D.	73,595	Osborn, Sidney P.*		24,728 D	39.9%	60.1%	39.9%	60.1%

Note: An asterisk (*) denotes incumbent. **In 1990 neither major party candidate won an absolute majority, therefore a runoff election was held February 26,1991; the vote above is for the February runoff. In the November 1990 election, a total of 1,055,406 votes were cast as follows: 523,984 (49.6%) Republican (Fife Symington); 519,691 (49.2%) Democratic (Terry Goddard); 11,731 (1.1%) Other. In past elections, the other vote included: 1986 - 224,085 Independent (Bill Schulz). The term of office for Arizona's Governor was increased from two to four years effective with the 1970 election.

POSTWAR VOTE FOR SENATOR

Year	Total Vote	Republican Vote	Republican Candidate	Democratic Vote	Democratic Candidate	Other Vote	Rep.-Dem. Plurality	Total Vote Rep.	Total Vote Dem.	Major Vote Rep.	Major Vote Dem.
2022	2,572,294	1,196,308	Masters, Blake	1,322,027	Kelly, Mark*	53,959	125,719 D	46.5%	51.4%	47.5%	52.5%
2020S**	3,355,317	1,637,661	McSally, Martha*	1,716,467	Kelly, Mark	1,189	78,806 D	48.8%	51.2%	48.8%	51.2%
2018	2,384,308	1,135,200	McSally, Martha	1,191,100	Sinema, Kyrsten	58,008	55,900 D	47.6%	50.0%	48.8%	51.2%
2016	2,530,730	1,359,267	McCain, John S. III*	1,031,245	Kirkpatrick, Ann	140,218	328,022 R	53.7%	40.7%	56.9%	43.1%
2012	2,243,422	1,104,457	Flake, Jeff	1,036,542	Carmona, Richard	102,423	67,915 R	49.2%	46.2%	51.6%	48.4%
2010	1,708,484	1,005,615	McCain, John S. III*	592,011	Glassman, Rodney	110,858	413,604 R	58.9%	34.7%	62.9%	37.1%
2006	1,526,782	814,293	Kyl, Jon*	664,141	Pederson, Jim	48,243	150,257 R	53.3%	43.5%	55.1%	44.9%
2004	1,961,677	1,505,372	McCain, John S. III*	404,507	Starky, Stuart Marc	51,798	1,100,865 R	76.7%	20.6%	78.8%	21.2%
2000	1,397,076	1,108,196	Kyl, Jon*			288,880	1,108,196 R	79.3%		100.0%	
1998	1,013,280	696,577	McCain, John S. III*	275,224	Ranger, Ed	41,479	421,353 R	68.7%	27.2%	71.7%	28.3%
1994	1,119,060	600,999	Kyl, Jon	442,510	Coppersmith, Sam G.	75,551	158,489 R	53.7%	39.5%	57.6%	42.4%
1992**	1,382,051	771,395	McCain, John S. III*	436,321	Sargent, Claire	174,335	335,074 R	55.8%	31.6%	63.9%	36.1%
1988	1,164,539	478,060	DeGreen, Keith	660,403	DeConcini, Dennis*	26,076	182,343 D	41.1%	56.7%	42.0%	58.0%
1986	862,921	521,850	McCain, John S. III	340,965	Kimball, Richard	106	180,885 R	60.5%	39.5%	60.5%	39.5%
1982	723,885	291,749	Dunn, Pete	411,970	DeConcini, Dennis*	20,166	120,221 D	40.3%	56.9%	41.5%	58.5%
1980	874,178	432,371	Goldwater, Barry M. Sr.*	422,972	Schulz, Bill	18,835	9,399 R	49.5%	48.4%	50.5%	49.5%
1976	741,210	321,236	Steiger, Sam	400,334	DeConcini, Dennis	19,640	79,098 D	43.3%	54.0%	44.5%	55.5%
1974	549,919	320,396	Goldwater, Barry M. Sr.*	229,523	Marshall, Jonathan		90,873 R	58.3%	41.7%	58.3%	41.7%
1970	407,796	228,284	Fannin, Paul*	179,512	Grossman, Sam		48,772 R	56.0%	44.0%	56.0%	44.0%
1968	479,945	274,607	Goldwater, Barry M. Sr.	205,338	Elson, Roy L.		69,269 R	57.2%	42.8%	57.2%	42.8%
1964	468,788	241,084	Fannin, Paul	227,704	Elson, Roy L.		13,380 R	51.4%	48.6%	51.4%	48.6%
1962	362,605	163,388	Mecham, Evan	199,217	Hayden, Carl*		35,829 D	45.1%	54.9%	45.1%	54.9%
1958	293,623	164,593	Goldwater, Barry M. Sr.*	129,030	McFarland, Ernest W.		35,563 R	56.1%	43.9%	56.1%	43.9%
1956	278,263	107,447	Jones, Ross F.	170,816	Hayden, Carl*		63,369 D	38.6%	61.4%	38.6%	61.4%
1952	257,401	132,063	Goldwater, Barry M. Sr.	125,338	McFarland, Ernest W.*		6,725 R	51.3%	48.7%	51.3%	48.7%
1950	185,092	68,846	Brockett, Bruce	116,246	Hayden, Carl*		47,400 D	37.2%	62.8%	37.2%	62.8%
1946	116,239	35,022	Powers, Ward S.	80,415	McFarland, Ernest W.*	802	45,393 D	30.1%	69.2%	30.3%	69.7%

Note: An asterisk (*) denotes incumbent. **The 2020 election was for a short term to fill a vacancy. In past elections, the other vote included: 1992 - 145,361 Independent (Evan Mecham). The Democratic Party did not run a candidate in the 2000 Senate election.

ARIZONA
GOVERNOR 2022

2022 Census Population	County	Total Vote	Republican (Lake)	Democratic (Hobbs)	Other	Rep.-Dem. Plurality		Percentage			
								Total Vote		Major Vote	
								Rep.	Dem.	Rep.	Dem.
72,068	APACHE	26,614	8,870	17,739	5	8,869	D	33.3%	66.7%	33.3%	66.7%
125,866	COCHISE	46,666	27,481	19,137	48	8,344	R	58.9%	41.0%	58.9%	41.1%
144,552	COCONINO	54,727	20,298	34,389	40	14,091	D	37.1%	62.8%	37.1%	62.9%
54,198	GILA	22,450	14,763	7,674	13	7,089	R	65.8%	34.2%	65.8%	34.2%
39,011	GRAHAM	10,847	7,760	3,087	0	4,673	R	71.5%	28.5%	71.5%	28.5%
9,493	GREENLEE	2,446	1,526	920	0	606	R	62.4%	37.6%	62.4%	37.6%
21,195	LA PAZ	5,499	3,847	1,646	6	2,201	R	70.0%	29.9%	70.0%	30.0%
4,512,331	MARICOPA	1,543,535	752,714	790,352	469	37,638	D	48.8%	51.2%	48.8%	51.2%
213,678	MOHAVE	81,510	61,125	20,369	16	40,756	R	75.0%	25.0%	75.0%	25.0%
111,160	NAVAJO	40,416	22,340	18,058	18	4,282	R	55.3%	44.7%	55.3%	44.7%
1,052,466	PIMA	398,554	157,034	241,398	122	84,364	D	39.4%	60.6%	39.4%	60.6%
467,550	PINAL	143,821	83,773	60,019	29	23,754	R	58.2%	41.7%	58.3%	41.7%
46,451	SANTA CRUZ	13,099	4,371	8,724	4	4,353	D	33.4%	66.6%	33.4%	66.6%
237,378	YAVAPAI	123,190	78,832	44,316	42	34,516	R	64.0%	36.0%	64.0%	36.0%
214,121	YUMA	46,111	26,040	20,063	8	5,977	R	56.5%	43.5%	56.5%	43.5%
7,321,518	TOTAL	2,559,485	1,270,774	1,287,891	820	17,117	D	49.6%	50.3%	49.7%	50.3%

ARIZONA
SENATOR 2022

2020 Census Population	County	Total Vote	Republican (Masters)	Democratic (Kelly)	Other	Rep.-Dem. Plurality		Percentage			
								Total Vote		Major Vote	
								Rep.	Dem.	Rep.	Dem.
72,068	APACHE	26,719	8,163	18,005	551	9,842	D	30.6%	67.4%	31.2%	68.8%
125,866	COCHISE	46,991	25,539	20,002	1,450	5,537	R	54.3%	42.6%	56.1%	43.9%
144,552	COCONINO	55,058	18,697	35,149	1,212	16,452	D	34.0%	63.8%	34.7%	65.3%
54,198	GILA	22,544	13,958	7,984	602	5,974	R	61.9%	35.4%	63.6%	36.4%
39,011	GRAHAM	10,886	7,388	3,243	255	4,145	R	67.9%	29.8%	69.5%	30.5%
9,493	GREENLEE	2,462	1,392	970	100	422	R	56.5%	39.4%	58.9%	41.1%
21,195	LA PAZ	5,530	3,656	1,711	163	1,945	R	66.1%	30.9%	68.1%	31.9%
4,512,331	MARICOPA	1,551,226	710,491	809,573	31,162	99,082	D	45.8%	52.2%	46.7%	53.3%
213,678	MOHAVE	81,899	58,737	21,040	2,122	37,697	R	71.7%	25.7%	73.6%	26.4%
111,160	NAVAJO	40,630	20,970	18,724	936	2,246	R	51.6%	46.1%	52.8%	47.2%
1,052,466	PIMA	400,725	144,936	248,230	7,559	103,294	D	36.2%	61.9%	36.9%	63.1%
467,550	PINAL	144,486	78,820	62,009	3,657	16,811	R	54.6%	42.9%	56.0%	44.0%
46,451	SANTA CRUZ	13,186	3,892	8,988	306	5,096	D	29.5%	68.2%	30.2%	69.8%
237,378	YAVAPAI	123,651	75,752	45,258	2,641	30,494	R	61.3%	36.6%	62.6%	37.4%
214,121	YUMA	46,301	23,917	21,141	1,243	2,776	R	51.7%	45.7%	53.1%	46.9%
7,321,518	TOTAL	2,572,294	1,196,308	1,322,027	53,959	125,719	D	46.5%	51.4%	47.5%	52.5%

ARIZONA

HOUSE OF REPRESENTATIVES

CD	Year	Total Vote	Republican Vote	Republican Candidate	Democratic Vote	Democratic Candidate	Other Vote	Rep.-Dem. Plurality	Total Vote Rep.	Total Vote Dem.	Major Vote Rep.	Major Vote Dem.
1	2022	361,477	182,336	SCHWEIKERT, DAVID*	179,141	HODGE, JEVIN		3,195 R	50.4%	49.6%	50.4%	49.6%
1	2020	365,178	176,709	SHEDD, TIFFANY	188,469	O'HALLERAN, TOM*		11,760 D	48.4%	51.6%	48.4%	51.6%
1	2018	266,089	122,784	ROGERS, WENDY	143,240	O'HALLERAN, TOM*	65	20,456 D	46.1%	53.8%	46.2%	53.8%
1	2016	280,710	121,745	BABEU, PAUL	142,219	O'HALLERAN, TOM	16,746	20,474 D	43.4%	50.7%	46.1%	53.9%
1	2014	185,114	87,723	TOBIN, ANDY	97,391	KIRKPATRICK, ANN*		9,668 D	47.4%	52.6%	47.4%	52.6%
1	2012	251,595	113,594	PATON, JONATHAN	122,774	KIRKPATRICK, ANN	15,227	9,180 D	45.1%	48.8%	48.1%	51.9%
2	2022	323,396	174,169	CRANE, ELI	149,151	O'HALLERAN, TOM*	76	25,018 R	53.9%	46.1%	53.9%	46.1%
2	2020	380,920	170,975	MARTIN, BRANDON	209,945	KIRKPATRICK, ANN*		38,970 D	44.9%	55.1%	44.9%	55.1%
2	2018	294,152	133,083	PETERSON, LEA MARQUEZ	161,000	KIRKPATRICK, ANN	69	27,917 D	45.2%	54.7%	45.3%	54.7%
2	2016	315,679	179,806	MCSALLY, MARTHA*	135,873	HEINZ, MATT		43,933 R	57.0%	43.0%	57.0%	43.0%
2	2014	219,351	109,704	MCSALLY, MARTHA	109,543	BARBER, RON*	104	161 R	50.0%	49.9%	50.0%	50.0%
2	2012	292,279	144,884	MCSALLY, MARTHA	147,338	BARBER, RON*	57	2,454 D	49.6%	50.4%	49.6%	50.4%
3	2022	141,074	32,475	ZINK, JEFFREY NELSON	108,599	GALLEGO, RUBEN*		76,124 D	23.0%	77.0%	23.0%	77.0%
3	2020	269,837	95,594	WOOD, DANIEL	174,243	GRIJALVA, RAUL M.*		78,649 D	35.4%	64.6%	35.4%	64.6%
3	2018	179,518	64,868	PIERSON, NICHOLAS "NICK"	114,650	GRIJALVA, RAUL M.*		49,782 D	36.1%	63.9%	36.1%	63.9%
3	2016	151,035			148,973	GRIJALVA, RAUL M.*	2,062	148,973 D		98.6%		100.0%
3	2014	104,428	46,185	SAUCEDO MERCER, GABRIELLA	58,192	GRIJALVA, RAUL M.*	51	12,007 D	44.2%	55.7%	44.2%	55.8%
3	2012	168,698	62,663	SAUCEDO MERCER, GABRIELLA	98,468	GRIJALVA, RAUL M.*	7,567	35,805 D	37.1%	58.4%	38.9%	61.1%
4	2022	265,498	116,521	COOPER, KELLY	148,941	STANTON, GREG*	36	32,420 D	43.9%	56.1%	43.9%	56.1%
4	2020	398,486	278,002	GOSAR, PAUL*	120,484	DISANTO, DELINA		157,518 R	69.8%	30.2%	69.8%	30.2%
4	2018	277,035	188,842	GOSAR, PAUL*	84,521	BRILL, DAVID	3,672	104,321 R	68.2%	30.5%	69.1%	30.9%
4	2016	284,783	203,487	GOSAR, PAUL*	81,296	WEISSER, MIKEL		122,191 R	71.5%	28.5%	71.5%	28.5%
4	2014	175,179	122,560	GOSAR, PAUL*	45,179	WEISSER, MIKEL	7,440	77,381 R	70.0%	25.8%	73.1%	26.9%
4	2012	243,760	162,907	GOSAR, PAUL*	69,154	ROBINSON, JOHNNIE	11,699	93,753 R	66.8%	28.4%	70.2%	29.8%
5	2022	321,590	182,464	BIGGS, ANDY*	120,243	RAMOS, JAVIER	18,883	62,221 R	56.7%	37.4%	60.3%	39.7%
5	2020	445,585	262,414	BIGGS, ANDY*	183,171	GREENE, JOAN		79,243 R	58.9%	41.1%	58.9%	41.1%
5	2018	313,064	186,037	BIGGS, ANDY*	127,027	GREENE, JOAN		59,010 R	59.4%	40.6%	59.4%	40.6%
5	2016	320,124	205,184	BIGGS, ANDY	114,940	FUENTES, TALIA		90,244 R	64.1%	35.9%	64.1%	35.9%
5	2014	179,463	124,867	SALMON, MATT*	54,596	WOODS, JAMES ISSAC		70,271 R	69.6%	30.4%	69.6%	30.4%
5	2012	273,059	183,470	SALMON, MATT	89,589	MORGAN, SPENCER		93,881 R	67.2%	32.8%	67.2%	32.8%
6	2022	349,283	177,201	CISCOMANI, JUAN	171,969	ENGEL, KIRSTEN	113	5,232 R	50.7%	49.2%	50.7%	49.3%
6	2020	417,427	217,783	SCHWEIKERT, DAVID*	199,644	TIPIRNENI, HIRAL		18,139 R	52.2%	47.8%	52.2%	47.8%
6	2018	313,699	173,140	SCHWEIKERT, DAVID*	140,559	MALIK, ANITA		32,581 R	55.2%	44.8%	55.2%	44.8%
6	2016	324,444	201,578	SCHWEIKERT, DAVID*	122,866	WILLIAMSON, W. JOHN		78,712 R	62.1%	37.9%	62.1%	37.9%
6	2014	199,776	129,578	SCHWEIKERT, DAVID*	70,198	WILLIAMSON, W. JOHN		59,380 R	64.9%	35.1%	64.9%	35.1%
6	2012	293,177	179,706	SCHWEIKERT, DAVID*	97,666	JETTE, MATTHEW	15,805	82,040 R	61.3%	33.3%	64.8%	35.2%
7	2022	195,862	69,444	POZZOLO, LUIS	126,418	GRIJALVA, RAÚL M.*		56,974 D	35.5%	64.5%	35.5%	64.5%
7	2020	215,678	50,226	BARNETT, JOSH	165,452	GALLEGO, RUBEN*		115,226 D	23.3%	76.7%	23.3%	76.7%
7	2018	132,051			113,044	GALLEGO, RUBEN*	19,007	113,044 D		85.6%		100.0%
7	2016	158,811	39,286	NUNEZ, EVE	119,465	GALLEGO, RUBEN*	60	80,179 D	24.7%	75.2%	24.7%	75.3%
7	2014	72,452			54,235	GALLEGO, RUBEN	18,217	54,235 D		74.9%		100.0%
7	2012	127,827			104,489	PASTOR, ED*	23,338	104,489 D		81.7%		100.0%
8	2022	204,713	197,555	LESKO, DEBBIE*			7,158	197,555 R	96.5%		100.0%	
8	2020	425,449	254,633	LESKO, DEBBIE*	170,816	MUSCATO, MICHAEL ARCHANGEL		83,817 R	59.9%	40.1%	59.9%	40.1%
8	2018	304,417	168,835	LESKO, DEBBIE*	135,569	TIPIRNENI, HIRAL	13	33,266 R	55.5%	44.5%	55.5%	44.5%
8	2016	298,971	204,942	FRANKS, TRENT*			94,029	204,942 R	68.5%		100.0%	
8	2014	169,776	128,710	FRANKS, TRENT*			41,066	128,710 R	75.8%		100.0%	
8	2012	272,791	172,809	FRANKS, TRENT*	95,635	SCHARER, GENE	4,347	77,174 R	63.3%	35.1%	64.4%	35.6%
9	2022	197,185	192,796	GOSAR, PAUL*			4,389	192,796 R	97.8%		100.0%	
9	2020	352,274	135,180	GILES, DAVE	217,094	STANTON, GREG*		81,914 D	38.4%	61.6%	38.4%	61.6%
9	2018	261,245	101,662	FERRARA, STEPHEN L.	159,583	STANTON, GREG		57,921 D	38.9%	61.1%	38.9%	61.1%
9	2016	277,507	108,350	GILES, DAVE	169,055	SINEMA, KYRSTEN*	102	60,705 D	39.0%	60.9%	39.1%	60.9%
9	2014	162,062	67,841	ROGERS, WENDY	88,609	SINEMA, KYRSTEN*	5,612	20,768 D	41.9%	54.7%	43.4%	56.6%
9	2012	250,131	111,630	PARKER, VERNON B.	121,881	SINEMA, KYRSTEN	16,620	10,251 D	44.6%	48.7%	47.8%	52.2%
TOTAL	2022	2,360,078	1,324,961		1,004,462		30,655	320,499 R	56.1%	42.6%	56.9%	43.1%
TOTAL	2020	3,270,834	1,641,516		1,629,318			12,198 R	50.2%	49.8%	50.2%	49.8%
TOTAL	2018	2,341,270	1,139,251		1,179,193		22,826	39,942 D	48.7%	50.4%	49.1%	50.9%
TOTAL	2016	2,412,064	1,264,378		1,034,687		112,999	229,691 R	52.4%	42.9%	55.0%	45.0%
TOTAL	2014	1,467,601	817,168		577,943		72,490	239,225 R	55.7%	39.4%	58.6%	41.4%
TOTAL	2012	2,173,317	1,131,663		946,994		94,660	184,669 R	52.1%	43.6%	54.4%	45.6%

Note: An asterisk (*) denotes incumbent.

ARIZONA
GENERAL AND PRIMARY ELECTIONS

GENERAL ELECTIONS: OTHER VOTES

Senate	Other vote was 53,762 Libertarian (Marc Victor), 197 Write-In (Write-In)
House	Other vote was:
CD 2	76 Write-In (Chris Sarappo)
CD 4	36 Write-In (Stephan Jones)
CD 5	18,851 Independent (Clint Smith), 32 Write-In (Debra Jo Borden)
CD 6	71 Write-in (Avery Thornton), 42 Write-In (Frank Bertone)
CD 8	5,145 Write-In (Jeremy Spreitzer), 2,013 Write-In (Alixandria Guzman)
CD 9	3,531 Write-In (Richard Grayson), 858 Write-In (Tom T.)

2022 PRIMARY ELECTIONS: SUPPLEMENTARY INFORMATION

Primary	August 2, 2022	Registration (as of August 2, 2022)		4,173,748	Republican Democratic Libertarian Other	1,440,250 1,291,221 32,779 1,409,498

Primary Type — Semi-open—Registered Democrats and Republicans could vote only in their party's primary. But voters not registered with any political party could participate in either the Democratic or Republican primary.

	REPUBLICAN PRIMARIES			DEMOCRATIC PRIMARIES		
Senator	Masters, Blake	327,198	40.2%	Kelly, Mark*	589,400	100.0%
	Lamon, Jim	228,467	28.1%			
	Brnovich, Mark	144,092	17.7%			
	McGuire, Michael "Mick"	71,100	8.7%			
	Olson, Justin	41,985	5.2%			
	Bozic, David Samuel (Write-In)	138				
	Bertone, Frank (Write-In)	88				
	TOTAL	*813,068*		*TOTAL*	*589,400*	
Governor	Lake, Kari	398,860	48.0%	Hobbs, Katie	431,059	72.3%
	Taylor Robson, Karrin	358,682	43.1%	Lopez, Marco	136,090	22.8%
	Salmon, Matt	30,704	3.7%	Lieberman, Aaron	28,878	4.8%
	Neely, Scott David	25,876	3.1%			
	Tulliani Zen, Paola	17,281	2.1%			
	Roldan, Carlos (Write-In)	42				
	Schatz, Alex (Write-In)	39				
	Finerd, Patrick (Write-In)	24				
	TOTAL	*831,508*		*TOTAL*	*596,027*	
Congressional District 1	Schweikert, David*	52,067	43.6%	Hodge, Jevin	46,144	61.9%
	Norton, Elijah	39,435	33.0%	Metzendorf, Adam	28,267	37.9%
	Barnett, Josh	27,999	23.4%	DiSanto, Delina (Write-In)	175	0.2%
	TOTAL	*119,501*		*TOTAL*	*74,586*	
Congressional District 2	Crane, Eli	38,681	35.8%	O'Halleran, Tom*	71,391	100.0%
	Blackman, Walter	26,399	24.4%			
	DeLuzio, Mark	18,515	17.1%			
	Yates, Andy	7,467	6.9%			
	Moore, John William	7,327	6.8%			
	Krystofiak, Steven	5,905	5.5%			
	Watkins, Ron	3,810	3.5%			
	TOTAL	*108,104*		*TOTAL*	*71,391*	
Congressional District 3	Zink, Jeffrey Nelson	13,894	100.0%	Gallego, Ruben*	47,972	100.0%
	TOTAL	*13,894*		*TOTAL*	*47,972*	

ARIZONA
GENERAL AND PRIMARY ELECTIONS

	REPUBLICAN PRIMARIES			DEMOCRATIC PRIMARIES		
Congressional District 4	Cooper, Kelly	20,281	28.4%	Stanton, Greg*	61,319	100.0%
	Wheeless, Tanya Contreras	18,166	25.4%			
	Giles, Dave	13,348	18.7%			
	Lopez, Rene	10,149	14.2%			
	Davison, Jerone	9,502	13.3%			
	TOTAL	71,446		TOTAL	61,319	
Congressional District 5	Biggs, Andy*	98,114	99.5%	Ramos, Javier	50,647	100.0%
	Beall, Jim Paul (Write-In)	197	0.2%			
	Callan, Martin (Write-In)	193	0.2%			
	Boels, David (Write-In)	66	0.1%			
	TOTAL	98,570		TOTAL	50,647	
Congressional District 6	Ciscomani, Juan	49,559	47.1%	Engel, Kirsten	54,060	59.1%
	Martin, Brandon	21,987	20.9%	Hernandez, Daniel	31,815	34.8%
	Winn, Kathleen	19,635	18.7%	Anderson, Avery	5,639	6.2%
	Mayberry, Young	8,942	8.5%			
	Free, Lucretia	5,029	4.8%			
	Flayer, Jordan (Write-In)	32				
	TOTAL	105,184		TOTAL	91,514	
Congressional District 7	Pozzolo, Luis	20,413	69.0%	Grijalva, Raúl M.*	62,547	100.0%
	Becker, Nina	9,064	30.6%			
	Reetz, David "Rizzo" (Write-In)	103	0.3%			
	TOTAL	29,580		TOTAL	62,547	
Congressional District 8	Lesko, Debbie*	100,629	100.0%			
	TOTAL	100,629				
Congressional District 9	Gosar, Paul*	67,340	65.9%	Lucier, David (Write-In)	1,319	72.7%
	Kutz, Randy	13,387	13.1%	Scharer, Gene (Write-In)	496	27.3%
	Morgan, Adam	12,508	12.2%			
	Dowling, Sandra E.	8,851	8.7%			
	Harper, Jack (Write-In)	76	0.1%			
	TOTAL	102,162		TOTAL	1,815	

Note: An asterisk (*) denotes incumbent.

ARKANSAS

Statewide Races

In 2010, then-Rep. John Boozman was running in a crowded GOP primary as he sought a promotion from the House to the Senate. Though he declined to make one of the primary debates, he sent a surrogate with a well-known last name to stand in for him: Sarah Huckabee, the daughter of former Gov. Mike Huckabee. Boozman won the primary with an outright majority and easily captured the Senate seat in the general election. A dozen years later, as he sought a third term, Huckabee (who assumed the surname Sanders after her marriage) would join him at the top of the statewide ticket. Boozman won reelection 65%–31% and Huckabee Sanders won the open governorship by a somewhat lesser 63%–35% margin.

A historically Democratic state – in 2008, Barack Obama became the first Democrat to win the presidency without Arkansas since its admission to the Union – Republicans have made seismic gains in the state over the past dozen years. Broadly, Little Rock's Pulaski County and parts of the northwest have drifted Democratic but virtually everything else has reddened.

That trend was evident in 2022's results. In 2010, Boozman unseated then-Sen. Blanche Lincoln, a Democrat who had a base in eastern Arkansas. Despite his 20-point win over Lincoln, Boozman lost all six counties that touch the Mississippi River (the state's eastern border) – though this area is about half Black by composition, it is rural. In 2022, Boozman carried five of those six counties, only missing out on Phillips County (coincidentally Lincoln's home county). Meanwhile, Republican margins in the northwest have receded. Historically the area of the state most amenable to Republicanism – in 1974, future governor (and president) Bill Clinton lost a congressional race there – the northwest has relatively high college attainment rates and a growing Hispanic bloc. In 2010, Boozman, who then represented the area in the House, carried Benton County (the northwesternmost county and home to Walmart's corporate headquarters) by over 50 points. In 2022, Boozman did no better in Benton County than he did statewide. One county south, Boozman "only" carried Washington County (where the University of Arkansas is located) by nine points and Huckabee Sanders lost it by 481 votes.

Looking to 2024, even if Democrats continue to slide in the rurals, Washington County may flip blue: it gave Trump only a 50%–46% margin in 2020, this was clearly down from the 56%–40% that Mitt Romney received there eight years earlier.

House Races

Arkansas, which has had an entirely GOP four-member delegation since the 2012 elections, was uneventful on the House front: all incumbents were reelected by crushing margins. Since losing the seat in 2010, Democrats have occasionally targeted the Little Rock-based 2nd District. Republican redistricters strengthened Rep. French Hill's (R, AR-2) hand by splitting Little Rock's Black community among three districts. Term-limited Republican Gov. Asa Hutchinson, who seemed to think such a move was excessive, did not sign off on the map, although since he declined to veto the redistricting legislation, the map took effect without his signature.

ARKANSAS
Congressional districts first established for elections held in 2022
4 members

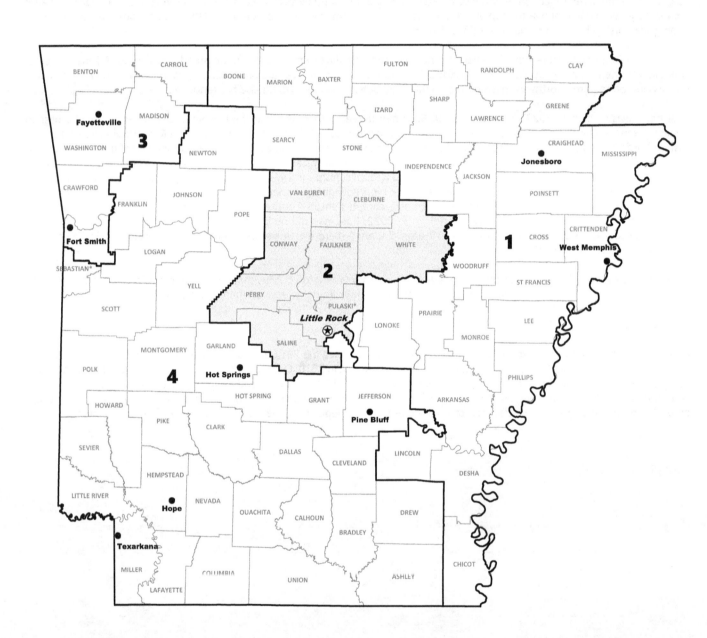

*Asterisk indicates a county whose boundaries include parts of two or more congressional districts.
CD 2 is highlighted for visibility.

ARKANSAS

GOVERNOR
Sarah Huckabee Sanders (R). Elected 2022 to a four-year term.

SENATORS (2 Republicans)
John Boozman (R). Reelected 2022 to a six-year term. Previously elected 2016, 2010.

Tom Cotton (R). Reelected 2020 to a six-year term. Previously elected 2014.

REPRESENTATIVES (4 Republicans)
1. Rick Crawford (R)
2. French Hill (R)
3. Steve Womack (R)
4. Bruce Westerman (R)

POSTWAR VOTE FOR PRESIDENT

Year	Total Vote	Republican Vote	Republican Candidate	Democratic Vote	Democratic Candidate	Other Vote	Rep.-Dem. Plurality	Total Vote Rep.	Total Vote Dem.	Major Vote Rep.	Major Vote Dem.
2020	1,219,069	760,647	Trump, Donald J.*	423,932	Biden, Joseph R. Jr.	34,490	336,715 R	62.4%	34.8%	64.2%	35.8%
2016**	1,130,676	684,872	Trump, Donald J.	380,494	Clinton, Hillary Rodham	65,310	304,378 R	60.6%	33.7%	64.3%	35.7%
2012	1,069,468	647,744	Romney, W. Mitt	394,409	Obama, Barack H.*	27,315	253,335 R	60.6%	36.9%	62.2%	37.8%
2008	1,086,617	638,017	McCain, John S. III	422,310	Obama, Barack H.	26,290	215,707 R	58.7%	38.9%	60.2%	39.8%
2004	1,054,945	572,898	Bush, George W.*	469,953	Kerry, John F.	12,094	102,945 R	54.3%	44.5%	54.9%	45.1%
2000**	921,781	472,940	Bush, George W.	422,768	Gore, Albert Jr.	26,073	50,172 R	51.3%	45.9%	52.8%	47.2%
1996**	884,262	325,416	Dole, Robert "Bob"	475,171	Clinton, Bill*	83,675	149,755 D	36.8%	53.7%	40.6%	59.4%
1992**	950,653	337,324	Bush, George H.*	505,823	Clinton, Bill	107,506	168,499 D	35.5%	53.2%	40.0%	60.0%
1988	827,738	466,578	Bush, George H.	349,237	Dukakis, Michael S.	11,923	117,341 R	56.4%	42.2%	57.2%	42.8%
1984	884,406	534,774	Reagan, Ronald*	338,646	Mondale, Walter F.	10,986	196,128 R	60.5%	38.3%	61.2%	38.8%
1980**	837,582	403,164	Reagan, Ronald	398,041	Carter, Jimmy*	36,377	5,123 R	48.1%	47.5%	50.3%	49.7%
1976	767,535	267,903	Ford, Gerald R.*	498,604	Carter, Jimmy	1,028	230,701 D	34.9%	65.0%	35.0%	65.0%
1972	651,320	448,541	Nixon, Richard M.*	199,892	McGovern, George S.	2,887	248,649 R	68.9%	30.7%	69.2%	30.8%
1968**	619,969	190,759	Nixon, Richard M.	188,228	Humphrey, Hubert Horatio Jr.	240,982	2,531 R#	30.8%	30.4%	50.3%	49.7%
1964	560,426	243,264	Goldwater, Barry M. Sr.	314,197	Johnson, Lyndon B.*	2,965	70,933 D	43.4%	56.1%	43.6%	56.4%
1960	428,509	184,508	Nixon, Richard M.	215,049	Kennedy, John F.	28,952	30,541 D	43.1%	50.2%	46.2%	53.8%
1956	406,572	186,287	Eisenhower, Dwight D.*	213,277	Stevenson, Adlai E. II	7,008	26,990 D	45.8%	52.5%	46.6%	53.4%
1952	404,800	177,155	Eisenhower, Dwight D.	226,300	Stevenson, Adlai E. II	1,345	49,145 D	43.8%	55.9%	43.9%	56.1%
1948**	242,475	50,959	Dewey, Thomas E.	149,659	Truman, Harry S.*	41,857	98,700 D	21.0%	61.7%	25.4%	74.6%

Note: An asterisk (*) denotes incumbent. A pound sign (#) in the plurality column indicates that the winner in 1968 did not run under the banner of either major party. **In past elections, the other vote included: 2016 - 29,949 Libertarian (Gary Johnson); 2000 - 13,421 Green (Ralph Nader); 1996 - 69,884 Reform (Ross Perot); 1992 - 99,132 Independent (Perot); 1980 - 22,468 Independent (John Anderson); 1968 - 240,982 American Independent (Wallace); 1948 - 40,068 States' Rights (Strom Thurmond). Wallace carried Arkansas in 1968 with 38.9 percent of the vote.

ARKANSAS

POSTWAR VOTE FOR GOVERNOR

Year	Total Vote	Republican Vote	Republican Candidate	Democratic Vote	Democratic Candidate	Other Vote	Rep.-Dem. Plurality	Total Vote Rep.	Total Vote Dem.	Major Vote Rep.	Major Vote Dem.
2022	907,037	571,105	Huckabee Sanders, Sarah	319,242	Jones, Chris	16,690	251,863 R	63.0%	35.2%	64.1%	35.9%
2018	891,509	582,406	Hutchinson, Asa*	283,218	Henderson, Jared K.	25,885	299,188 R	65.3%	31.8%	67.3%	32.7%
2014	848,592	470,429	Hutchinson, Asa	352,115	Ross, Mike	26,048	118,314 R	55.4%	41.5%	57.2%	42.8%
2010	781,333	262,784	Keet, Jim	503,336	Beebe, Mike D.*	15,213	240,552 D	33.6%	64.4%	34.3%	65.7%
2006	774,680	315,040	Hutchinson, Asa	430,765	Beebe, Mike D.	28,875	115,725 D	40.7%	55.6%	42.2%	57.8%
2002	805,696	427,082	Huckabee, Mike*	378,250	Fisher, Jimmie Lou	364	48,832 R	53.0%	46.9%	53.0%	47.0%
1998	728,619	430,919	Huckabee, Mike*	278,155	King, James	19,545	152,764 R	59.1%	38.2%	60.8%	39.2%
1994	716,840	287,904	Nelson, Sheffield	428,936	Tucker, Jim Guy*		141,032 D	40.2%	59.8%	40.2%	59.8%
1990	696,412	295,925	Nelson, Sheffield	400,386	Clinton, Bill*	101	104,461 D	42.5%	57.5%	42.5%	57.5%
1986**	688,551	248,427	White, Frank D.	439,882	Clinton, Bill*	242	191,455 D	36.1%	63.9%	36.1%	63.9%
1984	886,548	331,987	Freeman, Woody	554,561	Clinton, Bill*		222,574 D	37.4%	62.6%	37.4%	62.6%
1982	789,351	357,496	White, Frank D.*	431,855	Clinton, Bill		74,359 D	45.3%	54.7%	45.3%	54.7%
1980	838,925	435,684	White, Frank D.	403,241	Clinton, Bill*		32,443 R	51.9%	48.1%	51.9%	48.1%
1978	528,912	193,746	Lowe, A. Lynn	335,101	Clinton, Bill	65	141,355 D	36.6%	63.4%	36.6%	63.4%
1976	726,949	121,716	Griffith, Leon	605,083	Pryor, David H.*	150	483,367 D	16.7%	83.2%	16.7%	83.3%
1974	545,974	187,872	Coon, Ken	358,018	Pryor, David H.	84	170,146 D	34.4%	65.6%	34.4%	65.6%
1972	648,069	159,177	Blaylock, Len E.	488,892	Bumpers, Dale*		329,715 D	24.6%	75.4%	24.6%	75.4%
1970	608,198	196,418	Rockefeller, Winthrop*	375,648	Bumpers, Dale	36,132	179,230 D	32.3%	61.8%	34.3%	65.7%
1968	615,590	322,777	Rockefeller, Winthrop*	292,813	Crank, Marion		29,964 R	52.4%	47.6%	52.4%	47.6%
1966	563,527	306,324	Rockefeller, Winthrop	257,203	Johnson, James Douglas		49,121 R	54.4%	45.6%	54.4%	45.6%
1964	592,113	254,561	Rockefeller, Winthrop	337,489	Faubus, Orval E.*	63	82,928 D	43.0%	57.0%	43.0%	57.0%
1962	308,092	82,349	Ricketts, Willis	225,743	Faubus, Orval E.*		143,394 D	26.7%	73.3%	26.7%	73.3%
1960	421,985	129,921	Britt, Henry M.	292,064	Faubus, Orval E.*		162,143 D	30.8%	69.2%	30.8%	69.2%
1958	286,886	50,288	Johnson, George W.	236,598	Faubus, Orval E.*		186,310 D	17.5%	82.5%	17.5%	82.5%
1956	399,012	77,215	Mitchell, Roy	321,797	Faubus, Orval E.*		244,582 D	19.4%	80.6%	19.4%	80.6%
1954	335,176	127,004	Remmel, Pratt C.	208,121	Faubus, Orval E.	51	81,117 D	37.9%	62.1%	37.9%	62.1%
1952	391,592	49,292	Speck, Jefferson W.	342,292	Cherry, Francis	8	293,000 D	12.6%	87.4%	12.6%	87.4%
1950	317,081	50,303	Speck, Jefferson W.	266,778	McMath, Sidney S.*		216,475 D	15.9%	84.1%	15.9%	84.1%
1948	244,271	26,500	Black, Charles R.	217,771	McMath, Sidney S.		191,271 D	10.8%	89.2%	10.8%	89.2%
1946	152,162	24,133	Mills, W. T.	128,029	Laney, Ben*		103,896 D	15.9%	84.1%	15.9%	84.1%

Note: An asterisk (*) denotes incumbent. **The term of office for Arkansas Governor was increased from two to four years effective with the 1986 election.

POSTWAR VOTE FOR SENATOR

Year	Total Vote	Republican Vote	Republican Candidate	Democratic Vote	Democratic Candidate	Other Vote	Rep.-Dem. Plurality	Total Vote Rep.	Total Vote Dem.	Major Vote Rep.	Major Vote Dem.
2022	901,306	592,437	Boozman, John*	280,187	James, Natalie	28,682	312,250 R	65.7%	31.1%	67.9%	32.1%
2020**	1,193,261	793,871	Cotton, Tom*			399,390	793,871 R	66.5%		100.0%	
2016	1,107,522	661,984	Boozman, John*	400,602	Eldridge, Conner	44,936	261,382 R	59.8%	36.2%	62.3%	37.7%
2014	847,505	478,819	Cotton, Tom	334,174	Pryor, Mark*	34,512	144,645 R	56.5%	39.4%	58.9%	41.1%
2010	779,957	451,618	Boozman, John	288,156	Lincoln, Blanche L.*	40,183	163,462 R	57.9%	36.9%	61.0%	39.0%
2008**	1,011,754			804,678	Pryor, Mark*	207,076	804,678 D		79.5%		100.0%
2004	1,039,349	458,036	Holt, Jim L.	580,973	Lincoln, Blanche L.*	340	122,937 D	44.1%	55.9%	44.1%	55.9%
2002	803,959	370,653	Hutchinson, Tim*	433,306	Pryor, Mark		62,653 D	46.1%	53.9%	46.1%	53.9%
1998	700,644	295,870	Boozman, Fay	385,878	Lincoln, Blanche L.	18,896	90,008 D	42.2%	55.1%	43.4%	56.6%
1996	846,183	445,942	Hutchinson, Tim	400,241	Bryant, Winston		45,701 R	52.7%	47.3%	52.7%	47.3%
1992	920,008	366,373	Huckabee, Mike	553,635	Bumpers, Dale*		187,262 D	39.8%	60.2%	39.8%	60.2%
1990**	494,735			493,910	Pryor, David H.*	825	493,910 D		99.8%		100.0%
1986	695,487	262,313	Hutchinson, Asa	433,122	Bumpers, Dale*	52	170,809 D	37.7%	62.3%	37.7%	62.3%
1984	875,956	373,615	Bethune, Ed	502,341	Pryor, David H.*		128,726 D	42.7%	57.3%	42.7%	57.3%
1980	808,812	330,576	Clark, Bill	477,905	Bumpers, Dale*	331	147,329 D	40.9%	59.1%	40.9%	59.1%
1978	522,239	84,722	Kelly, Tom	399,916	Pryor, David H.	37,601	315,194 D	16.2%	76.6%	17.5%	82.5%
1974	543,082	82,026	Jones, John Harris	461,056	Bumpers, Dale		379,030 D	15.1%	84.9%	15.1%	84.9%
1972	634,636	248,238	Babbitt, Wayne H.	386,398	McClellan, John L.*		138,160 D	39.1%	60.9%	39.1%	60.9%
1968	591,704	241,739	Bernard, Charles T.	349,965	Fulbright, J. William*		108,226 D	40.9%	59.1%	40.9%	59.1%
1966**					McClellan, John L.*		D				
1962	312,880	98,013	Jones, Kenneth	214,867	Fulbright, J. William*		116,854 D	31.3%	68.7%	31.3%	68.7%
1960**					McClellan, John L.*		D				
1956	399,695	68,016	Henley, Ben C.	331,679	Fulbright, J. William*		263,663 D	17.0%	83.0%	17.0%	83.0%
1954	291,058			291,058	McClellan, John L.*		291,058 D		100.0%		100.0%
1950	302,582			302,582	Fulbright, J. William*		302,582 D		100.0%		100.0%
1948	231,922			216,401	McClellan, John L.*	15,521	216,401 D		93.3%		100.0%

Note: An asterisk (*) denotes incumbent. **In past elections, the other vote included: 2020 - 399,390 Libertarian (Ricky Harrington), and 2008 - 207,076 Green (Rebekah Kennedy), who finished second. In 1990 the vote for Senator David H. Pryor was not canvassed in seven counties because he was unopposed. Senator John L. McClellan was re-elected in 1960 and in 1966, but his vote was not canvassed in many counties. The Republican Party did not run a candidate in the 1948, 1950, 1954, 1960, 1966, 1990, and 2008 Senate elections. The Democratic Party did not run a candidate in the 2020 Senate election.

ARKANSAS
GOVERNOR 2022

2020 Census Population	County	Total Vote	Republican (Huckabee Sanders)	Democratic (Jones)	Other	Rep.-Dem. Plurality		Percentage Total Vote		Percentage Major Vote	
								Rep.	Dem.	Rep.	Dem.
17,468	ARKANSAS	4,489	3,197	1,231	61	1,966	R	71.2%	27.4%	72.2%	27.8%
19,602	ASHLEY	5,461	4,012	1,386	63	2,626	R	73.5%	25.4%	74.3%	25.7%
42,212	BAXTER	15,668	12,098	3,293	277	8,805	R	77.2%	21.0%	78.6%	21.4%
281,073	BENTON	90,897	55,907	33,000	1,990	22,907	R	61.5%	36.3%	62.9%	37.1%
37,552	BOONE	12,751	10,127	2,319	305	7,808	R	79.4%	18.2%	81.4%	18.6%
10,800	BRADLEY	2,636	1,764	846	26	918	R	66.9%	32.1%	67.6%	32.4%
5,221	CALHOUN	1,589	1,248	324	17	924	R	78.5%	20.4%	79.4%	20.6%
28,510	CARROLL	9,040	5,692	3,158	190	2,534	R	63.0%	34.9%	64.3%	35.7%
10,063	CHICOT	3,406	1,601	1,782	23	181	D	47.0%	52.3%	47.3%	52.7%
22,280	CLARK	6,167	3,492	2,589	86	903	R	56.6%	42.0%	57.4%	42.6%
14,558	CLAY	3,944	3,060	798	86	2,262	R	77.6%	20.2%	79.3%	20.7%
24,967	CLEBURNE	10,042	8,252	1,608	182	6,644	R	82.2%	16.0%	83.7%	16.3%
7,949	CLEVELAND	2,815	2,305	479	31	1,826	R	81.9%	17.0%	82.8%	17.2%
23,424	COLUMBIA	6,087	4,066	1,937	84	2,129	R	66.8%	31.8%	67.7%	32.3%
20,908	CONWAY	6,764	4,481	2,176	107	2,305	R	66.2%	32.2%	67.3%	32.7%
110,860	CRAIGHEAD	27,712	18,171	8,980	561	9,191	R	65.6%	32.4%	66.9%	33.1%
63,436	CRAWFORD	17,959	13,814	3,778	367	10,036	R	76.9%	21.0%	78.5%	21.5%
47,837	CRITTENDEN	10,752	5,295	5,294	163	1	R	49.2%	49.2%	50.0%	50.0%
16,401	CROSS	4,935	3,672	1,174	89	2,498	R	74.4%	23.8%	75.8%	24.2%
6,995	DALLAS	2,090	1,331	732	27	599	R	63.7%	35.0%	64.5%	35.5%
11,324	DESHA	3,110	1,611	1,464	35	147	R	51.8%	47.1%	52.4%	47.6%
18,244	DREW	5,312	3,380	1,871	61	1,509	R	63.6%	35.2%	64.4%	35.6%
126,340	FAULKNER	40,335	25,382	14,131	822	11,251	R	62.9%	35.0%	64.2%	35.8%
17,763	FRANKLIN	5,443	4,130	1,213	100	2,917	R	75.9%	22.3%	77.3%	22.7%
12,550	FULTON	3,984	3,045	834	105	2,211	R	76.4%	20.9%	78.5%	21.5%
99,945	GARLAND	33,340	22,225	10,493	622	11,732	R	66.7%	31.5%	67.9%	32.1%
18,332	GRANT	6,287	5,112	1,055	120	4,057	R	81.3%	16.8%	82.9%	17.1%
45,465	GREENE	11,562	8,982	2,330	250	6,652	R	77.7%	20.2%	79.4%	20.6%
21,504	HEMPSTEAD	4,685	3,311	1,316	58	1,995	R	70.7%	28.1%	71.6%	28.4%
33,867	HOT SPRING	9,939	7,230	2,528	181	4,702	R	72.7%	25.4%	74.1%	25.9%
13,225	HOWARD	3,642	2,580	1,000	62	1,580	R	70.8%	27.5%	72.1%	27.9%
37,914	INDEPENDENCE	10,585	8,077	2,316	192	5,761	R	76.3%	21.9%	77.7%	22.3%
13,679	IZARD	4,597	3,636	861	100	2,775	R	79.1%	18.7%	80.9%	19.1%
16,722	JACKSON	4,037	2,860	1,106	71	1,754	R	70.8%	27.4%	72.1%	27.9%
66,485	JEFFERSON	17,497	6,874	10,466	157	3,592	D	39.3%	59.8%	39.6%	60.4%
26,672	JOHNSON	7,010	5,071	1,791	148	3,280	R	72.3%	25.5%	73.9%	26.1%
6,612	LAFAYETTE	1,982	1,286	674	22	612	R	64.9%	34.0%	65.6%	34.4%
16,415	LAWRENCE	4,642	3,655	876	111	2,779	R	78.7%	18.9%	80.7%	19.3%
8,831	LEE	2,017	983	1,012	22	29	D	48.7%	50.2%	49.3%	50.7%
13,081	LINCOLN	2,777	2,015	730	32	1,285	R	72.6%	26.3%	73.4%	26.6%
12,275	LITTLE RIVER	3,815	2,906	835	74	2,071	R	76.2%	21.9%	77.7%	22.3%
21,501	LOGAN	6,258	4,854	1,265	139	3,589	R	77.6%	20.2%	79.3%	20.7%
73,667	LONOKE	22,370	16,603	5,287	480	11,316	R	74.2%	23.6%	75.8%	24.2%
16,674	MADISON	5,817	4,403	1,304	110	3,099	R	75.7%	22.4%	77.2%	22.8%
16,821	MARION	6,002	4,744	1,119	139	3,625	R	79.0%	18.6%	80.9%	19.1%
43,325	MILLER	11,268	8,571	2,523	174	6,048	R	76.1%	22.4%	77.3%	22.7%
40,449	MISSISSIPPI	8,693	5,401	3,092	200	2,309	R	62.1%	35.6%	63.6%	36.4%
6,680	MONROE	2,241	1,233	977	31	256	R	55.0%	43.6%	55.8%	44.2%
9,025	MONTGOMERY	3,121	2,471	578	72	1,893	R	79.2%	18.5%	81.0%	19.0%
8,258	NEVADA	2,464	1,658	780	26	878	R	67.3%	31.7%	68.0%	32.0%
7,771	NEWTON	3,080	2,440	557	83	1,883	R	79.2%	18.1%	81.4%	18.6%
23,384	OUACHITA	7,023	4,065	2,863	95	1,202	R	57.9%	40.8%	58.7%	41.3%
10,478	PERRY	3,818	2,873	871	74	2,002	R	75.2%	22.8%	76.7%	23.3%
17,639	PHILLIPS	4,366	1,892	2,415	59	523	D	43.3%	55.3%	43.9%	56.1%
10,736	PIKE	3,724	3,121	552	51	2,569	R	83.8%	14.8%	85.0%	15.0%
23,537	POINSETT	5,569	4,386	1,050	133	3,336	R	78.8%	18.9%	80.7%	19.3%
20,000	POLK	6,907	5,634	1,123	150	4,511	R	81.6%	16.3%	83.4%	16.6%
64,342	POPE	17,630	12,928	4,418	284	8,510	R	73.3%	25.1%	74.5%	25.5%
8,057	PRAIRIE	2,668	2,167	459	42	1,708	R	81.2%	17.2%	82.5%	17.5%
392,189	PULASKI	124,153	47,027	75,393	1,733	28,366	D	37.9%	60.7%	38.4%	61.6%

ARKANSAS
GOVERNOR 2022

2020 Census Population	County	Total Vote	Republican (Huckabee Sanders)	Democratic (Jones)	Other	Rep.-Dem. Plurality		Total Vote		Major Vote	
								Rep.	Dem.	Rep.	Dem.
18,036	RANDOLPH	5,357	4,201	1,026	130	3,175	R	78.4%	19.2%	80.4%	19.6%
123,287	SALINE	43,170	29,872	12,532	766	17,340	R	69.2%	29.0%	70.4%	29.6%
10,284	SCOTT	2,961	2,498	407	56	2,091	R	84.4%	13.7%	86.0%	14.0%
7,903	SEARCY	3,170	2,608	492	70	2,116	R	82.3%	15.5%	84.1%	15.9%
128,014	SEBASTIAN	34,376	22,939	10,734	703	12,205	R	66.7%	31.2%	68.1%	31.9%
17,018	SEVIER	3,663	2,825	784	54	2,041	R	77.1%	21.4%	78.3%	21.7%
17,579	SHARP	6,047	4,816	1,056	175	3,760	R	79.6%	17.5%	82.0%	18.0%
24,832	ST. FRANCIS	5,082	2,477	2,527	78	50	D	48.7%	49.7%	49.5%	50.5%
12,555	STONE	5,109	3,936	1,070	103	2,866	R	77.0%	20.9%	78.6%	21.4%
38,617	UNION	11,693	7,826	3,695	172	4,131	R	66.9%	31.6%	67.9%	32.1%
16,571	VAN BUREN	6,273	4,810	1,335	128	3,475	R	76.7%	21.3%	78.3%	21.7%
240,117	WASHINGTON	70,656	34,361	34,842	1,453	481	D	48.6%	49.3%	49.7%	50.3%
79,013	WHITE	23,125	18,010	4,613	502	13,397	R	77.9%	19.9%	79.6%	20.4%
6,307	WOODRUFF	2,092	1,347	695	50	652	R	64.4%	33.2%	66.0%	34.0%
21,367	YELL	5,289	4,172	1,022	95	3,150	R	78.9%	19.3%	80.3%	19.7%
3,025,394	TOTAL	907,037	571,105	319,242	16,690	251,863	R	63.0%	35.2%	64.1%	35.9%

ARKANSAS
HOUSE OF REPRESENTATIVES

CD	Year	Total Vote	Republican Vote	Republican Candidate	Democratic Vote	Democratic Candidate	Other Vote	Rep.-Dem. Plurality		Rep.	Dem.	Rep.	Dem.
1	2022	208,372	153,774	CRAWFORD, RICK*	54,598	HODGES, MONTE		99,176	R	73.8%	26.2%	73.8%	26.2%
1	2020	237,596	237,596	CRAWFORD, RICK*				237,596	R	100.0%		100.0%	
1	2018	201,245	138,757	CRAWFORD, RICK*	57,907	DESAI, CHINTAN	4,581	80,850	R	68.9%	28.8%	70.6%	29.4%
1	2016	241,047	183,866	CRAWFORD, RICK*			57,181	183,866	R	76.3%		100.0%	
1	2014	196,256	124,139	CRAWFORD, RICK*	63,555	MCPHERSON, JACKIE	8,562	60,584	R	63.3%	32.4%	66.1%	33.9%
1	2012	246,843	138,800	CRAWFORD, RICK*	96,601	ELLINGTON, SCOTT	11,442	42,199	R	56.2%	39.1%	59.0%	41.0%
2	2022	246,446	147,975	HILL, FRENCH*	86,887	HATHAWAY, QUINTESSA	11,584	61,088	R	60.0%	35.3%	63.0%	37.0%
2	2020	332,503	184,093	HILL, FRENCH*	148,410	ELLIOTT, JOYCE		35,683	R	55.4%	44.6%	55.4%	44.6%
2	2018	253,453	132,125	HILL, FRENCH*	116,135	TUCKER, CLARKE	5,193	15,990	R	52.1%	45.8%	53.2%	46.8%
2	2016	302,464	176,472	HILL, FRENCH*	111,347	CURRY, DIANNE	14,645	65,125	R	58.3%	36.8%	61.3%	38.7%
2	2014	237,330	123,073	HILL, FRENCH	103,477	HAYS, PATRICK	10,780	19,596	R	51.9%	43.6%	54.3%	45.7%
2	2012	286,598	158,175	GRIFFIN, TIM*	113,156	RULE, HERB	15,267	45,019	R	55.2%	39.5%	58.3%	41.7%
3	2022	223,588	142,401	WOMACK, STEVE*	73,541	MALLETT-HAYS, LAUREN	7,646	68,860	R	63.7%	32.9%	65.9%	34.1%
3	2020	334,262	214,960	WOMACK, STEVE*	106,325	WILLIAMS, CELESTE	12,977	108,635	R	64.3%	31.8%	66.9%	33.1%
3	2018	229,708	148,717	WOMACK, STEVE*	74,952	MAHONY, JOSHUA	6,039	73,765	R	64.7%	32.6%	66.5%	33.5%
3	2016	280,907	217,192	WOMACK, STEVE*			63,715	217,192	R	77.3%		100.0%	
3	2014	190,935	151,630	WOMACK, STEVE*			39,305	151,630	R	79.4%		100.0%	
3	2012	245,660	186,467	WOMACK, STEVE*			59,193	186,467	R	75.9%		100.0%	
4	2022	216,696	153,850	WESTERMAN, BRUCE*	56,745	WHITE, JOHN	6,101	97,105	R	71.0%	26.2%	73.1%	26.9%
4	2020	275,035	191,617	WESTERMAN, BRUCE*	75,750	HANSON, WILLIAM	7,668	115,867	R	69.7%	27.5%	71.7%	28.3%
4	2018	204,892	136,740	WESTERMAN, BRUCE*	63,984	SHAMEL, HAYDEN	4,168	72,756	R	66.7%	31.2%	68.1%	31.9%
4	2016	244,159	182,885	WESTERMAN, BRUCE*			61,274	182,885	R	74.9%		100.0%	
4	2014	206,131	110,789	WESTERMAN, BRUCE	87,742	WITT, JAMES LEE	7,600	23,047	R	53.7%	42.6%	55.8%	44.2%
4	2012	258,953	154,149	COTTON, TOM	95,013	JEFFRESS, GENE	9,791	59,136	R	59.5%	36.7%	61.9%	38.1%
TOTAL	2022	895,102	598,000		271,771		25,331	326,229	R	66.8%	30.4%	68.8%	31.2%
TOTAL	2020	1,179,396	828,266		330,485		20,645	497,781	R	70.2%	28.0%	71.5%	28.5%
TOTAL	2018	889,298	556,339		312,978		19,981	243,361	R	62.6%	35.2%	64.0%	36.0%
TOTAL	2016	1,068,577	760,415		111,347		196,815	649,068	R	71.2%	10.4%	87.2%	12.8%
TOTAL	2014	830,652	509,631		254,774		66,247	254,857	R	61.4%	30.7%	66.7%	33.3%
TOTAL	2012	1,038,054	637,591		304,770		95,693	332,821	R	61.4%	29.4%	67.7%	32.3%

Note: An asterisk (*) denotes incumbent.

ARKANSAS

GENERAL AND PRIMARY ELECTIONS

GENERAL ELECTIONS: OTHER VOTE

Governor	Other vote was 16,690 Libertarian (Ricky Harrington)
Senate	Other vote was 28,682 Libertarian (Kenneth Cates)
House	Other vote was:
CD 2	11,584 Libertarian (Michael White)
CD 3	7,646 Libertarian (Michael Kalagias)
CD 4	6,101 Libertarian (Gregory Maxwell)

2022 PRIMARY ELECTIONS: SUPPLEMENTARY INFORMATION

Primary	May 24, 2022	**Registration** (as of June 6, 2022, and includes inactive voters)	1,765,681	Republican	123,726
Primary Runoff	June 21, 2022			Democratic	88,508
				Libertarian	692
				Other	1,552,755

Primary Type   Open—Any registered voter could participate in either the Democratic or the Republican primary. However, if they participated in one party's primary they could not vote in the runoff of the other party.

	REPUBLICAN PRIMARIES			DEMOCRATIC PRIMARIES		
Senator	Boozman, John	201,677	58.0%	James, Natalie	49,722	54.1%
	Bequette, Jake	71,809	20.7%	Whitfield, Dan	28,319	30.8%
	Morgan, Jan	65,958	19.0%	Foster, Jack E.	13,891	15.1%
	Loftis, Heath	8,112	2.3%			
	TOTAL	347,556		TOTAL	91,932	
Governor	Huckabee Sanders, Sarah	289,249	83.1%	Jones, Chris	66,540	70.4%
	Washburn, Francis "Doc"	58,638	16.9%	Bland, Anthony "Tony"	9,055	9.6%
				Martin, Jay	7,731	8.2%
				Russell, James "Rus" III	6,421	6.8%
				Xayprasith-Mays, Supha	4,725	5.0%
	TOTAL	347,887		TOTAL	94,472	
Congressional District 1	Crawford, Rick*	64,102	74.6%			
	Smith, Brandt	11,981	13.9%			
	Shackelford, Jody	9,837	11.4%			
	TOTAL	85,920				
Congressional District 2	Hill, French*	49,488	58.5%			
	Reynolds, Conrad	35,078	41.5%			
	TOTAL	84,566				
Congressional District 3	Womack, Steve*	60,814	78.7%			
	Kumar, Neil	16,414	21.3%			
	TOTAL	77,228				
Congressional District 4						

Note: An asterisk (*) denotes incumbent.

CALIFORNIA

Statewide Races

In 2018, then-Lt. Gov. Gavin Newsom (D) ascended to the Golden State's top office. His 62% share was the highest that any Democratic candidate for governor had ever received in California's history. Then, in 2021, conservative activists, who were irritated by the governor's COVID-era restrictions (among other grievances), gathered enough signatures to force a recall election. Remarkably, turnout in the 2021 recall *increased* from the 2018 gubernatorial election – the total vote tally nudged up from 12.4 million to 12.8 million – but the verdict was identical: 62% voted to retain Newsom.

While no one doubted that Newsom would win a second term, the results were somewhat disappointing for Democrats. As turnout fell to 10.9 million, Newsom's share dropped to 59%. His declines were relatively tame in the more populous counties – two of the three counties where he improved were the Bay Area's Contra Costa and Marin – while his margins dropped by double-digits in some inland counties. In Lassen County, a northeastern county which was the home base of his GOP opponent, state Sen. Brian Dahle, his deficit grew from 55 to 69 percentage points.

One of the biggest disappointments for state Democrats was Orange County, a traditionally Republican but increasingly diverse, county bordering Los Angeles. In 2018, Orange County exemplified the "blue wave" that year better than anywhere else in California. Four years later, Newsom narrowly lost it.

Democratic Sen. Alex Padilla, who was appointed to replace Vice President Kamala Harris in the Senate, won a full term in his own right. He took 61%, faring slightly better than Newsom across the board.

House Races

After the 2020 census, California's redistricting commission was tasked with downsizing: with California's slow growth (thanks in part to high home prices), the state dropped from 53 to 52 seats – this was the first ever census where the state's delegation shrunk.

On the new map, the districts that got the most attention from national groups were in the Central Valley and on the periphery of the Los Angeles metro area. One of the closest House results in the nation came in CA-13, which was a Biden +11 open seat running between Fresno and Stockton. Though Democrats landed a strong recruit, Republican farmer John Duarte won by 564 votes.

Over the last few election cycles, two perpetual Democratic targets have been Republican Reps. David Valadao and Mike Garcia. The former has a Central Valley seat while the latter is based in northern Los Angeles County. Both received bluer districts but pulled off narrow wins. South of Los Angeles, two Orange County Republicans who were first elected in 2020, Young Kim and Michelle Steel, each won a second term.

Finally, in southern California, Democrats Julia Brownley, Katie Porter, and Mike Levin all had races that were somewhat competitive. Though all three Democrats outspent their opponents and were ultimately reelected, they each won by single-digit margins in seats that Biden would have carried by double-digits in 2020.

CALIFORNIA

Congressional districts first established for elections held in 2022

52 members

*Asterisk indicates a county whose boundaries include parts of two or more congressional districts.

CDs 4, 19, and 20 are highlighted for visibility. See Insets for Bay and Los Angeles-San Diego areas.

CALIFORNIA

Greater Los Angeles, San Diego Areas

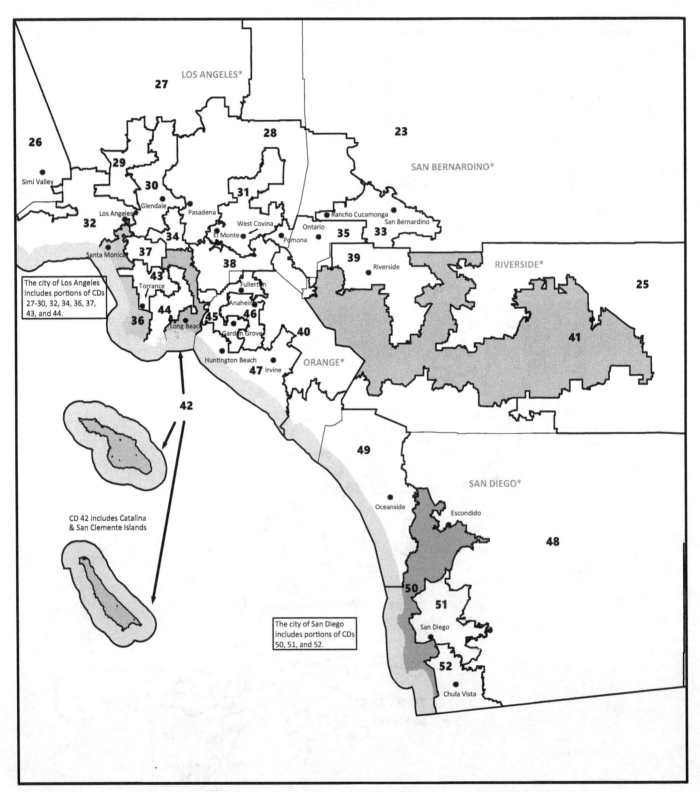

*Asterisk indicates a county whose boundaries include parts of two or more congressional districts.
CDs 36, 41, 42, and 50 are highlighted for visibility.

CALIFORNIA
Greater San Francisco Bay Area

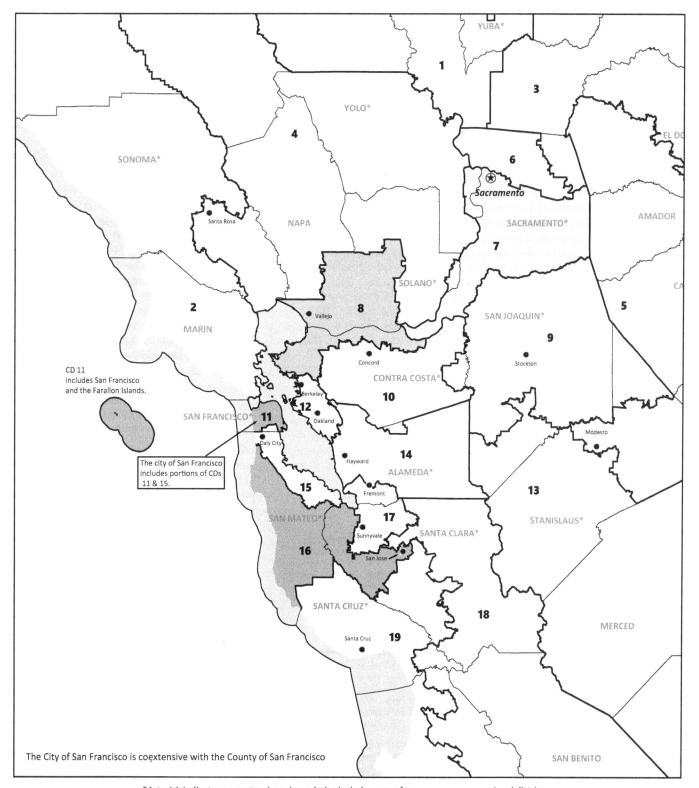

*Asterisk indicates a county whose boundaries include parts of two or more congressional districts.

CDs 7, 8, 11 and 16 are highlighted for visibility.

CALIFORNIA

GOVERNOR
Gavin Newsom (D). Reelected 2022 to a four-year term. Previously elected 2018.

SENATORS (2 Democrats)
Dianne Feinstein (D). Reelected 2018 to a six-year term. Previously elected 2012, 2006, 2000, 1994, and 1992 to fill the remaining two years of the term vacated when Senator Pete Wilson (R) was elected governor in November 1990.

Alex Padilla (D). In dual elections, elected 2022 in a special election to complete his term in the 117th Congress, and elected 2022 to a full six-year term. Appointed by the governor December 22, 2020, and sworn in January 20, 2021, to complete the term vacated by Kamala D. Harris following her election as vice president.

REPRESENTATIVES (12 Republicans, 40 Democrats)
1. Doug LaMalfa (R)
2. Jared Huffman (D)
3. Kevin Kiley (R)
4. Mike Thompson (D)
5. Tom McClintock (R)
6. Ami Bera (D)
7. Doris Matsui (D)
8. John Garamendi (D)
9. Josh Harder (D)
10. Mark DeSaulnier (D)
11. Nancy Pelosi (D)
12. Barbara Lee (D)
13. John Duarte (R)
14. Eric Swalwell (D)
15. Kevin Mullin (D)
16. Anna G. Eshoo (D)
17. Ro Khanna (D)
18. Zoe Lofgren (D)
19. Jimmy Panetta (D)
20. Kevin McCarthy (R)
21. Jim Costa (D)
22. David Valadao (R)
23. Jay Obernolte (R)
24. Salud Carbajal (D)
25. Raul Ruiz (D)
26. Julia Brownley (D)
27. Mike Garcia (R)
28. Judy Chu (D)
29. Tony Cardenas (D)
30. Adam B. Schiff (D)
31. Grace Flores Napolitano (D)
32. Brad Sherman (D)
33. Pete Aguilar (D)
34. Jimmy Gomez (D)
35. Norma J. Torres (D)
36. Ted Lieu (D)
37. Sydney Kamlager (D)
38. Linda J. Sánchez (D)
39. Mark A. Takano (D)
40. Young Kim (R)
41. Ken Calvert (R)
42. Robert Garcia (D)
43. Maxine Waters (D)
44. Nanette Diaz Barragan (D)
45. Michelle Steel (R)
46. Lou Correa (D)
47. Katie Porter (D)
48. Darrell Issa (R)
49. Mike Levin (D)
50. Scott Peters (D)
51. Sara Jacobs (D)
52. Juan Vargas (D)

POSTWAR VOTE FOR PRESIDENT

| | | Republican | | | Democratic | Other | Rep.-Dem. | Total Vote | | Major Vote | |
| | | | | | | | | Percentage | | | |
Year	Total Vote	Vote	Candidate	Vote	Candidate	Vote	Plurality	Rep.	Dem.	Rep.	Dem.
2020	17,500,881	6,006,429	Trump, Donald J.*	11,110,250	Biden, Joseph R. Jr.	384,202	5,103,821 D	34.3%	63.5%	35.1%	64.9%
2016**	14,181,595	4,483,810	Trump, Donald J.	8,753,788	Clinton, Hillary Rodham	943,997	4,269,978 D	31.6%	61.7%	33.9%	66.1%
2012	13,038,547	4,839,958	Romney, W. Mitt	7,854,285	Obama, Barack H.*	344,304	3,014,327 D	37.1%	60.2%	38.1%	61.9%
2008	13,531,900	5,011,781	McCain, John S. III	8,274,473	Obama, Barack H.	275,646	3,262,692 D	37.0%	61.0%	37.7%	62.3%
2004	12,421,852	5,509,826	Bush, George W.*	6,745,485	Kerry, John F.	166,541	1,235,659 D	44.4%	54.3%	45.0%	55.0%
2000**	10,965,856	4,567,429	Bush, George W.	5,861,203	Gore, Albert Jr.	537,224	1,293,774 D	41.7%	53.4%	43.8%	56.2%
1996**	10,019,484	3,828,380	Dole, Robert "Bob"	5,119,835	Clinton, Bill*	1,071,269	1,291,455 D	38.2%	51.1%	42.8%	57.2%
1992**	11,131,721	3,630,574	Bush, George H.*	5,121,325	Clinton, Bill	2,379,822	1,490,751 D	32.6%	46.0%	41.5%	58.5%
1988	9,887,065	5,054,917	Bush, George H.	4,702,233	Dukakis, Michael S.	129,915	352,684 R	51.1%	47.6%	51.8%	48.2%
1984	9,505,423	5,467,009	Reagan, Ronald*	3,922,519	Mondale, Walter F.	115,895	1,544,490 R	57.5%	41.3%	58.2%	41.8%
1980**	8,587,063	4,524,858	Reagan, Ronald	3,083,661	Carter, Jimmy*	978,544	1,441,197 R	52.7%	35.9%	59.5%	40.5%
1976	7,867,117	3,882,244	Ford, Gerald R.*	3,742,284	Carter, Jimmy	242,589	139,960 R	49.3%	47.6%	50.9%	49.1%
1972	8,367,862	4,602,096	Nixon, Richard M.*	3,475,847	McGovern, George S.	289,919	1,126,249 R	55.0%	41.5%	57.0%	43.0%
1968**	7,251,587	3,467,664	Nixon, Richard M.	3,244,318	Humphrey, Hubert Horatio Jr.	539,605	223,346 R	47.8%	44.7%	51.7%	48.3%
1964	7,057,586	2,879,108	Goldwater, Barry M. Sr.	4,171,877	Johnson, Lyndon B.*	6,601	1,292,769 D	40.8%	59.1%	40.8%	59.2%
1960	6,506,578	3,259,722	Nixon, Richard M.	3,224,099	Kennedy, John F.	22,757	35,623 R	50.1%	49.6%	50.3%	49.7%
1956	5,466,355	3,027,668	Eisenhower, Dwight D.*	2,420,135	Stevenson, Adlai E. II	18,552	607,533 R	55.4%	44.3%	55.6%	44.4%
1952	5,141,849	2,897,310	Eisenhower, Dwight D.	2,197,548	Stevenson, Adlai E. II	46,991	699,762 R	56.3%	42.7%	56.9%	43.1%
1948	4,021,538	1,895,269	Dewey, Thomas E.	1,913,134	Truman, Harry S.*	213,135	17,865 D	47.1%	47.6%	49.8%	50.2%

Note: An asterisk (*) denotes incumbent. **In past elections, the other vote included: 2016 - 478,500 Libertarian (Gary Johnson); 2000 - 418,707 Green (Ralph Nader); 1996 - 697,847 Reform (Ross Perot); 1992 - 2,296,006 Independent (Perot); 1980 - 739,833 Independent (John Anderson); 1968 - 487,270 American Independent (George Wallace).

CALIFORNIA

POSTWAR VOTE FOR GOVERNOR

		Republican		Democratic		Other Vote	Rep.-Dem. Plurality	Percentage			
								Total Vote		Major Vote	
Year	Total Vote	Vote	Candidate	Vote	Candidate			Rep.	Dem.	Rep.	Dem.
2022	10,933,009	4,462,910	Dahle, Brian	6,470,099	Newsom, Gavin*		2,007,189 D	40.8%	59.2%	40.8%	59.2%
2018	12,464,235	4,742,825	Cox, John H.	7,721,410	Newsom, Gavin		2,978,585 D	38.1%	61.9%	38.1%	61.9%
2014	7,317,581	2,929,213	Kashkari, Neel	4,388,368	Brown, Edmund G. Jr.*		1,459,155 D	40.0%	60.0%	40.0%	60.0%
2010	10,095,185	4,127,391	Whitman, Meg	5,428,149	Brown, Edmund G. Jr.	539,645	1,300,758 D	40.9%	53.8%	43.2%	56.8%
2006	8,679,416	4,850,157	Schwarzenegger, Arnold*	3,376,732	Angelides, Phil	452,527	1,473,425 R	55.9%	38.9%	59.0%	41.0%
2003S**	8,657,915	4,206,284	Schwarzenegger, Arnold	2,724,874	Bustamante, Cruz	1,726,757	1,481,410 R	48.6%	31.5%	60.7%	39.3%
2002	7,476,311	3,169,801	Simon, Bill	3,533,490	Davis, Gray*	773,020	363,689 D	42.4%	47.3%	47.3%	52.7%
1998	8,385,196	3,218,030	Lungren, Dan	4,860,702	Davis, Gray	306,464	1,642,672 D	38.4%	58.0%	39.8%	60.2%
1994	8,665,375	4,781,766	Wilson, Pete*	3,519,799	Brown, Kathleen	363,810	1,261,967 R	55.2%	40.6%	57.6%	42.4%
1990	7,699,467	3,791,904	Wilson, Pete	3,525,197	Feinstein, Dianne	382,366	266,707 R	49.2%	45.8%	51.8%	48.2%
1986	7,443,551	4,506,601	Deukmejian, George*	2,781,714	Bradley, Tom	155,236	1,724,887 R	60.5%	37.4%	61.8%	38.2%
1982	7,876,698	3,881,014	Deukmejian, George	3,787,669	Bradley, Tom	208,015	93,345 R	49.3%	48.1%	50.6%	49.4%
1978	6,922,378	2,526,534	Younger, Evelle J.	3,878,812	Brown, Edmund G. Jr.*	517,032	1,352,278 D	36.5%	56.0%	39.4%	60.6%
1974	6,248,070	2,952,954	Flournoy, Houston I.	3,131,648	Brown, Edmund G. Jr.	163,468	178,694 D	47.3%	50.1%	48.5%	51.5%
1970	6,510,272	3,439,664	Reagan, Ronald*	2,938,807	Unruh, Jess	131,801	500,857 R	52.8%	45.1%	53.9%	46.1%
1966	6,503,445	3,742,913	Reagan, Ronald	2,749,174	Brown, Edmund G.*	11,358	993,739 R	57.6%	42.3%	57.7%	42.3%
1962	5,853,270	2,740,351	Nixon, Richard M.	3,037,109	Brown, Edmund G.*	75,810	296,758 D	46.8%	51.9%	47.4%	52.6%
1958	5,255,777	2,110,911	Knowland, William F.	3,140,076	Brown, Edmund G.	4,790	1,029,165 D	40.2%	59.7%	40.2%	59.8%
1954	4,030,368	2,290,519	Knight, Goodwin J.*	1,739,368	Graves, Richard Perrin	481	551,151 R	56.8%	43.2%	56.8%	43.2%
1950	3,796,090	2,461,754	Warren, Earl*	1,333,856	Roosevelt, James	480	1,127,898 R	64.8%	35.1%	64.9%	35.1%
1946**	2,738,978	2,344,542	Warren, Earl*			394,436	2,344,542 R	85.6%		100.0%	

Note: An asterisk (*) denotes incumbent. **The 2003 election was for a short term to fill a vacancy created by voter approval of a measure to remove Governor Gray Davis (D) from office. The measure passed by a vote of 4,976,274 votes (55.4 percent) for recall to 4,007,783 (44.6 percent) against recall. In the same election, a total of 135 candidates ran for the right to succeed Davis. No primary election was held to cull the field. All candidates, regardless of party, ran together on the same ballot. The winner, Arnold Schwarzenegger, is listed as the Republican candidate. The leading Democratic vote-getter, Cruz Bustamante, is listed as the Democratic candidate. The percentages given are for Schwarzenegger and Bustamante. The leading "Other" candidate was Republican Tom McClintock, who received 1,161,287 votes (13.4 percent of the total). The percentage columns are for Schwarzenegger and Bustamante and do not include additional candidates. In 1946 the Republican candidate won both major party nominations.

POSTWAR VOTE FOR SENATOR

		Republican		Democratic		Other Vote	Rep.-Dem. Plurality	Percentage			
								Total Vote		Major Vote	
Year	Total Vote	Vote	Candidate	Vote	Candidate			Rep.	Dem.	Rep.	Dem.
2022	10,843,641	4,222,025	Meuser, Mark P.	6,621,616	Padilla, Alex*		2,399,591 D	38.9%	61.1%	38.9%	61.1%
2022**	10,771,848	4,212,540	Meuser, Mark P.	6,559,308	Padilla, Alex*		2,346,768 D	39.1%	60.9%	39.1%	60.9%
2018**	11,113,364			6,019,422	Feinstein, Dianne*		1,11,13,364 D		54.2%		100.0%
2016**	12,244,170			7,542,753	Harris, Kamala D.		1,22,44,170 D		61.6%		100.0%
2012	12,578,511	4,713,887	Emken, Elizabeth	7,864,624	Feinstein, Dianne*		3,150,737 D	37.5%	62.5%	37.5%	62.5%
2010	9,999,860	4,217,386	Fiorina, Carly	5,218,137	Boxer, Barbara*	564,337	1,000,751 D	42.2%	52.2%	44.7%	55.3%
2006	8,541,476	2,990,822	Mountjoy, Dick	5,076,289	Feinstein, Dianne*	474,365	2,085,467 D	35.0%	59.4%	37.1%	62.9%
2004	12,053,295	4,555,922	Jones, Bill	6,955,728	Boxer, Barbara*	541,645	2,399,806 D	37.8%	57.7%	39.6%	60.4%
2000	10,623,614	3,886,853	Campbell, Tom	5,932,522	Feinstein, Dianne*	804,239	2,045,669 D	36.6%	55.8%	39.6%	60.4%
1998	8,314,953	3,576,351	Fong, Matt	4,411,705	Boxer, Barbara*	326,897	835,354 D	43.0%	53.1%	44.8%	55.2%
1994	8,514,089	3,817,025	Huffington, Michael	3,979,152	Feinstein, Dianne*	717,912	162,127 D	44.8%	46.7%	49.0%	51.0%
1992**	10,799,703	4,644,182	Sargent, Claire	5,173,467	Boxer, Barbara	982,054	529,285 D	43.0%	47.9%	47.3%	52.7%
1992S	10,782,743	4,093,501	Seymour, John*	5,853,651	Feinstein, Dianne	835,591	1,760,150 D	38.0%	54.3%	41.2%	58.8%
1988	9,743,598	5,143,409	Wilson, Pete*	4,287,253	McCarthy, Leo T.	312,936	856,156 R	52.8%	44.0%	54.5%	45.5%
1986	7,398,522	3,541,804	Zschau, Ed	3,646,672	Cranston, Alan*	210,046	104,868 D	47.9%	49.3%	49.3%	50.7%
1982	7,805,538	4,022,565	Wilson, Pete	3,494,968	Brown, Edmund G. Jr.	288,005	527,597 R	51.5%	44.8%	53.5%	46.5%
1980	8,327,481	3,093,426	Gann, Paul	4,705,399	Cranston, Alan*	528,656	1,611,973 D	37.1%	56.5%	39.7%	60.3%
1976	7,472,268	3,748,973	Hayakawa, S. I.	3,502,862	Tunney, John V.*	220,433	246,111 R	50.2%	46.9%	51.7%	48.3%
1974	6,102,432	2,210,267	Richardson, H. L.	3,693,160	Cranston, Alan*	199,005	1,482,893 D	36.2%	60.5%	37.4%	62.6%
1970	6,492,157	2,877,617	Murphy, George*	3,496,558	Tunney, John V.	117,982	618,941 D	44.3%	53.9%	45.1%	54.9%
1968	7,102,465	3,329,148	Rafferty, Max	3,680,352	Cranston, Alan	92,965	351,204 D	46.9%	51.8%	47.5%	52.5%
1964	7,041,821	3,628,555	Murphy, George	3,411,912	Salinger, Pierre*	1,354	216,643 R	51.5%	48.5%	51.5%	48.5%
1962	5,647,952	3,180,483	Kuchel, Thomas H.*	2,452,839	Richards, Richard	14,630	727,644 R	56.3%	43.4%	56.5%	43.5%
1958	5,135,221	2,204,337	Knight, Goodwin J.	2,927,693	Engle, Clair	3,191	723,356 D	42.9%	57.0%	43.0%	57.0%
1956	5,361,467	2,892,918	Kuchel, Thomas H.*	2,445,816	Richards, Richard	22,733	447,102 R	54.0%	45.6%	54.2%	45.8%
1954S**	3,929,668	2,090,836	Kuchel, Thomas H.*	1,788,071	Yorty, Samuel W.	50,761	302,765 R	53.2%	45.5%	53.9%	46.1%
1952**	4,542,548	3,982,448	Knowland, William F.*			560,100	3,982,448 R	87.7%		100.0%	
1950	3,686,315	2,183,454	Nixon, Richard M.	1,502,507	Douglas, Helen Gahagan	354	680,947 R	59.2%	40.8%	59.2%	40.8%
1946	2,639,465	1,428,067	Knowland, William F.*	1,167,161	Rogers, Will Jr.	44,237	260,906 R	54.1%	44.2%	55.0%	45.0%

Note: An asterisk (*) denotes incumbent. **In 2022, there was a special election to fill the rest of the six-year term that Kamala Harris (D) was elected to in 2016. In 2018, California's jungle primary sent two Democrats to the general election, with the results as follows: 6,019,422 Dianne Feinstein (54.2%); 5,093,942 Kevin DeLeon (45.8%). Feinstein won by a plurality of 925,480 votes. In 2016, California's jungle primary also sent two Democrats to the general election, with the results as follows: 7,542,753 Kamala D. Harris (61.6%); 4,701,417 Loretta Sanchez (38.4%). Harris won by a plurality of 2,841,336 votes. In past elections, the other vote included: 1952 - 542,270 Progressive (Reuben W. Borough), who finished second. The Republican candidate that year (William F. Knowland) won both major party nominations. The 1954 election was for a short term to fill a vacancy, as was one of the 1992 elections.

CALIFORNIA
GOVERNOR 2022

2020 Census Population	County	Total Vote	Republican (Dahle)	Democratic (Newsom)	Other	Rep.-Dem. Plurality		Percentage Total Vote		Percentage Major Vote	
								Rep.	Dem.	Rep.	Dem.
1,671,168	ALAMEDA	487,969	100,923	387,046		286,123	D	20.7%	79.3%	20.7%	79.3%
1,136	ALPINE	619	256	363		107	D	41.4%	58.6%	41.4%	58.6%
40,131	AMADOR	18,655	12,628	6,027		6,601	R	67.7%	32.3%	67.7%	32.3%
219,114	BUTTE	72,441	40,939	31,502		9,437	R	56.5%	43.5%	56.5%	43.5%
46,038	CALAVERAS	21,240	14,137	7,103		7,034	R	66.6%	33.4%	66.6%	33.4%
21,605	COLUSA	5,562	4,009	1,553		2,456	R	72.1%	27.9%	72.1%	27.9%
1,155,188	CONTRA COSTA	388,503	123,132	265,371		142,239	D	31.7%	68.3%	31.7%	68.3%
27,972	DEL NORTE	8,375	5,111	3,264		1,847	R	61.0%	39.0%	61.0%	39.0%
193,913	EL DORADO	88,671	54,137	34,534		19,603	R	61.1%	38.9%	61.1%	38.9%
1,001,679	FRESNO	219,085	120,668	98,417		22,251	R	55.1%	44.9%	55.1%	44.9%
28,526	GLENN	7,930	6,000	1,930		4,070	R	75.7%	24.3%	75.7%	24.3%
135,819	HUMBOLDT	47,798	18,257	29,541		11,284	D	38.2%	61.8%	38.2%	61.8%
180,991	IMPERIAL	29,869	13,158	16,711		3,553	D	44.1%	55.9%	44.1%	55.9%
18,076	INYO	7,477	4,095	3,382		713	R	54.8%	45.2%	54.8%	45.2%
903,079	KERN	188,703	119,002	69,701		49,301	R	63.1%	36.9%	63.1%	36.9%
153,468	KINGS	26,912	17,523	9,389		8,134	R	65.1%	34.9%	65.1%	34.9%
64,614	LAKE	20,131	10,360	9,771		589	R	51.5%	48.5%	51.5%	48.5%
30,568	LASSEN	9,170	7,726	1,444		6,282	R	84.3%	15.7%	84.3%	15.7%
10,040,723	LOS ANGELES	2,389,227	769,174	1,620,053		850,879	D	32.2%	67.8%	32.2%	67.8%
157,915	MADERA	36,961	23,678	13,283		10,395	R	64.1%	35.9%	64.1%	35.9%
259,027	MARIN	119,064	23,775	95,289		71,514	D	20.0%	80.0%	20.0%	80.0%
17,246	MARIPOSA	7,840	4,896	2,944		1,952	R	62.4%	37.6%	62.4%	37.6%
86,919	MENDOCINO	30,394	11,363	19,031		7,668	D	37.4%	62.6%	37.4%	62.6%
279,313	MERCED	55,273	30,073	25,200		4,873	R	54.4%	45.6%	54.4%	45.6%
8,840	MODOC	3,412	2,725	687		2,038	R	79.9%	20.1%	79.9%	20.1%
14,362	MONO	4,569	2,076	2,493		417	D	45.4%	54.6%	45.4%	54.6%
434,621	MONTEREY	102,129	36,867	65,262		28,395	D	36.1%	63.9%	36.1%	63.9%
137,969	NAPA	50,108	17,671	32,437		14,766	D	35.3%	64.7%	35.3%	64.7%
100,191	NEVADA	50,737	24,082	26,655		2,573	D	47.5%	52.5%	47.5%	52.5%
3,177,905	ORANGE	956,940	492,734	464,206		28,528	R	51.5%	48.5%	51.5%	48.5%
401,405	PLACER	182,069	108,450	73,619		34,831	R	59.6%	40.4%	59.6%	40.4%
18,885	PLUMAS	8,633	5,550	3,083		2,467	R	64.3%	35.7%	64.3%	35.7%
2,483,726	RIVERSIDE	595,901	310,901	285,000		25,901	R	52.2%	47.8%	52.2%	47.8%
1,556,817	SACRAMENTO	477,613	202,933	274,680		71,747	D	42.5%	57.5%	42.5%	57.5%
63,266	SAN BENITO	19,578	9,150	10,428		1,278	D	46.7%	53.3%	46.7%	53.3%
2,185,317	SAN BERNARDINO	454,500	239,109	215,391		23,718	R	52.6%	47.4%	52.6%	47.4%
3,344,694	SAN DIEGO	1,029,228	455,107	574,121		119,014	D	44.2%	55.8%	44.2%	55.8%
882,417	SAN FRANCISCO	301,466	44,064	257,402		213,338	D	14.6%	85.4%	14.6%	85.4%
765,512	SAN JOAQUIN	177,325	91,827	85,498		6,329	R	51.8%	48.2%	51.8%	48.2%
284,085	SAN LUIS OBISPO	119,630	58,464	61,166		2,702	D	48.9%	51.1%	48.9%	51.1%
765,837	SAN MATEO	247,517	61,918	185,599		123,681	D	25.0%	75.0%	25.0%	75.0%
447,530	SANTA BARBARA	135,374	54,726	80,648		25,922	D	40.4%	59.6%	40.4%	59.6%
1,924,317	SANTA CLARA	541,895	162,518	379,377		216,859	D	30.0%	70.0%	30.0%	70.0%
273,524	SANTA CRUZ	104,169	25,052	79,117		54,065	D	24.0%	76.0%	24.0%	76.0%
180,772	SHASTA	68,520	49,913	18,607		31,306	R	72.8%	27.2%	72.8%	27.2%
3,009	SIERRA	1,543	1,014	529		485	R	65.7%	34.3%	65.7%	34.3%
43,732	SISKIYOU	17,723	11,397	6,326		5,071	R	64.3%	35.7%	64.3%	35.7%
449,107	SOLANO	130,619	52,850	77,769		24,919	D	40.5%	59.5%	40.5%	59.5%
494,527	SONOMA	197,454	57,413	140,041		82,628	D	29.1%	70.9%	29.1%	70.9%
552,693	STANISLAUS	130,967	75,656	55,311		20,345	R	57.8%	42.2%	57.8%	42.2%
97,287	SUTTER	28,106	19,024	9,082		9,942	R	67.7%	32.3%	67.7%	32.3%
65,316	TEHAMA	20,631	15,607	5,024		10,583	R	75.6%	24.4%	75.6%	24.4%
12,236	TRINITY	4,527	2,667	1,860		807	R	58.9%	41.1%	58.9%	41.1%
466,926	TULARE	91,326	58,053	33,273		24,780	R	63.6%	36.4%	63.6%	36.4%
54,761	TUOLUMNE	23,230	14,759	8,471		6,288	R	63.5%	36.5%	63.5%	36.5%
847,146	VENTURA	280,935	127,709	153,226		25,517	D	45.5%	54.5%	45.5%	54.5%
221,203	YOLO	67,135	22,807	44,328		21,521	D	34.0%	66.0%	34.0%	66.0%
79,182	YUBA	19,631	13,097	6,534		6,563	R	66.7%	33.3%	66.7%	33.3%
39,573,345	TOTAL	10,933,009	4,462,910	6,470,099		2,007,189	D	40.8%	59.2%	40.8%	59.2%

CALIFORNIA

2021 CALIFORNIA GUBERNATORIAL SPECIAL ELECTION

2020 Census Population	County	Total Vote	Larry Elder Republican	(*) (W) Gavin Newsom Democrat	Other Vote Other	Rep.-Dem. Plurality	Total Vote Rep.	Total Vote Dem.	Major Vote Rep.	Major Vote Dem.
1,671,168	ALAMEDA	720,879	68,410	465,901	186,568	397,491 D	9.5%	64.6%	12.8%	87.2%
1,136	ALPINE	681	157	354	170	197 D	23.1%	52.0%	30.7%	69.3%
40,131	AMADOR	21,562	8,862	6,957	5,743	1,905 R	41.1%	32.3%	56.0%	44.0%
219,114	BUTTE	90,894	28,705	36,128	26,061	7,423 D	31.6%	39.7%	44.3%	55.7%
46,038	CALAVERAS	25,346	10,660	8,320	6,366	2,340 R	42.1%	32.8%	56.2%	43.8%
21,605	COLUSA	6,752	2,574	2,027	2,151	547 R	38.1%	30.0%	55.9%	44.1%
1,155,188	CONTRA COSTA	564,947	91,262	324,747	148,938	233,485 D	16.2%	57.5%	21.9%	78.1%
27,972	DEL NORTE	9,879	4,094	3,505	2,280	589 R	41.4%	35.5%	53.9%	46.1%
193,913	EL DORADO	110,656	37,507	39,907	33,242	2,400 D	33.9%	36.1%	48.4%	51.6%
1,001,679	FRESNO	298,693	103,060	126,488	69,145	23,428 D	34.5%	42.3%	44.9%	55.1%
28,526	GLENN	9,656	4,202	2,485	2,969	1,717 R	43.5%	25.7%	62.8%	37.2%
135,819	HUMBOLDT	62,742	13,483	33,164	16,095	19,681 D	21.5%	52.9%	28.9%	71.1%
180,991	IMPERIAL	38,320	9,564	19,288	9,468	9,724 D	25.0%	50.3%	33.1%	66.9%
18,076	INYO	8,696	3,275	3,502	1,919	227 D	37.7%	40.3%	48.3%	51.7%
903,079	KERN	228,506	99,969	81,030	47,507	18,939 R	43.7%	35.5%	55.2%	44.8%
153,468	KINGS	34,558	15,577	11,242	7,739	4,335 R	45.1%	32.5%	58.1%	41.9%
64,614	LAKE	25,264	7,259	11,367	6,638	4,108 D	28.7%	45.0%	39.0%	61.0%
30,568	LASSEN	10,648	6,293	1,604	2,751	4,689 R	59.1%	15.1%	79.7%	20.3%
10,040,723	LOS ANGELES	3,564,724	648,067	2,077,859	838,798	1,429,792 D	18.2%	58.3%	23.8%	76.2%
157,915	MADERA	46,221	19,530	16,233	10,458	3,297 R	42.3%	35.1%	54.6%	45.4%
259,027	MARIN	161,819	15,901	108,599	37,319	92,698 D	9.8%	67.1%	12.8%	87.2%
17,246	MARIPOSA	9,847	4,086	3,376	2,385	710 R	41.5%	34.3%	54.8%	45.2%
86,919	MENDOCINO	40,486	7,799	22,093	10,594	14,294 D	19.3%	54.6%	26.1%	73.9%
279,313	MERCED	63,340	21,830	27,867	13,643	6,037 D	34.5%	44.0%	43.9%	56.1%
8,840	MODOC	3,557	1,753	730	1,074	1,023 R	49.3%	20.5%	70.6%	29.4%
14,362	MONO	5,970	1,690	2,805	1,475	1,115 D	28.3%	47.0%	37.6%	62.4%
434,621	MONTEREY	143,389	27,841	80,664	34,884	52,823 D	19.4%	56.3%	25.7%	74.3%
137,969	NAPA	68,265	12,613	38,948	16,704	26,335 D	18.5%	57.1%	24.5%	75.5%
100,191	NEVADA	64,341	16,546	29,851	17,944	13,305 D	25.7%	46.4%	35.7%	64.3%
3,177,905	ORANGE	1,324,113	423,224	586,457	314,432	163,233 D	32.0%	44.3%	41.9%	58.1%
401,405	PLACER	226,597	73,309	85,677	67,611	12,368 D	32.4%	37.8%	46.1%	53.9%
18,885	PLUMAS	10,227	3,918	3,408	2,901	510 R	38.3%	33.3%	53.5%	46.5%
2,483,726	RIVERSIDE	822,226	283,217	355,630	183,379	72,413 D	34.4%	43.3%	44.3%	55.7%
1,556,817	SACRAMENTO	651,674	147,776	329,952	173,946	182,176 D	22.7%	50.6%	30.9%	69.1%
63,266	SAN BENITO	26,686	6,848	12,718	7,120	5,870 D	25.7%	47.7%	35.0%	65.0%
2,185,317	SAN BERNARDINO	655,303	225,674	288,877	140,752	63,203 D	34.4%	44.1%	43.9%	56.1%
3,344,694	SAN DIEGO	1,437,629	355,417	674,670	407,542	319,253 D	24.7%	46.9%	34.5%	65.5%
882,417	SAN FRANCISCO	418,182	26,285	292,744	99,153	266,459 D	6.3%	70.0%	8.2%	91.8%
765,512	SAN JOAQUIN	231,385	68,230	105,405	57,750	37,175 D	29.5%	45.6%	39.3%	60.7%
284,085	SAN LUIS OBISPO	152,818	45,298	68,429	39,091	23,131 D	29.6%	44.8%	39.8%	60.2%
765,837	SAN MATEO	360,916	41,162	227,368	92,386	186,206 D	11.4%	63.0%	15.3%	84.7%
447,530	SANTA BARBARA	183,088	43,582	94,219	45,287	50,637 D	23.8%	51.5%	31.6%	68.4%
1,924,317	SANTA CLARA	790,875	105,590	468,851	216,434	363,261 D	13.4%	59.3%	18.4%	81.6%
273,524	SANTA CRUZ	146,433	17,494	90,874	38,065	73,380 D	11.9%	62.1%	16.1%	83.9%
180,772	SHASTA	82,541	36,022	22,592	23,927	13,430 R	43.6%	27.4%	61.5%	38.5%

CALIFORNIA

2021 CALIFORNIA GUBERNATORIAL SPECIAL ELECTION

2020 Census Population	County	Total Vote	Larry Elder Republican	(*) (W) Gavin Newsom Democrat	Other Vote Other	Rep.-Dem. Plurality		Total Vote Rep.	Total Vote Dem.	Major Vote Rep.	Major Vote Dem.
3,009	SIERRA	1,847	698	616	533	82	R	37.8%	33.4%	53.1%	46.9%
43,732	SISKIYOU	20,309	8,127	6,961	5,221	1,166	R	40.0%	34.3%	53.9%	46.1%
449,107	SOLANO	183,538	40,387	97,935	45,216	57,548	D	22.0%	53.4%	29.2%	70.8%
494,527	SONOMA	262,512	38,131	160,602	63,779	122,471	D	14.5%	61.2%	19.2%	80.8%
552,693	STANISLAUS	170,666	58,812	69,247	42,607	10,435	D	34.5%	40.6%	45.9%	54.1%
97,287	SUTTER	35,269	12,440	11,593	11,236	847	R	35.3%	32.9%	51.8%	48.2%
65,316	TEHAMA	25,012	11,529	6,386	7,097	5,143	R	46.1%	25.5%	64.4%	35.6%
12,236	TRINITY	5,422	1,770	2,106	1,546	336	D	32.6%	38.8%	45.7%	54.3%
466,926	TULARE	116,637	51,152	41,009	24,476	10,143	R	43.9%	35.2%	55.5%	44.5%
54,761	TUOLUMNE	28,024	11,374	9,850	6,800	1,524	R	40.6%	35.1%	53.6%	46.4%
847,146	VENTURA	373,903	108,043	182,470	83,390	74,427	D	28.9%	48.8%	37.2%	62.8%
221,203	YOLO	95,222	15,911	52,444	26,867	36,533	D	16.7%	55.1%	23.3%	76.7%
79,182	YUBA	25,968	9,878	7,961	8,129	1,917	R	38.0%	30.7%	55.4%	44.6%
	Votes Not Reported by County	0	0	0	0	0		0.0%	0.0%	0.0%	0.0%
39,573,345	TOTAL	15,305,660				4,146,391	D	23.3%	51.9%	31.0%	69.0%

CALIFORNIA

SENATOR 2022

2020 Census Population	County	Total Vote	Republican (Meuser)	Democratic (Padilla)	Other	Rep.-Dem. Plurality		Total Vote Rep.	Total Vote Dem.	Major Vote Rep.	Major Vote Dem.
1,671,168	ALAMEDA	477,583	94,283	383,300		289,017	D	19.7%	80.3%	19.7%	80.3%
1,136	ALPINE	612	240	372		132	D	39.2%	60.8%	39.2%	60.8%
40,131	AMADOR	18,439	11,917	6,522		5,395	R	64.6%	35.4%	64.6%	35.4%
219,114	BUTTE	71,650	38,183	33,467		4,716	R	53.3%	46.7%	53.3%	46.7%
46,038	CALAVERAS	21,064	13,415	7,649		5,766	R	63.7%	36.3%	63.7%	36.3%
21,605	COLUSA	5,458	3,651	1,807		1,844	R	66.9%	33.1%	66.9%	33.1%
1,155,188	CONTRA COSTA	383,453	116,122	267,331		151,209	D	30.3%	69.7%	30.3%	69.7%
27,972	DEL NORTE	8,252	4,852	3,400		1,452	R	58.8%	41.2%	58.8%	41.2%
193,913	EL DORADO	87,694	51,025	36,669		14,356	R	58.2%	41.8%	58.2%	41.8%
1,001,679	FRESNO	214,808	113,845	100,963		12,882	R	53.0%	47.0%	53.0%	47.0%
28,526	GLENN	7,834	5,600	2,234		3,366	R	71.5%	28.5%	71.5%	28.5%
135,819	HUMBOLDT	47,708	17,096	30,612		13,516	D	35.8%	64.2%	35.8%	64.2%
180,991	IMPERIAL	29,693	11,919	17,774		5,855	D	40.1%	59.9%	40.1%	59.9%
18,076	INYO	7,366	3,878	3,488		390	R	52.6%	47.4%	52.6%	47.4%
903,079	KERN	187,207	113,428	73,779		39,649	R	60.6%	39.4%	60.6%	39.4%
153,468	KINGS	26,600	16,533	10,067		6,466	R	62.2%	37.8%	62.2%	37.8%
64,614	LAKE	19,907	9,769	10,138		369	D	49.1%	50.9%	49.1%	50.9%
30,568	LASSEN	9,069	7,181	1,888		5,293	R	79.2%	20.8%	79.2%	20.8%
10,040,723	LOS ANGELES	2,386,219	715,913	1,670,306		954,393	D	30.0%	70.0%	30.0%	70.0%
157,915	MADERA	36,532	22,514	14,018		8,496	R	61.6%	38.4%	61.6%	38.4%
259,027	MARIN	117,822	22,326	95,496		73,170	D	18.9%	81.1%	18.9%	81.1%
17,246	MARIPOSA	7,753	4,703	3,050		1,653	R	60.7%	39.3%	60.7%	39.3%
86,919	MENDOCINO	30,151	10,406	19,745		9,339	D	34.5%	65.5%	34.5%	65.5%
279,313	MERCED	54,648	27,893	26,755		1,138	R	51.0%	49.0%	51.0%	49.0%
8,840	MODOC	3,354	2,552	802		1,750	R	76.1%	23.9%	76.1%	23.9%

CALIFORNIA
SENATOR 2022

2020 Census Population	County	Total Vote	Republican (Meuser)	Democratic (Padilla)	Other	Rep.-Dem. Plurality		Percentage Total Vote		Percentage Major Vote	
								Rep.	Dem.	Rep.	Dem.
14,362	MONO	4,519	1,925	2,594		669	D	42.6%	57.4%	42.6%	57.4%
434,621	MONTEREY	101,179	34,026	67,153		33,127	D	33.6%	66.4%	33.6%	66.4%
137,969	NAPA	49,200	16,549	32,651		16,102	D	33.6%	66.4%	33.6%	66.4%
100,191	NEVADA	50,376	22,478	27,898		5,420	D	44.6%	55.4%	44.6%	55.4%
3,177,905	ORANGE	968,679	489,185	479,494		9,691	R	50.5%	49.5%	50.5%	49.5%
401,405	PLACER	180,137	102,597	77,540		25,057	R	57.0%	43.0%	57.0%	43.0%
18,885	PLUMAS	8,558	5,153	3,405		1,748	R	60.2%	39.8%	60.2%	39.8%
2,483,726	RIVERSIDE	586,286	296,687	289,599		7,088	R	50.6%	49.4%	50.6%	49.4%
1,556,817	SACRAMENTO	472,042	188,925	283,117		94,192	D	40.0%	60.0%	40.0%	60.0%
63,266	SAN BENITO	19,384	8,368	11,016		2,648	D	43.2%	56.8%	43.2%	56.8%
2,185,317	SAN BERNARDINO	444,964	226,470	218,494		7,976	R	50.9%	49.1%	50.9%	49.1%
3,344,694	SAN DIEGO	1,018,311	432,027	586,284		154,257	D	42.4%	57.6%	42.4%	57.6%
882,417	SAN FRANCISCO	297,455	42,699	254,756		212,057	D	14.4%	85.6%	14.4%	85.6%
765,512	SAN JOAQUIN	175,367	85,078	90,289		5,211	D	48.5%	51.5%	48.5%	51.5%
284,085	SAN LUIS OBISPO	118,163	55,087	63,076		7,989	D	46.6%	53.4%	46.6%	53.4%
765,837	SAN MATEO	244,716	57,825	186,891		129,066	D	23.6%	76.4%	23.6%	76.4%
447,530	SANTA BARBARA	133,594	51,339	82,255		30,916	D	38.4%	61.6%	38.4%	61.6%
1,924,317	SANTA CLARA	536,401	153,249	383,152		229,903	D	28.6%	71.4%	28.6%	71.4%
273,524	SANTA CRUZ	103,485	22,810	80,675		57,865	D	22.0%	78.0%	22.0%	78.0%
180,772	SHASTA	67,555	46,750	20,805		25,945	R	69.2%	30.8%	69.2%	30.8%
3,009	SIERRA	1,545	973	572		401	R	63.0%	37.0%	63.0%	37.0%
43,732	SISKIYOU	17,499	10,607	6,892		3,715	R	60.6%	39.4%	60.6%	39.4%
449,107	SOLANO	129,760	49,443	80,317		30,874	D	38.1%	61.9%	38.1%	61.9%
494,527	SONOMA	195,179	51,982	143,197		91,215	D	26.6%	73.4%	26.6%	73.4%
552,693	STANISLAUS	128,653	70,792	57,861		12,931	R	55.0%	45.0%	55.0%	45.0%
97,287	SUTTER	27,624	17,827	9,797		8,030	R	64.5%	35.5%	64.5%	35.5%
65,316	TEHAMA	20,454	14,784	5,670		9,114	R	72.3%	27.7%	72.3%	27.7%
12,236	TRINITY	4,507	2,488	2,019		469	R	55.2%	44.8%	55.2%	44.8%
466,926	TULARE	90,574	55,359	35,215		20,144	R	61.1%	38.9%	61.1%	38.9%
54,761	TUOLUMNE	22,948	14,016	8,932		5,084	R	61.1%	38.9%	61.1%	38.9%
847,146	VENTURA	277,053	121,822	155,231		33,409	D	44.0%	56.0%	44.0%	56.0%
221,203	YOLO	67,116	21,022	46,094		25,072	D	31.3%	68.7%	31.3%	68.7%
79,182	YUBA	19,482	12,439	7,043		5,396	R	63.8%	36.2%	63.8%	36.2%
39,573,345	TOTAL	10,843,641	4,222,025	6,621,616		2,399,591	D	38.9%	61.1%	38.9%	61.1%

CALIFORNIA
HOUSE OF REPRESENTATIVES

CD	Year	Total Vote	Republican Vote	Republican Candidate	Democratic Vote	Democratic Candidate	Other Vote	Rep.-Dem. Plurality		Percentage Total Vote		Percentage Major Vote	
										Rep.	Dem.	Rep.	Dem.
1	2022	246,225	152,839	LAMALFA, DOUG*	93,386	STEINER, MAX		59,453	R	62.1%	37.9%	62.1%	37.9%
2	2022	308,749	79,029	BROWER, DOUGLAS	229,720	HUFFMAN, JARED*		150,691	D	25.6%	74.4%	25.6%	74.4%
3	2022	338,199	181,438	KILEY, KEVIN	156,761	JONES, KERMIT		24,677	R	53.6%	46.4%	53.6%	46.4%
4	2022	260,907	84,007	BROCK, MATT	176,900	THOMPSON, MIKE*		92,893	D	32.2%	67.8%	32.2%	67.8%
5	2022	283,030	173,524	MCCLINTOCK, TOM*	109,506	BARKLEY, MICHAEL J. "MIKE"		64,018	R	61.3%	38.7%	61.3%	38.7%
6	2022	216,383	95,325	HAMILTON, TAMIKA	121,058	BERA, AMI*		25,733	D	44.1%	55.9%	44.1%	55.9%
7	2022	220,651	70,033	SEMENENKO, MAX	150,618	MATSUI, DORIS*		80,585	D	31.7%	68.3%	31.7%	68.3%
8	2022	192,135	46,634	RECILE, RUDY	145,501	GARAMENDI, JOHN*		98,867	D	24.3%	75.7%	24.3%	75.7%
9	2022	174,400	78,802	PATTI, TOM	95,598	HARDER, JOSH*		16,796	D	45.2%	54.8%	45.2%	54.8%
10	2022	251,380			198,415	DESAULNIER, MARK*	52,965	198,415	D		78.9%		100.0%
11	2022	263,065	42,217	DENNIS, JOHN	220,848	PELOSI, NANCY*		178,631	D	16.0%	84.0%	16.0%	84.0%
12	2022	239,969	22,859	SLAUSON, STEPHEN	217,110	LEE, BARBARA*		194,251	D	9.5%	90.5%	9.5%	90.5%
13	2022	133,556	67,060	DUARTE, JOHN	66,496	GRAY, ADAM		564	R	50.2%	49.8%	50.2%	49.8%
14	2022	198,464	60,852	HAYDEN, ALISON	137,612	SWALWELL, ERIC*		76,760	D	30.7%	69.3%	30.7%	69.3%

CALIFORNIA

HOUSE OF REPRESENTATIVES

CD	Year	Total Vote	Republican Vote	Republican Candidate	Democratic Vote	Democratic Candidate	Other Vote	Rep.-Dem. Plurality	Total Vote Rep. %	Total Vote Dem. %	Major Vote Rep. %	Major Vote Dem. %
15	2022	194,874			108,077	MULLIN, KEVIN	86,797	108,077 D		55.5%		100.0%
16	2022	241,007			139,235	ESHOO, ANNA G.*	101,772	139,235 D		57.8%		100.0%
17	2022	180,253	52,400	TANDON, RITESH	127,853	KHANNA, RO*		75,453 D	29.1%	70.9%	29.1%	70.9%
18	2022	151,513	51,737	HERNANDEZ, PETER	99,776	LOFGREN, ZOE*		48,039 D	34.1%	65.9%	34.1%	65.9%
19	2022	283,310	88,816	GORMAN, JEFF	194,494	PANETTA, JIMMY*		105,678 D	31.3%	68.7%	31.3%	68.7%
20	2022	228,781	153,847	MCCARTHY, KEVIN*	74,934	WOOD, MARISA		78,913 R	67.2%	32.8%	67.2%	32.8%
21	2022	125,647	57,573	MAHER, MICHAEL	68,074	COSTA, JIM*		10,501 D	45.8%	54.2%	45.8%	54.2%
22	2022	102,856	52,994	VALADAO, DAVID*	49,862	SALAS, RUDY		3,132 R	51.5%	48.5%	51.5%	48.5%
23	2022	169,105	103,197	OBERNOLTE, JAY*	65,908	MARSHALL, DEREK		37,289 R	61.0%	39.0%	61.0%	39.0%
24	2022	262,552	103,533	ALLEN, BRADLEY "BRAD"	159,019	CARBAJAL, SALUD*		55,486 D	39.4%	60.6%	39.4%	60.6%
25	2022	152,742	65,101	HAWKINS, BRIAN E.	87,641	RUIZ, RAUL*		22,540 D	42.6%	57.4%	42.6%	57.4%
26	2022	246,789	112,214	JACOBS, MATT	134,575	BROWNLEY, JULIA*		22,361 D	45.5%	54.5%	45.5%	54.5%
27	2022	196,516	104,624	GARCIA, MIKE*	91,892	SMITH, CHRISTY		12,732 R	53.2%	46.8%	53.2%	46.8%
28	2022	226,557	76,495	HALLMAN, WES	150,062	CHU, JUDY*		73,567 D	33.8%	66.2%	33.8%	66.2%
29	2022	119,435			69,915	CARDENAS, TONY*	49,520	69,915 D		58.5%		100.0%
30	2022	211,068			150,100	SCHIFF, ADAM B.*	60,968	150,100 D		71.1%		100.0%
31	2022	153,625	62,153	MARTINEZ, DANIEL BOCIC	91,472	NAPOLITANO, GRACE FLORES*		29,319 D	40.5%	59.5%	40.5%	59.5%
32	2022	242,029	74,618	VOLOTZKY, LUCIE LAPOINTE	167,411	SHERMAN, BRAD*		92,793 D	30.8%	69.2%	30.8%	69.2%
33	2022	132,707	56,119	PORTER, JOHN MARK	76,588	AGUILAR, PETE*		20,469 D	42.3%	57.7%	42.3%	57.7%
34	2022	121,467			62,244	GOMEZ, JIMMY*	59,223	62,244 D		51.2%		100.0%
35	2022	130,953	55,832	CARGILE, MIKE	75,121	TORRES, NORMA*		19,289 D	42.6%	57.4%	42.6%	57.4%
36	2022	278,563	84,264	COLLINS, JOE E. III	194,299	LIEU, TED W.*		110,035 D	30.2%	69.8%	30.2%	69.8%
37	2022	131,880			84,338	KAMLAGER, SYDNEY	47,542	84,338 D		64.0%		100.0%
38	2022	174,311	73,051	CHING, ERIC J.	101,260	SANCHEZ, LINDA*		28,209 D	41.9%	58.1%	41.9%	58.1%
39	2022	131,597	55,701	SMITH, AJA	75,896	TAKANO, MARK A.*		20,195 D	42.3%	57.7%	42.3%	57.7%
40	2022	284,311	161,589	KIM, YOUNG*	122,722	MAHMOOD, ASIF		38,867 R	56.8%	43.2%	56.8%	43.2%
41	2022	236,638	123,869	CALVERT, KEN*	112,769	ROLLINS, WILL		11,100 R	52.3%	47.7%	52.3%	47.7%
42	2022	145,120	45,903	BRISCOE, JOHN	99,217	GARCIA, ROBERT		53,314 D	31.6%	68.4%	31.6%	68.4%
43	2022	123,447	27,985	NAVARRO, OMAR	95,462	WATERS, MAXINE*		67,477 D	22.7%	77.3%	22.7%	77.3%
44	2022	138,714	38,554	JONES, PAUL	100,160	BARRAGAN, NANETTE DIAZ*		61,606 D	27.8%	72.2%	27.8%	72.2%
45	2022	217,426	113,960	STEEL, MICHELLE*	103,466	CHEN, JAY		10,494 R	52.4%	47.6%	52.4%	47.6%
46	2022	126,298	48,257	GONZALES, CHRISTOPHER J.	78,041	CORREA, LOU*		29,784 D	38.2%	61.8%	38.2%	61.8%
47	2022	265,635	128,261	BAUGH, SCOTT	137,374	PORTER, KATIE*		9,113 D	48.3%	51.7%	48.3%	51.7%
48	2022	257,071	155,171	ISSA, DARRELL*	101,900	HOULAHAN, STEPHEN		53,271 R	60.4%	39.6%	60.4%	39.6%
49	2022	291,735	138,194	MARYOTT, BRIAN	153,541	LEVIN, MIKE*		15,347 D	47.4%	52.6%	47.4%	52.6%
50	2022	268,635	99,819	GUSTAFSON, COREY	168,816	PETERS, SCOTT*		68,997 D	37.2%	62.8%	37.2%	62.8%
51	2022	233,072	88,886	CAPLAN, STAN	144,186	JACOBS, SARA*		55,300 D	38.1%	61.9%	38.1%	61.9%
52	2022	151,016	50,330	GEFFENEY, TYLER	100,686	VARGAS, JUAN*		50,356 D	33.3%	66.7%	33.3%	66.7%
TOTAL	2022	10,656,368	3,859,666		6,337,915		458,787	2,478,249 D	36.2%	59.5%	37.8%	62.2%

Note: An asterisk (*) denotes incumbent.

CALIFORNIA

GENERAL AND PRIMARY ELECTIONS

2022 PRIMARY ELECTIONS: SUPPLEMENTARY INFORMATION

Primary June 7, 2022 **Registration** (as of May 23, 2022) 21,941,212

Party	Registration
Democratic	10,261,984
Republican	5,249,974
No Party Preference	4,983,013
American Independent	749,556
Libertarian	224,931
Peace and Freedom	117,314
Unknown	113,184
Green	92,570
Other	148,686

Primary Type Open—Any registered voter could participate in the "top two" primary, in which candidates of all parties (and independents) run together on the same ballot and the top two finishers in each primary race advanced to the general election.

CALIFORNIA

GENERAL AND PRIMARY ELECTIONS

	REPUBLICAN PRIMARIES			DEMOCRATIC PRIMARIES
	ALL-PARTY PRIMARIES			
Senator	Padilla, Alex* (Democrat)	3,725,544	54.1%	
	Meuser, Mark P. (Republican)	1,028,374	14.9%	
	Williams, Cordie (Republican)	474,321	6.9%	
	Elist, Jon (Republican)	289,716	4.2%	
	Smith, Chuck (Republican)	266,766	3.9%	
	Bradley, James (Republican)	235,788	3.4%	
	Pierce, Douglas (Democrat)	116,771	1.7%	
	Parker, John Thompson (Peace and Freedom)	105,477	1.5%	
	Liew, Sarah Sun (Republican)	76,994	1.1%	
	O'Dowd, Dan (Democrat)	74,916	1.1%	
	Agbede, Akinyemi (Democrat)	70,971	1.0%	
	Hall, Myron L. (Republican)	66,161	1.0%	
	Ursich, Timothy Jr. (Democrat)	58,348	0.8%	
	Lucero, Robert George Jr. (Republican)	53,398	0.8%	
	Conn, James Henry "Henk" (Green)	35,983	0.5%	
	Garcia, Eleanor (No Party Preference)	34,625	0.5%	
	Tapia, Carlos Guillermo (Republican)	33,870	0.5%	
	Elizondo, Pamela (Green)	31,981	0.5%	
	Petris, Enrique (Republican)	31,883	0.5%	
	Pirjada, Obaidul Huq (Democrat)	27,889	0.4%	
	Bradford, Daphne (No Party Preference)	26,900	0.4%	
	Grundmann, Don J. (No Party Preference)	10,181	0.1%	
	Jenkins, Deon D. (No Party Preference)	6,936	0.1%	
	TOTAL	6,883,793		
Governor	Newsom, Gavin* (Democrat)	3,945,728	55.9%	
	Dahle, Brian (Republican)	1,252,800	17.7%	
	Shellenberger, Michael (No Party Preference)	290,286	4.1%	
	Le Roux, Jenny Rae (Republican)	246,665	3.5%	
	Trimino, Anthony (Republican)	246,322	3.5%	
	Collins, Shawn (Republican)	173,083	2.5%	
	Rodriguez, Luis Javier (Green)	124,672	1.8%	
	Zacky, Leo S. (Republican)	94,521	1.3%	
	Williams, Major (Republican)	92,580	1.3%	
	Newman, Robert C. II (Republican)	82,849	1.2%	
	Ventresca, Joel (Democrat)	66,885	0.9%	
	Lozano, David (Republican)	66,542	0.9%	
	Anderson, Ronald A. (Republican)	53,554	0.8%	
	Senum, Reinette (No Party Preference)	53,015	0.8%	
	Perez-Serrato, Armando "Mando" (Democrat)	45,474	0.6%	
	Jones, Ron (Republican)	38,337	0.5%	
	Mercuri, Daniel (Republican)	36,396	0.5%	
	Collins, Heather (Green)	29,690	0.4%	
	Fanara, Anthony "Tony" (Democrat)	25,086	0.4%	
	Morales, Cristian Raul (Republican)	22,304	0.3%	
	Sortor, Lonnie (Republican)	21,044	0.3%	
	Schultz, Frederic C. (No Party Preference)	17,502	0.2%	
	Sanders, Woodrow "Woody" III (No Party Preference)	16,204	0.2%	
	Hanink, James G. (No Party Preference)	10,110	0.1%	
	Fiankan, Serge (No Party Preference)	6,201	0.1%	
	Zink, Bradley (No Party Preference)	5,997	0.1%	
	Scott, Jeff (Write-In) (Write-in)	13		
	Bhangoo, Gurinder (Write-In) (Write-in)	8		
	TOTAL	7,063,868		
Congressional District 1	LaMalfa, Doug* (Republican)	96,858	57.1%	
	Steiner, Max (Democrat)	55,549	32.8%	
	Geist, Tim (Republican)	11,408	6.7%	
	Yee, Rose Penelope (No Party Preference)	5,777	3.4%	
	TOTAL	169,592		

CALIFORNIA

GENERAL AND PRIMARY ELECTIONS

ALL-PARTY PRIMARIES

Congressional District 2	Huffman, Jared* (Democrat)	145,245	68.7%
	Brower, Douglas (Republican)	18,102	8.6%
	Coulombe, Chris (Republican)	17,498	8.3%
	Hampson, Beth (Democrat)	14,262	6.7%
	Ramirez, Archimedes (Republican)	12,202	5.8%
	Elizondo, Darian J. (Republican)	4,012	1.9%
	TOTAL	*211,321*	
Congressional District 3	Kiley, Kevin (Republican)	93,552	39.7%
	Jones, Kermit (Democrat)	91,217	38.7%
	Jones, Scott R. (Republican)	38,288	16.2%
	Peterson, David (Democrat)	12,675	5.4%
	TOTAL	*235,732*	
Congressional District 4	Thompson, Mike* (Democrat)	115,041	66.2%
	Brock, Matt (Republican)	28,260	16.3%
	Giblin, Scott (Republican)	16,914	9.7%
	Engdahl, Andrew David (Democrat)	8,634	5.0%
	Kishineff, Jason (No Party Preference)	2,477	1.4%
	Jones, Jimih L. (Republican)	2,363	1.4%
	Newman, Seth (Write-In) (Write-in)	15	
	TOTAL	*173,704*	
Congressional District 5	McClintock, Tom* (Republican)	87,010	45.5%
	Barkley, Michael J. "Mike" (Democrat)	64,285	33.6%
	Magsig, Nathan F. (Republican)	25,299	13.2%
	Wozniak, Steve (No Party Preference)	6,045	3.2%
	Main, David (Republican)	5,927	3.1%
	Obert, Kelsten Charles (Republican)	2,864	1.5%
	TOTAL	*191,430*	
Congressional District 6	Bera, Ami* (Democrat)	76,317	52.6%
	Hamilton, Tamika (Republican)	27,339	18.8%
	Daniels, Bret (Republican)	16,612	11.5%
	Bish, Chris (Republican)	11,421	7.9%
	Gorman, Mark (Democrat)	7,528	5.2%
	Black, Karla (Republican)	3,553	2.4%
	Langford, D. Keith Jr. (Republican)	2,272	1.6%
	Richardson, Chris (Write-In) (Write-in)	15	
	TOTAL	*145,057*	
Congressional District 7	Matsui, Doris* (Democrat)	94,896	63.2%
	Semenenko, Max (Republican)	42,728	28.5%
	Fremgen, Jimmy (Democrat)	12,550	8.4%
	TOTAL	*150,174*	
Congressional District 8	Garamendi, John* (Democrat)	72,333	63.1%
	Recile, Rudy (Republican)	23,518	20.5%
	Sudduth, Cheryl (Democrat)	11,378	9.9%
	Riley, Christopher (Democrat)	3,926	3.4%
	Rutsch, Edwin (Democrat)	3,268	2.9%
	Johnson, Demnlus (Write-In) (Write-in)	234	0.2%
	TOTAL	*114,657*	
Congressional District 9	Harder, Josh* (Democrat)	39,026	36.7%
	Patti, Tom (Republican)	30,843	29.0%
	Shoemaker, Jim (Republican)	15,443	14.5%
	Chima, Harpreet Singh (Democrat)	8,433	7.9%
	Madison, Jonathan (Republican)	5,992	5.6%
	Jafri, Khalid (Democrat)	3,174	3.0%
	Feng, Karena Apple (Democrat)	2,632	2.5%
	Andrews, Mark T. (No Party Preference)	758	0.7%
	TOTAL	*106,301*	

CALIFORNIA

GENERAL AND PRIMARY ELECTIONS

ALL-PARTY PRIMARIES

Congressional District 10	DeSaulnier, Mark* (Democrat)	124,787	84.0%
	Kerr, Michael Ernest (Green)	22,210	14.9%
	Piccinini, Katherine (Write-In) (Write-in)	1,638	1.1%
	TOTAL	148,635	
Congressional District 11	Pelosi, Nancy* (Democrat)	133,798	71.7%
	Dennis, John (Republican)	20,054	10.7%
	Buttar, Shahid (Democrat)	19,471	10.4%
	Del Castello, Eve (Republican)	7,319	3.9%
	Phillips, Jeffrey (Democrat)	3,595	1.9%
	Von Krieg, Bianca (Democrat)	2,499	1.3%
	TOTAL	186,736	
Congressional District 12	Lee, Barbara* (Democrat)	135,892	87.7%
	Slauson, Stephen (Republican)	8,274	5.3%
	Kaplan, Glenn (No Party Preference)	5,141	3.3%
	Wilson, Eric (Democrat)	3,753	2.4%
	Nuerge, Ned (Republican)	1,902	1.2%
	TOTAL	154,962	
Congressional District 13	Duarte, John (Republican)	26,163	34.2%
	Gray, Adam (Democrat)	23,784	31.1%
	Arballo, Phil (Democrat)	13,099	17.1%
	Giglio, David A. (Republican)	11,320	14.8%
	Martinez, Diego Javier (Republican)	2,026	2.7%
	TOTAL	76,392	
Congressional District 14	Swalwell, Eric* (Democrat)	77,120	63.6%
	Hayden, Alison (Republican)	12,503	10.3%
	Wong, Tom (Republican)	11,406	9.4%
	Iyer, Sri "Steve" (Republican)	10,829	8.9%
	Peters, James Andrew (Democrat)	6,216	5.1%
	Singh, Major (No Party Preference)	2,495	2.1%
	Simard, Liam Miguel (No Party Preference)	657	0.5%
	TOTAL	121,226	
Congressional District 15	Mullin, Kevin (Democrat)	58,806	41.1%
	Canepa, David J. (Democrat)	34,488	24.1%
	Mattammal, Gus (Republican)	23,625	16.5%
	Beach, Emily (Democrat)	20,816	14.6%
	Garrity, Jim (No Party Preference)	3,081	2.2%
	Watters, Andrew G. (Democrat)	1,551	1.1%
	Pataki, Ferenc (No Party Preference)	671	0.5%
	TOTAL	143,038	
Congressional District 16	Eshoo, Anna G.* (Democrat)	81,100	47.9%
	Kumar, Rishi (Democrat)	26,438	15.6%
	Ohtaki, Peter (Republican)	21,354	12.6%
	Fox, Richard B. (Republican)	13,187	7.8%
	Rading, Ajwang (Democrat)	11,418	6.7%
	Tanaka, Greg Lin (Democrat)	11,107	6.6%
	Solomon, Benjamin Thomas (Republican)	2,659	1.6%
	Fredrich, John Karl (No Party Preference)	2,120	1.3%
	Odekirk, Travis Andrew (Write-In) (Write-in)	2	
	TOTAL	169,385	
Congressional District 17	Khanna, Ro* (Democrat)	74,892	66.0%
	Tandon, Ritesh (Republican)	28,730	25.3%
	Forbes, Stephen (Democrat)	5,694	5.0%
	Ravul, Rao (Democrat)	2,394	2.1%
	Dehn, Joseph W. III (Libertarian)	1,836	1.6%
	TOTAL	113,546	

CALIFORNIA

GENERAL AND PRIMARY ELECTIONS

ALL-PARTY PRIMARIES

Congressional District 18	Lofgren, Zoe* (Democrat)	50,104	56.1%
	Hernandez, Peter (Republican)	27,935	31.3%
	Acevedo-Arreguin, Luis (Democrat)	11,253	12.6%
	TOTAL	89,292	
Congressional District 19	Panetta, Jimmy* (Democrat)	127,545	67.3%
	Gorman, Jeff (Republican)	44,181	23.3%
	Epperson, Dalila (Republican)	12,082	6.4%
	Deitch, Douglas (Democrat)	5,700	3.0%
	TOTAL	189,508	
Congressional District 20	McCarthy, Kevin* (Republican)	85,748	61.3%
	Wood, Marisa (Democrat)	33,511	24.0%
	Dewell, Ben (Democrat)	8,757	6.3%
	Davis, James (Republican)	6,382	4.6%
	Macauley, James (Republican)	5,488	3.9%
	TOTAL	139,886	
Congressional District 21	Costa, Jim* (Democrat)	33,850	47.0%
	Maher, Michael (Republican)	19,040	26.4%
	Stoll, Matt (Republican)	11,931	16.6%
	Garcia, Eric (Democrat)	7,239	10.0%
	TOTAL	72,060	
Congressional District 22	Salas, Rudy (Democrat)	25,337	45.2%
	Valadao, David* (Republican)	14,331	25.6%
	Mathys, Chris (Republican)	13,111	23.4%
	Medeiros, Adam (Republican)	3,250	5.8%
	TOTAL	56,029	
Congressional District 23	Obernolte, Jay* (Republican)	57,988	60.9%
	Marshall, Derek (Democrat)	20,776	21.8%
	Gomez, Blanca (Democrat)	16,516	17.3%
	TOTAL	95,280	
Congressional District 24	Carbajal, Salud* (Democrat)	111,199	60.0%
	Allen, Bradley "Brad" (Republican)	57,532	31.0%
	Weslander Quaid, Michele R. (No Party Preference)	13,880	7.5%
	Frankenfield, Jeff (No Party Preference)	2,732	1.5%
	TOTAL	185,343	
Congressional District 25	Ruiz, Raul* (Democrat)	55,315	56.4%
	Hawkins, Brian E. (Republican)	16,085	16.4%
	Tyson, Brian M. (Republican)	14,186	14.5%
	Gibson, James Francis (Republican)	6,059	6.2%
	Thakur, Albert "Burt" (Republican)	2,982	3.0%
	Truman, Ceci (Republican)	1,850	1.9%
	Reiss, Jonathan (Republican)	1,609	1.6%
	TOTAL	98,086	
Congressional District 26	Brownley, Julia* (Democrat)	91,535	54.3%
	Jacobs, Matt (Republican)	64,835	38.4%
	Taylor, Paul Nathan (Republican)	5,612	3.3%
	Goodman, Dave (No Party Preference)	3,950	2.3%
	Mikhail, Fadde (Republican)	2,775	1.6%
	TOTAL	168,707	
Congressional District 27	Garcia, Mike* (Republican)	57,469	47.1%
	Smith, Christy (Democrat)	45,675	37.4%
	Quartey, John Quaye II (Democrat)	8,303	6.8%
	Luevanos, Ruth (Democrat)	6,668	5.5%
	Rudnick, David (Republican)	2,648	2.2%
	Pierce, Mark (Republican)	1,352	1.1%
	TOTAL	122,115	

CALIFORNIA

GENERAL AND PRIMARY ELECTIONS

ALL-PARTY PRIMARIES

Congressional District 28	Chu, Judy* (Democrat)	90,395	63.0%
	Hallman, Wes (Republican)	41,955	29.2%
	Caronna, Dorothy (Democrat)	7,993	5.6%
	Depaolis, Giuliano "Gio" (No Party Preference)	3,100	2.2%
	TOTAL	143,443	
Congressional District 29	Cardenas, Tony* (Democrat)	47,941	56.7%
	Duenas, Angelica Maria (Democrat)	19,321	22.8%
	Carranza, Margarita Maria (Republican)	7,079	8.4%
	Miranda, Andy (Republican)	5,167	6.1%
	Melendez, Rudy (Republican)	5,057	6.0%
	TOTAL	84,565	
Congressional District 30	Schiff, Adam B.* (Democrat)	102,290	62.4%
	Pudlo, G. "Maebe A. Girl" (Democrat)	21,053	12.9%
	Kennedy, Ronda (Republican)	13,953	8.5%
	Gipson, Patrick Lee (Republican)	10,529	6.4%
	Nalbandian, Johnny (Republican)	7,693	4.7%
	Zuniga, Paloma (Republican)	2,614	1.6%
	Genovese, Sal (Democrat)	2,612	1.6%
	Meurer, William "Gunner" (Green)	1,598	1.0%
	Rodriguez, Tony (American Independent)	1,460	0.9%
	TOTAL	163,802	
Congressional District 31	Napolitano, Grace Flores* (Democrat)	49,415	55.5%
	Martinez, Daniel Bocic (Republican)	32,721	36.7%
	De Luca, Rocco Anthony (Democrat)	6,948	7.8%
	Levi, Erskine L. (Write-In) (Write-in)	17	
	TOTAL	89,101	
Congressional District 32	Sherman, Brad* (Democrat)	88,063	53.7%
	Volotzky, Lucie Lapointe (Republican)	32,342	19.7%
	Aazami, Shervin (Democrat)	15,036	9.2%
	Toomim, Melissa (Republican)	13,926	8.5%
	Rhodes, Aarika Samone (Democrat)	8,744	5.3%
	Potell, Jason (Democrat)	2,943	1.8%
	Rab, A. "Raji" (Democrat)	2,938	1.8%
	TOTAL	163,992	
Congressional District 33	Aguilar, Pete* (Democrat)	41,046	59.8%
	Porter, John Mark (Republican)	12,096	17.6%
	Gutierrez, Rex (Republican)	10,587	15.4%
	Richter, Ernest Harold (Republican)	4,878	7.1%
	TOTAL	68,607	
Congressional District 34	Gomez, Jimmy* (Democrat)	45,376	50.7%
	Kim, David (Democrat)	34,921	39.0%
	VonBuck, Clifton Rio Torrado (Republican)	9,150	10.2%
	TOTAL	89,447	
Congressional District 35	Torres, Norma* (Democrat)	37,554	54.3%
	Cargile, Mike (Republican)	17,431	25.2%
	Carcamo, Rafael (Republican)	7,619	11.0%
	Erbst, Bob (Republican)	3,480	5.0%
	Stevens, Lloyd A. (Democrat)	3,022	4.4%
	TOTAL	69,106	
Congressional District 36	Lieu, Ted W.* (Democrat)	122,969	67.1%
	Collins, Joe E. III (Republican)	24,553	13.4%
	Gates, Derrick R. (Republican)	10,263	5.6%
	Hakami, Ariana (Republican)	9,760	5.3%
	Ragge, Claire (Republican)	7,351	4.0%
	Obrien, Colin Kilpatrick (Democrat)	6,221	3.4%
	Williams, Steve (No Party Preference)	1,180	0.6%
	Jesuele, Matthew Vincent (No Party Preference)	976	0.5%
	TOTAL	183,273	

CALIFORNIA

GENERAL AND PRIMARY ELECTIONS

ALL-PARTY PRIMARIES

Congressional District 37	Kamlager, Sydney (Democrat)	42,628	43.7%
	Perry, Jan C. (Democrat)	17,993	18.5%
	Lee, Daniel W. (Democrat)	17,414	17.9%
	Mendoza, Sandra (Democrat)	8,017	8.2%
	Champion, Chris (Republican)	5,469	5.6%
	Fedalizo, Baltazar "Bong" (Republican)	3,520	3.6%
	Shure, Michael (Democrat)	2,469	2.5%
	TOTAL	*97,510*	
Congressional District 38	Sanchez, Linda* (Democrat)	58,586	58.7%
	Ching, Eric J. (Republican)	30,436	30.5%
	Sarega, John (Republican)	10,768	10.8%
	TOTAL	*99,790*	
Congressional District 39	Takano, Mark A.* (Democrat)	44,067	57.1%
	Smith, Aja (Republican)	9,751	12.6%
	Spinney, Bill (Republican)	7,421	9.6%
	Moreno, Tony (Republican)	5,527	7.2%
	Peterson, Art (Republican)	5,081	6.6%
	Minnella, John Lordsal (Republican)	3,662	4.7%
	Suarez, Emmanuel L. (Republican)	1,600	2.1%
	TOTAL	*77,109*	
Congressional District 40	Mahmood, Asif (Democrat)	74,607	40.9%
	Kim, Young* (Republican)	63,346	34.7%
	Raths, Greg G. (Republican)	42,404	23.2%
	Taurus, Nick (Republican)	2,193	1.2%
	TOTAL	*182,550*	
Congressional District 41	Calvert, Joseph W.* (Republican)	72,700	48.2%
	Rollins, Will (Democrat)	45,923	30.4%
	Kurani, Shrina (Democrat)	23,483	15.6%
	Lucio, John Michael (Republican)	6,880	4.6%
	Nevenic, Anna (No Party Preference)	1,862	1.2%
	TOTAL	*150,848*	
Congressional District 42	Garcia, Robert (Democrat)	43,406	46.7%
	Briscoe, John (Republican)	24,319	26.1%
	Garcia, Cristina (Democrat)	11,685	12.6%
	Mathews, Peter (Democrat)	3,415	3.7%
	Lopez, J. Nicole (Democrat)	3,164	3.4%
	Flores, Julio Cesar (Green)	2,491	2.7%
	Summerville, William Moses (Democrat)	2,301	2.5%
	Beltran, Joaquin (Democrat)	2,254	2.4%
	TOTAL	*93,035*	
Congressional District 43	Waters, Maxine* (Democrat)	55,889	74.3%
	Navarro, Omar (Republican)	8,927	11.9%
	Pratt, Allison (Republican)	5,489	7.3%
	Monestime, Jean M. (Democrat)	4,952	6.6%
	TOTAL	*75,257*	
Congressional District 44	Barragan, Nanette Diaz* (Democrat)	58,594	68.7%
	Jones, Paul (Republican)	20,569	24.1%
	Griffin, Morris F. (Democrat)	6,110	7.2%
	TOTAL	*85,273*	
Congressional District 45	Steel, Michelle* (Republican)	65,641	48.2%
	Chen, Jay (Democrat)	58,721	43.1%
	Pham, Long K. (Republican)	11,732	8.6%
	Shioura, Hilaire Fuji (Write-In) (Write-in)	6	
	TOTAL	*136,100*	

CALIFORNIA

GENERAL AND PRIMARY ELECTIONS

ALL-PARTY PRIMARIES

Congressional District 46	Correa, Lou* (Democrat)	37,311	49.1%
	Gonzales, Christopher J. (Republican)	11,823	15.6%
	Ortega, Mike (Democrat)	9,311	12.3%
	Nguyen, Mike (Republican)	9,162	12.1%
	Rocha, Felix Jr. (Republican)	7,084	9.3%
	Rushman, Ed (No Party Preference)	1,264	1.7%
	TOTAL	75,955	
Congressional District 47	Porter, Katie* (Democrat)	86,742	51.7%
	Baugh, Scott (Republican)	51,776	30.9%
	Phan West, Amy (Republican)	13,949	8.3%
	Burley, Brian (Republican)	11,952	7.1%
	Webber, Errol (Republican)	3,342	2.0%
	TOTAL	167,761	
Congressional District 48	Issa, Darrell* (Republican)	101,280	61.5%
	Houlahan, Stephen (Democrat)	45,740	27.8%
	Rascon, Matthew (Democrat)	14,983	9.1%
	Jahn, Lucinda KWH (No Party Preference)	2,614	1.6%
	TOTAL	164,617	
Congressional District 49	Levin, Mike* (Democrat)	92,211	48.9%
	Maryott, Brian (Republican)	35,805	19.0%
	Bartlett, Lisa A. (Republican)	20,163	10.7%
	Rodriguez, Christopher (Republican)	18,248	9.7%
	O'Neil, Josiah (Republican)	14,746	7.8%
	Smalley, Nadia B. (Democrat)	4,804	2.5%
	Taylor, Renee (Republican)	2,597	1.4%
	TOTAL	188,574	
Congressional District 50	Peters, Scott* (Democrat)	89,894	52.3%
	Gustafson, Corey (Republican)	51,312	29.9%
	Taitano, Kylie (Democrat)	16,065	9.4%
	Chiddick, David (Republican)	9,333	5.4%
	Schindler, Adam (No Party Preference)	5,168	3.0%
	TOTAL	171,772	
Congressional District 51	Jacobs, Sara* (Democrat)	91,329	60.5%
	Caplan, Stan (Republican)	56,183	37.2%
	Cortes, Jose (Peace and Freedom)	3,343	2.2%
	Holman Leak, Barrett (Write-In) (Write-in)	55	
	TOTAL	150,910	
Congressional District 52	Vargas, Juan* (Democrat)	56,827	59.1%
	Geffeney, Tyler (Republican)	29,348	30.5%
	Vazquez, Joaquin (Democrat)	9,965	10.4%
	TOTAL	96,140	

Note: An asterisk (*) denotes incumbent.

COLORADO

Statewide Races

In the years since Donald Trump descended from the escalator of Trump Tower to announce his first presidential campaign, few states have moved as sharply against Republicans as Colorado. In 2020, Joe Biden's 55%–41% margin in the state represented the best showing for a Democratic presidential nominee since 1964. Two years later, Colorado seemed as blue as ever.

Colorado Democrats' strong 2022 performance was not necessarily for lack of GOP effort. Republican voters in Colorado seemed to put their collective best foot forward when it came to nominating candidates. University of Colorado Regent Heidi Ganahl, the only statewide Republican remaining in office as 2022 began, won the GOP nomination. Despite some Democratic meddling on behalf of a more far-right candidate, Republicans nominated businessman Joe O'Dea for the state's Senate contest.

But statewide Democrats cleaned up. Gov. Jared Polis, a Democrat with some libertarian stances, was reelected by 19 points, nearly doubling his 11-point margin from 2018. Polis took 82% in Denver and won all three suburban counties that surround it by more than 20 points apiece. Polis' strength was also visible along the southern fringes of the Denver metro area. A decade ago, Douglas County, which has the highest median household income in the state, used to routinely deliver landslide margins to statewide Republicans – Polis came within a percentage point of carrying it. Just to the south of Douglas County, Colorado Springs' El Paso County has gotten more competitive. Despite its longtime image as an anti-tax, socially conservative hub, Polis only lost El Paso County 51%–47%.

Despite O'Dea's relatively moderate profile, Sen. Michael Bennet (D) secured a third full term in office. Though Bennet was favored, his win was surprisingly robust, as his 56%–41% margin was stronger than Biden's 2020 showing in Colorado.

House Races

For the post-2020 redistricting cycle, two changes came to Colorado. The first change came as the result of a 2018 ballot measure: that year, voters approved an amendment that created an independent redistricting commission. The second change was numerical: the state was awarded an eighth seat.

The new CO-8 appeared in the northern Denver metro area. It paired much of blue Adams County, which has a 40% Hispanic population, with the majority of Greeley's Weld County, which retains a red lean. State Rep. Yadira Caraveo (D) came out on the winning side of the tug-of-war against GOP state Sen. Barbara Kirkmeyer.

One of the biggest surprises of Election Night came in the 3rd District. Though first-term Rep. Lauren Boebert had a reputation as a far-right bomb thrower, redistricting did little to alter the character of her Trump +8 Western Slope district, and she was considered a favorite. But Boebert beat Democratic challenger Adam Frisch, a former Aspen mayor, by only 546 votes out of the roughly 327,000 cast in the district. Though a less polarizing Republican would have certainly won by more, Boebert was likely not helped by the statewide Democratic tide – according to analyst Drew Savicki, Polis carried the 3rd by a few points.

COLORADO

Congressional districts first established for elections held in 2022

8 members

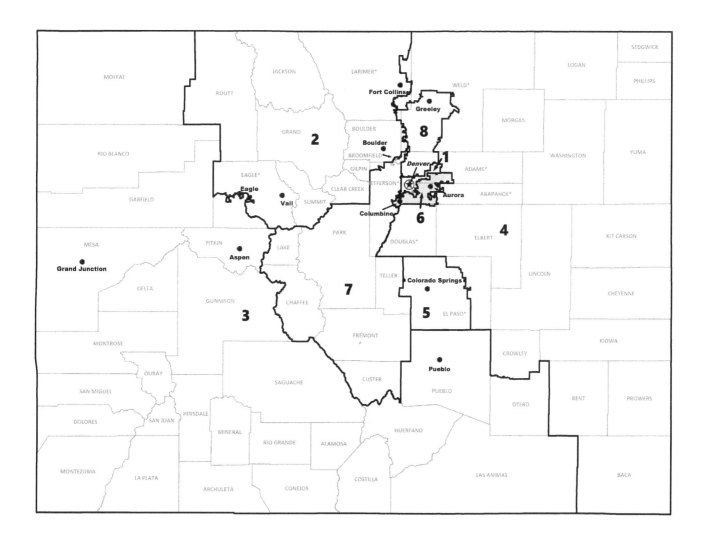

*Asterisk indicates a county whose boundaries include parts of two or more congressional districts.

CDs 1 and 6 are highlighted for visibility. See Inset for Denver area.

COLORADO

Greater Denver Area

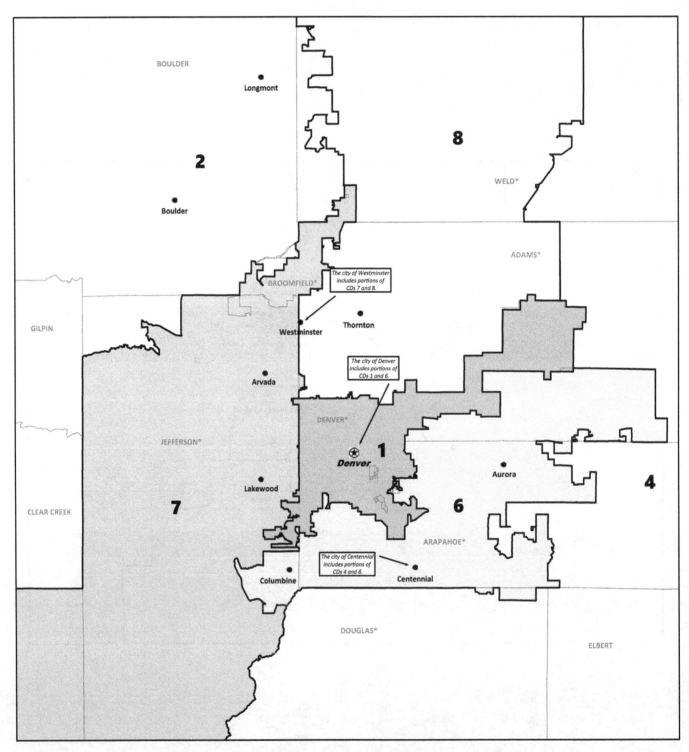

*Asterisk indicates a county whose boundaries include parts of two or more congressional districts.
CDs 1, 6 and 7 are highlighted for visibility.

COLORADO

GOVERNOR
Jared Polis (D). Reelected 2022 to a four-year term. Previously elected 2018.

SENATORS (1 Democrats)
Michael F. Bennet (D). Reelected 2022 to a six-year term. Sworn in as senator January 22, 2009, to fill the vacancy created by the resignation of Ken Salazar (D) to become U.S. secretary of interior, and elected 2010 and 2016.

John Hickenlooper (D). Elected 2020 to a six-year term.

REPRESENTATIVES (3 Republicans, 5 Democrats)
1. Diana L. DeGette (D)
2. Joseph "Joe" Neguse (D)
3. Lauren Boebert (R)
4. Ken Buck (R)
5. Doug Lamborn (R)
6. Jason Crow (D)
7. Brittany Pettersen (D)
8. Yadira Caraveo (D)

POSTWAR VOTE FOR PRESIDENT

		Republican		Democratic		Other Vote	Rep.-Dem. Plurality	Percentage			
								Total Vote		Major Vote	
Year	Total Vote	Vote	Candidate	Vote	Candidate			Rep.	Dem.	Rep.	Dem.
2020	3,256,980	1,364,607	Trump, Donald J.*	1,804,352	Biden, Joseph R. Jr.	88,021	439,745 D	41.9%	55.4%	43.1%	56.9%
2016**	2,780,247	1,202,484	Trump, Donald J.	1,338,870	Clinton, Hillary Rodham	238,893	136,386 D	43.3%	48.2%	47.3%	52.7%
2012	2,569,522	1,185,243	Romney, W. Mitt	1,323,102	Obama, Barack H.*	61,177	137,859 D	46.1%	51.5%	47.3%	52.7%
2008	2,401,462	1,073,629	McCain, John S. III	1,288,633	Obama, Barack H.	39,200	215,004 D	44.7%	53.7%	45.4%	54.6%
2004	2,130,330	1,101,255	Bush, George W.*	1,001,732	Kerry, John F.	27,343	99,523 R	51.7%	47.0%	52.4%	47.6%
2000**	1,741,368	883,748	Bush, George W.	738,227	Gore, Albert Jr.	119,393	145,521 R	50.8%	42.4%	54.5%	45.5%
1996**	1,510,704	691,848	Dole, Robert "Bob"	671,152	Clinton, Bill*	147,704	20,696 R	45.8%	44.4%	50.8%	49.2%
1992**	1,569,180	562,850	Bush, George H.*	629,681	Clinton, Bill	376,649	66,831 D	35.9%	40.1%	47.2%	52.8%
1988	1,372,394	728,177	Bush, George H.	621,453	Dukakis, Michael S.	22,764	106,724 R	53.1%	45.3%	54.0%	46.0%
1984	1,295,380	821,817	Reagan, Ronald*	454,975	Mondale, Walter F.	18,588	366,842 R	63.4%	35.1%	64.4%	35.6%
1980**	1,184,415	652,264	Reagan, Ronald	367,973	Carter, Jimmy*	164,178	284,291 R	55.1%	31.1%	63.9%	36.1%
1976	1,081,554	584,367	Ford, Gerald R.*	460,353	Carter, Jimmy	36,834	124,014 R	54.0%	42.6%	55.9%	44.1%
1972	953,884	597,189	Nixon, Richard M.*	329,980	McGovern, George S.	26,715	267,209 R	62.6%	34.6%	64.4%	35.6%
1968**	811,199	409,345	Nixon, Richard M.	335,174	Humphrey, Hubert Horatio Jr.	66,680	74,171 R	50.5%	41.3%	55.0%	45.0%
1964	776,986	296,767	Goldwater, Barry M. Sr.	476,024	Johnson, Lyndon B.*	4,195	179,257 D	38.2%	61.3%	38.4%	61.6%
1960	736,236	402,242	Nixon, Richard M.	330,629	Kennedy, John F.	3,365	71,613 R	54.6%	44.9%	54.9%	45.1%
1956	657,074	394,479	Eisenhower, Dwight D.*	257,997	Stevenson, Adlai E. II	4,598	136,482 R	60.0%	39.3%	60.5%	39.5%
1952	630,103	379,782	Eisenhower, Dwight D.	245,504	Stevenson, Adlai E. II	4,817	134,278 R	60.3%	39.0%	60.7%	39.3%
1948	515,237	239,714	Dewey, Thomas E.	267,288	Truman, Harry S.*	8,235	27,574 D	46.5%	51.9%	47.3%	52.7%

Note: An asterisk (*) denotes incumbent. **In past elections, the other vote included: 2016 - 144,121 Libertarian (Gary Johnson); 2000 - 91,434 Green (Ralph Nader); 1996 - 99,629 Reform (Ross Perot); 1992 - 366,010 Independent (Perot); 1980 - 130,633 Independent (John Anderson); 1968 - 60,813 American Independent (George Wallace).

COLORADO

POSTWAR VOTE FOR GOVERNOR

Year	Total Vote	Republican Vote	Republican Candidate	Democratic Vote	Democratic Candidate	Other Vote	Rep.-Dem. Plurality		Total Vote Rep.	Total Vote Dem.	Major Vote Rep.	Major Vote Dem.
2022	2,508,770	983,040	Ganahl, Heidi	1,468,481	Polis, Jared*	57,249	485,441	D	39.2%	58.5%	40.1%	59.9%
2018	2,525,062	1,080,801	Stapleton, Walker	1,348,888	Polis, Jared	95,373	268,087	D	42.8%	53.4%	44.5%	55.5%
2014	2,041,607	938,195	Beauprez, Bob	1,006,433	Hickenlooper, John*	96,979	68,238	D	46.0%	49.3%	48.2%	51.8%
2010**	1,788,001	199,062	Maes, Dan	912,189	Hickenlooper, John	676,750	713,127	D	11.1%	51.0%	17.9%	82.1%
2006	1,558,387	625,886	Beauprez, Bob	888,096	Ritter, Bill Jr.	44,405	262,210	D	40.2%	57.0%	41.3%	58.7%
2002	1,412,602	884,583	Owens, Bill*	475,373	Heath, Rollie	52,646	409,210	R	62.6%	33.7%	65.0%	35.0%
1998	1,323,530	649,688	Owens, Bill	639,358	Schoettler, Gail	34,484	10,330	R	49.1%	48.3%	50.4%	49.6%
1994	1,116,307	432,042	Benson, Bruce	619,205	Romer, Roy*	65,060	187,163	D	38.7%	55.5%	41.1%	58.9%
1990	1,011,272	358,403	Andrews, John	626,032	Romer, Roy*	26,837	267,629	D	35.4%	61.9%	36.4%	63.6%
1986	1,058,928	434,420	Strickland, Ted	616,325	Romer, Roy	8,183	181,905	D	41.0%	58.2%	41.3%	58.7%
1982	956,021	302,740	Fuhr, John D.	627,960	Lamm, Richard D.*	25,321	325,220	D	31.7%	65.7%	32.5%	67.5%
1978	823,807	317,292	Strickland, Ted	483,985	Lamm, Richard D.*	22,530	166,693	D	38.5%	58.7%	39.6%	60.4%
1974	828,968	378,907	Vanderhoof, John D.*	441,199	Lamm, Richard D.	8,862	62,292	D	45.7%	53.2%	46.2%	53.8%
1970	668,496	350,690	Love, John A.*	302,432	Hogan, Mark	15,374	48,258	R	52.5%	45.2%	53.7%	46.3%
1966	660,063	356,730	Love, John A.*	287,132	Knous, Robert L.	16,201	69,598	R	54.0%	43.5%	55.4%	44.6%
1962	616,481	349,342	Love, John A.	262,890	McNichols, Stephen L.R.*	4,249	86,452	R	56.7%	42.6%	57.1%	42.9%
1958**	549,808	228,643	Burch, Palmer L.	321,165	McNichols, Stephen L.R.*		92,522	D	41.6%	58.4%	41.6%	58.4%
1956	645,233	313,950	Brotzman, Donald G.	331,283	McNichols, Stephen L.R.		17,333	D	48.7%	51.3%	48.7%	51.3%
1954	489,540	227,335	Brotzman, Donald G.	262,205	Johnson, Edwin C.		34,870	D	46.4%	53.6%	46.4%	53.6%
1952	613,034	349,924	Thornton, Dan*	260,044	Metzger, John W.	3,066	89,880	R	57.1%	42.4%	57.4%	42.6%
1950	450,994	236,472	Thornton, Dan	212,976	Johnson, Walter W.	1,546	23,496	R	52.4%	47.2%	52.6%	47.4%
1948	501,680	168,928	Hamil, David A.	332,752	Knous, William Lee*		163,824	D	33.7%	66.3%	33.7%	66.3%
1946	335,087	160,483	Lavington, Leon E.	174,604	Knous, William Lee		14,121	D	47.9%	52.1%	47.9%	52.1%

Note: An asterisk (*) denotes incumbent. **In past elections, the other vote included: 2010 - 651,232 American Constitution (Tom Tancredo), who finished second. The term of office of Colorado's Governor was increased from two to four years effective with the 1958 election.

POSTWAR VOTE FOR SENATOR

Year	Total Vote	Republican Vote	Republican Candidate	Democratic Vote	Democratic Candidate	Other Vote	Rep.-Dem. Plurality		Total Vote Rep.	Total Vote Dem.	Major Vote Rep.	Major Vote Dem.
2022	2,500,130	1,031,693	O'Dea, Joe	1,397,170	Bennet, Michael F.*	71,267	365,477	D	41.3%	55.9%	42.5%	57.5%
2020	3,235,659	1,429,492	Gardner, Cory*	1,731,114	Hickenlooper, John	75,053	301,622	D	44.2%	53.5%	45.2%	54.8%
2016	2,743,029	1,215,318	Glenn, Darryl	1,370,710	Bennet, Michael F.*	157,001	155,392	D	44.3%	50.0%	47.0%	53.0%
2014	2,041,058	983,891	Gardner, Cory	944,203	Udall, Mark*	112,964	39,688	R	48.2%	46.3%	51.0%	49.0%
2010	1,777,464	824,789	Buck, Ken	854,685	Bennet, Michael F.*	97,990	29,896	D	46.4%	48.1%	49.1%	50.9%
2008	2,331,712	990,784	Schaffer, Bob	1,231,049	Udall, Mark	109,879	240,265	D	42.5%	52.8%	44.6%	55.4%
2004	2,107,554	980,668	Coors, Pete	1,081,188	Salazar, Ken	45,698	100,520	D	46.5%	51.3%	47.6%	52.4%
2002	1,416,082	717,893	Allard, Wayne*	648,130	Strickland, Tom	50,059	69,763	R	50.7%	45.8%	52.6%	47.4%
1998	1,327,235	829,370	Campbell, Ben Nighthorse*	464,754	Lamm, Dottie	33,111	364,616	R	62.5%	35.0%	64.1%	35.9%
1996	1,469,611	750,325	Allard, Wayne	677,600	Strickland, Tom	41,686	72,725	R	51.1%	46.1%	52.5%	47.5%
1992	1,552,289	662,893	Considine, Terry	803,725	Campbell, Ben Nighthorse	85,671	140,832	D	42.7%	51.8%	45.2%	54.8%
1990	1,022,027	569,048	Brown, Hank	425,746	Heath, Josie	27,233	143,302	R	55.7%	41.7%	57.2%	42.8%
1986	1,060,765	512,994	Kramer, Ken	529,449	Wirth, Timothy E.	18,322	16,455	D	48.4%	49.9%	49.2%	50.8%
1984	1,297,809	833,821	Armstrong, William L.*	449,327	Dick, Nancy	14,661	384,494	R	64.2%	34.6%	65.0%	35.0%
1980	1,173,646	571,295	Buchanan, Mary E.	590,501	Hart, Gary W.*	11,850	19,206	D	48.7%	50.3%	49.2%	50.8%
1978	819,150	480,596	Armstrong, William L.	330,247	Haskell, Floyd K.*	8,307	150,349	R	58.7%	40.3%	59.3%	40.7%
1974	824,166	325,508	Dominick, Peter H.*	471,691	Hart, Gary W.	26,967	146,183	D	39.5%	57.2%	40.8%	59.2%
1972	926,093	447,957	Alott, Gordon Llewellyn*	457,545	Haskell, Floyd K.	20,591	9,588	D	48.4%	49.4%	49.5%	50.5%
1968	785,536	459,952	Dominick, Peter H.*	325,584	McNichols, Stephen L.R.		134,368	R	58.6%	41.4%	58.6%	41.4%
1966	634,837	368,307	Alott, Gordon Llewellyn*	266,198	Romer, Roy	332	102,109	R	58.0%	41.9%	58.0%	42.0%
1962	613,444	328,655	Dominick, Peter H.	279,586	Carroll, John Albert*	5,203	49,069	R	53.6%	45.6%	54.0%	46.0%
1960	727,633	389,428	Alott, Gordon Llewellyn*	334,854	Knous, Robert L.	3,351	54,574	R	53.5%	46.0%	53.8%	46.2%
1956	636,974	317,102	Thornton, Dan	319,872	Carroll, John Albert		2,770	D	49.8%	50.2%	49.8%	50.2%
1954	484,188	248,502	Alott, Gordon Llewellyn	235,686	Carroll, John Albert		12,816	R	51.3%	48.7%	51.3%	48.7%
1950	450,176	239,734	Millikin, Eugene D.*	210,442	Carroll, John Albert		29,292	R	53.3%	46.7%	53.3%	46.7%
1948	510,121	165,069	Nicholson, Will F.	340,719	Johnson, Edwin C.*	4,333	175,650	D	32.4%	66.8%	32.6%	67.4%

Note: An asterisk (*) denotes incumbent.

COLORADO
GOVERNOR 2022

2020 Census Population	County	Total Vote	Republican (Ganahl)	Democratic (Polis)	Other	Rep.-Dem. Plurality		Percentage			
								Total Vote		Major Vote	
								Rep.	Dem.	Rep.	Dem.
519,315	ADAMS	167,618	63,960	99,625	4,033	35,665	D	38.2%	59.4%	39.1%	60.9%
16,423	ALAMOSA	5,920	2,674	3,022	224	348	D	45.2%	51.0%	46.9%	53.1%
657,609	ARAPAHOE	257,121	89,656	162,304	5,161	72,648	D	34.9%	63.1%	35.6%	64.4%
14,179	ARCHULETA	7,808	3,961	3,641	206	320	R	50.7%	46.6%	52.1%	47.9%
3,594	BACA	1,747	1,103	298	346	805	R	63.1%	17.1%	78.7%	21.3%
5,548	BENT	1,830	1,091	627	112	464	R	59.6%	34.3%	63.5%	36.5%
327,381	BOULDER	165,076	30,454	132,173	2,449	101,719	D	18.4%	80.1%	18.7%	81.3%
70,811	BROOMFIELD	37,479	11,796	25,006	677	13,210	D	31.5%	66.7%	32.1%	67.9%
20,513	CHAFFEE	11,749	4,646	6,807	296	2,161	D	39.5%	57.9%	40.6%	59.4%
1,833	CHEYENNE	915	758	115	42	643	R	82.8%	12.6%	86.8%	13.2%
9,734	CLEAR CREEK	5,180	1,919	3,118	143	1,199	D	37.0%	60.2%	38.1%	61.9%
8,240	CONEJOS	3,450	1,702	1,659	89	43	R	49.3%	48.1%	50.6%	49.4%
3,918	COSTILLA	1,676	507	1,120	49	613	D	30.3%	66.8%	31.2%	68.8%
6,156	CROWLEY	1,378	861	405	112	456	R	62.5%	29.4%	68.0%	32.0%
5,127	CUSTER	3,341	2,103	1,140	98	963	R	62.9%	34.1%	64.8%	35.2%
31,373	DELTA	15,917	9,753	5,651	513	4,102	R	61.3%	35.5%	63.3%	36.7%
729,348	DENVER	284,419	46,046	234,250	4,123	188,204	D	16.2%	82.4%	16.4%	83.6%
2,067	DOLORES	1,299	806	348	145	458	R	62.0%	26.8%	69.8%	30.2%
353,316	DOUGLAS	190,688	94,312	93,022	3,354	1,290	R	49.5%	48.8%	50.3%	49.7%
55,196	EAGLE	22,218	6,661	15,230	327	8,569	D	30.0%	68.5%	30.4%	69.6%
724,738	EL PASO	285,019	144,384	133,447	7,188	10,937	R	50.7%	46.8%	52.0%	48.0%
26,896	ELBERT	16,277	11,618	4,118	541	7,500	R	71.4%	25.3%	73.8%	26.2%
48,031	FREMONT	19,964	12,087	7,165	712	4,922	R	60.5%	35.9%	62.8%	37.2%
60,213	GARFIELD	24,537	10,444	13,443	650	2,999	D	42.6%	54.8%	43.7%	56.3%
6,293	GILPIN	3,417	1,302	2,023	92	721	D	38.1%	59.2%	39.2%	60.8%
15,783	GRAND	8,006	3,649	4,162	195	513	D	45.6%	52.0%	46.7%	53.3%
17,600	GUNNISON	9,135	2,733	6,184	218	3,451	D	29.9%	67.7%	30.6%	69.4%
828	HINSDALE	511	251	246	14	5	R	49.1%	48.1%	50.5%	49.5%
6,969	HUERFANO	3,859	1,656	2,102	101	446	D	42.9%	54.5%	44.1%	55.9%
1,397	JACKSON	682	526	140	16	386	R	77.1%	20.5%	79.0%	21.0%
584,699	JEFFERSON	300,158	108,638	185,398	6,122	76,760	D	36.2%	61.8%	36.9%	63.1%
1,414	KIOWA	759	562	99	98	463	R	74.0%	13.0%	85.0%	15.0%
7,078	KIT CARSON	3,026	2,465	475	86	1,990	R	81.5%	15.7%	83.8%	16.2%
56,432	LA PLATA	29,704	10,689	18,350	665	7,661	D	36.0%	61.8%	36.8%	63.2%
8,165	LAKE	2,975	991	1,899	85	908	D	33.3%	63.8%	34.3%	65.7%
359,303	LARIMER	176,322	66,749	105,588	3,985	38,839	D	37.9%	59.9%	38.7%	61.3%
14,578	LAS ANIMAS	6,691	3,071	3,411	209	340	D	45.9%	51.0%	47.4%	52.6%
5,742	LINCOLN	2,100	1,608	390	102	1,218	R	76.6%	18.6%	80.5%	19.5%
22,227	LOGAN	8,256	5,925	1,860	471	4,065	R	71.8%	22.5%	76.1%	23.9%
155,037	MESA	73,550	40,376	30,571	2,603	9,805	R	54.9%	41.6%	56.9%	43.1%
775	MINERAL	708	362	320	26	42	R	51.1%	45.2%	53.1%	46.9%
13,290	MOFFAT	5,418	4,174	1,058	186	3,116	R	77.0%	19.5%	79.8%	20.2%
26,288	MONTEZUMA	12,520	6,772	5,187	561	1,585	R	54.1%	41.4%	56.6%	43.4%
43,000	MONTROSE	20,899	12,835	7,529	535	5,306	R	61.4%	36.0%	63.0%	37.0%
29,042	MORGAN	10,151	7,090	2,679	382	4,411	R	69.8%	26.4%	72.6%	27.4%
18,335	OTERO	7,245	4,053	2,951	241	1,102	R	55.9%	40.7%	57.9%	42.1%
4,987	OURAY	3,566	1,255	2,242	69	987	D	35.2%	62.9%	35.9%	64.1%
19,031	PARK	10,050	5,271	4,463	316	808	R	52.4%	44.4%	54.2%	45.8%
4,264	PHILLIPS	1,969	1,519	384	66	1,135	R	77.1%	19.5%	79.8%	20.2%
17,683	PITKIN	9,576	1,907	7,565	104	5,658	D	19.9%	79.0%	20.1%	79.9%
12,206	PROWERS	4,286	2,847	1,139	300	1,708	R	66.4%	26.6%	71.4%	28.6%
169,155	PUEBLO	67,511	28,645	36,602	2,264	7,957	D	42.4%	54.2%	43.9%	56.1%
6,321	RIO BLANCO	3,053	2,408	507	138	1,901	R	78.9%	16.6%	82.6%	17.4%
11,268	RIO GRANDE	4,955	2,485	2,140	330	345	R	50.2%	43.2%	53.7%	46.3%
25,796	ROUTT	13,873	4,415	9,238	220	4,823	D	31.8%	66.6%	32.3%	67.7%
6,858	SAGUACHE	2,766	1,061	1,580	125	519	D	38.4%	57.1%	40.2%	59.8%
733	SAN JUAN	540	154	372	14	218	D	28.5%	68.9%	29.3%	70.7%
8,187	SAN MIGUEL	4,086	815	3,199	72	2,384	D	19.9%	78.3%	20.3%	79.7%
2,255	SEDGWICK	1,162	807	312	43	495	R	69.4%	26.9%	72.1%	27.9%
31,083	SUMMIT	14,275	3,650	10,383	242	6,733	D	25.6%	72.7%	26.0%	74.0%

COLORADO
GOVERNOR 2022

2020 Census Population	County	Total Vote	Republican (Ganahl)	Democratic (Polis)	Other	Rep.-Dem. Plurality		Percentage			
								Total Vote		Major Vote	
								Rep.	Dem.	Rep.	Dem.
25,563	TELLER	13,549	8,430	4,843	276	3,587	R	62.2%	35.7%	63.5%	36.5%
4,932	WASHINGTON	2,389	1,971	314	104	1,657	R	82.5%	13.1%	86.3%	13.7%
327,077	WELD	128,482	72,542	52,186	3,754	20,356	R	56.5%	40.6%	58.2%	41.8%
10,035	YUMA	3,964	3,079	656	229	2,423	R	77.7%	16.5%	82.4%	17.6%
5,783,268	TOTAL	2,508,770	983,040	1,468,481	57,249	485,441	D	39.2%	58.5%	40.1%	59.9%

COLORADO
SENATOR 2022

2020 Census Population	County	Total Vote	Republican (O'Dea)	Democratic (Bennet)	Other	Rep.-Dem. Plurality		Percentage			
								Total Vote		Major Vote	
								Rep.	Dem.	Rep.	Dem.
519,315	ADAMS	159,287	63,586	90,483	5,218	26,897	D	39.9%	56.8%	41.3%	58.7%
16,423	ALAMOSA	5,929	2,734	2,999	196	265	D	46.1%	50.6%	47.7%	52.3%
657,609	ARAPAHOE	257,317	96,033	154,678	6,606	58,645	D	37.3%	60.1%	38.3%	61.7%
14,179	ARCHULETA	7,820	4,099	3,428	293	671	R	52.4%	43.8%	54.5%	45.5%
3,594	BACA	1,745	1,303	371	71	932	R	74.7%	21.3%	77.8%	22.2%
5,548	BENT	1,810	1,104	640	66	464	R	61.0%	35.4%	63.3%	36.7%
327,381	BOULDER	165,428	33,858	128,227	3,343	94,369	D	20.5%	77.5%	20.9%	79.1%
70,811	BROOMFIELD	37,542	12,975	23,617	950	10,642	D	34.6%	62.9%	35.5%	64.5%
20,513	CHAFFEE	11,800	4,854	6,607	339	1,753	D	41.1%	56.0%	42.4%	57.6%
1,833	CHEYENNE	917	763	120	34	643	R	83.2%	13.1%	86.4%	13.6%
9,734	CLEAR CREEK	5,181	2,040	2,966	175	926	D	39.4%	57.2%	40.8%	59.2%
8,240	CONEJOS	3,447	1,704	1,669	74	35	R	49.4%	48.4%	50.5%	49.5%
3,918	COSTILLA	1,686	518	1,108	60	590	D	30.7%	65.7%	31.9%	68.1%
6,156	CROWLEY	1,375	849	432	94	417	R	61.7%	31.4%	66.3%	33.7%
5,127	CUSTER	3,328	2,112	1,061	155	1,051	R	63.5%	31.9%	66.6%	33.4%
31,373	DELTA	15,914	9,901	5,400	613	4,501	R	62.2%	33.9%	64.7%	35.3%
729,348	DENVER	285,128	51,582	228,419	5,127	176,837	D	18.1%	80.1%	18.4%	81.6%
2,067	DOLORES	1,285	873	353	59	520	R	67.9%	27.5%	71.2%	28.8%
353,316	DOUGLAS	190,908	100,978	85,173	4,757	15,805	R	52.9%	44.6%	54.2%	45.8%
55,196	EAGLE	22,193	7,776	13,960	457	6,184	D	35.0%	62.9%	35.8%	64.2%
724,738	EL PASO	284,314	149,995	124,024	10,295	25,971	R	52.8%	43.6%	54.7%	45.3%
26,896	ELBERT	16,254	11,897	3,824	533	8,073	R	73.2%	23.5%	75.7%	24.3%
48,031	FREMONT	19,988	12,285	6,802	901	5,483	R	61.5%	34.0%	64.4%	35.6%
60,213	GARFIELD	24,515	10,924	12,777	814	1,853	D	44.6%	52.1%	46.1%	53.9%
6,293	GILPIN	3,414	1,385	1,914	115	529	D	40.6%	56.1%	42.0%	58.0%
15,783	GRAND	7,985	3,824	3,912	249	88	D	47.9%	49.0%	49.4%	50.6%
17,600	GUNNISON	9,164	2,905	5,993	266	3,088	D	31.7%	65.4%	32.6%	67.4%
828	HINSDALE	517	272	223	22	49	R	52.6%	43.1%	54.9%	45.1%
6,969	HUERFANO	3,850	1,705	2,011	134	306	D	44.3%	52.2%	45.9%	54.1%
1,397	JACKSON	685	496	151	38	345	R	72.4%	22.0%	76.7%	23.3%
584,699	JEFFERSON	300,356	115,978	176,378	8,000	60,400	D	38.6%	58.7%	39.7%	60.3%
1,414	KIOWA	749	602	120	27	482	R	80.4%	16.0%	83.4%	16.6%
7,078	KIT CARSON	3,028	2,408	531	89	1,877	R	79.5%	17.5%	81.9%	18.1%
56,432	LA PLATA	29,729	11,231	17,711	787	6,480	D	37.8%	59.6%	38.8%	61.2%
8,165	LAKE	2,995	1,067	1,812	116	745	D	35.6%	60.5%	37.1%	62.9%
359,303	LARIMER	175,278	69,573	100,466	5,239	30,893	D	39.7%	57.3%	40.9%	59.1%
14,578	LAS ANIMAS	6,673	3,166	3,291	216	125	D	47.4%	49.3%	49.0%	51.0%
5,742	LINCOLN	2,106	1,624	401	81	1,223	R	77.1%	19.0%	80.2%	19.8%
22,227	LOGAN	8,263	5,980	1,954	329	4,026	R	72.4%	23.6%	75.4%	24.6%
155,037	MESA	73,435	41,766	28,732	2,937	13,034	R	56.9%	39.1%	59.2%	40.8%

COLORADO
SENATOR 2022

2020 Census Population	County	Total Vote	Republican (O'Dea)	Democratic (Bennet)	Other	Rep.-Dem. Plurality	Total Vote Rep.	Total Vote Dem.	Major Vote Rep.	Major Vote Dem.
775	MINERAL	709	369	310	30	59 R	52.0%	43.7%	54.3%	45.7%
13,290	MOFFAT	5,397	4,150	1,069	178	3,081 R	76.9%	19.8%	79.5%	20.5%
26,288	MONTEZUMA	12,509	6,960	5,072	477	1,888 R	55.6%	40.5%	57.8%	42.2%
43,000	MONTROSE	20,830	12,894	7,255	681	5,639 R	61.9%	34.8%	64.0%	36.0%
29,042	MORGAN	10,169	7,000	2,786	383	4,214 R	68.8%	27.4%	71.5%	28.5%
18,335	OTERO	7,236	3,958	3,052	226	906 R	54.7%	42.2%	56.5%	43.5%
4,987	OURAY	3,566	1,327	2,160	79	833 D	37.2%	60.6%	38.1%	61.9%
19,031	PARK	10,043	5,390	4,234	419	1,156 R	53.7%	42.2%	56.0%	44.0%
4,264	PHILLIPS	1,981	1,503	400	78	1,103 R	75.9%	20.2%	79.0%	21.0%
17,683	PITKIN	9,581	2,281	7,157	143	4,876 D	23.8%	74.7%	24.2%	75.8%
12,206	PROWERS	4,277	2,956	1,172	149	1,784 R	69.1%	27.4%	71.6%	28.4%
169,155	PUEBLO	67,349	29,493	35,581	2,275	6,088 D	43.8%	52.8%	45.3%	54.7%
6,321	RIO BLANCO	3,021	2,391	525	105	1,866 R	79.1%	17.4%	82.0%	18.0%
11,268	RIO GRANDE	4,944	2,625	2,136	183	489 R	53.1%	43.2%	55.1%	44.9%
25,796	ROUTT	13,867	4,836	8,737	294	3,901 D	34.9%	63.0%	35.6%	64.4%
6,858	SAGUACHE	2,771	1,070	1,577	124	507 D	38.6%	56.9%	40.4%	59.6%
733	SAN JUAN	538	164	350	24	186 D	30.5%	65.1%	31.9%	68.1%
8,187	SAN MIGUEL	4,083	888	3,110	85	2,222 D	21.7%	76.2%	22.2%	77.8%
2,255	SEDGWICK	1,162	807	308	47	499 R	69.4%	26.5%	72.4%	27.6%
31,083	SUMMIT	14,243	4,211	9,710	322	5,499 D	29.6%	68.2%	30.2%	69.8%
25,563	TELLER	13,557	8,602	4,515	440	4,087 R	63.5%	33.3%	65.6%	34.4%
4,932	WASHINGTON	2,402	1,964	347	91	1,617 R	81.8%	14.4%	85.0%	15.0%
327,077	WELD	128,590	74,043	50,129	4,418	23,914 R	57.6%	39.0%	59.6%	40.4%
10,035	YUMA	3,967	3,086	740	141	2,346 R	77.8%	18.7%	80.7%	19.3%
5,783,268	TOTAL	2,500,130	1,031,693	1,397,170	71,267	365,477 D	41.3%	55.9%	42.5%	57.5%

COLORADO
HOUSE OF REPRESENTATIVES

CD	Year	Total Vote	Republican Vote	Republican Candidate	Democratic Vote	Democratic Candidate	Other Vote	Rep.-Dem. Plurality	Total Vote Rep.	Total Vote Dem.	Major Vote Rep.	Major Vote Dem.
1	2022	282,686	49,530	QUALTERI, JENNIFER	226,929	DEGETTE, DIANA L.*	6,227	177,399 D	17.5%	80.3%	17.9%	82.1%
2	2022	348,839	97,700	DAWSON, MARSHALL	244,107	NEGUSE, JOSEPH "JOE"*	7,032	146,407 D	28.0%	70.0%	28.6%	71.4%
3	2022	327,285	163,839	BOEBERT, LAUREN*	163,293	FRISCH, ADAM	153	546 R	50.1%	49.9%	50.1%	49.9%
4	2022	354,513	216,024	BUCK, KEN*	129,619	MCCORKLE, IKE	8,870	86,405 R	60.9%	36.6%	62.5%	37.5%
5	2022	277,964	155,528	LAMBORN, DOUG*	111,978	TORRES, DAVID	10,458	43,550 R	56.0%	40.3%	58.1%	41.9%
6	2022	280,755	105,084	MONAHAN, STEVEN	170,140	CROW, JASON*	5,531	65,056 D	37.4%	60.6%	38.2%	61.8%
7	2022	363,601	150,510	AADLAND, ERIK	204,984	PETTERSEN, BRITTANY	8,107	54,474 D	41.4%	56.4%	42.3%	57.7%
8	2022	236,501	112,745	KIRKMEYER, BARBARA	114,377	CARAVEO, YADIRA	9,379	1,632 D	47.7%	48.4%	49.6%	50.4%
TOTAL	2022	2,472,144	1,050,960		1,365,427		55,757	314,467 D	42.5%	55.2%	43.5%	56.5%

Note: An asterisk (*) denotes incumbent.

COLORADO

GENERAL AND PRIMARY ELECTIONS

GENERAL ELECTIONS: OTHER VOTES

Governor	Other vote was 28,939 Libertarian (Kevin Ruskusky), 21,623 American Constitution (Danielle Neuschwanger), 6,687 Unity (Paul Fiorino)
Senate	Other vote was 43,534 Libertarian (Brian Peotter), 16,379 Unity (T.J. Cole), 11,354 Approval Voting Party (Frank Atwood)
House	Other vote was:
CD 1	6,157 Libertarian (John Kittleson), 70 Write-In (Iris Boswell)
CD 2	2,876 Unaffiliated (Steve Yurash), 2,188 American Constitution (Gary Nation), 1,968 Unity Party America (Tim Wolf)
CD 3	74 Write-In (John Keil), 71 Write-In (Kristin Skowronski), 8 Write-In (Richard Tetu)
CD 4	8,870 American Constitution (Ryan McGonigal)
CD 5	7,079 Libertarian (Brian Flanagan), 3,370 American Constitution (Christopher Mitchell), 9 Write-In (Matthew Feigenbaum)
CD 6	5,531 Libertarian (Eric Mulder)
CD 7	6,187 Libertarian (Ross Klopf), 1,828 Unity (Critter Milton), 92 Write-In (JP Lujan)
CD 8	9,280 Libertarian (Richard Ward), 99 Write-In (Tim Long)

2022 PRIMARY ELECTIONS: SUPPLEMENTARY INFORMATION

Primary	June 28, 2022	**Registration** (as of June 1, 2022 – includes 459,555 inactive registrants)	4,252,358	Democratic Republican Libertarian American Constitution Green Approval Voting Unity Unaffiliated	1,187,511 1,061,956 48,954 14,152 10,396 4,589 3,714 1,921,086
Primary Type	Semi-open—Registered Democrats and Republicans could vote only in their party's primary. Any other registered voter could participate in either the Democratic or Republican primary but in the process had to declare his or her affiliation with that party.				

	REPUBLICAN PRIMARIES			DEMOCRATIC PRIMARIES		
Senator	O'Dea, Joe Hanks, Ron TOTAL	345,060 288,483 633,543	54.5% 45.5%	Bennet, Michael F.* TOTAL	516,985 516,985	100.0%
Governor	Ganahl, Heidi Lopez, Greg TOTAL	341,157 292,187 633,344	53.9% 46.1%	Polis, Jared* TOTAL	523,489 523,489	100.0%
Congressional District 1	Qualteri, Jennifer TOTAL	18,568 18,568	100.0%	DeGette, Diana L.* Walia, Neal TOTAL	79,391 18,472 97,863	81.1% 18.9%
Congressional District 2	Dawson, Marshall TOTAL	43,164 43,164	100.0%	Neguse, Joseph "Joe"* TOTAL	91,793 91,793	100.0%
Congressional District 3	Boebert, Lauren* Coram, Don TOTAL	86,322 44,486 130,808	66.0% 34.0%	Frisch, Adam Sandoval Tafoya, Soledad Walker, Alex TOTAL	25,751 25,462 9,504 60,717	42.4% 41.9% 15.7%
Congressional District 4	Buck, Ken* Lewis, Robert TOTAL	90,091 31,593 121,684	74.0% 26.0%	McCorkle, Ike TOTAL	42,244 42,244	100.0%

COLORADO

GENERAL AND PRIMARY ELECTIONS

	REPUBLICAN PRIMARIES			DEMOCRATIC PRIMARIES		
Congressional District 5	Lamborn, Doug*	46,178	47.3%	Torres, David	24,413	54.7%
	Williams, Dave	32,669	33.5%	Colombe, Michael C.	20,237	45.3%
	Keltie, Rebecca	12,631	12.9%			
	Heaton, Andrew	6,121	6.3%			
	TOTAL	97,599		TOTAL	44,650	
Congressional District 6	Monahan, Steven	47,556	100.0%	Crow, Jason*	61,074	100.0%
	TOTAL	47,556		TOTAL	61,074	
Congressional District 7	Aadland, Erik	43,469	47.9%	Pettersen, Brittany	71,497	100.0%
	Reichert, Tim	32,583	35.9%			
	Imer, Laurel	14,665	16.2%			
	TOTAL	90,717		TOTAL	71,497	
Congressional District 8	Kirkmeyer, Barbara	22,724	39.0%	Caraveo, Yadira	38,837	100.0%
	Kulmann, Jan	13,398	23.0%			
	Saine, Lori A.	12,357	21.2%			
	Allcorn, Tyler	9,743	16.7%			
	TOTAL	58,222		TOTAL	38,837	

Note: An asterisk (*) denotes incumbent.

CONNECTICUT

Statewide Races

2022 was more straight-ticket than some recent election cycles in the Nutmeg State. In 2018, for example, as Sen. Chris Murphy (D) won reelection by 20 points, now-Gov. Ned Lamont (D) won the open-seat governorship by just three points. Running for a second term, Lamont faced a rematch with Trump-aligned businessman Bob Stefanowski and won by a considerably more comfortable 56%–43%. Lamont's 2022 win represented the biggest victory for a Democrat in a Connecticut gubernatorial race since 1986. Meanwhile, Democratic Sen. Richard Blumenthal, who was last on the ballot in 2016 and won by nearly 30 points that year, saw his crossover appeal lessen – he ran only slightly ahead of Lamont.

Both statewide Democrats carried six of the state's eight counties – each losing Litchfield and Windham counties, on either side of the state's northern border. Some of Lamont's biggest gains – and Blumenthal's least severe declines – came in the Hartford area and Fairfield County, with the latter being home to the state's upscale "Gold Coast" region. Meanwhile, the New Haven area, as well as the eastern counties of New London and Tolland, voted Democratic but saw some pro-Republican trends.

House Races

After a longer-than-necessary process, redistricting ended up in the hands of the Connecticut state Supreme Court, which produced a minimal-change map. Since 2008, the state has sent five Democrats to the House.

Republicans have occasionally targeted the 5th District, which takes up a swath of the state west of Hartford, only to consistently come up just short. This was the case in 2022: Rep. Jahana Hayes (D, CT-5) received a serious challenge from GOP state Sen. George Logan, but prevailed by less than a point.

On paper, the 2nd District, which is the geographic eastern half of the state, is another comparatively marginal Connecticut seat. But the parochial Rep. Joe Courtney has proved to be a formidable Democratic incumbent. Initially elected in the anti-George W. Bush 2006 midterm, Courtney was one of 30 Democrats that flipped GOP-held seats that year – after the 2022 cycle, was the only one from that group who is still serving in the House.

Elsewhere, the most Democratic seats in the state are districts 1 and 4, which contain Hartford and the Gold Coast, respectively. Additionally, Rep. Rosa DeLauro, the most senior member of the delegation (and who sometimes makes waves with her fashion choices), represents the New Haven-based 3rd District. DeLauro would be a heavy favorite if she seeks an 18th term in 2024, although her margins have dropped in recent cycles.

CONNECTICUT

Congressional districts first established for elections held in 2022

5 members

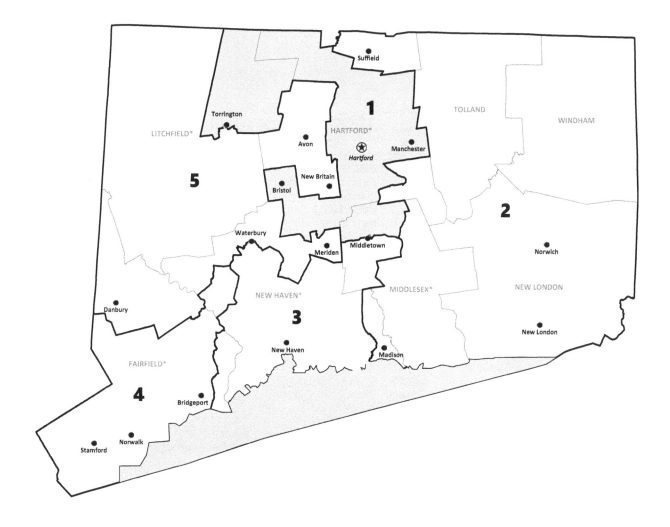

*Asterisk indicates a (now-abolished) county whose boundaries include parts of two or more congressional districts.

CD 1 is highlighted for visibility.

CONNECTICUT

GOVERNOR
Ned Lamont (D). Reelected 2022 to a four-year term. Previously elected 2018.

SENATORS (2 Democrats)
Richard Blumenthal (D). Reelected 2022 to a six-year term. Previously elected 2016, 2010.

Christopher Murphy (D). Reelected 2018 to a six-year term. Previously elected 2012.

REPRESENTATIVES (5 Democrats)
1. John B. Larson (D)
2. Joe Courtney (D)
3. Rosa L. DeLauro (D)
4. Jim Himes (D)
5. Jahana Hayes (D)

POSTWAR VOTE FOR PRESIDENT

Year	Total Vote	Republican Vote	Republican Candidate	Democratic Vote	Democratic Candidate	Other Vote	Rep.-Dem. Plurality	Total Vote Rep.	Total Vote Dem.	Major Vote Rep.	Major Vote Dem.
2020	1,823,857	714,717	Trump, Donald J.*	1,080,831	Biden, Joseph R. Jr.	28,309	366,114 D	39.2%	59.3%	39.8%	60.2%
2016**	1,644,920	673,215	Trump, Donald J.	897,572	Clinton, Hillary Rodham	74,133	224,357 D	40.9%	54.6%	42.9%	57.1%
2012	1,558,960	634,892	Romney, W. Mitt	905,083	Obama, Barack H.*	18,985	270,191 D	40.7%	58.1%	41.2%	58.8%
2008	1,646,792	629,428	McCain, John S. III	997,772	Obama, Barack H.	19,592	368,344 D	38.2%	60.6%	38.7%	61.3%
2004	1,578,769	693,826	Bush, George W.*	857,488	Kerry, John F.	27,455	163,662 D	43.9%	54.3%	44.7%	55.3%
2000**	1,459,525	561,094	Bush, George W.	816,015	Gore, Albert Jr.	82,416	254,921 D	38.4%	55.9%	40.7%	59.3%
1996**	1,392,614	483,109	Dole, Robert "Bob"	735,740	Clinton, Bill*	173,765	252,631 D	34.7%	52.8%	39.6%	60.4%
1992**	1,616,332	578,313	Bush, George H.*	682,318	Clinton, Bill	355,701	104,005 D	35.8%	42.2%	45.9%	54.1%
1988	1,443,394	750,241	Bush, George H.	676,584	Dukakis, Michael S.	16,569	73,657 R	52.0%	46.9%	52.6%	47.4%
1984	1,466,900	890,877	Reagan, Ronald*	569,597	Mondale, Walter F.	6,426	321,280 R	60.7%	38.8%	61.0%	39.0%
1980**	1,406,285	677,210	Reagan, Ronald	541,732	Carter, Jimmy*	187,343	135,478 R	48.2%	38.5%	55.6%	44.4%
1976	1,381,526	719,261	Ford, Gerald R.*	647,895	Carter, Jimmy	14,370	71,366 R	52.1%	46.9%	52.6%	47.4%
1972	1,384,277	810,763	Nixon, Richard M.*	555,498	McGovern, George S.	18,016	255,265 R	58.6%	40.1%	59.3%	40.7%
1968**	1,256,232	556,721	Nixon, Richard M.	621,561	Humphrey, Hubert Horatio Jr.	77,950	64,840 D	44.3%	49.5%	47.2%	52.8%
1964	1,218,578	390,996	Goldwater, Barry M. Sr.	826,269	Johnson, Lyndon B.*	1,313	435,273 D	32.1%	67.8%	32.1%	67.9%
1960	1,222,883	565,813	Nixon, Richard M.	657,055	Kennedy, John F.	15	91,242 D	46.3%	53.7%	46.3%	53.7%
1956	1,117,121	711,837	Eisenhower, Dwight D.*	405,079	Stevenson, Adlai E. II	205	306,758 R	63.7%	36.3%	63.7%	36.3%
1952	1,096,911	611,012	Eisenhower, Dwight D.	481,649	Stevenson, Adlai E. II	4,250	129,363 R	55.7%	43.9%	55.9%	44.1%
1948	883,518	437,754	Dewey, Thomas E.	423,297	Truman, Harry S.*	22,467	14,457 R	49.5%	47.9%	50.8%	49.2%

Note: An asterisk (*) denotes incumbent. **In past elections, the other vote included: 2016 - 48,676 Libertarian (Gary Johnson); 2000 - 64,452 Green (Ralph Nader); 1996 - 139,523 Reform (Ross Perot); 1992 - 348,771 Independent (Perot); 1980 - 171,807 Independent (John Anderson); 1968 - 76,650 American Independent (George Wallace).

CONNECTICUT

POSTWAR VOTE FOR GOVERNOR

		Republican		Democratic		Other Vote	Rep.-Dem. Plurality	Percentage			
								Total Vote		Major Vote	
Year	Total Vote	Vote	Candidate	Vote	Candidate			Rep.	Dem.	Rep.	Dem.
2022	1,268,898	546,209	Stefanowski, Bob	710,191	Lamont, Ned*	12,498	163,982 D	43.0%	56.0%	43.5%	56.5%
2018	1,406,803	650,138	Stefanowski, Bob	694,510	Lamont, Ned	62,155	44,372 D	46.2%	49.4%	48.4%	51.6%
2014	1,092,773	526,295	Foley, Tom C.	554,314	Malloy, Dan*	12,164	28,019 D	48.2%	50.7%	48.7%	51.3%
2010	1,145,799	560,874	Foley, Tom C.	567,278	Malloy, Dan	17,647	6,404 D	49.0%	49.5%	49.7%	50.3%
2006	1,123,466	710,048	Rell, M. Jodi*	398,220	DeStefano, John Jr.	15,198	311,828 R	63.2%	35.4%	64.1%	35.9%
2002	1,022,998	573,958	Rowland, John G.*	448,984	Curry, Bill	56	124,974 R	56.1%	43.9%	56.1%	43.9%
1998	999,537	628,707	Rowland, John G.*	354,187	Kennelly, Barbara B.	16,643	274,520 R	62.9%	35.4%	64.0%	36.0%
1994**	1,147,084	415,201	Rowland, John G.	375,133	Curry, Bill	356,750	40,068 R	36.2%	32.7%	52.5%	47.5%
1990**	1,142,101	427,840	Rowland, John G.	237,641	Morrison, Bruce A.	476,620	190,199 R#	37.5%	20.8%	64.3%	35.7%
1986	993,692	408,489	Belaga, Julie D.	575,638	O'Neill, William A.*	9,565	167,149 D	41.1%	57.9%	41.5%	58.5%
1982	1,083,876	497,773	Rome, Lewis B.	578,264	O'Neill, William A.*	7,839	80,491 D	45.9%	53.4%	46.3%	53.7%
1978	1,036,608	422,316	Sarasin, Ronald A.	613,109	Grasso, Ella T.*	1,183	190,793 D	40.7%	59.1%	40.8%	59.2%
1974	1,102,773	440,169	Steele, Robert H.	643,490	Grasso, Ella T.	19,114	203,321 D	39.9%	58.4%	40.6%	59.4%
1970	1,082,797	582,160	Meskill, Thomas J.	500,561	Daddario, Emilio Q.	76	81,599 R	53.8%	46.2%	53.8%	46.2%
1966	1,008,557	446,536	Gengras, E. Clayton	561,599	Dempsey, John N.*	422	115,063 D	44.3%	55.7%	44.3%	55.7%
1962	1,031,902	482,852	Alsop, John	549,027	Dempsey, John N.*	23	66,175 D	46.8%	53.2%	46.8%	53.2%
1958	974,509	360,644	Zeller, Fred R.	607,012	Ribicoff, Abraham A.*	6,853	246,368 D	37.0%	62.3%	37.3%	62.7%
1954	936,753	460,528	Lodge, John D.*	463,643	Ribicoff, Abraham A.	12,582	3,115 D	49.2%	49.5%	49.8%	50.2%
1950**	878,735	436,418	Lodge, John D.	419,404	Bowles, Chester*	22,913	17,014 R	49.7%	47.7%	51.0%	49.0%
1948	875,620	429,071	Shannon, James C.*	431,746	Bowles, Chester	14,803	2,675 D	49.0%	49.3%	49.8%	50.2%
1946	683,831	371,852	McConaughy, James L.	276,335	Snow, Wilbert*	35,644	95,517 R	54.4%	40.4%	57.4%	42.6%

Note: An asterisk (*) denotes incumbent. A pound sign (#) in the plurality column indicates that the winner in 1990 did not run under the banner of either major party. **In past elections, the other vote included: 1994 - 216,585 A Connecticut Party (Elaine Strong Groark); 130,128 Independent (Tom Scott); 1990 - 460,576 A Connecticut Party (Lowell P. Weicker Jr.). Weicker won the 1990 election with 40.4 percent of the total vote and a plurality of 32,736 votes. The term of office for Connecticut's Governor was increased from two to four years effective with the 1950 election.

CONNECTICUT

POSTWAR VOTE FOR SENATOR

		Republican		Democratic		Other Vote	Rep.-Dem. Plurality	Percentage			
								Total Vote		Major Vote	
Year	Total Vote	Vote	Candidate	Vote	Candidate			Rep.	Dem.	Rep.	Dem.
2022	1,259,887	535,943	Levy, Leora R.	723,864	Blumenthal, Richard*	80	187,921 D	42.5%	57.5%	42.5%	57.5%
2018	1,386,840	545,717	Corey, Matthew M.	825,579	Murphy, Christopher S.*	15,544	279,862 D	39.3%	59.5%	39.8%	60.2%
2016	1,596,276	552,621	Carter, Dan	1,008,714	Blumenthal, Richard*	34,941	456,093 D	34.6%	63.2%	35.4%	64.6%
2012	1,511,764	651,089	McMahon, Linda E.	828,761	Murphy, Christopher S.	31,914	177,672 D	43.1%	54.8%	44.0%	56.0%
2010	1,153,115	498,341	McMahon, Linda E.	636,040	Blumenthal, Richard	18,734	137,699 D	43.2%	55.2%	43.9%	56.1%
2006**	1,134,780	109,198	Achlesinger, Alan	450,844	Lamont, Ned	574,738	341,646 D#	9.6%	39.7%	19.5%	80.5%
2004	1,424,726	457,749	Orchulli, Jack	945,347	Dodd, Christopher J.*	21,630	487,598 D	32.1%	66.4%	32.6%	67.4%
2000	1,311,261	448,077	Giordano, Phil	828,902	Lieberman, Joseph L*	34,282	380,825 D	34.2%	63.2%	35.1%	64.9%
1998	964,457	312,177	Franks, Gary A.	628,306	Dodd, Christopher J.*	23,974	316,129 D	32.4%	65.1%	33.2%	66.8%
1994	1,079,767	334,833	Labriola, Jerry Jr.	723,842	Lieberman, Joseph L*	21,092	389,009 D	31.0%	67.0%	31.6%	68.4%
1992	1,500,709	572,036	Johnson, Brook	882,569	Dodd, Christopher J.*	46,104	310,533 D	38.1%	58.8%	39.3%	60.7%
1988	1,383,526	678,454	Weicker, Lowell P. Jr.*	688,499	Lieberman, Joseph I.	16,573	10,045 D	49.0%	49.8%	49.6%	50.4%
1986	976,933	340,438	Eddy, Roger W.	632,695	Dodd, Christopher J.*	3,800	292,257 D	34.8%	64.8%	35.0%	65.0%
1982	1,083,613	545,987	Weicker, Lowell P. Jr.*	499,146	Moffett, Anthony T.	38,480	46,841 R	50.4%	46.1%	52.2%	47.8%
1980	1,356,075	581,884	Buckley, James L.	763,969	Dodd, Christopher J.	10,222	182,085 D	42.9%	56.3%	43.2%	56.8%
1976	1,361,666	785,683	Weicker, Lowell P. Jr.*	561,018	Schaffer, Gloria	14,965	224,665 R	57.7%	41.2%	58.3%	41.7%
1974	1,084,918	372,055	Brannen, James H.	690,820	Ribicoff, Abraham A.*	22,043	318,765 D	34.3%	63.7%	35.0%	65.0%
1970**	1,089,353	454,721	Weicker, Lowell P. Jr.	368,111	Duffey, Joseph D.	266,521	86,610 R	41.7%	33.8%	55.3%	44.7%
1968	1,206,537	551,455	May, Edwin H. Jr.	655,043	Ribicoff, Abraham A.*	39	103,588 D	45.7%	54.3%	45.7%	54.3%
1964	1,208,163	426,939	Lodge, Henry Cabot Jr.	781,008	Dodd, Thomas J.*	216	354,069 D	35.3%	64.6%	35.3%	64.7%
1962	1,029,301	501,694	Seely-Brown, Horace Jr.	527,522	Ribicoff, Abraham A.	85	25,828 D	48.7%	51.3%	48.7%	51.3%
1958	965,463	410,622	Purtell, William A.*	554,841	Dodd, Thomas J.		144,219 D	42.5%	57.5%	42.5%	57.5%
1956	1,113,819	610,829	Bush, Prescott S.*	479,460	Dodd, Thomas J.	23,530	131,369 R	54.8%	43.0%	56.0%	44.0%
1952	1,093,467	573,854	Purtell, William A.	485,066	Benton, William*	34,547	88,788 R	52.5%	44.4%	54.2%	45.8%
1952S**	1,093,268	559,465	Bush, Prescott S.	530,505	Ribicoff, Abraham A.	3,298	28,960 R	51.2%	48.5%	51.3%	48.7%
1950	877,827	409,053	Talbot, Joseph E.	453,646	McMahon, Brien*	15,128	44,593 D	46.6%	51.7%	47.4%	52.6%
1950S**	877,135	430,311	Bush, Prescott S.	431,413	Benton, William	15,411	1,102 D	49.1%	49.2%	49.9%	50.1%
1946	682,921	381,328	Baldwin, Raymond E.*	276,424	Tone, Joseph M.	25,169	104,904 R	55.8%	40.5%	58.0%	42.0%

Note: An asterisk (*) denotes incumbent. A pound sign (#) in the plurality column indicates that the winner in 2006 did not run under the banner of either major party. **In past elections, the other vote included: 2006 - 564,095 Connecticut For Lieberman (Joseph I. Lieberman); 1970 - 266,497 Independent (Thomas J. Dodd). Lieberman won the 2006 election with 49.7 percent of the vote and a plurality of 113,251 votes. One each of the 1950 and 1952 elections were for short terms to fill a vacancy.

CONNECTICUT
GOVERNOR 2022

2020 Census Population	County	Total Vote	Republican (Stefanowski)	Democratic (Lamont)	Other	Rep.-Dem. Plurality	Percentage Total Vote Rep.	Dem.	Major Vote Rep.	Dem.
942,596	FAIRFIELD	316,356	128,447	185,848	2,061	57,401 D	40.6%	58.7%	40.9%	59.1%
891,590	HARTFORD	310,643	122,060	185,228	3,355	63,168 D	39.3%	59.6%	39.7%	60.3%
180,429	LITCHFIELD	81,668	44,282	36,525	861	7,757 R	54.2%	44.7%	54.8%	45.2%
162,611	MIDDLESEX	74,836	32,942	41,061	833	8,119 D	44.0%	54.9%	44.5%	55.5%
854,873	NEW HAVEN	286,023	126,138	157,141	2,744	31,003 D	44.1%	54.9%	44.5%	55.5%
265,342	NEW LONDON	100,147	43,902	54,838	1,407	10,936 D	43.8%	54.8%	44.5%	55.5%
150,866	TOLLAND	59,872	27,748	31,369	755	3,621 D	46.3%	52.4%	46.9%	53.1%
116,984	WINDHAM	39,353	20,690	18,181	482	2,509 R	52.6%	46.2%	53.2%	46.8%
3,565,291	TOTAL	1,268,898	546,209	710,191	12,498	163,982 D	43.0%	56.0%	43.5%	56.5%

CONNECTICUT
SENATOR 2022

2020 Census Population	County	Total Vote	Republican (Levy)	Democratic (Blumenthal)	Other	Rep.-Dem. Plurality	Percentage Total Vote Rep.	Dem.	Major Vote Rep.	Dem.
942,596	FAIRFIELD	313,462	126,757	186,698	7	59,941 D	40.4%	59.6%	40.4%	59.6%
891,590	HARTFORD	308,834	119,280	189,512	42	70,232 D	38.6%	61.4%	38.6%	61.4%
180,429	LITCHFIELD	81,142	43,788	37,345	9	6,443 R	54.0%	46.0%	54.0%	46.0%
162,611	MIDDLESEX	74,346	32,430	41,911	5	9,481 D	43.6%	56.4%	43.6%	56.4%
854,873	NEW HAVEN	283,839	122,770	161,063	6	38,293 D	43.3%	56.7%	43.3%	56.7%
265,342	NEW LONDON	99,552	42,835	56,711	6	13,876 D	43.0%	57.0%	43.0%	57.0%
150,866	TOLLAND	59,563	27,431	32,129	3	4,698 D	46.1%	53.9%	46.1%	53.9%
116,984	WINDHAM	39,149	20,652	18,495	2	2,157 R	52.8%	47.2%	52.8%	47.2%
3,565,291	TOTAL	1,259,887	535,943	723,864	80	187,921 D	42.5%	57.5%	42.5%	57.5%

CONNECTICUT
HOUSE OF REPRESENTATIVES

CD	Year	Total Vote	Republican Vote	Candidate	Democratic Vote	Candidate	Other Vote	Rep.-Dem. Plurality	Total Vote Rep.	Dem.	Major Vote Rep.	Dem.
1	2022	243,913	91,506	LAZOR, LAWRENCE "LARRY"	149,556	LARSON, JOHN B.*	2,851	58,050 D	37.5%	61.3%	38.0%	62.0%
1	2020	349,237	122,111	FAY, MARY	222,668	LARSON, JOHN B.*	4,458	100,557 D	35.0%	63.8%	35.4%	64.6%
1	2018	274,140	96,024	NYE, JENNIFER	175,087	LARSON, JOHN B.*	3,029	79,063 D	35.0%	63.9%	35.4%	64.6%
1	2016	312,925	105,674	COREY, MATTHEW M.	200,686	LARSON, JOHN B.*	6,565	95,012 D	33.8%	64.1%	34.5%	65.5%
1	2014	217,881	78,609	COREY, MATTHEW M.	135,825	LARSON, JOHN B.*	3,447	57,216 D	36.1%	62.3%	36.7%	63.3%
1	2012	297,061	82,321	DECKER, JOHN HENRY	206,973	LARSON, JOHN B.*	7,767	124,652 D	27.7%	69.7%	28.5%	71.5%
2	2022	285,031	114,506	FRANCE, MIKE	165,946	COURTNEY, JOE*	4,579	51,440 D	40.2%	58.2%	40.8%	59.2%
2	2020	367,347	140,356	ANDERSON, JUSTIN	218,119	COURTNEY, JOE*	8,872	77,763 D	38.2%	59.4%	39.2%	60.8%
2	2018	289,114	102,483	POSTEMSKI, DANNY	179,731	COURTNEY, JOE*	6,900	77,248 D	35.4%	62.2%	36.3%	63.7%
2	2016	330,257	111,149	NOVAK, DARIA	208,818	COURTNEY, JOE*	10,290	97,669 D	33.7%	63.2%	34.7%	65.3%
2	2014	227,936	80,837	HOPKINS-CAVANAGH, LORI	141,948	COURTNEY, JOE*	5,151	61,111 D	35.5%	62.3%	36.3%	63.7%
2	2012	299,960	88,103	FORMICA, PAUL	204,708	COURTNEY, JOE*	7,149	116,605 D	29.4%	68.2%	30.1%	69.9%
3	2022	242,651	98,704	DENARDIS, LESLEY	137,924	DELAURO, ROSA L.*	6,023	39,220 D	40.7%	56.8%	41.7%	58.3%
3	2020	346,103	137,598	STREICKER, MARGARET	203,265	DELAURO, ROSA L.*	5,240	65,667 D	39.8%	58.7%	40.4%	59.6%
3	2018	270,239	95,667	CADENA, ANGEL LUIS JR.	174,572	DELAURO, ROSA L.*		78,905 D	35.4%	64.6%	35.4%	64.6%
3	2016	309,379	95,786	CADENA, ANGEL LUIS JR.	213,572	DELAURO, ROSA L.*	21	117,786 D	31.0%	69.0%	31.0%	69.0%
3	2014	209,939	69,454	BROWN, JAMES E.	140,485	DELAURO, ROSA L.*		71,031 D	33.1%	66.9%	33.1%	66.9%
3	2012	291,301	73,726	WINSLEY, WAYNE	217,573	DELAURO, ROSA L.*	2	143,847 D	25.3%	74.7%	25.3%	74.7%

CONNECTICUT

HOUSE OF REPRESENTATIVES

			Republican		Democratic		Other Vote	Rep.-Dem. Plurality	Percentage			
									Total Vote		Major Vote	
CD	Year	Total Vote	Vote	Candidate	Vote	Candidate			Rep.	Dem.	Rep.	Dem.
4	2022	236,084	95,822	STEVENSON, JAYME	140,262	HIMES, JIM*		44,440 D	40.6%	59.4%	40.6%	59.4%
4	2020	360,716	130,627	RIDDLE, JONATHAN	224,432	HIMES, JIM*	5,657	93,805 D	36.2%	62.2%	36.8%	63.2%
4	2018	275,651	106,921	ARORA, HARRY	168,726	HIMES, JIM*	4	61,805 D	38.8%	61.2%	38.8%	61.2%
4	2016	313,540	125,724	SHABAN, JOHN	187,811	HIMES, JIM*	5	62,087 D	40.1%	59.9%	40.1%	59.9%
4	2014	198,800	91,922	DEBICELLA, DAN	106,873	HIMES, JIM*	5	14,951 D	46.2%	53.8%	46.2%	53.8%
4	2012	293,432	117,503	OBSITNIK, STEVE	175,929	HIMES, JIM*		58,426 D	40.0%	60.0%	40.0%	60.0%
5	2022	253,672	125,834	LOGAN, GEORGE	127,838	HAYES, JAHANA*		2,004 D	49.6%	50.4%	49.6%	50.4%
5	2020	349,524	151,988	SULLIVAN, DAVID XAVIER	192,484	HAYES, JAHANA*	5,052	40,496 D	43.5%	55.1%	44.1%	55.9%
5	2018	270,664	119,426	SANTOS, MANNY	151,225	HAYES, JAHANA	13	31,799 D	44.1%	55.9%	44.1%	55.9%
5	2016	309,082	129,801	COPE, CLAY	179,252	ESTY, ELIZABETH*	29	49,451 D	42.0%	58.0%	42.0%	58.0%
5	2014	213,301	97,767	GREENBERG, MARK	113,564	ESTY, ELIZABETH*	1,970	15,797 D	45.8%	53.2%	46.3%	53.7%
5	2012	284,757	138,637	RORABACK, ANDREW	146,098	ESTY, ELIZABETH	22	7,461 D	48.7%	51.3%	48.7%	51.3%
TOTAL	2022	1,261,351	526,372		721,526		13,453	195,154 D	41.7%	57.2%	42.2%	57.8%
TOTAL	2020	1,772,927	682,680		1,060,968		29,279	378,288 D	38.5%	59.8%	39.2%	60.8%
TOTAL	2018	1,379,808	520,521		849,341		9,946	328,820 D	37.7%	61.6%	38.0%	62.0%
TOTAL	2016	1,575,183	568,134		990,139		16,910	422,005 D	36.1%	62.9%	36.5%	63.5%
TOTAL	2014	1,067,857	418,589		638,695		10,573	220,106 D	39.2%	59.8%	39.6%	60.4%
TOTAL	2012	1,466,511	500,290		951,281		14,940	450,991 D	34.1%	64.9%	34.5%	65.5%

Note: An asterisk (*) denotes incumbent.

CONNECTICUT

GENERAL AND PRIMARY ELECTIONS

GENERAL ELECTIONS: OTHER VOTES

Governor Other vote was 12,400 Independent (Robert Hotaling), 98 Write-In (Michelle Bicking)

Senate Other vote was 80 Write-In (Write-In)

House Other vote was:

CD 1 2,851 Green (Mary Sanders)
CD 2 2,439 Green (Kevin Blacker), 2,140 Libertrian (William Hall)
CD 3 4,056 Independent (Amy Chai), 1,967 Green (Justin Paglino)

2022 PRIMARY ELECTIONS: SUPPLEMENTARY INFORMATION

Primary	August 9, 2022	**Registration** (as of October 26, 2021 – includes 117,825 inactive registrants)	2,472,466	Democrat	905,268
				Republican	497,981
				Other	41,151
				Unaffiliated	1,028,066

Primary Type Closed—Only registered Democrats and Republicans could vote in their party's primary.

CONNECTICUT
GENERAL AND PRIMARY ELECTIONS

	REPUBLICAN PRIMARIES			DEMOCRATIC PRIMARIES	
Senator	Levy, Leora R.	46,774	50.6%	Blumenthal, Richard*	Unopposed
	Klarides, Themis	37,003	40.0%		
	Lumaj, Peter	8,665	9.4%		
	TOTAL	92,442			
Congressional District 1					
Congressional District 2					
Congressional District 3					
Congressional District 4	Stevenson, Jayme	9,962	60.3%	Himes, Jim*	Unopposed
	Goldstein, Michael Ted	6,555	39.7%		
	TOTAL	16,517			
Congressional District 5					

Note: An asterisk (*) denotes incumbent.

DELAWARE

Statewide and House Races

Lacking a senatorial or gubernatorial race, President Joe Biden's home state got little attention in 2022. The First State's sole statewide race was its At-Large seat in the House, where Democrat Lisa Blunt Rochester won a fourth term. Blunt Rochester was first elected in 2016, replacing then-Rep. John Carney (D), who ran for (and won) the governorship.

Though she won by nearly 13 points, Blunt Rochester's 2022 performance was her weakest so far – something that may have to do with lack of Democratic enthusiasm during a sleepy midterm in the state. She carried Wilmington's New Castle County two-to-one while narrowly losing Dover's Kent County, in the middle of the state, and taking 43% in Sussex County, which makes up the southern third of the county. New Castle County, which bumps up against the Philadelphia metro area, usually casts a majority of Delaware's vote, as it did in 2022 (53% of state ballots were cast there). When Blunt Rochester's statewide margins were more robust, as in 2018 and 2020, she carried Kent County.

DELAWARE

One member At Large

DELAWARE

GOVERNOR
John C. Carney Jr. (D). Reelected 2020 to a four-year term. Previously elected 2016.

SENATORS (2 Democrats)
Thomas R. Carper (D). Reelected 2018 to a six-year term. Previously elected 2012, 2006, and 2000.

Christopher A. Coons (D). Reelected 2020 to a six-year term. Previously elected 2014 and 2010 in a special election.

REPRESENTATIVE (1 Democrat)
At Large. Lisa Blunt Rochester (D)

POSTWAR VOTE FOR PRESIDENT

Year	Total Vote	Republican Vote	Republican Candidate	Democratic Vote	Democratic Candidate	Other Vote	Rep.-Dem. Plurality	Total Vote Rep.	Total Vote Dem.	Major Vote Rep.	Major Vote Dem.
2020	504,346	200,603	Trump, Donald J.*	296,268	Joseph R. Biden Jr.	7,475	95,665 D	39.8%	58.7%	40.4%	59.6%
2016**	443,814	185,127	Trump, Donald J.	235,603	Clinton, Hillary Rodham	23,084	50,476 D	41.7%	53.1%	44.0%	56.0%
2012	413,921	165,484	Romney, W. Mitt	242,584	Obama, Barack H.*	5,853	77,100 D	40.0%	58.6%	40.6%	59.4%
2008	412,412	152,374	McCain, John S. III	255,459	Obama, Barack H.	4,579	103,085 D	36.9%	61.9%	37.4%	62.6%
2004	375,190	171,660	Bush, George W.*	200,152	Kerry, John F.	3,378	28,492 D	45.8%	53.3%	46.2%	53.8%
2000**	327,622	137,288	Bush, George W.	180,068	Gore, Albert Jr.	10,266	42,780 D	41.9%	55.0%	43.3%	56.7%
1996**	271,084	99,062	Dole, Robert "Bob"	140,355	Clinton, Bill*	31,667	41,293 D	36.5%	51.8%	41.4%	58.6%
1992**	289,735	102,313	Bush, George H.*	126,054	Clinton, Bill	61,368	23,741 D	35.3%	43.5%	44.8%	55.2%
1988	249,891	139,639	Bush, George H.	108,647	Dukakis, Michael S.	1,605	30,992 R	55.9%	43.5%	56.2%	43.8%
1984	254,572	152,190	Reagan, Ronald*	101,656	Mondale, Walter F.	726	50,534 R	59.8%	39.9%	60.0%	40.0%
1980**	235,900	111,252	Reagan, Ronald	105,754	Carter, Jimmy*	18,894	5,498 R	47.2%	44.8%	51.3%	48.7%
1976	235,834	109,831	Ford, Gerald R.*	122,596	Carter, Jimmy	3,407	12,765 D	46.6%	52.0%	47.3%	52.7%
1972	235,516	140,357	Nixon, Richard M.*	92,283	McGovern, George S.	2,876	48,074 R	59.6%	39.2%	60.3%	39.7%
1968**	214,367	96,714	Nixon, Richard M.	89,194	Humphrey, Hubert Horatio Jr.	28,459	7,520 R	45.1%	41.6%	52.0%	48.0%
1964	201,320	78,078	Goldwater, Barry M. Sr.	122,704	Johnson, Lyndon B.*	538	44,626 D	38.8%	60.9%	38.9%	61.1%
1960	196,683	96,373	Nixon, Richard M.	99,590	Kennedy, John F.	720	3,217 D	49.0%	50.6%	49.2%	50.8%
1956	177,988	98,057	Eisenhower, Dwight D.*	79,421	Stevenson, Adlai E. II	510	18,636 R	55.1%	44.6%	55.3%	44.7%
1952	174,025	90,059	Eisenhower, Dwight D.	83,315	Stevenson, Adlai E. II	651	6,744 R	51.8%	47.9%	51.9%	48.1%
1948	139,073	69,588	Dewey, Thomas E.	67,813	Truman, Harry S.*	1,672	1,775 R	50.0%	48.8%	50.6%	49.4%

Note: An asterisk (*) denotes incumbent. **In past elections, the other vote included: 2016 - 14,757 Libertarian (Gary Johnson); 2000 - 8,307 Green (Ralph Nader); 1996 - 28,719 Reform (Ross Perot); 1992 - 59,213 Independent (Perot); 1980 - 16,288 Independent (John Anderson); 1968 - 28,459 American Independent (George Wallace).

DELAWARE

POSTWAR VOTE FOR GOVERNOR

Year	Total Vote	Republican Vote	Republican Candidate	Democratic Vote	Democratic Candidate	Other Vote	Rep.-Dem. Plurality	Percentage Total Vote Rep.	Percentage Total Vote Dem.	Percentage Major Vote Rep.	Percentage Major Vote Dem.
2020	492,635	190,312	Murray, Julianne	292,903	Carney, John C. Jr.*	9,420	102,591 D	38.6%	59.5%	39.4%	60.6%
2016	425,812	166,852	Bonini, Colin	248,404	Carney, John C. Jr.	10,556	81,552 D	39.2%	58.3%	40.2%	59.8%
2012	398,033	113,793	Cragg, Jeffrey	275,993	Markell, Jack*	8,247	162,200 D	28.6%	69.3%	29.2%	70.8%
2008	395,204	126,662	Lee, William Swain	266,861	Markell, Jack	1,681	140,199 D	32.0%	67.5%	32.2%	67.8%
2004	365,008	167,115	Lee, William Swain	185,687	Minner, Ruth Ann*	12,206	18,572 D	45.8%	50.9%	47.4%	52.6%
2000	323,688	128,603	Burris, John M.	191,695	Minner, Ruth Ann	3,390	63,092 D	39.7%	59.2%	40.2%	59.8%
1996	271,122	82,654	Rzewnicki, Janet C.	188,300	Carper, Thomas R.*	168	105,646 D	30.5%	69.5%	30.5%	69.5%
1992	277,058	90,725	Scott, B. Gary	179,365	Carper, Thomas R.	6,968	88,640 D	32.7%	64.7%	33.6%	66.4%
1988	239,969	169,733	Castle, Michael N.*	70,236	Kreshtoll, Jacob		99,497 R	70.7%	29.3%	70.7%	29.3%
1984	243,565	135,250	Castle, Michael N.	108,315	Quillen, William T.		26,935 R	55.5%	44.5%	55.5%	44.5%
1980	225,081	159,004	du Pont, Pierre S. IV*	64,217	Gordy, William J.	1,860	94,787 R	70.6%	28.5%	71.2%	28.8%
1976	229,563	130,531	du Pont, Pierre S. IV	97,480	Tribbitt, Sherman W.*	1,552	33,051 R	56.9%	42.5%	57.2%	42.8%
1972	228,722	109,583	Peterson, Russell W*	117,274	Tribbitt, Sherman W.	1,865	7,691 D	47.9%	51.3%	48.3%	51.7%
1968	206,834	104,474	Peterson, Russell W.	102,360	Terry, Charles L. Jr.*		2,114 R	50.5%	49.5%	50.5%	49.5%
1964	200,171	97,374	Buckson, David P.	102,797	Terry, Charles L. Jr.		5,423 D	48.6%	51.4%	48.6%	51.4%
1960	194,835	94,043	Rollins, John W.	100,792	Carvel, Elbert N.		6,749 D	48.3%	51.7%	48.3%	51.7%
1956	177,012	91,965	Boggs, James Caleb*	85,047	McConnell, J. H. Tyler		6,918 R	52.0%	48.0%	52.0%	48.0%
1952	170,749	88,977	Boggs, James Caleb	81,772	Carvel, Elbert N.*		7,205 R	52.1%	47.9%	52.1%	47.9%
1948	140,335	64,996	George, Hyland P.	75,339	Carvel, Elbert N.		10,343 D	46.3%	53.7%	46.3%	53.7%

Note: An asterisk (*) denotes incumbent.

POSTWAR VOTE FOR SENATOR

Year	Total Vote	Republican Vote	Republican Candidate	Democratic Vote	Democratic Candidate	Other Vote	Rep.-Dem. Plurality	Percentage Total Vote Rep.	Percentage Total Vote Dem.	Percentage Major Vote Rep.	Percentage Major Vote Dem.
2020	490,935	186,054	Witzke, Lauren	291,804	Coons, Christopher A.*	13,077	105,750 D	37.9%	59.4%	38.9%	61.1%
2018	362,606	137,127	Arlett, Robert	217,385	Carper, Thomas R*	8,094	80,258 D	37.8%	60.0%	38.7%	61.3%
2014	234,038	98,823	Wade, Kevin	130,655	Coons, Christopher A.*	4,560	31,832 D	42.2%	55.8%	43.1%	56.9%
2012	399,607	115,700	Wade, Kevin	265,415	Carper, Thomas R*	18,492	149,715 D	29.0%	66.4%	30.4%	69.6%
2010S**	307,402	123,053	O'Donnell, Christine	174,012	Coons, Christopher A.	10,337	50,959 D	40.0%	56.6%	41.4%	58.6%
2008	398,134	140,595	O'Donnell, Christine	257,539	Biden, Joseph R. Jr.*		116,944 D	35.3%	64.7%	35.3%	64.7%
2006	254,099	69,734	Ting, Jan	170,567	Carper, Thomas R*	13,798	100,833 D	27.4%	67.1%	29.0%	71.0%
2002	232,314	94,793	Clatworthy, Raymond J.	135,253	Biden, Joseph R. Jr.*	2,268	40,460 D	40.8%	58.2%	41.2%	58.8%
2000	327,017	142,891	Roth, William V.*	181,566	Carper, Thomas R.	2,560	38,675 D	43.7%	55.5%	44.0%	56.0%
1996	275,591	105,088	Clatworthy, Raymond J.	165,465	Biden, Joseph R. Jr.*	5,038	60,377 D	38.1%	60.0%	38.8%	61.2%
1994	199,029	111,088	Roth, William V.*	84,554	Oberly, Charles M.	3,387	26,534 R	55.8%	42.5%	56.8%	43.2%
1990	180,152	64,554	Brady, M. Jane	112,918	Biden, Joseph R. Jr.*	2,680	48,364 D	35.8%	62.7%	36.4%	63.6%
1988	243,493	151,115	Roth, William V.*	92,378	Woo, S. B.		58,737 R	62.1%	37.9%	62.1%	37.9%
1984	245,932	98,101	Burris, John M.	147,831	Biden, Joseph R. Jr.*		49,730 D	39.9%	60.1%	39.9%	60.1%
1982	190,960	105,357	Roth, William V.*	84,413	Levinson, David N.	1,190	20,944 R	55.2%	44.2%	55.5%	44.5%
1978	162,072	66,479	Baxter, James H.	93,930	Biden, Joseph R. Jr.*	1,663	27,451 D	41.0%	58.0%	41.4%	58.6%
1976	224,859	125,502	Roth, William V.*	98,055	Maloney, Thomas C.	1,302	27,447 R	55.8%	43.6%	56.1%	43.9%
1972	229,828	112,844	Boggs, James Caleb*	116,006	Biden, Joseph R. Jr.	978	3,162 D	49.1%	50.5%	49.3%	50.7%
1970	161,439	94,979	Roth, William V.	64,740	Zimmerman, Jacob	1,720	30,239 R	58.8%	40.1%	59.5%	40.5%
1966	164,531	97,268	Boggs, James Caleb*	67,263	Tunnell, James M. Jr.		30,005 R	59.1%	40.9%	59.1%	40.9%
1964	200,703	103,782	Williams, John J.*	96,850	Carvel, Elbert N.	71	6,932 R	51.7%	48.3%	51.7%	48.3%
1960	194,964	98,874	Boggs, James Caleb	96,090	Frear, J. Allen Jr.*		2,784 R	50.7%	49.3%	50.7%	49.3%
1958	154,432	82,280	Williams, John J.*	72,152	Carvel, Elbert N.		10,128 R	53.3%	46.7%	53.3%	46.7%
1954	144,900	62,389	Warburton, Herbert B.	82,511	Frear, J. Allen Jr.*		20,122 D	43.1%	56.9%	43.1%	56.9%
1952	170,705	93,020	Williams, John J.*	77,685	du Pont Bayard, Alexis I.		15,335 R	54.5%	45.5%	54.5%	45.5%
1948	141,362	68,246	Buck, Clayton Douglass*	71,888	Frear, J. Allen Jr.	1,228	3,642 D	48.3%	50.9%	48.7%	51.3%
1946	113,513	62,603	Williams, John J.	50,910	Tunnell, James M.*		11,693 R	55.2%	44.8%	55.2%	44.8%

Note: An asterisk (*) denotes incumbent. **The 2010 election was for a short term to fill a vacancy.

DELAWARE

HOUSE OF REPRESENTATIVES

			Republican		Democratic		Other Vote	Rep.-Dem. Plurality	Percentage			
									Total Vote		Major Vote	
CD	Year	Total Vote	Vote	Candidate	Vote	Candidate			Rep.	Dem.	Rep.	Dem.
At Large	2022	321,649	138,201	MURPHY, LEE H.	178,416	ROCHESTER, LISA BLUNT*	5,032	40,215 D	43.0%	55.5%	43.6%	56.4%
At Large	2020	488,270	196,392	MURPHY, LEE H.	281,382	ROCHESTER, LISA BLUNT*	10,496	84,990 D	40.2%	57.6%	41.1%	58.9%
At Large	2018	353,814	125,384	WALKER, SCOTT	227,353	ROCHESTER, LISA BLUNT*	1,077	101,969 D	35.4%	64.3%	35.5%	64.5%
At Large	2016	420,682	172,301	REIGLE, HANS	233,554	ROCHESTER, LISA BLUNT	14,827	61,253 D	41.0%	55.5%	42.5%	57.5%
At Large	2014	231,617	85,146	IZZO, ROSE	137,251	CARNEY, JOHN C. JR.*	9,220	52,105 D	36.8%	59.3%	38.3%	61.7%
At Large	2012	388,059	129,757	KOVACH, THOMAS H.	249,933	CARNEY, JOHN C. JR.*	8,369	120,176 D	33.4%	64.4%	34.2%	65.8%
At Large	2010	305,636	125,442	URQUHART, GLEN	173,543	CARNEY, JOHN C. JR.	6,651	48,101 D	41.0%	56.8%	42.0%	58.0%
At Large	2008	385,457	235,437	CASTLE, MICHAEL N.*	146,434	HARTLEY-NAGLE, KAREN	3,586	89,003 R	61.1%	38.0%	61.7%	38.3%
At Large	2006	251,694	143,897	CASTLE, MICHAEL N.*	97,565	SPIVACK, DENNIS	10,232	46,332 R	57.2%	38.8%	59.6%	40.4%
At Large	2004	356,045	245,978	CASTLE, MICHAEL N.*	105,716	DONNELLY, PAUL	4,351	140,262 R	69.1%	29.7%	69.9%	30.1%
At Large	2002	228,405	164,605	CASTLE, MICHAEL N.*	61,011	MILLER, MICHAEL C.	2,789	103,594 R	72.1%	26.7%	73.0%	27.0%
At Large	2000	313,171	211,797	CASTLE, MICHAEL N.*	96,488	MILLER, MICHAEL C.	4,886	115,309 R	67.6%	30.8%	68.7%	31.3%
At Large	1998	180,527	119,811	CASTLE, MICHAEL N.*	57,446	WILLIAMS, DENNIS E.	3,270	62,365 R	66.4%	31.8%	67.6%	32.4%
At Large	1996	266,836	185,576	CASTLE, MICHAEL N.*	73,253	WILLIAMS, DENNIS E.	8,007	112,323 R	69.5%	27.5%	71.7%	28.3%
At Large	1994	195,037	137,960	CASTLE, MICHAEL N.*	51,803	DESANTIS, CAROL ANN	5,274	86,157 R	70.7%	26.6%	72.7%	27.3%
At Large	1992	276,157	153,037	CASTLE, MICHAEL N.	117,426	WOO, S. B.	5,694	35,611 R	55.4%	42.5%	56.6%	43.4%
At Large	1990	177,432	58,037	WILLIAMS, RALPH O.	116,274	CARPER, THOMAS R.*	3,121	58,237 D	32.7%	65.5%	33.3%	66.7%
At Large	1988	234,517	76,179	KRAPF, JAMES P.	158,338	CARPER, THOMAS R.*		82,159 D	32.5%	67.5%	32.5%	67.5%
At Large	1986	160,757	53,767	NEUBERGER, THOMAS S.	106,351	CARPER, THOMAS R.*	639	52,584 D	33.4%	66.2%	33.6%	66.4%
At Large	1984	243,014	100,650	DUPONT, ELISE	142,070	CARPER, THOMAS R.*	294	41,420 D	41.4%	58.5%	41.5%	58.5%
At Large	1982	188,064	87,153	EVANS, THOMAS B.*	98,533	CARPER, THOMAS R.	2,378	11,380 D	46.3%	52.4%	46.9%	53.1%
At Large	1980	216,629	133,842	EVANS, THOMAS B.*	81,227	MAXWELL, ROBERT L.	1,560	52,615 R	61.8%	37.5%	62.2%	37.8%
At Large	1978	157,566	91,689	EVANS, THOMAS B.*	64,863	HINDES, GARY E.	1,014	26,826 R	58.2%	41.2%	58.6%	41.4%
At Large	1976	214,799	110,677	EVANS, THOMAS B.	102,431	SHIPLEY, SAMUEL L.	1,691	8,246 R	51.5%	47.7%	51.9%	48.1%
At Large	1974	160,328	93,826	DU PONT, PIERRE S. IV*	63,490	SOLES, JAMES	3,012	30,336 R	58.5%	39.6%	59.6%	40.4%
At Large	1972	225,851	141,237	DU PONT, PIERRE S. IV*	83,230	HANDLOFF, NORMA	1,384	58,007 R	62.5%	36.9%	62.9%	37.1%
At Large	1970	160,313	86,125	DU PONT, PIERRE S. IV	71,429	DANIELLO, JOHN D.	2,759	14,696 R	53.7%	44.6%	54.7%	45.3%
At Large	1968	200,820	117,827	ROTH, WILLIAM V.*	82,993	MCDOWELL, HARRIS B. JR.		34,834 R	58.7%	41.3%	58.7%	41.3%
At Large	1966	163,093	90,961	ROTH, WILLIAM V.	72,132	MCDOWELL, HARRIS B. JR.*		18,829 R	55.8%	44.2%	55.8%	44.2%
At Large	1964	198,691	86,254	SNOWDEN, JAMES H.	112,361	MCDOWELL, HARRIS B. JR.*	76	26,107 D	43.4%	56.6%	43.4%	56.6%
At Large	1962	153,356	71,934	WILLIAMS, WILMER F.	81,166	MCDOWELL, HARRIS B. JR.*	256	9,232 D	46.9%	52.9%	47.0%	53.0%
At Large	1960	194,564	96,337	MCKINSTRY, JAMES T.	98,227	MCDOWELL, HARRIS B. JR.*		1,890 D	49.5%	50.5%	49.5%	50.5%
At Large	1958	152,896	76,099	HASKELL, HARRY G. JR.*	76,797	MCDOWELL, HARRIS B. JR.*		698 D	49.8%	50.2%	49.8%	50.2%
At Large	1956	176,182	91,538	HASKELL, HARRY G. JR.	84,644	MCDOWELL, HARRIS B. JR.*		6,894 R	52.0%	48.0%	52.0%	48.0%
At Large	1954	144,236	65,035	MARTIN, LILLIAN I.	79,201	MCDOWELL, HARRIS B. JR.		14,166 D	45.1%	54.9%	45.1%	54.9%
At Large	1952	170,015	88,285	WARBURTON, H. B.	81,730	SCANNELL, JOSEPH S.		6,555 R	51.9%	48.1%	51.9%	48.1%
At Large	1950	129,404	73,313	BOGGS, JAMES CALEB*	56,091	WINCHESTER, H. M.		17,222 R	56.7%	43.3%	56.7%	43.3%
At Large	1948	140,535	71,127	BOGGS, JAMES CALEB*	68,909	MCGUIGAN, J. CARL	499	2,218 R	50.6%	49.0%	50.8%	49.2%
At Large	1946	112,621	63,516	BOGGS, JAMES CALEB	49,105	TRAYNOR, PHILIP A.*		14,411 R	56.4%	43.6%	56.4%	43.6%

Note: An asterisk (*) denotes incumbent.

DELAWARE

GENERAL AND PRIMARY ELECTIONS

GENERAL ELECTIONS: OTHER VOTES

House Other vote was:

At Large 3,074 Libertarian (Cody McNutt), 1,958 Non Partisan (David Rogers)

DELAWARE
GENERAL AND PRIMARY ELECTIONS

2022 PRIMARY ELECTIONS: SUPPLEMENTARY INFORMATION

Primary	September 13, 2022	**Registration** (as of September 1, 2022)	760,788	Democratic	362,002
				Republican	209,358
				Independent	9,988
				Libertarian	2,185
				Green	737
				Other	4,205
				Nonpartisan	1,177
				Unaffiliated	171,136

Primary Type Closed—Only registered Democrats and Republicans could vote in their party's primary.

	REPUBLICAN PRIMARIES		DEMOCRATIC PRIMARIES	
Congressional At Large	Murphy, Lee H.	Unopposed	Rochester, Lisa Blunt*	Unopposed

Note: An asterisk (*) denotes incumbent.

FLORIDA

Statewide Races

Despite the differing national environments, one constant of the 2010, 2014, and 2018 midterms were close Republican victories in Florida gubernatorial contests. While 2022 again resulted in a Republican win, the margin was not close: Gov. Ron DeSantis was reelected by a margin of 1.5 million votes. DeSantis spent much of his first term seemingly positioning himself for a national run – both legislatively and rhetorically, he opposed all things "woke."

Minutes after polls closed on Election Night, Miami-Dade County reported the lion's share of its votes. After giving the Democratic nominees 20-point margins in the previous two gubernatorial contests, DeSantis was ahead by about ten points there. The rest of the state did not look better for Democrats: overall, DeSantis beat former Gov. (and then-current Rep.) Charlie Crist by a 59%–40% margin.

Other than Miami-Dade, DeSantis flipped six counties that Joe Biden carried two years earlier: Palm Beach, another South Florida county; Pinellas and Hillsborough, on either side of Tampa Bay; Orange and Osceola, in the Orlando area; and Jacksonville's Duval. In Crist's last gubernatorial run – he won the office in 2006 as a Republican but ran unsuccessfully as a Democrat in 2014 – he carried his home county, Pinellas, by a 52%–41% margin, an impressive showing in this typically marginal county. But by 2022, even the voters who knew him best were not enthusiastic about Crist: DeSantis carried Pinellas 55%–45%.

Republican Sen. Marco Rubio was also up for reelection in 2022. He drew a respectable Democratic challenger in Rep. Val Demings, a Black woman who, prior to her time in Congress, led the Orlando Police Department. Still, Rubio won 58%–41%. The sole county that produced a split outcome was Palm Beach, which went 51%–48% for DeSantis but went to Demings by roughly half a percentage point.

House Races

Florida, where Republicans have had unified control of state government for a generation, became the scene of an unlikely redistricting fight. Given the state's strong population growth, its House delegation was slated to expand from 27 to 28 members. When maps were proposed, DeSantis vetoed the plans produced by his own party's legislative leaders. DeSantis pushed through his own plan, which was a gerrymander aimed at increasing the GOP's advantage in the delegation to 20–8, up from their existing 16–11 edge. The governor's plan worked as intended.

In the panhandle, Democratic Rep. Al Lawson saw his district dismantled – it was 46% Black and ran horizontally from Tallahassee to Jacksonville. Lawson ran against Republican Rep. Neal Dunn but lost 60%–40% in a redder seat. Republicans also gained Crist's Pinellas County-based 13th District, as well as Democratic Rep. Stephanie Murphy's open 7th District.

With DeSantis atop the ticket, the Republican tide in Florida was so strong that it cut into Democratic territory. In FL-9, a seat that is roughly half Hispanic by composition, veteran Democratic Rep. Darren Soto won by only seven points. In South Florida's open 23rd District, Democrats landed a strong recruit in Jared Moskowitz, who won by just over three points. According to state analyst Matthew Isbell's calculations, both FL-9 and FL-23 were districts that Biden would have carried in 2020 but voted for DeSantis by single-digit margins.

FLORIDA

Congressional districts first established for elections held in 2022

28 members

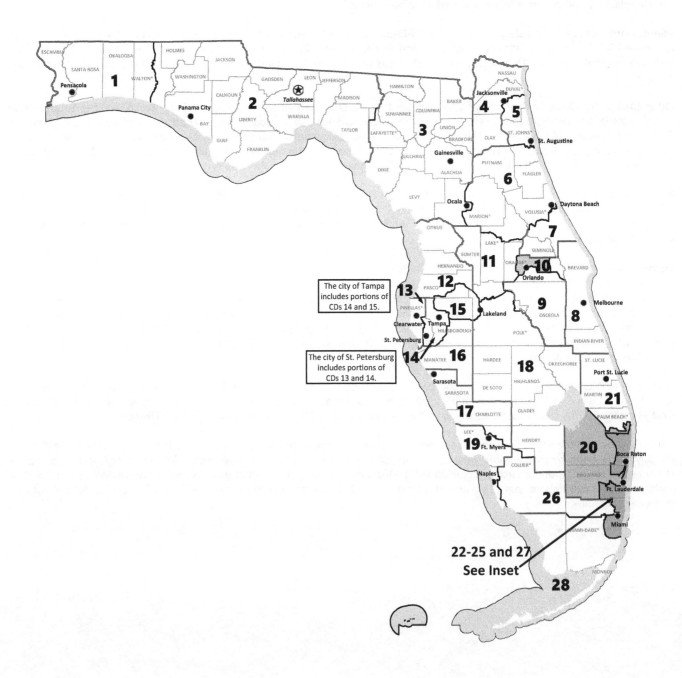

*Asterisk indicates a county whose boundaries include parts of two or more congressional districts.
CDs 10 and 20 are highlighted for visibility. See inset for Miami area: 22, 23, 24, 25, and 27.

FLORIDA

Greater Miami, Fort Lauderdale, West Palm Beach Area

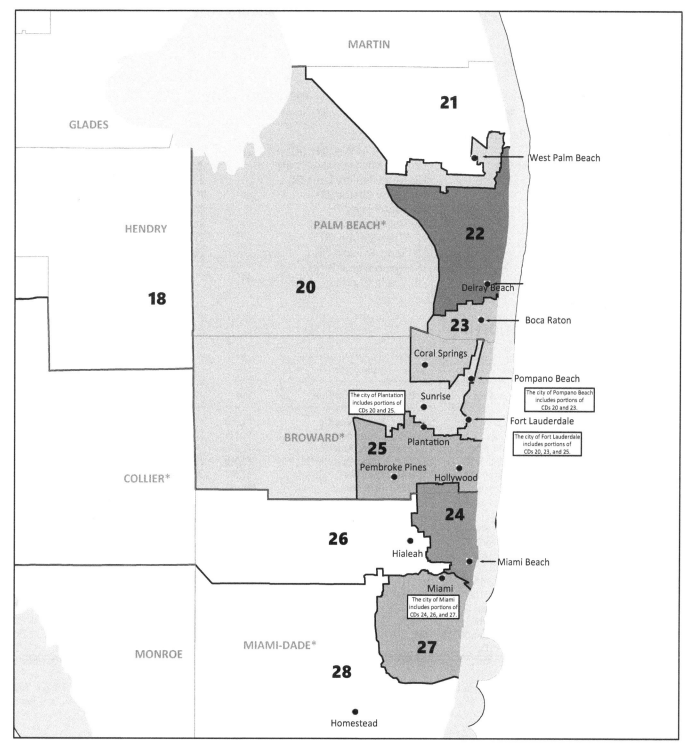

*Asterisk indicates a county whose boundaries include parts of two or more congressional districts.
CDs 20, 22, 23, 24, 25 and 27 are highlighted for visibility.

FLORIDA

GOVERNOR
Ron DeSantis (R). Reelected 2022 to a four-year term. Previously elected 2018.

SENATORS (2 Republicans)
Rick Scott (R). Elected 2018 to a six-year term.

Marco Rubio (R). Reelected 2022 to a six-year term. Previously elected 2016, 2010.

REPRESENTATIVES (20 Republicans, 8 Democrats)
1. Matt Gaetz (R)
2. Neal Dunn (R)
3. Kat Cammack (R)
4. Aaron Bean (R)
5. John Rutherford (R)
6. Michael Waltz (R)
7. Cory Mills (R)
8. Bill Posey (R)
9. Darren Soto (D)
10. Maxwell Frost (D)
11. Daniel A. Webster (R)
12. Gus Michael Bilirakis (R)
13. Anna Paulina Luna (R)
14. Kathy Castor (D)
15. Laurel Lee (R)
16. Vern Buchanan (R)
17. Greg Steube (R)
18. Scott Franklin (R)
19. Byron Donalds (R)
20. Sheila Cherfilus-McCormick (D)
21. Brian Mast (R)
22. Lois Frankel (D)
23. Jared Evan Moskowitz (D)
24. Frederica S. Wilson (D)
25. Debbie Wasserman-Schultz (D)
26. Mario Diaz-Balart (R)
27. Maria Elvira Salazar (R)
28. Carlos Giménez (R)

POSTWAR VOTE FOR PRESIDENT

Year	Total Vote	Republican Vote	Republican Candidate	Democratic Vote	Democratic Candidate	Other Vote	Rep.-Dem. Plurality	Total Vote Rep.	Total Vote Dem.	Major Vote Rep.	Major Vote Dem.
2020	11,067,456	5,668,731	Trump, Donald J.*	5,297,045	Biden, Joseph R. Jr.	101,680	371,686 R	51.2%	47.9%	51.7%	48.3%
2016**	9,420,039	4,617,886	Trump, Donald J.	4,504,975	Clinton, Hillary Rodham	297,178	112,911 R	49.0%	47.8%	50.6%	49.4%
2012	8,474,179	4,163,447	Romney, W. Mitt	4,237,756	Obama, Barack H.*	72,976	74,309 D	49.1%	50.0%	49.6%	50.4%
2008	8,390,744	4,045,624	McCain, John S. III	4,282,074	Obama, Barack H.	63,046	236,450 D	48.2%	51.0%	48.6%	51.4%
2004	7,609,810	3,964,522	Bush, George W.*	3,583,544	Kerry, John F.	61,744	380,978 R	52.1%	47.1%	52.5%	47.5%
2000**	5,963,110	2,912,790	Bush, George W.	2,912,253	Gore, Albert Jr.	138,067	537 R	48.8%	48.8%	50.0%	50.0%
1996**	5,303,794	2,244,536	Dole, Robert "Bob"	2,546,870	Clinton, Bill	512,388	302,334 D	42.3%	48.0%	46.8%	53.2%
1992**	5,314,392	2,173,310	Bush, George H.*	2,072,698	Clinton, Bill	1,068,384	100,612 R	40.9%	39.0%	51.2%	48.8%
1988	4,302,313	2,618,885	Bush, George H.	1,656,701	Dukakis, Michael S.	26,727	962,184 R	60.9%	38.5%	61.3%	38.7%
1984	4,180,051	2,730,350	Reagan, Ronald*	1,448,816	Mondale, Walter F.	885	1,281,534 R	65.3%	34.7%	65.3%	34.7%
1980**	3,686,930	2,046,951	Reagan, Ronald	1,419,475	Carter, Jimmy*	220,504	627,476 R	55.5%	38.5%	59.1%	40.9%
1976	3,150,631	1,469,531	Ford, Gerald R.*	1,636,000	Carter, Jimmy	45,100	166,469 D	46.6%	51.9%	47.3%	52.7%
1972	2,583,283	1,857,759	Nixon, Richard M.*	718,117	McGovern, George S.	7,407	1,139,642 R	71.9%	27.8%	72.1%	27.9%
1968**	2,187,805	886,804	Nixon, Richard M.	676,794	Humphrey, Hubert Horatio Jr.	624,207	210,010 R	40.5%	30.9%	56.7%	43.3%
1964	1,854,481	905,941	Goldwater, Barry M. Sr.	948,540	Johnson, Lyndon B.*		42,599 D	48.9%	51.1%	48.9%	51.1%
1960	1,544,176	795,476	Nixon, Richard M.	748,700	Kennedy, John F.		46,776 R	51.5%	48.5%	51.5%	48.5%
1956	1,125,762	643,849	Eisenhower, Dwight D.*	480,371	Stevenson, Adlai E. II	1,542	163,478 R	57.2%	42.7%	57.3%	42.7%
1952	989,337	544,036	Eisenhower, Dwight D.	444,950	Stevenson, Adlai E. II	351	99,086 R	55.0%	45.0%	55.0%	45.0%
1948**	577,643	194,280	Dewey, Thomas E.	281,988	Truman, Harry S.*	101,375	87,708 D	33.6%	48.8%	40.8%	59.2%

Note: An asterisk (*) denotes incumbent. **In past elections, the other vote included: 2016 - 207,043 (Gary Johnson); 2000 - 97,488 Green (Ralph Nader); 1996 - 483,870 Reform (Ross Perot); 1992 - 1,053,067 Independent (Perot); 1980 - 189,692 Independent (John Anderson); 1968 - 624,207 American Independent (George Wallace); 1948 - 89,755 States' Rights (Strom Thurmond).

FLORIDA

POSTWAR VOTE FOR GOVERNOR

Year	Total Vote	Republican Vote	Republican Candidate	Democratic Vote	Democratic Candidate	Other Vote	Rep.-Dem. Plurality	Total Vote Rep.	Total Vote Dem.	Major Vote Rep.	Major Vote Dem.
2022	7,771,399	4,614,210	DeSantis, Ron*	3,106,313	Crist, Charlie	50,876	1,507,897 R	59.4%	40.0%	59.8%	40.2%
2018	8,220,561	4,076,186	DeSantis, Ron	4,043,723	Gillum, Andrew	100,652	32,463 R	49.6%	49.2%	50.2%	49.8%
2014	5,951,561	2,865,343	Scott, Rick*	2,801,198	Crist, Charlie	285,020	64,145 R	48.1%	47.1%	50.6%	49.4%
2010	5,359,735	2,619,335	Scott, Rick	2,557,785	Sink, Alex	182,615	61,550 R	48.9%	47.7%	50.6%	49.4%
2006	4,829,270	2,519,845	Crist, Charlie	2,178,289	Davis, Jim	131,136	341,556 R	52.2%	45.1%	53.6%	46.4%
2002	5,100,581	2,856,845	Bush, Jeb*	2,201,427	McBride, Bill	42,309	655,418 R	56.0%	43.2%	56.5%	43.5%
1998	3,964,441	2,191,105	Bush, Jeb	1,773,054	MacKay, Buddy	282	418,051 R	55.3%	44.7%	55.3%	44.7%
1994	4,206,659	2,071,068	Bush, Jeb	2,135,008	Chiles, Lawton*	583	63,940 D	49.2%	50.8%	49.2%	50.8%
1990	3,530,871	1,535,068	Martinez, Bob*	1,995,206	Chiles, Lawton	597	460,138 D	43.5%	56.5%	43.5%	56.5%
1986	3,386,171	1,847,525	Martinez, Bob	1,538,620	Pajcic, Steve	26	308,905 R	54.6%	45.4%	54.6%	45.4%
1982	2,688,566	949,013	Bafalis, L. A.	1,739,553	Graham, Bob*		790,540 D	35.3%	64.7%	35.3%	64.7%
1978	2,530,468	1,123,888	Eckerd, Jack M.	1,406,580	Graham, Bob		282,692 D	44.4%	55.6%	44.4%	55.6%
1974	1,828,392	709,438	Thomas, Jerry	1,118,954	Askew, Reubin*		409,516 D	38.8%	61.2%	38.8%	61.2%
1970	1,730,813	746,243	Kirk, Claude R. Jr.*	984,305	Askew, Reubin	265	238,062 D	43.1%	56.9%	43.1%	56.9%
1966	1,489,661	821,190	Kirk, Claude R. Jr.	668,233	High, Robert King	238	152,957 R	55.1%	44.9%	55.1%	44.9%
1964**	1,663,481	686,297	Holley, Charles R.	933,554	Burns, Haydon	43,630	247,257 D	41.3%	56.1%	42.4%	57.6%
1960	1,419,343	569,936	Petersen, George C.	849,407	Bryant, Farris		279,471 D	40.2%	59.8%	40.2%	59.8%
1956	1,014,733	266,980	Washburn, William A. Jr.	747,753	Collins, Leroy*		480,773 D	26.3%	73.7%	26.3%	73.7%
1954S**	357,783	69,852	Watson, J. Tom	287,769	Collins, Leroy	162	217,917 D	19.5%	80.4%	19.5%	80.5%
1952	834,518	210,009	Swan, Harry S.	624,463	McCarty, Daniel T.	46	414,454 D	25.2%	74.8%	25.2%	74.8%
1948	457,638	76,153	Acker, Bert L.	381,459	Warren, Fuller	26	305,306 D	16.6%	83.4%	16.6%	83.4%

Note: An asterisk (*) denotes incumbent. **The 1964 election was for a two-year term to permit shifting the vote for governor to non-presidential years. The 1954 election was for a short term to fill a vacancy.

POSTWAR VOTE FOR SENATOR

Year	Total Vote	Republican Vote	Republican Candidate	Democratic Vote	Democratic Candidate	Other Vote	Rep.-Dem. Plurality	Total Vote Rep.	Total Vote Dem.	Major Vote Rep.	Major Vote Dem.
2022	7,758,014	4,474,847	Rubio, Marco*	3,201,522	Demings, Val B.	81,645	1,273,325 R	57.7%	41.3%	58.3%	41.7%
2018	8,190,005	4,099,505	Scott, Rick	4,089,472	Nelson, Bill*	1,028	10,033 R	50.1%	49.9%	50.1%	49.9%
2016	9,301,820	4,835,191	Rubio, Marco*	4,122,088	Murphy, Patrick	344,541	713,103 R	52.0%	44.3%	54.0%	46.0%
2012	8,189,946	3,458,267	Mack, Connie IV	4,523,451	Nelson, Bill*	208,228	1,065,184 D	42.2%	55.2%	43.3%	56.7%
2010**	5,411,106	2,645,743	Rubio, Marco	1,092,936	Meek, Kendrick B.	1,672,427	1,552,807 R	48.9%	20.2%	70.8%	29.2%
2006	4,793,534	1,826,127	Harris, Katherine	2,890,548	Nelson, "Bill"*	76,859	1,064,421 D	38.1%	60.3%	38.7%	61.3%
2004	7,429,894	3,672,864	Martinez, Mel	3,590,201	Castor, Betty	166,829	82,663 R	49.4%	48.3%	50.6%	49.4%
2000	5,856,731	2,705,348	McCollum, Bill	2,989,487	Nelson, "Bill"	161,896	284,139 D	46.2%	51.0%	47.5%	52.5%
1998	3,900,162	1,463,755	Crist, Charlie	2,436,407	Graham, Bob*		972,652 D	37.5%	62.5%	37.5%	62.5%
1994	4,106,176	2,894,726	Mack, Connie III*	1,210,412	Rodham, Hugh E.	1,038	1,684,314 R	70.5%	29.5%	70.5%	29.5%
1992	4,962,290	1,716,025	Grant, Bill	3,245,565	Graham, Bob*	220	1,529,060 D	34.6%	65.4%	34.6%	65.4%
1988	4,068,209	2,051,071	Mack, Connie III	2,016,553	MacKay, Buddy	585	34,518 R	50.4%	49.6%	50.4%	49.6%
1986	3,429,996	1,552,376	Hawkins, Paula*	1,877,543	Graham, Bob	77	325,167 D	45.3%	54.7%	45.3%	54.7%
1982	2,653,419	1,015,330	Poole, Van B.	1,637,667	Chiles, Lawton*	422	622,337 D	38.3%	61.7%	38.3%	61.7%
1980	3,528,028	1,822,460	Hawkins, Paula	1,705,409	Gunter, Bill	159	117,051 R	51.7%	48.3%	51.7%	48.3%
1976	2,857,534	1,057,886	Grady, John	1,799,518	Chiles, Lawton*	130	741,632 D	37.0%	63.0%	37.0%	63.0%
1974**	1,800,539	736,674	Eckerd, Jack M.	781,031	Stone, Richard	282,834	44,357 D	40.9%	43.4%	48.5%	51.5%
1970	1,675,570	772,817	Cramer, William C.	902,438	Chiles, Lawton	123	129,621 D	46.1%	53.9%	46.1%	53.9%
1968	2,024,136	1,131,499	Gurney, Edward J.	892,637	Collins, Leroy		238,862 R	55.9%	44.1%	55.9%	44.1%
1964	1,560,337	562,212	Kirk, Claude R. Jr.	997,585	Holland, Spessard L.*	540	435,373 D	36.0%	63.9%	36.0%	64.0%
1962	939,207	281,381	Rupert, Emerson H.	657,633	Smathers, George A.*	193	376,252 D	30.0%	70.0%	30.0%	70.0%
1958	542,069	155,956	Hyzer, Leland	386,113	Holland, Spessard L.*		230,157 D	28.8%	71.2%	28.8%	71.2%
1956	655,418			655,418	Smathers, George A.*		655,418 D		100.0%		100.0%
1952	617,800			616,665	Holland, Spessard L.*	1,135	616,665 D		99.8%		100.0%
1950	313,487	74,228	Booth, John P.	238,987	Smathers, George A.	272	164,759 D	23.7%	76.2%	23.7%	76.3%
1946	198,645	42,413	Schad, J. Harry	156,232	Holland, Spessard L.		113,819 D	21.4%	78.6%	21.4%	78.6%

Note: An asterisk (*) denotes incumbent. **In past elections, the other vote included: 2010 - 1,607,549 Independent (Charlie Crist), who placed second; 1974 - 282,659 American (John Grady). The Republican Party did not run a candidate in the 1952 and 1956 Senate elections.

FLORIDA
GOVERNOR 2022

2020 Census Population	County	Total Vote	Republican (DeSantis)	Democratic (Crist)	Other	Rep.-Dem. Plurality		Percentage Total Vote		Percentage Major Vote	
								Rep.	Dem.	Rep.	Dem.
270,032	ALACHUA	95,901	40,321	54,796	784	14,475	D	42.0%	57.1%	42.4%	57.6%
29,434	BAKER	10,725	9,594	1,092	39	8,502	R	89.5%	10.2%	89.8%	10.2%
173,469	BAY	67,093	52,590	14,091	412	38,499	R	78.4%	21.0%	78.9%	21.1%
28,568	BRADFORD	10,267	8,346	1,852	69	6,494	R	81.3%	18.0%	81.8%	18.2%
607,014	BREVARD	267,453	170,562	95,131	1,760	75,431	R	63.8%	35.6%	64.2%	35.8%
1,955,251	BROWARD	598,607	251,238	343,286	4,083	92,048	D	42.0%	57.3%	42.3%	57.7%
14,062	CALHOUN	4,858	4,180	657	21	3,523	R	86.0%	13.5%	86.4%	13.6%
191,064	CHARLOTTE	92,706	65,357	27,005	344	38,352	R	70.5%	29.1%	70.8%	29.2%
151,369	CITRUS	75,826	56,283	19,100	443	37,183	R	74.2%	25.2%	74.7%	25.3%
220,763	CLAY	90,119	67,292	22,187	640	45,105	R	74.7%	24.6%	75.2%	24.8%
387,966	COLLIER	163,759	117,477	45,815	467	71,662	R	71.7%	28.0%	71.9%	28.1%
72,154	COLUMBIA	23,727	18,790	4,789	148	14,001	R	79.2%	20.2%	79.7%	20.3%
38,079	DESOTO	8,701	6,637	2,023	41	4,614	R	76.3%	23.3%	76.6%	23.4%
16,919	DIXIE	6,179	5,394	735	50	4,659	R	87.3%	11.9%	88.0%	12.0%
961,793	DUVAL	329,319	182,569	143,837	2,913	38,732	R	55.4%	43.7%	55.9%	44.1%
319,784	ESCAMBIA	115,737	74,608	40,076	1,053	34,532	R	64.5%	34.6%	65.1%	34.9%
116,416	FLAGLER	58,696	39,183	19,177	336	20,006	R	66.8%	32.7%	67.1%	32.9%
12,286	FRANKLIN	5,442	4,003	1,406	33	2,597	R	73.6%	25.8%	74.0%	26.0%
45,669	GADSDEN	17,426	6,511	10,805	110	4,294	D	37.4%	62.0%	37.6%	62.4%
18,716	GILCHRIST	7,868	6,806	1,017	45	5,789	R	86.5%	12.9%	87.0%	13.0%
13,948	GLADES	3,829	3,091	721	17	2,370	R	80.7%	18.8%	81.1%	18.9%
14,474	GULF	6,425	5,150	1,247	28	3,903	R	80.2%	19.4%	80.5%	19.5%
14,449	HAMILTON	4,293	3,145	1,120	28	2,025	R	73.3%	26.1%	73.7%	26.3%
26,938	HARDEE	5,536	4,558	949	29	3,609	R	82.3%	17.1%	82.8%	17.2%
42,033	HENDRY	8,261	6,134	2,052	75	4,082	R	74.3%	24.8%	74.9%	25.1%
196,043	HERNANDO	80,415	56,247	23,700	468	32,547	R	69.9%	29.5%	70.4%	29.6%
107,017	HIGHLANDS	39,825	29,518	9,994	313	19,524	R	74.1%	25.1%	74.7%	25.3%
1,473,380	HILLSBOROUGH	483,514	261,936	217,349	4,229	44,587	R	54.2%	45.0%	54.7%	45.3%
19,703	HOLMES	6,782	6,214	533	35	5,681	R	91.6%	7.9%	92.1%	7.9%
161,546	INDIAN RIVER	77,400	52,269	24,744	387	27,525	R	67.5%	32.0%	67.9%	32.1%
47,080	JACKSON	16,326	12,412	3,835	79	8,577	R	76.0%	23.5%	76.4%	23.6%
14,288	JEFFERSON	7,127	4,310	2,776	41	1,534	R	60.5%	39.0%	60.8%	39.2%
8,315	LAFAYETTE	2,918	2,617	294	7	2,323	R	89.7%	10.1%	89.9%	10.1%
371,792	LAKE	160,160	106,578	52,579	1,003	53,999	R	66.5%	32.8%	67.0%	33.0%
777,411	LEE	275,239	189,335	84,739	1,165	104,596	R	68.8%	30.8%	69.1%	30.9%
294,412	LEON	117,751	49,244	67,535	972	18,291	D	41.8%	57.4%	42.2%	57.8%
41,797	LEVY	17,914	14,049	3,758	107	10,291	R	78.4%	21.0%	78.9%	21.1%
8,393	LIBERTY	2,617	2,234	371	12	1,863	R	85.4%	14.2%	85.8%	14.2%
18,524	MADISON	6,981	4,661	2,293	27	2,368	R	66.8%	32.8%	67.0%	33.0%
407,576	MANATEE	171,730	111,109	59,801	820	51,308	R	64.7%	34.8%	65.0%	35.0%
369,231	MARION	156,050	108,027	47,129	894	60,898	R	69.2%	30.2%	69.6%	30.4%
161,980	MARTIN	77,667	53,595	23,748	324	29,847	R	69.0%	30.6%	69.3%	30.7%
2,721,256	MIAMI-DADE	711,851	393,532	312,972	5,347	80,560	R	55.3%	44.0%	55.7%	44.3%
74,150	MONROE	34,004	20,479	13,314	211	7,165	R	60.2%	39.2%	60.6%	39.4%
89,773	NASSAU	47,764	36,551	10,973	240	25,578	R	76.5%	23.0%	76.9%	23.1%
212,140	OKALOOSA	81,008	61,715	18,569	724	43,146	R	76.2%	22.9%	76.9%	23.1%
42,326	OKEECHOBEE	10,886	8,746	2,079	61	6,667	R	80.3%	19.1%	80.8%	19.2%
1,396,795	ORANGE	407,230	187,653	216,221	3,356	28,568	D	46.1%	53.1%	46.5%	53.5%
378,454	OSCEOLA	102,825	54,330	47,387	1,108	6,943	R	52.8%	46.1%	53.4%	46.6%
1,502,034	PALM BEACH	543,788	278,454	262,655	2,679	15,799	R	51.2%	48.3%	51.5%	48.5%
560,435	PASCO	224,980	148,083	75,342	1,555	72,741	R	65.8%	33.5%	66.3%	33.7%
979,919	PINELLAS	423,494	231,284	189,563	2,647	41,721	R	54.6%	44.8%	55.0%	45.0%
732,435	POLK	230,017	148,254	80,172	1,591	68,082	R	64.5%	34.9%	64.9%	35.1%
74,925	PUTNAM	26,593	20,217	6,196	180	14,021	R	76.0%	23.3%	76.5%	23.5%
186,294	SANTA ROSA	75,698	60,091	15,096	511	44,995	R	79.4%	19.9%	79.9%	20.1%
437,909	SARASOTA	218,897	133,354	84,614	929	48,740	R	60.9%	38.7%	61.2%	38.8%
473,544	SEMINOLE	183,201	102,191	79,664	1,346	22,527	R	55.8%	43.5%	56.2%	43.8%
268,905	ST. JOHNS	144,654	101,066	42,873	715	58,193	R	69.9%	29.6%	70.2%	29.8%
331,983	ST. LUCIE	121,993	72,354	49,009	630	23,345	R	59.3%	40.2%	59.6%	40.4%
134,623	SUMTER	89,464	65,496	23,718	250	41,778	R	73.2%	26.5%	73.4%	26.6%

FLORIDA
GOVERNOR 2022

2020 Census Population	County	Total Vote	Republican (DeSantis)	Democratic (Crist)	Other	Rep.-Dem. Plurality		Percentage			
								Total Vote		Major Vote	
								Rep.	Dem.	Rep.	Dem.
44,525	SUWANNEE	16,367	13,649	2,650	68	10,999	R	83.4%	16.2%	83.7%	16.3%
21,546	TAYLOR	7,622	6,308	1,276	38	5,032	R	82.8%	16.7%	83.2%	16.8%
14,998	UNION	4,558	3,995	544	19	3,451	R	87.6%	11.9%	88.0%	12.0%
558,323	VOLUSIA	226,246	144,768	79,965	1,513	64,803	R	64.0%	35.3%	64.4%	35.6%
34,178	WAKULLA	15,063	11,033	3,920	110	7,113	R	73.2%	26.0%	73.8%	26.2%
75,397	WALTON	34,901	28,647	6,112	142	22,535	R	82.1%	17.5%	82.4%	17.6%
25,722	WASHINGTON	9,126	7,786	1,285	55	6,501	R	85.3%	14.1%	85.8%	14.2%
21,593,727	TOTAL	7,771,399	4,614,210	3,106,313	50,876	1,507,897	R	59.4%	40.0%	59.8%	40.2%

FLORIDA
SENATOR 2022

2020 Census Population	County	Total Vote	Republican (Rubio)	Democratic (Demings)	Other	Rep.-Dem. Plurality		Percentage			
								Total Vote		Major Vote	
								Rep.	Dem.	Rep.	Dem.
270,032	ALACHUA	95,734	39,220	55,439	1,075	16,219	D	41.0%	57.9%	41.4%	58.6%
29,434	BAKER	10,692	9,431	1,181	80	8,250	R	88.2%	11.0%	88.9%	11.1%
173,469	BAY	66,956	51,657	14,547	752	37,110	R	77.2%	21.7%	78.0%	22.0%
28,568	BRADFORD	10,210	8,156	1,942	112	6,214	R	79.9%	19.0%	80.8%	19.2%
607,014	BREVARD	267,163	165,233	98,978	2,952	66,255	R	61.8%	37.0%	62.5%	37.5%
1,955,251	BROWARD	598,046	238,962	353,575	5,509	114,613	D	40.0%	59.1%	40.3%	59.7%
14,062	CALHOUN	4,832	4,067	700	65	3,367	R	84.2%	14.5%	85.3%	14.7%
191,064	CHARLOTTE	92,448	63,845	27,757	846	36,088	R	69.1%	30.0%	69.7%	30.3%
151,369	CITRUS	75,668	55,087	19,634	947	35,453	R	72.8%	25.9%	73.7%	26.3%
220,763	CLAY	90,049	65,972	23,054	1,023	42,918	R	73.3%	25.6%	74.1%	25.9%
387,966	COLLIER	163,489	116,050	46,537	902	69,513	R	71.0%	28.5%	71.4%	28.6%
72,154	COLUMBIA	23,655	18,344	5,070	241	13,274	R	77.5%	21.4%	78.3%	21.7%
38,079	DESOTO	8,659	6,469	2,097	93	4,372	R	74.7%	24.2%	75.5%	24.5%
16,919	DIXIE	6,134	5,225	826	83	4,399	R	85.2%	13.5%	86.3%	13.7%
961,793	DUVAL	328,841	177,401	147,646	3,794	29,755	R	53.9%	44.9%	54.6%	45.4%
319,784	ESCAMBIA	115,496	73,225	40,790	1,481	32,435	R	63.4%	35.3%	64.2%	35.8%
116,416	FLAGLER	58,621	37,934	20,204	483	17,730	R	64.7%	34.5%	65.2%	34.8%
12,286	FRANKLIN	5,418	3,885	1,471	62	2,414	R	71.7%	27.2%	72.5%	27.5%
45,669	GADSDEN	17,384	6,086	11,113	185	5,027	D	35.0%	63.9%	35.4%	64.6%
18,716	GILCHRIST	7,846	6,657	1,087	102	5,570	R	84.8%	13.9%	86.0%	14.0%
13,948	GLADES	3,818	3,026	764	28	2,262	R	79.3%	20.0%	79.8%	20.2%
14,474	GULF	6,419	5,069	1,295	55	3,774	R	79.0%	20.2%	79.7%	20.3%
14,449	HAMILTON	4,282	3,030	1,215	37	1,815	R	70.8%	28.4%	71.4%	28.6%
26,938	HARDEE	5,522	4,480	981	61	3,499	R	81.1%	17.8%	82.0%	18.0%
42,033	HENDRY	8,233	6,008	2,121	104	3,887	R	73.0%	25.8%	73.9%	26.1%
196,043	HERNANDO	80,149	54,822	24,298	1,029	30,524	R	68.4%	30.3%	69.3%	30.7%
107,017	HIGHLANDS	39,731	28,777	10,480	474	18,297	R	72.4%	26.4%	73.3%	26.7%
1,473,380	HILLSBOROUGH	482,343	253,495	222,378	6,470	31,117	R	52.6%	46.1%	53.3%	46.7%
19,703	HOLMES	6,770	6,151	556	63	5,595	R	90.9%	8.2%	91.7%	8.3%
161,546	INDIAN RIVER	77,192	50,878	25,613	701	25,265	R	65.9%	33.2%	66.5%	33.5%
47,080	JACKSON	16,279	12,188	3,956	135	8,232	R	74.9%	24.3%	75.5%	24.5%
14,288	JEFFERSON	7,124	4,137	2,929	58	1,208	R	58.1%	41.1%	58.5%	41.5%
8,315	LAFAYETTE	2,907	2,521	348	38	2,173	R	86.7%	12.0%	87.9%	12.1%
371,792	LAKE	160,013	103,103	55,377	1,533	47,726	R	64.4%	34.6%	65.1%	34.9%
777,411	LEE	274,510	185,123	87,108	2,279	98,015	R	67.4%	31.7%	68.0%	32.0%

FLORIDA
SENATOR 2022

2020 Census Population	County	Total Vote	Republican (Rubio)	Democratic (Demings)	Other	Rep.-Dem. Plurality		Total Vote Rep.	Total Vote Dem.	Major Vote Rep.	Major Vote Dem.
294,412	LEON	117,487	46,511	69,677	1,299	23,166	D	39.6%	59.3%	40.0%	60.0%
41,797	LEVY	17,865	13,690	3,944	231	9,746	R	76.6%	22.1%	77.6%	22.4%
8,393	LIBERTY	2,602	2,164	405	33	1,759	R	83.2%	15.6%	84.2%	15.8%
18,524	MADISON	6,976	4,476	2,442	58	2,034	R	64.2%	35.0%	64.7%	35.3%
407,576	MANATEE	171,394	108,234	61,423	1,737	46,811	R	63.1%	35.8%	63.8%	36.2%
369,231	MARION	155,791	104,655	49,698	1,438	54,957	R	67.2%	31.9%	67.8%	32.2%
161,980	MARTIN	77,564	52,312	24,639	613	27,673	R	67.4%	31.8%	68.0%	32.0%
2,721,256	MIAMI-DADE	711,715	386,251	318,978	6,486	67,273	R	54.3%	44.8%	54.8%	45.2%
74,150	MONROE	33,972	19,897	13,756	319	6,141	R	58.6%	40.5%	59.1%	40.9%
89,773	NASSAU	47,713	35,944	11,337	432	24,607	R	75.3%	23.8%	76.0%	24.0%
212,140	OKALOOSA	80,789	60,808	18,851	1,130	41,957	R	75.3%	23.3%	76.3%	23.7%
42,326	OKEECHOBEE	10,863	8,532	2,218	113	6,314	R	78.5%	20.4%	79.4%	20.6%
1,396,795	ORANGE	407,053	177,105	225,569	4,379	48,464	D	43.5%	55.4%	44.0%	56.0%
378,454	OSCEOLA	102,693	51,422	49,907	1,364	1,515	R	50.1%	48.6%	50.7%	49.3%
1,502,034	PALM BEACH	542,618	267,715	269,839	5,064	2,124	D	49.3%	49.7%	49.8%	50.2%
560,435	PASCO	224,441	143,760	77,664	3,017	66,096	R	64.1%	34.6%	64.9%	35.1%
979,919	PINELLAS	422,047	223,747	192,058	6,242	31,689	R	53.0%	45.5%	53.8%	46.2%
732,435	POLK	229,498	144,548	82,261	2,689	62,287	R	63.0%	35.8%	63.7%	36.3%
74,925	PUTNAM	26,540	19,812	6,450	278	13,362	R	74.6%	24.3%	75.4%	24.6%
186,294	SANTA ROSA	75,570	59,111	15,554	905	43,557	R	78.2%	20.6%	79.2%	20.8%
437,909	SARASOTA	218,416	129,865	86,618	1,933	43,247	R	59.5%	39.7%	60.0%	40.0%
473,544	SEMINOLE	183,028	97,761	83,285	1,982	14,476	R	53.4%	45.5%	54.0%	46.0%
268,905	ST. JOHNS	144,371	98,564	44,371	1,436	54,193	R	68.3%	30.7%	69.0%	31.0%
331,983	ST. LUCIE	121,824	69,924	50,851	1,049	19,073	R	57.4%	41.7%	57.9%	42.1%
134,623	SUMTER	89,317	63,806	25,010	501	38,796	R	71.4%	28.0%	71.8%	28.2%
44,525	SUWANNEE	16,306	13,125	3,018	163	10,107	R	80.5%	18.5%	81.3%	18.7%
21,546	TAYLOR	7,617	6,063	1,495	59	4,568	R	79.6%	19.6%	80.2%	19.8%
14,998	UNION	4,539	3,917	580	42	3,337	R	86.3%	12.8%	87.1%	12.9%
558,323	VOLUSIA	225,862	139,085	84,543	2,234	54,542	R	61.6%	37.4%	62.2%	37.8%
34,178	WAKULLA	14,998	10,485	4,343	170	6,142	R	69.9%	29.0%	70.7%	29.3%
75,397	WALTON	34,817	28,203	6,326	288	21,877	R	81.0%	18.2%	81.7%	18.3%
25,722	WASHINGTON	9,095	7,641	1,345	109	6,296	R	84.0%	14.8%	85.0%	15.0%
21,593,727	TOTAL	7,758,014	4,474,847	3,201,522	81,645	1,273,325	R	57.7%	41.3%	58.3%	41.7%

FLORIDA
HOUSE OF REPRESENTATIVES

CD	Year	Total Vote	Republican Vote	Republican Candidate	Democratic Vote	Democratic Candidate	Other Vote	Rep.-Dem. Plurality		Total Vote Rep.	Total Vote Dem.	Major Vote Rep.	Major Vote Dem.
1	2022	290,816	197,349	GAETZ, MATT*	93,467	JONES, REBEKAH		103,882	R	67.9%	32.1%	67.9%	32.1%
1	2020	438,562	283,352	GAETZ, MATT*	149,172	EHR, PHIL	6,038	134,180	R	64.6%	34.0%	65.5%	34.5%
1	2018	322,388	216,189	GAETZ, MATT*	106,199	ZIMMERMAN, JENNIFER M.		109,990	R	67.1%	32.9%	67.1%	32.9%
1	2016	369,186	255,107	GAETZ, MATT	114,079	SPECHT, STEVEN		141,028	R	69.1%	30.9%	69.1%	30.9%
1	2014	235,343	165,086	MILLER, JEFF*	54,976	BRYAN, JAMES "JIM"	15,281	110,110	R	70.1%	23.4%	75.0%	25.0%
1	2012	342,594	238,440	MILLER, JEFF*	92,961	BRYAN, JAMES "JIM"	11,193	145,479	R	69.6%	27.1%	71.9%	28.1%
2	2022	301,389	180,236	DUNN, NEAL	121,153	LAWSON, AL*		59,083	R	59.8%	40.2%	59.8%	40.2%
2	2020**	311,999	305,337	DUNN, NEAL*			6,662	305,337	R	97.9%		100.0%	
2	2018**	295,568	199,335	DUNN, NEAL*	96,233	RACKLEFF, BOB		103,102	R	67.4%	32.6%	67.4%	32.6%
2	2016**	343,362	231,163	DUNN, NEAL	102,801	DARTLAND, WALTER	9,398	128,362	R	67.3%	29.9%	69.2%	30.8%
2	2014	249,780	123,262	SOUTHERLAND, STEVE*	126,096	GRAHAM, GWEN	422	2,834	D	49.3%	50.5%	49.4%	50.6%
2	2012	333,718	175,856	SOUTHERLAND, STEVE*	157,634	LAWSON, AL	228	18,222	R	52.7%	47.2%	52.7%	47.3%

FLORIDA
HOUSE OF REPRESENTATIVES

CD	Year	Total Vote	Republican Vote	Republican Candidate	Democratic Vote	Democratic Candidate	Other Vote	Rep.-Dem. Plurality	Total Vote Rep.	Total Vote Dem.	Major Vote Rep.	Major Vote Dem.
3	2022	284,893	178,101	CAMMACK, KAT*	103,382	HAWK, DANIELLE	3,410	74,719 R	62.5%	36.3%	63.3%	36.7%
3	2020**	390,401	223,075	CAMMACK, KAT	167,326	CHRISTENSEN, ADAM		55,749 R	57.1%	42.9%	57.1%	42.9%
3	2018**	306,496	176,616	YOHO, TED*	129,880	HAYES HINSON, YVONNE		46,736 R	57.6%	42.4%	57.6%	42.4%
3	2016**	342,700	193,843	YOHO, TED*	136,338	MCGURN, KENNETH "KEN"	12,519	57,505 R	56.6%	39.8%	58.7%	41.3%
3	2014	228,809	148,691	YOHO, TED*	73,910	WHEELER, MARIHELEN HADDOCK	6,208	74,781 R	65.0%	32.3%	66.8%	33.2%
3	2012	315,669	204,331	YOHO, TED	102,468	GAILLOT, J.R.	8,870	101,863 R	64.7%	32.5%	66.6%	33.4%
4	2022	274,103	165,696	BEAN, AARON	108,402	HOLLOWAY, LASHONDA "L.J."	5	57,294 R	60.5%	39.5%	60.5%	39.5%
4	2020**	504,940	308,497	RUTHERFORD, JOHN*	196,423	DEEGAN, DONNA	20	112,074 R	61.1%	38.9%	61.1%	38.9%
4	2018**	381,249	248,420	RUTHERFORD, JOHN*	123,351	SELMONT, GEORGE "GES"	9,478	125,069 R	65.2%	32.4%	66.8%	33.2%
4	2016**	409,662	287,509	RUTHERFORD, JOHN	113,088	BRUDERLY, DAVID E.	9,065	174,421 R	70.2%	27.6%	71.8%	28.2%
4	2014	227,253	177,887	CRENSHAW, ANDER*			49,366	177,887 R	78.3%		100.0%	
4	2012	315,470	239,988	CRENSHAW, ANDER*			75,482	239,988 R	76.1%		100.0%	
5	2022		Unopposed	RUTHERFORD, JOHN*								
5	2020**	336,973	117,510	ADLER, GARY	219,463	LAWSON, AL*		101,953 D	34.9%	65.1%	34.9%	65.1%
5	2018**	270,326	89,799	FULLER, VIRGINIA	180,527	LAWSON, AL*		90,728 D	33.2%	66.8%	33.2%	66.8%
5	2016**	302,874	108,325	SCURRY-SMITH, GLOREATHA "GLO"	194,549	LAWSON, AL		86,224 D	35.8%	64.2%	35.8%	64.2%
5	2014	171,577	59,237	SCURRY-SMITH, GLOREATHA "GLO"	112,340	BROWN, CORRINE*		53,103 D	34.5%	65.5%	34.5%	65.5%
5	2012	269,153	70,700	KOLB, LEANNE	190,472	BROWN, CORRINE*	7,981	119,772 D	26.3%	70.8%	27.1%	72.9%
6	2022	300,755	226,548	WALTZ, MICHAEL*			74,207	226,548 R	75.3%		100.0%	
6	2020**	437,856	265,393	WALTZ, MICHAEL*	172,305	CURTIS, CLINT	158	93,088 R	60.6%	39.4%	60.6%	39.4%
6	2018**	333,649	187,891	WALTZ, MICHAEL	145,758	SODERBERG, NANCY		42,133 R	56.3%	43.7%	56.3%	43.7%
6	2016**	364,570	213,519	DESANTIS, RON*	151,051	MCCULLOUGH, WILLIAM "BILL"		62,468 R	58.6%	41.4%	58.6%	41.4%
6	2014	265,817	166,254	DESANTIS, RON*	99,563	COX, DAVID		66,691 R	62.5%	37.5%	62.5%	37.5%
6	2012	342,451	195,962	DESANTIS, RON	146,489	BEAVEN, HEATHER		49,473 R	57.2%	42.8%	57.2%	42.8%
7	2022	304,055	177,966	MILLS, CORY	126,079	GREEN, KAREN	10	51,887 R	58.5%	41.5%	58.5%	41.5%
7	2020**	406,449	175,750	VALENTIN, LEO	224,946	MURPHY, STEPHANIE*	5,753	49,196 D	43.2%	55.3%	43.9%	56.1%
7	2018**	317,398	134,285	MILLER, MIKE	183,113	MURPHY, STEPHANIE*		48,828 D	42.3%	57.7%	42.3%	57.7%
7	2016**	353,655	171,583	MICA, JOHN L.*	182,039	MURPHY, STEPHANIE	33	10,456 D	48.5%	51.5%	48.5%	51.5%
7	2014	227,164	144,474	MICA, JOHN L.*	73,011	NEUMAN, WESLEY RYAN "WES"	9,679	71,463 R	63.6%	32.1%	66.4%	33.6%
7	2012	316,010	185,518	MICA, JOHN L.*	130,479	KENDALL, JASON H.	13	55,039 R	58.7%	41.3%	58.7%	41.3%
8	2022	342,208	222,128	POSEY, BILL*	120,080	TERRY, JOANNE		102,048 R	64.9%	35.1%	64.9%	35.1%
8	2020	459,788	282,093	POSEY, BILL*	177,695	KENNEDY, JIM		104,398 R	61.4%	38.6%	61.4%	38.6%
8	2018	360,527	218,112	POSEY, BILL*	142,415	PATEL, SANJAY		75,697 R	60.5%	39.5%	60.5%	39.5%
8	2016	390,561	246,483	POSEY, BILL*	127,127	WESTBROOK, CORRY	16,951	119,356 R	63.1%	32.5%	66.0%	34.0%
8	2014	274,513	180,728	POSEY, BILL*	93,724	ROTHBLATT, GABRIEL	61	87,004 R	65.8%	34.1%	65.9%	34.1%
8	2012	348,909	205,432	POSEY, BILL*	130,870	ROBERTS, SHANNON	12,607	74,562 R	58.9%	37.5%	61.1%	38.9%
9	2022	202,368	93,827	MOORE, SCOTTY	108,541	SOTO, DARREN*		14,714 D	46.4%	53.6%	46.4%	53.6%
9	2020**	429,638	188,889	OLSON, WILLIAM P. "BILL"	240,724	SOTO, DARREN*	25	51,835 D	44.0%	56.0%	44.0%	56.0%
9	2018**	296,737	124,565	LIEBNITZKY, WAYNE	172,172	SOTO, DARREN*		47,607 D	42.0%	58.0%	42.0%	58.0%
9	2016**	339,761	144,450	LIEBNITZKY, WAYNE	195,311	SOTO, DARREN		50,861 D	42.5%	57.5%	42.5%	57.5%
9	2014	173,878	74,963	PLATT, CAROL	93,850	GRAYSON, ALAN*	5,065	18,887 D	43.1%	54.0%	44.4%	55.6%
9	2012	263,747	98,856	LONG, TODD	164,891	GRAYSON, ALAN		66,035 D	37.5%	62.5%	37.5%	62.5%
10	2022	199,910	78,844	WIMBISH, CALVIN B.	117,955	FROST, MAXWELL ALEJANDRO	3,111	39,111 D	39.4%	59.0%	40.1%	59.9%
10	2020**	376,397	136,889	FRANCOIS, VENNIA	239,434	DEMINGS, VAL B.*	74	102,545 D	36.4%	63.6%	36.4%	63.6%
10	2018**		Unopposed			DEMINGS, VAL B.*						
10	2016**	305,989	107,498	LOWE, THUY "TWEE"	198,491	DEMINGS, VAL B.		90,993 D	35.1%	64.9%	35.1%	64.9%
10	2014	232,574	143,128	WEBSTER, DANIEL A.*	89,426	MCKENNA, MICHAEL PATRICK	20	53,702 R	61.5%	38.5%	61.5%	38.5%
10	2012	318,269	164,649	WEBSTER, DANIEL A.*	153,574	DEMINGS, VAL B.	46	11,075 R	51.7%	48.3%	51.7%	48.3%
11	2022	326,609	205,995	WEBSTER, DANIEL A.*	115,647	MUNNS, SHANTE	4,967	90,348 R	63.1%	35.4%	64.0%	36.0%
11	2020**	475,073	316,979	WEBSTER, DANIEL A.*	158,094	COTTRELL, DANA		158,885 R	66.7%	33.3%	66.7%	33.3%
11	2018**	367,506	239,395	WEBSTER, DANIEL A.*	128,053	COTTRELL, DANA	58	111,342 R	65.1%	34.8%	65.2%	34.8%
11	2016**	394,719	258,016	WEBSTER, DANIEL A.	124,713	KOLLER, DAVID C.	11,990	133,303 R	65.4%	31.6%	67.4%	32.6%
11	2014	272,294	181,508	NUGENT, RICHARD B.*	90,786	KOLLER, DAVID C.		90,722 R	66.7%	33.3%	66.7%	33.3%
11	2012	338,663	218,360	NUGENT, RICHARD B.*	120,303	WERDER, H. DAVID		98,057 R	64.5%	35.5%	64.5%	35.5%
12	2022	321,995	226,601	BILIRAKIS, GUS MICHAEL*	95,390	WALKER, KIMBERLY H.	4	131,211 R	70.4%	29.6%	70.4%	29.6%
12	2020**	453,135	284,941	BILIRAKIS, GUS MICHAEL*	168,194	WALKER, KIMBERLY H.		116,747 R	62.9%	37.1%	62.9%	37.1%
12	2018**	334,918	194,564	BILIRAKIS, GUS MICHAEL*	132,844	HUNTER, CHRIS	7,510	61,720 R	58.1%	39.7%	59.4%	40.6%
12	2016**	369,669	253,559	BILIRAKIS, GUS MICHAEL*	116,110	TAGER, ROBERT MATTHEW		137,449 R	68.6%	31.4%	68.6%	31.4%
12	2014		Unopposed	BILIRAKIS, GUS MICHAEL*								
12	2012	330,167	209,604	BILIRAKIS, GUS MICHAEL*	108,770	SNOW, JONATHAN MICHAEL	11,793	100,834 R	63.5%	32.9%	65.8%	34.2%

FLORIDA
HOUSE OF REPRESENTATIVES

| | | | Republican | | Democratic | | Other | Rep.-Dem. | Total Vote | | Major Vote | |
| | | | | | | | Vote | Plurality | | | | |
CD	Year	Total Vote	Vote	Candidate	Vote	Candidate			Rep.	Dem.	Rep.	Dem.
13	2022	341,546	181,487	PAULINA LUNA, ANNA	153,876	LYNN, ERIC	6,183	27,611 R	53.1%	45.1%	54.1%	45.9%
13	2020**	406,125	190,713	PAULINA LUNA, ANNA	215,405	CRIST, CHARLIE*	7	24,692 D	47.0%	53.0%	47.0%	53.0%
13	2018**	316,971	134,254	BUCK, GEORGE	182,717	CRIST, CHARLIE*		48,463 D	42.4%	57.6%	42.4%	57.6%
13	2016**	355,842	171,149	JOLLY, DAVID W.*	184,693	CRIST, CHARLIE		13,544 D	48.1%	51.9%	48.1%	51.9%
13	2014	223,576	168,172	JOLLY, DAVID W.*			55,404	168,172 R	75.2%		100.0%	
13	2012	329,347	189,605	YOUNG, C.W. BILL*	139,742	EHRLICH, JESSICA		49,863 R	57.6%	42.4%	57.6%	42.4%
14	2022	263,164	113,427	JUDGE, JAMES	149,737	CASTOR, KATHY*		36,310 D	43.1%	56.9%	43.1%	56.9%
14	2020**	372,136	147,896	QUINN, CHRISTINE	224,240	CASTOR, KATHY*		76,344 D	39.7%	60.3%	39.7%	60.3%
14	2018**		Unopposed			CASTOR, KATHY*						
14	2016**	316,877	121,088	QUINN, CHRISTINE	195,789	CASTOR, KATHY*		74,701 D	38.2%	61.8%	38.2%	61.8%
14	2014		Unopposed			CASTOR, KATHY*						
14	2012	280,601	83,480	OTERO, EVELIO "EJ"	197,121	CASTOR, KATHY*		113,641 D	29.8%	70.2%	29.8%	70.2%
15	2022	248,054	145,219	LEE, LAUREL	102,835	COHN, ALAN MICHAEL		42,384 R	58.5%	41.5%	58.5%	41.5%
15	2020**	390,671	216,374	FRANKLIN, SCOTT	174,297	COHN, ALAN MICHAEL		42,077 R	55.4%	44.6%	55.4%	44.6%
15	2018**	285,532	151,380	SPANO, ROSS	134,132	CARLSON, KRISTEN	20	17,248 R	53.0%	47.0%	53.0%	47.0%
15	2016**	318,474	182,999	ROSS, DENNIS A.*	135,475	LANGE, JIM		47,524 R	57.5%	42.5%	57.5%	42.5%
15	2014	213,582	128,750	ROSS, DENNIS A.*	84,832	COHN, ALAN MICHAEL		43,918 R	60.3%	39.7%	60.3%	39.7%
15	2012		Unopposed	ROSS, DENNIS A.								
16	2022	305,358	189,762	BUCHANAN, VERN*	115,575	SCHNEIDER, JAN	21	74,187 R	62.1%	37.8%	62.1%	37.9%
16	2020**	484,684	269,001	BUCHANAN, VERN*	215,683	GOOD, MARGARET ELIZABETH ROWELL		53,318 R	55.5%	44.5%	55.5%	44.5%
16	2018**	361,946	197,483	BUCHANAN, VERN*	164,463	SHAPIRO, DAVID		33,020 R	54.6%	45.4%	54.6%	45.4%
16	2016**	385,916	230,654	BUCHANAN, VERN*	155,262	SCHNEIDER, JAN		75,392 R	59.8%	40.2%	59.8%	40.2%
16	2014	274,829	169,126	BUCHANAN, VERN*	105,483	LAWRENCE, HENRY	220	63,643 R	61.5%	38.4%	61.6%	38.4%
16	2012	349,076	187,147	BUCHANAN, VERN*	161,929	FITZGERALD, KEITH		25,218 R	53.6%	46.4%	53.6%	46.4%
17	2022	348,506	222,483	STEUBE, GREG*	123,798	KALE, ANDREA DORIA	2,225	98,685 R	63.8%	35.5%	64.2%	35.8%
17	2020**	412,397	266,514	STEUBE, GREG*	140,487	ELLISON, ALLEN	5,396	126,027 R	64.6%	34.1%	65.5%	34.5%
17	2018**	310,520	193,326	STEUBE, GREG	117,194	ELLISON, ALLEN		76,132 R	62.3%	37.7%	62.3%	37.7%
17	2016**	338,675	209,348	ROONEY, TOM*	115,974	FREEMAN, APRIL	13,353	93,374 R	61.8%	34.2%	64.4%	35.6%
17	2014	223,756	141,493	ROONEY, TOM*	82,263	BRONSON, WILLIAM		59,230 R	63.2%	36.8%	63.2%	36.8%
17	2012	282,271	165,488	ROONEY, TOM*	116,766	BRONSON, WILLIAM	17	48,722 R	58.6%	41.4%	58.6%	41.4%
18	2022	224,234	167,429	FRANKLIN, SCOTT*			56,805	167,429 R	74.7%		100.0%	
18	2020**	449,720	253,286	MAST, BRIAN*	186,674	KEITH, PAMELA "PAM"	9,760	66,612 R	56.3%	41.5%	57.6%	42.4%
18	2018**	342,359	185,905	MAST, BRIAN*	156,454	BAER, LAUREN		29,451 R	54.3%	45.7%	54.3%	45.7%
18	2016**	375,918	201,488	MAST, BRIAN	161,918	PERKINS, RANDY	12,512	39,570 R	53.6%	43.1%	55.4%	44.6%
18	2014	253,374	101,896	DOMINO, CARL J.	151,478	MURPHY, PATRICK*		49,582 D	40.2%	59.8%	40.2%	59.8%
18	2012	330,665	164,353	WEST, ALLEN*	166,257	MURPHY, PATRICK	55	1,904 D	49.7%	50.3%	49.7%	50.3%
19	2022	313,274	213,035	DONALDS, BYRON*	100,226	BANYAI, CINDY LYN	13	112,809 R	68.0%	32.0%	68.0%	32.0%
19	2020	444,589	272,440	DONALDS, BYRON	172,146	BANYAI, CINDY LYN	3	100,294 R	61.3%	38.7%	61.3%	38.7%
19	2018	339,607	211,465	ROONEY, FRANCIS*	128,106	HOLDEN, DAVID	36	83,359 R	62.3%	37.7%	62.3%	37.7%
19	2016	363,166	239,225	ROONEY, FRANCIS	123,812	NEELD, ROBERT M.	129	115,413 R	65.9%	34.1%	65.9%	34.1%
19	2014	246,861	159,354	CLAWSON, CURT J.*	80,824	FREEMAN, APRIL	6,683	78,530 R	64.6%	32.7%	66.3%	33.7%
19	2012	306,216	189,833	RADEL, TREY	109,746	ROACH, JIM	6,637	80,087 R	62.0%	35.8%	63.4%	36.6%
20	2022	188,366	52,151	CLARK, DREW MONTEZ	136,215	CHERFILUS-MCCORMICK, SHEILA*		84,064 D	27.7%	72.3%	27.7%	72.3%
20	2020**	322,409	68,748	MUSSELWHITE, GREG	253,661	HASTINGS, ALCEE L.*		184,913 D	21.3%	78.7%	21.3%	78.7%
20	2018**	202,824			202,659	HASTINGS, ALCEE L.*	165	202,659 D		99.9%		100.0%
20	2016**	277,560	54,646	STEIN, GARY	222,914	HASTINGS, ALCEE L.*		168,268 D	19.7%	80.3%	19.7%	80.3%
20	2014	157,466	28,968	BONNER, JAY	128,498	HASTINGS, ALCEE L.*		99,530 D	18.4%	81.6%	18.4%	81.6%
20	2012	244,285			214,727	HASTINGS, ALCEE L.*	29,558	214,727 D		87.9%		100.0%
21	2022	328,505	208,614	MAST, BRIAN*	119,891	BALDERRAMOS ROBINSON, CORINNA		88,723 R	63.5%	36.5%	63.5%	36.5%
21	2020**	403,093	157,612	LOOMER, LAURA	237,925	FRANKEL, LOIS*	7,556	80,313 D	39.1%	59.0%	39.8%	60.2%
21	2018**		Unopposed			FRANKEL, LOIS*						
21	2016**	335,861	118,038	SPAIN, PAUL DOUGLAS	210,606	FRANKEL, LOIS	7,217	92,568 D	35.1%	62.7%	35.9%	64.1%
21	2014	153,970			153,395	DEUTCH, TED*	575	153,395 D		99.6%		100.0%
21	2012	284,400			221,263	DEUTCH, TED*	63,137	221,263 D		77.8%		100.0%
22	2022	272,204	122,194	FRANZESE, DAN	150,010	FRANKEL, LOIS*		27,816 D	44.9%	55.1%	44.9%	55.1%
22	2020**	402,317	166,553	PRUDEN, JAMES "JIM"	235,764	DEUTCH, TED*		69,211 D	41.4%	58.6%	41.4%	58.6%
22	2018**	297,683	113,049	KIMAZ, NICHOLAS	184,634	DEUTCH, TED*		71,585 D	38.0%	62.0%	38.0%	62.0%
22	2016**	337,850	138,737	MCGEE, ANDREA LEIGH	199,113	DEUTCH, TED		60,376 D	41.1%	58.9%	41.1%	58.9%
22	2014	216,096	90,685	SPAIN, PAUL DOUGLAS	125,404	FRANKEL, LOIS*	7	34,719 D	42.0%	58.0%	42.0%	58.0%
22	2012	313,071	142,050	HASNER, ADAM	171,021	FRANKEL, LOIS		28,971 D	45.4%	54.6%	45.4%	54.6%

FLORIDA
HOUSE OF REPRESENTATIVES

CD	Year	Total Vote	Republican Vote	Republican Candidate	Democratic Vote	Democratic Candidate	Other Vote	Rep.-Dem. Plurality	Total Vote Rep.	Total Vote Dem.	Major Vote Rep.	Major Vote Dem.
23	2022	279,049	130,681	BUDD, JOE	143,951	MOSKOWITZ, JARED	4,417	13,270 D	46.8%	51.6%	47.6%	52.4%
23	2020**	380,196	158,874	SPALDING, CARLA	221,239	WASSERMAN-SCHULTZ, DEBBIE*	83	62,365 D	41.8%	58.2%	41.8%	58.2%
23	2018**	276,366	99,446	KAUFMAN, JOSEPH "JOE"	161,611	WASSERMAN-SCHULTZ, DEBBIE*	15,309	62,165 D	36.0%	58.5%	38.1%	61.9%
23	2016**	323,120	130,818	KAUFMAN, JOSEPH "JOE"	183,225	WASSERMAN-SCHULTZ, DEBBIE*	9,077	52,407 D	40.5%	56.7%	41.7%	58.3%
23	2014	164,788	61,519	KAUFMAN, JOSEPH "JOE"	103,269	WASSERMAN-SCHULTZ, DEBBIE*		41,750 D	37.3%	62.7%	37.3%	62.7%
23	2012	275,430	98,096	HARRINGTON, KAREN	174,205	WASSERMAN-SCHULTZ, DEBBIE*	3,129	76,109 D	35.6%	63.2%	36.0%	64.0%
24	2022	185,891	52,449	NAVARRO, JESUS G.	133,442	WILSON, FREDERICA S.*		80,993 D	28.2%	71.8%	28.2%	71.8%
24	2020**	289,638	59,084	SPICER, LAVERN	218,825	WILSON, FREDERICA S.*	11,729	159,741 D	20.4%	75.6%	21.3%	78.7%
24	2018**		Unopposed			WILSON, FREDERICA S.*						
24	2016**		Unopposed			WILSON, FREDERICA S.*						
24	2014	149,918	15,239	NEREE, DUFIRSTSON	129,192	WILSON, FREDERICA S.*	5,487	113,953 D	10.2%	86.2%	10.6%	89.4%
24	2012		Unopposed			WILSON, FREDERICA S.						
25	2022	234,352	105,239	SPALDING, CARLA	129,113	WASSERMAN-SCHULTZ, DEBBIE*		23,874 D	44.9%	55.1%	44.9%	55.1%
25	2020**		Unopposed	DIAZ-BALART, MARIO*								
25	2018**	212,845	128,672	DIAZ-BALART, MARIO*	84,173	FLORES, MARY BARZEE		44,499 R	60.5%	39.5%	60.5%	39.5%
25	2016**	253,240	157,921	DIAZ-BALART, MARIO*	95,319	VALDES, ALINA		62,602 R	62.4%	37.6%	62.4%	37.6%
25	2014		Unopposed	DIAZ-BALART, MARIO*								
25	2012	200,229	151,466	DIAZ-BALART, MARIO*			48,763	151,466 R	75.6%		100.0%	
26	2022	202,108	143,240	DIAZ-BALART, MARIO*	58,868	OLIVO, CHRISTINE ALEXANDRIA		84,372 R	70.9%	29.1%	70.9%	29.1%
26	2020**	342,630	177,223	GIMENEZ, CARLOS	165,407	MUCARSEL-POWELL, DEBBIE*		11,816 R	51.7%	48.3%	51.7%	48.3%
26	2018**	235,475	115,678	CURBELO, CARLOS*	119,797	MUCARSEL-POWELL, DEBBIE		4,119 D	49.1%	50.9%	49.1%	50.9%
26	2016**	280,542	148,547	CURBELO, CARLOS*	115,493	GARCIA, JOE	16,502	33,054 R	53.0%	41.2%	56.3%	43.7%
26	2014	161,337	83,031	CURBELO, CARLOS	78,306	GARCIA, JOE*		4,725 R	51.5%	48.5%	51.5%	48.5%
26	2012	252,957	108,820	RIVERA, DAVID*	135,694	GARCIA, JOE	8,443	26,874 D	43.0%	53.6%	44.5%	55.5%
27	2022	237,442	136,038	SALAZAR, MARIA ELVIRA*	101,404	TADDEO, ANNETTE		34,634 R	57.3%	42.7%	57.3%	42.7%
27	2020**	342,975	176,141	SALAZAR, MARIA ELVIRA	166,758	SHALALA, DONNA*	76	9,383 R	51.4%	48.6%	51.4%	48.6%
27	2018**	252,586	115,588	SALAZAR, MARIA ELVIRA	130,743	SHALALA, DONNA	6,255	15,155 D	45.8%	51.8%	46.9%	53.1%
27	2016**	287,677	157,917	ROS-LEHTINEN, ILEANA*	129,760	FUHRMAN, SCOTT		28,157 R	54.9%	45.1%	54.9%	45.1%
27	2014		Unopposed	ROS-LEHTINEN, ILEANA*								
27	2012	230,171	138,488	ROS-LEHTINEN, ILEANA*	85,020	YEVANCEY, MANNY	6,663	53,468 R	60.2%	36.9%	62.0%	38.0%
28	2022	211,150	134,457	GIMENEZ, CARLOS*	76,665	ASENCIO, ROBERT	28	57,792 R	63.7%	36.3%	63.7%	36.3%
TOTAL	2022	7,332,304	4,271,196		2,905,702		155,406	1,365,494 R	58.3%	39.6%	59.5%	40.5%
TOTAL	2020	10,464,791	5,469,164		4,942,287		53,340	526,877 R	52.3%	47.2%	52.5%	47.5%
TOTAL	2018	7,021,476	3,675,417		3,307,228		38,831	368,189 R	52.3%	47.1%	52.6%	47.4%
TOTAL	2016	8,837,426	4,733,630		3,985,050		118,746	748,580 R	53.6%	45.1%	54.3%	45.7%
TOTAL	2014	4,998,555	2,713,451		2,130,626		154,478	582,825 R	54.3%	42.6%	56.0%	44.0%
TOTAL	2012	7,513,539	3,826,522		3,392,402		294,615	434,120 R	50.9%	45.2%	53.0%	47.0%

Note: An asterisk (*) denotes incumbent.

FLORIDA

GENERAL AND PRIMARY ELECTIONS

GENERAL ELECTIONS: OTHER VOTES

Governor	Other vote was 31,577 No party Affiliation (Carmen Gimenez), 19,299 Libertarian (Hector Roos)
Senate	Other vote was 32,177 Libertarian (Dennis Misigoy), 31,816 No Party Affiliation (Steven Grant), 17,385 No Party Affiliation (Tuan Nguyen), 267 Write-In (Write-In)
House	Other vote was:
CD 3	3,410 No Party Affiliation (Linda Brooks)
CD 4	5 Write-In (Gary Koniz)
CD 6	74,207 Libertarian (Joseph Hannoush)
CD 7	10 Write-In (Cardon Pompey)
CD 10	2,001 No Party Affiliation (Jason Holic), 1,110 No Party Affiliation (Usha Jain)
CD 11	4,967 No Party Affiliation (Kevin Porter)
CD 12	4 Write-In (Charles Smith)
CD 13	6,163 Libertarian (Frank Craft), 17 Write-In (Dwight Young), 3 Write-In (Jacob Curnow)
CD 16	21 Write-In (Ralph Hartman)
CD 17	2,225 No Party Affiliation (Theodore Murray)
CD 18	56,647 No Party Affiliation (Keith Hayden), 158 Write-In (Leonard Serratore)
CD 19	13 Write-In (Patrick Post)
CD 23	3,079 No Party Affiliation (Christine Scott), 1,338 No Party Affiliation (Mark Napier)
CD 28	28 Write-In (Jeremiah Schaffer)

2022 PRIMARY ELECTIONS: SUPPLEMENTARY INFORMATION

Primary	August 23, 2022	**Registration** (as of July 31, 2022)	14,325,606	Republican	5,194,845
				Democratic	4,963,930
				Other Parties	257,491
				No Party Affiliation	3,909,340

Primary Type Closed—Only registered Democrats and Republicans could vote in their party's primary, with the exception of races where there were to be no other candidates (including write-ins) on the general election ballot. Then, the contested primary would be open to all voters.

FLORIDA

GENERAL AND PRIMARY ELECTIONS

	REPUBLICAN PRIMARIES	DEMOCRATIC PRIMARIES		
Senator		Demings, Val B.	1,263,706	84.3%
		Rush, Brian	94,185	6.3%
		Sanchez, William	84,576	5.6%
		De La Fuente, Ricardo	56,749	3.8%
		TOTAL	*1,499,216*	
Governor		Crist, Charlie	904,524	59.7%
		Fried, Nicole "Nikki"	535,480	35.3%
		Daniel, Cadence	38,198	2.5%
		Wilis, Robert L.	36,786	2.4%
		TOTAL	*1,514,988*	

FLORIDA

GENERAL AND PRIMARY ELECTIONS

	REPUBLICAN PRIMARIES			DEMOCRATIC PRIMARIES		
Congressional District 1	Gaetz, Matt*	73,374	69.7%	Jones, Rebekah	21,875	62.6%
	Lombardo, Mark	25,720	24.4%	Schiller, Margaret "Peggy"	13,091	37.4%
	Merk, Gregory Charles	6,170	5.9%			
	TOTAL	105,264		TOTAL	34,966	
Congressional District 2						
Congressional District 3	Cammack, Kat*	63,279	85.2%	Hawk, Danielle	37,181	67.6%
	Waters, Justin	11,022	14.8%	Wells, Tom	17,799	32.4%
	TOTAL	74,301		TOTAL	54,980	
Congressional District 4	Bean, Aaron	49,060	68.1%	Holloway, LaShonda "L.J."	29,352	50.2%
	Aguilar, Erick Javier	18,605	25.8%	Hill, Anthony "Tony"	29,145	49.8%
	Chuba, Jon	4,388	6.1%			
	TOTAL	72,053		TOTAL	58,497	
Congressional District 5	Rutherford, John*	87,720	65.7%			
	Macie, Mara H.	23,607	17.7%			
	Lopez, Leigha "Luna"	22,283	16.7%			
	TOTAL	133,610				
Congressional District 6	Waltz, Michael*	65,694	77.4%			
	Davis, Charles E.	19,175	22.6%			
	TOTAL	84,869				
Congressional District 7	Mills, Cory	27,757	37.9%	Green, Karen	23,051	44.9%
	Sabatini, Anthony	17,332	23.7%	Krulick, Al	10,787	21.0%
	Duke, Brady	11,221	15.3%	Fernandez, Hilsia "Tatiana"	10,261	20.0%
	Edwards, Ted	4,259	5.8%	Pastrana, Allek	7,289	14.2%
	Roberts, Russell "Rusty"	4,031	5.5%			
	Benfield, Erika	3,964	5.4%			
	Sturgill, Scott	3,094	4.2%			
	Santos, Al	1,504	2.1%			
	TOTAL	73,162		TOTAL	51,388	
Congressional District 8				Terry, Joanne	29,542	54.6%
				Dodge, Danelle	24,592	45.4%
				TOTAL	54,134	
Congressional District 9	Moore, Scotty	16,971	55.9%			
	Castillo, Jose Alfredo	7,537	24.8%			
	Morales, Adianis	3,969	13.1%			
	Ortiz, Sergio E.	1,900	6.3%			
	TOTAL	30,377				
Congressional District 10	Wimbish, Calvin B.	121,030	88.9%	Frost, Maxwell Alejandro	19,288	34.8%
	Le, Tuan	3,601	2.6%	Bracy, Randolph	13,677	24.7%
	Weed, Peter	3,541	2.6%	Grayson, Alan	8,526	15.4%
	Lowe, Thuy "Twee"	3,201	2.4%	Brown, Corrine	5,274	9.5%
	Montague, Willie	3,176	2.3%	Jackson, Natalie	3,872	7.0%
	Jones, Lateresa	1,614	1.2%	Tachon, Teresa	1,301	2.3%
				Boone, Jeffrey	1,181	2.1%
				Gray, Terence R.	1,032	1.9%
				Achenbach, Jack	714	1.3%
				Muneer, Khalid	604	1.1%
	TOTAL	136,163		TOTAL	55,469	
Congressional District 11	Webster, Daniel A.*	43,469	51.0%			
	Loomer, Laura	37,647	44.2%			
	Soriano, Gavriel E.	4,072	4.8%			
	TOTAL	85,188				

FLORIDA

GENERAL AND PRIMARY ELECTIONS

	REPUBLICAN PRIMARIES			DEMOCRATIC PRIMARIES		
Congressional District 12	Bilirakis, Gus Michael*	67,189	79.7%			
	Martin, Jack	7,790	9.2%			
	Leiser, Chris	4,000	4.7%			
	Perras, Brian	3,217	3.8%			
	Preskitt, Sif	2,142	2.5%			
	TOTAL	84,338				
Congressional District 13	Paulina Luna, Anna	37,156	44.5%			
	Hayslett, Kevin	28,108	33.6%			
	Makki, Amanda	14,159	17.0%			
	Quinn, Christine	2,510	3.0%			
	Kheireddine, Moneer	1,599	1.9%			
	TOTAL	83,532				
Congressional District 14	Judge, James	20,466	53.1%	Castor, Kathy*	62,562	90.3%
	Torres, Jerry	11,398	29.6%	Bradley, Christopher	6,684	9.7%
	Nashagh, Samar "Sam"	6,650	17.3%			
	TOTAL	38,514		TOTAL	69,246	
Congressional District 15	Lee, Laurel	22,481	41.5%	Cohn, Alan Michael	14,928	33.1%
	Stargel, Kelli	15,072	27.8%	Brown, Gavin	10,034	22.3%
	Toledo, Jackie	6,307	11.6%	Geller, Eddie	9,859	21.9%
	Grimes, Demetries Andrew	5,629	10.4%	Ramirez, Cesar	7,817	17.3%
	McGovern, Kevin "Mac"	4,713	8.7%	Vanhorn, William	2,435	5.4%
	TOTAL	54,202		TOTAL	45,073	
Congressional District 16	Buchanan, Vern*	64,028	86.2%			
	Hyde, Martin	10,219	13.8%			
	TOTAL	74,247				
Congressional District 17						
Congressional District 18	Franklin, Scott*	44,927	73.1%			
	Raybon, Jennifer	6,606	10.7%			
	Schmeling, Wendy June	4,099	6.7%			
	Hartpence, Kenneth James "Kenny"	3,999	6.5%			
	Tarazona, Eduardo G. "Eddie"	1,864	3.0%			
	TOTAL	61,495				
Congressional District 19	Donalds, Byron	76,192	83.7%			
	Huff, Jim	14,795	16.3%			
	TOTAL	90,987				
Congressional District 20				Cherfilus-McCormick, Sheila*	47,601	65.6%
				Holness, Dale V.C.	20,783	28.6%
				Omphroy, Anika	4,197	5.8%
				TOTAL	72,581	
Congressional District 21	Mast, Brian*	56,535	78.1%			
	Buongiorno, Jeffrey	8,850	12.2%			
	Martz, Melissa	6,186	8.5%			
	Skrbic, Ljubo	853	1.2%			
	TOTAL	72,424				
Congressional District 22	Franzese, Dan	11,972	34.7%			
	Adeimy, Deborah	11,842	34.3%			
	Dorilas, Rod	6,594	19.1%			
	Arianas, Peter Steven	2,082	6.0%			
	Lawlor, Carrie	2,055	5.9%			
	TOTAL	34,545				

FLORIDA

GENERAL AND PRIMARY ELECTIONS

	REPUBLICAN PRIMARIES			DEMOCRATIC PRIMARIES		
Congressional District 23	Budd, Joe	12,592	37.6%	Moskowitz, Jared	38,822	61.1%
	Pruden, James "Jim"	7,399	22.1%	Sorensen, Ben	13,012	20.5%
	Swaffar, Darlene	3,872	11.6%	Holzhauer, Hava	5,276	8.3%
	McLaughlin, Christy	3,832	11.4%	Ellison, Allen	3,960	6.2%
	Chess, Steven	2,840	8.5%	Trout, W. Michael "Mike"	1,390	2.2%
	Weinstein, Ira	2,297	6.9%	Hamilton, Michaelangelo Collins	1,064	1.7%
	Perrone, Myles	639	1.9%			
	TOTAL	33,471		TOTAL	63,524	
Congressional District 24	Navarro, Jesus G.	6,373	64.5%	Wilson, Frederica S.*	56,776	89.3%
	Spicer, Lavern	3,506	35.5%	Harris, Kevin Corey	6,816	10.7%
	TOTAL	9,879		TOTAL	63,592	
Congressional District 25	Spalding, Carla	16,425	71.6%	Wasserman-Schultz, Debbie*	50,554	89.0%
	Young, Rubin	6,511	28.4%	Millwee, Robert	6,241	11.0%
	TOTAL	22,936		TOTAL	56,795	
Congressional District 26	Diaz-Balart, Mario*	36,861	84.3%			
	Aquino, Darren Dione	6,885	15.7%			
	TOTAL	43,746				
Congressional District 27	Salazar, Maria Elvira*	33,760	80.8%	Taddeo, Annette	27,015	67.8%
	Polo, Frank E.	8,023	19.2%	Russell, Ken	10,337	25.9%
				Montalvo, Angel	2,493	6.3%
	TOTAL	41,783		TOTAL	39,845	
Congressional District 28	Gimenez, Carlos	28,762	73.4%	Asencio, Robert	18,504	69.2%
	Garin, Carlos	6,048	15.4%	Paredes, Juan	8,217	30.8%
	Miller, K.W.	4,395	11.2%			
	TOTAL	39,205		TOTAL	26,721	

Note: An asterisk (*) denotes incumbent.

GEORGIA

Statewide Races

In 2018, Donald Trump endorsed then-Secretary of State Brian Kemp in Georgia's open-seat gubernatorial race. In a nationally watched contest, Kemp defeated Democrat Stacey Abrams. But in office, Kemp clashed with Trump on multiple occasions, most notably by refusing to help Trump subvert the results of the 2020 election in his state. With Trump's backing, former Sen. David Perdue challenged Kemp in the primary – but he went nowhere. Kemp won renomination by 52 points and carried every county. Trump had better luck in the Senate primary: his choice, retired professional football player Herschel Walker, easily won the nomination. On the Democratic side, Sen. Raphael Warnock ran for a full term and Abrams tried for a rematch against Kemp.

With Kemp's incumbency – and the fact that he was perceived to be "free" of Trump – Abrams struggled to gain traction. Kemp was reelected with 53%. Compared to their first bout, Kemp flipped several rural counties. Though he didn't entirely set the clock back, his metropolitan numbers were also impressive for a Trump-era Republican. In 2012, Cobb and Gwinnett counties, a pair of fast-growing suburban counties on either side of Atlanta, aggregately gave Republican Mitt Romney 55%, but by 2020, Trump slid to just 41% – Kemp got that number back up to 46%.

In the Senate race, Warnock ran a top-tier campaign while Walker was weighed down by personal baggage. On Election Day, Warnock finished first, but with just under 50%, forcing a runoff, which he won by three points. In suburban Atlanta, Walker ran markedly behind Kemp – in the aforementioned Cobb County, he took just 40% in the runoff. South of Atlanta, Warnock came within a point of flipping Fayette County, a historically GOP-leaning suburban area. Compared to his initial election, in a 2021 runoff, Warnock slid in much of rural Georgia, but he carried the exact same 30 counties.

House Races

Despite Georgia's overall pro-Democratic trend, Republicans controlled the legislature after 2020. For 2012, Georgia Republicans drew a 14-seat map that was meant to elect ten Republicans and four Democrats. But later in the decade, districts 6 and 7, both in Atlanta's northern suburbs, flipped from red to blue – Democrats claimed the former in 2018 and the latter in 2020. The trends in the 6th District were especially rapid: eight years after it gave Romney 61%, in 2012, Joe Biden carried it by 11 points.

The Republicans' solution was to take back the 6th District while conceding the 7th District. The 6th District was redrawn to include all of Forsyth County – though GOP margins have lessened there, Democrats usually struggled to break 35%. The new 6th District elected Republican Rich McCormick in a landslide. Meanwhile, 7th District Democratic Rep. Carolyn Bourdeaux lost a primary to Lucy McBath, the displaced 6th District incumbent. In the general election, McBath had no trouble winning this Gwinnett County-based seat.

The sole Democratic seat outside of metro Atlanta is the southwestern 2nd District – with a rural flavor, it includes Plains, the hometown of Georgia's most beloved son, Jimmy Carter. Republicans didn't get their preferred nominee against veteran Democrat Sanford Bishop, who won with 55%.

In addition to flipping the reconfigured 6th District, Republicans easily held the eight other Trump-won seats on the map.

GEORGIA

Congressional districts first established for elections held in 2022

14 members

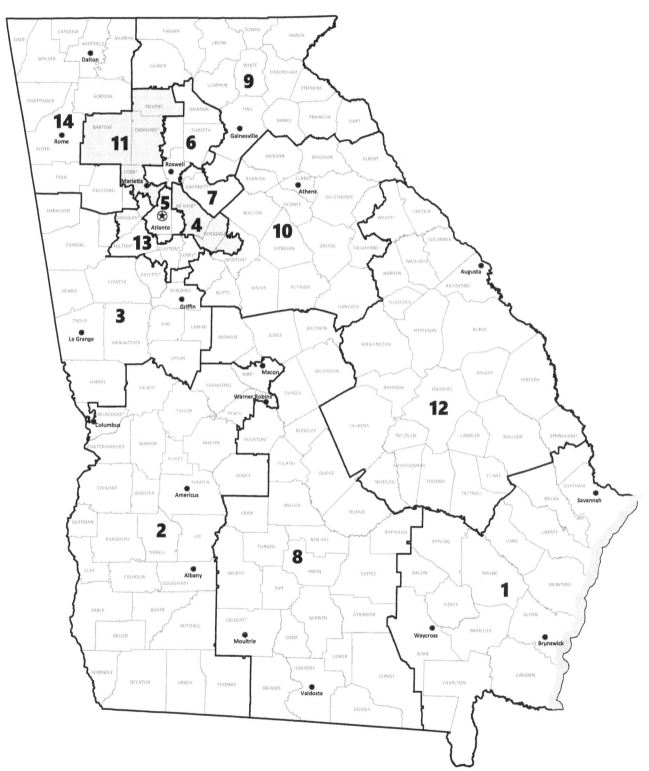

* Asterisk indicates a county whose boundaries include parts of two or more congressional districts.

CDs 4 and 11 are highlighted for visibility. See Inset for Atlanta area.

GEORGIA

Greater Atlanta Area

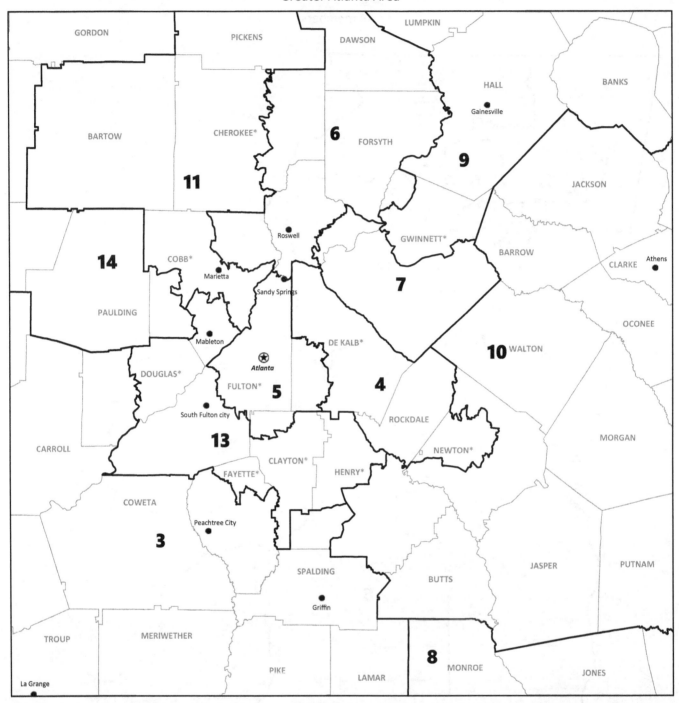

* Asterisk indicates a county whose boundaries include parts of two or more congressional districts.

GEORGIA

GOVERNOR
Brian Kemp (R). Reelected 2022 to a four-year term. Previously elected 2018.

SENATORS (2 Democrats)
Raphael Warnock (D). Reelected 2022 to a six-year term. Elected 2021 in a special election runoff to complete the term of Johnny Isakson (R), who resigned December 31, 2019, due to health concerns. The governor had appointed Kelly Loeffler (R) to the seat on December 4, 2019, until the special election could be held.

Jon Ossoff (D). Elected 2021 in a special election runoff for a six-year term.

REPRESENTATIVES (9 Republicans, 5 Democrats)
1. Earl Leroy "Buddy" Carter (R)
2. Sanford Bishop (D)
3. Drew Ferguson (R)
4. Henry C. "Hank" Johnson (D)
5. Nikema Williams (D)
6. Richard McCormick (R)
7. Lucy McBath (D)
8. Austin Scott (R)
9. Andrew Clyde (R)
10. Mike Collins (R)
11. Barry Loudermilk (R)
12. Rick W. Allen (R)
13. David Scott (D)
14. Marjorie Taylor Greene (R)

POSTWAR VOTE FOR PRESIDENT

		Republican		Democratic		Other Vote	Rep.-Dem. Plurality	Total Vote		Major Vote	
Year	Total Vote	Vote	Candidate	Vote	Candidate			Rep.	Dem.	Rep.	Dem.
2020	4,999,960	2,461,854	Trump, Donald J.*	2,473,633	Biden, Joseph R. Jr.	64,473	11,779 D	49.2%	49.5%	49.9%	50.1%
2016**	4,114,732	2,089,104	Trump, Donald J.	1,877,963	Clinton, Hillary Rodham	147,665	211,141 R	50.8%	45.6%	52.7%	47.3%
2012	3,900,050	2,078,688	Romney, W. Mitt	1,773,827	Obama, Barack H.*	47,535	304,861 R	53.3%	45.5%	54.0%	46.0%
2008	3,924,486	2,048,759	McCain, John S. III	1,844,123	Obama, Barack H.	31,604	204,636 R	52.2%	47.0%	52.6%	47.4%
2004	3,301,875	1,914,254	Bush, George W.*	1,366,149	Kerry, John F.	21,472	548,105 R	58.0%	41.4%	58.4%	41.6%
2000**	2,596,645	1,419,720	Bush, George W.	1,116,230	Gore, Albert Jr.	60,695	303,490 R	54.7%	43.0%	56.0%	44.0%
1996**	2,299,071	1,080,843	Dole, Robert "Bob"	1,053,849	Clinton, Bill*	164,379	26,994 R	47.0%	45.8%	50.6%	49.4%
1992**	2,321,125	995,252	Bush, George H.*	1,008,966	Clinton, Bill	316,907	13,714 D	42.9%	43.5%	49.7%	50.3%
1988	1,812,672	1,081,331	Bush, George H.	717,792	Dukakis, Michael S.	13,549	363,539 R	59.7%	39.6%	60.1%	39.9%
1984	1,776,120	1,068,722	Reagan, Ronald*	706,628	Mondale, Walter F.	770	362,094 R	60.2%	39.8%	60.2%	39.8%
1980**	1,596,695	654,168	Reagan, Ronald	890,733	Carter, Jimmy*	51,794	236,565 D	41.0%	55.8%	42.3%	57.7%
1976	1,467,458	483,743	Ford, Gerald R.*	979,409	Carter, Jimmy	4,306	495,666 D	33.0%	66.7%	33.1%	66.9%
1972	1,174,772	881,496	Nixon, Richard M.*	289,529	McGovern, George S.	3,747	591,967 R	75.0%	24.6%	75.3%	24.7%
1968**	1,250,266	380,111	Nixon, Richard M.	334,440	Humphrey, Hubert Horatio Jr.	535,715	45,671 R#	30.4%	26.7%	53.2%	46.8%
1964	1,139,335	616,584	Goldwater, Barry M. Sr.	522,556	Johnson, Lyndon B.*	195	94,028 R	54.1%	45.9%	54.1%	45.9%
1960	733,349	274,472	Nixon, Richard M.	458,638	Kennedy, John F.	239	184,166 D	37.4%	62.5%	37.4%	62.6%
1956	669,655	222,778	Eisenhower, Dwight D.*	444,688	Stevenson, Adlai E. II	2,189	221,910 D	33.3%	66.4%	33.4%	66.6%
1952	655,785	198,961	Eisenhower, Dwight D.	456,823	Stevenson, Adlai E. II	1	257,862 D	30.3%	69.7%	30.3%	69.7%
1948**	418,844	76,691	Dewey, Thomas E.	254,646	Truman, Harry S.*	87,507	177,955 D	18.3%	60.8%	23.1%	76.9%

Note: An asterisk (*) denotes incumbent. A pound sign (#) in the plurality column indicates that the winner in 1968 did not run under the banner of either major party. **In past elections, the other vote included: 2016-125,306 Libertarian (Gary Johnson); 2000 -13,273 Green (Ralph Nader); 1996 -146,337 Reform (Ross Perot); 1992 - 309,657 Independent (Perot); 1980 - 36,055 Independent (John Anderson); 1968 - 535,550 American Independent (George Wallace); 1948 - 85,135 States' Rights (Strom Thurmond, who placed second statewide). Wallace carried Georgia in 1968 with 42.8 percent of the vote.

GEORGIA

POSTWAR VOTE FOR GOVERNOR

Year	Total Vote	Republican Vote	Republican Candidate	Democratic Vote	Democratic Candidate	Other Vote	Rep.-Dem. Plurality	Total Vote Rep.	Total Vote Dem.	Major Vote Rep.	Major Vote Dem.
2022	3,953,408	2,111,572	Kemp, Brian*	1,813,673	Abrams, Stacey	28,163	297,899 R	53.4%	45.9%	53.8%	46.2%
2018	3,939,409	1,978,408	Kemp, Brian	1,923,685	Abrams, Stacey	37,316	54,723 R	50.2%	48.8%	50.7%	49.3%
2014	2,550,648	1,345,237	Deal, Nathan*	1,144,794	Carter, Jason J.	60,617	200,443 R	52.7%	44.9%	54.0%	46.0%
2010	2,576,161	1,365,832	Deal, Nathan	1,107,011	Barnes, Roy E.	103,318	258,821 R	53.0%	43.0%	55.2%	44.8%
2006	2,122,258	1,229,724	Perdue, Sonny*	811,049	Taylor, Mark	81,485	418,675 R	57.9%	38.2%	60.3%	39.7%
2002	2,027,177	1,041,700	Perdue, Sonny	937,070	Barnes, Roy E.*	48,407	104,630 R	51.4%	46.2%	52.6%	47.4%
1998	1,792,808	790,201	Millner, Guy	941,076	Barnes, Roy E.	61,531	150,875 D	44.1%	52.5%	45.6%	54.4%
1994	1,545,328	756,371	Millner, Guy	788,926	Miller, Zell*	31	32,555 D	48.9%	51.1%	48.9%	51.1%
1990	1,449,682	645,625	Isakson, Johnny	766,662	Miller, Zell	37,395	121,037 D	44.5%	52.9%	45.7%	54.3%
1986	1,175,114	346,512	Davis, Guy	828,465	Harris, Joe Frank*	137	481,953 D	29.5%	70.5%	29.5%	70.5%
1982	1,169,043	434,496	Bell, Robert H.	734,092	Harris, Joe Frank	455	299,596 D	37.2%	62.8%	37.2%	62.8%
1978	662,862	128,139	Cook, Rodney M.	534,572	Busbee, George*	151	406,433 D	19.3%	80.6%	19.3%	80.7%
1974	936,438	289,113	Thompson, Ronnie	646,777	Busbee, George	548	357,664 D	30.9%	69.1%	30.9%	69.1%
1970	1,046,663	424,983	Suit, Hal	620,419	Carter, Jimmy	1,261	195,436 D	40.6%	59.3%	40.7%	59.3%
1966**	975,019	453,665	Callaway, Howard H.	450,626	Maddox, Lester	70,728	3,039 R	46.5%	46.2%	50.2%	49.8%
1962	311,691			311,524	Sanders, Carl E.	167	311,524 D		99.9%		100.0%
1958	168,497			168,414	Vandiver, S. Ernest	83	168,414 D		100.0%		100.0%
1954	331,966			331,899	Griffin, S. Marvin	67	331,899 D		100.0%		100.0%
1950	234,430			230,771	Talmadge, Herman E.*	3,659	230,771 D		98.4%		100.0%
1948S**	363,764			354,712	Talmadge, Herman E.	9,052	354,712 D		97.5%		100.0%
1946	146,191			144,067	Talmadge, Eugene	2,124	144,067 D		98.5%		100.0%

Note: An asterisk (*) denotes incumbent. **In 1966 in the absence of a majority for any candidate, the State Legislature elected Democrat Lester Maddox to a four-year term. The 1948 election was for a short term to fill a vacancy. The Republican Party did not run a candidate in the 1946, 1948, 1950, 1954, 1958, and 1962 gubernatorial elections.

GEORGIA

POSTWAR VOTE FOR SENATOR

Year	Total Vote	Republican Vote	Republican Candidate	Democratic Vote	Democratic Candidate	Other Vote	Rep.-Dem. Plurality	Total Vote Rep.	Total Vote Dem.	Major Vote Rep.	Major Vote Dem.
2022**	3,935,924	1,908,442	Walker, Herschel	1,946,117	Warnock, Raphael*	81,365	37,675 D	48.5%	49.4%	49.5%	50.5%
2022**	3,541,877	1,721,244	Walker, Herschel	1,820,633	Warnock, Raphael*		99,389 D	48.6%	51.4%	48.6%	51.4%
2021S**	4,484,954	2,195,841	Loeffler, Kelly*	2,289,113	Warnock, Raphael		93,272 D	49.0%	51.0%	49.0%	51.0%
2021**	4,484,902	2,214,979	Perdue, David A.*	2,269,923	Ossoff, Jon		54,944 D	49.4%	50.6%	49.4%	50.6%
2020S**	4,914,361	1,273,214	Loeffler, Kelly*	1,617,035	Warnock, Raphael	2,024,112	47,808 R	49.3%	48.4%	50.5%	49.5%
2020**	4,952,175	2,462,617	Perdue, David A.*	2,374,519	Ossoff, Jon	115,039	88,098 R	49.7%	47.9%	50.9%	49.1%
2016	3,898,605	2,135,806	Isakson, Johnny*	1,599,726	Barksdale, Jim	163,073	536,080 R	54.8%	41.0%	57.2%	42.8%
2014	2,567,805	1,358,088	Perdue, David A.	1,160,811	Nunn, Michelle	48,906	197,277 R	52.9%	45.2%	53.9%	46.1%
2010	2,555,258	1,489,904	Isakson, Johnny*	996,516	Thurmond, Michael	68,838	493,388 R	58.3%	39.0%	59.9%	40.1%
2008**	3,752,485	1,867,097	Chambliss, Saxby*	1,757,393	Martin, Jim	127,995	109,704 R	49.8%	46.8%	51.5%	48.5%
2008**	2,137,956	1,228,033	Chambliss, Saxby*	909,923	Martin, Jim		318,110 R	57.4%	42.6%	57.4%	42.6%
2004	3,220,981	1,864,202	Isakson, Johnny	1,287,690	Majette, Denise L.	69,089	576,512 R	57.9%	40.0%	59.1%	40.9%
2002	2,030,608	1,071,464	Chambliss, Saxby	932,156	Cleland, Max*	26,988	139,308 R	52.8%	45.9%	53.5%	46.5%
2000S**	2,428,510	920,478	Mattingly, Mack F.	1,413,224	Miller, Zell*	94,808	492,746 D	37.9%	58.2%	39.4%	60.6%
1998	1,753,911	918,540	Coverdell, Paul*	791,904	Coles, Michael	43,467	126,636 R	52.4%	45.2%	53.7%	46.3%
1996	2,259,232	1,073,969	Millner, Guy	1,103,993	Cleland, Max	81,270	30,024 D	47.5%	48.9%	49.3%	50.7%
1992**	2,251,587	1,073,282	Coverdell, Paul	1,108,416	Fowler, Wyche Jr.*	69,889	35,134 D	47.7%	49.2%	49.2%	50.8%
1992**	1,253,991	635,114	Coverdell, Paul	618,877	Fowler, Wyche Jr.*		16,237 R	50.6%	49.4%	50.6%	49.4%
1990	1,033,517			1,033,439	Nunn, Sam*	78	1,033,439 D		100.0%		100.0%
1986	1,225,008	601,241	Mattingly, Mack F.*	623,707	Fowler, Wyche Jr.	60	22,466 D	49.1%	50.9%	49.1%	50.9%
1984	1,681,344	337,196	Hicks, John Michael	1,344,104	Nunn, Sam*	44	1,006,908 D	20.1%	79.9%	20.1%	79.9%
1980	1,580,340	803,686	Mattingly, Mack F.	776,143	Talmadge, Herman E.*	511	27,543 R	50.9%	49.1%	50.9%	49.1%
1978	645,164	108,808	Stokes, John W.	536,320	Nunn, Sam*	36	427,512 D	16.9%	83.1%	16.9%	83.1%
1974	874,555	246,866	Johnson, Jerry R.	627,376	Talmadge, Herman E.*	313	380,510 D	28.2%	71.7%	28.2%	71.8%
1972	1,178,708	542,331	Thompson, S. Fletcher	635,970	Nunn, Sam	407	93,639 D	46.0%	54.0%	46.0%	54.0%
1968	1,141,889	256,796	Patton, E. Earl	885,093	Talmadge, Herman E.*		628,297 D	22.5%	77.5%	22.5%	77.5%
1966	631,330			631,002	Russell, Richard Brevard Jr.*	328	631,002 D		99.9%		100.0%
1962	306,250			306,250	Talmadge, Herman E.*		306,250 D		100.0%		100.0%
1960	576,495			576,140	Russell, Richard Brevard Jr.*	355	576,140 D		99.9%		100.0%
1956	541,267			541,094	Talmadge, Herman E.	173	576,140 D		100.0%		100.0%
1954	333,936			333,917	Russell, Richard Brevard Jr.*	19	333,917 D		100.0%		100.0%
1950	261,293			261,290	George, Walter F.*	3	261,290 D		100.0%		100.0%
1948	362,504			362,104	Russell, Richard Brevard Jr.*	400	362,104 D		99.9%		100.0%

Note: An asterisk (*) denotes incumbent. **The 2000 and 2021 special elections were for short terms to fill a vacancy. In 1992, 2008, 2020, and 2022, no candidate drew a majority of the general election vote required by state law, forcing runoff elections. In each case, the general election vote is presented first and the runoff vote second. The runoffs following the 2022 general and special elections were held on June 21, 2022. The 2020 runoff was held on January 5, 2021; the 2008 runoff was held December 2; the 1992 runoff took place on November 24. The 2020 special election other vote includes Republican and Democratic candidates who ran on the same ballot, and they are included in the calculations for plurality and major vote. The Republican Party did not run a candidate in the 1948, 1950, 1954, 1956, 1960, 1962, 1966, and 1990 Senate elections.

GEORGIA
GOVERNOR 2022

2020 Census Population	County	Total Vote	Republican (Kemp)	Democratic (Abrams)	Other	Rep.-Dem. Plurality	Percentage			
							Total Vote		Major Vote	
							Rep.	Dem.	Rep.	Dem.
18,413	APPLING	6,703	5,552	1,131	20	4,421 R	82.8%	16.9%	83.1%	16.9%
8,182	ATKINSON	2,246	1,767	467	12	1,300 R	78.7%	20.8%	79.1%	20.9%
11,177	BACON	3,721	3,312	393	16	2,919 R	89.0%	10.6%	89.4%	10.6%
3,025	BAKER	1,258	755	500	3	255 R	60.0%	39.7%	60.2%	39.8%
44,986	BALDWIN	15,002	7,987	6,913	102	1,074 R	53.2%	46.1%	53.6%	46.4%
19,354	BANKS	7,326	6,651	607	68	6,044 R	90.8%	8.3%	91.6%	8.4%
83,976	BARROW	29,430	21,833	7,309	288	14,524 R	74.2%	24.8%	74.9%	25.1%
108,306	BARTOW	39,997	31,528	8,137	332	23,391 R	78.8%	20.3%	79.5%	20.5%
16,651	BEN HILL	5,118	3,412	1,680	26	1,732 R	66.7%	32.8%	67.0%	33.0%
19,478	BERRIEN	6,019	5,209	772	38	4,437 R	86.5%	12.8%	87.1%	12.9%
153,494	BIBB	54,200	22,396	31,514	290	9,118 D	41.3%	58.1%	41.5%	58.5%
12,938	BLECKLEY	4,805	3,886	883	36	3,003 R	80.9%	18.4%	81.5%	18.5%
19,171	BRANTLEY	5,859	5,416	393	50	5,023 R	92.4%	6.7%	93.2%	6.8%
15,354	BROOKS	5,642	3,644	1,959	39	1,685 R	64.6%	34.7%	65.0%	35.0%
40,081	BRYAN	17,006	12,188	4,676	142	7,512 R	71.7%	27.5%	72.3%	27.7%
80,548	BULLOCH	23,591	16,067	7,352	172	8,715 R	68.1%	31.2%	68.6%	31.4%
22,380	BURKE	8,467	4,685	3,720	62	965 R	55.3%	43.9%	55.7%	44.3%
25,209	BUTTS	9,695	7,223	2,420	52	4,803 R	74.5%	25.0%	74.9%	25.1%
6,180	CALHOUN	1,715	793	919	3	126 D	46.2%	53.6%	46.3%	53.7%
54,907	CAMDEN	17,945	12,494	5,264	187	7,230 R	69.6%	29.3%	70.4%	29.6%
10,840	CANDLER	3,562	2,666	885	11	1,781 R	74.8%	24.8%	75.1%	24.9%
120,634	CARROLL	43,727	32,095	11,258	374	20,837 R	73.4%	25.7%	74.0%	26.0%
67,906	CATOOSA	24,503	20,009	4,255	239	15,754 R	81.7%	17.4%	82.5%	17.5%
13,529	CHARLTON	3,405	2,654	728	23	1,926 R	77.9%	21.4%	78.5%	21.5%
289,676	CHATHAM	106,329	46,593	58,978	758	12,385 D	43.8%	55.5%	44.1%	55.9%
10,969	CHATTAHOOCHEE	1,020	583	427	10	156 R	57.2%	41.9%	57.7%	42.3%
24,828	CHATTOOGA	7,712	6,471	1,192	49	5,279 R	83.9%	15.5%	84.4%	15.6%
260,752	CHEROKEE	120,374	89,322	29,893	1,159	59,429 R	74.2%	24.8%	74.9%	25.1%
128,658	CLARKE	40,316	13,091	26,901	324	13,810 D	32.5%	66.7%	32.7%	67.3%
2,828	CLAY	1,126	570	553	3	17 R	50.6%	49.1%	50.8%	49.2%
293,733	CLAYTON	84,136	11,306	72,399	431	61,093 D	13.4%	86.0%	13.5%	86.5%
6,631	CLINCH	2,114	1,668	433	13	1,235 R	78.9%	20.5%	79.4%	20.6%
761,438	COBB	312,215	147,698	161,872	2,645	14,174 D	47.3%	51.8%	47.7%	52.3%
43,422	COFFEE	11,905	8,818	3,021	66	5,797 R	74.1%	25.4%	74.5%	25.5%
45,819	COLQUITT	·12,598	9,860	2,684	54	7,176 R	78.3%	21.3%	78.6%	21.4%
157,742	COLUMBIA	64,572	43,437	20,617	518	22,820 R	67.3%	31.9%	67.8%	32.2%
17,306	COOK	5,557	4,138	1,387	32	2,751 R	74.5%	25.0%	74.9%	25.1%
149,354	COWETA	63,726	45,376	17,847	503	27,529 R	71.2%	28.0%	71.8%	28.2%
12,449	CRAWFORD	4,835	3,633	1,171	31	2,462 R	75.1%	24.2%	75.6%	24.4%
22,355	CRISP	6,322	4,296	2,013	13	2,283 R	68.0%	31.8%	68.1%	31.9%
16,147	DADE	5,844	4,969	807	68	4,162 R	85.0%	13.8%	86.0%	14.0%
26,411	DAWSON	13,978	12,010	1,827	141	10,183 R	85.9%	13.1%	86.8%	13.2%
26,412	DECATUR	8,883	5,659	3,191	33	2,468 R	63.7%	35.9%	63.9%	36.1%
759,228	DEKALB	298,229	54,522	241,901	1,806	187,379 D	18.3%	81.1%	18.4%	81.6%
20,571	DODGE	6,630	5,087	1,518	25	3,569 R	76.7%	22.9%	77.0%	23.0%
13,370	DOOLY	3,286	1,860	1,416	10	444 R	56.6%	43.1%	56.8%	43.2%
88,673	DOUGHERTY	26,709	8,524	18,091	94	9,567 D	31.9%	67.7%	32.0%	68.0%
147,078	DOUGLAS	52,930	19,719	32,858	353	13,139 D	37.3%	62.1%	37.5%	62.5%
10,176	EARLY	3,908	2,321	1,576	11	745 R	59.4%	40.3%	59.6%	40.4%
4,014	ECHOLS	1,065	956	94	15	862 R	89.8%	8.8%	91.0%	9.0%
64,955	EFFINGHAM	25,398	19,553	5,603	242	13,950 R	77.0%	22.1%	77.7%	22.3%
19,251	ELBERT	7,324	5,369	1,916	39	3,453 R	73.3%	26.2%	73.7%	26.3%
22,756	EMANUEL	7,562	5,505	2,024	33	3,481 R	72.8%	26.8%	73.1%	26.9%
10,671	EVANS	3,361	2,467	882	12	1,585 R	73.4%	26.2%	73.7%	26.3%
26,404	FANNIN	12,637	10,752	1,796	89	8,956 R	85.1%	14.2%	85.7%	14.3%
114,984	FAYETTE	60,346	34,116	25,769	461	8,347 R	56.5%	42.7%	57.0%	43.0%
98,711	FLOYD	32,078	23,930	7,855	293	16,075 R	74.6%	24.5%	75.3%	24.7%
246,592	FORSYTH	102,446	74,116	27,434	896	46,682 R	72.3%	26.8%	73.0%	27.0%
23,468	FRANKLIN	8,739	7,734	948	57	6,786 R	88.5%	10.8%	89.1%	10.9%
1,067,116	FULTON	419,884	128,167	289,085	2,632	160,918 D	30.5%	68.8%	30.7%	69.3%

GEORGIA
GOVERNOR 2022

2020 Census Population	County	Total Vote	Republican (Kemp)	Democratic (Abrams)	Other	Rep.-Dem. Plurality	Percentage Total Vote		Percentage Major Vote	
							Rep.	Dem.	Rep.	Dem.
31,594	GILMER	14,086	11,952	2,010	124	9,942 R	84.9%	14.3%	85.6%	14.4%
2,979	GLASCOCK	1,305	1,211	89	5	1,122 R	92.8%	6.8%	93.2%	6.8%
85,660	GLYNN	33,279	22,245	10,779	255	11,466 R	66.8%	32.4%	67.4%	32.6%
58,167	GORDON	18,907	16,003	2,743	161	13,260 R	84.6%	14.5%	85.4%	14.6%
24,623	GRADY	8,341	5,884	2,422	35	3,462 R	70.5%	29.0%	70.8%	29.2%
18,499	GREENE	10,508	7,402	3,060	46	4,342 R	70.4%	29.1%	70.8%	29.2%
938,995	GWINNETT	299,482	133,076	164,051	2,355	30,975 D	44.4%	54.8%	44.8%	55.2%
45,414	HABERSHAM	16,990	14,513	2,322	155	12,191 R	85.4%	13.7%	86.2%	13.8%
205,525	HALL	73,516	56,573	16,299	644	40,274 R	77.0%	22.2%	77.6%	22.4%
8,475	HANCOCK	3,402	1,073	2,313	16	1,240 D	31.5%	68.0%	31.7%	68.3%
29,955	HARALSON	11,651	10,398	1,166	87	9,232 R	89.2%	10.0%	89.9%	10.1%
35,486	HARRIS	17,039	12,924	4,008	107	8,916 R	75.8%	23.5%	76.3%	23.7%
26,360	HART	10,560	8,426	2,039	95	6,387 R	79.8%	19.3%	80.5%	19.5%
11,988	HEARD	4,463	3,858	568	37	3,290 R	86.4%	12.7%	87.2%	12.8%
236,549	HENRY	95,568	36,392	58,643	533	22,251 D	38.1%	61.4%	38.3%	61.7%
158,726	HOUSTON	59,210	34,842	23,928	440	10,914 R	58.8%	40.4%	59.3%	40.7%
9,500	IRWIN	3,418	2,695	702	21	1,993 R	78.8%	20.5%	79.3%	20.7%
73,881	JACKSON	31,881	26,223	5,420	238	20,803 R	82.3%	17.0%	82.9%	17.1%
14,302	JASPER	6,574	5,237	1,286	51	3,951 R	79.7%	19.6%	80.3%	19.7%
15,125	JEFF DAVIS	4,543	3,865	646	32	3,219 R	85.1%	14.2%	85.7%	14.3%
15,385	JEFFERSON	6,278	3,162	3,089	27	73 R	50.4%	49.2%	50.6%	49.4%
8,646	JENKINS	2,774	1,893	871	10	1,022 R	68.2%	31.4%	68.5%	31.5%
9,643	JOHNSON	3,383	2,504	867	12	1,637 R	74.0%	25.6%	74.3%	25.7%
28,837	JONES	12,312	8,583	3,657	72	4,926 R	69.7%	29.7%	70.1%	29.9%
19,190	LAMAR	7,755	5,736	1,963	56	3,773 R	74.0%	25.3%	74.5%	25.5%
10,437	LANIER	2,638	1,932	691	15	1,241 R	73.2%	26.2%	73.7%	26.3%
47,683	LAURENS	18,550	12,508	5,973	69	6,535 R	67.4%	32.2%	67.7%	32.3%
30,110	LEE	13,587	10,094	3,413	80	6,681 R	74.3%	25.1%	74.7%	25.3%
61,455	LIBERTY	15,415	6,069	9,235	111	3,166 D	39.4%	59.9%	39.7%	60.3%
7,950	LINCOLN	3,982	2,966	992	24	1,974 R	74.5%	24.9%	74.9%	25.1%
19,662	LONG	4,426	2,944	1,443	39	1,501 R	66.5%	32.6%	67.1%	32.9%
117,727	LOWNDES	34,760	21,256	13,275	229	7,981 R	61.2%	38.2%	61.6%	38.4%
33,986	LUMPKIN	12,737	10,525	2,070	142	8,455 R	82.6%	16.3%	83.6%	16.4%
12,909	MACON	3,778	1,551	2,209	18	658 D	41.1%	58.5%	41.2%	58.8%
30,038	MADISON	12,554	9,955	2,500	99	7,455 R	79.3%	19.9%	79.9%	20.1%
8,365	MARION	2,846	1,868	954	24	914 R	65.6%	33.5%	66.2%	33.8%
21,323	MCDUFFIE	8,317	5,283	2,978	56	2,305 R	63.5%	35.8%	64.0%	36.0%
14,450	MCINTOSH	5,517	3,570	1,923	24	1,647 R	64.7%	34.9%	65.0%	35.0%
21,224	MERIWETHER	8,908	5,704	3,160	44	2,544 R	64.0%	35.5%	64.4%	35.6%
5,715	MILLER	2,164	1,689	462	13	1,227 R	78.0%	21.3%	78.5%	21.5%
21,822	MITCHELL	7,052	4,197	2,829	26	1,368 R	59.5%	40.1%	59.7%	40.3%
27,741	MONROE	13,718	10,314	3,315	89	6,999 R	75.2%	24.2%	75.7%	24.3%
9,220	MONTGOMERY	3,226	2,545	670	11	1,875 R	78.9%	20.8%	79.2%	20.8%
19,443	MORGAN	10,326	7,764	2,473	89	5,291 R	75.2%	23.9%	75.8%	24.2%
40,213	MURRAY	11,533	10,290	1,160	83	9,130 R	89.2%	10.1%	89.9%	10.1%
196,062	MUSCOGEE	59,462	23,925	35,149	388	11,224 D	40.2%	59.1%	40.5%	59.5%
112,454	NEWTON	42,876	19,094	23,531	251	4,437 D	44.5%	54.9%	44.8%	55.2%
40,604	OCONEE	22,478	16,553	5,783	142	10,770 R	73.6%	25.7%	74.1%	25.9%
15,350	OGLETHORPE	6,811	4,998	1,766	47	3,232 R	73.4%	25.9%	73.9%	26.1%
170,215	PAULDING	67,004	43,992	22,427	585	21,565 R	65.7%	33.5%	66.2%	33.8%
27,676	PEACH	10,039	5,542	4,431	66	1,111 R	55.2%	44.1%	55.6%	44.4%
32,843	PICKENS	15,086	12,937	2,041	108	10,896 R	85.8%	13.5%	86.4%	13.6%
19,569	PIERCE	7,177	6,462	674	41	5,788 R	90.0%	9.4%	90.6%	9.4%
19,118	PIKE	9,431	8,303	1,075	53	7,228 R	88.0%	11.4%	88.5%	11.5%
42,733	POLK	13,640	11,117	2,427	96	8,690 R	81.5%	17.8%	82.1%	17.9%
11,161	PULASKI	3,374	2,452	905	17	1,547 R	72.7%	26.8%	73.0%	27.0%
22,216	PUTNAM	10,237	7,689	2,497	51	5,192 R	75.1%	24.4%	75.5%	24.5%
2,307	QUITMAN	906	555	350	1	205 R	61.3%	38.6%	61.3%	38.7%
17,280	RABUN	8,262	6,766	1,415	81	5,351 R	81.9%	17.1%	82.7%	17.3%
6,779	RANDOLPH	2,565	1,243	1,317	5	74 D	48.5%	51.3%	48.6%	51.4%

GEORGIA
GOVERNOR 2022

2020 Census Population	County	Total Vote	Republican (Kemp)	Democratic (Abrams)	Other	Rep.-Dem. Plurality	Percentage Total Vote Rep.	Percentage Total Vote Dem.	Percentage Major Vote Rep.	Percentage Major Vote Dem.
203,065	RICHMOND	64,156	21,602	42,130	424	20,528 D	33.7%	65.7%	33.9%	66.1%
91,261	ROCKDALE	34,908	9,938	24,756	214	14,818 D	28.5%	70.9%	28.6%	71.4%
5,259	SCHLEY	1,876	1,526	339	11	1,187 R	81.3%	18.1%	81.8%	18.2%
13,982	SCREVEN	5,313	3,422	1,872	19	1,550 R	64.4%	35.2%	64.6%	35.4%
8,080	SEMINOLE	3,045	2,255	773	17	1,482 R	74.1%	25.4%	74.5%	25.5%
67,028	SPALDING	24,395	15,090	9,146	159	5,944 R	61.9%	37.5%	62.3%	37.7%
25,999	STEPHENS	9,400	7,818	1,501	81	6,317 R	83.2%	16.0%	83.9%	16.1%
6,545	STEWART	1,573	673	895	5	222 D	42.8%	56.9%	42.9%	57.1%
29,468	SUMTER	9,605	4,921	4,650	34	271 R	51.2%	48.4%	51.4%	48.6%
6,214	TALBOT	2,864	1,214	1,628	22	414 D	42.4%	56.8%	42.7%	57.3%
1,530	TALIAFERRO	807	327	477	3	150 D	40.5%	59.1%	40.7%	59.3%
25,210	TATTNALL	6,527	5,123	1,359	45	3,764 R	78.5%	20.8%	79.0%	21.0%
8,026	TAYLOR	3,216	2,137	1,069	10	1,068 R	66.4%	33.2%	66.7%	33.3%
15,797	TELFAIR	3,413	2,433	960	20	1,473 R	71.3%	28.1%	71.7%	28.3%
8,523	TERRELL	3,656	1,795	1,840	21	45 D	49.1%	50.3%	49.4%	50.6%
44,518	THOMAS	17,287	11,062	6,138	87	4,924 R	64.0%	35.5%	64.3%	35.7%
40,742	TIFT	13,044	9,418	3,546	80	5,872 R	72.2%	27.2%	72.6%	27.4%
26,865	TOOMBS	8,486	6,522	1,920	44	4,602 R	76.9%	22.6%	77.3%	22.7%
12,156	TOWNS	7,180	6,066	1,052	62	5,014 R	84.5%	14.7%	85.2%	14.8%
6,939	TREUTLEN	2,449	1,764	677	8	1,087 R	72.0%	27.6%	72.3%	27.7%
69,842	TROUP	23,256	14,864	8,262	130	6,602 R	63.9%	35.5%	64.3%	35.7%
8,011	TURNER	3,099	1,994	1,083	22	911 R	64.3%	34.9%	64.8%	35.2%
8,131	TWIGGS	3,540	1,980	1,542	18	438 R	55.9%	43.6%	56.2%	43.8%
24,838	UNION	14,312	12,123	2,070	119	10,053 R	84.7%	14.5%	85.4%	14.6%
26,417	UPSON	10,135	7,096	2,969	70	4,127 R	70.0%	29.3%	70.5%	29.5%
69,992	WALKER	22,117	18,414	3,505	198	14,909 R	83.3%	15.8%	84.0%	16.0%
95,403	WALTON	42,452	32,567	9,573	312	22,994 R	76.7%	22.6%	77.3%	22.7%
35,858	WARE	10,752	7,855	2,828	69	5,027 R	73.1%	26.3%	73.5%	26.5%
5,263	WARREN	2,157	1,063	1,081	13	18 D	49.3%	50.1%	49.6%	50.4%
20,428	WASHINGTON	7,794	4,098	3,665	31	433 R	52.6%	47.0%	52.8%	47.2%
30,017	WAYNE	10,025	8,170	1,796	59	6,374 R	81.5%	17.9%	82.0%	18.0%
2,611	WEBSTER	1,136	708	425	3	283 R	62.3%	37.4%	62.5%	37.5%
7,840	WHEELER	1,826	1,318	501	7	817 R	72.2%	27.4%	72.5%	27.5%
31,092	WHITE	12,730	10,999	1,618	113	9,381 R	86.4%	12.7%	87.2%	12.8%
104,680	WHITFIELD	27,014	20,919	5,874	221	15,045 R	77.4%	21.7%	78.1%	21.9%
8,587	WILCOX	2,621	1,998	613	10	1,385 R	76.2%	23.4%	76.5%	23.5%
9,807	WILKES	4,148	2,545	1,583	20	962 R	61.4%	38.2%	61.7%	38.3%
8,982	WILKINSON	4,056	2,366	1,673	17	693 R	58.3%	41.2%	58.6%	41.4%
20,259	WORTH	7,395	5,649	1,716	30	3,933 R	76.4%	23.2%	76.7%	23.3%
10,658,276	TOTAL	3,953,408	2,111,572	1,813,673	28,163	297,899 R	53.4%	45.9%	53.8%	46.2%

GEORGIA
SENATOR 2022

2020 Census Population	County	Total Vote	Republican (Walker)	Democratic (Warnock)	Other	Rep.-Dem. Plurality	Total Vote Rep.	Total Vote Dem.	Major Vote Rep.	Major Vote Dem.
18,413	APPLING	6,669	5,344	1,260	65	4,084 R	80.1%	18.9%	80.9%	19.1%
8,182	ATKINSON	2,238	1,709	502	27	1,207 R	76.4%	22.4%	77.3%	22.7%
11,177	BACON	3,710	3,204	458	48	2,746 R	86.4%	12.3%	87.5%	12.5%
3,025	BAKER	1,249	711	526	12	185 R	56.9%	42.1%	57.5%	42.5%
44,986	BALDWIN	14,957	7,416	7,327	214	89 R	49.6%	49.0%	50.3%	49.7%
19,354	BANKS	7,293	6,362	772	159	5,590 R	87.2%	10.6%	89.2%	10.8%
83,976	BARROW	29,273	20,136	8,244	893	11,892 R	68.8%	28.2%	71.0%	29.0%
108,306	BARTOW	39,763	29,361	9,349	1,053	20,012 R	73.8%	23.5%	75.8%	24.2%
16,651	BEN HILL	5,075	3,235	1,767	73	1,468 R	63.7%	34.8%	64.7%	35.3%
19,478	BERRIEN	5,990	5,002	909	79	4,093 R	83.5%	15.2%	84.6%	15.4%
153,494	BIBB	54,007	20,203	33,105	699	12,902 D	37.4%	61.3%	37.9%	62.1%
12,938	BLECKLEY	4,791	3,675	1,039	77	2,636 R	76.7%	21.7%	78.0%	22.0%
19,171	BRANTLEY	5,846	5,275	477	94	4,798 R	90.2%	8.2%	91.7%	8.3%
15,354	BROOKS	5,604	3,528	1,999	77	1,529 R	63.0%	35.7%	63.8%	36.2%
40,081	BRYAN	16,926	11,143	5,404	379	5,739 R	65.8%	31.9%	67.3%	32.7%
80,548	BULLOCH	23,469	14,858	8,195	416	6,663 R	63.3%	34.9%	64.5%	35.5%
22,380	BURKE	8,449	4,462	3,885	102	577 R	52.8%	46.0%	53.5%	46.5%
25,209	BUTTS	9,632	6,784	2,666	182	4,118 R	70.4%	27.7%	71.8%	28.2%
6,180	CALHOUN	1,698	724	963	11	239 D	42.6%	56.7%	42.9%	57.1%
54,907	CAMDEN	17,873	11,698	5,758	417	5,940 R	65.5%	32.2%	67.0%	33.0%
10,840	CANDLER	3,553	2,552	950	51	1,602 R	71.8%	26.7%	72.9%	27.1%
120,634	CARROLL	43,507	29,838	12,582	1,087	17,256 R	68.6%	28.9%	70.3%	29.7%
67,906	CATOOSA	24,402	18,562	5,282	558	13,280 R	76.1%	21.6%	77.8%	22.2%
13,529	CHARLTON	3,387	2,552	780	55	1,772 R	75.3%	23.0%	76.6%	23.4%
289,676	CHATHAM	106,001	41,189	62,996	1,816	21,807 D	38.9%	59.4%	39.5%	60.5%
10,969	CHATTAHOOCHEE	1,015	538	453	24	85 R	53.0%	44.6%	54.3%	45.7%
24,828	CHATTOOGA	7,663	5,977	1,514	172	4,463 R	78.0%	19.8%	79.8%	20.2%
260,752	CHEROKEE	119,631	80,811	34,987	3,833	45,824 R	67.6%	29.2%	69.8%	30.2%
128,658	CLARKE	40,176	10,810	28,566	800	17,756 D	26.9%	71.1%	27.5%	72.5%
2,828	CLAY	1,120	528	572	20	44 D	47.1%	51.1%	48.0%	52.0%
293,733	CLAYTON	83,952	9,450	73,412	1,090	63,962 D	11.3%	87.4%	11.4%	88.6%
6,631	CLINCH	2,104	1,630	439	35	1,191 R	77.5%	20.9%	78.8%	21.2%
761,438	COBB	310,652	125,795	176,385	8,472	50,590 D	40.5%	56.8%	41.6%	58.4%
43,422	COFFEE	11,852	8,447	3,216	189	5,231 R	71.3%	27.1%	72.4%	27.6%
45,819	COLQUITT	12,548	9,390	2,966	192	6,424 R	74.8%	23.6%	76.0%	24.0%
157,742	COLUMBIA	64,394	40,172	22,965	1,257	17,207 R	62.4%	35.7%	63.6%	36.4%
17,306	COOK	5,537	3,944	1,497	96	2,447 R	71.2%	27.0%	72.5%	27.5%
149,354	COWETA	63,355	41,512	20,169	1,674	21,343 R	65.5%	31.8%	67.3%	32.7%
12,449	CRAWFORD	4,816	3,440	1,298	78	2,142 R	71.4%	27.0%	72.6%	27.4%
22,355	CRISP	6,306	4,058	2,164	84	1,894 R	64.4%	34.3%	65.2%	34.8%
16,147	DADE	5,821	4,698	996	127	3,702 R	80.7%	17.1%	82.5%	17.5%
26,411	DAWSON	13,870	11,185	2,277	408	8,908 R	80.6%	16.4%	83.1%	16.9%
26,412	DECATUR	8,839	5,433	3,303	103	2,130 R	61.5%	37.4%	62.2%	37.8%
759,228	DEKALB	297,570	41,951	250,761	4,858	208,810 D	14.1%	84.3%	14.3%	85.7%
20,571	DODGE	6,608	4,895	1,640	73	3,255 R	74.1%	24.8%	74.9%	25.1%
13,370	DOOLY	3,277	1,784	1,461	32	323 R	54.4%	44.6%	55.0%	45.0%
88,673	DOUGHERTY	26,614	7,755	18,603	256	10,848 D	29.1%	69.9%	29.4%	70.6%
147,078	DOUGLAS	52,746	17,589	34,158	999	16,569 D	33.3%	64.8%	34.0%	66.0%
10,176	EARLY	3,887	2,209	1,650	28	559 R	56.8%	42.4%	57.2%	42.8%
4,014	ECHOLS	1,060	937	100	23	837 R	88.4%	9.4%	90.4%	9.6%
64,955	EFFINGHAM	25,308	18,231	6,473	604	11,758 R	72.0%	25.6%	73.8%	26.2%
19,251	ELBERT	7,302	5,135	2,077	90	3,058 R	70.3%	28.4%	71.2%	28.8%
22,756	EMANUEL	7,544	5,329	2,157	58	3,172 R	70.6%	28.6%	71.2%	28.8%
10,671	EVANS	3,336	2,314	968	54	1,346 R	69.4%	29.0%	70.5%	29.5%
26,404	FANNIN	12,556	10,036	2,230	290	7,806 R	79.9%	17.8%	81.8%	18.2%
114,984	FAYETTE	59,958	30,178	28,284	1,496	1,894 R	50.3%	47.2%	51.6%	48.4%
98,711	FLOYD	31,896	21,923	9,160	813	12,763 R	68.7%	28.7%	70.5%	29.5%
246,592	FORSYTH	101,853	66,013	32,852	2,988	33,161 R	64.8%	32.3%	66.8%	33.2%
23,468	FRANKLIN	8,704	7,374	1,166	164	6,208 R	84.7%	13.4%	86.3%	13.7%
1,067,116	FULTON	418,172	102,758	307,560	7,854	204,802 D	24.6%	73.5%	25.0%	75.0%

GEORGIA
SENATOR 2022

2020 Census Population	County	Total Vote	Republican (Walker)	Democratic (Warnock)	Other	Rep.-Dem. Plurality	Percentage Total Vote		Percentage Major Vote	
							Rep.	Dem.	Rep.	Dem.
31,594	GILMER	14,007	11,159	2,523	325	8,636 R	79.7%	18.0%	81.6%	18.4%
2,979	GLASCOCK	1,295	1,171	113	11	1,058 R	90.4%	8.7%	91.2%	8.8%
85,660	GLYNN	33,144	20,735	11,812	597	8,923 R	62.6%	35.6%	63.7%	36.3%
58,167	GORDON	18,787	14,955	3,357	475	11,598 R	79.6%	17.9%	81.7%	18.3%
24,623	GRADY	8,311	5,638	2,573	100	3,065 R	67.8%	31.0%	68.7%	31.3%
18,499	GREENE	10,424	6,741	3,527	156	3,214 R	64.7%	33.8%	65.7%	34.3%
938,995	GWINNETT	298,036	115,024	175,688	7,324	60,664 D	38.6%	58.9%	39.6%	60.4%
45,414	HABERSHAM	16,874	13,509	2,887	478	10,622 R	80.1%	17.1%	82.4%	17.6%
205,525	HALL	73,005	51,643	19,196	2,166	32,447 R	70.7%	26.3%	72.9%	27.1%
8,475	HANCOCK	3,392	989	2,373	30	1,384 D	29.2%	70.0%	29.4%	70.6%
29,955	HARALSON	11,595	9,789	1,498	308	8,291 R	84.4%	12.9%	86.7%	13.3%
35,486	HARRIS	16,956	12,072	4,546	338	7,526 R	71.2%	26.8%	72.6%	27.4%
26,360	HART	10,495	7,979	2,322	194	5,657 R	76.0%	22.1%	77.5%	22.5%
11,988	HEARD	4,441	3,673	675	93	2,998 R	82.7%	15.2%	84.5%	15.5%
236,549	HENRY	95,229	32,819	60,756	1,654	27,937 D	34.5%	63.8%	35.1%	64.9%
158,726	HOUSTON	58,991	32,239	25,657	1,095	6,582 R	54.7%	43.5%	55.7%	44.3%
9,500	IRWIN	3,404	2,601	757	46	1,844 R	76.4%	22.2%	77.5%	22.5%
73,881	JACKSON	31,706	24,379	6,504	823	17,875 R	76.9%	20.5%	78.9%	21.1%
14,302	JASPER	6,535	4,951	1,464	120	3,487 R	75.8%	22.4%	77.2%	22.8%
15,125	JEFF DAVIS	4,528	3,738	738	52	3,000 R	82.6%	16.3%	83.5%	16.5%
15,385	JEFFERSON	6,253	3,041	3,158	54	117 D	48.6%	50.5%	49.1%	50.9%
8,646	JENKINS	2,763	1,826	912	25	914 R	66.1%	33.0%	66.7%	33.3%
9,643	JOHNSON	3,370	2,484	869	17	1,615 R	73.7%	25.8%	74.1%	25.9%
28,837	JONES	12,270	8,089	3,990	191	4,099 R	65.9%	32.5%	67.0%	33.0%
19,190	LAMAR	7,713	5,416	2,139	158	3,277 R	70.2%	27.7%	71.7%	28.3%
10,437	LANIER	2,623	1,860	725	38	1,135 R	70.9%	27.6%	72.0%	28.0%
47,683	LAURENS	18,513	12,073	6,285	155	5,788 R	65.2%	33.9%	65.8%	34.2%
30,110	LEE	13,535	9,535	3,779	221	5,756 R	70.4%	27.9%	71.6%	28.4%
61,455	LIBERTY	15,369	5,490	9,615	264	4,125 D	35.7%	62.6%	36.3%	63.7%
7,950	LINCOLN	3,973	2,847	1,077	49	1,770 R	71.7%	27.1%	72.6%	27.4%
19,662	LONG	4,402	2,759	1,548	95	1,211 R	62.7%	35.2%	64.1%	35.9%
117,727	LOWNDES	34,612	20,213	13,849	550	6,364 R	58.4%	40.0%	59.3%	40.7%
33,986	LUMPKIN	12,673	9,765	2,539	369	7,226 R	77.1%	20.0%	79.4%	20.6%
12,909	MACON	3,761	1,460	2,269	32	809 D	38.8%	60.3%	39.2%	60.8%
30,038	MADISON	12,479	9,353	2,864	262	6,489 R	74.9%	23.0%	76.6%	23.4%
8,365	MARION	2,834	1,750	1,018	66	732 R	61.8%	35.9%	63.2%	36.8%
21,323	MCDUFFIE	8,301	5,067	3,103	131	1,964 R	61.0%	37.4%	62.0%	38.0%
14,450	MCINTOSH	5,487	3,344	2,048	95	1,296 R	60.9%	37.3%	62.0%	38.0%
21,224	MERIWETHER	8,874	5,336	3,363	175	1,973 R	60.1%	37.9%	61.3%	38.7%
5,715	MILLER	2,148	1,617	509	22	1,108 R	75.3%	23.7%	76.1%	23.9%
21,822	MITCHELL	7,020	3,986	2,953	81	1,033 R	56.8%	42.1%	57.4%	42.6%
27,741	MONROE	13,665	9,673	3,737	255	5,936 R	70.8%	27.3%	72.1%	27.9%
9,220	MONTGOMERY	3,226	2,450	742	34	1,708 R	75.9%	23.0%	76.8%	23.2%
19,443	MORGAN	10,258	7,322	2,762	174	4,560 R	71.4%	26.9%	72.6%	27.4%
40,213	MURRAY	11,469	9,737	1,533	199	8,204 R	84.9%	13.4%	86.4%	13.6%
196,062	MUSCOGEE	59,244	21,496	36,861	887	15,365 D	36.3%	62.2%	36.8%	63.2%
112,454	NEWTON	42,708	17,577	24,348	783	6,771 D	41.2%	57.0%	41.9%	58.1%
40,604	OCONEE	22,283	14,681	6,987	615	7,694 R	65.9%	31.4%	67.8%	32.2%
15,350	OGLETHORPE	6,786	4,638	1,996	152	2,642 R	68.3%	29.4%	69.9%	30.1%
170,215	PAULDING	66,713	40,689	24,389	1,635	16,300 R	61.0%	36.6%	62.5%	37.5%
27,676	PEACH	10,000	5,156	4,701	143	455 R	51.6%	47.0%	52.3%	47.7%
32,843	PICKENS	15,003	12,050	2,589	364	9,461 R	80.3%	17.3%	82.3%	17.7%
19,569	PIERCE	7,167	6,325	779	63	5,546 R	88.3%	10.9%	89.0%	11.0%
19,118	PIKE	9,396	7,948	1,257	191	6,691 R	84.6%	13.4%	86.3%	13.7%
42,733	POLK	13,563	10,426	2,794	343	7,632 R	76.9%	20.6%	78.9%	21.1%
11,161	PULASKI	3,366	2,319	1,002	45	1,317 R	68.9%	29.8%	69.8%	30.2%
22,216	PUTNAM	10,202	7,164	2,847	191	4,317 R	70.2%	27.9%	71.6%	28.4%
2,307	QUITMAN	902	511	378	13	133 R	56.7%	41.9%	57.5%	42.5%
17,280	RABUN	8,207	6,180	1,804	223	4,376 R	75.3%	22.0%	77.4%	22.6%
6,779	RANDOLPH	2,547	1,158	1,366	23	208 D	45.5%	53.6%	45.9%	54.1%

GEORGIA
SENATOR 2022

2020 Census Population	County	Total Vote	Republican (Walker)	Democratic (Warnock)	Other	Rep.-Dem. Plurality	Percentage			
							Total Vote		Major Vote	
							Rep.	Dem.	Rep.	Dem.
203,065	RICHMOND	63,938	19,491	43,567	880	24,076 D	30.5%	68.1%	30.9%	69.1%
91,261	ROCKDALE	34,774	8,722	25,478	574	16,756 D	25.1%	73.3%	25.5%	74.5%
5,259	SCHLEY	1,870	1,467	384	19	1,083 R	78.4%	20.5%	79.3%	20.7%
13,982	SCREVEN	5,285	3,203	2,009	73	1,194 R	60.6%	38.0%	61.5%	38.5%
8,080	SEMINOLE	3,023	2,152	827	44	1,325 R	71.2%	27.4%	72.2%	27.8%
67,028	SPALDING	24,262	13,966	9,761	535	4,205 R	57.6%	40.2%	58.9%	41.1%
25,999	STEPHENS	9,333	7,374	1,762	197	5,612 R	79.0%	18.9%	80.7%	19.3%
6,545	STEWART	1,567	638	916	13	278 D	40.7%	58.5%	41.1%	58.9%
29,468	SUMTER	9,580	4,590	4,894	96	304 D	47.9%	51.1%	48.4%	51.6%
6,214	TALBOT	2,849	1,118	1,688	43	570 D	39.2%	59.2%	39.8%	60.2%
1,530	TALIAFERRO	797	310	483	4	173 D	38.9%	60.6%	39.1%	60.9%
25,210	TATTNALL	6,500	4,866	1,525	109	3,341 R	74.9%	23.5%	76.1%	23.9%
8,026	TAYLOR	3,200	2,020	1,145	35	875 R	63.1%	35.8%	63.8%	36.2%
15,797	TELFAIR	3,400	2,340	1,032	28	1,308 R	68.8%	30.4%	69.4%	30.6%
8,523	TERRELL	3,638	1,695	1,904	39	209 D	46.6%	52.3%	47.1%	52.9%
44,518	THOMAS	17,180	10,481	6,436	263	4,045 R	61.0%	37.5%	62.0%	38.0%
40,742	TIFT	12,975	8,921	3,878	176	5,043 R	68.8%	29.9%	69.7%	30.3%
26,865	TOOMBS	8,460	6,298	2,062	100	4,236 R	74.4%	24.4%	75.3%	24.7%
12,156	TOWNS	7,109	5,568	1,362	179	4,206 R	78.3%	19.2%	80.3%	19.7%
6,939	TREUTLEN	2,444	1,721	711	12	1,010 R	70.4%	29.1%	70.8%	29.2%
69,842	TROUP	23,169	13,937	8,806	426	5,131 R	60.2%	38.0%	61.3%	38.7%
8,011	TURNER	3,086	1,892	1,152	42	740 R	61.3%	37.3%	62.2%	37.8%
8,131	TWIGGS	3,532	1,886	1,601	45	285 R	53.4%	45.3%	54.1%	45.9%
24,838	UNION	14,185	11,186	2,621	378	8,565 R	78.9%	18.5%	81.0%	19.0%
26,417	UPSON	10,064	6,685	3,173	206	3,512 R	66.4%	31.5%	67.8%	32.2%
69,992	WALKER	21,972	17,064	4,377	531	12,687 R	77.7%	19.9%	79.6%	20.4%
95,403	WALTON	42,259	30,553	10,702	1,004	19,851 R	72.3%	25.3%	74.1%	25.9%
35,858	WARE	10,704	7,567	2,976	161	4,591 R	70.7%	27.8%	71.8%	28.2%
5,263	WARREN	2,149	1,007	1,117	25	110 D	46.9%	52.0%	47.4%	52.6%
20,428	WASHINGTON	7,763	3,904	3,793	66	111 R	50.3%	48.9%	50.7%	49.3%
30,017	WAYNE	9,988	7,838	2,014	136	5,824 R	78.5%	20.2%	79.6%	20.4%
2,611	WEBSTER	1,125	676	442	7	234 R	60.1%	39.3%	60.5%	39.5%
7,840	WHEELER	1,817	1,266	534	17	732 R	69.7%	29.4%	70.3%	29.7%
31,092	WHITE	12,660	10,249	2,063	348	8,186 R	81.0%	16.3%	83.2%	16.8%
104,680	WHITFIELD	26,888	19,387	6,904	597	12,483 R	72.1%	25.7%	73.7%	26.3%
8,587	WILCOX	2,613	1,947	644	22	1,303 R	74.5%	24.6%	75.1%	24.9%
9,807	WILKES	4,128	2,402	1,680	46	722 R	58.2%	40.7%	58.8%	41.2%
8,982	WILKINSON	4,043	2,272	1,728	43	544 R	56.2%	42.7%	56.8%	43.2%
20,259	WORTH	7,358	5,416	1,842	100	3,574 R	73.6%	25.0%	74.6%	25.4%
10,658,276	TOTAL	3,935,924	1,908,442	1,946,117	81,365	37,675 D	48.5%	49.4%	49.5%	50.5%

GEORGIA
HOUSE OF REPRESENTATIVES

			Republican		Democratic		Other	Rep.-Dem.	Total Vote		Major Vote	
CD	Year	Total Vote	Vote	Candidate	Vote	Candidate	Vote	Plurality	Rep.	Dem.	Rep.	Dem.
1	2022	263,965	156,128	CARTER, EARL LEROY "BUDDY"*	107,837	HERRING, WADE		48,291 R	59.1%	40.9%	59.1%	40.9%
1	2020	324,695	189,457	CARTER, EARL LEROY "BUDDY"*	135,238	GRIGGS, JOYCE MARIE		54,219 R	58.3%	41.7%	58.3%	41.7%
1	2018	250,683	144,741	CARTER, EARL LEROY "BUDDY"*	105,942	RING, LISA		38,799 R	57.7%	42.3%	57.7%	42.3%
1	2016	211,112	210,243	CARTER, EARL LEROY "BUDDY"*			869	210,243 R	99.6%		100.0%	
1	2014	156,512	95,337	CARTER, EARL LEROY "BUDDY"	61,175	REESE, BRIAN CORWIN		34,162 R	60.9%	39.1%	60.9%	39.1%
1	2012	249,580	157,181	KINGSTON, JACK*	92,399	MESSINGER, LESLI		64,782 R	63.0%	37.0%	63.0%	37.0%
2	2022	241,340	108,665	WEST, CHRIS	132,675	BISHOP, SANFORD*		24,010 D	45.0%	55.0%	45.0%	55.0%
2	2020	273,017	111,620	COLE, DONALD EUGENE	161,397	BISHOP, SANFORD*		49,777 D	40.9%	59.1%	40.9%	59.1%
2	2018	229,171	92,472	WEST, HERMAN JR.	136,699	BISHOP, SANFORD*		44,227 D	40.4%	59.6%	40.4%	59.6%
2	2016	242,599	94,056	DUKE, GREG	148,543	BISHOP, SANFORD*		54,487 D	38.8%	61.2%	38.8%	61.2%
2	2014	162,900	66,537	DUKE, GREG	96,363	BISHOP, SANFORD*		29,826 D	40.8%	59.2%	40.8%	59.2%
2	2012	255,161	92,410	HOUSE, JOHN	162,751	BISHOP, SANFORD*		70,341 D	36.2%	63.8%	36.2%	63.8%
3	2022	310,581	213,524	FERGUSON, DREW*	97,057	ALMONORD, VAL		116,467 R	68.7%	31.3%	68.7%	31.3%
3	2020	371,318	241,526	FERGUSON, DREW*	129,792	ALMONORD, VAL		111,734 R	65.0%	35.0%	65.0%	35.0%
3	2018	293,006	191,996	FERGUSON, DREW*	101,010	ENDERLIN, CHUCK		90,986 R	65.5%	34.5%	65.5%	34.5%
3	2016	303,187	207,218	FERGUSON, DREW	95,969	PENDLEY, ANGELA		111,249 R	68.3%	31.7%	68.3%	31.7%
3	2014	156,277	156,277	WESTMORELAND, LYNN A.*				156,277 R	100.0%		100.0%	
3	2012	232,485	232,380	WESTMORELAND, LYNN A.*			105	232,380 R	100.0%		100.0%	
4	2022	275,634	59,302	CHAVEZ, JONATHAN	216,332	JOHNSON, HENRY C. "HANK" JR.*		157,030 D	21.5%	78.5%	21.5%	78.5%
4	2020	348,299	69,393	EZAMMUDEEN, JOHSIE CRUZ	278,906	JOHNSON, HENRY C. "HANK" JR.*		209,513 D	19.9%	80.1%	19.9%	80.1%
4	2018	288,809	61,092	PROFIT, JOE	227,717	JOHNSON, HENRY C. "HANK" JR.*		166,625 D	21.2%	78.8%	21.2%	78.8%
4	2016	290,739	70,593	ARMENDARIZ, VICTOR	220,146	JOHNSON, HENRY C. "HANK" JR.*		149,553 D	24.3%	75.7%	24.3%	75.7%
4	2014	161,320			161,211	JOHNSON, HENRY C. "HANK" JR.*	109	161,211 D		99.9%		100.0%
4	2012	283,962	75,041	VAUGHN, J. CHRIS	208,861	JOHNSON, HENRY C. "HANK" JR.*	60	133,820 D	26.4%	73.6%	26.4%	73.6%
5	2022	295,456	51,769	ZIMM, CHRISTIAN	243,687	WILLIAMS, NIKEMA*		191,918 D	17.5%	82.5%	17.5%	82.5%
5	2020	354,503	52,646	STANTON-KING, ANGELA	301,857	WILLIAMS, NIKEMA		249,211 D	14.9%	85.1%	14.9%	85.1%
5	2018	275,406			275,406	LEWIS, JOHN*		275,406 D		100.0%		100.0%
5	2016	300,549	46,768	BELL, DOUGLAS	253,781	LEWIS, JOHN*		207,013 D	15.6%	84.4%	15.6%	84.4%
5	2014	170,326			170,326	LEWIS, JOHN*		170,326 D		100.0%		100.0%
5	2012	277,689	43,335	STOPECK, HOWARD	234,330	LEWIS, JOHN*	24	190,995 D	15.6%	84.4%	15.6%	84.4%
6	2022	332,498	206,886	MCCORMICK, RICHARD DEAN	125,612	CHRISTIAN, BOB		81,274 R	62.2%	37.8%	62.2%	37.8%
6	2020	397,104	180,329	HANDEL, KAREN	216,775	MCBATH, LUCY KAY*		36,446 D	45.4%	54.6%	45.4%	54.6%
6	2018	317,032	156,875	HANDEL, KAREN*	160,139	MCBATH, LUCY KAY	18	3,264 D	49.5%	50.5%	49.5%	50.5%
6	2016	326,005	201,088	PRICE, THOMAS E.*	124,917	STOOKSBURY, RODNEY		76,171 R	61.7%	38.3%	61.7%	38.3%
6	2014	210,504	139,018	PRICE, THOMAS E.*	71,486	MONTIGEL, ROBERT		67,532 R	66.0%	34.0%	66.0%	34.0%
6	2012	294,034	189,669	PRICE, THOMAS E.*	104,365	KAZANOW, JEFF		85,304 R	64.5%	35.5%	64.5%	35.5%
7	2022	234,325	91,262	GONSALVES, MARK	143,063	MCBATH, LUCY KAY*		51,801 D	38.9%	61.1%	38.9%	61.1%
7	2020	371,464	180,564	MCCORMICK, RICHARD DEAN	190,900	BOURDEAUX, CAROLYN		10,336 D	48.6%	51.4%	48.6%	51.4%
7	2018	280,441	140,430	WOODALL, ROB*	140,011	BOURDEAUX, CAROLYN		419 R	50.1%	49.9%	50.1%	49.9%
7	2016	288,301	174,081	WOODALL, ROB*	114,220	MALIK, RASHID		59,861 R	60.4%	39.6%	60.4%	39.6%
7	2014	173,669	113,557	WOODALL, ROB*	60,112	WIGHT, THOMAS D.		53,445 R	65.4%	34.6%	65.4%	34.6%
7	2012	252,066	156,689	WOODALL, ROB*	95,377	REILLY, STEVE		61,312 R	62.2%	37.8%	62.2%	37.8%
8	2022	260,586	178,700	SCOTT, AUSTIN*	81,886	BUTLER, DARRIUS		96,814 R	68.6%	31.4%	68.6%	31.4%
8	2020	307,965	198,701	SCOTT, AUSTIN*	109,264	HOLLIDAY, LINDSAY DOZIER		89,437 R	64.5%	35.5%	64.5%	35.5%
8	2018	198,716	198,152	SCOTT, AUSTIN*			564	198,152 R	99.7%		100.0%	
8	2016	257,208	173,983	SCOTT, AUSTIN*	83,225	HARRIS, JAMES NEAL		90,758 R	67.6%	32.4%	67.6%	32.4%
8	2014	130,057	129,938	SCOTT, AUSTIN*			119	129,938 R	99.9%		100.0%	
8	2012	197,789	197,789	SCOTT, AUSTIN*				197,789 R	100.0%		100.0%	
9	2022	294,138	212,820	CLYDE, ANDREW*	81,318	FORD, MICHAEL "MIKE"		131,502 R	72.4%	27.6%	72.4%	27.6%
9	2020	372,547	292,750	CLYDE, ANDREW	79,797	PANDY, DEVIN D.		212,953 R	78.6%	21.4%	78.6%	21.4%
9	2018	282,578	224,661	COLLINS, DOUG*	57,912	MCCALL, JOSHUA BRAXTON	5	166,749 R	79.5%	20.5%	79.5%	20.5%
9	2016	256,535	256,535	COLLINS, DOUG*				256,535 R	100.0%		100.0%	
9	2014	181,047	146,059	COLLINS, DOUG*	34,988	VOGEL, DAVID D.		111,071 R	80.7%	19.3%	80.7%	19.3%
9	2012	252,153	192,101	COLLINS, DOUG	60,052	COOLEY, JODY		132,049 R	76.2%	23.8%	76.2%	23.8%
10	2022	307,630	198,523	COLLINS, MIKE A.	109,107	JOHNSON-GREEN, TABITHA A.		89,416 R	64.5%	35.5%	64.5%	35.5%
10	2020	378,446	235,810	HICE, JODY*	142,636	JOHNSON-GREEN, TABITHA A.		93,174 R	62.3%	37.7%	62.3%	37.7%
10	2018	302,735	190,396	HICE, JODY*	112,339	JOHNSON-GREEN, TABITHA A.		78,057 R	62.9%	37.1%	62.9%	37.1%
10	2016	244,821	243,725	HICE, JODY*			1,096	243,725 R	99.6%		100.0%	
10	2014	196,480	130,703	HICE, JODY	65,777	DIOUS, IVORY KENNETH "KEN"		64,926 R	66.5%	33.5%	66.5%	33.5%
10	2012	211,466	211,065	BROUN, PAUL*			401	211,065 R	99.8%		100.0%	

GEORGIA
HOUSE OF REPRESENTATIVES

| | | | Republican | | Democratic | | | | Percentage | | | |
| | | | | | | | | | Total Vote | | Major Vote | |
CD	Year	Total Vote	Vote	Candidate	Vote	Candidate	Other Vote	Rep.-Dem. Plurality	Rep.	Dem.	Rep.	Dem.
11	2022	303,657	190,086	LOUDERMILK, BARRY*	113,571	DAZA, ANTONIO		76,515 R	62.6%	37.4%	62.6%	37.4%
11	2020	405,882	245,259	LOUDERMILK, BARRY*	160,623	BARRETT, DANA		84,636 R	60.4%	39.6%	60.4%	39.6%
11	2018	310,540	191,887	LOUDERMILK, BARRY*	118,653	BROADY, FLYNN D. JR.		73,234 R	61.8%	38.2%	61.8%	38.2%
11	2016	323,318	217,935	LOUDERMILK, BARRY*	105,383	WILSON, DON		112,552 R	67.4%	32.6%	67.4%	32.6%
11	2014	161,532	161,532	LOUDERMILK, BARRY				161,532 R	100.0%		100.0%	
11	2012	287,351	196,968	GINGREY, PHIL*	90,353	THOMPSON, PATRICK	30	106,615 R	68.5%	31.4%	68.6%	31.4%
12	2022	265,195	158,047	ALLEN, RICK	107,148	JOHNSON, ELIZABETH "LIZ"		50,899 R	59.6%	40.4%	59.6%	40.4%
12	2020	310,099	181,038	ALLEN, RICK*	129,061	JOHNSON, ELIZABETH "LIZ"		51,977 R	58.4%	41.6%	58.4%	41.6%
12	2018	250,492	148,986	ALLEN, RICK*	101,503	JOHNSON, FRANCYS	3	47,483 R	59.5%	40.5%	59.5%	40.5%
12	2016	258,912	159,492	ALLEN, RICK*	99,420	MCCRACKEN, PATRICIA "TRICIA"		60,072 R	61.6%	38.4%	61.6%	38.4%
12	2014	166,814	91,336	ALLEN, RICK*	75,478	BARROW, JOHN*		15,858 R	54.8%	45.2%	54.8%	45.2%
12	2012	259,121	119,973	ANDERSON, LEE	139,148	BARROW, JOHN*		19,175 D	46.3%	53.7%	46.3%	53.7%
13	2022	264,616	48,228	GONZALES, CAESAR	216,388	SCOTT, DAVID*		168,160 D	18.2%	81.8%	18.2%	81.8%
13	2020	360,521	81,476	HITES, BECKY E.	279,045	SCOTT, DAVID*		197,569 D	22.6%	77.4%	22.6%	77.4%
13	2018	293,010	69,760	CALLAHAN, DAVID	223,157	SCOTT, DAVID*	93	153,397 D	23.8%	76.2%	23.8%	76.2%
13	2016	252,833			252,833	SCOTT, DAVID*		252,833 D		100.0%		100.0%
13	2014	159,445			159,445	SCOTT, DAVID*		159,445 D		100.0%		100.0%
13	2012	281,538	79,550	MALIK, S.	201,988	SCOTT, DAVID*		122,438 D	28.3%	71.7%	28.3%	71.7%
14	2022	258,351	170,162	GREENE, MARJORIE TAYLOR*	88,189	FLOWERS, MARCUS		81,973 R	65.9%	34.1%	65.9%	34.1%
14	2020	307,625	229,827	GREENE, MARJORIE TAYLOR	77,798	VAN AUSDAL, KEVIN		152,029 R	74.7%	25.3%	74.7%	25.3%
14	2018	229,724	175,743	GRAVES, TOM*	53,981	FOSTER, STEVE LAMAR		121,762 R	76.5%	23.5%	76.5%	23.5%
14	2016	216,743	216,743	GRAVES, TOM*				216,743 R	100.0%		100.0%	
14	2014	118,782	118,782	GRAVES, TOM*				118,782 R	100.0%		100.0%	
14	2012	219,192	159,947	GRAVES, TOM*	59,245	GRANT, DANIEL "DANNY"		100,702 R	73.0%	27.0%	73.0%	27.0%
TOTAL	2022	3,907,972	2,044,102		1,863,870			180,232 R	52.3%	47.7%	52.3%	47.7%
TOTAL	2020	4,883,485	2,490,396		2,393,089			97,307 R	51.0%	49.0%	51.0%	49.0%
TOTAL	2018	3,802,343	1,987,191		1,814,469		683	172,722 R	52.3%	47.7%	52.3%	47.7%
TOTAL	2016	3,772,862	2,272,460		1,498,437		1,965	774,023 R	60.2%	39.7%	60.3%	39.7%
TOTAL	2014	2,305,665	1,349,076		956,361		228	392,715 R	58.5%	41.5%	58.5%	41.5%
TOTAL	2012	3,553,587	2,104,098		1,448,869		620	655,229 R	59.2%	40.8%	59.2%	40.8%

Note: An asterisk (*) denotes incumbent.

GEORGIA
GENERAL AND PRIMARY ELECTIONS

GENERAL ELECTIONS: OTHER VOTES

Governor — Other vote was 28,163 Libertarian (Shane Hazel)

Senate — Other vote was 81,365 Libertarian (Chase Oliver)

2020 PRIMARY ELECTIONS: SUPPLEMENTARY INFORMATION

Primary	May 24, 2022	**Registration** (as of May 24, 2022)	6,827,178	No Party Registration
Primary Runoff	June 21, 2022			
General Runoff	December 6, 2022			
Primary Type	Open—Any registered voter could participate in either the Democratic or the Republican primary, although if voters cast a ballot in one party's primary they could not participate in a primary runoff of the other party. Voters who did not participate in the primary could vote in either party's runoff.			

GEORGIA

GENERAL AND PRIMARY ELECTIONS

	REPUBLICAN PRIMARIES			DEMOCRATIC PRIMARIES		
Senator	Walker, Herschel	803,560	68.2%	Warnock, Raphael*	702,610	96.0%
	Black, Gary	157,370	13.4%	Johnson-Shealey, Tamara	28,984	4.0%
	Saddler, Latham	104,471	8.9%			
	Clark, Josh	46,693	4.0%			
	King, Kelvin	37,930	3.2%			
	McColumn, Jonathan "Jon"	28,601	2.4%			
	TOTAL	1,178,625		TOTAL	731,594	
Governor	Kemp, Brian*	888,078	73.7%	Abrams, Stacey	727,168	100.0%
	Perdue, David A.	262,389	21.8%			
	Taylor, Kandiss	41,232	3.4%			
	Davis, Catherine	9,788	0.8%			
	Williams, Tom	3,255	0.3%			
	TOTAL	1,204,742		TOTAL	727,168	
Congressional District 1	Carter, Earl Leroy "Buddy"*	80,757	100.0%	Griggs, Joyce Marie	21,891	48.6%
				Herring, Wade	17,118	38.0%
				Munroe, Michelle L.	6,043	13.4%
	TOTAL	80,757		TOTAL	45,052	
				PRIMARY RUNOFF		
				Herring, Wade	12,880	61.9%
				Griggs, Joyce Marie	7,918	38.1%
				TOTAL	20,798	
Congressional District 2	Hunt, Jeremy	22,923	37.0%	Bishop, Sanford*	54,991	93.5%
	West, Chris	18,658	30.1%	O'Hara, Joe	3,814	6.5%
	Johnson, Wayne	11,574	18.7%			
	Childs, Vivian L.	3,986	6.4%			
	Robertson, Richard	2,832	4.6%			
	Whitehead, Paul	2,037	3.3%			
	TOTAL	62,010		TOTAL	58,805	
	PRIMARY RUNOFF					
	West, Chris	14,622	51.3%			
	Hunt, Jeremy	13,875	48.7%			
	TOTAL	28,497				
Congressional District 3	Ferguson, Drew*	96,314	82.7%	Almonord, Val	32,207	100.0%
	Craig, Jared	20,175	17.3%			
	TOTAL	116,489		TOTAL	32,207	
Congressional District 4	Chavez, Jonathan	21,924	78.3%	Johnson, Henry C. "Hank" Jr.*	84,773	100.0%
	Ivy, Surrea	6,078	21.7%			
	TOTAL	28,002		TOTAL	84,773	
Congressional District 5	Zimm, Christian	21,540	100.0%	Williams, Nikema*	78,440	86.3%
				Stovall, Valencia	8,701	9.6%
				Macbagito, Charlotte	3,791	4.2%
	TOTAL	21,540		TOTAL	90,932	

GEORGIA
GENERAL AND PRIMARY ELECTIONS

	REPUBLICAN PRIMARIES			DEMOCRATIC PRIMARIES		
Congressional District 6	McCormick, Richard Dean	48,967	43.1%	Christian, Bob	18,776	55.5%
	Evans, Jake	26,160	23.0%	White, Wayne	15,025	44.5%
	Staples, Mallory	10,178	9.0%			
	Hanson, Meagan	9,539	8.4%			
	Yu, Eugene	7,411	6.5%			
	Harbin, Blake	4,171	3.7%			
	Gatewood, Byron	3,358	3.0%			
	Voyles, Suzi	2,646	2.3%			
	Smith, Paulette	1,123	1.0%			
	TOTAL	113,553		TOTAL	33,801	
	PRIMARY RUNOFF					
	McCormick, Richard Dean	27,455	66.5%			
	Evans, Jake	13,808	33.5%			
	TOTAL	41,263				
Congressional District 7	Corbin, Michael	18,637	41.1%	McBath, Lucy Kay*	33,607	63.1%
	Gonsalves, Mark	12,477	27.5%	Bourdeaux, Carolyn	16,310	30.6%
	McCoy, Lisa	6,380	14.1%	McLeod, Donna	3,352	6.3%
	West, Mary	4,370	9.6%			
	Nyghtstorm, Y. G.	3,510	7.7%			
	TOTAL	45,374		TOTAL	53,269	
	PRIMARY RUNOFF					
	Gonsalves, Mark	8,591	70.1%			
	Corbin, Michael	3,666	29.9%			
	TOTAL	12,257				
Congressional District 8	Scott, Austin*	90,426	100.0%	Butler, Darrius	30,655	100.0%
	TOTAL	90,426		TOTAL	30,655	
Congressional District 9	Clyde, Andrew*	90,535	76.4%	Ford, Michael "Mike"	21,434	100.0%
	Souther, Ben	17,922	15.1%			
	Boggus, Michael Shane	4,230	3.6%			
	Howard, J. Gregory	3,463	2.9%			
	London, John	2,359	2.0%			
	TOTAL	118,509		TOTAL	21,434	
Congressional District 10	Collins, Mike A.	28,741	25.6%	Johnson-Green, Tabitha A.	15,821	42.0%
	Jones, Vernon J.	24,165	21.5%	Fore, Jessica Allison	7,257	19.2%
	Barr, Timothy	16,007	14.3%	Hatcher, Phyllis	7,120	18.9%
	Broun, Paul	14,901	13.3%	Oduwole, Femi	4,427	11.7%
	Curry, David	10,557	9.4%	Walton, Paul	3,077	8.2%
	Sims, Alan	7,388	6.6%			
	McMain, Marc	5,222	4.7%			
	Swan, Mitchell	5,184	4.6%			
	TOTAL	112,165		TOTAL	37,702	
	PRIMARY RUNOFF			**PRIMARY RUNOFF**		
	Collins, Mike A.	30,536	74.5%	Johnson-Green, Tabitha A.	9,070	64.4%
	Jones, Vernon J.	10,469	25.5%	Fore, Jessica Allison	5,024	35.6%
	TOTAL	41,005		TOTAL	14,094	
Congressional District 11	Loudermilk, Barry*	99,073	100.0%	Daza, Antonio	33,470	100.0%
	TOTAL	99,073		TOTAL	33,470	
Congressional District 12	Allen, Rick*	81,151	100.0%	Johnson, Elizabeth "Liz"	44,537	100.0%
	TOTAL	81,151		TOTAL	44,537	

GEORGIA

GENERAL AND PRIMARY ELECTIONS

		REPUBLICAN PRIMARIES			DEMOCRATIC PRIMARIES	
Congressional District 13	Gonzales, Caesar	12,659	57.2%	Scott, David*	60,544	65.7%
	Plotky, Calina	5,022	22.7%	Baker, Mark	11,581	12.6%
	Hawkins, Dominika	4,450	20.1%	Driscoll, Shastity	10,906	11.8%
				Fort, Vincent	9,108	9.9%
	TOTAL	22,131		TOTAL	92,139	
Congressional District 14	Greene, Marjorie Taylor*	72,215	69.5%	Flowers, Marcus	20,082	74.7%
	Strahan, Jennifer	17,595	16.9%	Davis, Wendy	5,141	19.1%
	Cunningham, Eric	6,390	6.2%	McCormack, Holly	1,662	6.2%
	Haygood, James	3,790	3.6%			
	Lutin, Charles	2,304	2.2%			
	Synstelien, Seth	1,547	1.5%			
	TOTAL	103,841		TOTAL	26,885	

Note: An asterisk (*) denotes incumbent.

HAWAII

Statewide Races

The Aloha State seemed to be as Democratic as it ever was in 2022. Sen. Brian Schatz (D), who was (somewhat unexpectedly) appointed in 2012 after the death of the nine-term Democratic Sen. Dan Inouye, easily won a second full term. As he did in his 2014 special and 2016 regular elections, Schatz won by a margin of more than 40 points and carried every county. Considering he turned 50 shortly before the 2022 general election and has a decade of seniority, Schatz could easily have a long Senatorial career.

Republicans fared better in the gubernatorial race, but still decisively lost. Gov. David Ige (D) was term-limited, leaving the governor's mansion open. The Democratic primary drew several well-known names: 2nd District Rep. Kai Kahele, who tried to return home after a single term in Congress, and former state First Lady Vicky Cayetano made the race. But the landslide winner was Lt. Gov. Josh Green, who garnered the most institutional support.

In the general election, Green faced another lieutenant governor: Republican Duke Aiona, who held the state's second-highest job from 2003 to 2011. But Green won with the same 63% that Ige received four years earlier. 2022 marked Aiona's third attempt at the governorship – he was also the GOP nominee in 2010 and 2014 – and it was his worst performance. Still, in a state where the GOP bench is severely lacking, one must give Aiona some credit as a "team player" for continuing to run under the party banner.

House Races

Hawaii's two districts barely changed in redistricting and are safely Democratic. In the 1st District, which is entirely confined to Honolulu County, Rep. Ed Case won by nearly 50 points. Case is on his second tour of duty in the House – he represented the 2nd District from 2003 to 2006 before coming back in 2018. With Kahele running for governor, the 2nd District, which takes in the balance of the state's geography, saw a multi-way Democratic primary. But state Sen. Jill Tokuda ran with the Congressional Progressive Caucus's endorsement and took nearly 60 percent. In 2018, Tokuda finished a close second to Green in the primary for lieutenant governor (Hawaii politics, at least at the federal and state levels, tends to feature a recurring cast of characters). Tokuda's 62%–35% margin in the general election was comfortable, but represented a decline from Kahele's performance two years earlier – perhaps with her incumbency, Tokuda's 2024 showing will be even stronger.

HAWAII
Congressional districts first established for elections held in 2022
2 members

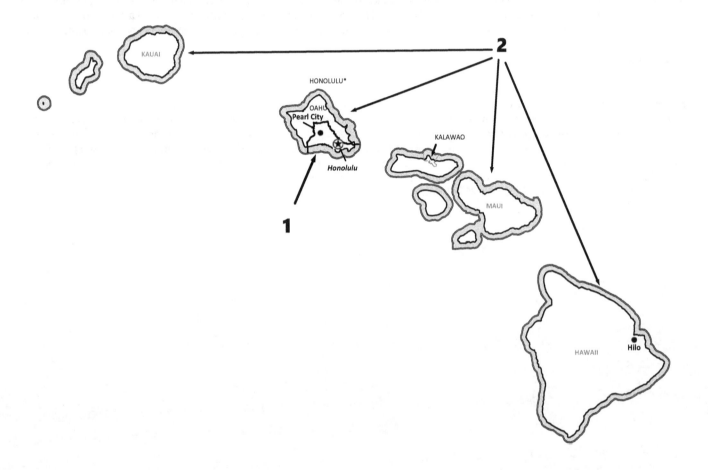

The County of Honolulu includes the City of Honolulu and the rest of the island of Oahu.

*Asterisk indicates a county whose boundaries include parts of two or more congressional districts.

Hawaii includes more islands to the west of those that are illustrated on this map; they are in CD 2.

HAWAII

GOVERNOR
Josh Green (D). Elected 2022 to a four-year term.

SENATORS (2 Democrats)
Mazie K. Hirono (D). Reelected 2018 to a six-year term. Previously elected 2012.

Brian Schatz (D). Reelected 2022 to a six-year term. Previously elected 2016, and elected November 4, 2014, in a special election following the death of Senator Daniel K. Inouye. Schatz was initially appointed December 27, 2012, to fill the vacancy.

REPRESENTATIVES (2 Democrats)
1. Ed Case (D)
2. Jill Tokuda (D)

POSTWAR VOTE FOR PRESIDENT

Year	Total Vote	Republican Vote	Republican Candidate	Democratic Vote	Democratic Candidate	Other Vote	Rep.-Dem. Plurality	Total Vote Rep.	Total Vote Dem.	Major Vote Rep.	Major Vote Dem.
2020	574,469	196,864	Trump, Donald J.*	366,130	Biden, Joseph R. Jr.	11,475	169,266 D	34.3%	63.7%	35.0%	65.0%
2016**	428,937	128,847	Trump, Donald J.	266,891	Clinton, Hillary Rodham	33,199	138,044 D	30.0%	62.2%	32.6%	67.4%
2012	434,697	121,015	Romney, W. Mitt	306,658	Obama, Barack H.*	7,024	185,643 D	27.8%	70.5%	28.3%	71.7%
2008	453,568	120,566	McCain, John S. III	325,871	Obama, Barack H.	7,131	205,305 D	26.6%	71.8%	27.0%	73.0%
2004	429,013	194,191	Bush, George W.*	231,708	Kerry, John F.	3,114	37,517 D	45.3%	54.0%	45.6%	54.4%
2000**	367,951	137,845	Bush, George W.	205,286	Gore, Albert Jr.	24,820	67,441 D	37.5%	55.8%	40.2%	59.8%
1996**	360,120	113,943	Dole, Robert "Bob"	205,012	Clinton, Bill*	41,165	91,069 D	31.6%	56.9%	35.7%	64.3%
1992**	372,842	136,822	Bush, George H.*	179,310	Clinton, Bill	56,710	42,488 D	36.7%	48.1%	43.3%	56.7%
1988	354,461	158,625	Bush, George H.	192,364	Dukakis, Michael S.	3,472	33,739 D	44.8%	54.3%	45.2%	54.8%
1984	335,846	185,050	Reagan, Ronald*	147,154	Mondale, Walter F.	3,642	37,896 R	55.1%	43.8%	55.7%	44.3%
1980**	303,287	130,112	Reagan, Ronald	135,879	Carter, Jimmy*	37,296	5,767 D	42.9%	44.8%	48.9%	51.1%
1976	291,301	140,003	Ford, Gerald R.*	147,375	Carter, Jimmy	3,923	7,372 D	48.1%	50.6%	48.7%	51.3%
1972	270,274	168,865	Nixon, Richard M.*	101,409	McGovern, George S.		67,456 R	62.5%	37.5%	62.5%	37.5%
1968**	236,218	91,425	Nixon, Richard M.	141,324	Humphrey, Hubert Horatio Jr.	3,469	49,899 D	38.7%	59.8%	39.3%	60.7%
1964	207,271	44,022	Goldwater, Barry M. Sr.	163,249	Johnson, Lyndon B.*		119,227 D	21.2%	78.8%	21.2%	78.8%
1960	184,705	92,295	Nixon, Richard M.	92,410	Kennedy, John F.		115 D	50.0%	50.0%	50.0%	50.0%

Note: An asterisk (*) denotes incumbent. **In past elections, the other vote included: 2016 - 15,954 Libertarian (Gary Johnson); 2000 - 21,623 Green (Ralph Nader); 1996 - 27,358 Reform (Ross Perot); 1992 - 53,003 Independent (Perot); 1980 - 32,021 Independent (John Anderson); 1968 - 3,469 American Independent (George Wallace). Hawaii was formally admitted as a state in August 1959.

HAWAII

POSTWAR VOTE FOR GOVERNOR

Year	Total Vote	Republican Vote	Republican Candidate	Democratic Vote	Democratic Candidate	Other Vote	Rep.-Dem.	Total Vote Rep.	Total Vote Dem.	Major Vote Rep.	Major Vote Dem.
2022	413,262	152,237	Aiona, Duke	261,025	Green, Josh		108,788 D	36.8%	63.2%	36.8%	63.2%
2018	390,843	131,719	Tupola, Andria	244,934	Ige, David Yutaka*	14,190	113,215 D	33.7%	62.7%	35.0%	65.0%
2014	366,210	135,775	Aiona, Duke	181,106	Ige, David Yutaka	49,329	45,331 D	37.1%	49.5%	42.8%	57.2%
2010	382,563	157,311	Aiona, Duke	222,724	Abercrombie, Neil	2,528	65,413 D	41.1%	58.2%	41.4%	58.6%
2006	344,315	215,313	Lingle, Linda*	121,717	Iwase, Randy	7,285	93,596 R	62.5%	35.4%	63.9%	36.1%
2002	382,110	197,009	Lingle, Linda	179,647	Hirono, Mazie K.	5,454	17,362 R	51.6%	47.0%	52.3%	47.7%
1998	407,556	198,952	Lingle, Linda	204,206	Cayetano, Benjamin J.*	4,398	5,254 D	48.8%	50.1%	49.3%	50.7%
1994**	369,013	107,908	Saiki, Patricia	134,978	Cayetano, Benjamin J.	126,127	27,070 D	29.2%	36.6%	44.4%	55.6%
1990	340,132	131,310	Hemmings, Fred	203,491	Waihee, John*	5,331	72,181 D	38.6%	59.8%	39.2%	60.8%
1986	334,115	160,460	Anderson, D. G.	173,655	Waihee, John		13,195 D	48.0%	52.0%	48.0%	52.0%
1982**	311,853	81,507	Anderson, D. G.	141,043	Ariyoshi, George R.*	89,303	59,536 D	26.1%	45.2%	36.6%	63.4%
1978	281,587	124,610	Leopold, John	153,394	Ariyoshi, George R.*	3,583	28,784 D	44.3%	54.5%	44.8%	55.2%
1974	249,650	113,388	Crossley, Randolph	136,262	Ariyoshi, George R.		22,874 D	45.4%	54.6%	45.4%	54.6%
1970	239,061	101,249	King, Samuel P.	137,812	Burns, John A.*		36,563 D	42.4%	57.6%	42.4%	57.6%
1966	213,164	104,324	Crossley, Randolph	108,840	Burns, John A.*		4,516 D	48.9%	51.1%	48.9%	51.1%
1962	196,015	81,707	Quinn, Willam F.*	114,308	Burns, John A.		32,601 D	41.7%	58.3%	41.7%	58.3%
1959**	168,662	86,213	Quinn, Willam F.	82,074	Burns, John A.	375	4,139 R	51.1%	48.7%	51.2%	48.8%

Note: An asterisk (*) denotes incumbent. **In past elections, the other vote included: 1994 -113,158 Best Party (Frank F. Fasi); 1982 - 89,303 Independent Democrat (Fasi). In both 1982 and 1994, Fasi finished second. The 1959 election was for a short term pending the regular vote in 1962.

POSTWAR VOTE FOR SENATOR

Year	Total Vote	Republican Vote	Republican Candidate	Democratic Vote	Democratic Candidate	Other Vote	Rep.-Dem. Plurality	Total Vote Rep.	Total Vote Dem.	Major Vote Rep.	Major Vote Dem.
2022	408,517	106,358	McDermott, Bob	290,894	Schatz, Brian*	11,265	184,536 D	26.0%	71.2%	26.8%	73.2%
2018	388,351	112,035	Curtis, Ron	276,316	Hirono, Mazie K.*		164,281 D	28.8%	71.2%	28.8%	71.2%
2016	416,562	92,653	Carroll, John S.	306,604	Schatz, Brian*	17,305	213,951 D	22.2%	73.6%	23.2%	76.8%
2014S**	353,774	98,006	Cavasso, Cam	246,827	Schatz, Brian*	8,941	148,821 D	27.7%	69.8%	28.4%	71.6%
2012	430,910	161,091	Lingle, Linda	269,819	Hirono, Mazie K.		108,728 D	37.4%	62.6%	37.4%	62.6%
2010	370,660	79,954	Cavasso, Cam	277,289	Inouye, Daniel K.*	13,417	197,335 D	21.6%	74.8%	22.4%	77.6%
2006	342,842	126,097	Thielen, Cynthia	210,330	Akaka, Daniel K.*	6,415	84,233 D	36.8%	61.3%	37.5%	62.5%
2004	415,347	87,172	Cavasso, Cam	313,629	Inouye, Daniel K.*	14,546	226,457 D	21.0%	75.5%	21.7%	78.3%
2000	345,623	84,701	Carroll, John	251,215	Akaka, Daniel K.*	9,707	166,514 D	24.5%	72.7%	25.2%	74.8%
1998	398,124	70,964	Young, Crystal	315,252	Inouye, Daniel K.*	11,908	244,288 D	17.8%	79.2%	18.4%	81.6%
1994	356,902	86,320	Hustace, Maria M.	256,189	Akaka, Daniel K.*	14,393	169,869 D	24.2%	71.8%	25.2%	74.8%
1992**	363,662	97,928	Reed, Rick	208,266	Inouye, Daniel K.*	57,468	110,338 D	26.9%	57.3%	32.0%	68.0%
1990S**	349,666	155,978	Saiki, Patricia	188,901	Akaka, Daniel K.	4,787	32,923 D	44.6%	54.0%	45.2%	54.8%
1988	323,876	66,987	Hustace, Maria M.	247,941	Matsunaga, Spark M.*	8,948	180,954 D	20.7%	76.6%	21.3%	78.7%
1986	328,797	86,910	Hutchinson, Frank	241,887	Inouye, Daniel K.*		154,977 D	26.4%	73.6%	26.4%	73.6%
1982	306,410	52,071	Brown, Clarence J.	245,386	Matsunaga, Spark M.*	8,953	193,315 D	17.0%	80.1%	17.5%	82.5%
1980	288,006	53,068	Brown, Cooper	224,485	Inouye, Daniel K.*	10,453	171,417 D	18.4%	77.9%	19.1%	80.9%
1976	302,092	122,724	Quinn, Willam F.	162,305	Matsunaga, Spark M.	17,063	39,581 D	40.6%	53.7%	43.1%	56.9%
1974**	250,221			207,454	Inouye, Daniel K.*	42,767	207,454 D		82.9%		100.0%
1970	240,760	124,163	Fong, Hiram L.*	116,597	Heftel, Cecil		7,566 R	51.6%	48.4%	51.6%	48.4%
1968	226,927	34,008	Thiessen, Wayne C.	189,248	Inouye, Daniel K.*	3,671	155,240 D	15.0%	83.4%	15.2%	84.8%
1964	208,814	110,747	Fong, Hiram L.*	96,789	Gill, Thomas P.	1,278	13,958 R	53.0%	46.4%	53.4%	46.6%
1962	196,361	60,067	Dillingham, Ben	136,294	Inouye, Daniel K.		76,227 D	30.6%	69.4%	30.6%	69.4%
1959**	163,875	79,123	Tsukiyama, Wilfred C.	83,700	Long, Oren E.	1,052	4,577 D	48.3%	51.1%	48.6%	51.4%
1959	164,808	87,161	Fong, Hiram L.	77,647	Fasi, Frank F.		9,514 R	52.9%	47.1%	52.9%	47.1%

Note: An asterisk (*) denotes incumbent. **In past elections, the other vote was: 1992 - 49,921 Green (Linda B. Martin); 1974 - 42,767 Peoples (James D. Kimmel), who finished second. The 1990 and 2014 elections were for a short term to fill a vacancy. The two 1959 elections were held to indeterminate terms and the Senate later determined by lot that Senator Long would serve a short term, Senator Fong a long term. The Republican Party did not run a Senate candidate in the 1974 election.

HAWAII
GOVERNOR 2022

2020 Census Population	County	Total Vote	Republican (Aiona)	Democratic (Green)	Other	Rep.-Dem. Plurality	Percentage			
							Total Vote		Major Vote	
							Rep.	Dem.	Rep.	Dem.
201,959	HAWAII	64,022	21,870	42,152		20,282 D	34.2%	65.8%	34.2%	65.8%
971,975	HONOLULU	273,543	102,968	170,575		67,607 D	37.6%	62.4%	37.6%	62.4%
72,456	KAUAI	24,018	9,722	14,296		4,574 D	40.5%	59.5%	40.5%	59.5%
167,641	MAUI	51,679	17,677	34,002		16,325 D	34.2%	65.8%	34.2%	65.8%
1,414,031	TOTAL	413,262	152,237	261,025		108,788 D	36.8%	63.2%	36.8%	63.2%

HAWAII
SENATOR 2022

2020 Census Population	County	Total Vote	Republican (McDermott)	Democratic (Schatz)	Other	Rep.-Dem. Plurality	Percentage			
							Total Vote		Major Vote	
							Rep.	Dem.	Rep.	Dem.
201,959	HAWAII	63,234	15,156	46,096	1,982	30,940 D	24.0%	72.9%	24.7%	75.3%
971,975	HONOLULU	270,991	74,265	190,178	6,548	115,913 D	27.4%	70.2%	28.1%	71.9%
72,456	KAUAI	23,449	5,711	16,974	764	11,263 D	24.4%	72.4%	25.2%	74.8%
167,641	MAUI	50,843	11,226	37,646	1,971	26,420 D	22.1%	74.0%	23.0%	77.0%
1,414,031	TOTAL	408,517	106,358	290,894	11,265	184,536 D	26.0%	71.2%	26.8%	73.2%

HAWAII
HOUSE OF REPRESENTATIVES

CD	Year	Total Vote	Republican		Democratic		Other Vote	Rep.-Dem. Plurality	Percentage			
			Vote	Candidate	Vote	Candidate			Total Vote		Major Vote	
									Rep.	Dem.	Rep.	Dem.
1	2022	194,763	51,217	KRESS, CONRAD	143,546	CASE, EDWARD E.*		92,329 D	26.3%	73.7%	26.3%	73.7%
1	2020	254,433	71,188	CURTIS, RON	183,245	CASE, EDWARD E.*		112,057 D	28.0%	72.0%	28.0%	72.0%
1	2018	184,211	42,498	CAVASSO, CAM	134,650	CASE, EDWARD E.	7,063	92,152 D	23.1%	73.1%	24.0%	76.0%
1	2016	202,357	45,958	OSTROV, SHIRLENE D. "SHIRL"	145,417	HANABUSA, COLLEEN	10,982	99,459 D	22.7%	71.9%	24.0%	76.0%
1	2014	179,844	86,454	DJOU, CHARLES	93,390	TAKAI, MARK		6,936 D	48.1%	51.9%	48.1%	51.9%
1	2012	213,329	96,824	DJOU, CHARLES	116,505	HANABUSA, COLLEEN*		19,681 D	45.4%	54.6%	45.4%	54.6%
2	2022	206,411	72,874	AKANA, JOSEPH S.	128,407	TOKUDA, JILL N.	5,130	55,533 D	35.3%	62.2%	36.2%	63.8%
2	2020	272,102	84,027	AKANA, JOSEPH S.	171,517	KAHELE, KAIAL'I	16,558	87,490 D	30.9%	63.0%	32.9%	67.1%
2	2018	198,121	44,850	EVANS, BRIAN	153,271	GABBARD, TULSI*		108,421 D	22.6%	77.4%	22.6%	77.4%
2	2016	210,516	39,668	KAAIHUE, ANGELA AULANI	170,848	GABBARD, TULSI*		131,180 D	18.8%	81.2%	18.8%	81.2%
2	2014	180,333	33,630	CROWLEY, KAWIKA	142,010	GABBARD, TULSI*	4,693	108,380 D	18.6%	78.7%	19.1%	80.9%
2	2012	209,210	40,707	CROWLEY, KAWIKA	168,503	GABBARD, TULSI		127,796 D	19.5%	80.5%	19.5%	80.5%
TOTAL	2022	401,174	124,091		271,953		5,130	147,862 D	30.9%	67.8%	31.3%	68.7%
TOTAL	2020	526,535	155,215		354,762		16,558	199,547 D	29.5%	67.4%	30.4%	69.6%
TOTAL	2018	382,332	87,348		287,921		7,063	200,573 D	22.8%	75.3%	23.3%	76.7%
TOTAL	2016	412,873	85,626		316,265		10,982	230,639 D	20.7%	76.6%	21.3%	78.7%
TOTAL	2014	360,177	120,084		235,400		4,693	115,316 D	33.3%	65.4%	33.8%	66.2%
TOTAL	2012	422,539	137,531		285,008			147,477 D	32.5%	67.5%	32.5%	67.5%

Note: An asterisk (*) denotes incumbent.

HAWAII

GENERAL AND PRIMARY ELECTIONS

GENERAL ELECTIONS: OTHER VOTES

Senate	Other vote was 4,915 Libertarian (Feena Bonoan), 4,142 Green (Emma Pohlman), 2,208 Aloha Aina (Dan Decker)
House	Other vote was:
CD 2	5,130 Libertarian (Michelle Tippens)

2022 PRIMARY ELECTIONS: SUPPLEMENTARY INFORMATION

Primary	August 13, 2022	Registration (as of August 13, 2022)		853,874	No Party Registration
Primary Type	Open—Any registered voter could participate in the party primary of his or her choice.				

	REPUBLICAN PRIMARIES			DEMOCRATIC PRIMARIES		
Senator	McDermott, Bob	25,686	39.6%	Schatz, Brian*	228,595	93.6%
	Dalhouse, Timothy	17,158	26.4%	Tataii, Steve	15,725	6.4%
	Christian, Wallyn Kanoelani	9,497	14.6%			
	Bond, Steven R.	6,407	9.9%			
	LaVonne, Asia	6,187	9.5%			
	TOTAL	64,935		TOTAL	244,320	
Governor	Aiona, Duke	37,608	49.6%	Green, Josh	158,161	62.9%
	Penn, BJ	19,817	26.1%	Cayetano, Vicky	52,447	20.9%
	Cordery, Gary	8,258	10.9%	Kahele, Kaiali'i	37,738	15.0%
	Tsuneyoshi, Heidi	7,255	9.6%	Tanabe, Van K.	1,236	0.5%
	Mariano, Lynn Barry	903	1.2%	Kim, Richard Y.	991	0.4%
	Morgan, Paul	796	1.0%	Bourgoin, David L.	590	0.2%
	Kahau, Keline	469	0.6%	Lewman, Clyde	249	0.1%
	Woods, Walter	438	0.6%			
	Paskowitz, Moses	189	0.2%			
	Hawat, George	140	0.2%			
	TOTAL	75,873		TOTAL	251,412	
Congressional District 1	Kress, Conrad	13,449	50.4%	Case, Edward E.*	100,667	83.2%
	Reyes, Arturo P. "Art"	7,465	28.0%	Alcubilla, Sergio	20,364	16.8%
	Largey, Patrick	5,785	21.7%			
	TOTAL	26,699		TOTAL	121,031	
Congressional District 2	Akana, Joseph S.	28,200	83.9%	Tokuda, Jill N.	62,275	57.6%
	Webster, Joseph E. "Joe"	5,403	16.1%	Branco, Patrick Pihana	27,057	25.0%
				Yoshida, Kyle	6,624	6.1%
				Schultz, Brendan	6,115	5.7%
				Gi, Nicole	3,937	3.6%
				Sparks, Steven B.	2,137	2.0%
	TOTAL	33,603		TOTAL	108,145	

Note: An asterisk (*) denotes incumbent.

IDAHO

Statewide Races

In the ruby red Gem State, Republicans dominate statewide politics – which can sometimes lead to intrafactional primaries. In 2018, then-Lt. Gov. Brad Little, with support from much of his party's establishment wing, won a competitive GOP gubernatorial primary. Little governed as a mainstream conservative, but he was frequently frustrated by his lieutenant governor, Janice McGeachin (the two offices are elected separately in Idaho). McGeachin, who allegedly had ties to right-wing militia groups, made a habit of rescinding Little's executive orders, namely his COVID-related measures, when the governor was travelling outside of Idaho. When Little returned from his trips, he would undo McGeachin's changes, but their friction came to a head when McGeachin announced she'd challenge Little in the primary for governor.

McGeachin was not Little's sole primary challenger, but she was the most prominent. Still, most Idaho Republicans were clearly content with the governor: in an eight-way primary, Little claimed 53%. In carrying most of the state's counties, Little posted especially strong performances in Boise's Ada County and in the Mormon-heavy east. McGeachin, though she lived in the east, carried four counties in North Idaho – the region has become a far-right political Mecca.

In the general election, Little increased his share to just over 60%, losing only Blaine County – home of the Sun Valley Ski resort, it is often the only county that Democrats carry in general elections. The Democratic nominee, Stephen Heidt, took 20% but a prominent independent candidate finished close behind. Ammon Bundy, an anti-government activist whose family first came to the nation's attention in 2014 during a standoff with the Bureau of Land Management, took 17%. In fact, Bundy got more votes than Heidt in 34 of the state's 44 counties – most of the counties where Heidt received more votes had a major city.

Vis-à-vis the gubernatorial race, the Senate contest was comparatively drama-free. Republican Sen. Mike Crapo easily won a fifth term, although his 61%–29% win represented the smallest margin of his Senatorial career. Scott Cleveland, an independent who ran to Crapo's right, likely drew many of his nearly 50,000 votes from Republicans who would have otherwise gone with the incumbent. In addition to Blaine, Crapo lost Teton County, which is in the orbit of the touristy Jackson Hole area.

House Races

Idaho's redistricting commission, which handles line-drawing, only needed to shift 35,000 residents between the state's two districts. District 2, represented by veteran Rep. Mike Simpson (R), is the most heavily Mormon district outside of Utah – it includes the eastern half of the state plus most of Boise proper. District 1, held by GOP Rep. Russ Fulcher, pairs the remainder of Ada County with the western and northern parts of the state. Democrats held the 1st District for a term after the 2008 elections, but the Idaho seats are otherwise safe Republican turf.

IDAHO

Congressional districts first established for elections held in 2022

2 members

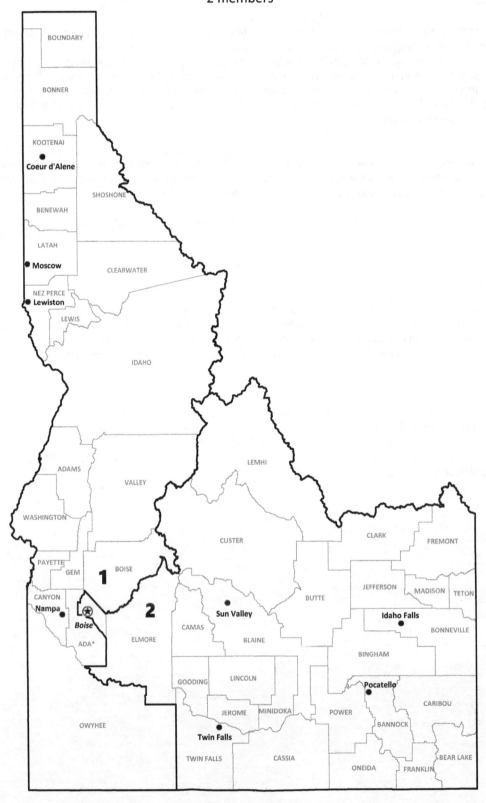

* Asterisk indicates a county whose boundaries include parts of two or more congressional districts.

IDAHO

GOVERNOR
Brad Little (R). Reelected 2022 to a four-year term. Previously elected 2018.

SENATORS (2 Republicans)
Michael D. Crapo (R). Reelected 2022 to a six-year term. Previously elected 2016, 2010, 2004, 1998.

Jim Risch (R). Reelected 2020 to a six-year term. Previously elected 2014, 2008.

REPRESENTATIVES (2 Republicans)
1. Russ M. Fulcher (R)
2. Michael K. Simpson (R)

POSTWAR VOTE FOR PRESIDENT

Year	Total Vote	Republican Vote	Republican Candidate	Democratic Vote	Democratic Candidate	Other Vote	Rep.-Dem. Plurality	Total Vote Rep.	Total Vote Dem.	Major Vote Rep.	Major Vote Dem.
2020	867,934	554,119	Trump, Donald J.*	287,021	Biden, Joseph R. Jr.	26,794	267,098 R	63.8%	33.1%	65.9%	34.1%
2016**	690,255	409,055	Trump, Donald J.	189,765	Clinton, Hillary Rodham	91,435	219,290 R	59.3%	27.5%	68.3%	31.7%
2012	652,346	420,911	Romney, W. Mitt	212,787	Obama, Barack H.*	18,648	208,124 R	64.5%	32.6%	66.4%	33.6%
2008	655,122	403,012	McCain, John S. III	236,440	Obama, Barack H.	15,670	166,572 R	61.5%	36.1%	63.0%	37.0%
2004	598,447	409,235	Bush, George W.*	181,098	Kerry, John F.	8,114	228,137 R	68.4%	30.3%	69.3%	30.7%
2000**	501,621	336,937	Bush, George W.	138,637	Gore, Albert Jr.	26,047	198,300 R	67.2%	27.6%	70.8%	29.2%
1996**	491,719	256,595	Dole, Robert "Bob"	165,443	Clinton, Bill*	69,681	91,152 R	52.2%	33.6%	60.8%	39.2%
1992**	482,142	202,645	Bush, George H.*	137,013	Clinton, Bill	142,484	65,632 R	42.0%	28.4%	59.7%	40.3%
1988	408,968	253,881	Bush, George H.	147,272	Dukakis, Michael S.	7,815	106,609 R	62.1%	36.0%	63.3%	36.7%
1984	411,144	297,523	Reagan, Ronald*	108,510	Mondale, Walter F.	5,111	189,013 R	72.4%	26.4%	73.3%	26.7%
1980**	437,431	290,699	Reagan, Ronald	110,192	Carter, Jimmy*	36,540	180,507 R	66.5%	25.2%	72.5%	27.5%
1976	344,071	204,151	Ford, Gerald R.*	126,549	Carter, Jimmy	13,371	77,602 R	59.3%	36.8%	61.7%	38.3%
1972	310,379	199,384	Nixon, Richard M.*	80,826	McGovern, George S.	30,169	118,558 R	64.2%	26.0%	71.2%	28.8%
1968**	291,183	165,369	Nixon, Richard M.	89,273	Humphrey, Hubert Horatio Jr.	36,541	76,096 R	56.8%	30.7%	64.9%	35.1%
1964	292,477	143,557	Goldwater, Barry M. Sr.	148,920	Johnson, Lyndon B.*		5,363 D	49.1%	50.9%	49.1%	50.9%
1960	300,450	161,597	Nixon, Richard M.	138,853	Kennedy, John F.		22,744 R	53.8%	46.2%	53.8%	46.2%
1956	272,989	166,979	Eisenhower, Dwight D.*	105,868	Stevenson, Adlai E. II	142	61,111 R	61.2%	38.8%	61.2%	38.8%
1952	276,254	180,707	Eisenhower, Dwight D.	95,081	Stevenson, Adlai E. II	466	85,626 R	65.4%	34.4%	65.5%	34.5%
1948	214,816	101,514	Dewey, Thomas E.	107,370	Truman, Harry S.*	5,932	5,856 D	47.3%	50.0%	48.6%	51.4%

Note: An asterisk (*) denotes incumbent. **In past elections, the other vote included: 2016 - 46,476 Independent (Evan McMullin), 28,331 Libertarian (Johnson); 2000 -12,292 Green (Ralph Nader); 1996 - 62,518 Reform (Ross Perot); 1992 -130,395 Independent (Perot); 1980 - 27,058 Independent (John Anderson); 1968 - 36,541 American Independent (George Wallace).

IDAHO

POSTWAR VOTE FOR GOVERNOR

		Republican		Democratic		Other Vote	Rep.-Dem. Plurality	Percentage			
								Total Vote		Major Vote	
Year	Total Vote	Vote	Candidate	Vote	Candidate			Rep.	Dem.	Rep.	Dem.
2022	592,624	358,598	Little, Brad*	120,160	Heidt, Stephen	113,866	238,438 R	60.5%	20.3%	74.9%	25.1%
2018	605,131	361,661	Little, Brad	231,081	Jordan, Paulette	12,389	130,580 R	59.8%	38.2%	61.0%	39.0%
2014	439,830	235,405	Otter, C. L. "Butch"*	169,556	Balukoff, A.J.	34,869	65,849 R	53.5%	38.6%	58.1%	41.9%
2010	452,535	267,483	Otter, C. L. "Butch"*	148,680	Allred, Keith	36,372	118,803 R	59.1%	32.9%	64.3%	35.7%
2006	450,850	237,437	Otter, C. L. "Butch"	198,845	Brady, Jerry M.	14,568	38,592 R	52.7%	44.1%	54.4%	45.6%
2002	411,477	231,566	Kempthorne, Dirk*	171,711	Brady, Jerry M.	8,200	59,855 R	56.3%	41.7%	57.4%	42.6%
1998	381,248	258,095	Kempthorne, Dirk	110,815	Huntley, Robert C.	12,338	147,280 R	67.7%	29.1%	70.0%	30.0%
1994	413,346	216,123	Batt, Phil	181,363	Echohawk, Larry	15,860	34,760 R	52.3%	43.9%	54.4%	45.6%
1990	320,610	101,937	Fairchild, Roger	218,673	Andrus, Cecil D.*		116,736 D	31.8%	68.2%	31.8%	68.2%
1986	387,426	189,794	Leroy, David H.	193,429	Andrus, Cecil D.	4,203	3,635 D	49.0%	49.9%	49.5%	50.5%
1982	326,522	161,157	Batt, Phil	165,365	Evans, John V.*		4,208 D	49.4%	50.6%	49.4%	50.6%
1978	288,566	114,149	Larsen, Allan	169,540	Evans, John V.*	4,877	55,391 D	39.6%	58.8%	40.2%	59.8%
1974	259,632	68,731	Murphy, Jack M.	184,142	Andrus, Cecil D.*	6,759	115,411 D	26.5%	70.9%	27.2%	72.8%
1970	245,112	117,108	Samuelson, Don*	128,004	Andrus, Cecil D.		10,896 D	47.8%	52.2%	47.8%	52.2%
1966**	252,593	104,586	Samuelson, Don	93,744	Andrus, Cecil D.	54,263	10,842 R	41.4%	37.1%	52.7%	47.3%
1962	255,454	139,578	Smylie, Robert E.*	115,876	Smith, Vernon K.		23,702 R	54.6%	45.4%	54.6%	45.4%
1958	239,046	121,810	Smylie, Robert E.*	117,236	Derr, A. M.		4,574 R	51.0%	49.0%	51.0%	49.0%
1954	228,685	124,038	Smylie, Robert E.	104,647	Hamilton, Clark		19,391 R	54.2%	45.8%	54.2%	45.8%
1950	204,792	107,642	Jordan, Len B.	97,150	Wright, Calvin E.		10,492 R	52.6%	47.4%	52.6%	47.4%
1946	181,364	102,233	Robins, Charles A.	79,131	Williams, Arnold*		23,102 R	56.4%	43.6%	56.4%	43.6%

Note: An asterisk (*) denotes incumbent. **In past elections, the Other Vote included: 1966 - 30,913 Independent (Perry Swisher).

POSTWAR VOTE FOR SENATOR

		Republican		Democratic		Other Vote	Rep.-Dem. Plurality	Percentage			
								Total Vote		Major Vote	
Year	Total Vote	Vote	Candidate	Vote	Candidate			Rep.	Dem.	Rep.	Dem.
2022	590,890	358,539	Crapo, Michael D.*	169,808	Roth, David	62,543	188,731 R	60.7%	28.7%	67.9%	32.1%
2020	859,827	538,446	Risch, Jim*	285,864	Jordan, Paulette	35,517	252,582 R	62.6%	33.2%	65.3%	34.7%
2016	678,943	449,017	Crapo, Michael D.*	188,249	Sturgill, Jerry	41,677	260,768 R	66.1%	27.7%	70.5%	29.5%
2014	437,170	285,596	Risch, Jim*	151,574	Mitchell, Nels		134,022 R	65.3%	34.7%	65.3%	34.7%
2010	449,530	319,953	Crapo, Michael D.*	112,057	Sullivan, P. Tom	17,520	207,896 R	71.2%	24.9%	74.1%	25.9%
2008	644,780	371,744	Risch, Jim	219,903	Larocco, Larry	53,133	151,841 R	57.7%	34.1%	62.8%	37.2%
2004**	503,932	499,796	Crapo, Michael D.*			4,136	499,796 R	99.2%		100.0%	
2002	408,544	266,215	Craig, Larry E.*	132,975	Blinken, Alan	9,354	133,240 R	65.2%	32.5%	66.7%	33.3%
1998	378,174	262,966	Crapo, Michael D.	107,375	Mauk, Bill	7,833	155,591 R	69.5%	28.4%	71.0%	29.0%
1996	497,233	283,532	Craig, Larry E.*	198,422	Minnick, Walt	15,279	85,110 R	57.0%	39.9%	58.8%	41.2%
1992	478,504	270,468	Kempthorne, Dirk	208,036	Stallings, Richard		62,432 R	56.5%	43.5%	56.5%	43.5%
1990	315,936	193,641	Craig, Larry E.	122,295	Twilegar, Ron J.		71,346 R	61.3%	38.7%	61.3%	38.7%
1986	382,024	196,958	Symms, Steven D.*	185,066	Evans, John V.		11,892 R	51.6%	48.4%	51.6%	48.4%
1984	406,168	293,193	McClure, James A.*	105,591	Busch, Peter M.	7,384	187,602 R	72.2%	26.0%	73.5%	26.5%
1980	439,647	218,701	Symms, Steven D.	214,439	Church, Frank*	6,507	4,262 R	49.7%	48.8%	50.5%	49.5%
1978	284,047	194,412	McClure, James A.*	89,635	Jensen, Dwight		104,777 R	68.4%	31.6%	68.4%	31.6%
1974	258,847	109,072	Smith, Robert L.	145,140	Church, Frank*	4,635	36,068 D	42.1%	56.1%	42.9%	57.1%
1972	309,602	161,804	McClure, James A.	140,913	Davis, William E. Bud	6,885	20,891 R	52.3%	45.5%	53.5%	46.5%
1968	287,876	114,394	Hansen, George V.	173,482	Church, Frank*		59,088 D	39.7%	60.3%	39.7%	60.3%
1966	252,456	139,819	Jordan, Len B.*	112,637	Harding, Ralph R.		27,182 R	55.4%	44.6%	55.4%	44.6%
1962	258,786	117,129	Hawley, Jack	141,657	Church, Frank*		24,528 D	45.3%	54.7%	45.3%	54.7%
1962S**	257,677	131,279	Jordan, Len B.*	126,398	Pfost, Gracie B.		4,881 R	50.9%	49.1%	50.9%	49.1%
1960	292,096	152,648	Dworshak, Henry C.*	139,448	McLaughlin, R. F.		13,200 R	52.3%	47.7%	52.3%	47.7%
1956	265,292	102,781	Welker, Herman*	149,096	Church, Frank	13,415	46,315 D	38.7%	56.2%	40.8%	59.2%
1954	226,408	142,269	Dworshak, Henry C.*	84,139	Taylor, Glen H.		58,130 R	62.8%	37.2%	62.8%	37.2%
1950	201,417	124,237	Welker, Herman	77,180	Clark, D. Worth		47,057 R	61.7%	38.3%	61.7%	38.3%
1950S**	201,700	104,608	Dworshak, Henry C.	97,092	Burtenshaw, Claude		7,516 R	51.9%	48.1%	51.9%	48.1%
1948	214,188	103,868	Dworshak, Henry C.*	107,000	Miller, Bert H.	3,320	3,132 D	48.5%	50.0%	49.3%	50.7%
1946S**	180,152	105,523	Dworshak, Henry C.	74,629	Donart, George E.		30,894 R	58.6%	41.4%	58.6%	41.4%

Note: An asterisk (*) denotes incumbent. **In 2004 there was no candidate on the Democratic line. A write-in candidate, who was a Democrat, received 4,136 votes, which is listed in the Other Vote column. The 1946 election and one each of the 1950 and 1962 elections were for short terms to fill vacancies.

IDAHO
GOVERNOR 2022

2020 Census Population	County	Total Vote	Republican (Little)	Democratic (Heidt)	Other	Rep.-Dem. Plurality	Percentage Total Vote		Percentage Major Vote	
							Rep.	Dem.	Rep.	Dem.
487,154	ADA	185,229	105,276	53,693	26,260	51,583 R	56.8%	29.0%	66.2%	33.8%
4,337	ADAMS	2,020	1,287	239	494	1,048 R	63.7%	11.8%	84.3%	15.7%
88,233	BANNOCK	25,501	14,945	7,006	3,550	7,939 R	58.6%	27.5%	68.1%	31.9%
6,148	BEAR LAKE	2,266	1,412	140	714	1,272 R	62.3%	6.2%	91.0%	9.0%
9,339	BENEWAH	3,454	2,097	397	960	1,700 R	60.7%	11.5%	84.1%	15.9%
46,990	BINGHAM	12,384	8,750	1,277	2,357	7,473 R	70.7%	10.3%	87.3%	12.7%
23,021	BLAINE	9,720	4,022	5,149	549	1,127 D	41.4%	53.0%	43.9%	56.1%
7,908	BOISE	3,444	1,932	453	1,059	1,479 R	56.1%	13.2%	81.0%	19.0%
46,173	BONNER	20,794	12,136	3,121	5,537	9,015 R	58.4%	15.0%	79.5%	20.5%
119,890	BONNEVILLE	35,487	24,525	5,310	5,652	19,215 R	69.1%	15.0%	82.2%	17.8%
12,296	BOUNDARY	5,239	3,084	437	1,718	2,647 R	58.9%	8.3%	87.6%	12.4%
2,606	BUTTE	1,009	635	74	300	561 R	62.9%	7.3%	89.6%	10.4%
1,113	CAMAS	517	337	61	119	276 R	65.2%	11.8%	84.7%	15.3%
232,022	CANYON	58,329	34,316	9,236	14,777	25,080 R	58.8%	15.8%	78.8%	21.2%
7,191	CARIBOU	2,120	1,495	142	483	1,353 R	70.5%	6.7%	91.3%	8.7%
24,062	CASSIA	5,802	4,074	371	1,357	3,703 R	70.2%	6.4%	91.7%	8.3%
839	CLARK	208	145	12	51	133 R	69.7%	5.8%	92.4%	7.6%
8,781	CLEARWATER	3,121	2,220	368	533	1,852 R	71.1%	11.8%	85.8%	14.2%
4,360	CUSTER	2,036	1,228	232	576	996 R	60.3%	11.4%	84.1%	15.9%
27,562	ELMORE	6,630	4,260	1,023	1,347	3,237 R	64.3%	15.4%	80.6%	19.4%
13,961	FRANKLIN	4,337	2,744	213	1,380	2,531 R	63.3%	4.9%	92.8%	7.2%
13,090	FREMONT	4,262	3,073	347	842	2,726 R	72.1%	8.1%	89.9%	10.1%
18,279	GEM	7,631	4,582	599	2,450	3,983 R	60.0%	7.8%	88.4%	11.6%
15,206	GOODING	4,051	2,458	430	1,163	2,028 R	60.7%	10.6%	85.1%	14.9%
16,739	IDAHO	7,470	4,840	638	1,992	4,202 R	64.8%	8.5%	88.4%	11.6%
30,082	JEFFERSON	9,089	6,591	580	1,918	6,011 R	72.5%	6.4%	91.9%	8.1%
24,424	JEROME	4,858	3,161	540	1,157	2,621 R	65.1%	11.1%	85.4%	14.6%
167,496	KOOTENAI	62,296	38,296	9,299	14,701	28,997 R	61.5%	14.9%	80.5%	19.5%
40,220	LATAH	14,973	8,256	5,043	1,674	3,213 R	55.1%	33.7%	62.1%	37.9%
8,086	LEMHI	3,660	2,465	421	774	2,044 R	67.3%	11.5%	85.4%	14.6%
3,845	LEWIS	1,361	1,013	123	225	890 R	74.4%	9.0%	89.2%	10.8%
5,343	LINCOLN	1,321	841	152	328	689 R	63.7%	11.5%	84.7%	15.3%
39,703	MADISON	8,405	6,037	694	1,674	5,343 R	71.8%	8.3%	89.7%	10.3%
21,102	MINIDOKA	4,721	3,222	399	1,100	2,823 R	68.2%	8.5%	89.0%	11.0%
40,563	NEZ PERCE	13,412	9,252	2,659	1,501	6,593 R	69.0%	19.8%	77.7%	22.3%
4,572	ONEIDA	1,627	1,031	70	526	961 R	63.4%	4.3%	93.6%	6.4%
11,868	OWYHEE	3,290	1,881	300	1,109	1,581 R	57.2%	9.1%	86.2%	13.8%
24,110	PAYETTE	7,609	4,874	723	2,012	4,151 R	64.1%	9.5%	87.1%	12.9%
7,700	POWER	1,972	1,411	297	264	1,114 R	71.6%	15.1%	82.6%	17.4%
12,957	SHOSHONE	4,128	2,614	767	747	1,847 R	63.3%	18.6%	77.3%	22.7%
12,218	TETON	4,692	2,169	1,989	534	180 R	46.2%	42.4%	52.2%	47.8%
87,142	TWIN FALLS	22,993	13,884	3,428	5,681	10,456 R	60.4%	14.9%	80.2%	19.8%
11,527	VALLEY	5,232	3,211	1,344	677	1,867 R	61.4%	25.7%	70.5%	29.5%
10,252	WASHINGTON	3,924	2,516	364	1,044	2,152 R	64.1%	9.3%	87.4%	12.6%
1,800,510	TOTAL	592,624	358,598	120,160	113,866	238,438 R	60.5%	20.3%	74.9%	25.1%

IDAHO
SENATOR 2022

2020 Census Population	County	Total Vote	Republican (Crapo)	Democratic (Roth)	Other	Rep.-Dem. Plurality		Percentage			
								Total Vote		Major Vote	
								Rep.	Dem.	Rep.	Dem.
487,154	ADA	184,521	87,579	76,656	20,286	10,923	R	47.5%	41.5%	53.3%	46.7%
4,337	ADAMS	2,011	1,425	367	219	1,058	R	70.9%	18.2%	79.5%	20.5%
88,233	BANNOCK	25,443	14,480	9,054	1,909	5,426	R	56.9%	35.6%	61.5%	38.5%
6,148	BEAR LAKE	2,244	1,871	196	177	1,675	R	83.4%	8.7%	90.5%	9.5%
9,339	BENEWAH	3,464	2,662	503	299	2,159	R	76.8%	14.5%	84.1%	15.9%
46,990	BINGHAM	12,310	9,491	1,750	1,069	7,741	R	77.1%	14.2%	84.4%	15.6%
23,021	BLAINE	9,689	3,121	6,006	562	2,885	D	32.2%	62.0%	34.2%	65.8%
7,908	BOISE	3,437	2,172	673	592	1,499	R	63.2%	19.6%	76.3%	23.7%
46,173	BONNER	20,761	13,348	5,467	1,946	7,881	R	64.3%	26.3%	70.9%	29.1%
119,890	BONNEVILLE	35,439	24,579	7,866	2,994	16,713	R	69.4%	22.2%	75.8%	24.2%
12,296	BOUNDARY	5,200	3,939	732	529	3,207	R	75.8%	14.1%	84.3%	15.7%
2,606	BUTTE	993	783	114	96	669	R	78.9%	11.5%	87.3%	12.7%
1,113	CAMAS	516	367	95	54	272	R	71.1%	18.4%	79.4%	20.6%
232,022	CANYON	58,229	36,558	12,961	8,710	23,597	R	62.8%	22.3%	73.8%	26.2%
7,191	CARIBOU	2,116	1,735	205	176	1,530	R	82.0%	9.7%	89.4%	10.6%
24,062	CASSIA	5,796	4,619	584	593	4,035	R	79.7%	10.1%	88.8%	11.2%
839	CLARK	206	161	19	26	142	R	78.2%	9.2%	89.4%	10.6%
8,781	CLEARWATER	3,120	2,389	526	205	1,863	R	76.6%	16.9%	82.0%	18.0%
4,360	CUSTER	2,009	1,447	359	203	1,088	R	72.0%	17.9%	80.1%	19.9%
27,562	ELMORE	6,605	4,380	1,334	891	3,046	R	66.3%	20.2%	76.7%	23.3%
13,961	FRANKLIN	4,305	3,588	302	415	3,286	R	83.3%	7.0%	92.2%	7.8%
13,090	FREMONT	4,240	3,399	480	361	2,919	R	80.2%	11.3%	87.6%	12.4%
18,279	GEM	7,571	5,118	1,076	1,377	4,042	R	67.6%	14.2%	82.6%	17.4%
15,206	GOODING	4,047	2,941	609	497	2,332	R	72.7%	15.0%	82.8%	17.2%
16,739	IDAHO	7,465	5,741	962	762	4,779	R	76.9%	12.9%	85.6%	14.4%
30,082	JEFFERSON	9,094	7,396	836	862	6,560	R	81.3%	9.2%	89.8%	10.2%
24,424	JEROME	4,865	3,506	803	556	2,703	R	72.1%	16.5%	81.4%	18.6%
167,496	KOOTENAI	62,239	42,115	13,404	6,720	28,711	R	67.7%	21.5%	75.9%	24.1%
40,220	LATAH	14,984	7,484	6,881	619	603	R	49.9%	45.9%	52.1%	47.9%
8,086	LEMHI	3,654	2,690	674	290	2,016	R	73.6%	18.4%	80.0%	20.0%
3,845	LEWIS	1,359	1,097	176	86	921	R	80.7%	13.0%	86.2%	13.8%
5,343	LINCOLN	1,314	978	221	115	757	R	74.4%	16.8%	81.6%	18.4%
39,703	MADISON	8,276	6,533	972	771	5,561	R	78.9%	11.7%	87.0%	13.0%
21,102	MINIDOKA	4,712	3,623	592	497	3,031	R	76.9%	12.6%	86.0%	14.0%
40,563	NEZ PERCE	13,446	8,986	3,628	832	5,358	R	66.8%	27.0%	71.2%	28.8%
4,572	ONEIDA	1,601	1,330	117	154	1,213	R	83.1%	7.3%	91.9%	8.1%
11,868	OWYHEE	3,275	2,376	411	488	1,965	R	72.5%	12.5%	85.3%	14.7%
24,110	PAYETTE	7,587	5,509	1,079	999	4,430	R	72.6%	14.2%	83.6%	16.4%
7,700	POWER	1,972	1,428	420	124	1,008	R	72.4%	21.3%	77.3%	22.7%
12,957	SHOSHONE	4,109	2,858	1,005	246	1,853	R	69.6%	24.5%	74.0%	26.0%
12,218	TETON	4,686	2,100	2,375	211	275	D	44.8%	50.7%	46.9%	53.1%
87,142	TWIN FALLS	22,863	14,914	4,780	3,169	10,134	R	65.2%	20.9%	75.7%	24.3%
11,527	VALLEY	5,220	2,829	1,974	417	855	R	54.2%	37.8%	58.9%	41.1%
10,252	WASHINGTON	3,897	2,894	564	439	2,330	R	74.3%	14.5%	83.7%	16.3%
1,800,510	TOTAL	590,890	358,539	169,808	62,543	188,731	R	60.7%	28.7%	67.9%	32.1%

IDAHO

HOUSE OF REPRESENTATIVES

CD	Year	Total Vote	Republican Vote	Republican Candidate	Democratic Vote	Democratic Candidate	Other Vote	Rep.-Dem. Plurality	Total Vote Rep.	Total Vote Dem.	Major Vote Rep.	Major Vote Dem.
1	2022	312,442	222,901	FULCHER, RUSSELL M.*	82,261	PETERSON, KAYLEE	7,280	140,640 R	71.3%	26.3%	73.0%	27.0%
1	2020	458,576	310,736	FULCHER, RUSSELL M.*	131,380	SOTO, RUDY	16,460	179,356 R	67.8%	28.6%	70.3%	29.7%
1	2018	315,069	197,719	FULCHER, RUSSELL M.	96,922	MCNEIL, CRISTINA	20,428	100,797 R	62.8%	30.8%	67.1%	32.9%
1	2016	355,357	242,252	LABRADOR, RAUL R.*	113,052	PIOTROWSKI, JAMES	53	129,200 R	68.2%	31.8%	68.2%	31.8%
1	2014	220,864	143,580	LABRADOR, RAUL R.*	77,277	RINGO, SHIRLEY G.	7	66,303 R	65.0%	35.0%	65.0%	35.0%
1	2012	316,724	199,402	LABRADOR, RAUL R.*	97,450	FARRIS, JIMMY	19,872	101,952 R	63.0%	30.8%	67.2%	32.8%
2	2022	271,186	172,450	SIMPSON, MICHAEL K.*	98,736	NORMAN, WENDY		73,714 R	63.6%	36.4%	63.6%	36.4%
2	2020	391,333	250,669	SIMPSON, MICHAEL K.*	124,151	SWISHER, AARON	16,513	126,518 R	64.1%	31.7%	66.9%	33.1%
2	2018	280,655	170,274	SIMPSON, MICHAEL K.*	110,381	SWISHER, AARON		59,893 R	60.7%	39.3%	60.7%	39.3%
2	2016	326,237	205,292	SIMPSON, MICHAEL K.*	95,940	MARTINEZ, JENNIFER	25,005	109,352 R	62.9%	29.4%	68.2%	31.8%
2	2014	214,293	131,492	SIMPSON, MICHAEL K.*	82,801	STALLINGS, RICHARD		48,691 R	61.4%	38.6%	61.4%	38.6%
2	2012	318,494	207,412	SIMPSON, MICHAEL K.*	110,847	LEFAVOUR, NICOLE	235	96,565 R	65.1%	34.8%	65.2%	34.8%
TOTAL	2022	583,628	395,351		180,997		7,280	214,354 R	67.7%	31.0%	68.6%	31.4%
TOTAL	2020	849,909	561,405		255,531		32,973	305,874 R	66.1%	30.1%	68.7%	31.3%
TOTAL	2018	595,724	367,993		207,303		20,428	160,690 R	61.8%	34.8%	64.0%	36.0%
TOTAL	2016	681,594	447,544		208,992		25,058	238,552 R	65.7%	30.7%	68.2%	31.8%
TOTAL	2014	435,157	275,072		160,078		7	114,994 R	63.2%	36.8%	63.2%	36.8%
TOTAL	2012	635,218	406,814		208,297		20,107	198,517 R	64.0%	32.8%	66.1%	33.9%

Note: An asterisk (*) denotes incumbent.

IDAHO

GENERAL AND PRIMARY ELECTIONS

GENERAL ELECTIONS: OTHER VOTES

Governor Other vote was 101,835 Independent (Ammon Bundy), 6,714 Libertarian (Paul Sand), 5,250 Constitution (Chantyrose Davison), 67 Write-In (Write-In)

Senate Other vote was 49,917 Independent (Scott Cleveland), 8,500 Constitution (Ray Writz), 4,126 Libertarian (Idaho Sierra Law)

House Other vote was:

CD 1 7,280 Libertarian (Darian Drake)

2022 PRIMARY ELECTIONS: SUPPLEMENTARY INFORMATION

Primary	May 17, 2022	**Registration** (as of May 1, 2022)	995,474	Republican	550,873
				Democratic	129,758
				Libertarian	10,963
				Constitution	3,875
				Unaffiliated	550,873

Primary Type Semi-Open—Registered Democrats and unaffiliated voters could participate in the Democratic primary. Only registered Republicans could vote in the Republican primary.

IDAHO

GENERAL AND PRIMARY ELECTIONS

	REPUBLICAN PRIMARIES			DEMOCRATIC PRIMARIES		
Senator	Crapo, Michael D.	177,906	67.1%	Roth, David	19,160	57.8%
	Trotter, Scott	27,699	10.5%	Pursley, Benjamin "Ben"	13,987	42.2%
	Bourn, Brenda	21,612	8.2%			
	Turnbull, Ramont	20,883	7.9%			
	Fleming, Natalie M.	16,902	6.4%			
	TOTAL	265,002		TOTAL	33,147	
Governor	Little, Brad	148,843	52.8%	Heidt, Stephen	25,088	78.8%
	McGeachin, Janice	90,857	32.2%	Rognstad, Shelby (Write-In)	6,736	21.2%
	Humphreys, Edward R.	30,878	11.0%	Reilly, David (Write-In)	21	0.1%
	Bradshaw, Steven R.	5,470	1.9%			
	Jackson, Ashley	3,172	1.1%			
	Marie, Lisa	1,120	0.4%			
	Cannady, Ben	804	0.3%			
	Usabel, Cody	680	0.2%			
	TOTAL	281,824		TOTAL	31,845	
Congressional District 1	Fulcher, Russell M.	126,528	100.0%	Peterson, Kaylee	15,057	100.0%
	TOTAL	126,528		TOTAL	15,057	
Congressional District 2	Simpson, Michael K.*	67,177	54.6%	Norman, Wendy	17,150	100.0%
	Smith, Bryan D.	40,267	32.7%			
	Christensen, Flint L.	7,113	5.8%			
	Porter, Chris	6,357	5.2%			
	Levy, Daniel Algiers Lucas	2,185	1.8%			
	TOTAL	123,099		TOTAL	17,150	

Note: An asterisk (*) denotes incumbent.

ILLINOIS

Statewide Races

The 2022 election went about as well as it could have for Democrats in the Land of Lincoln: it was the first midterm cycle since 2002 where they won both the governorship and the Senate seat that was up.

Sen. Tammy Duckworth was unopposed in her primary while Gov. J. B. Pritzker only garnered token opposition. Both incumbents were Democrats seeking a second term to their respective offices. In the six-way Republican primary, the Democratic Governors Association ran ads boosting state Sen. Darren Bailey, a downstate conservative. Bailey, who one GOP member of the delegation noted seemed a better fit for Missouri than Illinois, won the primary decisively. In the lower-profile Senate primary, Republicans nominated Kathy Salvi.

In the general election, Pritzker's 12.5-point margin was a few points lower than the 15-point margin he won by 2018. But in 2018, a conservative third-party candidate, state Sen. Sam McCann took 4%, which likely came disproportionately from then-Gov. Bruce Rauner's (R) share. Indeed, in both 2018 and 2022, Pritzker took just under 55% while Bailey's 43% was up 4 points from Rauner's 39%. Compared to 2018, though, Pritzker saw every county south of the state capital in Springfield shift heavily against him – although, again, unlike 2018, there was no conservative independent candidate taking votes from the Republican in 2022.

In the Senate race, Duckworth won by a larger 15-point margin. Duckworth carried all 13 counties that voted for Pritzker while adding Jackson County (Southern Illinois University) and Winnebago's Rockford County. By securing reelection, she broke a curse of sorts. Before 2022, her seat had not reelected an incumbent since 1986.

House Races

For the second decade in a row, the task of redistricting in Illinois fell to a Democratic trifecta – and for the fifth decade in a row, the state was slated to lose representation. With the delegation set to shrink from 18 to 17 members, Democrats enacted a gerrymander that ultimately increased their advantage from 13-5 to 14-3.

National Democrats undoubtedly appreciated Rep. Adam Kinzinger's (R) stances against Trump and his service on the January 6th Select Committee. But the Democratic mappers back home in Illinois were not going to give him special treatment – their priority was maximizing seats for their own party. Kinzinger retired, and his seat was eliminated.

Democrats targeted GOP Rep. Rodney Davis, a mainstream Republican who held the light red 13th District, which ran from the East St. Louis area to Urbana. After his seat was made much bluer, Davis opted to run in the adjacent, and dark red 15th District – he lost a primary against the much more Trump-aligned Rep. Mary Miller.

Democrats also shored up their marginal seats. They gave Rep. Lauren Underwood, in the outer reaches of Chicagoland, a firmer seat and finessed the 17th District, a marginal seat that borders Iowa, so that it would be less amenable to Republicans. In a move that didn't have as much to do with pure partisanship, legislators created a second heavily Hispanic seat by reconfiguring the 3rd District (the existing 4th District was already majority-Hispanic).

ILLINOIS

Congressional districts first established for elections held in 2022

17 members

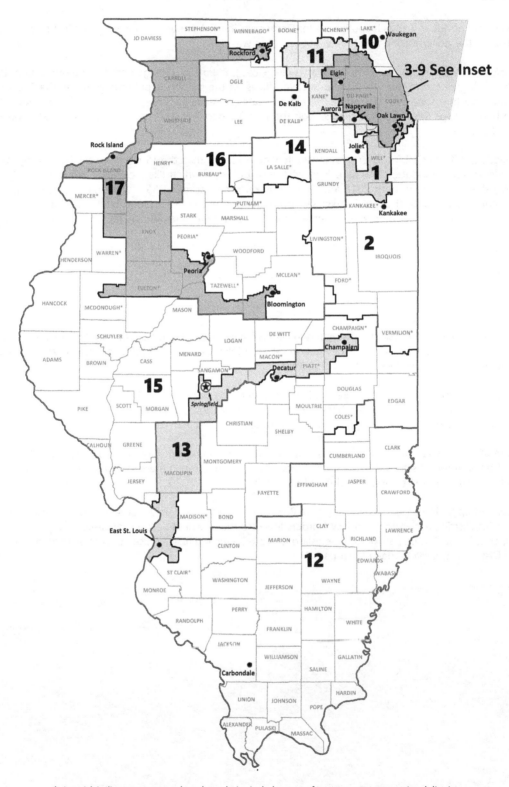

* Asterisk indicates a county whose boundaries include parts of two or more congressional districts.
CDs 1, 11, 13, and 17 are highlighted for visibility. See Inset for Chicago area.

ILLINOIS
Greater Chicago Area

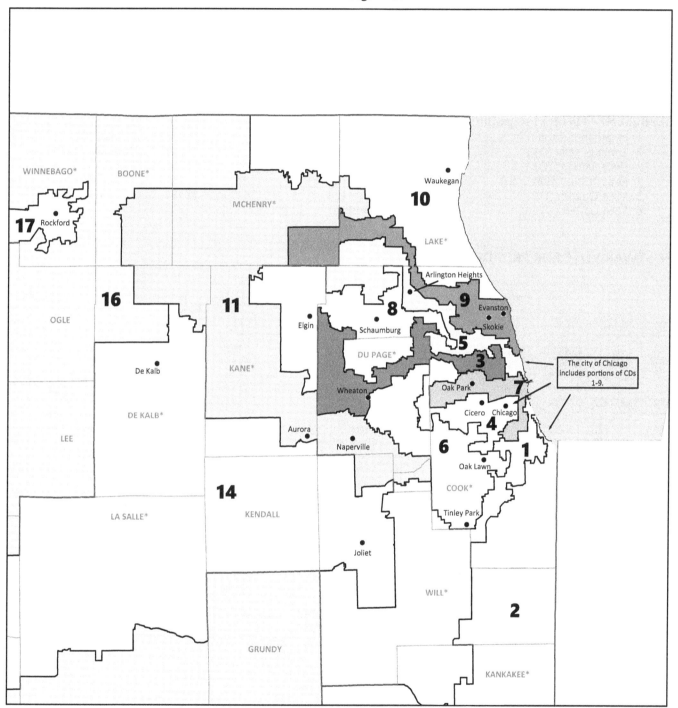

* Asterisk indicates a county whose boundaries include parts of two or more congressional districts.
CDs 3, 5, 7, 9, 11, and 16 are highlighted for visibility.

ILLINOIS

GOVERNOR
Jay "J. B." Pritzker (D). Reelected 2022 to a four-year term. Previously elected 2018.

SENATORS (2 Democrats)
Richard J. Durbin (D). Reelected 2020 to a six-year term. Previously elected 2014, 2008, 2002, 1996.

Tammy Duckworth (D). Reelected 2022 to a six-year term. Previously elected 2016.

REPRESENTATIVES (3 Republicans, 14 Democrats)
1. Jonathan Jackson (D)
2. Robin L. Kelly (D)
3. Delia Ramirez (D)
4. Jesús "Chuy" Garcia (D)
5. Mike Quigley (D)
6. Sean Casten (D)
7. Danny K. Davis (D)
8. Raja Krishnamoorthi (D)
9. Janice D. "Jan" Schakowsky (D)
10. Brad Schneider (D)
11. Bill Foster (D)
12. Mike Bost (R)
13. Nikki Budzinski (D)
14. Lauren Underwood (D)
15. Mary Miller (R)
16. Darin LaHood (R)
17. Eric Sorensen (D)

POSTWAR VOTE FOR PRESIDENT

Year	Total Vote	Republican Vote	Republican Candidate	Democratic Vote	Democratic Candidate	Other Vote	Rep.-Dem. Plurality	Total Vote Rep.	Total Vote Dem.	Major Vote Rep.	Major Vote Dem.
2020	6,033,744	2,446,891	Trump, Donald J.*	3,471,915	Biden, Joseph R. Jr.	114,938	1,025,024 D	40.6%	57.5%	41.3%	58.7%
2016**	5,536,424	2,146,015	Trump, Donald J.	3,090,729	Clinton, Hillary Rodham	299,680	944,714 D	38.8%	55.8%	41.0%	59.0%
2012	5,242,014	2,135,216	Romney, W. Mitt	3,019,512	Obama, Barack H.*	87,286	884,296 D	40.7%	57.6%	41.4%	58.6%
2008	5,522,371	2,031,179	McCain, John S. III	3,419,348	Obama, Barack H.	71,844	1,388,169 D	36.8%	61.9%	37.3%	62.7%
2004	5,274,322	2,345,946	Bush, George W.*	2,891,550	Kerry, John F.	36,826	545,604 D	44.5%	54.8%	44.8%	55.2%
2000**	4,742,123	2,019,421	Bush, George W.	2,589,026	Gore, Albert Jr.	133,676	569,605 D	42.6%	54.6%	43.8%	56.2%
1996**	4,311,391	1,587,021	Dole, Robert "Bob"	2,341,744	Clinton, Bill*	382,626	754,723 D	36.8%	54.3%	40.4%	59.6%
1992**	5,050,157	1,734,096	Bush, George H.*	2,453,350	Clinton, Bill	862,711	719,254 D	34.3%	48.6%	41.4%	58.6%
1988	4,559,120	2,310,939	Bush, George H.	2,215,940	Dukakis, Michael S.	32,241	94,999 R	50.7%	48.6%	51.0%	49.0%
1984	4,819,088	2,707,103	Reagan, Ronald*	2,086,499	Mondale, Walter F.	25,486	620,604 R	56.2%	43.3%	56.5%	43.5%
1980**	4,749,721	2,358,049	Reagan, Ronald	1,981,413	Carter, Jimmy*	410,259	376,636 R	49.6%	41.7%	54.3%	45.7%
1976	4,718,914	2,364,269	Ford, Gerald R.*	2,271,295	Carter, Jimmy	83,350	92,974 R	50.1%	48.1%	51.0%	49.0%
1972	4,723,236	2,788,179	Nixon, Richard M.*	1,913,472	McGovern, George S.	21,585	874,707 R	59.0%	40.5%	59.3%	40.7%
1968**	4,619,749	2,174,774	Nixon, Richard M.	2,039,814	Humphrey, Hubert Horatio Jr.	405,161	134,960 R	47.1%	44.2%	51.6%	48.4%
1964	4,702,841	1,905,946	Goldwater, Barry M. Sr.	2,796,833	Johnson, Lyndon B.*	62	890,887 D	40.5%	59.5%	40.5%	59.5%
1960	4,757,409	2,368,988	Nixon, Richard M.	2,377,846	Kennedy, John F.	10,575	8,858 D	49.8%	50.0%	49.9%	50.1%
1956	4,407,407	2,623,327	Eisenhower, Dwight D.*	1,775,682	Stevenson, Adlai E. II	8,398	847,645 R	59.5%	40.3%	59.6%	40.4%
1952	4,481,058	2,457,327	Eisenhower, Dwight D.	2,013,920	Stevenson, Adlai E. II	9,811	443,407 R	54.8%	44.9%	55.0%	45.0%
1948	3,984,046	1,961,103	Dewey, Thomas E.	1,994,715	Truman, Harry S.*	28,228	33,612 D	49.2%	50.1%	49.6%	50.4%

Note: An asterisk (*) denotes incumbent. **In past elections, the other vote included: 2016 - 209,596 Libertarian (Gary Johnson); 2000 - 103,759 Green (Ralph Nader); 1996 - 346,408 Reform (Ross Perot); 1992 - 840,515 Independent (Perot); 1980 - 346,754 Independent (John Anderson); 1968 - 390,958 American Independent (George Wallace).

ILLINOIS

POSTWAR VOTE FOR GOVERNOR

Year	Total Vote	Republican Vote	Republican Candidate	Democratic Vote	Democratic Candidate	Other Vote	Rep.-Dem. Plurality	Total Vote % Rep.	Total Vote % Dem.	Major Vote % Rep.	Major Vote % Dem.
2022	4,104,774	1,739,095	Bailey, Darren	2,253,748	Pritzker, Jay "J.B."*	111,931	514,653 D	42.4%	54.9%	43.6%	56.4%
2018	4,547,657	1,765,751	Rauner, Bruce	2,479,746	Pritzker, Jay "J. B."	302,160	713,995 D	38.8%	54.5%	41.6%	58.4%
2014	3,627,690	1,823,627	Rauner, Bruce	1,681,343	Quinn, Pat*	122,720	142,284 R	50.3%	46.3%	52.0%	48.0%
2010	3,729,989	1,713,385	Brady, Bill	1,745,219	Quinn, Pat*	271,385	31,834 D	45.9%	46.8%	49.5%	50.5%
2006**	3,487,989	1,369,315	Topinka, Judy Baar	1,736,731	Blagojevich, Rod R.*	381,943	367,416 D	39.3%	49.8%	44.1%	55.9%
2002	3,538,891	1,594,960	Ryan, Jim	1,847,040	Blagojevich, Rod R.	96,891	252,080 D	45.1%	52.2%	46.3%	53.7%
1998	3,358,705	1,714,094	Ryan, George H.	1,594,191	Poshard, Glenn	50,420	119,903 R	51.0%	47.5%	51.8%	48.2%
1994	3,106,566	1,984,318	Edgar, Jim*	1,069,850	Netsch, Dawn C.	52,398	914,468 R	63.9%	34.4%	65.0%	35.0%
1990	3,257,410	1,653,126	Edgar, Jim	1,569,217	Hartigan, Neil F.	35,067	83,909 R	50.7%	48.2%	51.3%	48.7%
1986**	3,143,978	1,655,849	Thompson, James R.*	208,830	(See note)	1,279,299	1,447,019 R	52.7%	6.6%	88.8%	11.2%
1982	3,673,681	1,816,101	Thompson, James R.*	1,811,027	Stevenson, Adlai E. II	46,553	5,074 R	49.4%	49.3%	50.1%	49.9%
1978	3,150,095	1,859,684	Thompson, James R.*	1,263,134	Bakalis, Michael	27,277	596,550 R	59.0%	40.1%	59.6%	40.4%
1976**	4,635,728	3,000,395	Thompson, James R.	1,606,989	Howlett, Michael J.	28,344	1,393,406 R	64.7%	34.7%	65.1%	34.9%
1972	4,678,802	2,293,809	Ogilvie, Richard B.*	2,371,301	Walker, Daniel	13,692	77,492 D	49.0%	50.7%	49.2%	50.8%
1968	4,506,000	2,307,295	Ogilvie, Richard B.	2,179,501	Shapiro, Samuel H.	19,204	127,794 R	51.2%	48.4%	51.4%	48.6%
1964	4,657,500	2,239,095	Percy, Charles H.	2,418,394	Kerner, Otto*	11	179,299 D	48.1%	51.9%	48.1%	51.9%
1960	4,674,187	2,070,479	Stratton, William G.*	2,594,731	Kerner, Otto	8,977	524,252 D	44.3%	55.5%	44.4%	55.6%
1956	4,314,611	2,171,786	Stratton, William G.*	2,134,909	Austin, Richard B.	7,916	36,877 R	50.3%	49.5%	50.4%	49.6%
1952	4,415,864	2,317,363	Stratton, William G.	2,089,721	Dixon, Sherwood	8,780	227,642 R	52.5%	47.3%	52.6%	47.4%
1948	3,940,257	1,678,007	Green, Dwight H.*	2,250,074	Stevenson, Adlai E. II	12,176	572,067 D	42.6%	57.1%	42.7%	57.3%

Note: An asterisk (*) denotes incumbent. **In past elections, the other vote included: 2006 - 361,336 Green (Rich Whitney); 1986 - 1,256,626 Illinois Solidarity (Adlai E. Stevenson III). In 1986, there was no Democratic candidate for governor on the ballot. Mark Fairchild, a supporter of Lyndon H. LaRouche Jr., was the "paired" Democratic candidate for Lt. Governor and the Democratic vote was cast for this ticket of "no name" and Fairchild. Running on the Illinois Solidarity line, Stevenson finished second with 40.0% of the vote. The 1976 vote was for a two-year term to permit shifting the election for Governor to non-presidential years.

POSTWAR VOTE FOR SENATOR

Year	Total Vote	Republican Vote	Republican Candidate	Democratic Vote	Democratic Candidate	Other Vote	Rep.-Dem. Plurality	Total Vote % Rep.	Total Vote % Dem.	Major Vote % Rep.	Major Vote % Dem.
2022	4,100,739	1,701,055	Salvi, Kathy	2,329,136	Duckworth, Tammy*	70,548	628,081 D	41.5%	56.8%	42.2%	57.8%
2020	5,968,901	2,319,870	Curran, Mark	3,278,930	Durbin, Richard J.*	370,101	959,060 D	38.9%	54.9%	41.4%	58.6%
2016	5,491,878	2,184,692	Kirk, Mark Steven*	3,012,940	Duckworth, Tammy	294,246	828,248 D	39.8%	54.9%	42.0%	58.0%
2014	3,603,519	1,538,522	Oberweis, James D.	1,929,637	Durbin, Richard J.*	135,360	391,115 D	42.7%	53.5%	44.4%	55.6%
2010	3,704,473	1,778,698	Kirk, Mark Steven	1,719,478	Giannoulias, Alexander	206,297	59,220 R	48.0%	46.4%	50.8%	49.2%
2010S**	3,545,984	1,677,729	Kirk, Mark Steven	1,641,486	Giannoulias, Alexander	226,769	36,243 R	47.3%	46.3%	50.5%	49.5%
2008	5,329,884	1,520,621	Sauerberg, Steve	3,615,844	Durbin, Richard J.*	193,419	2,095,223 D	28.5%	67.8%	29.6%	70.4%
2004	5,141,520	1,390,690	Keyes, Alan	3,597,456	Obama, Barack H.	153,374	2,206,766 D	27.0%	70.0%	27.9%	72.1%
2002	3,486,851	1,325,703	Durkin, Jim	2,103,766	Durbin, Richard J.*	57,382	778,063 D	38.0%	60.3%	38.7%	61.3%
1998	3,395,033	1,709,041	Fitzgerald, Peter G.	1,610,496	Moseley-Braun, Carol*	75,496	98,545 R	50.3%	47.4%	51.5%	48.5%
1996	4,250,722	1,728,824	Salvi, Al	2,384,028	Durbin, Richard J.	137,870	655,204 D	40.7%	56.1%	42.0%	58.0%
1992	4,939,558	2,126,833	Williamson, Richard S.	2,631,229	Moseley-Braun, Carol	181,496	504,396 D	43.1%	53.3%	44.7%	55.3%
1990	3,251,005	1,135,628	Martin, Lynn	2,115,377	Simon, Paul*		979,749 D	34.9%	65.1%	34.9%	65.1%
1986	3,122,883	1,053,734	Koehler, Judy	2,033,783	Dixon, Alan J.*	35,366	980,049 D	33.7%	65.1%	34.1%	65.9%
1984	4,787,473	2,308,039	Percy, Charles H.*	2,397,303	Simon, Paul	82,131	89,264 D	48.2%	50.1%	49.1%	50.9%
1980	4,580,029	1,946,296	O'Neal, David C.	2,565,302	Dixon, Alan J.	68,431	619,006 D	42.5%	56.0%	43.1%	56.9%
1978	3,184,764	1,698,711	Percy, Charles H.*	1,448,187	Seith, Alex	37,866	250,524 R	53.3%	45.5%	54.0%	46.0%
1974	2,914,666	1,084,884	Burditt, George M.	1,811,496	Stevenson, Adlai E. II*	18,286	726,612 D	37.2%	62.2%	37.5%	62.5%
1972	4,608,380	2,867,078	Percy, Charles H.*	1,721,031	Pucinski, Roman C.	20,271	1,146,047 R	62.2%	37.3%	62.5%	37.5%
1970S**	3,599,272	1,519,718	Smith, Ralph T.*	2,065,054	Stevenson, Adlai E. II	14,500	545,336 D	42.2%	57.4%	42.4%	57.6%
1968	4,449,757	2,358,947	Dirksen, Everett McKinley*	2,073,242	Clark, William G.	17,568	285,705 R	53.0%	46.6%	53.2%	46.8%
1966	3,822,725	2,100,449	Percy, Charles H.	1,678,147	Douglas, Paul H.*	44,129	422,302 R	54.9%	43.9%	55.6%	44.4%
1962	3,709,216	1,961,202	Dirksen, Everett McKinley*	1,748,007	Yates, Sidney R.	7	213,195 R	52.9%	47.1%	52.9%	47.1%
1960	4,632,796	2,093,846	Witwer, Samuel W.	2,530,943	Douglas, Paul H.*	8,007	437,097 D	45.2%	54.6%	45.3%	54.7%
1956	4,264,830	2,307,352	Dirksen, Everett McKinley*	1,949,883	Stengel, Richard	7,595	357,469 R	54.1%	45.7%	54.2%	45.8%
1954	3,368,025	1,563,683	Meek, Joseph T.	1,804,338	Douglas, Paul H.*	4	240,655 D	46.4%	53.6%	46.4%	53.6%
1950	3,622,673	1,951,984	Dirksen, Everett McKinley	1,657,630	Lucas, Scott W.*	13,059	294,354 R	53.9%	45.8%	54.1%	45.9%
1948	3,900,285	1,740,026	Brooks, C. Wayland*	2,147,754	Douglas, Paul H.	12,505	407,728 D	44.6%	55.1%	44.8%	55.2%

Note: An asterisk (*) denotes incumbent. **The 1970 election and one of the 2010 elections were for a short term to fill a vacancy.

ILLINOIS
GOVERNOR 2022

2020 Census Population	County	Total Vote	Republican (Bailey)	Democratic (Pritzker)	Other	Rep.-Dem. Plurality	Total Vote Rep.	Total Vote Dem.	Major Vote Rep.	Major Vote Dem.
65,494	ADAMS	25,015	19,474	5,033	508	14,441 R	77.8%	20.1%	79.5%	20.5%
5,704	ALEXANDER	1,709	989	699	21	290 R	57.9%	40.9%	58.6%	41.4%
16,461	BOND	6,497	4,611	1,687	199	2,924 R	71.0%	26.0%	73.2%	26.8%
53,626	BOONE	17,654	10,246	6,803	605	3,443 R	58.0%	38.5%	60.1%	39.9%
6,594	BROWN	1,929	1,595	305	29	1,290 R	82.7%	15.8%	83.9%	16.1%
32,633	BUREAU	12,773	7,738	4,636	399	3,102 R	60.6%	36.3%	62.5%	37.5%
4,727	CALHOUN	2,406	1,749	588	69	1,161 R	72.7%	24.4%	74.8%	25.2%
14,311	CARROLL	6,023	3,966	1,868	189	2,098 R	65.8%	31.0%	68.0%	32.0%
12,062	CASS	3,993	2,782	1,098	113	1,684 R	69.7%	27.5%	71.7%	28.3%
209,084	CHAMPAIGN	67,970	26,061	40,011	1,898	13,950 D	38.3%	58.9%	39.4%	60.6%
32,292	CHRISTIAN	12,532	8,635	3,466	431	5,169 R	68.9%	27.7%	71.4%	28.6%
15,410	CLARK	6,393	5,071	1,217	105	3,854 R	79.3%	19.0%	80.6%	19.4%
13,201	CLAY	5,832	4,963	782	87	4,181 R	85.1%	13.4%	86.4%	13.6%
37,592	CLINTON	14,894	11,423	3,114	357	8,309 R	76.7%	20.9%	78.6%	21.4%
50,655	COLES	16,591	10,622	5,547	422	5,075 R	64.0%	33.4%	65.7%	34.3%
5,141,687	COOK	1,442,785	344,902	1,065,445	32,438	720,543 D	23.9%	73.8%	24.5%	75.5%
18,657	CRAWFORD	7,030	5,439	1,377	214	4,062 R	77.4%	19.6%	79.8%	20.2%
10,781	CUMBERLAND	4,802	3,830	867	105	2,963 R	79.8%	18.1%	81.5%	18.5%
15,623	DE WITT	6,145	4,352	1,599	194	2,753 R	70.8%	26.0%	73.1%	26.9%
105,059	DEKALB	34,432	16,119	17,047	1,266	928 D	46.8%	49.5%	48.6%	51.4%
19,465	DOUGLAS	6,512	4,778	1,555	179	3,223 R	73.4%	23.9%	75.4%	24.6%
921,485	DU PAGE	340,309	138,667	190,601	11,041	51,934 D	40.7%	56.0%	42.1%	57.9%
17,161	EDGAR	6,156	4,624	1,367	165	3,257 R	75.1%	22.2%	77.2%	22.8%
6,390	EDWARDS	2,824	2,488	296	40	2,192 R	88.1%	10.5%	89.4%	10.6%
34,043	EFFINGHAM	15,992	13,072	2,609	311	10,463 R	81.7%	16.3%	83.4%	16.6%
21,360	FAYETTE	8,069	6,627	1,290	152	5,337 R	82.1%	16.0%	83.7%	16.3%
12,962	FORD	5,168	3,776	1,230	162	2,546 R	73.1%	23.8%	75.4%	24.6%
38,474	FRANKLIN	13,733	10,442	2,952	339	7,490 R	76.0%	21.5%	78.0%	22.0%
34,314	FULTON	13,167	7,794	4,924	449	2,870 R	59.2%	37.4%	61.3%	38.7%
4,819	GALLATIN	2,232	1,716	445	71	1,271 R	76.9%	19.9%	79.4%	20.6%
12,965	GREENE	4,591	3,550	951	90	2,599 R	77.3%	20.7%	78.9%	21.1%
51,218	GRUNDY	19,409	11,733	6,966	710	4,767 R	60.5%	35.9%	62.7%	37.3%
8,122	HAMILTON	3,454	2,819	577	58	2,242 R	81.6%	16.7%	83.0%	17.0%
17,709	HANCOCK	7,248	5,619	1,438	191	4,181 R	77.5%	19.8%	79.6%	20.4%
3,836	HARDIN	1,683	1,339	284	60	1,055 R	79.6%	16.9%	82.5%	17.5%
6,643	HENDERSON	2,960	1,980	883	97	1,097 R	66.9%	29.8%	69.2%	30.8%
48,932	HENRY	19,723	12,155	6,949	619	5,206 R	61.6%	35.2%	63.6%	36.4%
27,127	IROQUOIS	10,532	8,334	1,948	250	6,386 R	79.1%	18.5%	81.1%	18.9%
56,609	JACKSON	17,121	8,372	8,303	446	69 R	48.9%	48.5%	50.2%	49.8%
9,619	JASPER	4,661	3,943	645	73	3,298 R	84.6%	13.8%	85.9%	14.1%
37,706	JEFFERSON	13,212	10,096	2,821	295	7,275 R	76.4%	21.4%	78.2%	21.8%
21,812	JERSEY	9,413	6,971	2,174	268	4,797 R	74.1%	23.1%	76.2%	23.8%
21,246	JO DAVIESS	9,526	5,486	3,754	286	1,732 R	57.6%	39.4%	59.4%	40.6%
12,518	JOHNSON	4,841	3,878	868	95	3,010 R	80.1%	17.9%	81.7%	18.3%
533,112	KANE	157,759	68,064	84,777	4,918	16,713 D	43.1%	53.7%	44.5%	55.5%
109,762	KANKAKEE	35,244	20,842	13,287	1,115	7,555 R	59.1%	37.7%	61.1%	38.9%
129,522	KENDALL	45,208	21,457	22,218	1,533	761 D	47.5%	49.1%	49.1%	50.9%
49,610	KNOX	17,598	9,597	7,486	515	2,111 R	54.5%	42.5%	56.2%	43.8%
108,823	LA SALLE	39,664	21,781	16,558	1,325	5,223 R	54.9%	41.7%	56.8%	43.2%
695,969	LAKE	228,629	83,724	137,912	6,993	54,188 D	36.6%	60.3%	37.8%	62.2%
15,666	LAWRENCE	5,113	4,094	909	110	3,185 R	80.1%	17.8%	81.8%	18.2%
34,037	LEE	12,204	7,220	4,599	385	2,621 R	59.2%	37.7%	61.1%	38.9%
35,684	LIVINGSTON	12,923	9,315	3,253	355	6,062 R	72.1%	25.2%	74.1%	25.9%
28,651	LOGAN	9,720	6,741	2,724	255	4,017 R	69.4%	28.0%	71.2%	28.8%
103,995	MACON	35,590	20,764	13,873	953	6,891 R	58.3%	39.0%	59.9%	40.1%
44,932	MACOUPIN	18,121	12,047	5,575	499	6,472 R	66.5%	30.8%	68.4%	31.6%
263,254	MADISON	98,134	55,205	39,856	3,073	15,349 R	56.3%	40.6%	58.1%	41.9%
37,255	MARION	13,005	9,860	2,859	286	7,001 R	75.8%	22.0%	77.5%	22.5%
11,448	MARSHALL	4,749	3,166	1,463	120	1,703 R	66.7%	30.8%	68.4%	31.6%
13,352	MASON	4,998	3,361	1,468	169	1,893 R	67.2%	29.4%	69.6%	30.4%

ILLINOIS
GOVERNOR 2022

2020 Census Population	County	Total Vote	Republican (Bailey)	Democratic (Pritzker)	Other	Rep.-Dem. Plurality	Percentage Total Vote Rep.	Dem.	Major Vote Rep.	Dem.
13,759	MASSAC	4,884	3,734	1,047	103	2,687 R	76.5%	21.4%	78.1%	21.9%
29,617	MCDONOUGH	9,460	5,945	3,269	246	2,676 R	62.8%	34.6%	64.5%	35.5%
308,253	MCHENRY	116,171	56,839	55,134	4,198	1,705 R	48.9%	47.5%	50.8%	49.2%
171,285	MCLEAN	64,859	31,125	31,930	1,804	805 D	48.0%	49.2%	49.4%	50.6%
12,202	MENARD	5,281	3,548	1,567	166	1,981 R	67.2%	29.7%	69.4%	30.6%
15,472	MERCER	6,785	4,238	2,297	250	1,941 R	62.5%	33.9%	64.9%	35.1%
34,748	MONROE	15,718	10,656	4,609	453	6,047 R	67.8%	29.3%	69.8%	30.2%
28,385	MONTGOMERY	10,754	7,395	3,030	329	4,365 R	68.8%	28.2%	70.9%	29.1%
33,554	MORGAN	11,042	7,314	3,459	269	3,855 R	66.2%	31.3%	67.9%	32.1%
14,551	MOULTRIE	5,304	3,919	1,250	135	2,669 R	73.9%	23.6%	75.8%	24.2%
50,723	OGLE	19,530	12,400	6,518	612	5,882 R	63.5%	33.4%	65.5%	34.5%
178,639	PEORIA	59,024	28,164	29,195	1,665	1,031 D	47.7%	49.5%	49.1%	50.9%
20,914	PERRY	7,829	5,804	1,828	197	3,976 R	74.1%	23.3%	76.0%	24.0%
16,363	PIATT	7,667	4,785	2,597	285	2,188 R	62.4%	33.9%	64.8%	35.2%
15,582	PIKE	6,081	4,968	975	138	3,993 R	81.7%	16.0%	83.6%	16.4%
4,209	POPE	1,690	1,361	304	25	1,057 R	80.5%	18.0%	81.7%	18.3%
5,323	PULASKI	2,029	1,404	584	41	820 R	69.2%	28.8%	70.6%	29.4%
5,752	PUTNAM	2,798	1,622	1,080	96	542 R	58.0%	38.6%	60.0%	40.0%
31,763	RANDOLPH	11,433	8,092	2,999	342	5,093 R	70.8%	26.2%	73.0%	27.0%
15,537	RICHLAND	6,315	4,950	1,188	177	3,762 R	78.4%	18.8%	80.6%	19.4%
141,879	ROCK ISLAND	48,203	21,130	25,663	1,410	4,533 D	43.8%	53.2%	45.2%	54.8%
23,520	SALINE	8,192	6,241	1,751	200	4,490 R	76.2%	21.4%	78.1%	21.9%
194,375	SANGAMON	79,487	39,166	38,161	2,160	1,005 R	49.3%	48.0%	50.6%	49.4%
6,777	SCHUYLER	3,226	2,307	817	102	1,490 R	71.5%	25.3%	73.8%	26.2%
4,953	SCOTT	2,116	1,702	378	36	1,324 R	80.4%	17.9%	81.8%	18.2%
21,646	SHELBY	9,777	7,654	1,890	233	5,764 R	78.3%	19.3%	80.2%	19.8%
259,303	ST. CLAIR	88,773	41,154	45,071	2,548	3,917 D	46.4%	50.8%	47.7%	52.3%
5,346	STARK	2,327	1,645	593	89	1,052 R	70.7%	25.5%	73.5%	26.5%
44,482	STEPHENSON	16,743	9,897	6,303	543	3,594 R	59.1%	37.6%	61.1%	38.9%
131,789	TAZEWELL	51,435	32,484	17,424	1,527	15,060 R	63.2%	33.9%	65.1%	34.9%
16,660	UNION	7,019	4,988	1,839	192	3,149 R	71.1%	26.2%	73.1%	26.9%
75,598	VERMILION	22,056	14,674	6,738	644	7,936 R	66.5%	30.5%	68.5%	31.5%
11,511	WABASH	4,076	3,288	730	58	2,558 R	80.7%	17.9%	81.8%	18.2%
16,819	WARREN	5,941	3,764	2,024	153	1,740 R	63.4%	34.1%	65.0%	35.0%
13,882	WASHINGTON	6,080	4,739	1,182	159	3,557 R	77.9%	19.4%	80.0%	20.0%
16,222	WAYNE	6,904	6,140	651	113	5,489 R	88.9%	9.4%	90.4%	9.6%
13,544	WHITE	5,764	4,766	878	120	3,888 R	82.7%	15.2%	84.4%	15.6%
55,173	WHITESIDE	20,057	11,090	8,335	632	2,755 R	55.3%	41.6%	57.1%	42.9%
691,843	WILL	233,151	108,464	117,475	7,212	9,011 D	46.5%	50.4%	48.0%	52.0%
66,668	WILLIAMSON	25,133	17,723	6,821	589	10,902 R	70.5%	27.1%	72.2%	27.8%
282,447	WINNEBAGO	88,077	43,492	41,987	2,598	1,505 R	49.4%	47.7%	50.9%	49.1%
38,482	WOODFORD	16,983	12,260	4,341	382	7,919 R	72.2%	25.6%	73.9%	26.1%
12,662,810	TOTAL	4,104,774	1,739,095	2,253,748	111,931	514,653 D	42.4%	54.9%	43.6%	56.4%

ILLINOIS
SENATOR 2022

2020 Census Population	County	Total Vote	Republican (Salvi)	Democratic (Duckworth)	Other	Rep.-Dem. Plurality	Percentage Total Vote		Major Vote	
							Rep.	Dem.	Rep.	Dem.
65,494	ADAMS	24,961	18,341	6,244	376	12,097 R	73.5%	25.0%	74.6%	25.4%
5,704	ALEXANDER	1,707	930	764	13	166 R	54.5%	44.8%	54.9%	45.1%
16,461	BOND	6,403	4,193	2,061	149	2,132 R	65.5%	32.2%	67.0%	33.0%
53,626	BOONE	17,532	10,157	7,022	353	3,135 R	57.9%	40.1%	59.1%	40.9%
6,594	BROWN	1,911	1,475	394	42	1,081 R	77.2%	20.6%	78.9%	21.1%
32,633	BUREAU	12,678	7,429	5,028	221	2,401 R	58.6%	39.7%	59.6%	40.4%
4,727	CALHOUN	2,333	1,485	789	59	696 R	63.7%	33.8%	65.3%	34.7%
14,311	CARROLL	5,956	3,804	2,039	113	1,765 R	63.9%	34.2%	65.1%	34.9%
12,062	CASS	3,935	2,581	1,260	94	1,321 R	65.6%	32.0%	67.2%	32.8%
209,084	CHAMPAIGN	67,855	25,791	40,756	1,308	14,965 D	38.0%	60.1%	38.8%	61.2%
32,292	CHRISTIAN	12,429	8,222	3,865	342	4,357 R	66.2%	31.1%	68.0%	32.0%
15,410	CLARK	6,320	4,745	1,480	95	3,265 R	75.1%	23.4%	76.2%	23.8%
13,201	CLAY	5,738	4,554	1,082	102	3,472 R	79.4%	18.9%	80.8%	19.2%
37,592	CLINTON	14,808	10,662	3,856	290	6,806 R	72.0%	26.0%	73.4%	26.6%
50,655	COLES	16,500	10,270	5,924	306	4,346 R	62.2%	35.9%	63.4%	36.6%
5,141,687	COOK	1,441,909	341,447	1,080,175	20,287	738,728 D	23.7%	74.9%	24.0%	76.0%
18,657	CRAWFORD	6,948	5,100	1,685	163	3,415 R	73.4%	24.3%	75.2%	24.8%
10,781	CUMBERLAND	4,763	3,607	1,077	79	2,530 R	75.7%	22.6%	77.0%	23.0%
15,623	DE WITT	6,086	4,152	1,784	150	2,368 R	68.2%	29.3%	69.9%	30.1%
105,059	DEKALB	34,513	16,063	17,688	762	1,625 D	46.5%	51.3%	47.6%	52.4%
19,465	DOUGLAS	6,462	4,529	1,801	132	2,728 R	70.1%	27.9%	71.5%	28.5%
921,485	DU PAGE	341,740	141,316	194,606	5,818	53,290 D	41.4%	56.9%	42.1%	57.9%
17,161	EDGAR	6,057	4,361	1,583	113	2,778 R	72.0%	26.1%	73.4%	26.6%
6,390	EDWARDS	2,784	2,280	448	56	1,832 R	81.9%	16.1%	83.6%	16.4%
34,043	EFFINGHAM	15,854	12,409	3,190	255	9,219 R	78.3%	20.1%	79.5%	20.5%
21,360	FAYETTE	8,012	6,190	1,678	144	4,512 R	77.3%	20.9%	78.7%	21.3%
12,962	FORD	5,142	3,621	1,386	135	2,235 R	70.4%	27.0%	72.3%	27.7%
38,474	FRANKLIN	13,696	9,545	3,908	243	5,637 R	69.7%	28.5%	71.0%	29.0%
34,314	FULTON	13,015	7,009	5,685	321	1,324 R	53.9%	43.7%	55.2%	44.8%
4,819	GALLATIN	2,166	1,373	753	40	620 R	63.4%	34.8%	64.6%	35.4%
12,965	GREENE	4,523	3,297	1,144	82	2,153 R	72.9%	25.3%	74.2%	25.8%
51,218	GRUNDY	19,370	11,266	7,685	419	3,581 R	58.2%	39.7%	59.4%	40.6%
8,122	HAMILTON	3,401	2,502	844	55	1,658 R	73.6%	24.8%	74.8%	25.2%
17,709	HANCOCK	7,212	5,177	1,875	160	3,302 R	71.8%	26.0%	73.4%	26.6%
3,836	HARDIN	1,650	1,220	402	28	818 R	73.9%	24.4%	75.2%	24.8%
6,643	HENDERSON	2,912	1,813	1,020	79	793 R	62.3%	35.0%	64.0%	36.0%
48,932	HENRY	19,661	11,833	7,430	398	4,403 R	60.2%	37.8%	61.4%	38.6%
27,127	IROQUOIS	10,449	8,018	2,222	209	5,796 R	76.7%	21.3%	78.3%	21.7%
56,609	JACKSON	17,110	7,693	9,109	308	1,416 D	45.0%	53.2%	45.8%	54.2%
9,619	JASPER	4,575	3,645	860	70	2,785 R	79.7%	18.8%	80.9%	19.1%
37,706	JEFFERSON	13,145	9,163	3,731	251	5,432 R	69.7%	28.4%	71.1%	28.9%
21,812	JERSEY	9,273	6,402	2,648	223	3,754 R	69.0%	28.6%	70.7%	29.3%
21,246	JO DAVIESS	9,469	5,355	3,943	171	1,412 R	56.6%	41.6%	57.6%	42.4%
12,518	JOHNSON	4,813	3,690	1,052	71	2,638 R	76.7%	21.9%	77.8%	22.2%
533,112	KANE	157,941	68,771	86,477	2,693	17,706 D	43.5%	54.8%	44.3%	55.7%
109,762	KANKAKEE	35,156	19,522	14,819	815	4,703 R	55.5%	42.2%	56.8%	43.2%
129,522	KENDALL	45,286	21,294	23,151	841	1,857 D	47.0%	51.1%	47.9%	52.1%
49,610	KNOX	17,568	9,130	8,072	366	1,058 R	52.0%	45.9%	53.1%	46.9%
108,823	LA SALLE	39,604	20,804	18,076	724	2,728 R	52.5%	45.6%	53.5%	46.5%
695,969	LAKE	229,516	87,529	138,584	3,403	51,055 D	38.1%	60.4%	38.7%	61.3%
15,666	LAWRENCE	5,027	3,745	1,178	104	2,567 R	74.5%	23.4%	76.1%	23.9%
34,037	LEE	12,012	7,113	4,685	214	2,428 R	59.2%	39.0%	60.3%	39.7%
35,684	LIVINGSTON	12,810	9,020	3,554	236	5,466 R	70.4%	27.7%	71.7%	28.3%
28,651	LOGAN	9,679	6,508	2,887	284	3,621 R	67.2%	29.8%	69.3%	30.7%
103,995	MACON	35,282	20,042	14,573	667	5,469 R	56.8%	41.3%	57.9%	42.1%
44,932	MACOUPIN	17,768	11,025	6,377	366	4,648 R	62.0%	35.9%	63.4%	36.6%
263,254	MADISON	98,150	51,858	44,273	2,019	7,585 R	52.8%	45.1%	53.9%	46.1%
37,255	MARION	12,926	9,272	3,407	247	5,865 R	71.7%	26.4%	73.1%	26.9%
11,448	MARSHALL	4,738	2,997	1,641	100	1,356 R	63.3%	34.6%	64.6%	35.4%
13,352	MASON	4,968	3,135	1,739	94	1,396 R	63.1%	35.0%	64.3%	35.7%

ILLINOIS
SENATOR 2022

2020 Census Population	County	Total Vote	Republican (Salvi)	Democratic (Duckworth)	Other	Rep.-Dem. Plurality	Percentage Total Vote		Percentage Major Vote	
							Rep.	Dem.	Rep.	Dem.
13,759	MASSAC	4,862	3,474	1,317	71	2,157 R	71.5%	27.1%	72.5%	27.5%
29,617	MCDONOUGH	9,390	5,434	3,793	163	1,641 R	57.9%	40.4%	58.9%	41.1%
308,253	MCHENRY	116,519	57,974	56,054	2,491	1,920 R	49.8%	48.1%	50.8%	49.2%
171,285	MCLEAN	64,848	31,353	32,188	1,307	835 D	48.3%	49.6%	49.3%	50.7%
12,202	MENARD	5,285	3,469	1,655	161	1,814 R	65.6%	31.3%	67.7%	32.3%
15,472	MERCER	6,738	3,945	2,559	234	1,386 R	58.5%	38.0%	60.7%	39.3%
34,748	MONROE	15,703	10,240	5,197	266	5,043 R	65.2%	33.1%	66.3%	33.7%
28,385	MONTGOMERY	10,604	6,954	3,407	243	3,547 R	65.6%	32.1%	67.1%	32.9%
33,554	MORGAN	11,027	7,120	3,656	251	3,464 R	64.6%	33.2%	66.1%	33.9%
14,551	MOULTRIE	5,265	3,694	1,448	123	2,246 R	70.2%	27.5%	71.8%	28.2%
50,723	OGLE	19,415	12,105	6,920	390	5,185 R	62.3%	35.6%	63.6%	36.4%
178,639	PEORIA	59,035	27,071	30,889	1,075	3,818 D	45.9%	52.3%	46.7%	53.3%
20,914	PERRY	7,770	5,205	2,433	132	2,772 R	67.0%	31.3%	68.1%	31.9%
16,363	PIATT	7,617	4,657	2,783	177	1,874 R	61.1%	36.5%	62.6%	37.4%
15,582	PIKE	6,029	4,611	1,308	110	3,303 R	76.5%	21.7%	77.9%	22.1%
4,209	POPE	1,646	1,265	357	24	908 R	76.9%	21.7%	78.0%	22.0%
5,323	PULASKI	1,988	1,231	730	27	501 R	61.9%	36.7%	62.8%	37.2%
5,752	PUTNAM	2,750	1,464	1,233	53	231 R	53.2%	44.8%	54.3%	45.7%
31,763	RANDOLPH	11,363	7,611	3,527	225	4,084 R	67.0%	31.0%	68.3%	31.7%
15,537	RICHLAND	6,205	4,608	1,462	135	3,146 R	74.3%	23.6%	75.9%	24.1%
141,879	ROCK ISLAND	48,006	20,548	26,469	989	5,921 D	42.8%	55.1%	43.7%	56.3%
23,520	SALINE	8,051	5,554	2,358	139	3,196 R	69.0%	29.3%	70.2%	29.8%
194,375	SANGAMON	79,720	39,389	38,056	2,275	1,333 R	49.4%	47.7%	50.9%	49.1%
6,777	SCHUYLER	3,127	2,027	1,007	93	1,020 R	64.8%	32.2%	66.8%	33.2%
4,953	SCOTT	2,083	1,588	465	30	1,123 R	76.2%	22.3%	77.4%	22.6%
21,646	SHELBY	9,677	7,177	2,304	196	4,873 R	74.2%	23.8%	75.7%	24.3%
259,303	ST. CLAIR	88,788	39,335	47,634	1,819	8,299 D	44.3%	53.6%	45.2%	54.8%
5,346	STARK	2,314	1,499	742	73	757 R	64.8%	32.1%	66.9%	33.1%
44,482	STEPHENSON	16,660	9,393	6,914	353	2,479 R	56.4%	41.5%	57.6%	42.4%
131,789	TAZEWELL	51,261	31,135	19,021	1,105	12,114 R	60.7%	37.1%	62.1%	37.9%
16,660	UNION	6,973	4,514	2,319	140	2,195 R	64.7%	33.3%	66.1%	33.9%
75,598	VERMILION	21,973	14,135	7,445	393	6,690 R	64.3%	33.9%	65.5%	34.5%
11,511	WABASH	4,041	3,083	899	59	2,184 R	76.3%	22.2%	77.4%	22.6%
16,819	WARREN	5,861	3,545	2,198	118	1,347 R	60.5%	37.5%	61.7%	38.3%
13,882	WASHINGTON	5,977	4,424	1,425	128	2,999 R	74.0%	23.8%	75.6%	24.4%
16,222	WAYNE	6,770	5,610	1,056	104	4,554 R	82.9%	15.6%	84.2%	15.8%
13,544	WHITE	5,679	4,316	1,275	88	3,041 R	76.0%	22.5%	77.2%	22.8%
55,173	WHITESIDE	19,953	10,792	8,772	389	2,020 R	54.1%	44.0%	55.2%	44.8%
691,843	WILL	233,477	107,581	122,189	3,707	14,608 D	46.1%	52.3%	46.8%	53.2%
66,668	WILLIAMSON	25,136	16,665	8,067	404	8,598 R	66.3%	32.1%	67.4%	32.6%
282,447	WINNEBAGO	88,060	42,972	43,384	1,704	412 D	48.8%	49.3%	49.8%	50.2%
38,482	WOODFORD	16,886	11,808	4,752	326	7,056 R	69.9%	28.1%	71.3%	28.7%
12,662,810	TOTAL	4,100,739	1,701,055	2,329,136	70,548	628,081 D	41.5%	56.8%	42.2%	57.8%

ILLINOIS
HOUSE OF REPRESENTATIVES

| | | | Republican | | Democratic | | Other | Rep.-Dem. | Percentage Total Vote | | Major Vote | |
									Rep.	Dem.	Rep.	Dem.
CD	Year	Total Vote	Vote	Candidate	Vote	Candidate	Vote	Plurality				
1	2022	237,425	78,258	CARLSON, ERIC	159,142	JACKSON, JONATHAN L.	25	80,884 D	33.0%	67.0%	33.0%	67.0%
1	2020	325,123	85,027	WHITE, PHILANISE	239,943	RUSH, BOBBY L.*	153	154,916 D	26.2%	73.8%	26.2%	73.8%
1	2018	257,885	50,960	TILLMAN, JIMMY LEE II	189,560	RUSH, BOBBY L.*	17,365	138,600 D	19.8%	73.5%	21.2%	78.8%
1	2016	315,862	81,817	DEUSER, AUGUST (O'NEILL)	234,037	RUSH, BOBBY L.*	8	152,220 D	25.9%	74.1%	25.9%	74.1%
1	2014	222,017	59,749	TILLMAN, JIMMY LEE II	162,268	RUSH, BOBBY L.*		102,519 D	26.9%	73.1%	26.9%	73.1%
1	2012	320,844	83,989	PELOQUIN, DONALD E.	236,854	RUSH, BOBBY L.*	1	152,865 D	26.2%	73.8%	26.2%	73.8%
2	2022	209,175	68,761	LYNCH, THOMAS	140,414	KELLY, ROBIN L.*		71,653 D	32.9%	67.1%	32.9%	67.1%
2	2020	298,038	63,142	RABORN, THERESA	234,896	KELLY, ROBIN L.*		171,754 D	21.2%	78.8%	21.2%	78.8%
2	2018	235,251	44,567	MERKLE, DAVID	190,684	KELLY, ROBIN L.*		146,117 D	18.9%	81.1%	18.9%	81.1%
2	2016	294,522	59,471	MORROW, JOHN F.	235,051	KELLY, ROBIN L.*		175,580 D	20.2%	79.8%	20.2%	79.8%
2	2014	204,266	43,799	WALLACE, ERIC M.	160,337	KELLY, ROBIN L.*	130	116,538 D	21.4%	78.5%	21.5%	78.5%
2	2012	297,712	69,115	WOODWORTH, BRIAN	188,303	JACKSON, JESSE L. JR.*	40,294	119,188 D	23.2%	63.3%	26.8%	73.2%
3	2022	177,759	55,995	BURAU, JUSTIN	121,764	RAMIREZ, DELIA		65,769 D	31.5%	68.5%	31.5%	68.5%
3	2020	306,848	133,851	FRICILONE, MIKE	172,997	NEWMAN, MARIE		39,146 D	43.6%	56.4%	43.6%	56.4%
3	2018	223,334	57,885	JONES, ARTHUR J.	163,053	LIPINSKI, DANIEL WILLIAM*	2,396	105,168 D	25.9%	73.0%	26.2%	73.8%
3	2016	225,411			225,320	LIPINSKI, DANIEL WILLIAM*	91	225,320 D		100.0%		100.0%
3	2014	180,855	64,091	BRANNIGAN, SHARON M.	116,764	LIPINSKI, DANIEL WILLIAM*		52,673 D	35.4%	64.6%	35.4%	64.6%
3	2012	246,398	77,653	GRABOWSKI, RICHARD	168,738	LIPINSKI, DANIEL WILLIAM*	7	91,085 D	31.5%	68.5%	31.5%	68.5%
4	2022	133,047	37,352	FALAKOS, JAMES	91,036	GARCIA, JESUS "CHUY"*	4,659	53,684 D	28.1%	68.4%	29.1%	70.9%
4	2020	222,737	35,518	SOLORIO, JESUS	187,219	GARCIA, JESUS "CHUY"*		151,701 D	15.9%	84.1%	15.9%	84.1%
4	2018	166,189	22,294	LORCH, MARK WAYNE	143,895	GARCIA, JESUS "CHUY"		121,601 D	13.4%	86.6%	13.4%	86.6%
4	2016	171,297			171,297	GUTIERREZ, LUIS V.*		171,297 D		100.0%		100.0%
4	2014	101,944	22,278	CONCEPCION, HECTOR	79,666	GUTIERREZ, LUIS V.*		57,388 D	21.9%	78.1%	21.9%	78.1%
4	2012	160,509	27,279	CONCEPCION, HECTOR	133,226	GUTIERREZ, LUIS V.*	4	105,947 D	17.0%	83.0%	17.0%	83.0%
5	2022	274,550	79,112	HANSON, TOM	190,999	QUIGLEY, MIKE*	4,439	111,887 D	28.8%	69.6%	29.3%	70.7%
5	2020	361,271	96,200	HANSON, TOM	255,661	QUIGLEY, MIKE*	9,410	159,461 D	26.6%	70.8%	27.3%	72.7%
5	2018	279,131	65,134	HANSON, TOM	213,992	QUIGLEY, MIKE*	5	148,858 D	23.3%	76.7%	23.3%	76.7%
5	2016	313,724	86,222	KOLBER, VINCENT A. "VINCE"	212,842	QUIGLEY, MIKE*	14,660	126,620 D	27.5%	67.8%	28.8%	71.2%
5	2014	184,019	56,350	KOLBER, VINCENT A. "VINCE"	116,364	QUIGLEY, MIKE*	11,305	60,014 D	30.6%	63.2%	32.6%	67.4%
5	2012	270,377	77,289	SCHMITT, DAN	177,729	QUIGLEY, MIKE*	15,359	100,440 D	28.6%	65.7%	30.3%	69.7%
6	2022	276,859	126,351	PEKAU, KEITH	150,496	CASTEN, SEAN*	12	24,145 D	45.6%	54.4%	45.6%	54.4%
6	2020	404,747	183,891	IVES, JEANNE	213,777	CASTEN, SEAN*	7,079	29,886 D	45.4%	52.8%	46.2%	53.8%
6	2018	315,446	146,445	ROSKAM, PETER J.*	169,001	CASTEN, SEAN		22,556 D	46.4%	53.6%	46.4%	53.6%
6	2016	352,146	208,555	ROSKAM, PETER J.*	143,591	HOWLAND, AMANDA		64,964 R	59.2%	40.8%	59.2%	40.8%
6	2014	238,752	160,287	ROSKAM, PETER J.*	78,465	MASON, MICHAEL		81,822 R	67.1%	32.9%	67.1%	32.9%
6	2012	326,129	193,138	ROSKAM, PETER J.*	132,991	COOLIDGE, LESLIE		60,147 R	59.2%	40.8%	59.2%	40.8%
7	2022	167,746	83	KOPPIE, CHAD	167,650	DAVIS, DANNY K.*	13	167,567 D		99.9%		100.0%
7	2020	310,128	41,390	CAMERON, CRAIG	249,383	DAVIS, DANNY K.*	19,355	207,993 D	13.3%	80.4%	14.2%	85.8%
7	2018	246,243	30,497	CAMERON, CRAIG	215,746	DAVIS, DANNY K.*		185,249 D	12.4%	87.6%	12.4%	87.6%
7	2016	297,466	46,882	LEEF, JEFFREY A	250,584	DAVIS, DANNY K.*		203,702 D	15.8%	84.2%	15.8%	84.2%
7	2014	182,278	27,168	BUMPERS, ROBERT L.	155,110	DAVIS, DANNY K.*		127,942 D	14.9%	85.1%	14.9%	85.1%
7	2012	286,435	31,466	ZAK, RITA	242,439	DAVIS, DANNY K.*	12,530	210,973 D	11.0%	84.6%	11.5%	88.5%
8	2022	207,215	89,335	DARGIS, CHRIS	117,880	KRISHNAMOORTHI, RAJA*		28,545 D	43.1%	56.9%	43.1%	56.9%
8	2020	254,578			186,251	KRISHNAMOORTHI, RAJA*	68,327	186,251 D		73.2%		100.0%
8	2018	197,127	67,073	DIGANVKER, JITENDRA "JD"	130,054	KRISHNAMOORTHI, RAJA*		62,981 D	34.0%	66.0%	34.0%	66.0%
8	2016	248,571	103,617	DICIANNI, PETER "PETE"	144,954	KRISHNAMOORTHI, RAJA		41,337 D	41.7%	58.3%	41.7%	58.3%
8	2014	151,056	66,878	KAIFESH, LAWRENCE JOSEPH "LARRY"	84,178	DUCKWORTH, TAMMY*		17,300 D	44.3%	55.7%	44.3%	55.7%
8	2012	225,066	101,860	WALSH, JOE*	123,206	DUCKWORTH, TAMMY		21,346 D	45.3%	54.7%	45.3%	54.7%
9	2022	250,530	70,915	RICE, MAXWELL	179,615	SCHAKOWSKY, JANICE D. "JAN"*		108,700 D	28.3%	71.7%	28.3%	71.7%
9	2020	369,170	107,125	SANGARI, SARGIS	262,045	SCHAKOWSKY, JANICE D. "JAN"*		154,920 D	29.0%	71.0%	29.0%	71.0%
9	2018	290,351	76,983	ELLESON, JOHN D.	213,368	SCHAKOWSKY, JANICE D. "JAN"*		136,385 D	26.5%	73.5%	26.5%	73.5%
9	2016	326,948	109,550	LASONDE, JOAN MCCARTHY	217,306	SCHAKOWSKY, JANICE D. "JAN"*	92	107,756 D	33.5%	66.5%	33.5%	66.5%
9	2014	213,450	72,384	ATANUS, SUSANNE	141,000	SCHAKOWSKY, JANICE D. "JAN"*	66	68,616 D	33.9%	66.1%	33.9%	66.1%
9	2012	293,807	98,924	WOLFE, TIMOTHY	194,869	SCHAKOWSKY, JANICE D. "JAN"*	14	95,945 D	33.7%	66.3%	33.7%	66.3%
10	2022	242,165	89,599	SEVERINO, JOSEPH	152,566	SCHNEIDER, BRAD*		62,967 D	37.0%	63.0%	37.0%	63.0%
10	2020	316,874	114,442	MUKHERJEE, VALERIE RAMIREZ	202,402	SCHNEIDER, BRAD*	30	87,960 D	36.1%	63.9%	36.1%	63.9%
10	2018	238,664	82,124	BENNETT, DOUGLAS R.	156,540	SCHNEIDER, BRAD*		74,416 D	34.4%	65.6%	34.4%	65.6%
10	2016	285,996	135,535	DOLD, ROBERT*	150,435	SCHNEIDER, BRAD	26	14,900 D	47.4%	52.6%	47.4%	52.6%
10	2014	187,128	95,992	DOLD, ROBERT	91,136	SCHNEIDER, BRAD*		4,856 R	51.3%	48.7%	51.3%	48.7%
10	2012	264,454	130,564	DOLD, ROBERT*	133,890	SCHNEIDER, BRAD		3,326 D	49.4%	50.6%	49.4%	50.6%

ILLINOIS
HOUSE OF REPRESENTATIVES

CD	Year	Total Vote	Republican Vote	Republican Candidate	Democratic Vote	Democratic Candidate	Other Vote	Rep.-Dem. Plurality	Total Vote Rep.	Total Vote Dem.	Major Vote Rep.	Major Vote Dem.
11	2022	264,241	115,069	LAUF, CATALINA	149,172	FOSTER, BILL*		34,103 D	43.5%	56.5%	43.5%	56.5%
11	2020	307,377	112,807	LAIB, RICK	194,557	FOSTER, BILL*	13	81,750 D	36.7%	63.3%	36.7%	63.3%
11	2018	227,765	82,358	STELLA, DOMINICK J. "NICK"	145,407	FOSTER, BILL*		63,049 D	36.2%	63.8%	36.2%	63.8%
11	2016	275,573	108,995	KHOURI, TONIA	166,578	FOSTER, BILL*		57,583 D	39.6%	60.4%	39.6%	60.4%
11	2014	174,772	81,335	SENGER, DARLENE	93,436	FOSTER, BILL*	1	12,101 D	46.5%	53.5%	46.5%	53.5%
11	2012	254,295	105,348	BIGGERT, JUDY*	148,928	FOSTER, BILL	19	43,580 D	41.4%	58.6%	41.4%	58.6%
12	2022	291,171	218,379	BOST, MIKE*	72,791	MARKEL, HOMER "CHIP"	1	145,588 R	75.0%	25.0%	75.0%	25.0%
12	2020	322,416	194,839	BOST, MIKE*	127,577	LENZI, RAYMOND		67,262 R	60.4%	39.6%	60.4%	39.6%
12	2018	261,543	134,884	BOST, MIKE*	118,724	KELLY, BRENDAN	7,935	16,160 R	51.6%	45.4%	53.2%	46.8%
12	2016	313,002	169,976	BOST, MIKE*	124,246	BARICEVIC, CHARLES "C.J."	18,780	45,730 R	54.3%	39.7%	57.8%	42.2%
12	2014	209,738	110,038	BOST, MIKE	87,860	ENYART, WILLIAM*	11,840	22,178 R	52.5%	41.9%	55.6%	44.4%
12	2012	303,949	129,902	PLUMMER, JASON	157,000	ENYART, WILLIAM	17,047	27,098 D	42.7%	51.7%	45.3%	54.7%
13	2022	250,450	108,646	DEERING, REGAN	141,788	BUDZINSKI, NIKKI	16	33,142 D	43.4%	56.6%	43.4%	56.6%
13	2020	333,021	181,373	DAVIS, RODNEY L.*	151,648	DIRKSEN LONDRIGAN, BETSY		29,725 R	54.5%	45.5%	54.5%	45.5%
13	2018	270,981	136,516	DAVIS, RODNEY L.*	134,458	DIRKSEN LONDRIGAN, BETSY	7	2,058 R	50.4%	49.6%	50.4%	49.6%
13	2016	314,394	187,583	DAVIS, RODNEY L.*	126,811	WICKLUND, MARK D.		60,772 R	59.7%	40.3%	59.7%	40.3%
13	2014	210,272	123,337	DAVIS, RODNEY L.*	86,935	CALLIS, ANN E.		36,402 R	58.7%	41.3%	58.7%	41.3%
13	2012	294,385	137,034	DAVIS, RODNEY L.	136,032	GILL, DAVID M.	21,319	1,002 R	46.5%	46.2%	50.2%	49.8%
14	2022	236,600	108,451	GRYDER, SCOTT	128,141	UNDERWOOD, LAUREN*	8	19,690 D	45.8%	54.2%	45.8%	54.2%
14	2020	401,052	197,835	OBERWEIS, JIM	203,209	UNDERWOOD, LAUREN*	8	5,374 D	49.3%	50.7%	49.3%	50.7%
14	2018	297,199	141,164	HULTGREN, RANDY M.*	156,035	UNDERWOOD, LAUREN		14,871 D	47.5%	52.5%	47.5%	52.5%
14	2016	338,097	200,508	HULTGREN, RANDY M.*	137,589	WALZ, JIM		62,919 R	59.3%	40.7%	59.3%	40.7%
14	2014	222,230	145,369	HULTGREN, RANDY M.*	76,861	ANDERSON, DENNIS		68,508 R	65.4%	34.6%	65.4%	34.6%
14	2012	301,954	177,603	HULTGREN, RANDY M.*	124,351	ANDERSON, DENNIS		53,252 R	58.8%	41.2%	58.8%	41.2%
15	2022	299,403	213,007	MILLER, MARY*	86,396	LANGE, PAUL J.		126,611 R	71.1%	28.9%	71.1%	28.9%
15	2020	333,506	244,947	MILLER, MARY	88,559	WEAVER, ERIKA		156,388 R	73.4%	26.6%	73.4%	26.6%
15	2018	255,608	181,294	SHIMKUS, JOHN M.*	74,309	GAITHER, KEVIN	5	106,985 R	70.9%	29.1%	70.9%	29.1%
15	2016	274,554	274,554	SHIMKUS, JOHN M.*				274,554 R	100.0%		100.0%	
15	2014	221,926	166,274	SHIMKUS, JOHN M.*	55,652	THORSLAND, ERIC		110,622 R	74.9%	25.1%	74.9%	25.1%
15	2012	299,937	205,775	SHIMKUS, JOHN M.*	94,162	MICHAEL, ANGELA		111,613 R	68.6%	31.4%	68.6%	31.4%
16	2022	297,946	197,621	LAHOOD, DARIN*	100,325	HADERLEIN, ELIZABETH "LISA"		97,296 R	66.3%	33.7%	66.3%	33.7%
16	2020	338,159	218,839	KINZINGER, ADAM*	119,313	BRZOZOWSKI, DANI	7	99,526 R	64.7%	35.3%	64.7%	35.3%
16	2018	255,825	151,254	KINZINGER, ADAM*	104,569	DADY, SARA	2	46,685 R	59.1%	40.9%	59.1%	40.9%
16	2016	259,853	259,722	KINZINGER, ADAM*			131	259,722 R	99.9%		100.0%	
16	2014	217,198	153,388	KINZINGER, ADAM*	63,810	OLSEN, RANDALL WAYNE		89,578 R	70.6%	29.4%	70.6%	29.4%
16	2012	294,090	181,789	KINZINGER, ADAM*	112,301	ROHL, WANDA		69,488 R	61.8%	38.2%	61.8%	38.2%
17	2022	233,123	111,931	KING, ESTHER JOY	121,186	SORENSEN, ERIC	6	9,255 D	48.0%	52.0%	48.0%	52.0%
17	2020	299,895	143,863	KING, ESTHER JOY	156,011	BUSTOS, CHERI*	21	12,148 D	48.0%	52.0%	48.0%	52.0%
17	2018	229,749	87,090	FAWELL, BILL	142,659	BUSTOS, CHERI*		55,569 D	37.9%	62.1%	37.9%	62.1%
17	2016	287,068	113,943	HARLAN, PATRICK	173,125	BUSTOS, CHERI*		59,182 D	39.7%	60.3%	39.7%	60.3%
17	2014	199,361	88,785	SCHILLING, BOBBY	110,560	BUSTOS, CHERI*	16	21,775 D	44.5%	55.5%	44.5%	55.5%
17	2012	288,161	134,623	SCHILLING, BOBBY*	153,519	BUSTOS, CHERI	19	18,896 D	46.7%	53.3%	46.7%	53.3%
18	2020	371,879	261,840	LAHOOD, DARIN*	110,039	PETRILLI, GEORGE		151,801 R	70.4%	29.6%	70.4%	29.6%
18	2018	291,413	195,927	LAHOOD, DARIN*	95,486	RODRIGUEZ, JUNIUS		100,441 R	67.2%	32.8%	67.2%	32.8%
18	2016	347,283	250,506	LAHOOD, DARIN*	96,770	RODRIGUEZ, JUNIUS	7	153,736 R	72.1%	27.9%	72.1%	27.9%
18	2014	246,740	184,363	SCHOCK, AARON*	62,377	MILLER, DARREL ERVIN		121,986 R	74.7%	25.3%	74.7%	25.3%
18	2012	329,631	244,467	SCHOCK, AARON*	85,164	WATERWORTH, STEVE		159,303 R	74.2%	25.8%	74.2%	25.8%
TOTAL	2022	4,049,405	1,768,865		2,271,361		9,179	502,496 D	43.7%	56.1%	43.8%	56.2%
TOTAL	2020	5,876,819	2,416,929		3,355,487		104,403	938,558 D	41.1%	57.1%	41.9%	58.1%
TOTAL	2018	4,539,704	1,754,449		2,757,540		27,715	1,003,091 D	38.6%	60.7%	38.9%	61.1%
TOTAL	2016	5,241,767	2,397,436		2,810,536		33,795	413,100 D	45.7%	53.6%	46.0%	54.0%
TOTAL	2014	3,568,002	1,721,865		1,822,779		23,358	100,914 D	48.3%	51.1%	48.6%	51.4%
TOTAL	2012	5,058,133	2,207,818		2,743,702		106,613	535,884 D	43.6%	54.2%	44.6%	55.4%

Note: An asterisk (*) denotes incumbent.

ILLINOIS

GENERAL AND PRIMARY ELECTIONS

GENERAL ELECTIONS: OTHER VOTES

Governor	Other vote was 111,850 Libertarian (Scott Schluter), 28 Independent (Emily Johnson), 28 Independent (Shon-Tiyon Horton), 18 Independent (Elizabeth Sebesta), 7 Write-In (Michael Kinney)
Senate	Other vote was 68,671 Libertarian (William Redpath), 1877 Write-In (Write-In)
House	Other vote was:
CD 1	Independent (Tori Nicholson), 12 Write-In (Babette Peyton)
CD 4	4,605 Working Class (Edward Hershey), 54 Write-In (Alicia Martinez)
CD 5	4,439 Independent (Jerico Cruz)
CD 6	12 Write-In (Arthur Jones)
CD 7	10 Write-In (Roger Romanelli), 3 Write-In (Joshua Loyd)
CD 12	1 Write-In (Nancy Foster)
CD 13	16 Write-In (Nancy Foster)
CD 14	8 Independent (Barry Wilson)
CD 17	6 Write-In (Brrad Ahrens)

2022 PRIMARY ELECTIONS: SUPPLEMENTARY INFORMATION

Primary	June 28, 2022	Registration (as of March 17, 2020)	8,116,720	No Party Registration
Primary Type	Open—Any registered voter could participate in the primary of either party.			

	REPUBLICAN PRIMARIES			DEMOCRATIC PRIMARIES		
Senator	Salvi, Kathy	216,007	30.2%	Duckworth, Tammy*	856,720	100.0%
	Hubbard, Peggy	177,180	24.8%			
	Dubiel, Matthew "Matt"	90,538	12.7%			
	Chlebek, Casey	76,213	10.7%			
	Piton, Robert "Bobby"	65,461	9.2%			
	Williams, Anthony W.	52,890	7.4%			
	Tillman, Jimmy Lee II	36,342	5.1%			
	TOTAL	714,631		TOTAL	856,720	
Governor	Bailey, Darren	458,102	57.5%	Pritzker, Jay "J.B."*	810,989	91.9%
	Sullivan, Jesse	125,094	15.7%	Miles, Beverly	71,704	8.1%
	Irvin, Richard	119,592	15.0%			
	Rabine, Gary	52,194	6.5%			
	Schimpf, Paul	34,676	4.4%			
	Solomon, Max	7,371	0.9%			
	TOTAL	797,029		TOTAL	882,693	

ILLINOIS

GENERAL AND PRIMARY ELECTIONS

	REPUBLICAN PRIMARIES			DEMOCRATIC PRIMARIES		
Congressional District 1	Carlson, Eric	10,755	40.5%	Jackson, Jonathan L.	21,607	28.2%
	Regnier, Jeff	10,375	39.0%	Dowell, Pat	14,594	19.0%
	Young, Geno	3,853	14.5%	Norington-Reaves, Karin	10,825	14.1%
	White, Philanise	1,598	6.0%	Collins, Jacqueline "Jacqui"	9,299	12.1%
				Butler, Chris	4,141	5.4%
				Cole, Jahmal	4,045	5.3%
				Swain, Jonathan T.	2,554	3.3%
				Thompson, Michael A.	1,680	2.2%
				Williams, Charise A.	1,601	2.1%
				Goodrum, Cassandra	1,422	1.9%
				Lewis, Marcus	901	1.2%
				Palmer, Robert	899	1.2%
				Pippion McGriff, Nykea	892	1.2%
				Rosner, Terre Layng	780	1.0%
				Matthews, Ameena	686	0.9%
				Birgans, Kirby	511	0.7%
				DeJoie, Steven	251	0.3%
	TOTAL	26,581		TOTAL	76,688	
Congressional District 2	Lynch, Thomas	10,289	37.2%	Kelly, Robin L.*	56,606	100.0%
	Cultra, Shane	9,869	35.7%			
	Ramos, Ashley	7,524	27.2%			
	TOTAL	27,682		TOTAL	56,606	
Congressional District 3	Burau, Justin	18,997	100.0%	Ramirez, Delia	37,296	66.4%
				Villegas, Gilbert	12,990	23.1%
				Chehade, Iymen	3,719	6.6%
				Aguirre, Juan Enrique	2,175	3.9%
	TOTAL	18,997		TOTAL	56,180	
Congressional District 4	Falakos, James	12,192	100.0%	Garcia, Jesus "Chuy"*	37,499	100.0%
	TOTAL	12,192		TOTAL	37,499	
Congressional District 5	Hanson, Tom	14,806	55.4%	Quigley, Mike*	82,490	100.0%
	McGonigal, Malgorzata	11,916	44.6%			
	Rowder, Frank	2				
	TOTAL	26,724		TOTAL	82,490	
Congressional District 6	Pekau, Keith	20,178	38.7%	Casten, Sean*	45,654	67.7%
	Grasso, Gary	14,150	27.2%	Newman, Marie	19,726	29.2%
	Conforti, Niki	5,947	11.4%	Hughes, Charles M.	2,085	3.1%
	O'Shea, Catherine	5,243	10.1%			
	Kaspar, Scott	3,573	6.9%			
	Cruz, Robert "Rob"	3,003	5.8%			
	TOTAL	52,094		TOTAL	67,465	
Congressional District 7				Davis, Danny K.*	39,230	51.9%
				Collins, Kina	34,574	45.7%
				Mendenhall, Denarvis	1,808	2.4%
				TOTAL	75,612	
Congressional District 8	Dargis, Chris	11,055	32.0%	Krishnamoorthi, Raja*	29,933	70.3%
	Wood, Phillip Owen	6,529	18.9%	Ahmed, Junaid	12,627	29.7%
	Kopsaftis, Peter	6,101	17.6%			
	Kolodziej, Karen	6,017	17.4%			
	Koppie, Chad	4,886	14.1%			
	TOTAL	34,588		TOTAL	42,560	
Congressional District 9	Rice, Maxwell	22,751	100.0%	Schakowsky, Janice D. "Jan"*	76,956	100.0%
	TOTAL	22,751		TOTAL	76,956	
Congressional District 10	Severino, Joseph	33,708	100.0%	Schneider, Brad*	52,624	100.0%
	TOTAL	33,708		TOTAL	52,624	

ILLINOIS

GENERAL AND PRIMARY ELECTIONS

	REPUBLICAN PRIMARIES			DEMOCRATIC PRIMARIES		
Congressional District 11	Lauf, Catalina	15,360	31.0%	Foster, Bill*	44,096	100.0%
	Evans, Jerry	11,158	22.5%			
	Carroll, Mark Joseph	9,955	20.1%			
	Hathaway-Altman, Susan	6,017	12.1%			
	Miller, Cassandra Tanner	3,730	7.5%			
	Heeg, Andrea	3,334	6.7%			
	TOTAL	49,554		TOTAL	44,096	
Congressional District 12	Bost, Mike*	88,681	100.0%	Markel, Homer "Chip"	11,068	56.7%
				Qualls, Joshua	8,438	43.3%
	TOTAL	88,681		TOTAL	19,506	
Congressional District 13	Deering, Regan	14,885	34.6%	Budzinski, Nikki	31,593	75.6%
	Reising, Jesse	14,184	32.9%	Palmer, David	10,216	24.4%
	Hausman, Matt	10,289	23.9%			
	Martin, Terry	3,694	8.6%			
	TOTAL	43,052		TOTAL	41,809	
Congressional District 14	Gryder, Scott	13,998	30.9%	Underwood, Lauren*	37,780	100.0%
	Marter, James T.	10,950	24.2%			
	Koolidge, Mike	9,378	20.7%			
	Lombardi, Jack	6,372	14.1%			
	Milton, Jaime	4,612	10.2%			
	TOTAL	45,310		TOTAL	37,780	
Congressional District 15	Miller, Mary*	64,549	57.4%	Lange, Paul J.	21,433	100.0%
	Davis, Rodney L.	47,852	42.6%			
	TOTAL	112,401		TOTAL	21,433	
Congressional District 16	LaHood, Darin*	56,582	66.4%			
	Peters, Walt	11,278	13.2%			
	Guillemette, JoAnne	10,476	12.3%			
	Rebresh, Michael	6,911	8.1%			
	TOTAL	85,247				
Congressional District 17	King, Esther Joy	31,065	68.5%	Sorensen, Eric	14,702	37.7%
	Helmick, Charles William "Charlie"	14,274	31.5%	Wallace, Litesa	9,103	23.3%
				Logemann, Jonathan	5,628	14.4%
				Normoyle, Angie	4,818	12.4%
				Williams, Marsha	2,701	6.9%
				McGowan, Jacqueline	2,040	5.2%
				Thomas, Kermit	11	
				McNeely, Linda	3	
	TOTAL	45,339		TOTAL	39,006	

Note: An asterisk (*) denotes incumbent.

INDIANA

Statewide Races

The Hoosier State, which holds its gubernatorial races in presidential years, had a Senate contest as its highest-profile race on the ballot in 2022. But Indiana's Senate race was among the most straightforward contests in the nation.

Sen. Todd Young, a Republican acceptable to most factions of the party, ran for a second term in 2022. Neither Young nor the Democratic nominee, Hammond Mayor Tom McDermott, had any opposition in their primaries. The general campaign received minimal attention from the national parties, and Young won 59%–38%. McDermott carried his home county, Lake, as well as Indianapolis's Marion County and Bloomington's Monroe County. The other 89 counties voted Republican.

The northern Indianapolis suburbs – specifically those that make up Hamilton County – have seen some pro-Democratic trends but the area remains Republican-leaning. While Young's margin in Hamilton County was down 10 percentage points from 2016, he still carried it by 14 points. Conversely, Young's largest gains came in the southern part of the state, an area that has historically been friendlier to Democrats. In 2016, Young lost Perry County, with a population of just under 20,000, by a 50%–45% margin – it was the sole county along the Ohio River (the state's southern border) that he lost. Six years later, Perry County voted 62%-36% for the Republican.

House Races

Indiana Republicans entered the cycle with a 7-2 advantage in the state's eight-member delegation. Republican mappers basically opted for a status quo map.

There was no question that Democratic Rep. Andre Carson would retain a safely blue Indianapolis seat. But there was some doubt about what Republicans would do with Democratic Rep. Frank Mrvan's light blue 1st District, based in the Calumet Region. Traditionally one of the most Democratic regions of the state, the lean of this blue-collar seat has become less pronounced. While Republican mappers could have "cracked" the seat, they opted to make only small changes – perhaps in the hope that the general trends of the area would continue to push it their way.

And the GOP mappers were vindicated, at least to some degree. For the first time in decades, national Republicans prioritized IN-1. In what became one of the most expensive House races, Republican Jennifer Ruth Green, a Black woman with a background in the military, gave Mrvan, who is from a well-known political family in the area, a serious race. But Mrvan prevailed 53%–47%.

While GOP legislators left the 1st District basically untouched, they sought to strengthen Republican Rep. Victoria Spartz's hand. Spartz's 5th District contained the aforementioned Hamilton County. In 2020, she was first elected in an open-seat contest, winning 50%–46%, a result much closer than in any of the state's other Republican-held seats. At its southern end, Spartz's original district had a section of Indianapolis proper, which made up a quarter of the district and gave her less than 35% in 2020. Those Indianapolis precincts were removed, and the district picked up Muncie's Delaware County. Spartz still had the closest margin of the state's seven Republican members, but this time she won with over 60%.

INDIANA

Congressional districts first established for elections held in 2022

9 members

* Asterisk indicates a county whose boundaries include parts of two or more congressional districts.

INDIANA

GOVERNOR
Eric Holcomb (R). Reelected 2020 to a four-year term. Previously elected 2016.

SENATORS (2 Republicans)
Mike Braun (R). Elected 2018 to a six-year term.

Todd Young (R). Reelected 2022 to a six-year term. Previously elected 2016.

REPRESENTATIVES (7 Republicans, 2 Democrats)
1. Frank J. Mrvan (D)
2. Rudy Yakym (R)
3. James "Jim" Banks (R)
4. James "Jim" Baird (R)
5. Victoria Spartz (R)
6. Gregory "Greg" Pence (R)
7. Andre D. Carson (D)
8. Larry D. Bucshon (R)
9. Erin Houchin (R)

POSTWAR VOTE FOR PRESIDENT

Year	Total Vote	Republican Vote	Republican Candidate	Democratic Vote	Democratic Candidate	Other Vote	Rep.-Dem. Plurality	Total Vote Rep.	Total Vote Dem.	Major Vote Rep.	Major Vote Dem.
2020	3,033,121	1,729,519	Trump, Donald J.*	1,242,416	Biden, Joseph R. Jr.	61,186	487,103 R	57.0%	41.0%	58.2%	41.8%
2016**	2,734,958	1,557,286	Trump, Donald J.	1,033,126	Clinton, Hillary Rodham	144,546	524,160 R	56.9%	37.8%	60.1%	39.9%
2012	2,624,534	1,420,543	Romney, W. Mitt	1,152,887	Obama, Barack H.*	51,104	267,656 R	54.1%	43.9%	55.2%	44.8%
2008	2,751,054	1,345,648	McCain, John S. III	1,374,039	Obama, Barack H.	31,367	28,391 D	48.9%	49.9%	49.5%	50.5%
2004	2,468,002	1,479,438	Bush, George W.*	969,011	Kerry, John F.	19,553	510,427 R	59.9%	39.3%	60.4%	39.6%
2000**	2,199,305	1,245,836	Bush, George W.	901,980	Gore, Albert Jr.	51,489	343,856 R	56.6%	41.0%	58.0%	42.0%
1996**	2,135,842	1,006,693	Dole, Robert "Bob"	887,424	Clinton, Bill*	241,725	119,269 R	47.1%	41.5%	53.1%	46.9%
1992**	2,305,871	989,375	Bush, George H.*	848,420	Clinton, Bill	468,076	140,955 R	42.9%	36.8%	53.8%	46.2%
1988	2,168,621	1,297,763	Bush, George H.	860,643	Dukakis, Michael S.	10,215	437,120 R	59.8%	39.7%	60.1%	39.9%
1984	2,233,069	1,377,230	Reagan, Ronald*	841,481	Mondale, Walter F.	14,358	535,749 R	61.7%	37.7%	62.1%	37.9%
1980**	2,242,033	1,255,656	Reagan, Ronald	844,197	Carter, Jimmy*	142,180	411,459 R	56.0%	37.7%	59.8%	40.2%
1976	2,220,362	1,183,958	Ford, Gerald R.*	1,014,714	Carter, Jimmy	21,690	169,244 R	53.3%	45.7%	53.8%	46.2%
1972	2,125,529	1,405,154	Nixon, Richard M.*	708,568	McGovern, George S.	11,807	696,586 R	66.1%	33.3%	66.5%	33.5%
1968**	2,123,597	1,067,885	Nixon, Richard M.	806,659	Humphrey, Hubert Horatio Jr.	249,053	261,226 R	50.3%	38.0%	57.0%	43.0%
1964	2,091,606	911,118	Goldwater, Barry M. Sr.	1,170,848	Johnson, Lyndon B.*	9,640	259,730 D	43.6%	56.0%	43.8%	56.2%
1960	2,135,360	1,175,120	Nixon, Richard M.	952,358	Kennedy, John F.	7,882	222,762 R	55.0%	44.6%	55.2%	44.8%
1956	1,974,607	1,182,811	Eisenhower, Dwight D.*	783,908	Stevenson, Adlai E. II	7,888	398,903 R	59.9%	39.7%	60.1%	39.9%
1952	1,955,049	1,136,259	Eisenhower, Dwight D.	801,530	Stevenson, Adlai E. II	17,260	334,729 R	58.1%	41.0%	58.6%	41.4%
1948	1,656,212	821,079	Dewey, Thomas E.	807,831	Truman, Harry S.*	27,302	13,248 R	49.6%	48.8%	50.4%	49.6%

Note: An asterisk (*) denotes incumbent. **In past elections, the other vote included: 2016 -133,993 Libertarian (Gary Johnson); 2000 -18,531 Green (Ralph Nader); 1996 - 224,299 Reform (Ross Perot); 1992 - 455,934 Independent (Perot); 1980 - 111,639 Independent (John Anderson); 1968 - 243,108 American Independent (George Wallace).

INDIANA

POSTWAR VOTE FOR GOVERNOR

Year	Total Vote	Republican Vote	Republican Candidate	Democratic Vote	Democratic Candidate	Other Vote	Rep.-Dem. Plurality	Percentage Total Vote Rep.	Percentage Total Vote Dem.	Percentage Major Vote Rep.	Percentage Major Vote Dem.
2020**	3,020,388	1,706,727	Holcomb, Eric*	968,094	Myers, Woodrow	345,567	738,633 R	56.5%	32.1%	63.8%	36.2%
2016	2,719,968	1,397,396	Holcomb, Eric	1,235,503	Gregg, John R.	87,069	161,893 R	51.4%	45.4%	53.1%	46.9%
2012	2,577,329	1,275,424	Pence, Mike	1,200,016	Gregg, John R.	101,889	75,408 R	49.5%	46.6%	51.5%	48.5%
2008	2,703,752	1,563,885	Daniels, Mitch*	1,082,463	Thompson, Jill Long	57,404	481,422 R	57.8%	40.0%	59.1%	40.9%
2004	2,448,498	1,302,912	Daniels, Mitch	1,113,900	Kernan, Joseph E.	31,686	189,012 R	53.2%	45.5%	53.9%	46.1%
2000	2,179,413	908,285	McIntosh, David M.	1,232,525	O'Bannon, Frank*	38,603	324,240 D	41.7%	56.6%	42.4%	57.6%
1996	2,110,047	986,982	Goldsmith, Stephen	1,087,128	O'Bannon, Frank	35,937	100,146 D	46.8%	51.5%	47.6%	52.4%
1992	2,229,116	822,533	Pearson, Linley E.	1,382,151	Bayh, Evan*	24,432	559,618 D	36.9%	62.0%	37.3%	62.7%
1988	2,140,781	1,002,207	Mutz, John M.	1,138,574	Bayh, Evan		136,367 D	46.8%	53.2%	46.8%	53.2%
1984	2,197,988	1,146,497	Orr, Robert D.*	1,036,922	Townsend, W. Wayne	14,569	109,575 R	52.2%	47.2%	52.5%	47.5%
1980	2,178,403	1,257,383	Orr, Robert D.	913,116	Hillenbrand, John A.	7,904	344,267 R	57.7%	41.9%	57.9%	42.1%
1976	2,175,324	1,236,555	Bowen, Otis R.*	927,243	Conrad, Larry A.	11,526	309,312 R	56.8%	42.6%	57.1%	42.9%
1972	2,120,847	1,203,903	Bowen, Otis R.	900,489	Welsh, Matthew E.	16,455	303,414 R	56.8%	42.5%	57.2%	42.8%
1968	2,049,063	1,080,262	Whitcomb, Edgar D.	965,816	Rock, Robert L.	2,985	114,446 R	52.7%	47.1%	52.8%	47.2%
1964	2,073,058	901,342	Ristine, Richard O.	1,164,763	Branigin, Roger D.	6,953	263,421 D	43.5%	56.2%	43.6%	56.4%
1960	2,128,965	1,049,540	Parker, Crawford F.	1,072,717	Welsh, Matthew E.	6,708	23,177 D	49.3%	50.4%	49.5%	50.5%
1956	1,954,290	1,086,868	Handley, Harold W.	859,393	Tucker, Ralph	8,029	227,475 R	55.6%	44.0%	55.8%	44.2%
1952	1,931,869	1,075,685	Craig, George N.	841,984	Watkins, John A.	14,200	233,701 R	55.7%	43.6%	56.1%	43.9%
1948	1,652,321	745,892	Creighton, Hobart	884,995	Schricker, Henry F.	21,434	139,103 D	45.1%	53.6%	45.7%	54.3%

Note: An asterisk (*) denotes incumbent. **In past elections, the other vote included: 2020 – 345,567 Libertarian (Donald Rainwater).

POSTWAR VOTE FOR SENATOR

Year	Total Vote	Republican Vote	Republican Candidate	Democratic Vote	Democratic Candidate	Other Vote	Rep.-Dem. Plurality	Percentage Total Vote Rep.	Percentage Total Vote Dem.	Percentage Major Vote Rep.	Percentage Major Vote Dem.
2022	1,860,154	1,090,390	Young, Todd*	704,480	McDermott, Thomas M. Jr.	65,284	385,910 R	58.6%	37.9%	60.8%	39.2%
2018	2,282,565	1,158,000	Braun, Mike	1,023,553	Donnelly, Joseph S.*	101,012	134,447 R	50.7%	44.8%	53.1%	46.9%
2016	2,732,546	1,423,991	Young, Todd	1,158,947	Bayh, Evan	149,608	265,044 R	52.1%	42.4%	55.1%	44.9%
2012	2,560,102	1,133,621	Mourdock, Richard E.	1,281,181	Donnelly, Joseph S.	145,300	147,560 D	44.3%	50.0%	46.9%	53.1%
2010	1,744,481	952,116	Coats, Daniel R.	697,775	Ellsworth, Brad	94,590	254,341 R	54.6%	40.0%	57.7%	42.3%
2006**	1,341,111	1,171,553	Lugar, Richard G.*			169,558	1,171,553 R	87.4%		100.0%	
2004	2,428,233	903,913	Scott, Marvin B.	1,496,976	Bayh, Evan*	27,344	593,063 D	37.2%	61.6%	37.6%	62.4%
2000	2,145,209	1,427,944	Lugar, Richard G.*	683,273	Johnson, David L.	33,992	744,671 R	66.6%	31.9%	67.6%	32.4%
1998	1,588,617	552,732	Helmke, Paul	1,012,244	Bayh, Evan	23,641	459,512 D	34.8%	63.7%	35.3%	64.7%
1994	1,543,568	1,039,625	Lugar, Richard G.*	470,799	Jontz, Jim	33,144	568,826 R	67.4%	30.5%	68.8%	31.2%
1992	2,211,426	1,267,972	Coats, Daniel R.*	900,148	Hogsett, Joseph H.	43,306	367,824 R	57.3%	40.7%	58.5%	41.5%
1990S**	1,504,302	806,048	Coats, Daniel R.	696,639	Hill, Baron P.	1,615	109,409 R	53.6%	46.3%	53.6%	46.4%
1988	2,099,303	1,430,525	Lugar, Richard G.*	668,778	Wickes, Jack		761,747 R	68.1%	31.9%	68.1%	31.9%
1986	1,545,563	936,143	Quayle, John Danforth*	595,192	Long, Jill Lynette	14,228	340,951 R	60.6%	38.5%	61.1%	38.9%
1982	1,817,287	978,301	Lugar, Richard G.*	828,400	Fithian, Floyd	10,586	149,901 R	53.8%	45.6%	54.1%	45.9%
1980	2,198,376	1,182,414	Quayle, John Danforth	1,015,962	Bayh, Birch Evan*		166,452 R	53.8%	46.2%	53.8%	46.2%
1976	2,171,187	1,275,833	Lugar, Richard G.	878,522	Hartke, R. Vance*	16,832	397,311 R	58.8%	40.5%	59.2%	40.8%
1974	1,752,978	814,117	Lugar, Richard G.	889,269	Bayh, Birch Evan*	49,592	75,152 D	46.4%	50.7%	47.8%	52.2%
1970	1,737,697	866,707	Roudebush, Richard	870,990	Hartke, R. Vance*		4,283 D	49.9%	50.1%	49.9%	50.1%
1968	2,053,118	988,571	Ruckelshaus, William	1,060,456	Bayh, Birch Evan*	4,091	71,885 D	48.1%	51.7%	48.2%	51.8%
1964	2,076,963	941,519	Bontrager, D. Russell	1,128,505	Hartke, R. Vance*	6,939	186,986 D	45.3%	54.3%	45.5%	54.5%
1962	1,800,038	894,547	Capehart, Homer E.*	905,491	Bayh, Birch Evan		10,944 D	49.7%	50.3%	49.7%	50.3%
1958	1,724,598	731,635	Handley, Harold W.	973,636	Hartke, R. Vance	19,327	242,001 D	42.4%	56.5%	42.9%	57.1%
1956	1,963,986	1,084,262	Capehart, Homer E.*	871,781	Wickard, Claude R.	7,943	212,481 R	55.2%	44.4%	55.4%	44.6%
1952	1,946,118	1,020,605	Jenner, William E.*	911,169	Schricker, Henry F.	14,344	109,436 R	52.4%	46.8%	52.8%	47.2%
1950	1,598,724	844,303	Capehart, Homer E.*	741,025	Campbell, Alex M.	13,396	103,278 R	52.8%	46.4%	53.3%	46.7%
1946	1,347,434	739,809	Jenner, William E.	584,288	Townsend, M. Clifford	23,337	155,521 R	54.9%	43.4%	55.9%	44.1%

Note: An asterisk (*) denotes incumbent. **In past elections, the other vote included: 2006 - 168,820 Libertarian (Steve Osborn), who finished second. The 1990 election was for a short term to fill a vacancy. The Democratic Party did not run a candidate in the 2006 Senate election.

INDIANA
SENATOR 2022

2020 Census Population	County	Total Vote	Republican (Young)	Democratic (McDermott)	Other	Rep.-Dem. Plurality	Percentage Total Vote Rep.	Dem.	Major Vote Rep.	Dem.
35,820	ADAMS	8,950	6,914	1,841	195	5,073 R	77.3%	20.6%	79.0%	21.0%
380,342	ALLEN	101,697	59,128	39,913	2,656	19,215 R	58.1%	39.2%	59.7%	40.3%
83,784	BARTHOLOMEW	22,504	13,827	7,623	1,054	6,204 R	61.4%	33.9%	64.5%	35.5%
8,758	BENTON	2,467	1,938	469	60	1,469 R	78.6%	19.0%	80.5%	19.5%
11,746	BLACKFORD	3,394	2,500	740	154	1,760 R	73.7%	21.8%	77.2%	22.8%
68,257	BOONE	24,806	14,178	9,159	1,469	5,019 R	57.2%	36.9%	60.8%	39.2%
15,150	BROWN	6,355	3,796	2,113	446	1,683 R	59.7%	33.2%	64.2%	35.8%
20,278	CARROLL	6,181	4,644	1,267	270	3,377 R	75.1%	20.5%	78.6%	21.4%
37,701	CASS	8,588	6,250	2,081	257	4,169 R	72.8%	24.2%	75.0%	25.0%
118,841	CLARK	36,429	22,389	13,061	979	9,328 R	61.5%	35.9%	63.2%	36.8%
26,255	CLAY	7,642	5,885	1,507	250	4,378 R	77.0%	19.7%	79.6%	20.4%
32,464	CLINTON	7,293	5,362	1,606	325	3,756 R	73.5%	22.0%	77.0%	23.0%
10,589	CRAWFORD	3,705	2,630	983	92	1,647 R	71.0%	26.5%	72.8%	27.2%
33,346	DAVIESS	6,987	5,754	1,059	174	4,695 R	82.4%	15.2%	84.5%	15.5%
49,577	DEARBORN	14,267	11,309	2,628	330	8,681 R	79.3%	18.4%	81.1%	18.9%
26,603	DECATUR	8,050	6,184	1,381	485	4,803 R	76.8%	17.2%	81.7%	18.3%
43,616	DEKALB	11,732	8,584	2,773	375	5,811 R	73.2%	23.6%	75.6%	24.4%
114,291	DELAWARE	30,078	17,162	11,867	1,049	5,295 R	57.1%	39.5%	59.1%	40.9%
42,729	DUBOIS	13,715	9,906	3,502	307	6,404 R	72.2%	25.5%	73.9%	26.1%
206,556	ELKHART	44,652	30,852	12,635	1,165	18,217 R	69.1%	28.3%	70.9%	29.1%
23,123	FAYETTE	6,164	4,720	1,274	170	3,446 R	76.6%	20.7%	78.7%	21.3%
78,823	FLOYD	26,912	15,948	10,313	651	5,635 R	59.3%	38.3%	60.7%	39.3%
16,351	FOUNTAIN	4,983	3,891	945	147	2,946 R	78.1%	19.0%	80.5%	19.5%
22,764	FRANKLIN	7,367	5,923	1,236	208	4,687 R	80.4%	16.8%	82.7%	17.3%
20,009	FULTON	5,520	4,224	1,162	134	3,062 R	76.5%	21.1%	78.4%	21.6%
33,649	GIBSON	9,998	7,612	2,205	181	5,407 R	76.1%	22.1%	77.5%	22.5%
65,786	GRANT	15,809	11,383	3,927	499	7,456 R	72.0%	24.8%	74.4%	25.6%
31,924	GREENE	9,446	7,033	2,098	315	4,935 R	74.5%	22.2%	77.0%	23.0%
340,425	HAMILTON	129,226	70,412	52,873	5,941	17,539 R	54.5%	40.9%	57.1%	42.9%
78,664	HANCOCK	23,945	15,455	6,685	1,805	8,770 R	64.5%	27.9%	69.8%	30.2%
40,728	HARRISON	13,832	10,150	3,315	367	6,835 R	73.4%	24.0%	75.4%	24.6%
171,484	HENDRICKS	48,576	28,965	16,404	3,207	12,561 R	59.6%	33.8%	63.8%	36.2%
48,132	HENRY	13,498	9,388	3,338	772	6,050 R	69.6%	24.7%	73.8%	26.2%
82,746	HOWARD	24,846	16,738	7,289	819	9,449 R	67.4%	29.3%	69.7%	30.3%
36,589	HUNTINGTON	11,307	8,465	2,508	334	5,957 R	74.9%	22.2%	77.1%	22.9%
44,263	JACKSON	11,240	8,612	2,219	409	6,393 R	76.6%	19.7%	79.5%	20.5%
33,615	JASPER	9,238	7,050	1,982	206	5,068 R	76.3%	21.5%	78.1%	21.9%
20,424	JAY	5,410	4,084	1,182	144	2,902 R	75.5%	21.8%	77.6%	22.4%
32,430	JEFFERSON	9,803	6,503	3,059	241	3,444 R	66.3%	31.2%	68.0%	32.0%
27,777	JENNINGS	7,941	5,992	1,532	417	4,460 R	75.5%	19.3%	79.6%	20.4%
159,025	JOHNSON	44,887	29,129	13,080	2,678	16,049 R	64.9%	29.1%	69.0%	31.0%
36,718	KNOX	10,114	7,468	2,369	277	5,099 R	73.8%	23.4%	75.9%	24.1%
79,574	KOSCIUSKO	22,951	18,033	3,996	922	14,037 R	78.6%	17.4%	81.9%	18.1%
110,084	LA PORTE	31,962	17,279	13,920	763	3,359 R	54.1%	43.6%	55.4%	44.6%
39,598	LAGRANGE	6,599	5,223	1,229	147	3,994 R	79.1%	18.6%	81.0%	19.0%
486,289	LAKE	133,693	57,426	73,866	2,401	16,440 D	43.0%	55.3%	43.7%	56.3%
45,472	LAWRENCE	12,772	9,700	2,622	450	7,078 R	75.9%	20.5%	78.7%	21.3%
129,911	MADISON	35,836	21,536	12,470	1,830	9,066 R	60.1%	34.8%	63.3%	36.7%
963,666	MARION	223,706	78,138	136,473	9,095	58,335 D	34.9%	61.0%	36.4%	63.6%
46,235	MARSHALL	12,781	9,471	2,979	331	6,492 R	74.1%	23.3%	76.1%	23.9%
10,273	MARTIN	3,495	2,691	666	138	2,025 R	77.0%	19.1%	80.2%	19.8%
35,487	MIAMI	8,519	6,524	1,713	282	4,811 R	76.6%	20.1%	79.2%	20.8%
148,408	MONROE	40,236	14,286	24,777	1,173	10,491 D	35.5%	61.6%	36.6%	63.4%
38,394	MONTGOMERY	9,753	7,063	2,219	471	4,844 R	72.4%	22.8%	76.1%	23.9%
70,648	MORGAN	21,265	15,004	4,366	1,895	10,638 R	70.6%	20.5%	77.5%	22.5%
14,008	NEWTON	3,982	3,032	837	113	2,195 R	76.1%	21.0%	78.4%	21.6%
47,851	NOBLE	11,476	8,696	2,425	355	6,271 R	75.8%	21.1%	78.2%	21.8%
5,869	OHIO	1,921	1,458	422	41	1,036 R	75.9%	22.0%	77.6%	22.4%
19,663	ORANGE	5,382	4,083	1,132	167	2,951 R	75.9%	21.0%	78.3%	21.7%
20,846	OWEN	6,173	4,230	1,518	425	2,712 R	68.5%	24.6%	73.6%	26.4%

INDIANA
SENATOR 2022

2020 Census Population	County	Total Vote	Republican (Young)	Democratic (McDermott)	Other	Rep.-Dem. Plurality	Total Vote Rep.	Total Vote Dem.	Major Vote Rep.	Major Vote Dem.
16,948	PARKE	4,481	3,469	873	139	2,596 R	77.4%	19.5%	79.9%	20.1%
19,281	PERRY	6,223	3,838	2,233	152	1,605 R	61.7%	35.9%	63.2%	36.8%
12,430	PIKE	3,645	2,771	806	68	1,965 R	76.0%	22.1%	77.5%	22.5%
171,029	PORTER	57,981	30,158	26,643	1,180	3,515 R	52.0%	46.0%	53.1%	46.9%
25,449	POSEY	8,727	6,316	2,224	187	4,092 R	72.4%	25.5%	74.0%	26.0%
12,335	PULASKI	3,735	2,847	784	104	2,063 R	76.2%	21.0%	78.4%	21.6%
37,798	PUTNAM	9,928	6,954	2,254	720	4,700 R	70.0%	22.7%	75.5%	24.5%
24,657	RANDOLPH	6,886	5,235	1,426	225	3,809 R	76.0%	20.7%	78.6%	21.4%
28,378	RIPLEY	8,332	6,608	1,475	249	5,133 R	79.3%	17.7%	81.8%	18.2%
16,614	RUSH	4,863	3,586	965	312	2,621 R	73.7%	19.8%	78.8%	21.2%
23,964	SCOTT	6,832	4,782	1,864	186	2,918 R	70.0%	27.3%	72.0%	28.0%
44,860	SHELBY	11,510	7,991	2,704	815	5,287 R	69.4%	23.5%	74.7%	25.3%
20,274	SPENCER	7,598	5,347	2,087	164	3,260 R	70.4%	27.5%	71.9%	28.1%
271,994	ST. JOSEPH	71,671	37,276	33,013	1,382	4,263 R	52.0%	46.1%	53.0%	47.0%
23,028	STARKE	6,870	4,955	1,724	191	3,231 R	72.1%	25.1%	74.2%	25.8%
34,693	STEUBEN	9,676	6,921	2,479	276	4,442 R	71.5%	25.6%	73.6%	26.4%
20,707	SULLIVAN	6,318	4,544	1,564	210	2,980 R	71.9%	24.8%	74.4%	25.6%
10,775	SWITZERLAND	2,643	1,956	608	79	1,348 R	74.0%	23.0%	76.3%	23.7%
195,403	TIPPECANOE	38,658	19,616	17,984	1,058	1,632 R	50.7%	46.5%	52.2%	47.8%
15,174	TIPTON	5,260	3,822	1,148	290	2,674 R	72.7%	21.8%	76.9%	23.1%
7,057	UNION	2,486	1,946	472	68	1,474 R	78.3%	19.0%	80.5%	19.5%
181,713	VANDERBURGH	47,116	27,255	18,886	975	8,369 R	57.8%	40.1%	59.1%	40.9%
15,510	VERMILLION	5,060	3,386	1,541	133	1,845 R	66.9%	30.5%	68.7%	31.3%
107,030	VIGO	26,861	15,559	10,639	663	4,920 R	57.9%	39.6%	59.4%	40.6%
31,045	WABASH	9,855	7,530	2,046	279	5,484 R	76.4%	20.8%	78.6%	21.4%
8,278	WARREN	2,814	2,187	544	83	1,643 R	77.7%	19.3%	80.1%	19.9%
63,226	WARRICK	20,106	13,456	6,251	399	7,205 R	66.9%	31.1%	68.3%	31.7%
28,117	WASHINGTON	7,978	6,119	1,615	244	4,504 R	76.7%	20.2%	79.1%	20.9%
65,916	WAYNE	16,590	10,875	5,176	539	5,699 R	65.6%	31.2%	67.8%	32.2%
28,395	WELLS	9,146	7,317	1,576	253	5,741 R	80.0%	17.2%	82.3%	17.7%
24,105	WHITE	6,729	4,972	1,601	156	3,371 R	73.9%	23.8%	75.6%	24.4%
34,042	WHITLEY	11,520	8,586	2,442	492	6,144 R	74.5%	21.2%	77.9%	22.1%
6,744,653	TOTAL	1,860,154	1,090,390	704,480	65,284	385,910 R	58.6%	37.9%	60.8%	39.2%

INDIANA
HOUSE OF REPRESENTATIVES

CD	Year	Total Vote	Republican Vote	Republican Candidate	Democratic Vote	Democratic Candidate	Other Vote	Rep.-Dem. Plurality	Total Vote Rep.	Total Vote Dem.	Major Vote Rep.	Major Vote Dem.
1	2022	213,207	100,542	GREEN, JENNIFER-RUTH	112,656	MRVAN, FRANK J.*	9	12,114 D	47.2%	52.8%	47.2%	52.8%
1	2020	326,948	132,247	LEYVA, MARK J.	185,180	MRVAN, FRANK J.	9,521	52,933 D	40.4%	56.6%	41.7%	58.3%
1	2018	245,209	85,594	LEYVA, MARK J.	159,611	VISCLOSKY, PETER J.*	4	74,017 D	34.9%	65.1%	34.9%	65.1%
1	2016	254,583			207,515	VISCLOSKY, PETER J.*	47,068	207,515 D		81.5%		100.0%
1	2014	142,293	51,000	LEYVA, MARK J.	86,579	VISCLOSKY, PETER J.*	4,714	35,579 D	35.8%	60.8%	37.1%	62.9%
1	2012	279,034	91,291	PHELPS, JOEL	187,743	VISCLOSKY, PETER J.*		96,452 D	32.7%	67.3%	32.7%	67.3%
2	2022	194,373	125,537	YAKYM, RUDOLPH "RUDY" III	62,955	STEURY, PAUL D.	5,881	62,582 R	64.6%	32.4%	66.6%	33.4%
2	2020	298,568	183,601	WALORSKI, JACKIE*	114,967	HACKETT, PATRICIA "PAT"		68,634 R	61.5%	38.5%	61.5%	38.5%
2	2018	228,889	125,499	WALORSKI, JACKIE*	103,363	HALL, MEL	27	22,136 R	54.8%	45.2%	54.8%	45.2%
2	2016	277,357	164,355	WALORSKI, JACKIE*	102,401	COLEMAN, LYNN C.	10,601	61,954 R	59.3%	36.9%	61.6%	38.4%
2	2014	145,200	85,583	WALORSKI, JACKIE*	55,590	BOCK, JOE	4,027	29,993 R	58.9%	38.3%	60.6%	39.4%
2	2012	273,475	134,033	WALORSKI, JACKIE	130,113	MULLEN, BRENDAN	9,329	3,920 R	49.0%	47.6%	50.7%	49.3%

INDIANA

HOUSE OF REPRESENTATIVES

CD	Year	Total Vote	Republican Vote	Republican Candidate	Democratic Vote	Democratic Candidate	Other Vote	Rep.-Dem. Plurality	Total Vote Rep.	Total Vote Dem.	Major Vote Rep.	Major Vote Dem.
3	2022	201,542	131,579	BANKS, JAMES "JIM"*	60,577	SNYDER, GARY L.	9,386	71,002 R	65.3%	30.1%	68.5%	31.5%
3	2020	325,751	220,989	BANKS, JAMES "JIM"*	104,762	COLDIRON, CHIP		116,227 R	67.8%	32.2%	67.8%	32.2%
3	2018	245,537	158,927	BANKS, JAMES "JIM"*	86,610	TRITCH, COURTNEY		72,317 R	64.7%	35.3%	64.7%	35.3%
3	2016	287,247	201,396	BANKS, JAMES "JIM"	66,023	SCHRADER, THOMAS ALLEN	19,828	135,373 R	70.1%	23.0%	75.3%	24.7%
3	2014	148,793	102,889	STUTZMAN, MARLIN A.*	39,771	KUHNLE, JUSTIN	6,133	63,118 R	69.1%	26.7%	72.1%	27.9%
3	2012	280,235	187,872	STUTZMAN, MARLIN A.*	92,363	BOYD, KEVIN		95,509 R	67.0%	33.0%	67.0%	33.0%
4	2022	197,698	134,864	BAIRD, JAMES "JIM"*	62,834	DAY, ROGER D.		72,030 R	68.2%	31.8%	68.2%	31.8%
4	2020	338,515	225,531	BAIRD, JAMES "JIM"*	112,984	MACKEY, JOSEPH "JOE"		112,547 R	66.6%	33.4%	66.6%	33.4%
4	2018	244,363	156,539	BAIRD, JAMES "JIM"	87,824	BECK, TOBI		68,715 R	64.1%	35.9%	64.1%	35.9%
4	2016	299,434	193,412	ROKITA, TODD*	91,256	DALE, JOHN	14,766	102,156 R	64.6%	30.5%	67.9%	32.1%
4	2014	142,054	94,998	ROKITA, TODD*	47,056	DALE, JOHN		47,942 R	66.9%	33.1%	66.9%	33.1%
4	2012	272,268	168,688	ROKITA, TODD*	93,015	NELSON, TARA E.	10,565	75,673 R	62.0%	34.2%	64.5%	35.5%
5	2022	240,009	146,575	SPARTZ, VICTORIA*	93,434	LAKE, JEANNINE		53,141 R	61.1%	38.9%	61.1%	38.9%
5	2020	416,226	208,212	SPARTZ, VICTORIA	191,226	HALE, CHRISTINA	16,788	16,986 R	50.0%	45.9%	52.1%	47.9%
5	2018	317,177	180,035	BROOKS, SUSAN*	137,142	THORNTON, DIERDRE "DEE"		42,893 R	56.8%	43.2%	56.8%	43.2%
5	2016	361,135	221,957	BROOKS, SUSAN*	123,849	DEMAREE, ANGELA	15,329	98,108 R	61.5%	34.3%	64.2%	35.8%
5	2014	161,440	105,277	BROOKS, SUSAN*	49,756	DENNEY, SHAWN A.	6,407	55,521 R	65.2%	30.8%	67.9%	32.1%
5	2012	333,359	194,570	BROOKS, SUSAN	125,347	RESKE, SCOTT	13,442	69,223 R	58.4%	37.6%	60.8%	39.2%
6	2022	193,524	130,686	PENCE, GREGORY "GREG"*	62,838	WIRTH, CYNTHIA "CINDE"		67,848 R	67.5%	32.5%	67.5%	32.5%
6	2020	328,213	225,319	PENCE, GREGORY "GREG"*	91,103	LAKE, JEANNINE	11,791	134,216 R	68.7%	27.8%	71.2%	28.8%
6	2018	241,726	154,260	PENCE, GREGORY "GREG"	79,430	LAKE, JEANNINE	8,036	74,830 R	63.8%	32.9%	66.0%	34.0%
6	2016	296,385	204,920	MESSER, LUKE*	79,135	WELSH, BARRY A.	12,330	125,785 R	69.1%	26.7%	72.1%	27.9%
6	2014	155,071	102,187	MESSER, LUKE*	45,509	HEITZMAN, SUSAN HALL	7,375	56,678 R	65.9%	29.3%	69.2%	30.8%
6	2012	275,253	162,613	MESSER, LUKE	96,678	BOOKOUT, BRAD	15,962	65,935 R	59.1%	35.1%	62.7%	37.3%
7	2022	175,180	53,631	GRABOVSKY, ANGELA	117,309	CARSON, ANDRE D.*	4,240	63,678 D	30.6%	67.0%	31.4%	68.6%
7	2020	282,568	106,146	SMITH, SUSAN MARIE	176,422	CARSON, ANDRE D.*		70,276 D	37.6%	62.4%	37.6%	62.4%
7	2018	217,596	76,457	HARMON, WAYNE E. "GUNNY"	141,139	CARSON, ANDRE D.*		64,682 D	35.1%	64.9%	35.1%	64.9%
7	2016	264,670	94,456	PING, CATHERINE "CAT"	158,739	CARSON, ANDRE D.*	11,475	64,283 D	35.7%	60.0%	37.3%	62.7%
7	2014	112,261	46,887	PING, CATHERINE "CAT"	61,443	CARSON, ANDRE D.*	3,931	14,556 D	41.8%	54.7%	43.3%	56.7%
7	2012	257,950	95,828	MAY, CARLOS	162,122	CARSON, ANDRE D.*		66,294 D	37.1%	62.9%	37.1%	62.9%
8	2022	216,040	141,995	BUCSHON, LARRY D.*	68,109	MCCORMICK, RAY	5,936	73,886 R	65.7%	31.5%	67.6%	32.4%
8	2020	320,617	214,643	BUCSHON, LARRY D.*	95,691	MARSILI, E. THOMASINA	10,283	118,952 R	66.9%	29.8%	69.2%	30.8%
8	2018	244,291	157,396	BUCSHON, LARRY D.*	86,895	TANOOS, WILLIAM		70,501 R	64.4%	35.6%	64.4%	35.6%
8	2016	294,713	187,702	BUCSHON, LARRY D.*	93,356	DRAKE, RON	13,655	94,346 R	63.7%	31.7%	66.8%	33.2%
8	2014	171,315	103,344	BUCSHON, LARRY D.	61,384	SPANGLER, TOM	6,587	41,960 R	60.3%	35.8%	62.7%	37.3%
8	2012	283,992	151,533	BUCSHON, LARRY D.*	122,325	CROOKS, DAVE	10,134	29,208 R	53.4%	43.1%	55.3%	44.7%
9	2022	225,276	143,166	HOUCHIN, ERIN	75,700	FYFE, MATTHEW	6,410	67,466 R	63.6%	33.6%	65.4%	34.6%
9	2020	359,038	222,057	HOLLINGSWORTH, TREY*	122,566	RUFF, ANDY	14,415	99,491 R	61.8%	34.1%	64.4%	35.6%
9	2018	271,361	153,271	HOLLINGSWORTH, TREY*	118,090	WATSON, LIZ		35,181 R	56.5%	43.5%	56.5%	43.5%
9	2016	322,843	174,791	HOLLINGSWORTH, TREY	130,627	YODER, SHELLI	17,425	44,164 R	54.1%	40.5%	57.2%	42.8%
9	2014	162,387	101,594	YOUNG, TODD*	55,016	BAILEY, BILL	5,777	46,578 R	62.6%	33.9%	64.9%	35.1%
9	2012	298,180	165,332	YOUNG, TODD*	132,848	YODER, SHELLI		32,484 R	55.4%	44.6%	55.4%	44.6%
TOTAL	2022	1,856,849	1,108,575		716,412		31,862	392,163 R	59.7%	38.6%	60.7%	39.3%
TOTAL	2020	2,996,444	1,738,745		1,194,901		62,798	543,844 R	58.0%	39.9%	59.3%	40.7%
TOTAL	2018	2,256,149	1,247,978		1,000,104		8,067	247,874 R	55.3%	44.3%	55.5%	44.5%
TOTAL	2016	2,658,367	1,442,989		1,052,901		162,477	390,088 R	54.3%	39.6%	57.8%	42.2%
TOTAL	2014	1,340,814	793,759		502,104		44,951	291,655 R	59.2%	37.4%	61.3%	38.7%
TOTAL	2012	2,553,746	1,351,760		1,142,554		59,432	209,206 R	52.9%	44.7%	54.2%	45.8%

Note: An asterisk (*) denotes incumbent.

INDIANA

GENERAL AND PRIMARY ELECTIONS

GENERAL ELECTIONS: OTHER VOTES

Senate	Other vote was 63,823 Libertarian (James Sceniak), 1,461 Write-In (Write-In)
House	Other vote was:
CD 1	9 Independent (William Powers)
CD 2	5,870 Libertarian (William Henry), 11 Independent (Mike Hubbard)
CD 7	4,240 Libertarian (Gavin Maple)
CD 8	5,936 Libertarian (Andrew Horning)
CD 9	6,374 Libertarian (Tonya Millis), 36 Green (Jacob Bailey)

2022 PRIMARY ELECTIONS: SUPPLEMENTARY INFORMATION

Primary	May 3, 2022	Registration (as of May 3, 2022)		4,738,816	No Party Registration
Primary Type	Open—Any registered voter could participate in the primary of either party, although he or she could be challenged based on party affiliation. When a voter is challenged, they must execute a statement saying that they voted for a majority of the party's candidates in the previous general election. If they did not vote in the previous general election, they must indicate that they will vote for a majority of the party's candidates in the next general election.				

	REPUBLICAN PRIMARIES			DEMOCRATIC PRIMARIES		
Senator	Young, Todd	372,738	100.0%	McDermott, Thomas M. Jr.	173,466	100.0%
	TOTAL	372,738		TOTAL	173,466	
Congressional District 1	Green, Jennifer-Ruth	14,616	47.1%	Mrvan, Frank J.*	34,489	86.4%
	Milo, Blair E.	6,964	22.4%	Fantin, Richard E.	5,413	13.6%
	Leyva, Mark J.	4,173	13.5%			
	Pappas, Nicholas	2,409	7.8%			
	Lucas, Martin	1,114	3.6%			
	Ruiz, Ben	1,054	3.4%			
	Storer, Aaron	692	2.2%			
	TOTAL	31,022		TOTAL	39,902	
Congressional District 2	Walorski, Jackie*	36,928	100.0%	Steury, Paul D.	11,708	100.0%
	TOTAL	36,928		TOTAL	11,708	
Congressional District 3	Banks, James "Jim"*	54,033	100.0%	Snyder, Gary L.	6,794	56.2%
				Calkins, Aaron "A.J."	2,894	23.9%
				Beachy, Phillip	2,400	19.9%
	TOTAL	54,033		TOTAL	12,088	
Congressional District 4	Baird, James "Jim"*	50,342	100.0%	Day, Roger D.	5,680	68.2%
				Pollchik, Howard Joseph	2,648	31.8%
	TOTAL	50,342		TOTAL	8,328	
Congressional District 5	Spartz, Victoria*	47,128	100.0%	Lee Lake, Jeannine	10,192	60.0%
				Hall, Matthew L.	6,799	40.0%
	TOTAL	47,128		TOTAL	16,991	
Congressional District 6	Pence, Gregory "Greg"*	44,893	77.6%	Wirth, Cynthia "Cinde"	9,057	73.1%
	Alspach, James Dean	12,923	22.4%	Holland, George Thomas	3,337	26.9%
	TOTAL	57,816		TOTAL	12,394	

INDIANA

GENERAL AND PRIMARY ELECTIONS

	REPUBLICAN PRIMARIES			DEMOCRATIC PRIMARIES		
Congressional District 7	Grabovsky, Angela	6,886	53.6%	Carson, Andre D.*	36,242	93.9%
	Johnson, Russell Scott "Rusty"	2,185	17.0%	Godfrey, Curtis	1,526	4.0%
	Pace, Jennifer	1,556	12.1%	Pullins, Pierre Quincy	830	2.2%
	Allen, Bill	1,505	11.7%			
	Walters, Gerald	722	5.6%			
	TOTAL	*12,854*		*TOTAL*	*38,598*	
Congressional District 8	Bucshon, Larry D.*	47,557	100.0%	Mccormick, Ray	16,465	69.7%
				Dhahir, Adnan	4,429	18.7%
				Priest, Peter F.H. II	2,731	11.6%
	TOTAL	*47,557*		*TOTAL*	*23,625*	
Congressional District 9	Houchin, Erin	21,697	37.2%	Dorris, Dale William II	30,233,023	99.9%
	Sodrel, Mike	15,008	25.7%	Fyfe, Matthew	12,240	
	Barnes-Israel, Stu	12,193	20.9%	Asare, Isak	6,305	
	Baker, Jim	2,946	5.1%			
	Davisson, J. Michael	1,597	2.7%			
	Schansberg, D. Eric	1,559	2.7%			
	Tibbs, Brian	1,461	2.5%			
	Thomas, William Joseph "Bill"	956	1.6%			
	Heiwig, Dan	919	1.6%			
	TOTAL	*58,336*		*TOTAL*	*30,251,568*	

Note: An asterisk (*) denotes incumbent.

IOWA

Statewide Races

2022 could be described as a banner cycle for Iowa Republicans: as Gov. Kim Reynolds won her second full term as governor, Sen. Chuck Grassley was reelected to an eighth term. While both Republicans won by double-digit margins, the 2022 result represented something of a break with precedent, as it was a rare cycle where Grassley was not the best-performing Republican on the ticket.

Democrats seemed to have an obvious recruit against Grassley in former Rep. Abby Finkenauer, who was narrowly defeated in 2020 after representing eastern Iowa for a term. But Mike Franken, a retired Navy vice admiral and unsuccessful candidate in the 2020 Senate primary, won the primary 55%–40%. In the general election, Franken matched Grassley's fundraising and probably benefitted from grumblings about the incumbent's age: though Grassley seemed to be in good health, he was standing for reelection at age 89.

Grassley secured an eighth term, but his 56%–44% margin represented the closest reelection result of his career. In 2010 and 2016, Johnson County, home of the University of Iowa, was the sole county that voted against Grassley – in 2022, four others joined it. Linn (Cedar Rapids) and Black Hawk (Waterloo) flipped against Grassley, as did Polk (Des Moines) and Story (Ames) counties. Compared to 2016, Dallas County, which is just west of Des Moines and has seen suburban growth, swung the most against Grassley, as his 65%-31% margin dropped to 53%–47%.

In the gubernatorial race, Reynolds, who aligned herself closely with Donald Trump, won by an even heftier margin, 58%–40%. The Democratic nominee, Deidre DeJear, carried just four counties. Perhaps more than anything else, Reynold's win illustrated how red rural Iowa had become. In 2014, her Republican predecessor, longtime Gov. Terry Branstad, was reelected to his final term as governor by a 22-point margin statewide. In his landslide reelection, Branstad took more than 70% in 27 counties – in 2022, Reynolds doubled that, taking over 70% in 55 counties.

House Races

Since the 1970s, Iowa's maps have been drawn by the nonpartisan Legislative Services Agency. Although the legislature can vote down its plans, it has traditionally deferred to the LSA. With complete control of state government, Iowa Republicans played some hardball, though.

The state's existing map featured four Trump-won districts: Districts 1–3, in the east and south, were marginal, while District 4, in the northwest, gave Trump a 27-point margin. Initially, the LSA produced a map that created two Biden-won seats – legislative Republicans voted that down. After going back to the drawing board, the LSA produced a status quo map.

Going into 2022, the sole Democrat in the state's delegation was two-term Rep. Cindy Axne. Republicans scored a serious recruit in state Sen. Zach Nunn, who flipped the seat by just over 2,000 votes. Axne carried Des Moines's Polk County, which made up over the 61% of the district, by 14 points but lost the other counties. The two Republican incumbents in eastern Iowa won by single-digit margins and 4th District Republican Rep. Randy Feenstra was reelected easily. With Axne's defeat, Iowa's federal delegation was all-Republican for the first time since the 1954 elections.

IOWA

Congressional districts first established for elections held in 2022

4 members

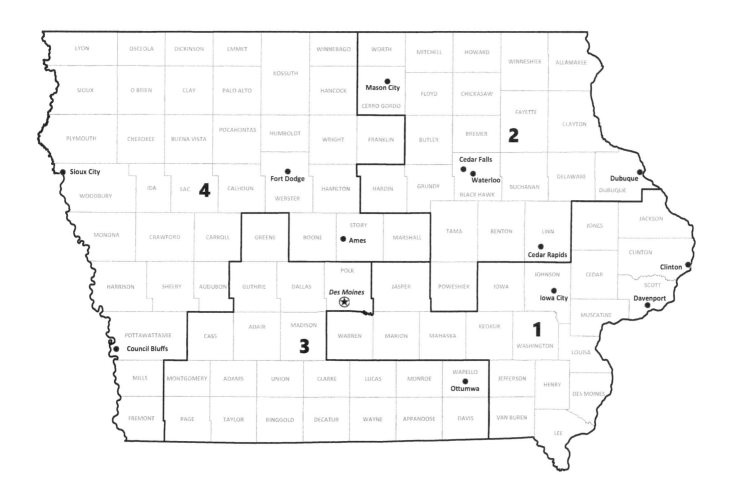

IOWA

GOVERNOR
Kim Reynolds (R). Reelected 2022 to a four-year term. Previously elected 2018. Assumed office May 24, 2017, to serve the remainder of the term vacated by the resignation of Terry E. Branstad to become the U.S. ambassador to China.

SENATORS (2 Republicans)
Joni Ernst (R). Reelected 2020 to a six-year term. Previously elected 2014.

Chuck E. Grassley (R). Reelected 2022 to a six-year term. Previously elected 2016, 2010, 2004, 1998, 1992, 1986, 1980.

REPRESENTATIVES (4 Republicans)
1. Mariannette Miller-Meeks (R)
2. Ashley Hinson (R)
3. Zachary Nunn (R)
4. Randy Feenstra (R)

POSTWAR VOTE FOR PRESIDENT

Year	Total Vote	Republican Vote	Republican Candidate	Democratic Vote	Democratic Candidate	Other Vote	Rep.-Dem. Plurality	Total Vote Rep.	Total Vote Dem.	Major Vote Rep.	Major Vote Dem.
2020	1,690,871	897,672	Trump, Donald J.*	759,061	Biden, Joseph R. Jr.	34,138	138,611 R	53.1%	44.9%	54.2%	45.8%
2016**	1,566,031	800,983	Trump, Donald J.	653,669	Clinton, Hillary Rodham	111,379	147,314 R	51.1%	41.7%	55.1%	44.9%
2012	1,582,180	730,617	Romney, W. Mitt	822,544	Obama, Barack H.*	29,019	91,927 D	46.2%	52.0%	47.0%	53.0%
2008	1,537,123	682,379	McCain, John S. III	828,940	Obama, Barack H.	25,804	146,561 D	44.4%	53.9%	45.2%	54.8%
2004	1,506,908	751,957	Bush, George W.*	741,898	Kerry, John F.	13,053	10,059 R	49.9%	49.2%	50.3%	49.7%
2000**	1,315,563	634,373	Bush, George W.	638,517	Gore, Albert Jr.	42,673	4,144 D	48.2%	48.5%	49.8%	50.2%
1996**	1,234,075	492,644	Dole, Robert "Bob"	620,258	Clinton, Bill*	121,173	127,614 D	39.9%	50.3%	44.3%	55.7%
1992**	1,354,607	504,891	Bush, George H.*	586,353	Clinton, Bill	263,363	81,462 D	37.3%	43.3%	46.3%	53.7%
1988	1,225,614	545,355	Bush, George H.	670,557	Dukakis, Michael S.	9,702	125,202 D	44.5%	54.7%	44.9%	55.1%
1984	1,319,805	703,088	Reagan, Ronald*	605,620	Mondale, Walter F.	11,097	97,468 R	53.3%	45.9%	53.7%	46.3%
1980**	1,317,661	676,026	Reagan, Ronald	508,672	Carter, Jimmy*	132,963	167,354 R	51.3%	38.6%	57.1%	42.9%
1976	1,279,306	632,863	Ford, Gerald R.*	619,931	Carter, Jimmy	26,512	12,932 R	49.5%	48.5%	50.5%	49.5%
1972	1,225,944	706,207	Nixon, Richard M.*	496,206	McGovern, George S.	23,531	210,001 R	57.6%	40.5%	58.7%	41.3%
1968**	1,167,931	619,106	Nixon, Richard M.	476,699	Humphrey, Hubert Horatio Jr.	72,126	142,407 R	53.0%	40.8%	56.5%	43.5%
1964	1,184,539	449,148	Goldwater, Barry M. Sr.	733,030	Johnson, Lyndon B.*	2,361	283,882 D	37.9%	61.9%	38.0%	62.0%
1960	1,273,810	722,381	Nixon, Richard M.	550,565	Kennedy, John F.	864	171,816 R	56.7%	43.2%	56.7%	43.3%
1956	1,234,564	729,187	Eisenhower, Dwight D.*	501,858	Stevenson, Adlai E. II	3,519	227,329 R	59.1%	40.7%	59.2%	40.8%
1952	1,268,773	808,906	Eisenhower, Dwight D.	451,513	Stevenson, Adlai E. II	8,354	357,393 R	63.8%	35.6%	64.2%	35.8%
1948	1,038,264	494,018	Dewey, Thomas E.	522,380	Truman, Harry S.*	21,866	28,362 D	47.6%	50.3%	48.6%	51.4%

Note: An asterisk (*) denotes incumbent. **In past elections, the other vote included: 2016 - 59,186 Libertarian (Gary Johnson); 2000 - 29,374 Green (Ralph Nader); 1996 -105,159 Reform (Ross Perot); 1992 - 253,468 Independent (Perot); 1980 - 115,633 Independent (John Anderson); 1968 - 66,422 American Independent (George Wallace).

IOWA

POSTWAR VOTE FOR GOVERNOR

Year	Total Vote	Republican Vote	Candidate	Democratic Vote	Candidate	Other Vote	Rep.-Dem. Plurality	Total Vote Rep.	Total Vote Dem.	Major Vote Rep.	Major Vote Dem.
2022	1,221,864	709,198	Reynolds, Kim*	482,950	DeJear, Deidre	29,716	226,248 R	58.0%	39.5%	59.5%	40.5%
2018	1,327,638	667,275	Reynolds, Kim*	630,986	Hubbell, Fred	29,377	36,289 R	50.3%	47.5%	51.4%	48.6%
2014	1,129,057	666,032	Branstad, Terry E.*	420,787	Hatch, Jack	42,238	245,245 R	59.0%	37.3%	61.3%	38.7%
2010	1,122,013	592,494	Branstad, Terry E.*	484,798	Culver, Chet*	44,721	107,696 R	52.8%	43.2%	55.0%	45.0%
2006	1,053,255	467,425	Nussle, Jim	569,021	Culver, Chet	16,809	101,596 D	44.4%	54.0%	45.1%	54.9%
2002	1,025,802	456,612	Gross, Doug	540,449	Vilsack, Tom*	28,741	83,837 D	44.5%	52.7%	45.8%	54.2%
1998	956,418	444,787	Lightfoot, Jim Ross	500,231	Vilsack, Tom	11,400	55,444 D	46.5%	52.3%	47.1%	52.9%
1994	997,248	566,395	Branstad, Terry E.*	414,453	Campbell, Bonnie J.	16,400	151,942 R	56.8%	41.6%	57.7%	42.3%
1990	976,483	591,852	Branstad, Terry E.*	379,372	Avenson, Donald D.	5,259	212,480 R	60.6%	38.9%	60.9%	39.1%
1986	910,623	472,712	Branstad, Terry E.*	436,987	Junkins, Lowell L.	924	35,725 R	51.9%	48.0%	52.0%	48.0%
1982	1,038,229	548,313	Branstad, Terry E.*	483,291	Conlin, Roxanne	6,625	65,022 R	52.8%	46.5%	53.2%	46.8%
1978	843,190	491,713	Ray, Robert E.*	345,519	Fitzgerald, Jerome D.	5,958	146,194 R	58.3%	41.0%	58.7%	41.3%
1974**	920,458	534,518	Ray, Robert E.*	377,553	Schaben, James F.	8,387	156,965 R	58.1%	41.0%	58.6%	41.4%
1972	1,210,222	707,177	Ray, Robert E.*	487,282	Franzenburg, Paul	15,763	219,895 R	58.4%	40.3%	59.2%	40.8%
1970	791,241	403,394	Ray, Robert E.*	368,911	Fulton, Robert	18,936	34,483 R	51.0%	46.6%	52.2%	47.8%
1968	1,135,988	613,827	Ray, Robert E.	521,216	Franzenburg, Paul	945	92,611 R	54.0%	45.9%	54.1%	45.9%
1966	893,175	394,518	Murray, William G.	494,259	Hughes, Harold E.*	4,398	99,741 D	44.2%	55.3%	44.4%	55.6%
1964	1,167,734	365,131	Hultman, Evan	794,610	Hughes, Harold E.*	7,993	429,479 D	31.3%	68.0%	31.5%	68.5%
1962	819,854	388,955	Erbe, Norman A.*	430,899	Hughes, Harold E.		41,944 D	47.4%	52.6%	47.4%	52.6%
1960	1,237,089	645,026	Erbe, Norman A.	592,063	McManus, E. J.		52,963 R	52.1%	47.9%	52.1%	47.9%
1958	859,095	394,071	Murray, William G.	465,024	Loveless, Herschel C.*		70,953 D	45.9%	54.1%	45.9%	54.1%
1956	1,204,235	587,383	Hoegh, Leo A.*	616,852	Loveless, Herschel C.		29,469 D	48.8%	51.2%	48.8%	51.2%
1954	848,592	435,944	Hoegh, Leo A.	410,255	Herring, Clyde E.	2,393	25,689 R	51.4%	48.3%	51.5%	48.5%
1952	1,230,045	638,388	Beardsley, William*	587,671	Loveless, Herschel C.	3,986	50,717 R	51.9%	47.8%	52.1%	47.9%
1950	857,213	506,642	Beardsley, William*	347,176	Gillette, Lester S.	3,395	159,466 R	59.1%	40.5%	59.3%	40.7%
1948	994,833	553,900	Beardsley, William	434,432	Switzer, Carroll O.	6,501	119,468 R	55.7%	43.7%	56.0%	44.0%
1946	631,681	362,592	Blue, Robert D.	266,190	Miles, Frank	2,899	96,402 R	57.4%	42.1%	57.7%	42.3%

Note: An asterisk (*) denotes incumbent. **The term of office of Iowa's Governor was increased from two to four years effective with the 1974 election.

POSTWAR VOTE FOR SENATOR

Year	Total Vote	Republican Vote	Candidate	Democratic Vote	Candidate	Other Vote	Rep.-Dem. Plurality	Total Vote Rep.	Total Vote Dem.	Major Vote Rep.	Major Vote Dem.
2022	1,216,646	681,501	Grassley, Charles E.*	533,330	Franken, Michael	1,815	148,171 R	56.0%	43.8%	56.1%	43.9%
2020	1,671,828	864,997	Ernst, Joni*	754,859	Greenfield, Theresa	51,972	110,138 R	51.7%	45.2%	53.4%	46.6%
2016	1,541,036	926,007	Grassley, Charles E.*	549,460	Judge, Patty	65,569	376,547 R	60.1%	35.7%	62.8%	37.2%
2014	1,129,700	588,575	Ernst, Joni	494,370	Braley, Bruce	46,755	94,205 R	52.1%	43.8%	54.3%	45.7%
2010	1,116,063	718,215	Grassley, Charles E.*	371,686	Conlin, Roxanne	26,162	346,529 R	64.4%	33.3%	65.9%	34.1%
2008	1,502,918	560,006	Reed, Christopher	941,665	Harkin, Tom*	1,247	381,659 D	37.3%	62.7%	37.3%	62.7%
2004	1,479,228	1,038,175	Grassley, Charles E.*	412,365	Small, Arthur A.	28,688	625,810 R	70.2%	27.9%	71.6%	28.4%
2002	1,023,075	447,892	Ganske, Greg	554,278	Harkin, Tom*	20,905	106,386 D	43.8%	54.2%	44.7%	55.3%
1998	947,907	648,480	Grassley, Charles E.*	289,049	Osterberg, David	10,378	359,431 R	68.4%	30.5%	69.2%	30.8%
1996	1,224,054	571,807	Lightfoot, Jim Ross	634,166	Harkin, Tom*	18,081	62,359 D	46.7%	51.8%	47.4%	52.6%
1992	1,292,494	899,761	Grassley, Charles E.*	351,561	Lloyd-Jones, Jean	41,172	548,200 R	69.6%	27.2%	71.9%	28.1%
1990	983,933	446,869	Tauke, Tom	535,975	Harkin, Tom*	1,089	89,106 D	45.4%	54.5%	45.5%	54.5%
1986	891,762	588,880	Grassley, Charles E.*	299,406	Roehrick, John P.	3,476	289,474 R	66.0%	33.6%	66.3%	33.7%
1984	1,292,700	564,381	Jepsen, Roger W.*	716,883	Harkin, Tom	11,436	152,502 D	43.7%	55.5%	44.0%	56.0%
1980	1,277,034	683,014	Grassley, Charles E.	581,545	Culver, John C.*	12,475	101,469 R	53.5%	45.5%	54.0%	46.0%
1978	824,654	421,598	Jepsen, Roger W.	395,066	Clark, Richard*	7,990	26,532 R	51.1%	47.9%	51.6%	48.4%
1974	889,561	420,546	Stanley, David M.	462,947	Culver, John C.	6,068	42,401 D	47.3%	52.0%	47.6%	52.4%
1972	1,203,333	530,525	Miller, Jack*	662,637	Clark, Richard	10,171	132,112 D	44.1%	55.1%	44.5%	55.5%
1968	1,144,086	568,469	Stanley, David M.	574,884	Hughes, Harold E.	733	6,415 D	49.7%	50.2%	49.7%	50.3%
1966	857,496	522,339	Miller, Jack*	324,114	Smith, E. B.	11,043	198,225 R	60.9%	37.8%	61.7%	38.3%
1962	807,972	431,364	Hickenlooper, Bourke B.*	376,602	Smith, E. B.	6	54,762 R	53.4%	46.6%	53.4%	46.6%
1960	1,237,582	642,463	Miller, Jack	595,119	Loveless, Herschel C.		47,344 R	51.9%	48.1%	51.9%	48.1%
1956	1,178,655	635,499	Hickenlooper, Bourke B.*	543,156	Evans, R. M.		92,343 R	53.9%	46.1%	53.9%	46.1%
1954	847,355	442,409	Martin, Thomas E.	402,712	Gillette, Guy M.*	2,234	39,697 R	52.2%	47.5%	52.3%	47.7%
1950	858,523	470,613	Hickenlooper, Bourke B.*	383,766	Loveland, Albert J.	4,144	86,847 R	54.8%	44.7%	55.1%	44.9%
1948	1,000,412	415,778	Wilson, George*	578,226	Gillette, Guy M.	6,408	162,448 D	41.6%	57.8%	41.8%	58.2%

Note: An asterisk (*) denotes incumbent.

IOWA
GOVERNOR 2022

2020 Census Population	County	Total Vote	Republican (Reynolds)	Democratic (DeJear)	Other	Rep.-Dem. Plurality		Percentage			
								Total Vote		Major Vote	
								Rep.	Dem.	Rep.	Dem.
7,170	ADAIR	3,174	2,333	761	80	1,572	R	73.5%	24.0%	75.4%	24.6%
3,604	ADAMS	1,673	1,241	381	51	860	R	74.2%	22.8%	76.5%	23.5%
13,678	ALLAMAKEE	5,794	4,100	1,579	115	2,521	R	70.8%	27.3%	72.2%	27.8%
12,450	APPANOOSE	4,700	3,432	1,134	134	2,298	R	73.0%	24.1%	75.2%	24.8%
5,506	AUDUBON	2,451	1,757	661	33	1,096	R	71.7%	27.0%	72.7%	27.3%
25,689	BENTON	11,346	7,745	3,292	309	4,453	R	68.3%	29.0%	70.2%	29.8%
131,305	BLACK HAWK	47,140	24,236	21,585	1,319	2,651	R	51.4%	45.8%	52.9%	47.1%
26,284	BOONE	11,204	6,813	4,065	326	2,748	R	60.8%	36.3%	62.6%	37.4%
25,119	BREMER	11,090	6,989	3,820	281	3,169	R	63.0%	34.4%	64.7%	35.3%
21,204	BUCHANAN	8,217	5,356	2,650	211	2,706	R	65.2%	32.3%	66.9%	33.1%
19,526	BUENA VISTA	5,145	3,745	1,299	101	2,446	R	72.8%	25.2%	74.2%	25.8%
14,455	BUTLER	6,066	4,501	1,429	136	3,072	R	74.2%	23.6%	75.9%	24.1%
9,677	CALHOUN	3,980	3,021	870	89	2,151	R	75.9%	21.9%	77.6%	22.4%
20,168	CARROLL	8,252	6,261	1,854	137	4,407	R	75.9%	22.5%	77.2%	22.8%
12,813	CASS	5,272	3,864	1,299	109	2,565	R	73.3%	24.6%	74.8%	25.2%
18,697	CEDAR	7,938	4,996	2,734	208	2,262	R	62.9%	34.4%	64.6%	35.4%
42,479	CERRO GORDO	17,097	9,607	7,096	394	2,511	R	56.2%	41.5%	57.5%	42.5%
11,262	CHEROKEE	4,577	3,579	911	87	2,668	R	78.2%	19.9%	79.7%	20.3%
11,923	CHICKASAW	4,939	3,570	1,292	77	2,278	R	72.3%	26.2%	73.4%	26.6%
9,388	CLARKE	3,392	2,494	824	74	1,670	R	73.5%	24.3%	75.2%	24.8%
16,001	CLAY	6,474	4,805	1,536	133	3,269	R	74.2%	23.7%	75.8%	24.2%
17,560	CLAYTON	7,372	5,110	2,105	157	3,005	R	69.3%	28.6%	70.8%	29.2%
46,418	CLINTON	16,894	10,173	6,406	315	3,767	R	60.2%	37.9%	61.4%	38.6%
16,783	CRAWFORD	4,466	3,504	876	86	2,628	R	78.5%	19.6%	80.0%	20.0%
94,355	DALLAS	44,609	24,403	19,272	934	5,131	R	54.7%	43.2%	55.9%	44.1%
9,006	DAVIS	3,029	2,338	626	65	1,712	R	77.2%	20.7%	78.9%	21.1%
7,866	DECATUR	2,793	2,081	651	61	1,430	R	74.5%	23.3%	76.2%	23.8%
16,992	DELAWARE	7,647	5,632	1,871	144	3,761	R	73.6%	24.5%	75.1%	24.9%
38,952	DES MOINES	13,488	7,929	5,184	375	2,745	R	58.8%	38.4%	60.5%	39.5%
17,330	DICKINSON	8,284	6,062	2,078	144	3,984	R	73.2%	25.1%	74.5%	25.5%
97,411	DUBUQUE	38,821	22,035	15,774	1,012	6,261	R	56.8%	40.6%	58.3%	41.7%
9,178	EMMET	3,397	2,525	803	69	1,722	R	74.3%	23.6%	75.9%	24.1%
19,665	FAYETTE	7,538	5,032	2,328	178	2,704	R	66.8%	30.9%	68.4%	31.6%
15,643	FLOYD	5,757	3,657	1,953	147	1,704	R	63.5%	33.9%	65.2%	34.8%
10,075	FRANKLIN	3,622	2,676	881	65	1,795	R	73.9%	24.3%	75.2%	24.8%
6,976	FREMONT	2,635	1,987	600	48	1,387	R	75.4%	22.8%	76.8%	23.2%
8,905	GREENE	3,632	2,473	1,078	81	1,395	R	68.1%	29.7%	69.6%	30.4%
12,262	GRUNDY	5,378	4,033	1,229	116	2,804	R	75.0%	22.9%	76.6%	23.4%
10,709	GUTHRIE	5,037	3,619	1,275	143	2,344	R	71.8%	25.3%	73.9%	26.1%
14,785	HAMILTON	5,743	3,914	1,704	125	2,210	R	68.2%	29.7%	69.7%	30.3%
10,620	HANCOCK	4,388	3,302	1,009	77	2,293	R	75.3%	23.0%	76.6%	23.4%
16,817	HARDIN	6,598	4,645	1,793	160	2,852	R	70.4%	27.2%	72.1%	27.9%
14,088	HARRISON	5,532	4,069	1,325	130	2,744	R	73.6%	24.0%	75.4%	24.6%
19,962	HENRY	6,963	4,837	1,987	139	2,850	R	69.5%	28.5%	70.9%	29.1%
9,170	HOWARD	3,388	2,310	1,010	68	1,300	R	68.2%	29.8%	69.6%	30.4%
9,559	HUMBOLDT	3,876	3,016	796	64	2,220	R	77.8%	20.5%	79.1%	20.9%
6,874	IDA	2,753	2,239	468	46	1,771	R	81.3%	17.0%	82.7%	17.3%
16,214	IOWA	7,479	5,001	2,299	179	2,702	R	66.9%	30.7%	68.5%	31.5%
19,474	JACKSON	7,783	5,260	2,278	245	2,982	R	67.6%	29.3%	69.8%	30.2%
37,262	JASPER	15,013	9,552	5,019	442	4,533	R	63.6%	33.4%	65.6%	34.4%
18,371	JEFFERSON	6,660	3,449	3,086	125	363	R	51.8%	46.3%	52.8%	47.2%
151,503	JOHNSON	63,638	18,413	43,686	1,539	25,273	D	28.9%	68.6%	29.7%	70.3%
20,742	JONES	8,176	5,285	2,678	213	2,607	R	64.6%	32.8%	66.4%	33.6%
10,273	KEOKUK	3,841	2,953	837	51	2,116	R	76.9%	21.8%	77.9%	22.1%
14,813	KOSSUTH	6,736	5,030	1,592	114	3,438	R	74.7%	23.6%	76.0%	24.0%
33,690	LEE	11,465	7,182	4,032	251	3,150	R	62.6%	35.2%	64.0%	36.0%
227,870	LINN	93,499	42,887	47,539	3,073	4,652	D	45.9%	50.8%	47.4%	52.6%
11,014	LOUISA	3,523	2,578	864	81	1,714	R	73.2%	24.5%	74.9%	25.1%
8,625	LUCAS	3,453	2,599	782	72	1,817	R	75.3%	22.6%	76.9%	23.1%
11,753	LYON	4,999	4,438	534	27	3,904	R	88.8%	10.7%	89.3%	10.7%

IOWA
GOVERNOR 2022

2020 Census Population	County	Total Vote	Republican (Reynolds)	Democratic (DeJear)	Other	RepDem. Plurality		Percentage			
								Total Vote		Major Vote	
								Rep.	Dem.	Rep.	Dem.
16,431	MADISON	7,559	5,307	2,077	175	3,230	R	70.2%	27.5%	71.9%	28.1%
22,084	MAHASKA	8,129	6,299	1,667	163	4,632	R	77.5%	20.5%	79.1%	20.9%
33,379	MARION	14,364	10,237	3,808	319	6,429	R	71.3%	26.5%	72.9%	27.1%
39,366	MARSHALL	12,390	7,544	4,584	262	2,960	R	60.9%	37.0%	62.2%	37.8%
15,143	MILLS	5,649	4,034	1,487	128	2,547	R	71.4%	26.3%	73.1%	26.9%
10,609	MITCHELL	4,252	2,899	1,263	90	1,636	R	68.2%	29.7%	69.7%	30.3%
8,634	MONONA	3,335	2,555	718	62	1,837	R	76.6%	21.5%	78.1%	21.9%
7,717	MONROE	2,966	2,266	635	65	1,631	R	76.4%	21.4%	78.1%	21.9%
9,924	MONTGOMERY	3,554	2,602	871	81	1,731	R	73.2%	24.5%	74.9%	25.1%
42,655	MUSCATINE	13,231	7,902	4,950	379	2,952	R	59.7%	37.4%	61.5%	38.5%
13,782	O'BRIEN	5,396	4,541	776	79	3,765	R	84.2%	14.4%	85.4%	14.6%
5,960	OSCEOLA	2,305	2,018	245	42	1,773	R	87.5%	10.6%	89.2%	10.8%
15,126	PAGE	5,103	3,796	1,192	115	2,604	R	74.4%	23.4%	76.1%	23.9%
8,880	PALO ALTO	3,602	2,706	829	67	1,877	R	75.1%	23.0%	76.5%	23.5%
25,240	PLYMOUTH	9,823	8,027	1,643	153	6,384	R	81.7%	16.7%	83.0%	17.0%
6,608	POCAHONTAS	2,860	2,269	532	59	1,737	R	79.3%	18.6%	81.0%	19.0%
492,228	POLK	190,999	85,542	100,312	5,145	14,770	D	44.8%	52.5%	46.0%	54.0%
93,310	POTTAWATTAMIE	29,080	18,152	10,318	610	7,834	R	62.4%	35.5%	63.8%	36.2%
18,620	POWESHIEK	7,628	4,491	2,957	180	1,534	R	58.9%	38.8%	60.3%	39.7%
4,907	RINGGOLD	2,080	1,574	456	50	1,118	R	75.7%	21.9%	77.5%	22.5%
9,731	SAC	3,960	3,135	754	71	2,381	R	79.2%	19.0%	80.6%	19.4%
173,287	SCOTT	63,742	34,604	27,530	1,608	7,074	R	54.3%	43.2%	55.7%	44.3%
11,476	SHELBY	4,697	3,570	1,023	104	2,547	R	76.0%	21.8%	77.7%	22.3%
34,874	SIOUX	14,190	12,790	1,280	120	11,510	R	90.1%	9.0%	90.9%	9.1%
97,573	STORY	36,972	16,214	19,876	882	3,662	D	43.9%	53.8%	44.9%	55.1%
16,853	TAMA	6,634	4,389	2,053	192	2,336	R	66.2%	30.9%	68.1%	31.9%
6,138	TAYLOR	2,298	1,850	405	43	1,445	R	80.5%	17.6%	82.0%	18.0%
12,249	UNION	4,581	3,180	1,278	123	1,902	R	69.4%	27.9%	71.3%	28.7%
7,036	VAN BUREN	2,801	2,189	568	44	1,621	R	78.2%	20.3%	79.4%	20.6%
34,994	WAPELLO	10,510	6,822	3,397	291	3,425	R	64.9%	32.3%	66.8%	33.2%
51,792	WARREN	23,837	14,631	8,531	675	6,100	R	61.4%	35.8%	63.2%	36.8%
21,999	WASHINGTON	8,805	5,692	2,937	176	2,755	R	64.6%	33.4%	66.0%	34.0%
6,448	WAYNE	2,383	1,939	406	38	1,533	R	81.4%	17.0%	82.7%	17.3%
35,813	WEBSTER	12,051	8,028	3,774	249	4,254	R	66.6%	31.3%	68.0%	32.0%
10,339	WINNEBAGO	4,399	2,991	1,301	107	1,690	R	68.0%	29.6%	69.7%	30.3%
20,000	WINNESHIEK	9,677	5,530	3,974	173	1,556	R	57.1%	41.1%	58.2%	41.8%
103,240	WOODBURY	28,656	18,982	9,053	621	9,929	R	66.2%	31.6%	67.7%	32.3%
7,395	WORTH	3,253	2,123	1,039	91	1,084	R	65.3%	31.9%	67.1%	32.9%
12,547	WRIGHT	4,287	3,105	1,071	111	2,034	R	72.4%	25.0%	74.4%	25.6%
3,161,850	TOTAL	1,221,864	709,198	482,950	29,716	226,248	R	58.0%	39.5%	59.5%	40.5%

IOWA
SENATOR 2022

2020 Census Population	County	Total Vote	Republican (Grassley)	Democratic (Franken)	Other	Rep.-Dem. Plurality		Percentage			
								Total Vote		Major Vote	
								Rep.	Dem.	Rep.	Dem.
7,170	ADAIR	3,169	2,279	887	3	1,392	R	71.9%	28.0%	72.0%	28.0%
3,604	ADAMS	1,637	1,167	467	3	700	R	71.3%	28.5%	71.4%	28.6%
13,678	ALLAMAKEE	5,742	3,806	1,934	2	1,872	R	66.3%	33.7%	66.3%	33.7%
12,450	APPANOOSE	4,711	3,357	1,349	5	2,008	R	71.3%	28.6%	71.3%	28.7%
5,506	AUDUBON	2,425	1,661	760	4	901	R	68.5%	31.3%	68.6%	31.4%

IOWA
SENATOR 2022

2020 Census Population	County	Total Vote	Republican (Grassley)	Democratic (Franken)	Other	Rep.-Dem. Plurality	Percentage Total Vote Rep.	Dem.	Major Vote Rep.	Dem.
25,689	BENTON	11,346	7,502	3,823	21	3,679 R	66.1%	33.7%	66.2%	33.8%
131,305	BLACK HAWK	47,223	23,133	24,036	54	903 D	49.0%	50.9%	49.0%	51.0%
26,284	BOONE	11,094	6,456	4,618	20	1,838 R	58.2%	41.6%	58.3%	41.7%
25,119	BREMER	10,992	6,641	4,345	6	2,296 R	60.4%	39.5%	60.4%	39.6%
21,204	BUCHANAN	8,166	5,085	3,071	10	2,014 R	62.3%	37.6%	62.3%	37.7%
19,526	BUENA VISTA	5,053	3,530	1,518	5	2,012 R	69.9%	30.0%	69.9%	30.1%
14,455	BUTLER	6,009	4,334	1,669	6	2,665 R	72.1%	27.8%	72.2%	27.8%
9,677	CALHOUN	3,886	2,853	1,027	6	1,826 R	73.4%	26.4%	73.5%	26.5%
20,168	CARROLL	8,110	5,773	2,327	10	3,446 R	71.2%	28.7%	71.3%	28.7%
12,813	CASS	5,209	3,698	1,502	9	2,196 R	71.0%	28.8%	71.1%	28.9%
18,697	CEDAR	7,917	4,806	3,106	5	1,700 R	60.7%	39.2%	60.7%	39.3%
42,479	CERRO GORDO	16,927	9,260	7,644	23	1,616 R	54.7%	45.2%	54.8%	45.2%
11,262	CHEROKEE	4,500	3,338	1,159	3	2,179 R	74.2%	25.8%	74.2%	25.8%
11,923	CHICKASAW	4,945	3,276	1,665	4	1,611 R	66.2%	33.7%	66.3%	33.7%
9,388	CLARKE	3,343	2,332	1,005	6	1,327 R	69.8%	30.1%	69.9%	30.1%
16,001	CLAY	6,383	4,578	1,795	10	2,783 R	71.7%	28.1%	71.8%	28.2%
17,560	CLAYTON	7,360	4,839	2,512	9	2,327 R	65.7%	34.1%	65.8%	34.2%
46,418	CLINTON	16,823	9,595	7,213	15	2,382 R	57.0%	42.9%	57.1%	42.9%
16,783	CRAWFORD	4,394	3,289	1,101	4	2,188 R	74.9%	25.1%	74.9%	25.1%
94,355	DALLAS	44,103	23,286	20,757	60	2,529 R	52.8%	47.1%	52.9%	47.1%
9,006	DAVIS	2,973	2,206	764	3	1,442 R	74.2%	25.7%	74.3%	25.7%
7,866	DECATUR	2,745	1,944	794	7	1,150 R	70.8%	28.9%	71.0%	29.0%
16,992	DELAWARE	7,639	5,423	2,210	6	3,213 R	71.0%	28.9%	71.0%	29.0%
38,952	DES MOINES	13,206	7,353	5,836	17	1,517 R	55.7%	44.2%	55.8%	44.2%
17,330	DICKINSON	8,286	5,821	2,459	6	3,362 R	70.3%	29.7%	70.3%	29.7%
97,411	DUBUQUE	38,823	20,762	18,020	41	2,742 R	53.5%	46.4%	53.5%	46.5%
9,178	EMMET	3,328	2,391	935	2	1,456 R	71.8%	28.1%	71.9%	28.1%
19,665	FAYETTE	7,536	4,784	2,744	8	2,040 R	63.5%	36.4%	63.5%	36.5%
15,643	FLOYD	5,717	3,465	2,247	5	1,218 R	60.6%	39.3%	60.7%	39.3%
10,075	FRANKLIN	3,588	2,558	1,025	5	1,533 R	71.3%	28.6%	71.4%	28.6%
6,976	FREMONT	2,600	1,861	735	4	1,126 R	71.6%	28.3%	71.7%	28.3%
8,905	GREENE	3,569	2,340	1,218	11	1,122 R	65.6%	34.1%	65.8%	34.2%
12,262	GRUNDY	5,378	3,909	1,462	7	2,447 R	72.7%	27.2%	72.8%	27.2%
10,709	GUTHRIE	5,013	3,448	1,549	16	1,899 R	68.8%	30.9%	69.0%	31.0%
14,785	HAMILTON	5,707	3,757	1,945	5	1,812 R	65.8%	34.1%	65.9%	34.1%
10,620	HANCOCK	4,350	3,148	1,194	8	1,954 R	72.4%	27.4%	72.5%	27.5%
16,817	HARDIN	6,591	4,539	2,044	8	2,495 R	68.9%	31.0%	69.0%	31.0%
14,088	HARRISON	5,463	3,889	1,548	26	2,341 R	71.2%	28.3%	71.5%	28.5%
19,962	HENRY	6,870	4,602	2,261	7	2,341 R	67.0%	32.9%	67.1%	32.9%
9,170	HOWARD	3,353	2,126	1,221	6	905 R	63.4%	36.4%	63.5%	36.5%
9,559	HUMBOLDT	3,830	2,896	931	3	1,965 R	75.6%	24.3%	75.7%	24.3%
6,874	IDA	2,726	2,130	588	8	1,542 R	78.1%	21.6%	78.4%	21.6%
16,214	IOWA	7,357	4,803	2,539	15	2,264 R	65.3%	34.5%	65.4%	34.6%
19,474	JACKSON	7,639	4,816	2,816	7	2,000 R	63.0%	36.9%	63.1%	36.9%
37,262	JASPER	14,979	9,298	5,658	23	3,640 R	62.1%	37.8%	62.2%	37.8%
18,371	JEFFERSON	6,489	3,263	3,214	12	49 R	50.3%	49.5%	50.4%	49.6%
151,503	JOHNSON	63,723	18,245	45,416	62	27,171 D	28.6%	71.3%	28.7%	71.3%
20,742	JONES	8,173	5,118	3,041	14	2,077 R	62.6%	37.2%	62.7%	37.3%
10,273	KEOKUK	3,766	2,811	949	6	1,862 R	74.6%	25.2%	74.8%	25.2%
14,813	KOSSUTH	6,715	4,781	1,925	9	2,856 R	71.2%	28.7%	71.3%	28.7%
33,690	LEE	11,453	6,964	4,476	13	2,488 R	60.8%	39.1%	60.9%	39.1%
227,370	LINN	93,682	42,551	51,008	123	8,457 D	45.4%	54.4%	45.5%	54.5%
11,014	LOUISA	3,482	2,441	1,038	3	1,403 R	70.1%	29.8%	70.2%	29.8%
8,625	LUCAS	3,460	2,513	937	10	1,576 R	72.6%	27.1%	72.8%	27.2%
11,753	LYON	4,940	4,277	662	1	3,615 R	86.6%	13.4%	86.6%	13.4%
16,431	MADISON	7,485	5,064	2,405	16	2,659 R	67.7%	32.1%	67.8%	32.2%
22,084	MAHASKA	7,993	6,049	1,936	8	4,113 R	75.7%	24.2%	75.8%	24.2%
33,379	MARION	14,160	9,799	4,341	20	5,458 R	69.2%	30.7%	69.3%	30.7%
39,366	MARSHALL	12,383	7,307	5,060	16	2,247 R	59.0%	40.9%	59.1%	40.9%
15,143	MILLS	5,602	3,937	1,654	11	2,283 R	70.3%	29.5%	70.4%	29.6%

IOWA
SENATOR 2022

2020 Census Population	County	Total Vote	Republican (Grassley)	Democratic (Franken)	Other	Rep.-Dem. Plurality	Percentage Total Vote Rep.	Dem.	Major Vote Rep.	Dem.
10,609	MITCHELL	4,246	2,761	1,479	6	1,282 R	65.0%	34.8%	65.1%	34.9%
8,634	MONONA	3,264	2,376	879	9	1,497 R	72.8%	26.9%	73.0%	27.0%
7,717	MONROE	2,903	2,135	762	6	1,373 R	73.5%	26.2%	73.7%	26.3%
9,924	MONTGOMERY	3,518	2,509	1,004	5	1,505 R	71.3%	28.5%	71.4%	28.6%
42,655	MUSCATINE	13,193	7,623	5,550	20	2,073 R	57.8%	42.1%	57.9%	42.1%
13,782	O'BRIEN	5,336	4,361	972	3	3,389 R	81.7%	18.2%	81.8%	18.2%
5,960	OSCEOLA	2,272	1,923	346	3	1,577 R	84.6%	15.2%	84.8%	15.2%
15,126	PAGE	5,104	3,707	1,385	12	2,322 R	72.6%	27.1%	72.8%	27.2%
8,880	PALO ALTO	3,586	2,586	994	6	1,592 R	72.1%	27.7%	72.2%	27.8%
25,240	PLYMOUTH	9,716	7,650	2,053	13	5,597 R	78.7%	21.1%	78.8%	21.2%
6,608	POCAHONTAS	2,820	2,158	658	4	1,500 R	76.5%	23.3%	76.6%	23.4%
492,228	POLK	191,134	83,279	107,478	377	24,199 D	43.6%	56.2%	43.7%	56.3%
93,310	POTTAWATTAMIE	29,008	17,785	11,173	50	6,612 R	61.3%	38.5%	61.4%	38.6%
18,620	POWESHIEK	7,511	4,325	3,174	12	1,151 R	57.6%	42.3%	57.7%	42.3%
4,907	RINGGOLD	2,043	1,484	556	3	928 R	72.6%	27.2%	72.7%	27.3%
9,731	SAC	3,921	2,999	914	8	2,085 R	76.5%	23.3%	76.6%	23.4%
173,287	SCOTT	63,706	32,955	30,655	96	2,300 R	51.7%	48.1%	51.8%	48.2%
11,476	SHELBY	4,620	3,401	1,213	6	2,188 R	73.6%	26.3%	73.7%	26.3%
34,874	SIOUX	14,107	12,398	1,694	15	10,704 R	87.9%	12.0%	88.0%	12.0%
97,573	STORY	36,958	15,870	21,022	66	5,152 D	42.9%	56.9%	43.0%	57.0%
16,853	TAMA	6,624	4,241	2,373	10	1,868 R	64.0%	35.8%	64.1%	35.9%
6,138	TAYLOR	2,255	1,764	487	4	1,277 R	78.2%	21.6%	78.4%	21.6%
12,249	UNION	4,506	3,035	1,464	7	1,571 R	67.4%	32.5%	67.5%	32.5%
7,036	VAN BUREN	2,774	2,097	671	6	1,426 R	75.6%	24.2%	75.8%	24.2%
34,994	WAPELLO	10,448	6,601	3,837	10	2,764 R	63.2%	36.7%	63.2%	36.8%
51,792	WARREN	23,738	14,052	9,634	52	4,418 R	59.2%	40.6%	59.3%	40.7%
21,999	WASHINGTON	8,691	5,450	3,235	6	2,215 R	62.7%	37.2%	62.8%	37.2%
6,448	WAYNE	2,378	1,860	514	4	1,346 R	78.2%	21.6%	78.3%	21.7%
35,813	WEBSTER	11,965	7,704	4,244	17	3,460 R	64.4%	35.5%	64.5%	35.5%
10,339	WINNEBAGO	4,362	2,881	1,478	3	1,403 R	66.0%	33.9%	66.1%	33.9%
20,000	WINNESHIEK	9,586	5,094	4,477	15	617 R	53.1%	46.7%	53.2%	46.8%
103,240	WOODBURY	28,636	18,161	10,409	66	7,752 R	63.4%	36.3%	63.6%	36.4%
7,395	WORTH	3,219	2,031	1,183	5	848 R	63.1%	36.8%	63.2%	36.8%
12,547	WRIGHT	4,259	2,982	1,268	9	1,714 R	70.0%	29.8%	70.2%	29.8%
3,161,850	TOTAL	1,216,646	681,501	533,330	1,815	148,171 R	56.0%	43.8%	56.1%	43.9%

IOWA
HOUSE OF REPRESENTATIVES

CD	Year	Total Vote	Republican Vote	Republican Candidate	Democratic Vote	Democratic Candidate	Other Vote	Rep.-Dem. Plurality	Total Vote Rep.	Dem.	Major Vote Rep.	Dem.
1	2022	305,380	162,947	MILLER-MEEKS, MARIANNETTE*	142,173	BOHANNAN, CHRISTINA	260	20,774 R	53.4%	46.6%	53.4%	46.6%
1	2020	413,869	212,088	HINSON, ASHLEY	201,347	FINKENAUER, ABBY*	434	10,741 R	51.2%	48.6%	51.3%	48.7%
1	2018	334,243	153,442	BLUM, ROD*	170,342	FINKENAUER, ABBY	10,459	16,900 D	45.9%	51.0%	47.4%	52.6%
1	2016	384,977	206,903	BLUM, ROD*	177,403	VERNON, MONICA	671	29,500 R	53.7%	46.1%	53.8%	46.2%
1	2014	289,306	147,762	BLUM, ROD	141,145	MURPHY, PAT	399	6,617 R	51.1%	48.8%	51.1%	48.9%
1	2012	390,849	162,465	LANGE, BENJAMIN M.	222,422	BRALEY, BRUCE*	5,962	59,957 D	41.6%	56.9%	42.2%	57.8%
2	2022	318,399	172,181	HINSON, ASHLEY*	145,940	MATHIS, LIZ	278	26,241 R	54.1%	45.8%	54.1%	45.9%
2	2020	394,625	196,964	MILLER-MEEKS, MARIANNETTE	196,958	HART, RITA	703	6 R	49.9%	49.9%	50.0%	50.0%
2	2018	312,913	133,287	PETERS, CHRISTOPHER	171,446	LOEBSACK, DAVID*	8,180	38,159 D	42.6%	54.8%	43.7%	56.3%
2	2016	370,032	170,933	PETERS, CHRISTOPHER	198,571	LOEBSACK, DAVID*	528	27,638 D	46.2%	53.7%	46.3%	53.7%
2	2014	273,329	129,455	MILLER-MEEKS, MARIANNETTE	143,431	LOEBSACK, DAVID*	443	13,976 D	47.4%	52.5%	47.4%	52.6%
2	2012	381,275	161,977	ARCHER, JOHN	211,863	LOEBSACK, DAVID*	7,435	49,886 D	42.5%	55.6%	43.3%	56.7%

IOWA
HOUSE OF REPRESENTATIVES

			Republican		Democratic		Other Vote	Rep.-Dem. Plurality	Percentage			
									Total Vote		Major Vote	
CD	Year	Total Vote	Vote	Candidate	Vote	Candidate			Rep.	Dem.	Rep.	Dem.
3	2022	310,913	156,262	NUNN, ZACH	154,117	AXNE, CINDY*	534	2,145 R	50.3%	49.6%	50.3%	49.7%
3	2020	447,947	212,997	YOUNG, DAVID	219,205	AXNE, CINDY*	15,745	6,208 D	47.5%	48.9%	49.3%	50.7%
3	2018	356,241	167,933	YOUNG, DAVID*	175,642	AXNE, CINDY	12,666	7,709 D	47.1%	49.3%	48.9%	51.1%
3	2016	390,287	208,598	YOUNG, DAVID*	155,002	MOWRER, JIM	26,687	53,596 R	53.4%	39.7%	57.4%	42.6%
3	2014	282,066	148,814	YOUNG, DAVID	119,109	APPEL, STACI	14,143	29,705 R	52.8%	42.2%	55.5%	44.5%
3	2012	386,842	202,000	LATHAM, TOM*	168,632	BOSWELL, LEONARD L.	16,210	33,368 R	52.2%	43.6%	54.5%	45.5%
4	2022	277,008	186,467	FEENSTRA, RANDY*	84,230	MELTON, RYAN	6,311	102,237 R	67.3%	30.4%	68.9%	31.1%
4	2020	383,022	237,369	FEENSTRA, RANDY	144,761	SCHOLTEN, JAMES	892	92,608 R	62.0%	37.8%	62.1%	37.9%
4	2018	313,251	157,676	KING, STEVE*	147,246	SCHOLTEN, JAMES	8,329	10,430 R	50.3%	47.0%	51.7%	48.3%
4	2016	370,259	226,719	KING, STEVE*	142,993	WEAVER, KIM	547	83,726 R	61.2%	38.6%	61.3%	38.7%
4	2014	275,633	169,834	KING, STEVE*	105,504	MOWRER, JIM	295	64,330 R	61.6%	38.3%	61.7%	38.3%
4	2012	377,883	200,063	KING, STEVE*	169,470	VILSACK, CHRISTIE	8,350	30,593 R	52.9%	44.8%	54.1%	45.9%
TOTAL	2022	1,211,700	677,857		526,460		7,383	151,397 R	55.9%	43.4%	56.3%	43.7%
TOTAL	2020	1,639,463	859,418		762,271		17,774	97,147 R	52.4%	46.5%	53.0%	47.0%
TOTAL	2018	1,316,648	612,338		664,676		39,634	52,338 D	46.5%	50.5%	48.0%	52.0%
TOTAL	2016	1,515,555	813,153		673,969		28,433	139,184 R	53.7%	44.5%	54.7%	45.3%
TOTAL	2014	1,120,334	595,865		509,189		15,280	86,676 R	53.2%	45.4%	53.9%	46.1%
TOTAL	2012	1,536,849	726,505		772,387		37,957	45,882 D	47.3%	50.3%	48.5%	51.5%

Note: An asterisk (*) denotes incumbent.

IOWA
GENERAL AND PRIMARY ELECTIONS

GENERAL ELECTIONS: OTHER VOTES

Governor — Other vote was 28,998 Libertarian (Rick Stewart), 718 Write-In (Write-In)

Senate — Other vote was 1,815 Write-In (Write-Ins)

House — Other vote was:

- CD 1: 260 Write-In (Write-In)
- CD 2: 278 Write-In (Write-In)
- CD 3: 534 Write-In (Write-In)
- CD 4: 6,035 Libertarian (Bryan Holder), 276 Write-In (Write-In)

2022 PRIMARY ELECTIONS: SUPPLEMENTARY INFORMATION

Primary	June 7, 2022	Registration (as of June 1, 2022 – includes 107,319 inactive registrants)	2,213,606	Republican	737,141
				Democratic	700,339
				No Party	755,840
				Other	20,286

Primary Type — Semi-open—Registered Democrats and Republicans could vote only in their party's primary, although any registered voter (including those not affiliated with either party) could participate in either party's primary by changing his or her registration to that party on primary day.

IOWA

GENERAL AND PRIMARY ELECTIONS

	REPUBLICAN PRIMARIES			DEMOCRATIC PRIMARIES		
Senator	Grassley, Charles E.*	143,634	73.3%	Franken, Michael	86,527	55.2%
	Carlin, Jim	51,891	26.5%	Finkenauer, Abby	62,581	39.9%
	Write-In	312	0.2%	Hurst, Glenn	7,571	4.8%
				Write-In	158	0.1%
	TOTAL	195,837		TOTAL	156,837	
Governor	Reynolds, Kim*	185,293	99.0%	DeJear, Deidre	145,555	99.5%
	Write-In	1,808	1.0%	Write-In	801	0.5%
	TOTAL	187,101		TOTAL	146,356	
Congressional District 1	Miller-Meeks, Mariannette*	41,260	98.7%	Bohannan, Christina	37,475	99.7%
	Write-In	546	1.3%	Write-In	110	0.3%
	TOTAL	41,806		TOTAL	37,585	
Congressional District 2	Hinson, Ashley*	39,897	99.3%	Mathis, Liz	40,737	99.6%
	Write-In	284	0.7%	Write-In	150	0.4%
	TOTAL	40,181		TOTAL	40,887	
Congressional District 3	Nunn, Zach	30,502	65.8%	Axne, Cindy*	47,710	99.5%
	Hasso, Nicole	8,991	19.4%	Write-In	252	0.5%
	Leffler, Gary	6,800	14.7%			
	Write-In	89	0.2%			
	TOTAL	46,382		TOTAL	47,962	
Congressional District 4	Feenstra, Randy*	51,271	98.9%	Melton, Ryan	20,794	99.7%
	Write-In	596	1.1%	Write-In	69	0.3%
	TOTAL	51,867		TOTAL	20,863	

Note: An asterisk (*) denotes incumbent.

KANSAS

Statewide Races

The biggest contest in Kansas in 2022 was a test of Democratic Gov. Laura Kelly's staying power. In 2018, running against a toxic Republican nominee, she won 48%–43%. Would typically red Kansas want four more years of a Democratic governor?

During her term, Kelly often kept above-water approval ratings. State Attorney General Derek Schmidt seemed a formidable opponent on paper, but once he got the GOP nomination, ran an underwhelming campaign. As with her 2018 campaign, Kelly cultivated a postpartisan image by getting prominent Republicans to vouch for her. Bill Graves, a popular 90s-era Republican governor, who Schmidt began his career working for, backed Kelly.

This was all enough for Kelly to prevail on Election Day – she was reelected by a little over two points. Schmidt was likely hurt by the presence of state Sen. Dennis Pyle, a Republican who ran as an independent, but Kelly came close to winning a majority of the vote anyway (she got 49.5%). While Kelly performed slightly worse in most counties her second time around, she expanded her margin in populous Johnson County (the Kansas City suburbs) to 59%–39% and held Wichita's Sedgewick County 50%–47%. In 2018, her best county was Douglas, home of the University of Kansas, in Lawrence – in 2022, her three-to-one margin there held.

Kansas, by the way, also had a Senate race, although the result was never in question. Republican Sen. Jerry Moran won a third term by a 60%–37% margin. As with his first two races, he lost Douglas County and Wyandotte County – the latter includes Kansas's part of Kansas City proper. But realignment seemed to be catching up to Moran: he lost a third county this time, Johnson. In 2016, he carried it 55%–39%, but lost it 49%–48% in 2022. Gov. Laura Kelly's strong showing in the area likely boosted Democratic nominee Mark Holland. But Moran gained ground in much of rural Kansas. In 2016, he cleared 90% in just one county, Wallace, on the Colorado border. In 2022, he repeated that feat in Wallace, and added five other counties, all in the rural west.

House Races

With a legislative supermajority, Kansas Republicans overrode a veto from Kelly to enact their preferred map. Democrats were hopeful that the state Supreme Court, where a majority of judges were appointed by Democratic governors, would intervene – but that was not in the cards.

One of Republicans' main goals was to weaken 3rd District Rep. Sharice Davids, the only Democrat in the four-member delegation. Though the district kept all of Johnson County, it traded parts of deep blue Wyandotte County for some rural counties. With that change, Biden's 2020 share in the district dropped from 54% to 51%. Running in a more marginal seat, Davids faced a rematch with Republican Amanda Adkins. But Davids expanded her margin of victory, winning 55%–43%, up from her 54%–44% result in 2020.

KANSAS
Congressional districts first established for elections held in 2022
4 members

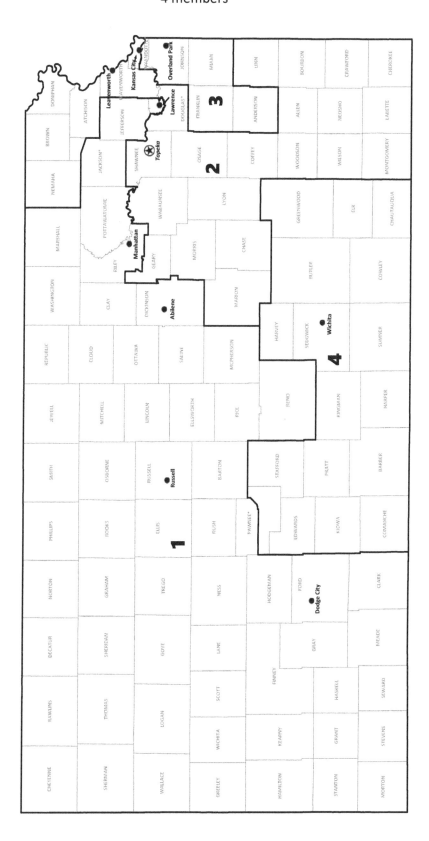

* Asterisk indicates a county whose boundaries include parts of two or more congressional districts.

KANSAS

GOVERNOR
Laura Kelly (D). Reelected 2022 to a four-year term. Previously elected 2018.

SENATORS (2 Republicans)
Jerry Moran (R). Reelected 2022 to a six-year term. Previously elected 2016, 2010.

Roger Marshall (R). Elected 2020 to a six-year term.

REPRESENTATIVES (3 Republicans, 1 Democrat)
1. Tracey Mann (R)
2. Jake LaTurner (R)
3. Sharice Davids (D)
4. Ron Estes (R)

POSTWAR VOTE FOR PRESIDENT

Year	Total Vote	Republican Vote	Republican Candidate	Democratic Vote	Democratic Candidate	Other Vote	Rep.-Dem. Plurality	Total Vote Rep.	Total Vote Dem.	Major Vote Rep.	Major Vote Dem.
2020	1,373,986	771,406	Trump, Donald J.*	570,323	Biden, Joseph R. Jr.	32,257	201,083 R	56.1%	41.5%	57.5%	42.5%
2016**	1,184,402	671,018	Trump, Donald J.	427,005	Clinton, Hillary Rodham	86,379	244,013 R	56.7%	36.1%	61.1%	38.9%
2012	1,159,971	692,634	Romney, W. Mitt	440,726	Obama, Barack H.*	26,611	251,908 R	59.7%	38.0%	61.1%	38.9%
2008	1,235,872	699,655	McCain, John S. III	514,765	Obama, Barack H.	21,452	184,890 R	56.6%	41.7%	57.6%	42.4%
2004	1,187,756	736,456	Bush, George W.*	434,993	Kerry, John F.	16,307	301,463 R	62.0%	36.6%	62.9%	37.1%
2000**	1,072,218	622,332	Bush, George W.	399,276	Gore, Albert Jr.	50,610	223,056 R	58.0%	37.2%	60.9%	39.1%
1996**	1,074,300	583,245	Dole, Robert "Bob"	387,659	Clinton, Bill*	103,396	195,586 R	54.3%	36.1%	60.1%	39.9%
1992**	1,157,335	449,951	Bush, George H.*	390,434	Clinton, Bill	316,950	59,517 R	38.9%	33.7%	53.5%	46.5%
1988	993,044	554,049	Bush, George H.	422,636	Dukakis, Michael S.	16,359	131,413 R	55.8%	42.6%	56.7%	43.3%
1984	1,021,991	677,296	Reagan, Ronald*	333,149	Mondale, Walter F.	11,546	344,147 R	66.3%	32.6%	67.0%	33.0%
1980**	979,795	566,812	Reagan, Ronald	326,150	Carter, Jimmy*	86,833	240,662 R	57.9%	33.3%	63.5%	36.5%
1976	957,845	502,752	Ford, Gerald R.*	430,421	Carter, Jimmy	24,672	72,331 R	52.5%	44.9%	53.9%	46.1%
1972	916,095	619,812	Nixon, Richard M.*	270,287	McGovern, George S.	25,996	349,525 R	67.7%	29.5%	69.6%	30.4%
1968**	872,783	478,674	Nixon, Richard M.	302,996	Humphrey, Hubert Horatio Jr.	91,113	175,678 R	54.8%	34.7%	61.2%	38.8%
1964	857,901	386,579	Goldwater, Barry M. Sr.	464,028	Johnson, Lyndon B.*	7,294	77,449 D	45.1%	54.1%	45.4%	54.6%
1960	928,825	561,474	Nixon, Richard M.	363,213	Kennedy, John F.	4,138	198,261 R	60.4%	39.1%	60.7%	39.3%
1956	866,243	566,878	Eisenhower, Dwight D.*	296,317	Stevenson, Adlai E. II	3,048	270,561 R	65.4%	34.2%	65.7%	34.3%
1952	896,166	616,302	Eisenhower, Dwight D.	273,296	Stevenson, Adlai E. II	6,568	343,006 R	68.8%	30.5%	69.3%	30.7%
1948	788,819	423,039	Dewey, Thomas E.	351,902	Truman, Harry S.*	13,878	71,137 R	53.6%	44.6%	54.6%	45.4%

Note: An asterisk (*) denotes incumbent. **In past elections, the other vote included: 2016 - 55,406 Libertarian (Gary Johnson); 2000 - 36,086 Green (Ralph Nader); 1996 - 92,639 Reform (Ross Perot); 1992 - 312,358 Independent (Perot); 1980 - 68,231 Independent (John Anderson); 1968 - 88,921 American Independent (George Wallace).

KANSAS

POSTWAR VOTE FOR GOVERNOR

Year	Total Vote	Republican Vote	Republican Candidate	Democratic Vote	Democratic Candidate	Other Vote	Rep.-Dem. Plurality	Total Vote Rep.	Total Vote Dem.	Major Vote Rep.	Major Vote Dem.
2022	1,008,998	477,591	Schmidt, Derek	499,849	Kelly, Laura*	31,558	22,258 D	47.3%	49.5%	48.9%	51.1%
2018	1,055,060	453,030	Kobach, Kris W.	506,509	Kelly, Laura	95,521	53,479 D	42.9%	48.0%	47.2%	52.8%
2014	869,502	433,196	Brownback, Sam*	401,100	Davis, Paul	35,206	32,096 R	49.8%	46.1%	51.9%	48.1%
2010	838,790	530,760	Brownback, Sam	270,166	Holland, Tom	37,864	260,594 R	63.3%	32.2%	66.3%	33.7%
2006	849,700	343,586	Barnett, Jim	491,993	Sebelius, Kathleen*	14,121	148,407 D	40.4%	57.9%	41.1%	58.9%
2002	835,692	376,830	Shallenburger, Tim	441,858	Sebelius, Kathleen	17,004	65,028 D	45.1%	52.9%	46.0%	54.0%
1998	742,665	544,882	Graves, Bill*	168,243	Sawyer, Tom	29,540	376,639 R	73.4%	22.7%	76.4%	23.6%
1994	821,030	526,113	Graves, Bill	294,733	Slattery, Jim	184	231,380 R	64.1%	35.9%	64.1%	35.9%
1990	783,325	333,589	Hayden, Mike*	380,609	Finney, Joan	69,127	47,020 D	42.6%	48.6%	46.7%	53.3%
1986	840,605	436,267	Hayden, Mike	404,338	Docking, Thomas R.		31,929 R	51.9%	48.1%	51.9%	48.1%
1982	763,263	339,356	Hardage, Sam	405,772	Carlin, John*	18,135	66,416 D	44.5%	53.2%	45.5%	54.5%
1978	736,246	348,015	Bennett, Robert F.*	363,835	Carlin, John	24,396	15,820 D	47.3%	49.4%	48.9%	51.1%
1974**	783,875	387,792	Bennett, Robert F.	384,115	Miller, Vern	11,968	3,677 R	49.5%	49.0%	50.2%	49.8%
1972	921,550	341,438	Kay, Morris	571,256	Docking, Robert*	8,856	229,818 D	37.1%	62.0%	37.4%	62.6%
1970	745,196	333,227	Frizzell, Kent	404,611	Docking, Robert*	7,358	71,384 D	44.7%	54.3%	45.2%	54.8%
1968	862,473	410,673	Harman, Rick	447,269	Docking, Robert*	4,531	36,596 D	47.6%	51.9%	47.9%	52.1%
1966	692,955	304,325	Avery, William H.*	380,030	Docking, Robert	8,600	75,705 D	43.9%	54.8%	44.5%	55.5%
1964	850,414	432,667	Avery, William H.	400,264	Wiles, Harry G.	17,483	32,403 R	50.9%	47.1%	51.9%	48.1%
1962	638,798	341,257	Anderson, John Jr.*	291,285	Saffels, Dale E.	6,256	49,972 R	53.4%	45.6%	54.0%	46.0%
1960	922,522	511,534	Anderson, John Jr.	402,261	Docking, George*	8,727	109,273 R	55.4%	43.6%	56.0%	44.0%
1958	735,939	313,036	Reed, Clyde M.	415,506	Docking, George*	7,397	102,470 D	42.5%	56.5%	43.0%	57.0%
1956	864,935	364,340	Shaw, Warren W.	479,701	Docking, George	20,894	115,361 D	42.1%	55.5%	43.2%	56.8%
1954	622,633	329,868	Hall, Fred	286,218	Docking, George	6,547	43,650 R	53.0%	46.0%	53.5%	46.5%
1952	872,139	491,338	Arn, Edward F.*	363,482	Rooney, Charles	17,319	127,856 R	56.3%	41.7%	57.5%	42.5%
1950	619,310	333,001	Arn, Edward F.	275,494	Anderson, Kenneth T.	10,815	57,507 R	53.8%	44.5%	54.7%	45.3%
1948	760,407	433,396	Carlson, Frank*	307,485	Carpenter, Randolph	19,526	125,911 R	57.0%	40.4%	58.5%	41.5%
1946	577,694	309,064	Carlson, Frank	254,283	Woodring, Harry H.	14,347	54,781 R	53.5%	44.0%	54.9%	45.1%

Note: An asterisk (*) denotes incumbent. **The term of office of Kansas's governor was increased from two to four years effective with the 1974 election.

POSTWAR VOTE FOR SENATOR

Year	Total Vote	Republican Vote	Republican Candidate	Democratic Vote	Democratic Candidate	Other Vote	Rep.-Dem. Plurality	Total Vote Rep.	Total Vote Dem.	Major Vote Rep.	Major Vote Dem.
2022	1,004,956	602,976	Moran, Jerry*	372,214	Holland, Mark R.	29,766	230,762 R	60.0%	37.0%	61.8%	38.2%
2020	1,367,755	727,962	Marshall, Roger	571,530	Bollier, Barbara	68,263	156,432 R	53.2%	41.8%	56.0%	44.0%
2016	1,177,922	732,376	Moran, Jerry*	379,740	Wiesner, Patrick	65,806	352,636 R	62.2%	32.2%	65.9%	34.1%
2014**	866,191	460,350	Roberts, Pat*			405,841	460,350 R	53.1%		100.0%	
2010	837,692	587,175	Moran, Jerry	220,971	Johnston, Lisa	29,546	366,204 R	70.1%	26.4%	72.7%	27.3%
2008	1,210,690	727,121	Roberts, Pat*	441,399	Slattery, Jim	42,170	285,722 R	60.1%	36.5%	62.2%	37.8%
2004	1,129,022	780,863	Brownback, Sam*	310,337	Jones, Lee	37,822	470,526 R	69.2%	27.5%	71.6%	28.4%
2002	776,850	641,075	Roberts, Pat*			135,775	641,075 R	82.5%		100.0%	
1998	727,236	474,639	Brownback, Sam*	229,718	Feleciano, Paul Jr.	22,879	244,921 R	65.3%	31.6%	67.4%	32.6%
1996	1,052,300	652,677	Roberts, Pat	362,380	Thompson, Sally	37,243	290,297 R	62.0%	34.4%	64.3%	35.7%
1996S**	1,064,716	574,021	Brownback, Sam	461,344	Docking, Jill	29,351	112,677 R	53.9%	43.3%	55.4%	44.6%
1992	1,126,447	706,246	Dole, Robert "Bob"*	349,525	O'Dell, Gloria	70,676	356,721 R	62.7%	31.0%	66.9%	33.1%
1990	786,235	578,605	Kassebaum, Nancy Landon*	207,491	Williams, Dick	139	371,114 R	73.6%	26.4%	73.6%	26.4%
1986	823,566	576,902	Dole, Robert "Bob"*	246,664	MacDonald, Guy		330,238 R	70.0%	30.0%	70.0%	30.0%
1984	996,729	757,402	Kassebaum, Nancy Landon*	211,664	Maher, James R.	27,663	545,738 R	76.0%	21.2%	78.2%	21.8%
1980	938,957	598,686	Dole, Robert "Bob"*	340,271	Simpson, John		258,415 R	63.8%	36.2%	63.8%	36.2%
1978	748,839	403,354	Kassebaum, Nancy Landon	317,602	Roy, William R.	27,883	85,752 R	53.9%	42.4%	55.9%	44.1%
1974	794,437	403,983	Dole, Robert "Bob"*	390,451	Roy, William R.	3	13,532 R	50.9%	49.1%	50.9%	49.1%
1972	871,702	622,591	Pearson, James B.*	200,764	Tetzlaff, Arch O.	48,347	421,827 R	71.4%	23.0%	75.6%	24.4%
1968	817,096	490,911	Dole, Robert "Bob"	315,911	Robinson, William I.	10,274	175,000 R	60.1%	38.7%	60.8%	39.2%
1966	671,345	350,077	Pearson, James B.*	303,223	Breeding, J. Floyd	18,045	46,854 R	52.1%	45.2%	53.6%	46.4%
1962	622,232	388,500	Carlson, Frank*	223,630	Smith, K. L.	10,102	164,870 R	62.4%	35.9%	63.5%	36.5%
1962S**	613,250	344,689	Pearson, James B.*	260,756	Aylward, Paul L.	7,805	83,933 R	56.2%	42.5%	56.9%	43.1%
1960	888,550	485,499	Schoeppel, Andrew F.*	388,859	Theis, Frank	14,198	96,640 R	54.6%	43.8%	55.5%	44.5%
1956	825,280	477,822	Carlson, Frank*	333,939	Hart, George	13,519	143,883 R	57.9%	40.5%	58.9%	41.1%
1954	618,063	348,144	Schoeppel, Andrew F.*	258,575	McGill, George	11,344	89,569 R	56.3%	41.8%	57.4%	42.6%
1950	619,104	335,880	Carlson, Frank*	271,365	Aiken, Paul	11,859	64,515 R	54.3%	43.8%	55.3%	44.7%
1948	716,342	393,412	Schoeppel, Andrew F.	305,987	McGill, George	16,943	87,425 R	54.9%	42.7%	56.3%	43.7%

Note: An asterisk (*) denotes incumbent. **In past elections, the other vote included: 2014 - 368,372 Independent (Greg Orman). One of the 1996 and 1962 elections was for a short term to fill a vacancy. The Democratic Party did not run a candidate in the 2002 and 2014 Senate elections.

KANSAS
GOVERNOR 2022

2020 Census Population	County	Total Vote	Republican (Schmidt)	Democratic (Kelly)	Other	Rep.-Dem. Plurality	Percentage Total Vote Rep.	Dem.	Major Vote Rep.	Dem.
12,340	ALLEN	4,138	2,424	1,579	135	845 R	58.6%	38.2%	60.6%	39.4%
7,875	ANDERSON	2,908	1,899	835	174	1,064 R	65.3%	28.7%	69.5%	30.5%
16,081	ATCHISON	5,480	2,929	2,185	366	744 R	53.4%	39.9%	57.3%	42.7%
4,406	BARBER	1,745	1,261	403	81	858 R	72.3%	23.1%	75.8%	24.2%
25,721	BARTON	8,095	5,026	2,645	424	2,381 R	62.1%	32.7%	65.5%	34.5%
14,570	BOURBON	4,839	3,155	1,474	210	1,681 R	65.2%	30.5%	68.2%	31.8%
9,572	BROWN	3,367	1,837	1,180	350	657 R	54.6%	35.0%	60.9%	39.1%
67,021	BUTLER	23,756	13,867	9,042	847	4,825 R	58.4%	38.1%	60.5%	39.5%
2,664	CHASE	1,185	692	463	30	229 R	58.4%	39.1%	59.9%	40.1%
3,251	CHAUTAUQUA	1,182	960	200	22	760 R	81.2%	16.9%	82.8%	17.2%
19,935	CHEROKEE	6,433	4,378	1,833	222	2,545 R	68.1%	28.5%	70.5%	29.5%
2,662	CHEYENNE	1,018	785	207	26	578 R	77.1%	20.3%	79.1%	20.9%
1,998	CLARK	852	565	220	67	345 R	66.3%	25.8%	72.0%	28.0%
8,006	CLAY	3,301	2,051	1,105	145	946 R	62.1%	33.5%	65.0%	35.0%
8,780	CLOUD	3,205	2,103	1,014	88	1,089 R	65.6%	31.6%	67.5%	32.5%
8,181	COFFEY	3,443	2,251	1,049	143	1,202 R	65.4%	30.5%	68.2%	31.8%
1,696	COMANCHE	744	514	188	42	326 R	69.1%	25.3%	73.2%	26.8%
34,915	COWLEY	10,671	5,898	4,327	446	1,571 R	55.3%	40.5%	57.7%	42.3%
38,845	CRAWFORD	11,834	6,033	5,432	369	601 R	51.0%	45.9%	52.6%	47.4%
2,832	DECATUR	1,132	803	283	46	520 R	70.9%	25.0%	73.9%	26.1%
18,466	DICKINSON	6,943	4,253	2,414	276	1,839 R	61.3%	34.8%	63.8%	36.2%
7,616	DONIPHAN	2,644	1,773	648	223	1,125 R	67.1%	24.5%	73.2%	26.8%
122,663	DOUGLAS	47,396	10,634	35,796	966	25,162 D	22.4%	75.5%	22.9%	77.1%
2,799	EDWARDS	1,093	725	333	35	392 R	66.3%	30.5%	68.5%	31.5%
2,542	ELK	1,076	750	283	43	467 R	69.7%	26.3%	72.6%	27.4%
28,555	ELLIS	10,552	5,968	4,248	336	1,720 R	56.6%	40.3%	58.4%	41.6%
6,103	ELLSWORTH	2,238	1,269	866	103	403 R	56.7%	38.7%	59.4%	40.6%
36,362	FINNEY	7,191	4,021	2,924	246	1,097 R	55.9%	40.7%	57.9%	42.1%
33,385	FORD	5,994	3,410	2,348	236	1,062 R	56.9%	39.2%	59.2%	40.8%
25,578	FRANKLIN	9,535	5,374	3,823	338	1,551 R	56.4%	40.1%	58.4%	41.6%
31,094	GEARY	6,075	2,758	3,094	223	336 D	45.4%	50.9%	47.1%	52.9%
2,640	GOVE	1,161	866	248	47	618 R	74.6%	21.4%	77.7%	22.3%
2,490	GRAHAM	1,033	709	280	44	429 R	68.6%	27.1%	71.7%	28.3%
7,099	GRANT	1,613	1,055	489	69	566 R	65.4%	30.3%	68.3%	31.7%
5,953	GRAY	1,718	1,222	428	68	794 R	71.1%	24.9%	74.1%	25.9%
1,230	GREELEY	453	312	114	27	198 R	68.9%	25.2%	73.2%	26.8%
5,999	GREENWOOD	2,320	1,483	753	84	730 R	63.9%	32.5%	66.3%	33.7%
2,526	HAMILTON	605	401	175	29	226 R	66.3%	28.9%	69.6%	30.4%
5,428	HARPER	1,979	1,314	577	88	737 R	66.4%	29.2%	69.5%	30.5%
34,487	HARVEY	12,917	6,279	6,206	432	73 R	48.6%	48.0%	50.3%	49.7%
3,957	HASKELL	994	715	250	29	465 R	71.9%	25.2%	74.1%	25.9%
1,788	HODGEMAN	807	594	181	32	413 R	73.6%	22.4%	76.6%	23.4%
13,166	JACKSON	5,089	2,670	2,081	338	589 R	52.5%	40.9%	56.2%	43.8%
19,128	JEFFERSON	7,622	3,939	3,380	303	559 R	51.7%	44.3%	53.8%	46.2%
2,881	JEWELL	1,208	861	268	79	593 R	71.3%	22.2%	76.3%	23.7%
604,162	JOHNSON	262,697	102,162	155,104	5,431	52,942 D	38.9%	59.0%	39.7%	60.3%
3,822	KEARNY	957	694	220	43	474 R	72.5%	23.0%	75.9%	24.1%
7,189	KINGMAN	3,100	1,997	971	132	1,026 R	64.4%	31.3%	67.3%	32.7%
2,478	KIOWA	944	662	234	48	428 R	70.1%	24.8%	73.9%	26.1%
19,583	LABETTE	5,927	3,470	2,287	170	1,183 R	58.5%	38.6%	60.3%	39.7%
1,541	LANE	681	487	164	30	323 R	71.5%	24.1%	74.8%	25.2%
81,920	LEAVENWORTH	26,893	13,419	12,480	994	939 R	49.9%	46.4%	51.8%	48.2%
2,963	LINCOLN	1,204	803	344	57	459 R	66.7%	28.6%	70.0%	30.0%
9,727	LINN	3,723	2,576	979	168	1,597 R	69.2%	26.3%	72.5%	27.5%
2,801	LOGAN	1,105	818	237	50	581 R	74.0%	21.4%	77.5%	22.5%
33,227	LYON	10,128	4,411	5,380	337	969 D	43.6%	53.1%	45.1%	54.9%
11,916	MARION	4,815	2,935	1,709	171	1,226 R	61.0%	35.5%	63.2%	36.8%
9,723	MARSHALL	3,899	2,157	1,523	219	634 R	55.3%	39.1%	58.6%	41.4%
28,614	MCPHERSON	11,044	6,509	4,158	377	2,351 R	58.9%	37.6%	61.0%	39.0%
4,025	MEADE	1,312	951	309	52	642 R	72.5%	23.6%	75.5%	24.5%

KANSAS
GOVERNOR 2022

2020 Census Population	County	Total Vote	Republican (Schmidt)	Democratic (Kelly)	Other	Rep.-Dem. Plurality	Percentage Total Vote		Percentage Major Vote	
							Rep.	Dem.	Rep.	Dem.
34,386	MIAMI	13,494	7,993	5,050	451	2,943 R	59.2%	37.4%	61.3%	38.7%
5,981	MITCHELL	2,375	1,577	718	80	859 R	66.4%	30.2%	68.7%	31.3%
31,784	MONTGOMERY	9,611	6,567	2,746	298	3,821 R	68.3%	28.6%	70.5%	29.5%
5,625	MORRIS	2,244	1,227	942	75	285 R	54.7%	42.0%	56.6%	43.4%
2,555	MORTON	808	606	167	35	439 R	75.0%	20.7%	78.4%	21.6%
10,266	NEMAHA	4,609	2,957	1,276	376	1,681 R	64.2%	27.7%	69.9%	30.1%
15,964	NEOSHO	5,106	3,053	1,854	199	1,199 R	59.8%	36.3%	62.2%	37.8%
2,754	NESS	1,157	900	208	49	692 R	77.8%	18.0%	81.2%	18.8%
5,363	NORTON	1,799	1,244	473	82	771 R	69.1%	26.3%	72.5%	27.5%
15,990	OSAGE	6,285	3,582	2,449	254	1,133 R	57.0%	39.0%	59.4%	40.6%
3,418	OSBORNE	1,440	937	394	109	543 R	65.1%	27.4%	70.4%	29.6%
5,722	OTTAWA	2,388	1,592	695	101	897 R	66.7%	29.1%	69.6%	30.4%
6,390	PAWNEE	2,155	1,207	827	121	380 R	56.0%	38.4%	59.3%	40.7%
5,242	PHILLIPS	2,187	1,647	465	75	1,182 R	75.3%	21.3%	78.0%	22.0%
24,491	POTTAWATOMIE	10,503	6,245	3,789	469	2,456 R	59.5%	36.1%	62.2%	37.8%
9,132	PRATT	3,128	1,841	1,168	119	673 R	58.9%	37.3%	61.2%	38.8%
2,540	RAWLINS	1,148	808	308	32	500 R	70.4%	26.8%	72.4%	27.6%
61,963	RENO	20,776	11,083	8,813	880	2,270 R	53.3%	42.4%	55.7%	44.3%
4,645	REPUBLIC	1,970	1,396	494	80	902 R	70.9%	25.1%	73.9%	26.1%
9,555	RICE	3,112	1,858	985	269	873 R	59.7%	31.7%	65.4%	34.6%
73,637	RILEY	18,195	6,849	10,849	497	4,000 D	37.6%	59.6%	38.7%	61.3%
4,908	ROOKS	2,104	1,488	541	75	947 R	70.7%	25.7%	73.3%	26.7%
3,055	RUSH	1,328	852	390	86	462 R	64.2%	29.4%	68.6%	31.4%
6,861	RUSSELL	2,717	1,698	886	133	812 R	62.5%	32.6%	65.7%	34.3%
54,203	SALINE	17,731	9,124	8,036	571	1,088 R	51.5%	45.3%	53.2%	46.8%
4,818	SCOTT	1,699	1,279	346	74	933 R	75.3%	20.4%	78.7%	21.3%
516,642	SEDGWICK	155,206	72,884	77,727	4,595	4,843 D	47.0%	50.1%	48.4%	51.6%
21,130	SEWARD	2,944	1,726	1,104	114	622 R	58.6%	37.5%	61.0%	39.0%
176,967	SHAWNEE	65,914	24,882	39,312	1,720	14,430 D	37.7%	59.6%	38.8%	61.2%
2,527	SHERIDAN	1,112	863	197	52	666 R	77.6%	17.7%	81.4%	18.6%
5,916	SHERMAN	2,052	1,485	484	83	1,001 R	72.4%	23.6%	75.4%	24.6%
3,588	SMITH	1,645	1,163	403	79	760 R	70.7%	24.5%	74.3%	25.7%
4,163	STAFFORD	1,571	1,039	458	74	581 R	66.1%	29.2%	69.4%	30.6%
1,983	STANTON	517	373	124	20	249 R	72.1%	24.0%	75.1%	24.9%
5,468	STEVENS	1,401	1,037	302	62	735 R	74.0%	21.6%	77.4%	22.6%
22,826	SUMNER	7,890	4,592	2,926	372	1,666 R	58.2%	37.1%	61.1%	38.9%
7,756	THOMAS	2,888	1,995	782	111	1,213 R	69.1%	27.1%	71.8%	28.2%
2,809	TREGO	1,263	856	342	65	514 R	67.8%	27.1%	71.5%	28.5%
6,942	WABAUNSEE	3,353	1,977	1,257	119	720 R	59.0%	37.5%	61.1%	38.9%
1,520	WALLACE	672	560	78	34	482 R	83.3%	11.6%	87.8%	12.2%
5,393	WASHINGTON	2,257	1,677	511	69	1,166 R	74.3%	22.6%	76.6%	23.4%
2,112	WICHITA	712	548	138	26	410 R	77.0%	19.4%	79.9%	20.1%
8,512	WILSON	3,290	2,405	769	116	1,636 R	73.1%	23.4%	75.8%	24.2%
3,147	WOODSON	1,185	833	324	28	509 R	70.3%	27.3%	72.0%	28.0%
165,303	WYANDOTTE	35,044	10,249	23,772	1,023	13,523 D	29.2%	67.8%	30.1%	69.9%
2,914,929	TOTAL	1,008,998	477,591	499,849	31,558	22,258 D	47.3%	49.5%	48.9%	51.1%

KANSAS
SENATOR 2022

2020 Census Population	County	Total Vote	Republican (Moran)	Democratic (Holland)	Other	Rep.-Dem. Plurality	Percentage Total Vote Rep.	Dem.	Major Vote Rep.	Dem.
12,340	ALLEN	4,122	3,014	984	124	2,030 R	73.1%	23.9%	75.4%	24.6%
7,875	ANDERSON	2,901	2,291	505	105	1,786 R	79.0%	17.4%	81.9%	18.1%
16,081	ATCHISON	5,486	3,936	1,413	137	2,523 R	71.7%	25.8%	73.6%	26.4%
4,406	BARBER	1,737	1,521	169	47	1,352 R	87.6%	9.7%	90.0%	10.0%
25,721	BARTON	8,072	6,626	1,232	214	5,394 R	82.1%	15.3%	84.3%	15.7%
14,570	BOURBON	4,787	3,561	1,050	176	2,511 R	74.4%	21.9%	77.2%	22.8%
9,572	BROWN	3,353	2,588	646	119	1,942 R	77.2%	19.3%	80.0%	20.0%
67,021	BUTLER	23,675	16,962	5,987	726	10,975 R	71.6%	25.3%	73.9%	26.1%
2,664	CHASE	1,177	898	245	34	653 R	76.3%	20.8%	78.6%	21.4%
3,251	CHAUTAUQUA	1,173	991	151	31	840 R	84.5%	12.9%	86.8%	13.2%
19,935	CHEROKEE	6,407	4,716	1,492	199	3,224 R	73.6%	23.3%	76.0%	24.0%
2,662	CHEYENNE	1,039	903	112	24	791 R	86.9%	10.8%	89.0%	11.0%
1,998	CLARK	854	725	95	34	630 R	84.9%	11.1%	88.4%	11.6%
8,006	CLAY	3,297	2,711	479	107	2,232 R	82.2%	14.5%	85.0%	15.0%
8,780	CLOUD	3,209	2,575	530	104	2,045 R	80.2%	16.5%	82.9%	17.1%
8,181	COFFEY	3,437	2,733	574	130	2,159 R	79.5%	16.7%	82.6%	17.4%
1,696	COMANCHE	744	652	67	25	585 R	87.6%	9.0%	90.7%	9.3%
34,915	COWLEY	10,611	7,362	2,867	382	4,495 R	69.4%	27.0%	72.0%	28.0%
38,845	CRAWFORD	11,797	7,154	4,276	367	2,878 R	60.6%	36.2%	62.6%	37.4%
2,832	DECATUR	1,129	986	114	29	872 R	87.3%	10.1%	89.6%	10.4%
18,466	DICKINSON	6,912	5,446	1,239	227	4,207 R	78.8%	17.9%	81.5%	18.5%
7,616	DONIPHAN	2,638	2,159	405	74	1,754 R	81.8%	15.4%	84.2%	15.8%
122,663	DOUGLAS	47,161	14,501	31,415	1,245	16,914 D	30.7%	66.6%	31.6%	68.4%
2,799	EDWARDS	1,089	923	139	27	784 R	84.8%	12.8%	86.9%	13.1%
2,542	ELK	1,062	891	132	39	759 R	83.9%	12.4%	87.1%	12.9%
28,555	ELLIS	10,518	7,920	2,236	362	5,684 R	75.3%	21.3%	78.0%	22.0%
6,103	ELLSWORTH	2,244	1,821	359	64	1,462 R	81.1%	16.0%	83.5%	16.5%
36,362	FINNEY	7,160	5,162	1,793	205	3,369 R	72.1%	25.0%	74.2%	25.8%
33,385	FORD	5,966	4,350	1,452	164	2,898 R	72.9%	24.3%	75.0%	25.0%
25,578	FRANKLIN	9,512	6,678	2,505	329	4,173 R	70.2%	26.3%	72.7%	27.3%
31,094	GEARY	6,051	3,799	2,038	214	1,761 R	62.8%	33.7%	65.1%	34.9%
2,640	GOVE	1,156	1,049	86	21	963 R	90.7%	7.4%	92.4%	7.6%
2,490	GRAHAM	1,002	845	109	48	736 R	84.3%	10.9%	88.6%	11.4%
7,099	GRANT	1,606	1,362	206	38	1,156 R	84.8%	12.8%	86.9%	13.1%
5,953	GRAY	1,702	1,476	179	47	1,297 R	86.7%	10.5%	89.2%	10.8%
1,230	GREELEY	453	402	38	13	364 R	88.7%	8.4%	91.4%	8.6%
5,999	GREENWOOD	2,312	1,863	371	78	1,492 R	80.6%	16.0%	83.4%	16.6%
2,526	HAMILTON	599	529	63	7	466 R	88.3%	10.5%	89.4%	10.6%
5,428	HARPER	1,973	1,665	248	60	1,417 R	84.4%	12.6%	87.0%	13.0%
34,487	HARVEY	12,809	8,127	4,325	357	3,802 R	63.4%	33.8%	65.3%	34.7%
3,957	HASKELL	986	862	103	21	759 R	87.4%	10.4%	89.3%	10.7%
1,788	HODGEMAN	794	700	78	16	622 R	88.2%	9.8%	90.0%	10.0%
13,166	JACKSON	5,105	3,791	1,122	192	2,669 R	74.3%	22.0%	77.2%	22.8%
19,128	JEFFERSON	7,594	5,208	2,160	226	3,048 R	68.6%	28.4%	70.7%	29.3%
2,881	JEWELL	1,205	1,055	117	33	938 R	87.6%	9.7%	90.0%	10.0%
604,162	JOHNSON	262,051	125,715	129,199	7,137	3,484 D	48.0%	49.3%	49.3%	50.7%
3,822	KEARNY	951	847	85	19	762 R	89.1%	8.9%	90.9%	9.1%
7,189	KINGMAN	3,094	2,527	500	67	2,027 R	81.7%	16.2%	83.5%	16.5%
2,478	KIOWA	936	825	82	29	743 R	88.1%	8.8%	91.0%	9.0%
19,583	LABETTE	5,932	4,021	1,725	186	2,296 R	67.8%	29.1%	70.0%	30.0%
1,541	LANE	672	596	57	19	539 R	88.7%	8.5%	91.3%	8.7%
81,920	LEAVENWORTH	26,857	16,570	9,444	843	7,126 R	61.7%	35.2%	63.7%	36.3%
2,963	LINCOLN	1,198	1,020	128	50	892 R	85.1%	10.7%	88.9%	11.1%
9,727	LINN	3,715	3,017	593	105	2,424 R	81.2%	16.0%	83.6%	16.4%
2,801	LOGAN	1,086	979	82	25	897 R	90.1%	7.6%	92.3%	7.7%
33,227	LYON	10,052	6,203	3,549	300	2,654 R	61.7%	35.3%	63.6%	36.4%
11,916	MARION	4,813	3,801	901	111	2,900 R	79.0%	18.7%	80.8%	19.2%
9,723	MARSHALL	3,885	3,043	755	87	2,288 R	78.3%	19.4%	80.1%	19.9%
28,614	MCPHERSON	11,154	8,268	2,593	293	5,675 R	74.1%	23.2%	76.1%	23.9%
4,025	MEADE	1,311	1,154	123	34	1,031 R	88.0%	9.4%	90.4%	9.6%

KANSAS
SENATOR 2022

2020 Census Population	County	Total Vote	Republican (Moran)	Democratic (Holland)	Other	Rep.-Dem. Plurality	Percentage Total Vote Rep.	Dem.	Major Vote Rep.	Dem.
34,386	MIAMI	13,453	9,475	3,574	404	5,901 R	70.4%	26.6%	72.6%	27.4%
5,981	MITCHELL	2,372	2,023	291	58	1,732 R	85.3%	12.3%	87.4%	12.6%
31,784	MONTGOMERY	9,516	7,117	2,105	294	5,012 R	74.8%	22.1%	77.2%	22.8%
5,625	MORRIS	2,229	1,724	436	69	1,288 R	77.3%	19.6%	79.8%	20.2%
2,555	MORTON	792	696	62	34	634 R	87.9%	7.8%	91.8%	8.2%
10,266	NEMAHA	4,579	3,931	543	105	3,388 R	85.8%	11.9%	87.9%	12.1%
15,964	NEOSHO	5,100	3,751	1,194	155	2,557 R	73.5%	23.4%	75.9%	24.1%
2,754	NESS	1,152	1,057	64	31	993 R	91.8%	5.6%	94.3%	5.7%
5,363	NORTON	1,792	1,551	200	41	1,351 R	86.6%	11.2%	88.6%	11.4%
15,990	OSAGE	6,250	4,716	1,320	214	3,396 R	75.5%	21.1%	78.1%	21.9%
3,418	OSBORNE	1,439	1,245	133	61	1,112 R	86.5%	9.2%	90.3%	9.7%
5,722	OTTAWA	2,375	1,986	280	109	1,706 R	83.6%	11.8%	87.6%	12.4%
6,390	PAWNEE	2,145	1,691	376	78	1,315 R	78.8%	17.5%	81.8%	18.2%
5,242	PHILLIPS	2,199	1,988	156	55	1,832 R	90.4%	7.1%	92.7%	7.3%
24,491	POTTAWATOMIE	10,452	8,113	2,073	266	6,040 R	77.6%	19.8%	79.6%	20.4%
9,132	PRATT	3,109	2,419	591	99	1,828 R	77.8%	19.0%	80.4%	19.6%
2,540	RAWLINS	1,155	1,010	109	36	901 R	87.4%	9.4%	90.3%	9.7%
61,963	RENO	20,643	14,459	5,467	717	8,992 R	70.0%	26.5%	72.6%	27.4%
4,645	REPUBLIC	1,966	1,647	244	75	1,403 R	83.8%	12.4%	87.1%	12.9%
9,555	RICE	3,096	2,510	494	92	2,016 R	81.1%	16.0%	83.6%	16.4%
73,637	RILEY	18,150	9,761	7,950	439	1,811 R	53.8%	43.8%	55.1%	44.9%
4,908	ROOKS	2,085	1,775	183	127	1,592 R	85.1%	8.8%	90.7%	9.3%
3,055	RUSH	1,334	1,157	130	47	1,027 R	86.7%	9.7%	89.9%	10.1%
6,861	RUSSELL	2,691	2,263	327	101	1,936 R	84.1%	12.2%	87.4%	12.6%
54,203	SALINE	17,620	12,174	4,780	666	7,394 R	69.1%	27.1%	71.8%	28.2%
4,818	SCOTT	1,703	1,517	131	55	1,386 R	89.1%	7.7%	92.1%	7.9%
516,642	SEDGWICK	154,117	90,856	58,815	4,446	32,041 R	59.0%	38.2%	60.7%	39.3%
21,130	SEWARD	2,941	2,127	722	92	1,405 R	72.3%	24.5%	74.7%	25.3%
176,967	SHAWNEE	65,636	35,517	28,051	2,068	7,466 R	54.1%	42.7%	55.9%	44.1%
2,527	SHERIDAN	1,049	954	65	30	889 R	90.9%	6.2%	93.6%	6.4%
5,916	SHERMAN	2,045	1,726	227	92	1,499 R	84.4%	11.1%	88.4%	11.6%
3,588	SMITH	1,641	1,410	171	60	1,239 R	85.9%	10.4%	89.2%	10.8%
4,163	STAFFORD	1,570	1,320	189	61	1,131 R	84.1%	12.0%	87.5%	12.5%
1,983	STANTON	509	453	41	15	412 R	89.0%	8.1%	91.7%	8.3%
5,468	STEVENS	1,397	1,256	115	26	1,141 R	89.9%	8.2%	91.6%	8.4%
22,826	SUMNER	7,869	5,896	1,692	281	4,204 R	74.9%	21.5%	77.7%	22.3%
7,756	THOMAS	2,886	2,457	355	74	2,102 R	85.1%	12.3%	87.4%	12.6%
2,809	TREGO	1,262	1,105	123	34	982 R	87.6%	9.7%	90.0%	10.0%
6,942	WABAUNSEE	3,342	2,625	596	121	2,029 R	78.5%	17.8%	81.5%	18.5%
1,520	WALLACE	672	618	30	24	588 R	92.0%	4.5%	95.4%	4.6%
5,393	WASHINGTON	2,240	2,014	190	36	1,824 R	89.9%	8.5%	91.4%	8.6%
2,112	WICHITA	713	627	64	22	563 R	87.9%	9.0%	90.7%	9.3%
8,512	WILSON	3,322	2,705	535	82	2,170 R	81.4%	16.1%	83.5%	16.5%
3,147	WOODSON	1,180	938	187	55	751 R	79.5%	15.8%	83.4%	16.6%
165,303	WYANDOTTE	34,845	12,541	21,111	1,193	8,570 D	36.0%	60.6%	37.3%	62.7%
2,914,929	TOTAL	1,004,956	602,976	372,214	29,766	230,762 R	60.0%	37.0%	61.8%	38.2%

KANSAS

HOUSE OF REPRESENTATIVES

CD	Year	Total Vote	Republican Vote	Republican Candidate	Democratic Vote	Democratic Candidate	Other Vote	Rep.-Dem. Plurality	Percentage Total Vote Rep.	Percentage Total Vote Dem.	Percentage Major Vote Rep.	Percentage Major Vote Dem.
1	2022	238,425	161,333	MANN, TRACEY*	77,092	BEARD, JAMES "JIMMY"		84,241 R	67.7%	32.3%	67.7%	32.3%
1	2020	292,622	208,229	MANN, TRACEY	84,393	BARNETT, KALI		123,836 R	71.2%	28.8%	71.2%	28.8%
1	2018	224,640	153,082	MARSHALL, ROGER*	71,558	LAPOLICE, ALAN		81,524 R	68.1%	31.9%	68.1%	31.9%
1	2016	257,971	169,992	MARSHALL, ROGER			87,979	169,992 R	65.9%		100.0%	
1	2014	204,161	138,764	HUELSKAMP, TIM*	65,397	SHEROW, JAMES E.		73,367 R	68.0%	32.0%	68.0%	32.0%
1	2012	211,337	211,337	HUELSKAMP, TIM*				211,337 R	100.0%		100.0%	
2	2022	233,358	134,506	LATURNER, JAKE*	98,852	SCHMIDT, PATRICK		35,654 R	57.6%	42.4%	57.6%	42.4%
2	2020	336,315	185,464	LATURNER, JAKE	136,650	DE LA ISLA, MICHELLE	14,201	48,814 R	55.1%	40.6%	57.6%	42.4%
2	2018	264,688	126,098	WATKINS, STEVE	123,859	DAVIS, PAUL	14,731	2,239 R	47.6%	46.8%	50.4%	49.6%
2	2016	297,401	181,228	JENKINS, LYNN*	96,840	POTTER, BRITANI	19,333	84,388 R	60.9%	32.6%	65.2%	34.8%
2	2014	225,686	128,742	JENKINS, LYNN*	87,153	WAKEFIELD, MARGIE	9,791	41,589 R	57.0%	38.6%	59.6%	40.4%
2	2012	293,718	167,463	JENKINS, LYNN*	113,735	SCHLINGENSIEPEN, TOBIAS	12,520	53,728 R	57.0%	38.7%	59.6%	40.4%
3	2022	301,294	128,839	ADKINS, AMANDA L.	165,527	DAVIDS, SHARICE*	6,928	36,688 D	42.8%	54.9%	43.8%	56.2%
3	2020	410,418	178,773	ADKINS, AMANDA L.	220,049	DAVIDS, SHARICE*	11,596	41,276 D	43.6%	53.6%	44.8%	55.2%
3	2018	318,301	139,762	YODER, KEVIN*	170,518	DAVIDS, SHARICE	8,021	30,756 D	43.9%	53.6%	45.0%	55.0%
3	2016	343,113	176,022	YODER, KEVIN*	139,300	SIDIE, JAY	27,791	36,722 R	51.3%	40.6%	55.8%	44.2%
3	2014	224,077	134,493	YODER, KEVIN*	89,584	KULTALA, KELLY		44,909 R	60.0%	40.0%	60.0%	40.0%
3	2012	293,762	201,087	YODER, KEVIN*			92,675	201,087 R	68.5%		100.0%	
4	2022	228,740	144,889	ESTES, RON*	83,851	HERNANDEZ, BOB		61,038 R	63.3%	36.7%	63.3%	36.7%
4	2020	319,598	203,432	ESTES, RON*	116,166	LOMBARD, LAURA		87,266 R	63.7%	36.3%	63.7%	36.3%
4	2018	242,693	144,248	ESTES, RON*	98,445	THOMPSON, JAMES A.		45,803 R	59.4%	40.6%	59.4%	40.6%
4	2016	275,251	166,998	POMPEO, MIKE*	81,495	GIROUX, DANIEL B.	26,758	85,503 R	60.7%	29.6%	67.2%	32.8%
4	2014	208,153	138,757	POMPEO, MIKE*	69,396	SCHUCKMAN, PERRY		69,361 R	66.7%	33.3%	66.7%	33.3%
4	2012	258,922	161,094	POMPEO, MIKE*	81,770	TILLMAN, ROBERT	16,058	79,324 R	62.2%	31.6%	66.3%	33.7%
TOTAL	2022	1,001,817	569,567		425,322		6,928	144,245 R	56.9%	42.5%	57.2%	42.8%
TOTAL	2020	1,358,953	775,898		557,258		25,797	218,640 R	57.1%	41.0%	58.2%	41.8%
TOTAL	2018	1,050,322	563,190		464,380		22,752	98,810 R	53.6%	44.2%	54.8%	45.2%
TOTAL	2016	1,173,736	694,240		317,635		161,861	376,605 R	59.1%	27.1%	68.6%	31.4%
TOTAL	2014	862,077	540,756		311,530		9,791	229,226 R	62.7%	36.1%	63.4%	36.6%
TOTAL	2012	1,057,739	740,981		195,505		121,253	545,476 R	70.1%	18.5%	79.1%	20.9%

Note: An asterisk (*) denotes incumbent.

KANSAS

GENERAL AND PRIMARY ELECTIONS

GENERAL ELECTIONS: OTHER VOTES

Governor	Other vote was 20,452 Independent (Dennis Pyle), 11,106 Libertarian (Seth Cordell)
Senate	29,766 Libertarian (David Graham)
House	Other vote was:
CD 3	6,928 Libertarian (Steven Hohe)

2022 PRIMARY ELECTIONS: SUPPLEMENTARY INFORMATION

Primary	August 2, 2022	**Registration** (as of July 1, 2022)	1,935,534	Republican	851,882
				Democratic	495,574
				Libertarian	22,207
				Unaffiliated	565,871

Primary Type — Semi-open—Registered Democrats and Republicans could vote only in their party's primary. "Unaffiliated" voters could participate in either primary, although they had to change their registration to that party on primary day.

KANSAS

GENERAL AND PRIMARY ELECTIONS

	REPUBLICAN PRIMARIES			DEMOCRATIC PRIMARIES		
Senator	Moran, Jerry*	383,332	80.5%	Holland, Mark R.	101,429	38.1%
	Farr, Joan	93,016	19.5%	Buskirk, Paul	53,750	20.2%
				Wiesner, Patrick	47,034	17.6%
				Andra, Mike	33,464	12.6%
				Klingenberg, Robert	21,413	8.0%
				Soetaert, Michael	9,464	3.6%
	TOTAL	476,348		TOTAL	266,554	
Governor	Schmidt, Derek	373,524	80.6%	Kelly, Laura*	270,968	93.8%
	Briggs, Arlyn	89,898	19.4%	Karnowski, Richard S.	17,802	6.2%
	TOTAL	463,422		TOTAL	288,770	
Congressional District 1	Mann, Tracey*	117,899	100.0%	Beard, James "Jimmy"	42,589	100.0%
	TOTAL	117,899		TOTAL	42,589	
Congressional District 2	LaTurner, Jake*	94,578	100.0%	Schmidt, Patrick	54,439	100.0%
	TOTAL	94,578		TOTAL	54,439	
Congressional District 3	Adkins, Amanda L.	96,896	77.2%	Davids, Sharice*	103,945	100.0%
	McCaughrean, John A.	28,573	22.8%			
	TOTAL	125,469		TOTAL	103,945	
Congressional District 4	Estes, Ron*	102,915	100.0%	Hernandez, Bob	42,222	100.0%
	TOTAL	102,915		TOTAL	42,222	

Note: An asterisk (*) denotes incumbent.

KENTUCKY

Statewide Races

Kentucky, which holds its gubernatorial races in the odd-numbered years preceding presidential election years, saw a rather uneventful Senate race. Republicans prevailed, with Sen. Rand Paul winning a third term.

Though Paul's libertarian-tinged Republicanism seems a somewhat curious fit for a state that is rather dependent on the federal government, his partisan label has been enough for voters to give him clear majorities. In 2022, against Democratic state Rep. Charles Booker, Paul carried all but three of the state's 120 counties. Louisville's Jefferson County, the state's richest source of Democratic votes, gave Booker 59%, while Lexington's Fayette County gave him a slightly higher 61%. Jefferson and Fayette were the state's only Biden-won counties. In addition to that pair, Booker carried Franklin County, where the state capital of Frankfort is located, by five points. Eastern Kentucky voted heavily against Booker, but his performance in many coalfields counties were no worse, or even marginally better, than what Amy McGrath, the party's nominee for the other seat in 2020, got – without Trump leading the ticket, it's possible GOP enthusiasm was down there.

Even as much of the state has lurched rightward, the region that often gives Republicans their best margins is the south-central part of the state – essentially, an area straddling the Cumberland and Mississippi plateaus. Eight of Paul's ten best counties were in that area, and he took over 85% in each.

House Races

For the first time since their party's establishment in 1854, Kentucky Republicans entered a redistricting cycle with control of both houses of the state legislature. Though the state has a Democratic governor, Kentucky law only requires the legislature to muster a simple majority to override vetoes.

The sole Democrat in the Bluegrass State's six-member delegation was the retiring Rep. John Yarmuth. Yarmuth won the 3rd District, which is essentially coterminous with Jefferson County, in 2006. Republicans could have theoretically drawn themselves a new seat by "cracking" Louisville multiple ways. But the legislature – reportedly with Sen. Mitch McConnell's blessing – opted against making drastic changes. Yarmuth endorsed Democratic state Sen. Morgan McGarvey. In his primary, McGarvey took 63% against state Rep. Attica Scott. In November, he took about the same share against a Republican.

Of the state's five GOP-held seats, only the Lexington-centric 6th District has been somewhat shaky for Republicans. Rep. Andy Barr (R) got to office in 2012 by ousting a Democratic incumbent 51%–47%. After two easier races, he had a competitive race with Amy McGrath in 2018 (this was before she ran statewide). As the GOP lost control of Congress in 2018, Barr won reelection 51%–48% – while he lost Fayette and Franklin counties, he carried all the district's Appalachian counties by double-digits. Democrats did not prioritize the 6th District in 2020. But to insulate Barr from future challenges, Republican mappers removed Franklin County from the district. In 2022, Barr was also helped by drawing an exceptionally weak Democratic challenger in Geoff Young, who praised Russian leader Vladimir Putin. As top state Democrats disowned Young, Barr won by 29 points, his strongest reelection margin to date.

KENTUCKY
Congressional districts first established for elections held in 2022
6 members

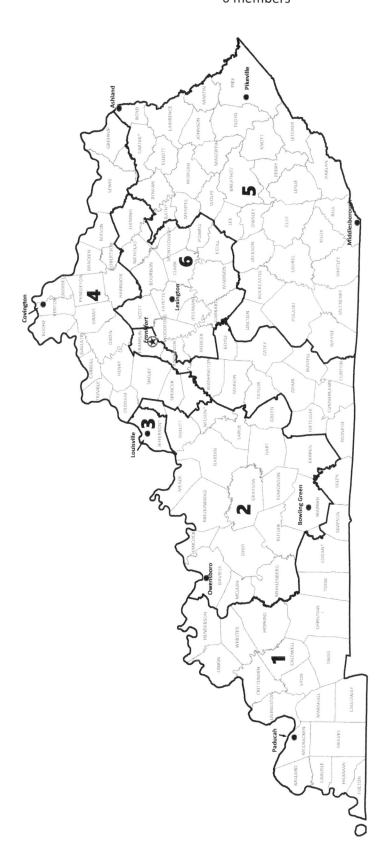

* Asterisk indicates a county whose boundaries include parts of two or more congressional districts.

KENTUCKY

GOVERNOR
Andy Beshear (D). Elected 2019 to a four-year term.

SENATORS (2 Republicans)
Mitch McConnell (R). Reelected 2020 to a six-year term. Previously elected 2014, 2008, 2002, 1996, 1990, 1984.

Rand Paul (R). Reelected 2022 to a six-year term. Previously elected 2016, 2010.

REPRESENTATIVES (5 Republicans, 1 Democrat)
1. James R. Comer (R)
2. Brett Guthrie (R)
3. Morgan McGarvey (D)
4. Thomas Massie (R)
5. Harold "Hal" Rogers (R)
6. Garland "Andy" Barr (R)

POSTWAR VOTE FOR PRESIDENT

Year	Total Vote	Republican Vote	Republican Candidate	Democratic Vote	Democratic Candidate	Other Vote	Rep.-Dem. Plurality	Total Vote Rep.	Total Vote Dem.	Major Vote Rep.	Major Vote Dem.
2020	2,136,768	1,326,646	Trump, Donald J.*	772,474	Biden, Joseph R. Jr.	37,648	554,172 R	62.1%	36.2%	63.2%	36.8%
2016**	1,924,149	1,202,971	Trump, Donald J.	628,854	Clinton, Hillary Rodham	92,324	574,117 R	62.5%	32.7%	65.7%	34.3%
2012	1,797,212	1,087,190	Romney, W. Mitt	679,370	Obama, Barack H.*	30,652	407,820 R	60.5%	37.8%	61.5%	38.5%
2008	1,826,620	1,048,462	McCain, John S. III	751,985	Obama, Barack H.	26,173	296,477 R	57.4%	41.2%	58.2%	41.8%
2004	1,795,882	1,069,439	Bush, George W.*	712,733	Kerry, John F.	13,710	356,706 R	59.5%	39.7%	60.0%	40.0%
2000**	1,544,187	872,492	Bush, George W.	638,898	Gore, Albert Jr.	32,797	233,594 R	56.5%	41.4%	57.7%	42.3%
1996**	1,388,708	623,283	Dole, Robert "Bob"	636,614	Clinton, Bill*	128,811	13,331 D	44.9%	45.8%	49.5%	50.5%
1992**	1,492,900	617,178	Bush, George H.*	665,104	Clinton, Bill	210,618	47,926 D	41.3%	44.6%	48.1%	51.9%
1988	1,322,517	734,281	Bush, George H.	580,368	Dukakis, Michael S.	7,868	153,913 R	55.5%	43.9%	55.9%	44.1%
1984	1,369,345	821,702	Reagan, Ronald*	539,539	Mondale, Walter F.	8,104	282,163 R	60.0%	39.4%	60.4%	39.6%
1980**	1,294,627	635,274	Reagan, Ronald	616,417	Carter, Jimmy*	42,936	18,857 R	49.1%	47.6%	50.8%	49.2%
1976	1,167,142	531,852	Ford, Gerald R.*	615,717	Carter, Jimmy	19,573	83,865 D	45.6%	52.8%	46.3%	53.7%
1972	1,067,499	676,446	Nixon, Richard M.*	371,159	McGovern, George S.	19,894	305,287 R	63.4%	34.8%	64.6%	35.4%
1968**	1,055,893	462,411	Nixon, Richard M.	397,541	Humphrey, Hubert Horatio Jr.	195,941	64,870 R	43.8%	37.6%	53.8%	46.2%
1964	1,046,105	372,977	Goldwater, Barry M. Sr.	669,659	Johnson, Lyndon B.*	3,469	296,682 D	35.7%	64.0%	35.8%	64.2%
1960	1,124,462	602,607	Nixon, Richard M.	521,855	Kennedy, John F.		80,752 R	53.6%	46.4%	53.6%	46.4%
1956	1,053,805	572,192	Eisenhower, Dwight D.*	476,453	Stevenson, Adlai E. II	5,160	95,739 R	54.3%	45.2%	54.6%	45.4%
1952	993,148	495,029	Eisenhower, Dwight D.	495,729	Stevenson, Adlai E. II	2,390	700 D	49.8%	49.9%	50.0%	50.0%
1948	822,658	341,210	Dewey, Thomas E.	466,756	Truman, Harry S.*	14,692	125,546 D	41.5%	56.7%	42.2%	57.8%

Note: An asterisk (*) denotes incumbent. **In past elections, the other vote included: 2016 - 53,752 Independent (Gary Johnson); 2000 - 23,192 Green (Ralph Nader); 1996 - 120,396 Reform (Ross Perot); 1992 - 203,944 Independent (Perot); 1980 - 31,127 Independent (John Anderson); 1968 - 193,098 American Independent (George Wallace).

KENTUCKY

POSTWAR VOTE FOR GOVERNOR

Year	Total Vote	Republican Vote	Republican Candidate	Democratic Vote	Democratic Candidate	Other Vote	Rep.-Dem. Plurality	Total Vote Rep.	Total Vote Dem.	Major Vote Rep.	Major Vote Dem.
2019	1,443,123	704,754	Bevin, Matt G.*	709,890	Beshear, Andy	28,479	5,136 D	48.8%	49.2%	49.8%	50.2%
2015	973,692	511,374	Bevin, Matt G.	426,620	Conway, Jack	35,698	84,754 R	52.5%	43.8%	54.5%	45.5%
2011	833,139	294,034	Williams, David Lynn	464,245	Beshear, Steven L.*	74,860	170,211 D	35.3%	55.7%	38.8%	61.2%
2007	1,055,325	435,773	Fletcher, Ernest*	619,552	Beshear, Steven L.		183,779 D	41.3%	58.7%	41.3%	58.7%
2003	1,083,443	596,284	Fletcher, Ernest	487,159	Chandler, Ben		109,125 R	55.0%	45.0%	55.0%	45.0%
1999**	580,074	128,788	Martin, Peppy	352,099	Patton, Paul E.*	99,187	223,311 D	22.2%	60.7%	26.8%	73.2%
1995	983,979	479,227	Forgy, Larry	500,787	Patton, Paul E.	3,965	21,560 D	48.7%	50.9%	48.9%	51.1%
1991	834,920	294,452	Harper, John	540,468	Jones, Brereton C.		246,016 D	35.3%	64.7%	35.3%	64.7%
1987	777,815	273,141	Harper, John	504,674	Wilkinson, Wallace G.		231,533 D	35.1%	64.9%	35.1%	64.9%
1983	1,030,628	454,650	Bunning, Jim	561,674	Collins, Martha Layne	14,304	107,024 D	44.1%	54.5%	44.7%	55.3%
1979	939,366	381,278	Nunn, Louie B.	558,088	Brown, J. Y. Jr.		176,810 D	40.6%	59.4%	40.6%	59.4%
1975	748,157	277,998	Gable, Robert E.	470,159	Carroll, Julian*		192,161 D	37.2%	62.8%	37.2%	62.8%
1971	930,792	412,653	Emberton, Thomas	470,722	Ford, Wendell H.	47,417	58,069 D	44.3%	50.6%	46.7%	53.3%
1967	886,146	453,323	Nunn, Louie B.	425,674	Ward, Henry	7,149	27,649 R	51.2%	48.0%	51.6%	48.4%
1963	886,047	436,496	Nunn, Louie B.	449,551	Breathitt, Edward T.		13,055 D	49.3%	50.7%	49.3%	50.7%
1959	853,005	336,456	Robsion, John M. Jr.	516,549	Combs, Bert T.		180,093 D	39.4%	60.6%	39.4%	60.6%
1955	778,488	322,671	Denney, Edwin R.	451,647	Chandler, Happy	4,170	128,976 D	41.4%	58.0%	41.7%	58.3%
1951	634,359	288,014	Siler, Eugene	346,345	Wetherby, Lawrence W.		58,331 D	45.4%	54.6%	45.4%	54.6%
1947	675,551	287,756	Dummit, Eldon S.	387,795	Clements, Earle C.		100,039 D	42.6%	57.4%	42.6%	57.4%

Note: An asterisk (*) denotes incumbent. **In past elections, the other vote included: 1999 - 88,930 Reform (Gatewood Galbraith).

POSTWAR VOTE FOR SENATOR

Year	Total Vote	Republican Vote	Republican Candidate	Democratic Vote	Democratic Candidate	Other Vote	Rep.-Dem. Plurality	Total Vote Rep.	Total Vote Dem.	Major Vote Rep.	Major Vote Dem.
2022	1,477,830	913,326	Paul, Rand*	564,311	Booker, Charles	193	349,015 R	61.8%	38.2%	61.8%	38.2%
2020	2,135,057	1,233,315	McConnell, Mitch*	816,257	McGrath, Amy	85,485	417,058 R	57.8%	38.2%	60.2%	39.8%
2016	1,903,465	1,090,177	Paul, Rand*	813,246	Gray, Jim	42	276,931 R	57.3%	42.7%	57.3%	42.7%
2014	1,435,868	806,787	McConnell, Mitch*	584,698	Grimes, Alison Lundergan	44,383	222,089 R	56.2%	40.7%	58.0%	42.0%
2010	1,356,468	755,411	Paul, Rand	599,843	Conway, Jack	1,214	155,568 R	55.7%	44.2%	55.7%	44.3%
2008	1,800,821	953,816	McConnell, Mitch*	847,005	Lunsford, Bruce		106,811 R	53.0%	47.0%	53.0%	47.0%
2004	1,724,362	873,507	Bunning, Jim*	850,855	Mongiardo, Frank Daniel		22,652 R	50.7%	49.3%	50.7%	49.3%
2002	1,131,475	731,679	McConnell, Mitch*	399,634	Weinberg, Lois Combs	162	332,045 R	64.7%	35.3%	64.7%	35.3%
1998	1,145,414	569,817	Bunning, Jim	563,051	Baesler, Scott	12,546	6,766 R	49.7%	49.2%	50.3%	49.7%
1996	1,307,046	724,794	McConnell, Mitch*	560,012	Beshear, Steven L.	22,240	164,782 R	55.5%	42.8%	56.4%	43.6%
1992	1,330,858	476,604	Williams, David Lynn	836,888	Ford, Wendell H.*	17,366	360,284 D	35.8%	62.9%	36.3%	63.7%
1990	916,010	478,034	McConnell, Mitch*	437,976	Sloane, Harvey		40,058 R	52.2%	47.8%	52.2%	47.8%
1986	677,280	173,330	Andrews, Jackson M.	503,775	Ford, Wendell H.*	175	330,445 D	25.6%	74.4%	25.6%	74.4%
1984	1,292,407	644,990	McConnell, Mitch	639,721	Huddleston, Walter*	7,696	5,269 R	49.9%	49.5%	50.2%	49.8%
1980	1,106,890	386,029	Foust, Mary Louise	720,861	Ford, Wendell H.*		334,832 D	34.9%	65.1%	34.9%	65.1%
1978	476,783	175,766	Guenthner, Louie	290,730	Huddleston, Walter*	10,287	114,964 D	36.9%	61.0%	37.7%	62.3%
1974	745,994	328,982	Cook, Marlow W.*	399,406	Ford, Wendell H.	17,606	70,424 D	44.1%	53.5%	45.2%	54.8%
1972	1,037,861	494,337	Nunn, Louie B.	528,550	Huddleston, Walter	14,974	34,213 D	47.6%	50.9%	48.3%	51.7%
1968	942,865	484,260	Cook, Marlow W.	448,960	Peden, Katherine	9,645	35,300 R	51.4%	47.6%	51.9%	48.1%
1966	749,884	483,805	Cooper, John Sherman*	266,079	Brown, John Young		217,726 R	64.5%	35.5%	64.5%	35.5%
1962	820,088	432,648	Morton, Thruston B.*	387,440	Wyatt, Wilson W.		45,208 R	52.8%	47.2%	52.8%	47.2%
1960	1,088,377	644,087	Cooper, John Sherman*	444,290	Johnson, Keen		199,797 R	59.2%	40.8%	59.2%	40.8%
1956	1,006,825	506,903	Morton, Thruston B.	499,922	Clements, Earle C.*		6,981 R	50.3%	49.7%	50.3%	49.7%
1956S**	1,011,645	538,505	Cooper, John Sherman	473,140	Wetherby, Lawrence W.		65,365 R	53.2%	46.8%	53.2%	46.8%
1954	797,057	362,948	Cooper, John Sherman*	434,109	Barkley, Alben W.		71,161 D	45.5%	54.5%	45.5%	54.5%
1952S**	960,228	494,576	Cooper, John Sherman	465,652	Underwood, Thomas R.		28,924 R	51.5%	48.5%	51.5%	48.5%
1950	612,617	278,368	Dawson, Charles I.	334,249	Clements, Earle C.		55,881 D	45.4%	54.6%	45.4%	54.6%
1948	794,469	383,776	Cooper, John Sherman*	408,256	Chapman, Virgil	2,437	24,480 D	48.3%	51.4%	48.5%	51.5%
1946S**	615,119	327,652	Cooper, John Sherman	285,829	Brown, John Young	1,638	41,823 R	53.3%	46.5%	53.4%	46.6%

Note: An asterisk (*) denotes incumbent. **The elections in 1946 and 1952 as well as one in 1956 were for short terms to fill vacancies.

KENTUCKY
SENATOR 2022

2020 Census Population	County	Total Vote	Republican (Paul)	Democratic (Booker)	Other	Rep.-Dem. Plurality	Percentage			
							Total Vote		Major Vote	
							Rep.	Dem.	Rep.	Dem.
19,260	ADAIR	6,324	5,249	1,075		4,174 R	83.0%	17.0%	83.0%	17.0%
21,429	ALLEN	6,102	4,931	1,171		3,760 R	80.8%	19.2%	80.8%	19.2%
22,827	ANDERSON	9,378	6,687	2,691		3,996 R	71.3%	28.7%	71.3%	28.7%
7,885	BALLARD	3,127	2,488	639		1,849 R	79.6%	20.4%	79.6%	20.4%
44,408	BARREN	14,143	10,298	3,845		6,453 R	72.8%	27.2%	72.8%	27.2%
12,521	BATH	4,233	2,827	1,404	2	1,423 R	66.8%	33.2%	66.8%	33.2%
25,981	BELL	6,795	5,420	1,375		4,045 R	79.8%	20.2%	79.8%	20.2%
133,897	BOONE	45,318	30,898	14,409	11	16,489 R	68.2%	31.8%	68.2%	31.8%
19,811	BOURBON	6,818	4,381	2,429	8	1,952 R	64.3%	35.6%	64.3%	35.7%
46,668	BOYD	14,169	9,071	5,098		3,973 R	64.0%	36.0%	64.0%	36.0%
30,137	BOYLE	10,326	6,304	4,021	1	2,283 R	61.0%	38.9%	61.1%	38.9%
8,303	BRACKEN	3,234	2,478	756		1,722 R	76.6%	23.4%	76.6%	23.4%
12,587	BREATHITT	3,552	2,285	1,267		1,018 R	64.3%	35.7%	64.3%	35.7%
20,572	BRECKINRIDGE	6,799	5,076	1,723		3,353 R	74.7%	25.3%	74.7%	25.3%
82,027	BULLITT	24,842	17,945	6,895	2	11,050 R	72.2%	27.8%	72.2%	27.8%
12,925	BUTLER	4,195	3,429	766		2,663 R	81.7%	18.3%	81.7%	18.3%
12,777	CALDWELL	4,684	3,580	1,104		2,476 R	76.4%	23.6%	76.4%	23.6%
39,206	CALLOWAY	11,841	7,906	3,934	1	3,972 R	66.8%	33.2%	66.8%	33.2%
93,597	CAMPBELL	35,664	20,849	14,812	3	6,037 R	58.5%	41.5%	58.5%	41.5%
4,773	CARLISLE	2,128	1,750	377	1	1,373 R	82.2%	17.7%	82.3%	17.7%
10,645	CARROLL	2,878	1,992	886		1,106 R	69.2%	30.8%	69.2%	30.8%
26,756	CARTER	8,176	5,792	2,383	1	3,409 R	70.8%	29.1%	70.9%	29.1%
16,227	CASEY	5,148	4,396	751	1	3,645 R	85.4%	14.6%	85.4%	14.6%
70,447	CHRISTIAN	15,465	10,255	5,210		5,045 R	66.3%	33.7%	66.3%	33.7%
36,413	CLARK	12,805	8,270	4,533	2	3,737 R	64.6%	35.4%	64.6%	35.4%
19,892	CLAY	4,925	4,238	687		3,551 R	86.1%	13.9%	86.1%	13.9%
10,253	CLINTON	3,425	3,016	409		2,607 R	88.1%	11.9%	88.1%	11.9%
8,809	CRITTENDEN	3,074	2,540	534		2,006 R	82.6%	17.4%	82.6%	17.4%
6,613	CUMBERLAND	2,478	2,123	355		1,768 R	85.7%	14.3%	85.7%	14.3%
101,862	DAVIESS	32,906	20,998	11,906	2	9,092 R	63.8%	36.2%	63.8%	36.2%
12,187	EDMONSON	4,266	3,309	957		2,352 R	77.6%	22.4%	77.6%	22.4%
7,549	ELLIOTT	2,064	1,406	658		748 R	68.1%	31.9%	68.1%	31.9%
14,154	ESTILL	4,621	3,511	1,110		2,401 R	76.0%	24.0%	76.0%	24.0%
323,890	FAYETTE	106,550	42,041	64,467	42	22,426 D	39.5%	60.5%	39.5%	60.5%
14,596	FLEMING	5,057	3,803	1,254		2,549 R	75.2%	24.8%	75.2%	24.8%
35,516	FLOYD	11,637	7,636	4,000	1	3,636 R	65.6%	34.4%	65.6%	34.4%
51,137	FRANKLIN	20,162	9,570	10,589	3	1,019 D	47.5%	52.5%	47.5%	52.5%
5,977	FULTON	1,532	1,087	445		642 R	71.0%	29.0%	71.0%	29.0%
8,916	GALLATIN	3,012	2,224	788		1,436 R	73.8%	26.2%	73.8%	26.2%
17,742	GARRARD	5,907	4,560	1,347		3,213 R	77.2%	22.8%	77.2%	22.8%
25,116	GRANT	7,441	5,847	1,592	2	4,255 R	78.6%	21.4%	78.6%	21.4%
37,298	GRAVES	12,093	9,514	2,575	4	6,939 R	78.7%	21.3%	78.7%	21.3%
26,514	GRAYSON	7,917	6,229	1,687	1	4,542 R	78.7%	21.3%	78.7%	21.3%
10,978	GREEN	4,313	3,650	655		3,003 R	84.8%	15.2%	84.8%	15.2%
35,101	GREENUP	12,634	8,899	3,735		5,164 R	70.4%	29.6%	70.4%	29.6%
8,732	HANCOCK	3,257	2,223	1,034		1,189 R	68.3%	31.7%	68.3%	31.7%
111,419	HARDIN	30,886	19,413	11,459	14	7,954 R	62.9%	37.1%	62.9%	37.1%
26,005	HARLAN	7,719	6,386	1,333		5,053 R	82.7%	17.3%	82.7%	17.3%
18,946	HARRISON	6,659	4,624	2,030	5	2,594 R	69.4%	30.5%	69.5%	30.5%
19,092	HART	6,226	4,624	1,602		3,022 R	74.3%	25.7%	74.3%	25.7%
45,206	HENDERSON	13,998	8,765	5,233		3,532 R	62.6%	37.4%	62.6%	37.4%
16,195	HENRY	6,039	4,228	1,810	1	2,418 R	70.0%	30.0%	70.0%	30.0%
4,365	HICKMAN	1,547	1,264	283		981 R	81.7%	18.3%	81.7%	18.3%
44,706	HOPKINS	14,796	10,592	4,204		6,388 R	71.6%	28.4%	71.6%	28.4%
13,363	JACKSON	3,668	3,283	385		2,898 R	89.5%	10.5%	89.5%	10.5%
768,182	JEFFERSON	277,888	113,726	164,131	31	50,405 D	40.9%	59.1%	40.9%	59.1%
54,401	JESSAMINE	17,301	11,569	5,732		5,837 R	66.9%	33.1%	66.9%	33.1%
22,187	JOHNSON	5,643	4,559	1,084		3,475 R	80.8%	19.2%	80.8%	19.2%
167,308	KENTON	51,158	30,057	21,096	5	8,961 R	58.8%	41.2%	58.8%	41.2%
14,796	KNOTT	4,792	3,252	1,540		1,712 R	67.9%	32.1%	67.9%	32.1%

KENTUCKY
SENATOR 2022

2020 Census Population	County	Total Vote	Republican (Paul)	Democratic (Booker)	Other	Rep.-Dem. Plurality	Percentage Total Vote		Percentage Major Vote	
							Rep.	Dem.	Rep.	Dem.
31,143	KNOX	7,977	6,457	1,516	4	4,941 R	80.9%	19.0%	81.0%	19.0%
14,459	LARUE	5,205	3,955	1,250		2,705 R	76.0%	24.0%	76.0%	24.0%
60,974	LAUREL	17,571	14,474	3,096	1	11,378 R	82.4%	17.6%	82.4%	17.6%
15,289	LAWRENCE	4,127	3,179	948		2,231 R	77.0%	23.0%	77.0%	23.0%
7,356	LEE	2,071	1,648	423		1,225 R	79.6%	20.4%	79.6%	20.4%
9,850	LESLIE	2,881	2,509	371	1	2,138 R	87.1%	12.9%	87.1%	12.9%
21,497	LETCHER	5,727	3,873	1,854		2,019 R	67.6%	32.4%	67.6%	32.4%
13,270	LEWIS	3,831	3,259	572		2,687 R	85.1%	14.9%	85.1%	14.9%
24,593	LINCOLN	7,403	5,687	1,715	1	3,972 R	76.8%	23.2%	76.8%	23.2%
9,210	LIVINGSTON	3,216	2,609	606	1	2,003 R	81.1%	18.8%	81.2%	18.8%
27,161	LOGAN	8,508	6,240	2,268		3,972 R	73.3%	26.7%	73.3%	26.7%
8,180	LYON	3,230	2,356	874		1,482 R	72.9%	27.1%	72.9%	27.1%
93,427	MADISON	30,019	18,593	11,420	6	7,173 R	61.9%	38.0%	61.9%	38.1%
12,144	MAGOFFIN	4,876	3,404	1,472		1,932 R	69.8%	30.2%	69.8%	30.2%
19,342	MARION	5,896	3,782	2,112	2	1,670 R	64.1%	35.8%	64.2%	35.8%
31,193	MARSHALL	12,930	9,875	3,054	1	6,821 R	76.4%	23.6%	76.4%	23.6%
11,150	MARTIN	2,599	2,241	358		1,883 R	86.2%	13.8%	86.2%	13.8%
17,094	MASON	5,806	3,879	1,927		1,952 R	66.8%	33.2%	66.8%	33.2%
65,549	MCCRACKEN	22,762	15,294	7,466	2	7,828 R	67.2%	32.8%	67.2%	32.8%
17,287	MCCREARY	4,367	3,738	629		3,109 R	85.6%	14.4%	85.6%	14.4%
9,216	MCLEAN	3,634	2,760	874		1,886 R	75.9%	24.1%	75.9%	24.1%
28,744	MEADE	9,555	6,881	2,672	2	4,209 R	72.0%	28.0%	72.0%	28.0%
6,515	MENIFEE	2,265	1,586	679		907 R	70.0%	30.0%	70.0%	30.0%
22,066	MERCER	8,288	5,980	2,308		3,672 R	72.2%	27.8%	72.2%	27.8%
10,080	METCALFE	3,999	3,047	952		2,095 R	76.2%	23.8%	76.2%	23.8%
10,684	MONROE	3,807	3,356	451		2,905 R	88.2%	11.8%	88.2%	11.8%
28,279	MONTGOMERY	8,986	6,152	2,834		3,318 R	68.5%	31.5%	68.5%	31.5%
13,368	MORGAN	4,021	2,894	1,127		1,767 R	72.0%	28.0%	72.0%	28.0%
30,607	MUHLENBERG	10,200	7,062	3,137	1	3,925 R	69.2%	30.8%	69.2%	30.8%
46,384	NELSON	16,993	11,205	5,787	1	5,418 R	65.9%	34.1%	65.9%	34.1%
7,296	NICHOLAS	2,473	1,649	824		825 R	66.7%	33.3%	66.7%	33.3%
24,040	OHIO	7,278	5,617	1,660	1	3,957 R	77.2%	22.8%	77.2%	22.8%
66,836	OLDHAM	26,297	15,998	10,295	4	5,703 R	60.8%	39.1%	60.8%	39.2%
10,938	OWEN	3,895	2,937	958		1,979 R	75.4%	24.6%	75.4%	24.6%
4,419	OWSLEY	1,759	1,467	292		1,175 R	83.4%	16.6%	83.4%	16.6%
14,585	PENDLETON	4,892	3,841	1,051		2,790 R	78.5%	21.5%	78.5%	21.5%
25,655	PERRY	7,462	5,212	2,250		2,962 R	69.8%	30.2%	69.8%	30.2%
57,756	PIKE	15,735	11,667	4,067	1	7,600 R	74.1%	25.8%	74.2%	25.8%
12,430	POWELL	3,592	2,503	1,089		1,414 R	69.7%	30.3%	69.7%	30.3%
65,247	PULASKI	21,177	17,000	4,177		12,823 R	80.3%	19.7%	80.3%	19.7%
2,114	ROBERTSON	979	684	295		389 R	69.9%	30.1%	69.9%	30.1%
16,696	ROCKCASTLE	4,781	4,020	761		3,259 R	84.1%	15.9%	84.1%	15.9%
24,470	ROWAN	7,416	4,235	3,180	1	1,055 R	57.1%	42.9%	57.1%	42.9%
17,993	RUSSELL	6,407	5,422	985		4,437 R	84.6%	15.4%	84.6%	15.4%
57,473	SCOTT	20,503	12,302	8,198	3	4,104 R	60.0%	40.0%	60.0%	40.0%
49,463	SHELBY	17,806	11,606	6,194	6	5,412 R	65.2%	34.8%	65.2%	34.8%
18,716	SIMPSON	5,738	3,975	1,763		2,212 R	69.3%	30.7%	69.3%	30.7%
19,404	SPENCER	7,734	5,844	1,889	1	3,955 R	75.6%	24.4%	75.6%	24.4%
25,824	TAYLOR	8,996	6,751	2,244	1	4,507 R	75.0%	24.9%	75.1%	24.9%
12,303	TODD	3,495	2,681	814		1,867 R	76.7%	23.3%	76.7%	23.3%
14,711	TRIGG	5,455	4,057	1,396	2	2,661 R	74.4%	25.6%	74.4%	25.6%
8,492	TRIMBLE	3,190	2,394	795	1	1,599 R	75.0%	24.9%	75.1%	24.9%
14,384	UNION	4,881	3,688	1,193		2,495 R	75.6%	24.4%	75.6%	24.4%
133,825	WARREN	38,358	22,951	15,403	4	7,548 R	59.8%	40.2%	59.8%	40.2%
12,179	WASHINGTON	4,956	3,492	1,464		2,028 R	70.5%	29.5%	70.5%	29.5%
20,334	WAYNE	6,331	5,021	1,310		3,711 R	79.3%	20.7%	79.3%	20.7%
12,954	WEBSTER	4,212	3,158	1,054		2,104 R	75.0%	25.0%	75.0%	25.0%
36,409	WHITLEY	10,043	8,221	1,822		6,399 R	81.9%	18.1%	81.9%	18.1%
7,155	WOLFE	2,253	1,400	853		547 R	62.1%	37.9%	62.1%	37.9%
26,877	WOODFORD	11,251	6,227	5,023	1	1,204 R	55.3%	44.6%	55.4%	44.6%
4,478,171	TOTAL	1,477,830	913,326	564,311	193	349,015 R	61.8%	38.2%	61.8%	38.2%

KENTUCKY

HOUSE OF REPRESENTATIVES

CD	Year	Total Vote	Republican Vote	Republican Candidate	Democratic Vote	Democratic Candidate	Other Vote	Rep.-Dem. Plurality	Total Vote Rep.	Total Vote Dem.	Major Vote Rep.	Major Vote Dem.
1	2022	245,858	184,157	COMER, JAMES R.*	61,701	AUSBROOKS, JIMMY		122,456 R	74.9%	25.1%	74.9%	25.1%
1	2020	328,470	246,329	COMER, JAMES R.*	82,141	RHODES, JAMES		164,188 R	75.0%	25.0%	75.0%	25.0%
1	2018	251,016	172,167	COMER, JAMES R.*	78,849	WALKER, PAUL		93,318 R	68.6%	31.4%	68.6%	31.4%
1	2016	299,001	216,959	COMER, JAMES R.	81,710	GASKINS, SAM	332	135,249 R	72.6%	27.3%	72.6%	27.4%
1	2014	236,618	173,022	WHITFIELD, EDWARD*	63,596	HATCHETT, CHARLES KENDALL		109,426 R	73.1%	26.9%	73.1%	26.9%
1	2012	287,155	199,956	WHITFIELD, EDWARD*	87,199	HATCHETT, CHARLES KENDALL		112,757 R	69.6%	30.4%	69.6%	30.4%
2	2022	237,256	170,487	GUTHRIE, BRETT*	66,769	LINDERMAN, HANK		103,718 R	71.9%	28.1%	71.9%	28.1%
2	2020	360,399	255,735	GUTHRIE, BRETT*	94,643	LINDERMAN, HANK	10,021	161,092 R	71.0%	26.3%	73.0%	27.0%
2	2018	257,345	171,700	GUTHRIE, BRETT*	79,964	LINDERMAN, HANK	5,681	91,736 R	66.7%	31.1%	68.2%	31.8%
2	2016	251,825	251,825	GUTHRIE, BRETT*				251,825 R	100.0%		100.0%	
2	2014	226,834	156,936	GUTHRIE, BRETT*	69,898	LEACH, RON		87,038 R	69.2%	30.8%	69.2%	30.8%
2	2012	282,267	181,508	GUTHRIE, BRETT*	89,541	WILLIAMS, DAVID LYNN	11,218	91,967 R	64.3%	31.7%	67.0%	33.0%
3	2022	259,587	98,637	RAY, STUART	160,920	MCGARVEY, MORGAN	30	62,283 D	38.0%	62.0%	38.0%	62.0%
3	2020	368,097	137,425	PALAZZO, RHONDA	230,672	YARMUTH, JOHN*		93,247 D	37.3%	62.7%	37.3%	62.7%
3	2018	278,720	101,930	GLISSON, VICKIE	173,002	YARMUTH, JOHN*	3,788	71,072 D	36.6%	62.1%	37.1%	62.9%
3	2016	334,494	122,093	BRATCHER, HAROLD	212,401	YARMUTH, JOHN*		90,308 D	36.5%	63.5%	36.5%	63.5%
3	2014	247,355	87,981	MACFARLANE, MICHAEL	157,056	YARMUTH, JOHN*	2,318	69,075 D	35.6%	63.5%	35.9%	64.1%
3	2012	322,656	111,452	WICKER, BROOKS	206,385	YARMUTH, JOHN*	4,819	94,933 D	34.5%	64.0%	35.1%	64.9%
4	2022	257,629	167,541	MASSIE, THOMAS*	79,977	LEHMAN, MATTHEW	10,111	87,564 R	65.0%	31.0%	67.7%	32.3%
4	2020	382,509	256,613	MASSIE, THOMAS*	125,896	OWENSBY, ALEXANDRA		130,717 R	67.1%	32.9%	67.1%	32.9%
4	2018	261,812	162,946	MASSIE, THOMAS*	90,536	HALL, SETH	8,330	72,410 R	62.2%	34.6%	64.3%	35.7%
4	2016	327,987	233,922	MASSIE, THOMAS*	94,065	SIDLE, CALVIN		139,857 R	71.3%	28.7%	71.3%	28.7%
4	2014	222,158	150,464	MASSIE, THOMAS*	71,694	NEWBERRY, PETER		78,770 R	67.7%	32.3%	67.7%	32.3%
4	2012	299,444	186,036	MASSIE, THOMAS*	104,734	ADKINS, WILLIAM R. "BILL"	8,674	81,302 R	62.1%	35.0%	64.0%	36.0%
5	2022	216,270	177,712	ROGERS, HAROLD "HAL"*	38,549	HALBLEIB, CONOR	9	139,163 R	82.2%	17.8%	82.2%	17.8%
5	2020	297,970	250,914	ROGERS, HAROLD "HAL"*	47,056	BEST, MATTHEW RYAN		203,858 R	84.2%	15.8%	84.2%	15.8%
5	2018	218,017	172,093	ROGERS, HAROLD "HAL"*	45,890	STEPP, KENNETH	34	126,203 R	78.9%	21.0%	78.9%	21.1%
5	2016	221,242	221,242	ROGERS, HAROLD "HAL"*				221,242 R	100.0%		100.0%	
5	2014	218,967	171,350	ROGERS, HAROLD "HAL"*	47,617	STEPP, KENNETH		123,733 R	78.3%	21.7%	78.3%	21.7%
5	2012	250,855	195,408	ROGERS, HAROLD "HAL"*	55,447	STEPP, KENNETH		139,961 R	77.9%	22.1%	77.9%	22.1%
6	2022	246,818	154,762	BARR, ANDY GARLAND*	83,005	YOUNG, GEOFFREY M. "GEOFF"	9,051	71,757 R	62.7%	33.6%	65.1%	34.9%
6	2020	378,450	216,948	BARR, ANDY GARLAND*	155,011	HICKS, JOSH	6,491	61,937 R	57.3%	41.0%	58.3%	41.7%
6	2018	302,888	154,468	BARR, GARLAND "ANDY"*	144,736	MCGRATH, AMY	3,684	9,732 R	51.0%	47.8%	51.6%	48.4%
6	2016	330,827	202,099	BARR, GARLAND "ANDY"*	128,728	KEMPER, NANCY JO		73,371 R	61.1%	38.9%	61.1%	38.9%
6	2014	245,694	147,404	BARR, GARLAND "ANDY"*	98,290	JENSEN, ELISABETH		49,114 R	60.0%	40.0%	60.0%	40.0%
6	2012	303,000	153,222	BARR, GARLAND "ANDY"	141,438	CHANDLER, BEN*	8,340	11,784 R	50.6%	46.7%	52.0%	48.0%
TOTAL	2022	1,463,418	953,296		490,921		19,201	462,375 R	65.1%	33.5%	66.0%	34.0%
TOTAL	2020	2,115,895	1,363,964		735,419		16,512	628,545 R	64.5%	34.8%	65.0%	35.0%
TOTAL	2018	1,569,798	935,304		612,977		21,517	322,327 R	59.6%	39.0%	60.4%	39.6%
TOTAL	2016	1,765,376	1,248,140		516,904		332	731,236 R	70.7%	29.3%	70.7%	29.3%
TOTAL	2014	1,397,626	887,157		508,151		2,318	379,006 R	63.5%	36.4%	63.6%	36.4%
TOTAL	2012	1,745,377	1,027,582		684,744		33,051	342,838 R	58.9%	39.2%	60.0%	40.0%

Note: An asterisk (*) denotes incumbent.

KENTUCKY

GENERAL AND PRIMARY ELECTIONS

GENERAL ELECTIONS: OTHER VOTES

Senate	Other vote was 145 Write-In (Charles Thomason), 48 Write-In (Billy Wilson)
House	Other vote was:
CD 3	30 Write-In (Daniel Cobble)
CD 4	10,111 Independent (Ethan Osborne)
CD 5	9 Write-In (Stephan Mazur)
CD 6	8,970 Write-In (Maurice Cravens), 81 Write-In (Maxwell Froedge)

2022 PRIMARY ELECTIONS: SUPPLEMENTARY INFORMATION

Primary	May 17, 2022	Registration (as of May 15, 2022)	3,564,550	Democratic	1,612,323
				Republican	1,608,203
				Other	189,054
				Independent	136,294
				Libertarian	14,960
				Green	2,090
				Constitution	1,077
				Reform	167
				Social Workers	382

Primary Type Closed—Only registered Democrats and Republicans could vote in their party's primary.

	REPUBLICAN PRIMARIES			DEMOCRATIC PRIMARIES		
Senator	Paul, Rand*	333,051	86.4%	Booker, Charles	214,245	73.3%
	Fredrick, Valerie "Dr. Val"	14,018	3.6%	Blanton, Joshua Wesley Sr.	30,980	10.6%
	Hamilton, Paull V.	13,473	3.5%	Merrill, John	28,931	9.9%
	Blankenship, Arnold	10,092	2.6%	Gao, Ruth	18,154	6.2%
	Stainfield, Tami L.	9,526	2.5%			
	Schiess, John	5,538	1.4%			
	TOTAL	385,698		TOTAL	292,310	
Congressional District 1						
Congressional District 2	Guthrie, Brett	52,265	78.1%	Linderman, Hank	20,174	58.2%
	Watts, Lee	11,996	17.9%	Compton, William Dakota	14,465	41.8%
	Feher, Brent	2,681	4.0%			
	TOTAL	66,942		TOTAL	34,639	
Congressional District 3	Ray, Stuart	9,703	29.5%	McGarvey, Morgan	52,157	63.3%
	Palazzo, Rhonda	9,645	29.4%	Scott, Attica	30,183	36.7%
	Craven, Mike	6,488	19.7%			
	Puccetti, Gregory Peter	2,980	9.1%			
	Cobble, Daniel	1,539	4.7%			
	Gregory, Justin	1,293	3.9%			
	Barrios Moreno, Darien D.	1,212	3.7%			
	TOTAL	32,860		TOTAL	82,340	
Congressional District 4	Massie, Thomas	50,301	75.2%			
	Wirth, Claire	10,521	15.7%			
	McDowell, Alyssa Dara	3,446	5.2%			
	Washington, George	2,606	3.9%			
	TOTAL	66,874				

KENTUCKY
GENERAL AND PRIMARY ELECTIONS

	REPUBLICAN PRIMARIES			DEMOCRATIC PRIMARIES		
Congressional District 5	Rogers, Harold "Hal"	77,050	82.6%			
	Serrano, Gerardo	5,460	5.9%			
	Andrews, Jeannette	4,160	4.5%			
	Monhollen, Brandon	3,831	4.1%			
	Van Dam, Richard	2,784	3.0%			
	TOTAL	*93,285*				
Congressional District 6	Barr, Andy Garland	47,660	87.8%	Young, Geoffrey M. "Geoff"	25,722	51.7%
	Petteys, Derek	6,593	12.2%	Preece, Christopher	24,007	48.3%
	TOTAL	*54,253*		*TOTAL*	*49,729*	

Note: An asterisk (*) denotes incumbent.

LOUISIANA

Statewide Races

In recent years, Louisiana, with a colorful political tradition, has seen more action in its odd-year gubernatorial races than in its federal elections. The 2022 cycle followed suit: as with 2020, Louisiana voters gave an incumbent Republican senator an outright win.

The 2022 primary in Louisiana drew about a dozen candidates, but the well-funded Sen. John Kennedy was never considered vulnerable. In Louisiana, all candidates run on the same primary ballot and a runoff ensues if no one secures a majority. No major Republicans challenged the incumbent, while two main Democratic contenders emerged, each with differing styles. Luke Mixon, a white moderate, fashioned himself in the mold of Democratic Gov. John Bel Edwards – he was a military veteran who took a nuanced position on abortion rights. Meanwhile, Gary Chambers, a Black man, ran as a more strident progressive. In 2021, he placed a strong third in a special election for the Black-majority 2nd District, running especially well with white liberals in New Orleans.

On Election Day, Kennedy took 62%, easily surpassing the 50%+1 threshold needed to win outright. Along with another minor Republican, the GOP share of the primary was just over 63%. Chambers finished ahead of Mixon, though neither claimed more than 20% of the vote.

The result was a near-perfect repeat of 2020's Senate result: that year, Sen. Bill Cassidy (R) won outright with 59% and combined with another lesser Republican for 61%. Both Cassidy and Kennedy placed first in 63 of 64 parishes, only missing Orleans Parish (coterminous with the city of New Orleans). In each case, the weakest Republican-won parish was St. John the Baptist, just up the Mississippi River from New Orleans. Thanks to split Democratic opposition, both Republican incumbents carried it with pluralities of less than 40%. Generally, Kennedy performed a few points better than Cassidy across the board. One exception was East Baton Rouge, the site of the state capitol that the famed Huey Long built nearly 100 years ago. Though Democratic candidates won the aggregate vote there both years, Kennedy got the same 46% plurality as Cassidy did.

House Races

Louisiana, with six districts, was among the last states to pass a new map in 2022. Republicans have held a 5-1 advantage in the state's delegation since the 2012 elections. Republicans, who had close to a legislative supermajority, passed what amounted to a minimal-change plan – aside from adjusting for population shifts, they deferred to the incumbents in making some parochial changes. Edwards, who was under some pressure to leverage his position as governor to fight for an additional Democratic-leaning seat, vetoed the map. But Republican leadership mustered enough votes to override Edwards' veto and enact their plan.

None of the six districts were even remotely competitive between the two parties. In the southwestern 3rd District, there was a somewhat notable intraparty contest. Republican Rep. Clay Higgins, who had a penchant for generating controversy, drew a challenge from fellow Republican Holden Hoggatt, who suggested he'd have a more cooperative style. Though Hoggatt got endorsements from several of the area's former representatives, he took just 11% to Higgins's 64%.

LOUISIANA

Congressional districts first established for elections held in 2022

6 members

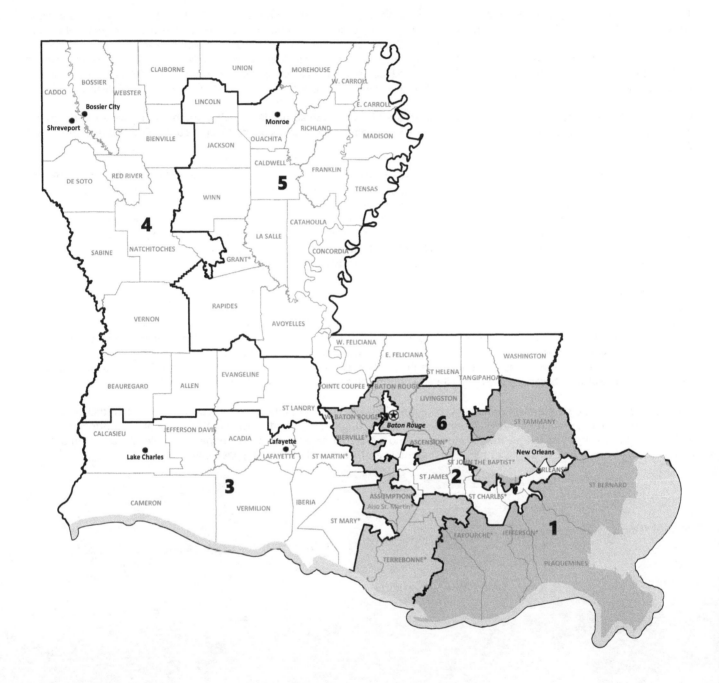

The county equivalent in Louisiana is known as a parish.

* Asterisk indicates a parish whose boundaries include parts of two or more congressional districts.

CDs 1 and 6 are highlighted for visibility. St. Martin Parish consists of two areas.

LOUISIANA

GOVERNOR
John Bel Edwards (D). Reelected 2019 to a four-year term. Previously elected 2015.

SENATORS (2 Republicans)
Bill Cassidy (R). Reelected 2020 to a six-year term. Previously elected 2014.

John Neely Kennedy (R). Reelected 2022 to a six-year term. Previously elected 2016.

REPRESENTATIVES (5 Republicans, 1 Democrat)
1. Steve Scalise (R)
2. Troy Carter (D)
3. Clay Higgins (R)
4. Mike Johnson (R)
5. Julia Letlow (R)
6. Garret Graves (R)

POSTWAR VOTE FOR PRESIDENT

| | | Republican | | Democratic | | Other Vote | Rep.-Dem. Plurality | Percentage | | | |
| | | | | | | | | Total Vote | | Major Vote | |
Year	Total Vote	Vote	Candidate	Vote	Candidate			Rep.	Dem.	Rep.	Dem.
2020	2,148,062	1,255,776	Trump, Donald J.*	856,034	Biden, Joseph R. Jr.	36,252	399,742 R	58.5%	39.9%	59.5%	40.5%
2016**	2,029,032	1,178,638	Trump, Donald J.	780,154	Clinton, Hillary Rodham	70,240	398,484 R	58.1%	38.4%	60.2%	39.8%
2012	1,994,065	1,152,262	Romney, W. Mitt	809,141	Obama, Barack H.*	32,662	343,121 R	57.8%	40.6%	58.7%	41.3%
2008	1,960,761	1,148,275	McCain, John S. III	782,989	Obama, Barack H.	29,497	365,286 R	58.6%	39.9%	59.5%	40.5%
2004	1,943,106	1,102,169	Bush, George W.*	820,299	Kerry, John F.	20,638	281,870 R	56.7%	42.2%	57.3%	42.7%
2000**	1,765,656	927,871	Bush, George W.	792,344	Gore, Albert Jr.	45,441	135,527 R	52.6%	44.9%	53.9%	46.1%
1996**	1,783,959	712,586	Dole, Robert "Bob"	927,837	Clinton, Bill*	143,536	215,251 D	39.9%	52.0%	43.4%	56.6%
1992**	1,790,017	733,386	Bush, George H.*	815,971	Clinton, Bill	240,660	82,585 D	41.0%	45.6%	47.3%	52.7%
1988	1,628,202	883,702	Bush, George H.	717,460	Dukakis, Michael S.	27,040	166,242 R	54.3%	44.1%	55.2%	44.8%
1984	1,706,822	1,037,299	Reagan, Ronald*	651,586	Mondale, Walter F.	17,937	385,713 R	60.8%	38.2%	61.4%	38.6%
1980**	1,548,591	792,853	Reagan, Ronald	708,453	Carter, Jimmy*	47,285	84,400 R	51.2%	45.7%	52.8%	47.2%
1976	1,278,539	587,446	Ford, Gerald R.*	661,365	Carter, Jimmy	29,728	73,919 D	45.9%	51.7%	47.0%	53.0%
1972	1,051,491	686,852	Nixon, Richard M.*	298,142	McGovern, George S.	66,497	388,710 R	65.3%	28.4%	69.7%	30.3%
1968**	1,097,450	257,535	Nixon, Richard M.	309,615	Humphrey, Hubert Horatio Jr.	530,300	52,080 D#	23.5%	28.2%	45.4%	54.6%
1964	896,293	509,225	Goldwater, Barry M. Sr.	387,068	Johnson, Lyndon B.*		122,157 R	56.8%	43.2%	56.8%	43.2%
1960**	807,891	230,980	Nixon, Richard M.	407,339	Kennedy, John F.	169,572	176,359 D	28.6%	50.4%	36.2%	63.8%
1956	617,544	329,047	Eisenhower, Dwight D.*	243,977	Stevenson, Adlai E. II	44,520	85,070 R	53.3%	39.5%	57.4%	42.6%
1952	651,952	306,925	Eisenhower, Dwight D.	345,027	Stevenson, Adlai E. II		38,102 D	47.1%	52.9%	47.1%	52.9%
1948**	416,336	72,657	Dewey, Thomas E.	136,344	Truman, Harry S.*	207,335	63,687 D#	17.5%	32.7%	34.8%	65.2%

Note: An asterisk (*) denotes incumbent. A pound sign (#) in the plurality column indicates that the winner in 1948 and 1968 did not run under the banner of either major party.
**In past elections, the other vote included: 2016 - 37,978 Libertarian (Gary Johnson); 2000 - 20,473 Green (Ralph Nader); 1996 - 123,293 Reform (Ross Perot); 1992 - 211,478 Independent (Perot); 1980 - 26,345 Independent (John Anderson); 1968 - 530,300 American Independent (George Wallace); 1960 - 169,572 Unpledged Independent Electors; 1948 - 204,290 States' Rights (Strom Thurmond). Wallace carried Louisiana in 1968 with 48.3% of the vote. Thurmond won the state in 1948 with 49.1%.

LOUISIANA

POSTWAR VOTE FOR GOVERNOR

Year	Total Vote	Republican Vote	Republican Candidate	Democratic Vote	Democratic Candidate	Other Vote	Rep.-Dem. Plurality	Total Vote Rep.	Total Vote Dem.	Major Vote Rep.	Major Vote Dem.
2019**	1,508,784	734,286	Rispone, Eddie	774,498	Edwards, John Bel*		40,212 D	48.7%	51.3%	48.7%	51.3%
2015**	1,152,864	505,940	Vitter, David B.	646,924	Edwards, John Bel		140,984 D	43.9%	56.1%	43.9%	56.1%
2011	1,023,163	673,239	Jindal, Bobby*	182,925	Hollis, Tara	166,999	490,314 R	65.8%	17.9%	78.6%	21.4%
2007**	1,297,840	699,275	Jindal, Bobby	226,476	Boasso, Walter J.	372,089	472,799 R	53.9%	17.5%	75.5%	24.5%
2003**	1,407,842	676,484	Jindal, Bobby	731,358	Kathleen, Babineaux		54,874 D	48.1%	51.9%	48.1%	51.9%
1999	1,295,205	805,203	Foster, Mike*	382,445	Jefferson, William J.	107,557	422,758 R	62.2%	29.5%	67.8%	32.2%
1995**	1,550,360	984,499	Foster, Mike	565,861	Fields, Cleo		418,638 R	63.5%	36.5%	63.5%	36.5%
1991**	1,728,040	671,009	Duke, David E.	1,057,031	Edwards, Edwin W.		386,022 D	38.8%	61.2%	38.8%	61.2%
1987**	1,558,730	287,780	Livingston, Bob	516,078	Roemer, Charles	754,872	228,298 D	18.5%	33.1%	35.8%	64.2%
1983	1,615,905	588,508	Treen, David Conner*	1,006,561	Edwards, Edwin W.	20,836	418,053 D	36.4%	62.3%	36.9%	63.1%
1979**	1,371,825	690,691	Treen, David Conner	681,134	Lambert, Louis		9,557 R	50.3%	49.7%	50.3%	49.7%
1975	430,095			430,095	Edwards, Edwin W.*		430,095 D		100.0%		100.0%
1972	1,121,570	480,424	Treen, David Conner	641,146	Edwards, Edwin W.		160,722 D	42.8%	57.2%	42.8%	57.2%
1968	372,762		430,095 R	372,762	McKeithen, John J.*		372,762 D		100.0%		100.0%
1964	773,390	297,753	Lyons, Charlton H. Sr.	469,589	McKeithen, John J.	6,048	171,836 D	38.5%	60.7%	38.8%	61.2%
1960	506,562	86,135	Grevemberg, F. C.	407,907	Davis, Jimmie H.	12,520	321,772 D	17.0%	80.5%	17.4%	82.6%
1956	172,291			172,291	Long, Earl K.		172,291 D		100.0%		100.0%
1952	118,723			118,723	Kennon, Robert F.		118,723 D		100.0%		100.0%
1948	76,566			76,566	Long, Earl K.		76,566 D		100.0%		100.0%

Note: An asterisk (*) denotes incumbent. **Since the 1970s, Louisiana has had a two-tier election system for governor in which all candidates, regardless of party, run together in an open election. A candidate who wins a majority of the vote is elected. If no candidate receives 50%, a runoff is held between the top two finishers. The results of the runoff are listed in this chart for 1979, 1991, 1995, 2003, 2015, and 2019. In elections that did not require a runoff, the leading Democratic and Republican candidates are listed with their votes from the first-round, open election. The votes for other candidates are listed in the "Other Vote" column, regardless of whether they were Democratic, Republican, or Independent. In past elections, the other vote included: 2007 - 186,682 No Party (John Georges), 161,665 Democrat (Foster Campbell); 1987 - 437,801 Democrat (Edwin W. Edwards). In 1987, Edwards withdrew after finishing second in the initial round of voting. Democrat Charles Roemer finished first with 33.1% and with Edwards's withdrawal, no runoff was held. The major party vote percentages are calculated for the top vote-getter for each party only; it does not include additional members of the same party. The Republican Party did not run a candidate in the 1948, 1952, 1956, 1968, and 1975 gubernatorial elections.

LOUISIANA

POSTWAR VOTE FOR SENATOR

		Republican		Democratic		Other Vote	Rep.-Dem. Plurality	Percentage			
								Total Vote		Major Vote	
Year	Total Vote	Vote	Candidate	Vote	Candidate			Rep.	Dem.	Rep.	Dem.
2022	1,383,290	851,568	Kennedy, John Neely*	246,933	Chambers, Gary	284,789	604,635 R	61.6%	34.0%	64.4%	35.6%
2020	2,071,543	1,228,908	Cassidy, Bill*	394,049	Perkins, Adrian	448,586	834,859 R	61.2%	35.3%	63.4%	36.6%
2016**	884,007	536,191	Kennedy, John Neely	347,816	Campbell, Foster		188,375 R	60.7%	39.3%	60.7%	39.3%
2014**	1,273,589	712,379	Cassidy, Bill	561,210	Landrieu, Mary L.*		151,169 R	55.9%	44.1%	55.9%	44.1%
2010	1,264,994	715,415	Vitter, David B.*	476,572	Melancon, Charlie R.	73,007	238,843 R	56.6%	37.7%	60.0%	40.0%
2008	1,896,574	867,177	Kennedy, John	988,298	Landrieu, Mary L.*	41,099	121,121 D	45.7%	52.1%	46.7%	53.3%
2004**	1,848,056	943,014	Vitter, David B.	542,150	John, Chris	362,892	400,864 R	51.0%	29.3%	63.5%	36.5%
2002**	1,235,296	596,642	Terrell, Suzanne Haik	638,654	Landrieu, Mary L.*		42,012 D	48.3%	51.7%	48.3%	51.7%
1998	969,165	306,616	Donelon, Jim	620,502	Breaux, John B.*	42,047	313,886 D	31.6%	64.0%	33.1%	66.9%
1996**	1,700,102	847,157	Jenkins, Louis E. "Woody" Jr.	852,945	Landrieu, Mary L.		5,788 D	49.8%	50.2%	49.8%	50.2%
1992	843,037	69,986	Stockstill, Lyle	616,021	Breaux, John B.*	157,030	546,035 D	8.3%	73.1%	10.2%	89.8%
1990	1,396,113	607,391	Duke, David E.	752,902	Johnston, J. Bennett*	35,820	145,511 D	43.5%	53.9%	44.7%	55.3%
1986**	1,369,897	646,311	Moore, W. Henson	723,586	Breaux, John B.		77,275 D	47.2%	52.8%	47.2%	52.8%
1984	977,473	86,546	Ross, Robert M.	838,181	Johnston, J. Bennett*	52,746	751,635 D	8.9%	85.7%	9.4%	90.6%
1980**	843,362	13,739	Bardwell, Jerry C.	484,770	Long, Russell B.*	342,504	471,031 D	1.6%	57.6%		100.0%
1978**	839,669			498,773	Johnston, J. Bennett*	340,896	498,773 D		59.4%		100.0%
1974	434,643			434,643	Long, Russell B.*		434,643 D		100.0%		100.0%
1972**	1,084,904	206,846	Toledano, Ben C.	598,987	Johnston, J. Bennett	279,071	392,141 D	19.1%	55.2%	25.7%	74.3%
1968	518,586			518,586	Long, Russell B.*		518,586 D		100.0%		100.0%
1966	437,695			437,695	Ellender, Allen J.*		437,695 D		100.0%		100.0%
1962	421,904	103,066	O'Hearn, Taylor Walters	318,838	Long, Russell B.*		215,772 D	24.4%	75.6%	24.4%	75.6%
1960	541,928	109,698	Reese, George W. Jr.	432,228	Ellender, Allen J.*	2	322,530 D	20.2%	79.8%	20.2%	79.8%
1956	335,564			335,564	Long, Russell B.*		335,564 D		100.0%		100.0%
1954	207,115			207,115	Ellender, Allen J.*		207,115 D		100.0%		100.0%
1950	251,838	30,931	Gerth, Charles S.	220,907	Long, Russell B.*		189,976 D	12.3%	87.7%	12.3%	87.7%
1948	330,324			330,315	Ellender, Allen J.	9	330,315 D		100.0%		100.0%
1948S**	407,685	102,339	Clarke, Clem S.	305,346	Long, Russell B.		203,007 D	25.1%	74.9%	25.1%	74.9%

Note: An asterisk (*) denotes incumbent. **In 2008 and 2010, Louisiana used the more typical system of party primaries followed by a general election to fill seats in Congress. Since 1978, all other Senate seats were decided in open elections in which candidates of all parties ran together on the same ballot. If no candidate won a majority of the vote in the first round, a runoff was held between the top two vote-getters, regardless of party. The Senate elections in 1986, 1996, 2002, 2014, and 2016 were decided by a runoff, with the results of the runoff listed in this chart. In elections that did not require a runoff, the leading Democratic and Republican candidates are listed with their votes in the first-round, open election. The votes for other candidates are listed in the "Other Vote" column, regardless of whether they were Democratic, Republican, or Independent. In past elections, the other vote included: 2004 - 275,821 Democrat (John Kennedy); 1980 - 325,922 Democrat (Louis Jenkins) and 1978 - 340,896 Democrat (Louis Jenkins); 1972 - 250,161 Independent (John J. McKeithen), who finished second. One of the 1948 elections was for a short term to fill a vacancy. The major party vote percentages are calculated for the top vote-getter for each party only; it does not include additional members of the same party. The Republican Party did not run a candidate in Senate elections in 1948, 1954, 1956, 1966, 1968, 1974, and 1978.

LOUISIANA

SENATOR 2022

2020 Census Population	Parish	Total Vote	Republican (Kennedy)	Democratic (Chambers)	Other	Rep.-Dem. Plurality	Percentage			
							Total Vote		Major Vote	
							Rep.	Dem.	Rep.	Dem.
61,989	ACADIA	19,647	15,864	1,687	2,096	14,177 R	80.7%	8.6%	90.4%	9.6%
25,676	ALLEN	6,386	5,033	541	812	4,492 R	78.8%	8.5%	90.3%	9.7%
127,103	ASCENSION	40,776	27,149	6,370	7,257	20,779 R	66.6%	15.6%	81.0%	19.0%
21,818	ASSUMPTION	7,655	5,126	1,256	1,273	3,870 R	67.0%	16.4%	80.3%	19.7%
40,123	AVOYELLES	11,422	8,102	936	2,384	7,166 R	70.9%	8.2%	89.6%	10.4%

LOUISIANA
SENATOR 2022

2020 Census Population	Parish	Total Vote	Republican (Kennedy)	Democratic (Chambers)	Other	Rep.-Dem. Plurality	Percentage Total Vote		Percentage Major Vote	
							Rep.	Dem.	Rep.	Dem.
37,596	BEAUREGARD	10,830	8,979	622	1,229	8,357 R	82.9%	5.7%	93.5%	6.5%
13,206	BIENVILLE	4,769	2,704	957	1,108	1,747 R	56.7%	20.1%	73.9%	26.1%
127,361	BOSSIER	32,181	23,910	3,751	4,520	20,159 R	74.3%	11.7%	86.4%	13.6%
239,555	CADDO	66,349	33,687	15,902	16,760	17,785 R	50.8%	24.0%	67.9%	32.1%
203,807	CALCASIEU	53,673	36,865	7,401	9,407	29,464 R	68.7%	13.8%	83.3%	16.7%
9,922	CALDWELL	3,219	2,738	151	330	2,587 R	85.1%	4.7%	94.8%	5.2%
6,937	CAMERON	2,447	2,158	52	237	2,106 R	88.2%	2.1%	97.6%	2.4%
9,463	CATAHOULA	3,568	2,590	411	567	2,179 R	72.6%	11.5%	86.3%	13.7%
15,679	CLAIBORNE	4,425	2,898	811	716	2,087 R	65.5%	18.3%	78.1%	21.9%
19,192	CONCORDIA	5,947	3,912	781	1,254	3,131 R	65.8%	13.1%	83.4%	16.6%
27,557	DE SOTO	9,247	6,284	1,236	1,727	5,048 R	68.0%	13.4%	83.6%	16.4%
439,143	EAST BATON ROUGE	137,079	63,024	41,303	32,752	21,721 R	46.0%	30.1%	60.4%	39.6%
6,839	EAST CARROLL	1,983	833	630	520	203 R	42.0%	31.8%	56.9%	43.1%
19,155	EAST FELICIANA	7,430	4,560	1,630	1,240	2,930 R	61.4%	21.9%	73.7%	26.3%
33,372	EVANGELINE	11,116	7,841	1,524	1,751	6,317 R	70.5%	13.7%	83.7%	16.3%
20,001	FRANKLIN	6,149	4,871	582	696	4,289 R	79.2%	9.5%	89.3%	10.7%
22,450	GRANT	6,350	5,550	250	550	5,300 R	87.4%	3.9%	95.7%	4.3%
69,594	IBERIA	19,632	13,796	2,908	2,928	10,888 R	70.3%	14.8%	82.6%	17.4%
32,528	IBERVILLE	12,154	6,196	3,696	2,262	2,500 R	51.0%	30.4%	62.6%	37.4%
15,757	JACKSON	5,670	4,045	655	970	3,390 R	71.3%	11.6%	86.1%	13.9%
432,282	JEFFERSON	118,183	68,954	19,705	29,524	49,249 R	58.3%	16.7%	77.8%	22.2%
31,440	JEFFERSON DAVIS	10,109	7,965	885	1,259	7,080 R	78.8%	8.8%	90.0%	10.0%
14,910	LA SALLE	4,983	4,486	141	356	4,345 R	90.0%	2.8%	97.0%	3.0%
244,823	LAFAYETTE	72,444	48,435	11,967	12,042	36,468 R	66.9%	16.5%	80.2%	19.8%
97,658	LAFOURCHE	30,177	24,016	2,032	4,129	21,984 R	79.6%	6.7%	92.2%	7.8%
46,719	LINCOLN	12,583	8,155	1,869	2,559	6,286 R	64.8%	14.9%	81.4%	18.6%
141,300	LIVINGSTON	42,271	35,213	2,469	4,589	32,744 R	83.3%	5.8%	93.4%	6.6%
10,897	MADISON	2,726	1,419	697	610	722 R	52.1%	25.6%	67.1%	32.9%
24,816	MOREHOUSE	7,189	4,455	1,336	1,398	3,119 R	62.0%	18.6%	76.9%	23.1%
38,093	NATCHITOCHES	10,294	6,600	1,607	2,087	4,993 R	64.1%	15.6%	80.4%	19.6%
390,214	ORLEANS	110,985	17,931	45,713	47,341	27,782 D	16.2%	41.2%	28.2%	71.8%
153,043	OUACHITA	43,052	28,727	6,239	8,086	22,488 R	66.7%	14.5%	82.2%	17.8%
23,189	PLAQUEMINES	7,869	5,398	1,101	1,370	4,297 R	68.6%	14.0%	83.1%	16.9%
21,756	POINTE COUPEE	9,631	6,039	1,727	1,865	4,312 R	62.7%	17.9%	77.8%	22.2%
129,661	RAPIDES	39,079	27,110	5,384	6,585	21,726 R	69.4%	13.8%	83.4%	16.6%
8,425	RED RIVER	2,488	1,714	379	395	1,335 R	68.9%	15.2%	81.9%	18.1%
20,095	RICHLAND	6,719	4,771	935	1,013	3,836 R	71.0%	13.9%	83.6%	16.4%
23,944	SABINE	7,488	6,316	444	728	5,872 R	84.3%	5.9%	93.4%	6.6%
47,373	ST. BERNARD	10,739	6,950	1,708	2,081	5,242 R	64.7%	15.9%	80.3%	19.7%
53,228	ST. CHARLES	18,016	11,876	2,663	3,477	9,213 R	65.9%	14.8%	81.7%	18.3%
10,142	ST. HELENA	4,170	2,034	925	1,211	1,109 R	48.8%	22.2%	68.7%	31.3%
21,046	ST. JAMES	8,838	4,468	1,385	2,985	3,083 R	50.6%	15.7%	76.3%	23.7%
42,809	ST. JOHN THE BAPTIST	11,643	4,457	3,475	3,711	982 R	38.3%	29.8%	56.2%	43.8%
82,041	ST. LANDRY	26,942	16,217	5,507	5,218	10,710 R	60.2%	20.4%	74.7%	25.3%
53,436	ST. MARTIN	17,144	12,317	2,527	2,300	9,790 R	71.8%	14.7%	83.0%	17.0%

LOUISIANA
SENATOR 2022

2020 Census Population	Parish	Total Vote	Republican (Kennedy)	Democratic (Chambers)	Other	Rep.-Dem. Plurality	Total Vote Rep.	Total Vote Dem.	Major Vote Rep.	Major Vote Dem.
49,119	ST. MARY	14,461	9,755	2,289	2,417	7,466 R	67.5%	15.8%	81.0%	19.0%
261,693	ST. TAMMANY	94,655	68,694	8,520	17,441	60,174 R	72.6%	9.0%	89.0%	11.0%
135,267	TANGIPAHOA	35,489	24,754	4,402	6,333	20,352 R	69.8%	12.4%	84.9%	15.1%
4,301	TENSAS	1,652	900	380	372	520 R	54.5%	23.0%	70.3%	29.7%
110,262	TERREBONNE	27,366	20,731	2,362	4,273	18,369 R	75.8%	8.6%	89.8%	10.2%
22,151	UNION	7,680	6,070	574	1,036	5,496 R	79.0%	7.5%	91.4%	8.6%
59,529	VERMILION	17,953	14,573	1,321	2,059	13,252 R	81.2%	7.4%	91.7%	8.3%
47,214	VERNON	11,239	9,413	658	1,168	8,755 R	83.8%	5.9%	93.5%	6.5%
46,248	WASHINGTON	13,171	9,020	2,034	2,117	6,986 R	68.5%	15.4%	81.6%	18.4%
38,281	WEBSTER	11,990	8,188	1,931	1,871	6,257 R	68.3%	16.1%	80.9%	19.1%
26,549	WEST BATON ROUGE	10,104	5,815	2,607	1,682	3,208 R	57.6%	25.8%	69.0%	31.0%
10,831	WEST CARROLL	3,389	2,964	165	260	2,799 R	87.5%	4.9%	94.7%	5.3%
15,615	WEST FELICIANA	4,277	2,800	430	1,047	2,370 R	65.5%	10.1%	86.7%	13.3%
13,859	WINN	3,998	3,153	397	448	2,756 R	78.9%	9.9%	88.8%	11.2%
4,650,082	TOTAL	1,383,290	851,568	246,933	284,789	604,635 R	61.6%	17.9%	77.5%	22.5%

LOUISIANA
HOUSE OF REPRESENTATIVES

CD	Year	Total Vote	Rep. Vote	Republican Candidate	Dem. Vote	Democratic Candidate	Other Vote	Rep.-Dem. Plurality	Total Vote Rep.	Total Vote Dem.	Major Vote Rep.	Major Vote Dem.
1	2022	244,044	177,670	SCALISE, STEVE*	61,467	DARLING, KATIE	4,907	116,203 R	72.8%	25.2%	74.3%	25.7%
1	2020	374,369	270,330	SCALISE, STEVE*	94,730	DUGAS, LEE ANN	9,309	175,600 R	72.2%	25.3%	74.1%	25.9%
1	2018	269,325	192,555	SCALISE, STEVE*	44,273	SAVOIE, TAMMY	32,497	148,282 R	71.5%	16.4%	81.3%	18.7%
1	2016	326,788	243,645	SCALISE, STEVE*	41,840	DUGAS, LEE ANN	41,303	201,805 R	74.6%	12.8%	85.3%	14.7%
1	2014	244,004	189,250	SCALISE, STEVE*	24,761	MENDOZA, M.V. "VINNY"	29,993	164,489 R	77.6%	10.1%	88.4%	11.6%
1	2012	290,410	193,496	SCALISE, STEVE*	61,703	MENDOZA, M.V. VINNY	35,211	131,793 R	66.6%	21.2%	75.8%	24.2%
2	2022	205,047	46,927	LUX, DANIEL ANTHONY "DAN"	158,120	CARTER, TROY A.*		111,193 D	22.9%	77.1%	22.9%	77.1%
2	2020	316,982	47,575	SCHILLING, DAVID M.	201,636	RICHMOND, CEDRIC*	67,771	154,061 D	15.0%	63.6%	19.1%	80.9%
2	2018	235,982			190,182	RICHMOND, CEDRIC*	45,800	190,182 D		80.6%		100.0%
2	2016	284,269			198,289	RICHMOND, CEDRIC*	85,980	198,289 D		69.8%		100.0%
2	2014	221,570			152,201	RICHMOND, CEDRIC*	69,369	152,201 D		68.7%		100.0%
2	2012	287,354	38,801	BAILEY, DWAYNE	158,501	RICHMOND, CEDRIC*	90,052	119,700 D	13.5%	55.2%	19.7%	80.3%
3	2022	224,552	144,423	HIGGINS, CLAY*	23,641	LEBLANC, LESSIE OLIVIA	56,488	120,782 R	64.3%	10.5%	85.9%	14.1%
3	2020	340,120	230,480	HIGGINS, CLAY*	60,852	HARRIS, BRAYLON	48,788	169,628 R	67.8%	17.9%	79.1%	20.9%
3	2018	245,943	136,876	HIGGINS, CLAY*	43,729	METHVIN, MILDRED "MIMI"	65,338	93,147 R	55.7%	17.8%	75.8%	24.2%
3	2016	320,454	91,532	ANGELLE, SCOTT A.	28,385	HEBERT, JACOB "DORIAN PHIBIAN"	200,537	63,147 R	28.6%	8.9%	76.3%	23.7%
3	2014	236,268	185,867	BOUSTANY, CHARLES W. JR.*			50,401	185,867 R	78.7%		100.0%	
3	2012	311,393	139,123	BOUSTANY, CHARLES W. JR.	67,070	RICHARD, RON	105,200	72,053 R	44.7%	21.5%	67.5%	32.5%
4	2022		Unopposed	JOHNSON, MIKE*								
4	2020	306,578	185,265	JOHNSON, MIKE*	78,157	HOUSTON, KENNY	43,156	107,108 R	60.4%	25.5%	70.3%	29.7%
4	2018	216,872	139,326	JOHNSON, MIKE*	72,934	TRUNDLE, RYAN	4,612	66,392 R	64.2%	33.6%	65.6%	34.4%
4	2016	285,985	70,580	JOHNSON, MIKE	80,593	JONES, MARSHALL	134,812	10,013 D	24.7%	28.2%	46.7%	53.3%
4	2014	207,919	152,683	FLEMING, JOHN*			55,236	152,683 R	73.4%		100.0%	
4	2012	249,531	187,894	FLEMING, JOHN*			61,637	187,894 R	75.3%		100.0%	
5	2022	223,553	151,080	LETLOW, JULIA*	35,149	DANTZLER, OSCAR "OMAR"	37,324	115,931 R	67.6%	15.7%	81.1%	18.9%
5	2020	309,556	102,533	LETLOW, LUKE J.	50,812	CHRISTOPHE, SANDRA "CANDY"	156,211	51,721 R	33.1%	16.4%	66.9%	33.1%
5	2018	223,946	149,018	ABRAHAM, RALPH LEE*	67,118	FLEENOR, JESSEE CARLTON	7,810	81,900 R	66.5%	30.0%	68.9%	31.1%
5	2016	255,662	208,545	ABRAHAM, RALPH LEE*			47,117	208,545 R	81.6%		100.0%	
5	2014	239,551	55,489	ABRAHAM, RALPH LEE	67,611	MAYO, JAMIE	116,451	12,122 D	23.2%	28.2%	45.1%	54.9%
5	2012	260,216	202,536	ALEXANDER, RODNEY*			57,680	202,536 R	77.8%		100.0%	

LOUISIANA

HOUSE OF REPRESENTATIVES

CD	Year	Total Vote	Republican Vote	Republican Candidate	Democratic Vote	Democratic Candidate	Other Vote	Rep.-Dem. Plurality	Total Vote Rep.	Total Vote Dem.	Major Vote Rep.	Major Vote Dem.
6	2022	235,928	189,684	GRAVES, GARRET*			46,244	189,684 R	80.4%		100.0%	
6	2020	373,996	265,706	GRAVES, GARRET*	95,541	WILLIAMS, DARTANYON A.	12,749	170,165 R	71.0%	25.5%	73.6%	26.4%
6	2018	268,525	186,553	GRAVES, GARRET*	55,089	DEWITT, JUSTIN	26,883	131,464 R	69.5%	20.5%	77.2%	22.8%
6	2016	331,098	207,483	GRAVES, GARRET*	49,380	LIEBERMAN, RICHARD	74,235	158,103 R	62.7%	14.9%	80.8%	19.2%
6	2014	258,479	70,715	GRAVES, GARRET	77,866	EDWARDS, EDWIN W.	109,898	7,151 D	27.4%	30.1%	47.6%	52.4%
6	2012	306,713	243,553	CASSIDY, BILL*			63,160	243,553 R	79.4%		100.0%	
TOTAL	2022	1,133,124	709,784		278,377		144,963	431,407 R	62.6%	24.6%	71.8%	28.2%
TOTAL	2020	2,021,601	1,101,889		581,728		337,984	520,161 R	54.5%	28.8%	65.4%	34.6%
TOTAL	2018	1,460,593	804,328		473,325		182,940	331,003 R	55.1%	32.4%	63.0%	37.0%
TOTAL	2016	1,804,256	821,785		398,487		583,984	423,298 R	45.5%	22.1%	67.3%	32.7%
TOTAL	2014	1,407,791	654,004		322,439		431,348	331,565 R	46.5%	22.9%	67.0%	33.0%
TOTAL	2012	1,705,617	1,005,403		287,274		412,940	718,129 R	58.9%	16.8%	77.8%	22.2%

Note: An asterisk (*) denotes incumbent.

LOUISIANA

GENERAL AND PRIMARY ELECTIONS

GENERAL ELECTIONS: OTHER VOTES

Senate — Other vote was 182,887 Democrat (Luke Mixon), 31,568 Democrat (Syrita Steib), 25,275 Independent (Devin Graham), 11,910 Independent (M.V. Mendoza), 9,378 No Party Affiliation (Beryl Billiot), 7,767 Democrat (Salvador Rodriguez), 5,388 Independent (Bradley McMorris), 4,865 Libertarian (Aaron Sigler), 2,753 Other (Xan John), 1,676 Democrat (William Olson), 1,322 Other (Thomas Wenn).

House — Other vote was:

- **CD 1**: 4,907 Libertarian (Howard Kearney)
- **CD 3**: 23,641 Democrat (Lessie Leblanc), 21,172 Democrat (Tia LeBrun), 4,012 Republican (Thomas Payne), 3,255 Independent (Gloria Wiggins), 1,955 Republican (Jacob Shaheen), 1,620 Libertarian (Guy McLendon)
- **CD 5**: 19,383 Democrat (Walter Huff), 12,159 Republican (Allen Guillory), 5,782 Republican (Hunter Pullen)
- **CD 6**: 30,709 Libertarian (Rufus Craig), 15,535 Republican (Brian Belzer)

2022 PRIMARY ELECTIONS: SUPPLEMENTARY INFORMATION

Primary	November 8, 2022 (Congress First-Round Vote)	**Registration** (as of November 1, 2022)	3,016,626	Democratic	1,189,716
Primary Runoff	December 2, 2022 (Congress Second-Round Vote)			Republican	1,007,718
				Other Parties	819,192

Primary Type — Open—For governor and other federal offices, Louisiana has a two-tier electoral system open to all voters, with a first round of voting (sometimes called an open or "jungle" primary) that features candidates from all parties running together on the same ballot. A candidate who wins a majority of the vote in the first round is elected. Otherwise, there is a runoff held several weeks later between the top two finishers.

MAINE

Statewide Races

In 2020, Maine's biggest non-presidential contest, its Senate race, was among the cycle's most heartbreaking disappointments for national Democrats. After trailing in virtually every poll, Sen. Susan Collins, who is the nearest modern-day equivalent to the old school liberal Republicans who used to dominate New England, was reelected. As Joe Biden carried Maine by nine points, Collins became the only senator to win a state that voted for the opposing party's presidential nominee.

Maine did not have a Senate race in 2022, but the result was more satisfying for Democrats. Gov. Janet Mills won reelection by 13 points, the best showing for a Democratic gubernatorial nominee since 1982.

Mills's predecessor as governor, Paul LePage, a bombastic Republican who spent time as a bartender in Florida after leaving office in 2019, tried to mount a comeback. But Maine voters were content with Mills at the helm: she won 56%–43%, up from her 51%–43% margin in 2018. There was some continuity in the returns: Mills carried the same nine counties as she did four years earlier. She won the eight counties that supported Biden in 2020, all of which are located near the state's coastline, and added her home county, Franklin. Mills' biggest improvement came in Portland's Cumberland County, where she upped her share from 61% to 69%. In his successful campaigns, LePage relied on heavy margins in northern Maine – compared to the coastal counties, the area has a more working-class flavor. LePage carried Aroostook County, the state's northernmost county and home to a large French-Canadian bloc, 58%–41%, for instance.

House Races

In 2021, Mills signed off on a map that made small changes to the state's two districts. The southern 1st District takes in Cumberland County and a selection of other coastal counties, while the 2nd District is the balance of the state. As the former saw faster population growth, it needed to shed about 23,000 residents. Though only a handful of municipalities changed districts, the most notable change was the capital, Augusta – it was moved from ME-1 to ME-2.

In the 1st District, seven-term Democratic Rep. Chellie Pingree had little to worry about. She was reelected by 26 points, matching Mills's performance in the district.

Mills was not the only prominent Maine Democrat facing their predecessor. In the 2nd District, Democratic Rep. Jared Golden, a 40-year-old Marine Corps veteran, faced a rematch with the man he ousted in 2018, former Republican Rep. Bruce Poliquin. In their first bout, Poliquin placed first but took less than 50%. But Golden benefitted from Maine's then-new ranked choice voting system – if a first-place finisher takes less than a majority, ballots are reallocated until a candidate clears 50% – to win by a point.

In office, Golden joined the moderate Blue Dog Coalition and cast himself as an independent-minded Democrat. In one ad, while eating lobster, he declared that, because of his work, "Maine common sense is back on the table in Washington." Golden won his rematch with Poliquin by a more decisive 53%–47%.

MAINE
Congressional districts first established for elections held in 2022
2 members

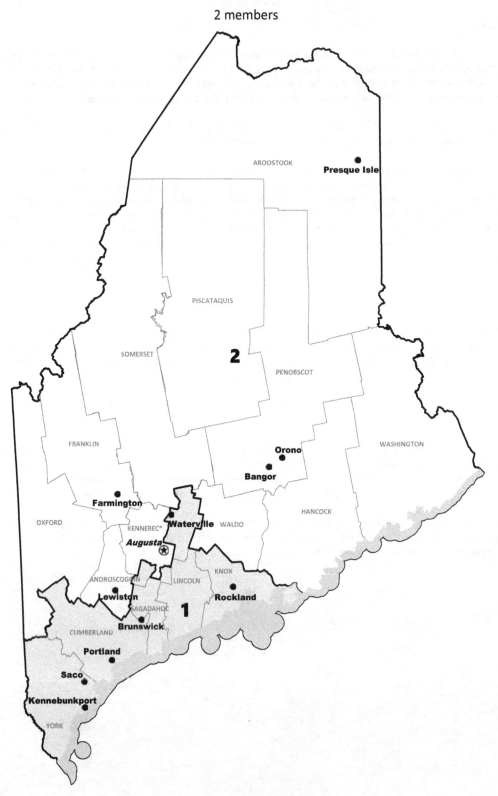

* Asterisk indicates a county whose boundaries include parts of two or more congressional districts.
CD 1 is highlighted for visibility.

MAINE

GOVERNOR
Janet T. Mills (D). Reelected 2022 to a four-year term. Previously elected 2018.

SENATORS (1 Republican, 1 Independent)
Susan M. Collins (R). Reelected 2020 to a six-year term. Previously elected 2014, 2008, 2002, 1996.

Angus S. King Jr. (I). Reelected 2018 to a six-year term. Previously elected 2012.

REPRESENTATIVES (2 Democrats)
1. Chellie Pingree (D)
2. Jared Golden (D)

POSTWAR VOTE FOR PRESIDENT

		Republican		Democratic		Other Vote	Rep.-Dem. Plurality	Percentage			
								Total Vote		Major Vote	
Year	Total Vote	Vote	Candidate	Vote	Candidate			Rep.	Dem.	Rep.	Dem.
2020	819,461	360,737	Trump, Donald J.*	435,072	Biden, Joseph R. Jr.	23,652	74,335 D	44.0%	53.1%	45.3%	54.7%
2016**	747,927	335,593	Trump, Donald J.	357,735	Clinton, Hillary Rodham	54,599	22,142 D	44.9%	47.8%	48.4%	51.6%
2012	713,180	292,276	Romney, W. Mitt	401,306	Obama, Barack H.*	19,598	109,030 D	41.0%	56.3%	42.1%	57.9%
2008	731,163	295,273	McCain, John S. III	421,923	Obama, Barack H.	13,967	126,650 D	40.4%	57.7%	41.2%	58.8%
2004	740,752	330,201	Bush, George W.*	396,842	Kerry, John F.	13,709	66,641 D	44.6%	53.6%	45.4%	54.6%
2000**	651,817	286,616	Bush, George W.	319,951	Gore, Albert Jr.	45,250	33,335 D	44.0%	49.1%	47.3%	52.7%
1996**	605,897	186,378	Dole, Robert "Bob"	312,788	Clinton, Bill*	106,731	126,410 D	30.8%	51.6%	37.3%	62.7%
1992**	679,499	206,504	Bush, George H.*	263,420	Clinton, Bill	209,575	56,916 D	30.4%	38.8%	43.9%	56.1%
1988	555,035	307,131	Bush, George H.	243,569	Dukakis, Michael S.	4,335	63,562 R	55.3%	43.9%	55.8%	44.2%
1984	553,144	336,500	Reagan, Ronald*	214,515	Mondale, Walter F.	2,129	121,985 R	60.8%	38.8%	61.1%	38.9%
1980**	523,011	238,522	Reagan, Ronald	220,974	Carter, Jimmy*	63,515	17,548 R	45.6%	42.3%	51.9%	48.1%
1976	483,216	236,320	Ford, Gerald R.*	232,279	Carter, Jimmy	14,617	4,041 R	48.9%	48.1%	50.4%	49.6%
1972	417,042	256,458	Nixon, Richard M.*	160,584	McGovern, George S.		95,874 R	61.5%	38.5%	61.5%	38.5%
1968**	392,936	169,254	Nixon, Richard M.	217,312	Humphrey, Hubert Horatio Jr.	6,370	48,058 D	43.1%	55.3%	43.8%	56.2%
1964	380,965	118,701	Goldwater, Barry M. Sr.	262,264	Johnson, Lyndon B.*		143,563 D	31.2%	68.8%	31.2%	68.8%
1960	421,767	240,608	Nixon, Richard M.	181,159	Kennedy, John F.		59,449 R	57.0%	43.0%	57.0%	43.0%
1956	351,706	249,238	Eisenhower, Dwight D.*	102,468	Stevenson, Adlai E. II		146,770 R	70.9%	29.1%	70.9%	29.1%
1952	351,786	232,353	Eisenhower, Dwight D.	118,806	Stevenson, Adlai E. II	627	113,547 R	66.0%	33.8%	66.2%	33.8%
1948	264,787	150,234	Dewey, Thomas E.	111,916	Truman, Harry S.*	2,637	38,318 R	56.7%	42.3%	57.3%	42.7%

Note: An asterisk (*) denotes incumbent. **In past elections, the other vote included: 2016 - 38,105 Libertarian (Gary Johnson); 2000 - 37,127 Green (Ralph Nader); 1996 - 85,970 Reform (Ross Perot); 1992 - 206,820 Independent (Perot), who placed second; 1980 - 53,327 Independent (John Anderson); 1968 - 6,370 American Independent (George Wallace). Under Maine's unique system of distributing electoral votes, Republican Donald J. Trump won a single electoral vote in 2016 to Hillary Rodham Clinton's three, and a single electoral vote in 2020 to Joseph R. Biden Jr.'s three.

MAINE

POSTWAR VOTE FOR GOVERNOR

		Republican		Democratic		Other Vote	Rep.-Dem. Plurality	Percentage			
								Total Vote		Major Vote	
Year	Total Vote	Vote	Candidate	Vote	Candidate			Rep.	Dem.	Rep.	Dem.
2022	676,819	287,304	LePage, Paul R.	376,934	Mills, Janet T.*	12,581	89,630 D	42.4%	55.7%	43.3%	56.7%
2018	630,667	272,311	Moody, Shawn H.	320,962	Mills, Janet T.	37,394	48,651 D	43.2%	50.9%	45.9%	54.1%
2014	611,227	294,519	LePage, Paul R.*	265,114	Michaud, Michael H.	51,594	29,405 R	48.2%	43.4%	52.6%	47.4%
2010**	572,766	218,065	LePage, Paul R.	109,387	Mitchell, Elizabeth H. "Libby"	245,314	108,678 R	38.1%	19.1%	66.6%	33.4%
2006**	550,865	166,425	Woodcock, Chandler E.	209,927	Baldacci, John*	174,513	43,502 D	30.2%	38.1%	44.2%	55.8%
2002	505,190	209,496	Cianchette, Peter E.	238,179	Baldacci, John	57,515	28,683 D	41.5%	47.1%	46.8%	53.2%
1998**	421,009	79,716	Longley, James B. Jr.	50,506	Connolly, Thomas J.	290,787	29,210 R#	18.9%	12.0%	61.2%	38.8%
1994**	511,308	117,990	Collins, Susan M.	172,951	Brennan, Joseph E.	220,367	54,961 D#	23.1%	33.8%	40.6%	59.4%
1990	522,492	243,766	McKernan, John R.*	230,038	Brennan, Joseph E.	48,688	13,728 R	46.7%	44.0%	51.4%	48.6%
1986**	426,861	170,312	McKernan, John R.	128,744	Tierney, James	127,805	41,568 R	39.9%	30.2%	56.9%	43.1%
1982	460,295	172,949	Cragin, Charles L.	281,066	Brennan, Joseph E.*	6,280	108,117 D	37.6%	61.1%	38.1%	61.9%
1978**	370,258	126,862	Palmer, Linwood E.	176,493	Brennan, Joseph E.	66,903	49,631 D	34.3%	47.7%	41.8%	58.2%
1974**	363,945	84,176	Erwin, James S.	132,219	Mitchell, George J.	147,550	48,043 D#	23.1%	36.3%	38.9%	61.1%
1970	325,386	162,248	Erwin, James S.	163,138	Curtis, Kenneth M.*		890 D	49.9%	50.1%	49.9%	50.1%
1966	323,838	151,802	Reed, John H.*	172,036	Curtis, Kenneth M.		20,234 D	46.9%	53.1%	46.9%	53.1%
1962	292,725	146,604	Reed, John H.*	146,121	Dolloff, Maynard C.		483 R	50.1%	49.9%	50.1%	49.9%
1960S**	417,215	219,768	Reed, John H.	197,447	Coffin, Frank M.		22,321 R	52.7%	47.3%	52.7%	47.3%
1958**	280,245	134,572	Hildreth, Horace A.	145,673	Clauson, Clinton A.		11,101 D	48.0%	52.0%	48.0%	52.0%
1956	304,649	124,395	Trafton, Willis A. Jr.	180,254	Muskie, Edmund S.*		55,859 D	40.8%	59.2%	40.8%	59.2%
1954	248,971	113,298	Cross, Burton M.*	135,673	Muskie, Edmund S.		22,375 D	45.5%	54.5%	45.5%	54.5%
1952	248,441	128,532	Cross, Burton M.	82,538	Oliver, James C.	37,371	45,994 R	51.7%	33.2%	60.9%	39.1%
1950	241,177	145,823	Payne, Frederick G.*	94,304	Grant, Earle S.	1,050	51,519 R	60.5%	39.1%	60.7%	39.3%
1948	222,500	145,956	Payne, Frederick G.	76,544	Lausier, Louis B.		69,412 R	65.6%	34.4%	65.6%	34.4%
1946	179,951	110,327	Hildreth, Horace A.	69,624	Clark, F. Davis		40,703 R	61.3%	38.7%	61.3%	38.7%

Note: An asterisk (*) denotes incumbent. A pound sign (#) in the plurality column indicates that the winners in 1974, 1994, and 1998 were independents. **In past elections, the other vote included: 2010 - 208, 270 Independent (Eliot R. Cutler), who placed second; 2006 - 118,715 Independent Maine Course (Barbara Merrill); 1998 - 246,772 Independent (Angus King), who was re-elected with 58.6% of the total vote; 1994 -180, 829 Independent (King), who was elected with 35.4% of the total vote; 1986 - 64,317 Independent (Sherry F. Huber), 63,474 Independent (John E. Menario); 1978 - 65,889 Independent (Herman C. Frankland); 1974 - 142,464 Independent (James B. Longley), who was elected with 39.1% of the total vote. The 1960 election was for a short term to fill a vacancy. The term of office of Maine's Governor was increased from two to four years effective with the 1958 election.

MAINE

POSTWAR VOTE FOR SENATOR

Year	Total Vote	Republican Vote	Republican Candidate	Democratic Vote	Democratic Candidate	Other Vote	Rep.-Dem. Plurality	Total Vote Rep.	Total Vote Dem.	Major Vote Rep.	Major Vote Dem.
2020	819,183	417,645	Collins, Susan M.*	347,223	Gideon, Sara	54,315	70,422 R	51.0%	42.4%	54.6%	45.4%
2018**	634,409	223,502	Brakey, Eric	66,268	Ringelstein, Zak	344,639	157,234 R#	35.2%	10.4%	77.1%	22.9%
2014	604,008	413,495	Collins, Susan M.*	190,244	Bellows, Shenna	269	223,251 R	68.5%	31.5%	68.5%	31.5%
2012**	700,599	215,399	Summers, Charles E.	92,900	Dill, Cynthia Ann	392,300	122,499 R#	30.7%	13.3%	69.9%	30.1%
2008	724,430	444,300	Collins, Susan M.*	279,510	Allen, Tom	620	164,790 R	61.3%	38.6%	61.4%	38.6%
2006	543,981	402,598	Snowe, Olympia J.*	111,984	Bright, Jean Hay	29,399	290,614 R	74.0%	20.6%	78.2%	21.8%
2002	504,899	295,041	Collins, Susan M.*	209,858	Pingree, Chellie		85,183 R	58.4%	41.6%	58.4%	41.6%
2000	634,872	437,689	Snowe, Olympia J.*	197,183	Lawrence, Mark W.		240,506 R	68.9%	31.1%	68.9%	31.1%
1996	606,777	298,422	Collins, Susan M.	266,226	Brennan, Joseph E.	42,129	32,196 R	49.2%	43.9%	52.9%	47.1%
1994	511,733	308,244	Snowe, Olympia J.	186,042	Andrews, Thomas H.	17,447	122,202 R	60.2%	36.4%	62.4%	37.6%
1990	520,320	319,167	Cohen, William S.*	201,053	Rolde, Neil	100	118,114 R	61.3%	38.6%	61.4%	38.6%
1988	557,375	104,758	Wyman, Jasper S.	452,590	Mitchell, George J.*	27	347,832 D	18.8%	81.2%	18.8%	81.2%
1984	551,406	404,414	Cohen, William S.*	142,626	Mitchell, Elizabeth H. "Libby"	4,366	261,788 R	73.3%	25.9%	73.9%	26.1%
1982	459,715	179,882	Emery, David F.	279,819	Mitchell, George J.	14	99,937 D	39.1%	60.9%	39.1%	60.9%
1978	375,172	212,294	Cohen, William S.	127,327	Hathaway, William D.*	35,551	84,967 R	56.6%	33.9%	62.5%	37.5%
1976	486,254	193,489	Monks, Robert A.G.	292,704	Muskie, Edmund S.*	61	99,215 D	39.8%	60.2%	39.8%	60.2%
1972	421,310	197,040	Smith, Margaret Chase*	224,270	Hathaway, William D.		27,230 D	46.8%	53.2%	46.8%	53.2%
1970	323,860	123,906	Bishop, Neil S.	199,954	Muskie, Edmund S.*		76,048 D	38.3%	61.7%	38.3%	61.7%
1966	319,535	188,291	Smith, Margaret Chase*	131,136	Violette, Elmer H.	108	57,155 R	58.9%	41.0%	58.9%	41.1%
1964	380,551	127,040	McIntire, Clifford G.	253,511	Muskie, Edmund S.*		126,471 D	33.4%	66.6%	33.4%	66.6%
1960	416,699	256,890	Smith, Margaret Chase*	159,809	Cormier, Lucia M.		97,081 R	61.6%	38.4%	61.6%	38.4%
1958	284,364	111,522	Payne, Frederick G.*	172,842	Muskie, Edmund S.		61,320 D	39.2%	60.8%	39.2%	60.8%
1954	246,605	144,530	Smith, Margaret Chase*	102,075	Fullam, Paul A.		42,455 R	58.6%	41.4%	58.6%	41.4%
1952	237,164	139,205	Payne, Frederick G.	82,665	Dube, Roger P.	15,294	56,540 R	58.7%	34.9%	62.7%	37.3%
1948	223,256	159,182	Smith, Margaret Chase	64,074	Scolten, Adrian H.		95,108 R	71.3%	28.7%	71.3%	28.7%
1946	175,014	111,215	Brewster, Ralph O.*	63,799	MacDonald, Peter M.		47,416 R	63.5%	36.5%	63.5%	36.5%

Note: An asterisk (*) denotes incumbent. A pound sign (#) in the plurality column indicates that the winner in 2012 and 2018 was an independent. **In past elections, the other vote included: 2018 - 344,575 Independent (Angus King), who received 54.3% of the total vote and was elected with a plurality of 121,073 votes; 2012 - 370,580 Independent (King), who received 52.9% of the total vote and was elected with a plurality of 155,181 votes.

MAINE

GOVERNOR 2022

2020 Census Population	County	Total Vote	Republican (LePage)	Democratic (Mills)	Other	Rep.-Dem. Plurality	Total Vote Rep.	Total Vote Dem.	Major Vote Rep.	Major Vote Dem.
108,421	ANDROSCOGGIN	47,019	23,220	22,915	884	305 R	49.4%	48.7%	50.3%	49.7%
67,059	AROOSTOOK	28,632	16,530	11,587	515	4,943 R	57.7%	40.5%	58.8%	41.2%
295,766	CUMBERLAND	161,851	47,201	112,188	2,462	64,987 D	29.2%	69.3%	29.6%	70.4%
30,320	FRANKLIN	14,928	7,179	7,406	343	227 D	48.1%	49.6%	49.2%	50.8%
55,212	HANCOCK	30,539	12,527	17,446	566	4,919 D	41.0%	57.1%	41.8%	58.2%
122,609	KENNEBEC	60,346	28,368	30,838	1,140	2,470 D	47.0%	51.1%	47.9%	52.1%
39,899	KNOX	22,256	8,430	13,441	385	5,011 D	37.9%	60.4%	38.5%	61.5%
34,773	LINCOLN	20,946	8,744	11,853	349	3,109 D	41.7%	56.6%	42.5%	57.5%
58,150	OXFORD	27,735	14,229	12,875	631	1,354 R	51.3%	46.4%	52.5%	47.5%
152,403	PENOBSCOT	68,643	35,496	31,844	1,303	3,652 R	51.7%	46.4%	52.7%	47.3%

MAINE

GOVERNOR 2022

2020 Census Population	County	Total Vote	Republican (LePage)	Democratic (Mills)	Other	Rep.-Dem. Plurality		Percentage			
								Total Vote		Major Vote	
								Rep.	Dem.	Rep.	Dem.
16,843	PISCATAQUIS	8,216	4,960	3,098	158	1,862	R	60.4%	37.7%	61.6%	38.4%
35,986	SAGADAHOC	20,842	8,049	12,414	379	4,365	D	38.6%	59.6%	39.3%	60.7%
50,658	SOMERSET	22,816	13,233	9,083	500	4,150	R	58.0%	39.8%	59.3%	40.7%
39,833	WALDO	21,007	9,099	11,508	400	2,409	D	43.3%	54.8%	44.2%	55.8%
31,523	WASHINGTON	14,777	8,160	6,064	553	2,096	R	55.2%	41.0%	57.4%	42.6%
208,640	YORK	104,428	41,662	60,772	1,994	19,110	D	39.9%	58.2%	40.7%	59.3%
	Votes Not Reported by County	1,838	217	1,602	19	1,385	D	11.8%	87.2%	11.9%	88.1%
1,348,095	TOTAL	676,819	287,304	376,934	12,581	89,630	D	42.4%	55.7%	43.3%	56.7%

MAINE

HOUSE OF REPRESENTATIVES

CD	Year	Total Vote	Republican		Democratic		Other Vote	Rep.-Dem. Plurality		Percentage			
			Vote	Candidate	Vote	Candidate				Total Vote		Major Vote	
										Rep.	Dem.	Rep.	Dem.
1	2022	349,176	129,263	THELANDER, EDWIN	219,753	PINGREE, CHELLIE	160	90,490	D	37.0%	62.9%	37.0%	63.0%
1	2020	436,027	165,008	ALLEN, JAY THOMAS	271,004	PINGREE, CHELLIE*	15	105,996	D	37.8%	62.2%	37.8%	62.2%
1	2018	342,053	111,188	HOLBROOK, MARK I.	201,195	PINGREE, CHELLIE*	29,670	90,007	D	32.5%	58.8%	35.6%	64.4%
1	2016	392,391	164,569	HOLBROOK, MARK I.	227,546	PINGREE, CHELLIE*	276	62,977	D	41.9%	58.0%	42.0%	58.0%
1	2014	308,898	94,751	MISIUK, ISAAC J.	186,674	PINGREE, CHELLIE*	27,473	91,923	D	30.7%	60.4%	33.7%	66.3%
1	2012	364,803	128,440	COURTNEY, JONATHAN T.E.	236,363	PINGREE, CHELLIE*		107,923	D	35.2%	64.8%	35.2%	64.8%
2	2022	316,382	141,260	POLIQUIN, BRUCE L.	153,074	GOLDEN, JARED	22,048	11,814	D	44.6%	48.4%	48.0%	52.0%
2	2020	373,235	175,228	CRAFTS, DALE JOHN	197,974	GOLDEN, JARED*	33	22,746	D	46.9%	53.0%	47.0%	53.0%
2	2018	289,624	134,184	POLIQUIN, BRUCE L.*	132,013	GOLDEN, JARED	23,427	2,171	R	46.3%	45.6%	50.4%	49.6%
2	2016	352,183	192,878	POLIQUIN, BRUCE L.*	159,081	CAIN, EMILY ANN	224	33,797	R	54.8%	45.2%	54.8%	45.2%
2	2014	283,448	133,308	POLIQUIN, BRUCE L.	118,556	CAIN, EMILY ANN	31,584	14,752	R	47.0%	41.8%	52.9%	47.1%
2	2012	328,998	137,542	RAYE, KEVIN L.	191,456	MICHAUD, MICHAEL H.*		53,914	D	41.8%	58.2%	41.8%	58.2%
TOTAL	2022	665,558	270,523		372,827		22,208	102,304	D	40.6%	56.0%	42.0%	58.0%
TOTAL	2020	809,262	340,236		468,978		48	128,742	D	42.0%	58.0%	42.0%	58.0%
TOTAL	2018	631,677	245,372		333,208		53,097	87,836	D	38.8%	52.7%	42.4%	57.6%
TOTAL	2016	744,574	357,447		386,627		500	29,180	D	48.0%	51.9%	48.0%	52.0%
TOTAL	2014	592,346	228,059		305,230		59,057	77,171	D	38.5%	51.5%	42.8%	57.2%
TOTAL	2012	693,801	265,982		427,819			161,837	D	38.3%	61.7%	38.3%	61.7%

Note: An asterisk (*) denotes incumbent.

MAINE

GENERAL AND PRIMARY ELECTIONS

GENERAL ELECTIONS: OTHER VOTES

Governor   Other vote was 12,581 Independent (Sam Hunkler)

House   Other vote was:

    CD 1   160 Write-In (Scattered Write-Ins)

    CD 2   21,655 Independent (Tiffany Bond), 393 Write-In (Scattered Write-Ins)

MAINE

GENERAL AND PRIMARY ELECTIONS

2022 PRIMARY ELECTIONS: SUPPLEMENTARY INFORMATION

Primary	July 14, 2022	**Registration** (as of July 10, 2022 – includes 2,563 inactive registrants)	1,117,145	Democratic Republican Green Independent Libertarian Unenrolled	396,601 314,469 42,013 665 360,041

Primary Type Semi-open—Registered voters in a political party could participate only in their party's primary. "Unenrolled" and new voters could vote in either party's primary by enrolling in that party on primary day.

	REPUBLICAN PRIMARIES			DEMOCRATIC PRIMARIES		
Governor	LePage, Paul R. Write-In *TOTAL*	59,713 5,971 *65,684*	90.9% 9.1%	Mills, Janet T.* Write-In *TOTAL*	69,422 4,889 *74,311*	93.4% 6.6%
Congressional District 1	Thelander, Edwin *TOTAL*	22,346 *22,346*	100.0%	Pingree, Chellie* *TOTAL*	43,007 *43,007*	100.0%
Congressional District 2	Poliquin, Bruce L. Caruso, Elizabeth Michelle *TOTAL*	22,149 14,699 *36,848*	60.1% 39.9%	Golden, Jared* *TOTAL*	25,684 *25,684*	100.0%

Note: An asterisk (*) denotes incumbent.

MARYLAND

Statewide Races

In Maryland, the most visible 2022 contest was the race for governor. If Larry Hogan, a popular moderate Republican who typically scored high approval ratings even with Democrats, had been allowed to seek a third term, he would have been a formidable general election candidate. But under Maryland law, he was barred from running in 2022, giving Democrats a top pick-up opportunity.

The early Democratic frontrunner was state Comptroller Peter Franchot. When Franchot won a fourth term as Comptroller in 2018, he got more votes than any other statewide candidate. But Franchot, when campaigning for a promotion, was not especially charismatic on the stump. Later entrants who would become notable contenders were Thomas Perez and Wes Moore. Moore won the primary with just over 32%. He ran well in the Baltimore area and took nearly 50% in Prince George's County, a large Black-majority county east of the nation's capital.

Already underdogs to hold the governorship in normally blue Maryland, Republicans did not prioritize electability when choosing a nominee. They nominated far-right state Delegate Dan Cox, a Trump candidate, over Hogan's choice.

Hogan did not make an endorsement in the general election and Moore heavily outspent Cox. In the primary, Moore won with 32.4% of the vote – in the general election, he won by a 32.4-point margin. Moore carried the same ten localities that Joe Biden won two years earlier. Notably, in Cox's home county, Frederick, a blue-trending county north of Montgomery, Moore's 10.3-point margin represented a slight increase from Biden's 9.7-point margin.

In the Senate race, which almost seemed like an afterthought, Democratic Sen. Chris Van Hollen won a second term by 32 points. In almost every county, his margin was within a few points of Moore's.

House Races

In Maryland, a state with a notoriously ugly eight-seat map, Democrats passed a map containing eight Biden-won seats, up from seven on the outgoing map. Legislators enacted it over Hogan's veto. Litigation followed, with Fair Maps Maryland, an anti-gerrymandering group led by Hogan, challenging the maps. A state judge agreed with the plaintiffs. Rather than appealing the ruling, Democratic legislators produced a visually cleaner map that contained seven Biden-won seats. Under the second plan, the Eastern Shore-based 1st District stayed a Trump-won seat. Democrats also made the 6th District, which pairs part of Montgomery County with western Maryland, more competitive. These concessions were enough for Hogan, who signed the new map.

With a more marginal seat, Democratic Rep. Dave Trone won reelection in the 6th District by a 55%–45% margin, essentially matching Biden's showing there in 2020. None of the other Democratic-held seats were especially competitive. As national Democrats wrote off the race, 1st District Republican Andy Harris received as spirited challenge from Democrat Heather Mizeur. A former state legislator from Montgomery County, with a liberal record, Mizeur moved to the Eastern Shore and, on the campaign trail, took on a more moderate tone. In a district that Trump carried 56%–42% in 2020, Harris won by a lesser 54%–43%.

MARYLAND
Congressional districts first established for elections held in 2022
8 members

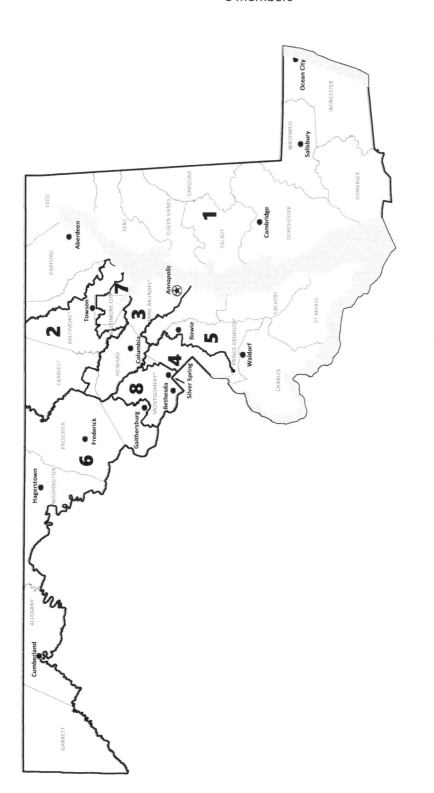

The city of Baltimore City is an independent city that is treated as a county equivalent.

*Asterisk indicates a county whose boundaries include parts of two or more congressional districts.

MARYLAND

GOVERNOR
Larry Hogan (R). Reelected 2022 to a four-year term. Previously elected 2018, 2014.

SENATORS (2 Democrats)
Benjamin L. Cardin (D). Reelected 2018 to a six-year term. Previously elected 2012, 2006.

Chris Van Hollen Jr. (D). Reelected 2022 to a six-year term. Previously elected 2016.

REPRESENTATIVES (1 Republican, 7 Democrats)
1. Andy Harris (R)
2. C. A. Dutch Ruppersberger (D)
3. John P. Sarbanes (D)
4. Glenn Ivey (D)
5. Steny H. Hoyer (D)
6. David Trone (D)
7. Kweisi Mfume (D)
8. Jamie Raskin (D)

POSTWAR VOTE FOR PRESIDENT

Year	Total Vote	Republican Vote	Republican Candidate	Democratic Vote	Democratic Candidate	Other Vote	Rep.-Dem. Plurality	Total Vote Rep.	Total Vote Dem.	Major Vote Rep.	Major Vote Dem.
2020	3,037,030	976,414	Trump, Donald J.*	1,985,023	Biden, Joseph R. Jr.	75,593	1,008,609 D	32.2%	65.4%	33.0%	67.0%
2016**	2,781,446	943,169	Trump, Donald J.	1,677,928	Clinton, Hillary Rodham	160,349	734,759 D	33.9%	60.3%	36.0%	64.0%
2012	2,707,327	971,869	Romney, W. Mitt	1,677,844	Obama, Barack H.*	57,614	705,975 D	35.9%	62.0%	36.7%	63.3%
2008	2,631,596	959,862	McCain, John S. III	1,629,467	Obama, Barack H.	42,267	669,605 D	36.5%	61.9%	37.1%	62.9%
2004	2,386,678	1,024,703	Bush, George W.*	1,334,493	Kerry, John F.	27,482	309,790 D	42.9%	55.9%	43.4%	56.6%
2000**	2,020,480	813,797	Bush, George W.	1,140,782	Gore, Albert Jr.	65,901	326,985 D	40.3%	56.5%	41.6%	58.4%
1996**	1,780,870	681,530	Dole, Robert "Bob"	966,207	Clinton, Bill*	133,133	284,677 D	38.3%	54.3%	41.4%	58.6%
1992**	1,985,046	707,094	Bush, George H.*	988,571	Clinton, Bill	289,381	281,477 D	35.6%	49.8%	41.7%	58.3%
1988	1,714,358	876,167	Bush, George H.	826,304	Dukakis, Michael S.	11,887	49,863 R	51.1%	48.2%	51.5%	48.5%
1984	1,675,873	879,918	Reagan, Ronald*	787,935	Mondale, Walter F.	8,020	91,983 R	52.5%	47.0%	52.8%	47.2%
1980**	1,540,496	680,606	Reagan, Ronald	726,161	Carter, Jimmy*	133,729	45,555 D	44.2%	47.1%	48.4%	51.6%
1976	1,439,897	672,661	Ford, Gerald R.*	759,612	Carter, Jimmy	7,624	86,951 D	46.7%	52.8%	47.0%	53.0%
1972	1,353,812	829,305	Nixon, Richard M.*	505,781	McGovern, George S.	18,726	323,524 R	61.3%	37.4%	62.1%	37.9%
1968**	1,235,039	517,995	Nixon, Richard M.	538,310	Humphrey, Hubert Horatio Jr.	178,734	20,315 D	41.9%	43.6%	49.0%	51.0%
1964	1,116,457	385,495	Goldwater, Barry M. Sr.	730,912	Johnson, Lyndon B.*	50	345,417 D	34.5%	65.5%	34.5%	65.5%
1960	1,055,349	489,538	Nixon, Richard M.	565,808	Kennedy, John F.	3	76,270 D	46.4%	53.6%	46.4%	53.6%
1956	932,827	559,738	Eisenhower, Dwight D.*	372,613	Stevenson, Adlai E. II	476	187,125 R	60.0%	39.9%	60.0%	40.0%
1952	902,074	499,424	Eisenhower, Dwight D.	395,337	Stevenson, Adlai E. II	7,313	104,087 R	55.4%	43.8%	55.8%	44.2%
1948	596,748	294,814	Dewey, Thomas E.	286,521	Truman, Harry S.*	15,413	8,293 R	49.4%	48.0%	50.7%	49.3%

Note: An asterisk (*) denotes incumbent. **In past elections, the other vote included: 2016 - 79,605 Libertarian (Gary Johnson); 2000 - 53,768 Green (Ralph Nader); 1996 - 115,812 Reform (Ross Perot); 1992 - 281,414 Independent (Perot); 1980 - 119,537 Independent (John Anderson); 1968 - 178,734 American Independent (George Wallace).

MARYLAND

POSTWAR VOTE FOR GOVERNOR

Year	Total Vote	Republican Vote	Republican Candidate	Democratic Vote	Democratic Candidate	Other Vote	Rep.-Dem. Plurality	Total Vote Rep.	Total Vote Dem.	Major Vote Rep.	Major Vote Dem.
2022	2,005,223	644,000	Cox, Dan	1,293,944	Moore, Wes	67,279	649,944 D	32.1%	64.5%	33.2%	66.8%
2018	2,304,512	1,275,644	Hogan, Larry*	1,002,639	Jealous, Ben	26,229	273,005 R	55.4%	43.5%	56.0%	44.0%
2014	1,733,177	884,400	Hogan, Larry	818,890	Brown, Anthony G.	29,887	65,510 R	51.0%	47.2%	51.9%	48.1%
2010	1,857,880	776,319	Ehrlich, Robert L. "Bob" Jr.	1,044,961	O'Malley, Martin*	36,600	268,642 D	41.8%	56.2%	42.6%	57.4%
2006	1,788,316	825,464	Ehrlich, Robert L. "Bob" Jr.*	942,279	O'Malley, Martin	20,573	116,815 D	46.2%	52.7%	46.7%	53.3%
2002	1,706,179	879,592	Ehrlich, Robert L. "Bob" Jr.	813,422	Townsend, Kathleen Kennedy	13,165	66,170 R	51.6%	47.7%	52.0%	48.0%
1998	1,535,978	688,357	Sauerbrey, Ellen R.	846,972	Glendening, Parris N.*	649	158,615 D	44.8%	55.1%	44.8%	55.2%
1994	1,410,300	702,101	Sauerbrey, Ellen R.	708,094	Glendening, Parris N.	105	5,993 D	49.8%	50.2%	49.8%	50.2%
1990	1,111,088	446,980	Shepard, William S.	664,015	Schaefer, William D.*	93	217,035 D	40.2%	59.8%	40.2%	59.8%
1986	1,101,476	194,185	Mooney, Thomas J.	907,291	Schaefer, William D.		713,106 D	17.6%	82.4%	17.6%	82.4%
1982	1,139,149	432,826	Pascal, Robert A.	705,910	Hughes, Harry R.*	413	273,084 D	38.0%	62.0%	38.0%	62.0%
1978	1,011,963	293,635	Beall, John Glenn Jr.	718,328	Hughes, Harry R.		424,693 D	29.0%	71.0%	29.0%	71.0%
1974	949,097	346,449	Gore, Louise	602,648	Mandel, Marvin*		256,199 D	36.5%	63.5%	36.5%	63.5%
1970	973,099	314,336	Blair, C. Stanley	639,579	Mandel, Marvin*	19,184	325,243 D	32.3%	65.7%	33.0%	67.0%
1966	919,760	455,318	Agnew, Spiro T.	373,543	Mahoney, George P.	90,899	81,775 R	49.5%	40.6%	54.9%	45.1%
1962	769,347	341,271	Small, Frank Jr.	428,071	Tawes, J. Millard*	5	86,800 D	44.4%	55.6%	44.4%	55.6%
1958	763,234	278,173	Devereux, James Patrick	485,061	Tawes, J. Millard		206,888 D	36.4%	63.6%	36.4%	63.6%
1954	700,484	381,451	McKeldin, Theodore R.*	319,033	Byrd, Harry Clifton		62,418 R	54.5%	45.5%	54.5%	45.5%
1950	645,631	369,807	McKeldin, Theodore R.	275,824	Lane, William Preston*		93,983 R	57.3%	42.7%	57.3%	42.7%
1946	489,836	221,752	McKeldin, Theodore R.	268,084	Lane, William Preston		46,332 D	45.3%	54.7%	45.3%	54.7%

Note: An asterisk (*) denotes incumbent.

POSTWAR VOTE FOR SENATOR

Year	Total Vote	Republican Vote	Republican Candidate	Democratic Vote	Democratic Candidate	Other Vote	Rep.-Dem. Plurality	Total Vote Rep.	Total Vote Dem.	Major Vote Rep.	Major Vote Dem.
2022	2,002,336	682,293	Chaffee, Chris	1,316,897	Van Hollen, Chris Jr.*	3,146	634,604 D	34.1%	65.8%	34.1%	65.9%
2018	2,299,889	697,017	Campbell, Tony	1,491,614	Cardin, Benjamin L.*	111,258	794,597 D	30.3%	64.9%	31.8%	68.2%
2016	2,726,170	972,557	Szeliga, Kathy	1,659,907	Van Hollen, Chris Jr.	93,706	687,350 D	35.7%	60.9%	36.9%	63.1%
2012**	2,633,234	693,291	Bongino, Daniel John	1,474,028	Cardin, Benjamin L.*	465,915	780,737 D	26.3%	56.0%	32.0%	68.0%
2010	1,833,858	655,666	Wartotz, Eric	1,140,531	Mikulski, Barbara A.*	37,661	484,865 D	35.8%	62.2%	36.5%	63.5%
2006	1,781,139	787,182	Steele, Michael	965,477	Cardin, Benjamin L.	28,480	178,295 D	44.2%	54.2%	44.9%	55.1%
2004	2,323,183	783,055	Pipkin, Edward J.	1,504,691	Mikulski, Barbara A.*	35,437	721,636 D	33.7%	64.8%	34.2%	65.8%
2000	1,946,898	715,178	Rappaport, Paul H.	1,230,013	Sarbanes, Paul S.*	1,707	514,835 D	36.7%	63.2%	36.8%	63.2%
1998	1,507,447	444,637	Pierpont, Ross Z.	1,062,810	Mikulski, Barbara A.*		618,173 D	29.5%	70.5%	29.5%	70.5%
1994	1,369,104	559,908	Brock, William E.	809,125	Sarbanes, Paul S.*	71	249,217 D	40.9%	59.1%	40.9%	59.1%
1992	1,841,735	533,688	Keyes, Alan	1,307,610	Mikulski, Barbara A.*	437	773,922 D	29.0%	71.0%	29.0%	71.0%
1988	1,617,065	617,537	Keyes, Alan	999,166	Sarbanes, Paul S.*	362	381,629 D	38.2%	61.8%	38.2%	61.8%
1986	1,112,637	437,411	Chavez, Linda	675,225	Mikulski, Barbara A.	1	237,814 D	39.3%	60.7%	39.3%	60.7%
1982	1,114,690	407,334	Hogan, Lawrence J.	707,356	Sarbanes, Paul S.*		300,022 D	36.5%	63.5%	36.5%	63.5%
1980	1,286,088	850,970	Mathias, Charles McCurdy Jr.*	435,118	Conroy, Edward T.		415,852 R	66.2%	33.8%	66.2%	33.8%
1976	1,365,568	530,439	Beall, John Glenn Jr.*	772,101	Sarbanes, Paul S.	63,028	241,662 D	38.8%	56.5%	40.7%	59.3%
1974	877,786	503,223	Mathias, Charles McCurdy Jr.*	374,563	Mikulski, Barbara A.		128,660 R	57.3%	42.7%	57.3%	42.7%
1970	956,370	484,960	Beall, John Glenn Jr.	460,422	Tydings, Joseph D.*	10,988	24,538 R	50.7%	48.1%	51.3%	48.7%
1968**	1,133,727	541,893	Mathias, Charles McCurdy Jr.	443,367	Brewster, Daniel B.*	148,467	98,526 R	47.8%	39.1%	55.0%	45.0%
1964	1,081,049	402,393	Beall, James Glenn*	678,649	Tydings, Joseph D.	7	276,256 D	37.2%	62.8%	37.2%	62.8%
1962	708,855	269,131	Miller, Edward T.	439,723	Brewster, Daniel B.	1	170,592 D	38.0%	62.0%	38.0%	62.0%
1958	749,291	382,021	Beall, James Glenn*	367,270	D'Alesandro, Thomas Jr.		14,751 R	51.0%	49.0%	51.0%	49.0%
1956	892,167	473,059	Butler, John Marshall*	419,108	Mahoney, George P.		53,951 R	53.0%	47.0%	53.0%	47.0%
1952	856,193	449,823	Beall, James Glenn	406,370	Mahoney, George P.		43,453 R	52.5%	47.5%	52.5%	47.5%
1950	615,614	326,291	Butler, John Marshall	283,180	Tydings, Millard E.*	6,143	43,111 R	53.0%	46.0%	53.5%	46.5%
1946	472,232	235,000	Markey, David John	237,232	O'Conor, Herbert R.		2,232 D	49.8%	50.2%	49.8%	50.2%

Note: An asterisk (*) denotes incumbent. **In past elections, the other vote included: 2012 - 430,934 Independent (S. Rob Sobhani); 1968 - 148,467 Independent (George P. Mahoney).

MARYLAND
GOVERNOR 2022

2020 Census Population	County	Total Vote	Republican (Cox)	Democratic (Moore)	Other	Rep.-Dem. Plurality		Total Vote Rep.	Total Vote Dem.	Major Vote Rep.	Major Vote Dem.
70,473	ALLEGANY	21,697	14,145	6,796	756	7,349	R	65.2%	31.3%	67.5%	32.5%
580,939	ANNE ARUNDEL	216,023	83,823	123,929	8,271	40,106	D	38.8%	57.4%	40.3%	59.7%
828,241	BALTIMORE	270,912	88,971	172,494	9,447	83,523	D	32.8%	63.7%	34.0%	66.0%
591,025	BALTIMORE CITY	145,009	12,309	126,768	5,932	114,459	D	8.5%	87.4%	8.9%	91.1%
92,797	CALVERT	37,577	19,668	16,757	1,152	2,911	R	52.3%	44.6%	54.0%	46.0%
33,496	CAROLINE	10,729	6,869	3,447	413	3,422	R	64.0%	32.1%	66.6%	33.4%
168,996	CARROLL	71,887	40,683	28,117	3,087	12,566	R	56.6%	39.1%	59.1%	40.9%
103,108	CECIL	33,067	19,873	11,992	1,202	7,881	R	60.1%	36.3%	62.4%	37.6%
164,018	CHARLES	54,510	15,830	37,367	1,313	21,537	D	29.0%	68.6%	29.8%	70.2%
31,955	DORCHESTER	11,493	6,377	4,715	401	1,662	R	55.5%	41.0%	57.5%	42.5%
261,206	FREDERICK	106,608	46,040	56,992	3,576	10,952	D	43.2%	53.5%	44.7%	55.3%
29,058	GARRETT	11,305	8,381	2,507	417	5,874	R	74.1%	22.2%	77.0%	23.0%
256,399	HARFORD	103,346	53,962	45,222	4,162	8,740	R	52.2%	43.8%	54.4%	45.6%
327,213	HOWARD	130,291	34,514	91,031	4,746	56,517	D	26.5%	69.9%	27.5%	72.5%
19,455	KENT	8,463	3,791	4,394	278	603	D	44.8%	51.9%	46.3%	53.7%
1,051,715	MONTGOMERY	343,371	64,507	269,072	9,792	204,565	D	18.8%	78.4%	19.3%	80.7%
907,925	PRINCE GEORGES	240,908	20,045	214,971	5,892	194,926	D	8.3%	89.2%	8.5%	91.5%
50,635	QUEEN ANNES	22,899	13,123	8,913	863	4,210	R	57.3%	38.9%	59.6%	40.4%
25,663	SOMERSET	6,829	4,128	2,491	210	1,637	R	60.4%	36.5%	62.4%	37.6%
113,763	ST. MARYS	37,703	21,150	15,057	1,496	6,093	R	56.1%	39.9%	58.4%	41.6%
37,249	TALBOT	17,646	7,935	9,116	595	1,181	D	45.0%	51.7%	46.5%	53.5%
151,544	WASHINGTON	48,853	28,547	18,727	1,579	9,820	R	58.4%	38.3%	60.4%	39.6%
103,987	WICOMICO	30,296	15,362	13,873	1,061	1,489	R	50.7%	45.8%	52.5%	47.5%
52,568	WORCESTER	23,801	13,967	9,196	638	4,771	R	58.7%	38.6%	60.3%	39.7%
6,053,428	TOTAL	2,005,223	644,000	1,293,944	67,279	649,944	D	32.1%	64.5%	33.2%	66.8%

MARYLAND
SENATOR 2022

2020 Census Population	County	Total Vote	Republican (Chaffee)	Democratic (Van Hollen)	Other	Rep.-Dem. Plurality		Total Vote Rep.	Total Vote Dem.	Major Vote Rep.	Major Vote Dem.
70,473	ALLEGANY	21,587	14,326	7,244	17	7,082	R	66.4%	33.6%	66.4%	33.6%
580,939	ANNE ARUNDEL	215,544	91,471	123,696	377	32,225	D	42.4%	57.4%	42.5%	57.5%
828,241	BALTIMORE	273,126	97,307	175,417	402	78,110	D	35.6%	64.2%	35.7%	64.3%
591,025	BALTIMORE CITY	143,386	13,849	129,257	280	115,408	D	9.7%	90.1%	9.7%	90.3%
92,797	CALVERT	37,426	20,382	17,007	37	3,375	R	54.5%	45.4%	54.5%	45.5%
33,496	CAROLINE	10,656	7,054	3,586	16	3,468	R	66.2%	33.7%	66.3%	33.7%
168,996	CARROLL	71,626	43,761	27,775	90	15,986	R	61.1%	38.8%	61.2%	38.8%
103,108	CECIL	32,913	20,725	12,132	56	8,593	R	63.0%	36.9%	63.1%	36.9%
164,018	CHARLES	54,574	16,207	38,270	97	22,063	D	29.7%	70.1%	29.8%	70.2%
31,955	DORCHESTER	11,473	6,511	4,947	15	1,564	R	56.8%	43.1%	56.8%	43.2%
261,206	FREDERICK	106,233	47,406	58,708	119	11,302	D	44.6%	55.3%	44.7%	55.3%
29,058	GARRETT	11,262	8,647	2,608	7	6,039	R	76.8%	23.2%	76.8%	23.2%
256,399	HARFORD	103,136	57,713	45,273	150	12,440	R	56.0%	43.9%	56.0%	44.0%
327,213	HOWARD	130,052	37,617	92,205	230	54,588	D	28.9%	70.9%	29.0%	71.0%
19,455	KENT	8,425	3,950	4,461	14	511	D	46.9%	52.9%	47.0%	53.0%
1,051,715	MONTGOMERY	343,072	65,956	276,482	634	210,526	D	19.2%	80.6%	19.3%	80.7%
907,925	PRINCE GEORGES	240,251	21,127	218,726	398	197,599	D	8.8%	91.0%	8.8%	91.2%
50,635	QUEEN ANNES	22,805	14,064	8,710	31	5,354	R	61.7%	38.2%	61.8%	38.2%
25,663	SOMERSET	6,807	4,146	2,656	5	1,490	R	60.9%	39.0%	61.0%	39.0%
113,763	ST. MARYS	37,568	21,869	15,656	43	6,213	R	58.2%	41.7%	58.3%	41.7%

MARYLAND
SENATOR 2022

2020 Census Population	County	Total Vote	Republican (Chaffee)	Democratic (Van Hollen)	Other	Rep.-Dem. Plurality	Total Vote Rep.	Total Vote Dem.	Major Vote Rep.	Major Vote Dem.
37,249	TALBOT	17,589	8,548	9,028	13	480 D	48.6%	51.3%	48.6%	51.4%
151,544	WASHINGTON	48,556	29,072	19,420	64	9,652 R	59.9%	40.0%	60.0%	40.0%
103,987	WICOMICO	30,432	16,104	14,296	32	1,808 R	52.9%	47.0%	53.0%	47.0%
52,568	WORCESTER	23,837	14,481	9,337	19	5,144 R	60.8%	39.2%	60.8%	39.2%
6,053,428	TOTAL	2,002,336	682,293	1,316,897	3,146	634,604 D	34.1%	65.8%	34.1%	65.9%

MARYLAND
HOUSE OF REPRESENTATIVES

CD	Year	Total Vote	Rep. Vote	Republican Candidate	Dem. Vote	Democratic Candidate	Other Vote	Rep.-Dem. Plurality	Total Rep.	Total Dem.	Major Rep.	Major Dem.
1	2022	293,358	159,673	HARRIS, ANDY*	126,511	MIZEUR, HEATHER	7,174	33,162 R	54.4%	43.1%	55.8%	44.2%
1	2020	395,524	250,901	HARRIS, ANDY*	143,877	MASON, MIA	746	107,024 R	63.4%	36.4%	63.6%	36.4%
1	2018	306,186	183,662	HARRIS, ANDY*	116,631	COLVIN, JESSE	5,893	67,031 R	60.0%	38.1%	61.2%	38.8%
1	2016	362,097	242,574	HARRIS, ANDY*	103,622	WERNER, JOSEPH	15,901	138,952 R	67.0%	28.6%	70.1%	29.9%
1	2014	250,418	176,342	HARRIS, ANDY*	73,843	TILGHMAN, BILL	233	102,499 R	70.4%	29.5%	70.5%	29.5%
1	2012	337,760	214,204	HARRIS, ANDY*	92,812	ROSEN, WENDY	30,744	121,392 R	63.4%	27.5%	69.8%	30.2%
2	2022	268,434	109,075	AMBROSE, NICOLEE	158,998	RUPPERSBERGER, C. A. DUTCH*	361	49,923 D	40.6%	59.2%	40.7%	59.3%
2	2020	332,026	106,355	SALLING, JOHNNY RAY	224,836	RUPPERSBERGER, C. A. DUTCH*	835	118,481 D	32.0%	67.7%	32.1%	67.9%
2	2018	253,302	77,782	MATORY, LIZ	167,201	RUPPERSBERGER, C. A. DUTCH*	8,319	89,419 D	30.7%	66.0%	31.7%	68.3%
2	2016	309,480	102,577	MCDONOUGH, PATRICK L.	192,183	RUPPERSBERGER, C. A. DUTCH*	14,720	89,606 D	33.1%	62.1%	34.8%	65.2%
2	2014	196,354	70,411	BANACH, DAVID	120,412	RUPPERSBERGER, C. A. DUTCH*	5,531	50,001 D	35.9%	61.3%	36.9%	63.1%
2	2012	295,940	92,071	JACOBS, NANCY C.	194,088	RUPPERSBERGER, C. A. DUTCH*	9,781	102,017 D	31.1%	65.6%	32.2%	67.8%
3	2022	291,602	115,801	MORGAN, YURIPZY	175,514	SARBANES, JOHN P.*	287	59,713 D	39.7%	60.2%	39.8%	60.2%
3	2020	373,206	112,117	ANTHONY, CHARLES	260,358	SARBANES, JOHN P.*	731	148,241 D	30.0%	69.8%	30.1%	69.9%
3	2018	292,880	82,774	ANTHONY, CHARLES	202,407	SARBANES, JOHN P.*	7,699	119,633 D	28.3%	69.1%	29.0%	71.0%
3	2016	339,675	115,048	PLASTER, MARK	214,640	SARBANES, JOHN P.*	9,987	99,592 D	33.9%	63.2%	34.9%	65.1%
3	2014	215,946	87,029	LONG, CHARLES A.	128,594	SARBANES, JOHN P.*	323	41,565 D	40.3%	59.5%	40.4%	59.6%
3	2012	319,859	94,549	KNOWLES, ERIC DELANO	213,747	SARBANES, JOHN P.*	11,563	119,198 D	29.6%	66.8%	30.7%	69.3%
4	2022	160,009	15,441	WARNER, JEFF	144,168	IVEY, GLENN F.	400	128,727 D	9.7%	90.1%	9.7%	90.3%
4	2020	354,529	71,671	MCDERMOTT, GEORGE E.	282,119	BROWN, ANTHONY G.*	739	210,448 D	20.2%	79.6%	20.3%	79.7%
4	2018	268,583	53,327	MCDERMOTT, GEORGE E.	209,642	BROWN, ANTHONY G.*	5,614	156,315 D	19.9%	78.1%	20.3%	79.7%
4	2016	320,650	68,670	MCDERMOTT, GEORGE E.	237,501	BROWN, ANTHONY G.	14,479	168,831 D	21.4%	74.1%	22.4%	77.6%
4	2014	191,837	54,217	HOYT, NANCY	134,628	EDWARDS, DONNA*	2,992	80,411 D	28.3%	70.2%	28.7%	71.3%
4	2012	311,512	64,560	LOUDON, FAITH M.	240,385	EDWARDS, DONNA*	6,567	175,825 D	20.7%	77.2%	21.2%	78.8%
5	2022	276,920	94,000	PALOMBI, CHRISTOPHER	182,478	HOYER, STENY H.*	442	88,478 D	33.9%	65.9%	34.0%	66.0%
5	2020	398,839	123,525	PALOMBI, CHRISTOPHER	274,210	HOYER, STENY H.*	1,104	150,685 D	31.0%	68.8%	31.1%	68.9%
5	2018	304,209	82,361	DEVINE, WILLIAM A. III	213,796	HOYER, STENY H.*	8,052	131,435 D	27.1%	70.3%	27.8%	72.2%
5	2016	360,634	105,931	ARNESS, MARK KENNETH	242,989	HOYER, STENY H.*	11,714	137,058 D	29.4%	67.4%	30.4%	69.6%
5	2014	226,040	80,752	CHAFFEE, CHRIS	144,725	HOYER, STENY H.*	563	63,973 D	35.7%	64.0%	35.8%	64.2%
5	2012	343,820	95,271	O'DONNELL, TONY	238,618	HOYER, STENY H.*	9,931	143,347 D	27.7%	69.4%	28.5%	71.5%
6	2022	256,398	115,771	PARROTT, NEIL CONRAD	140,295	TRONE, DAVID*	332	24,524 D	45.2%	54.7%	45.2%	54.8%
6	2020	366,434	143,599	PARROTT, NEIL CONRAD	215,540	TRONE, DAVID*	7,295	71,941 D	39.2%	58.8%	40.0%	60.0%
6	2018	277,084	105,209	HOEBER, AMIE	163,346	TRONE, DAVID	8,529	58,137 D	38.0%	59.0%	39.2%	60.8%
6	2016	331,973	133,081	HOEBER, AMIE	185,770	DELANEY, JOHN*	13,122	52,689 D	40.1%	56.0%	41.7%	58.3%
6	2014	190,536	91,930	BONGINO, DANIEL JOHN	94,704	DELANEY, JOHN*	3,902	2,774 D	48.2%	49.7%	49.3%	50.7%
6	2012	309,549	117,313	BARTLETT, ROSCOE G.*	181,921	DELANEY, JOHN	10,315	64,608 D	37.9%	58.8%	39.2%	60.8%
7	2022	184,801	32,737	COLLIER, SCOTT M.	151,640	MFUME, KWEISI*	424	118,903 D	17.7%	82.1%	17.8%	82.2%
7	2020	330,998	92,825	KLACIK, KIMBERLY	237,084	MFUME, KWEISI*	1,089	144,259 D	28.0%	71.6%	28.1%	71.9%
7	2018	264,710	56,266	DAVIS, RICHMOND	202,345	CUMMINGS, ELIJAH E.*	6,099	146,079 D	21.3%	76.4%	21.8%	78.2%
7	2016	318,912	69,556	VAUGHN, CORROGAN R.	238,838	CUMMINGS, ELIJAH E.*	10,518	169,282 D	21.8%	74.9%	22.6%	77.4%
7	2014	206,809	55,860	VAUGHN, CORROGAN R.	144,639	CUMMINGS, ELIJAH E.*	6,310	88,779 D	27.0%	69.9%	27.9%	72.1%
7	2012	323,818	67,405	MIRABILE, FRANK C.	247,770	CUMMINGS, ELIJAH E.*	8,643	180,365 D	20.8%	76.5%	21.4%	78.6%

MARYLAND

HOUSE OF REPRESENTATIVES

CD	Year	Total Vote	Republican Vote	Republican Candidate	Democratic Vote	Democratic Candidate	Other Vote	Rep.-Dem. Plurality	Total Vote Rep.	Total Vote Dem.	Major Vote Rep.	Major Vote Dem.
8	2022	264,206	47,965	COLL, GREGORY THOMAS	211,842	RASKIN, JAMIE*	4,399	163,877 D	18.2%	80.2%	18.5%	81.5%
8	2020	402,614	127,157	COLL, GREGORY THOMAS	274,716	RASKIN, JAMIE*	741	147,559 D	31.6%	68.2%	31.6%	68.4%
8	2018	319,330	96,525	WALSH, JOHN	217,679	RASKIN, JAMIE*	5,126	121,154 D	30.2%	68.2%	30.7%	69.3%
8	2016	364,324	124,651	COX, DAN	220,657	RASKIN, JAMIE	19,016	96,006 D	34.2%	60.6%	36.1%	63.9%
8	2014	225,097	87,859	WALLACE, DAVE	136,722	VAN HOLLEN, CHRIS JR.*	516	48,863 D	39.0%	60.7%	39.1%	60.9%
8	2012	343,256	113,033	TIMMERMAN, KENNETH R.	217,531	VAN HOLLEN, CHRIS JR.*	12,692	104,498 D	32.9%	63.4%	34.2%	65.8%
TOTAL	2022	1,995,728	690,463		1,291,446		13,819	600,983 D	34.6%	64.7%	34.8%	65.2%
TOTAL	2020	2,954,170	1,028,150		1,912,740		13,280	884,590 D	34.8%	64.7%	35.0%	65.0%
TOTAL	2018	2,286,284	737,906		1,493,047		55,331	755,141 D	32.3%	65.3%	33.1%	66.9%
TOTAL	2016	2,707,745	962,088		1,636,200		109,457	674,112 D	35.5%	60.4%	37.0%	63.0%
TOTAL	2014	1,703,037	704,400		978,267		20,370	273,867 D	41.4%	57.4%	41.9%	58.1%
TOTAL	2012	2,585,514	858,406		1,626,872		100,236	768,466 D	33.2%	62.9%	34.5%	65.5%

Note: An asterisk (*) denotes incumbent.

MARYLAND

GENERAL AND PRIMARY ELECTIONS

GENERAL ELECTIONS: OTHER VOTES

Governor — Other vote was 30,101 Libertarian (David Lashar), 17,154 Working Class (David Harding), 14,580 Green (Nancy Wallace), 5,444 Write-In (Write-In)

Senate — Other vote was 3,146 Write-In (Write-Ins)

House — Other vote was:

CD 1	6,924 Libertarian (Daniel Thibeault), 250 Write-In (Scattered Write-Ins)
CD 2	361 Write-In (Scattered Write-Ins)
CD 3	287 Write-In (Scattered Write-Ins)
CD 4	400 Write-In (Scattered Write-Ins)
CD 5	442 Write-In (Scattered Write-Ins)
CD 6	332 Write-In (Scattered Write-Ins)
CD 7	424 Write-In (Scattered Write-Ins)
CD 8	4,125 Libertarian (Andres Garcia), 274 Write-In (Scattered Write-Ins)

2022 PRIMARY ELECTIONS: SUPPLEMENTARY INFORMATION

Primary July 19, 2022

Registration (as of July 19, 2022) 3,778,905

Democratic	2,227,703
Republican	987,476
Libertarian	10,396
Green	4,086
Working Class Party	2,456
Other	22,901
Unaffiliated	523,887

Primary Type Closed—Only registered Democrats and Republicans could vote in their party's primary.

MARYLAND

GENERAL AND PRIMARY ELECTIONS

	REPUBLICAN PRIMARIES			DEMOCRATIC PRIMARIES		
Senator	Chaffee, Chris	50,514	20.4%	Van Hollen, Chris Jr.*	535,014	80.8%
	Friend, Lorie R.	35,714	14.5%	Smith, Michelle L.	127,089	19.2%
	Thormann, John	33,290	13.5%			
	Perez, Joseph	26,359	10.7%			
	Davis, George	21,095	8.5%			
	Tarantin, James	20,514	8.3%			
	Hawkins, Reba A.	18,057	7.3%			
	McGreevey, Jon	18,057	7.3%			
	Puglisi, Todd A.	13,550	5.5%			
	Eze, Nnabu	9,917	4.0%			
	TOTAL	247,067		TOTAL	662,103	
Governor	Cox, Dan	153,423	52.0%	Moore, Wes	217,524	32.4%
	Schulz, Kelly	128,302	43.5%	Perez, Tom	202,175	30.1%
	Ficker, Robin	8,268	2.8%	Franchot, Peter	141,586	21.1%
	Werner, Joseph	5,075	1.7%	Baker, Rushern L. III	26,594	4.0%
				Gansler, Doug	25,481	3.8%
				King, John B. Jr.	24,882	3.7%
				Jain, Ashwani	13,784	2.1%
				Baron, Jon	11,880	1.8%
				Segal, Jerome "Jerry"	4,276	0.6%
				Jaffe, Ralph	2,978	0.4%
	TOTAL	295,068		TOTAL	671,160	
Congressional District 1	Harris, Andy*	67,933	100.0%	Mizeur, Heather	34,549	68.8%
				Harden, R. David	15,683	31.2%
	TOTAL	67,933		TOTAL	50,232	
Congressional District 2	Ambrose, Nicolee	12,201	32.3%	Ruppersberger, C. A. Dutch*	62,896	75.5%
	Wallace, Dave	7,643	20.2%	Croom, George	8,465	10.2%
	Geppi, Michael A.	5,595	14.8%	Dent, Marques	7,728	9.3%
	Flowers, Bernard "Berney"	4,983	13.2%	Fusha, Liri	4,218	5.1%
	McNulty, Ellen "EJ"	4,204	11.1%			
	Griffin, Lance	3,192	8.4%			
	TOTAL	37,818		TOTAL	83,307	
Congressional District 3	Morgan, Yuripzy	13,198	33.6%	Sarbanes, John P.*	63,790	84.6%
	Kelley, Joe	8,924	22.7%	Beardsley, Ben R.	6,854	9.1%
	Pitocco, Antonio Patrizio	8,041	20.5%	Pretot, Jake	4,728	6.3%
	Harris, Thomas E. "Pinkston"	4,966	12.6%			
	Torres, Amal	4,171	10.6%			
	TOTAL	39,300		TOTAL	75,372	
Congressional District 4	Warner, Jeff	2,414	58.7%	Ivey, Glenn F.	42,791	51.8%
	McDermott, George E.	1,091	26.5%	Edwards, Donna	29,114	35.2%
	Loeb, Eric	607	14.8%	Angel, Angela	4,678	5.7%
				Allison, Tammy	1,726	2.1%
				Shelton, Kim A.	1,354	1.6%
				Holmes, Greg	1,024	1.2%
				Curtis, James Levi Jr.	763	0.9%
				Fogg, Matthew	663	0.8%
				McGhee, Robert K.	549	0.7%
	TOTAL	4,112		TOTAL	82,662	
Congressional District 5	Palombi, Christopher	24,423	67.5%	Hoyer, Steny H.*	68,729	71.3%
	Hoffman, Vanessa Marie	3,538	9.8%	Wilkes, Mckayla	18,403	19.1%
	Villanova, Tannis	2,445	6.8%	Washington, Keith	9,222	9.6%
	Lemon, Michael S.	1,818	5.0%			
	Jarboe-Duley, Toni	1,578	4.4%			
	Stevens, Patrick Lucky	1,344	3.7%			
	Cubero, Bryan DuVal	1,024	2.8%			
	TOTAL	36,170		TOTAL	96,354	

MARYLAND

GENERAL AND PRIMARY ELECTIONS

	REPUBLICAN PRIMARIES			DEMOCRATIC PRIMARIES		
Congressional District 6	Parrott, Neil Conrad	31,665	62.6%	Trone, David*	44,370	79.0%
	Foldi, Matthew	7,497	14.8%	Smilowitz, Ben	8,995	16.0%
	Roca, Mariela	3,858	7.6%	Gluck, George	2,789	5.0%
	Black, Colt M.	3,789	7.5%			
	Jenkins, Jonathan	3,406	6.7%			
	Poissonnier, Robert	400	0.8%			
	TOTAL	50,615		TOTAL	56,154	
Congressional District 7	Collier, Scott M.	2,873	34.6%	Mfume, Kweisi*	80,118	85.2%
	Sigley, Lorrie A.	2,245	27.1%	Davis, Tashi Kimandus	7,141	7.6%
	Pearson, Michael T.	1,906	23.0%	McNeal, Wayne	4,890	5.2%
	Bly, Raymond J.	1,271	15.3%	El, Elihu "Eli"	1,885	2.0%
	TOTAL	8,295		TOTAL	94,034	
Congressional District 8	Coll, Gregory Thomas	11,445	83.6%	Raskin, Jamie*	109,055	93.9%
	Yadeta, Michael	2,245	16.4%	Odulate, Andalib	7,075	6.1%
	TOTAL	13,690		TOTAL	116,130	

Note: An asterisk (*) denotes incumbent.

MASSACHUSETTS

Statewide Races

In its 2022 gubernatorial race, Massachusetts was essentially the New England version of Maryland: both deep blue states had popular, anti-Trump Republican governors who easily rode out the pro-Democratic 2018 cycle – but neither was on the ballot four years later.

First elected governor in 2014, Gov. Charlie Baker emerged as a leading moderate Republican. A Trump critic, Baker's approval ratings were often in the 70s in public polls, and he won reelection with two-thirds of the vote in 2018. In Boston proper, which has not given a Republican presidential nominee over 25 percent since 1988, he took nearly 50%.

But some of Baker's fellow Republicans were not as impressed with his postpartisanship. Before the governor declared his 2022 plans, he drew a primary challenger in State Rep. Geoff Diehl. In 2018, Diehl was the party's nominee against Democratic Sen. Elizabeth Warren – he took 36% but at least managed to carry his home county, Plymouth. Diehl quickly secured Trump's endorsement. In the Bay State, fewer than one in ten voters are registered Republicans. As Trump's endorsement seemed likely to carry weight with that bloc, Baker would have been reliant on independent voters backing him in a potential primary (the state's partisan primaries are open to unaffiliated voters). Shortly before Christmas 2021, Baker announced he would not run for reelection.

With Baker out, several top-tier Democratic prospects gave the race a look. But state Attorney General Maura Healey eventually won the Democratic primary in what amounted to a coronation. State Sen. Sonia Chang-Diaz, the only other candidate, dropped out before the early September primary but did so too late for her name to be removed from the ballot. Healey won with 85%.

In the general election, Massachusetts voters were not eager to support a Trump-aligned Republican. Healey led by wide margins in every public poll and eventually prevailed by 29 points, the best showing for a Democratic gubernatorial nominee since 1986. Plymouth was again Diehl's best county, but this time, he lost it by nine points. As an aside, Healey had some of the more memorable campaign items of the cycle. Before her time in public office, she played basketball professionally – her campaign put out buttons that read "My governor is a baller."

House Races

With nine Democratic-held seats, Massachusetts has the largest one-party delegation in the House. The legislature passed a plan that made few changes to the previous map, and Baker signed off on it. The most marginal district was the 9th, which includes the iconic, hook-shaped Cape Cod peninsula. Rep. Bill Keating (D, MA-9) won 59%–41%. On the other side of the commonwealth, western Massachusetts's 1st District offered a measure of intrigue. Rep. Richard Neal, the House delegation's most senior member and the sitting chairman of the powerful Ways and Means Committee, had a Republican opponent for the first time since 2010. Would Republicans be able to make much headway against Neal? The result, as most observers suspected, was "no." Neal won an 18th term by 23 points, matching Joe Biden's 2020 margin in the district.

MASSACHUSETTS
Congressional districts first established for elections held in 2022
9 members

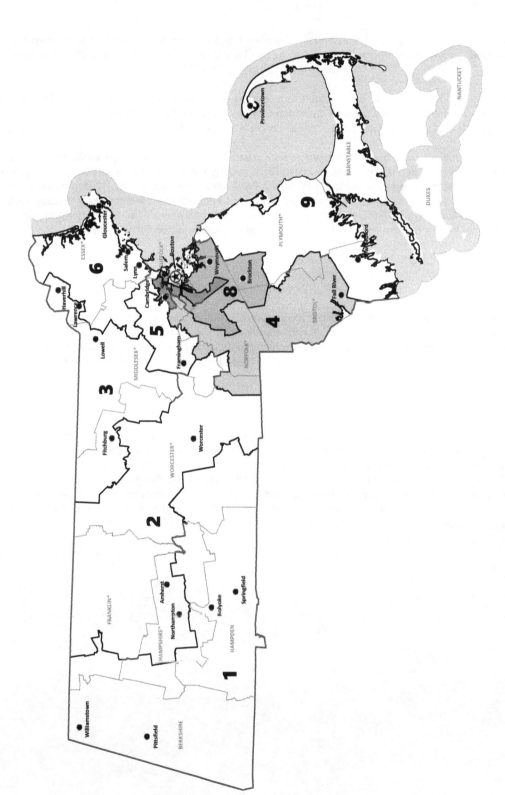

*Asterisk indicates a county whose boundaries include parts of two or more congressional districts.

CDs 4, 7, and 8 are highlighted for visibility. See Inset for Boston area.

MASSACHUSETTS

Greater Boston Area

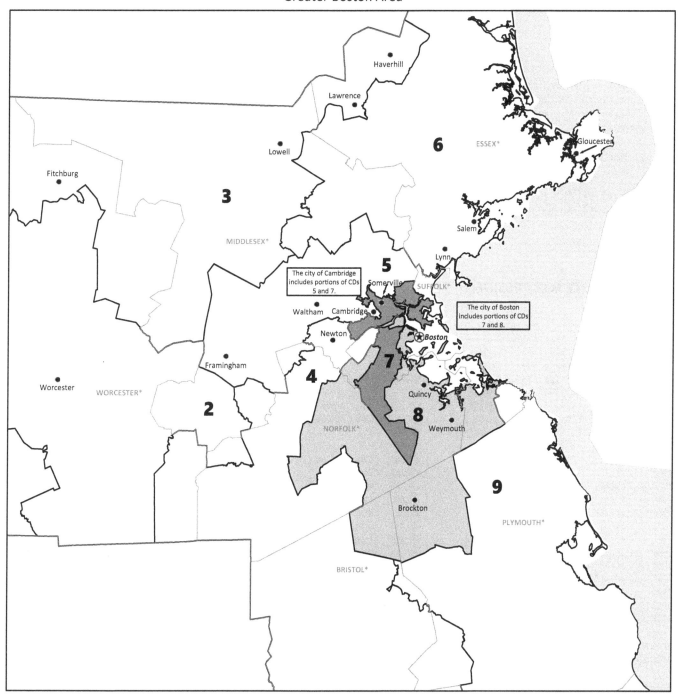

* Asterisk indicates a county whose boundaries include parts of two or more congressional districts.
CDs 7 and 8 are highlighted for visibility.

MASSACHUSETTS

GOVERNOR
Maura Healey (D). Elected 2022 to a four-year term.

SENATORS (2 Democrats)
Edward J. Markey (D). Reelected 2020 to a full six-year term. Previously elected 2014. First elected June 25, 2013, to serve the remainder of the term vacated by the January 2013 resignation of John Kerry to become secretary of state. William "Mo" Cowan (D) had been appointed on January 30, 2013, to fill the vacant seat until the June 2013 special election.

Elizabeth Warren (D). Reelected 2018 to a six-year term. Previously elected 2012.

REPRESENTATIVES (9 Democrats)
1. Richard E. Neal (D)
2. James McGovern (D)
3. Lori Trahan (D)
4. Jake Auchincloss (D)
5. Katherine M. Clark (D)
6. Seth Moulton (D)
7. Ayanna Pressley (D)
8. Stephen F. Lynch (D)
9. William Richard Keating (D)

POSTWAR VOTE FOR PRESIDENT

		Republican		Democratic		Other Vote	Rep.-Dem. Plurality	Percentage			
								Total Vote		Major Vote	
Year	Total Vote	Vote	Candidate	Vote	Candidate			Rep.	Dem.	Rep.	Dem.
2020	3,631,402	1,167,202	Trump, Donald J.*	2,382,202	Biden, Joseph R. Jr.	81,998	1,215,000 D	32.1%	65.6%	32.9%	67.1%
2016**	3,325,046	1,090,893	Trump, Donald J.	1,995,196	Clinton, Hillary Rodham	238,957	904,303 D	32.8%	60.0%	35.3%	64.7%
2012	3,167,767	1,188,314	Romney, W. Mitt	1,921,290	Obama, Barack H.*	58,163	732,976 D	37.5%	60.7%	38.2%	61.8%
2008	3,080,985	1,108,854	McCain, John S. III	1,904,097	Obama, Barack H.	68,034	795,243 D	36.0%	61.8%	36.8%	63.2%
2004	2,912,388	1,071,109	Bush, George W.*	1,803,800	Kerry, John F.	37,479	732,691 D	36.8%	61.9%	37.3%	62.7%
2000**	2,702,984	878,502	Bush, George W.	1,616,487	Gore, Albert Jr.	207,995	737,985 D	32.5%	59.8%	35.2%	64.8%
1996**	2,556,785	718,107	Dole, Robert "Bob"	1,571,763	Clinton, Bill*	266,915	853,656 D	28.1%	61.5%	31.4%	68.6%
1992**	2,773,700	805,049	Bush, George H.*	1,318,662	Clinton, Bill	649,989	513,613 D	29.0%	47.5%	37.9%	62.1%
1988	2,632,805	1,194,635	Bush, George H.	1,401,415	Dukakis, Michael S.	36,755	206,780 D	45.4%	53.2%	46.0%	54.0%
1984	2,559,453	1,310,936	Reagan, Ronald*	1,239,606	Mondale, Walter F.	8,911	71,330 R	51.2%	48.4%	51.4%	48.6%
1980**	2,524,298	1,057,631	Reagan, Ronald	1,053,802	Carter, Jimmy*	412,865	3,829 R	41.9%	41.7%	50.1%	49.9%
1976	2,547,558	1,030,276	Ford, Gerald R.*	1,429,475	Carter, Jimmy	87,807	399,199 D	40.4%	56.1%	41.9%	58.1%
1972	2,458,756	1,112,078	Nixon, Richard M.*	1,332,540	McGovern, George S.	14,138	220,462 D	45.2%	54.2%	45.5%	54.5%
1968**	2,331,752	766,844	Nixon, Richard M.	1,469,218	Humphrey, Hubert Horatio Jr.	95,690	702,374 D	32.9%	63.0%	34.3%	65.7%
1964	2,344,798	549,727	Goldwater, Barry M. Sr.	1,786,422	Johnson, Lyndon B.*	8,649	1,236,695 D	23.4%	76.2%	23.5%	76.5%
1960	2,469,480	976,750	Nixon, Richard M.	1,487,174	Kennedy, John F.	5,556	510,424 D	39.6%	60.2%	39.6%	60.4%
1956	2,348,506	1,393,197	Eisenhower, Dwight D.*	948,190	Stevenson, Adlai E. II	7,119	445,007 R	59.3%	40.4%	59.5%	40.5%
1952	2,383,398	1,292,325	Eisenhower, Dwight D.	1,083,525	Stevenson, Adlai E. II	7,548	208,800 R	54.2%	45.5%	54.4%	45.6%
1948	2,107,146	909,370	Dewey, Thomas E.	1,151,788	Truman, Harry S.*	43,988	242,418 D	43.2%	54.7%	44.1%	55.9%

Note: An asterisk (*) denotes incumbent. **In past elections, the other vote included: 2016 - 138,018 Libertarian (Gary Johnson); 2000 - 173,564 Green (Ralph Nader); 1996 - 227,217 Reform (Ross Perot); 1992 - 630,731 Independent (Perot); 1980 - 382,539 Independent (John Anderson); 1968 - 87,088 American Independent (George Wallace).

MASSACHUSETTS

POSTWAR VOTE FOR GOVERNOR

Year	Total Vote	Republican Vote	Republican Candidate	Democratic Vote	Democratic Candidate	Other Vote	Rep.-Dem. Plurality	Total Vote Rep. %	Total Vote Dem. %	Major Vote Rep. %	Major Vote Dem. %
2022	2,485,796	859,343	Diehl, Geoff	1,584,403	Healey, Maura	42,050	725,060 D	34.6%	63.7%	35.2%	64.8%
2018	2,674,615	1,781,341	Baker, Charles D.*	885,770	Gonzalez, Jay	7,504	895,571 R	66.6%	33.1%	66.8%	33.2%
2014	2,158,326	1,044,573	Baker, Charles D.	1,004,408	Coakley, Martha	109,345	40,165 R	48.4%	46.5%	51.0%	49.0%
2010	2,297,039	964,866	Baker, Charles D.	1,112,283	Patrick, Deval*	219,890	147,417 D	42.0%	48.4%	46.5%	53.5%
2006	2,219,779	784,342	Healey, Kerry	1,234,984	Patrick, Deval	200,453	450,642 D	35.3%	55.6%	38.8%	61.2%
2002	2,194,179	1,091,988	Romney, W. Mitt	985,981	O'Brien, Shannon P.	116,210	106,007 R	49.8%	44.9%	52.6%	47.4%
1998	1,903,336	967,160	Cellucci, Argeo Paul*	901,843	Harshbarger, Scott	34,333	65,317 R	50.8%	47.4%	51.7%	48.3%
1994	2,255,150	1,599,141	Weld, William F.*	636,138	Roosevelt, Mark	19,871	963,003 R	70.9%	28.2%	71.5%	28.5%
1990	2,342,927	1,175,817	Weld, William F.	1,099,878	Silber, John	67,232	75,939 R	50.2%	46.9%	51.7%	48.3%
1986	1,684,079	525,364	Kariotis, George	1,157,786	Dukakis, Michael S.*	929	632,422 D	31.2%	68.7%	31.2%	68.8%
1982	2,050,254	749,679	Sears, John W.	1,219,109	Dukakis, Michael S.	81,466	469,430 D	36.6%	59.5%	38.1%	61.9%
1978	1,962,251	926,072	Hatch, Francis W.	1,030,294	King, Edward J.	5,885	104,222 D	47.2%	52.5%	47.3%	52.7%
1974	1,854,798	784,353	Sargent, Francis W.*	992,284	Dukakis, Michael S.	78,161	207,931 D	42.3%	53.5%	44.1%	55.9%
1970	1,867,906	1,058,623	Sargent, Francis W.*	799,269	White, Kevin H.	10,014	259,354 R	56.7%	42.8%	57.0%	43.0%
1966**	2,041,177	1,277,358	Volpe, John A.*	752,720	McCormack, Edward J.	11,099	524,638 R	62.6%	36.9%	62.9%	37.1%
1964	2,340,130	1,176,462	Volpe, John A.	1,153,416	Bellotti, Francis X.	10,252	23,046 R	50.3%	49.3%	50.5%	49.5%
1962	2,109,089	1,047,891	Volpe, John A.*	1,053,322	Peabody, Endicott	7,876	5,431 D	49.7%	49.9%	49.9%	50.1%
1960	2,417,133	1,269,295	Volpe, John A.	1,130,810	Ward, Joseph D.	17,028	138,485 R	52.5%	46.8%	52.9%	47.1%
1958	1,899,117	818,463	Gibbons, Charles	1,067,020	Furcolo, Foster*	13,634	248,557 D	43.1%	56.2%	43.4%	56.6%
1956	2,339,884	1,096,759	Whittier, Sumner G.	1,234,618	Furcolo, Foster	8,507	137,859 D	46.9%	52.8%	47.0%	53.0%
1954	1,903,774	985,339	Herter, Christian A.*	910,087	Murphy, Robert F.	8,348	75,252 R	51.8%	47.8%	52.0%	48.0%
1952	2,356,298	1,175,955	Herter, Christian A.	1,161,499	Dever, Paul A.*	18,844	14,456 R	49.9%	49.3%	50.3%	49.7%
1950	1,910,180	824,069	Coolidge, Arthur W.	1,074,570	Dever, Paul A.*	11,541	250,501 D	43.1%	56.3%	43.4%	56.6%
1948	2,099,250	849,895	Bradford, Robert F.*	1,239,247	Dever, Paul A.	10,108	389,352 D	40.5%	59.0%	40.7%	59.3%
1946	1,683,452	911,152	Bradford, Robert F.	762,743	Tobin, Maurice J.*	9,557	148,409 R	54.1%	45.3%	54.4%	45.6%

Note: An asterisk (*) denotes incumbent. **The term of office of Massachusetts's governor was increased from two to four years effective with the 1966 election.

POSTWAR VOTE FOR SENATOR

Year	Total Vote	Republican Vote	Republican Candidate	Democratic Vote	Democratic Candidate	Other Vote	Rep.-Dem. Plurality	Total Vote Rep. %	Total Vote Dem. %	Major Vote Rep. %	Major Vote Dem. %
2020	3,564,136	1,177,765	O'Connor, Kevin	2,357,809	Markey, Edward J.*	28,562	1,180,044 D	33.0%	66.2%	33.3%	66.7%
2018	2,707,090	979,210	Diehl, Geoff	1,633,371	Warren, Elizabeth*	94,509	654,161 D	36.2%	60.3%	37.5%	62.5%
2014	2,084,972	791,950	Herr, Brian J.	1,289,944	Markey, Edward J.*	3,078	497,994 D	38.0%	61.9%	38.0%	62.0%
2013S**	1,177,790	525,307	Gomez, Gabriel E.	645,429	Markey, Edward J.	7,054	120,122 D	44.6%	54.8%	44.9%	55.1%
2012	3,156,553	1,458,048	Brown, Scott P.*	1,696,346	Warren, Elizabeth	2,159	238,298 D	46.2%	53.7%	46.2%	53.8%
2010S**	2,252,582	1,168,178	Brown, Scott P.	1,060,861	Coakley, Martha	23,543	107,317 R	51.9%	47.1%	52.4%	47.6%
2008	2,994,247	926,044	Beatty, Jeffrey K.	1,971,974	Kerry, John F.*	96,229	1,045,930 D	30.9%	65.9%	32.0%	68.0%
2006	2,165,490	661,532	Chase, Kenneth G.	1,500,738	Kennedy, Edward M.*	3,220	839,206 D	30.5%	69.3%	30.6%	69.4%
2002**	2,006,758			1,605,976	Kerry, John F.*	400,782	1,605,976 D		80.0%		100.0%
2000**	2,599,420	334,341	Robinson, Jack E. III	1,889,494	Kennedy, Edward M.*	375,585	1,555,153 D	12.9%	72.7%	15.0%	85.0%
1996	2,555,886	1,142,837	Weld, William F.	1,334,345	Kerry, John F.*	78,704	191,508 D	44.7%	52.2%	46.1%	53.9%
1994	2,179,964	894,005	Romney, W. Mitt	1,266,011	Kennedy, Edward M.*	19,948	372,006 D	41.0%	58.1%	41.4%	58.6%
1990	2,316,212	992,917	Rappaport, Jim	1,321,712	Kerry, John F.*	1,583	328,795 D	42.9%	57.1%	42.9%	57.1%
1988	2,606,225	884,267	Malone, Joseph D.	1,693,344	Kennedy, Edward M.*	28,614	809,077 D	33.9%	65.0%	34.3%	65.7%
1984	2,530,195	1,136,806	Shamie, Raymond	1,392,981	Kerry, John F.	408	256,175 D	44.9%	55.1%	44.9%	55.1%
1982	2,050,769	784,602	Shamie, Raymond	1,247,084	Kennedy, Edward M.*	19,083	462,482 D	38.3%	60.8%	38.6%	61.4%
1978	1,985,700	890,584	Brooke, Edward W. III*	1,093,283	Tsongas, Paul E.	1,833	202,699 D	44.8%	55.1%	44.9%	55.1%
1976	2,491,255	722,641	Robertson, Michael	1,726,657	Kennedy, Edward M.*	41,957	1,004,016 D	29.0%	69.3%	29.5%	70.5%
1972	2,370,676	1,505,932	Brooke, Edward W. III*	823,278	Droney, John J.	41,466	682,654 R	63.5%	34.7%	64.7%	35.3%
1970	1,935,607	715,978	Spaulding, Josiah A.	1,202,856	Kennedy, Edward M.*	16,773	486,878 D	37.0%	62.1%	37.3%	62.7%
1966	1,999,949	1,213,473	Brooke, Edward W. III	774,761	Peabody, Endicott	11,715	438,712 R	60.7%	38.7%	61.0%	39.0%
1964	2,312,028	587,663	Whitmore, Howard Jr.	1,716,907	Kennedy, Edward M.*	7,458	1,129,244 D	25.4%	74.3%	25.5%	74.5%
1962S**	2,097,085	877,669	Lodge, George C.	1,162,611	Kennedy, Edward M.	56,805	284,942 D	41.9%	55.4%	43.0%	57.0%
1960	2,417,813	1,358,556	Saltonstall, Leverett*	1,050,725	O'Connor, Thomas J. Jr.	8,532	307,831 R	56.2%	43.5%	56.4%	43.6%
1958	1,862,041	488,318	Celeste, Vincent J.	1,362,926	Kennedy, John F.*	10,797	874,608 D	26.2%	73.2%	26.4%	73.6%
1954	1,892,710	956,605	Saltonstall, Leverett*	927,899	Furcolo, Foster	8,206	28,706 R	50.5%	49.0%	50.8%	49.2%
1952	2,360,425	1,141,247	Lodge, Henry Cabot Jr.*	1,211,984	Kennedy, John F.	7,194	70,737 D	48.3%	51.3%	48.5%	51.5%
1948	2,055,798	1,088,475	Saltonstall, Leverett*	954,398	Fitzgerald, John I.	12,925	134,077 R	52.9%	46.4%	53.3%	46.7%
1946	1,662,063	989,736	Lodge, Henry Cabot Jr.	660,200	Walsh, David I.*	12,127	329,536 R	59.5%	39.7%	60.0%	40.0%

Note: An asterisk (*) denotes incumbent. **In past elections, the other vote included: 2002 - 369,807 Libertarian (Michael E. Cloud); 2000 - 308,748 Libertarian (Carla Howell). The Republican Party did not run a candidate in the 2002 Senate election. The 1962, 2010, and 2013 elections were for short terms to fill a vacancy; the 2010 election was held in January 2010.

MASSACHUSETTS
GOVERNOR 2022

2020 Census Population	County	Total Vote	Republican (Diehl)	Democratic (Healey)	Other	Rep.-Dem. Plurality	Total Vote Rep.	Total Vote Dem.	Major Vote Rep.	Major Vote Dem.
213,558	BARNSTABLE	117,842	46,011	70,163	1,668	24,152 D	39.0%	59.5%	39.6%	60.4%
125,118	BERKSHIRE	49,030	13,205	34,898	927	21,693 D	26.9%	71.2%	27.5%	72.5%
566,571	BRISTOL	183,390	81,033	98,969	3,388	17,936 D	44.2%	54.0%	45.0%	55.0%
17,365	DUKES	9,343	2,011	7,185	147	5,174 D	21.5%	76.9%	21.9%	78.1%
790,584	ESSEX	286,816	104,400	177,760	4,656	73,360 D	36.4%	62.0%	37.0%	63.0%
70,350	FRANKLIN	31,615	8,788	22,287	540	13,499 D	27.8%	70.5%	28.3%	71.7%
467,210	HAMPDEN	138,239	60,203	75,523	2,513	15,320 D	43.5%	54.6%	44.4%	55.6%
161,026	HAMPSHIRE	64,838	17,138	46,679	1,021	29,541 D	26.4%	72.0%	26.9%	73.1%
1,613,205	MIDDLESEX	605,766	169,707	426,054	10,005	256,347 D	28.0%	70.3%	28.5%	71.5%
11,444	NANTUCKET	4,903	1,553	3,262	88	1,709 D	31.7%	66.5%	32.3%	67.7%
708,325	NORFOLK	284,985	96,607	183,795	4,583	87,188 D	33.9%	64.5%	34.5%	65.5%
522,420	PLYMOUTH	214,794	95,669	115,810	3,315	20,141 D	44.5%	53.9%	45.2%	54.8%
803,156	SUFFOLK	201,428	38,886	159,232	3,310	120,346 D	19.3%	79.1%	19.6%	80.4%
832,339	WORCESTER	292,807	124,132	162,786	5,889	38,654 D	42.4%	55.6%	43.3%	56.7%
6,902,671	TOTAL	2,485,796	859,343	1,584,403	42,050	725,060 D	34.6%	63.7%	35.2%	64.8%

MASSACHUSETTS
HOUSE OF REPRESENTATIVES

CD	Year	Total Vote	Rep. Vote	Republican Candidate	Dem. Vote	Democratic Candidate	Other Vote	Rep.-Dem. Plurality	Total Rep.	Total Dem.	Major Rep.	Major Dem.
1	2022	256,399	98,386	MARTILLI, DEAN JAMES	157,635	NEAL, RICHARD E.*	378	59,249 D	38.4%	61.5%	38.4%	61.6%
1	2020	285,332			275,376	NEAL, RICHARD E.*	9,956	275,376 D		96.5%		100.0%
1	2018	216,900			211,790	NEAL, RICHARD E.*	5,110	211,790 D		97.6%		100.0%
1	2016	321,539			235,803	NEAL, RICHARD E.*	85,736	235,803 D		73.3%		100.0%
1	2014	171,110			167,612	NEAL, RICHARD E.*	3,498	167,612 D		98.0%		100.0%
1	2012	266,133			261,936	NEAL, RICHARD E.*	4,197	261,936 D		98.4%		100.0%
2	2022	272,871	91,956	SOSSA-PAQUETTE, JEFFREY ALLEN	180,639	MCGOVERN, JAMES*	276	88,683 D	33.7%	66.2%	33.7%	66.3%
2	2020	382,452	132,220	LOVVORN, TRACY LYN	249,854	MCGOVERN, JAMES*	378	117,634 D	34.6%	65.3%	34.6%	65.4%
2	2018	284,893	93,391	LOVVORN, TRACY LYN	191,332	MCGOVERN, JAMES*	170	97,941 D	32.8%	67.2%	32.8%	67.2%
2	2016	280,411			275,487	MCGOVERN, JAMES*	4,924	275,487 D		98.2%		100.0%
2	2014	172,745			169,640	MCGOVERN, JAMES*	3,105	169,640 D		98.2%		100.0%
2	2012	263,335			259,257	MCGOVERN, JAMES*	4,078	259,257 D		98.5%		100.0%
3	2022	243,301	88,585	TRAN, DEAN	154,496	TRAHAN, LORI*	220	65,911 D	36.4%	63.5%	36.4%	63.6%
3	2020	293,539			286,896	TRAHAN, LORI*	6,643	286,896 D		97.7%		100.0%
3	2018	279,327	93,445	GREEN, RICK	173,175	TRAHAN, LORI	12,707	79,730 D	33.5%	62.0%	35.0%	65.0%
3	2016	344,592	107,519	WOFFORD, ROSEANN EHRHARD	236,713	TSONGAS, NICOLA S.*	360	129,194 D	31.2%	68.7%	31.2%	68.8%
3	2014	220,946	81,638	WOFFORD, ROSEANN EHRHARD	139,104	TSONGAS, NICOLA S.*	204	57,466 D	36.9%	63.0%	37.0%	63.0%
3	2012	321,753	109,372	GOLNIK, JONATHAN A.	212,119	TSONGAS, NICOLA S.*	262	102,747 D	34.0%	65.9%	34.0%	66.0%
4	2022	208,279			201,882	AUCHINCLOSS, JAKE*	6,397	201,882 D		96.9%		100.0%
4	2020	412,823	160,474	HALL, JULIE	251,102	AUCHINCLOSS, JAKE	1,247	90,628 D	38.9%	60.8%	39.0%	61.0%
4	2018	251,016			245,289	KENNEDY, JOSEPH PATRICK III*	5,727	245,289 D		97.7%		100.0%
4	2016	379,213	113,055	ROSA, DAVID A.	265,823	KENNEDY, JOSEPH PATRICK III*	335	152,768 D	29.8%	70.1%	29.8%	70.2%
4	2014	188,098			184,158	KENNEDY, JOSEPH PATRICK III*	3,940	184,158 D		97.9%		100.0%
4	2012	362,245	129,936	BIELAT, SEAN	221,303	KENNEDY, JOSEPH PATRICK III	11,006	91,367 D	35.9%	61.1%	37.0%	63.0%
5	2022	275,671	71,491	COLARUSSO, CAROLINE	203,994	CLARK, KATHERINE M.*	186	132,503 D	25.9%	74.0%	26.0%	74.0%
5	2020	396,183	101,351	COLARUSSO, CAROLINE	294,427	CLARK, KATHERINE M.*	405	193,076 D	25.6%	74.3%	25.6%	74.4%
5	2018	311,324	74,856	HUGO, JOHN	236,243	CLARK, KATHERINE M.*	225	161,387 D	24.0%	75.9%	24.1%	75.9%
5	2016	289,807			285,606	CLARK, KATHERINE M.*	4,201	285,606 D		98.6%		100.0%
5	2014	185,260			182,100	CLARK, KATHERINE M.*	3,160	182,100 D		98.3%		100.0%
5	2012	341,109	82,944	TIERNEY, TOM	257,490	MARKEY, EDWARD J.*	675	174,546 D	24.3%	75.5%	24.4%	75.6%

MASSACHUSETTS
HOUSE OF REPRESENTATIVES

			Republican		Democratic		Other Vote	Rep.-Dem. Plurality	Percentage			
									Total Vote		Major Vote	
CD	Year	Total Vote	Vote	Candidate	Vote	Candidate			Rep.	Dem.	Rep.	Dem.
6	2022	315,081	110,770	MAY, ROBERT JR.	198,119	MOULTON, SETH*	6,192	87,349 D	35.2%	62.9%	35.9%	64.1%
6	2020	437,677	150,695	MORAN, JOHN PAUL	286,377	MOULTON, SETH*	605	135,682 D	34.4%	65.4%	34.5%	65.5%
6	2018	333,975	104,798	SCHNEIDER, JOSEPH S.	217,703	MOULTON, SETH*	11,474	112,905 D	31.4%	65.2%	32.5%	67.5%
6	2016	314,055			308,923	MOULTON, SETH*	5,132	308,923 D		98.4%		100.0%
6	2014	272,219	111,989	TISEI, RICHARD	149,638	MOULTON, SETH	10,592	37,649 D	41.1%	55.0%	42.8%	57.2%
6	2012	374,807	176,612	TISEI, RICHARD	180,942	TIERNEY, JOHN F.*	17,253	4,330 D	47.1%	48.3%	49.4%	50.6%
7	2022	179,511	27,129	PALMER, DONNIE DIONICIO JR.	151,825	PRESSLEY, AYANNA*	557	124,696 D	15.1%	84.6%	15.2%	84.8%
7	2020	308,650			267,362	PRESSLEY, AYANNA*	41,288	267,362 D		86.6%		100.0%
7	2018	220,411			216,559	PRESSLEY, AYANNA	3,852	216,559 D		98.3%		100.0%
7	2016	256,911			253,354	CAPUANO, MICHAEL E.*	3,557	253,354 D		98.6%		100.0%
7	2014	144,546			142,133	CAPUANO, MICHAEL E.*	2,413	142,133 D		98.3%		100.0%
7	2012	252,836			210,794	CAPUANO, MICHAEL E.*	42,042	210,794 D		83.4%		100.0%
8	2022	272,564	82,126	BURKE, ROBERT G.	189,987	LYNCH, STEPHEN F.*	451	107,861 D	30.1%	69.7%	30.2%	69.8%
8	2020	385,401			310,940	LYNCH, STEPHEN F.*	74,461	310,940 D		80.7%		100.0%
8	2018	263,307			259,159	LYNCH, STEPHEN F.*	4,148	259,159 D		98.4%		100.0%
8	2016	374,265	102,744	BURKE, WILLIAM	271,019	LYNCH, STEPHEN F.*	502	168,275 D	27.5%	72.4%	27.5%	72.5%
8	2014	203,351			200,644	LYNCH, STEPHEN F.*	2,707	200,644 D		98.7%		100.0%
8	2012	346,811	82,242	SELVAGGI, JOE	263,999	LYNCH, STEPHEN F.*	570	181,757 D	23.7%	76.1%	23.8%	76.2%
9	2022	334,320	136,347	BROWN, JESSE G.	197,823	KEATING, WILLIAM RICHARD*	150	61,476 D	40.8%	59.2%	40.8%	59.2%
9	2020	424,601	154,261	BRADY, HELEN	260,262	KEATING, WILLIAM RICHARD*	10,078	106,001 D	36.3%	61.3%	37.2%	62.8%
9	2018	323,928	131,463	TEDESCHI, PETER D.	192,347	KEATING, WILLIAM RICHARD*	118	60,884 D	40.6%	59.4%	40.6%	59.4%
9	2016	379,895	127,803	ALLIEGRO, MARK C.	211,790	KEATING, WILLIAM RICHARD*	40,302	83,987 D	33.6%	55.7%	37.6%	62.4%
9	2014	255,541	114,971	CHAPMAN, JOHN C.	140,413	KEATING, WILLIAM RICHARD*	157	25,442 D	45.0%	54.9%	45.0%	55.0%
9	2012	362,405	116,531	SHELDON, CHRISTOPHER	212,754	KEATING, WILLIAM RICHARD*	33,120	96,223 D	32.2%	58.7%	35.4%	64.6%
TOTAL	2022	2,357,997	706,790		1,636,400		14,807	929,610 D	30.0%	69.4%	30.2%	69.8%
TOTAL	2020	3,326,658	699,001		2,482,596		145,061	1,783,595 D	21.0%	74.6%	22.0%	78.0%
TOTAL	2018	2,485,081	497,953		1,943,597		43,531	1,445,644 D	20.0%	78.2%	20.4%	79.6%
TOTAL	2016	2,940,688	451,121		2,344,518		145,049	1,893,397 D	15.3%	79.7%	16.1%	83.9%
TOTAL	2014	1,813,816	308,598		1,475,442		29,776	1,166,844 D	17.0%	81.3%	17.3%	82.7%
TOTAL	2012	2,891,434	697,637		2,080,594		113,203	1,382,957 D	24.1%	72.0%	25.1%	74.9%

Note: An asterisk (*) denotes incumbent.

MASSACHUSETTS
GENERAL AND PRIMARY ELECTIONS

GENERAL ELECTIONS: OTHER VOTES

Governor   Other vote was 39,244 Libertarian (Kevin Reed), 2,806 Write-in (Write-in)

House   Other vote was:

CD 1   378 Write-in (Scattered Write-Ins)
CD 2   276 Write-in (Scattered Write-Ins)
CD 3   220 Write-in (Scattered Write-Ins)
CD 4   6,397 Write-in (Scattered Write-Ins)
CD 5   186 Write-in (Scattered Write-Ins)
CD 6   5,995 Unenrolled (Mark Tashjian), 197 Write-in (Scattered Write-Ins)
CD 7   557 Write-in (Scattered Write-Ins)
CD 8   451 Write-in (Scattered Write-Ins)
CD 9   150 Write-in (Scattered Write-Ins)

MASSACHUSETTS

GENERAL AND PRIMARY ELECTIONS

2022 PRIMARY ELECTIONS: SUPPLEMENTARY INFORMATION

Primary	September 20, 2022	**Registration** (as of August 27, 2022)	4,838,359	Democratic	1,434,356
				Republican	436,379
				Other	56,356
				Unenrolled (Independent)	2,911,268

Primary Type Semi-open—Registered Democrats and Republicans could vote only in their party's primary. "Unrolled" voters could participate in either party's primary.

	REPUBLICAN PRIMARIES			DEMOCRATIC PRIMARIES		
Governor	Diehl, Geoff	149,800	55.3%	Healey, Maura	642,092	85.3%
	Doughty, Chris	120,418	44.4%	Chang-Diaz, Sonia Rosa	108,574	14.4%
	Write In	769	0.3%	Write In	1,972	0.3%
	TOTAL	270,987		TOTAL	752,638	
Congressional District 1	Martilli, Dean James	23,256	99.2%	Neal, Richard E.*	71,928	99.2%
	Scattered Write-Ins	194	0.8%	Scattered Write-Ins	606	0.8%
	TOTAL	23,450		TOTAL	72,534	
Congressional District 2	Sossa-Paquette, Jeffrey Allen	22,675	99.4%	McGovern, James*	69,839	99.7%
	Scattered Write-Ins	140	0.6%	Scattered Write-Ins	216	0.3%
	TOTAL	22,815		TOTAL	70,055	
Congressional District 3	Tran, Dean	24,087	99.3%	Trahan, Lori*	64,190	99.6%
	Scattered Write-Ins	180	0.7%	Scattered Write-Ins	283	0.4%
	TOTAL	24,267		TOTAL	64,473	
Congressional District 4	Scattered Write-Ins	1,457	57.2%	Auchincloss, Jake*	67,738	99.3%
	Cannata, David B. (Write-In)	1,091	42.8%	Scattered Write-Ins	481	0.7%
	TOTAL	2,548		TOTAL	68,219	
Congressional District 5	Colarusso, Caroline	16,184	99.0%	Clark, Katherine M.*	84,845	99.6%
	Scattered Write-Ins	161	1.0%	Scattered Write-Ins	329	0.4%
	TOTAL	16,345		TOTAL	85,174	
Congressional District 6	May, Robert Jr.	29,503	99.2%	Moulton, Seth*	84,860	99.3%
	Scattered Write-Ins	240	0.8%	Scattered Write-Ins	597	0.7%
	TOTAL	29,743		TOTAL	85,457	
Congressional District 7	Palmer, Donnie Dionicio Jr.	4,657	97.6%	Pressley, Ayanna*	69,227	98.7%
	Scattered Write-Ins	114	2.4%	Scattered Write-Ins	893	1.3%
	TOTAL	4,771		TOTAL	70,120	
Congressional District 8	Burke, Robert G.	19,173	73.0%	Lynch, Stephen F.*	73,191	99.0%
	Rodrigues, Hamilton Soares	6,977	26.6%	Scattered Write-Ins	715	1.0%
	Scattered Write-Ins	124	0.5%			
	TOTAL	26,274		TOTAL	73,906	
Congressional District 9	Brown, Jesse G.	24,384	51.3%	Keating, William Richard*	81,530	99.7%
	Sullivan, Dan	23,002	48.4%	Scattered Write-Ins	228	0.3%
	Scattered Write-Ins	113	0.2%			
	TOTAL	47,499		TOTAL	81,758	

Note: An asterisk (*) denotes incumbent.

MICHIGAN

Statewide Races

In 2018, former state Sen. Gretchen Whitmer, who was still in her 40s but already had a notable career in state politics, won Michigan's open gubernatorial contest by just under ten points. During her term, she became a national figure, receiving some vice-presidential buzz in 2020.

Whitmer entered the 2022 cycle with positive approval ratings, although early polls suggested Republicans could be competitive. In what became something of an embarrassment for the state party, several declared Republicans did not submit enough petition signatures to appear on the primary ballot. Tudor Dixon, a conservative broadcaster, eventually won the primary with a 40% plurality.

Whitmer was reelected by just over ten points, a slightly better showing than her 2018 result. As with 2018, her best county was Ann Arbor's Washtenaw (home of the University of Michigan), not Detroit's Wayne, although she took over 70% of the vote in each. Just north of Wayne, suburban Oakland County, the state's second-largest county by population, continued its pro-Democratic movement. A decade ago, Democrats often posted just single-digit margins in Oakland County. Whitmer carried it 61%–38%. In historically Republican western Michigan, Whitmer continued to gain in Grand Rapids' Kent County, carrying it 54%–44% – this area was the heart of Gerald Ford's district when he served in Congress.

Whitmer's 2018 and 2020 maps were identical, with a few exceptions. In the northwest, she flipped Grand Traverse County and the smaller, adjacent Benzie County. These counties make up the state's "Cherry Coast," a politically blue-trending area known for producing a red fruit. The sole Whitmer-to-Dixon county was working-class Gogebic, on the Upper Peninsula.

During the campaign, Whitmer campaigned in support of Proposal 3, which would have amended the state constitution to enshrine abortion protections. It passed with 57%. All Whitmer-won counties voted in favor, as did several marginal Dixon-won counties.

House Races

In 2018, Michigan voters approved a measure that established a nonpartisan redistricting commission that would draw the state's lines after the 2020 census. The commission was tasked with drawing 13 seats, down from 14 on the outgoing map.

In central Michigan, the race for the Lansing-based 7th District was among the cycle's most costly. But Democratic Rep. Elissa Slotkin won by a comfortable 52%–46% in a seat that would have only given Joe Biden a single-point margin. Democratic Rep. Dan Kildee, whose district contains Flint, was also reelected in a marginal Biden-won seat. In western Michigan's 3rd District, Republican Peter Meijer, who supported Trump's impeachment, lost to a pro-Trump primary challenger, John Gibbs. Gibbs lost the general election to Democrat Hillary Scholten by a wider-than-expected 55%–42%.

A bright spot for Republicans was Macomb County's 10th District. Though he was favored, Republican John James won the seat by half a point – but the district gave statewide Democrats clear margins. After the election, James became the sole Black member of the state delegation. Though they are both plurality-Black by composition, the two districts containing Detroit proper, the 12th and 13th, elected Democrats Rashida Tlaib (an Arab American) and Shri Thanedar (an Indian American), respectively.

MICHIGAN
Congressional districts first established for elections held in 2022
13 members

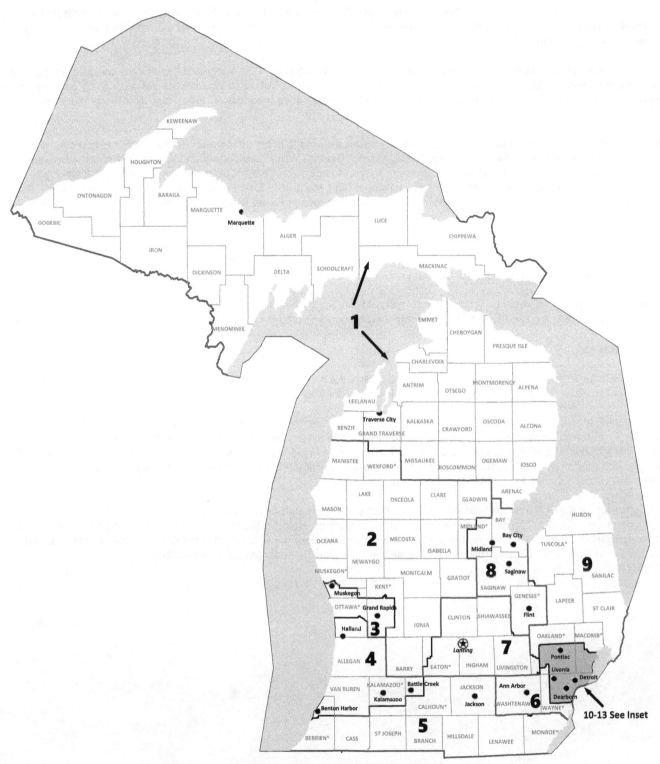

* Asterisk indicates a county whose boundaries include parts of two or more congressional districts.

See Inset for Detroit area.

MICHIGAN
Greater Detroit Area

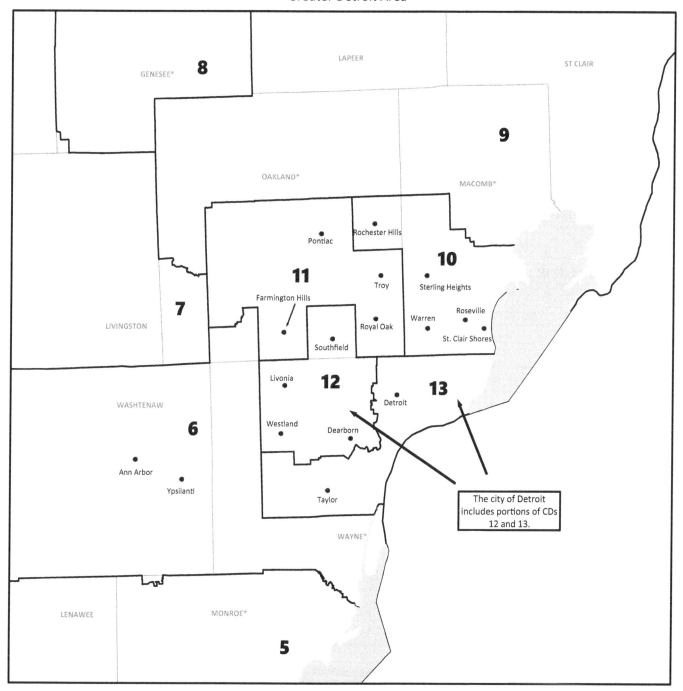

* Asterisk indicates a county whose boundaries include parts of two or more congressional districts.

MICHIGAN

GOVERNOR
Gretchen Whitmer (D). Reelected 2022 to a four-year term. Previously elected 2018.

SENATORS (2 Democrats)
Gary C. Peters (D). Reelected 2020 to a six-year term. Previously elected 2014.

Debbie Stabenow (D). Reelected 2018 to a six-year term. Previously elected 2012, 2006, 2000.

REPRESENTATIVES (6 Republicans, 7 Democrats)
1. Jack Bergman (R)
2. John Moolenaar (R)
3. Hillary Scholten (D)
4. Bill Huizenga (R)
5. Timothy Walberg (R)
6. Debbie Dingell (D)
7. Elissa Slotkin (D)
8. Daniel Kildee (D)
9. Lisa McClain (R)
10. John James (R)
11. Haley Stevens (D)
12. Rashida Tlaib (D)
13. Shri Thanedar (D)

POSTWAR VOTE FOR PRESIDENT

Year	Total Vote	Republican Vote	Republican Candidate	Democratic Vote	Democratic Candidate	Other Vote	Rep.-Dem. Plurality	Total Vote Rep.	Total Vote Dem.	Major Vote Rep.	Major Vote Dem.
2020	5,539,302	2,649,852	Trump, Donald J.*	2,804,040	Biden, Joseph R. Jr.	85,410	154,188 D	47.8%	50.6%	48.6%	51.4%
2016**	4,799,284	2,279,543	Trump, Donald J.	2,268,839	Clinton, Hillary Rodham	250,902	10,704 R	47.5%	47.3%	50.1%	49.9%
2012	4,730,961	2,115,256	Romney, W. Mitt	2,564,569	Obama, Barack H.*	51,136	449,313 D	44.7%	54.2%	45.2%	54.8%
2008	5,001,766	2,048,639	McCain, John S. III	2,872,579	Obama, Barack H.	80,548	823,940 D	41.0%	57.4%	41.6%	58.4%
2004	4,839,252	2,313,746	Bush, George W.*	2,479,183	Kerry, John F.	46,323	165,437 D	47.8%	51.2%	48.3%	51.7%
2000**	4,232,711	1,953,139	Bush, George W.	2,170,418	Gore, Albert Jr.	109,154	217,279 D	46.1%	51.3%	47.4%	52.6%
1996**	3,848,844	1,481,212	Dole, Robert "Bob"	1,989,653	Clinton, Bill*	377,979	508,441 D	38.5%	51.7%	42.7%	57.3%
1992**	4,274,673	1,554,940	Bush, George H.*	1,871,182	Clinton, Bill	848,551	316,242 D	36.4%	43.8%	45.4%	54.6%
1988	3,669,163	1,965,486	Bush, George H.	1,675,783	Dukakis, Michael S.	27,894	289,703 R	53.6%	45.7%	54.0%	46.0%
1984	3,801,658	2,251,571	Reagan, Ronald*	1,529,638	Mondale, Walter F.	20,449	721,933 R	59.2%	40.2%	59.5%	40.5%
1980**	3,909,725	1,915,225	Reagan, Ronald	1,661,532	Carter, Jimmy*	332,968	253,693 R	49.0%	42.5%	53.5%	46.5%
1976	3,653,749	1,893,742	Ford, Gerald R.*	1,696,714	Carter, Jimmy	63,293	197,028 R	51.8%	46.4%	52.7%	47.3%
1972	3,489,727	1,961,721	Nixon, Richard M.*	1,459,435	McGovern, George S.	68,571	502,286 R	56.2%	41.8%	57.3%	42.7%
1968**	3,306,250	1,370,665	Nixon, Richard M.	1,593,082	Humphrey, Hubert Horatio Jr.	342,503	222,417 D	41.5%	48.2%	46.2%	53.8%
1964	3,203,102	1,060,152	Goldwater, Barry M. Sr.	2,136,615	Johnson, Lyndon B.*	6,335	1,076,463 D	33.1%	66.7%	33.2%	66.8%
1960	3,318,097	1,620,428	Nixon, Richard M.	1,687,269	Kennedy, John F.	10,400	66,841 D	48.8%	50.9%	49.0%	51.0%
1956	3,080,468	1,713,647	Eisenhower, Dwight D.*	1,359,898	Stevenson, Adlai E. II	6,923	353,749 R	55.6%	44.1%	55.8%	44.2%
1952	2,798,592	1,551,529	Eisenhower, Dwight D.	1,230,657	Stevenson, Adlai E. II	16,406	320,872 R	55.4%	44.0%	55.8%	44.2%
1948	2,109,609	1,038,595	Dewey, Thomas E.	1,003,448	Truman, Harry S.*	67,566	35,147 R	49.2%	47.6%	50.9%	49.1%

Note: An asterisk (*) denotes incumbent **In past elections, the other vote included: 2016 - 172,136 Libertarian (Gary Johnson); 2000 - 84,165 Green (Ralph Nader); 1996 - 336,670 Reform (Ross Perot); 1992 - 824,813 Independent (Perot); 1980 - 275,223 Independent (John Anderson); 1968 - 331,968 American Independent (George Wallace).

MICHIGAN

POSTWAR VOTE FOR GOVERNOR

Year	Total Vote	Republican Vote	Republican Candidate	Democratic Vote	Democratic Candidate	Other Vote	Rep.-Dem. Plurality	Total Vote Rep.	Total Vote Dem.	Major Vote Rep.	Major Vote Dem.
2022	4,461,772	1,960,635	Dixon, Tudor	2,430,305	Whitmer, Gretchen*	70,832	469,670 D	43.9%	54.5%	44.7%	55.3%
2018	4,250,585	1,859,534	Schuette, Bill	2,266,193	Whitmer, Gretchen	124,858	406,659 D	43.7%	53.3%	45.1%	54.9%
2014	3,156,531	1,607,399	Snyder, Rick*	1,479,057	Schauer, Mark H.	70,075	128,342 R	50.9%	46.9%	52.1%	47.9%
2010	3,226,088	1,874,834	Snyder, Rick	1,287,320	Bernero, Virg	63,934	587,514 R	58.1%	39.9%	59.3%	40.7%
2006	3,801,256	1,608,086	DeVos, Dick	2,142,513	Granholm, Jennifer M.*	50,657	534,427 D	42.3%	56.4%	42.9%	57.1%
2002	3,177,565	1,506,104	Posthumus, Dick	1,633,796	Granholm, Jennifer M.	37,665	127,692 D	47.4%	51.4%	48.0%	52.0%
1998	3,027,104	1,883,005	Engler, John*	1,143,574	Fieger, Geoffrey	525	739,431 R	62.2%	37.8%	62.2%	37.8%
1994	3,089,077	1,899,101	Engler, John*	1,188,438	Wolpe, Howard	1,538	710,663 R	61.5%	38.5%	61.5%	38.5%
1990	2,564,563	1,276,134	Engler, John	1,258,539	Blanchard, James J.*	29,890	17,595 R	49.8%	49.1%	50.3%	49.7%
1986	2,396,564	753,647	Lucas, William	1,632,138	Blanchard, James J.*	10,779	878,491 D	31.4%	68.1%	31.6%	68.4%
1982	3,040,008	1,369,582	Headlee, Richard H.	1,561,291	Blanchard, James J.	109,135	191,709 D	45.1%	51.4%	46.7%	53.3%
1978	2,867,212	1,628,485	Milliken, William G.*	1,237,256	Fitzgerald, William	1,471	391,229 R	56.8%	43.2%	56.8%	43.2%
1974	2,657,020	1,356,865	Milliken, William G.*	1,242,250	Levin, Sander M.	57,905	114,615 R	51.1%	46.8%	52.2%	47.8%
1970	2,656,093	1,338,711	Milliken, William G.*	1,294,600	Levin, Sander M.	22,782	44,111 R	50.4%	48.7%	50.8%	49.2%
1966**	2,461,909	1,490,430	Romney, George W.*	963,383	Ferency, Zoltan A.	8,096	527,047 R	60.5%	39.1%	60.7%	39.3%
1964	3,158,102	1,764,355	Romney, George W.*	1,381,442	Staebler, Neil	12,305	382,913 R	55.9%	43.7%	56.1%	43.9%
1962	2,764,839	1,420,086	Romney, George W.	1,339,513	Swainson, John B.*	5,240	80,573 R	51.4%	48.4%	51.5%	48.5%
1960	3,255,991	1,602,022	Bagwell, Paul D.	1,643,634	Swainson, John B.	10,335	41,612 D	49.2%	50.5%	49.4%	50.6%
1958	2,312,184	1,078,089	Bagwell, Paul D.	1,225,533	Williams, G. Mennen*	8,562	147,444 D	46.6%	53.0%	46.8%	53.2%
1956	3,049,651	1,376,376	Cobo, Albert E.	1,666,689	Williams, G. Mennen*	6,586	290,313 D	45.1%	54.7%	45.2%	54.8%
1954	2,187,027	963,300	Leonard, Donald S.	1,216,308	Williams, G. Mennen*	7,419	253,008 D	44.0%	55.6%	44.2%	55.8%
1952	2,865,980	1,423,275	Alger, Fred M. Jr.	1,431,893	Williams, G. Mennen*	10,812	8,618 D	49.7%	50.0%	49.8%	50.2%
1950	1,879,382	933,998	Kelly, Harry F.	935,152	Williams, G. Mennen*	10,232	1,154 D	49.7%	49.8%	50.0%	50.0%
1948	2,113,122	964,810	Sigler, Kim*	1,128,664	Williams, G. Mennen	19,648	163,854 D	45.7%	53.4%	46.1%	53.9%
1946	1,665,475	1,003,878	Sigler, Kim	644,540	Van Wagoner, Murray D.	17,057	359,338 R	60.3%	38.7%	60.9%	39.1%

Note: An asterisk (*) denotes incumbent. **The term of office of Michigan's Governor was increased from two to four years effective with the 1966 election.

POSTWAR VOTE FOR SENATOR

Year	Total Vote	Republican Vote	Republican Candidate	Democratic Vote	Democratic Candidate	Other Vote	Rep.-Dem. Plurality	Total Vote Rep.	Total Vote Dem.	Major Vote Rep.	Major Vote Dem.
2020	5,479,720	2,642,233	James, John	2,734,568	Peters, Gary C.*	102,919	92,335 D	48.2%	49.9%	49.1%	50.9%
2018	4,237,271	1,938,818	James, John	2,214,478	Stabenow, Debbie*	83,975	275,660 D	45.8%	52.3%	46.7%	53.3%
2014	3,121,775	1,290,199	Land, Terri Lynn	1,704,936	Peters, Gary C.	126,640	414,737 D	41.3%	54.6%	43.1%	56.9%
2012	4,652,918	1,767,386	Hoekstra, Peter	2,735,826	Stabenow, Debbie*	149,706	968,440 D	38.0%	58.8%	39.2%	60.8%
2008	4,848,620	1,641,070	Hoogendyk, Jack Jr.	3,038,386	Levin, Carl*	169,164	1,397,316 D	33.8%	62.7%	35.1%	64.9%
2006	3,780,142	1,559,597	Bouchard, Michael	2,151,278	Stabenow, Debbie*	69,267	591,681 D	41.3%	56.9%	42.0%	58.0%
2002	3,129,287	1,185,545	Raczkowski, Andrew	1,896,614	Levin, Carl*	47,128	711,069 D	37.9%	60.6%	38.5%	61.5%
2000	4,167,685	1,994,693	Abraham, Spencer*	2,061,952	Stabenow, Debbie	111,040	67,259 D	47.9%	49.5%	49.2%	50.8%
1996	3,762,575	1,500,106	Romney, Ronna	2,195,738	Levin, Carl*	66,731	695,632 D	39.9%	58.4%	40.6%	59.4%
1994	3,043,385	1,578,770	Abraham, Spencer	1,300,960	Carr, M. Robert	163,655	277,810 R	51.9%	42.7%	54.8%	45.2%
1990	2,560,494	1,055,695	Schuette, Bill	1,471,753	Levin, Carl*	33,046	416,058 D	41.2%	57.5%	41.8%	58.2%
1988	3,505,985	1,348,219	Dunn, Jim	2,116,865	Riegle, Donald Wayne Jr.*	40,901	768,646 D	38.5%	60.4%	38.9%	61.1%
1984	3,700,938	1,745,302	Lousma, Jack	1,915,831	Levin, Carl*	39,805	170,529 D	47.2%	51.8%	47.7%	52.3%
1982	2,994,334	1,223,288	Ruppe, Philip E.	1,728,793	Riegle, Donald Wayne Jr.*	42,253	505,505 D	40.9%	57.7%	41.4%	58.6%
1978	2,846,630	1,362,165	Griffin, Robert P.*	1,484,193	Levin, Carl	272	122,028 D	47.9%	52.1%	47.9%	52.1%
1976	3,484,664	1,635,087	Esch, Marvin L.	1,831,031	Riegle, Donald Wayne Jr.	18,546	195,944 D	46.9%	52.5%	47.2%	52.8%
1972	3,406,906	1,781,065	Griffin, Robert P.*	1,577,178	Kelley, Frank J.	48,663	203,887 R	52.3%	46.3%	53.0%	47.0%
1970	2,610,763	858,438	Romney, Lenore	1,744,672	Hart, Philip A.*	7,653	886,234 D	32.9%	66.8%	33.0%	67.0%
1966	2,439,365	1,363,530	Griffin, Robert P.*	1,069,484	Williams, G. Mennen	6,351	294,046 R	55.9%	43.8%	56.0%	44.0%
1964	3,101,667	1,096,272	Peterson, Elly M.	1,996,912	Hart, Philip A.*	8,483	900,640 D	35.3%	64.4%	35.4%	64.6%
1960	3,226,647	1,548,873	Bentley, Alvin M.	1,669,179	McNamara, Patrick V.*	8,595	120,306 D	48.0%	51.7%	48.1%	51.9%
1958	2,271,644	1,046,963	Potter, Charles E.*	1,216,966	Hart, Philip A.	7,715	170,003 D	46.1%	53.6%	46.2%	53.8%
1954	2,144,840	1,049,420	Ferguson, Homer*	1,088,550	McNamara, Patrick V.	6,870	39,130 D	48.9%	50.8%	49.1%	50.9%
1952	2,821,133	1,428,352	Potter, Charles E.	1,383,416	Moody, Blair	9,365	44,936 R	50.6%	49.0%	50.8%	49.2%
1948	2,062,097	1,045,156	Ferguson, Homer*	1,000,329	Hook, Frank E.	16,612	44,827 R	50.7%	48.5%	51.1%	48.9%
1946	1,618,720	1,085,570	Vandenberg, Arthur H.*	517,923	Lee, James H.	15,227	567,647 R	67.1%	32.0%	67.7%	32.3%

Note: An asterisk (*) denotes incumbent.

MICHIGAN
GOVERNOR 2022

2020 Census Population	County	Total Vote	Republican (Dixon)	Democratic (Whitmer)	Other	Rep.-Dem. Plurality		Percentage			
								Total Vote		Major Vote	
								Rep.	Dem.	Rep.	Dem.
10,468	ALCONA	5,981	3,802	2,076	103	1,726	R	63.6%	34.7%	64.7%	35.3%
9,127	ALGER	4,326	2,258	1,984	84	274	R	52.2%	45.9%	53.2%	46.8%
118,523	ALLEGAN	57,342	33,590	22,802	950	10,788	R	58.6%	39.8%	59.6%	40.4%
28,433	ALPENA	13,980	7,920	5,779	281	2,141	R	56.7%	41.3%	57.8%	42.2%
23,435	ANTRIM	14,014	7,827	5,937	250	1,890	R	55.9%	42.4%	56.9%	43.1%
14,926	ARENAC	7,170	4,314	2,709	147	1,605	R	60.2%	37.8%	61.4%	38.6%
8,202	BARAGA	3,444	2,056	1,329	59	727	R	59.7%	38.6%	60.7%	39.3%
61,769	BARRY	30,697	18,547	11,552	598	6,995	R	60.4%	37.6%	61.6%	38.4%
103,283	BAY	49,209	23,448	24,783	978	1,335	D	47.6%	50.4%	48.6%	51.4%
17,846	BENZIE	10,689	5,064	5,446	179	382	D	47.4%	50.9%	48.2%	51.8%
153,540	BERRIEN	64,024	33,157	29,803	1,064	3,354	R	51.8%	46.5%	52.7%	47.3%
43,581	BRANCH	16,130	10,132	5,676	322	4,456	R	62.8%	35.2%	64.1%	35.9%
134,374	CALHOUN	51,576	25,694	24,916	966	778	R	49.8%	48.3%	50.8%	49.2%
51,901	CASS	20,353	12,666	7,350	337	5,316	R	62.2%	36.1%	63.3%	36.7%
26,199	CHARLEVOIX	14,669	7,667	6,728	274	939	R	52.3%	45.9%	53.3%	46.7%
25,310	CHEBOYGAN	13,334	7,707	5,357	270	2,350	R	57.8%	40.2%	59.0%	41.0%
37,399	CHIPPEWA	14,537	7,902	6,303	332	1,599	R	54.4%	43.4%	55.6%	44.4%
31,079	CLARE	13,198	7,850	5,057	291	2,793	R	59.5%	38.3%	60.8%	39.2%
79,912	CLINTON	41,204	19,904	20,664	636	760	D	48.3%	50.2%	49.1%	50.9%
14,076	CRAWFORD	6,531	3,728	2,655	148	1,073	R	57.1%	40.7%	58.4%	41.6%
35,868	DELTA	17,341	10,097	6,890	354	3,207	R	58.2%	39.7%	59.4%	40.6%
25,277	DICKINSON	11,986	7,446	4,310	230	3,136	R	62.1%	36.0%	63.3%	36.7%
110,494	EATON	53,558	23,828	28,806	924	4,978	D	44.5%	53.8%	45.3%	54.7%
33,587	EMMET	19,195	9,590	9,285	320	305	R	50.0%	48.4%	50.8%	49.2%
405,946	GENESEE	171,594	68,282	100,325	2,987	32,043	D	39.8%	58.5%	40.5%	59.5%
25,558	GLADWIN	12,025	7,357	4,422	246	2,935	R	61.2%	36.8%	62.5%	37.5%
14,313	GOGEBIC	6,466	3,413	2,940	113	473	R	52.8%	45.5%	53.7%	46.3%
93,397	GRAND TRAVERSE	52,302	24,005	27,396	901	3,391	D	45.9%	52.4%	46.7%	53.3%
40,801	GRATIOT	15,324	8,659	6,285	380	2,374	R	56.5%	41.0%	57.9%	42.1%
45,635	HILLSDALE	18,650	12,644	5,575	431	7,069	R	67.8%	29.9%	69.4%	30.6%
35,666	HOUGHTON	15,480	8,128	7,030	322	1,098	R	52.5%	45.4%	53.6%	46.4%
30,999	HURON	15,006	9,395	5,310	301	4,085	R	62.6%	35.4%	63.9%	36.1%
292,346	INGHAM	119,042	34,869	82,408	1,765	47,539	D	29.3%	69.2%	29.7%	70.3%
64,832	IONIA	27,008	15,786	10,645	577	5,141	R	58.4%	39.4%	59.7%	40.3%
25,206	IOSCO	12,631	7,111	5,266	254	1,845	R	56.3%	41.7%	57.5%	42.5%
11,105	IRON	5,620	3,282	2,236	102	1,046	R	58.4%	39.8%	59.5%	40.5%
69,485	ISABELLA	23,957	10,927	12,581	449	1,654	D	45.6%	52.5%	46.5%	53.5%
158,744	JACKSON	64,705	34,439	29,011	1,255	5,428	R	53.2%	44.8%	54.3%	45.7%
265,478	KALAMAZOO	116,776	42,436	72,516	1,824	30,080	D	36.3%	62.1%	36.9%	63.1%
18,149	KALKASKA	8,854	5,616	3,009	229	2,607	R	63.4%	34.0%	65.1%	34.9%
658,027	KENT	299,872	132,172	162,899	4,801	30,727	D	44.1%	54.3%	44.8%	55.2%
2,136	KEWEENAW	1,390	701	666	23	35	R	50.4%	47.9%	51.3%	48.7%
11,793	LAKE	5,260	3,055	2,081	124	974	R	58.1%	39.6%	59.5%	40.5%
87,739	LAPEER	43,802	26,940	15,983	879	10,957	R	61.5%	36.5%	62.8%	37.2%
21,848	LEELANAU	15,474	6,752	8,540	182	1,788	D	43.6%	55.2%	44.2%	55.8%
98,686	LENAWEE	42,857	23,796	18,248	813	5,548	R	55.5%	42.6%	56.6%	43.4%
192,671	LIVINGSTON	108,839	60,494	46,524	1,821	13,970	R	55.6%	42.7%	56.5%	43.5%
6,223	LUCE	2,366	1,520	786	60	734	R	64.2%	33.2%	65.9%	34.1%
10,825	MACKINAC	5,999	3,325	2,567	107	758	R	55.4%	42.8%	56.4%	43.6%
876,216	MACOMB	384,544	179,258	199,277	6,009	20,019	D	46.6%	51.8%	47.4%	52.6%
24,650	MANISTEE	12,646	6,364	6,026	256	338	R	50.3%	47.7%	51.4%	48.6%
66,996	MARQUETTE	31,369	11,967	18,880	522	6,913	D	38.1%	60.2%	38.8%	61.2%
29,227	MASON	14,761	8,018	6,419	324	1,599	R	54.3%	43.5%	55.5%	44.5%
43,589	MECOSTA	17,510	10,262	6,867	381	3,395	R	58.6%	39.2%	59.9%	40.1%
22,828	MENOMINEE	9,676	6,129	3,347	200	2,782	R	63.3%	34.6%	64.7%	35.3%
83,251	MIDLAND	41,224	20,964	19,497	763	1,467	R	50.9%	47.3%	51.8%	48.2%
15,152	MISSAUKEE	7,448	5,306	1,995	147	3,311	R	71.2%	26.8%	72.7%	27.3%
151,003	MONROE	68,997	38,312	29,482	1,203	8,830	R	55.5%	42.7%	56.5%	43.5%
64,068	MONTCALM	26,395	16,165	9,622	608	6,543	R	61.2%	36.5%	62.7%	37.3%
9,377	MONTMORENCY	5,119	3,301	1,701	117	1,600	R	64.5%	33.2%	66.0%	34.0%

MICHIGAN
GOVERNOR 2022

2020 Census Population	County	Total Vote	Republican (Dixon)	Democratic (Whitmer)	Other	Rep.-Dem. Plurality		Percentage Total Vote		Percentage Major Vote	
								Rep.	Dem.	Rep.	Dem.
173,436	MUSKEGON	73,836	33,121	39,269	1,446	6,148	D	44.9%	53.2%	45.8%	54.2%
49,187	NEWAYGO	22,761	14,879	7,417	465	7,462	R	65.4%	32.6%	66.7%	33.3%
1,258,791	OAKLAND	630,205	238,448	383,895	7,862	145,447	D	37.8%	60.9%	38.3%	61.7%
26,517	OCEANA	12,086	7,012	4,820	254	2,192	R	58.0%	39.9%	59.3%	40.7%
21,096	OGEMAW	9,892	6,151	3,532	209	2,619	R	62.2%	35.7%	63.5%	36.5%
5,718	ONTONAGON	3,259	1,862	1,319	78	543	R	57.1%	40.5%	58.5%	41.5%
23,505	OSCEOLA	10,379	6,954	3,174	251	3,780	R	67.0%	30.6%	68.7%	31.3%
8,276	OSCODA	4,012	2,553	1,355	104	1,198	R	63.6%	33.8%	65.3%	34.7%
24,763	OTSEGO	12,505	7,422	4,818	265	2,604	R	59.4%	38.5%	60.6%	39.4%
292,753	OTTAWA	146,432	85,361	58,952	2,119	26,409	R	58.3%	40.3%	59.1%	40.9%
12,629	PRESQUE ISLE	7,298	4,165	2,981	152	1,184	R	57.1%	40.8%	58.3%	41.7%
24,186	ROSCOMMON	12,951	7,391	5,284	276	2,107	R	57.1%	40.8%	58.3%	41.7%
190,495	SAGINAW	81,550	37,002	43,219	1,329	6,217	D	45.4%	53.0%	46.1%	53.9%
41,226	SANILAC	18,804	12,473	5,967	364	6,506	R	66.3%	31.7%	67.6%	32.4%
8,141	SCHOOLCRAFT	3,888	2,264	1,527	97	737	R	58.2%	39.3%	59.7%	40.3%
68,221	SHIAWASSEE	32,402	16,969	14,730	703	2,239	R	52.4%	45.5%	53.5%	46.5%
159,595	ST. CLAIR	74,505	42,731	30,170	1,604	12,561	R	57.4%	40.5%	58.6%	41.4%
61,116	ST. JOSEPH	21,910	13,059	8,402	449	4,657	R	59.6%	38.3%	60.8%	39.2%
52,220	TUSCOLA	24,007	15,078	8,418	511	6,660	R	62.8%	35.1%	64.2%	35.8%
75,817	VAN BUREN	31,922	15,974	15,347	601	627	R	50.0%	48.1%	51.0%	49.0%
367,335	WASHTENAW	180,848	42,804	135,904	2,140	93,100	D	23.7%	75.1%	24.0%	76.0%
1,747,584	WAYNE	645,739	180,487	457,601	7,651	277,114	D	28.0%	70.9%	28.3%	71.7%
33,744	WEXFORD	15,105	9,131	5,645	329	3,486	R	60.5%	37.4%	61.8%	38.2%
9,998,925	TOTAL	4,461,772	1,960,635	2,430,305	70,832	469,670	D	43.9%	54.5%	44.7%	55.3%

MICHIGAN
HOUSE OF REPRESENTATIVES

CD	Year	Total Vote	Republican Vote	Republican Candidate	Democratic Vote	Democratic Candidate	Other Vote	Rep.-Dem. Plurality		Percentage Total Vote		Percentage Major Vote	
										Rep.	Dem.	Rep.	Dem.
1	2022	388,599	233,094	BERGMAN, JACK*	145,403	LORINSER, BOB	10,102	87,691	R	60.0%	37.4%	61.6%	38.4%
1	2020	416,219	256,581	BERGMAN, JACK*	153,328	FERGUSON, DANA ALAN	6,310	103,253	R	61.6%	36.8%	62.6%	37.4%
1	2018	332,497	187,251	BERGMAN, JACK*	145,246	MORGAN, MATTHEW		42,005	R	56.3%	43.7%	56.3%	43.7%
1	2016	360,271	197,777	BERGMAN, JACK	144,334	JOHNSON, LONNIE BARTON "LON"	18,160	53,443	R	54.9%	40.1%	57.8%	42.2%
1	2014	250,131	130,414	BENISHEK, DAN*	113,263	CANNON, JERRY	6,454	17,151	R	52.1%	45.3%	53.5%	46.5%
1	2012	347,037	167,060	BENISHEK, DAN*	165,179	MCDOWELL, GARY	14,798	1,881	R	48.1%	47.6%	50.3%	49.7%
2	2022	339,521	216,222	MOOLENAAR, JOHN*	116,452	HILLIARD, JEROME "JERRY"	6,847	99,770	R	63.7%	34.3%	65.0%	35.0%
2	2020	403,247	238,711	HUIZENGA, BILL*	154,122	BERGHOEF, BRYAN	10,414	84,589	R	59.2%	38.2%	60.8%	39.2%
2	2018	305,463	168,970	HUIZENGA, BILL*	131,254	DAVIDSON, ROB	5,239	37,716	R	55.3%	43.0%	56.3%	43.7%
2	2016	339,328	212,508	HUIZENGA, BILL*	110,391	MURPHY, DENNIS B.	16,429	102,117	R	62.6%	32.5%	65.8%	34.2%
2	2014	213,072	135,568	HUIZENGA, BILL*	70,851	VANDERSTELT, DEAN	6,653	64,717	R	63.6%	33.3%	65.7%	34.3%
2	2012	318,267	194,653	HUIZENGA, BILL*	108,973	GERMAN, WILLIE JR.	14,641	85,680	R	61.2%	34.2%	64.1%	35.9%
3	2022	338,988	142,229	GIBBS, JOHN	185,989	SCHOLTEN, HILLARY	10,770	43,760	D	42.0%	54.9%	43.3%	56.7%
3	2020	403,419	213,649	MEIJER, PETER	189,769	SCHOLTEN, HILLARY	1	23,880	R	53.0%	47.0%	53.0%	47.0%
3	2018**	310,740	169,107	AMASH, JUSTIN*	134,185	ALBRO, CATHY	7,448	34,922	R	54.4%	43.2%	55.8%	44.2%
3	2016	342,365	203,545	AMASH, JUSTIN*	128,400	SMITH, DOUGLAS	10,420	75,145	R	59.5%	37.5%	61.3%	38.7%
3	2014	217,165	125,754	AMASH, JUSTIN*	84,720	GOODRICH, BOB	6,691	41,034	R	57.9%	39.0%	59.7%	40.3%
3	2012	326,283	171,675	AMASH, JUSTIN*	144,108	PESTKA, STEVE	10,500	27,567	R	52.6%	44.2%	54.4%	45.6%

MICHIGAN

HOUSE OF REPRESENTATIVES

			Republican		Democratic		Other Vote	Rep.-Dem. Plurality	Total Vote		Major Vote	
CD	Year	Total Vote	Vote	Candidate	Vote	Candidate			Rep.	Dem.	Rep.	Dem.
4	2022	338,348	183,936	HUIZENGA, BILL*	143,690	ALFONSO, JOSEPH	10,722	40,246 R	54.4%	42.5%	56.1%	43.9%
4	2020	373,245	242,621	MOOLENAAR, JOHN*	120,802	HILLIARD, JEROME "JERRY"	9,822	121,819 R	65.0%	32.4%	66.8%	33.2%
4	2018	285,050	178,510	MOOLENAAR, JOHN*	106,540	HILLIARD, JEROME "JERRY"		71,970 R	62.6%	37.4%	62.6%	37.4%
4	2016	315,751	194,572	MOOLENAAR, JOHN*	101,277	WIRTH, DEBRA FREIDELL	19,902	93,295 R	61.6%	32.1%	65.8%	34.2%
4	2014	219,423	123,962	MOOLENAAR, JOHN	85,777	HOLMES, JEFF	9,684	38,185 R	56.5%	39.1%	59.1%	40.9%
4	2012	312,949	197,386	CAMP, DAVE*	104,996	WIRTH, DEBRA FREIDELL	10,567	92,390 R	63.1%	33.6%	65.3%	34.7%
5	2022	317,258	198,020	WALBERG, TIMOTHY*	110,946	GOLDBERG, BART	8,292	87,074 R	62.4%	35.0%	64.1%	35.9%
5	2020	361,032	150,772	KELLY, TIMOTHY P.	196,599	KILDEE, DANIEL*	13,661	45,827 D	41.8%	54.5%	43.4%	56.6%
5	2018	276,413	99,265	WINES, TRAVIS	164,502	KILDEE, DANIEL*	12,646	65,237 D	35.9%	59.5%	37.6%	62.4%
5	2016	319,291	112,102	HARDWICK, ALLEN	195,279	KILDEE, DANIEL*	11,910	83,177 D	35.1%	61.2%	36.5%	63.5%
5	2014	222,138	69,222	HARDWICK, ALLEN	148,182	KILDEE, DANIEL*	4,734	78,960 D	31.2%	66.7%	31.8%	68.2%
5	2012	330,146	103,931	SLEZAK, JIM	214,531	KILDEE, DANIEL	11,684	110,600 D	31.5%	65.0%	32.6%	67.4%
6	2022	366,927	125,167	WILLIAMS, WHITTNEY	241,759	DINGELL, DEBBIE*	1	116,592 D	34.1%	65.9%	34.1%	65.9%
6	2020	378,980	211,496	UPTON, FRED*	152,085	HOADLEY, JON	15,399	59,411 R	55.8%	40.1%	58.2%	41.8%
6	2018	293,438	147,436	UPTON, FRED*	134,082	LONGJOHN, MATT	11,920	13,354 R	50.2%	45.7%	52.4%	47.6%
6	2016	329,565	193,259	UPTON, FRED*	119,980	CLEMENTS, PAUL C.	16,326	73,279 R	58.6%	36.4%	61.7%	38.3%
6	2014	208,976	116,801	UPTON, FRED*	84,391	CLEMENTS, PAUL C.	7,784	32,410 R	55.9%	40.4%	58.1%	41.9%
6	2012	320,475	174,955	UPTON, FRED*	136,563	O'BRIEN, MIKE	8,957	38,392 R	54.6%	42.6%	56.2%	43.8%
7	2022	372,708	172,624	BARRETT, TOM	192,809	SLOTKIN, ELISSA*	7,275	20,185 D	46.3%	51.7%	47.2%	52.8%
7	2020	387,267	227,524	WALBERG, TIMOTHY*	159,743	DRISKELL, GRETCHEN D.		67,781 R	58.8%	41.2%	58.8%	41.2%
7	2018	295,060	158,730	WALBERG, TIMOTHY*	136,330	DRISKELL, GRETCHEN D.		22,400 R	53.8%	46.2%	53.8%	46.2%
7	2016	334,807	184,321	WALBERG, TIMOTHY*	134,010	DRISKELL, GRETCHEN D.	16,476	50,311 R	55.1%	40.0%	57.9%	42.1%
7	2014	223,685	119,564	WALBERG, TIMOTHY*	92,083	BYRNES, PAM	12,038	27,481 R	53.5%	41.2%	56.5%	43.5%
7	2012	318,069	169,668	WALBERG, TIMOTHY*	136,849	HASKELL, KURT R.	11,552	32,819 R	53.3%	43.0%	55.4%	44.6%
8	2022	335,829	143,850	JUNGE, PAUL	178,322	KILDEE, DANIEL*	13,657	34,472 D	42.8%	53.1%	44.7%	55.3%
8	2020	428,344	202,525	JUNGE, PAUL	217,922	SLOTKIN, ELISSA*	7,897	15,397 D	47.3%	50.9%	48.2%	51.8%
8	2018	341,593	159,782	BISHOP, MIKE*	172,880	SLOTKIN, ELISSA	8,931	13,098 D	46.8%	50.6%	48.0%	52.0%
8	2016	366,968	205,629	BISHOP, MIKE*	143,791	SHKRELI, SUZANNA	17,548	61,838 R	56.0%	39.2%	58.8%	41.2%
8	2014	243,125	132,739	BISHOP, MIKE	102,269	SCHERTZING, ERIC	8,117	30,470 R	54.6%	42.1%	56.5%	43.5%
8	2012	345,054	202,217	ROGERS, MIKE*	128,657	ENDERLE, LANCE	14,180	73,560 R	58.6%	37.3%	61.1%	38.9%
9	2022	372,922	238,300	MCCLAIN, LISA*	123,702	JAYE, BRIAN	10,920	114,598 R	63.9%	33.2%	65.8%	34.2%
9	2020	399,117	153,296	LANGWORTHY, CHARLES JOHN	230,318	LEVIN, ANDY*	15,503	77,022 D	38.4%	57.7%	40.0%	60.0%
9	2018	304,563	112,123	STEARNS, CANDIUS	181,734	LEVIN, ANDY	10,706	69,611 D	36.8%	59.7%	38.2%	61.8%
9	2016	344,775	128,937	MORSE, CHRISTOPHER R.	199,661	LEVIN, SANDER M.*	16,177	70,724 D	37.4%	57.9%	39.2%	60.8%
9	2014	225,757	81,470	BRIKHO, GEORGE	136,342	LEVIN, SANDER M.*	7,945	54,872 D	36.1%	60.4%	37.4%	62.6%
9	2012	337,316	114,760	VOLARIC, DON	208,846	LEVIN, SANDER M.*	13,710	94,086 D	34.0%	61.9%	35.5%	64.5%
10	2022	326,237	159,202	JAMES, JOHN	157,602	MARLINGA, CARL	9,433	1,600 R	48.8%	48.3%	50.3%	49.7%
10	2020	409,786	271,607	MCCLAIN, LISA	138,179	BIZON, KIMBERLY		133,428 R	66.3%	33.7%	66.3%	33.7%
10	2018	303,064	182,808	MITCHELL, PAUL*	106,061	BIZON, KIMBERLY	14,195	76,747 R	60.3%	35.0%	63.3%	36.7%
10	2016	340,983	215,132	MITCHELL, PAUL	110,112	ACCAVITTI, FRANK JR.	15,739	105,020 R	63.1%	32.3%	66.1%	33.9%
10	2014	228,692	157,069	MILLER, CANDICE S.*	67,143	STADLER, CHUCK	4,480	89,926 R	68.7%	29.4%	70.1%	29.9%
10	2012	328,612	226,075	MILLER, CANDICE S.*	97,734	STADLER, CHUCK	4,803	128,341 R	68.8%	29.7%	69.8%	30.2%
11	2022	366,179	141,642	AMBROSE, MARK	224,537	STEVENS, HALEY*		82,895 D	38.7%	61.3%	38.7%	61.3%
11	2020	450,473	215,405	ESSHAKI, ERIC	226,128	STEVENS, HALEY*	8,940	10,723 D	47.8%	50.2%	48.8%	51.2%
11	2018	350,901	158,463	EPSTEIN, LENA	181,912	STEVENS, HALEY	10,526	23,449 D	45.2%	51.8%	46.6%	53.4%
11	2016	379,488	200,872	TROTT, DAVE A.*	152,461	KUMAR, ANIL	26,155	48,411 R	52.9%	40.2%	56.9%	43.1%
11	2014	251,238	140,435	TROTT, DAVE A.	101,681	MCKENZIE, BOBBY	9,122	38,754 R	55.9%	40.5%	58.0%	42.0%
11	2012	358,139	181,788	BENTIVOLIO, KERRY	158,879	TAJ, SYED	17,472	22,909 R	50.8%	44.4%	53.4%	46.6%
12	2022	277,577	72,888	ELLIOTT, STEVEN	196,643	TLAIB, RASHIDA*	8,046	123,755 D	26.3%	70.8%	27.0%	73.0%
12	2020	383,823	117,719	JONES, JEFF	254,957	DINGELL, DEBBIE*	11,147	137,238 D	30.7%	66.4%	31.6%	68.4%
12	2018	294,628	85,115	JONES, JEFF	200,588	DINGELL, DEBBIE*	8,925	115,473 D	28.9%	68.1%	29.8%	70.2%
12	2016	328,542	96,104	JONES, JEFF	211,378	DINGELL, DEBBIE*	21,060	115,274 D	29.3%	64.3%	31.3%	68.7%
12	2014	206,660	64,716	BOWMAN, TERRENCE "TERRY"	134,346	DINGELL, DEBBIE	7,598	69,630 D	31.3%	65.0%	32.5%	67.5%
12	2012	319,223	92,472	KALLGREN, CYNTHIA	216,884	DINGELL, JOHN D. JR.*	9,867	124,412 D	29.0%	67.9%	29.9%	70.1%
13	2022	234,444	56,187	BIVINGS, MARTELL	166,650	THANEDAR, SHRI	11,607	110,463 D	24.0%	71.1%	25.2%	74.8%
13	2020	285,885	53,311	DUDENHOEFER, DAVID ANTHONY	223,205	TLAIB, RASHIDA*	9,369	169,894 D	18.6%	78.1%	19.3%	80.7%
13	2018	196,299			165,355	TLAIB, RASHIDA	30,944	165,355 D		84.2%		100.0%
13	2016	257,797	40,541	GORMAN, JEFF	198,771	CONYERS, JOHN JR.*	18,485	158,230 D	15.7%	77.1%	16.9%	83.1%
13	2014	166,947	27,234	GORMAN, JEFF	132,710	CONYERS, JOHN JR.*	7,003	105,476 D	16.3%	79.5%	17.0%	83.0%
13	2012	284,270	38,769	SAWICKI, HARRY	235,336	CONYERS, JOHN JR.*	10,165	196,567 D	13.6%	82.8%	14.1%	85.9%

MICHIGAN
HOUSE OF REPRESENTATIVES

CD	Year	Total Vote	Republican Vote	Republican Candidate	Democratic Vote	Democratic Candidate	Other Vote	Rep.-Dem. Plurality	Total Vote Rep.	Total Vote Dem.	Major Vote Rep.	Major Vote Dem.
14	2020	342,303	62,664	PATRICK, ROBERT VANCE	271,370	LAWRENCE, BRENDA*	8,269	208,706 D	18.3%	79.3%	18.8%	81.2%
14	2018	264,994	45,899	HERSCHFUS, MARC S.	214,334	LAWRENCE, BRENDA*	4,761	168,435 D	17.3%	80.9%	17.6%	82.4%
14	2016	310,974	58,103	KLAUSNER, HOWARD	244,135	LAWRENCE, BRENDA*	8,736	186,032 D	18.7%	78.5%	19.2%	80.8%
14	2014	212,468	41,801	BARR, CHRISTINA	165,272	LAWRENCE, BRENDA	5,395	123,471 D	19.7%	77.8%	20.2%	79.8%
14	2012	328,792	51,395	HAULER, JOHN	270,450	PETERS, GARY C.*	6,947	219,055 D	15.6%	82.3%	16.0%	84.0%
TOTAL	2022	4,375,537	2,083,361		2,184,504		107,672	101,143 D	47.6%	49.9%	48.8%	51.2%
TOTAL	2020	5,423,140	2,617,881		2,688,527		116,732	70,646 D	48.3%	49.6%	49.3%	50.7%
TOTAL	2018	4,154,703	1,853,459		2,175,003		126,241	321,544 D	44.6%	52.4%	46.0%	54.0%
TOTAL	2016	4,670,905	2,243,402		2,193,980		233,523	49,422 R	48.0%	47.0%	50.6%	49.4%
TOTAL	2014	3,089,477	1,466,749		1,519,030		103,698	52,281 D	47.5%	49.2%	49.1%	50.9%
TOTAL	2012	4,574,632	2,086,804		2,327,985		159,843	241,181 D	45.6%	50.9%	47.3%	52.7%

Note: An asterisk (*) denotes incumbent.

MICHIGAN
GENERAL AND PRIMARY ELECTIONS

GENERAL ELECTIONS: OTHER VOTES

Governor — Other vote was 38,800 Libertarian (Mary Buzuma), 16,246 U.S. Taxpayers (Donna Brandenburg), 10,766 Green (Kevin Hogan), 4,973 Natural Law (Daryl Simpson), 47 Write-In (Write-Ins)

House — Other vote was:

- CD 1: 5,510 Working Class (Liz Hakola), 4,592 Libertarian (Andrew Gale)
- CD 2: 6,847 Libertarian (Nathan Hewer)
- CD 3: 6,634 Libertarian (Jamie Lewis), 4,136 Working Class (Louis Palus)
- CD 4: 8,478 Libertarian (Lorence Wenke), 2,244 U.S. Taxpayers (Curtis Clark)
- CD 5: 5,129 Libertarian (Norman Peterson), 3,162 U.S. Taxpayers (Ezra Scott), 1 Write-In (Michael Johnson)
- CD 6: 1 Write-In (Frank Acosta)
- CD 7: 7,275 Libertarian (Leah Dailey)
- CD 8: 9,077 Working Class (Kathy Goodwin), 4,580 Libertarian (David Canny)
- CD 9: 6,571 Working Class (Jim Walkowicz), 4,349 Libertarian (Jacob Kelts)
- CD 10: 5,905 Working Class (Andrea Kirby), 3,524 Libertarian (Mike Saliba), 4 Write-In (Darko Martinovski)
- CD 12: 8,046 Working Class (Gary Walkowicz)
- CD 13: 8,833 Working Class (Simone Coleman), 2,769 U.S. Taxpayers (Christopher Dardzinski), 3 Write-In (Brenda Sanders), 1 Write-In (Rogelio Landin), 1 Write-In (Ronald Cole)

2022 PRIMARY ELECTIONS: SUPPLEMENTARY INFORMATION

Primary: August 2, 2022

Registration (as of July 2022 – includes 917,002 inactive registrants): 8,119,949 — No Party Registration

Primary Type: Open—Any registered voter could participate in the primary of either party.

MICHIGAN

GENERAL AND PRIMARY ELECTIONS

	REPUBLICAN PRIMARIES			DEMOCRATIC PRIMARIES		
Governor	Dixon, Tudor	436,350	39.7%	Whitmer, Gretchen*	938,382	100.0%
	Rinke, Kevin	236,306	21.5%			
	Soldano, Garrett	192,442	17.5%			
	Kelley, Ryan D.	165,587	15.1%			
	Rebandt, Ralph	45,046	4.1%			
	Craig, James Elmer (Write-In)	23,521	2.1%			
	Adkisson, Elizabeth Ann (Write-In)	11				
	Blackburn, Justin Paul (Write-In)	10				
	TOTAL	1,099,273		TOTAL	938,382	
Congressional District 1	Bergman, Jack*	111,911	100.0%	Lorinser, Bob	67,251	100.0%
	McDonell, David John (Write-In)	6				
	TOTAL	111,917		TOTAL	67,251	
Congressional District 2	Moolenaar, John*	77,394	65.2%	Hilliard, Jerome "Jerry"	40,952	100.0%
	Norton, Thomas John	41,273	34.8%			
	Gonzales, Jericho Joel (Write-In)	37				
	TOTAL	118,704		TOTAL	40,952	
Congressional District 3	Gibbs, John	54,136	51.8%	Scholten, Hillary	59,661	100.0%
	Meijer, Peter*	50,440	48.2%			
	TOTAL	104,576		TOTAL	59,661	
Congressional District 4	Huizenga, Bill*	88,851	100.0%	Alfonso, Joseph (Write-In)	10,992	100.0%
	TOTAL	88,851		TOTAL	10,992	
Congressional District 5	Walberg, Timothy*	67,582	67.2%	Goldberg, Bart	39,971	100.0%
	O'Donnell, Sherry	32,886	32.7%			
	Ferszt, Elizabeth A.(Write-In)	66	0.1%			
	Trouten, Bryan (Write-In)	31				
	TOTAL	100,565		TOTAL	39,971	
Congressional District 6	Williams, Whittney	30,564	53.7%	Dingell, Debbie*	102,859	100.0%
	Kolanagireddy, Hima	26,371	46.3%			
	TOTAL	56,935		TOTAL	102,859	
Congressional District 7	Barrett, Tom	75,491	96.0%	Slotkin, Elissa*	77,826	100.0%
	Hagg, Jacob "Jake"(Write-In)	3,108	4.0%			
	TOTAL	78,599		TOTAL	77,826	
Congressional District 8	Junge, Paul	42,363	53.7%	Kildee, Daniel*	70,791	100.0%
	Seely, Matthew	18,658	23.6%			
	Miller, Candice	17,879	22.7%			
	TOTAL	78,900		TOTAL	70,791	
Congressional District 9	McClain, Lisa*	97,017	78.7%	Jaye, Brian	48,802	100.0%
	Donovan, Michelle R.E.	26,215	21.3%			
	TOTAL	123,232		TOTAL	48,802	
Congressional District 10	James, John	63,417	86.3%	Marlinga, Carl	32,653	47.8%
	Marcinkewciz, Tony	10,079	13.7%	Powell, Rhonda	11,396	16.7%
				Rogensues, Angela	9,503	13.9%
				Arraf, Huwaida	8,846	13.0%
				Yanez, Henry	5,891	8.6%
	TOTAL	73,496		TOTAL	68,289	
Congressional District 11	Ambrose, Mark	42,270	70.5%	Stevens, Haley*	70,508	59.9%
	DenOtter, Matthew	17,702	29.5%	Levin, Andy	47,117	40.1%
	TOTAL	59,972		TOTAL	117,625	

MICHIGAN

GENERAL AND PRIMARY ELECTIONS

	REPUBLICAN PRIMARIES			DEMOCRATIC PRIMARIES		
Congressional District 12	Elliott, Steven	14,431	52.9%	Tlaib, Rashida*	61,635	63.8%
	Hooper, James	9,651	35.4%	Winfrey, Janice	21,636	22.4%
	Nehme, Hassan	3,196	11.7%	Garrett, Mykale "Kelly"	8,334	8.6%
				Jackson, Shanelle	4,927	5.1%
	TOTAL	27,278		TOTAL	96,532	
Congressional District 13	Bivings, Martell	19,618	100.0%	Thanedar, Shri	22,314	28.3%
				Hollier, Adam	18,517	23.5%
				Roberson, Portia	13,318	16.9%
				Conyers, John III	6,778	8.6%
				Gay-Dagnogo, Sherry	6,440	8.2%
				McPhail, Sharon	5,043	6.4%
				Griffie, Michael	3,636	4.6%
				Riddle, Sam	1,841	2.3%
				Rutledge, Lorrie	916	1.2%
				Landin, Rogelio (Write-In)	3	
				Tan, Boratha	3	
	TOTAL	19,618		TOTAL	78,809	

Note: An asterisk (*) denotes incumbent.

MINNESOTA

Statewide Races

Before the 2010 elections, Minnesota Democrats had been locked out of their state's governor's mansion for nearly a generation – from 1990 to 2006, they had lost five consecutive elections. But in 2010, Democrats finally won the governorship with then-former Sen. Mark Dayton. By 2022, Gov. Tim Walz's reelection win marked the fourth consecutive Democratic gubernatorial victory in Minnesota.

In 2018, Walz, then a congressman representing an Obama-to-Trump district in southern Minnesota, ran for governor. Though Minnesota governors are not term-limited, Dayton retired after serving two terms. In a pro-Democratic year, Walz won 54%–42%, up from Dayton's 50%–45% showing from 2014. As he doubled Dayton's margin of victory, Walz made significant improvements in the Twin Cities metro, but slid in almost every rural county. This trend would persist in 2022.

In Minnesota, both parties hold pre-primary conventions, where, if a candidate has sufficient support they earned the party's endorsement, although unsuccessful convention candidates can still compete in the statewide primary. Republican state Sen. Scott Jensen, with a base in Carver County, a blue-trending but still red-leaning suburb of the Twin Cities, earned the GOP endorsement at a convention and had little competition in the primary. In his primary, the incumbent Walz only had token opposition.

While Walz's performance slipped from his 2018 showing, his nearly eight-point margin was still slightly stronger than what Joe Biden carried Minnesota by two years earlier. Hennepin County, which houses Minneapolis and is by far the state's most populous county, gave Walz a 44-percentage point margin up from his 38-point edge in 2018 – in fact, Walz's 250,620 raw vote margin there more than accounted for his 192,408-vote statewide advantage.

Outside of the Twin Cities, the only two counties where Walz improved on his 2018 showings were Cook, at the very tip of the state's northeastern Arrowhead Region, and Rochester's Olmsted. After voting against Dayton twice, Walz carried Olmsted by double-digits in both of his campaigns. Still, rural Minnesota continued to sour on Walz. Norman County, in the northwest, was tied in 2018's gubernatorial race – in 2022, Jensen carried it 58%–37%.

House Races

Though Democrats took a legislative trifecta after the 2022 elections, going into the redistricting process, Republicans controlled the state Senate, giving them a seat at the table. As the legislature deadlocked, redistricting in Minnesota fell to the courts for, at least, the fifth consecutive decade. The court's plan was not a radical departure from the status quo: in the eight-member delegation, four Democrats held Biden-won seats while four Republicans held Trump-won seats.

The most marginal district was the 2nd – over 60% of its residents are in Dakota County, just south of the Twin Cities. Democrat Angie Craig earned a third term by winning a rematch with Republican Tyler Kistner. Craig was likely helped by Walz, who carried the district 53%–45%. In August, Republican Brad Finstad won a special election to the 1st District (Walz's old seat) by four points. As an incumbent, though, Finstad had an easier race, winning 54%–42%, as Jensen carried the district.

MINNESOTA
Congressional districts first established for elections held in 2022
8 members

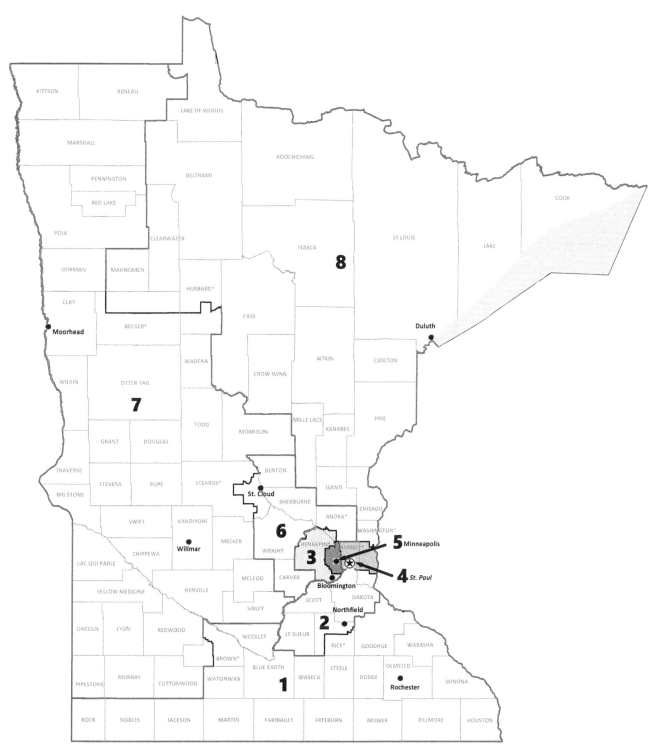

* Asterisk indicates a county whose boundaries include parts of two or more congressional districts.
CDs 3, 4, and 5 are highlighted for visibility. See Inset for Minneapolis area.

MINNESOTA
Minneapolis-St. Paul Area

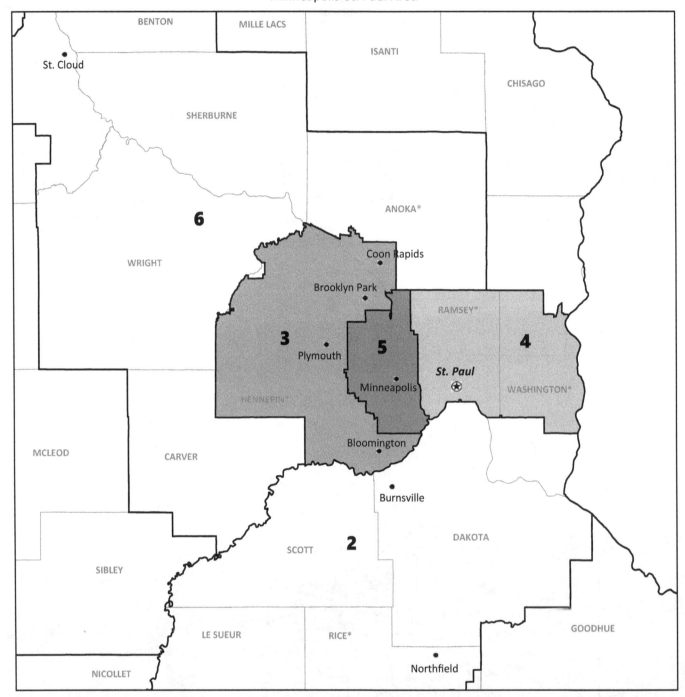

* Asterisk indicates a county whose boundaries include parts of two or more congressional districts.

CDs 3, 4, and 5 are highlighted for visibility.

MINNESOTA

GOVERNOR
Timothy J. Walz (D). Reelected 2022 to a four-year term. Previously elected 2018.

SENATORS (2 Democrats)
Tina Smith (D). Reelected 2020 to a six-year term. Appointed January 3, 2018, to complete the term vacated by Al Franken (D), who resigned January 2, 2018, following sexual assault allegations against him. Smith was elected the last two years of Franken's term in the November 6, 2018, special election.

Amy Klobuchar (D). Reelected 2018 to a six-year term. Previously elected 2012, 2006.

REPRESENTATIVES (4 Republicans, 4 Democrats)
1. Brad Finstad (R)
2. Angie Craig (D)
3. Dean Phillips (D)
4. Betty McCollum (D)
5. Ilhan Omar (D)
6. Tom Emmer (R)
7. Michelle Fischbach (R)
8. Pete Stauber (R)

POSTWAR VOTE FOR PRESIDENT

| | | Republican | | Democratic | | Other Vote | Rep.-Dem. Plurality | Percentage | | | |
| | | | | | | | | Total Vote | | Major Vote | |
Year	Total Vote	Vote	Candidate	Vote	Candidate			Rep.	Dem.	Rep.	Dem.
2020	3,277,171	1,484,065	Trump, Donald J.*	1,717,077	Biden, Joseph R. Jr.	76,029	233,012 D	45.3%	52.4%	46.4%	53.6%
2016**	2,944,813	1,322,951	Trump, Donald J.	1,367,716	Clinton, Hillary Rodham	254,146	44,765 D	44.9%	46.4%	49.2%	50.8%
2012	2,936,561	1,320,225	Romney, W. Mitt	1,546,167	Obama, Barack H.*	70,169	225,942 D	45.0%	52.7%	46.1%	53.9%
2008	2,910,369	1,275,409	McCain, John S. III	1,573,354	Obama, Barack H.	61,606	297,945 D	43.8%	54.1%	44.8%	55.2%
2004	2,828,387	1,346,695	Bush, George W.*	1,445,014	Kerry, John F.	36,678	98,319 D	47.6%	51.1%	48.2%	51.8%
2000**	2,438,685	1,109,659	Bush, George W.	1,168,266	Gore, Albert Jr.	160,760	58,607 D	45.5%	47.9%	48.7%	51.3%
1996**	2,192,640	766,476	Dole, Robert "Bob"	1,120,438	Clinton, Bill*	305,726	353,962 D	35.0%	51.1%	40.6%	59.4%
1992**	2,347,948	747,841	Bush, George H.*	1,020,997	Clinton, Bill	579,110	273,156 D	31.9%	43.5%	42.3%	57.7%
1988	2,096,790	962,337	Bush, George H.	1,109,471	Dukakis, Michael S.	24,982	147,134 D	45.9%	52.9%	46.4%	53.6%
1984	2,084,449	1,032,603	Reagan, Ronald*	1,036,364	Mondale, Walter F.	15,482	3,761 D	49.5%	49.7%	49.9%	50.1%
1980**	2,051,980	873,268	Reagan, Ronald	954,174	Carter, Jimmy*	224,538	80,906 D	42.6%	46.5%	47.8%	52.2%
1976	1,949,931	819,395	Ford, Gerald R.*	1,070,440	Carter, Jimmy	60,096	251,045 D	42.0%	54.9%	43.4%	56.6%
1972	1,741,652	898,269	Nixon, Richard M.*	802,346	McGovern, George S.	41,037	95,923 R	51.6%	46.1%	52.8%	47.2%
1968**	1,588,506	658,643	Nixon, Richard M.	857,738	Humphrey, Hubert Horatio Jr.	72,125	199,095 D	41.5%	54.0%	43.4%	56.6%
1964	1,554,462	559,624	Goldwater, Barry M. Sr.	991,117	Johnson, Lyndon B.*	3,721	431,493 D	36.0%	63.8%	36.1%	63.9%
1960	1,541,887	757,915	Nixon, Richard M.	779,933	Kennedy, John F.	4,039	22,018 D	49.2%	50.6%	49.3%	50.7%
1956	1,340,005	719,302	Eisenhower, Dwight D.*	617,525	Stevenson, Adlai E. II	3,178	101,777 R	53.7%	46.1%	53.8%	46.2%
1952	1,379,483	763,211	Eisenhower, Dwight D.	608,458	Stevenson, Adlai E. II	7,814	154,753 R	55.3%	44.1%	55.6%	44.4%
1948	1,212,226	483,617	Dewey, Thomas E.	692,966	Truman, Harry S.*	35,643	209,349 D	39.9%	57.2%	41.1%	58.9%

Note: An asterisk (*) denotes incumbent. **In past elections, the other vote included: 2016 - 112,972 Libertarian (Gary Johnson); 2000 - 126,696 Green (Nader); 1996 - 257,704 Reform (Ross Perot); 1992 - 562,506 Independent (Perot); 1980 - 174,990 Independent (John Anderson); 1968 - 68,931 American Independent (George Wallace).

MINNESOTA

POSTWAR VOTE FOR GOVERNOR

Year	Total Vote	Republican Vote	Republican Candidate	Democratic Vote	Democratic Candidate	Other Vote	Rep.-Dem. Plurality	Total Vote Rep.	Total Vote Dem.	Major Vote Rep.	Major Vote Dem.
2022	2,510,661	1,119,941	Jensen, Scott	1,312,349	Walz, Timothy J.*	78,371	192,408 D	44.6%	52.3%	46.0%	54.0%
2018	2,587,287	1,097,705	Johnson, Jeff	1,393,096	Walz, Timothy J.	96,486	295,391 D	42.4%	53.8%	44.1%	55.9%
2014	1,975,406	879,257	Johnson, Jeff	989,113	Dayton, Mark*	107,036	109,856 D	44.5%	50.1%	47.1%	52.9%
2010**	2,107,021	910,462	Emmer, Tom	919,232	Dayton, Mark	277,327	8,770 D	43.2%	43.6%	49.8%	50.2%
2006	2,202,937	1,028,568	Pawlenty, Tim*	1,007,460	Hatch, Mike	166,909	21,108 R	46.7%	45.7%	50.5%	49.5%
2002**	2,252,473	999,473	Pawlenty, Tim	821,268	Moe, Roger D.	431,732	178,205 R	44.4%	36.5%	54.9%	45.1%
1998**	2,090,518	716,880	Coleman, Norm	587,060	Humphrey, Hubert Horatio "Skip" III	786,578	129,820 R#	34.3%	28.1%	55.0%	45.0%
1994	1,765,590	1,094,165	Carlson, Arne*	589,344	Marty, John	82,081	504,821 R	62.0%	33.4%	65.0%	35.0%
1990	1,806,777	895,988	Carlson, Arne	836,218	Perpich, Rudy*	74,571	59,770 R	49.6%	46.3%	51.7%	48.3%
1986	1,415,989	606,755	Ludeman, Cal R.	790,138	Perpich, Rudy*	19,096	183,383 D	42.9%	55.8%	43.4%	56.6%
1982	1,789,539	715,796	Whitney, Wheelock	1,049,104	Perpich, Rudy*	24,639	333,308 D	40.0%	58.6%	40.6%	59.4%
1978	1,585,702	830,019	Quie, Albert H.	718,244	Perpich, Rudy*	37,439	111,775 R	52.3%	45.3%	53.6%	46.4%
1974	1,252,898	367,722	Johnson, John W.	786,787	Anderson, Wendell R.*	98,389	419,065 D	29.3%	62.8%	31.9%	68.1%
1970	1,365,443	621,780	Head, Douglas M.	737,921	Anderson, Wendell R.	5,742	116,141 D	45.5%	54.0%	45.7%	54.3%
1966	1,295,058	680,593	Levander, Harold	607,943	Rolvaag, Karl F.*	6,522	72,650 R	52.6%	46.9%	52.8%	47.2%
1962**	1,246,904	619,751	Andersen, Elmer L.*	619,842	Rolvaag, Karl F.	7,311	91 D	49.7%	49.7%	50.0%	50.0%
1960	1,550,265	783,813	Andersen, Elmer L.	760,934	Freeman, Orville L.	5,518	22,879 R	50.6%	49.1%	50.7%	49.3%
1958	1,159,915	490,731	MacKinnon, George	658,326	Freeman, Orville L.*	10,858	167,595 D	42.3%	56.8%	42.7%	57.3%
1956	1,422,161	685,196	Nelsen, Ancher	731,180	Freeman, Orville L.*	5,785	45,984 D	48.2%	51.4%	48.4%	51.6%
1954	1,151,417	538,865	Anderson, C. Elmer*	607,099	Freeman, Orville L.	5,453	68,234 D	46.8%	52.7%	47.0%	53.0%
1952	1,418,869	785,125	Anderson, C. Elmer	624,480	Freeman, Orville L.	9,264	160,645 R	55.3%	44.0%	55.7%	44.3%
1950	1,046,632	635,800	Youngdahl, Luther W.*	400,637	Peterson, Harry H.	10,195	235,163 R	60.7%	38.3%	61.3%	38.7%
1948	1,210,874	643,572	Youngdahl, Luther W.*	545,746	Halsted, Charles L.	21,556	97,826 R	53.1%	45.1%	54.1%	45.9%
1946	880,348	519,067	Youngdahl, Luther W.	349,565	Barker, Harold H.	11,716	169,502 R	59.0%	39.7%	59.8%	40.2%

Note: An asterisk (*) denotes incumbent. A pound sign (#) in the plurality column indicates that the winner in 1998 ran on the Reform Party line. **In past elections, the other vote included: 2010 - 251,487 Independence (Tom Horner); 2002 - 364,534 Independence (Timothy J. Penny); 1998 – 773,403 Reform (Jesse Ventura), who was elected with 37.0% of the total vote and a plurality of 56,523 votes. The term of office of Minnesota's Governor was increased from two to four years effective with the 1962 election.

MINNESOTA

POSTWAR VOTE FOR SENATOR

		Republican		Democratic		Other Vote	Rep.-Dem. Plurality	Percentage			
								Total Vote		Major Vote	
Year	Total Vote	Vote	Candidate	Vote	Candidate			Rep.	Dem.	Rep.	Dem.
2020	3,214,256	1,398,145	Lewis, Jason	1,566,522	Smith, Tina*	249,589	168,377 D	43.5%	48.7%	47.2%	52.8%
2018S**	2,587,356	1,095,777	Housley, Karin	1,370,540	Smith, Tina*	121,039	274,763 D	42.4%	53.0%	44.4%	55.6%
2018	2,596,879	940,437	Newberger, James	1,566,174	Klobuchar, Amy*	90,268	625,737 D	36.2%	60.3%	37.5%	62.5%
2014	1,981,528	850,227	McFadden, Mike	1,053,205	Franken, Al*	78,096	202,978 D	42.9%	53.2%	44.7%	55.3%
2012	2,843,207	867,974	Bills, Kurt	1,854,595	Klobuchar, Amy*	120,638	986,621 D	30.5%	65.2%	31.9%	68.1%
2008**	2,887,646	1,212,317	Coleman, Norm*	1,212,629	Franken, Al	462,700	312 D	42.0%	42.0%	50.0%	50.0%
2006	2,202,772	835,653	Kennedy, Mark	1,278,849	Klobuchar, Amy	88,270	443,196 D	37.9%	58.1%	39.5%	60.5%
2002**	2,254,639	1,116,697	Coleman, Norm	1,067,246	Mondale, Walter F.	70,696	49,451 R	49.5%	47.3%	51.1%	48.9%
2000	2,419,520	1,047,474	Grams, Rod*	1,181,553	Dayton, Mark	190,493	134,079 D	43.3%	48.8%	47.0%	53.0%
1996	2,183,062	901,282	Boschwitz, Rudy	1,098,493	Wellstone, Paul D.*	183,287	197,211 D	41.3%	50.3%	45.1%	54.9%
1994	1,772,929	869,653	Grams, Rod	781,860	Wynia, Ann	121,416	87,793 R	49.1%	44.1%	52.7%	47.3%
1990	1,808,045	864,375	Boschwitz, Rudy*	911,999	Wellstone, Paul D.	31,671	47,624 D	47.8%	50.4%	48.7%	51.3%
1988	2,093,953	1,176,210	Durenberger, David*	856,694	Humphrey, Hubert Horatio "Skip" III	61,049	319,516 R	56.2%	40.9%	57.9%	42.1%
1984	2,066,143	1,199,926	Boschwitz, Rudy*	852,844	Growe, Joan Anderson	13,373	347,082 R	58.1%	41.3%	58.5%	41.5%
1982	1,804,676	949,207	Durenberger, David*	840,401	Dayton, Mark	15,068	108,806 R	52.6%	46.6%	53.0%	47.0%
1978	1,580,778	894,092	Boschwitz, Rudy	638,375	Anderson, Wendell R.*	48,311	255,717 R	56.6%	40.4%	58.3%	41.7%
1978S**	1,560,724	957,908	Durenberger, David	538,675	Short, Robert E.	64,141	419,233 R	61.4%	34.5%	64.0%	36.0%
1976	1,912,068	478,611	Brekke, Gerald W.	1,290,736	Humphrey, Hubert Horatio Jr.*	142,721	812,125 D	25.0%	67.5%	27.1%	72.9%
1972	1,731,653	742,121	Hansen, Philip	981,340	Mondale, Walter F.*	8,192	239,219 D	42.9%	56.7%	43.1%	56.9%
1970	1,364,887	568,025	MacGregor, Clark	788,256	Humphrey, Hubert Horatio Jr.	8,606	220,231 D	41.6%	57.8%	41.9%	58.1%
1966	1,271,426	574,868	Forsythe, Robert A.	685,840	Mondale, Walter F.	10,718	110,972 D	45.2%	53.9%	45.6%	54.4%
1964	1,543,600	605,933	Whitney, Wheelock	931,363	McCarthy, Eugene J.*	6,304	325,430 D	39.3%	60.3%	39.4%	60.6%
1960	1,536,839	648,586	Peterson, P. Kenneth	884,168	Humphrey, Hubert Horatio Jr.*	4,085	235,582 D	42.2%	57.5%	42.3%	57.7%
1958	1,150,883	536,629	Thye, Edward J.	608,847	McCarthy, Eugene J.	5,407	72,218 D	46.6%	52.9%	46.8%	53.2%
1954	1,138,952	479,619	Bjornson, Val	642,193	Humphrey, Hubert Horatio Jr.*	17,140	162,574 D	42.1%	56.4%	42.8%	57.2%
1952	1,387,419	785,649	Thye, Edward J.*	590,011	Carlson, William E.	11,759	195,638 R	56.6%	42.5%	57.1%	42.9%
1948	1,217,250	482,801	Ball, Joseph H.*	729,494	Humphrey, Hubert Horatio Jr.	4,955	246,693 D	39.7%	59.9%	39.8%	60.2%
1946	878,731	517,775	Thye, Edward J.	349,520	Jorgenson, Theodore	11,436	168,255 R	58.9%	39.8%	59.7%	40.3%

Note: An asterisk (*) denotes incumbent. **In past elections, the other vote included: 2008 - 437,505 Independence (Dean Barkley). In October 2002 the Democratic incumbent, Paul Wellstone, was killed in an airplane crash. Walter F. Mondale was named to replace him on the general election ballot. One of the 1978 elections and one of the 2018 elections was for a short term to fill a vacancy.

MINNESOTA
GOVERNOR 2022

2020 Census Population	County	Total Vote	Republican (Jensen)	Democratic (Walz)	Other	Rep.-Dem. Plurality	Percentage			
							Total Vote		Major Vote	
							Rep.	Dem.	Rep.	Dem.
15,950	AITKIN	8,434	5,110	3,030	294	2,080 R	60.6%	35.9%	62.8%	37.2%
358,093	ANOKA	156,313	76,587	74,515	5,211	2,072 R	49.0%	47.7%	50.7%	49.3%
34,547	BECKER	14,747	9,486	4,738	523	4,748 R	64.3%	32.1%	66.7%	33.3%
47,343	BELTRAMI	18,085	9,248	8,124	713	1,124 R	51.1%	44.9%	53.2%	46.8%
41,022	BENTON	16,387	10,495	5,244	648	5,251 R	64.0%	32.0%	66.7%	33.3%
4,997	BIG STONE	2,438	1,492	863	83	629 R	61.2%	35.4%	63.4%	36.6%
67,798	BLUE EARTH	26,509	11,904	13,783	822	1,879 D	44.9%	52.0%	46.3%	53.7%
25,016	BROWN	11,648	7,439	3,915	294	3,524 R	63.9%	33.6%	65.5%	34.5%
36,007	CARLTON	15,896	7,274	7,913	709	639 D	45.8%	49.8%	47.9%	52.1%
105,614	CARVER	54,214	28,078	24,888	1,248	3,190 R	51.8%	45.9%	53.0%	47.0%

MINNESOTA
GOVERNOR 2022

2020 Census Population	County	Total Vote	Republican (Jensen)	Democratic (Walz)	Other	Rep.-Dem. Plurality	Percentage Total Vote Rep.	Dem.	Major Vote Rep.	Dem.
29,924	CASS	15,217	9,626	5,071	520	4,555 R	63.3%	33.3%	65.5%	34.5%
11,794	CHIPPEWA	4,930	3,115	1,676	139	1,439 R	63.2%	34.0%	65.0%	35.0%
56,834	CHISAGO	25,925	15,647	9,321	957	6,326 R	60.4%	36.0%	62.7%	37.3%
64,269	CLAY	22,241	10,199	11,139	903	940 D	45.9%	50.1%	47.8%	52.2%
8,825	CLEARWATER	3,569	2,550	879	140	1,671 R	71.4%	24.6%	74.4%	25.6%
5,463	COOK	3,221	958	2,171	92	1,213 D	29.7%	67.4%	30.6%	69.4%
11,207	COTTONWOOD	4,619	3,087	1,363	169	1,724 R	66.8%	29.5%	69.4%	30.6%
65,351	CROW WING	32,656	20,188	11,388	1,080	8,800 R	61.8%	34.9%	63.9%	36.1%
430,141	DAKOTA	200,613	83,220	112,003	5,390	28,783 D	41.5%	55.8%	42.6%	57.4%
21,004	DODGE	9,421	5,855	3,287	279	2,568 R	62.1%	34.9%	64.0%	36.0%
38,331	DOUGLAS	19,710	12,797	6,358	555	6,439 R	64.9%	32.3%	66.8%	33.2%
13,661	FARIBAULT	6,028	3,846	2,000	182	1,846 R	63.8%	33.2%	65.8%	34.2%
21,098	FILLMORE	9,501	5,432	3,809	260	1,623 R	57.2%	40.1%	58.8%	41.2%
30,302	FREEBORN	13,034	7,262	5,350	422	1,912 R	55.7%	41.0%	57.6%	42.4%
46,450	GOODHUE	23,104	12,407	9,940	757	2,467 R	53.7%	43.0%	55.5%	44.5%
6,004	GRANT	2,953	1,771	1,054	128	717 R	60.0%	35.7%	62.7%	37.3%
1,268,070	HENNEPIN	575,529	154,393	405,013	16,123	250,620 D	26.8%	70.4%	27.6%	72.4%
18,623	HOUSTON	8,745	4,874	3,604	267	1,270 R	55.7%	41.2%	57.5%	42.5%
21,626	HUBBARD	10,649	6,590	3,672	387	2,918 R	61.9%	34.5%	64.2%	35.8%
40,788	ISANTI	18,862	12,271	5,778	813	6,493 R	65.1%	30.6%	68.0%	32.0%
45,217	ITASCA	21,373	11,488	9,017	868	2,471 R	53.8%	42.2%	56.0%	44.0%
9,843	JACKSON	4,560	3,055	1,350	155	1,705 R	67.0%	29.6%	69.4%	30.6%
16,383	KANABEC	7,160	4,582	2,277	301	2,305 R	64.0%	31.8%	66.8%	33.2%
43,152	KANDIYOHI	18,233	11,281	6,421	531	4,860 R	61.9%	35.2%	63.7%	36.3%
4,295	KITTSON	1,926	1,160	689	77	471 R	60.2%	35.8%	62.7%	37.3%
12,223	KOOCHICHING	5,227	2,953	2,058	216	895 R	56.5%	39.4%	58.9%	41.1%
6,623	LAC QUI PARLE	3,150	1,935	1,102	113	833 R	61.4%	35.0%	63.7%	36.3%
10,704	LAKE	5,661	2,501	2,970	190	469 D	44.2%	52.5%	45.7%	54.3%
3,755	LAKE OF THE WOODS	1,828	1,297	473	58	824 R	71.0%	25.9%	73.3%	26.7%
28,953	LE SUEUR	13,217	8,184	4,591	442	3,593 R	61.9%	34.7%	64.1%	35.9%
5,646	LINCOLN	2,440	1,653	710	77	943 R	67.7%	29.1%	70.0%	30.0%
25,363	LYON	9,800	6,267	3,264	269	3,003 R	63.9%	33.3%	65.8%	34.2%
5,527	MAHNOMEN	1,648	898	651	99	247 R	54.5%	39.5%	58.0%	42.0%
9,335	MARSHALL	4,067	2,970	954	143	2,016 R	73.0%	23.5%	75.7%	24.3%
19,696	MARTIN	8,374	5,644	2,471	259	3,173 R	67.4%	29.5%	69.6%	30.4%
35,959	MCLEOD	16,457	10,768	5,171	518	5,597 R	65.4%	31.4%	67.6%	32.4%
23,267	MEEKER	10,814	7,249	3,214	351	4,035 R	67.0%	29.7%	69.3%	30.7%
26,396	MILLE LACS	11,078	7,209	3,390	479	3,819 R	65.1%	30.6%	68.0%	32.0%
33,477	MORRISON	15,458	11,529	3,451	478	8,078 R	74.6%	22.3%	77.0%	23.0%
40,053	MOWER	14,112	7,043	6,573	496	470 R	49.9%	46.6%	51.7%	48.3%
8,194	MURRAY	3,915	2,729	1,051	135	1,678 R	69.7%	26.8%	72.2%	27.8%
34,332	NICOLLET	15,309	6,962	7,929	418	967 D	45.5%	51.8%	46.8%	53.2%
21,624	NOBLES	6,082	4,013	1,854	215	2,159 R	66.0%	30.5%	68.4%	31.6%
6,363	NORMAN	2,504	1,448	929	127	519 R	57.8%	37.1%	60.9%	39.1%
158,737	OLMSTED	68,121	29,068	37,471	1,582	8,403 D	42.7%	55.0%	43.7%	56.3%
58,991	OTTER TAIL	28,518	18,618	8,950	950	9,668 R	65.3%	31.4%	67.5%	32.5%
14,130	PENNINGTON	5,461	3,464	1,734	263	1,730 R	63.4%	31.8%	66.6%	33.4%
29,702	PINE	12,393	7,601	4,290	502	3,311 R	61.3%	34.6%	63.9%	36.1%
9,088	PIPESTONE	3,809	2,819	872	118	1,947 R	74.0%	22.9%	76.4%	23.6%
31,371	POLK	10,934	7,180	3,400	354	3,780 R	65.7%	31.1%	67.9%	32.1%
11,296	POPE	5,673	3,549	1,970	154	1,579 R	62.6%	34.7%	64.3%	35.7%
550,844	RAMSEY	218,077	54,771	155,850	7,456	101,079 D	25.1%	71.5%	26.0%	74.0%
4,063	RED LAKE	1,602	1,047	483	72	564 R	65.4%	30.1%	68.4%	31.6%
15,174	REDWOOD	6,439	4,581	1,698	160	2,883 R	71.1%	26.4%	73.0%	27.0%
14,540	RENVILLE	6,297	4,192	1,883	222	2,309 R	66.6%	29.9%	69.0%	31.0%
66,997	RICE	28,379	13,182	14,252	945	1,070 D	46.4%	50.2%	48.0%	52.0%
9,327	ROCK	4,139	2,877	1,139	123	1,738 R	69.5%	27.5%	71.6%	28.4%
15,140	ROSEAU	6,501	4,783	1,535	183	3,248 R	73.6%	23.6%	75.7%	24.3%
149,681	SCOTT	67,960	35,289	30,870	1,801	4,419 R	51.9%	45.4%	53.3%	46.7%
97,678	SHERBURNE	41,621	26,517	13,697	1,407	12,820 R	63.7%	32.9%	65.9%	34.1%

MINNESOTA
GOVERNOR 2022

2020 Census Population	County	Total Vote	Republican (Jensen)	Democratic (Walz)	Other	Rep.-Dem. Plurality	Percentage Total Vote Rep.	Dem.	Major Vote Rep.	Dem.
14,884	SIBLEY	6,620	4,519	1,907	194	2,612 R	68.3%	28.8%	70.3%	29.7%
199,427	ST. LOUIS	92,840	35,372	53,551	3,917	18,179 D	38.1%	57.7%	39.8%	60.2%
161,104	STEARNS	65,485	39,171	24,162	2,152	15,009 R	59.8%	36.9%	61.8%	38.2%
36,721	STEELE	16,539	9,485	6,498	556	2,987 R	57.3%	39.3%	59.3%	40.7%
9,790	STEVENS	4,033	2,437	1,490	106	947 R	60.4%	36.9%	62.1%	37.9%
9,262	SWIFT	3,917	2,409	1,389	119	1,020 R	61.5%	35.5%	63.4%	36.6%
24,675	TODD	10,859	7,780	2,649	430	5,131 R	71.6%	24.4%	74.6%	25.4%
3,262	TRAVERSE	1,548	968	519	61	449 R	62.5%	33.5%	65.1%	34.9%
21,644	WABASHA	10,731	6,366	4,020	345	2,346 R	59.3%	37.5%	61.3%	38.7%
13,737	WADENA	5,983	4,260	1,511	212	2,749 R	71.2%	25.3%	73.8%	26.2%
18,603	WASECA	8,383	5,212	2,843	328	2,369 R	62.2%	33.9%	64.7%	35.3%
263,775	WASHINGTON	130,714	56,472	70,814	3,428	14,342 D	43.2%	54.2%	44.4%	55.6%
10,854	WATONWAN	3,868	2,325	1,445	98	880 R	60.1%	37.4%	61.7%	38.3%
6,202	WILKIN	2,592	1,783	704	105	1,079 R	68.8%	27.2%	71.7%	28.3%
50,590	WINONA	20,450	9,913	9,889	648	24 R	48.5%	48.4%	50.1%	49.9%
138,975	WRIGHT	66,223	40,993	23,116	2,114	17,877 R	61.9%	34.9%	63.9%	36.1%
9,699	YELLOW MEDICINE	4,361	2,919	1,299	143	1,620 R	66.9%	29.8%	69.2%	30.8%
5,652,495	TOTAL	2,510,661	1,119,941	1,312,349	78,371	192,408 D	44.6%	52.3%	46.0%	54.0%

MINNESOTA
HOUSE OF REPRESENTATIVES

CD	Year	Total Vote	Republican Vote	Republican Candidate	Democratic Vote	Democratic Candidate	Other Vote	Rep.-Dem. Plurality	Total Vote Rep.	Dem.	Major Vote Rep.	Dem.
1	2022	296,547	159,621	FINSTAD, BRAD	125,457	ETTINGER, JEFF	11,469	34,164 R	53.8%	42.3%	56.0%	44.0%
1	2020	368,856	179,234	HAGEDORN, JAMES "JIM"*	167,890	FEEHAN, DAN	21,732	11,344 R	48.6%	45.5%	51.6%	48.4%
1	2018	291,661	146,200	HAGEDORN, JAMES "JIM"	144,885	FEEHAN, DAN	576	1,315 R	50.1%	49.7%	50.2%	49.8%
1	2016	335,877	166,526	HAGEDORN, JAMES "JIM"	169,074	WALZ, TIMOTHY J.*	277	2,548 D	49.6%	50.3%	49.6%	50.4%
1	2014	226,695	103,536	HAGEDORN, JAMES "JIM"	122,851	WALZ, TIMOTHY J.*	308	19,315 D	45.7%	54.2%	45.7%	54.3%
1	2012	335,880	142,164	QUIST, ALLEN	193,211	WALZ, TIMOTHY J.*	505	51,047 D	42.3%	57.5%	42.4%	57.6%
2	2022	325,472	148,576	KISTNER, TYLER	165,583	CRAIG, ANGIE	11,313	17,007 D	45.6%	50.9%	47.3%	52.7%
2	2020	424,512	194,954	KISTNER, TYLER	204,534	CRAIG, ANGIE*	25,024	9,580 D	45.9%	48.2%	48.8%	51.2%
2	2018	337,968	159,344	LEWIS, JASON*	177,958	CRAIG, ANGIE	666	18,614 D	47.1%	52.7%	47.2%	52.8%
2	2016	370,514	173,970	LEWIS, JASON	167,315	CRAIG, ANGIE	29,229	6,655 R	47.0%	45.2%	51.0%	49.0%
2	2014	245,848	137,778	KLINE, JOHN*	95,565	OBERMUELLER, MIKE	12,505	42,213 R	56.0%	38.9%	59.0%	41.0%
2	2012	358,446	193,587	KLINE, JOHN*	164,338	OBERMUELLER, MIKE	521	29,249 R	54.0%	45.8%	54.1%	45.9%
3	2022	333,921	134,797	WEILER, TOM	198,883	PHILLIPS, DEAN	241	64,086 D	40.4%	59.6%	40.4%	59.6%
3	2020	443,603	196,625	QUALLS, KENDALL	246,666	PHILLIPS, DEAN*	312	50,041 D	44.3%	55.6%	44.4%	55.6%
3	2018	363,949	160,839	PAULSEN, ERIK*	202,404	PHILLIPS, DEAN	706	41,565 D	44.2%	55.6%	44.3%	55.7%
3	2016	393,464	223,077	PAULSEN, ERIK*	169,243	BONOFF, TERRI E.	1,144	53,834 R	56.7%	43.0%	56.9%	43.1%
3	2014	269,585	167,515	PAULSEN, ERIK*	101,846	SUND, SHARON	224	65,669 R	62.1%	37.8%	62.2%	37.8%
3	2012	382,705	222,335	PAULSEN, ERIK*	159,937	BARNES, BRIAN	433	62,398 R	58.1%	41.8%	58.2%	41.8%
4	2022	295,973	95,493	LOR XIONG, MAY	200,055	MCCOLLUM, BETTY*	425	104,562 D	32.3%	67.6%	32.3%	67.7%
4	2020	389,114	112,730	RECHTZIGEL, GENE	245,813	MCCOLLUM, BETTY*	30,571	133,083 D	29.0%	63.2%	31.4%	68.6%
4	2018	328,614	97,747	RYAN, GREG	216,865	MCCOLLUM, BETTY*	14,002	119,118 D	29.7%	66.0%	31.1%	68.9%
4	2016	351,944	121,032	RYAN, GREG	203,299	MCCOLLUM, BETTY*	27,613	82,267 D	34.4%	57.8%	37.3%	62.7%
4	2014	241,637	79,492	WAHLGREN, SHARNA	147,857	MCCOLLUM, BETTY*	14,288	68,365 D	32.9%	61.2%	35.0%	65.0%
4	2012	347,991	109,659	HERNANDEZ, TONY	216,685	MCCOLLUM, BETTY*	21,647	107,026 D	31.5%	62.3%	33.6%	66.4%
5	2022	288,206	70,702	DAVIS, CICELY	214,224	OMAR, ILHAN	3,280	143,522 D	24.5%	74.3%	24.8%	75.2%
5	2020	398,229	102,878	JOHNSON, LACY	255,924	OMAR, ILHAN*	39,427	153,046 D	25.8%	64.3%	28.7%	71.3%
5	2018	343,358	74,440	ZIELINSKI, JENNIFER	267,703	OMAR, ILHAN	1,215	193,263 D	21.7%	78.0%	21.8%	78.2%
5	2016	361,882	80,660	DRAKE, FRANK NELSON	249,964	ELLISON, KEITH*	31,258	169,304 D	22.3%	69.1%	24.4%	75.6%
5	2014	236,010	56,577	DAGGETT, DOUG J.	167,079	ELLISON, KEITH*	12,354	110,502 D	24.0%	70.8%	25.3%	74.7%
5	2012	351,969	88,753	FIELDS, CHRIS	262,102	ELLISON, KEITH*	1,114	173,349 D	25.2%	74.5%	25.3%	74.7%

MINNESOTA

HOUSE OF REPRESENTATIVES

CD	Year	Total Vote	Republican Vote	Republican Candidate	Democratic Vote	Democratic Candidate	Other Vote	Rep.-Dem. Plurality	Total Vote Rep.	Total Vote Dem.	Major Vote Rep.	Major Vote Dem.
6	2022	319,767	198,145	EMMER, TOM	120,852	HENDRICKS, JEANNE	770	77,293 R	62.0%	37.8%	62.1%	37.9%
6	2020	412,307	270,901	EMMER, TOM*	140,853	ZAHRADKA, TAWNJA	553	130,048 R	65.7%	34.2%	65.8%	34.2%
6	2018	315,726	192,931	EMMER, TOM*	122,332	TODD, IAN	463	70,599 R	61.1%	38.7%	61.2%	38.8%
6	2016	358,924	235,380	EMMER, TOM*	123,008	SNYDER, DAVID	536	112,372 R	65.6%	34.3%	65.7%	34.3%
6	2014	236,846	133,328	EMMER, TOM	90,926	PERSKE, JOE	12,592	42,402 R	56.3%	38.4%	59.5%	40.5%
6	2012	355,153	179,240	BACHMANN, MICHELE*	174,944	GRAVES, JIM	969	4,296 R	50.5%	49.3%	50.6%	49.4%
7	2022	305,866	204,766	FISCHBACH, MICHELLE	84,455	ABAHSAIN, JILL	16,645	120,311 R	66.9%	27.6%	70.8%	29.2%
7	2020	363,477	194,066	FISCHBACH, MICHELLE	144,840	PETERSON, COLLIN C.*	24,571	49,226 R	53.4%	39.8%	57.3%	42.7%
7	2018	281,509	134,668	HUGHES, DAVE	146,672	PETERSON, COLLIN C.*	169	12,004 D	47.8%	52.1%	47.9%	52.1%
7	2016	330,848	156,952	HUGHES, DAVE	173,589	PETERSON, COLLIN C.*	307	16,637 D	47.4%	52.5%	47.5%	52.5%
7	2014	240,835	109,955	WESTROM, TORREY NORMAN	130,546	PETERSON, COLLIN C.*	334	20,591 D	45.7%	54.2%	45.7%	54.3%
7	2012	327,576	114,151	BYBERG, LEE	197,791	PETERSON, COLLIN C.*	15,634	83,640 D	34.8%	60.4%	36.6%	63.4%
8	2022	330,080	188,755	STAUBER, PETE	141,009	SCHULTZ, JEN	316	47,746 R	57.2%	42.7%	57.2%	42.8%
8	2020	393,711	223,432	STAUBER, PETE*	147,853	NYSTROM, QUINN REABE	22,426	75,579 R	56.8%	37.6%	60.2%	39.8%
8	2018	314,211	159,364	STAUBER, PETE	141,950	RADINOVICH, JOSEPH "JOE"	12,897	17,414 R	50.7%	45.2%	52.9%	47.1%
8	2016	356,979	177,089	MILLS, STEWART	179,098	NOLAN, RICHARD M.*	792	2,009 D	49.6%	50.2%	49.7%	50.3%
8	2014	266,083	125,358	MILLS, STEWART	129,090	NOLAN, RICHARD M.*	11,635	3,732 D	47.1%	48.5%	49.3%	50.7%
8	2012	353,663	160,520	CRAVAACK, CHIP*	191,976	NOLAN, RICHARD M.	1,167	31,456 D	45.4%	54.3%	45.5%	54.5%
TOTAL	2022	2,495,832	1,200,855		1,250,518		44,459	49,663 D	48.1%	50.1%	49.0%	51.0%
TOTAL	2020	3,193,809	1,474,820		1,554,373		164,616	79,553 D	46.2%	48.7%	48.7%	51.3%
TOTAL	2018	2,576,996	1,125,533		1,420,769		30,694	295,236 D	43.7%	55.1%	44.2%	55.8%
TOTAL	2016	2,860,432	1,334,686		1,434,590		91,156	99,904 D	46.7%	50.2%	48.2%	51.8%
TOTAL	2014	1,963,539	913,539		985,760		64,240	72,221 D	46.5%	50.2%	48.1%	51.9%
TOTAL	2012	2,813,383	1,210,409		1,560,984		41,990	350,575 D	43.0%	55.5%	43.7%	56.3%

Note: An asterisk (*) denotes incumbent.

MINNESOTA

GENERAL AND PRIMARY ELECTIONS

GENERAL ELECTIONS: OTHER VOTES

Governor — Other vote was 29,346 Legal Marijuana Now (James McCaskel), 22,599 Grassroots – Legalize Cannabis (Steve Patterson), 18,156 Independence-Alliance (Hugh McTavish), 7,241 Socialist Workers Party (Gabrielle Prosser), 1,029 Write-In (Write-Ins)

House — Other vote was:

CD 1 — 6,389 Legal Marijuana Now (Richard Reisdorf), 4,943 Grassroots - Legalize Cannabis (Brian Abrahamson), 137 Write-In (Write-Ins)

CD 2 — 10,728 Legal Marijuana Now (Paula Overby), 585 Write-In (Write-Ins)

CD 3 — 241 Write-In (Write-Ins)

CD 4 — 425 Write-In (Write-Ins)

CD 5 — 3,280 Write-In (Write-Ins)

CD 6 — 770 Write-In (Write-Ins)

CD 7 — 16,421 Legal Marijuana Now (Travis Johnson), 224 Write-In (Write-Ins)

CD 8 — 316 Write-In (Write-Ins)

MINNESOTA

GENERAL AND PRIMARY ELECTIONS

2022 PRIMARY ELECTIONS: SUPPLEMENTARY INFORMATION

Primary	August 9, 2022	**Registration** (as of June 1, 2022)	3,559,251	No Party Registration
Primary Type	Open—Any registered voter could participate in the party primary of their choice.			

	REPUBLICAN PRIMARIES			DEMOCRATIC PRIMARIES		
Governor	Jensen, Scott	288,499	89.3%	Walz, Timothy J.*	416,973	96.5%
	Lacey, Joyce Lynne	21,308	6.6%	Savior, Olé	14,950	3.5%
	Carney, Bob "Again" Jr.	13,213	4.1%			
	TOTAL	*323,020*		*TOTAL*	*431,923*	
Congressional District 1						
Congressional District 2						
Congressional District 3						
Congressional District 4	Lor Xiong, May	9,574	44.1%	McCollum, Betty*	58,043	83.4%
	Silver, Jerry	7,399	34.1%	Badhasso, Amane	10,557	15.2%
	Rechtzigel, Gene	4,753	21.9%	Moghul, Fasil	997	1.4%
	TOTAL	*21,726*		*TOTAL*	*69,597*	
Congressional District 5	Davis, Cicely	4,765	48.0%	Omar, Ilhan*	57,683	50.3%
	White, Royce Alexaner	3,689	37.2%	Samuels, Don	55,217	48.2%
	Gaskin, Guy T.	1,476	14.9%	Schluter, Nate	671	0.6%
				Kern, Aliena Jeanene "A.J."	519	0.5%
				Ross, Albert	477	0.4%
	TOTAL	*9,930*		*TOTAL*	*114,567*	
Congressional District 6						
Congressional District 7	Fischbach, Michelle*	59,429	100.0%	Abahsain, Jill	14,352	59.0%
				Gruenhagen, Alycia R.	9,972	41.0%
	TOTAL	*59,429*		*TOTAL*	*24,324*	
Congressional District 8	Stauber, Pete*	51,410	91.0%	Schultz, Jen	38,545	86.1%
	Welty, Harry Robb	5,075	9.0%	Munter, John	6,199	13.9%
	TOTAL	*56,485*		*TOTAL*	*44,744*	

Note: An asterisk (*) denotes incumbent.

MISSISSIPPI

Statewide Races

Neither of Mississippi's Senate seats were up in 2022 and the state holds its gubernatorial races in the odd-numbered years preceding presidential election years.

House Races

After the 2000 census, Mississippi dropped from five districts down to four. Since then, its four districts have seen only minor changes.

In statewide elections, Democrats typically only carry the 2nd District, which includes Mississippi's Delta and the state capital of Jackson. Democrat Bennie Thompson has represented the district since 1993 – before chairing the January 6th Select Committee, he had a relatively low-key profile. Though Thompson, as he always does, won comfortably, his margin hinted at low enthusiasm from Black voters: in a district that is close to two-thirds Black by composition, Thompson took 60%.

None of Mississippi's three Republican-held seats would have given Joe Biden over 40% of the vote in 2020. All saw sleepy general elections in 2022, but two hosted notable primaries.

In the 3rd District, which is a wide swath of central Mississippi, first-term Rep. Michael Guest only narrowly led challenger Michael Cassidy in the early June primary. Guest stressed his fiscal conservative credentials, but his vote to establish a committee investigating the January 6th insurrection gave Cassidy fodder. In the runoff, though, Cassidy underwhelmed, and Guest got a boost from *Congressional Leadership Fund*, a super PAC with ties to then-House Minority Leader Kevin McCarthy. Guest won the runoff two-to-one.

In the 4th District, which contains the state's portion of the Gulf Coast, six-term Rep. Steve Palazzo lost renomination. In 2021, a House Ethics Committee report found evidence that strongly suggested Palazzo misspent campaign funds. Palazzo placed first in the seven-way primary but took less than one-third of the vote. Jackson County sheriff Mike Ezell won the ensuing runoff 54%–46%.

MISSISSIPPI

Congressional districts first established for elections held in 2022

4 members

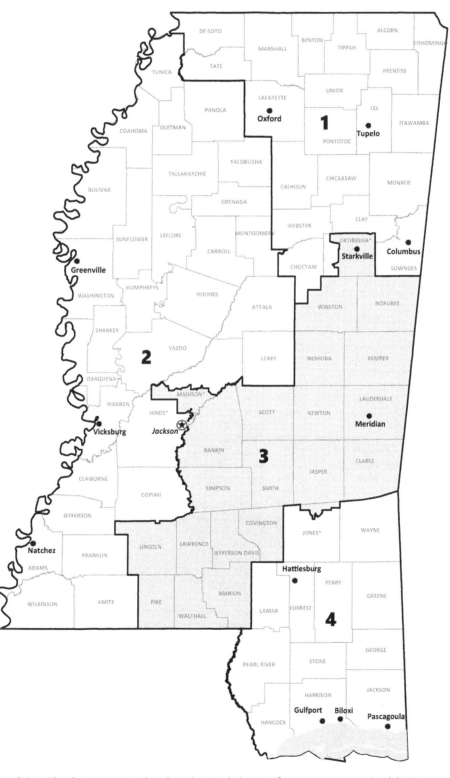

* Asterisk indicates a county whose boundaries include parts of two or more congressional districts.

CD 3 is highlighted for visibility.

MISSISSIPPI

GOVERNOR
Tate Reeves (R). Elected 2019 to a four-year term.

SENATORS (2 Republicans)
Cindy Hyde-Smith (R). Reelected 2020 to a six-year term. Appointed by the governor as interim senator following the April 1, 2018, resignation of W. Thad Cochran (R) due to health issues. Hyde-Smith was sworn in April 9, 2018, and was elected to fill the final two years of Cochran's term in the in the November 27, 2018, special election runoff.

Roger F. Wicker (R). Reelected 2018 to a six-year term. Previously elected 2012 and 2008 to fill the final four years of the term vacated by the December 2007 resignation of C. Trent Lott. Wicker had been appointed to fill the vacancy and was sworn in as senator on December 31, 2007.

REPRESENTATIVES (3 Republicans, 1 Democrat)
1. Mike Ezell (R)
2. Bennie Thompson (D)
3. Michael Guest (R)
4. Steven Palazzo (R)

POSTWAR VOTE FOR PRESIDENT

		Republican		Democratic		Other Vote	Rep.-Dem. Plurality	Percentage			
								Total Vote		Major Vote	
Year	Total Vote	Vote	Candidate	Vote	Candidate			Rep.	Dem.	Rep.	Dem.
2020	1,313,759	756,764	Trump, Donald J.*	539,398	Biden, Joseph R. Jr.	17,597	217,366 R	57.6%	41.1%	58.4%	41.6%
2016**	1,209,357	700,714	Trump, Donald J.	485,131	Clinton, Hillary Rodham	23,512	215,583 R	57.9%	40.1%	59.1%	40.9%
2012	1,285,584	710,746	Romney, W. Mitt	562,949	Obama, Barack H.*	11,889	147,797 R	55.3%	43.8%	55.8%	44.2%
2008	1,289,865	724,597	McCain, John S. III	554,662	Obama, Barack H.	10,606	169,935 R	56.2%	43.0%	56.6%	43.4%
2004	1,152,145	684,981	Bush, George W.*	458,094	Kerry, John F.	9,070	226,887 R	59.5%	39.8%	59.9%	40.1%
2000**	994,184	572,844	Bush, George W.	404,614	Gore, Albert Jr.	16,726	168,230 R	57.6%	40.7%	58.6%	41.4%
1996**	893,857	439,838	Dole, Robert "Bob"	394,022	Clinton, Bill*	59,997	45,816 R	49.2%	44.1%	52.7%	47.3%
1992**	981,793	487,793	Bush, George H.*	400,258	Clinton, Bill	93,742	87,535 R	49.7%	40.8%	54.9%	45.1%
1988	931,527	557,890	Bush, George H.	363,921	Dukakis, Michael S.	9,716	193,969 R	59.9%	39.1%	60.5%	39.5%
1984	941,104	582,377	Reagan, Ronald*	352,192	Mondale, Walter F.	6,535	230,185 R	61.9%	37.4%	62.3%	37.7%
1980**	892,620	441,089	Reagan, Ronald	429,281	Carter, Jimmy*	22,250	11,808 R	49.4%	48.1%	50.7%	49.3%
1976	769,361	366,846	Ford, Gerald R.*	381,309	Carter, Jimmy	21,206	14,463 D	47.7%	49.6%	49.0%	51.0%
1972	645,963	505,125	Nixon, Richard M.*	126,782	McGovern, George S.	14,056	378,343 R	78.2%	19.6%	79.9%	20.1%
1968**	654,509	88,516	Nixon, Richard M.	150,644	Humphrey, Hubert Horatio Jr.	415,349	62,128 D#	13.5%	23.0%	37.0%	63.0%
1964	409,146	356,528	Goldwater, Barry M. Sr.	52,618	Johnson, Lyndon B.*		303,910 R	87.1%	12.9%	87.1%	12.9%
1960**	298,171	73,561	Nixon, Richard M.	108,362	Kennedy, John F.	116,248	34,801 D#	24.7%	36.3%	40.4%	59.6%
1956	248,104	60,685	Eisenhower, Dwight D.*	144,453	Stevenson, Adlai E. II	42,966	83,768 D	24.5%	58.2%	29.6%	70.4%
1952	285,532	112,966	Eisenhower, Dwight D.	172,566	Stevenson, Adlai E. II		59,600 D	39.6%	60.4%	39.6%	60.4%
1948**	192,190	5,043	Dewey, Thomas E.	19,384	Truman, Harry S.*	167,763	14,041 D#	2.6%	10.1%	20.6%	79.4%

Note: An asterisk (*) denotes incumbent. A pound sign (#) indicates that the state was carried by a third party candidate or independent electoral state. **In past elections, the other vote included: 2016 - 14,435 Libertarian (Gary Johnson); 2000 - 8,122 Green (Ralph Nader); 1996 - 52,222 Reform (Ross Perot); 1992 - 85,626 Independent (Perot); 1980 - 12,036 Independent (John Anderson); 1968 - 415,349 American Independent (George Wallace); 1960 -116,248 Unpledged Independent Democratic electors; 1948 - 167,538 States' Rights (Strom Thurmond). Thurmond won Mississippi in 1948 with 87.2 percent of the vote. The slate of Unpledged Independent Democratic electors carried the state in 1960 with 39.0 percent. Wallace won Mississippi in 1968 with 63.5 percent of the vote.

MISSISSIPPI

POSTWAR VOTE FOR GOVERNOR

Year	Total Vote	Republican Vote	Republican Candidate	Democratic Vote	Democratic Candidate	Other Vote	Rep.-Dem.	Total Vote Rep.	Total Vote Dem.	Major Vote Rep.	Major Vote Dem.
2019	884,911	459,396	Reeves, Tate	414,368	Hood, Jim	11,147	45,028 R	51.9%	46.8%	52.6%	47.4%
2015	725,207	480,399	Bryant, Phil*	234,858	Gray, Robert	9,950	245,541 R	66.2%	32.4%	67.2%	32.8%
2011	893,468	544,851	Bryant, Phil	348,617	DuPree, Johnny L.		196,234 R	61.0%	39.0%	61.0%	39.0%
2007	744,039	430,807	Barbour, Haley*	313,232	Eaves, John Arthur Jr.		117,575 R	57.9%	42.1%	57.9%	42.1%
2003	894,487	470,404	Barbour, Haley	409,787	Musgrove, Ronnie*	14,296	60,617 R	52.6%	45.8%	53.4%	46.6%
1999**	763,938	370,691	Parker, Mike	379,034	Musgrove, Ronnie	14,213	8,343 D	48.5%	49.6%	49.4%	50.6%
1995	819,471	455,261	Fordice, Kirk*	364,210	Molpus, Dick		91,051 R	55.6%	44.4%	55.6%	44.4%
1991	711,188	361,500	Fordice, Kirk	338,435	Mabus, Ray*	11,253	23,065 R	50.8%	47.6%	51.6%	48.4%
1987	721,695	336,006	Reed, Jack R.	385,689	Mabus, Ray		49,683 D	46.6%	53.4%	46.6%	53.4%
1983	742,737	288,764	Bramlett, Leon	409,209	Allain, William A.	44,764	120,445 D	38.9%	55.1%	41.4%	58.6%
1979	677,322	263,702	Carmichael, Gil	413,620	Winter, William		149,918 D	38.9%	61.1%	38.9%	61.1%
1975	708,033	319,632	Carmichael, Gil	369,568	Finch, Cliff	18,833	49,936 D	45.1%	52.2%	46.4%	53.6%
1971**	780,537			601,122	Waller, William L.	179,415	601,122 D		77.0%		100.0%
1967	448,696	133,378	Phillips, Rubel L.	315,318	Williams, John Bell		181,940 D	29.7%	70.3%	29.7%	70.3%
1963	363,971	138,515	Phillips, Rubel L.	225,456	Johnson, Paul B. Jr.		86,941 D	38.1%	61.9%	38.1%	61.9%
1959	57,671			57,671	Barnett, Ross R.		57,671 D		100.0%		100.0%
1955	40,707			40,707	Coleman, James P.		40,707 D		100.0%		100.0%
1951	43,422			43,422	White, Hugh L.		43,422 D		100.0%		100.0%
1947	166,095			161,993	Wright, Fielding L.	4,102	161,993 D		97.5%		100.0%

Note: An asterisk (*) denotes incumbent. **In past elections, the other vote included: 1971 - 172,762 Independent (Charles Evers), who finished second. In 1999, no candidate received a majority of the vote. Democrat Ronnie Musgrove was elected in January 2000 by the Mississippi House of Representatives. The Republican Party did not run a gubernatorial candidate in 1947, 1951, 1955, 1959, and 1971.

POSTWAR VOTE FOR SENATOR

Year	Total Vote	Republican Vote	Republican Candidate	Democratic Vote	Democratic Candidate	Other Vote	Rep.-Dem. Plurality	Total Vote Rep.	Total Vote Dem.	Major Vote Rep.	Major Vote Dem.
2020	1,311,354	709,511	Hyde-Smith, Cindy*	578,691	Espy, Mike	23,152	130,820 R	54.1%	44.1%	55.1%	44.9%
2018	936,215	547,619	Wicker, Roger F.*	369,567	Baria, David	19,029	178,052 R	58.5%	39.5%	59.7%	40.3%
2018S**	907,588	486,769	Hyde-Smith, Cindy*	420,819	Espy, Mike		65,950 R	53.6%	46.4%	53.6%	46.4%
2014	631,858	378,481	Cochran, W. Thad*	239,439	Childers, Travis	13,938	139,042 R	59.9%	37.9%	61.3%	38.7%
2012	1,241,568	709,626	Wicker, Roger F.*	503,467	Gore, Albert N. Jr.	28,475	206,159 R	57.2%	40.6%	58.5%	41.5%
2008S	1,243,473	683,409	Wicker, Roger F.*	560,064	Musgrove, Ronnie		123,345 R	55.0%	45.0%	55.0%	45.0%
2008	1,247,026	766,111	Cochran, W. Thad*	480,915	Fleming, Erik R.		285,196 R	61.4%	38.6%	61.4%	38.6%
2006	610,921	388,399	Lott, C. Trent*	213,000	Fleming, Erik R.	9,522	175,399 R	63.6%	34.9%	64.6%	35.4%
2002**	630,495	533,269	Cochran, W. Thad*			97,226	533,269 R	84.6%		100.0%	
2000	994,144	654,941	Lott, C. Trent*	314,090	Brown, Troy	25,113	340,851 R	65.9%	31.6%	67.6%	32.4%
1996	878,662	624,154	Cochran, W. Thad*	240,647	Hunt, James W. "Bootie"	13,861	383,507 R	71.0%	27.4%	72.2%	27.8%
1994	608,085	418,333	Lott, C. Trent*	189,752	Harper, Ken		228,581 R	68.8%	31.2%	68.8%	31.2%
1990	274,244	274,244	Cochran, W. Thad*				274,244 R	100.0%		100.0%	
1988	946,719	510,380	Lott, C. Trent	436,339	Dowdy, Wayne		74,041 R	53.9%	46.1%	53.9%	46.1%
1984	952,240	580,314	Cochran, W. Thad*	371,926	Winter, William		208,388 R	60.9%	39.1%	60.9%	39.1%
1982	645,026	230,927	Barbour, Haley	414,099	Stennis, John*		183,172 D	35.8%	64.2%	35.8%	64.2%
1978**	583,936	263,089	Cochran, W. Thad	185,454	Dantin, Maurice	135,393	77,635 R	45.1%	31.8%	58.7%	41.3%
1976	554,433			554,433	Stennis, John*		554,433 D		100.0%		100.0%
1972	645,746	249,779	Carmichael, Gil	375,102	Eastland, James O.*	20,865	125,323 D	38.7%	58.1%	40.0%	60.0%
1970**	324,215			286,622	Stennis, John*	37,593	286,622 D		88.4%		100.0%
1966	394,541	105,652	Walker, Prentiss	258,248	Eastland, James O.*	30,641	152,596 D	26.8%	65.5%	29.0%	71.0%
1964	343,364			343,364	Stennis, John*		343,364 D		100.0%		100.0%
1960	266,148	21,807	Moore, Joe A.	244,341	Eastland, James O.*		222,534 D	8.2%	91.8%	8.2%	91.8%
1958	61,039			61,039	Stennis, John*		61,039 D		100.0%		100.0%
1954	105,526	4,678	White, James A.	100,848	Eastland, James O.*		96,170 D	4.4%	95.6%	4.4%	95.6%
1952	233,919			233,919	Stennis, John*		233,919 D		100.0%		100.0%
1948	151,478			151,478	Eastland, James O.*		151,478 D		100.0%		100.0%
1947S**	193,086					193,086					
1946	46,747			46,747	Bilbo, Theodore G.*		46,747 D		100.0%		100.0%

Note: An asterisk (*) denotes incumbent. **In past elections, the other vote included: 2002 - 97,226 Reform (Shawn O'Hara), who finished second; 1978 - 133,646 Independent (Charles Evers). The 1947 election and one each of the 2008 and 2018 elections were for short terms to fill a vacancy. The results from the latter two elections reflect the outcomes of runoffs. In 1947, John Stennis received 52,068 votes (26.9 percent of the total vote) and won the election with a plurality of 6,343 votes. Other candidates that year included: 45,725 W. M. Colmer; 43,642 Forrest B. Jackson; 27,159 Paul B. Johnson; 24,492 John E. Rankin. The Republican Party did not run a candidate in Senate elections in 1946, 1948, 1952, 1958, 1964, 1970, and 1976. The Democratic Party did not run a candidate in Senate elections in 1990 and 2002.

MISSISSIPPI

HOUSE OF REPRESENTATIVES

			Republican		Democratic		Other Vote	Rep.-Dem. Plurality	Percentage			
									Total Vote		Major Vote	
CD	Year	Total Vote	Vote	Candidate	Vote	Candidate			Rep.	Dem.	Rep.	Dem.
1	2022	167,389	122,151	KELLY, TRENT*	45,238	BLACK, DIANNE		76,913 R	73.0%	27.0%	73.0%	27.0%
1	2020	332,795	228,787	KELLY, TRENT*	104,008	ELIASON, ANTONIA		124,779 R	68.7%	31.3%	68.7%	31.3%
1	2018	236,521	158,245	KELLY, TRENT*	76,601	WADKINS, RANDY	1,675	81,644 R	66.9%	32.4%	67.4%	32.6%
1	2016	300,423	206,455	KELLY, TRENT*	83,947	OWENS, JACOB	10,021	122,508 R	68.7%	27.9%	71.1%	28.9%
1	2014	151,111	102,622	NUNNELEE, ALAN*	43,713	DICKEY, RON E.	4,776	58,909 R	67.9%	28.9%	70.1%	29.9%
1	2012	309,177	186,760	NUNNELEE, ALAN*	114,076	MORRIS, BRAD	8,341	72,684 R	60.4%	36.9%	62.1%	37.9%
2	2022	180,169	71,884	FLOWERS, BRIAN	108,285	THOMPSON, BENNIE*		36,401 D	39.9%	60.1%	39.9%	60.1%
2	2020	297,234	101,010	FLOWERS, BRIAN	196,224	THOMPSON, BENNIE*		95,214 D	34.0%	66.0%	34.0%	66.0%
2	2018	221,379			158,921	THOMPSON, BENNIE*	62,458	158,921 D		71.8%		100.0%
2	2016	286,626	83,542	BOUIE, JOHN II	192,343	THOMPSON, BENNIE*	10,741	108,801 D	29.1%	67.1%	30.3%	69.7%
2	2014	148,646			100,688	THOMPSON, BENNIE*	47,958	100,688 D		67.7%		100.0%
2	2012	320,244	99,160	MARCY, BILL	214,978	THOMPSON, BENNIE*	6,106	115,818 D	31.0%	67.1%	31.6%	68.4%
3	2022	187,284	132,481	GUEST, MICHAEL*			54,803	132,481 R	70.7%		100.0%	
3	2020	341,846	221,064	GUEST, MICHAEL*	120,782	BENFORD, DOROTHY		100,282 R	64.7%	35.3%	64.7%	35.3%
3	2018	257,271	160,284	GUEST, MICHAEL	94,461	EVANS, MICHAEL	2,526	65,823 R	62.3%	36.7%	62.9%	37.1%
3	2016	316,445	209,490	HARPER, GREGG*	96,101	QUINN, DENNIS C.	10,854	113,389 R	66.2%	30.4%	68.6%	31.4%
3	2014	170,946	117,771	HARPER, GREGG*	47,744	MAGEE, DOUGLAS MACARTHUR "DOUG"	5,431	70,027 R	68.9%	27.9%	71.2%	28.8%
3	2012	293,322	234,717	HARPER, GREGG*			58,605	234,717 R	80.0%		100.0%	
4	2022	174,258	127,813	EZELL, MIKE	42,876	DUPREE, JOHNNY L.	3,569	84,937 R	73.3%	24.6%	74.9%	25.1%
4	2020	255,971	255,971	PALAZZO, STEVEN*				255,971 R	100.0%		100.0%	
4	2018	223,732	152,633	PALAZZO, STEVEN*	68,787	ANDERSON, JERAMEY	2,312	83,846 R	68.2%	30.7%	68.9%	31.1%
4	2016	278,779	181,323	PALAZZO, STEVEN*	77,505	GLADNEY, MARK	19,951	103,818 R	65.0%	27.8%	70.1%	29.9%
4	2014	155,576	108,776	PALAZZO, STEVEN*	37,869	MOORE, MATT	8,931	70,907 R	69.9%	24.3%	74.2%	25.8%
4	2012	285,432	182,998	PALAZZO, STEVEN*	82,344	MOORE, MATT	20,090	100,654 R	64.1%	28.8%	69.0%	31.0%
TOTAL	2022	709,100	454,329		196,399		58,372	257,930 R	64.1%	27.7%	69.8%	30.2%
TOTAL	2020	1,227,846	806,832		421,014			385,818 R	65.7%	34.3%	65.7%	34.3%
TOTAL	2018	938,903	471,162		398,770		68,971	72,392 R	50.2%	42.5%	54.2%	45.8%
TOTAL	2016	1,182,273	680,810		449,896		51,567	230,914 R	57.6%	38.1%	60.2%	39.8%
TOTAL	2014	626,279	329,169		230,014		67,096	99,155 R	52.6%	36.7%	58.9%	41.1%
TOTAL	2012	1,208,175	703,635		411,398		93,142	292,237 R	58.2%	34.1%	63.1%	36.9%

Note: An asterisk (*) denotes incumbent.

MISSISSIPPI

GENERAL AND PRIMARY ELECTIONS

GENERAL ELECTIONS: OTHER VOTES

House   Other vote was:

CD 4   3,569 Libertarian (Alden Johnson)

2022 PRIMARY ELECTIONS: SUPPLEMENTARY INFORMATION

Primary	June 7, 2022	**Registration** (as of June 2022)	1,918,343	No Party Registration
Primary Runoff	June 28, 2022			
Primary Type	Open—Any registered voter could participate in the party primary of his or her choice. But any voter who cast a ballot in the primary of one party could not vote in the runoff of the other party.			

MISSISSIPPI

GENERAL AND PRIMARY ELECTIONS

	REPUBLICAN PRIMARIES			DEMOCRATIC PRIMARIES		
Congressional District 1	Kelly, Trent*	27,447	89.8%	Black, Dianne	8,268	79.0%
	Strauss, Mark David	3,109	10.2%	Avery, Hunter	2,203	21.0%
	TOTAL	30,556		TOTAL	10,471	
Congressional District 2	Flowers, Brian	6,087	43.2%	Thompson, Bennie*	49,907	96.3%
	Eller, Ronald	4,564	32.4%	Kerner, Gerald "Jerry"	1,927	3.7%
	Carson, Michael	2,966	21.0%			
	Johnson, Stanford	487	3.5%			
	TOTAL	14,104		TOTAL	51,834	
	PRIMARY RUNOFF					
	Flowers, Brian	6,224	58.5%			
	Eller, Ronald	4,418	41.5%			
	TOTAL	10,642				
Congressional District 3	Guest, Michael*	23,675	47.5%			
	Cassidy, Michael	23,407	46.9%			
	Griffin, Thomas B.	2,785	5.6%			
	TOTAL	49,867				
	PRIMARY RUNOFF					
	Guest, Michael*	47,007	67.4%			
	Cassidy, Michael	22,713	32.6%			
	TOTAL	69,720				
Congressional District 4	Palazzo, Steven*	16,387	31.5%	DuPree, Johnny L.	9,952	84.9%
	Ezell, Mike	13,020	25.0%	Sellers, David	1,766	15.1%
	Wagner, Clay	11,698	22.5%			
	Wiggins, Brice	4,859	9.3%			
	Boyanton, Carl	3,224	6.2%			
	Brooks, Raymond N.	2,405	4.6%			
	Peterson, Kidron	449	0.9%			
	TOTAL	52,042		TOTAL	11,718	
	PRIMARY RUNOFF					
	Ezell, Mike	31,225	53.8%			
	Palazzo, Steven*	26,849	46.2%			
	TOTAL	58,074				

Note: An asterisk (*) denotes incumbent.

MISSOURI

Statewide Races

In 2022, the Show-Me State saw an open-seat contest for Senate. Once a prime presidential bellwether, Missouri has moved sharply rightward in the years since 2008, when Barack Obama became the first presidential nominee since 1956 to win the White House without it.

In March 2021, two-term Republican Sen. Roy Blunt announced he would not run in 2022, when his seat came up. Blunt easily made the jump from the House to the Senate in 2010 but was held to a three-point margin in 2016 by then-Missouri Secretary of State Jason Kander (D). With the Biden administration unpopular in Missouri, though, Republicans were heavy favorites to hold Blunt's seat – as long as they didn't run a toxic nominee, which was not inevitable.

In Missouri, there was no shortage of ambitious Republicans who considered the race. Two members of the House delegation, 4th District Rep. Vicki Hartzler and 7th District Rep. Billy Long, as well as state Attorney General Eric Schmitt were among a crowded field of contenders. But another name, that was notable for the wrong reasons, was former Gov. Eric Greitens. Elected in 2016, he resigned in 2018 when faced with domestic abuse allegations. Though he was leading in some polls, anti-Greitens forces took to the airwaves late in the primary campaign. Trump, in a written endorsement that was claimed by multiple candidates, simply telegraphed his support for "Eric." But Greitens took just 19% and carried only three counties, all in the southwestern Bootheel. Hartzler, placing second, carried her district but not much else. Schmitt won with 46%. Democrats, meanwhile, opted for Trudy Busch Valentine, from a well-known brewing family, over veteran Lucas Kunce, who ran as a progressive.

The general election lined up with expectations: Schmitt, who was up by a dozen or so points in most polls, won 55%–42%. Busch Valentine carried Kansas City's Jackson County, Columbia's Boone County, as well as the duo of St. Louis City and County. Schmitt took everything else, clearing 70% of the vote in 85 of the 114 counties. Busch Valentine came close to carrying Clay and Platte counties, which are suburban communities north of Kansas City.

House Races

Despite protests from many of its more conservative members, the GOP-dominated Missouri legislature passed a map that was designed to preserve Republicans' 6-2 advantage in the state delegation. It would have theoretically been possible to increase the GOP's advantage to 7-1 by splitting Jackson County among several districts – but Republican mappers may have deemed that too risky.

Republicans also sought to protect Rep. Ann Wagner. Holding the suburban St. Louis 2nd District, she was first elected in 2012. Wagner was easily reelected in 2014 and 2016 but had a close call in 2018. In 2020, as her district was about evenly split in the presidential race, she won 52%–45% – noticeably ahead of Trump, but not the type of landslide margin that she used to get. As Wagner's seat added two exurban counties in the remap, she won 55%–43%.

MISSOURI

Congressional districts first established for elections held in 2022

8 members

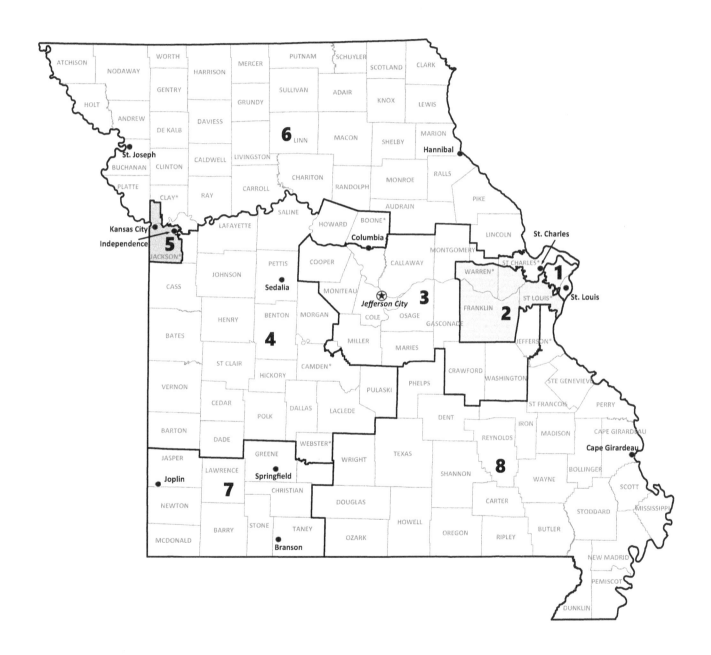

The city of St. Louis is an independent city that is treated as a county equivalent; so is Kansas City for voting purposes.

* Asterisk indicates a county whose boundaries include parts of two or more congressional districts.

CDs 1, 2, and 5 are highlighted for visibility.

MISSOURI

GOVERNOR
Mike Parson (R). Reelected 2020 to a four-year term. Sworn in June 1, 2018, to fill the seat vacated by Eric Greitens (R), who resigned May 29, 2018, due to allegations of sexual misconduct and misuse of voter data during the 2016 election.

SENATORS (2 Republicans)
Eric Schmitt (R). Elected 2022 to a six-year term.

Josh Hawley (R). Elected 2018 to a six-year term.

REPRESENTATIVES (6 Republicans, 2 Democrats)
1. Cori Bush (D)
2. Ann Wagner (R)
3. Blaine Luetkemeyer (R)
4. Mark Alford (R)
5. Emanuel Cleaver II (D)
6. Samuel B. Graves Jr. (R)
7. Eric Burlison (R)
8. Jason Smith (R)

POSTWAR VOTE FOR PRESIDENT

Year	Total Vote	Republican Vote	Republican Candidate	Democratic Vote	Democratic Candidate	Other Vote	Rep.-Dem. Plurality	Total Vote Rep.	Total Vote Dem.	Major Vote Rep.	Major Vote Dem.
2020	3,025,962	1,718,736	Trump, Donald J.*	1,253,014	Biden, Joseph R. Jr.	54,212	465,722 R	56.8%	41.4%	57.8%	42.2%
2016	2,808,605	1,594,511	Trump, Donald J.	1,071,068	Clinton, Hillary Rodham	143,026	523,443 R	56.8%	38.1%	59.8%	40.2%
2012	2,757,323	1,482,440	Romney, W. Mitt	1,223,796	Obama, Barack H.*	51,087	258,644 R	53.8%	44.4%	54.8%	45.2%
2008	2,925,205	1,445,814	McCain, John S. III	1,441,911	Obama, Barack H.	37,480	3,903 R	49.4%	49.3%	50.1%	49.9%
2004	2,731,364	1,455,713	Bush, George W.*	1,259,171	Kerry, John F.	16,480	196,542 R	53.3%	46.1%	53.6%	46.4%
2000**	2,359,892	1,189,924	Bush, George W.	1,111,138	Gore, Albert Jr.	58,830	78,786 R	50.4%	47.1%	51.7%	48.3%
1996**	2,158,065	890,016	Dole, Robert "Bob"	1,025,935	Clinton, Bill*	242,114	135,919 D	41.2%	47.5%	46.5%	53.5%
1992**	2,391,565	811,159	Bush, George H.*	1,053,873	Clinton, Bill	526,533	242,714 D	33.9%	44.1%	43.5%	56.5%
1988	2,093,713	1,084,953	Bush, George H.	1,001,619	Dukakis, Michael S.	7,141	83,334 R	51.8%	47.8%	52.0%	48.0%
1984	2,122,783	1,274,188	Reagan, Ronald*	848,583	Mondale, Walter F.	12	425,605 R	60.0%	40.0%	60.0%	40.0%
1980**	2,099,824	1,074,181	Reagan, Ronald	931,182	Carter, Jimmy*	94,461	142,999 R	51.2%	44.3%	53.6%	46.4%
1976	1,953,600	927,443	Ford, Gerald R.*	998,387	Carter, Jimmy	27,770	70,944 D	47.5%	51.1%	48.2%	51.8%
1972	1,855,803	1,153,852	Nixon, Richard M.*	697,147	McGovern, George S.	4,804	456,705 R	62.2%	37.6%	62.3%	37.7%
1968**	1,809,502	811,932	Nixon, Richard M.	791,444	Humphrey, Hubert Horatio Jr.	206,126	20,488 R	44.9%	43.7%	50.6%	49.4%
1964	1,817,879	653,535	Goldwater, Barry M. Sr.	1,164,344	Johnson, Lyndon B.*		510,809 D	36.0%	64.0%	36.0%	64.0%
1960	1,934,422	962,221	Nixon, Richard M.	972,201	Kennedy, John F.		9,980 D	49.7%	50.3%	49.7%	50.3%
1956	1,832,562	914,289	Eisenhower, Dwight D.*	918,273	Stevenson, Adlai E. II		3,984 D	49.9%	50.1%	49.9%	50.1%
1952	1,892,062	959,429	Eisenhower, Dwight D.	929,830	Stevenson, Adlai E. II	2,803	29,599 R	50.7%	49.1%	50.8%	49.2%
1948	1,578,628	655,039	Dewey, Thomas E.	917,315	Truman, Harry S.*	6,274	262,276 D	41.5%	58.1%	41.7%	58.3%

Note: An asterisk (*) denotes incumbent. **In past elections, the other vote included: 2000 - 38,515 Green (Ralph Nader); 1996 - 217,188 Reform (Ross Perot); 1992 - 518,741 Independent (Perot); 1980 - 77,920 Independent (John Anderson); 1968 - 206,126 American Independent (George Wallace).

MISSOURI

POSTWAR VOTE FOR GOVERNOR

Year	Total Vote	Republican Vote	Republican Candidate	Democratic Vote	Democratic Candidate	Other Vote	Rep.-Dem. Plurality	Total Vote Rep.	Total Vote Dem.	Major Vote Rep.	Major Vote Dem.
2020**	3,012,287	1,720,202	Parson, Mike*	1,225,771	Galloway, Nicole	66,314	494,431 R	57.1%	40.7%	58.4%	41.6%
2016	2,803,046	1,433,397	Greitens, Eric	1,277,360	Koster, Chris	92,289	156,037 R	51.1%	45.6%	52.9%	47.1%
2012	2,727,883	1,160,265	Spence, David "Dave"	1,494,056	Nixon, Jay W.*	73,562	333,791 D	42.5%	54.8%	43.7%	56.3%
2008	2,877,778	1,136,364	Hulshof, Kenny	1,680,611	Nixon, Jay W.	60,803	544,247 D	39.5%	58.4%	40.3%	59.7%
2004	2,719,599	1,382,419	Blunt, Matt	1,301,442	McCaskill, Claire	35,738	80,977 R	50.8%	47.9%	51.5%	48.5%
2000	2,346,830	1,131,307	Talent, James M.	1,152,752	Holden, Bob	62,771	21,445 D	48.2%	49.1%	49.5%	50.5%
1996	2,142,518	866,268	Kelly, Margaret	1,224,801	Carnahan, Mel*	51,449	358,533 D	40.4%	57.2%	41.4%	58.6%
1992	2,343,999	968,574	Webster, William L.	1,375,425	Carnahan, Mel		406,851 D	41.3%	58.7%	41.3%	58.7%
1988	2,085,928	1,339,531	Ashcroft, John*	724,919	Hearnes, Betty C.	21,478	614,612 R	64.2%	34.8%	64.9%	35.1%
1984	2,108,210	1,194,506	Ashcroft, John	913,700	Rothman, Kenneth J.	4	280,806 R	56.7%	43.3%	56.7%	43.3%
1980	2,088,028	1,098,950	Bond, Kit	981,884	Teasdale, Joseph P.*	7,194	117,066 R	52.6%	47.0%	52.8%	47.2%
1976	1,933,575	958,110	Bond, Kit*	971,184	Teasdale, Joseph P.	4,281	13,074 D	49.6%	50.2%	49.7%	50.3%
1972	1,865,683	1,029,451	Bond, Kit	832,751	Dowd, Edward L.	3,481	196,700 R	55.2%	44.6%	55.3%	44.7%
1968	1,764,602	691,797	Roos, Lawrence K.	1,072,805	Hearnes, Warren E.*		381,008 D	39.2%	60.8%	39.2%	60.8%
1964	1,789,600	678,949	Shepley, Ethan A.H.	1,110,651	Hearnes, Warren E.		431,702 D	37.9%	62.1%	37.9%	62.1%
1960	1,887,326	792,131	Farmer, Edward G.	1,095,195	Dalton, John M.		303,064 D	42.0%	58.0%	42.0%	58.0%
1956	1,808,338	866,810	Hocker, Lon	941,528	Blair, James T. Jr.		74,718 D	47.9%	52.1%	47.9%	52.1%
1952	1,870,998	886,270	Elliott, Howard	983,169	Donnelly, Phil M.	1,559	96,899 D	47.4%	52.5%	47.4%	52.6%
1948	1,567,338	670,064	Thompson, Murray E.	893,092	Smith, Forrest	4,182	223,028 D	42.8%	57.0%	42.9%	57.1%

Note: An asterisk (*) denotes incumbent. **Mike Parson, formerly the leiutenant governor, became governor in 2018 following the resignation of Eric Greitens.

POSTWAR VOTE FOR SENATOR

Year	Total Vote	Republican Vote	Republican Candidate	Democratic Vote	Democratic Candidate	Other Vote	Rep.-Dem. Plurality	Total Vote Rep.	Total Vote Dem.	Major Vote Rep.	Major Vote Dem.
2022	2,069,130	1,146,966	Schmitt, Eric	872,694	Busch Valentine, Trudy	49,470	274,272 R	55.4%	42.2%	56.8%	43.2%
2018	2,442,289	1,254,927	Hawley, Josh	1,112,935	McCaskill, Claire*	74,427	141,992 R	51.4%	45.6%	53.0%	47.0%
2016	2,802,641	1,378,458	Blunt, Roy*	1,300,200	Kander, Jason	123,983	78,258 R	49.2%	46.4%	51.5%	48.5%
2012	2,725,793	1,066,159	Akin, Todd	1,494,125	McCaskill, Claire*	165,509	427,966 D	39.1%	54.8%	41.6%	58.4%
2010	1,943,899	1,054,160	Blunt, Roy	789,736	Carnahan, Robin	100,003	264,424 R	54.2%	40.6%	57.2%	42.8%
2006	2,128,459	1,006,941	Talent, James M.*	1,055,255	McCaskill, Claire	66,263	48,314 D	47.3%	49.6%	48.8%	51.2%
2004	2,706,402	1,518,089	Bond, Kit*	1,158,261	Farmer, Nancy	30,052	359,828 R	56.1%	42.8%	56.7%	43.3%
2002S**	1,877,620	935,032	Talent, James M.	913,778	Carnahan, Jean*	28,810	21,254 R	49.8%	48.7%	50.6%	49.4%
2000**	2,361,586	1,142,852	Ashcroft, John*	1,191,812	Carnahan, Mel	26,922	48,960 D	48.4%	50.5%	49.0%	51.0%
1998	1,576,857	830,625	Bond, Kit*	690,208	Nixon, Jay W.	56,024	140,417 R	52.7%	43.8%	54.6%	45.4%
1994	1,775,116	1,060,149	Ashcroft, John	633,697	Wheat, Alan	81,270	426,452 R	59.7%	35.7%	62.6%	37.4%
1992	2,354,925	1,221,901	Bond, Kit*	1,057,967	Rothman-Serot, Geri	75,057	163,934 R	51.9%	44.9%	53.6%	46.4%
1988	2,078,875	1,407,416	Danforth, John C.*	660,045	Nixon, Jay W.	11,414	747,371 R	67.7%	31.8%	68.1%	31.9%
1986	1,477,327	777,612	Bond, Kit	699,624	Woods, Harriett	91	77,988 R	52.6%	47.4%	52.6%	47.4%
1982	1,543,521	784,876	Danforth, John C.*	758,629	Woods, Harriett	16	26,247 R	50.8%	49.1%	50.9%	49.1%
1980	2,066,965	985,399	McNary, Gene	1,074,859	Eagleton, Thomas F.*	6,707	89,460 D	47.7%	52.0%	47.8%	52.2%
1976	1,914,777	1,090,067	Danforth, John C.	813,571	Hearnes, Warren E.	11,139	276,496 R	56.9%	42.5%	57.3%	42.7%
1974	1,224,303	480,900	Curtis, Thomas B.	735,433	Eagleton, Thomas F.*	7,970	254,533 D	39.3%	60.1%	39.5%	60.5%
1970	1,283,912	617,903	Danforth, John C.	655,431	Symington, Stuart*	10,578	37,528 D	48.1%	51.0%	48.5%	51.5%
1968	1,737,958	850,544	Curtis, Thomas B.	887,414	Eagleton, Thomas F.		36,870 D	48.9%	51.1%	48.9%	51.1%
1964	1,783,043	596,377	Bradshaw, Jean Paul	1,186,666	Symington, Stuart*		590,289 D	33.4%	66.6%	33.4%	66.6%
1962	1,222,259	555,330	Kemper, Crosby	666,929	Long, Edward V.*		111,599 D	45.4%	54.6%	45.4%	54.6%
1960S**	1,880,232	880,576	Hocker, Lon	999,656	Long, Edward V.		119,080 D	46.8%	53.2%	46.8%	53.2%
1958	1,173,930	393,847	Palmer, Hazel	780,083	Symington, Stuart*		386,236 D	33.5%	66.5%	33.5%	66.5%
1956	1,800,984	785,048	Douglas, Herbert	1,015,936	Hennings, Thomas Carey Jr.*		230,888 D	43.6%	56.4%	43.6%	56.4%
1952	1,868,083	858,170	Kem, James P.*	1,008,523	Symington, Stuart	1,390	150,353 D	45.9%	54.0%	46.0%	54.0%
1950	1,279,631	593,139	Donnell, Forrest C.*	685,732	Hennings, Thomas Carey Jr.	760	92,593 D	46.4%	53.6%	46.4%	53.6%
1946	1,084,100	572,556	Kem, James P.	511,544	Briggs, Frank		61,012 R	52.8%	47.2%	52.8%	47.2%

Note: An asterisk (*) denotes incumbent. **In 2000, the Democratic candidate, Mel Carnahan, was killed in an airplane crash in October but his name remained on the ballot and he won the election in November. Subsequently, his widow, Jean Carnahan, was appointed to fill the seat until an election could be held in 2002 for the remaining four years of the term. The 1960 and 2002 elections were for short terms to fill a vacancy.

MISSOURI
SENATOR 2022

2020 Census Population	County City	Total Vote	Republican (Schmitt)	Democratic (Busch Valentine)	Other	Rep.-Dem. Plurality	Percentage Total Vote Rep.	Dem.	Major Vote Rep.	Dem.
25,278	ADAIR	7,071	4,423	2,460	188	1,963 R	62.6%	34.8%	64.3%	35.7%
17,771	ANDREW	6,727	4,885	1,657	185	3,228 R	72.6%	24.6%	74.7%	25.3%
5,143	ATCHISON	1,910	1,468	392	50	1,076 R	76.9%	20.5%	78.9%	21.1%
25,393	AUDRAIN	7,469	5,209	2,069	191	3,140 R	69.7%	27.7%	71.6%	28.4%
35,938	BARRY	10,973	8,537	2,046	390	6,491 R	77.8%	18.6%	80.7%	19.3%
11,769	BARTON	4,326	3,654	586	86	3,068 R	84.5%	13.5%	86.2%	13.8%
16,194	BATES	5,766	4,227	1,362	177	2,865 R	73.3%	23.6%	75.6%	24.4%
19,564	BENTON	7,728	5,717	1,773	238	3,944 R	74.0%	22.9%	76.3%	23.7%
12,127	BOLLINGER	4,168	3,589	507	72	3,082 R	86.1%	12.2%	87.6%	12.4%
181,054	BOONE	63,110	25,940	35,608	1,562	9,668 D	41.1%	56.4%	42.1%	57.9%
87,334	BUCHANAN	24,570	14,828	8,884	858	5,944 R	60.4%	36.2%	62.5%	37.5%
42,597	BUTLER	11,519	9,345	1,872	302	7,473 R	81.1%	16.3%	83.3%	16.7%
9,047	CALDWELL	3,432	2,588	745	99	1,843 R	75.4%	21.7%	77.6%	22.4%
44,733	CALLAWAY	15,003	9,917	4,622	464	5,295 R	66.1%	30.8%	68.2%	31.8%
46,511	CAMDEN	18,289	13,380	4,384	525	8,996 R	73.2%	24.0%	75.3%	24.7%
79,067	CAPE GIRARDEAU	27,888	20,511	6,650	727	13,861 R	73.5%	23.8%	75.5%	24.5%
8,693	CARROLL	3,359	2,610	685	64	1,925 R	77.7%	20.4%	79.2%	20.8%
5,959	CARTER	1,911	1,578	298	35	1,280 R	82.6%	15.6%	84.1%	15.9%
106,355	CASS	39,799	24,848	13,927	1,024	10,921 R	62.4%	35.0%	64.1%	35.9%
14,434	CEDAR	5,149	3,962	929	258	3,033 R	76.9%	18.0%	81.0%	19.0%
7,434	CHARITON	2,813	2,083	667	63	1,416 R	74.0%	23.7%	75.7%	24.3%
89,131	CHRISTIAN	33,300	24,206	8,070	1,024	16,136 R	72.7%	24.2%	75.0%	25.0%
6,818	CLARK	2,349	1,738	535	76	1,203 R	74.0%	22.8%	76.5%	23.5%
251,367	CLAY	87,406	43,210	41,987	2,209	1,223 R	49.4%	48.0%	50.7%	49.3%
20,421	CLINTON	7,569	5,147	2,219	203	2,928 R	68.0%	29.3%	69.9%	30.1%
76,845	COLE	28,538	18,289	9,487	762	8,802 R	64.1%	33.2%	65.8%	34.2%
17,725	COOPER	6,128	4,198	1,737	193	2,461 R	68.5%	28.3%	70.7%	29.3%
23,941	CRAWFORD	7,603	5,822	1,610	171	4,212 R	76.6%	21.2%	78.3%	21.7%
7,583	DADE	2,997	2,395	501	101	1,894 R	79.9%	16.7%	82.7%	17.3%
16,938	DALLAS	5,752	4,449	1,097	206	3,352 R	77.3%	19.1%	80.2%	19.8%
8,263	DAVIESS	2,709	2,029	608	72	1,421 R	74.9%	22.4%	76.9%	23.1%
12,609	DEKALB	3,394	2,575	700	119	1,875 R	75.9%	20.6%	78.6%	21.4%
15,583	DENT	5,014	4,030	822	162	3,208 R	80.4%	16.4%	83.1%	16.9%
13,210	DOUGLAS	5,032	4,101	780	151	3,321 R	81.5%	15.5%	84.0%	16.0%
29,020	DUNKLIN	6,220	4,906	1,167	147	3,739 R	78.9%	18.8%	80.8%	19.2%
104,241	FRANKLIN	37,088	25,089	11,139	860	13,950 R	67.6%	30.0%	69.3%	30.7%
14,756	GASCONADE	5,712	4,306	1,299	107	3,007 R	75.4%	22.7%	76.8%	23.2%
6,584	GENTRY	2,325	1,748	528	49	1,220 R	75.2%	22.7%	76.8%	23.2%
294,249	GREENE	98,011	55,499	39,211	3,301	16,288 R	56.6%	40.0%	58.6%	41.4%
9,808	GRUNDY	3,226	2,514	641	71	1,873 R	77.9%	19.9%	79.7%	20.3%
8,352	HARRISON	2,736	2,237	445	54	1,792 R	81.8%	16.3%	83.4%	16.6%
21,895	HENRY	7,528	5,232	2,084	212	3,148 R	69.5%	27.7%	71.5%	28.5%
9,613	HICKORY	3,668	2,747	796	125	1,951 R	74.9%	21.7%	77.5%	22.5%
4,406	HOLT	1,671	1,383	262	26	1,121 R	82.8%	15.7%	84.1%	15.9%
10,029	HOWARD	3,872	2,529	1,212	131	1,317 R	65.3%	31.3%	67.6%	32.4%
40,182	HOWELL	13,298	10,336	2,452	510	7,884 R	77.7%	18.4%	80.8%	19.2%
10,144	IRON	3,072	2,246	747	79	1,499 R	73.1%	24.3%	75.0%	25.0%
704,043	JACKSON	130,597	64,471	62,895	3,231	1,576 R	49.4%	48.2%	50.6%	49.4%
121,694	JASPER	34,699	25,183	8,500	1,016	16,683 R	72.6%	24.5%	74.8%	25.2%
225,564	JEFFERSON	79,438	48,881	28,670	1,887	20,211 R	61.5%	36.1%	63.0%	37.0%
54,125	JOHNSON	15,672	10,019	5,134	519	4,885 R	63.9%	32.8%	66.1%	33.9%
	KANSAS CITY	86,004	16,353	68,143	1,508	51,790 D	19.0%	79.2%	19.4%	80.6%
3,964	KNOX	1,366	996	317	53	679 R	72.9%	23.2%	75.9%	24.1%
35,808	LACLEDE	11,351	9,018	1,948	385	7,070 R	79.4%	17.2%	82.2%	17.8%
32,813	LAFAYETTE	12,030	8,233	3,525	272	4,708 R	68.4%	29.3%	70.0%	30.0%
38,474	LAWRENCE	12,561	9,834	2,316	411	7,518 R	78.3%	18.4%	80.9%	19.1%
9,762	LEWIS	3,152	2,339	716	97	1,623 R	74.2%	22.7%	76.6%	23.4%
59,525	LINCOLN	19,873	14,099	5,202	572	8,897 R	70.9%	26.2%	73.0%	27.0%
11,914	LINN	4,131	2,915	1,129	87	1,786 R	70.6%	27.3%	72.1%	27.9%
15,277	LIVINGSTON	4,743	3,523	1,131	89	2,392 R	74.3%	23.8%	75.7%	24.3%

MISSOURI
SENATOR 2022

2020 Census Population	County City	Total Vote	Republican (Schmitt)	Democratic (Busch Valentine)	Other	Rep.-Dem. Plurality	Percentage Total Vote Rep.	Dem.	Major Vote Rep.	Dem.
15,121	MACON	5,588	4,264	1,174	150	3,090 R	76.3%	21.0%	78.4%	21.6%
12,109	MADISON	3,720	2,907	721	92	2,186 R	78.1%	19.4%	80.1%	19.9%
8,707	MARIES	3,454	2,737	652	65	2,085 R	79.2%	18.9%	80.8%	19.2%
28,568	MARION	8,693	6,254	2,197	242	4,057 R	71.9%	25.3%	74.0%	26.0%
22,872	MCDONALD	6,091	5,001	887	203	4,114 R	82.1%	14.6%	84.9%	15.1%
3,621	MERCER	1,264	1,028	213	23	815 R	81.3%	16.9%	82.8%	17.2%
25,729	MILLER	8,739	6,889	1,574	276	5,315 R	78.8%	18.0%	81.4%	18.6%
13,128	MISSISSIPPI	2,896	2,237	592	67	1,645 R	77.2%	20.4%	79.1%	20.9%
16,139	MONITEAU	5,128	3,903	1,088	137	2,815 R	76.1%	21.2%	78.2%	21.8%
8,664	MONROE	3,158	2,344	739	75	1,605 R	74.2%	23.4%	76.0%	24.0%
11,607	MONTGOMERY	4,085	2,990	1,015	80	1,975 R	73.2%	24.8%	74.7%	25.3%
20,699	MORGAN	6,951	5,150	1,584	217	3,566 R	74.1%	22.8%	76.5%	23.5%
17,036	NEW MADRID	4,412	3,347	964	101	2,383 R	75.9%	21.8%	77.6%	22.4%
58,379	NEWTON	19,937	15,565	3,878	494	11,687 R	78.1%	19.5%	80.1%	19.9%
22,111	NODAWAY	7,061	4,757	2,156	148	2,601 R	67.4%	30.5%	68.8%	31.2%
10,544	OREGON	3,071	2,391	571	109	1,820 R	77.9%	18.6%	80.7%	19.3%
13,655	OSAGE	5,533	4,587	856	90	3,731 R	82.9%	15.5%	84.3%	15.7%
9,172	OZARK	3,699	2,960	610	129	2,350 R	80.0%	16.5%	82.9%	17.1%
15,677	PEMISCOT	3,217	2,457	707	53	1,750 R	76.4%	22.0%	77.7%	22.3%
19,115	PERRY	6,340	5,113	1,101	126	4,012 R	80.6%	17.4%	82.3%	17.7%
42,397	PETTIS	13,152	9,032	3,677	443	5,355 R	68.7%	28.0%	71.1%	28.9%
44,628	PHELPS	13,618	9,268	4,001	349	5,267 R	68.1%	29.4%	69.8%	30.2%
18,318	PIKE	5,167	3,738	1,299	130	2,439 R	72.3%	25.1%	74.2%	25.8%
105,025	PLATTE	41,120	20,304	19,918	898	386 R	49.4%	48.4%	50.5%	49.5%
32,287	POLK	10,563	7,948	2,184	431	5,764 R	75.2%	20.7%	78.4%	21.6%
52,603	PULASKI	9,313	6,703	2,224	386	4,479 R	72.0%	23.9%	75.1%	24.9%
4,697	PUTNAM	1,714	1,379	287	48	1,092 R	80.5%	16.7%	82.8%	17.2%
10,319	RALLS	3,982	2,917	935	130	1,982 R	73.3%	23.5%	75.7%	24.3%
24,732	RANDOLPH	7,424	5,242	1,954	228	3,288 R	70.6%	26.3%	72.8%	27.2%
23,069	RAY	7,939	5,286	2,403	250	2,883 R	66.6%	30.3%	68.7%	31.3%
6,283	REYNOLDS	2,396	1,817	512	67	1,305 R	75.8%	21.4%	78.0%	22.0%
13,271	RIPLEY	3,735	3,005	609	121	2,396 R	80.5%	16.3%	83.1%	16.9%
22,725	SALINE	6,278	4,030	2,079	169	1,951 R	64.2%	33.1%	66.0%	34.0%
4,669	SCHUYLER	1,530	1,182	304	44	878 R	77.3%	19.9%	79.5%	20.5%
4,912	SCOTLAND	1,360	1,010	305	45	705 R	74.3%	22.4%	76.8%	23.2%
38,256	SCOTT	11,625	9,210	2,161	254	7,049 R	79.2%	18.6%	81.0%	19.0%
8,165	SHANNON	2,910	2,243	586	81	1,657 R	77.1%	20.1%	79.3%	20.7%
5,940	SHELBY	2,298	1,753	479	66	1,274 R	76.3%	20.8%	78.5%	21.5%
403,742	ST. CHARLES	150,979	83,559	64,552	2,868	19,007 R	55.3%	42.8%	56.4%	43.6%
9,432	ST. CLAIR	3,692	2,711	835	146	1,876 R	73.4%	22.6%	76.5%	23.5%
67,449	ST. FRANCOIS	18,238	12,552	5,197	489	7,355 R	68.8%	28.5%	70.7%	29.3%
995,221	ST. LOUIS	369,628	137,197	226,772	5,659	89,575 D	37.1%	61.4%	37.7%	62.3%
298,643	ST. LOUIS CITY	84,096	12,835	69,839	1,422	57,004 D	15.3%	83.0%	15.5%	84.5%
17,948	STE. GENEVIEVE	6,640	4,329	2,181	130	2,148 R	65.2%	32.8%	66.5%	33.5%
29,021	STODDARD	8,637	7,320	1,145	172	6,175 R	84.8%	13.3%	86.5%	13.5%
32,092	STONE	13,809	10,784	2,662	363	8,122 R	78.1%	19.3%	80.2%	19.8%
6,064	SULLIVAN	1,744	1,360	344	40	1,016 R	78.0%	19.7%	79.8%	20.2%
56,286	TANEY	17,795	13,734	3,542	519	10,192 R	77.2%	19.9%	79.5%	20.5%
25,433	TEXAS	8,257	6,621	1,337	299	5,284 R	80.2%	16.2%	83.2%	16.8%
20,570	VERNON	6,156	4,620	1,325	211	3,295 R	75.0%	21.5%	77.7%	22.3%
35,864	WARREN	13,172	9,103	3,768	301	5,335 R	69.1%	28.6%	70.7%	29.3%
24,746	WASHINGTON	6,934	5,267	1,498	169	3,769 R	76.0%	21.6%	77.9%	22.1%
12,852	WAYNE	4,064	3,374	605	85	2,769 R	83.0%	14.9%	84.8%	15.2%
39,714	WEBSTER	14,206	10,667	3,008	531	7,659 R	75.1%	21.2%	78.0%	22.0%
2,016	WORTH	863	651	184	28	467 R	75.4%	21.3%	78.0%	22.0%
18,393	WRIGHT	6,244	5,210	819	215	4,391 R	83.4%	13.1%	86.4%	13.6%
6,149,506	TOTAL	2,069,130	1,146,966	872,694	49,470	274,272 R	55.4%	42.2%	56.8%	43.2%

MISSOURI
HOUSE OF REPRESENTATIVES

			Republican		Democratic		Other Vote	Rep.-Dem. Plurality	Percentage			
									Total Vote		Major Vote	
CD	Year	Total Vote	Vote	Candidate	Vote	Candidate			Rep.	Dem.	Rep.	Dem.
1	2022	220,958	53,767	JONES, ANDREW	160,999	BUSH, CORI*	6,192	107,232 D	24.3%	72.9%	25.0%	75.0%
1	2020	316,171	59,940	ROGERS, ANTHONY	249,087	BUSH, CORI	7,144	189,147 D	19.0%	78.8%	19.4%	80.6%
1	2018	274,375	45,867	VROMAN, ROBERT	219,781	CLAY, WILLIAM LACY JR.*	8,727	173,914 D	16.7%	80.1%	17.3%	82.7%
1	2016	314,024	62,714	BAILEY, STEVEN G.	236,993	CLAY, WILLIAM LACY JR.*	14,317	174,279 D	20.0%	75.5%	20.9%	79.1%
1	2014	163,494	35,273	ELDER, DANIEL J.	119,315	CLAY, WILLIAM LACY JR.*	8,906	84,042 D	21.6%	73.0%	22.8%	77.2%
1	2012	340,583	60,832	HAMLIN, ROBYN	267,927	CLAY, WILLIAM LACY JR.*	11,824	207,095 D	17.9%	78.7%	18.5%	81.5%
2	2022	315,666	173,277	WAGNER, ANN*	135,895	GUNBY, PATRICIA "TRISH"	6,494	37,382 R	54.9%	43.1%	56.0%	44.0%
2	2020	449,348	233,157	WAGNER, ANN*	204,540	SCHUPP, JILL DARLYNE	11,651	28,617 R	51.9%	45.5%	53.3%	46.7%
2	2018	376,066	192,477	WAGNER, ANN*	177,611	VANOSTRAN, CORT	5,978	14,866 R	51.2%	47.2%	52.0%	48.0%
2	2016	413,296	241,954	WAGNER, ANN*	155,689	OTTO, BILL	15,653	86,265 R	58.5%	37.7%	60.8%	39.2%
2	2014	231,117	148,191	WAGNER, ANN*	75,384	LIEBER, ARTHUR	7,542	72,807 R	64.1%	32.6%	66.3%	33.7%
2	2012	394,448	236,971	WAGNER, ANN	146,272	KOENEN, GLENN	11,205	90,699 R	60.1%	37.1%	61.8%	38.2%
3	2022	277,597	180,746	LUETKEMEYER, BLAINE*	96,851	MANN, BETHANY		83,895 R	65.1%	34.9%	65.1%	34.9%
3	2020	407,348	282,866	LUETKEMEYER, BLAINE*	116,095	REZABEK, MEGAN	8,387	166,771 R	69.4%	28.5%	70.9%	29.1%
3	2018	324,608	211,243	LUETKEMEYER, BLAINE*	106,589	GEPPERT, KATY	6,776	104,654 R	65.1%	32.8%	66.5%	33.5%
3	2016	368,333	249,865	LUETKEMEYER, BLAINE*	102,891	MILLER, KEVIN	15,577	146,974 R	67.8%	27.9%	70.8%	29.2%
3	2014	191,620	130,940	LUETKEMEYER, BLAINE*	52,021	DENTON, COURTNEY	8,659	78,919 R	68.3%	27.1%	71.6%	28.4%
3	2012	338,385	214,843	LUETKEMEYER, BLAINE*	111,189	MAYER, ERIC C.	12,353	103,654 R	63.5%	32.9%	65.9%	34.1%
4	2022	255,079	181,890	ALFORD, MARK	67,069	TRUMAN, JACK	6,120	114,821 R	71.3%	26.3%	73.1%	26.9%
4	2020	362,836	245,247	HARTZLER, VICKY*	107,635	SIMMONS, LINDSEY NICOLE	9,954	137,612 R	67.6%	29.7%	69.5%	30.5%
4	2018	293,316	190,138	HARTZLER, VICKY*	95,968	HOAGENSON, RENEE	7,210	94,170 R	64.8%	32.7%	66.5%	33.5%
4	2016	332,234	225,348	HARTZLER, VICKY*	92,510	CHRISTENSEN, GORDON	14,376	132,838 R	67.8%	27.8%	70.9%	29.1%
4	2014	176,286	120,014	HARTZLER, VICKY*	46,464	IRVIN, NATE A.	9,808	73,550 R	68.1%	26.4%	72.1%	27.9%
4	2012	318,723	192,237	HARTZLER, VICKY*	113,120	HENSLEY, TERESA	13,366	79,117 R	60.3%	35.5%	63.0%	37.0%
5	2022	230,555	84,008	TURK, JACOB	140,688	CLEAVER, EMANUEL II*	5,859	56,680 D	36.4%	61.0%	37.4%	62.6%
5	2020	352,430	135,934	DERKS, RYAN	207,180	CLEAVER, EMANUEL II*	9,316	71,246 D	38.6%	58.8%	39.6%	60.4%
5	2018	283,785	101,069	TURK, JACOB	175,019	CLEAVER, EMANUEL II*	7,697	73,950 D	35.6%	61.7%	36.6%	63.4%
5	2016	324,270	123,771	TURK, JACOB	190,766	CLEAVER, EMANUEL II*	9,733	66,995 D	38.2%	58.8%	39.4%	60.6%
5	2014	153,635	69,071	TURK, JACOB	79,256	CLEAVER, EMANUEL II*	5,308	10,185 D	45.0%	51.6%	46.6%	53.4%
5	2012	330,942	122,149	TURK, JACOB	200,290	CLEAVER, EMANUEL II*	8,503	78,141 D	36.9%	60.5%	37.9%	62.1%
6	2022	262,892	184,865	GRAVES, SAMUEL B. JR.*	72,253	MARTIN, HENRY	5,774	112,612 R	70.3%	27.5%	71.9%	28.1%
6	2020	385,779	258,709	GRAVES, SAMUEL B. JR.*	118,926	ROSS, GENA	8,144	139,783 R	67.1%	30.8%	68.5%	31.5%
6	2018	305,409	199,796	GRAVES, SAMUEL B. JR.*	97,660	MARTIN, HENRY	7,953	102,136 R	65.4%	32.0%	67.2%	32.8%
6	2016	350,444	238,388	GRAVES, SAMUEL B. JR.*	99,692	BLACKWELL, DAVID M.	12,364	138,696 R	68.0%	28.4%	70.5%	29.5%
6	2014	186,970	124,616	GRAVES, SAMUEL B. JR.*	55,157	HEDGE, W.A. "BILL"	7,197	69,459 R	66.7%	29.5%	69.3%	30.7%
6	2012	333,688	216,906	GRAVES, SAMUEL B. JR.*	108,503	YARBER, KYLE	8,279	108,403 R	65.0%	32.5%	66.7%	33.3%
7	2022	251,947	178,592	BURLISON, ERIC	67,485	RADAKER-SHEAFER, KRISTEN	5,870	111,107 R	70.9%	26.8%	72.6%	27.4%
7	2020	369,283	254,318	LONG, BILLY*	98,111	MONTSENY, TERESA	16,854	156,207 R	68.9%	26.6%	72.2%	27.8%
7	2018	296,455	196,343	LONG, BILLY*	89,190	SCHOOLCRAFT, JAMIE	10,922	107,153 R	66.2%	30.1%	68.8%	31.2%
7	2016	338,607	228,692	LONG, BILLY*	92,756	WILLIAMS, GENEVIEVE	17,159	135,936 R	67.5%	27.4%	71.1%	28.9%
7	2014	163,957	104,054	LONG, BILLY*	47,282	EVANS, JIM	12,621	56,772 R	63.5%	28.8%	68.8%	31.2%
7	2012	318,740	203,565	LONG, BILLY*	98,498	EVANS, JIM	16,677	105,067 R	63.9%	30.9%	67.4%	32.6%
8	2022	245,395	186,472	SMITH, JASON*	53,738	MCCALLIAN, RANDI	5,185	132,734 R	76.0%	21.9%	77.6%	22.4%
8	2020	330,226	253,811	SMITH, JASON*	70,561	ELLIS, KATHY	5,854	183,250 R	76.9%	21.4%	78.2%	21.8%
8	2018	264,399	194,042	SMITH, JASON*	66,151	ELLIS, KATHY	4,206	127,891 R	73.4%	25.0%	74.6%	25.4%
8	2016	308,871	229,792	SMITH, JASON*	70,009	COWELL, DAVE	9,070	159,783 R	74.4%	22.7%	76.6%	23.4%
8	2014	159,224	106,124	SMITH, JASON*	38,721	STOCKER, BARBARA HAMILL	14,379	67,403 R	66.7%	24.3%	73.3%	26.7%
8	2012	300,391	216,083	EMERSON, JO ANN*	73,755	RUSHIN, JACK	10,553	142,328 R	71.9%	24.6%	74.6%	25.4%
TOTAL	2022	2,060,089	1,223,617		794,978		41,494	428,639 R	59.4%	38.6%	60.6%	39.4%
TOTAL	2020	2,973,421	1,723,982		1,172,135		77,304	551,847 R	58.0%	39.4%	59.5%	40.5%
TOTAL	2018	2,418,413	1,330,975		1,027,969		59,469	303,006 R	55.0%	42.5%	56.4%	43.6%
TOTAL	2016	2,750,079	1,600,524		1,041,306		108,249	559,218 R	58.2%	37.9%	60.6%	39.4%
TOTAL	2014	1,426,303	838,283		513,600		74,420	324,683 R	58.8%	36.0%	62.0%	38.0%
TOTAL	2012	2,675,900	1,463,586		1,119,554		92,760	344,032 R	54.7%	41.8%	56.7%	43.3%

Note: An asterisk (*) denotes incumbent.

MISSOURI

GENERAL AND PRIMARY ELECTIONS

GENERAL ELECTIONS: OTHER VOTES

Senate	Other vote was 34,821 Libertarian (Jonathan Dine), 14,608 Constitution (Paul Venable), 41 Write-In (Write-Ins)
House	Other vote was:
CD 1	6,192 Libertarian (George Zsidisin)
CD 2	6,494 Libertarian (Bill Slantz)
CD 3	0 Write-In (Thomas Clapp)
CD 4	6,117 Libertarian (Randall Langkraehr), 1 Write-In (Darrell McClanahan), 1 Write-In (David Haave), 1 Write-In (Wyatt Parsons)
CD 5	5,859 Libertarian (Robin Dominick)
CD 6	5,774 Libertarian (Edward Maidment)
CD 7	5,869 Libertarian (Kevin Craig), 1 Write-In (Roger Rekate)
CD 8	5,185 Libertarian (Jim Higgins)

2022 PRIMARY ELECTIONS: SUPPLEMENTARY INFORMATION

Primary	August 2, 2022	**Registration** (as of November 1, 2022)		4,286,342	No Party Registration
Primary Type	Open—Any registered voter could participate in the party primary of his or her choice.				

	REPUBLICAN PRIMARIES			**DEMOCRATIC PRIMARIES**		
Senator	Schmitt, Eric	299,282	45.6%	Busch Valentine, Trudy	158,957	43.2%
	Hartzler, Vicky	144,903	22.1%	Kunce, Lucas	141,203	38.3%
	Greitens, Eric	124,155	18.9%	Toder, Spencer	17,465	4.7%
	Long, Billy	32,603	5.0%	Wright, Carla "Coffee"	14,438	3.9%
	McCloskey, Mark	19,540	3.0%	Ross, Gena	8,749	2.4%
	Schatz, Dave	7,509	1.1%	Kelly, Jewel	6,464	1.8%
	Lewis, Patrick	6,085	0.9%	Rolen, Lewis	5,247	1.4%
	Vaughn, Curtis D.	3,451	0.5%	Kelly, Pat	5,002	1.4%
	Mcelroy, Eric James	2,805	0.4%	Harris, Ronald William	4,074	1.1%
	Allen, Robert	2,111	0.3%	Shipp, Joshua	3,334	0.9%
	Gardner, C.W.	2,044	0.3%	Taylor, Clarence "Clay"	3,322	0.9%
	Sims, Dave	1,949	0.3%			
	Mowinski, Bernie	1,602	0.2%			
	Porter, Deshon	1,574	0.2%			
	McClanahan, Darrell Leon III	1,139	0.2%			
	Joiner, Rickey	1,084	0.2%			
	Olson, Robert	1,081	0.2%			
	Chilton, Dennis Lee	755	0.1%			
	Breyfogle, Russel Pealer Jr.	685	0.1%			
	Schepers, Kevin C.	681	0.1%			
	Tunnell, Hartford	637	0.1%			
	TOTAL	655,675		TOTAL	368,255	
Congressional District 1	Jones, Andrew	6,937	42.4%	Bush, Cori*	65,326	69.5%
	Jordan, Steven	5,153	31.5%	Roberts, Steve	25,015	26.6%
	Mitchell-Riley, Laura	4,260	26.1%	Daniels, Michael	1,683	1.8%
				Harshaw, Ron	1,065	1.1%
				Childress, Earl	929	1.0%
	TOTAL	16,350		TOTAL	94,018	

MISSOURI

GENERAL AND PRIMARY ELECTIONS

	REPUBLICAN PRIMARIES			DEMOCRATIC PRIMARIES		
Congressional District 2	Wagner, Ann*	54,440	67.1%	Gunby, Patricia "Trish"	50,457	85.2%
	Salvatore, Tony	12,516	15.4%	Reed, Raymond "Ray"	8,741	14.8%
	Smith, Wesley	7,317	9.0%			
	Berry, Paul III	6,888	8.5%			
	TOTAL	81,161		TOTAL	59,198	
Congressional District 3	Luetkemeyer, Blaine*	66,430	69.6%	Mann, Bethany	22,638	62.2%
	Wilkinson, Brandon	15,796	16.5%	Karlen, Jon	7,349	20.2%
	Hill, Dustin	11,610	12.2%	Daly, Andrew	5,184	14.3%
	Skwira, Richard Jr.	1,616	1.7%	Durrwachter, Dylan	1,197	3.3%
	TOTAL	95,452		TOTAL	36,368	
Congressional District 4	Alford, Mark	36,981	35.2%	Truman, Jack	25,641	100.0%
	Brattin, Richard "Rick"	22,509	21.4%			
	Bruce, Kalena	16,677	15.9%			
	Burks, Taylor	10,624	10.1%			
	Irwin, William "Bill"	9,648	9.2%			
	Campbell, Jim "Soupy"	4,642	4.4%			
	Labrue, Kyle Stonner	4,026	3.8%			
	TOTAL	105,107		TOTAL	25,641	
Congressional District 5	Turk, Jacob	20,475	51.8%	Cleaver, Emanuel II*	60,399	85.6%
	Barham, Jerry	13,246	33.5%	Salazar, Maite Gabrielle	10,147	14.4%
	Young, Herschel	5,833	14.7%			
	TOTAL	39,554		TOTAL	70,546	
Congressional District 6	Graves, Samuel B. Jr.*	72,996	75.7%	Martin, Henry	13,488	46.2%
	Ryan, Christopher	7,848	8.1%	West, Charles	9,761	33.4%
	Kleinmeyer, Brandon	7,414	7.7%	Howard, Michael	5,959	20.4%
	Shultz, Dakota	5,902	6.1%			
	Dady, John	2,309	2.4%			
	TOTAL	96,469		TOTAL	29,208	
Congressional District 7	Burlison, Eric	39,443	38.2%	Radaker-Sheafer, Kristen	13,680	63.3%
	Wasson, Jay	23,253	22.5%	Woodman, John M.	5,493	25.4%
	Bryant, Alex	18,522	17.9%	Lockwood, Bryce F.	2,430	11.2%
	Moon, Mike	8,957	8.7%			
	Alexander, Sam	5,665	5.5%			
	Richards, Audrey	3,095	3.0%			
	Walker, Paul D.	3,028	2.9%			
	Lombardi-Olive, Camille	1,363	1.3%			
	TOTAL	103,326		TOTAL	21,603	
Congressional District 8	Smith, Jason*	78,342	82.0%	McCallian, Randi	16,691	100.0%
	Turner, Jacob	17,242	18.0%			
	TOTAL	95,584		TOTAL	16,691	

Note: An asterisk (*) denotes incumbent.

MONTANA

Statewide Races

Neither of Montana's Senate seats were up in 2022, and its voters elect governors in presidential years.

House Races

For 2022, Montana, an At-Large state since the 1992 elections, regained its second district. Though the GOP enjoyed unified control of state government for the first time in nearly two decades, redistricting in Montana is handled by an independent, bipartisan commission. From the days of Woodrow Wilson's presidency until the 1990 elections, Montana was divided vertically between two districts. During those years, a western district spanned the Idaho border and took in (roughly) a third of the state's geography, while the rest of the state was put into a more expansive eastern seat. Going into 2022, the expectation was that the commission would adapt a similar configuration – and it did.

The western district, labeled MT-1, was the more politically marginal of the pair: in 2020, Donald Trump carried Montana 57%–41% but would have only posted a 52%–45% margin in the new 1st District. The presence of the state's two largest Democratic vote banks, Missoula County (home of the University of Montana) and Gallatin County (Bozeman), in the district helped keep it somewhat marginal.

The early frontrunner was Republican Ryan Zinke, who was elected to the At-Large seat in 2014 and held it until he was tapped to serve as Trump's Interior Secretary, in 2017. But Zinke, despite a Trump endorsement, did not get a free pass in the primary. State Sen. Al Olszewski reminded voters of Zinke's less-than ideal departure from the Trump administration – the subject of numerous ethics investigations, he resigned after less than two years on the job. Olszewski came close to denying Zinke the nomination, losing 42%–40%. Flathead County (Kalispell) was the county that cast the most votes in the primary, and it happened to be where both leading candidates hailed from – it gave Olszewski a 48%–32% margin.

In the general election, Zinke faced Democrat Monica Tranel, a lawyer who was an Olympic champion rower in the 1990s. As with the primary, Zinke underwhelmed: he won by just three points, taking less than 50%. Tranel ran well in Gallatin and Missoula counties but may have been hurt by poor outreach to Native Americans. Glacier County, which contains the Blackfeet Reservation, gave Tranel a 17-point margin, down from the 31-point margin Joe Biden got there in 2020.

Republican Matt Rosendale, an anti-establishment conservative who held the old At-Large seat, ran in the deep red 2nd District. In an intriguing result, Rosendale took 57% but an independent outpolled the Democratic nominee. Gary Buchanan ran as a centrist independent and got the endorsement of Republican Marc Racicot, a popular former governor. Buchanan took 22% districtwide to Democrat Penny Ronning's 20%. Buchanan outpolled Ronning in Lewis and Clark County (Helena) and Yellowstone County (Billings) but finished behind her in most counties that contain Native American reservations.

MONTANA
Congressional districts first established for elections held in 2022
2 members

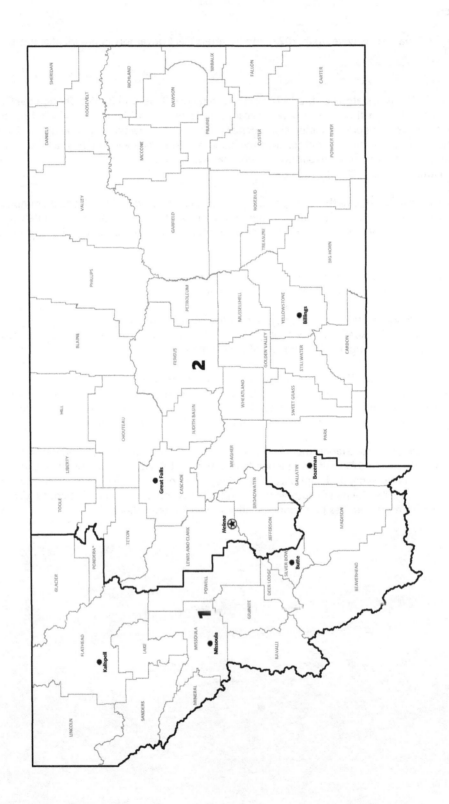

* Asterisk indicates a county whose boundaries include parts of two or more congressional districts.

MONTANA

GOVERNOR
Greg Gianforte (R). Elected 2020 to a four-year term.

SENATORS (1 Democrat, 1 Republican)
Steve Daines (R). Reelected 2020 to a six-year term. Previously elected 2014.

Jon Tester (D). Reelected 2018 to a six-year term. Previously elected 2012, 2006.

REPRESENTATIVE (2 Republicans)
1. Ryan K. Zinke (R)
2. Matt Rosendale (R)

POSTWAR VOTE FOR PRESIDENT

Year	Total Vote	Republican Vote	Republican Candidate	Democratic Vote	Democratic Candidate	Other Vote	Rep.-Dem. Plurality	Total Vote Rep.	Total Vote Dem.	Major Vote Rep.	Major Vote Dem.
2020	603,674	343,602	Trump, Donald J.*	244,786	Biden, Joseph R. Jr.	15,286	98,816 R	56.9%	40.5%	58.4%	41.6%
2016**	497,147	279,240	Trump, Donald J.	177,709	Clinton, Hillary Rodham	40,198	101,531 R	56.2%	35.7%	61.1%	38.9%
2012	484,048	267,928	Romney, W. Mitt	201,839	Obama, Barack H.*	14,281	66,089 R	55.4%	41.7%	57.0%	43.0%
2008	490,302	242,763	McCain, John S. III	231,667	Obama, Barack H.	15,872	11,096 R	49.5%	47.2%	51.2%	48.8%
2004	450,445	266,063	Bush, George W.*	173,710	Kerry, John F.	10,672	92,353 R	59.1%	38.6%	60.5%	39.5%
2000**	410,997	240,178	Bush, George W.	137,126	Gore, Albert Jr.	33,693	103,052 R	58.4%	33.4%	63.7%	36.3%
1996**	407,261	179,652	Dole, Robert "Bob"	167,922	Clinton, Bill*	59,687	11,730 R	44.1%	41.2%	51.7%	48.3%
1992**	410,611	144,207	Bush, George H.*	154,507	Clinton, Bill	111,897	10,300 D	35.1%	37.6%	48.3%	51.7%
1988	365,674	190,412	Bush, George H.	168,936	Dukakis, Michael S.	6,326	21,476 R	52.1%	46.2%	53.0%	47.0%
1984	384,377	232,450	Reagan, Ronald*	146,742	Mondale, Walter F.	5,185	85,708 R	60.5%	38.2%	61.3%	38.7%
1980**	363,952	206,814	Reagan, Ronald	118,032	Carter, Jimmy*	39,106	88,782 R	56.8%	32.4%	63.7%	36.3%
1976	328,734	173,703	Ford, Gerald R.*	149,259	Carter, Jimmy	5,772	24,444 R	52.8%	45.4%	53.8%	46.2%
1972	317,603	183,976	Nixon, Richard M.*	120,197	McGovern, George S.	13,430	63,779 R	57.9%	37.8%	60.5%	39.5%
1968**	274,404	138,835	Nixon, Richard M.	114,117	Humphrey, Hubert Horatio Jr.	21,452	24,718 R	50.6%	41.6%	54.9%	45.1%
1964	278,628	113,032	Goldwater, Barry M. Sr.	164,246	Johnson, Lyndon B.*	1,350	51,214 D	40.6%	58.9%	40.8%	59.2%
1960	277,579	141,841	Nixon, Richard M.	134,891	Kennedy, John F.	847	6,950 R	51.1%	48.6%	51.3%	48.7%
1956	271,171	154,933	Eisenhower, Dwight D.*	116,238	Stevenson, Adlai E. II		38,695 R	57.1%	42.9%	57.1%	42.9%
1952	265,037	157,394	Eisenhower, Dwight D.	106,213	Stevenson, Adlai E. II	1,430	51,181 R	59.4%	40.1%	59.7%	40.3%
1948	224,278	96,770	Dewey, Thomas E.	119,071	Truman, Harry S.*	8,437	22,301 D	43.1%	53.1%	44.8%	55.2%

Note: An asterisk (*) denotes incumbent. **In past elections, the other vote included: 2016 - 28,037 Libertarian (Gary Johnson); 2000 - 24,437 Green (Ralph Nader); 1996 - 55,229 Reform (Ross Perot); 1992 - 107,225 Independent (Perot); 1980 - 29,281 Independent (John Anderson); 1968 - 20,015 American Independent (George Wallace).

MONTANA

POSTWAR VOTE FOR GOVERNOR

Year	Total Vote	Republican Vote	Republican Candidate	Democratic Vote	Democratic Candidate	Other Vote	Rep.-Dem. Plurality	Total Vote Rep.	Total Vote Dem.	Major Vote Rep.	Major Vote Dem.
2020	603,587	328,548	Gianforte, Greg	250,860	Cooney, Mike	24,179	77,688 R	54.4%	41.6%	56.7%	43.3%
2016	509,360	236,115	Gianforte, Greg	255,933	Bullock, Steve*	17,312	19,818 D	46.4%	50.2%	48.0%	52.0%
2012	483,489	228,879	Hill, Rick	236,450	Bullock, Steve	18,160	7,571 D	47.3%	48.9%	49.2%	50.8%
2008	486,734	158,268	Brown, Roy	318,670	Schweitzer, Brian*	9,796	160,402 D	32.5%	65.5%	33.2%	66.8%
2004	446,146	205,313	Brown, Bob	225,016	Schweitzer, Brian	15,817	19,703 D	46.0%	50.4%	47.7%	52.3%
2000	410,192	209,135	Martz, Judy	193,131	O'Keefe, Mark	7,926	16,004 R	51.0%	47.1%	52.0%	48.0%
1996**	405,175	320,768	Racicot, Marc*	84,407	Jacobson, Judy		236,361 R	79.2%	20.8%	79.2%	20.8%
1992	407,842	209,401	Racicot, Marc	198,421	Bradley, Dorothy	20	10,980 R	51.3%	48.7%	51.3%	48.7%
1988	367,021	190,604	Stephens, Stan	169,313	Judge, Thomas L.	7,104	21,291 R	51.9%	46.1%	53.0%	47.0%
1984	378,970	100,070	Goodover, Pat M.	266,578	Schwinden, Ted*	12,322	166,508 D	26.4%	70.3%	27.3%	72.7%
1980	360,470	160,896	Ramirez, Jack	199,574	Schwinden, Ted		38,678 D	44.6%	55.4%	44.6%	55.4%
1976	316,720	115,848	Woodahl, Robert	195,420	Judge, Thomas L.*	5,452	79,572 D	36.6%	61.7%	37.2%	62.8%
1972	318,754	146,231	Smith, Ed	172,523	Judge, Thomas L.		26,292 D	45.9%	54.1%	45.9%	54.1%
1968	278,112	116,432	Babcock, Tim M.*	150,481	Anderson, Forrest H.	11,199	34,049 D	41.9%	54.1%	43.6%	56.4%
1964	280,975	144,113	Babcock, Tim M.	136,862	Renne, Roland		7,251 R	51.3%	48.7%	51.3%	48.7%
1960	279,881	154,230	Nutter, Donald G.	125,651	Cannon, Paul		28,579 R	55.1%	44.9%	55.1%	44.9%
1956	270,366	138,878	Aronson, John Hugo*	131,488	Olsen, Arnold		7,390 R	51.4%	48.6%	51.4%	48.6%
1952	263,792	134,423	Aronson, John Hugo	129,369	Bonner, John W.*		5,054 R	51.0%	49.0%	51.0%	49.0%
1948	222,964	97,792	Ford, Samuel C.*	124,267	Bonner, John W.	905	26,475 D	43.9%	55.7%	44.0%	56.0%

Note: An asterisk (*) denotes incumbent. **In 1996, the Democratic vote total included 7,936 absentee ballots cast for the party's initial gubernatorial candidate, Chet Blaylock, who died that October.

POSTWAR VOTE FOR SENATOR

Year	Total Vote	Republican Vote	Republican Candidate	Democratic Vote	Democratic Candidate	Other Vote	Rep.-Dem. Plurality	Total Vote Rep.	Total Vote Dem.	Major Vote Rep.	Major Vote Dem.
2020	605,637	333,174	Daines, Steve*	272,463	Bullock, Steve		60,711 R	55.0%	45.0%	55.0%	45.0%
2018	504,384	235,963	Rosendale, Matt	253,876	Tester, Jon*	14,545	17,913 D	46.8%	50.3%	48.2%	51.8%
2014	369,826	213,709	Daines, Steve	148,184	Curtis, Amanda	7,933	65,525 R	57.8%	40.1%	59.1%	40.9%
2012	486,066	218,051	Rehberg, Dennis "Denny"	236,123	Tester, Jon*	31,892	18,072 D	44.9%	48.6%	48.0%	52.0%
2008	477,658	129,369	Kelleher, Bob	348,289	Baucus, Max S.*		218,920 D	27.1%	72.9%	27.1%	72.9%
2006	406,505	196,283	Burns, Conrad*	199,845	Tester, Jon	10,377	3,562 D	48.3%	49.2%	49.6%	50.4%
2002	326,537	103,611	Taylor, Mike	204,853	Baucus, Max S.*	18,073	101,242 D	31.7%	62.7%	33.6%	66.4%
2000	411,601	208,082	Burns, Conrad*	194,430	Schweitzer, Brian	9,089	13,652 R	50.6%	47.2%	51.7%	48.3%
1996	407,490	182,111	Rehberg, Dennis "Denny"	201,935	Baucus, Max S.*	23,444	19,824 D	44.7%	49.6%	47.4%	52.6%
1994	350,409	218,542	Burns, Conrad*	131,845	Mudd, Jack	22	86,697 R	62.4%	37.6%	62.4%	37.6%
1990	319,336	93,836	Kolstad, Allen C.	217,563	Baucus, Max S.*	7,937	123,727 D	29.4%	68.1%	30.1%	69.9%
1988	365,254	189,445	Burns, Conrad	175,809	Melcher, John*		13,636 R	51.9%	48.1%	51.9%	48.1%
1984	379,155	154,308	Cozzens, Chuck	215,704	Baucus, Max S.*	9,143	61,396 D	40.7%	56.9%	41.7%	58.3%
1982	321,062	133,789	Williams, Larry	174,861	Melcher, John*	12,412	41,072 D	41.7%	54.5%	43.3%	56.7%
1978	287,942	127,589	Williams, Larry	160,353	Baucus, Max S.		32,764 D	44.3%	55.7%	44.3%	55.7%
1976	321,445	115,213	Burger, Stanley C.	206,232	Melcher, John		91,019 D	35.8%	64.2%	35.8%	64.2%
1972	314,925	151,316	Hibbard, Henry S.	163,609	Metcalf, Lee*		12,293 D	48.0%	52.0%	48.0%	52.0%
1970	247,869	97,809	Wallace, Harold E.	150,060	Mansfield, Mike*		52,251 D	39.5%	60.5%	39.5%	60.5%
1966	259,863	121,697	Babcock, Tim M.	138,166	Metcalf, Lee*		16,469 D	46.8%	53.2%	46.8%	53.2%
1964	280,010	99,367	Blewett, Alex	180,643	Mansfield, Mike*		81,276 D	35.5%	64.5%	35.5%	64.5%
1960	276,612	136,281	Fjare, Orvin B.	140,331	Metcalf, Lee		4,050 D	49.3%	50.7%	49.3%	50.7%
1958	229,483	54,573	Welch, Lou W.	174,910	Mansfield, Mike*		120,337 D	23.8%	76.2%	23.8%	76.2%
1954	227,454	112,863	D'Ewart, Wesley A.	114,591	Murray, James E.*		1,728 D	49.6%	50.4%	49.6%	50.4%
1952	262,297	127,360	Ecton, Zales N.*	133,109	Mansfield, Mike	1,828	5,749 D	48.6%	50.7%	48.9%	51.1%
1948	221,003	94,458	Davis, Tom J.	125,193	Murray, James E.*	1,352	30,735 D	42.7%	56.6%	43.0%	57.0%
1946	190,566	101,901	Ecton, Zales N.	86,476	Erickson, Leif	2,189	15,425 R	53.5%	45.4%	54.1%	45.9%

Note: An asterisk (*) denotes incumbent.

MONTANA
HOUSE OF REPRESENTATIVES

| | | | Republican | | Democratic | | Other | Rep.-Dem. | Percentage Total Vote | | Major Vote | |
| | | | | | | | | | | | | |
CD	Year	Total Vote	Vote	Candidate	Vote	Candidate	Vote	Plurality	Rep.	Dem.	Rep.	Dem.
1	2022	247,960	123,102	ZINKE, RYAN	115,265	TRANEL, MONICA	9,593	7,837 R	49.6%	46.5%	51.6%	48.4%
2	2022	215,672	121,979	ROSENDALE, MATT*	43,480	RONNING, PENNY	50,213	78,499 R	56.6%	20.2%	73.7%	26.3%
TOTAL	2022	463,632	245,081		158,745		59,806	86,336 R	52.9%	34.2%	60.7%	39.3%

Note: An asterisk (*) denotes incumbent.

MONTANA
GENERAL AND PRIMARY ELECTIONS

GENERAL ELECTIONS: OTHER VOTES

House Other vote was:
CD 1   9,593 Libertarian (John Lamb)
CD 2   47,195 Independent (Gary Buchanan), 3,018 Libertarian (Sam Rankin)

2022 PRIMARY ELECTIONS: SUPPLEMENTARY INFORMATION

Primary June 7, 2022 **Registration** (as of June 7, 2022) 743,710 No Party Registration

Primary Type Open—Any registered voter could participate in the party primary of his or her choice.

	REPUBLICAN PRIMARIES			DEMOCRATIC PRIMARIES		
Congressional District 1	Zinke, Ryan	35,601	41.7%	Tranel, Monica	37,138	64.9%
	Olszewski, Albert	33,927	39.7%	Neumann, Cora	15,396	26.9%
	Todd, Mary	8,915	10.4%	Winter, Thomas	4,723	8.2%
	Jette, Matt	4,973	5.8%			
	Heuer, Mitch	1,953	2.3%			
	TOTAL	85,369		TOTAL	57,257	
Congressional District 2	Rosendale, Matt*	73,453	75.7%	Ronning, Penny	21,983	58.5%
	Austin, Kyle	11,930	12.3%	Sweeney, Mark	8,586	22.8%
	Walking Child, Charles A.	5,909	6.1%	Wiliams, Skylar	7,029	18.7%
	Boyette, James	5,712	5.9%			
	TOTAL	97,004		TOTAL	37,598	

Note: An asterisk (*) denotes incumbent.

NEBRASKA

Statewide Races

With neither of its Senate seats up in 2022, Nebraska's top contest was for governor, although there was little question Republicans would continue their winning streak (they have prevailed in every contest since 1998). In 2014, businessperson Pete Ricketts, who would serve two terms as governor, won a crowded Republican primary with just 27% of the vote. With Ricketts term-limited, another competitive primary seemed likely.

In 2021, Donald Trump endorsed agribusiness executive Charles Herbster. Though Herbster was leading in early polls, he was eventually weighed down by allegations of sexual misconduct. Ricketts, a conservative, endorsed University of Nebraska Regent Jim Pillen while state Sen. Brad Lindstrom courted moderates. Pillen finished first, with 34% – he carried Lincoln's Lancaster County and ran well in his home area, in the northeast. Herbster placed second, with 30%, while Lindstrom, who found support in metro Omaha but struggled in the rural areas, came in third, with 26%.

The general election was less eventful: Pillen defeated state Sen. Carol Blood, the Democratic nominee, by a 59%–36% margin. Shortly after Pillen took office, Republican Sen. Ben Sasse stepped down – Pillen, perhaps with the primary campaign in mind, appointed Ricketts to the seat. Looking to 2024, Nebraska will host a "double barrel" Senate contest: Ricketts will have to run in a special election, while Republican Sen. Deb Fischer's seat has a regularly scheduled election.

House Races

Nebraska's unicameral, nonpartisan legislature passed a map that Ricketts signed. Of the state's three seats, the Omaha-based 2nd district is the most competitive – though it got redder in redistricting, it would have still favored Joe Biden 52%–46% in 2020. Republicans appended all or parts of two red counties to Douglas County, a Biden +11 county that contains over 80% of the 2nd District's population. Still, Republican Don Bacon, who was first elected in 2016 and has never won reelection by more than five points, continued his winning streak, beating state Sen. Tony Vargas by less than three points.

In late June, Republican Mike Flood got to the House in what was likely an illegal special election in the 1st District: elected to finish a former member's term representing the old district, the June special election was held under the lines that were meant to take effect in November. Still, the election was the first among a string of post-Roe special elections where Democrats overperformed. Though the seat contains a selection of rural counties, Lancaster County punched above its weight, limiting Flood's margin to five points against state Sen. Patty Pansing Brooks, the Democratic nominee. In the November election, which featured a family feud of sorts – Ricketts backed Flood while the state's first lady backed Pansing Brooks – Flood won by 16 points.

The rural 3rd District, which includes western Nebraska, continued to expand in redistricting: it contains all or parts of 80 counties, more than any other district. Rep. Adrian Smith's 78% share was a bit better than the 75% that Trump would have carried the district with in 2020.

NEBRASKA
Congressional districts first established for elections held in 2022
3 members

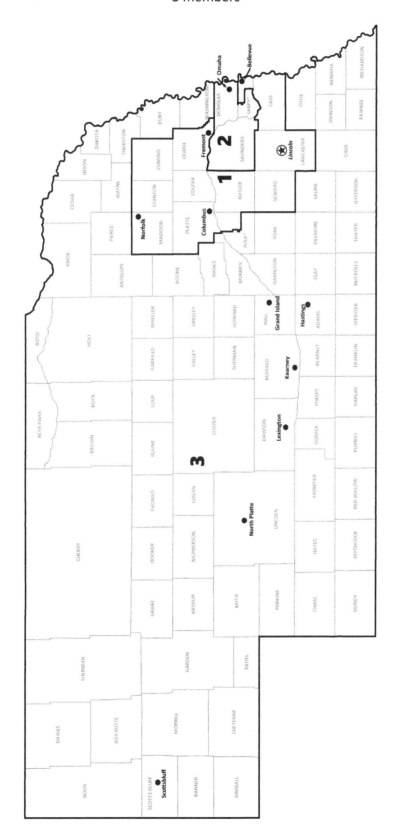

* Asterisk indicates a county whose boundaries include parts of two or more congressional districts.

NEBRASKA

GOVERNOR
Jim Pillen (R). Elected 2022 to a four-year term.

SENATORS (1 Republican)
Deb Fischer (R). Reelected 2018 to a six-year term. Previously elected 2012.

Pete Ricketts (R). Appointed by the governor on January 12, 2023, and sworn in January 23, 2023, to fill the vacancy created by the resignation of Ben Sasse to become president of the University of Florida, and elected in 2020, 2014. Ricketts has declared candidacy for the special election that will be held on November 5, 2024, to fill the last two years of the six-year term that Ben Sasse was elected to.

REPRESENTATIVES (3 Republicans)
1. Mike Flood (R)   2. Don Bacon (R)   3. Adrian Smith (R)

POSTWAR VOTE FOR PRESIDENT

Year	Total Vote	Republican Vote	Republican Candidate	Democratic Vote	Democratic Candidate	Other Vote	Rep.-Dem. Plurality	Total Vote Rep.	Total Vote Dem.	Major Vote Rep.	Major Vote Dem.
2020	956,383	556,846	Trump, Donald J.*	374,583	Biden, Joseph R. Jr.	24,954	182,263 R	58.2%	39.2%	59.8%	40.2%
2016**	844,227	495,961	Trump, Donald J.	284,494	Clinton, Hillary Rodham	63,772	211,467 R	58.7%	33.7%	63.5%	36.5%
2012	794,379	475,064	Romney, W. Mitt	302,081	Obama, Barack H.*	17,234	172,983 R	59.8%	38.0%	61.1%	38.9%
2008	801,281	452,979	McCain, John S. III	333,319	Obama, Barack H.	14,983	119,660 R	56.5%	41.6%	57.6%	42.4%
2004	778,186	512,814	Bush, George W.*	254,328	Kerry, John F.	11,044	258,486 R	65.9%	32.7%	66.8%	33.2%
2000**	697,019	433,862	Bush, George W.	231,780	Gore, Albert Jr.	31,377	202,082 R	62.2%	33.3%	65.2%	34.8%
1996**	677,415	363,467	Dole, Robert "Bob"	236,761	Clinton, Bill*	77,187	126,706 R	53.7%	35.0%	60.6%	39.4%
1992**	737,546	343,678	Bush, George H.*	216,864	Clinton, Bill	177,004	126,814 R	46.6%	29.4%	61.3%	38.7%
1988	661,465	397,956	Bush, George H.	259,235	Dukakis, Michael S.	4,274	138,721 R	60.2%	39.2%	60.6%	39.4%
1984	652,090	460,054	Reagan, Ronald*	187,866	Mondale, Walter F.	4,170	272,188 R	70.6%	28.8%	71.0%	29.0%
1980**	640,854	419,937	Reagan, Ronald	166,851	Carter, Jimmy*	54,066	253,086 R	65.5%	26.0%	71.6%	28.4%
1976	607,668	359,705	Ford, Gerald R.*	233,692	Carter, Jimmy	14,271	126,013 R	59.2%	38.5%	60.6%	39.4%
1972	576,289	406,298	Nixon, Richard M.*	169,991	McGovern, George S.		236,307 R	70.5%	29.5%	70.5%	29.5%
1968**	536,851	321,163	Nixon, Richard M.	170,784	Humphrey, Hubert Horatio Jr.	44,904	150,379 R	59.8%	31.8%	65.3%	34.7%
1964	584,154	276,847	Goldwater, Barry M. Sr.	307,307	Johnson, Lyndon B.*		30,460 D	47.4%	52.6%	47.4%	52.6%
1960	613,095	380,553	Nixon, Richard M.	232,542	Kennedy, John F.		148,011 R	62.1%	37.9%	62.1%	37.9%
1956	577,137	378,108	Eisenhower, Dwight D.*	199,029	Stevenson, Adlai E. II		179,079 R	65.5%	34.5%	65.5%	34.5%
1952	609,660	421,603	Eisenhower, Dwight D.	188,057	Stevenson, Adlai E. II		233,546 R	69.2%	30.8%	69.2%	30.8%
1948	488,940	264,774	Dewey, Thomas E.	224,165	Truman, Harry S.*	1	40,609 R	54.2%	45.8%	54.2%	45.8%

Note: An asterisk (*) denotes incumbent. **In past elections, the other vote included: 2016 - 38,946 Libertarian (Gary Johnson); 2000 - 24,540 Green (Ralph Nader); 1996 - 71,278 Reform (Ross Perot); 1992 - 174,104 Independent (Perot); 1980 - 44,993 Independent (John Anderson); 1968 - 44,904 American Independent (George Wallace).

NEBRASKA

POSTWAR VOTE FOR GOVERNOR

| Year | Total Vote | Republican | | Democratic | | Other Vote | Rep.-Dem. Plurality | Percentage | | | |
| | | Vote | Candidate | Vote | Candidate | | | Total Vote | | Major Vote | |
								Rep.	Dem.	Rep.	Dem.
2022	672,593	398,334	Pillen, Jim	242,006	Blood, Carol	32,253	156,328 R	59.2%	36.0%	62.2%	37.8%
2018	697,981	411,812	Ricketts, Pete*	286,169	Krist, Bob		125,643 R	59.0%	41.0%	59.0%	41.0%
2014	540,202	308,751	Ricketts, Pete	211,905	Hassebrook, Chuck	19,546	96,846 R	57.2%	39.2%	59.3%	40.7%
2010	487,988	360,645	Heineman, Dave*	127,343	Meister, Mike		233,302 R	73.9%	26.1%	73.9%	26.1%
2006	593,357	435,507	Heineman, Dave*	145,115	Hahn, David	12,735	290,392 R	73.4%	24.5%	75.0%	25.0%
2002	480,991	330,349	Johanns, Mike*	132,348	Dean, Stormy	18,294	198,001 R	68.7%	27.5%	71.4%	28.6%
1998	545,238	293,910	Johanns, Mike	250,678	Hoppner, Bill	650	43,232 R	53.9%	46.0%	54.0%	46.0%
1994	579,561	148,230	Spence, Gene	423,270	Nelson, Earl "Ben"*	8,061	275,040 D	25.6%	73.0%	25.9%	74.1%
1990	586,542	288,741	Orr, Kay*	292,771	Nelson, Earl "Ben"	5,030	4,030 D	49.2%	49.9%	49.7%	50.3%
1986	564,422	298,325	Orr, Kay	265,156	Boosalis, Helen	941	33,169 R	52.9%	47.0%	52.9%	47.1%
1982	547,902	270,203	Thone, Charles*	277,436	Kerrey, Bob	263	7,233 D	49.3%	50.6%	49.3%	50.7%
1978	492,423	275,473	Thone, Charles	216,754	Whelan, Gerald T.	196	58,719 R	55.9%	44.0%	56.0%	44.0%
1974	451,306	159,780	Marvel, Richard D.	267,012	Exon, J. James*	24,514	107,232 D	35.4%	59.2%	37.4%	62.6%
1970	461,619	201,994	Tiemann, Norbert T.*	248,552	Exon, J. James	11,073	46,558 D	43.8%	53.8%	44.8%	55.2%
1966**	486,396	299,245	Tiemann, Norbert T.	186,985	Sorensen, Philip C.	166	112,260 R	61.5%	38.4%	61.5%	38.5%
1964	578,090	231,029	Burney, Dwight W.	347,026	Morrison, Frank B.*	35	115,997 D	40.0%	60.0%	40.0%	60.0%
1962	464,585	221,885	Seaton, Fred A.	242,669	Morrison, Frank B.*	31	20,784 D	47.8%	52.2%	47.8%	52.2%
1960	598,971	287,302	Cooper, John R.	311,344	Morrison, Frank B.	325	24,042 D	48.0%	52.0%	48.0%	52.0%
1958	421,067	209,705	Anderson, Victor E.*	211,345	Brooks, Ralph G.	17	1,640 D	49.8%	50.2%	49.8%	50.2%
1956	567,916	308,285	Anderson, Victor E.*	228,048	Sorrell, Frank	31,583	80,237 R	54.3%	40.2%	57.5%	42.5%
1954	414,841	250,080	Anderson, Victor E.	164,753	Ritchie, William	8	85,327 R	60.3%	39.7%	60.3%	39.7%
1952	594,814	365,409	Crosby, Robert B.	229,400	Raecke, Walter R.	5	136,009 R	61.4%	38.6%	61.4%	38.6%
1950	449,728	247,089	Peterson, Val*	202,638	Raecke, Walter R.	1	44,451 R	54.9%	45.1%	54.9%	45.1%
1948	476,352	286,119	Peterson, Val*	190,214	Sorrell, Frank	19	95,905 R	60.1%	39.9%	60.1%	39.9%
1946	380,835	249,468	Peterson, Val	131,367	Sorrell, Frank		118,101 R	65.5%	34.5%	65.5%	34.5%

Note: An asterisk (*) denotes incumbent. **The term of office of Nebraska's governor was increased from two to four years effective with the 1966 election.

POSTWAR VOTE FOR SENATOR

| Year | Total Vote | Republican | | Democratic | | Other Vote | Rep.-Dem. Plurality | Percentage | | | |
| | | Vote | Candidate | Vote | Candidate | | | Total Vote | | Major Vote | |
								Rep.	Dem.	Rep.	Dem.
2020	930,012	583,507	Sasse, Ben*	227,191	Janicek, Chris	119,314	356,316 R	62.7%	24.4%	72.0%	28.0%
2018	698,883	403,151	Fischer, Deb*	269,917	Raybould, Jane	25,815	133,234 R	57.7%	38.6%	59.9%	40.1%
2014	540,337	347,636	Sasse, Ben	170,127	Domina, David A.	22,574	177,509 R	64.3%	31.5%	67.1%	32.9%
2012	788,572	455,593	Fischer, Deb	332,979	Kerrey, Bob		122,614 R	57.8%	42.2%	57.8%	42.2%
2008	792,511	455,854	Johanns, Mike	317,456	Kleeb, Scott	19,201	138,398 R	57.5%	40.1%	58.9%	41.1%
2006	592,316	213,928	Ricketts, Pete	378,388	Nelson, Earl "Ben"*		164,460 D	36.1%	63.9%	36.1%	63.9%
2002	480,217	397,438	Hagel, Chuck*	70,290	Matulka, Charlie A.	12,489	327,148 R	82.8%	14.6%	85.0%	15.0%
2000	692,344	337,967	Stenberg, Don	353,097	Nelson, Earl "Ben"	1,280	15,130 D	48.8%	51.0%	48.9%	51.1%
1996	676,789	379,933	Hagel, Chuck	281,904	Nelson, Earl "Ben"	14,952	98,029 R	56.1%	41.7%	57.4%	42.6%
1994	579,205	260,668	Stoney, Jan	317,297	Kerrey, Bob*	1,240	56,629 D	45.0%	54.8%	45.1%	54.9%
1990	593,828	243,013	Daub, Harold J.	349,779	Exon, J. James*	1,036	106,766 D	40.9%	58.9%	41.0%	59.0%
1988	667,860	278,250	Karnes, David*	378,717	Kerrey, Bob	10,893	100,467 D	41.7%	56.7%	42.4%	57.6%
1984	639,668	307,147	Hoch, Nancy	332,217	Exon, J. James*	304	25,070 D	48.0%	51.9%	48.0%	52.0%
1982	545,647	155,760	Keck, Jim	363,350	Zorinsky, Edward*	26,537	207,590 D	28.5%	66.6%	30.0%	70.0%
1978	494,368	159,806	Shasteen, Donald	334,276	Exon, J. James	286	174,470 D	32.3%	67.6%	32.3%	67.7%
1976	598,314	284,284	McCollister, John Y.	313,809	Zorinsky, Edward	221	29,525 D	47.5%	52.4%	47.5%	52.5%
1972	568,580	301,841	Curtis, Carl T.*	265,922	Carpenter, Terry	817	35,919 R	53.1%	46.8%	53.2%	46.8%
1970	458,966	240,894	Hruska, Roman L.*	217,681	Morrison, Frank B.	391	23,213 R	52.5%	47.4%	52.5%	47.5%
1966	485,101	296,116	Curtis, Carl T.*	187,950	Morrison, Frank B.	1,035	108,166 R	61.0%	38.7%	61.2%	38.8%
1964	563,401	345,772	Hruska, Roman L.*	217,605	Arndt, Raymond W.	24	128,167 R	61.4%	38.6%	61.4%	38.6%
1960	598,743	352,748	Curtis, Carl T.*	245,837	Conrad, Robert B.	158	106,911 R	58.9%	41.1%	58.9%	41.1%
1958	417,385	232,227	Hruska, Roman L.*	185,152	Morrison, Frank B.	6	47,075 R	55.6%	44.4%	55.6%	44.4%
1954	418,691	255,695	Curtis, Carl T.	162,990	Neville, Keith	6	92,705 R	61.1%	38.9%	61.1%	38.9%
1954S**	411,225	250,341	Hruska, Roman L.	160,881	Green, James F.	3	89,460 R	60.9%	39.1%	60.9%	39.1%
1952	591,749	408,971	Butler, Hugh*	164,660	Long, Stanley D.	18,118	244,311 R	69.1%	27.8%	71.3%	28.7%
1952S**	581,750	369,841	Griswold, Dwight	211,898	Ritchie, William	11	157,943 R	63.6%	36.4%	63.6%	36.4%
1948	471,895	267,575	Wherry, Kenneth S.*	204,320	Carpenter, Terry		63,255 R	56.7%	43.3%	56.7%	43.3%
1946	382,959	271,208	Butler, Hugh*	111,751	Mekota, John E.		159,457 R	70.8%	29.2%	70.8%	29.2%

Note: An asterisk (*) denotes incumbent. **One each of the 1952 and 1954 elections was for a short term to fill a vacancy.

NEBRASKA
GOVERNOR 2022

2020 Census Population	County	Total Vote	Republican (Pillen)	Democratic (Blood)	Other	Rep.-Dem. Plurality	Total Vote Rep.	Total Vote Dem.	Major Vote Rep.	Major Vote Dem.
31,243	ADAMS	10,403	6,973	2,821	609	4,152 R	67.0%	27.1%	71.2%	28.8%
6,297	ANTELOPE	2,482	2,026	241	215	1,785 R	81.6%	9.7%	89.4%	10.6%
467	ARTHUR	250	220	13	17	207 R	88.0%	5.2%	94.4%	5.6%
752	BANNER	369	316	29	24	287 R	85.6%	7.9%	91.6%	8.4%
464	BLAINE	206	169	23	14	146 R	82.0%	11.2%	88.0%	12.0%
5,185	BOONE	2,599	2,026	393	180	1,633 R	78.0%	15.1%	83.8%	16.2%
10,774	BOX BUTTE	3,369	2,462	761	146	1,701 R	73.1%	22.6%	76.4%	23.6%
1,923	BOYD	904	739	99	66	640 R	81.7%	11.0%	88.2%	11.8%
2,963	BROWN	1,216	938	159	119	779 R	77.1%	13.1%	85.5%	14.5%
49,819	BUFFALO	16,049	11,233	3,946	870	7,287 R	70.0%	24.6%	74.0%	26.0%
6,476	BURT	2,807	2,030	638	139	1,392 R	72.3%	22.7%	76.1%	23.9%
8,037	BUTLER	3,533	2,773	585	175	2,188 R	78.5%	16.6%	82.6%	17.4%
26,338	CASS	11,405	7,462	3,317	626	4,145 R	65.4%	29.1%	69.2%	30.8%
8,397	CEDAR	3,860	3,107	466	287	2,641 R	80.5%	12.1%	87.0%	13.0%
3,941	CHASE	1,531	1,296	176	59	1,120 R	84.7%	11.5%	88.0%	12.0%
5,687	CHERRY	2,552	1,984	240	328	1,744 R	77.7%	9.4%	89.2%	10.8%
8,812	CHEYENNE	3,344	2,688	456	200	2,232 R	80.4%	13.6%	85.5%	14.5%
6,213	CLAY	2,762	2,175	405	182	1,770 R	78.7%	14.7%	84.3%	15.7%
10,656	COLFAX	2,430	1,892	445	93	1,447 R	77.9%	18.3%	81.0%	19.0%
8,848	CUMING	3,210	2,589	509	112	2,080 R	80.7%	15.9%	83.6%	16.4%
10,790	CUSTER	4,410	3,562	561	287	3,001 R	80.8%	12.7%	86.4%	13.6%
20,007	DAKOTA	3,608	2,525	931	152	1,594 R	70.0%	25.8%	73.1%	26.9%
8,548	DAWES	3,198	2,158	821	219	1,337 R	67.5%	25.7%	72.4%	27.6%
23,508	DAWSON	5,639	4,303	1,035	301	3,268 R	76.3%	18.4%	80.6%	19.4%
1,819	DEUEL	733	612	76	45	536 R	83.5%	10.4%	89.0%	11.0%
5,623	DIXON	2,254	1,710	406	138	1,304 R	75.9%	18.0%	80.8%	19.2%
36,585	DODGE	11,566	7,682	3,302	582	4,380 R	66.4%	28.5%	69.9%	30.1%
572,163	DOUGLAS	191,492	87,136	96,628	7,728	9,492 D	45.5%	50.5%	47.4%	52.6%
1,689	DUNDY	762	650	75	37	575 R	85.3%	9.8%	89.7%	10.3%
5,460	FILLMORE	2,430	1,859	491	80	1,368 R	76.5%	20.2%	79.1%	20.9%
2,978	FRANKLIN	1,193	976	159	58	817 R	81.8%	13.3%	86.0%	14.0%
2,627	FRONTIER	1,083	895	142	46	753 R	82.6%	13.1%	86.3%	13.7%
4,667	FURNAS	1,878	1,524	241	113	1,283 R	81.2%	12.8%	86.3%	13.7%
21,546	GAGE	8,032	5,317	2,357	358	2,960 R	66.2%	29.3%	69.3%	30.7%
1,835	GARDEN	894	736	109	49	627 R	82.3%	12.2%	87.1%	12.9%
1,979	GARFIELD	773	628	80	65	548 R	81.2%	10.3%	88.7%	11.3%
1,985	GOSPER	842	676	127	39	549 R	80.3%	15.1%	84.2%	15.8%
619	GRANT	282	253	18	11	235 R	89.7%	6.4%	93.4%	6.6%
2,356	GREELEY	1,044	766	194	84	572 R	73.4%	18.6%	79.8%	20.2%
61,373	HALL	15,298	10,223	4,145	930	6,078 R	66.8%	27.1%	71.2%	28.8%
9,364	HAMILTON	4,125	3,128	757	240	2,371 R	75.8%	18.4%	80.5%	19.5%
3,390	HARLAN	1,423	1,109	234	80	875 R	77.9%	16.4%	82.6%	17.4%
922	HAYES	394	341	23	30	318 R	86.5%	5.8%	93.7%	6.3%
2,767	HITCHCOCK	1,066	844	120	102	724 R	79.2%	11.3%	87.6%	12.4%
10,063	HOLT	3,982	3,125	431	426	2,694 R	78.5%	10.8%	87.9%	12.1%
689	HOOKER	375	300	62	13	238 R	80.0%	16.5%	82.9%	17.1%
6,467	HOWARD	2,456	1,853	442	161	1,411 R	75.4%	18.0%	80.7%	19.3%
7,042	JEFFERSON	2,689	1,916	634	139	1,282 R	71.3%	23.6%	75.1%	24.9%
5,083	JOHNSON	1,631	1,061	467	103	594 R	65.1%	28.6%	69.4%	30.6%
6,503	KEARNEY	2,572	1,981	448	143	1,533 R	77.0%	17.4%	81.6%	18.4%
8,031	KEITH	2,918	2,337	456	125	1,881 R	80.1%	15.6%	83.7%	16.3%
811	KEYA PAHA	420	318	37	65	281 R	75.7%	8.8%	89.6%	10.4%
3,656	KIMBALL	1,335	1,115	158	62	957 R	83.5%	11.8%	87.6%	12.4%
8,339	KNOX	3,721	2,922	586	213	2,336 R	78.5%	15.7%	83.3%	16.7%
320,285	LANCASTER	114,858	52,769	57,424	4,665	4,655 D	45.9%	50.0%	47.9%	52.1%
34,915	LINCOLN	12,151	9,029	2,481	641	6,548 R	74.3%	20.4%	78.4%	21.6%
743	LOGAN	337	290	22	25	268 R	86.1%	6.5%	92.9%	7.1%
671	LOUP	339	255	48	36	207 R	75.2%	14.2%	84.2%	15.8%
35,160	MADISON	11,733	9,108	2,035	590	7,073 R	77.6%	17.3%	81.7%	18.3%
493	MCPHERSON	223	188	24	11	164 R	84.3%	10.8%	88.7%	11.3%

NEBRASKA
GOVERNOR 2022

2020 Census Population	County	Total Vote	Republican (Pillen)	Democratic (Blood)	Other	Rep.-Dem. Plurality		Percentage			
								Total Vote		Major Vote	
								Rep.	Dem.	Rep.	Dem.
7,753	MERRICK	3,347	2,629	516	202	2,113	R	78.5%	15.4%	83.6%	16.4%
4,623	MORRILL	1,963	1,543	255	165	1,288	R	78.6%	13.0%	85.8%	14.2%
3,527	NANCE	1,281	923	260	98	663	R	72.1%	20.3%	78.0%	22.0%
6,968	NEMAHA	2,347	1,655	571	121	1,084	R	70.5%	24.3%	74.3%	25.7%
4,138	NUCKOLLS	1,593	1,276	234	83	1,042	R	80.1%	14.7%	84.5%	15.5%
16,034	OTOE	5,797	3,920	1,593	284	2,327	R	67.6%	27.5%	71.1%	28.9%
2,618	PAWNEE	1,083	817	224	42	593	R	75.4%	20.7%	78.5%	21.5%
2,897	PERKINS	1,113	918	135	60	783	R	82.5%	12.1%	87.2%	12.8%
9,034	PHELPS	3,694	3,012	509	173	2,503	R	81.5%	13.8%	85.5%	14.5%
7,166	PIERCE	2,892	2,463	288	141	2,175	R	85.2%	10.0%	89.5%	10.5%
33,479	PLATTE	11,159	9,103	1,695	361	7,408	R	81.6%	15.2%	84.3%	15.7%
5,220	POLK	2,064	1,658	321	85	1,337	R	80.3%	15.6%	83.8%	16.2%
10,725	RED WILLOW	4,006	3,174	608	224	2,566	R	79.2%	15.2%	83.9%	16.1%
7,870	RICHARDSON	2,971	1,987	766	218	1,221	R	66.9%	25.8%	72.2%	27.8%
1,354	ROCK	604	504	63	37	441	R	83.4%	10.4%	88.9%	11.1%
14,188	SALINE	3,787	2,388	1,188	211	1,200	R	63.1%	31.4%	66.8%	33.2%
188,134	SARPY	64,794	35,821	26,039	2,934	9,782	R	55.3%	40.2%	57.9%	42.1%
21,699	SAUNDERS	9,658	6,842	2,316	500	4,526	R	70.8%	24.0%	74.7%	25.3%
35,583	SCOTTS BLUFF	9,886	7,125	2,259	502	4,866	R	72.1%	22.9%	75.9%	24.1%
17,336	SEWARD	6,760	4,921	1,556	283	3,365	R	72.8%	23.0%	76.0%	24.0%
5,256	SHERIDAN	1,877	1,349	226	302	1,123	R	71.9%	12.0%	85.7%	14.3%
2,999	SHERMAN	1,250	896	246	108	650	R	71.7%	19.7%	78.5%	21.5%
1,160	SIOUX	534	427	56	51	371	R	80.0%	10.5%	88.4%	11.6%
5,901	STANTON	2,467	1,967	340	160	1,627	R	79.7%	13.8%	85.3%	14.7%
5,000	THAYER	2,192	1,707	373	112	1,334	R	77.9%	17.0%	82.1%	17.9%
724	THOMAS	318	265	29	24	236	R	83.3%	9.1%	90.1%	9.9%
7,231	THURSTON	1,294	824	424	46	400	R	63.7%	32.8%	66.0%	34.0%
4,149	VALLEY	1,810	1,414	278	118	1,136	R	78.1%	15.4%	83.6%	16.4%
20,880	WASHINGTON	8,853	6,244	2,227	382	4,017	R	70.5%	25.2%	73.7%	26.3%
9,468	WAYNE	3,053	2,215	685	153	1,530	R	72.6%	22.4%	76.4%	23.6%
3,494	WEBSTER	1,313	1,021	207	85	814	R	77.8%	15.8%	83.1%	16.9%
781	WHEELER	353	227	39	87	188	R	64.3%	11.0%	85.3%	14.7%
13,694	YORK	5,040	3,821	971	248	2,850	R	75.8%	19.3%	79.7%	20.3%
1,937,926	TOTAL	672,593	398,334	242,006	32,253	156,328	R	59.2%	36.0%	62.2%	37.8%

NEBRASKA
HOUSE OF REPRESENTATIVES

CD	Year	Total Vote	Republican		Democratic		Other Vote	Rep.-Dem. Plurality		Percentage			
			Vote	Candidate	Vote	Candidate				Total Vote		Major Vote	
										Rep.	Dem.	Rep.	Dem.
1	2022	223,165	129,236	FLOOD, MIKE*	93,929	PANSING BROOKS, PATTY		35,307	R	57.9%	42.1%	57.9%	42.1%
1	2020	317,566	189,006	FORTENBERRY, JEFF*	119,622	BOLZ, KATE	8,938	69,384	R	59.5%	37.7%	61.2%	38.8%
1	2018	234,781	141,712	FORTENBERRY, JEFF*	93,069	MCCLURE, JESSICA		48,643	R	60.4%	39.6%	60.4%	39.6%
1	2016	273,238	189,771	FORTENBERRY, JEFF*	83,467	WIK, DANIEL M.		106,304	R	69.5%	30.5%	69.5%	30.5%
1	2014	179,057	123,219	FORTENBERRY, JEFF*	55,838	CRAWFORD, DENNIS P.		67,381	R	68.8%	31.2%	68.8%	31.2%
1	2012	256,095	174,889	FORTENBERRY, JEFF*	81,206	REIMAN, KOREY L.		93,683	R	68.3%	31.7%	68.3%	31.7%
2	2022	219,470	112,663	BACON, DON*	106,807	VARGAS, ANTHONY "TONY"		5,856	R	51.3%	48.7%	51.3%	48.7%
2	2020	336,962	171,071	BACON, DON*	155,706	EASTMAN, KARA	10,185	15,365	R	50.8%	46.2%	52.4%	47.6%
2	2018	248,485	126,715	BACON, DON*	121,770	EASTMAN, KARA		4,945	R	51.0%	49.0%	51.0%	49.0%
2	2016	288,308	141,066	BACON, DON	137,602	ASHFORD, BRAD*	9,640	3,464	R	48.9%	47.7%	50.6%	49.4%
2	2014	171,509	78,157	TERRY, LEE*	83,872	ASHFORD, BRAD	9,480	5,715	D	45.6%	48.9%	48.2%	51.8%
2	2012	263,731	133,964	TERRY, LEE*	129,767	EWING, JOHN W. JR.		4,197	R	50.8%	49.2%	50.8%	49.2%

NEBRASKA

HOUSE OF REPRESENTATIVES

CD	Year	Total Vote	Republican Vote	Republican Candidate	Democratic Vote	Democratic Candidate	Other Vote	Rep.-Dem. Plurality	Total Vote Rep. %	Total Vote Dem. %	Major Vote Rep. %	Major Vote Dem. %
3	2022	220,552	172,700	SMITH, ADRIAN*	34,836	ELSE, DAVID J.	13,016	137,864 R	78.3%	15.8%	83.2%	16.8%
3	2020	286,770	225,157	SMITH, ADRIAN*	50,690	ELWORTH, MARK G. JR.	10,923	174,467 R	78.5%	17.7%	81.6%	18.4%
3	2018	213,304	163,650	SMITH, ADRIAN*	49,654	THEOBALD, PAUL		113,996 R	76.7%	23.3%	76.7%	23.3%
3	2016	226,907	226,907	SMITH, ADRIAN*				226,907 R	100.0%		100.0%	
3	2014	184,964	139,440	SMITH, ADRIAN*	45,524	SULLIVAN, MARK		93,916 R	75.4%	24.6%	75.4%	24.6%
3	2012	252,689	187,423	SMITH, ADRIAN*	65,266	SULLIVAN, MARK		122,157 R	74.2%	25.8%	74.2%	25.8%
TOTAL	2022	663,187	414,599		235,572		13,016	179,027 R	62.5%	35.5%	63.8%	36.2%
TOTAL	2020	941,298	585,234		326,018		30,046	259,216 R	62.2%	34.6%	64.2%	35.8%
TOTAL	2018	696,570	432,077		264,493			167,584 R	62.0%	38.0%	62.0%	38.0%
TOTAL	2016	788,453	557,744		221,069		9,640	336,675 R	70.7%	28.0%	71.6%	28.4%
TOTAL	2014	535,530	340,816		185,234		9,480	155,582 R	63.6%	34.6%	64.8%	35.2%
TOTAL	2012	772,515	496,276		276,239			220,037 R	64.2%	35.8%	64.2%	35.8%

Note: An asterisk (*) denotes incumbent.

NEBRASKA

GENERAL AND PRIMARY ELECTIONS

GENERAL ELECTIONS: OTHER VOTES

Governor — Other vote was 26,455 Libertarian (Scott Zimmerman), 5,798 Write-In (Scattered Write-Ins)

House — Other vote was:

CD 3 — 13,016 Legal Marijuana Now (Mark Elworth)

2022 PRIMARY ELECTIONS: SUPPLEMENTARY INFORMATION

Primary — May 10, 2022

Registration (as of May 3, 2022) — 1,216,336

Republican	602,410
Democratic	346,526
Libertarian	18,267
Other	2,333
Nonpartisan	1,237,672

Primary Type — Closed—Registered Democrats and Republicans could vote only in their party's primary. Voters registered as Nonpartisan could participate in either party's primary for the Senate and House (but not for governor). As for president, each party sets its own rules on primary participation.

	REPUBLICAN PRIMARIES			DEMOCRATIC PRIMARIES		
Governor	Pillen, Jim	91,555	33.9%	Blood, Carol	88,859	88.7%
	Herbster, Charles W.	80,771	29.9%	Harris, Roy A.	11,267	11.3%
	Lindstrom, Brett	70,554	26.1%			
	Thibodeau, Theresa	16,432	6.1%			
	Ridenour, Breland	4,685	1.7%			
	Connely, Michael	2,838	1.1%			
	Carpenter, Donna Nicole	1,536	0.6%			
	McNinch, Lela L.	1,192	0.4%			
	Wentz, Troy	708	0.3%			
	TOTAL	270,271		TOTAL	100,126	

NEBRASKA

GENERAL AND PRIMARY ELECTIONS

	REPUBLICAN PRIMARIES			DEMOCRATIC PRIMARIES		
Congressional District 1	Flood, Mike*	61,265	73.9%	Pansing Brooks, Patty	31,808	86.5%
	Fortenberry, Jeff	9,807	11.8%	Zakaria, Jazari Kual "Joseph"	4,944	13.5%
	Weaver, John Glen	5,470	6.6%			
	Connely, Thireena Yuki	3,353	4.0%			
	Huffman, Curtis D.	3,062	3.7%			
	TOTAL	*82,957*		*TOTAL*	*36,752*	
Congressional District 2	Bacon, Don*	53,824	77.1%	Vargas, Anthony "Tony"	31,930	68.6%
	Kuehl, Steve	15,945	22.9%	Shelton, Alisha	14,585	31.4%
	TOTAL	*69,769*		*TOTAL*	*46,515*	
Congressional District 3	Smith, Adrian*	89,453	76.0%	Else, David J.	8,701	52.2%
	Calhoun, Mike	28,243	24.0%	Wik, Daniel M.	7,968	47.8%
	TOTAL	*117,696*		*TOTAL*	*16,669*	

Note: An asterisk (*) denotes incumbent.

NEVADA

Statewide Races

In Nevada, two first-term statewide Democrats sought reelection in 2022. Though Joe Biden carried Nevada in 2020, the state has not exhibited the same pro-Democratic trend that, say, next door Arizona has: while Biden improved several percentage points over Hillary Clinton's showing in Arizona, both Democrats carried Nevada by the same about 2.5 points. The Nevada economy is also heavily reliant on tourism – after the in-power Democrats had imposed COVID restrictions, it seemed possible the electorate would be in a rebellious mood.

In 2016, Democrat Catherine Cortez Masto, a former state Attorney General, won a race to succeed former Senate Majority Leader Harry Reid (D), who retired after representing the state for 30 years. In beating a strong Republican 47%–45%, she became the first Latina elected to the chamber. Six years later, national Republicans backed Cortez Masto's successor as state Attorney General, Adam Laxalt, who easily won the nomination. Compared to other GOP nominees in key states, Laxalt was a decent recruit, but he made some gaffes. In this socially libertarian state, Cortez Masto ran on her support for abortion rights and reached out to the Hispanic community.

Though Laxalt had a slight lead in most polls, Cortez Masto was reelected 49%–48%. As voting got underway, the Las Vegas' Culinary Workers Local 226 – arguably the state's most influential union – was firing on all cylinders as its members worked to turn out Democrats. Cortez Masto carried Las Vegas's Clark County, which usually casts two-thirds of the statewide vote, by almost eight points. A decade ago, conventional wisdom was what successful statewide Democrats needed to carry Clark by at least ten points. So how did Cortez Masto win? Reno's Washoe County, the second most populous county, has picked up some slack for Democrats. In 2016, Cortez Masto lost Washoe County by 1,683 votes – six years later, her 8,615-vote margin there provided her statewide margin of victory.

In the gubernatorial race, Democrat Steve Sisolak lost his job by less than two percentage points. In terms of candidate quality, Sisolak's opponent, Clark County Sheriff Joe Lombardo, seemed a cut above Laxalt. Compared to his 2018 result, Sisolak improved in some of the staunchly Republican, but lightly populated, rural "Cow Counties" – but his margin in Clark County was more than halved, dropping from 13 points to less than six.

House Races

Though he lost his seat, one of Sisolak's legacies that Democrats came to appreciate in 2022 was the congressional map he signed. With unified control of state government, Democrats sought to lock in their 3-1 edge in the state delegation.

On the outgoing map, NV-1, a safely blue seat in urban Las Vegas, was sandwiched between Districts 3 and 4, which were more marginal, Democratic-held seats based in suburban Clark County. District 2, the sole GOP-held seat, was Washoe County and a handful of cow counties. Democratic legislators left NV-2 unchanged, but "unpacked" NV-1 to make NV-3 and NV-4 bluer. The gerrymander worked as intended: as NV-2 voted heavily Republican, the three Clark County-based districts reelected their Democratic incumbents by mid-single-digit margins.

NEVADA

Congressional districts first established for elections held in 2022

4 members

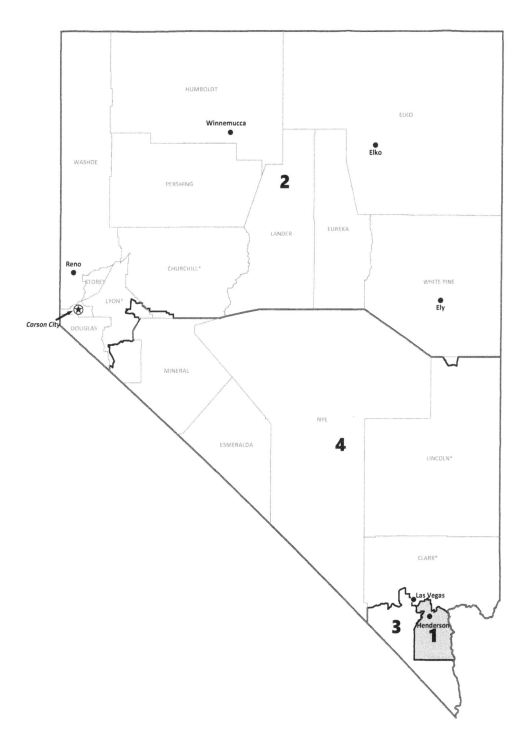

The city of Carson City is an independent city that is treated as a county equivalent; the label is included only for the city.

* Asterisk indicates a county whose boundaries include parts of two or more congressional districts.

NEVADA

GOVERNOR
Joe Lombardo (R). Elected 2022 to a four-year term.

SENATORS (2 Democrats)
Jacky Rosen (D). Elected 2018 to a six-year term.

Catherine Cortez Masto (D). Reelected 2022 to a six-year term. Previously elected 2016.

REPRESENTATIVES (1 Republican, 3 Democrats)
1. Dina Titus (D)
2. Mark Amodei (R)
3. Susie Lee (D)
4. Steven A. Horsford (D)

POSTWAR VOTE FOR PRESIDENT

Year	Total Vote	Republican Vote	Republican Candidate	Democratic Vote	Democratic Candidate	Other Vote	Rep.-Dem. Plurality	Total Vote Rep.	Total Vote Dem.	Major Vote Rep.	Major Vote Dem.
2020	1,405,376	669,890	Trump, Donald J.*	703,486	Biden, Joseph R. Jr.	32,000	33,596 D	47.7%	50.1%	48.8%	51.2%
2016**	1,125,385	512,058	Trump, Donald J.	539,260	Clinton, Hillary Rodham	74,067	27,202 D	45.5%	47.9%	48.7%	51.3%
2012	1,014,918	463,567	Romney, W. Mitt	531,373	Obama, Barack H.*	19,978	67,806 D	45.7%	52.4%	46.6%	53.4%
2008	967,848	412,827	McCain, John S. III	533,736	Obama, Barack H.	21,285	120,909 D	42.7%	55.1%	43.6%	56.4%
2004	829,587	418,690	Bush, George W.*	397,190	Kerry, John F.	13,707	21,500 R	50.5%	47.9%	51.3%	48.7%
2000**	608,970	301,575	Bush, George W.	279,978	Gore, Albert Jr.	27,417	21,597 R	49.5%	46.0%	51.9%	48.1%
1996**	464,279	199,244	Dole, Robert "Bob"	203,974	Clinton, Bill*	61,061	4,730 D	42.9%	43.9%	49.4%	50.6%
1992**	506,318	175,828	Bush, George H.*	189,148	Clinton, Bill	141,342	13,320 D	34.7%	37.4%	48.2%	51.8%
1988	350,067	206,040	Bush, George H.	132,738	Dukakis, Michael S.	11,289	73,302 R	58.9%	37.9%	60.8%	39.2%
1984	286,667	188,770	Reagan, Ronald*	91,655	Mondale, Walter F.	6,242	97,115 R	65.8%	32.0%	67.3%	32.7%
1980**	247,885	155,017	Reagan, Ronald	66,666	Carter, Jimmy*	26,202	88,351 R	62.5%	26.9%	69.9%	30.1%
1976	201,876	101,273	Ford, Gerald R.*	92,479	Carter, Jimmy	8,124	8,794 R	50.2%	45.8%	52.3%	47.7%
1972	181,766	115,750	Nixon, Richard M.*	66,016	McGovern, George S.		49,734 R	63.7%	36.3%	63.7%	36.3%
1968**	154,218	73,188	Nixon, Richard M.	60,598	Humphrey, Hubert Horatio Jr.	20,432	12,590 R	47.5%	39.3%	54.7%	45.3%
1964	135,433	56,094	Goldwater, Barry M. Sr.	79,339	Johnson, Lyndon B.*		23,245 D	41.4%	58.6%	41.4%	58.6%
1960	107,267	52,387	Nixon, Richard M.	54,880	Kennedy, John F.		2,493 D	48.8%	51.2%	48.8%	51.2%
1956	96,689	56,049	Eisenhower, Dwight D.*	40,640	Stevenson, Adlai E. II		15,409 R	58.0%	42.0%	58.0%	42.0%
1952	82,190	50,502	Eisenhower, Dwight D.	31,688	Stevenson, Adlai E. II		18,814 R	61.4%	38.6%	61.4%	38.6%
1948	62,117	29,357	Dewey, Thomas E.	31,291	Truman, Harry S.*	1,469	1,934 D	47.3%	50.4%	48.4%	51.6%

Note: An asterisk (*) denotes incumbent. **In past elections, the other vote included: 2016 - 37,384 Libertarian (Gary Johnson); 2000 - 15,008 Green (Ralph Nader); 1996 - 43,986 Reform (Ross Perot); 1992 - 132,580 Independent (Perot); 1980 - 17,651 Independent (John Anderson); 1968 - 20,432 American Independent (George Wallace).

NEVADA

POSTWAR VOTE FOR GOVERNOR

		Republican		Democratic		Other Vote	Rep.-Dem. Plurality	Percentage			
								Total Vote		Major Vote	
Year	Total Vote	Vote	Candidate	Vote	Candidate			Rep.	Dem.	Rep.	Dem.
2022	1,019,071	497,377	Lombardo, Joe	481,991	Sisolak, Steve*	39,703	15,386 R	48.8%	47.3%	50.8%	49.2%
2018	971,799	440,320	Laxalt, Adam	480,007	Sisolak, Steve	51,472	39,687 D	45.3%	49.4%	47.8%	52.2%
2014	547,349	386,340	Sandoval, Brian*	130,722	Goodman, Robert "Bob"	30,287	255,618 R	70.6%	23.9%	74.7%	25.3%
2010	716,529	382,350	Sandoval, Brian	298,171	Reid, Rory	36,008	84,179 R	53.4%	41.6%	56.2%	43.8%
2006	582,158	279,003	Gibbons, James A. "Jim"	255,684	Titus, Dina	47,471	23,319 R	47.9%	43.9%	52.2%	47.8%
2002	504,079	344,001	Guinn, Kenny*	110,935	Neal, Joe	49,143	233,066 R	68.2%	22.0%	75.6%	24.4%
1998	433,630	223,892	Guinn, Kenny	182,281	Jones, Jan Laverty	27,457	41,611 R	51.6%	42.0%	55.1%	44.9%
1994	379,676	156,875	Gibbons, James A. "Jim"	200,026	Miller, Robert J.*	22,775	43,151 D	41.3%	52.7%	44.0%	56.0%
1990	320,743	95,789	Gallaway, Jim	207,878	Miller, Robert J.*	17,076	112,089 D	29.9%	64.8%	31.5%	68.5%
1986	260,375	65,081	Cafferata, Patty	187,268	Bryan, Richard H.*	8,026	122,187 D	25.0%	71.9%	25.8%	74.2%
1982	239,751	100,104	List, Robert F.*	128,132	Bryan, Richard H.	11,515	28,028 D	41.8%	53.4%	43.9%	56.1%
1978	192,445	108,097	List, Robert F.	76,361	Rose, Robert E.	7,987	31,736 R	56.2%	39.7%	58.6%	41.4%
1974**	169,358	28,959	Crumpler, Shirley	114,114	O'Callaghan, Mike*	26,285	85,155 D	17.1%	67.4%	20.2%	79.8%
1970	146,991	64,400	Fike, Ed	70,697	O'Callaghan, Mike	11,894	6,297 D	43.8%	48.1%	47.7%	52.3%
1966	137,677	71,807	Laxalt, Paul	65,870	Sawyer, Grant*		5,937 R	52.2%	47.8%	52.2%	47.8%
1962	96,929	32,145	Gragson, Oran K.	64,784	Sawyer, Grant*		32,639 D	33.2%	66.8%	33.2%	66.8%
1958	84,889	34,025	Russell, Charles H.*	50,864	Sawyer, Grant		16,839 D	40.1%	59.9%	40.1%	59.9%
1954	78,462	41,665	Russell, Charles H.*	36,797	Pittman, Vail		4,868 R	53.1%	46.9%	53.1%	46.9%
1950	61,773	35,609	Russell, Charles H.	26,164	Pittman, Vail*		9,445 R	57.6%	42.4%	57.6%	42.4%
1946	49,902	21,247	Jepson, Melvin E.	28,655	Pittman, Vail		7,408 D	42.6%	57.4%	42.6%	57.4%

Note: An asterisk (*) denotes incumbent. **In past elections, the other vote included: 1974 - 26,285 Independent American (James Ray Houston).

POSTWAR VOTE FOR SENATOR

		Republican		Democratic		Other Vote	Rep.-Dem. Plurality	Percentage			
								Total Vote		Major Vote	
Year	Total Vote	Vote	Candidate	Vote	Candidate			Rep.	Dem.	Rep.	Dem.
2022	1,020,850	490,388	Laxalt, Adam	498,316	Masto, Catherine Cortez*	32,146	7,928 D	48.0%	48.8%	49.6%	50.4%
2018	972,132	441,202	Heller, Dean*	490,071	Rosen, Jacky	40,859	48,869 D	45.4%	50.4%	47.4%	52.6%
2016	1,108,294	495,079	Heck, Joe	521,994	Masto, Catherine Cortez	91,221	26,915 D	44.7%	47.1%	48.7%	51.3%
2012	997,805	457,656	Heller, Dean*	446,080	Berkley, Shelley	94,069	11,576 R	45.9%	44.7%	50.6%	49.4%
2010	721,404	321,361	Angle, Sharron E.	362,785	Reid, Harry*	37,258	41,424 D	44.5%	50.3%	47.0%	53.0%
2006	582,572	322,501	Ensign, John*	238,796	Carter, Jack	21,275	83,705 R	55.4%	41.0%	57.5%	42.5%
2004	810,068	284,640	Ziser, Richard	494,805	Reid, Harry*	30,623	210,165 D	35.1%	61.1%	36.5%	63.5%
2000	600,250	330,687	Ensign, John	238,260	Bernstein, Ed	31,303	92,427 R	55.1%	39.7%	58.1%	41.9%
1998	435,790	208,222	Ensign, John	208,650	Reid, Harry*	18,918	428 D	47.8%	47.9%	49.9%	50.1%
1994	380,530	156,020	Furman, Hal	193,804	Bryan, Richard H.*	30,706	37,784 D	41.0%	50.9%	44.6%	55.4%
1992	495,887	199,413	Dahl, Demar	253,150	Reid, Harry*	43,324	53,737 D	40.2%	51.0%	44.1%	55.9%
1988	349,649	161,336	Hecht, Jacob Chic*	175,548	Bryan, Richard H.	12,765	14,212 D	46.1%	50.2%	47.9%	52.1%
1986	261,932	116,606	Santini, James	130,955	Reid, Harry	14,371	14,349 D	44.5%	50.0%	47.1%	52.9%
1982	240,394	120,377	Hecht, Jacob Chic	114,720	Cannon, Howard W.*	5,297	5,657 R	50.1%	47.7%	51.2%	48.8%
1980	246,436	144,224	Laxalt, Paul*	92,129	Gojack, Mary	10,083	52,095 R	58.5%	37.4%	61.0%	39.0%
1976	201,980	63,471	Towell, David	127,295	Cannon, Howard W.*	11,214	63,824 D	31.4%	63.0%	33.3%	66.7%
1974	169,473	79,605	Laxalt, Paul	78,981	Reid, Harry	10,887	624 R	47.0%	46.6%	50.2%	49.8%
1970	147,768	60,838	Raggio, William J.	85,187	Cannon, Howard W.*	1,743	24,349 D	41.2%	57.6%	41.7%	58.3%
1968	152,690	69,068	Fike, Ed	83,622	Bible, Alan Harvey*		14,554 D	45.2%	54.8%	45.2%	54.8%
1964	134,624	67,288	Laxalt, Paul	67,336	Cannon, Howard W.*		48 D	50.0%	50.0%	50.0%	50.0%
1962	97,192	33,749	Wright, William B.	63,443	Bible, Alan Harvey*		29,694 D	34.7%	65.3%	34.7%	65.3%
1958	84,492	35,760	Malone, George W.*	48,732	Cannon, Howard W.		12,972 D	42.3%	57.7%	42.3%	57.7%
1956	96,389	45,712	Young, Cliff	50,677	Bible, Alan Harvey*		4,965 D	47.4%	52.6%	47.4%	52.6%
1954S**	77,513	32,470	Brown, Ernest S.	45,043	Bible, Alan Harvey		12,573 D	41.9%	58.1%	41.9%	58.1%
1952	81,090	41,906	Malone, George W.*	39,184	Mechling, Thomas B.		2,722 R	51.7%	48.3%	51.7%	48.3%
1950	61,762	25,933	Marshall, George E.	35,829	McCarran, Patrick A.*		9,896 D	42.0%	58.0%	42.0%	58.0%
1946	50,354	27,801	Malone, George W.	22,553	Bunker, Berkeley L.		5,248 R	55.2%	44.8%	55.2%	44.8%

Note: An asterisk (*) denotes incumbent. **The 1954 election was for a short term to fill a vacancy.

NEVADA
GOVERNOR 2022

2020 Census Population	County	Total Vote	Republican (Lombardo)	Democratic (Sisolak)	Other	Rep.-Dem. Plurality	Percentage Total Vote Rep.	Dem.	Major Vote Rep.	Dem.
56,347	CARSON CITY	23,665	12,721	9,822	1,122	2,899 R	53.8%	41.5%	56.4%	43.6%
25,044	CHURCHILL	9,865	7,020	2,223	622	4,797 R	71.2%	22.5%	75.9%	24.1%
2,285,328	CLARK	680,355	308,760	347,397	24,198	38,637 D	45.4%	51.1%	47.1%	52.9%
49,225	DOUGLAS	29,154	19,070	9,014	1,070	10,056 R	65.4%	30.9%	67.9%	32.1%
52,804	ELKO	16,183	12,173	2,923	1,087	9,250 R	75.2%	18.1%	80.6%	19.4%
875	ESMERALDA	453	338	64	51	274 R	74.6%	14.1%	84.1%	15.9%
2,043	EUREKA	782	681	61	40	620 R	87.1%	7.8%	91.8%	8.2%
16,841	HUMBOLDT	6,109	4,488	1,201	420	3,287 R	73.5%	19.7%	78.9%	21.1%
5,520	LANDER	2,208	1,678	316	214	1,362 R	76.0%	14.3%	84.2%	15.8%
5,183	LINCOLN	2,160	1,710	264	186	1,446 R	79.2%	12.2%	86.6%	13.4%
58,186	LYON	23,601	16,338	5,960	1,303	10,378 R	69.2%	25.3%	73.3%	26.7%
4,531	MINERAL	1,893	1,138	613	142	525 R	60.1%	32.4%	65.0%	35.0%
47,174	NYE	20,815	13,824	5,813	1,178	8,011 R	66.4%	27.9%	70.4%	29.6%
6,770	PERSHING	1,774	1,286	384	104	902 R	72.5%	21.6%	77.0%	23.0%
4,173	STOREY	2,562	1,748	678	136	1,070 R	68.2%	26.5%	72.1%	27.9%
475,286	WASHOE	194,042	91,862	94,646	7,534	2,784 D	47.3%	48.8%	49.3%	50.7%
9,543	WHITE PINE	3,450	2,542	612	296	1,930 R	73.7%	17.7%	80.6%	19.4%
3,104,873	TOTAL	1,019,071	497,377	481,991	39,703	15,386 R	48.8%	47.3%	50.8%	49.2%

NEVADA
SENATOR 2022

2020 Census Population	County	Total Vote	Republican (Laxalt)	Democratic (Masto)	Other	Rep.-Dem. Plurality	Percentage Total Vote Rep.	Dem.	Major Vote Rep.	Dem.
56,347	CARSON CITY	23,694	12,451	10,337	906	2,114 R	52.5%	43.6%	54.6%	45.4%
25,044	CHURCHILL	9,880	7,032	2,423	425	4,609 R	71.2%	24.5%	74.4%	25.6%
2,285,328	CLARK	681,798	304,133	357,275	20,390	53,142 D	44.6%	52.4%	46.0%	54.0%
49,225	DOUGLAS	29,169	18,890	9,466	813	9,424 R	64.8%	32.5%	66.6%	33.4%
52,804	ELKO	16,191	12,180	3,286	725	8,894 R	75.2%	20.3%	78.8%	21.2%
875	ESMERALDA	454	344	68	42	276 R	75.8%	15.0%	83.5%	16.5%
2,043	EUREKA	781	671	73	37	598 R	85.9%	9.3%	90.2%	9.8%
16,841	HUMBOLDT	6,112	4,456	1,358	298	3,098 R	72.9%	22.2%	76.6%	23.4%
5,520	LANDER	2,212	1,673	387	152	1,286 R	75.6%	17.5%	81.2%	18.8%
5,183	LINCOLN	2,157	1,727	321	109	1,406 R	80.1%	14.9%	84.3%	15.7%
58,186	LYON	23,616	16,293	6,244	1,079	10,049 R	69.0%	26.4%	72.3%	27.7%
4,531	MINERAL	1,894	1,124	660	110	464 R	59.3%	34.8%	63.0%	37.0%
47,174	NYE	20,823	13,833	5,957	1,033	7,876 R	66.4%	28.6%	69.9%	30.1%
6,770	PERSHING	1,777	1,272	419	86	853 R	71.6%	23.6%	75.2%	24.8%
4,173	STOREY	2,561	1,728	721	112	1,007 R	67.5%	28.2%	70.6%	29.4%
475,286	WASHOE	194,280	90,002	98,617	5,661	8,615 D	46.3%	50.8%	47.7%	52.3%
9,543	WHITE PINE	3,451	2,579	704	168	1,875 R	74.7%	20.4%	78.6%	21.4%
3,104,873	TOTAL	1,020,850	490,388	498,316	32,146	7,928 D	48.0%	48.8%	49.6%	50.4%

NEVADA

HOUSE OF REPRESENTATIVES

CD	Year	Total Vote	Republican Vote	Republican Candidate	Democratic Vote	Democratic Candidate	Other Vote	Rep.-Dem. Plurality	Total Vote Rep.	Total Vote Dem.	Major Vote Rep.	Major Vote Dem.
1	2022	224,349	103,115	ROBERTSON, MARK	115,700	TITUS, DINA*	5,534	12,585 D	46.0%	51.6%	47.1%	52.9%
1	2020	223,213	74,490	BENTLEY, JOYCE	137,868	TITUS, DINA*	10,855	63,378 D	33.4%	61.8%	35.1%	64.9%
1	2018	152,201	46,978	BENTLEY, JOYCE	100,707	TITUS, DINA*	4,516	53,729 D	30.9%	66.2%	31.8%	68.2%
1	2016	188,352	54,174	PERRY, MARY	116,537	TITUS, DINA*	17,641	62,363 D	28.8%	61.9%	31.7%	68.3%
1	2014	80,299	30,413	TEIJEIRO, ANNETTE	45,643	TITUS, DINA*	4,243	15,230 D	37.9%	56.8%	40.0%	60.0%
1	2012	179,278	56,521	EDWARDS, CHRIS	113,967	TITUS, DINA	8,790	57,446 D	31.5%	63.6%	33.2%	66.8%
2	2022	310,498	185,467	AMODEI, MARK*	117,371	KRAUSE, ELIZABETH MERCEDES	7,660	68,096 R	59.7%	37.8%	61.2%	38.8%
2	2020	382,673	216,078	AMODEI, MARK*	155,780	ACKERMAN, PATRICIA GERALDENE	10,815	60,298 R	56.5%	40.7%	58.1%	41.9%
2	2018	287,537	167,435	AMODEI, MARK*	120,102	KOBLE, CLINT		47,333 R	58.2%	41.8%	58.2%	41.8%
2	2016	313,336	182,676	AMODEI, MARK*	115,722	EVANS, H.D. "CHIP"	14,938	66,954 R	58.3%	36.9%	61.2%	38.8%
2	2014	186,210	122,402	AMODEI, MARK*	52,016	SPEES, KRISTEN	11,792	70,386 R	65.7%	27.9%	70.2%	29.8%
2	2012	281,449	162,213	AMODEI, MARK*	102,019	KOEPNICK, SAMUEL	17,217	60,194 R	57.6%	36.2%	61.4%	38.6%
3	2022	252,169	121,083	BECKER, APRIL	131,086	LEE, SUSIE*		10,003 D	48.0%	52.0%	48.0%	52.0%
3	2020	417,252	190,975	RODIMER, DAN "BIG DAN"	203,421	LEE, SUSIE*	22,856	12,446 D	45.8%	48.8%	48.4%	51.6%
3	2018	286,168	122,566	TARKANIAN, DANNY	148,501	LEE, SUSIE	15,101	25,935 D	42.8%	51.9%	45.2%	54.8%
3	2016	310,963	142,926	TARKANIAN, DANNY	146,869	ROSEN, JACKY	21,168	3,943 D	46.0%	47.2%	49.3%	50.7%
3	2014	145,719	88,528	HECK, JOE*	52,644	BILBRAY, ERIN	4,547	35,884 R	60.8%	36.1%	62.7%	37.3%
3	2012	272,523	137,244	HECK, JOE*	116,823	OCEGUERA, JOHN	18,456	20,421 R	50.4%	42.9%	54.0%	46.0%
4	2022	222,487	105,870	PETERS, SAMUEL JAMES	116,617	HORSFORD, STEVEN A.*		10,747 D	47.6%	52.4%	47.6%	52.4%
4	2020	332,469	152,284	MARCHANT, JIM	168,457	HORSFORD, STEVEN A.*	11,728	16,173 D	45.8%	50.7%	47.5%	52.5%
4	2018	234,868	102,748	HARDY, CRESENT	121,962	HORSFORD, STEVEN A.	10,158	19,214 D	43.7%	51.9%	45.7%	54.3%
4	2016	265,846	118,328	HARDY, CRESENT*	128,985	KIHUEN, RUBEN	18,533	10,657 D	44.5%	48.5%	47.8%	52.2%
4	2014	130,781	63,466	HARDY, CRESENT	59,844	HORSFORD, STEVEN A.*	7,471	3,622 R	48.5%	45.8%	51.5%	48.5%
4	2012	240,492	101,261	TARKANIAN, DANNY	120,501	HORSFORD, STEVEN A.	18,730	19,240 D	42.1%	50.1%	45.7%	54.3%
TOTAL	2022	1,009,503	515,535		480,774		13,194	34,761 R	51.1%	47.6%	51.7%	48.3%
TOTAL	2020	1,355,607	633,827		665,526		56,254	31,699 D	46.8%	49.1%	48.8%	51.2%
TOTAL	2018	960,774	439,727		491,272		29,775	51,545 D	45.8%	51.1%	47.2%	52.8%
TOTAL	2016	1,078,497	498,104		508,113		72,280	10,009 D	46.2%	47.1%	49.5%	50.5%
TOTAL	2014	543,009	304,809		210,147		28,053	94,662 R	56.1%	38.7%	59.2%	40.8%
TOTAL	2012	973,742	457,239		453,310		63,193	3,929 R	47.0%	46.6%	50.2%	49.8%

Note: An asterisk (*) denotes incumbent.

NEVADA

GENERAL AND PRIMARY ELECTIONS

GENERAL ELECTIONS: OTHER VOTES

Governor   Other vote was 14,919 Libertarian (Brandon Davis), 14,866 Other (None of Candidates), 9,918 Independent American (Ed Bridges)

Senate   12,441 Other (None of These Candidates), 8,075 No Party Preference (Barry Lindemann), 6,422 Libertarian (Neil Scott), 5,208 Independent American (Barry Rubinson)

House   Other vote was:

CD 1   5,534 Libertarian (Ken Cavanaugh)

CD 2   4,194 Independent American (Russell Best), 3,466 Libertarian (Darryl Baber)

NEVADA

GENERAL AND PRIMARY ELECTIONS

2022 PRIMARY ELECTIONS: SUPPLEMENTARY INFORMATION

Primary	June 14, 2022	**Registration** (as of June 2022 — includes 321,142 inactive voters)	2,163,903	Democratic Republican Independent American Libertarian Other Nonpartisan	720,835 640,801 96,040 21,074 56,214 628,939

Primary Type — Closed—Only registered Democrats and Republicans could vote in their party's primary.

	REPUBLICAN PRIMARIES			**DEMOCRATIC PRIMARIES**		
Senator	Laxalt, Adam	127,757	55.9%	Masto, Catherine Cortez*	159,694	90.9%
	Brown, Sam	78,206	34.2%	Reid, Corey	4,491	2.6%
	Mendenhall, Sharelle	6,946	3.0%	"None of These Candidates"	4,216	2.4%
	"None of These Candidates"	6,277	2.7%	Rheinhart, Allen	3,852	2.2%
	Conrad, William "Bill"	3,440	1.5%	Kasheta, Stephanie	3,487	2.0%
	Hockstedler, William	2,836	1.2%			
	Rodriguez, Paul	1,844	0.8%			
	Perkins, Tyler	850	0.4%			
	Poliak, Carlo	332	0.1%			
	TOTAL	228,488		TOTAL	175,740	
Governor	Lombardo, Joe	87,761	38.4%	Sisolak, Steve*	157,283	89.5%
	Gilbert, Joey	61,738	27.0%	Collins, Tom	12,051	6.9%
	Heller, Dean	32,087	14.0%	"None of These Candidates"	6,340	3.6%
	Lee, John J.	17,846	7.8%			
	Nohra, Guy	8,348	3.7%			
	Simon, Fred	6,856	3.0%			
	Heck, Thomas "Tom"	4,315	1.9%			
	"None of These Candidates"	4,219	1.8%			
	Hamilton, Eddie	1,293	0.6%			
	Whitley, Amber	1,238	0.5%			
	Walls, William "Dock"	833	0.4%			
	Evertsen, Gary	558	0.2%			
	Evans, Seven Achilles	475	0.2%			
	O'Brien, Edward E.	422	0.2%			
	Zilberberg, Barak	352	0.2%			
	Lusak, Stanleigh Harold	229	0.1%			
	TOTAL	228,570		TOTAL	175,674	
Congressional District 1	Robertson, Mark	12,375	30.1%	Titus, Dina*	33,565	79.8%
	Brog, David	7,226	17.6%	Vilela, Amy	8,482	20.2%
	Serrano, Carolina Andrea	7,050	17.1%			
	Hardy, Cresent	4,790	11.6%			
	Steel, Cynthia Dianne	4,782	11.6%			
	Adams, Jane	2,081	5.1%			
	Sholty, Morgun	1,998	4.9%			
	Turner, Jessie	845	2.1%			
	TOTAL	41,147		TOTAL	42,047	
Congressional District 2	Amodei, Mark*	49,779	54.9%	Krause, Elizabeth Mercedes	22,072	49.0%
	Tarkanian, Danny	29,563	32.6%	Hanifan, Tim	6,440	14.3%
	Beck, Joel	6,744	7.4%	Doucette, Michael	5,478	12.2%
	Sampson, Catherine Marie	3,010	3.3%	Joshi, Rahul	3,613	8.0%
	Nadell, Brian	1,614	1.8%	Hansen, Brian	3,276	7.3%
				Afzal, Joseph Edward "Joey"	3,117	6.9%
				Gorman, Gerold Lee	1,034	2.3%
	TOTAL	90,710		TOTAL	45,030	

NEVADA
GENERAL AND PRIMARY ELECTIONS

	REPUBLICAN PRIMARIES			DEMOCRATIC PRIMARIES		
Congressional District 3	Becker, April	28,260	64.9%	Lee, Susie*	37,069	89.7%
	Kovacs, John	4,857	11.1%	Hynes, Randell Scott "Randy"	4,265	10.3%
	Bossert, Clark	4,553	10.4%			
	Malgeri, Noah V.	3,981	9.1%			
	Goldberg, Albert Maxwell	1,920	4.4%			
	TOTAL	*43,571*		*TOTAL*	*41,334*	
Congressional District 4	Peters, Samuel James	20,956	47.7%	Horsford, Steven A.*	Unopposed	
	Black, Ann "Annie"	18,249	41.5%			
	Bonaventura, Chance	4,748	10.8%			
	TOTAL	*43,953*				

Note: An asterisk (*) denotes incumbent.

NEW HAMPSHIRE

Statewide Races

In late 2021, Republican Chris Sununu, who, a year earlier had won a third two-year term as governor of a blue state, shocked the political world by announcing he'd seek reelection instead of challenging first-term Democratic Sen. Maggie Hassan. In 2016, Hassan won her seat by ousting a Republican incumbent by 1,017 votes and seemed vulnerable.

Without Sununu, the two main Republican contenders that emerged in the September primary were state Senate President Chuck Morse and veteran Don Buldoc – national Republicans preferred the former, while the latter ran as a more Trump-aligned candidate. Shortly before the primary, in a move that seemed engineered to help Bolduc, the Senate Majority PAC, a group led by Senate Majority Leader Chuck Schumer (D) took to the airwaves hitting Morse. Bolduc won the primary 37%–36%.

As the Republicans campaigned against each other, Hassan projected a postpartisan image. Over the summer, she ran ads touting the results of a report published by the Lugar Center (named for a late Indiana Republican senator) that ranked her as the most bipartisan senator.

As the GOP nominee in a blue state, Bolduc had a change of heart: in the primary, he parroted Trump's election fraud claims – in the general election, he decided that the 2020 election was legitimate, after all. Hassan, who had been stockpiling funds during the primary season, outspent Bolduc by a factor of ten-to-one. Though some polls showed Bolduc with some late momentum, Senate Leadership Fund, a PAC linked to Senate Minority Leader Mitch McConnell (R), canceled its New Hampshire reservations – it was taken as a sign that national Republicans lacked confidence in the race.

Hassan won a second term by a surprisingly large 53%–44% vote, becoming the first Democrat in the popular vote era to win reelection to this seat. She carried eight of the state's ten counties, only missing Belknap (Laconia) and Coos, the state's least populous and northernmost county.

With Sununu out of the Senate race, he was a heavy favorite for reelection. Though his share was down from the 65% he took in 2020, Sununu won by a still-heavy 57%–41% margin over state Sen. Tom Sherman, who represented the Seacoast area. Sununu won every county but Grafton (containing Dartmouth College) and rural Cheshire.

House Races

New Hampshire, with two Democratic-held districts, was among the last states to pass a redistricting map. Legislative Republicans, in the majority, passed a plan essentially conceding the 2nd District to Democrats while turning the 1st District into a Republican seat. Sununu insisted that the current plan, with two single-digit Biden-won seats, be kept intact. The matter was kicked to the state Supreme Court, which took on Sununu's minimal-change mentality – the two districts have each had their basic shapes since the 1880s.

In the 1st District, which attracted considerable outside spending, Democratic Rep. Chris Pappas beat former Trump administration staffer Karoline Leavitt 54%–46%. In the 2nd District, veteran Democratic Rep. Annie Kuster won 56%–44% against Rob Burns, a frequent GOP candidate who beat out Sununu's choice in the primary.

NEW HAMPSHIRE

Congressional districts first established for elections held in 2022

2 members

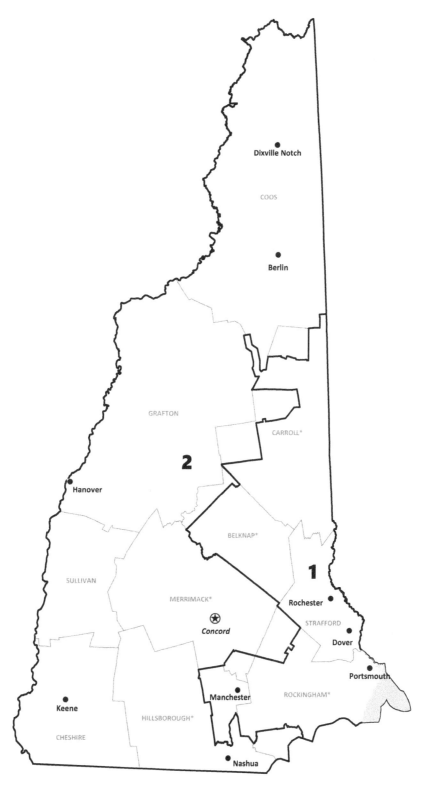

* Asterisk indicates a county whose boundaries include parts of two or more congressional districts.

NEW HAMPSHIRE

GOVERNOR
Chris Sununu (R). Reelected 2022 to a two-year term. Previously elected 2020, 2018, 2016.

SENATORS (2 Democrats)
Jeanne Shaheen (D). Reelected 2020 to a six-year term. Previously elected 2014, 2008.

Maggie Hassan (D). Reelected 2022 to a six-year term. Previously elected 2016.

REPRESENTATIVES (2 Democrats)
1. Chris Pappas (D)   2. Ann McLane Kuster (D)

POSTWAR VOTE FOR PRESIDENT

		Republican		Democratic		Other Vote	Rep.-Dem. Plurality	Percentage			
								Total Vote		Major Vote	
Year	Total Vote	Vote	Candidate	Vote	Candidate			Rep.	Dem.	Rep.	Dem.
2020	806,205	365,660	Trump, Donald J.*	424,937	Biden, Joseph R. Jr.	15,608	59,277 D	45.4%	52.7%	46.3%	53.7%
2016**	744,296	345,790	Trump, Donald J.	348,526	Clinton, Hillary Rodham	49,980	2,736 D	46.5%	46.8%	49.8%	50.2%
2012	710,972	329,918	Romney, W. Mitt	369,561	Obama, Barack H.*	11,493	39,643 D	46.4%	52.0%	47.2%	52.8%
2008	710,970	316,534	McCain, John S. III	384,826	Obama, Barack H.	9,610	68,292 D	44.5%	54.1%	45.1%	54.9%
2004	677,738	331,237	Bush, George W.*	340,511	Kerry, John F.	5,990	9,274 D	48.9%	50.2%	49.3%	50.7%
2000**	569,081	273,559	Bush, George W.	266,348	Gore, Albert Jr.	29,174	7,211 R	48.1%	46.8%	50.7%	49.3%
1996**	499,175	196,532	Dole, Robert "Bob"	246,214	Clinton, Bill*	56,429	49,682 D	39.4%	49.3%	44.4%	55.6%
1992**	537,943	202,484	Bush, George H.*	209,040	Clinton, Bill	126,419	6,556 D	37.6%	38.9%	49.2%	50.8%
1988	451,074	281,537	Bush, George H.	163,696	Dukakis, Michael S.	5,841	117,841 R	62.4%	36.3%	63.2%	36.8%
1984	389,066	267,051	Reagan, Ronald*	120,395	Mondale, Walter F.	1,620	146,656 R	68.6%	30.9%	68.9%	31.1%
1980**	383,990	221,705	Reagan, Ronald	108,864	Carter, Jimmy*	53,421	112,841 R	57.7%	28.4%	67.1%	32.9%
1976	339,618	185,935	Ford, Gerald R.*	147,635	Carter, Jimmy	6,048	38,300 R	54.7%	43.5%	55.7%	44.3%
1972	334,055	213,724	Nixon, Richard M.*	116,435	McGovern, George S.	3,896	97,289 R	64.0%	34.9%	64.7%	35.3%
1968**	297,298	154,903	Nixon, Richard M.	130,589	Humphrey, Hubert Horatio Jr.	11,806	24,314 R	52.1%	43.9%	54.3%	45.7%
1964	288,093	104,029	Goldwater, Barry M. Sr.	184,064	Johnson, Lyndon B.*		80,035 D	36.1%	63.9%	36.1%	63.9%
1960	295,761	157,989	Nixon, Richard M.	137,772	Kennedy, John F.		20,217 R	53.4%	46.6%	53.4%	46.6%
1956	266,994	176,519	Eisenhower, Dwight D.*	90,364	Stevenson, Adlai E. II	111	86,155 R	66.1%	33.8%	66.1%	33.9%
1952	272,950	166,287	Eisenhower, Dwight D.	106,663	Stevenson, Adlai E. II		59,624 R	60.9%	39.1%	60.9%	39.1%
1948	231,440	121,299	Dewey, Thomas E.	107,995	Truman, Harry S.*	2,146	13,304 R	52.4%	46.7%	52.9%	47.1%

Note: An asterisk (*) denotes incumbent. **In past elections, the other vote included: 2016 - 30,777 Libertarian (Gary Johnson); 2000 - 22,198 Green (Ralph Nader); 1996 - 48,390 Reform (Ross Perot); 1992 - 121,337 Independent (Perot); 1980 - 49,693 Independent (John Anderson); 1968 - 11,173 American Independent (George Wallace).

NEW HAMPSHIRE

POSTWAR VOTE FOR GOVERNOR

		Republican		Democratic		Other Vote	Rep.-Dem. Plurality	Percentage			
								Total Vote		Major Vote	
Year	Total Vote	Vote	Candidate	Vote	Candidate			Rep.	Dem.	Rep.	Dem.
2022	619,135	352,813	Sununu, Chris*	256,766	Sherman, Tom	9,556	96,047 R	57.0%	41.5%	57.9%	42.1%
2020	793,260	516,609	Sununu, Chris*	264,639	Feltes, Dan	12,012	251,970 R	65.1%	33.4%	66.1%	33.9%
2018	573,602	302,764	Sununu, Chris*	262,359	Kelly, Molly	8,479	40,405 R	52.8%	45.7%	53.6%	46.4%
2016	724,863	354,040	Sununu, Chris	337,589	Van Ostern, Colin	33,234	16,451 R	48.8%	46.6%	51.2%	48.8%
2014	486,183	230,610	Havenstein, Walter "Walt"	254,666	Hassan, Maggie*	907	24,056 D	47.4%	52.4%	47.5%	52.5%
2012	693,877	295,026	Lamontagne, Ovide M.	378,934	Hassan, Maggie	19,917	83,908 D	42.5%	54.6%	43.8%	56.2%
2010	456,588	205,616	Stephen, John A.	240,346	Lynch, John*	10,626	34,730 D	45.0%	52.6%	46.1%	53.9%
2008	682,910	188,555	Kenney, Joseph D.	479,042	Lynch, John*	15,313	290,487 D	27.6%	70.1%	28.2%	71.8%
2006	403,679	104,288	Coburn, Jim	298,760	Lynch, John*	631	194,472 D	25.8%	74.0%	25.9%	74.1%
2004	667,020	325,981	Benson, Craig*	340,299	Lynch, John	740	14,318 D	48.9%	51.0%	48.9%	51.1%
2002	442,976	259,663	Benson, Craig	169,277	Fernald, Mark D.	14,036	90,386 R	58.6%	38.2%	60.5%	39.5%
2000	564,953	246,952	Humphrey, Gordon John	275,038	Shaheen, Jeanne*	42,963	28,086 D	43.7%	48.7%	47.3%	52.7%
1998	318,940	98,473	Lucas, Jay	210,769	Shaheen, Jeanne*	9,698	112,296 D	30.9%	66.1%	31.8%	68.2%
1996	497,040	196,321	Lamontagne, Ovide M.	284,175	Shaheen, Jeanne	16,544	87,854 D	39.5%	57.2%	40.9%	59.1%
1994	311,882	218,134	Merrill, Steve*	79,686	King, Wayne D.	14,062	138,448 R	69.9%	25.6%	73.2%	26.8%
1992	516,170	289,170	Merrill, Steve	206,232	Arnesen, Deborah A.	20,768	82,938 R	56.0%	40.0%	58.4%	41.6%
1990	295,018	177,773	Gregg, Judd*	101,923	Grandmaison, J. Joseph	15,322	75,850 R	60.3%	34.5%	63.6%	36.4%
1988	441,923	267,064	Gregg, Judd	172,543	McEachern, Paul	2,316	94,521 R	60.4%	39.0%	60.8%	39.2%
1986	251,107	134,824	Sununu, John H.*	116,142	McEachern, Paul	141	18,682 R	53.7%	46.3%	53.7%	46.3%
1984	383,910	256,574	Sununu, John H.*	127,156	Spirou, Chris	180	129,418 R	66.8%	33.1%	66.9%	33.1%
1982	282,588	145,389	Sununu, John H.	132,317	Gallen, Hugh J.*	4,882	13,072 R	51.4%	46.8%	52.4%	47.6%
1980	384,031	156,178	Thomson, Meldrim Jr.	226,436	Gallen, Hugh J.*	1,417	70,258 D	40.7%	59.0%	40.8%	59.2%
1978	269,587	122,464	Thomson, Meldrim Jr.*	133,133	Gallen, Hugh J.	13,990	10,669 D	45.4%	49.4%	47.9%	52.1%
1976	342,669	197,589	Thomson, Meldrim Jr.*	145,015	Spanos, Harry V.	65	52,574 R	57.7%	42.3%	57.7%	42.3%
1974	226,665	115,933	Thomson, Meldrim Jr.*	110,591	Leonard, Richard W.	141	5,342 R	51.1%	48.8%	51.2%	48.8%
1972**	323,102	133,702	Thomson, Meldrim Jr.	126,107	Crowley, Roger J.	63,293	7,595 R	41.4%	39.0%	51.5%	48.5%
1970	222,441	102,298	Peterson, Walter R.*	98,098	Crowley, Roger J.	22,045	4,200 R	46.0%	44.1%	51.0%	49.0%
1968	285,342	149,902	Peterson, Walter R.	135,378	Bussiere, Emile R.	62	14,524 R	52.5%	47.4%	52.5%	47.5%
1966	233,642	107,259	Gregg, Hugh	125,882	King, John W.*	501	18,623 D	45.9%	53.9%	46.0%	54.0%
1964	285,863	94,824	Pillsbury, John	190,863	King, John W.*	176	96,039 D	33.2%	66.8%	33.2%	66.8%
1962	230,048	94,567	Pillsbury, John	135,481	King, John W.		40,914 D	41.1%	58.9%	41.1%	58.9%
1960	290,527	161,123	Powell, Wesley*	129,404	Boutin, Bernard L.		31,719 R	55.5%	44.5%	55.5%	44.5%
1958	206,745	106,790	Powell, Wesley	99,955	Boutin, Bernard L.		6,835 R	51.7%	48.3%	51.7%	48.3%
1956	258,695	141,578	Dwinell, Lane*	117,117	Shaw, John		24,461 R	54.7%	45.3%	54.7%	45.3%
1954	194,631	107,287	Dwinell, Lane	87,344	Shaw, John		19,943 R	55.1%	44.9%	55.1%	44.9%
1952	265,715	167,791	Gregg, Hugh	97,924	Craig, William H.		69,867 R	63.1%	36.9%	63.1%	36.9%
1950	191,239	108,907	Adams, Sherman*	82,258	Bingham, Robert P.	74	26,649 R	56.9%	43.0%	57.0%	43.0%
1948	222,571	116,212	Adams, Sherman	105,207	Hill, Herbert W.	1,152	11,005 R	52.2%	47.3%	52.5%	47.5%
1946	163,451	103,204	Dale, Charles M.	60,247	Keefe, F. Clyde		42,957 R	63.1%	36.9%	63.1%	36.9%

Note: An asterisk (*) denotes incumbent. **In past elections, the other vote included: 1972 - 63,199 Independent (Malcolm McLane).

NEW HAMPSHIRE

POSTWAR VOTE FOR SENATOR

Year	Total Vote	Republican Vote	Republican Candidate	Democratic Vote	Democratic Candidate	Other Vote	Rep.-Dem. Plurality	Total Vote Rep. %	Total Vote Dem. %	Major Vote Rep. %	Major Vote Dem. %
2022	620,975	275,928	Bolduc, Donald C.	332,193	Hassan, Maggie*	12,854	56,265 D	44.4%	53.5%	45.4%	54.6%
2020	795,914	326,229	Messner, Bryant	450,778	Shaheen, Jeanne*	18,907	124,549 D	41.0%	56.6%	42.0%	58.0%
2016	739,140	353,632	Ayotte, Kelly*	354,649	Hassan, Maggie	30,859	1,017 D	47.8%	48.0%	49.9%	50.1%
2014	488,159	235,347	Brown, Scott P.	251,184	Shaheen, Jeanne*	1,628	15,837 D	48.2%	51.5%	48.4%	51.6%
2010	455,149	273,218	Ayotte, Kelly	167,545	Hodes, Paul W.	14,386	105,673 R	60.0%	36.8%	62.0%	38.0%
2008	694,787	314,403	Sununu, John E.*	358,438	Shaheen, Jeanne	21,946	44,035 D	45.3%	51.6%	46.7%	53.3%
2004	657,086	434,847	Gregg, Judd*	221,549	Haddock, Doris R. "GrannyD"	690	213,298 R	66.2%	33.7%	66.2%	33.8%
2002	447,135	227,229	Sununu, John E.	207,478	Shaheen, Jeanne	12,428	19,751 R	50.8%	46.4%	52.3%	47.7%
1998	314,956	213,477	Gregg, Judd*	88,883	Condodemetraky, George	12,596	124,594 R	67.8%	28.2%	70.6%	29.4%
1996	491,966	242,304	Smith, Robert C.*	227,397	Swett, Dick	22,265	14,907 R	49.3%	46.2%	51.6%	48.4%
1992	518,416	249,591	Gregg, Judd	234,982	Rauh, John	33,843	14,609 R	48.1%	45.3%	51.5%	48.5%
1990	291,393	189,792	Smith, Robert C.	91,299	Durkin, John A.	10,302	98,493 R	65.1%	31.3%	67.5%	32.5%
1986	244,797	154,090	Rudman, Warren B.*	79,225	Peabody, Endicott	11,482	74,865 R	62.9%	32.4%	66.0%	34.0%
1984	384,406	225,828	Humphrey, Gordon John*	157,447	D'Amours, Norman E.	1,131	68,381 R	58.7%	41.0%	58.9%	41.1%
1980	375,060	195,559	Rudman, Warren B.	179,455	Durkin, John A.*	46	16,104 R	52.1%	47.8%	52.1%	47.9%
1978	263,779	133,745	Humphrey, Gordon John	127,945	McIntyre, Thomas J.*	2,089	5,800 R	50.7%	48.5%	51.1%	48.9%
1975S**	262,682	113,007	Wyman, Louis C.	140,778	Durkin, John A.	8,897	27,771 D	43.0%	53.6%	44.5%	55.5%
1974**	223,363	110,926	Wyman, Louis C.	110,924	Durkin, John A.	1,513	2 R	49.7%	49.7%	50.0%	50.0%
1972	324,354	139,852	Powell, Wesley	184,495	McIntyre, Thomas J.*	7	44,643 D	43.1%	56.9%	43.1%	56.9%
1968	286,989	170,163	Cotton, Norris R.*	116,816	King, John W.	10	53,347 R	59.3%	40.7%	59.3%	40.7%
1966	229,305	105,241	Thyng, Harrison R.	123,888	McIntyre, Thomas J.*	176	18,647 D	45.9%	54.0%	45.9%	54.1%
1962	224,479	134,035	Cotton, Norris R.*	90,444	Catalfo, Alfred Jr.		43,591 R	59.7%	40.3%	59.7%	40.3%
1962S**	224,811	107,199	Bass, Perkins	117,612	McIntyre, Thomas J.		10,413 D	47.7%	52.3%	47.7%	52.3%
1960	287,545	173,521	Bridges, Styles*	114,024	Hill, Herbert W.		59,497 R	60.3%	39.7%	60.3%	39.7%
1956	251,943	161,424	Cotton, Norris R.*	90,519	Pickett, Laurence M.		70,905 R	64.1%	35.9%	64.1%	35.9%
1954	194,536	117,150	Bridges, Styles*	77,386	Morin, Gerard L.		39,764 R	60.2%	39.8%	60.2%	39.8%
1954S**	189,558	114,068	Cotton, Norris R.	75,490	Betley, Stanley J.		38,578 R	60.2%	39.8%	60.2%	39.8%
1950	190,573	106,142	Tobey, Charles W.*	72,473	Kelley, Emmet J.	11,958	33,669 R	55.7%	38.0%	59.4%	40.6%
1948	222,898	129,600	Bridges, Styles*	91,760	Fortin, Alfred E.	1,538	37,840 R	58.1%	41.2%	58.5%	41.5%

Note: An asterisk (*) denotes incumbent. **Following the closely contested 1974 election, neither candidate was seated and the 1975 special election was held for the remaining years of that term. One each of the 1954 and 1962 elections was for a short term to fill a vacancy.

NEW HAMPSHIRE

GOVERNOR 2022

2020 Census Population	County	Total Vote	Republican (Sununu)	Democratic (Sherman)	Other	Rep.-Dem. Plurality	Total Vote Rep. %	Total Vote Dem. %	Major Vote Rep. %	Major Vote Dem. %
61,528	BELKNAP	30,353	20,499	9,429	425	11,070 R	67.5%	31.1%	68.5%	31.5%
49,228	CARROLL	27,202	16,554	10,306	342	6,248 R	60.9%	37.9%	61.6%	38.4%
76,422	CHESHIRE	33,909	16,503	16,890	516	387 D	48.7%	49.8%	49.4%	50.6%
31,691	COOS	12,805	8,251	4,194	360	4,057 R	64.4%	32.8%	66.3%	33.7%
90,008	GRAFTON	42,586	20,427	21,483	676	1,056 D	48.0%	50.4%	48.7%	51.3%
417,553	HILLSBOROUGH	171,866	99,608	69,673	2,585	29,935 R	58.0%	40.5%	58.8%	41.2%
151,915	MERRIMACK	70,752	38,669	30,835	1,248	7,834 R	54.7%	43.6%	55.6%	44.4%
310,982	ROCKINGHAM	154,018	92,043	59,759	2,216	32,284 R	59.8%	38.8%	60.6%	39.4%
130,860	STRAFFORD	56,524	29,100	26,495	929	2,605 R	51.5%	46.9%	52.3%	47.7%
43,259	SULLIVAN	19,120	11,159	7,702	259	3,457 R	58.4%	40.3%	59.2%	40.8%
1,363,446	TOTAL	619,135	352,813	256,766	9,556	96,047 R	57.0%	41.5%	57.9%	42.1%

NEW HAMPSHIRE
SENATOR 2022

2020 Census Population	County	Total Vote	Republican (Bolduc)	Democratic (Hassan)	Other	Rep.-Dem. Plurality	Percentage Total Vote Rep.	Dem.	Major Vote Rep.	Dem.
61,528	BELKNAP	30,797	16,591	13,669	537	2,922 R	53.9%	44.4%	54.8%	45.2%
49,228	CARROLL	27,137	13,014	13,708	415	694 D	48.0%	50.5%	48.7%	51.3%
76,422	CHESHIRE	34,008	13,241	20,083	684	6,842 D	38.9%	59.1%	39.7%	60.3%
31,691	COOS	12,903	6,491	6,059	353	432 R	50.3%	47.0%	51.7%	48.3%
90,008	GRAFTON	42,772	15,544	26,337	891	10,793 D	36.3%	61.6%	37.1%	62.9%
417,553	HILLSBOROUGH	172,376	76,862	91,776	3,738	14,914 D	44.6%	53.2%	45.6%	54.4%
151,915	MERRIMACK	70,858	29,965	39,367	1,526	9,402 D	42.3%	55.6%	43.2%	56.8%
310,982	ROCKINGHAM	154,387	73,244	78,047	3,096	4,803 D	47.4%	50.6%	48.4%	51.6%
130,860	STRAFFORD	56,618	22,217	33,240	1,161	11,023 D	39.2%	58.7%	40.1%	59.9%
43,259	SULLIVAN	19,119	8,759	9,907	453	1,148 D	45.8%	51.8%	46.9%	53.1%
1,363,446	TOTAL	620,975	275,928	332,193	12,854	56,265 D	44.4%	53.5%	45.4%	54.6%

NEW HAMPSHIRE
HOUSE OF REPRESENTATIVES

CD	Year	Total Vote	Republican Vote	Candidate	Democratic Vote	Candidate	Other Vote	Rep.-Dem. Plurality	Total Vote Rep.	Dem.	Major Vote Rep.	Dem.
1	2022	309,962	142,229	LEAVITT, KAROLINE	167,391	PAPPAS, CHRIS*	342	25,162 D	45.9%	54.0%	45.9%	54.1%
1	2020	400,661	185,159	MOWERS, MATT	205,606	PAPPAS, CHRIS*	9,896	20,447 D	46.2%	51.3%	47.4%	52.6%
1	2018	291,039	130,996	EDWARDS, EDDIE	155,884	PAPPAS, CHRIS	4,159	24,888 D	45.0%	53.6%	45.7%	54.3%
1	2016	365,984	157,176	GUINTA, FRANK C.*	162,080	SHEA-PORTER, CAROL	46,728	4,904 D	42.9%	44.3%	49.2%	50.8%
1	2014	242,736	125,508	GUINTA, FRANK C.	116,769	SHEA-PORTER, CAROL*	459	8,739 R	51.7%	48.1%	51.8%	48.2%
1	2012	345,022	158,659	GUINTA, FRANK C.*	171,650	SHEA-PORTER, CAROL	14,713	12,991 D	46.0%	49.8%	48.0%	52.0%
2	2022	307,584	135,579	BURNS, ROBERT	171,636	KUSTER, ANN MCLANE*	369	36,057 D	44.1%	55.8%	44.1%	55.9%
2	2020	386,441	168,886	NEGRON, STEVEN	208,289	KUSTER, ANN MCLANE*	9,266	39,403 D	43.7%	53.9%	44.8%	55.2%
2	2018	279,705	117,990	NEGRON, STEVEN	155,358	KUSTER, ANN MCLANE*	6,357	37,368 D	42.2%	55.5%	43.2%	56.8%
2	2016	350,793	158,973	LAWRENCE, JAMES "JIM"	174,495	KUSTER, ANN MCLANE*	17,325	15,522 D	45.3%	49.7%	47.7%	52.3%
2	2014	238,184	106,871	GARCIA, MARILINDA	130,700	KUSTER, ANN MCLANE*	613	23,829 D	44.9%	54.9%	45.0%	55.0%
2	2012	337,394	152,977	BASS, CHARLES*	169,275	KUSTER, ANN MCLANE	15,142	16,298 D	45.3%	50.2%	47.5%	52.5%
TOTAL	2022	617,546	277,808		339,027		711	61,219 D	45.0%	54.9%	45.0%	55.0%
TOTAL	2020	787,102	354,045		413,895		19,162	59,850 D	45.0%	52.6%	46.1%	53.9%
TOTAL	2018	570,744	248,986		311,242		10,516	62,256 D	43.6%	54.5%	44.4%	55.6%
TOTAL	2016	716,777	316,149		336,575		64,053	20,426 D	44.1%	47.0%	48.4%	51.6%
TOTAL	2014	480,920	232,379		247,469		1,072	15,090 D	48.3%	51.5%	48.4%	51.6%
TOTAL	2012	682,416	311,636		340,925		29,855	29,289 D	45.7%	50.0%	47.8%	52.2%

Note: An asterisk (*) denotes incumbent.

NEW HAMPSHIRE

GENERAL AND PRIMARY ELECTIONS

GENERAL ELECTIONS: OTHER VOTES

Governor Other vote was 5,071 Libertarian (Kelly Halldorson), 2,772 Libertarian (Karlyn Borysenko), 1,713 Write-In; Write-Ins (Scattered Write-Ins)

Senate Other vote was 12,390 Libertarian (Jeremy Kauffman), 464 Write-In; Write-Ins (Scattered Write-Ins)

House Other vote was:
- CD 1   342 Write-In; Write-Ins (Scattered Write-Ins)
- CD 2   369 Write-In; Write-Ins (Scattered Write-Ins)

2022 PRIMARY ELECTIONS: SUPPLEMENTARY INFORMATION

Primary September 13, 2022   **Registration** (as of September 13, 2022)   1,890,775   Republican / Democratic / Undeclared

Primary Type Semi-open—Registered Democrats and Republicans could vote only in their party's primary. "Undeclared" voters could participate in either party's primary but must declare affiliation at the polls.

	REPUBLICAN PRIMARIES			DEMOCRATIC PRIMARIES		
Senator	Bolduc, Donald C.	52,629	36.9%	Hassan, Maggie*	88,146	93.8%
	Morse, Chuck	50,929	35.7%	Krautmann, Paul	3,629	3.9%
	Smith, Kevin H.	16,621	11.7%	Riggieri, John	1,680	1.8%
	Mansharamani, Vikram	10,690	7.5%	Scattered Write-Ins (Write-In)	546	0.6%
	Fenton, Bruce	6,381	4.5%			
	Berman, John L.	961	0.7%			
	Martin, Andy	920	0.6%			
	Sivalingam, Tejasinha	832	0.6%			
	Lamare, Dennis	773	0.5%			
	Laplante, Edmond	723	0.5%			
	Scattered Write-Ins (Write-In)	623	0.4%			
	Beloin, Gerard	521	0.4%			
	TOTAL	142,603		TOTAL	94,001	
Governor	Sununu, Chris*	113,443	78.5%	Sherman, Tom	83,205	97.1%
	Testerman, Karen	14,473	10.0%	Scattered Write-Ins (Write-In)	2,503	2.9%
	Riley, Thaddeus	11,107	7.7%			
	Acciard, Julian	2,906	2.0%			
	Lewis, Jay	1,318	0.9%			
	Mcmenamon, Richard	817	0.6%			
	Scattered Write-Ins (Write-In)	374	0.3%			
	TOTAL	144,438		TOTAL	85,708	
Congressional District 1	Leavitt, Karoline	25,931	34.4%	Pappas, Chris*	41,990	99.1%
	Mowers, Matt	19,072	25.3%	Scattered Write-Ins (Write-In)	381	0.9%
	Huff Brown, Gail	12,999	17.2%			
	Prescott, Russell	7,551	10.0%			
	Baxter, Tim	6,970	9.2%			
	Maxwell, Mary	673	0.9%			
	Rondeau, Kevin	610	0.8%			
	Towne, Gilead R	466	0.6%			
	Scattered Write-Ins (Write-In)	440	0.6%			
	Kilbane, Mark	347	0.5%			
	Alciere, Tom	342	0.5%			
	TOTAL	75,401		TOTAL	42,371	

NEW HAMPSHIRE

GENERAL AND PRIMARY ELECTIONS

	REPUBLICAN PRIMARIES			DEMOCRATIC PRIMARIES		
Congressional District 2	Burns, Robert	21,065	33.0%	Kuster, Ann McLane*	48,630	99.3%
	Hansel, George	19,024	29.8%	Scattered Write-Ins (Write-In)	324	0.7%
	Williams, Lily Tang	15,729	24.6%			
	Black, Scott	2,211	3.5%			
	Mercer, Jay	2,085	3.3%			
	Poirier, Dean A.	2,047	3.2%			
	Callis, Michael	1,133	1.8%			
	Scattered Write-Ins (Write-In)	574	0.9%			
	TOTAL	*63,868*		*TOTAL*	*48,954*	

Note: An asterisk (*) denotes incumbent.

NEW JERSEY

Statewide Races

Neither of the Garden State's Senate seats were up in 2022, but in 2021, its odd-year gubernatorial election represented one of the more impressive Republican statewide overpeformances of the Biden era.

In 2017, Democrat Phil Murphy, who served as Barack Obama's first Ambassador to Germany, succeeded Republican Chris Christie; Christie's popularity peaked around the time of his 2013 reelection, but his image with the electorate had eroded considerably since. Against Christie's lieutenant governor, Kim Guadagno, Murphy won 56%–42%. While Murphy's win boosted Democratic morale heading into the 2018 midterms, the overall trendline may have been telling: Murphy's percentage margin was no better than Hillary Clinton's 55%–41% spread from 2016.

In 2021, the runner-up from the 2017 Republican primary, former state Sen. Jack Ciattarelli, got the party's nomination. Though Murphy led in every public poll, he rarely took more than 50% of the vote. On Election Day, most undecided voters seemed to break decisively towards Ciattarelli: though Murphy became the first New Jersey Democratic governor to win reelection since 1977, he did so by just a 51%–48% margin. Statewide, Ciattarelli earned nearly as many votes (1,255,185) as Christie did (1,278,932) in his 2013 landslide.

Murphy's slump was especially pronounced in South Jersey, the most culturally "southern" part of the state: In 2017, he carried the version of the 2nd District that was in place at the time (taking in Atlantic City), 50%–48% – but according to the New Jersey Globe's Joey Fox, lost it 59%–40% four years later. Still, in the economically better-off parts of North Jersey, Murphy saw only small declines, or in some cases, improvements from his 2017 showing – the latter was the case in Hunterdon and Somerset counties.

House Races

In New Jersey, redistricting is handled by a bipartisan commission. After the 2010 census, the commission passed a map that Republicans favored. In a Democratic-leaning state, a tied 6-6 delegation was elected in 2012, although Democrats had taken a substantial 9-3 advantage by the end of the decade. The commission's ultimate reasoning seemed to be simple: the Republicans got their preferred map last time, so it's the Democrats turn this time.

Under the Democratic-drafted plan, Murphy, while taking a 51% share statewide, would have carried nine of 12 districts (on the outgoing map, he would have carried only six). Democratic Reps. Josh Gottheimer, Andy Kim, and Mikie Sherrill had districts that voted for Ciattarelli in 2021 but found themselves in Murphy-won seats after the new lines were drawn – all three were reelected by double-digit margins in 2022.

To shore up their other members, Democrats had to throw one of their own, 7th District Rep. Tom Malinowski, under the bus. In 2020, he narrowly won reelection in a contest against state Sen. Tom Kean Jr., the son of a popular 1980s-era governor. After 2021, Malinowski's standing was hurt as reports surfaced that he had improperly traded stocks. Malinowski kept the race competitive, but in a seat that went to Biden by four points and Ciattarelli by 13, Kean won by about three points.

NEW JERSEY

Congressional districts first established for elections held in 2022

12 members

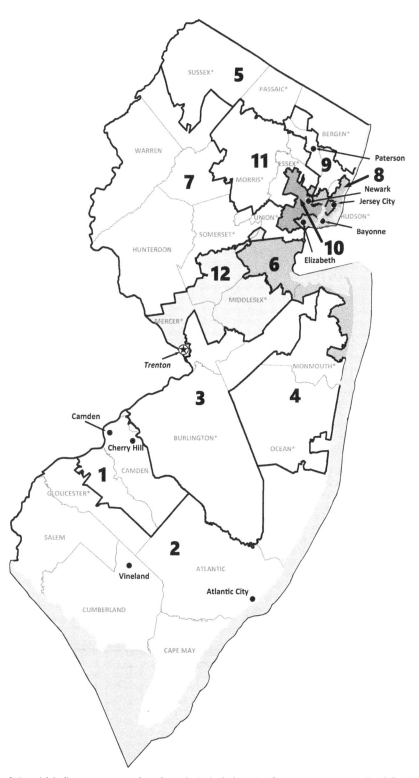

* Asterisk indicates a county whose boundaries include parts of two or more congressional districts.
CDs 6, 8, 10 and 12 are highlighted for visibility. See Inset for New Jersey Gateway area.

NEW JERSEY

Northern New Jersey Gateway Area

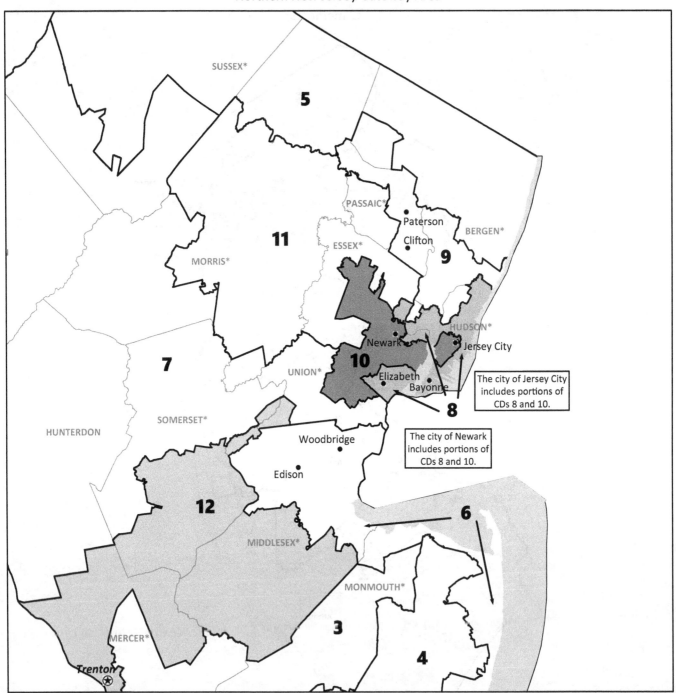

CDs 8, 10, and 12 are highlighted for visibility.
* Asterisk indicates a county whose boundaries include parts of two or more congressional districts.

NEW JERSEY

GOVERNOR
Philip Murphy (D). Reelected 2021 to a four-year term. Previously elected 2017.

SENATORS (2 Democrats)
Cory Booker (D). Reelected 2020 to a six-year term. Previously elected 2014 and October 16, 2013, to serve the remainder of the term vacated by the June 2013 death of Frank Lautenberg (D). Jeff Chiesa (R) had been appointed June 6, 2013, to fill the vacant seat until the October 2013 special election.

Robert Menendez (D). Reelected 2018 to a six-year term. Previously elected 2012, 2006.

REPRESENTATIVES (3 Republicans, 9 Democrats)
1. Donald Norcross (D)
2. Jeff Van Drew (R)
3. Andy Kim (D)
4. Christopher H. Smith (R)
5. Joshua S. Gottheimer (D)
6. Frank Pallone (D)
7. Thomas Kean Jr. (R)
8. Robert Menendez Jr. (D)
9. William J. Pascrell Jr. (D)
10. Donald M. Payne Jr. (D)
11. Mikie Sherrill (D)
12. Bonnie Watson Coleman (D)

POSTWAR VOTE FOR PRESIDENT

Year	Total Vote	Republican Vote	Republican Candidate	Democratic Vote	Democratic Candidate	Other Vote	Rep.-Dem. Plurality	Total Vote Rep.	Total Vote Dem.	Major Vote Rep.	Major Vote Dem.
2020	4,549,353	1,883,274	Trump, Donald J.*	2,608,335	Biden, Joseph R. Jr.	57,744	725,061 D	41.4%	57.3%	41.9%	58.1%
2016**	3,874,046	1,601,933	Trump, Donald J.	2,148,278	Clinton, Hillary Rodham	123,835	546,345 D	41.4%	55.5%	42.7%	57.3%
2012	3,640,292	1,477,568	Romney, W. Mitt	2,125,101	Obama, Barack H.*	37,623	647,533 D	40.6%	58.4%	41.0%	59.0%
2008	3,868,237	1,613,207	McCain, John S. III	2,215,422	Obama, Barack H.	39,608	602,215 D	41.7%	57.3%	42.1%	57.9%
2004	3,611,691	1,670,003	Bush, George W.*	1,911,430	Kerry, John F.	30,258	241,427 D	46.2%	52.9%	46.6%	53.4%
2000**	3,187,226	1,284,173	Bush, George W.	1,788,850	Gore, Albert Jr.	114,203	504,677 D	40.3%	56.1%	41.8%	58.2%
1996**	3,075,807	1,103,078	Dole, Robert "Bob"	1,652,329	Clinton, Bill*	320,400	549,251 D	35.9%	53.7%	40.0%	60.0%
1992**	3,343,594	1,356,865	Bush, George H.*	1,436,206	Clinton, Bill	550,523	79,341 D	40.6%	43.0%	48.6%	51.4%
1988	3,099,553	1,743,192	Bush, George H.	1,320,352	Dukakis, Michael S.	36,009	422,840 R	56.2%	42.6%	56.9%	43.1%
1984	3,217,862	1,933,630	Reagan, Ronald*	1,261,323	Mondale, Walter F.	22,909	672,307 R	60.1%	39.2%	60.5%	39.5%
1980**	2,975,684	1,546,557	Reagan, Ronald	1,147,364	Carter, Jimmy*	281,763	399,193 R	52.0%	38.6%	57.4%	42.6%
1976	3,014,472	1,509,688	Ford, Gerald R.*	1,444,653	Carter, Jimmy	60,131	65,035 R	50.1%	47.9%	51.1%	48.9%
1972	2,997,229	1,845,502	Nixon, Richard M.*	1,102,211	McGovern, George S.	49,516	743,291 R	61.6%	36.8%	62.6%	37.4%
1968**	2,875,395	1,325,467	Nixon, Richard M.	1,264,206	Humphrey, Hubert Horatio Jr.	285,722	61,261 R	46.1%	44.0%	51.2%	48.8%
1964	2,847,663	964,174	Goldwater, Barry M. Sr.	1,868,231	Johnson, Lyndon B.*	15,258	904,057 D	33.9%	65.6%	34.0%	66.0%
1960	2,773,111	1,363,324	Nixon, Richard M.	1,385,415	Kennedy, John F.	24,372	22,091 D	49.2%	50.0%	49.6%	50.4%
1956	2,484,312	1,606,942	Eisenhower, Dwight D.*	850,337	Stevenson, Adlai E. II	27,033	756,605 R	64.7%	34.2%	65.4%	34.6%
1952	2,418,554	1,373,613	Eisenhower, Dwight D.	1,015,902	Stevenson, Adlai E. II	29,039	357,711 R	56.8%	42.0%	57.5%	42.5%
1948	1,949,555	981,124	Dewey, Thomas E.	895,455	Truman, Harry S.*	72,976	85,669 R	50.3%	45.9%	52.3%	47.7%

Note: An asterisk (*) denotes incumbent. **In past elections, the other vote included: 2016 - 72,477 Libertarian (Gary Johnson); 2000 - 94,554 Green (Ralph Nader); 1996 - 262,134 Reform (Ross Perot); 1992 - 521,829 Independent (Perot); 1980 - 234,632 Independent (John Anderson); 1968 - 262,187 American Independent (George Wallace).

NEW JERSEY

POSTWAR VOTE FOR GOVERNOR

		Republican		Democratic		Other Vote	Rep.-Dem. Plurality	Percentage			
								Total Vote		Major Vote	
Year	Total Vote	Vote	Candidate	Vote	Candidate			Rep.	Dem.	Rep.	Dem.
2021	2,614,886	1,255,185	Ciattarelli, Jack	1,339,471	Murphy, Philip*	20,230	84,286 D	48.0%	51.2%	48.4%	51.6%
2017	2,147,415	899,583	Guadagno, Kim	1,203,110	Murphy, Philip	44,722	303,527 D	41.9%	56.0%	42.8%	57.2%
2013	2,120,866	1,278,932	Christie, Chris*	809,978	Buono, Barbara	31,956	468,954 R	60.3%	38.2%	61.2%	38.8%
2009	2,423,792	1,174,445	Christie, Chris	1,087,731	Corzine, Jon S.*	161,616	86,714 R	48.5%	44.9%	51.9%	48.1%
2005	2,290,099	985,271	Forrester, Doug	1,224,551	Corzine, Jon S.	80,277	239,280 D	43.0%	53.5%	44.6%	55.4%
2001	2,227,165	928,174	Schundler, Bret	1,256,853	McGreevey, James	42,138	328,679 D	41.7%	56.4%	42.5%	57.5%
1997	2,418,344	1,133,394	Whitman, Christine T.*	1,107,968	McGreevey, James	176,982	25,426 R	46.9%	45.8%	50.6%	49.4%
1993	2,505,964	1,236,124	Whitman, Christine T.	1,210,031	Florio, James J.*	59,809	26,093 R	49.3%	48.3%	50.5%	49.5%
1989	2,253,800	838,553	Courter, James A.	1,379,973	Florio, James J.	35,274	541,420 D	37.2%	61.2%	37.8%	62.2%
1985	1,972,624	1,372,631	Kean, Thomas H.*	578,402	Shapiro, Peter	21,591	794,229 R	69.6%	29.3%	70.4%	29.6%
1981	2,317,239	1,145,999	Kean, Thomas H.	1,144,202	Florio, James J.	27,038	1,797 R	49.5%	49.4%	50.0%	50.0%
1977	2,126,264	888,880	Bateman, Raymond H.	1,184,564	Byrne, Brendan T.*	52,820	295,684 D	41.8%	55.7%	42.9%	57.1%
1973	2,122,010	676,235	Sandman, Charles W.	1,414,613	Byrne, Brendan T.	31,162	738,378 D	31.9%	66.7%	32.3%	67.7%
1969	2,366,606	1,411,905	Cahill, William T.	911,003	Meyner, Robert B.	43,698	500,902 R	59.7%	38.5%	60.8%	39.2%
1965	2,229,583	915,996	Dumont, Wayne Jr.	1,279,568	Hughes, Richard J.*	34,019	363,572 D	41.1%	57.4%	41.7%	58.3%
1961	2,152,662	1,049,274	Mitchell, James P.	1,084,194	Hughes, Richard J.	19,194	34,920 D	48.7%	50.4%	49.2%	50.8%
1957	2,018,488	897,321	Forbes, Malcolm Stevenson Sr.	1,101,130	Meyner, Robert B.*	20,037	203,809 D	44.5%	54.6%	44.9%	55.1%
1953	1,810,812	809,068	Troast, Paul L.	962,710	Meyner, Robert B.	39,034	153,642 D	44.7%	53.2%	45.7%	54.3%
1949**	1,718,788	885,882	Driscoll, Alfred Eastlack*	810,022	Wene, Elmer H.	22,884	75,860 R	51.5%	47.1%	52.2%	47.8%
1946	1,414,527	807,378	Driscoll, Alfred Eastlack	585,960	Hansen, Lewis G.	21,189	221,418 R	57.1%	41.4%	57.9%	42.1%

Note: An asterisk (*) denotes incumbent. **The term of office of New Jersey's Governor was increased from three to four years effective with the 1949 election.

POSTWAR VOTE FOR SENATOR

		Republican		Democratic		Other Vote	Rep.-Dem. Plurality	Percentage			
								Total Vote		Major Vote	
Year	Total Vote	Vote	Candidate	Vote	Candidate			Rep.	Dem.	Rep.	Dem.
2020	4,440,440	1,817,052	Mehta, Rikin	2,541,178	Booker, Cory*	82,210	724,126 D	40.9%	57.2%	41.7%	58.3%
2018	3,169,310	1,357,355	Hugin, Robert "Bob"	1,711,654	Menendez, Robert*	100,301	354,299 D	42.8%	54.0%	44.2%	55.8%
2014	1,869,535	791,297	Bell, Jeffrey	1,043,866	Booker, Cory*	34,372	252,569 D	42.3%	55.8%	43.1%	56.9%
2013S**	1,348,659	593,684	Lonegan, Steven M.	740,742	Booker, Cory	14,233	147,058 D	44.0%	54.9%	44.5%	55.5%
2012	3,374,668	1,329,405	Kyrillos, Joe	1,985,783	Menendez, Robert*	59,480	656,378 D	39.4%	58.8%	40.1%	59.9%
2008	3,482,445	1,461,025	Zimmer, Dick	1,951,218	Lautenberg, Frank R.*	70,202	490,193 D	42.0%	56.0%	42.8%	57.2%
2006	2,250,070	997,775	Kean, Tom Jr.	1,200,843	Menendez, Robert*	51,452	203,068 D	44.3%	53.4%	45.4%	54.6%
2002	2,112,604	928,439	Forrester, Douglas R.	1,138,193	Lautenberg, Frank R.	45,972	209,754 D	43.9%	53.9%	44.9%	55.1%
2000	3,015,662	1,420,267	Franks, Bob	1,511,237	Corzine, Jon S.	84,158	90,970 D	47.1%	50.1%	48.4%	51.6%
1996	2,884,106	1,227,817	Zimmer, Dick	1,519,328	Torricelli, Robert G.	136,961	291,511 D	42.6%	52.7%	44.7%	55.3%
1994	2,054,887	966,244	Haytaian, Garabed	1,033,487	Lautenberg, Frank R.*	55,156	67,243 D	47.0%	50.3%	48.3%	51.7%
1990	1,938,454	918,874	Whitman, Christine T.	977,810	Bradley, Bill Warren*	41,770	58,936 D	47.4%	50.4%	48.4%	51.6%
1988	2,987,634	1,349,937	Dawkins, Peter M.	1,599,905	Lautenberg, Frank R.*	37,792	249,968 D	45.2%	53.6%	45.8%	54.2%
1984	3,096,456	1,080,100	Mochary, Mary V.	1,986,644	Bradley, Bill Warren*	29,712	906,544 D	34.9%	64.2%	35.2%	64.8%
1982	2,193,945	1,047,626	Fenwick, Millicent	1,117,549	Lautenberg, Frank R.	28,770	69,923 D	47.8%	50.9%	48.4%	51.6%
1978	1,957,515	844,200	Bell, Jeffrey	1,082,960	Bradley, Bill Warren	30,355	238,760 D	43.1%	55.3%	43.8%	56.2%
1976	2,771,387	1,054,505	Norcross, David F.	1,681,140	Williams, Harrison A. Jr.*	35,742	626,635 D	38.0%	60.7%	38.5%	61.5%
1972	2,791,907	1,743,854	Case, Clifford P.*	963,573	Kerbs, Paul J.	84,480	780,281 R	62.5%	34.5%	64.4%	35.6%
1970	2,142,105	903,026	Gross, Nelson G.	1,157,074	Williams, Harrison A. Jr.*	82,005	254,048 D	42.2%	54.0%	43.8%	56.2%
1966	2,130,688	1,278,843	Case, Clifford P.*	788,021	Wilentz, Warren W.	63,824	490,822 R	60.0%	37.0%	61.9%	38.1%
1964	2,709,575	1,011,280	Shanley, Bernard M.	1,677,515	Williams, Harrison A. Jr.*	20,780	666,235 D	37.3%	61.9%	37.6%	62.4%
1960	2,664,556	1,483,832	Case, Clifford*	1,151,385	Lord, Thorn	29,339	332,447 R	55.7%	43.2%	56.3%	43.7%
1958	1,881,329	882,287	Kean, Robert Winthrop	966,832	Williams, Harrison A. Jr.	32,210	84,545 D	46.9%	51.4%	47.7%	52.3%
1954	1,770,557	861,528	Case, Clifford P.*	858,158	Howell, Charles R.	50,871	3,370 R	48.7%	48.5%	50.1%	49.9%
1952	2,318,232	1,286,782	Smith, H. Alexander*	1,011,187	Alexander, Archibald S.	20,263	275,595 R	55.5%	43.6%	56.0%	44.0%
1948	1,869,882	934,720	Hendrickson, Robert C.	884,414	Alexander, Archibald S.	50,748	50,306 R	50.0%	47.3%	51.4%	48.6%
1946	1,367,155	799,808	Smith, H. Alexander*	548,458	Brunner, George E.	18,889	251,350 R	58.5%	40.1%	59.3%	40.7%

Note: An asterisk (*) denotes incumbent. **The 2013 election was for a short term to fill a vacancy.

NEW JERSEY

2021 NEW JERSEY GUBERNATORIAL GENERAL

2020 Census Population	County	Total Vote	Jack Ciattarelli Republican	(*) (W) Philip Murphy Democrat	Madelyn Hoffman Green	Gregg Mele Libertarian	Joanne Kuniansky Socialist Workers Party	Rep.-Dem. Plurality	Total Vote Rep.	Total Vote Dem.	Major Vote Rep.	Major Vote Dem.
264,448	ATLANTIC	81,308	44,977	35,736	296	215	84	9,241 R	55.3%	44.0%	55.7%	44.3%
935,393	BERGEN	276,350	129,644	145,150	618	520	418	15,506 D	46.9%	52.5%	47.2%	52.8%
446,432	BURLINGTON	155,547	71,772	82,877	294	433	171	11,105 D	46.1%	53.3%	46.4%	53.6%
507,282	CAMDEN	149,392	56,016	92,162	431	592	191	36,146 D	37.5%	61.7%	37.8%	62.2%
92,211	CAPE MAY	38,661	24,260	14,183	89	72	57	10,077 R	62.8%	36.7%	63.1%	36.9%
149,350	CUMBERLAND	32,029	17,794	13,978	129	88	40	3,816 R	55.6%	43.6%	56.0%	44.0%
799,943	ESSEX	179,167	45,542	132,520	475	321	309	86,978 D	25.4%	74.0%	25.6%	74.4%
292,421	GLOUCESTER	100,748	54,976	44,959	300	364	149	10,017 R	54.6%	44.6%	55.0%	45.0%
672,831	HUDSON	119,715	30,443	88,066	433	444	329	57,623 D	25.4%	73.6%	25.7%	74.3%
124,506	HUNTERDON	56,784	33,459	22,820	221	188	96	10,639 R	58.9%	40.2%	59.5%	40.5%
368,145	MERCER	101,625	34,617	66,151	329	372	156	31,534 D	34.1%	65.1%	34.4%	65.6%
826,735	MIDDLESEX	208,758	90,297	116,352	970	682	457	26,055 D	43.3%	55.7%	43.7%	56.3%
619,973	MONMOUTH	239,788	141,100	96,664	996	678	350	44,436 R	58.8%	40.3%	59.3%	40.7%
492,937	MORRIS	185,923	102,769	81,915	600	481	158	20,854 R	55.3%	44.1%	55.6%	44.4%
610,498	OCEAN	215,810	145,756	68,615	534	671	234	77,141 R	67.5%	31.8%	68.0%	32.0%
501,429	PASSAIC	112,324	53,551	57,812	383	369	209	4,261 D	47.7%	51.5%	48.1%	51.9%
62,367	SALEM	19,691	12,620	6,893	76	81	21	5,727 R	64.1%	35.0%	64.7%	35.3%
329,964	SOMERSET	113,672	54,264	58,585	311	373	139	4,321 D	47.7%	51.5%	48.1%	51.9%
140,677	SUSSEX	54,319	36,310	17,346	316	255	92	18,964 R	66.8%	31.9%	67.7%	32.3%
557,237	UNION	136,318	51,279	83,913	436	404	286	32,634 D	37.6%	61.6%	37.9%	62.1%
	Votes not included in the average elector vote	0	0	0	0	0	0	0	0.0%	0.0%	0.0%	0.0%
105,503	WARREN	36,957	23,739	12,774	213	165	66	10,965 R	64.2%	34.6%	65.0%	35.0%
8,900,282	TOTAL	2,614,886						84,286 D	48.0%	51.2%	48.4%	51.6%

NEW JERSEY

HOUSE OF REPRESENTATIVES

CD	Year	Total Vote	Republican Vote	Republican Candidate	Democratic Vote	Democratic Candidate	Other Vote	Rep.-Dem. Plurality	Total Vote Rep.	Total Vote Dem.	Major Vote Rep.	Major Vote Dem.
1	2022	223,884	78,794	GUSTAFSON, CLAIRE	139,559	NORCROSS, DONALD*	5,531	60,765 D	35.2%	62.3%	36.1%	63.9%
1	2020	385,030	144,463	GUSTAFSON, CLAIRE	240,567	NORCROSS, DONALD*		96,104 D	37.5%	62.5%	37.5%	62.5%
1	2018	263,418	87,617	DILKS, PAUL	169,628	NORCROSS, DONALD*	6,173	82,011 D	33.3%	64.4%	34.1%	65.9%
1	2016	305,473	112,388	PATTERSON, BOB	183,231	NORCROSS, DONALD*	9,854	70,843 D	36.8%	60.0%	38.0%	62.0%
1	2014	162,492	64,073	COBB, GARRY W.	93,315	NORCROSS, DONALD	5,104	29,242 D	39.4%	57.4%	40.7%	59.3%
1	2012	308,519	92,459	HORTON, GREGORY W.	210,470	ANDREWS, ROBERT E.*	5,590	118,011 D	30.0%	68.2%	30.5%	69.5%
2	2022	236,484	139,217	VAN DREW, JEFF*	94,522	ALEXANDER, TIM	2,745	44,695 R	58.9%	40.0%	59.6%	40.4%
2	2020	376,547	195,526	VAN DREW, JEFF*	173,849	KENNEDY, AMY	7,172	21,677 R	51.9%	46.2%	52.9%	47.1%
2	2018	258,363	116,866	GROSSMAN, SETH	136,685	VAN DREW, JEFF	4,812	19,819 D	45.2%	52.9%	46.1%	53.9%
2	2016	297,795	176,338	LOBIONDO, FRANK A.*	110,838	COLE, DAVID H.	10,619	65,500 R	59.2%	37.2%	61.4%	38.6%
2	2014	177,148	108,875	LOBIONDO, FRANK A.*	66,026	HUGHES, WILLIAM J. JR.	2,247	42,849 R	61.5%	37.3%	62.2%	37.8%
2	2012	289,072	166,679	LOBIONDO, FRANK A.*	116,463	SHOBER, CASSANDRA	5,930	50,216 R	57.7%	40.3%	58.9%	41.1%
3	2022	271,376	118,415	HEALEY, BOB	150,498	KIM, ANDY*	2,463	32,083 D	43.6%	55.5%	44.0%	56.0%
3	2020	431,762	196,327	RICHTER, DAVID	229,840	KIM, ANDY*	5,595	33,513 D	45.5%	53.2%	46.1%	53.9%
3	2018	306,875	149,500	MACARTHUR, TOM*	153,473	KIM, ANDY	3,902	3,973 D	48.7%	50.0%	49.3%	50.7%
3	2016	328,060	194,596	MACARTHUR, TOM*	127,526	LAVERGNE, FREDERICK JOHN	5,938	67,070 R	59.3%	38.9%	60.4%	39.6%
3	2014	186,103	100,471	MACARTHUR, TOM	82,537	BELGARD, AIMEE	3,095	17,934 R	54.0%	44.4%	54.9%	45.1%
3	2012	324,406	174,257	RUNYAN, JON*	145,509	ADLER, SHELLEY	4,640	28,748 R	53.7%	44.9%	54.5%	45.5%

NEW JERSEY
HOUSE OF REPRESENTATIVES

| | | | Republican | | Democratic | | Other | Rep.-Dem. | Percentage | | | |
| | | | | | | | | | Total Vote | | Major Vote | |
CD	Year	Total Vote	Vote	Candidate	Vote	Candidate	Vote	Plurality	Rep.	Dem.	Rep.	Dem.
4	2022	258,962	173,288	SMITH, CHRISTOPHER H.*	81,233	JENKINS, MATTHEW	4,441	92,055 R	66.9%	31.4%	68.1%	31.9%
4	2020	424,368	254,103	SMITH, CHRISTOPHER H.*	162,420	SCHMID, STEPHANIE	7,845	91,683 R	59.9%	38.3%	61.0%	39.0%
4	2018	294,348	163,065	SMITH, CHRISTOPHER H.*	126,766	WELLE, JOSH	4,517	36,299 R	55.4%	43.1%	56.3%	43.7%
4	2016	332,684	211,992	SMITH, CHRISTOPHER H.*	111,532	PHILLIPSON, LORNA	9,160	100,460 R	63.7%	33.5%	65.5%	34.5%
4	2014	174,849	118,826	SMITH, CHRISTOPHER H.*	54,415	SCOLAVINO, RUBEN	1,608	64,411 R	68.0%	31.1%	68.6%	31.4%
4	2012	306,249	195,146	SMITH, CHRISTOPHER H.*	107,992	FROELICH, BRIAN P.	3,111	87,154 R	63.7%	35.3%	64.4%	35.6%
5	2022	265,943	117,873	PALLOTTA, FRANK	145,559	GOTTHEIMER, JOSHUA S.*	2,511	27,686 D	44.3%	54.7%	44.7%	55.3%
5	2020	423,636	193,333	PALLOTTA, FRANK	225,175	GOTTHEIMER, JOSHUA S.*	5,128	31,842 D	45.6%	53.2%	46.2%	53.8%
5	2018	301,823	128,255	MCCANN, JOHN J. JR.	169,546	GOTTHEIMER, JOSHUA S.*	4,022	41,291 D	42.5%	56.2%	43.1%	56.9%
5	2016	337,701	157,690	GARRETT, SCOTT*	172,587	GOTTHEIMER, JOSHUA S.	7,424	14,897 D	46.7%	51.1%	47.7%	52.3%
5	2014	188,921	104,678	GARRETT, SCOTT*	81,808	CHO, ROY	2,435	22,870 R	55.4%	43.3%	56.1%	43.9%
5	2012	304,377	167,503	GARRETT, SCOTT*	130,102	GUSSEN, ADAM	6,772	37,401 R	55.0%	42.7%	56.3%	43.7%
6	2022	184,919	75,839	KILEY, SUSAN M.	106,238	PALLONE, FRANK JR.*	2,842	30,399 D	41.0%	57.5%	41.7%	58.3%
6	2020	326,408	126,760	ONUOHA, CHRISTIAN	199,648	PALLONE, FRANK JR.*		72,888 D	38.8%	61.2%	38.8%	61.2%
6	2018	221,195	80,443	PEZZULLO, RICHARD J.	140,752	PALLONE, FRANK JR.*		60,309 D	36.4%	63.6%	36.4%	63.6%
6	2016	263,435	91,908	SONNEK-SCHMELZ, BRENT	167,895	PALLONE, FRANK JR.*	3,632	75,987 D	34.9%	63.7%	35.4%	64.6%
6	2014	120,457	46,891	WILKINSON, ANTHONY E.	72,190	PALLONE, FRANK JR.*	1,376	25,299 D	38.9%	59.9%	39.4%	60.6%
6	2012	239,638	84,360	LITTLE, ANNA C.	151,782	PALLONE, FRANK JR.*	3,496	67,422 D	35.2%	63.3%	35.7%	64.3%
7	2022	310,093	159,392	KEAN, THOMAS H.	150,701	MALINOWSKI, TOM*		8,691 R	51.4%	48.6%	51.4%	48.6%
7	2020	433,947	214,318	KEAN, THOMAS H.	219,629	MALINOWSKI, TOM*		5,311 D	49.4%	50.6%	49.4%	50.6%
7	2018	322,742	150,785	LANCE, LEONARD*	166,985	MALINOWSKI, TOM	4,972	16,200 D	46.7%	51.7%	47.5%	52.5%
7	2016	343,635	185,850	LANCE, LEONARD*	148,188	JACOB, PETER	9,597	37,662 R	54.1%	43.1%	55.6%	44.4%
7	2014	175,997	104,287	LANCE, LEONARD*	68,232	KOVACH, JANICE	3,478	36,055 R	59.3%	38.8%	60.4%	39.6%
7	2012	307,395	175,704	LANCE, LEONARD*	123,090	CHIVUKULA, UPENDRA J.	8,601	52,614 R	57.2%	40.0%	58.8%	41.2%
8	2022	106,473	24,957	ARROYO, MARCOS	78,382	MENENDEZ, ROBERT J.	3,134	53,425 D	23.4%	73.6%	24.2%	75.8%
8	2020	238,773	58,686	MUSHNICK, JASON TODD	176,758	SIRES, ALBIO*	3,329	118,072 D	24.6%	74.0%	24.9%	75.1%
8	2018	153,455	28,725	MUNIZ, JOHN	119,881	SIRES, ALBIO*	4,849	91,156 D	18.7%	78.1%	19.3%	80.7%
8	2016	174,889	32,337	KHAN, AGHA	134,733	SIRES, ALBIO*	7,819	102,396 D	18.5%	77.0%	19.4%	80.6%
8	2014	79,518	15,141	TISCORNIA, JUDE ANTHONY	61,510	SIRES, ALBIO*	2,867	46,369 D	19.0%	77.4%	19.8%	80.2%
8	2012	167,800	31,767	KARCZEWSKI, MARIA	130,857	SIRES, ALBIO*	5,176	99,090 D	18.9%	78.0%	19.5%	80.5%
9	2022	149,984	65,365	PREMPEH, WILLIAM SREBOE	82,457	PASCRELL, WILLIAM J. JR.*	2,162	17,092 D	43.6%	55.0%	44.2%	55.8%
9	2020	309,542	98,629	PREMPEH, WILLIAM SREBOE	203,674	PASCRELL, WILLIAM J. JR.*	7,239	105,045 D	31.9%	65.8%	32.6%	67.4%
9	2018	200,416	57,854	FISHER, ERIC	140,832	PASCRELL, WILLIAM J. JR.*	1,730	82,978 D	28.9%	70.3%	29.1%	70.9%
9	2016	233,242	65,376	CASTILLO, HECTOR L.	162,642	PASCRELL, WILLIAM J. JR.*	5,224	97,266 D	28.0%	69.7%	28.7%	71.3%
9	2014	120,459	36,246	PAUL, DIERDRE	82,498	PASCRELL, WILLIAM J. JR.*	1,715	46,252 D	30.1%	68.5%	30.5%	69.5%
9	2012	220,148	55,094	BOTEACH, SHMULEY	162,834	PASCRELL, WILLIAM J. JR.*	2,220	107,740 D	25.0%	74.0%	25.3%	74.7%
10	2022	129,707	25,993	PINCKNEY, DAVID H.	100,710	PAYNE, DONALD M. JR.*	3,004	74,717 D	20.0%	77.6%	20.5%	79.5%
10	2020	290,009	40,298	ZINONE, JENNIFER	241,522	PAYNE, DONALD M. JR.*	8,189	201,224 D	13.9%	83.3%	14.3%	85.7%
10	2018	200,159	20,191	KHAN, AGHA	175,253	PAYNE, DONALD M. JR.*	4,715	155,062 D	10.1%	87.6%	10.3%	89.7%
10	2016	222,771	26,450	PINCKNEY, DAVID H.	190,856	PAYNE, DONALD M. JR.*	5,465	164,406 D	11.9%	85.7%	12.2%	87.8%
10	2014	112,123	14,154	DENTLEY, YOLANDA	95,734	PAYNE, DONALD M. JR.*	2,235	81,580 D	12.6%	85.4%	12.9%	87.1%
10	2012	230,060	24,271	KELEMEN, BRIAN C.	201,435	PAYNE, DONALD M. JR.	4,354	177,164 D	10.5%	87.6%	10.8%	89.2%
11	2022	273,664	109,952	DEGROOT, PAUL	161,436	SHERRILL, MIKIE	2,276	51,484 D	40.2%	59.0%	40.5%	59.5%
11	2020	441,176	206,013	BECCHI, ROSEMARY	235,163	SHERRILL, MIKIE*		29,150 D	46.7%	53.3%	46.7%	53.3%
11	2018	323,574	136,322	WEBBER, JAY	183,684	SHERRILL, MIKIE	3,568	47,362 D	42.1%	56.8%	42.6%	57.4%
11	2016	334,992	194,299	FRELINGHUYSEN, RODNEY*	130,162	WENZEL, JOSEPH M.	10,531	64,137 R	58.0%	38.9%	59.9%	40.1%
11	2014	174,932	109,455	FRELINGHUYSEN, RODNEY*	65,477	DUNEC, MARK S.		43,978 R	62.6%	37.4%	62.6%	37.4%
11	2012	309,899	182,239	FRELINGHUYSEN, RODNEY*	123,935	ARVANITES, JOHN	3,725	58,304 R	58.8%	40.0%	59.5%	40.5%
12	2022	198,227	71,175	MAYFIELD, DARIUS	125,127	COLEMAN, BONNIE WATSON*	1,925	53,952 D	35.9%	63.1%	36.3%	63.7%
12	2020	351,725	114,591	RAZZOLI, MARK	230,883	COLEMAN, BONNIE WATSON*	6,251	116,292 D	32.6%	65.6%	33.2%	66.8%
12	2018	252,375	79,041	KIPNIS, DARYL	173,334	COLEMAN, BONNIE WATSON*		94,293 D	31.3%	68.7%	31.3%	68.7%
12	2016	288,634	92,407	UCCIO, STEVEN J.	181,430	COLEMAN, BONNIE WATSON*	14,797	89,023 D	32.0%	62.9%	33.7%	66.3%
12	2014	148,366	54,168	ECK, ALIETA	90,430	COLEMAN, BONNIE WATSON	3,768	36,262 D	36.5%	61.0%	37.5%	62.5%
12	2012	274,391	80,907	BECK, ERIC A.	189,938	HOLT, RUSH D.*	3,546	109,031 D	29.5%	69.2%	29.9%	70.1%
TOTAL	2022	2,609,716	1,160,260		1,416,422		33,034	256,162 D	44.5%	54.3%	45.0%	55.0%
TOTAL	2020	4,432,923	1,843,047		2,539,128		50,748	696,081 D	41.6%	57.3%	42.1%	57.9%
TOTAL	2018	3,098,743	1,198,664		1,856,819		43,260	658,155 D	38.7%	59.9%	39.2%	60.8%
TOTAL	2016	3,463,311	1,541,631		1,821,620		100,060	279,989 D	44.5%	52.6%	45.8%	54.2%
TOTAL	2014	1,821,365	877,265		914,172		29,928	36,907 D	48.2%	50.2%	49.0%	51.0%
TOTAL	2012	3,281,954	1,430,386		1,794,407		57,161	364,021 D	43.6%	54.7%	44.4%	55.6%

Note: An asterisk (*) denotes incumbent.

NEW JERSEY

GENERAL AND PRIMARY ELECTIONS

GENERAL ELECTIONS: OTHER VOTES

Governor (2021)	Other vote was 8,450 Green (Madelyn Hoffman), 7,768 Libertarian (Gregg Mele), 4,012 Socialist Workers Party (Joanne Kuniansky)
House	Other vote was:
CD 1	3,343 For the People (Patricia Kline), 1,546 Libertarian (Isaiah Fletcher), 642 Cannon Fire (Allen Cannon)
CD 2	1,825 Libertarian (Michael Gallo), 920 Other (Anthony Sanchez)
CD 3	1,347 Libertarian (Christopher Russomanno), 1,116 God Save America (Gregory Sobocinski)
CD 4	1,902 Libertarian (Jason Cullen), 905 Other (Hank Schroeder), 437 Independent (Pam Daniels)
CD 5	1,193 Libertarian (Jeremy Marcus), 700 Together We Stand (Trevor Ferrigno), 618 American Values (Louis Vellucci)
CD 6	1,361 Libertarian (Tara Fisher), 947 Other (Inder Soni), 534 Other (Eric Antisell)
CD 8	1,016 Socialist Workers Party (Joanne Kuniansky), 758 Libertarian (Dan Delaney), 714 Other (David Cook), 400 Labor (Pablo Olivera), 246 Truth and Merit (John Salierno)
CD 9	1,054 Libertarian (Sean Armstrong), 1,108 Socialist Workers Party (Lea Sherman)
CD 10	1,989 Jobs and Justice (Cynthia Johnson), 634 Libertarian (Kendal Ludden), 381 The Mahali Party (Clenard Childress)
CD 11	2,276 Libertarian (Joseph Biasco)
CD 12	1,925 Libertarian (C. Lynn Genrich)

2022 PRIMARY ELECTIONS: SUPPLEMENTARY INFORMATION

Primary	July 7, 2022	**Registration** (as of June 1, 2022)	6,445,397	Democratic	2,508,456
				Republican	1,490,261
				Libertarian	22,676
				Conservative	15,722
				U.S. Constitution	15,325
				Green	11,651
				Socialist	7,772
				Natural Law	6,263
				Reform	1,782
				Unaffiliated	2,365,489

Primary Type Semi-open—Registered Democrats and Republicans could vote only in their party's primary. "Unaffiliated" voters could participate in either party's primary if they were willing to become a member of that party.

	REPUBLICAN PRIMARIES			DEMOCRATIC PRIMARIES		
Congressional District 1	Gustafson, Claire	13,134	69.0%	Norcross, Donald*	43,910	76.9%
	Galdo, Damon	5,908	31.0%	DeSantis, Mario	13,210	23.1%
	TOTAL	19,042		TOTAL	57,120	
Congressional District 2	Van Drew, Jeff*	33,278	86.1%	Alexander, Tim	13,418	61.0%
	Barker, John	3,040	7.9%	Rush, Carolyn	8,586	39.0%
	Pignatelli, Sean	2,314	6.0%			
	TOTAL	38,632		TOTAL	22,004	
Congressional District 3	Healey, Bob	16,626	52.8%	Kim, Andy*	36,143	92.9%
	Smith, Ian A.	12,052	38.3%	Hendler, Reuven	2,777	7.1%
	Ferrara, Nicholas J.	2,786	8.9%			
	TOTAL	31,464		TOTAL	38,920	

NEW JERSEY

GENERAL AND PRIMARY ELECTIONS

	REPUBLICAN PRIMARIES			DEMOCRATIC PRIMARIES		
Congressional District 4	Smith, Christopher H.*	32,049	57.6%	Jenkins, Matthew	19,428	100.0%
	Crispi, Mike	20,600	37.0%			
	Gray, Steve	2,230	4.0%			
	Blasi, Mike	733	1.3%			
	TOTAL	55,612		TOTAL	19,428	
Congressional District 5	Pallotta, Frank	14,497	51.1%	Gottheimer, Joshua S.*	19,051	100.0%
	De Gregorio, Nick	12,788	45.1%			
	Skenderi, Sab	622	2.2%			
	Schneiderman, Fred	451	1.6%			
	TOTAL	28,358		TOTAL	19,051	
Congressional District 6	Kiley, Susan M.	9,722	57.0%	Pallone, Frank Jr.*	28,241	100.0%
	Mehta, Rikin	4,535	26.6%			
	Toomey, Thomas	2,798	16.4%			
	TOTAL	17,055		TOTAL	28,241	
Congressional District 7	Kean, Thomas H.	24,106	45.7%	Malinowski, Tom*	34,442	94.4%
	Rizzo, Philip	12,481	23.7%	Bacon, Roger	2,042	5.6%
	Peterson, Erik	8,102	15.4%			
	Flora, John P.	2,907	5.5%			
	Isemann, John Henry	2,576	4.9%			
	Dorlon, Kevin	2,176	4.1%			
	Schwab, Sterling I.	414	0.8%			
	TOTAL	52,762		TOTAL	36,484	
Congressional District 8	Arroyo, Marcos	2,617	100.0%	Menendez, Robert J.	23,844	84.0%
				Ocampo Grajales, David	3,118	11.0%
				Roseborough-Eberhard, Andrea "Ane"	1,417	5.0%
	TOTAL	2,617		TOTAL	28,379	
Congressional District 9	Prempeh, William Sreboe	9,494	100.0%	Pascrell, William J. Jr.*	14,713	100.0%
	TOTAL	9,494		TOTAL	14,713	
Congressional District 10	Pinckney, David H.	3,272	82.6%	Payne, Donald M. Jr.*	26,342	83.6%
	Stewart, Garth	687	17.4%	Oakley, Imani	3,230	10.3%
				Khalfani, Akil	1,926	6.1%
	TOTAL	3,959		TOTAL	31,498	
Congressional District 11	DeGroot, Paul	12,057	38.3%	Sherrill, Mikie*	32,277	100.0%
	Selen, Tayfun	11,766	37.3%			
	Anderson, Toby	6,022	19.1%			
	McAndrew, Ruth	1,255	4.0%			
	Halter, Alexander	417	1.3%			
	TOTAL	31,517		TOTAL	32,277	
Congressional District 12	Mayfield, Darius	12,944	100.0%	Coleman, Bonnie Watson*	34,253	100.0%
	TOTAL	12,944		TOTAL	34,253	

Note: An asterisk (*) denotes incumbent.

NEW MEXICO

Statewide Races

In 2022, New Mexico had a gubernatorial race that looked a lot like its 2020 race for Senate.

In 2018, then-Rep. Michelle Lujan Grisham (D) left her Albuquerque-centric 1st District to run in the open-seat race for governor. She defeated fellow Rep. Steve Pearce (R) by 14 points. In office, Lujan Grisham kept decent approval ratings and, in 2020, was named as a possible Vice-Presidential pick for then-nominee Joe Biden. In 2021, she got unfavorable press when it was reported that she paid over $60,000 in a settlement with a former staffer who alleged sexual misconduct during a staff meeting (the governor denied the allegations).

Meanwhile, Republicans needed a candidate. Their sole member of the House delegation did not seem likely to run for governor, and all sitting statewide officials were Democrats. Though they lost the contest, New Mexico's 2020 Senate result was still encouraging for Republicans. As Biden carried the state by 11 points, Mark Ronchetti, a Republican well-known for his years as a local weatherman, held then-Rep. Ben Ray Lujan, a Democrat who was running for a promotion, to a 52%–46% margin. In late 2021, Ronchetti announced he'd challenge Lujan Grisham.

Lujan Grisham led in most public polls, though often by single-digit margins – which was exactly how the race ended up on Election Day. In something of an anticlimactic result, the topline result was unchanged from 2020: Ronchetti lost 52%–46%. Against Lujan Grisham, he carried the same 19 counties that he did two years earlier and narrowly flipped Socorro County, a scenic, but relatively sparsely populated, county in the middle of the state. But Democratic strength in the large counties basically held: Albuquerque's Bernalillo County, which casts a third of the statewide vote, gave Ronchetti the same 40.6% as it did in 2020.

House Races

As New Mexico was set to remain at three seats after the 2020 census, Democrats, with the governorship and both chambers of the legislature, controlled the line-drawing process.

Since the 2008 elections, Democrats have continuously held districts 1 (Albuquerque) and 3 (Santa Fe and the rural north) but have only sporadically won District 2, which pairs Las Cruces with the southeastern oilfields of "Little Texas." Democrats lost the 2nd District in 2010, after holding it for a term but regained it with Xochitl Torres Small, a moderate Blue Dog, in 2018. But as Donald Trump carried NM-2 by a dozen points in 2020, Torres Small lost a rematch with Yvette Herrell, a strident conservative.

Instead of trying to keep their 2-1 advantage intact, Democratic mappers went for a 3-0 plan. Though this entailed making Districts 1 and 3 more competitive, they transferred Democratic voters into NM-2 and split up Little Texas. It worked. The redrawn 2nd District would have gone 52%–46% for Biden in 2020 – the change was enough to enable Democratic challenger Gabe Vasquez to unseat Herrell by less than a point. The Democratic incumbents in the other two seats each won with more than 55% of the vote.

NEW MEXICO
Congressional districts first established for elections held in 2022
3 members

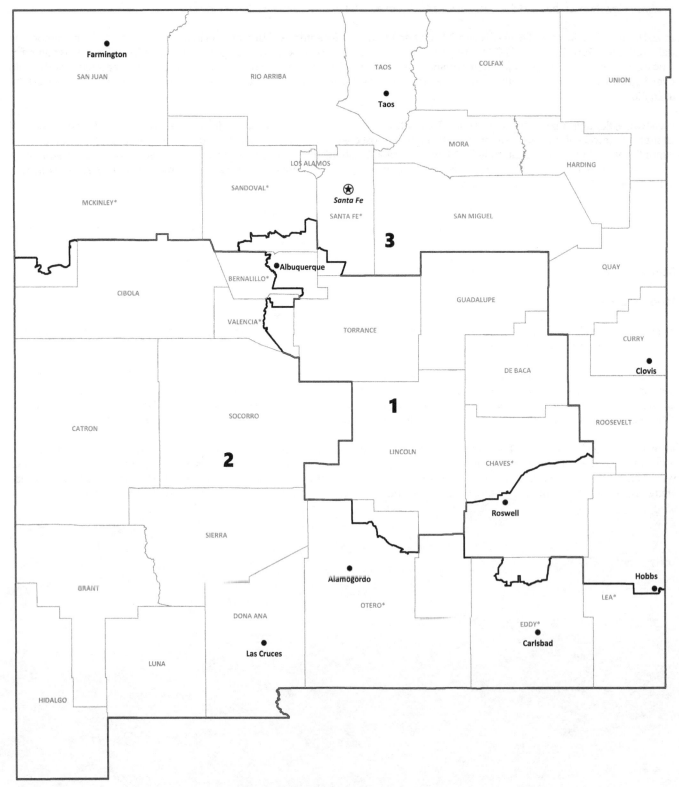

* Asterisk indicates a county whose boundaries include parts of two or more congressional districts.

NEW MEXICO

GOVERNOR
Michelle Lujan Grisham (D). Reelected 2022 to a four-year term. Previously elected 2018.

SENATORS (2 Democrats)
Martin Heinrich (D). Reelected 2018 to a six-year term. Previously elected 2012.

Ben Ray Luján (D). Elected 2020 to a six-year term.

REPRESENTATIVES (3 Democrats)
1. Melanie Stansbury (D)
2. Gabe Vasquez (D)
3. Teresa Leger Fernandez (D)

POSTWAR VOTE FOR PRESIDENT

		Republican		Democratic		Other Vote	Rep.-Dem. Plurality	Percentage			
								Total Vote		Major Vote	
Year	Total Vote	Vote	Candidate	Vote	Candidate			Rep.	Dem.	Rep.	Dem.
2020	923,965	401,894	Trump, Donald J.*	501,614	Biden, Joseph R. Jr.	20,457	99,720 D	43.5%	54.3%	44.5%	55.5%
2016**	798,319	319,667	Trump, Donald J.	385,234	Clinton, Hillary Rodham	93,418	65,567 D	40.0%	48.3%	45.3%	54.7%
2012	783,757	335,788	Romney, W. Mitt	415,335	Obama, Barack H.*	32,634	79,547 D	42.8%	53.0%	44.7%	55.3%
2008	830,158	346,832	McCain, John S. III	472,422	Obama, Barack H.	10,904	125,590 D	41.8%	56.9%	42.3%	57.7%
2004	756,304	376,930	Bush, George W.*	370,942	Kerry, John F.	8,432	5,988 R	49.8%	49.0%	50.4%	49.6%
2000**	598,605	286,417	Bush, George W.	286,783	Gore, Albert Jr.	25,405	366 D	47.8%	47.9%	50.0%	50.0%
1996**	556,074	232,751	Dole, Robert "Bob"	273,495	Clinton, Bill*	49,828	40,744 D	41.9%	49.2%	46.0%	54.0%
1992**	569,986	212,824	Bush, George H.*	261,617	Clinton, Bill	95,545	48,793 D	37.3%	45.9%	44.9%	55.1%
1988	521,287	270,341	Bush, George H.	244,497	Dukakis, Michael S.	6,449	25,844 R	51.9%	46.9%	52.5%	47.5%
1984	514,370	307,101	Reagan, Ronald*	201,769	Mondale, Walter F.	5,500	105,332 R	59.7%	39.2%	60.3%	39.7%
1980**	456,971	250,779	Reagan, Ronald	167,826	Carter, Jimmy*	38,366	82,953 R	54.9%	36.7%	59.9%	40.1%
1976	418,409	211,419	Ford, Gerald R.*	201,148	Carter, Jimmy	5,842	10,271 R	50.5%	48.1%	51.2%	48.8%
1972	386,241	235,606	Nixon, Richard M.*	141,084	McGovern, George S.	9,551	94,522 R	61.0%	36.5%	62.5%	37.5%
1968**	327,350	169,692	Nixon, Richard M.	130,081	Humphrey, Hubert Horatio Jr.	27,577	39,611 R	51.8%	39.7%	56.6%	43.4%
1964	328,645	132,838	Goldwater, Barry M. Sr.	194,015	Johnson, Lyndon B.*	1,792	61,177 D	40.4%	59.0%	40.6%	59.4%
1960	311,107	153,733	Nixon, Richard M.	156,027	Kennedy, John F.	1,347	2,294 D	49.4%	50.2%	49.6%	50.4%
1956	253,926	146,788	Eisenhower, Dwight D.*	106,098	Stevenson, Adlai E. II	1,040	40,690 R	57.8%	41.8%	58.0%	42.0%
1952	238,608	132,170	Eisenhower, Dwight D.	105,661	Stevenson, Adlai E. II	777	26,509 R	55.4%	44.3%	55.6%	44.4%
1948	187,063	80,303	Dewey, Thomas E.	105,464	Truman, Harry S.*	1,296	25,161 D	42.9%	56.4%	43.2%	56.8%

Note: An asterisk (*) denotes incumbent. **In past elections, the other vote included: 2016 - 74,541 Libertarian (Gary Johnson); 2000 - 21,251 Green (Ralph Nader); 1996 - 32,257 Reform (Ross Perot); 1992 - 91,895 Independent (Perot); 1980 - 29,459 Independent (John Anderson); 1968 - 25,737 American Independent (George Wallace).

NEW MEXICO

POSTWAR VOTE FOR GOVERNOR

		Republican		Democratic		Other Vote	Rep.-Dem. Plurality	Percentage			
								Total Vote		Major Vote	
Year	Total Vote	Vote	Candidate	Vote	Candidate			Rep.	Dem.	Rep.	Dem.
2022	712,256	324,701	Ronchetti, Mark V.	370,168	Grisham, Michelle Lujan*	17,387	45,467 D	45.6%	52.0%	46.7%	53.3%
2018	696,459	298,091	Pearce, Steve	398,368	Grisham, Michelle Lujan		100,277 D	42.8%	57.2%	42.8%	57.2%
2014	512,805	293,443	Martinez, Susana*	219,362	King, Gary K.		74,081 R	57.2%	42.8%	57.2%	42.8%
2010	602,827	321,219	Martinez, Susana	280,614	Denish, Diane D.	994	40,605 R	53.3%	46.5%	53.4%	46.6%
2006	559,170	174,364	Dendahl, John	384,806	Richardson, Bill*		210,442 D	31.2%	68.8%	31.2%	68.8%
2002	484,233	189,074	Sanchez, John A.	268,693	Richardson, Bill	26,466	79,619 D	39.0%	55.5%	41.3%	58.7%
1998	498,703	271,948	Johnson, Gary E.*	226,755	Chavez, Martin J.		45,193 R	54.5%	45.5%	54.5%	45.5%
1994**	467,621	232,945	Johnson, Gary E.	186,686	King, Bruce*	47,990	46,259 R	49.8%	39.9%	55.5%	44.5%
1990	411,232	185,692	Bond, Frank	224,564	King, Bruce	976	38,872 D	45.2%	54.6%	45.3%	54.7%
1986	394,833	209,455	Carruthers, Garrey E.	185,378	Powell, Ray B.		24,077 R	53.0%	47.0%	53.0%	47.0%
1982	407,466	191,626	Irick, John B.	215,840	Anaya, Toney		24,214 D	47.0%	53.0%	47.0%	53.0%
1978	345,577	170,848	Skeen, Joseph R.	174,631	King, Bruce	98	3,783 D	49.4%	50.5%	49.5%	50.5%
1974	328,742	160,430	Skeen, Joseph R.	164,172	Apodaca, Jerry	4,140	3,742 D	48.8%	49.9%	49.4%	50.6%
1970**	290,375	134,640	Domenici, Peter V.	148,835	King, Bruce	6,900	14,195 D	46.4%	51.3%	47.5%	52.5%
1968	318,975	160,140	Cargo, David F.*	157,230	Chavez, Fabian	1,605	2,910 R	50.2%	49.3%	50.5%	49.5%
1966	260,232	134,625	Cargo, David F.	125,587	Lusk, T. E.	20	9,038 R	51.7%	48.3%	51.7%	48.3%
1964	318,042	126,540	Tucker, Merle H.	191,497	Campbell, Jack M.*	5	64,957 D	39.8%	60.2%	39.8%	60.2%
1962	247,135	116,184	Mechem, Edwin L.*	130,933	Campbell, Jack M.	18	14,749 D	47.0%	53.0%	47.0%	53.0%
1960	305,542	153,765	Mechem, Edwin L.	151,777	Burroughs, John*		1,988 R	50.3%	49.7%	50.3%	49.7%
1958	205,048	101,567	Mechem, Edwin L.*	103,481	Burroughs, John		1,914 D	49.5%	50.5%	49.5%	50.5%
1956	251,751	131,488	Mechem, Edwin L.	120,263	Simms, John F. Jr.*		11,225 R	52.2%	47.8%	52.2%	47.8%
1954	193,956	83,373	Stockton, Alvin	110,583	Simms, John F. Jr.		27,210 D	43.0%	57.0%	43.0%	57.0%
1952	240,150	129,116	Mechem, Edwin L.*	111,034	Grantham, Everett		18,082 R	53.8%	46.2%	53.8%	46.2%
1950	180,205	96,846	Mechem, Edwin L.	83,359	Miles, John E.		13,487 R	53.7%	46.3%	53.7%	46.3%
1948	189,992	86,023	Lujan, Manuel	103,969	Mabry, Thomas J.*		17,946 D	45.3%	54.7%	45.3%	54.7%
1946	132,630	62,575	Safford, Edward L.	70,055	Mabry, Thomas J.		7,480 D	47.2%	52.8%	47.2%	52.8%

Note: An asterisk (*) denotes incumbent. **In past elections, the other vote included: 1994 - 47,990 Green (Roberto Mondragon). The term of New Mexico's Governor was increased from two to four years effective with the 1970 election.

POSTWAR VOTE FOR SENATOR

		Republican		Democratic		Other Vote	Rep.-Dem. Plurality	Percentage			
								Total Vote		Major Vote	
Year	Total Vote	Vote	Candidate	Vote	Candidate			Rep.	Dem.	Rep.	Dem.
2020	917,237	418,483	Ronchetti, Mark	474,483	Lujan, Ben Ray	24,271	56,000 D	45.6%	51.7%	46.9%	53.1%
2018**	697,012	212,813	Rich, Mick	376,998	Heinrich, Martin*	107,201	164,185 D	30.5%	54.1%	36.1%	63.9%
2014	515,506	229,097	Weh, Allen	286,409	Udall, Tom*		57,312 D	44.4%	55.6%	44.4%	55.6%
2012	775,792	351,259	Wilson, Heather A.	395,717	Heinrich, Martin	28,816	44,458 D	45.3%	51.0%	47.0%	53.0%
2008	823,650	318,522	Pearce, Steve	505,128	Udall, Tom		186,606 D	38.7%	61.3%	38.7%	61.3%
2006	558,550	163,826	McCulloch, Allen	394,365	Bingaman, Jeff*	359	230,539 D	29.3%	70.6%	29.3%	70.7%
2002	483,340	314,301	Domenici, Peter V.*	169,039	Tristani, Gloria		145,262 R	65.0%	35.0%	65.0%	35.0%
2000	589,526	225,517	Redmond, Bill	363,744	Bingaman, Jeff*	265	138,227 D	38.3%	61.7%	38.3%	61.7%
1996	551,821	357,171	Domenici, Peter V.*	164,356	Trujillo, Art	30,294	192,815 R	64.7%	29.8%	68.5%	31.5%
1994	463,196	213,025	McMillan, Colin R.	249,989	Bingaman, Jeff*	182	36,964 D	46.0%	54.0%	46.0%	54.0%
1990	406,938	296,712	Domenici, Peter V.*	110,033	Benavides, Tom R.	193	186,679 R	72.9%	27.0%	72.9%	27.1%
1988	508,598	186,579	Valentine, William	321,983	Bingaman, Jeff*	36	135,404 D	36.7%	63.3%	36.7%	63.3%
1984	502,634	361,371	Domenici, Peter V.*	141,253	Pratt, Judith A.	10	220,118 R	71.9%	28.1%	71.9%	28.1%
1982	404,810	187,128	Schmitt, Harrison*	217,682	Bingaman, Jeff		30,554 D	46.2%	53.8%	46.2%	53.8%
1978	343,554	183,442	Domenici, Peter V.*	160,045	Anaya, Toney	67	23,397 R	53.4%	46.6%	53.4%	46.6%
1976	413,141	234,681	Schmitt, Harrison	176,382	Montoya, Joseph M.*	2,078	58,299 R	56.8%	42.7%	57.1%	42.9%
1972	378,330	204,253	Domenici, Peter V.	173,815	Daniels, Jack	262	30,438 R	54.0%	45.9%	54.0%	46.0%
1970	289,906	135,004	Carter, Anderson	151,486	Montoya, Joseph M.*	3,416	16,482 D	46.6%	52.3%	47.1%	52.9%
1966	258,203	120,988	Carter, Anderson	137,205	Anderson, Clinton P.*	10	16,217 D	46.9%	53.1%	46.9%	53.1%
1964	325,774	147,562	Mechem, Edwin L.	178,209	Montoya, Joseph M.	3	30,647 D	45.3%	54.7%	45.3%	54.7%
1960	300,551	109,897	Colwes, William	190,654	Anderson, Clinton P.*		80,757 D	36.6%	63.4%	36.6%	63.4%
1958	203,323	75,827	Atchley, Forrest S.	127,496	Chavez, Dennis*		51,669 D	37.3%	62.7%	37.3%	62.7%
1954	194,422	83,071	Mechem, Edwin L.	111,351	Anderson, Clinton P.*		28,280 D	42.7%	57.3%	42.7%	57.3%
1952	239,711	117,168	Hurley, Patrick J.	122,543	Chavez, Dennis*		5,375 D	48.9%	51.1%	48.9%	51.1%
1948	188,495	80,226	Hurley, Patrick J.	108,269	Anderson, Clinton P.		28,043 D	42.6%	57.4%	42.6%	57.4%
1946	133,282	64,632	Hurley, Patrick J.	68,650	Chavez, Dennis*		4,018 D	48.5%	51.5%	48.5%	51.5%

Note: An asterisk (*) denotes incumbent. **In past elections, the other vote included: 2018 - Libertarian 107,201 (Gary Johnson).

NEW MEXICO
GOVERNOR 2022

2020 Census Population	County	Total Vote	Republican (Ronchetti)	Democratic (Grisham)	Other	Rep.-Dem. Plurality		Percentage Total Vote Rep.	Dem.	Percentage Major Vote Rep.	Dem.
680,099	BERNALILLO	245,300	99,639	141,177	4,484	41,538	D	40.6%	57.6%	41.4%	58.6%
3,547	CATRON	2,022	1,493	471	58	1,022	R	73.8%	23.3%	76.0%	24.0%
64,554	CHAVES	16,326	11,884	4,063	379	7,821	R	72.8%	24.9%	74.5%	25.5%
26,641	CIBOLA	6,870	3,230	3,418	222	188	D	47.0%	49.8%	48.6%	51.4%
11,933	COLFAX	4,909	2,719	2,053	137	666	R	55.4%	41.8%	57.0%	43.0%
48,765	CURRY	10,248	7,092	2,516	640	4,576	R	69.2%	24.6%	73.8%	26.2%
1,745	DE BACA	758	566	167	25	399	R	74.7%	22.0%	77.2%	22.8%
218,700	DONA ANA	57,724	23,213	32,147	2,364	8,934	D	40.2%	55.7%	41.9%	58.1%
58,630	EDDY	16,716	12,996	3,376	344	9,620	R	77.7%	20.2%	79.4%	20.6%
26,971	GRANT	11,696	5,217	6,185	294	968	D	44.6%	52.9%	45.8%	54.2%
4,298	GUADALUPE	1,741	784	915	42	131	D	45.0%	52.6%	46.1%	53.9%
621	HARDING	419	280	129	10	151	R	66.8%	30.8%	68.5%	31.5%
4,193	HIDALGO	1,624	914	645	65	269	R	56.3%	39.7%	58.6%	41.4%
71,104	LEA	14,008	11,542	2,104	362	9,438	R	82.4%	15.0%	84.6%	15.4%
19,639	LINCOLN	8,355	5,778	2,334	243	3,444	R	69.2%	27.9%	71.2%	28.8%
19,514	LOS ALAMOS	10,148	3,751	6,192	205	2,441	D	37.0%	61.0%	37.7%	62.3%
23,697	LUNA	5,889	3,250	2,445	194	805	R	55.2%	41.5%	57.1%	42.9%
71,446	MCKINLEY	19,481	5,799	12,910	772	7,111	D	29.8%	66.3%	31.0%	69.0%
4,530	MORA	2,457	832	1,584	41	752	D	33.9%	64.5%	34.4%	65.6%
67,603	OTERO	17,642	11,182	5,852	608	5,330	R	63.4%	33.2%	65.6%	34.4%
8,248	QUAY	3,027	2,104	803	120	1,301	R	69.5%	26.5%	72.4%	27.6%
38,954	RIO ARRIBA	12,961	4,729	8,037	195	3,308	D	36.5%	62.0%	37.0%	63.0%
18,414	ROOSEVELT	4,662	3,177	1,087	398	2,090	R	68.1%	23.3%	74.5%	25.5%
122,909	SAN JUAN	40,054	25,574	12,849	1,631	12,725	R	63.8%	32.1%	66.6%	33.4%
27,258	SAN MIGUEL	9,468	2,785	6,531	152	3,746	D	29.4%	69.0%	29.9%	70.1%
147,724	SANDOVAL	61,235	29,337	30,789	1,109	1,452	D	47.9%	50.3%	48.8%	51.2%
150,930	SANTA FE	69,602	16,287	52,447	868	36,160	D	23.4%	75.4%	23.7%	76.3%
10,835	SIERRA	4,919	3,001	1,780	138	1,221	R	61.0%	36.2%	62.8%	37.2%
16,588	SOCORRO	6,140	2,988	2,950	202	38	R	48.7%	48.0%	50.3%	49.7%
32,827	TAOS	13,348	2,964	10,188	196	7,224	D	22.2%	76.3%	22.5%	77.5%
15,491	TORRANCE	5,544	3,712	1,588	244	2,124	R	67.0%	28.6%	70.0%	30.0%
4,056	UNION	1,500	1,101	328	71	773	R	73.4%	21.9%	77.0%	23.0%
76,940	VALENCIA	25,463	14,781	10,108	574	4,673	R	58.0%	39.7%	59.4%	40.6%
2,099,404	TOTAL	712,256	324,701	370,168	17,387	45,467	D	45.6%	52.0%	46.7%	53.3%

NEW MEXICO
HOUSE OF REPRESENTATIVES

CD	Year	Total Vote	Republican Vote	Republican Candidate	Democratic Vote	Democratic Candidate	Other Vote	Rep.-Dem. Plurality		Total Vote Rep.	Dem.	Major Vote Rep.	Dem.
1	2022	280,671	124,151	GARCIA HOLMES, MICHELLE	156,462	STANSBURY, MELANIE ANN*	58	32,311	D	44.2%	55.7%	44.2%	55.8%
1	2020	321,290	134,337	HOLMES, MICHELLE GARCIA	186,953	HAALAND, DEBRA*		52,616	D	41.8%	58.2%	41.8%	58.2%
1	2018	249,162	90,507	ARNOLD-JONES, JANICE E.	147,336	HAALAND, DEBRA	11,319	56,829	D	36.3%	59.1%	38.1%	61.9%
1	2016	277,967	96,879	PRIEM, RICHARD G.	181,088	GRISHAM, MICHELLE LUJAN*		84,209	D	34.9%	65.1%	34.9%	65.1%
1	2014	180,032	74,558	FRESE, MICHAEL H.	105,474	GRISHAM, MICHELLE LUJAN*		30,916	D	41.4%	58.6%	41.4%	58.6%
1	2012	275,856	112,473	ARNOLD-JONES, JANICE E.	162,924	GRISHAM, MICHELLE LUJAN	459	50,451	D	40.8%	59.1%	40.8%	59.2%
2	2022	192,673	95,636	HERRELL, YVETTE*	96,986	VASQUEZ, GABRIEL "GABE"	51	1,350	D	49.6%	50.3%	49.6%	50.4%
2	2020	264,946	142,283	HERRELL, YVETTE	122,546	TORRES SMALL, XOCHITL*	117	19,737	R	53.7%	46.3%	53.7%	46.3%
2	2018	199,256	97,767	HERRELL, YVETTE	101,489	TORRES SMALL, XOCHITL		3,722	D	49.1%	50.9%	49.1%	50.9%
2	2016	228,817	143,515	PEARCE, STEVE*	85,232	SOULES, MERRIE LEE	70	58,283	R	62.7%	37.2%	62.7%	37.3%
2	2014	147,777	95,209	PEARCE, STEVE*	52,499	LARA, ROXANNE "ROCKY"	69	42,710	R	64.4%	35.5%	64.5%	35.5%
2	2012	225,515	133,180	PEARCE, STEVE*	92,162	ERHARD, EVELYN MADRID	173	41,018	R	59.1%	40.9%	59.1%	40.9%

NEW MEXICO

HOUSE OF REPRESENTATIVES

CD	Year	Total Vote	Republican Vote	Republican Candidate	Democratic Vote	Democratic Candidate	Other Vote	Rep.-Dem. Plurality	Total Vote Rep.	Total Vote Dem.	Major Vote Rep.	Major Vote Dem.
3	2022	230,782	96,565	MARTINEZ JOHNSON, ALEXIS	134,217	FERNANDEZ, TERESA LEGER*		37,652 D	41.8%	58.2%	41.8%	58.2%
3	2020	317,448	131,166	JOHNSON, ALEXIS M.	186,282	FERNANDEZ, TERESA LEGER		55,116 D	41.3%	58.7%	41.3%	58.7%
3	2018	244,893	76,427	MCFALL, JERALD	155,201	LUJAN, BEN RAY*	13,265	78,774 D	31.2%	63.4%	33.0%	67.0%
3	2016	273,342	102,730	ROMERO, MICHAEL H.	170,612	LUJAN, BEN RAY*		67,882 D	37.6%	62.4%	37.6%	62.4%
3	2014	184,076	70,775	BYRD, JEFFERSON L.	113,249	LUJAN, BEN RAY*	52	42,474 D	38.4%	61.5%	38.5%	61.5%
3	2012	264,719	97,616	BYRD, JEFFERSON L.	167,103	LUJAN, BEN RAY*		69,487 D	36.9%	63.1%	36.9%	63.1%
TOTAL	2022	704,126	316,352		387,665		109	71,313 D	44.9%	55.1%	44.9%	55.1%
TOTAL	2020	903,684	407,786		495,781		117	87,995 D	45.1%	54.9%	45.1%	54.9%
TOTAL	2018	693,311	264,701		404,026		24,584	139,325 D	38.2%	58.3%	39.6%	60.4%
TOTAL	2016	780,126	343,124		436,932		70	93,808 D	44.0%	56.0%	44.0%	56.0%
TOTAL	2014	511,885	240,542		271,222		121	30,680 D	47.0%	53.0%	47.0%	53.0%
TOTAL	2012	766,090	343,269		422,189		632	78,920 D	44.8%	55.1%	44.8%	55.2%

Note: An asterisk (*) denotes incumbent.

NEW MEXICO

GENERAL AND PRIMARY ELECTIONS

GENERAL ELECTIONS: OTHER VOTES

Governor   Other vote was 17,387 Libertarian (Karen Bedonie)

House   Other vote was:

    CD 1   58 Write-In (Victoria Gonzales)
    CD 2   51 Write-In (Eliseo Luna)

2022 PRIMARY ELECTIONS: SUPPLEMENTARY INFORMATION

Primary   June 7, 2022   **Registration** (as of May 31, 2022)   1,348,632

Democratic	598,811
Republican	417,165
Other	14,019
Libertarian	14,248
No Party, Independent, Declined to State	304,389

Primary Type   Closed—Only registered Democrats and Republicans could vote in their party's primary.

	REPUBLICAN PRIMARIES			DEMOCRATIC PRIMARIES		
Governor	Ronchetti, Mark V.	68,658	58.4%	Grisham, Michelle Lujan*	125,238	100.0%
	Dow, Rebecca L.	18,185	15.5%			
	Zanetti, Gregory Joseph	16,394	13.9%			
	Block, Jay C.	12,469	10.6%			
	Maharg, Ethel R.	1,845	1.6%			
	TOTAL	117,551		TOTAL	125,238	
Congressional District 1	Garcia Holmes, Michelle	25,822	58.7%	Stansbury, Melanie Ann	44,223	100.0%
	Sanchez, Louie	18,171	41.3%			
	TOTAL	43,993		TOTAL	44,223	

NEW MEXICO

GENERAL AND PRIMARY ELECTIONS

	REPUBLICAN PRIMARIES			DEMOCRATIC PRIMARIES		
Congressional District 2	Herrell, Yvette*	28,623	100.0%	Vasquez, Gabriel "Gabe"	24,010	76.1%
				Patel, Darshan Nilesh	7,534	23.9%
	TOTAL	*28,623*		*TOTAL*	*31,544*	
Congressional District 3	Martinez Johnson, Alexis	28,729	100.0%	Fernandez, Teresa Leger*	46,940	100.0%
	TOTAL	*28,729*		*TOTAL*	*46,940*	

Note: An asterisk (*) denotes incumbent.

NEW YORK

Statewide Races

If, in early 2022, an elections analyst could travel through time to get a sneak peek at any state's November results and chose New York, they would have had good reason to assume that national Republicans often-discussed "red wave" had materialized. But that, of course, was not the case. That New York experienced a localized "red wave" in its top races as Democrats beat expectations in adjacent states spoke to the state-by-state nature of the 2022 midterms.

After the resignation of three-term Democratic Gov. Andrew Cuomo, in 2021, then-Lt. Gov. Kathy Hochul, a Democrat from Buffalo, ascended to the state's top job. Running as a center-left Democrat, she won the party's nomination with 67% over two New York City-area candidates.

In the general election, Hochul was criticized for running a weak campaign and faced a credible opponent in Republican Rep. Lee Zeldin, who represented the Long Island-based 1st District. As Zeldin relentlessly hit Democrats on crime, Hochul seemed taken off guard. Hochul won by a margin of just 53%–47%. Compared to Cuomo's showing four years earlier, some of Hochul's biggest declines came in New York City itself: in 2018, its five boroughs collectively gave Cuomo an 82%–15% margin – they favored Hochul only 70%–30%. One exception to the pro-Republican trend was the state capital area. The only two counties that Hochul carried that Cuomo didn't were Columbia and Schenectady, near Albany (Cuomo was not beloved by state employees).

The Republican current in New York also took a toll on Senate Majority Leader Chuck Schumer's performance. Until 2022, he was a chronic overperformer: when he was last up, in 2016, he won 71%–27% and carried 57 of the state's 62 counties. Though he fared better than Hochul, his 57%–43% margin was the weakest for a Democratic Senate nominee in New York since 2000.

House Races

New York voters established an independent redistricting commission via referendum, but the legislature was not obligated to accept its maps. Hochul vowed to play hardball. With a Democratic legislature, she signed what became known to political observers as the "Hochulmander." The 26-seat map featured 22 Biden-won seats, packing Republicans into four safe seats. But the state Court of Appeals overturned the map – importantly, it did not give legislators a second bite at the apple, appointing its own special master to draw the lines.

Under the court-approved plan, Democrats won only a 15-11 advantage. Zeldin's coattails helped Republicans flip two Biden-won Long Island seats, Districts 3 and 4 – the former of which elected the infamous George Santos. North of the city, Republicans notched a satisfying win by narrowly defeating Rep. Sean Patrick Maloney, then the chair of the Democratic Congressional Campaign Committee. Going further Upstate, Republicans flipped the newly drawn 19th and held the Syracuse-based 22nd. The Hudson Valley's 18th District was a rare marginal seat that went to Democrats – Rep. Pat Ryan won a high-profile August special election and did not take his November race for granted. Finally, in a notable member-vs-member Democratic primary that featured two committee chairs, Rep. Jerrold Nadler beat Rep. Carolyn Maloney in Manhattan's 12th District.

NEW YORK

Congressional districts first established for elections held in 2022

26 members

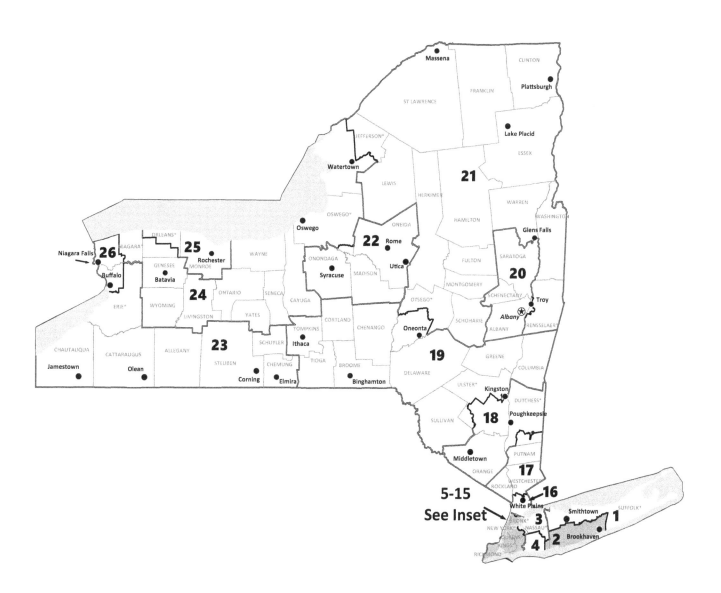

* Asterisk indicates a county whose boundaries include parts of two or more congressional districts.

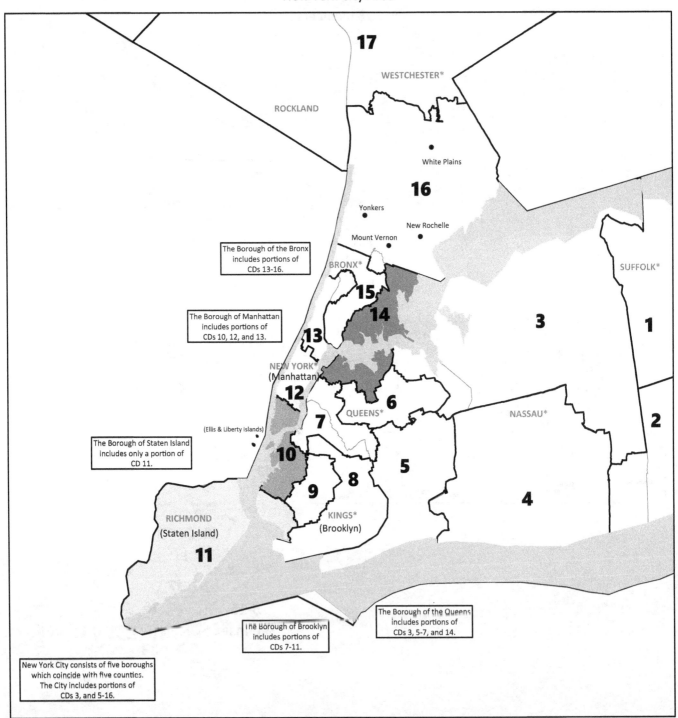

NEW YORK

GOVERNOR
Kathy Hochul (D). Elected 2022 to a four-year term. Formerly lieutenant governor, assumed office August 24, 2021, after Andrew Cuomo's resignation following sexual harassment allegations.

SENATORS (2 Democrats)
Kirsten E. Gillibrand (D). Reelected 2018 to a six-year term. Previously elected 2012 and 2010 to fill the remaining two years of the term vacated by Hillary Rodham Clinton (D), who resigned in January 2009 to become U.S. secretary of state. Gillibrand sworn in as senator January 27, 2009, shortly after the vacancy occurred.

Charles E. Schumer (D). Reelected 2022 to a six-year term. Previously elected 2016, 2010, 2004, 1998.

REPRESENTATIVES (11 Republicans, 15 Democrats)
1. Nick LaLota (R)
2. Andrew Garbarino (R)
3. George Santos (R)
4. Anthony D'Esposito (R)
5. Gregory W. Meeks (D)
6. Grace Meng (D)
7. Nydia Velazquez (D)
8. Hakeem Jeffries (D)
9. Yvette D. Clarke (D)
10. Daniel Goldman (D)
11. Nicole Malliotakis (R)
12. Jerrold Nadler (D)
13. Adriano Espaillat (D)
14. Alexandria Ocasio-Cortez (D)
15. Ritchie Torres (D)
16. Jamaal Bowman (D)
17. Michael Lawler (R)
18. Pat Ryan (D)
19. Marcus Molinaro (R)
20. Paul D. Tonko (D)
21. Elise Stefanik (R)
22. Brandon Williams (R)
23. Nicholas A. Langworthy (R)
24. Claudia Tenney (R)
25. Joseph D. Morelle (D)
26. Brian M. Higgins (D)

POSTWAR VOTE FOR PRESIDENT

Year	Total Vote	Republican Vote	Republican Candidate	Democratic Vote	Democratic Candidate	Other Vote	Rep.-Dem. Plurality	Total Vote Rep.	Total Vote Dem.	Major Vote Rep.	Major Vote Dem.
2020	8,616,861	3,251,997	Trump, Donald J.*	5,244,886	Biden, Joseph R. Jr.	119,978	1,992,889 D	37.7%	60.9%	38.3%	61.7%
2016**	7,721,442	2,819,533	Trump, Donald J.	4,556,118	Clinton, Hillary Rodham	345,791	1,736,585 D	36.5%	59.0%	38.2%	61.8%
2012	7,081,159	2,490,431	Romney, W. Mitt	4,485,741	Obama, Barack H.*	104,987	1,995,310 D	35.2%	63.3%	35.7%	64.3%
2008	7,640,931	2,752,771	McCain, John S. III	4,804,945	Obama, Barack H.	83,215	2,052,174 D	36.0%	62.9%	36.4%	63.6%
2004	7,391,036	2,962,567	Bush, George W.*	4,314,280	Kerry, John F.	114,189	1,351,713 D	40.1%	58.4%	40.7%	59.3%
2000**	6,821,999	2,403,374	Bush, George W.	4,107,697	Gore, Albert Jr.	310,928	1,704,323 D	35.2%	60.2%	36.9%	63.1%
1996**	6,316,129	1,933,492	Dole, Robert "Bob"	3,756,177	Clinton, Bill*	626,460	1,822,685 D	30.6%	59.5%	34.0%	66.0%
1992**	6,926,925	2,346,649	Bush, George H.*	3,444,450	Clinton, Bill	1,135,826	1,097,801 D	33.9%	49.7%	40.5%	59.5%
1988	6,485,683	3,081,871	Bush, George H.	3,347,882	Dukakis, Michael S.	55,930	266,011 D	47.5%	51.6%	47.9%	52.1%
1984	6,806,810	3,664,763	Reagan, Ronald*	3,119,609	Mondale, Walter F.	22,438	545,154 R	53.8%	45.8%	54.0%	46.0%
1980**	6,201,959	2,893,831	Reagan, Ronald	2,728,372	Carter, Jimmy*	579,756	165,459 R	46.7%	44.0%	51.5%	48.5%
1976	6,534,170	3,100,791	Ford, Gerald R.*	3,389,558	Carter, Jimmy	43,821	288,767 D	47.5%	51.9%	47.8%	52.2%
1972	7,165,919	4,192,778	Nixon, Richard M.*	2,951,084	McGovern, George S.	22,057	1,241,694 R	58.5%	41.2%	58.7%	41.3%
1968**	6,791,688	3,007,932	Nixon, Richard M.	3,378,470	Humphrey, Hubert Horatio Jr.	405,286	370,538 D	44.3%	49.7%	47.1%	52.9%
1964	7,166,275	2,243,559	Goldwater, Barry M. Sr.	4,913,102	Johnson, Lyndon B.*	9,614	2,669,543 D	31.3%	68.6%	31.3%	68.7%
1960	7,291,079	3,446,419	Nixon, Richard M.	3,830,085	Kennedy, John F.	14,575	383,666 D	47.3%	52.5%	47.4%	52.6%
1956	7,095,971	4,345,506	Eisenhower, Dwight D.*	2,747,944	Stevenson, Adlai E. II	2,521	1,597,562 R	61.2%	38.7%	61.3%	38.7%
1952	7,128,239	3,952,813	Eisenhower, Dwight D.	3,104,601	Stevenson, Adlai E. II	70,825	848,212 R	55.5%	43.6%	56.0%	44.0%
1948**	6,177,337	2,841,163	Dewey, Thomas E.	2,780,204	Truman, Harry S.*	555,970	60,959 R	46.0%	45.0%	50.5%	49.5%

Note: An asterisk (*) denotes incumbent. **In past elections, the other vote included: 2016 - 176,598 Libertarian (Gary Johnson); 2000 - 244,030 Green (Ralph Nader); 1996 - 503,458 Reform (Ross Perot); 1992 - 1,090,721 Independent (Perot); 1980 - 467,801 Independent (John Anderson); 1968 - 358,864 American Independent (George Wallace); 1948 - 509,559 Progressive (Henry Wallace).

NEW YORK

POSTWAR VOTE FOR GOVERNOR

Year	Total Vote	Republican Vote	Republican Candidate	Democratic Vote	Democratic Candidate	Other Vote	Rep.-Dem. Plurality	Total Vote Rep. %	Total Vote Dem. %	Major Vote Rep. %	Major Vote Dem. %
2022	5,912,286	2,762,581	Zeldin, Lee M.	3,140,415	Hochul, Kathy Courtney*	9,290	377,834 D	46.7%	53.1%	46.8%	53.2%
2018	6,104,477	2,207,602	Molinaro, Marcus	3,635,340	Cuomo, Andrew M.*	261,535	1,427,738 D	36.2%	59.6%	37.8%	62.2%
2014	3,819,086	1,537,077	Astorino, Rob	2,069,480	Cuomo, Andrew M.*	212,529	532,403 D	40.2%	54.2%	42.6%	57.4%
2010	4,658,825	1,548,184	Paladino, Carl	2,911,721	Cuomo, Andrew M.	198,920	1,363,537 D	33.2%	62.5%	34.7%	65.3%
2006	4,437,220	1,274,335	Faso, John	3,086,709	Spitzer, Eliot	76,176	1,812,374 D	28.7%	69.6%	29.2%	70.8%
2002**	4,579,078	2,262,255	Pataki, George E.*	1,534,064	McCall, H. Carl	782,759	728,191 R	49.4%	33.5%	59.6%	40.4%
1998	4,735,236	2,571,991	Pataki, George E.*	1,570,317	Vallone, Peter F.	592,928	1,001,674 R	54.3%	33.2%	62.1%	37.9%
1994	5,208,762	2,538,702	Pataki, George E.	2,364,904	Cuomo, Mario M.*	305,156	173,798 R	48.7%	45.4%	51.8%	48.2%
1990**	4,056,896	865,948	Rinfret, Pierre A.	2,157,087	Cuomo, Mario M.*	1,033,861	1,291,139 D	21.3%	53.2%	28.6%	71.4%
1986	4,294,124	1,363,810	O'Rourke, Andrew P.	2,775,229	Cuomo, Mario M.*	155,085	1,411,419 D	31.8%	64.6%	32.9%	67.1%
1982	5,254,891	2,494,827	Lehrman, Lew	2,675,213	Cuomo, Mario M.	84,851	180,386 D	47.5%	50.9%	48.3%	51.7%
1978	4,768,820	2,156,404	Duryea, Perry B.	2,429,272	Carey, Hugh L.*	183,144	272,868 D	45.2%	50.9%	47.0%	53.0%
1974	5,293,176	2,219,667	Wilson, Malcolm*	3,028,503	Carey, Hugh L.	45,006	808,836 D	41.9%	57.2%	42.3%	57.7%
1970	6,013,064	3,151,432	Rockefeller, Nelson A.*	2,421,426	Goldberg, Arthur J.	440,206	730,006 R	52.4%	40.3%	56.5%	43.5%
1966**	6,006,246	2,690,626	Rockefeller, Nelson A.*	2,298,363	O'Connor, Frank	1,017,257	392,263 R	44.8%	38.3%	53.9%	46.1%
1962	5,805,631	3,081,587	Rockefeller, Nelson A.*	2,552,418	Morgenthau, Robert M.	171,626	529,169 R	53.1%	44.0%	54.7%	45.3%
1958	5,712,665	3,126,929	Rockefeller, Nelson A.	2,553,895	Harriman, Averell*	31,841	573,034 R	54.7%	44.7%	55.0%	45.0%
1954	5,161,942	2,549,613	Ives, Irving M.	2,560,738	Harriman, Averell	51,591	11,125 D	49.4%	49.6%	49.9%	50.1%
1950	5,308,889	2,819,523	Dewey, Thomas E.*	2,246,855	Lynch, Walter A.	242,511	572,668 R	53.1%	42.3%	55.7%	44.3%
1946	4,964,552	2,825,633	Dewey, Thomas E.*	2,138,482	Mead, James M.	437	687,151 R	56.9%	43.1%	56.9%	43.1%

Note: An asterisk (*) denotes incumbent. On August 24, 2021, Kathy C. Hochul took the office as governor of New York after Andrew M. Cuomo's resignation. **In past elections, the other vote included: 2002 - 654,016 Independence (B. Thomas Golisano); 1990 - 827,614 Conservative (Herbert I. London); 1966 - 510,023 Conservative (Paul L. Adams), 507,234 Liberal (Franklin Roosevelt Jr.).

POSTWAR VOTE FOR SENATOR

Year	Total Vote	Republican Vote	Republican Candidate	Democratic Vote	Democratic Candidate	Other Vote	Rep.-Dem. Plurality	Total Vote Rep. %	Total Vote Dem. %	Major Vote Rep. %	Major Vote Dem. %
2022	5,852,707	2,501,151	Pinion, Joe	3,320,561	Schumer, Charles E.*	30,995	819,410 D	42.7%	56.7%	43.0%	57.0%
2018	6,059,023	1,998,220	Farley, Chele C.	4,056,931	Gillibrand, Kirsten E.*	3,872	2,058,711 D	33.0%	67.0%	33.0%	67.0%
2016	7,396,305	2,009,355	Long, Wendy	5,221,945	Schumer, Charles E.*	165,005	3,212,590 D	27.2%	70.6%	27.8%	72.2%
2012	6,679,678	1,758,702	Long, Wendy	4,822,330	Gillibrand, Kirsten E.*	98,646	3,063,628 D	26.3%	72.2%	26.7%	73.3%
2010	4,596,796	1,480,423	Townsend, Jay	3,047,880	Schumer, Charles E.*	68,493	1,567,457 D	32.2%	66.3%	32.7%	67.3%
2010S**	4,508,771	1,582,693	DioGuardi, Joseph J.	2,837,684	Gillibrand, Kirsten E.*	88,394	1,254,991 D	35.1%	62.9%	35.8%	64.2%
2006	4,490,053	1,392,189	Spencer, John	3,008,428	Clinton, Hillary Rodham*	89,436	1,616,239 D	31.0%	67.0%	31.6%	68.4%
2004	6,702,875	1,625,069	Mills, Howard D.	4,769,824	Schumer, Charles E.*	307,982	3,144,755 D	24.2%	71.2%	25.4%	74.6%
2000	6,779,839	2,915,730	Lazio, Rick A.	3,747,310	Clinton, Hillary Rodham	116,799	831,580 D	43.0%	55.3%	43.8%	56.2%
1998	4,670,805	2,058,988	D'Amato, Alfonse M.*	2,551,065	Schumer, Charles E.	60,752	492,077 D	44.1%	54.6%	44.7%	55.3%
1994	4,794,601	1,988,308	Castro, Bernadette	2,646,541	Moynihan, Daniel Patrick*	159,752	658,233 D	41.5%	55.2%	42.9%	57.1%
1992	6,458,826	3,166,994	D'Amato, Alfonse M.*	3,086,200	Abrams, Robert	205,632	80,794 R	49.0%	47.8%	50.6%	49.4%
1988	6,040,980	1,875,784	McMillan, Robert	4,048,649	Moynihan, Daniel Patrick*	116,547	2,172,865 D	31.1%	67.0%	31.7%	68.3%
1986	4,179,447	2,378,197	D'Amato, Alfonse M.*	1,723,216	Green, Mark J.	78,034	654,981 R	56.9%	41.2%	58.0%	42.0%
1982	4,967,729	1,696,766	Sullivan, Florence M.	3,232,146	Moynihan, Daniel Patrick*	38,817	1,535,380 D	34.2%	65.1%	34.4%	65.6%
1980**	6,014,914	2,699,652	D'Amato, Alfonse M.	2,618,661	Holtzman, Elizabeth	696,601	80,991 R	44.9%	43.5%	50.8%	49.2%
1976	6,319,755	2,836,633	Buckley, James L.*	3,422,594	Moynihan, Daniel Patrick	60,528	585,961 D	44.9%	54.2%	45.3%	54.7%
1974	5,163,600	2,340,188	Javits, Jacob K.*	1,973,781	Clark, Ramsey	849,631	366,407 R	45.3%	38.2%	54.2%	45.8%
1970**	5,904,782	1,434,472	Goodell, Charles E.*	2,171,232	Ottinger, Richard L.	2,299,078	736,760 D#	24.3%	36.8%	39.8%	60.2%
1968**	6,574,415	3,269,772	Javits, Jacob K.*	2,150,695	O'Dwyer, Paul	1,153,948	1,119,077 R	49.7%	32.7%	60.3%	39.7%
1964	7,151,686	3,104,056	Keating, Kenneth B.*	3,823,749	Kennedy, Robert F.	223,881	719,693 D	43.4%	53.5%	44.8%	55.2%
1962	5,703,168	3,272,417	Javits, Jacob K.*	2,289,323	Donovan, James B.	141,428	983,094 R	57.4%	40.1%	58.8%	41.2%
1958	5,602,088	2,842,942	Keating, Kenneth B.	2,709,950	Hogan, Frank S.	49,196	132,992 R	50.7%	48.4%	51.2%	48.8%
1956	6,991,136	3,723,933	Javits, Jacob K.	3,265,159	Wagner, Robert Ferdinand	2,044	458,774 R	53.3%	46.7%	53.3%	46.7%
1952	6,980,259	3,853,934	Ives, Irving M.*	2,521,736	Cashmore, John	604,589	1,332,198 R	55.2%	36.1%	60.4%	39.6%
1950	5,228,403	2,367,353	Hanley, Joe F.	2,632,313	Lehman, Herbert H.*	228,737	264,960 D	45.3%	50.3%	47.4%	52.6%
1949S**	4,966,878	2,384,381	Dulles, John Foster	2,582,438	Lehman, Herbert H.	59	198,057 D	48.0%	52.0%	48.0%	52.0%
1946	4,867,564	2,559,365	Ives, Irving M.	2,308,112	Lehman, Herbert H.	87	251,253 R	52.6%	47.4%	52.6%	47.4%

Note: An asterisk (*) denotes incumbent. A pound sign (#) in the plurality column indicates that the winner in 1970 did not run under the banner of either major party. **In past elections, the other vote included: 1980 - 664,544 Liberal (Jacob K. Javits); 1970 - 2,288,190 Conservative (James L. Buckley); 1968 - 1,139,402 Conservative (Buckley). Buckley won the 1970 election with 38.8% of the total vote and a plurality of 116,958 votes. The 1949 election and one of the 2010 elections were for short terms to fill a vacancy.

NEW YORK
GOVERNOR 2022

2020 Census Population	County	Total Vote	Republican (Zeldin)	Democratic (Hochul)	Other	Rep.-Dem. Plurality		Percentage			
								Total Vote		Major Vote	
								Rep.	Dem.	Rep.	Dem.
305,817	ALBANY	116,965	47,545	69,035	385	21,490	D	40.6%	59.0%	40.8%	59.2%
46,118	ALLEGANY	15,888	11,974	3,868	46	8,106	R	75.4%	24.3%	75.6%	24.4%
1,414,324	BRONX	200,739	44,948	155,564	227	110,616	D	22.4%	77.5%	22.4%	77.6%
190,269	BROOME	68,230	38,343	29,799	88	8,544	R	56.2%	43.7%	56.3%	43.7%
76,112	CATTARAUGUS	26,091	18,265	7,795	31	10,470	R	70.0%	29.9%	70.1%	29.9%
76,524	CAYUGA	26,949	16,725	10,175	49	6,550	R	62.1%	37.8%	62.2%	37.8%
127,072	CHAUTAUQUA	43,561	28,268	15,237	56	13,031	R	64.9%	35.0%	65.0%	35.0%
83,466	CHEMUNG	27,910	18,364	9,474	72	8,890	R	65.8%	33.9%	66.0%	34.0%
47,229	CHENANGO	16,873	11,871	4,968	34	6,903	R	70.4%	29.4%	70.5%	29.5%
80,569	CLINTON	27,524	15,590	11,894	40	3,696	R	56.6%	43.2%	56.7%	43.3%
59,510	COLUMBIA	29,745	13,605	16,079	61	2,474	D	45.7%	54.1%	45.8%	54.2%
47,629	CORTLAND	16,149	9,294	6,812	43	2,482	R	57.6%	42.2%	57.7%	42.3%
44,120	DELAWARE	18,608	12,095	6,490	23	5,605	R	65.0%	34.9%	65.1%	34.9%
294,812	DUTCHESS	115,150	59,486	55,519	145	3,967	R	51.7%	48.2%	51.7%	48.3%
920,134	ERIE	341,309	160,004	180,626	679	20,622	D	46.9%	52.9%	47.0%	53.0%
36,913	ESSEX	15,536	8,522	6,992	22	1,530	R	54.9%	45.0%	54.9%	45.1%
50,088	FRANKLIN	15,197	9,180	6,003	14	3,177	R	60.4%	39.5%	60.5%	39.5%
53,413	FULTON	18,879	13,591	5,255	33	8,336	R	72.0%	27.8%	72.1%	27.9%
57,343	GENESEE	22,312	16,003	6,274	35	9,729	R	71.7%	28.1%	71.8%	28.2%
47,232	GREENE	20,165	12,492	7,651	22	4,841	R	61.9%	37.9%	62.0%	38.0%
4,418	HAMILTON	2,882	2,051	831		1,220	R	71.2%	28.8%	71.2%	28.8%
61,360	HERKIMER	22,318	16,529	5,753	36	10,776	R	74.1%	25.8%	74.2%	25.8%
109,309	JEFFERSON	31,766	22,523	9,204	39	13,319	R	70.9%	29.0%	71.0%	29.0%
2,556,145	KINGS	566,517	163,430	402,114	973	238,684	D	28.8%	71.0%	28.9%	71.1%
26,255	LEWIS	10,655	8,580	2,068	7	6,512	R	80.5%	19.4%	80.6%	19.4%
62,962	LIVINGSTON	24,350	16,168	8,136	46	8,032	R	66.4%	33.4%	66.5%	33.5%
70,899	MADISON	26,265	15,972	10,192	101	5,780	R	60.8%	38.8%	61.0%	39.0%
742,374	MONROE	275,938	126,637	148,751	550	22,114	D	45.9%	53.9%	46.0%	54.0%
49,299	MONTGOMERY	15,924	10,858	5,028	38	5,830	R	68.2%	31.6%	68.3%	31.7%
1,358,613	NASSAU	518,640	286,147	232,036	457	54,111	R	55.2%	44.7%	55.2%	44.8%
1,629,734	NEW YORK	453,311	80,159	372,149	1,003	291,990	D	17.7%	82.1%	17.7%	82.3%
209,653	NIAGARA	76,424	46,627	29,669	128	16,958	R	61.0%	38.8%	61.1%	38.9%
228,726	ONEIDA	75,519	49,991	25,358	170	24,633	R	66.2%	33.6%	66.3%	33.7%
460,793	ONONDAGA	169,977	78,239	91,410	328	13,171	D	46.0%	53.8%	46.1%	53.9%
110,132	ONTARIO	46,228	25,979	20,166	83	5,813	R	56.2%	43.6%	56.3%	43.7%
385,834	ORANGE	124,142	69,558	54,386	198	15,172	R	56.0%	43.8%	56.1%	43.9%
40,309	ORLEANS	13,688	10,376	3,292	20	7,084	R	75.8%	24.1%	75.9%	24.1%
117,203	OSWEGO	40,281	27,094	13,115	72	13,979	R	67.3%	32.6%	67.4%	32.6%
59,549	OTSEGO	22,102	13,255	8,795	52	4,460	R	60.0%	39.8%	60.1%	39.9%
98,405	PUTNAM	41,350	24,898	16,413	39	8,485	R	60.2%	39.7%	60.3%	39.7%
2,251,771	QUEENS	438,286	160,279	277,280	727	117,001	D	36.6%	63.3%	36.6%	63.4%
158,904	RENSSELAER	62,405	33,749	28,521	135	5,228	R	54.1%	45.7%	54.2%	45.8%
477,025	RICHMOND	141,133	93,818	47,135	180	46,683	R	66.5%	33.4%	66.6%	33.4%
326,189	ROCKLAND	109,029	61,018	47,854	157	13,164	R	56.0%	43.9%	56.0%	44.0%
230,555	SARATOGA	104,173	55,824	48,183	166	7,641	R	53.6%	46.3%	53.7%	46.3%
155,578	SCHENECTADY	54,552	26,772	27,632	148	860	D	49.1%	50.7%	49.2%	50.8%
31,021	SCHOHARIE	12,860	8,910	3,923	27	4,987	R	69.3%	30.5%	69.4%	30.6%
17,846	SCHUYLER	7,778	5,092	2,661	25	2,431	R	65.5%	34.2%	65.7%	34.3%
34,064	SENECA	11,577	7,002	4,551	24	2,451	R	60.5%	39.3%	60.6%	39.4%
107,699	ST. LAWRENCE	34,320	22,687	11,591	42	11,096	R	66.1%	33.8%	66.2%	33.8%
95,301	STEUBEN	34,608	24,886	9,666	56	15,220	R	71.9%	27.9%	72.0%	28.0%
1,477,528	SUFFOLK	566,491	330,337	235,736	418	94,601	R	58.3%	41.6%	58.4%	41.6%
75,624	SULLIVAN	24,787	15,009	9,759	19	5,250	R	60.6%	39.4%	60.6%	39.4%
48,245	TIOGA	19,015	12,871	6,117	27	6,754	R	67.7%	32.2%	67.8%	32.2%
102,377	TOMPKINS	35,032	9,630	25,319	83	15,689	D	27.5%	72.3%	27.6%	72.4%
177,798	ULSTER	78,069	33,347	44,583	139	11,236	D	42.7%	57.1%	42.8%	57.2%
64,057	WARREN	28,183	15,761	12,373	49	3,388	R	55.9%	43.9%	56.0%	44.0%
61,254	WASHINGTON	22,130	14,155	7,946	29	6,209	R	64.0%	35.9%	64.0%	36.0%
89,892	WAYNE	33,694	22,823	10,814	57	12,009	R	67.7%	32.1%	67.9%	32.1%
968,247	WESTCHESTER	328,519	130,035	198,202	282	68,167	D	39.6%	60.3%	39.6%	60.4%

NEW YORK
GOVERNOR 2022

2020 Census Population	County	Total Vote	Republican (Zeldin)	Democratic (Hochul)	Other	RepDem. Plurality		Percentage			
								Total Vote		Major Vote	
								Rep.	Dem.	Rep.	Dem.
39,858	WYOMING	15,297	11,978	3,292	27	8,686	R	78.3%	21.5%	78.4%	21.6%
24,867	YATES	8,291	5,362	2,901	28	2,461	R	64.7%	35.0%	64.9%	35.1%
19,456,366	TOTAL	5,912,286	2,762,581	3,140,415	9,290	377,834	D	46.7%	53.1%	46.8%	53.2%

NEW YORK
SENATOR 2022

2020 Census Population	County	Total Vote	Republican (Pinion)	Democratic (Schumer)	Other	RepDem. Plurality		Percentage			
								Total Vote		Major Vote	
								Rep.	Dem.	Rep.	Dem.
305,817	ALBANY	116,197	42,719	72,875	603	30,156	D	36.8%	62.7%	37.0%	63.0%
46,118	ALLEGANY	15,667	11,277	4,306	84	6,971	R	72.0%	27.5%	72.4%	27.6%
1,414,324	BRONX	196,567	37,130	158,433	1,004	121,303	D	18.9%	80.6%	19.0%	81.0%
190,269	BROOME	67,753	34,688	32,587	478	2,101	R	51.2%	48.1%	51.6%	48.4%
76,112	CATTARAUGUS	25,740	16,938	8,677	125	8,261	R	65.8%	33.7%	66.1%	33.9%
76,524	CAYUGA	26,798	15,139	11,527	132	3,612	R	56.5%	43.0%	56.8%	43.2%
127,072	CHAUTAUQUA	43,202	26,217	16,782	203	9,435	R	60.7%	38.8%	61.0%	39.0%
83,466	CHEMUNG	27,569	16,907	10,500	162	6,407	R	61.3%	38.1%	61.7%	38.3%
47,229	CHENANGO	16,711	10,805	5,778	128	5,027	R	64.7%	34.6%	65.2%	34.8%
80,569	CLINTON	27,303	13,792	13,341	170	451	R	50.5%	48.9%	50.8%	49.2%
59,510	COLUMBIA	29,543	12,633	16,812	98	4,179	D	42.8%	56.9%	42.9%	57.1%
47,629	CORTLAND	16,065	8,485	7,469	111	1,016	R	52.8%	46.5%	53.2%	46.8%
44,120	DELAWARE	18,460	11,316	7,041	103	4,275	R	61.3%	38.1%	61.6%	38.4%
294,812	DUTCHESS	114,276	56,353	57,306	617	953	D	49.3%	50.1%	49.6%	50.4%
920,134	ERIE	339,720	148,585	188,979	2,156	40,394	D	43.7%	55.6%	44.0%	56.0%
36,913	ESSEX	15,259	7,654	7,514	91	140	R	50.2%	49.2%	50.5%	49.5%
50,088	FRANKLIN	15,046	8,071	6,885	90	1,186	R	53.6%	45.8%	54.0%	46.0%
53,413	FULTON	18,433	12,191	6,121	121	6,070	R	66.1%	33.2%	66.6%	33.4%
57,343	GENESEE	22,088	14,897	7,056	135	7,841	R	67.4%	31.9%	67.9%	32.1%
47,232	GREENE	19,861	11,711	8,026	124	3,685	R	59.0%	40.4%	59.3%	40.7%
4,418	HAMILTON	2,823	1,838	969	16	869	R	65.1%	34.3%	65.5%	34.5%
61,360	HERKIMER	22,163	15,042	6,999	122	8,043	R	67.9%	31.6%	68.2%	31.8%
109,309	JEFFERSON	31,443	19,667	11,618	158	8,049	R	62.5%	36.9%	62.9%	37.1%
2,556,145	KINGS	557,005	129,692	423,867	3,446	294,175	D	23.3%	76.1%	23.4%	76.6%
26,255	LEWIS	10,410	7,372	3,001	37	4,371	R	70.8%	28.8%	71.1%	28.9%
62,962	LIVINGSTON	24,158	14,958	9,029	171	5,929	R	61.9%	37.4%	62.4%	37.6%
70,899	MADISON	26,189	14,573	11,440	176	3,133	R	55.6%	43.7%	56.0%	44.0%
742,374	MONROE	275,160	117,075	156,529	1,556	39,454	D	42.5%	56.9%	42.8%	57.2%
49,299	MONTGOMERY	15,632	9,764	5,783	85	3,981	R	62.5%	37.0%	62.8%	37.2%
1,358,613	NASSAU	514,658	265,004	248,186	1,468	16,818	R	51.5%	48.2%	51.6%	48.4%
1,629,734	NEW YORK	451,594	65,366	383,518	2,710	318,152	D	14.5%	84.9%	14.6%	85.4%
209,653	NIAGARA	75,611	43,261	31,950	400	11,311	R	57.2%	42.3%	57.5%	42.5%
228,726	ONEIDA	74,823	44,899	29,494	430	15,405	R	60.0%	39.4%	60.4%	39.6%
460,793	ONONDAGA	169,565	69,374	99,205	986	29,831	D	40.9%	58.5%	41.2%	58.8%
110,132	ONTARIO	45,983	24,104	21,626	253	2,478	R	52.4%	47.0%	52.7%	47.3%
385,834	ORANGE	122,260	63,292	58,364	604	4,928	R	51.8%	47.7%	52.0%	48.0%
40,309	ORLEANS	13,472	9,609	3,788	75	5,821	R	71.3%	28.1%	71.7%	28.3%
117,203	OSWEGO	39,968	24,802	14,909	257	9,893	R	62.1%	37.3%	62.5%	37.5%
59,549	OTSEGO	21,826	12,042	9,623	161	2,419	R	55.2%	44.1%	55.6%	44.4%
98,405	PUTNAM	41,050	23,863	17,019	168	6,844	R	58.1%	41.5%	58.4%	41.6%

NEW YORK

SENATOR 2022

2020 Census Population	County	Total Vote	Republican (Pinion)	Democratic (Schumer)	Other	Rep.-Dem. Plurality	Percentage			
							Total Vote		Major Vote	
							Rep.	Dem.	Rep.	Dem.
2,251,771	QUEENS	432,588	137,805	291,905	2,878	154,100 D	31.9%	67.5%	32.1%	67.9%
158,904	RENSSELAER	61,907	30,662	30,809	436	147 D	49.5%	49.8%	49.9%	50.1%
477,025	RICHMOND	139,664	88,015	50,985	664	37,030 R	63.0%	36.5%	63.3%	36.7%
326,189	ROCKLAND	103,893	51,183	52,298	412	1,115 D	49.3%	50.3%	49.5%	50.5%
230,555	SARATOGA	103,297	52,030	50,718	549	1,312 R	50.4%	49.1%	50.6%	49.4%
155,578	SCHENECTADY	53,929	24,440	29,124	365	4,684 D	45.3%	54.0%	45.6%	54.4%
31,021	SCHOHARIE	12,740	8,254	4,385	101	3,869 R	64.8%	34.4%	65.3%	34.7%
17,846	SCHUYLER	7,688	4,759	2,883	46	1,876 R	61.9%	37.5%	62.3%	37.7%
34,064	SENECA	11,502	6,375	5,035	92	1,340 R	55.4%	43.8%	55.9%	44.1%
107,699	ST. LAWRENCE	33,952	19,389	14,351	212	5,038 R	57.1%	42.3%	57.5%	42.5%
95,301	STEUBEN	34,260	23,456	10,616	188	12,840 R	68.5%	31.0%	68.8%	31.2%
1,477,528	SUFFOLK	560,257	311,254	246,789	2,214	64,465 R	55.6%	44.0%	55.8%	44.2%
75,624	SULLIVAN	24,345	13,385	10,800	160	2,585 R	55.0%	44.4%	55.3%	44.7%
48,245	TIOGA	18,847	11,981	6,743	123	5,238 R	63.6%	35.8%	64.0%	36.0%
102,377	TOMPKINS	35,153	8,956	25,928	269	16,972 D	25.5%	73.8%	25.7%	74.3%
177,798	ULSTER	77,503	31,327	45,660	516	14,333 D	40.4%	58.9%	40.7%	59.3%
64,057	WARREN	27,898	14,452	13,263	183	1,189 R	51.8%	47.5%	52.1%	47.9%
61,254	WASHINGTON	21,899	12,987	8,773	139	4,214 R	59.3%	40.1%	59.7%	40.3%
89,892	WAYNE	33,467	21,320	11,983	164	9,337 R	63.7%	35.8%	64.0%	36.0%
968,247	WESTCHESTER	326,523	119,891	205,496	1,136	85,605 D	36.7%	62.9%	36.8%	63.2%
39,858	WYOMING	15,116	11,191	3,838	87	7,353 R	74.0%	25.4%	74.5%	25.5%
24,867	YATES	8,228	4,934	3,247	47	1,687 R	60.0%	39.5%	60.3%	39.7%
19,456,366	TOTAL	5,852,707	2,501,151	3,320,561	30,995	819,410 D	42.7%	56.7%	43.0%	57.0%

NEW YORK

HOUSE OF REPRESENTATIVES

CD	Year	Total Vote	Republican		Democratic		Other Vote	Rep.-Dem. Plurality	Percentage			
									Total Vote		Major Vote	
			Vote	Candidate	Vote	Candidate			Rep.	Dem.	Rep.	Dem.
1	2022	318,995	177,040	LALOTA, NICHOLAS J. "NICK"	141,907	FLEMING, BRIDGET M	48	35,133 R	55.5%	44.5%	55.5%	44.5%
1	2020	357,346	199,763	ZELDIN, LEE M.*	157,484	GOROFF, NANCY	99	42,279 R	55.9%	44.1%	55.9%	44.1%
1	2018	270,053	139,027	ZELDIN, LEE M.*	127,991	GERSHON, PERRY	3,035	11,036 R	51.5%	47.4%	52.1%	47.9%
1	2016	323,890	188,499	ZELDIN, LEE M.*	135,278	THRONE-HOLST, ANNA	113	53,221 R	58.2%	41.8%	58.2%	41.8%
1	2014	172,865	94,035	ZELDIN, LEE M.	78,722	BISHOP, TIMOTHY H.*	108	15,313 R	54.4%	45.5%	54.4%	45.6%
1	2012	278,659	132,304	ALTSCHULER, RANDY	146,179	BISHOP, TIMOTHY H.*	176	13,875 D	47.5%	52.5%	47.5%	52.5%
2	2022	249,032	151,178	GARBARINO, ANDREW*	97,774	GORDON, JACKIE	80	53,404 R	60.7%	39.3%	60.7%	39.3%
2	2020	335,012	177,353	GARBARINO, ANDREW	154,123	GORDON, JACKIE	3,536	23,230 R	52.9%	46.0%	53.5%	46.5%
2	2018	241,217	128,078	KING, PETER T.*	113,074	GRECHEN SHIRLEY, LIUBA	65	15,004 R	53.1%	46.9%	53.1%	46.9%
2	2016	292,595	181,506	KING, PETER T.*	110,938	GREGORY, DUWAYNE	151	70,568 R	62.0%	37.9%	62.1%	37.9%
2	2014	139,330	95,177	KING, PETER T.*	41,814	MAHER, PATRICIA M.	2,339	53,363 R	68.3%	30.0%	69.5%	30.5%
2	2012	242,943	142,309	KING, PETER T.*	100,545	FALCONE, VIVIANNE	89	41,764 R	58.6%	41.4%	58.6%	41.4%
3	2022	271,331	145,824	DEVOLDER-SANTOS, GEORGE ANTHONY	125,404	ZIMMERMAN, ROBERT P.	103	20,420 R	53.7%	46.2%	53.8%	46.2%
3	2020	372,612	161,907	DEVOLDER-SANTOS, GEORGE ANTHONY	208,412	SUOZZI, THOMAS R.*	2,293	46,505 D	43.5%	55.9%	43.7%	56.3%
3	2018	267,062	109,514	DEBONO, DAN	157,456	SUOZZI, THOMAS R.*	92	47,942 D	41.0%	59.0%	41.0%	59.0%
3	2016	324,254	152,304	MARTINS, JACK M.	171,775	SUOZZI, THOMAS R.	175	19,471 D	47.0%	53.0%	47.0%	53.0%
3	2014	164,375	74,269	LALLY, GRANT M.	90,032	ISRAEL, STEVE J.*	74	15,763 D	45.2%	54.8%	45.2%	54.8%
3	2012	273,171	113,203	LABATE, STEPHEN	157,880	ISRAEL, STEVE J.*	2,088	44,677 D	41.4%	57.8%	41.8%	58.2%
4	2022	271,560	140,622	D'ESPOSITO, ANTHONY P.	130,871	GILLEN, LAURA A.	67	9,751 R	51.8%	48.2%	51.8%	48.2%
4	2020	355,912	153,007	TUMAN, DOUGLAS	199,762	RICE, KATHLEEN M.*	3,143	46,755 D	43.0%	56.1%	43.4%	56.6%
4	2018	260,206	100,571	BENNO, AMEER	159,535	RICE, KATHLEEN M.*	100	58,964 D	38.7%	61.3%	38.7%	61.3%
4	2016	313,000	126,438	GURFEIN, DAVID	186,423	RICE, KATHLEEN M.*	139	59,985 D	40.4%	59.6%	40.4%	59.6%
4	2014	170,099	80,127	BLAKEMAN, BRUCE	89,793	RICE, KATHLEEN M.	179	9,666 D	47.1%	52.8%	47.2%	52.8%
4	2012	265,300	85,693	BECKER, FRANCIS X. JR.	163,955	MCCARTHY, CAROLYN*	15,652	78,262 D	32.3%	61.8%	34.3%	65.7%

NEW YORK
HOUSE OF REPRESENTATIVES

									Percentage			
			Republican		Democratic		Other	Rep.-Dem.	Total Vote		Major Vote	
CD	Year	Total Vote	Vote	Candidate	Vote	Candidate	Vote	Plurality	Rep.	Dem.	Rep.	Dem.
5	2022	138,987	34,407	KING, PAUL	104,396	MEEKS, GREGORY W.*	184	69,989 D	24.8%	75.1%	24.8%	75.2%
5	2020	230,679			229,125	MEEKS, GREGORY W.*	1,554	229,125 D		99.3%		100.0%
5	2018	161,471			160,500	MEEKS, GREGORY W.*	971	160,500 D		99.4%		100.0%
5	2016	233,853	30,312	O'REILLY, MICHAEL	199,815	MEEKS, GREGORY W.*	3,726	169,503 D	13.0%	85.4%	13.2%	86.8%
5	2014	79,821			75,712	MEEKS, GREGORY W.*	4,109	75,712 D		94.9%		100.0%
5	2012	187,141	17,875	JENNINGS, ALLAN JR.	167,836	MEEKS, GREGORY W.*	1,430	149,961 D	9.6%	89.7%	9.6%	90.4%
6	2022	133,114	47,935	ZMICH, THOMAS	85,049	MENG, GRACE*	130	37,114 D	36.0%	63.9%	36.0%	64.0%
6	2020	233,914	74,829	ZMICH, THOMAS	158,862	MENG, GRACE*	223	84,033 D	32.0%	67.9%	32.0%	68.0%
6	2018	123,421			111,646	MENG, GRACE*	11,775	111,646 D		90.5%		100.0%
6	2016	189,433	50,617	MAIO, DANNIEL	136,506	MENG, GRACE*	2,310	85,889 D	26.7%	72.1%	27.1%	72.9%
6	2014	55,963			55,368	MENG, GRACE*	595	55,368 D		98.9%		100.0%
6	2012	164,374	50,846	HALLORAN, DANIEL	111,501	MENG, GRACE	2,027	60,655 D	30.9%	67.8%	31.3%	68.7%
7	2022	148,304	28,597	PAGAN, JUAN	119,473	VELAZQUEZ, NYDIA*	234	90,876 D	19.3%	80.6%	19.3%	80.7%
7	2020	225,453	32,520	KELLY, BRIAN	191,073	VELAZQUEZ, NYDIA*	1,860	158,553 D	14.4%	84.8%	14.5%	85.5%
7	2018	157,302			146,687	VELAZQUEZ, NYDIA*	10,615	146,687 D		93.3%		100.0%
7	2016	189,890	17,478	ROMAGUERA, ALLAN E.	172,146	VELAZQUEZ, NYDIA*	266	154,668 D	9.2%	90.7%	9.2%	90.8%
7	2014	63,812	5,713	FERNANDEZ, JOSE LUIS	56,593	VELAZQUEZ, NYDIA*	1,506	50,880 D	9.0%	88.7%	9.2%	90.8%
7	2012	152,111			143,930	VELAZQUEZ, NYDIA*	8,181	143,930 D		94.6%		100.0%
8	2022	138,330	39,060	DASHEVSKY, YURI	99,079	JEFFRIES, HAKEEM*	191	60,019 D	28.2%	71.6%	28.3%	71.7%
8	2020	277,169	42,007	WALLACE, GARFIELD	234,933	JEFFRIES, HAKEEM*	229	192,926 D	15.2%	84.8%	15.2%	84.8%
8	2018	191,567			180,376	JEFFRIES, HAKEEM*	11,191	180,376 D		94.2%		100.0%
8	2016	230,203			214,595	JEFFRIES, HAKEEM*	15,608	214,595 D		93.2%		100.0%
8	2014	83,999			77,255	JEFFRIES, HAKEEM*	6,744	77,255 D		92.0%		100.0%
8	2012	204,207	17,650	BELLONE, ALAN	184,039	JEFFRIES, HAKEEM	2,518	166,389 D	8.6%	90.1%	8.8%	91.2%
9	2022	143,853			116,970	CLARKE, YVETTE D.*	26,883	116,970 D		81.3%		100.0%
9	2020	277,248	43,950	JEAN-PIERRE, CONSTANTIN	230,221	CLARKE, YVETTE D.*	3,077	186,271 D	15.9%	83.0%	16.0%	84.0%
9	2018	203,423	20,901	GAYOT, LUTCHI	181,455	CLARKE, YVETTE D.*	1,067	160,554 D	10.3%	89.2%	10.3%	89.7%
9	2016	232,094			214,189	CLARKE, YVETTE D.*	17,905	214,189 D		92.3%		100.0%
9	2014	92,569			82,659	CLARKE, YVETTE D.*	9,910	82,659 D		89.3%		100.0%
9	2012	213,431	24,164	CAVANAGH, DANIEL	186,141	CLARKE, YVETTE D.*	3,126	161,977 D	11.3%	87.2%	11.5%	88.5%
10	2022	192,347	29,058	HAMDAN, BENINE	160,582	GOLDMAN, DANIEL	2,707	131,524 D	15.1%	83.5%	15.3%	84.7%
10	2020	276,976	66,889	BERNSTEIN, CATHY	206,310	NADLER, JERROLD*	3,777	139,421 D	24.1%	74.5%	24.5%	75.5%
10	2018	210,958	37,619	LEVIN, NAOMI	173,095	NADLER, JERROLD*	244	135,476 D	17.8%	82.1%	17.9%	82.1%
10	2016	246,525	53,857	ROSENTHAL, PHILIP	192,371	NADLER, JERROLD*	297	138,514 D	21.8%	78.0%	21.9%	78.1%
10	2014	101,881			89,080	NADLER, JERROLD*	12,801	89,080 D		87.4%		100.0%
10	2012	205,349	39,413	CHAN, MICHAEL	165,743	NADLER, JERROLD*	193	126,330 D	19.2%	80.7%	19.2%	80.8%
11	2022	188,099	115,992	MALLIOTAKIS, NICOLE*	71,801	ROSE, MAX	306	44,191 R	61.7%	38.2%	61.8%	38.2%
11	2020	293,314	155,608	MALLIOTAKIS, NICOLE	137,198	ROSE, MAX*	508	18,410 R	53.1%	46.8%	53.1%	46.9%
11	2018	192,173	89,441	DONOVAN, DANIEL M. JR.*	101,823	ROSE, MAX	909	12,382 D	46.5%	53.0%	46.8%	53.2%
11	2016	232,317	142,934	DONOVAN, DANIEL M. JR.*	85,257	REICHARD, RICHARD	4,126	57,677 R	61.5%	36.7%	62.6%	37.4%
11	2014	107,363	58,886	GRIMM, MICHAEL G.*	45,244	RECCHIA JR., DOMENIC M.	3,233	13,642 R	54.8%	42.1%	56.6%	43.4%
11	2012	197,635	103,118	GRIMM, MICHAEL G.*	92,430	MURPHY, MARK	2,087	10,688 R	52.2%	46.8%	52.7%	47.3%
12	2022	246,105	44,173	ZUMBLUSKAS, MICHAEL K.	200,890	NADLER, JERROLD*	1,042	156,717 D	17.9%	81.6%	18.0%	82.0%
12	2020	323,021	53,061	SANTIAGO-CANO, CARLOS	265,172	MALONEY, CAROLYN B.*	4,788	212,111 D	16.4%	82.1%	16.7%	83.3%
12	2018	251,877	30,446	RABIN, ELIOT	217,430	MALONEY, CAROLYN B.*	4,001	186,984 D	12.1%	86.3%	12.3%	87.7%
12	2016	294,071	49,399	ARDINI, ROBERT	244,358	MALONEY, CAROLYN B.*	314	194,959 D	16.8%	83.1%	16.8%	83.2%
12	2014	113,429	22,731	DI IORIO, NICHOLAS S. "NICK"	90,603	MALONEY, CAROLYN B.*	95	67,872 D	20.0%	79.9%	20.1%	79.9%
12	2012	241,426	46,841	WIGHT, CHRISTOPHER	194,370	MALONEY, CAROLYN B.*	215	147,529 D	19.4%	80.5%	19.4%	80.6%
13	2022	117,846			116,589	ESPAILLAT, ADRIANO*	1,257	116,589 D		98.9%		100.0%
13	2020	255,370	19,829	GWINN, LOVELYNN	231,841	ESPAILLAT, ADRIANO*	3,700	212,012 D	7.8%	90.8%	7.9%	92.1%
13	2018	190,688	10,268	BUTLER, JINEEA	180,035	ESPAILLAT, ADRIANO*	385	169,767 D	5.4%	94.4%	5.4%	94.6%
13	2016	233,737	16,089	EVANS, TONY	207,194	ESPAILLAT, ADRIANO	10,454	191,105 D	6.9%	88.6%	7.2%	92.8%
13	2014	78,353			68,396	RANGEL, CHARLES B.*	9,957	68,396 D		87.3%		100.0%
13	2012	192,913	12,147	SCHLEY, CRAIG	175,016	RANGEL, CHARLES B.*	5,750	162,869 D	6.3%	90.7%	6.5%	93.5%
14	2022	116,790	31,935	FORTE, TINA	82,453	OCASIO-CORTEZ, ALEXANDRIA*	2,402	50,518 D	27.3%	70.6%	27.9%	72.1%
14	2020	213,323	58,440	CUMMINGS, JOHN C.	152,661	OCASIO-CORTEZ, ALEXANDRIA*	2,222	94,221 D	27.4%	71.6%	27.7%	72.3%
14	2018	141,204	19,202	PAPPAS, ANTHONY	110,318	OCASIO-CORTEZ, ALEXANDRIA	11,684	91,116 D	13.6%	78.1%	14.8%	85.2%
14	2016	178,323	30,545	SPOTORNO, FRANK	147,587	CROWLEY, JOSEPH*	191	117,042 D	17.1%	82.8%	17.1%	82.9%
14	2014	57,204			50,352	CROWLEY, JOSEPH*	6,852	50,352 D		88.0%		100.0%
14	2012	145,190	21,755	GIBBONS, WILLIAM JR.	120,761	CROWLEY, JOSEPH*	2,674	99,006 D	15.0%	83.2%	15.3%	84.7%

NEW YORK

HOUSE OF REPRESENTATIVES

CD	Year	Total Vote	Republican Vote	Republican Candidate	Democratic Vote	Democratic Candidate	Other Vote	Rep.-Dem. Plurality	Total Vote Rep.	Total Vote Dem.	Major Vote Rep.	Major Vote Dem.
15	2022	92,390	15,882	SAPASKIS, STYLO ADONIS	76,406	TORRES, RITCHIE JOHN*	102	60,524 D	17.2%	82.7%	17.2%	82.8%
15	2020	191,037	21,221	DELICES, PATRICK	169,533	TORRES, RITCHIE JOHN	283	148,312 D	11.1%	88.7%	11.1%	88.9%
15	2018	129,751	5,205	GONZALEZ, JASON	124,469	SERRANO, JOSE E.*	77	119,264 D	4.0%	95.9%	4.0%	96.0%
15	2016	174,036	6,129	VEGA, ALEJANDRO	165,688	SERRANO, JOSE E.*	2,219	159,559 D	3.5%	95.2%	3.6%	96.4%
15	2014	56,563			54,906	SERRANO, JOSE E.*	1,657	54,906 D		97.1%		100.0%
15	2012	157,115	4,427	DELLA VALLE, FRANK	152,661	SERRANO, JOSE E.*	27	148,234 D	2.8%	97.2%	2.8%	97.2%
16	2022	207,928	74,156	FLISSER, MIRIAM L.	133,567	BOWMAN, JAMAAL*	205	59,411 D	35.7%	64.2%	35.7%	64.3%
16	2020	259,970			218,471	BOWMAN, JAMAAL	41,499	218,471 D		84.0%		100.0%
16	2018	183,356			182,044	ENGEL, ELIOT L.*	1,312	182,044 D		99.3%		100.0%
16	2016	222,230			209,857	ENGEL, ELIOT L.*	12,373	209,857 D		94.4%		100.0%
16	2014	100,391			99,658	ENGEL, ELIOT L.*	733	99,658 D		99.3%		100.0%
16	2012	236,553	53,935	MCLAUGHLIN, JOSEPH	179,562	ENGEL, ELIOT L.*	3,056	125,627 D	22.8%	75.9%	23.1%	76.9%
17	2022	285,430	143,550	LAWLER, MICHAEL V.	141,730	MALONEY, SEAN*	150	1,820 R	50.3%	49.7%	50.3%	49.7%
17	2020	332,852	117,307	MCARDLE-SCHULMAN, MAUREEN B.	197,353	JONES, MONDAIRE	18,192	80,046 D	35.2%	59.3%	37.3%	62.7%
17	2018	193,841			170,168	LOWEY, NITA M.*	23,673	170,168 D		87.8%		100.0%
17	2016	216,585			214,530	LOWEY, NITA M.*	2,055	214,530 D		99.1%		100.0%
17	2014	174,054	75,781	DAY, CHRIS	98,150	LOWEY, NITA M.*	123	22,369 D	43.5%	56.4%	43.6%	56.4%
17	2012	266,205	91,899	CARVIN, JOE	171,417	LOWEY, NITA M.*	2,889	79,518 D	34.5%	64.4%	34.9%	65.1%
18	2022	267,053	131,653	SCHMITT, COLIN J.	135,245	RYAN, PATRICK*	155	3,592 D	49.3%	50.6%	49.3%	50.7%
18	2020	335,545	145,098	FARLEY, CHELE C.	187,169	MALONEY, SEAN*	3,278	42,071 D	43.2%	55.8%	43.7%	56.3%
18	2018	251,690	112,035	O'DONNELL, JAMES	139,564	MALONEY, SEAN*	91	27,529 D	44.5%	55.5%	44.5%	55.5%
18	2016	291,527	129,369	OLIVA, PHIL	162,060	MALONEY, SEAN*	98	32,691 D	44.4%	55.6%	44.4%	55.6%
18	2014	179,091	85,660	HAYWORTH, NAN	88,993	MALONEY, SEAN*	4,438	3,333 D	47.8%	49.7%	49.0%	51.0%
18	2012	277,063	133,049	HAYWORTH, NAN*	143,845	MALONEY, SEAN	169	10,796 D	48.0%	51.9%	48.1%	51.9%
19	2022	287,618	146,004	MOLINARO, MARCUS	141,509	RILEY, JOSH	105	4,495 R	50.8%	49.2%	50.8%	49.2%
19	2020	352,771	151,475	VAN DE WATER, KYLE	192,100	DELGADO, ANTONIO*	9,196	40,625 D	42.9%	54.5%	44.1%	55.9%
19	2018	287,986	132,873	FASO, JOHN*	147,873	DELGADO, ANTONIO	7,240	15,000 D	46.1%	51.3%	47.3%	52.7%
19	2016	307,614	166,171	FASO, JOHN	141,224	TEACHOUT, ZEPHYR	219	24,947 R	54.0%	45.9%	54.1%	45.9%
19	2014	204,173	131,594	GIBSON, CHRISTOPHER P.*	72,470	ELDRIDGE, SEAN	109	59,124 R	64.5%	35.5%	64.5%	35.5%
19	2012	284,679	150,245	GIBSON, CHRISTOPHER P.*	134,295	SCHREIBMAN, JULIAN	139	15,950 R	52.8%	47.2%	52.8%	47.2%
20	2022	291,433	130,869	JOY, ELIZABETH L.	160,420	TONKO, PAUL D.*	144	29,551 D	44.9%	55.0%	44.9%	55.1%
20	2020	359,342	139,446	JOY, ELIZABETH L.	219,705	TONKO, PAUL D.*	191	80,259 D	38.8%	61.1%	38.8%	61.2%
20	2018	266,014	89,058	VITOLLO, FRANCIS JOSEPH	176,811	TONKO, PAUL D.*	145	87,753 D	33.5%	66.5%	33.5%	66.5%
20	2016	313,939	100,740	VITOLLO, FRANCIS JOSEPH	213,018	TONKO, PAUL D.*	181	112,278 D	32.1%	67.9%	32.1%	67.9%
20	2014	204,329	79,104	FISCHER, JIM	125,111	TONKO, PAUL D.*	114	46,007 D	38.7%	61.2%	38.7%	61.3%
20	2012	297,314	93,778	DIETERICH, ROBERT	203,401	TONKO, PAUL D.*	135	109,623 D	31.5%	68.4%	31.6%	68.4%
21	2022	285,095	168,579	STEFANIK, ELISE*	116,421	CASTELLI, MATT	95	52,158 R	59.1%	40.8%	59.2%	40.8%
21	2020	320,779	188,649	STEFANIK, ELISE*	131,992	COBB, TEDRA LYNN	138	56,657 R	58.8%	41.1%	58.8%	41.2%
21	2018	235,267	131,981	STEFANIK, ELISE*	99,791	COBB, TEDRA LYNN	3,495	32,190 R	56.1%	42.4%	56.9%	43.1%
21	2016	272,606	177,886	STEFANIK, ELISE*	82,161	DERRICK, MIKE	12,559	95,725 R	65.3%	30.1%	68.4%	31.6%
21	2014	174,668	96,226	STEFANIK, ELISE	59,063	WOOLF, AARON	19,379	37,163 R	55.1%	33.8%	62.0%	38.0%
21	2012	252,556	121,646	DOHENY, MATTHEW A.	126,631	OWENS, WILLIAM L. "BILL"*	4,279	4,985 D	48.2%	50.1%	49.0%	51.0%
22	2022	268,608	135,544	WILLIAMS, BRANDON M.	132,913	CONOLE, FRANCIS	151	2,631 R	50.5%	49.5%	50.5%	49.5%
22	2020	319,638	156,098	TENNEY, CLAUDIA	155,989	BRINDISI, ANTHONY*	7,551	109 R	48.8%	48.8%	50.0%	50.0%
22	2018	251,212	123,242	TENNEY, CLAUDIA*	127,715	BRINDISI, ANTHONY	255	4,473 D	49.1%	50.8%	49.1%	50.9%
22	2016	278,531	129,444	TENNEY, CLAUDIA	114,266	MYERS, KIM	34,821	15,178 R	46.5%	41.0%	53.1%	46.9%
22	2014	131,932	129,851	HANNA, RICHARD L.*			2,081	129,851 R	98.4%		100.0%	
22	2012	260,863	157,941	HANNA, RICHARD L.*	102,080	LAMB, DAN	842	55,861 R	60.5%	39.1%	60.7%	39.3%
23	2022	297,041	192,694	LANGWORTHY, NICK	104,114	DELLA PIA, MAX H.	233	88,580 R	64.9%	35.1%	64.9%	35.1%
23	2020	313,842	181,060	REED, THOMAS W. II*	129,014	MITRANO, TRACY	3,768	52,046 R	57.7%	41.1%	58.4%	41.6%
23	2018	240,374	130,323	REED, THOMAS W. II*	109,932	MITRANO, TRACY	119	20,391 R	54.2%	45.7%	54.2%	45.8%
23	2016	279,735	161,050	REED, THOMAS W. II*	118,584	PLUMB, JOHN	101	42,466 R	57.6%	42.4%	57.6%	42.4%
23	2014	183,481	113,130	REED, THOMAS W. II*	70,242	ROBERTSON, MARTHA	109	42,888 R	61.7%	38.3%	61.7%	38.3%
23	2012	265,282	137,669	REED, THOMAS W. II*	127,535	SHINAGAWA, NATE	78	10,134 R	51.9%	48.1%	51.9%	48.1%
24	2022	277,253	182,054	TENNEY, CLAUDIA*	95,028	HOLDEN, STEVEN	171	87,026 R	65.7%	34.3%	65.7%	34.3%
24	2020	343,624	182,567	KATKO, JOHN M.*	147,638	BALTER, DANA	13,419	34,929 R	53.1%	43.0%	55.3%	44.7%
24	2018	260,477	136,920	KATKO, JOHN M.*	123,226	BALTER, DANA	331	13,694 R	52.6%	47.3%	52.6%	47.4%
24	2016	302,115	182,761	KATKO, JOHN M.*	119,040	DEACON, COLLEEN	314	63,721 R	60.5%	39.4%	60.6%	39.4%
24	2014	199,222	118,474	KATKO, JOHN M.	80,304	MAFFEI, DANIEL B.*	444	38,170 R	59.5%	40.3%	59.6%	40.4%
24	2012	292,988	127,054	BUERKLE, ANN MARIE*	143,044	MAFFEI, DANIEL B.	22,890	15,990 D	43.4%	48.8%	47.0%	53.0%

NEW YORK
HOUSE OF REPRESENTATIVES

			Republican		Democratic		Other Vote	Rep.-Dem. Plurality	Percentage			
									Total Vote		Major Vote	
CD	Year	Total Vote	Vote	Candidate	Vote	Candidate			Rep.	Dem.	Rep.	Dem.
25	2022	282,344	130,190	SINGLETARY, LA'RON DSMOND	152,022	MORELLE, JOSEPH D.*	132	21,832 D	46.1%	53.8%	46.1%	53.9%
25	2020	348,098	136,198	MITRIS, GEORGE	206,396	MORELLE, JOSEPH D.*	5,504	70,198 D	39.1%	59.3%	39.8%	60.2%
25	2018	270,120	110,736	MAXWELL, JIM	159,244	MORELLE, JOSEPH D.	140	48,508 D	41.0%	59.0%	41.0%	59.0%
25	2016	325,831	142,650	ASSINI, MARK W.	182,950	SLAUGHTER, LOUISE M.*	231	40,300 D	43.8%	56.1%	43.8%	56.2%
25	2014	192,971	95,932	ASSINI, MARK W.	96,803	SLAUGHTER, LOUISE M.*	236	871 D	49.7%	50.2%	49.8%	50.2%
25	2012	313,452	133,389	BROOKS, MAGGIE	179,810	SLAUGHTER, LOUISE M.*	253	46,421 D	42.6%	57.4%	42.6%	57.4%
26	2022	245,371	88,339	SAMS, STEVEN L. II	156,883	HIGGINS, BRIAN M.*	149	68,544 D	36.0%	63.9%	36.0%	64.0%
26	2020	319,835	91,687	DONOVAN, RICKY THOMAS	223,276	HIGGINS, BRIAN M.*	4,872	131,589 D	28.7%	69.8%	29.1%	70.9%
26	2018	230,663	61,488	ZENO, RENEE MARIE	169,166	HIGGINS, BRIAN M.*	9	107,678 D	26.7%	73.3%	26.7%	73.3%
26	2016	288,679	73,377	SCHRATZ, SHELLY	215,289	HIGGINS, BRIAN M.*	13	141,912 D	25.4%	74.6%	25.4%	74.6%
26	2014	166,124	52,909	WEPPNER, KATHLEEN "KATHY"	113,210	HIGGINS, BRIAN M.*	5	60,301 D	31.8%	68.1%	31.9%	68.1%
26	2012	284,271	71,666	MADIGAN, MICHAEL H.	212,588	HIGGINS, BRIAN M.*	17	140,922 D	25.2%	74.8%	25.2%	74.8%
27	2020	383,608	229,044	JACOBS, CHRISTOPHER*	149,559	MCMURRAY, NATHAN D.	5,005	79,485 R	59.7%	39.0%	60.5%	39.5%
27	2018	285,300	140,146	COLLINS, CHRIS*	139,059	MCMURRAY, NATHAN D.	6,095	1,087 R	49.1%	48.7%	50.2%	49.8%
27	2016	328,809	220,885	COLLINS, CHRIS*	107,832	KASTENBAUM, DIANA	92	113,053 R	67.2%	32.8%	67.2%	32.8%
27	2014	203,645	144,675	COLLINS, CHRIS*	58,911	O'DONNELL, JIM	59	85,764 R	71.0%	28.9%	71.1%	28.9%
27	2012	317,534	161,220	COLLINS, CHRIS	156,219	HOCHUL, KATHY COURTNEY*	95	5,001 R	50.8%	49.2%	50.8%	49.2%
TOTAL	2022	5,762,257	2,525,335		3,199,496		37,426	674,161 D	43.8%	55.5%	44.1%	55.9%
TOTAL	2020	8,208,290	2,979,013		5,085,372		143,905	2,106,359 D	36.3%	62.0%	36.9%	63.1%
TOTAL	2018	5,948,673	1,859,074		3,990,483		99,116	2,131,409 D	31.3%	67.1%	31.8%	68.2%
TOTAL	2016	7,116,422	2,530,440		4,464,931		121,051	1,934,491 D	35.6%	62.7%	36.2%	63.8%
TOTAL	2014	3,651,707	1,554,274		2,009,444		87,989	455,170 D	42.6%	55.0%	43.6%	56.4%
TOTAL	2012	6,469,725	2,245,236		4,143,414		81,075	1,898,178 D	34.7%	64.0%	35.1%	64.9%

Note: An asterisk (*) denotes incumbent.

NEW YORK

GENERAL AND PRIMARY ELECTIONS

GENERAL ELECTIONS: OTHER VOTES

Governor	Other vote was 9,290 Write-In (Scattered Write-Ins)
Senate	Other vote was 26,844 LaRouche (Diane Sare), 4,151 Write-In (Scattered Write-Ins)
House	Other vote was:
CD 1	48 Write-In (Scattered Write-Ins)
CD 2	80 Write-In (Scattered Write-Ins)
CD 3	103 Write-In (Scattered Write-Ins)
CD 4	67 Write-In (Scattered Write-Ins)
CD 5	184 Write-In (Scattered Write-Ins)
CD 6	130 Write-In (Scattered Write-Ins)
CD 7	234 Write-In (Scattered Write-Ins)
CD 8	191 Write-In (Scattered Write-Ins)
CD 9	26,521 Conservative (Menachem Raitport), 362 Write-In (Scattered Write-Ins)
CD 10	1,260 Write-In (Scattered Write-Ins)
CD 11	306 Write-In (Scattered Write-Ins)
CD 12	631 Independent (Michael Itkis), 411 Write-In (Scattered Write-Ins)
CD 13	1,257 Write-In (Scattered Write-Ins)
CD 14	2,208 Conservative (Desi Cuellar), 194 Write-In (Scattered Write-Ins)
CD 15	102 Write-In (Scattered Write-Ins)
CD 16	205 Write-In (Scattered Write-Ins)
CD 17	150 Write-In (Scattered Write-Ins)
CD 18	155 Write-In (Scattered Write-Ins)
CD 19	105 Write-In (Scattered Write-Ins)
CD 20	144 Write-In (Scattered Write-Ins)
CD 21	95 Write-In (Scattered Write-Ins)
CD 22	151 Write-In (Scattered Write-Ins)
CD 23	233 Write-In (Scattered Write-Ins)
CD 24	171 Write-In (Scattered Write-Ins)
CD 25	132 Write-In (Scattered Write-Ins)
CD 26	149 Write-In (Scattered Write-Ins)

2022 PRIMARY ELECTIONS: SUPPLEMENTARY INFORMATION

Primary	June 28, 2022	**Registration** (as of February 21, 2022 – includes 1,076,933 inactive registrants)		12,982,819	Democratic Republican Conservative Working Families Other Parties Unaffiliated	6,472,096 2,848,894 162,988 49,253 464,688 2,984,900

Primary Type Closed—Only registered Democrats and Republicans could vote in their party's primary.

	REPUBLICAN PRIMARIES			DEMOCRATIC PRIMARIES		
Senator	Pinion, Joe	Unopposed		Schumer, Charles E.*	Unopposed	
Governor	Zeldin, Lee M.	196,874	43.4%	Hochul, Kathy Courtney	607,928	67.4%
	Giuliani, Andrew	103,267	22.8%	Williams, Jumaane D.	173,872	19.3%
	Astorino, Rob	84,464	18.6%	Suozzi, Thomas R.	116,972	13.0%
	Wilson, Harry	66,736	14.7%	Scattered Write-Ins (Write-In)	3,730	0.4%
	Scattered Write-Ins (Write-In)	2,261	0.5%			
	TOTAL	453,602		TOTAL	902,502	

NEW YORK

GENERAL AND PRIMARY ELECTIONS

	REPUBLICAN PRIMARIES			DEMOCRATIC PRIMARIES		
Congressional District 1						
Congressional District 2	Garbarino, Andrew* Cornicelli, Robert Rakebrandt, Mike Scattered Write-Ins (Write-In) TOTAL	9,902 7,250 1,622 70 18,844	52.5% 38.5% 8.6% 0.4%			
Congressional District 3				Zimmerman, Robert P. Kaiman, Jon Lafazan, Joshua Alexander D'Arrigo, Melanie Rasool, Reema Scattered Write-Ins (Write-In) TOTAL	10,074 7,242 5,554 4,519 738 51 28,178	35.8% 25.7% 19.7% 16.0% 2.6% 0.2%
Congressional District 4						
Congressional District 5						
Congressional District 6						
Congressional District 7						
Congressional District 8						
Congressional District 9						
Congressional District 10						
Congressional District 11						
Congressional District 12						
Congressional District 13						
Congressional District 14						
Congressional District 15						
Congressional District 16				Bowman, Jamaal* Gashi, Vedat Parker, Catherine F. Jaffe, Mark Scattered Write-Ins TOTAL	21,643 10,009 7,503 608 36 39,799	54.4% 25.1% 18.9% 1.5% 0.1%

NEW YORK

GENERAL AND PRIMARY ELECTIONS

	REPUBLICAN PRIMARIES			DEMOCRATIC PRIMARIES		
Congressional District 17	Lawler, Michael V.	12,317	74.7%	Maloney, Sean*	24,535	66.3%
	Faulkner, William G.	1,958	11.9%	Biaggi, Alessandra	12,266	33.1%
	Falciglia, Charles J.	1,392	8.4%	Scattered Write-Ins	203	0.5%
	David, Shoshana M.	491	3.0%			
	Schrepel, Jack W.	188	1.1%			
	Scattered Write-Ins	139	0.8%			
	TOTAL	16,485		TOTAL	37,004	
Congressional District 18				Ryan, Patrick*	30,093	83.8%
				Mills, Aisha	4,730	13.2%
				Mugulusi, Moses R.	993	2.8%
				Scattered Write-Ins	108	0.3%
				TOTAL	35,924	
Congressional District 19				Riley, Josh	31,193	62.3%
				Cheney, Jamie	18,625	37.2%
				Scattered Write-Ins	229	0.5%
				TOTAL	50,047	
Congressional District 20				Tonko, Paul D.*	18,251	88.1%
				Rar, Rostislav	2,422	11.7%
				Scattered Write-Ins	54	0.3%
				TOTAL	20,727	
Congressional District 21				Castelli, Matt	19,319	80.8%
				Putori, Matt	4,528	18.9%
				Scattered Write-Ins	52	0.2%
				TOTAL	23,899	
Congressional District 22	Williams, Brandon M.	14,351	57.4%	Conole, Francis	10,971	39.5%
	Wells, Steven M.	10,501	42.0%	Klee Hood, Sarah	9,790	35.2%
	Scattered Write-Ins	141	0.6%	Roberts, Sam	3,662	13.2%
				Majok, Chol	3,315	11.9%
				Scattered Write-Ins	58	0.2%
	TOTAL	24,993		TOTAL	27,796	
Congressional District 23	Langworthy, Nick	24,450	51.3%			
	Paladino, Carl	22,603	47.5%			
	Scattered Write-Ins	570	1.2%			
	TOTAL	47,623				
Congressional District 24	Tenney, Claudia	17,630	53.7%			
	Fratto, Mario	13,150	40.0%			
	Phillips, George K.	1,967	6.0%			
	Scattered Write-Ins	105	0.3%			
	TOTAL	32,852				
Congressional District 25						
Congressional District 26				Higgins, Brian M.*	28,485	90.9%
				Egriu, Emin Eddie	2,731	8.7%
				Scattered Write-Ins	109	0.3%
				TOTAL	31,325	

Note: An asterisk (*) denotes incumbent.

NORTH CAROLINA

Statewide Races

With no gubernatorial contest, the 2022 Senate race in North Carolina ended just like most Senate races there have ended over the last several cycles: Republicans narrowly prevailed.

The early Republican frontrunner to replace retiring GOP Sen. Richard Burr was former Gov. Pat McCrory. But Donald Trump endorsed Rep. Ted Budd, who made electability an issue – in 2016, as Trump carried the state by four points, McCrory was narrowly ousted. Budd's stock rose, and he carried 99 of 100 counties, only barely missing Charlotte's Mecklenburg, where McCrory had served 14 years as mayor. After nominating, and losing with, a white man in 2020's Senate contest, Democrats wanted to try something new. They chose Cheri Beasley, a Black woman who led the state Supreme Court until her 2020 defeat. Though she lost that year, she received more raw votes than Joe Biden.

Though several Trump-endorsed candidates in competitive states flopped in 2022, Budd won by just over three points. Aside from rural whites making up a greater portion of the electorate, Budd was helped by a low minority turnout – somewhat ironic, considering why Democrats recruited Beasley. Beasley came within half a point of losing the redrawn 1st District, a rural northeastern district that is over 40% Black by composition. In 2020, Cal Cunningham, the Democratic nominee for Senate, would have carried the 2022 version of NC-1 by nearly nine points. Still, Democrats may consider investing more in western North Carolina. Eight of the top ten counties where Beasley most outperformed Biden were west of Charlotte, one of which was Asheville's Buncombe.

House Races

While it is most famous for basketball and barbeque, North Carolina is also known for its redistricting wars. Since 2010, it has had five House maps in place – and it is slated to get another for 2024. Without veto power over redistricting bills, Gov. Roy Cooper (D) couldn't stop his Republican legislature from passing a map. When Republicans drew a new 14-seat plan (the state gained a seat in the census), Democrats were only clear favorites in three districts. After litigation, the state Supreme Court, which had a liberal majority, drafted a new plan. Importantly, though, the court plan would only be in place for one election cycle – in 2022, control of the high court also flipped to Republicans.

On the court map, Biden and Trump would have carried seven districts apiece – and the 2022 House results ended up reflecting that split. The new 14th District appeared in the Charlotte area, and it went to the telegenic state Sen. Jeff Jackson (D). In the northeast, as NC-1 was about evenly split in the Senate race, Democratic state Sen. Don Davis won by an impressive five points. The closest district was the 13th, south of Raleigh. Democratic state Sen. Wiley Nickel beat a flawed Republican by a few points. In western North Carolina, state Sen. Chuck Edwards (R), a challenger who got a rare amount of institutional support, defeated the scandal-plagued first-term Rep. Madison Cawthorn in the primary. Cawthown may have put the 11th District seat at risk in the general election, but Edwards won by nine points.

NORTH CAROLINA

Congressional districts first established for elections held in 2022
14 members

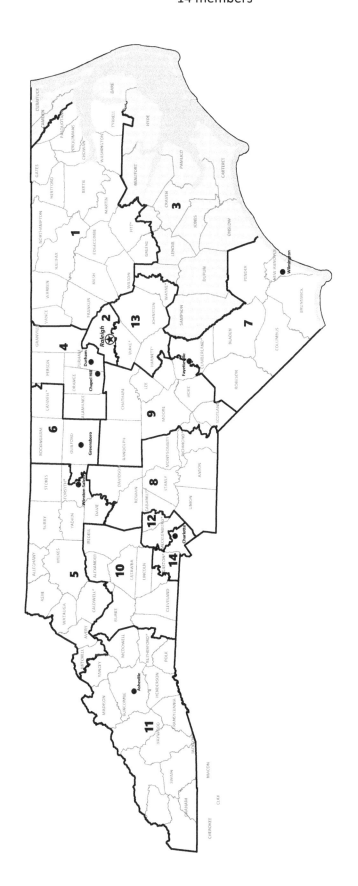

NORTH CAROLINA

GOVERNOR
Roy Cooper (D). Reelected 2020 to a four-year term. Previously elected 2016.

SENATORS (2 Republicans)
Ted Budd (R). Elected 2022 to a six-year term.

Thom Tillis (R). Reelected 2020 to a six-year term. Previously elected 2014.

REPRESENTATIVES (7 Republicans, 7 Democrats)
1. Donald Davis (D)
2. Deborah Ross (D)
3. Greg Murphy (R)
4. Valerie Foushee (D)
5. Virginia Ann Foxx (R)
6. Kathy Manning (D)
7. David Rouzer (R)
8. Dan Bishop (R)
9. Richard Hudson (R)
10. Patrick T. McHenry (R)
11. Chuck Edwards (R)
12. Alma S. Adams (D)
13. Wiley Nickel (D)
14. Jeff Jackson (D)

POSTWAR VOTE FOR PRESIDENT

Year	Total Vote	Republican Vote	Republican Candidate	Democratic Vote	Democratic Candidate	Other Vote	Rep.-Dem. Plurality	Total Vote Rep.	Total Vote Dem.	Major Vote Rep.	Major Vote Dem.
2020	5,524,804	2,758,775	Trump, Donald J.*	2,684,292	Biden, Joseph R. Jr.	81,737	74,483 R	49.9%	48.6%	50.7%	49.3%
2016**	4,741,564	2,362,631	Trump, Donald J.	2,189,316	Clinton, Hillary Rodham	189,617	173,315 R	49.8%	46.2%	51.9%	48.1%
2012	4,505,372	2,270,395	Romney, W. Mitt	2,178,391	Obama, Barack H.*	56,586	92,004 R	50.4%	48.4%	51.0%	49.0%
2008	4,310,789	2,128,474	McCain, John S. III	2,142,651	Obama, Barack H.	39,664	14,177 D	49.4%	49.7%	49.8%	50.2%
2004	3,501,007	1,961,166	Bush, George W.*	1,525,849	Kerry, John F.	13,992	435,317 R	56.0%	43.6%	56.2%	43.8%
2000	2,911,262	1,631,163	Bush, George W.	1,257,692	Gore, Albert Jr.	22,407	373,471 R	56.0%	43.2%	56.5%	43.5%
1996**	2,515,807	1,225,938	Dole, Robert "Bob"	1,107,849	Clinton, Bill*	182,020	118,089 R	48.7%	44.0%	52.5%	47.5%
1992**	2,611,850	1,134,661	Bush, George H.*	1,114,042	Clinton, Bill	363,147	20,619 R	43.4%	42.7%	50.5%	49.5%
1988	2,134,370	1,237,258	Bush, George H.	890,167	Dukakis, Michael S.	6,945	347,091 R	58.0%	41.7%	58.2%	41.8%
1984	2,175,361	1,346,481	Reagan, Ronald*	824,287	Mondale, Walter F.	4,593	522,194 R	61.9%	37.9%	62.0%	38.0%
1980**	1,855,833	915,018	Reagan, Ronald	875,635	Carter, Jimmy*	65,180	39,383 R	49.3%	47.2%	51.1%	48.9%
1976	1,677,914	741,960	Ford, Gerald R.*	926,365	Carter, Jimmy	9,589	184,405 D	44.2%	55.2%	44.5%	55.5%
1972	1,518,612	1,054,889	Nixon, Richard M.*	438,705	McGovern, George S.	25,018	616,184 R	69.5%	28.9%	70.6%	29.4%
1968**	1,587,493	627,192	Nixon, Richard M.	464,113	Humphrey, Hubert Horatio Jr.	496,188	163,079 R	39.5%	29.2%	57.5%	42.5%
1964	1,424,983	624,844	Goldwater, Barry M. Sr.	800,139	Johnson, Lyndon B.*		175,295 D	43.8%	56.2%	43.8%	56.2%
1960	1,368,556	655,420	Nixon, Richard M.	713,136	Kennedy, John F.		57,716 D	47.9%	52.1%	47.9%	52.1%
1956	1,165,592	575,062	Eisenhower, Dwight D.*	590,530	Stevenson, Adlai E. II		15,468 D	49.3%	50.7%	49.3%	50.7%
1952	1,210,910	558,107	Eisenhower, Dwight D.	652,803	Stevenson, Adlai E. II		94,696 D	46.1%	53.9%	46.1%	53.9%
1948**	791,209	258,572	Dewey, Thomas E.	459,070	Truman, Harry S.*	73,567	200,498 D	32.7%	58.0%	36.0%	64.0%

Note: An asterisk (*) denotes incumbent. **In past elections, the other vote included: 2016 - 130,126 Libertarian (Gary Johnson); 1996 - 168,059 Reform (Ross Perot); 1992 - 357,864 Independent (Perot); 1980 - 52,800 Independent (John Anderson); 1968 - 496,188 American Independent (George Wallace, who finished second); 1948 - 69,652 States' Rights (Strom Thurmond).

NORTH CAROLINA

POSTWAR VOTE FOR GOVERNOR

		Republican		Democratic		Other Vote	Rep.-Dem. Plurality	Percentage			
								Total Vote		Major Vote	
Year	Total Vote	Vote	Candidate	Vote	Candidate			Rep.	Dem.	Rep.	Dem.
2020	5,502,778	2,586,605	Forest, Dan	2,834,790	Cooper, Roy*	81,383	248,185 D	47.0%	51.5%	47.7%	52.3%
2016	4,711,014	2,298,880	McCrory, Pat*	2,309,157	Cooper, Roy	102,977	10,277 D	48.8%	49.0%	49.9%	50.1%
2012	4,468,295	2,440,707	McCrory, Pat	1,931,580	Dalton, Walter H.	96,008	509,127 R	54.6%	43.2%	55.8%	44.2%
2008	4,268,941	2,001,168	McCrory, Pat	2,146,189	Perdue, Bev	121,584	145,021 D	46.9%	50.3%	48.3%	51.7%
2004	3,486,688	1,495,021	Ballantine, Patrick J.	1,939,154	Easley, Mike*	52,513	444,133 D	42.9%	55.6%	43.5%	56.5%
2000	2,942,062	1,360,960	Vinroot, Richard	1,530,324	Easley, Mike	50,778	169,364 D	46.3%	52.0%	47.1%	52.9%
1996	2,566,185	1,097,053	Hayes, Robert "Robin"	1,436,638	Hunt, James B. Jr.*	32,494	339,585 D	42.8%	56.0%	43.3%	56.7%
1992	2,595,184	1,121,955	Gardner, James C.	1,368,246	Hunt, James B. Jr.	104,983	246,291 D	43.2%	52.7%	45.1%	54.9%
1988	2,180,205	1,222,338	Martin, James G.*	957,867	Jordan, Robert B.		264,471 R	56.1%	43.9%	56.1%	43.9%
1984	2,226,727	1,208,167	Martin, James G.	1,011,209	Edmisten, Rufus	7,351	196,958 R	54.3%	45.4%	54.4%	45.6%
1980	1,847,432	691,449	Lake, Beverly	1,143,145	Hunt, James B. Jr.*	12,838	451,696 D	37.4%	61.9%	37.7%	62.3%
1976	1,663,814	564,092	Flaherty, David T.	1,081,293	Hunt, James B. Jr.	18,429	517,201 D	33.9%	65.0%	34.3%	65.7%
1972	1,504,785	767,470	Holshouser, James E. Jr.	729,104	Bowles, Hargrove Skipper Jr.	8,211	38,366 R	51.0%	48.5%	51.3%	48.7%
1968	1,558,308	737,075	Gardner, James C.	821,233	Scott, Robert W.		84,158 D	47.3%	52.7%	47.3%	52.7%
1964	1,396,508	606,165	Gavin, Robert L.	790,343	Moore, Dan K.		184,178 D	43.4%	56.6%	43.4%	56.6%
1960	1,350,360	613,975	Gavin, Robert L.	735,248	Sanford, Terry	1,137	121,273 D	45.5%	54.4%	45.5%	54.5%
1956	1,135,859	375,379	Hayes, Kyle	760,480	Hodges, Luther H.		385,101 D	33.0%	67.0%	33.0%	67.0%
1952	1,179,635	383,329	Seawell, Herbert F. Jr.	796,306	Umstead, William B.		412,977 D	32.5%	67.5%	32.5%	67.5%
1948	780,525	206,166	Pritchard, George M.	570,995	Scott, W. Kerr	3,364	364,829 D	26.4%	73.2%	26.5%	73.5%

Note: An asterisk (*) denotes incumbent.

POSTWAR VOTE FOR SENATOR

		Republican		Democratic		Other Vote	Rep.-Dem. Plurality	Percentage			
								Total Vote		Major Vote	
Year	Total Vote	Vote	Candidate	Vote	Candidate			Rep.	Dem.	Rep.	Dem.
2022	3,773,924	1,905,786	Budd, Ted	1,784,049	Beasley, Cheri	84,089	121,737 R	50.5%	47.3%	51.6%	48.4%
2020	5,474,952	2,665,598	Tillis, Thom*	2,569,965	Cunningham, Cal	239,389	95,633 R	48.7%	46.9%	50.9%	49.1%
2016	4,691,133	2,395,376	Burr, Richard M.*	2,128,165	Ross, Deborah K.	167,592	267,211 R	51.1%	45.4%	53.0%	47.0%
2014	2,915,281	1,423,259	Tillis, Thom	1,377,651	Hagan, Kay*	114,371	45,608 R	48.8%	47.3%	50.8%	49.2%
2010	2,660,079	1,458,046	Burr, Richard M.*	1,145,074	Marshall, Elaine	56,959	312,972 R	54.8%	43.0%	56.0%	44.0%
2008	4,271,970	1,887,510	Dole, Elizabeth*	2,249,311	Hagan, Kay	135,149	361,801 D	44.2%	52.7%	45.6%	54.4%
2004	3,472,082	1,791,450	Burr, Richard M.	1,632,527	Bowles, Erskine B.	48,105	158,923 R	51.6%	47.0%	52.3%	47.7%
2002	2,331,181	1,248,664	Dole, Elizabeth	1,047,983	Bowles, Erskine B.	34,534	200,681 R	53.6%	45.0%	54.4%	45.6%
1998	2,012,143	945,943	Faircloth, Lauch*	1,029,237	Edwards, John	36,963	83,294 D	47.0%	51.2%	47.9%	52.1%
1996	2,556,456	1,345,833	Helms, Jesse*	1,173,875	Gantt, Harvey B.	36,748	171,958 R	52.6%	45.9%	53.4%	46.6%
1992	2,577,891	1,297,892	Faircloth, Lauch	1,194,015	Sanford, Terry*	85,984	103,877 R	50.3%	46.3%	52.1%	47.9%
1990	2,069,585	1,087,331	Helms, Jesse*	981,573	Gantt, Harvey B.	681	105,758 R	52.5%	47.4%	52.6%	47.4%
1986	1,591,330	767,668	Broyhill, James Thomas*	823,662	Sanford, Terry		55,994 D	48.2%	51.8%	48.2%	51.8%
1984	2,239,051	1,156,768	Helms, Jesse*	1,070,488	Hunt, James B. Jr.	11,795	86,280 R	51.7%	47.8%	51.9%	48.1%
1980	1,797,665	898,064	East, John P.	887,653	Morgan, Robert*	11,948	10,411 R	50.0%	49.4%	50.3%	49.7%
1978	1,135,814	619,151	Helms, Jesse*	516,663	Ingram, John		102,488 R	54.5%	45.5%	54.5%	45.5%
1974	1,020,367	377,618	Stevens, William E.	633,775	Morgan, Robert	8,974	256,157 D	37.0%	62.1%	37.3%	62.7%
1972	1,472,541	795,248	Helms, Jesse	677,293	Galifianakis, Nick		117,955 R	54.0%	46.0%	54.0%	46.0%
1968	1,437,340	566,934	Somers, Robert V.	870,406	Ervin, Sam James Jr.*		303,472 D	39.4%	60.6%	39.4%	60.6%
1966	901,978	400,502	Shallcross, John S.	501,440	Jordan, B. Everett*	36	100,938 D	44.4%	55.6%	44.4%	55.6%
1962	813,155	321,635	Greene, Claude L. Jr.	491,520	Ervin, Sam James Jr.*		169,885 D	39.6%	60.4%	39.6%	60.4%
1960	1,291,485	497,964	Hayes, Kyle	793,521	Jordan, B. Everett*		295,557 D	38.6%	61.4%	38.6%	61.4%
1958S**	616,469	184,977	Clarke, Richard C. Jr.	431,492	Jordan, B. Everett*		246,515 D	30.0%	70.0%	30.0%	70.0%
1956	1,098,828	367,475	Johnson, Joel A.	731,353	Ervin, Sam James Jr.*		363,878 D	33.4%	66.6%	33.4%	66.6%
1954	619,634	211,322	West, Paul C.	408,312	Scott, W. Kerr		196,990 D	34.1%	65.9%	34.1%	65.9%
1954S**	410,574			410,574	Ervin, Sam James Jr.*		410,574 D		100.0%		100.0%
1950	548,277	171,804	Leavitt, Halsey B.	376,473	Hoey, Clyde R.*		204,669 D	31.3%	68.7%	31.3%	68.7%
1950S**	544,924	177,753	Gavin, E. L.	364,912	Smith, Willis	2,259	187,159 D	32.6%	67.0%	32.8%	67.2%
1948	764,559	220,307	Wilkinson, John A.	540,762	Broughton, J. Melville*	3,490	320,455 D	28.8%	70.7%	28.9%	71.1%

Note: An asterisk (*) denotes incumbent. **One each of the 1950 and 1954 elections as well as the 1958 election were for short terms to fill vacancies. The Republican Party did not run a Senate candidate in the 1954 election for the short term.

NORTH CAROLINA
SENATOR 2022

2020 Census Population	County	Total Vote	Republican (Budd)	Democratic (Beasley)	Other	Rep.-Dem. Plurality	Percentage Total Vote Rep.	Dem.	Major Vote Rep.	Dem.
170,548	ALAMANCE	60,013	32,866	25,866	1,281	7,000 R	54.8%	43.1%	56.0%	44.0%
37,646	ALEXANDER	15,265	11,833	3,031	401	8,802 R	77.5%	19.9%	79.6%	20.4%
11,194	ALLEGHANY	5,021	3,648	1,249	124	2,399 R	72.7%	24.9%	74.5%	25.5%
24,584	ANSON	7,163	3,711	3,324	128	387 R	51.8%	46.4%	52.8%	47.2%
27,384	ASHE	11,817	8,371	3,172	274	5,199 R	70.8%	26.8%	72.5%	27.5%
17,610	AVERY	6,834	5,089	1,595	150	3,494 R	74.5%	23.3%	76.1%	23.9%
47,128	BEAUFORT	18,976	12,338	6,245	393	6,093 R	65.0%	32.9%	66.4%	33.6%
18,912	BERTIE	6,360	2,781	3,492	87	711 D	43.7%	54.9%	44.3%	55.7%
32,704	BLADEN	11,783	6,745	4,799	239	1,946 R	57.2%	40.7%	58.4%	41.6%
145,089	BRUNSWICK	73,093	44,911	26,685	1,497	18,226 R	61.4%	36.5%	62.7%	37.3%
262,365	BUNCOMBE	120,126	43,222	73,807	3,097	30,585 D	36.0%	61.4%	36.9%	63.1%
90,648	BURKE	29,978	20,456	8,847	675	11,609 R	68.2%	29.5%	69.8%	30.2%
218,090	CABARRUS	75,681	41,468	32,372	1,841	9,096 R	54.8%	42.8%	56.2%	43.8%
82,384	CALDWELL	27,908	20,900	6,404	604	14,496 R	74.9%	22.9%	76.5%	23.5%
10,941	CAMDEN	4,280	3,127	1,006	147	2,121 R	73.1%	23.5%	75.7%	24.3%
69,820	CARTERET	32,240	22,709	8,827	704	13,882 R	70.4%	27.4%	72.0%	28.0%
22,666	CASWELL	8,118	4,867	3,121	130	1,746 R	60.0%	38.4%	60.9%	39.1%
160,021	CATAWBA	55,566	38,252	16,076	1,238	22,176 R	68.8%	28.9%	70.4%	29.6%
75,255	CHATHAM	39,469	16,275	22,493	701	6,218 D	41.2%	57.0%	42.0%	58.0%
28,826	CHEROKEE	12,190	9,493	2,448	249	7,045 R	77.9%	20.1%	79.5%	20.5%
13,965	CHOWAN	5,520	3,360	2,048	112	1,312 R	60.9%	37.1%	62.1%	37.9%
11,339	CLAY	5,518	4,073	1,339	106	2,734 R	73.8%	24.3%	75.3%	24.7%
98,313	CLEVELAND	32,846	21,654	10,557	635	11,097 R	65.9%	32.1%	67.2%	32.8%
55,520	COLUMBUS	19,039	11,723	6,888	428	4,835 R	61.6%	36.2%	63.0%	37.0%
102,334	CRAVEN	36,985	21,981	14,101	903	7,880 R	59.4%	38.1%	60.9%	39.1%
335,139	CUMBERLAND	84,007	35,674	46,449	1,884	10,775 D	42.5%	55.3%	43.4%	56.6%
28,090	CURRITUCK	11,638	8,593	2,739	306	5,854 R	73.8%	23.5%	75.8%	24.2%
37,174	DARE	17,844	10,236	7,097	511	3,139 R	57.4%	39.8%	59.1%	40.9%
168,374	DAVIDSON	59,260	43,393	14,643	1,224	28,750 R	73.2%	24.7%	74.8%	25.2%
43,079	DAVIE	18,059	13,191	4,501	367	8,690 R	73.0%	24.9%	74.6%	25.4%
58,698	DUPLIN	15,210	9,852	5,071	287	4,781 R	64.8%	33.3%	66.0%	34.0%
322,388	DURHAM	128,097	22,107	103,630	2,360	81,523 D	17.3%	80.9%	17.6%	82.4%
51,354	EDGECOMBE	15,495	6,046	9,213	236	3,167 D	39.0%	59.5%	39.6%	60.4%
383,727	FORSYTH	134,818	58,350	73,524	2,944	15,174 D	43.3%	54.5%	44.2%	55.8%
70,319	FRANKLIN	27,630	15,292	11,701	637	3,591 R	55.3%	42.3%	56.7%	43.3%
225,802	GASTON	73,442	46,256	25,676	1,510	20,580 R	63.0%	35.0%	64.3%	35.7%
11,597	GATES	4,308	2,431	1,758	119	673 R	56.4%	40.8%	58.0%	42.0%
8,459	GRAHAM	3,543	2,791	639	113	2,152 R	78.8%	18.0%	81.4%	18.6%
60,836	GRANVILLE	22,241	11,770	9,950	521	1,820 R	52.9%	44.7%	54.2%	45.8%
21,085	GREENE	6,045	3,518	2,410	117	1,108 R	58.2%	39.9%	59.3%	40.7%
538,745	GUILFORD	187,236	74,544	108,688	4,004	34,144 D	39.8%	58.0%	40.7%	59.3%
49,911	HALIFAX	15,720	6,631	8,889	200	2,258 D	42.2%	56.5%	42.7%	57.3%
136,535	HARNETT	36,923	22,860	13,133	930	9,727 R	61.9%	35.6%	63.5%	36.5%
62,720	HAYWOOD	26,768	16,078	9,972	718	6,106 R	60.1%	37.3%	61.7%	38.3%
118,348	HENDERSON	51,165	29,798	20,167	1,200	9,631 R	58.2%	39.4%	59.6%	40.4%
23,594	HERTFORD	6,601	2,400	4,096	105	1,696 D	36.4%	62.1%	36.9%	63.1%
55,362	HOKE	13,100	5,594	7,118	388	1,524 D	42.7%	54.3%	44.0%	56.0%
4,988	HYDE	1,863	1,083	731	49	352 R	58.1%	39.2%	59.7%	40.3%
183,058	IREDELL	69,625	46,598	21,442	1,585	25,156 R	66.9%	30.8%	68.5%	31.5%
44,012	JACKSON	14,932	7,920	6,557	455	1,363 R	53.0%	43.9%	54.7%	45.3%
211,601	JOHNSTON	76,054	46,239	28,121	1,694	18,118 R	60.8%	37.0%	62.2%	37.8%
9,443	JONES	3,873	2,382	1,397	94	985 R	61.5%	36.1%	63.0%	37.0%
62,060	LEE	19,233	11,042	7,767	424	3,275 R	57.4%	40.4%	58.7%	41.3%
55,919	LENOIR	18,686	10,452	7,872	362	2,580 R	55.9%	42.1%	57.0%	43.0%
86,706	LINCOLN	36,285	26,130	9,418	737	16,712 R	72.0%	26.0%	73.5%	26.5%
36,140	MACON	15,744	10,698	4,617	429	6,081 R	67.9%	29.3%	69.9%	30.1%
21,893	MADISON	10,101	5,797	3,959	345	1,838 R	57.4%	39.2%	59.4%	40.6%
22,446	MARTIN	8,746	4,717	3,841	188	876 R	53.9%	43.9%	55.1%	44.9%
45,955	MCDOWELL	16,086	11,776	3,895	415	7,881 R	73.2%	24.2%	75.1%	24.9%
1,113,690	MECKLENBURG	360,294	117,742	234,787	7,765	117,045 D	32.7%	65.2%	33.4%	66.6%

NORTH CAROLINA
SENATOR 2022

2020 Census Population	County	Total Vote	Republican (Budd)	Democratic (Beasley)	Other	RepDem. Plurality	Percentage Total Vote Rep.	Percentage Total Vote Dem.	Percentage Major Vote Rep.	Percentage Major Vote Dem.
15,019	MITCHELL	6,533	5,024	1,354	155	3,670 R	76.9%	20.7%	78.8%	21.2%
27,282	MONTGOMERY	8,684	5,834	2,667	183	3,167 R	67.2%	30.7%	68.6%	31.4%
101,590	MOORE	42,316	26,874	14,586	856	12,288 R	63.5%	34.5%	64.8%	35.2%
94,450	NASH	35,739	18,796	16,401	542	2,395 R	52.6%	45.9%	53.4%	46.6%
235,705	NEW HANOVER	94,017	45,012	46,785	2,220	1,773 D	47.9%	49.8%	49.0%	51.0%
19,447	NORTHAMPTON	6,777	2,962	3,718	97	756 D	43.7%	54.9%	44.3%	55.7%
197,802	ONSLOW	44,013	29,106	13,544	1,363	15,562 R	66.1%	30.8%	68.2%	31.8%
148,696	ORANGE	66,553	14,213	51,125	1,215	36,912 D	21.4%	76.8%	21.8%	78.2%
12,791	PAMLICO	6,141	3,908	2,091	142	1,817 R	63.6%	34.0%	65.1%	34.9%
39,979	PASQUOTANK	14,161	7,304	6,468	389	836 R	51.6%	45.7%	53.0%	47.0%
63,617	PENDER	23,525	15,466	7,548	511	7,918 R	65.7%	32.1%	67.2%	32.8%
13,510	PERQUIMANS	5,468	3,813	1,557	98	2,256 R	69.7%	28.5%	71.0%	29.0%
39,630	PERSON	15,438	9,201	5,905	332	3,296 R	59.6%	38.2%	60.9%	39.1%
181,256	PITT	55,026	26,160	27,705	1,161	1,545 D	47.5%	50.3%	48.6%	51.4%
20,826	POLK	9,552	5,686	3,635	231	2,051 R	59.5%	38.1%	61.0%	39.0%
144,037	RANDOLPH	48,346	38,030	9,313	1,003	28,717 R	78.7%	19.3%	80.3%	19.7%
44,875	RICHMOND	12,596	7,317	5,016	263	2,301 R	58.1%	39.8%	59.3%	40.7%
130,397	ROBESON	27,050	15,732	10,736	582	4,996 R	58.2%	39.7%	59.4%	40.6%
91,290	ROCKINGHAM	32,566	21,617	10,110	839	11,507 R	66.4%	31.0%	68.1%	31.9%
142,730	ROWAN	48,197	32,766	14,282	1,149	18,484 R	68.0%	29.6%	69.6%	30.4%
67,294	RUTHERFORD	23,441	17,330	5,538	573	11,792 R	73.9%	23.6%	75.8%	24.2%
63,667	SAMPSON	17,879	11,574	6,045	260	5,529 R	64.7%	33.8%	65.7%	34.3%
34,802	SCOTLAND	9,519	4,922	4,359	238	563 R	51.7%	45.8%	53.0%	47.0%
63,091	STANLY	23,626	17,927	5,163	536	12,764 R	75.9%	21.9%	77.6%	22.4%
45,680	STOKES	18,205	13,915	3,803	487	10,112 R	76.4%	20.9%	78.5%	21.5%
71,897	SURRY	24,704	18,303	5,828	573	12,475 R	74.1%	23.6%	75.8%	24.2%
14,335	SWAIN	4,776	2,884	1,708	184	1,176 R	60.4%	35.8%	62.8%	37.2%
34,620	TRANSYLVANIA	16,170	8,832	6,867	471	1,965 R	54.6%	42.5%	56.3%	43.7%
4,005	TYRRELL	1,281	770	482	29	288 R	60.1%	37.6%	61.5%	38.5%
241,512	UNION	90,103	56,882	31,354	1,867	25,528 R	63.1%	34.8%	64.5%	35.5%
44,586	VANCE	12,967	5,620	7,097	250	1,477 D	43.3%	54.7%	44.2%	55.8%
1,118,126	WAKE	453,170	160,818	281,367	10,985	120,549 D	35.5%	62.1%	36.4%	63.6%
19,770	WARREN	7,183	2,753	4,344	86	1,591 D	38.3%	60.5%	38.8%	61.2%
11,580	WASHINGTON	4,075	1,996	2,002	77	6 D	49.0%	49.1%	49.9%	50.1%
56,449	WATAUGA	22,786	10,455	11,677	654	1,222 D	45.9%	51.2%	47.2%	52.8%
123,306	WAYNE	35,328	20,723	13,990	615	6,733 R	58.7%	39.6%	59.7%	40.3%
68,557	WILKES	24,546	19,294	4,770	482	14,524 R	78.6%	19.4%	80.2%	19.8%
82,008	WILSON	26,249	13,310	12,503	436	807 R	50.7%	47.6%	51.6%	48.4%
37,770	YADKIN	13,870	11,117	2,400	353	8,717 R	80.2%	17.3%	82.2%	17.8%
18,176	YANCEY	8,887	5,706	2,946	235	2,760 R	64.2%	33.1%	66.0%	34.0%
10,530,693	TOTAL	3,773,924	1,905,786	1,784,049	84,089	121,737 R	50.5%	47.3%	51.6%	48.4%

NORTH CAROLINA
HOUSE OF REPRESENTATIVES

			Republican		Democratic		Other	Rep.-Dem.	Total Vote		Major Vote	
CD	Year	Total Vote	Vote	Candidate	Vote	Candidate	Vote	Plurality	Rep.	Dem.	Rep.	Dem.
1	2022	257,776	122,780	SMITH, SANDY	134,996	DAVIS, DON		12,216 D	47.6%	52.4%	47.6%	52.4%
1**	2020	348,618	159,748	SMITH, SANDY	188,870	BUTTERFIELD, GEORGE K. "G. K."*		29,122 D	45.8%	54.2%	45.8%	54.2%
1**	2018	272,675	82,218	ALLISON, ROGER	190,457	BUTTERFIELD, GEORGE K. "G. K."*		108,239 D	30.2%	69.8%	30.2%	69.8%
1**	2016	350,699	101,567	DEW, H. POWELL JR.	240,661	BUTTERFIELD, GEORGE K. "G. K."*	8,471	139,094 D	29.0%	68.6%	29.7%	70.3%
1	2014	210,323	55,990	RICH, ARTHUR	154,333	BUTTERFIELD, GEORGE K. "G. K."*		98,343 D	26.6%	73.4%	26.6%	73.4%
1	2012	338,066	77,288	DILAURO, PETE	254,644	BUTTERFIELD, GEORGE K. "G. K."*	6,134	177,356 D	22.9%	75.3%	23.3%	76.7%
2	2022	294,869	104,155	VILLAVERDE, CHRISTINE E.	190,714	ROSS, DEBORAH K.*		86,559 D	35.3%	64.7%	35.3%	64.7%
2**	2020	495,345	172,544	SWAIN, ALAN	311,887	ROSS, DEBORAH K.	10,914	139,343 D	34.8%	63.0%	35.6%	64.4%
2**	2018	331,704	170,072	HOLDING, GEORGE*	151,977	COLEMAN, LINDA	9,655	18,095 R	51.3%	45.8%	52.8%	47.2%
2**	2016	390,567	221,485	HOLDING, GEORGE*	169,082	MCNEIL, JOHN P.		52,403 R	56.7%	43.3%	56.7%	43.3%
2	2014	207,607	122,128	ELLMERS, RENEE*	85,479	AIKEN, CLAY		36,649 R	58.8%	41.2%	58.8%	41.2%
2	2012	311,397	174,066	ELLMERS, RENEE*	128,973	WILKINS, STEVE	8,358	45,093 R	55.9%	41.4%	57.4%	42.6%
3	2022	248,898	166,520	MURPHY, GREG*	82,378	GASKINS, BARBARA D.		84,142 R	66.9%	33.1%	66.9%	33.1%
3**	2020	362,552	229,800	MURPHY, GREG*	132,752	FARROW, DARYL		97,048 R	63.4%	36.6%	63.4%	36.6%
3**	2018	187,901	187,901	JONES, WALTER B. JR.*				187,901 R	100.0%		100.0%	
3**	2016	323,701	217,531	JONES, WALTER B. JR.*	106,170	REEVES, ERNEST TYRONE		111,361 R	67.2%	32.8%	67.2%	32.8%
3	2014	205,597	139,415	JONES, WALTER B. JR.*	66,182	ADAME, MARSHALL		73,233 R	67.8%	32.2%	67.8%	32.2%
3	2012	309,885	195,571	JONES, WALTER B. JR.*	114,314	ANDERSON, ERIK		81,257 R	63.1%	36.9%	63.1%	36.9%
4	2022	291,425	96,442	GEELS, COURTNEY	194,983	FOUSHEE, VALERIE P.		98,541 D	33.1%	66.9%	33.1%	66.9%
4**	2020	493,719	161,298	THOMAS, ROBERT	332,421	PRICE, DAVID E.*		171,123 D	32.7%	67.3%	32.7%	67.3%
4**	2018	341,403	82,052	LOOR, STEVE VON	247,067	PRICE, DAVID E.*	12,284	165,015 D	24.0%	72.4%	24.9%	75.1%
4**	2016	409,541	130,161	GOOGE, SUE	279,380	PRICE, DAVID E.*		149,219 D	31.8%	68.2%	31.8%	68.2%
4	2014	227,362	57,416	WRIGHT, PAUL	169,946	PRICE, DAVID E.*		112,530 D	25.3%	74.7%	25.3%	74.7%
4	2012	348,485	88,951	D'ANNUNZIO, TIM	259,534	PRICE, DAVID E.*		170,583 D	25.5%	74.5%	25.5%	74.5%
5	2022	277,548	175,279	FOXX, VIRGINIA ANN*	102,269	PARRISH, KYLE		73,010 R	63.2%	36.8%	63.2%	36.8%
5**	2020	385,244	257,843	FOXX, VIRGINIA ANN*	119,846	BROWN, DAVID WILSON	7,555	137,997 R	66.9%	31.1%	68.3%	31.7%
5**	2018	280,385	159,917	FOXX, VIRGINIA ANN*	120,468	ADAMS, DENISE "DD"		39,449 R	57.0%	43.0%	57.0%	43.0%
5**	2016	355,512	207,625	FOXX, VIRGINIA ANN*	147,887	BRANNON, JOSHUA "JOSH"		59,738 R	58.4%	41.6%	58.4%	41.6%
5	2014	228,252	139,279	FOXX, VIRGINIA ANN*	88,973	BRANNON, JOSHUA "JOSH"		50,306 R	61.0%	39.0%	61.0%	39.0%
5	2012	349,197	200,945	FOXX, VIRGINIA ANN*	148,252	MOTSINGER, ELISABETH		52,693 R	57.5%	42.5%	57.5%	42.5%
6	2022	258,998	116,635	CASTELLI, CHRISTIAN	139,553	MANNING, KATHY*	2,810	22,918 D	45.0%	53.9%	45.5%	54.5%
6**	2020	407,129	153,598	HAYWOOD, JOSEPH "LEE"	253,531	MANNING, KATHY		99,933 D	37.7%	62.3%	37.7%	62.3%
6**	2018	284,360	160,709	WALKER, MARK*	123,651	WATTS, RYAN		37,058 R	56.5%	43.5%	56.5%	43.5%
6**	2016	351,150	207,983	WALKER, MARK*	143,167	GLIDEWELL, POWELL WATKINS "PETE" III		64,816 R	59.2%	40.8%	59.2%	40.8%
6	2014	251,070	147,312	WALKER, MARK	103,758	FJELD, LAURA		43,554 R	58.7%	41.3%	58.7%	41.3%
6	2012	364,583	222,116	COBLE, HOWARD*	142,467	FORIEST, TONY		79,649 R	60.9%	39.1%	60.9%	39.1%
7	2022	284,269	164,047	ROUZER, DAVID*	120,222	GRAHAM, CHARLES		43,825 R	57.7%	42.3%	57.7%	42.3%
7**	2020	452,208	272,443	ROUZER, DAVID*	179,045	WARD, CHRISTOPHER M.	720	93,398 R	60.2%	39.6%	60.3%	39.7%
7**	2018	282,312	156,809	ROUZER, DAVID*	120,838	HORTON, KYLE	4,665	35,971 R	55.5%	42.8%	56.5%	39.1%
7**	2016	347,706	211,801	ROUZER, DAVID*	135,905	CASTEEN, J. WESLEY		75,896 R	60.9%	39.1%	60.9%	39.1%
7	2014	226,504	134,431	ROUZER, DAVID	84,054	BARFIELD JR., JONATHAN	8,019	50,377 R	59.4%	37.1%	61.5%	38.5%
7	2012	336,736	168,041	ROUZER, DAVID	168,695	MCINTYRE, MIKE*		654 D	49.9%	50.1%	49.9%	50.1%
8	2022	263,190	183,998	BISHOP, DAN*	79,192	HUFFMAN, SCOTT		104,806 R	69.9%	30.1%	69.9%	30.1%
8**	2020	380,555	202,774	HUDSON, RICHARD*	177,781	TIMMONS-GOODSON, PATRICIA		24,993 R	53.3%	46.7%	53.3%	46.7%
8**	2018	255,521	141,402	HUDSON, RICHARD*	114,119	MCNEILL, FRANK		27,283 R	55.3%	44.7%	55.3%	44.7%
8**	2016	323,045	189,863	HUDSON, RICHARD*	133,182	MILLS, THOMAS		56,681 R	58.8%	41.2%	58.8%	41.2%
8	2014	187,422	121,568	HUDSON, RICHARD*	65,854	BLUE, ANTONIO		55,714 R	64.9%	35.1%	64.9%	35.1%
8	2012	302,280	160,695	HUDSON, RICHARD	137,139	KISSELL, LARRY*	4,446	23,556 R	53.2%	45.4%	54.0%	46.0%
9	2022	232,655	131,453	HUDSON, RICHARD*	101,202	CLARK, BEN		30,251 R	56.5%	43.5%	56.5%	43.5%
9**	2020	404,124	224,661	BISHOP, DAN*	179,463	WALLACE, CYNTHIA		45,198 R	55.6%	44.4%	55.6%	44.4%
9**	2018	282,717	139,246	HARRIS, MARK	138,341	MCCREADY, DANIEL "DAN"	5,130	905 R	49.3%	48.9%	50.2%	49.8%
9**	2016	332,493	193,452	PITTENGER, ROBERT*	139,041	CANO, CHRISTIAN		54,411 R	58.2%	41.8%	58.2%	41.8%
9	2014	173,668	163,080	PITTENGER, ROBERT*			10,588	163,080 R	93.9%		100.0%	
9	2012	375,690	194,537	PITTENGER, ROBERT	171,503	ROBERTS, JENNIFER	9,650	23,034 R	51.8%	45.7%	53.1%	46.9%
10	2022	268,207	194,681	MCHENRY, PATRICK T.*	73,174	GENANT, PAM	352	121,507 R	72.6%	27.3%	72.7%	27.3%
10**	2020	412,284	284,095	MCHENRY, PATRICK T.*	128,189	PARKER, DAVID		155,906 R	68.9%	31.1%	68.9%	31.1%
10**	2018	278,228	164,969	MCHENRY, PATRICK T.*	113,259	BROWN, DAVID WILSON		51,710 R	59.3%	40.7%	59.3%	40.7%
10**	2016	349,744	220,825	MCHENRY, PATRICK T.*	128,919	MILLARD, ANDY		91,906 R	63.1%	36.9%	63.1%	36.9%
10	2014	218,796	133,504	MCHENRY, PATRICK T.*	85,292	MACQUEEN IV, TATE		48,212 R	61.0%	39.0%	61.0%	39.0%
10	2012	334,849	190,826	MCHENRY, PATRICK T.*	144,023	KEEVER, PATRICIA R. "PATSY"		46,803 R	57.0%	43.0%	57.0%	43.0%

NORTH CAROLINA
HOUSE OF REPRESENTATIVES

			Republican		Democratic		Other	Rep.-Dem.	Percentage Total Vote		Major Vote	
CD	Year	Total Vote	Vote	Candidate	Vote	Candidate	Vote	Plurality	Rep.	Dem.	Rep.	Dem.
11	2022	323,912	174,232	EDWARDS, CHUCK	144,165	BEACH-FERRARA, JASMINE	5,515	30,067 R	53.8%	44.5%	54.7%	45.3%
11**	2020	450,145	245,351	CAWTHORN, MADISON	190,609	DAVIS, MORRIS "MOE"	14,185	54,742 R	54.5%	42.3%	56.3%	43.7%
11**	2018	300,666	178,012	MEADOWS, MARK*	116,508	PRICE, PHILLIP G.	6,146	61,504 R	59.2%	38.7%	60.4%	39.6%
11**	2016	359,508	230,405	MEADOWS, MARK*	129,103	BRYSON, FREDERICK "RICK"		101,302 R	64.1%	35.9%	64.1%	35.9%
11	2014	230,024	144,682	MEADOWS, MARK*	85,342	HILL, THOMAS		59,340 R	62.9%	37.1%	62.9%	37.1%
11	2012	331,426	190,319	MEADOWS, MARK	141,107	ROGERS, HAYDEN		49,212 R	57.4%	42.6%	57.4%	42.6%
12	2022	223,908	83,414	LEE, TYLER	140,494	ADAMS, ALMA S.*		57,080 D	37.3%	62.7%	37.3%	62.7%
12**	2020	341,457			341,457	ADAMS, ALMA S.*		341,457 D		100.0%		100.0%
12**	2018	279,138	75,164	WRIGHT, PAUL	203,974	ADAMS, ALMA S.*		128,810 D	26.9%	73.1%	26.9%	73.1%
12**	2016	349,300	115,185	THREATT, LEON	234,115	ADAMS, ALMA S.*		118,930 D	33.0%	67.0%	33.0%	67.0%
12	2014	172,664	42,568	COAKLEY, VINCE	130,096	ADAMS, ALMA S.		87,528 D	24.7%	75.3%	24.7%	75.3%
12	2012	310,908	63,317	BROSCH, JACK	247,591	WATT, MELVIN*		184,274 D	20.4%	79.6%	20.4%	79.6%
13	2022	277,346	134,256	HINES, BO	143,090	NICKEL, WILEY		8,834 D	48.4%	51.6%	48.4%	51.6%
13**	2020	391,865	267,181	BUDD, TED*	124,684	HUFFMAN, SCOTT		142,497 R	68.2%	31.8%	68.2%	31.8%
13**	2018	286,316	147,570	BUDD, TED*	130,402	MANNING, KATHY	8,344	17,168 R	51.5%	45.5%	53.1%	46.9%
13**	2016	355,492	199,443	BUDD, TED	156,049	DAVIS, BRUCE		43,394 R	56.1%	43.9%	56.1%	43.9%
13	2014	268,709	153,991	HOLDING, GEORGE*	114,718	CLEARY, BRENDA		39,273 R	57.3%	42.7%	57.3%	42.7%
13	2012	370,610	210,495	HOLDING, GEORGE	160,115	MALONE, CHARLES		50,380 R	56.8%	43.2%	56.8%	43.2%
14	2022	257,752	109,014	HARRIGAN, PAT	148,738	JACKSON, JEFF		39,724 D	42.3%	57.7%	42.3%	57.7%
TOTAL	2022	3,760,753	1,956,906		1,795,170		8,677	161,736 R	52.0%	47.7%	52.2%	47.8%
TOTAL	2020	5,325,245	2,631,336		2,660,535		33,374	29,199 D	49.4%	50.0%	49.7%	50.3%
TOTAL	2018	3,663,326	1,846,041		1,771,061		46,224	74,980 R	50.4%	48.3%	51.0%	49.0%
TOTAL	2016	4,598,458	2,447,326		2,142,661		8,471	304,665 R	53.2%	46.6%	53.3%	46.7%
TOTAL	2014	2,807,998	1,555,364		1,234,027		18,607	321,337 R	55.4%	43.9%	55.8%	44.2%
TOTAL	2012	4,384,112	2,137,167		2,218,357		28,588	81,190 D	48.7%	50.6%	49.1%	50.9%

Note: An asterisk (*) denotes incumbent.

NORTH CAROLINA
GENERAL AND PRIMARY ELECTIONS

GENERAL ELECTIONS: OTHER VOTES

Senate Other vote was 51,640 Libertarian (Shannon Bray), 29,934 Green (Matthew Hoh), 2,515 Write-In (Write-In)

House Other vote was:

CD 6   2,810 Libertarian (Thomas Watercott)
CD 10   242 Write-In (Write-In), 110 Write-In (Diana Jimison)
CD 11   7,555 Libertarian (David Coatney)

2022 PRIMARY ELECTIONS: SUPPLEMENTARY INFORMATION

Primary	May 17, 2022	**Registration** (as of May 17, 2022)	6,942,210	Democratic	2,493,492
Primary Runoff	July 26, 2022			Republican	2,198,612
				Green	0
				Constitution	0
				Libertarian	48,979
				Unaffiliated	2,532,944

Primary Type   Semi-open—Registered Democrats and Republicans could vote only in their party's primary. Unaffiliated voters could participate in the primary of any recognized party. However, if a voter cast a ballot in one party's primary, they could not participate in the runoff of another party.

NORTH CAROLINA
GENERAL AND PRIMARY ELECTIONS

	REPUBLICAN PRIMARIES			DEMOCRATIC PRIMARIES		
Senator	Budd, Ted	448,128	58.6%	Beasley, Cheri	501,766	81.1%
	McCrory, Pat	188,135	24.6%	Carr, James Lester Jr.	21,903	3.5%
	Walker, Mark	70,486	9.2%	Hammond, Alyssia Rose-Katherine	21,005	3.4%
	Eastman, Marjorie K.	22,535	2.9%	Williams, Marcus W.	17,446	2.8%
	Flaherty, David	7,265	1.0%	Johnson, Constance Lov	12,500	2.0%
	Harper, Kenneth Jabari Jr.	7,129	0.9%	Newton, Everette "Rett"	10,043	1.6%
	Banwart, Jennifer Alexis	3,088	0.4%	Booker, Chrelle	9,937	1.6%
	Moss, Charles Kenneth	2,920	0.4%	Magginis, Brendan	7,044	1.1%
	Bryant, Leonard L.	2,906	0.4%	Colon, Robert	6,904	1.1%
	Griffiths, Benjamin	2,870	0.4%	Antoine, Gregory	5,179	0.8%
	Tshiovo, Debora	2,741	0.4%	LaGrone, Tobias Everett	5,048	0.8%
	Brian, Lee	2,232	0.3%			
	Sibhatu, Lichia	2,191	0.3%			
	Bulecza, Andrew "Drew"	2,022	0.3%			
	TOTAL	764,648		TOTAL	618,775	
Congressional District 1	Smith, Sandy	13,621	31.4%	Davis, Don	42,693	63.2%
	Roberson, Sandy	11,603	26.7%	Smith, Erica D.	21,012	31.1%
	Strickland, Billy	6,050	13.9%	Spriggs, Jason Albert	2,123	3.1%
	Roberson, Brent	5,992	13.8%	Bishop, Jullian C. Sr.	1,752	2.6%
	Murphy, Brad	4,128	9.5%			
	Aiken, Will	1,285	3.0%			
	Reeves, Ernest Tyrone	523	1.2%			
	Williams, Henry II	202	0.5%			
	TOTAL	43,404		TOTAL	67,580	
Congressional District 2	Villaverde, Christine E.	19,650	55.1%	Ross, Deborah K.*	Unopposed	
	Ganorkar, Mahesh "Max"	9,133	25.6%			
	Safta, Adina	6,872	19.3%			
	TOTAL	35,655				
Congressional District 3	Murphy, Greg*	50,123	75.7%	Gaskins, Barbara D.	23,051	80.8%
	Cowden, Tony	9,332	14.1%	Swartz, Joe	5,495	19.2%
	Earhart, Eric	3,274	4.9%			
	Papastrat, George J.	1,789	2.7%			
	Friend, Brian Michael	1,698	2.6%			
	TOTAL	66,216		TOTAL	28,546	
Congressional District 4	Geels, Courtney	19,645	64.5%	Foushee, Valerie P.	40,806	46.1%
	Thomas, Robert	10,793	35.5%	Allam, Nida	32,731	37.0%
				Aiken, Clay	6,529	7.4%
				Ward, Ashley	4,767	5.4%
				Watkins, Richard L.	1,155	1.3%
				Cavalier, Crystal	1,116	1.3%
				Valentine, Stephen J.	1,023	1.2%
				Groom, Matt	435	0.5%
	TOTAL	30,438		TOTAL	88,562	
Congressional District 5	Foxx, Virginia Ann*	61,680	76.6%	Parrish, Kyle	Unopposed	
	Ackerman, Michael	18,868	23.4%			
	TOTAL	80,548				

NORTH CAROLINA

GENERAL AND PRIMARY ELECTIONS

	REPUBLICAN PRIMARIES			DEMOCRATIC PRIMARIES		
Congressional District 6	Castelli, Christian	15,450	36.2%	Manning, Kathy*	Unopposed	
	Haywood, Lee	14,390	33.7%			
	Contogiannis, Mary Ann	5,211	12.2%			
	Austin, Gerry	2,568	6.0%			
	Pichardo, Laura	1,889	4.4%			
	Boguslawski, Marvin	1,716	4.0%			
	Schuch, William "Bill"	1,452	3.4%			
	TOTAL	42,676				
Congressional District 7	Rouzer, David*	39,203	79.2%	Graham, Charles	13,054	31.2%
	Southworth-Beckwith, Max	10,300	20.8%	Evans, Charles E.	12,263	29.3%
				Miller, Steve	9,744	23.3%
				Midgette, Yushonda	6,738	16.1%
	TOTAL	49,503		TOTAL	41,799	
Congressional District 8	Bishop, Dan*	Unopposed		Huffman, Scott	Unopposed	
Congressional District 9	Hudson, Richard*	38,117	79.2%	Clark, Ben	Unopposed	
	Bucardo, Jennyfer	4,175	8.7%			
	Andriani, Mike	3,950	8.2%			
	Rios, Francisco	1,891	3.9%			
	TOTAL	48,133				
Congressional District 10	McHenry, Patrick T.*	49,973	68.1%	Genant, Pam	13,028	77.5%
	Robinson, Gary	11,671	15.9%	Felder, Michael	3,790	22.5%
	Magnotta, Michael	4,703	6.4%			
	Gregory, Jeff	3,649	5.0%			
	Speer, Richard	3,381	4.6%			
	TOTAL	73,377		TOTAL	16,818	
Congressional District 11	Edwards, Chuck	29,496	33.4%	Beach-Ferrara, Jasmine	32,478	59.7%
	Cawthorn, Madison*	28,112	31.9%	Dean, Katie	13,957	25.6%
	Burril, Matthew	8,341	9.5%	Carey, Jay	3,858	7.1%
	O'connell, Bruce	6,037	6.8%	Hess, Bo	2,082	3.8%
	Honeycutt, Rod	5,775	6.5%	Gutierrez, Marco	1,040	1.9%
	Woodhouse, Michele V.	4,668	5.3%	Lunsford, Bynum M.	1,002	1.8%
	Nevarez, Wendy Marie-Limbaugh	4,525	5.1%			
	Sluder, Kristie	1,304	1.5%			
	TOTAL	88,258		TOTAL	54,417	
Congressional District 12	Lee, Tyler	10,388	42.9%	Adams, Alma S.*	37,984	91.7%
	Huffman, Andrew	8,311	34.3%	Sharkey, John	3,460	8.3%
	Joseph, Nalini	5,543	22.9%			
	TOTAL	24,242		TOTAL	41,444	
Congressional District 13	Hines, Bo	17,602	32.1%	Nickel, Wiley	23,155	51.6%
	Barbour, DeVan	12,426	22.6%	Searcy, Sam	10,284	22.9%
	Daughtry, Kelly Kathleen	9,300	16.9%	Campbell Bowles, Jamie	4,217	9.4%
	Keirsey, Kent	6,223	11.3%	Click, Nathan	3,866	8.6%
	Ellmers, Renee	5,176	9.4%	Lee, Denton	3,311	7.4%
	Slotta, Chad	3,074	5.6%			
	Morel, Jessica	738	1.3%			
	Wolff, Kevin Alan	344	0.6%			
	TOTAL	54,883		TOTAL	44,833	

NORTH CAROLINA

GENERAL AND PRIMARY ELECTIONS

	REPUBLICAN PRIMARIES			DEMOCRATIC PRIMARIES		
Congressional	Harrigan, Pat	27,638	75.6%	Jackson, Jeff	34,724	86.1%
District 14	Simpson, Jonathan	8,909	24.4%	Mammadov, Ram	5,598	13.9%
	TOTAL	*36,547*		*TOTAL*	*40,322*	

Note: An asterisk (*) denotes incumbent.

NORTH DAKOTA

Statewide and House Races

As with 2020, Democrats were not much of a factor in solidly Republican North Dakota, but there was a surprisingly strong conservative protest vote.

Over his statewide career, one of the true electoral powerhouses in the Senate seemed to be Republican John Hoeven. In 2000, as a first-time candidate, he won the state's open-seat gubernatorial race 55%–45% over a strong Democrat. Four years later, he was reelected 71%–27% and won a third term in 2008 (at the time, there were no gubernatorial term limits) by an even stronger 74%–24%. In 2010, one of the state's Senate seats opened up. Hoeven entered the race and became the first Republican since 1980 to win a Senate race in North Dakota – he did so in a smashing fashion, upping his vote share to 76% and, for the first time in his career, carrying every county. Hoeven was up next in 2016. In his Senate reelection contest, he upped his margin yet again, winning by an astounding 78%–17%, although he failed to carry Sioux County (which is part of the Standing Rock Reservation). In 2022, could he keep expanding his margin?

The answer, as it turned out, was no, though the race was unlike his previous contests, in that it became something of a three-way race. Hoeven's share dropped to just over 56%, while Democrat Katrina Christiansen took 25% and Rick Becker, a Republican legislator who ran as a conservative independent, pulled 18%. Becker ran to Hoeven's right, tying the Republican incumbent to Joe Biden in his messaging. Hoeven still carried every county but Sioux and Rolette (which also includes a Native American reservation). An east versus west divide emerged between the two losing candidates: Christiansen outpolled Becker in all Minnesota border counties, but Becker took more votes in most counties west of Christiansen's home of Jamestown, in Stutsman County. In 2020, GOP Gov. Doug Burgum won comfortably, but his margin was similarly held down by a high volume of write-in votes in many conservative counties.

Republican Rep. Kelly Armstrong won a third term representing the state's At-Large district, but his only rival was an independent, not a Democrat. In 2018, beauty pageant contender Cara Mund became the first North Dakotan to be crowned Miss America. Citing the Supreme Court's ruling that overturned *Roe v. Wade*, she entered North Dakota's House race as an Independent – the Democrats subsequently withdrew their own nominee. Armstrong still prevailed 62%–38%, but it seems likely that, without a partisan label, Mund performed better than a Democratic candidate otherwise would have. Aside from Rolette and Sioux, she carried Fargo's Cass County, the state's most populous county, by two points.

NORTH DAKOTA
One member At Large

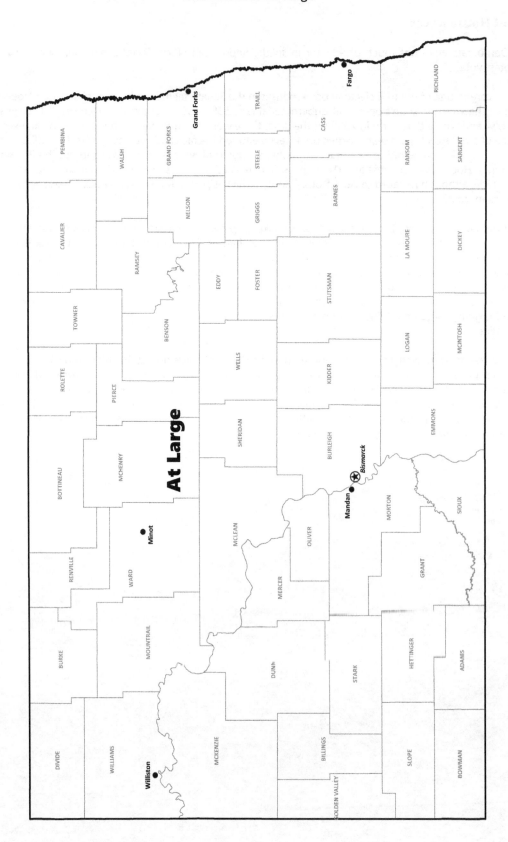

NORTH DAKOTA

GOVERNOR
Doug Burgum (R). Reelected 2020 to a four-year term. Previously elected 2016.

SENATORS (2 Republicans)
Kevin Cramer (R). Elected 2018 to a six-year term.

John Hoeven (R). Reelected 2022 to a six-year term. Previously elected 2016, 2010.

REPRESENTATIVES (1 Republican)
At Large. Kelly Armstrong (R)

POSTWAR VOTE FOR PRESIDENT

Year	Total Vote	Republican Vote	Republican Candidate	Democratic Vote	Democratic Candidate	Other Vote	Rep.-Dem. Plurality	Total Vote Rep.	Total Vote Dem.	Major Vote Rep.	Major Vote Dem.
2020	362,024	235,751	Trump, Donald J.*	115,042	Biden, Joseph R. Jr.	11,231	120,709 R	65.1%	31.8%	67.2%	32.8%
2016**	344,360	216,794	Trump, Donald J.	93,758	Clinton, Hillary Rodham	33,808	123,036 R	63.0%	27.2%	69.8%	30.2%
2012	322,627	188,163	Romney, W. Mitt	124,827	Obama, Barack H.*	9,637	63,336 R	58.3%	38.7%	60.1%	39.9%
2008	316,621	168,601	McCain, John S. III	141,278	Obama, Barack H.	6,742	27,323 R	53.3%	44.6%	54.4%	45.6%
2004	312,833	196,651	Bush, George W.*	111,052	Kerry, John F.	5,130	85,599 R	62.9%	35.5%	63.9%	36.1%
2000**	288,256	174,852	Bush, George W.	95,284	Gore, Albert Jr.	18,120	79,568 R	60.7%	33.1%	64.7%	35.3%
1996**	266,411	125,050	Dole, Robert "Bob"	106,905	Clinton, Bill*	34,456	18,145 R	46.9%	40.1%	53.9%	46.1%
1992**	308,133	136,244	Bush, George H.*	99,168	Clinton, Bill	72,721	37,076 R	44.2%	32.2%	57.9%	42.1%
1988	297,261	166,559	Bush, George H.	127,739	Dukakis, Michael S.	2,963	38,820 R	56.0%	43.0%	56.6%	43.4%
1984	308,971	200,336	Reagan, Ronald*	104,429	Mondale, Walter F.	4,206	95,907 R	64.8%	33.8%	65.7%	34.3%
1980**	301,545	193,695	Reagan, Ronald	79,189	Carter, Jimmy*	28,661	114,506 R	64.2%	26.3%	71.0%	29.0%
1976	297,188	153,470	Ford, Gerald R.*	136,078	Carter, Jimmy	7,640	17,392 R	51.6%	45.8%	53.0%	47.0%
1972	280,514	174,109	Nixon, Richard M.*	100,384	McGovern, George S.	6,021	73,725 R	62.1%	35.8%	63.4%	36.6%
1968**	247,882	138,669	Nixon, Richard M.	94,769	Humphrey, Hubert Horatio Jr.	14,444	43,900 R	55.9%	38.2%	59.4%	40.6%
1964	258,389	108,207	Goldwater, Barry M. Sr.	149,784	Johnson, Lyndon B.*	398	41,577 D	41.9%	58.0%	41.9%	58.1%
1960	278,431	154,310	Nixon, Richard M.	123,963	Kennedy, John F.	158	30,347 R	55.4%	44.5%	55.5%	44.5%
1956	253,991	156,766	Eisenhower, Dwight D.*	96,742	Stevenson, Adlai E. II	483	60,024 R	61.7%	38.1%	61.8%	38.2%
1952	270,127	191,712	Eisenhower, Dwight D.	76,694	Stevenson, Adlai E. II	1,721	115,018 R	71.0%	28.4%	71.4%	28.6%
1948	220,716	115,139	Dewey, Thomas E.	95,812	Truman, Harry S.*	9,765	19,327 R	52.2%	43.4%	54.6%	45.4%

Note: An asterisk (*) denotes incumbent. **In past elections, the other vote included: 2016 - 21,434 Libertarian (Gary Johnson); 2000 - 9,486 Green (Ralph Nader); 1996 - 32,515 Reform (Ross Perot); 1992 - 71,084 Independent (Perot); 1980 - 23,640 Independent (John Anderson); 1968 - 14,244 American Independent (George Wallace).

NORTH DAKOTA

POSTWAR VOTE FOR GOVERNOR

Year	Total Vote	Republican Vote	Republican Candidate	Democratic Vote	Democratic Candidate	Other Vote	Rep.-Dem. Plurality	Total Vote Rep.	Total Vote Dem.	Major Vote Rep.	Major Vote Dem.
2020	357,859	235,629	Burgum, Doug*	90,925	Lenz, Shelley	31,805	144,704 R	65.8%	25.4%	72.2%	27.8%
2016	339,601	259,863	Burgum, Doug	65,855	Nelson, Marvin E.	13,883	194,008 R	76.5%	19.4%	79.8%	20.2%
2012	317,812	200,526	Dalrymple, Jack*	109,047	Taylor, Ryan M.	8,239	91,479 R	63.1%	34.3%	64.8%	35.2%
2008	315,692	235,009	Hoeven, John*	74,279	Mathern, Tim	6,404	160,730 R	74.4%	23.5%	76.0%	24.0%
2004	309,873	220,803	Hoeven, John*	84,877	Satrom, Joe	4,193	135,926 R	71.3%	27.4%	72.2%	27.8%
2000	289,412	159,255	Hoeven, John	130,144	Heitkamp, Heidi	13	29,111 R	55.0%	45.0%	55.0%	45.0%
1996	264,298	174,937	Schafer, Edward T.*	89,349	Kaldor, Lee	12	85,588 R	66.2%	33.8%	66.2%	33.8%
1992	304,861	176,398	Schafer, Edward T.	123,845	Spaeth, Nicholas	4,618	52,553 R	57.9%	40.6%	58.8%	41.2%
1988	299,080	119,986	Mallberg, Leon L.	179,094	Sinner, George A.*		59,108 D	40.1%	59.9%	40.1%	59.9%
1984	314,382	140,460	Olson, Allen I.*	173,922	Sinner, George A.		33,462 D	44.7%	55.3%	44.7%	55.3%
1980	302,621	162,230	Olson, Allen I.	140,391	Link, Arthur A.*		21,839 R	53.6%	46.4%	53.6%	46.4%
1976	297,249	138,321	Elkin, Richard	153,309	Link, Arthur A.*	5,619	14,988 D	46.5%	51.6%	47.4%	52.6%
1972	281,931	138,032	Davis, John E.	143,899	Link, Arthur A.		5,867 D	49.0%	51.0%	49.0%	51.0%
1968	247,998	108,380	McCarney, Robert P.	135,955	Guy, William L.*	3,663	27,575 D	43.7%	54.8%	44.4%	55.6%
1964**	262,661	116,247	Halcrow, Don	146,414	Guy, William L.*		30,167 D	44.3%	55.7%	44.3%	55.7%
1962	228,509	113,251	Andrews, Mark	115,258	Guy, William L.*		2,007 D	49.6%	50.4%	49.6%	50.4%
1960	275,375	122,486	Dahl, C. P.	136,148	Guy, William L.	16,741	13,662 D	44.5%	49.4%	47.4%	52.6%
1958	210,599	111,836	Davis, John E.*	98,763	Lord, John F.		13,073 R	53.1%	46.9%	53.1%	46.9%
1956	252,435	147,566	Davis, John E.	104,869	Warner, Wallace E.		42,697 R	58.5%	41.5%	58.5%	41.5%
1954	193,501	124,253	Brunsdale, Norman*	69,248	Bymers, Cornelius		55,005 R	64.2%	35.8%	64.2%	35.8%
1952	253,934	199,944	Brunsdale, Norman*	53,990	Johnson, Ole S.		145,954 R	78.7%	21.3%	78.7%	21.3%
1950	183,772	121,822	Brunsdale, Norman	61,950	Byerly, Clyde G.		59,872 R	66.3%	33.7%	66.3%	33.7%
1948	214,958	131,764	Aandahl, Fred G.*	80,655	Henry, Howard	2,539	51,109 R	61.3%	37.5%	62.0%	38.0%
1946	169,391	116,672	Aandahl, Fred G.*	52,719	Burdick, Quentin N.		63,953 R	68.9%	31.1%	68.9%	31.1%

Note: An asterisk (*) denotes incumbent. **The term of office of North Dakota's Governor was increased from two to four years effective with the 1964 election.

NORTH DAKOTA

POSTWAR VOTE FOR SENATOR

		Republican		Democratic		Other Vote	Rep.-Dem. Plurality	Percentage			
								Total Vote		Major Vote	
Year	Total Vote	Vote	Candidate	Vote	Candidate			Rep.	Dem.	Rep.	Dem.
2022	240,140	135,474	Hoeven, John*	59,995	Christiansen, Katrina	44,671	75,479 R	56.4%	25.0%	69.3%	30.7%
2018	326,138	179,720	Cramer, Kevin	144,376	Heitkamp, Heidi*	2,042	35,344 R	55.1%	44.3%	55.5%	44.5%
2016	342,501	268,788	Hoeven, John*	58,116	Glassheim, Eliot	15,597	210,672 R	78.5%	17.0%	82.2%	17.8%
2012	320,851	158,282	Berg, Rick	161,163	Heitkamp, Heidi	1,406	2,881 D	49.3%	50.2%	49.5%	50.5%
2010	238,812	181,689	Hoeven, John	52,955	Potter, Tracy	4,168	128,734 R	76.1%	22.2%	77.4%	22.6%
2006	218,152	64,417	Grotberg, Dwight	150,146	Conrad, Kent*	3,589	85,729 D	29.5%	68.8%	30.0%	70.0%
2004	310,696	98,553	Liffrig, Mike G.	212,143	Dorgan, Byron L.*		113,590 D	31.7%	68.3%	31.7%	68.3%
2000	287,539	111,069	Sand, Duane	176,470	Conrad, Kent*		65,401 D	38.6%	61.4%	38.6%	61.4%
1998	213,358	75,013	Nalewaja, Donna	134,747	Dorgan, Byron L.*	3,598	59,734 D	35.2%	63.2%	35.8%	64.2%
1994	236,547	99,390	Clayburg, Ben	137,157	Conrad, Kent*		37,767 D	42.0%	58.0%	42.0%	58.0%
1992	303,957	118,162	Sydness, Steve	179,347	Dorgan, Byron L.	6,448	61,185 D	38.9%	59.0%	39.7%	60.3%
1992S**	163,311	55,194	Dalrymple, Jack	103,246	Conrad, Kent*	4,871	48,052 D	33.8%	63.2%	34.8%	65.2%
1988	289,170	112,937	Striden, Earl	171,899	Burdick, Quentin N.*	4,334	58,962 D	39.1%	59.4%	39.6%	60.4%
1986	288,998	141,797	Andrews, Mark*	143,932	Conrad, Kent	3,269	2,135 D	49.1%	49.8%	49.6%	50.4%
1982	262,465	89,304	Knorr, Gene	164,873	Burdick, Quentin N.*	8,288	75,569 D	34.0%	62.8%	35.1%	64.9%
1980	299,272	210,347	Andrews, Mark	86,658	Johanneson, Kent	2,267	123,689 R	70.3%	29.0%	70.8%	29.2%
1976	283,062	103,466	Stroup, Richard	175,772	Burdick, Quentin N.*	3,824	72,306 D	36.6%	62.1%	37.1%	62.9%
1974	235,661	114,117	Young, Milton R.*	113,931	Guy, William L.	7,613	186 R	48.4%	48.3%	50.0%	50.0%
1970	219,560	82,996	Kleppe, Tom	134,519	Burdick, Quentin N.*	2,045	51,523 D	37.8%	61.3%	38.2%	61.8%
1968	239,776	154,968	Young, Milton R.*	80,815	Lashkowitz, Herschel	3,993	74,153 R	64.6%	33.7%	65.7%	34.3%
1964	258,945	109,681	Kleppe, Tom	149,264	Burdick, Quentin N.*		39,583 D	42.4%	57.6%	42.4%	57.6%
1962	223,737	135,705	Young, Milton R.*	88,032	Lanier, William		47,673 R	60.7%	39.3%	60.7%	39.3%
1960S**	210,349	103,475	Davis, John E.	104,593	Burdick, Quentin N.	2,281	1,118 D	49.2%	49.7%	49.7%	50.3%
1958	204,635	117,070	Langer, William*	84,892	Vendsel, Raymond	2,673	32,178 R	57.2%	41.5%	58.0%	42.0%
1956	244,161	155,305	Young, Milton R.*	87,919	Burdick, Quentin N.	937	67,386 R	63.6%	36.0%	63.9%	36.1%
1952**	237,995	157,907	Langer, William*	55,347	Morrison, Harold A.	24,741	102,560 R	66.3%	23.3%	74.0%	26.0%
1950	186,716	126,209	Young, Milton R.*	60,507	O'Brien, Harry		65,702 R	67.6%	32.4%	67.6%	32.4%
1946**	165,382	88,210	Langer, William*	38,368	Larson, Abner B.	38,804	49,842 R	53.3%	23.2%	69.7%	30.3%
1946S**	136,852	75,998	Young, Milton R.*	37,507	Lanier, William	23,347	38,491 R	55.5%	27.4%	67.0%	33.0%

Note: An asterisk (*) denotes incumbent. **In past elections, the other vote included: 1952 - 24,741 Independent (Fred G. Aandahl); 1946 - 38,804 Independent (Arthur E. Thompson), who finished second; 1946 Special - 20,848 Independent (Gerald P. Nye). One of the 1992 elections was for a short term to fill a vacancy and the special election was held in December. The 1946 and 1960 special elections were held in June for short terms to fill vacancies.

NORTH DAKOTA

SENATOR 2022

2020 Census Population	County	Total Vote	Republican (Hoeven)	Democratic (Christiansen)	Other	Rep.-Dem. Plurality	Percentage			
							Total Vote		Major Vote	
							Rep.	Dem.	Rep.	Dem.
2,206	ADAMS	929	651	126	152	525 R	70.1%	13.6%	83.8%	16.2%
10,405	BARNES	3,888	2,314	978	596	1,336 R	59.5%	25.2%	70.3%	29.7%
6,827	BENSON	1,480	749	470	261	279 R	50.6%	31.8%	61.4%	38.6%
928	BILLINGS	537	381	48	108	333 R	70.9%	8.9%	88.8%	11.2%
6,263	BOTTINEAU	2,853	1,803	463	587	1,340 R	63.2%	16.2%	79.6%	20.4%
3,008	BOWMAN	1,356	1,003	126	227	877 R	74.0%	9.3%	88.8%	11.2%
2,106	BURKE	777	494	62	221	432 R	63.6%	8.0%	88.8%	11.2%
95,997	BURLEIGH	35,413	18,759	7,654	9,000	11,105 R	53.0%	21.6%	71.0%	29.0%
182,946	CASS	53,872	26,520	21,360	5,992	5,160 R	49.2%	39.6%	55.4%	44.6%
3,762	CAVALIER	1,570	1,123	267	180	856 R	71.5%	17.0%	80.8%	19.2%

NORTH DAKOTA
SENATOR 2022

2020 Census Population	County	Total Vote	Republican (Hoeven)	Democratic (Christiansen)	Other	Rep.-Dem. Plurality	Percentage Total Vote Rep.	Dem.	Major Vote Rep.	Dem.
4,874	DICKEY	1,782	1,211	335	236	876 R	68.0%	18.8%	78.3%	21.7%
2,261	DIVIDE	1,024	657	161	206	496 R	64.2%	15.7%	80.3%	19.7%
4,425	DUNN	1,653	1,107	189	357	918 R	67.0%	11.4%	85.4%	14.6%
2,292	EDDY	936	543	204	189	339 R	58.0%	21.8%	72.7%	27.3%
3,245	EMMONS	1,542	915	106	521	809 R	59.3%	6.9%	89.6%	10.4%
3,207	FOSTER	1,259	798	198	263	600 R	63.4%	15.7%	80.1%	19.9%
1,753	GOLDEN VALLEY	778	551	78	149	473 R	70.8%	10.0%	87.6%	12.4%
69,247	GRAND FORKS	18,887	9,954	6,474	2,459	3,480 R	52.7%	34.3%	60.6%	39.4%
2,268	GRANT	1,114	755	103	256	652 R	67.8%	9.2%	88.0%	12.0%
2,236	GRIGGS	994	656	178	160	478 R	66.0%	17.9%	78.7%	21.3%
2,501	HETTINGER	1,037	718	113	206	605 R	69.2%	10.9%	86.4%	13.6%
2,478	KIDDER	1,061	657	119	285	538 R	61.9%	11.2%	84.7%	15.3%
4,034	LA MOURE	1,646	1,124	313	209	811 R	68.3%	19.0%	78.2%	21.8%
1,844	LOGAN	821	541	68	212	473 R	65.9%	8.3%	88.8%	11.2%
5,733	MCHENRY	2,158	1,265	297	596	968 R	58.6%	13.8%	81.0%	19.0%
2,498	MCINTOSH	1,105	780	123	202	657 R	70.6%	11.1%	86.4%	13.6%
15,330	MCKENZIE	3,207	2,229	407	571	1,822 R	69.5%	12.7%	84.6%	15.4%
9,447	MCLEAN	4,241	2,385	720	1,136	1,665 R	56.2%	17.0%	76.8%	23.2%
8,154	MERCER	3,583	2,213	429	941	1,784 R	61.8%	12.0%	83.8%	16.2%
31,469	MORTON	11,358	6,130	2,101	3,127	4,029 R	54.0%	18.5%	74.5%	25.5%
10,552	MOUNTRAIL	2,621	1,393	632	596	761 R	53.1%	24.1%	68.8%	31.2%
2,879	NELSON	1,518	963	362	193	601 R	63.4%	23.8%	72.7%	27.3%
1,965	OLIVER	833	509	82	242	427 R	61.1%	9.8%	86.1%	13.9%
6,801	PEMBINA	2,461	1,737	406	318	1,331 R	70.6%	16.5%	81.1%	18.9%
3,966	PIERCE	1,495	876	227	392	649 R	58.6%	15.2%	79.4%	20.6%
11,477	RAMSEY	4,017	2,424	890	703	1,534 R	60.3%	22.2%	73.1%	26.9%
5,219	RANSOM	1,821	1,045	527	249	518 R	57.4%	28.9%	66.5%	33.5%
2,317	RENVILLE	896	547	87	262	460 R	61.0%	9.7%	86.3%	13.7%
16,164	RICHLAND	5,966	3,756	1,411	799	2,345 R	63.0%	23.7%	72.7%	27.3%
14,096	ROLETTE	2,732	1,118	1,268	346	150 D	40.9%	46.4%	46.9%	53.1%
3,905	SARGENT	1,581	988	403	190	585 R	62.5%	25.5%	71.0%	29.0%
1,309	SHERIDAN	624	361	64	199	297 R	57.9%	10.3%	84.9%	15.1%
4,202	SIOUX	584	176	301	107	125 D	30.1%	51.5%	36.9%	63.1%
746	SLOPE	302	226	23	53	203 R	74.8%	7.6%	90.8%	9.2%
31,594	STARK	9,146	5,927	1,138	2,081	4,789 R	64.8%	12.4%	83.9%	16.1%
1,893	STEELE	790	469	222	99	247 R	59.4%	28.1%	67.9%	32.1%
20,701	STUTSMAN	6,724	3,862	1,533	1,329	2,329 R	57.4%	22.8%	71.6%	28.4%
2,182	TOWNER	855	550	178	127	372 R	64.3%	20.8%	75.5%	24.5%
8,057	TRAILL	2,972	1,795	822	355	973 R	60.4%	27.7%	68.6%	31.4%
10,637	WALSH	3,481	2,416	640	425	1,776 R	69.4%	18.4%	79.1%	20.9%
67,410	WARD	16,756	9,849	3,314	3,593	6,535 R	58.8%	19.8%	74.8%	25.2%
3,834	WELLS	1,695	923	225	547	698 R	54.5%	13.3%	80.4%	19.6%
37,963	WILLIAMS	7,409	4,578	970	1,861	3,608 R	61.8%	13.1%	82.5%	17.5%
763,613	TOTAL	240,140	135,474	59,995	44,671	75,479 R	56.4%	25.0%	69.3%	30.7%

NORTH DAKOTA HOUSE OF REPRESENTATIVES

			Republican		Democratic		Other Vote	Rep.-Dem. Plurality	Percentage			
									Total Vote		Major Vote	
CD	Year	Total Vote	Vote	Candidate	Vote	Candidate			Rep.	Dem.	Rep.	Dem.
At Large	2022	238,586	148,399	ARMSTRONG, KELLY*			90,187	148,399 R	62.2%		100.0%	
At Large	2020	355,598	245,229	ARMSTRONG, KELLY*	97,970	RAKNERUD, ZACHARY	12,399	147,259 R	69.0%	27.6%	71.5%	28.5%
At Large	2018	321,532	193,568	ARMSTRONG, KELLY	114,377	SCHNEIDER, MAC	13,587	79,191 R	60.2%	35.6%	62.9%	37.1%
At Large	2016	338,459	233,980	CRAMER, KEVIN*	80,377	IRON EYES, CHASE	24,102	153,603 R	69.1%	23.7%	74.4%	25.6%
At Large	2014	248,670	138,100	CRAMER, KEVIN*	95,678	SINNER, GEORGE	14,892	42,422 R	55.5%	38.5%	59.1%	40.9%
At Large	2012	316,071	173,433	CRAMER, KEVIN	131,869	GULLESON, PAM	10,769	41,564 R	54.9%	41.7%	56.8%	43.2%
At Large	2010	237,137	129,802	BERG, RICK	106,542	POMEROY, EARL*	793	23,260 R	54.7%	44.9%	54.9%	45.1%
At Large	2008	313,965	119,388	SAND, DUANE	194,577	POMEROY, EARL*		75,189 D	38.0%	62.0%	38.0%	62.0%
At Large	2006	217,621	74,687	MECHTEL, MATT	142,934	POMEROY, EARL*		68,247 D	34.3%	65.7%	34.3%	65.7%
At Large	2004	310,814	125,684	SAND, DUANE	185,130	POMEROY, EARL*		59,446 D	40.4%	59.6%	40.4%	59.6%
At Large	2002	231,030	109,957	CLAYBURGH, RICK	121,073	POMEROY, EARL*		11,116 D	47.6%	52.4%	47.6%	52.4%
At Large	2000	285,658	127,251	DORSO, JOHN	151,173	POMEROY, EARL*	7,234	23,922 D	44.5%	52.9%	45.7%	54.3%
At Large	1998	212,888	87,511	CRAMER, KEVIN	119,668	POMEROY, EARL*	5,709	32,157 D	41.1%	56.2%	42.2%	57.8%
At Large	1996	263,010	113,684	CRAMER, KEVIN	144,833	POMEROY, EARL*	4,493	31,149 D	43.2%	55.1%	44.0%	56.0%
At Large	1994	235,389	105,988	PORTER, GARY	123,134	POMEROY, EARL*	6,267	17,146 D	45.0%	52.3%	46.3%	53.7%
At Large	1992	297,898	117,442	KORSMO, JOHN T.	169,273	POMEROY, EARL	11,183	51,831 D	39.4%	56.8%	41.0%	59.0%
At Large	1990	233,979	81,443	SCHAFER, EDWARD T.	152,530	DORGAN, BYRON L.*	6	71,087 D	34.8%	65.2%	34.8%	65.2%
At Large	1988	299,982	84,475	SYDNESS, STEVE	212,583	DORGAN, BYRON L.*	2,924	128,108 D	28.2%	70.9%	28.4%	71.6%
At Large	1986	286,361	66,989	VINJE, SYVER	216,258	DORGAN, BYRON L.*	3,114	149,269 D	23.4%	75.5%	23.7%	76.3%
At Large	1984	308,729	65,761	ALTENBURG, LOIS I.	242,968	DORGAN, BYRON L.*		177,207 D	21.3%	78.7%	21.3%	78.7%
At Large	1982	260,499	72,241	JONES, KENT	186,534	DORGAN, BYRON L.*	1,724	114,293 D	27.7%	71.6%	27.9%	72.1%
At Large	1980	293,076	124,707	SMYKOWSKI, JIM	166,437	DORGAN, BYRON L.	1,932	41,730 D	42.6%	56.8%	42.8%	57.2%
At Large	1978	220,348	147,746	ANDREWS, MARK*	68,016	HAGEN, BRUCE	4,586	79,730 R	67.1%	30.9%	68.5%	31.5%
At Large	1976	289,881	181,018	ANDREWS, MARK*	104,263	OMDAHL, LLOYD B.	4,600	76,755 R	62.4%	36.0%	63.5%	36.5%
At Large	1974	233,688	130,184	ANDREWS, MARK*	103,504	DORGAN, BYRON L.		26,680 R	55.7%	44.3%	55.7%	44.3%
At Large	1972	268,721	195,360	ANDREWS, MARK*	72,850	ISTA, RICHARD	511	122,510 R	72.7%	27.1%	72.8%	27.2%

Note: An asterisk (*) denotes incumbent.

NORTH DAKOTA

GENERAL AND PRIMARY ELECTIONS

GENERAL ELECTIONS: OTHER VOTES

Senate   Other vote was 44,406 Independent (Rick Becker), 265 Write-In (Write-Ins)

House   Other vote was:

At Large   89,644 Independent (Cara Mund), 543 Write-In (Write-Ins)

2022 PRIMARY ELECTIONS: SUPPLEMENTARY INFORMATION

Primary   June 14, 2022   **Registration**   No Party Registration
(No Formal Registration)

Primary Type   Open—Any person of voting age (18 years old at the time of the primary election) could participate in the primary of either party. As of June 14, 2022, North Dakota's estimated voting-age population was 564,935.

NORTH DAKOTA

GENERAL AND PRIMARY ELECTIONS

	REPUBLICAN PRIMARIES			DEMOCRATIC PRIMARIES		
Senator	Hoeven, John*	59,529	77.8%	Christiansen, Katrina	17,187	76.8%
	Kuntz, Riley	16,400	21.4%	Steele, Michael J.	5,174	23.1%
	Scattered Write-Ins	557	0.7%	Scattered Write-Ins	24	0.1%
	TOTAL	76,486		TOTAL	22,385	
Congressional At Large	Armstrong, Kelly*	70,424	99.0%	Haugen, Mark	21,897	99.7%
	Scattered Write-Ins	709	1.0%	Scattered Write-Ins	57	0.3%
	TOTAL	71,133		TOTAL	21,954	

Note: An asterisk (*) denotes incumbent.

OHIO

Statewide Races

In 2022, Ohio's open-seat Senate race became its marquee contest. Two-term GOP Sen. Rob Portman's retirement precipitated a competitive Republican primary. The state's early May contest was among the first statewide primaries of the year, and the result was seen as a victory for former President Donald Trump. In April, Trump endorsed author and venture capitalist J. D. Vance, who successfully grabbed the populist mantle. In a field with five serious candidates, Vance won with just over 32 percent of the vote.

Ohio Democrats had long wanted Rep. Tim Ryan, with a base in the Youngstown area, to run statewide. Ryan finally took the plunge in 2022. Ryan heavily outraised Vance, as the latter relied heavily on outside groups to close the gap. It was enough for a Vance win, but he underperformed the eight-point spread that Ohio twice gave Trump. Still, Vance's 53%–47% margin was a near mirror image of the 2018 result, when Democratic Sen. Sherrod Brown was reelected to the state's other seat. Ryan underperformed Brown in all 88 counties but, in a sign of the changing Democratic coalition, came closest to matching him in Delaware and Warren counties, just north of Columbus and Cincinnati, respectively. Ryan lost those two, but only fared about a point worse than Brown in each. In another sign of the times, Vance carried the pair of Mahoning and Trumbull counties, which Ryan had long represented, by five points, about matching Trump's margin.

Ohio's contest for governor was not as much of a race. Republican Gov. Mike DeWine, a septuagenarian who has a longer and more varied electoral resume than virtually any other officeholder, was reelected by 25 points. Though populist Republicans were not excited about renominating him, he carried all but three counties against Dayton Mayor Nan Whaley (D) in the general election.

House Races

It is probably fair to say that Ohio had the nation's most convoluted redistricting process. With the legislature, state Supreme Court, and a newly established redistricting commission involved, Ohio enacted a plan that was not as harsh of a GOP gerrymander as the outgoing map was, but it still favored Republicans. The 15-seat map featured 11 Trump-won districts. Of the four Biden-won seats, only two were safely Democratic.

Given the hand they were dealt, though, House Democrats held up about as well as could be expected. To start, they won both marginal Biden seats. In OH-1, which linked Cincinnati proper with Warren County, Democrat Greg Landsman ousted veteran Republican Steve Chabot. Democrats also held the open 13th District, which centered on Akron.

Perhaps the most notable House result in Ohio was in the Toledo-based OH-9. Redistricting turned Democratic Rep. Marcy Kaptur's previously blue seat into one that would have favored Trump by three points. Republicans nominated J. R. Majewski, who made headlines in 2020 by transforming his lawn into a Trump banner. But after reports surfaced that Majewski embellished his military record, national Republicans abandoned him. Kaptur won by 13 points – when she was sworn in for a 21st term, she became the longest-serving woman in the House.

OHIO
Congressional districts first established for elections held in 2022
15 members

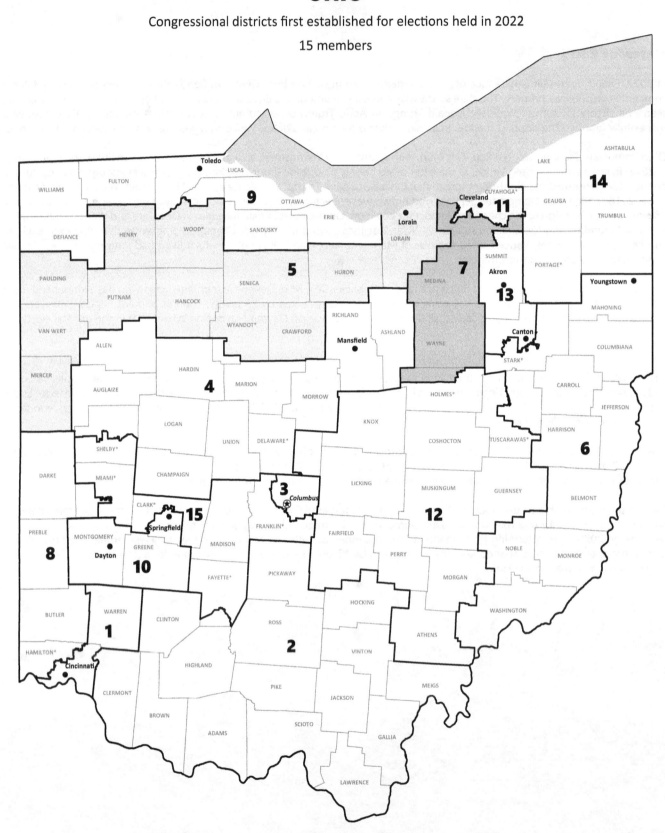

* Asterisk indicates a county whose boundaries include parts of two or more congressional districts.
CDs 5 and 7 are highlighted for visibility.

OHIO
Greater Cleveland Area

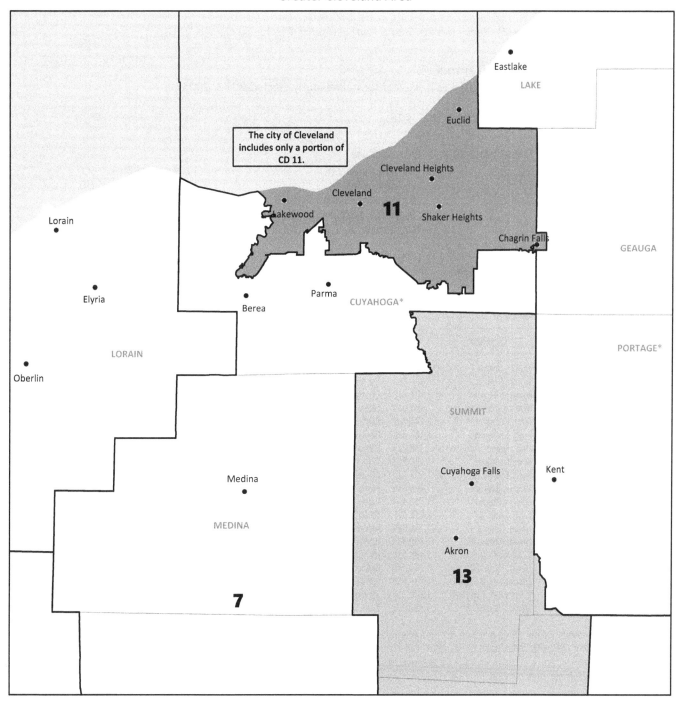

*Asterisk indicates a county whose boundaries include parts of two or more congressional districts.

CDs 11 and 13 are highlighted for visibility.

OHIO

GOVERNOR
Michael "Mike" DeWine (R). Reelected 2022 to a four-year term. Previously elected 2018.

SENATORS (1 Republican, 1 Democrat)
Sherrod Brown (D). Reelected 2018 to a six-year term. Previously elected 2012, 2006.

J. D. Vance (R). Elected 2022 to a six-year term.

REPRESENTATIVES (10 Republicans, 5 Democrats)
1. Greg Landsman (D)
2. Brad Wenstrup (R)
3. Joyce Beatty (D)
4. Jim Jordan (R)
5. Bob Latta (R)
6. Bill Johnson (R)
7. Max Miller (R)
8. Warren Davidson (R)
9. Marcy Kaptur (D)
10. Michael R. Turner (R)
11. Shontel Brown (D)
12. Troy Balderson (R)
13. Emilia Sykes (D)
14. David Joyce (R)
15. Mike Carey (R)

POSTWAR VOTE FOR PRESIDENT

Year	Total Vote	Republican Vote	Republican Candidate	Democratic Vote	Democratic Candidate	Other Vote	Rep.-Dem. Plurality	Total Vote Rep.	Total Vote Dem.	Major Vote Rep.	Major Vote Dem.
2020	5,922,202	3,154,834	Trump, Donald J.*	2,679,165	Biden, Joseph R. Jr.	88,203	475,669 R	53.3%	45.2%	54.1%	45.9%
2016**	5,496,487	2,841,005	Trump, Donald J.	2,394,164	Clinton, Hillary Rodham	261,318	446,841 R	51.7%	43.6%	54.3%	45.7%
2012	5,580,840	2,661,433	Romney, W. Mitt	2,827,710	Obama, Barack H.*	91,697	166,277 D	47.7%	50.7%	48.5%	51.5%
2008	5,708,350	2,677,820	McCain, John S. III	2,940,044	Obama, Barack H.	90,486	262,224 D	46.9%	51.5%	47.7%	52.3%
2004	5,627,908	2,859,768	Bush, George W.*	2,741,167	Kerry, John F.	26,973	118,601 R	50.8%	48.7%	51.1%	48.9%
2000**	4,701,998	2,350,363	Bush, George W.	2,183,628	Gore, Albert Jr.	168,007	166,735 R	50.0%	46.4%	51.8%	48.2%
1996**	4,534,434	1,859,883	Dole, Robert "Bob"	2,148,222	Clinton, Bill*	526,329	288,339 D	41.0%	47.4%	46.4%	53.6%
1992**	4,939,967	1,894,310	Bush, George H.*	1,984,942	Clinton, Bill	1,060,715	90,632 D	38.3%	40.2%	48.8%	51.2%
1988	4,393,699	2,416,549	Bush, George H.	1,939,629	Dukakis, Michael S.	37,521	476,920 R	55.0%	44.1%	55.5%	44.5%
1984	4,547,619	2,678,560	Reagan, Ronald*	1,825,440	Mondale, Walter F.	43,619	853,120 R	58.9%	40.1%	59.5%	40.5%
1980**	4,283,603	2,206,545	Reagan, Ronald	1,752,414	Carter, Jimmy*	324,644	454,131 R	51.5%	40.9%	55.7%	44.3%
1976	4,111,873	2,000,505	Ford, Gerald R.*	2,011,621	Carter, Jimmy	99,747	11,116 D	48.7%	48.9%	49.9%	50.1%
1972	4,094,787	2,441,827	Nixon, Richard M.*	1,558,889	McGovern, George S.	94,071	882,938 R	59.6%	38.1%	61.0%	39.0%
1968**	3,959,698	1,791,014	Nixon, Richard M.	1,700,586	Humphrey, Hubert Horatio Jr.	468,098	90,428 R	45.2%	42.9%	51.3%	48.7%
1964	3,969,196	1,470,865	Goldwater, Barry M. Sr.	2,498,331	Johnson, Lyndon B.*		1,027,466 D	37.1%	62.9%	37.1%	62.9%
1960	4,161,859	2,217,611	Nixon, Richard M.	1,944,248	Kennedy, John F.		273,363 R	53.3%	46.7%	53.3%	46.7%
1956	3,702,265	2,262,610	Eisenhower, Dwight D.*	1,439,655	Stevenson, Adlai E. II		822,955 R	61.1%	38.9%	61.1%	38.9%
1952	3,700,758	2,100,391	Eisenhower, Dwight D.	1,600,367	Stevenson, Adlai E. II		500,024 R	56.8%	43.2%	56.8%	43.2%
1948	2,936,071	1,445,684	Dewey, Thomas E.	1,452,791	Truman, Harry S.*	37,596	7,107 D	49.2%	49.5%	49.9%	50.1%

Note: An asterisk (*) denotes incumbent. **In past elections, the other vote included: 2016 - 174,498 Libertarian (Gary Johnson); 2000 - 117,799 Green (Ralph Nader); 1996 - 483,207 Reform (Ross Perot); 1992 - 1,036,426 Independent (Perot); 1980 - 254,472 Independent (John Anderson); 1968 - 467,495 American Independent (George Wallace).

OHIO

POSTWAR VOTE FOR GOVERNOR

Year	Total Vote	Republican Vote	Republican Candidate	Democratic Vote	Democratic Candidate	Other Vote	Rep.-Dem. Plurality	Total Vote Rep.	Total Vote Dem.	Major Vote Rep.	Major Vote Dem.
2022	4,134,877	2,580,424	DeWine, Michael "Mike"*	1,545,489	Whaley, Nan	8,964	1,034,935 R	62.4%	37.4%	62.5%	37.5%
2018	4,429,582	2,231,917	DeWine, Michael "Mike"	2,067,847	Cordray, Richard	129,818	164,070 R	50.4%	46.7%	51.9%	48.1%
2014	3,055,913	1,944,848	Kasich, John R.*	1,009,359	FitzGerald, Ed	101,706	935,489 R	63.6%	33.0%	65.8%	34.2%
2010	3,852,469	1,889,186	Kasich, John R.	1,812,059	Strickland, Ted*	151,224	77,127 R	49.0%	47.0%	51.0%	49.0%
2006	4,022,754	1,474,285	Blackwell, J. Kenneth	2,435,384	Strickland, Ted	113,085	961,099 D	36.6%	60.5%	37.7%	62.3%
2002	3,228,992	1,865,007	Taft, Robert Alphonso*	1,236,924	Hagan, Timothy	127,061	628,083 R	57.8%	38.3%	60.1%	39.9%
1998	3,354,213	1,678,721	Taft, Robert Alphonso	1,498,956	Fisher, Lee	176,536	179,765 R	50.0%	44.7%	52.8%	47.2%
1994	3,346,238	2,401,572	Voinovich, George*	835,849	Burch, Robert L.	108,817	1,565,723 R	71.8%	25.0%	74.2%	25.8%
1990	3,482,650	1,938,103	Voinovich, George	1,544,416	Celebrezze, Anthony J.	131	393,687 R	55.7%	44.3%	55.7%	44.3%
1986	3,066,611	1,207,264	Rhodes, James A.	1,858,372	Celeste, Richard F.*	975	651,108 D	39.4%	60.6%	39.4%	60.6%
1982	3,356,791	1,303,962	Brown, Clarence J. Jr.	1,981,952	Celeste, Richard F.	70,877	677,990 D	38.8%	59.0%	39.7%	60.3%
1978	2,843,351	1,402,167	Rhodes, James A.*	1,354,631	Celeste, Richard F.	86,553	47,536 R	49.3%	47.6%	50.9%	49.1%
1974	3,072,010	1,493,679	Rhodes, James A.	1,482,191	Gilligan, John J.*	96,140	11,488 R	48.6%	48.2%	50.2%	49.8%
1970	3,184,131	1,382,657	Cloud, Roger	1,725,560	Gilligan, John J.	75,914	342,903 D	43.4%	54.2%	44.5%	55.5%
1966	2,887,331	1,795,277	Rhodes, James A.*	1,092,054	Reams, Henry Frazier "Frazier" Jr.		703,223 R	62.2%	37.8%	62.2%	37.8%
1962	3,116,953	1,836,432	Rhodes, James A.	1,280,521	Disalle, Michael V.*		555,911 R	58.9%	41.1%	58.9%	41.1%
1958**	3,284,134	1,414,874	O'Neill, C. William*	1,869,260	Disalle, Michael V.		454,386 D	43.1%	56.9%	43.1%	56.9%
1956	3,542,091	1,984,988	O'Neill, C. William	1,557,103	Disalle, Michael V.		427,885 R	56.0%	44.0%	56.0%	44.0%
1954	2,597,790	1,192,528	Rhodes, James A.	1,405,262	Lausche, Frank J.*		212,734 D	45.9%	54.1%	45.9%	54.1%
1952	3,605,168	1,590,058	Taft, Charles P.	2,015,110	Lausche, Frank J.*		425,052 D	44.1%	55.9%	44.1%	55.9%
1950	2,892,819	1,370,570	Ebright, Don H.	1,522,249	Lausche, Frank J.*		151,679 D	47.4%	52.6%	47.4%	52.6%
1948	3,018,289	1,398,514	Herbert, Thomas J.*	1,619,775	Lausche, Frank J.		221,261 D	46.3%	53.7%	46.3%	53.7%
1946	2,303,750	1,166,550	Herbert, Thomas J.	1,125,997	Lausche, Frank J.*	11,203	40,553 R	50.6%	48.9%	50.9%	49.1%

Note: An asterisk (*) denotes incumbent. **The term of office of Ohio's Governor was increased from two to four years effective with the 1958 election.

POSTWAR VOTE FOR SENATOR

Year	Total Vote	Republican Vote	Republican Candidate	Democratic Vote	Democratic Candidate	Other Vote	Rep.-Dem. Plurality	Total Vote Rep.	Total Vote Dem.	Major Vote Rep.	Major Vote Dem.
2022	4,133,342	2,192,114	Vance, James David "J.D."	1,939,489	Ryan, Tim	1,739	252,625 R	53.0%	46.9%	53.1%	46.9%
2018	4,410,898	2,053,963	Renacci, Jim	2,355,923	Brown, Sherrod*	1,012	301,960 D	46.6%	53.4%	46.6%	53.4%
2016	5,374,164	3,118,567	Portman, Rob*	1,996,908	Strickland, Ted	258,689	1,121,659 R	58.0%	37.2%	61.0%	39.0%
2012	5,449,114	2,435,740	Mandel, Josh	2,762,757	Brown, Sherrod*	250,617	327,017 D	44.7%	50.7%	46.9%	53.1%
2010	3,815,098	2,168,742	Portman, Rob	1,503,297	Fisher, Lee	143,059	665,445 R	56.8%	39.4%	59.1%	40.9%
2006	4,019,236	1,761,037	DeWine, Michael "Mike"*	2,257,369	Brown, Sherrod	830	496,332 D	43.8%	56.2%	43.8%	56.2%
2004	5,426,196	3,464,651	Voinovich, George*	1,961,249	Fingerhut, Eric D.	296	1,503,402 R	63.9%	36.1%	63.9%	36.1%
2000	4,448,801	2,665,512	DeWine, Michael "Mike"*	1,595,066	Celeste, Theodore S.	188,223	1,070,446 R	59.9%	35.9%	62.6%	37.4%
1998	3,404,351	1,922,087	Voinovich, George	1,482,054	Boyle, Mary O.	210	440,033 R	56.5%	43.5%	56.5%	43.5%
1994	3,436,884	1,836,556	DeWine, Michael "Mike"	1,348,213	Hyatt, Joel	252,115	488,343 R	53.4%	39.2%	57.7%	42.3%
1992	4,793,953	2,028,300	DeWine, Michael "Mike"	2,444,419	Glenn, John H.*	321,234	416,119 D	42.3%	51.0%	45.3%	54.7%
1988	4,352,905	1,872,716	Voinovich, George	2,480,038	Metzenbaum, Howard M.*	151	607,322 D	43.0%	57.0%	43.0%	57.0%
1986	3,121,188	1,171,893	Kindness, Thomas N.	1,949,208	Glenn, John H.*	87	777,315 D	37.5%	62.5%	37.5%	62.5%
1982	3,395,463	1,396,790	Pfeifer, Paul E.	1,923,767	Metzenbaum, Howard M.*	74,906	526,977 D	41.1%	56.7%	42.1%	57.9%
1980	4,027,303	1,137,695	Betts, James E.	2,770,786	Glenn, John H.*	118,822	1,633,091 D	28.2%	68.8%	29.1%	70.9%
1976	3,920,613	1,823,774	Taft, Robert Alphonso*	1,941,113	Metzenbaum, Howard M.	155,726	117,339 D	46.5%	49.5%	48.4%	51.6%
1974	2,987,951	918,133	Perk, Ralph J.	1,930,670	Glenn, John H.	139,148	1,012,537 D	30.7%	64.6%	32.2%	67.8%
1970	3,151,274	1,565,682	Taft, Robert Alphonso	1,495,262	Metzenbaum, Howard M.	90,330	70,420 R	49.7%	47.4%	51.2%	48.8%
1968	3,743,121	1,928,964	Saxbe, William B.	1,814,152	Gilligan, John J.	5	114,812 R	51.5%	48.5%	51.5%	48.5%
1964	3,830,389	1,906,781	Taft, Robert Alphonso	1,923,608	Young, Stephen M.*		16,827 D	49.8%	50.2%	49.8%	50.2%
1962	2,995,105	1,151,292	Briley, John Marshall	1,843,813	Lausche, Frank J.*		692,521 D	38.4%	61.6%	38.4%	61.6%
1958	3,149,410	1,497,199	Bricker, John W.*	1,652,211	Young, Stephen M.		155,012 D	47.5%	52.5%	47.5%	52.5%
1956	3,525,499	1,660,910	Bender, George H.*	1,864,589	Lausche, Frank J.		203,679 D	47.1%	52.9%	47.1%	52.9%
1954S**	2,512,773	1,257,874	Bender, George H.	1,254,899	Burke, Thomas A.		2,975 R	50.1%	49.9%	50.1%	49.9%
1952	3,442,291	1,878,961	Bricker, John W.*	1,563,330	Disalle, Michael V.		315,631 R	54.6%	45.4%	54.6%	45.4%
1950	2,860,102	1,645,643	Taft, Robert Alphonso*	1,214,459	Ferguson, Joseph T.		431,184 R	57.5%	42.5%	57.5%	42.5%
1946	2,237,269	1,275,774	Bricker, John W.	947,610	Huffman, James W.	13,885	328,164 R	57.0%	42.4%	57.4%	42.6%
1946S**	2,123,526	1,193,942	Taft, Kingsley A.	929,584	Webber, Henry P.		264,358 R	56.2%	43.8%	56.2%	43.8%

Note: An asterisk (*) denotes incumbent. **One of the 1946 elections and the 1954 election were for short terms to fill a vacancy.

OHIO
GOVERNOR 2022

2020 Census Population	County	Total Vote	Republican (DeWine)	Democratic (Whaley)	Other	Rep.-Dem. Plurality		Percentage Total Vote		Percentage Major Vote	
								Rep.	Dem.	Rep.	Dem.
27,725	ADAMS	8,764	7,348	1,395	21	5,953	R	83.8%	15.9%	84.0%	16.0%
102,294	ALLEN	32,449	25,461	6,835	153	18,626	R	78.5%	21.1%	78.8%	21.2%
53,550	ASHLAND	18,344	14,510	3,729	105	10,781	R	79.1%	20.3%	79.6%	20.4%
97,260	ASHTABULA	30,573	20,903	9,621	49	11,282	R	68.4%	31.5%	68.5%	31.5%
65,267	ATHENS	19,081	8,920	10,155	6	1,235	D	46.7%	53.2%	46.8%	53.2%
45,702	AUGLAIZE	18,554	16,019	2,474	61	13,545	R	86.3%	13.3%	86.6%	13.4%
67,029	BELMONT	22,495	16,884	5,546	65	11,338	R	75.1%	24.7%	75.3%	24.7%
43,516	BROWN	14,144	11,658	2,372	114	9,286	R	82.4%	16.8%	83.1%	16.9%
384,046	BUTLER	128,448	90,063	38,186	199	51,877	R	70.1%	29.7%	70.2%	29.8%
26,902	CARROLL	10,073	8,074	1,969	30	6,105	R	80.2%	19.5%	80.4%	19.6%
38,950	CHAMPAIGN	14,369	11,324	2,962	83	8,362	R	78.8%	20.6%	79.3%	20.7%
134,171	CLARK	43,748	31,121	12,559	68	18,562	R	71.1%	28.7%	71.2%	28.8%
207,021	CLERMONT	80,178	59,153	20,888	137	38,265	R	73.8%	26.1%	73.9%	26.1%
42,021	CLINTON	14,102	11,479	2,583	40	8,896	R	81.4%	18.3%	81.6%	18.4%
101,939	COLUMBIANA	35,330	28,013	7,169	148	20,844	R	79.3%	20.3%	79.6%	20.4%
36,658	COSHOCTON	11,305	8,901	2,369	35	6,532	R	78.7%	21.0%	79.0%	21.0%
41,534	CRAWFORD	14,757	11,781	2,949	27	8,832	R	79.8%	20.0%	80.0%	20.0%
1,234,398	CUYAHOGA	410,267	175,697	234,076	494	58,379	D	42.8%	57.1%	42.9%	57.1%
51,136	DARKE	19,789	17,278	2,464	47	14,814	R	87.3%	12.5%	87.5%	12.5%
38,122	DEFIANCE	13,352	10,180	3,139	33	7,041	R	76.2%	23.5%	76.4%	23.6%
210,414	DELAWARE	98,812	62,733	35,942	137	26,791	R	63.5%	36.4%	63.6%	36.4%
74,370	ERIE	28,924	18,651	10,236	37	8,415	R	64.5%	35.4%	64.6%	35.4%
158,181	FAIRFIELD	58,988	41,017	17,842	129	23,175	R	69.5%	30.2%	69.7%	30.3%
28,561	FAYETTE	8,405	6,913	1,476	16	5,437	R	82.2%	17.6%	82.4%	17.6%
1,319,380	FRANKLIN	425,756	182,914	242,332	510	59,418	D	43.0%	56.9%	43.0%	57.0%
42,167	FULTON	16,367	13,008	3,324	35	9,684	R	79.5%	20.3%	79.6%	20.4%
29,909	GALLIA	9,006	7,229	1,677	100	5,552	R	80.3%	18.6%	81.2%	18.8%
93,749	GEAUGA	42,449	28,930	13,344	175	15,586	R	68.2%	31.4%	68.4%	31.6%
169,725	GREENE	65,992	45,528	20,367	97	25,161	R	69.0%	30.9%	69.1%	30.9%
38,918	GUERNSEY	12,155	9,486	2,530	139	6,956	R	78.0%	20.8%	78.9%	21.1%
818,738	HAMILTON	303,971	155,577	148,023	371	7,554	R	51.2%	48.7%	51.2%	48.8%
75,810	HANCOCK	27,216	20,975	6,127	114	14,848	R	77.1%	22.5%	77.4%	22.6%
31,407	HARDIN	8,965	7,210	1,717	38	5,493	R	80.4%	19.2%	80.8%	19.2%
15,059	HARRISON	5,165	4,079	1,072	14	3,007	R	79.0%	20.8%	79.2%	20.8%
26,991	HENRY	10,403	8,437	1,949	17	6,488	R	81.1%	18.7%	81.2%	18.8%
43,244	HIGHLAND	13,059	10,880	2,114	65	8,766	R	83.3%	16.2%	83.7%	16.3%
28,312	HOCKING	9,483	7,046	2,405	32	4,641	R	74.3%	25.4%	74.6%	25.4%
43,861	HOLMES	8,448	7,262	1,115	71	6,147	R	86.0%	13.2%	86.7%	13.3%
58,344	HURON	18,425	13,904	4,464	57	9,440	R	75.5%	24.2%	75.7%	24.3%
32,454	JACKSON	8,791	7,033	1,749	9	5,284	R	80.0%	19.9%	80.1%	19.9%
65,356	JEFFERSON	22,828	16,929	5,855	44	11,074	R	74.2%	25.6%	74.3%	25.7%
62,577	KNOX	22,953	17,349	5,525	79	11,824	R	75.6%	24.1%	75.8%	24.2%
230,796	LAKE	94,339	61,121	33,098	120	28,023	R	64.8%	35.1%	64.9%	35.1%
59,582	LAWRENCE	17,430	13,602	3,815	13	9,787	R	78.0%	21.9%	78.1%	21.9%
177,657	LICKING	66,168	46,881	19,143	144	27,738	R	70.9%	28.9%	71.0%	29.0%
45,788	LOGAN	16,413	13,553	2,777	83	10,776	R	82.6%	16.9%	83.0%	17.0%
310,712	LORAIN	110,831	66,289	44,314	228	21,975	R	59.8%	40.0%	59.9%	40.1%
427,945	LUCAS	132,954	72,214	60,516	224	11,698	R	54.3%	45.5%	54.4%	45.6%
44,946	MADISON	14,075	10,783	3,244	48	7,539	R	76.6%	23.0%	76.9%	23.1%
229,499	MAHONING	85,213	55,676	29,444	93	26,232	R	65.3%	34.6%	65.4%	34.6%
65,056	MARION	19,115	14,263	4,818	34	9,445	R	74.6%	25.2%	74.7%	25.3%
180,310	MEDINA	77,918	53,498	24,034	386	29,464	R	68.7%	30.8%	69.0%	31.0%
22,949	MEIGS	7,359	5,755	1,519	85	4,236	R	78.2%	20.6%	79.1%	20.9%
41,200	MERCER	17,675	15,403	2,230	42	13,173	R	87.1%	12.6%	87.4%	12.6%
107,451	MIAMI	42,240	33,709	8,452	79	25,257	R	79.8%	20.0%	80.0%	20.0%
13,654	MONROE	4,853	3,793	1,022	38	2,771	R	78.2%	21.1%	78.8%	21.2%
532,475	MONTGOMERY	187,104	110,672	76,154	278	34,518	R	59.1%	40.7%	59.2%	40.8%
14,529	MORGAN	4,772	3,808	958	6	2,850	R	79.8%	20.1%	79.9%	20.1%
35,419	MORROW	13,222	10,698	2,475	49	8,223	R	80.9%	18.7%	81.2%	18.8%
86,365	MUSKINGUM	27,344	21,064	6,230	50	14,834	R	77.0%	22.8%	77.2%	22.8%

OHIO
GOVERNOR 2022

2020 Census Population	County	Total Vote	Republican (DeWine)	Democratic (Whaley)	Other	Rep.-Dem. Plurality	Percentage Total Vote Rep.	Dem.	Major Vote Rep.	Dem.
14,439	NOBLE	4,592	3,785	778	29	3,007 R	82.4%	16.9%	82.9%	17.1%
40,643	OTTAWA	18,509	13,312	5,171	26	8,141 R	71.9%	27.9%	72.0%	28.0%
18,678	PAULDING	6,473	5,169	1,285	19	3,884 R	79.9%	19.9%	80.1%	19.9%
36,189	PERRY	11,828	9,263	2,515	50	6,748 R	78.3%	21.3%	78.6%	21.4%
58,684	PICKAWAY	19,545	15,209	4,289	47	10,920 R	77.8%	21.9%	78.0%	22.0%
27,846	PIKE	7,744	5,889	1,842	13	4,047 R	76.0%	23.8%	76.2%	23.8%
162,706	PORTAGE	60,416	37,634	22,665	117	14,969 R	62.3%	37.5%	62.4%	37.6%
40,907	PREBLE	15,717	13,172	2,504	41	10,668 R	83.8%	15.9%	84.0%	16.0%
33,863	PUTNAM	14,989	13,402	1,550	37	11,852 R	89.4%	10.3%	89.6%	10.4%
121,566	RICHLAND	41,497	30,899	10,429	169	20,470 R	74.5%	25.1%	74.8%	25.2%
76,585	ROSS	22,577	16,496	6,037	44	10,459 R	73.1%	26.7%	73.2%	26.8%
58,549	SANDUSKY	21,422	15,712	5,631	79	10,081 R	73.3%	26.3%	73.6%	26.4%
75,397	SCIOTO	21,005	15,934	5,048	23	10,886 R	75.9%	24.0%	75.9%	24.1%
55,227	SENECA	18,044	13,667	4,319	58	9,348 R	75.7%	23.9%	76.0%	24.0%
48,586	SHELBY	18,058	15,717	2,291	50	13,426 R	87.0%	12.7%	87.3%	12.7%
371,267	STARK	133,932	90,387	43,082	463	47,305 R	67.5%	32.2%	67.7%	32.3%
541,823	SUMMIT	198,341	105,776	92,205	360	13,571 R	53.3%	46.5%	53.4%	46.6%
198,183	TRUMBULL	72,747	48,459	24,163	125	24,296 R	66.6%	33.2%	66.7%	33.3%
92,063	TUSCARAWAS	30,165	22,296	7,685	184	14,611 R	73.9%	25.5%	74.4%	25.6%
59,309	UNION	25,382	18,387	6,918	77	11,469 R	72.4%	27.3%	72.7%	27.3%
28,311	VAN WERT	10,020	8,279	1,702	39	6,577 R	82.6%	17.0%	82.9%	17.1%
13,108	VINTON	3,971	3,111	832	28	2,279 R	78.3%	21.0%	78.9%	21.1%
235,882	WARREN	101,618	74,345	27,070	203	47,275 R	73.2%	26.6%	73.3%	26.7%
59,961	WASHINGTON	22,641	16,934	5,625	82	11,309 R	74.8%	24.8%	75.1%	24.9%
115,744	WAYNE	38,346	28,284	9,824	238	18,460 R	73.8%	25.6%	74.2%	25.8%
36,762	WILLIAMS	12,915	10,331	2,543	41	7,788 R	80.0%	19.7%	80.2%	19.8%
131,035	WOOD	48,554	31,399	17,060	95	14,339 R	64.7%	35.1%	64.8%	35.2%
21,773	WYANDOT	8,121	6,537	1,558	26	4,979 R	80.5%	19.2%	80.8%	19.2%
11,708,187	TOTAL	4,134,877	2,580,424	1,545,489	8,964	1,034,935 R	62.4%	37.4%	62.5%	37.5%

OHIO
SENATOR 2022

2020 Census Population	County	Total Vote	Republican (Vance)	Democratic (Ryan)	Other	Rep.-Dem. Plurality	Percentage Total Vote Rep.	Dem.	Major Vote Rep.	Dem.
27,725	ADAMS	8,726	6,749	1,976	1	4,773 R	77.3%	22.6%	77.4%	22.6%
102,294	ALLEN	32,666	23,229	9,428	9	13,801 R	71.1%	28.9%	71.1%	28.9%
53,550	ASHLAND	18,409	13,366	5,034	9	8,332 R	72.6%	27.3%	72.6%	27.4%
97,260	ASHTABULA	30,852	18,277	12,561	14	5,716 R	59.2%	40.7%	59.3%	40.7%
65,267	ATHENS	19,065	7,482	11,578	5	4,096 D	39.2%	60.7%	39.3%	60.7%
45,702	AUGLAIZE	18,671	15,022	3,641	8	11,381 R	80.5%	19.5%	80.5%	19.5%
67,029	BELMONT	22,530	15,169	7,356	5	7,813 R	67.3%	32.6%	67.3%	32.7%
43,516	BROWN	14,137	10,832	3,300	5	7,532 R	76.6%	23.3%	76.6%	23.4%
384,046	BUTLER	128,052	79,240	48,777	35	30,463 R	61.9%	38.1%	61.9%	38.1%
26,902	CARROLL	10,122	7,372	2,743	7	4,629 R	72.8%	27.1%	72.9%	27.1%
38,950	CHAMPAIGN	14,402	10,253	4,095	54	6,158 R	71.2%	28.4%	71.5%	28.5%
134,171	CLARK	44,282	27,131	17,141	10	9,990 R	61.3%	38.7%	61.3%	38.7%
207,021	CLERMONT	80,006	52,888	27,084	34	25,804 R	66.1%	33.9%	66.1%	33.9%
42,021	CLINTON	14,084	10,515	3,562	7	6,953 R	74.7%	25.3%	74.7%	25.3%
101,939	COLUMBIANA	35,545	24,829	10,705	11	14,124 R	69.9%	30.1%	69.9%	30.1%

OHIO
SENATOR 2022

2020 Census Population	County	Total Vote	Republican (Vance)	Democratic (Ryan)	Other	Rep.-Dem. Plurality	Percentage Total Vote		Major Vote	
							Rep.	Dem.	Rep.	Dem.
36,658	COSHOCTON	11,281	8,021	3,255	5	4,766 R	71.1%	28.9%	71.1%	28.9%
41,534	CRAWFORD	14,804	10,855	3,948	1	6,907 R	73.3%	26.7%	73.3%	26.7%
1,234,398	CUYAHOGA	408,543	131,427	277,039	77	145,612 D	32.2%	67.8%	32.2%	67.8%
51,136	DARKE	19,755	15,977	3,773	5	12,204 R	80.9%	19.1%	80.9%	19.1%
38,122	DEFIANCE	13,336	8,821	4,513	2	4,308 R	66.1%	33.8%	66.2%	33.8%
210,414	DELAWARE	98,885	52,539	46,319	27	6,220 R	53.1%	46.8%	53.1%	46.9%
74,370	ERIE	28,833	15,287	13,541	5	1,746 R	53.0%	47.0%	53.0%	47.0%
158,181	FAIRFIELD	59,258	35,926	23,305	27	12,621 R	60.6%	39.3%	60.7%	39.3%
28,561	FAYETTE	8,389	6,287	2,102		4,185 R	74.9%	25.1%	74.9%	25.1%
1,319,380	FRANKLIN	425,060	143,263	281,505	292	138,242 D	33.7%	66.2%	33.7%	66.3%
42,167	FULTON	16,207	10,906	5,299	2	5,607 R	67.3%	32.7%	67.3%	32.7%
29,909	GALLIA	9,114	6,993	2,116	5	4,877 R	76.7%	23.2%	76.8%	23.2%
93,749	GEAUGA	42,694	25,331	17,348	15	7,983 R	59.3%	40.6%	59.4%	40.6%
169,725	GREENE	65,716	39,189	26,490	37	12,699 R	59.6%	40.3%	59.7%	40.3%
38,918	GUERNSEY	12,192	8,678	3,505	9	5,173 R	71.2%	28.7%	71.2%	28.8%
818,738	HAMILTON	302,486	127,792	174,511	183	46,719 D	42.2%	57.7%	42.3%	57.7%
75,810	HANCOCK	27,088	18,357	8,717	14	9,640 R	67.8%	32.2%	67.8%	32.2%
31,407	HARDIN	8,997	6,521	2,471	5	4,050 R	72.5%	27.5%	72.5%	27.5%
15,059	HARRISON	5,172	3,721	1,451		2,270 R	71.9%	28.1%	71.9%	28.1%
26,991	HENRY	10,294	7,102	3,190	2	3,912 R	69.0%	31.0%	69.0%	31.0%
43,244	HIGHLAND	13,112	10,185	2,925	2	7,260 R	77.7%	22.3%	77.7%	22.3%
28,312	HOCKING	9,495	6,353	3,139	3	3,214 R	66.9%	33.1%	66.9%	33.1%
43,861	HOLMES	8,624	7,056	1,564	4	5,492 R	81.8%	18.1%	81.9%	18.1%
58,344	HURON	18,404	12,398	5,998	8	6,400 R	67.4%	32.6%	67.4%	32.6%
32,454	JACKSON	8,885	6,599	2,285	1	4,314 R	74.3%	25.7%	74.3%	25.7%
65,356	JEFFERSON	22,894	14,970	7,914	10	7,056 R	65.4%	34.6%	65.4%	34.6%
62,577	KNOX	23,080	16,104	6,969	7	9,135 R	69.8%	30.2%	69.8%	30.2%
230,796	LAKE	94,071	50,890	43,166	15	7,724 R	54.1%	45.9%	54.1%	45.9%
59,582	LAWRENCE	17,490	12,697	4,793		7,904 R	72.6%	27.4%	72.6%	27.4%
177,657	LICKING	66,371	41,566	24,774	31	16,792 R	62.6%	37.3%	62.7%	37.3%
45,788	LOGAN	16,454	12,551	3,898	5	8,653 R	76.3%	23.7%	76.3%	23.7%
310,712	LORAIN	111,727	54,488	57,191	48	2,703 D	48.8%	51.2%	48.8%	51.2%
427,945	LUCAS	131,765	53,009	78,727	29	25,718 D	40.2%	59.7%	40.2%	59.8%
44,946	MADISON	14,120	9,763	4,350	7	5,413 R	69.1%	30.8%	69.2%	30.8%
229,499	MAHONING	85,837	44,397	41,421	19	2,976 R	51.7%	48.3%	51.7%	48.3%
65,056	MARION	19,105	12,760	6,342	3	6,418 R	66.8%	33.2%	66.8%	33.2%
180,310	MEDINA	77,974	45,960	31,979	35	13,981 R	58.9%	41.0%	59.0%	41.0%
22,949	MEIGS	7,468	5,589	1,875	4	3,714 R	74.8%	25.1%	74.9%	25.1%
41,200	MERCER	17,782	14,390	3,389	3	11,001 R	80.9%	19.1%	80.9%	19.1%
107,451	MIAMI	42,131	30,114	11,993	24	18,121 R	71.5%	28.5%	71.5%	28.5%
13,654	MONROE	4,863	3,479	1,378	6	2,101 R	71.5%	28.3%	71.6%	28.4%
532,475	MONTGOMERY	186,002	91,382	94,512	108	3,130 D	49.1%	50.8%	49.2%	50.8%
14,529	MORGAN	4,811	3,494	1,317		2,177 R	72.6%	27.4%	72.6%	27.4%
35,419	MORROW	13,290	9,985	3,303	2	6,682 R	75.1%	24.9%	75.1%	24.9%
86,365	MUSKINGUM	27,307	18,664	8,638	5	10,026 R	68.3%	31.6%	68.4%	31.6%
14,439	NOBLE	4,606	3,519	1,083	4	2,436 R	76.4%	23.5%	76.5%	23.5%
40,643	OTTAWA	18,405	10,653	7,750	2	2,903 R	57.9%	42.1%	57.9%	42.1%
18,678	PAULDING	6,462	4,873	1,587	2	3,286 R	75.4%	24.6%	75.4%	24.6%
36,189	PERRY	11,935	8,557	3,342	36	5,215 R	71.7%	28.0%	71.9%	28.1%
58,684	PICKAWAY	19,562	13,859	5,696	7	8,163 R	70.8%	29.1%	70.9%	29.1%
27,846	PIKE	7,815	5,488	2,327		3,161 R	70.2%	29.8%	70.2%	29.8%
162,706	PORTAGE	60,481	32,274	28,175	32	4,099 R	53.4%	46.6%	53.4%	46.6%
40,907	PREBLE	15,694	12,156	3,533	5	8,623 R	77.5%	22.5%	77.5%	22.5%
33,863	PUTNAM	15,004	12,332	2,667	5	9,665 R	82.2%	17.8%	82.2%	17.8%
121,566	RICHLAND	41,732	28,812	12,904	16	15,908 R	69.0%	30.9%	69.1%	30.9%
76,585	ROSS	22,592	14,728	7,858	6	6,870 R	65.2%	34.8%	65.2%	34.8%
58,549	SANDUSKY	21,308	13,076	8,177	55	4,899 R	61.4%	38.4%	61.5%	38.5%
75,397	SCIOTO	21,069	14,656	6,411	2	8,245 R	69.6%	30.4%	69.6%	30.4%
55,227	SENECA	17,958	11,618	6,322	18	5,296 R	64.7%	35.2%	64.8%	35.2%
48,586	SHELBY	18,028	14,512	3,509	7	11,003 R	80.5%	19.5%	80.5%	19.5%

OHIO
SENATOR 2022

2020 Census Population	County	Total Vote	Republican (Vance)	Democratic (Ryan)	Other	Rep.-Dem. Plurality		Percentage			
								Total Vote		Major Vote	
								Rep.	Dem.	Rep.	Dem.
371,267	STARK	133,546	77,287	56,215	44	21,072	R	57.9%	42.1%	57.9%	42.1%
541,823	SUMMIT	199,897	86,724	113,111	62	26,387	D	43.4%	56.6%	43.4%	56.6%
198,183	TRUMBULL	73,000	39,082	33,890	28	5,192	R	53.5%	46.4%	53.6%	46.4%
92,063	TUSCARAWAS	30,350	20,072	10,267	11	9,805	R	66.1%	33.8%	66.2%	33.8%
59,309	UNION	25,399	16,320	9,075	4	7,245	R	64.3%	35.7%	64.3%	35.7%
28,311	VAN WERT	10,135	7,959	2,176		5,783	R	78.5%	21.5%	78.5%	21.5%
13,108	VINTON	4,016	2,986	1,028	2	1,958	R	74.4%	25.6%	74.4%	25.6%
235,882	WARREN	101,372	65,370	35,970	32	29,400	R	64.5%	35.5%	64.5%	35.5%
59,961	WASHINGTON	22,751	15,812	6,938	1	8,874	R	69.5%	30.5%	69.5%	30.5%
115,744	WAYNE	38,450	25,599	12,832	19	12,767	R	66.6%	33.4%	66.6%	33.4%
36,762	WILLIAMS	12,843	8,935	3,903	5	5,032	R	69.6%	30.4%	69.6%	30.4%
131,035	WOOD	48,148	24,854	23,269	25	1,585	R	51.6%	48.3%	51.6%	48.4%
21,773	WYANDOT	8,069	5,811	2,255	3	3,556	R	72.0%	27.9%	72.0%	28.0%
11,708,187	TOTAL	4,133,342	2,192,114	1,939,489	1,739	252,625	R	53.0%	46.9%	53.1%	46.9%

OHIO
HOUSE OF REPRESENTATIVES

CD	Year	Total Vote	Republican		Democratic		Other Vote	Rep.-Dem. Plurality		Percentage			
										Total Vote		Major Vote	
			Vote	Candidate	Vote	Candidate				Rep.	Dem.	Rep.	Dem.
1	2022	296,474	140,058	CHABOT, STEVE*	156,416	LANDSMAN, GREG		16,358	D	47.2%	52.8%	47.2%	52.8%
1	2020	385,285	199,560	CHABOT, STEVE*	172,022	SCHRODER, KATE	13,703	27,538	R	51.8%	44.6%	53.7%	46.3%
1	2018	300,871	154,409	CHABOT, STEVE*	141,118	PUREVAL, AFTAB	5,344	13,291	R	51.3%	46.9%	52.2%	47.8%
1	2016	354,788	210,014	CHABOT, STEVE*	144,644	YOUNG, MICHELE	130	65,370	R	59.2%	40.8%	59.2%	40.8%
1	2014	197,383	124,779	CHABOT, STEVE*	72,604	KUNDRATA, FRED		52,175	R	63.2%	36.8%	63.2%	36.8%
1	2012	349,716	201,907	CHABOT, STEVE*	131,490	SINNARD, JEFF	16,319	70,417	R	57.7%	37.6%	60.6%	39.4%
2	2022	257,862	192,117	WENSTRUP, BRAD*	65,745	MEADOWS, SAMANTHA		126,372	R	74.5%	25.5%	74.5%	25.5%
2	2020	377,248	230,430	WENSTRUP, BRAD*	146,781	CASTLE, JAMIE M.	37	83,649	R	61.1%	38.9%	61.1%	38.9%
2	2018	289,661	166,714	WENSTRUP, BRAD*	119,333	SCHILLER, JILL	3,614	47,381	R	57.6%	41.2%	58.3%	41.7%
2	2016	340,279	221,193	WENSTRUP, BRAD*	111,694	SMITH, WILLIAM	7,392	109,499	R	65.0%	32.8%	66.4%	33.6%
2	2014	201,111	132,658	WENSTRUP, BRAD*	68,453	TYSZKIEWICZ, MAREK		64,205	R	66.0%	34.0%	66.0%	34.0%
2	2012	331,381	194,299	WENSTRUP, BRAD	137,082	SMITH, WILLIAM		57,217	R	58.6%	41.4%	58.6%	41.4%
3	2022	258,797	76,455	STAHLEY, LEE	182,324	BEATTY, JOYCE*	18	105,869	D	29.5%	70.5%	29.5%	70.5%
3	2020	321,092	93,569	RICHARDSON, MARK FRANCIS	227,420	BEATTY, JOYCE*	103	133,851	D	29.1%	70.8%	29.2%	70.8%
3	2018	246,677	65,040	BURGESS, JAMES	181,575	BEATTY, JOYCE*	62	116,535	D	26.4%	73.6%	26.4%	73.6%
3	2016	291,351	91,560	ADAMS, JOHN	199,791	BEATTY, JOYCE*		108,231	D	31.4%	68.6%	31.4%	68.6%
3	2014	143,261	51,475	ADAMS, JOHN	91,769	BEATTY, JOYCE*	17	40,294	D	35.9%	64.1%	35.9%	64.1%
3	2012	295,938	77,903	LONG, CHRIS	201,921	BEATTY, JOYCE	16,114	124,018	D	26.3%	68.2%	27.8%	72.2%
4	2022	290,156	200,773	JORDAN, JIM*	89,383	WILSON, TAMIE		111,390	R	69.2%	30.8%	69.2%	30.8%
4	2020	347,626	235,875	JORDAN, JIM*	101,897	FRESHOUR, SHANNON	9,854	133,978	R	67.9%	29.3%	69.8%	30.2%
4	2018	257,405	167,993	JORDAN, JIM*	89,412	GARRETT, JANET		78,581	R	65.3%	34.7%	65.3%	34.7%
4	2016	309,208	210,227	JORDAN, JIM*	98,981	GARRETT, JANET		111,246	R	68.0%	32.0%	68.0%	32.0%
4	2014	186,072	125,907	JORDAN, JIM*	60,165	GARRETT, JANET		65,742	R	67.7%	32.3%	67.7%	32.3%
4	2012	312,998	182,643	JORDAN, JIM*	114,214	SLONE, JIM	16,141	68,429	R	58.4%	36.5%	61.5%	38.5%
5	2022	279,937	187,303	LATTA, BOB*	92,634	SWARTZ, CRAIG		94,669	R	66.9%	33.1%	66.9%	33.1%
5	2020	377,981	257,019	LATTA, BOB*	120,962	RUBANDO, NICK		136,057	R	68.0%	32.0%	68.0%	32.0%
5	2018	283,617	176,569	LATTA, BOB*	99,655	GALBRAITH, JOHN MICHAEL	7,393	76,914	R	62.3%	35.1%	63.9%	36.1%
5	2016	344,991	244,599	LATTA, BOB*	100,392	NEU, JAMES JR.		144,207	R	70.9%	29.1%	70.9%	29.1%
5	2014	202,300	134,449	LATTA, BOB*	58,507	FRY, ROBERT	9,344	75,942	R	66.5%	28.9%	69.7%	30.3%
5	2012	351,878	201,514	LATTA, BOB*	137,806	ZIMMANN, ANGELA	12,558	63,708	R	57.3%	39.2%	59.4%	40.6%

OHIO

HOUSE OF REPRESENTATIVES

			Republican		Democratic		Other Vote	Rep.-Dem. Plurality	Percentage			
									Total Vote		Major Vote	
CD	Year	Total Vote	Vote	Candidate	Vote	Candidate			Rep.	Dem.	Rep.	Dem.
6	2022	280,383	189,883	JOHNSON, BILL*	90,500	LYRAS, LOUIS GEORGE		99,383 R	67.7%	32.3%	67.7%	32.3%
6	2020	334,791	249,130	JOHNSON, BILL*	85,661	ROBERTS, SHAWNA		163,469 R	74.4%	25.6%	74.4%	25.6%
6	2018	249,490	172,774	JOHNSON, BILL*	76,716	ROBERTS, SHAWNA		96,058 R	69.3%	30.7%	69.3%	30.7%
6	2016	302,755	213,975	JOHNSON, BILL*	88,780	LORENTZ, MICHAEL L.		125,195 R	70.7%	29.3%	70.7%	29.3%
6	2014	190,652	111,026	JOHNSON, BILL*	73,561	GARRISON, JENNIFER	6,065	37,465 R	58.2%	38.6%	60.1%	39.9%
6	2012	308,980	164,536	JOHNSON, BILL*	144,444	WILSON, CHARLES A. JR.		20,092 R	53.3%	46.7%	53.3%	46.7%
7	2022	303,573	168,002	MILLER, MAX	135,485	DIEMER, MATTHEW	86	32,517 R	55.3%	44.6%	55.4%	44.6%
7	2020	350,549	236,607	GIBBS, BOB*	102,271	POTTER, QUENTIN	11,671	134,336 R	67.5%	29.2%	69.8%	30.2%
7	2018	260,653	153,117	GIBBS, BOB*	107,536	HARBAUGH, KEN		45,581 R	58.7%	41.3%	58.7%	41.3%
7	2016	309,553	198,221	GIBBS, BOB*	89,638	RICH, ROY	21,694	108,583 R	64.0%	29.0%	68.9%	31.1%
7	2014	143,959	143,959	GIBBS, BOB*				143,959 R	100.0%		100.0%	
7	2012	315,812	178,104	GIBBS, BOB*	137,708	HEALY-ABRAMS, JOYCE		40,396 R	56.4%	43.6%	56.4%	43.6%
8	2022	278,916	180,287	DAVIDSON, WARREN*	98,629	ENOCH, VANESSA		81,658 R	64.6%	35.4%	64.6%	35.4%
8	2020	357,157	246,277	DAVIDSON, WARREN*	110,766	ENOCH, VANESSA	114	135,511 R	69.0%	31.0%	69.0%	31.0%
8	2018	261,133	173,852	DAVIDSON, WARREN*	87,281	ENOCH, VANESSA		86,571 R	66.6%	33.4%	66.6%	33.4%
8	2016	325,506	223,833	DAVIDSON, WARREN*	87,794	FOUGHT, STEVEN	13,879	136,039 R	68.8%	27.0%	71.8%	28.2%
8	2014	188,330	126,539	BOEHNER, JOHN A.*	51,534	POETTER, TOM	10,257	75,005 R	67.2%	27.4%	71.1%	28.9%
8	2012	246,442	246,380	BOEHNER, JOHN A.*			62	246,380 R	100.0%		100.0%	
9	2022	266,017	115,362	MAJEWSKI, J.R.	150,655	KAPTUR, MARCY*		35,293 D	43.4%	56.6%	43.4%	56.6%
9	2020	301,752	111,385	WEBER, ROBERT MARION	190,328	KAPTUR, MARCY*	39	78,943 D	36.9%	63.1%	36.9%	63.1%
9	2018	231,937	74,670	KRAUS, STEVEN W.	157,219	KAPTUR, MARCY*	48	82,549 D	32.2%	67.8%	32.2%	67.8%
9	2016	282,398	88,427	LARSON, DONALD P.	193,966	KAPTUR, MARCY*	5	105,539 D	31.3%	68.7%	31.3%	68.7%
9	2014	160,715	51,704	MAY, RICHARD	108,870	KAPTUR, MARCY*	141	57,166 D	32.2%	67.7%	32.2%	67.8%
9	2012	298,166	68,666	WURZELBACHER, SAMUEL	217,775	KAPTUR, MARCY*	11,725	149,109 D	23.0%	73.0%	24.0%	76.0%
10	2022	272,961	168,327	TURNER, MICHAEL R.*	104,634	ESRATI, DAVID		63,693 R	61.7%	38.3%	61.7%	38.3%
10	2020	364,948	212,972	TURNER, MICHAEL R.*	151,976	TIMS, DESIREE		60,996 R	58.4%	41.6%	58.4%	41.6%
10	2018	281,726	157,554	TURNER, MICHAEL R.*	118,785	GASPER, THERESA	5,387	38,769 R	55.9%	42.2%	57.0%	43.0%
10	2016	336,602	215,724	TURNER, MICHAEL R.*	109,981	KLEPINGER, ROBERT	10,897	105,743 R	64.1%	32.7%	66.2%	33.8%
10	2014	200,606	130,752	TURNER, MICHAEL R.*	63,249	KLEPINGER, ROBERT	6,605	67,503 R	65.2%	31.5%	67.4%	32.6%
10	2012	349,671	208,201	TURNER, MICHAEL R.*	131,097	NEUHARDT, SHAREN SWARTZ	10,373	77,104 R	59.5%	37.5%	61.4%	38.6%
11	2022	215,710	47,988	BREWER, ERIC	167,722	BROWN, SHONTEL*		119,734 D	22.2%	77.8%	22.2%	77.8%
11	2020	302,421	60,323	GORE, LAVERNE	242,098	FUDGE, MARCIA L.*		181,775 D	19.9%	80.1%	19.9%	80.1%
11	2018	250,660	44,486	GOLDSTEIN, BEVERLY A.	206,138	FUDGE, MARCIA L.*	36	161,652 D	17.7%	82.2%	17.8%	82.2%
11	2016	302,686	59,769	GOLDSTEIN, BEVERLY A.	242,917	FUDGE, MARCIA L.*		183,148 D	19.7%	80.3%	19.7%	80.3%
11	2014	172,566	35,461	ZETZER, MARK	137,105	FUDGE, MARCIA L.*		101,644 D	20.5%	79.5%	20.5%	79.5%
11	2012	258,378			258,378	FUDGE, MARCIA L.*		258,378 D		100.0%		100.0%
12	2022	276,237	191,344	BALDERSON, TROY*	84,893	RIPPEL-ELTON, AMY		106,451 R	69.3%	30.7%	69.3%	30.7%
12	2020	437,672	241,790	BALDERSON, TROY*	182,847	SHEARER, ALAINA	13,035	58,943 R	55.2%	41.8%	56.9%	43.1%
12	2018	341,647	175,677	BALDERSON, TROY*	161,251	O'CONNOR, DANNY	4,719	14,426 R	51.4%	47.2%	52.1%	47.9%
12	2016	377,534	251,266	TIBERI, PAT*	112,638	ALBERTSON, ED	13,630	138,628 R	66.6%	29.8%	69.0%	31.0%
12	2014	221,081	150,573	TIBERI, PAT*	61,360	TIBBS, DAVID ARTHUR	9,148	89,213 R	68.1%	27.8%	71.0%	29.0%
12	2012	368,488	233,874	TIBERI, PAT*	134,614	REESE, JIM		99,260 R	63.5%	36.5%	63.5%	36.5%
13	2022	284,409	134,593	GILBERT, MADISON GESIOTTO	149,816	SYKES, EMILIA		15,223 D	47.3%	52.7%	47.3%	52.7%
13	2020	330,801	148,648	HAGAN, CHRISTINA	173,631	RYAN, TIM*	8,522	24,983 D	44.9%	52.5%	46.1%	53.9%
13	2018	251,370	98,047	DEPIZZO, CHRISTOPHER	153,323	RYAN, TIM*		55,276 D	39.0%	61.0%	39.0%	61.0%
13	2016	308,004	99,377	MORCKEL, RICHARD A.	208,610	RYAN, TIM*	17	109,233 D	32.3%	67.7%	32.3%	67.7%
13	2014	175,549	55,233	PEKAREK, THOMAS	120,230	RYAN, TIM*	86	64,997 D	31.5%	68.5%	31.5%	68.5%
13	2012	323,612	88,120	AGANA, MARISHA	235,492	RYAN, TIM*		147,372 D	27.2%	72.8%	27.2%	72.8%
14	2022	297,028	183,389	JOYCE, DAVID*	113,639	KILBOY, MATT		69,750 R	61.7%	38.3%	61.7%	38.3%
14	2020	397,450	238,864	JOYCE, DAVID*	158,586	MUERI, HILLARY O'CONNOR		80,278 R	60.1%	39.9%	60.1%	39.9%
14	2018	307,358	169,809	JOYCE, DAVID*	137,549	RADER, ELIZABETH "BETSY"		32,260 R	55.2%	44.8%	55.2%	44.8%
14	2016	350,269	219,191	JOYCE, DAVID*	130,907	WAGER, MICHAEL	171	88,284 R	62.6%	37.4%	62.6%	37.4%
14	2014	214,580	135,736	JOYCE, DAVID*	70,856	WAGER, MICHAEL	7,988	64,880 R	63.3%	33.0%	65.7%	34.3%
14	2012	339,884	183,660	JOYCE, DAVID	131,638	BLANCHARD, DALE VIRGIL	24,586	52,022 R	54.0%	38.7%	58.2%	41.8%
15	2022	251,251	143,112	CAREY, MIKE*	108,139	JOSEPHSON, GARY		34,973 R	57.0%	43.0%	57.0%	43.0%
15	2020	383,361	243,103	STIVERS, STEVE*	140,183	NEWBY, JOEL	75	102,920 R	63.4%	36.6%	63.4%	36.6%
15	2018	292,443	170,593	STIVERS, STEVE*	116,112	NEAL, RICK	5,738	54,481 R	58.3%	39.7%	59.5%	40.5%
15	2016	336,807	222,847	STIVERS, STEVE*	113,960	WHARTON, SCOTT		108,887 R	66.2%	33.8%	66.2%	33.8%
15	2014	194,621	128,496	STIVERS, STEVE*	66,125	WHARTON, SCOTT		62,371 R	66.0%	34.0%	66.0%	34.0%
15	2012	333,465	205,277	STIVERS, STEVE*	128,188	LANG, PAT		77,089 R	61.6%	38.4%	61.6%	38.4%

OHIO
HOUSE OF REPRESENTATIVES

			Republican		Democratic		Other Vote	Rep.-Dem. Plurality	Percentage			
									Total Vote		Major Vote	
CD	Year	Total Vote	Vote	Candidate	Vote	Candidate			Rep.	Dem.	Rep.	Dem.
16	2020	391,406	247,335	GONZALEZ, ANTHONY*	144,071	GODFREY, AARON		103,264 R	63.2%	36.8%	63.2%	36.8%
16	2018	299,710	170,029	GONZALEZ, ANTHONY	129,681	PALMER, SUSAN MORAN		40,348 R	56.7%	43.3%	56.7%	43.3%
16	2016	345,624	225,794	RENACCI, JIM*	119,830	MUNDY, KEITH		105,964 R	65.3%	34.7%	65.3%	34.7%
16	2014	207,375	132,176	RENACCI, JIM*	75,199	CROSSLAND, PETE		56,977 R	63.7%	36.3%	63.7%	36.3%
16	2012	355,771	185,167	RENACCI, JIM*	170,604	SUTTON, BETTY		14,563 R	52.0%	48.0%	52.0%	48.0%
TOTAL	2022	4,109,711	2,318,993		1,790,614		104	528,379 R	56.4%	43.6%	56.4%	43.6%
TOTAL	2020	5,761,540	3,252,887		2,451,500		57,153	801,387 R	56.5%	42.5%	57.0%	43.0%
TOTAL	2018	4,406,358	2,291,333		2,082,684		32,341	208,649 R	52.0%	47.3%	52.4%	47.6%
TOTAL	2016	5,218,355	2,996,017		2,154,523		67,815	841,494 R	57.4%	41.3%	58.2%	41.8%
TOTAL	2014	3,000,161	1,770,923		1,179,587		49,651	591,336 R	59.0%	39.3%	60.0%	40.0%
TOTAL	2012	5,140,580	2,620,251		2,412,451		107,878	207,800 R	51.0%	46.9%	52.1%	47.9%

Note: An asterisk (*) denotes incumbent.

OHIO
GENERAL AND PRIMARY ELECTIONS

GENERAL ELECTIONS: OTHER VOTES

Governor — Other vote was 8,082 Write-In (Marshall Usher), 574 Write-In (Timothy Grady), 231 Write-In (Renea Turner), 77 Write-In (Craig Patton)

Senate — Other vote was 702 Write-In (John Cheng), 403 Write-In (Shane Hoffman), 362 Write-In (LaShondra Tinsley), 194 Write-In (Stephen Faris), 78 Write-In (Matthew Esh)

House — Other vote was:
- CD 3: 18 Write-In (Alexander Amicucci)
- CD 7: 51 Write-In (Vince Licursi), 35 Write-In (Brian Kenderes)

2022 PRIMARY ELECTIONS: SUPPLEMENTARY INFORMATION

Primary May 3, 2022 **Registration** (as of May 3, 2022) 7,948,302 No Party Registration

Primary Type Open—Any registered voter could participate in the primary of either party. However, records are kept of voter participation in recent primaries, and voters who cast a ballot in one party's primary could be challenged if they attempted to participate in the other party's primary. They could be asked to sign an affidavit affirming the fact that they were voting in the opposing party's primary and would become identified with that party because of their primary ballot cast.

	REPUBLICAN PRIMARIES			DEMOCRATIC PRIMARIES		
Senator	Vance, James David "J.D."	344,736	32.2%	Ryan, Tim	359,941	69.6%
	Mandel, Josh	255,854	23.9%	Harper, Morgan	92,347	17.8%
	Dolan, Matt	249,239	23.3%	Johnson, Traci "TJ"	65,209	12.6%
	Gibbons, Mike	124,653	11.7%			
	Timken, Jane	62,779	5.9%			
	Pukita, Mark	22,692	2.1%			
	Patel, Neil	9,873	0.9%			
	TOTAL	1,069,826		TOTAL	517,497	

OHIO

GENERAL AND PRIMARY ELECTIONS

		REPUBLICAN PRIMARIES			DEMOCRATIC PRIMARIES	
Governor	DeWine, Michael "Mike"*	519,594	48.1%	Whaley, Nan	331,014	65.0%
	Renacci, Jim	302,494	28.0%	Cranley, John	178,132	35.0%
	Blystone, Joe	235,584	21.8%			
	Hood, Ron	22,411	2.1%			
	TOTAL	1,080,083		TOTAL	509,146	
Congressional District 1	Chabot, Steve*	45,450	100.0%	Landsman, Greg	28,330	100.0%
	TOTAL	45,450		TOTAL	28,330	
Congressional District 2	Wenstrup, Brad*	56,805	77.4%	Meadows, Samantha	11,694	72.0%
	Condit, Jim Jr.	9,250	12.6%	Darnowsky, Alan	4,541	28.0%
	Windisch, David	7,382	10.1%			
	TOTAL	73,437		TOTAL	16,235	
Congressional District 3	Stahley, Lee	30,250	100.0%	Beatty, Joyce*	48,241	100.0%
	TOTAL	30,250		TOTAL	48,241	
Congressional District 4	Jordan, Jim*	86,576	100.0%	Wilson, Tamie	10,804	51.5%
				Sites, Jeffrey Alan	10,160	48.5%
	TOTAL	86,576		TOTAL	20,964	
Congressional District 5	Latta, Bob*	69,981	100.0%	Swartz, Craig	14,590	55.3%
				Heberling, Martin III	11,812	44.7%
	TOTAL	69,981		TOTAL	26,402	
Congressional District 6	Johnson, Bill*	48,563	76.4%	Lyras, Louis George	8,579	31.3%
	Anderson, John	8,242	13.0%	Jones, Eric	6,931	25.3%
	Morgenstern, Michael	4,450	7.0%	Roberts, Shawna	6,825	24.9%
	Zelenitz, Gregory	2,316	3.6%	Alexander, Martin	5,043	18.4%
	TOTAL	63,571		TOTAL	27,378	
Congressional District 7	Miller, Max	43,158	71.8%	Diemer, Matthew	12,636	62.8%
	Schulz, Jonah	8,325	13.9%	Rader, Tristan	7,500	37.2%
	Gaddis, Charlie	5,581	9.3%			
	Alexander, Anthony Leon	3,033	5.0%			
	TOTAL	60,097		TOTAL	20,136	
Congressional District 8	Davidson, Warren*	50,372	72.4%	Enoch, Vanessa	18,290	100.0%
	Heimlich, Phil	19,230	27.6%			
	TOTAL	69,602		TOTAL	18,290	
Congressional District 9	Majewski, J.R.	21,666	35.7%	Kaptur, Marcy*	32,968	100.0%
	Riedel, Craig	18,861	31.0%			
	Gavarone, Theresa	17,337	28.5%			
	Deck, Beth	2,883	4.7%			
	TOTAL	60,747		TOTAL	32,968	
Congressional District 10	Turner, Michael R.*	63,336	100.0%	Esrati, David	10,324	31.5%
				Hardenbrook, Jeff	8,464	25.8%
				Stapleton, Baxter	8,373	25.5%
				Benjamin, Kirk	5,614	17.1%
	TOTAL	63,336		TOTAL	32,775	
Congressional District 11	Brewer, Eric	8,240	57.6%	Brown, Shontel*	44,841	66.3%
	Hemphill, James	6,062	42.4%	Turner, Nina	22,830	33.7%
	TOTAL	14,302		TOTAL	67,671	
Congressional District 12	Balderson, Troy*	66,181	82.3%	Rippel-Elton, Amy	12,712	56.7%
	Lape, Brandon Michael	14,196	17.7%	Fletcher, Michael	9,717	43.3%
	TOTAL	80,377		TOTAL	22,429	

OHIO

GENERAL AND PRIMARY ELECTIONS

	REPUBLICAN PRIMARIES			DEMOCRATIC PRIMARIES		
Congressional District 13	Gilbert, Madison Gesiotto	16,211	28.6%	Sykes, Emilia	36,251	100.0%
	Wheeler, Gregory	13,284	23.4%			
	Porter, Janet Folger	9,402	16.6%			
	Hawkins, Shay	6,468	11.4%			
	Saylor, Ryan	5,261	9.3%			
	Sabatucci, Dante	4,740	8.4%			
	King, Santana F.	1,338	2.4%			
	TOTAL	56,704		TOTAL	36,251	
Congressional District 14	Joyce, David*	58,042	75.7%	Kilboy, Matt	34,499	100.0%
	Awtrey, Patrick	12,296	16.0%			
	Cormack, Bevin	6,364	8.3%			
	TOTAL	76,702		TOTAL	34,499	
Congressional District 15	Carey, Mike*	48,938	100.0%	Josephson, Gary	9,047	100.0%
	TOTAL	48,938		TOTAL	9,047	

Note: An asterisk (*) denotes incumbent.

OKLAHOMA

Statewide Races

In presidential races, Oklahoma has long been one of Republicans' best states – Democrats have not even carried a county there since the 2000 election. But its gubernatorial races have been more competitive. In the state's 2014 and 2018 contests for governor, Republicans won by 15 and 12 points, respectively. The 2022 result was right in line with those last two contests.

As Joe Biden was deeply unpopular in Oklahoma, some public polls showed Republican Gov. Kevin Stitt only barely ahead of – or even trailing – his Democratic opponent, state Superintendent of Public Instruction Joy Hofmeister. Elected to the office in 2014 as a Republican, Hofmeister changed parties in 2021. In the general election, Hofmeister hit Stitt on educational and tribal issues – in an unusual endorsement, leaders from the five largest Native American nations in Oklahoma endorsed her, even as Stitt was a member of the Cherokee Nation himself. But Stitt, who ran on keeping Oklahoma open during the pandemic and against Biden, won 55%–42%, carrying 74 of the state's 77 counties.

As with his 2018 result, Stitt's worst county was Oklahoma County (containing Oklahoma City), where he took 42% both times he was on the ballot. Cleveland County, which is seeing Oklahoma City's suburbs spill into its borders, voted against Stitt for a second time, giving him 46%. After Tulsa County, the state's second most populous county, went 50%–47% for Stitt in 2018, he lost it by 415 votes in 2022 – both major party candidates were from this county. Meanwhile, traditionally Democratic eastern Oklahoma continued to trend right. In 2018, Stitt lost Muskogee County, where his Democratic opponent hailed from (it is also known as the home of country singer Carrie Underwood), by 1 vote. Four years later, Muskogee County matched the state, going 55%–42% for Stitt.

Sen. James Lankford's seat was scheduled to come up in 2022, but Sen. Jim Inhofe's resignation precipitated a special election, so both of Oklahoma's Senate seats were up – and both elected Republicans without much fanfare. Lankford won a second full term 64%–32%, carrying every county. Rep. Markwayne Mullin, representing the eastern 2nd District, won the GOP nomination to replace Inhofe. Democrats got a good recruit in former 5th District Rep. Kendra Horn (who shared a surname with their nominee for the other seat). The special election was somewhat more competitive: Mullin won 62%–35% but lost Oklahoma County by five points (Horn represented that area while in Congress).

House Races

With Republicans in charge of Oklahoma's remap, their central partisan objective was to strengthen their hold on the 5th District. In 2018, Horn upset an incumbent who seemed to be caught sleeping. Two years later, though, as Donald Trump carried the district by six points, Republican Stephanie Bice ousted Horn by a 52%–48% vote. Republicans split Oklahoma County three ways and added some exurban counties to the 5th District. Bice won a second term with 59% of the vote and Republicans held the other four seats by margins of more than 25 points.

OKLAHOMA
Congressional districts first established for elections held in 2022
5 members

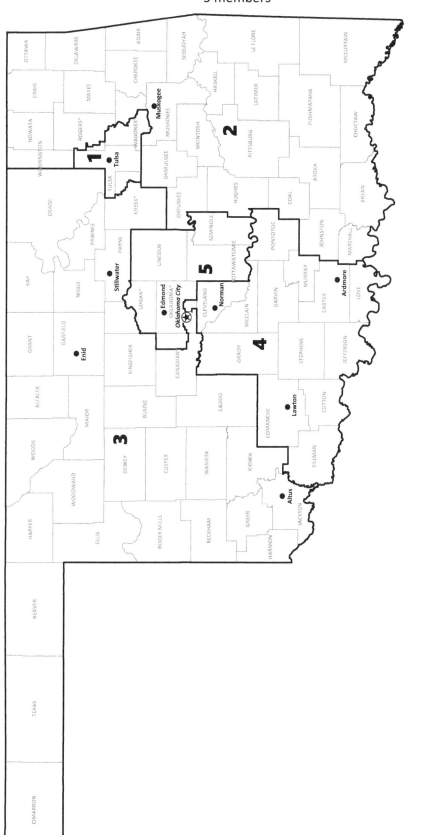

* Asterisk indicates a county whose boundaries include parts of two or more congressional districts.

OKLAHOMA

GOVERNOR
Kevin Stitt (R). Reelected 2022 to a four-year term. Previously elected 2018.

SENATORS (2 Republicans)
Markwayne Mullin (R). Elected 2022 in a special election to complete the final four years of the term vacated by James Inhofe (R), who resigned on January 3, 2023.

James Lankford (R). Reelected 2022 to a six-year term. Previously elected 2016, and 2014 to complete the final two years of the term vacated by Tom Coburn (R), who resigned January 3, 2015, after the recurrence of prostate cancer.

REPRESENTATIVES (5 Republicans)
1. Kevin Hern (R)
2. Josh Brecheen (R)
3. Frank D. Lucas (R)
4. Thomas J. Cole (R)
5. Stephanie Bice (R)

POSTWAR VOTE FOR PRESIDENT

Year	Total Vote	Republican Vote	Republican Candidate	Democratic Vote	Democratic Candidate	Other Vote	Rep.-Dem. Plurality	Total Vote Rep.	Total Vote Dem.	Major Vote Rep.	Major Vote Dem.
2020	1,560,699	1,020,280	Trump, Donald J.*	503,890	Biden, Joseph R. Jr.	36,529	516,390 R	65.4%	32.3%	66.9%	33.1%
2016**	1,452,992	949,136	Trump, Donald J.	420,375	Clinton, Hillary Rodham	83,481	528,761 R	65.3%	28.9%	69.3%	30.7%
2012	1,334,872	891,325	Romney, W. Mitt	443,547	Obama, Barack H.*		447,778 R	66.8%	33.2%	66.8%	33.2%
2008	1,462,661	960,165	McCain, John S. III	502,496	Obama, Barack H.		457,669 R	65.6%	34.4%	65.6%	34.4%
2004	1,463,758	959,792	Bush, George W.*	503,966	Kerry, John F.		455,826 R	65.6%	34.4%	65.6%	34.4%
2000	1,234,229	744,337	Bush, George W.	474,276	Gore, Albert Jr.	15,616	270,061 R	60.3%	38.4%	61.1%	38.9%
1996**	1,206,713	582,315	Dole, Robert "Bob"	488,105	Clinton, Bill*	136,293	94,210 R	48.3%	40.4%	54.4%	45.6%
1992**	1,390,359	592,929	Bush, George H.*	473,066	Clinton, Bill	324,364	119,863 R	42.6%	34.0%	55.6%	44.4%
1988	1,171,036	678,367	Bush, George H.	483,423	Dukakis, Michael S.	9,246	194,944 R	57.9%	41.3%	58.4%	41.6%
1984	1,255,676	861,530	Reagan, Ronald*	385,080	Mondale, Walter F.	9,066	476,450 R	68.6%	30.7%	69.1%	30.9%
1980**	1,149,708	695,570	Reagan, Ronald	402,026	Carter, Jimmy*	52,112	293,544 R	60.5%	35.0%	63.4%	36.6%
1976	1,092,251	545,708	Ford, Gerald R.*	532,442	Carter, Jimmy	14,101	13,266 R	50.0%	48.7%	50.6%	49.4%
1972	1,029,900	759,025	Nixon, Richard M.*	247,147	McGovern, George S.	23,728	511,878 R	73.7%	24.0%	75.4%	24.6%
1968**	943,086	449,697	Nixon, Richard M.	301,658	Humphrey, Hubert Horatio Jr.	191,731	148,039 R	47.7%	32.0%	59.9%	40.1%
1964	932,499	412,665	Goldwater, Barry M. Sr.	519,834	Johnson, Lyndon B.*		107,169 D	44.3%	55.7%	44.3%	55.7%
1960	903,150	533,039	Nixon, Richard M.	370,111	Kennedy, John F.		162,928 R	59.0%	41.0%	59.0%	41.0%
1956	859,350	473,769	Eisenhower, Dwight D.*	385,581	Stevenson, Adlai E. II		88,188 R	55.1%	44.9%	55.1%	44.9%
1952	948,984	518,045	Eisenhower, Dwight D.	430,939	Stevenson, Adlai E. II		87,106 R	54.6%	45.4%	54.6%	45.4%
1948	721,599	268,817	Dewey, Thomas E.	452,782	Truman, Harry S.*		183,965 D	37.3%	62.7%	37.3%	62.7%

Note: An asterisk (*) denotes incumbent. **In past elections, the other vote included: 2016 - 83,481 Libertarian (Gary Johnson); 1996 - 130,788 Reform (Ross Perot); 1992 - 319,878 Independent (Perot); 1980 - 38,284 Independent (John Anderson); 1968 - 191,731 American Independent (George Wallace).

OKLAHOMA

POSTWAR VOTE FOR GOVERNOR

Year	Total Vote	Republican Vote	Republican Candidate	Democratic Vote	Democratic Candidate	Other Vote	Rep.-Dem. Plurality	Total Vote Rep.	Total Vote Dem.	Major Vote Rep.	Major Vote Dem.
2022	1,153,284	639,484	Stitt, Kevin*	481,904	Hofmeister, Joy	31,896	157,580 R	55.4%	41.8%	57.0%	43.0%
2018	1,186,385	644,579	Stitt, Kevin	500,973	Edmondson, Drew	40,833	143,606 R	54.3%	42.2%	56.3%	43.7%
2014	824,831	460,298	Fallin, Mary*	338,239	Dorman, Joe	26,294	122,059 R	55.8%	41.0%	57.6%	42.4%
2010	1,034,767	625,506	Fallin, Mary	409,261	Askins, Jari		216,245 R	60.4%	39.6%	60.4%	39.6%
2006	926,462	310,327	Istook, Ernest J.	616,135	Henry, Brad*		305,808 D	33.5%	66.5%	33.5%	66.5%
2002**	1,035,620	441,277	Largent, Steve	448,143	Henry, Brad	146,200	6,866 D	42.6%	43.3%	49.6%	50.4%
1998	873,585	505,498	Keating, Frank*	357,552	Boyd, Laura	10,535	147,946 R	57.9%	40.9%	58.6%	41.4%
1994**	995,012	466,740	Keating, Frank	294,936	Mildren, Jack	233,336	171,804 R	46.9%	29.6%	61.3%	38.7%
1990	911,314	297,584	Price, Bill	523,196	Walters, David	90,534	225,612 D	32.7%	57.4%	36.3%	63.7%
1986	909,925	431,762	Bellmon, Henry Louis	405,295	Walters, David	72,868	26,467 R	47.5%	44.5%	51.6%	48.4%
1982	883,130	332,207	Daxon, Tom	548,159	Nigh, George*	2,764	215,952 D	37.6%	62.1%	37.7%	62.3%
1978	777,414	367,055	Shotts, Ron	402,240	Nigh, George	8,119	35,185 D	47.2%	51.7%	47.7%	52.3%
1974	804,842	290,459	Inhofe, James M.	514,383	Boren, David L.		223,924 D	36.1%	63.9%	36.1%	63.9%
1970	698,790	336,157	Bartlett, Dewey F.*	338,338	Hall, David	24,295	2,181 D	48.1%	48.4%	49.8%	50.2%
1966	677,258	377,078	Bartlett, Dewey F.	296,328	Moore, Preston J.	3,852	80,750 R	55.7%	43.8%	56.0%	44.0%
1962	709,763	392,316	Bellmon, Henry Louis	315,357	Atkinson, W. P.	2,090	76,959 R	55.3%	44.4%	55.4%	44.6%
1958	538,839	107,495	Ferguson, Phil	399,504	Edmondson, J. Howard	31,840	292,009 D	19.9%	74.1%	21.2%	78.8%
1954	609,194	251,808	Sparks, Reuben K.	357,386	Gary, Raymond		105,578 D	41.3%	58.7%	41.3%	58.7%
1950	644,276	313,205	Ferguson, Jo O.	329,308	Murray, Johnston	1,763	16,103 D	48.6%	51.1%	48.7%	51.3%
1946	494,599	227,426	Flynn, Olney F.	259,491	Turner, Roy J.	7,682	32,065 D	46.0%	52.5%	46.7%	53.3%

Note: An asterisk (*) denotes incumbent. **In past elections, the other vote included: 2002 - 146,200 Independent (Gary L. Richardson); 1994 - 233,336 Independent (Wes Watkins).

POSTWAR VOTE FOR SENATOR

Year	Total Vote	Republican Vote	Republican Candidate	Democratic Vote	Democratic Candidate	Other Vote	Rep.-Dem. Plurality	Total Vote Rep.	Total Vote Dem.	Major Vote Rep.	Major Vote Dem.
2022	1,150,732	739,960	Lankford, James*	369,370	Horn, Madison	41,402	370,590 R	64.3%	32.1%	66.7%	33.3%
2020	1,556,361	979,140	Inhofe, James M.*	509,763	Broyles, Abby	67,458	469,377 R	62.9%	32.8%	65.8%	34.2%
2016	1,448,047	980,892	Lankford, James*	355,911	Workman, Mike	111,244	624,981 R	67.7%	24.6%	73.4%	26.6%
2014	820,733	558,166	Inhofe, James M.*	234,307	Silverstein, Matthew Benjamin "Matt"	28,260	323,859 R	68.0%	28.5%	70.4%	29.6%
2014S**	820,890	557,002	Lankford, James	237,923	Johnson, Connie	25,965	319,079 R	67.9%	29.0%	70.1%	29.9%
2010	1,017,151	718,482	Coburn, Tom*	265,814	Rogers, Jim	32,855	452,668 R	70.6%	26.1%	73.0%	27.0%
2008	1,346,819	763,375	Inhofe, James M.*	527,736	Rice, Andrew	55,708	235,639 R	56.7%	39.2%	59.1%	40.9%
2004	1,446,846	763,433	Coburn, Tom	596,750	Carson, Brad	86,663	166,683 R	52.8%	41.2%	56.1%	43.9%
2002	1,018,424	583,579	Inhofe, James M.*	369,789	Walters, David	65,056	213,790 R	57.3%	36.3%	61.2%	38.8%
1998	859,713	570,682	Nickles, Don*	268,898	Carroll, Don E.	20,133	301,784 R	66.4%	31.3%	68.0%	32.0%
1996	1,183,150	670,610	Inhofe, James M.*	474,162	Boren, Jim	38,378	196,448 R	56.7%	40.1%	58.6%	41.4%
1994S**	982,430	542,390	Inhofe, James M.	392,488	McCurdy, Dave	47,552	149,902 R	55.2%	40.0%	58.0%	42.0%
1992	1,294,423	757,876	Nickles, Don*	494,350	Lewis, Steve	42,197	263,526 R	58.5%	38.2%	60.5%	39.5%
1990	884,498	148,814	Jones, Stephen	735,684	Boren, David L.*		586,870 D	16.8%	83.2%	16.8%	83.2%
1986	893,666	493,436	Nickles, Don*	400,230	Jones, James R.		93,206 R	55.2%	44.8%	55.2%	44.8%
1984	1,197,937	280,638	Crozier, Will E. Bill	906,131	Boren, David L.*	11,168	625,493 D	23.4%	75.6%	23.6%	76.4%
1980	1,098,294	587,252	Nickles, Don	478,283	Coats, Andrew	32,759	108,969 R	53.5%	43.5%	55.1%	44.9%
1978	754,264	247,857	Kamm, Robert B.	493,953	Boren, David L.	12,454	246,096 D	32.9%	65.5%	33.4%	66.6%
1974	791,809	390,997	Bellmon, Henry Louis*	387,162	Edmondson, Ed	13,650	3,835 R	49.4%	48.9%	50.2%	49.8%
1972	1,005,148	516,934	Bartlett, Dewey F.	478,212	Edmondson, Ed	10,002	38,722 R	51.4%	47.6%	51.9%	48.1%
1968	909,119	470,120	Bellmon, Henry Louis	419,658	Monroney, Almer Stillwell Mike*	19,341	50,462 R	51.7%	46.2%	52.8%	47.2%
1966	638,742	295,585	Patterson, Pat J.	343,157	Harris, Fred R.*		47,572 D	46.3%	53.7%	46.3%	53.7%
1964S**	912,174	445,392	Wilkinson, Bud	466,782	Harris, Fred R.		21,390 D	48.8%	51.2%	48.8%	51.2%
1962	664,712	307,966	Crawford, B. Hayden	353,890	Monroney, Almer Stillwell Mike*	2,856	45,924 D	46.3%	53.2%	46.5%	53.5%
1960	864,475	385,646	Crawford, B. Hayden	474,116	Kerr, Robert Samuel Sr.*	4,713	88,470 D	44.6%	54.8%	44.9%	55.1%
1956	831,142	371,146	McKeever, Douglas	459,996	Monroney, Almer Stillwell Mike*		88,850 D	44.7%	55.3%	44.7%	55.3%
1954	600,120	262,013	Mock, Fred M.	335,127	Kerr, Robert Samuel Sr.*	2,980	73,114 D	43.7%	55.8%	43.9%	56.1%
1950	631,177	285,224	Alexander, W. H.	345,953	Monroney, Almer Stillwell Mike		60,729 D	45.2%	54.8%	45.2%	54.8%
1948	708,931	265,169	Rizley, Ross	441,654	Kerr, Robert Samuel Sr.	2,108	176,485 D	37.4%	62.3%	37.5%	62.5%

Note: An asterisk (*) denotes incumbent. **The 1964, 1994, and 2014 elections were for short terms to fill vacancies.

OKLAHOMA
GOVERNOR 2022

							Percentage			
							Total Vote		Major Vote	
2020 Census Population	County	Total Vote	Republican (Stitt)	Democratic (Hofmeister)	Other	Rep.-Dem. Plurality	Rep.	Dem.	Rep.	Dem.
22,152	ADAIR	5,222	3,135	1,896	191	1,239 R	60.0%	36.3%	62.3%	37.7%
5,676	ALFALFA	1,735	1,287	385	63	902 R	74.2%	22.2%	77.0%	23.0%
13,789	ATOKA	3,921	2,790	1,011	120	1,779 R	71.2%	25.8%	73.4%	26.6%
5,290	BEAVER	1,698	1,382	249	67	1,133 R	81.4%	14.7%	84.7%	15.3%
21,827	BECKHAM	5,480	4,115	1,240	125	2,875 R	75.1%	22.6%	76.8%	23.2%
9,424	BLAINE	2,980	1,985	886	109	1,099 R	66.6%	29.7%	69.1%	30.9%
48,290	BRYAN	11,467	7,144	3,941	382	3,203 R	62.3%	34.4%	64.4%	35.6%
28,682	CADDO	7,062	4,166	2,668	228	1,498 R	59.0%	37.8%	61.0%	39.0%
149,690	CANADIAN	50,214	29,474	19,306	1,434	10,168 R	58.7%	38.4%	60.4%	39.6%
48,144	CARTER	13,408	8,621	4,332	455	4,289 R	64.3%	32.3%	66.6%	33.4%
48,761	CHEROKEE	13,545	6,660	6,481	404	179 R	49.2%	47.8%	50.7%	49.3%
14,665	CHOCTAW	4,050	2,798	1,084	168	1,714 R	69.1%	26.8%	72.1%	27.9%
2,128	CIMARRON	733	640	62	31	578 R	87.3%	8.5%	91.2%	8.8%
285,168	CLEVELAND	91,279	41,379	47,356	2,544	5,977 D	45.3%	51.9%	46.6%	53.4%
5,485	COAL	1,908	1,288	549	71	739 R	67.5%	28.8%	70.1%	29.9%
120,613	COMANCHE	23,580	12,219	10,293	1,068	1,926 R	51.8%	43.7%	54.3%	45.7%
5,636	COTTON	1,843	1,187	545	111	642 R	64.4%	29.6%	68.5%	31.5%
14,167	CRAIG	4,485	2,880	1,492	113	1,388 R	64.2%	33.3%	65.9%	34.1%
71,611	CREEK	22,350	15,015	6,816	519	8,199 R	67.2%	30.5%	68.8%	31.2%
28,960	CUSTER	7,492	4,853	2,461	178	2,392 R	64.8%	32.8%	66.4%	33.6%
43,194	DELAWARE	13,218	8,858	3,947	413	4,911 R	67.0%	29.9%	69.2%	30.8%
4,882	DEWEY	1,767	1,400	321	46	1,079 R	79.2%	18.2%	81.3%	18.7%
3,850	ELLIS	1,486	1,167	281	38	886 R	78.5%	18.9%	80.6%	19.4%
60,833	GARFIELD	16,214	10,800	4,960	454	5,840 R	66.6%	30.6%	68.5%	31.5%
27,750	GARVIN	8,122	5,589	2,296	237	3,293 R	68.8%	28.3%	70.9%	29.1%
56,146	GRADY	17,825	12,165	5,163	497	7,002 R	68.2%	29.0%	70.2%	29.8%
4,334	GRANT	1,599	1,181	375	43	806 R	73.9%	23.5%	75.9%	24.1%
5,714	GREER	1,342	902	394	46	508 R	67.2%	29.4%	69.6%	30.4%
2,638	HARMON	650	458	179	13	279 R	70.5%	27.5%	71.9%	28.1%
3,693	HARPER	1,168	809	317	42	492 R	69.3%	27.1%	71.8%	28.2%
12,650	HASKELL	3,392	2,337	985	70	1,352 R	68.9%	29.0%	70.3%	29.7%
13,312	HUGHES	3,545	2,352	1,093	100	1,259 R	66.3%	30.8%	68.3%	31.7%
24,467	JACKSON	5,502	3,857	1,450	195	2,407 R	70.1%	26.4%	72.7%	27.3%
5,999	JEFFERSON	1,613	1,098	444	71	654 R	68.1%	27.5%	71.2%	28.8%
11,075	JOHNSTON	2,963	1,986	867	110	1,119 R	67.0%	29.3%	69.6%	30.4%
43,528	KAY	12,532	7,927	4,204	401	3,723 R	63.3%	33.5%	65.3%	34.7%
15,796	KINGFISHER	4,883	3,647	1,121	115	2,526 R	74.7%	23.0%	76.5%	23.5%
8,695	KIOWA	2,461	1,648	764	49	884 R	67.0%	31.0%	68.3%	31.7%
10,065	LATIMER	3,064	1,985	960	119	1,025 R	64.8%	31.3%	67.4%	32.6%
49,861	LE FLORE	12,141	8,266	3,377	498	4,889 R	68.1%	27.8%	71.0%	29.0%
34,994	LINCOLN	11,098	7,587	3,131	380	4,456 R	68.4%	28.2%	70.8%	29.2%
48,284	LOGAN	17,019	11,086	5,517	416	5,569 R	65.1%	32.4%	66.8%	33.2%
10,291	LOVE	2,742	1,951	703	88	1,248 R	71.2%	25.6%	73.5%	26.5%
7,629	MAJOR	2,691	2,151	470	70	1,681 R	79.9%	17.5%	82.1%	17.9%
17,047	MARSHALL	4,391	2,958	1,312	121	1,646 R	67.4%	29.9%	69.3%	30.7%
41,139	MAYES	12,650	8,031	4,205	414	3,826 R	63.5%	33.2%	65.6%	34.4%
40,777	MCCLAIN	15,046	10,160	4,458	428	5,702 R	67.5%	29.6%	69.5%	30.5%
32,706	MCCURTAIN	8,248	5,566	2,311	371	3,255 R	67.5%	28.0%	70.7%	29.3%
19,679	MCINTOSH	6,476	4,028	2,300	148	1,728 R	62.2%	35.5%	63.7%	36.3%
14,116	MURRAY	4,251	2,718	1,398	135	1,320 R	63.9%	32.9%	66.0%	34.0%
68,022	MUSKOGEE	17,796	9,835	7,517	444	2,318 R	55.3%	42.2%	56.7%	43.3%
11,126	NOBLE	3,814	2,461	1,240	113	1,221 R	64.5%	32.5%	66.5%	33.5%
10,041	NOWATA	3,323	2,302	916	105	1,386 R	69.3%	27.6%	71.5%	28.5%
12,019	OKFUSKEE	2,945	1,785	1,067	93	718 R	60.6%	36.2%	62.6%	37.4%
799,370	OKLAHOMA	222,554	93,466	122,996	6,092	29,530 D	42.0%	55.3%	43.2%	56.8%
38,503	OKMULGEE	10,635	6,187	4,186	262	2,001 R	58.2%	39.4%	59.6%	40.4%
46,988	OSAGE	15,105	9,053	5,656	396	3,397 R	59.9%	37.4%	61.5%	38.5%
31,100	OTTAWA	7,688	4,718	2,649	321	2,069 R	61.4%	34.5%	64.0%	36.0%
16,396	PAWNEE	5,047	3,354	1,554	139	1,800 R	66.5%	30.8%	68.3%	31.7%
81,665	PAYNE	22,138	11,029	10,561	548	468 R	49.8%	47.7%	51.1%	48.9%

OKLAHOMA
GOVERNOR 2022

							Percentage			
							Total Vote		Major Vote	
2020 Census Population	County	Total Vote	Republican (Stitt)	Democratic (Hofmeister)	Other	Rep.-Dem. Plurality	Rep.	Dem.	Rep.	Dem.
43,654	PITTSBURG	12,691	8,322	3,973	396	4,349 R	65.6%	31.3%	67.7%	32.3%
38,275	PONTOTOC	11,205	5,748	5,068	389	680 R	51.3%	45.2%	53.1%	46.9%
72,862	POTTAWATOMIE	20,713	12,415	7,651	647	4,764 R	59.9%	36.9%	61.9%	38.1%
11,128	PUSHMATAHA	3,297	2,309	870	118	1,439 R	70.0%	26.4%	72.6%	27.4%
3,580	ROGER MILLS	1,320	1,092	191	37	901 R	82.7%	14.5%	85.1%	14.9%
92,825	ROGERS	33,933	22,581	10,527	825	12,054 R	66.5%	31.0%	68.2%	31.8%
24,230	SEMINOLE	5,861	3,642	2,050	169	1,592 R	62.1%	35.0%	64.0%	36.0%
41,449	SEQUOYAH	10,274	6,516	3,329	429	3,187 R	63.4%	32.4%	66.2%	33.8%
43,180	STEPHENS	13,116	8,957	3,580	579	5,377 R	68.3%	27.3%	71.4%	28.6%
19,803	TEXAS	3,658	2,806	712	140	2,094 R	76.7%	19.5%	79.8%	20.2%
7,232	TILLMAN	1,850	1,203	565	82	638 R	65.0%	30.5%	68.0%	32.0%
652,649	TULSA	194,095	94,981	95,396	3,718	415 D	48.9%	49.1%	49.9%	50.1%
81,685	WAGONER	26,870	17,434	8,846	590	8,588 R	64.9%	32.9%	66.3%	33.7%
51,566	WASHINGTON	17,151	11,152	5,578	421	5,574 R	65.0%	32.5%	66.7%	33.3%
10,928	WASHITA	3,575	2,633	841	101	1,792 R	73.7%	23.5%	75.8%	24.2%
8,763	WOODS	2,702	1,816	804	82	1,012 R	67.2%	29.8%	69.3%	30.7%
20,102	WOODWARD	5,377	4,001	1,225	151	2,776 R	74.4%	22.8%	76.6%	23.4%
3,964,443	TOTAL	1,153,284	639,484	481,904	31,896	157,580 R	55.4%	41.8%	57.0%	43.0%

OKLAHOMA
SENATOR 2022

							Percentage			
							Total Vote		Major Vote	
2020 Census Population	County	Total Vote	Republican (Lankford)	Democratic (Horn)	Other	Rep.-Dem. Plurality	Rep.	Dem.	Rep.	Dem.
22,152	ADAIR	5,195	3,652	1,376	167	2,276 R	70.3%	26.5%	72.6%	27.4%
5,676	ALFALFA	1,735	1,490	173	72	1,317 R	85.9%	10.0%	89.6%	10.4%
13,789	ATOKA	3,909	3,204	605	100	2,599 R	82.0%	15.5%	84.1%	15.9%
5,290	BEAVER	1,681	1,467	135	79	1,332 R	87.3%	8.0%	91.6%	8.4%
21,827	BECKHAM	5,468	4,508	807	153	3,701 R	82.4%	14.8%	84.8%	15.2%
9,424	BLAINE	2,969	2,303	538	128	1,765 R	77.6%	18.1%	81.1%	18.9%
48,290	BRYAN	11,451	8,743	2,330	378	6,413 R	76.4%	20.3%	79.0%	21.0%
28,682	CADDO	7,052	5,022	1,792	238	3,230 R	71.2%	25.4%	73.7%	26.3%
149,690	CANADIAN	50,097	34,207	13,867	2,023	20,340 R	68.3%	27.7%	71.2%	28.8%
48,144	CARTER	13,381	9,829	3,076	476	6,753 R	73.5%	23.0%	76.2%	23.8%
48,761	CHEROKEE	13,511	8,106	4,905	500	3,201 R	60.0%	36.3%	62.3%	37.7%
14,665	CHOCTAW	4,036	3,238	666	132	2,572 R	80.2%	16.5%	82.9%	17.1%
2,128	CIMARRON	729	651	38	40	613 R	89.3%	5.2%	94.5%	5.5%
285,168	CLEVELAND	91,085	49,400	38,150	3,535	11,250 R	54.2%	41.9%	56.4%	43.6%
5,485	COAL	1,885	1,497	333	55	1,164 R	79.4%	17.7%	81.8%	18.2%
120,613	COMANCHE	23,550	14,473	7,983	1,094	6,490 R	61.5%	33.9%	64.5%	35.5%
5,636	COTTON	1,843	1,498	252	93	1,246 R	81.3%	13.7%	85.6%	14.4%
14,167	CRAIG	4,472	3,338	975	159	2,363 R	74.6%	21.8%	77.4%	22.6%
71,611	CREEK	22,303	16,482	4,942	879	11,540 R	73.9%	22.2%	76.9%	23.1%
28,960	CUSTER	7,493	5,698	1,567	228	4,131 R	76.0%	20.9%	78.4%	21.6%
43,194	DELAWARE	13,191	10,101	2,724	366	7,377 R	76.6%	20.7%	78.8%	21.2%
4,882	DEWEY	1,764	1,534	160	70	1,374 R	87.0%	9.1%	90.6%	9.4%
3,850	ELLIS	1,486	1,297	152	37	1,145 R	87.3%	10.2%	89.5%	10.5%
60,833	GARFIELD	16,186	12,215	3,297	674	8,918 R	75.5%	20.4%	78.7%	21.3%
27,750	GARVIN	8,108	6,314	1,519	275	4,795 R	77.9%	18.7%	80.6%	19.4%

OKLAHOMA
SENATOR 2022

2020 Census Population	County	Total Vote	Republican (Lankford)	Democratic (Horn)	Other	Rep.-Dem. Plurality	Percentage Total Vote Rep.	Dem.	Major Vote Rep.	Dem.
56,146	GRADY	17,798	13,847	3,363	588	10,484 R	77.8%	18.9%	80.5%	19.5%
4,334	GRANT	1,596	1,321	207	68	1,114 R	82.8%	13.0%	86.5%	13.5%
5,714	GREER	1,342	1,049	241	52	808 R	78.2%	18.0%	81.3%	18.7%
2,638	HARMON	647	523	113	11	410 R	80.8%	17.5%	82.2%	17.8%
3,693	HARPER	1,166	998	111	57	887 R	85.6%	9.5%	90.0%	10.0%
12,650	HASKELL	3,385	2,675	633	77	2,042 R	79.0%	18.7%	80.9%	19.1%
13,312	HUGHES	3,538	2,666	722	150	1,944 R	75.4%	20.4%	78.7%	21.3%
24,467	JACKSON	5,497	4,372	912	213	3,460 R	79.5%	16.6%	82.7%	17.3%
5,999	JEFFERSON	1,608	1,281	253	74	1,028 R	79.7%	15.7%	83.5%	16.5%
11,075	JOHNSTON	2,958	2,373	490	95	1,883 R	80.2%	16.6%	82.9%	17.1%
43,528	KAY	12,506	8,993	3,039	474	5,954 R	71.9%	24.3%	74.7%	25.3%
15,796	KINGFISHER	4,875	4,062	627	186	3,435 R	83.3%	12.9%	86.6%	13.4%
8,695	KIOWA	2,458	1,916	496	46	1,420 R	77.9%	20.2%	79.4%	20.6%
10,065	LATIMER	3,057	2,332	601	124	1,731 R	76.3%	19.7%	79.5%	20.5%
49,861	LE FLORE	12,105	9,469	2,232	404	7,237 R	78.2%	18.4%	80.9%	19.1%
34,994	LINCOLN	11,084	8,648	1,980	456	6,668 R	78.0%	17.9%	81.4%	18.6%
48,284	LOGAN	16,979	12,310	3,985	684	8,325 R	72.5%	23.5%	75.5%	24.5%
10,291	LOVE	2,735	2,174	473	88	1,701 R	79.5%	17.3%	82.1%	17.9%
7,629	MAJOR	2,690	2,328	238	124	2,090 R	86.5%	8.8%	90.7%	9.3%
17,047	MARSHALL	4,388	3,484	788	116	2,696 R	79.4%	18.0%	81.6%	18.4%
41,139	MAYES	12,627	9,259	2,851	517	6,408 R	73.3%	22.6%	76.5%	23.5%
40,777	MCCLAIN	15,028	11,520	2,988	520	8,532 R	76.7%	19.9%	79.4%	20.6%
32,706	MCCURTAIN	8,230	6,644	1,326	260	5,318 R	80.7%	16.1%	83.4%	16.6%
19,679	MCINTOSH	6,444	4,587	1,676	181	2,911 R	71.2%	26.0%	73.2%	26.8%
14,116	MURRAY	4,242	3,242	833	167	2,409 R	76.4%	19.6%	79.6%	20.4%
68,022	MUSKOGEE	17,764	11,504	5,641	619	5,863 R	64.8%	31.8%	67.1%	32.9%
11,126	NOBLE	3,811	2,864	784	163	2,080 R	75.2%	20.6%	78.5%	21.5%
10,041	NOWATA	3,312	2,611	577	124	2,034 R	78.8%	17.4%	81.9%	18.1%
12,019	OKFUSKEE	2,937	2,085	727	125	1,358 R	71.0%	24.8%	74.1%	25.9%
799,370	OKLAHOMA	221,996	112,093	102,417	7,486	9,676 R	50.5%	46.1%	52.3%	47.7%
38,503	OKMULGEE	10,619	6,977	3,246	396	3,731 R	65.7%	30.6%	68.2%	31.8%
46,988	OSAGE	15,078	9,987	4,531	560	5,456 R	66.2%	30.1%	68.8%	31.2%
31,100	OTTAWA	7,670	5,534	1,842	294	3,692 R	72.2%	24.0%	75.0%	25.0%
16,396	PAWNEE	5,049	3,752	1,087	210	2,665 R	74.3%	21.5%	77.5%	22.5%
81,665	PAYNE	22,098	13,121	8,167	810	4,954 R	59.4%	37.0%	61.6%	38.4%
43,654	PITTSBURG	12,671	9,450	2,839	382	6,611 R	74.6%	22.4%	76.9%	23.1%
38,275	PONTOTOC	11,191	7,539	3,239	413	4,300 R	67.4%	28.9%	69.9%	30.1%
72,862	POTTAWATOMIE	20,684	14,484	5,383	817	9,101 R	70.0%	26.0%	72.9%	27.1%
11,128	PUSHMATAHA	3,282	2,656	532	94	2,124 R	80.9%	16.2%	83.3%	16.7%
3,580	ROGER MILLS	1,314	1,139	119	56	1,020 R	86.7%	9.1%	90.5%	9.5%
92,825	ROGERS	33,876	25,065	7,525	1,286	17,540 R	74.0%	22.2%	76.9%	23.1%
24,230	SEMINOLE	5,858	4,184	1,483	191	2,701 R	71.4%	25.3%	73.8%	26.2%
11,449	SEQUOYAH	10,244	7,669	2,224	351	5,445 R	74.9%	21.7%	77.5%	22.5%
43,180	STEPHENS	13,107	10,292	2,260	555	8,032 R	78.5%	17.2%	82.0%	18.0%
19,803	TEXAS	3,652	3,018	453	181	2,565 R	82.6%	12.4%	86.9%	13.1%
7,232	TILLMAN	1,844	1,444	330	70	1,114 R	78.3%	17.9%	81.4%	18.6%
652,649	TULSA	193,538	108,757	78,231	6,550	30,526 R	56.2%	40.4%	58.2%	41.8%
81,685	WAGONER	26,823	19,333	6,511	979	12,822 R	72.1%	24.3%	74.8%	25.2%
51,566	WASHINGTON	17,098	12,470	4,010	618	8,460 R	72.9%	23.5%	75.7%	24.3%
10,928	WASHITA	3,571	2,995	465	111	2,530 R	83.9%	13.0%	86.6%	13.4%
8,763	WOODS	2,699	2,149	468	82	1,681 R	79.6%	17.3%	82.1%	17.9%
20,102	WOODWARD	5,383	4,448	739	196	3,709 R	82.6%	13.7%	85.8%	14.2%
3,964,443	TOTAL	1,150,732	739,960	369,370	41,402	370,590 R	64.3%	32.1%	66.7%	33.3%

OKLAHOMA
SENATE SPECIAL 2022

2020 Census Population	County	Total Vote	(W) Markwayne Mullin Republican	Kendra Horn Democrat	Ray Woods Independent	Robert Murphy Libertarian	Rep.-Dem. Plurality	Percentage Total Vote Rep.	Dem.	Major Vote Rep.	Dem.
22,152	ADAIR	5,227	3,865	1,161	131	70	2,704 R	73.9%	22.2%	76.9%	23.1%
5,676	ALFALFA	1,733	1,450	240	22	21	1,210 R	83.7%	13.8%	85.8%	14.2%
13,789	ATOKA	3,923	3,211	624	54	34	2,587 R	81.9%	15.9%	83.7%	16.3%
5,290	BEAVER	1,690	1,482	151	38	19	1,331 R	87.7%	8.9%	90.8%	9.2%
21,827	BECKHAM	5,470	4,360	975	65	70	3,385 R	79.7%	17.8%	81.7%	18.3%
9,424	BLAINE	2,965	2,215	661	57	32	1,554 R	74.7%	22.3%	77.0%	23.0%
48,290	BRYAN	11,457	8,642	2,492	161	162	6,150 R	75.4%	21.8%	77.6%	22.4%
28,682	CADDO	7,052	4,689	2,170	104	89	2,519 R	66.5%	30.8%	68.4%	31.6%
149,690	CANADIAN	50,059	32,520	15,846	820	873	16,674 R	65.0%	31.7%	67.2%	32.8%
48,144	CARTER	13,385	9,669	3,302	215	199	6,367 R	72.2%	24.7%	74.5%	25.5%
48,761	CHEROKEE	13,517	7,944	5,124	245	204	2,820 R	58.8%	37.9%	60.8%	39.2%
14,665	CHOCTAW	4,040	3,242	689	58	51	2,553 R	80.2%	17.1%	82.5%	17.5%
2,128	CIMARRON	731	659	51	13	8	608 R	90.2%	7.0%	92.8%	7.2%
285,168	CLEVELAND	91,035	46,468	41,634	1,398	1,535	4,834 R	51.0%	45.7%	52.7%	47.3%
5,485	COAL	1,891	1,518	321	34	18	1,197 R	80.3%	17.0%	82.5%	17.5%
120,613	COMANCHE	23,500	13,850	8,661	496	493	5,189 R	58.9%	36.9%	61.5%	38.5%
5,636	COTTON	1,830	1,439	310	41	40	1,129 R	78.6%	16.9%	82.3%	17.7%
14,167	CRAIG	4,481	3,317	1,045	73	46	2,272 R	74.0%	23.3%	76.0%	24.0%
71,611	CREEK	22,304	16,245	5,386	340	333	10,859 R	72.8%	24.1%	75.1%	24.9%
28,960	CUSTER	7,487	5,350	1,939	91	107	3,411 R	71.5%	25.9%	73.4%	26.6%
43,194	DELAWARE	13,205	9,928	2,938	207	132	6,990 R	75.2%	22.2%	77.2%	22.8%
4,882	DEWEY	1,757	1,488	216	34	19	1,272 R	84.7%	12.3%	87.3%	12.7%
3,850	ELLIS	1,484	1,258	191	18	17	1,067 R	84.8%	12.9%	86.8%	13.2%
60,833	GARFIELD	16,181	11,766	3,908	285	222	7,858 R	72.7%	24.2%	75.1%	24.9%
27,750	GARVIN	8,114	6,112	1,779	119	104	4,333 R	75.3%	21.9%	77.5%	22.5%
56,146	GRADY	17,804	13,253	4,079	220	252	9,174 R	74.4%	22.9%	76.5%	23.5%
4,334	GRANT	1,594	1,267	271	25	31	996 R	79.5%	17.0%	82.4%	17.6%
5,714	GREER	1,339	1,011	289	26	13	722 R	75.5%	21.6%	77.8%	22.2%
2,638	HARMON	649	497	138	8	6	359 R	76.6%	21.3%	78.3%	21.7%
3,693	HARPER	1,167	982	139	21	25	843 R	84.1%	11.9%	87.6%	12.4%
12,650	HASKELL	3,386	2,645	676	39	26	1,969 R	78.1%	20.0%	79.6%	20.4%
13,312	HUGHES	3,548	2,603	837	61	47	1,766 R	73.4%	23.6%	75.7%	24.3%
24,467	JACKSON	5,486	4,262	1,044	77	103	3,218 R	77.7%	19.0%	80.3%	19.7%
5,999	JEFFERSON	1,599	1,269	278	32	20	991 R	79.4%	17.4%	82.0%	18.0%
11,075	JOHNSTON	2,961	2,357	513	55	36	1,844 R	79.6%	17.3%	82.1%	17.9%
43,528	KAY	12,499	8,662	3,434	225	178	5,228 R	69.3%	27.5%	71.6%	28.4%
15,796	KINGFISHER	4,873	3,942	808	66	57	3,134 R	80.9%	16.6%	83.0%	17.0%
8,695	KIOWA	2,455	1,794	615	25	21	1,179 R	73.1%	25.1%	74.5%	25.5%
10,065	LATIMER	3,063	2,341	636	49	37	1,705 R	76.4%	20.8%	78.6%	21.4%
49,861	LE FLORE	12,121	9,540	2,273	165	143	7,267 R	78.7%	18.8%	80.8%	19.2%
34,994	LINCOLN	11,085	8,379	2,374	179	153	6,005 R	75.6%	21.4%	77.9%	22.1%
48,284	LOGAN	16,977	11,904	4,548	246	279	7,356 R	70.1%	26.8%	72.4%	27.6%
10,291	LOVE	2,731	2,152	497	43	39	1,655 R	78.8%	18.2%	81.2%	18.8%
7,629	MAJOR	2,688	2,288	301	73	26	1,987 R	85.1%	11.2%	88.4%	11.6%
17,047	MARSHALL	4,385	3,436	832	61	56	2,604 R	78.4%	19.0%	80.5%	19.5%

OKLAHOMA
SENATE SPECIAL 2022

2020 Census Population	County	Total Vote	(W) Markwayne Mullin Republican	Kendra Horn Democrat	Ray Woods Independent	Robert Murphy Libertarian	Rep.-Dem. Plurality	Percentage Total Vote Rep.	Dem.	Major Vote Rep.	Dem.
41,139	MAYES	12,642	9,145	3,090	203	204	6,055 R	72.3%	24.4%	74.7%	25.3%
40,777	MCCLAIN	15,012	11,107	3,500	187	218	7,607 R	74.0%	23.3%	76.0%	24.0%
32,706	MCCURTAIN	8,256	6,703	1,345	119	89	5,358 R	81.2%	16.3%	83.3%	16.7%
19,679	MCINTOSH	6,460	4,485	1,803	95	77	2,682 R	69.4%	27.9%	71.3%	28.7%
14,116	MURRAY	4,248	3,153	973	61	61	2,180 R	74.2%	22.9%	76.4%	23.6%
68,022	MUSKOGEE	17,782	11,263	6,022	247	250	5,241 R	63.3%	33.9%	65.2%	34.8%
11,126	NOBLE	3,804	2,763	923	52	66	1,840 R	72.6%	24.3%	75.0%	25.0%
10,041	NOWATA	3,321	2,631	613	40	37	2,018 R	79.2%	18.5%	81.1%	18.9%
12,019	OKFUSKEE	2,938	2,063	788	47	40	1,275 R	70.2%	26.8%	72.4%	27.6%
799,370	OKLAHOMA	221,862	103,019	112,532	3,068	3,243	9,513 D	46.4%	50.7%	47.8%	52.2%
38,503	OKMULGEE	10,624	6,881	3,442	158	143	3,439 R	64.8%	32.4%	66.7%	33.3%
46,988	OSAGE	15,084	9,856	4,824	212	192	5,032 R	65.3%	32.0%	67.1%	32.9%
31,100	OTTAWA	7,678	5,510	1,911	141	116	3,599 R	71.8%	24.9%	74.2%	25.8%
16,396	PAWNEE	5,047	3,709	1,188	77	73	2,521 R	73.5%	23.5%	75.7%	24.3%
81,665	PAYNE	22,073	12,225	9,147	305	396	3,078 R	55.4%	41.4%	57.2%	42.8%
43,654	PITTSBURG	12,688	9,412	2,979	172	125	6,433 R	74.2%	23.5%	76.0%	24.0%
38,275	PONTOTOC	11,166	7,175	3,647	164	180	3,528 R	64.3%	32.7%	66.3%	33.7%
72,862	POTTAWATOMIE	20,675	13,787	6,227	365	296	7,560 R	66.7%	30.1%	68.9%	31.1%
11,128	PUSHMATAHA	3,287	2,683	532	36	36	2,151 R	81.6%	16.2%	83.5%	16.5%
3,580	ROGER MILLS	1,317	1,120	160	20	17	960 R	85.0%	12.1%	87.5%	12.5%
92,825	ROGERS	33,894	24,637	8,221	491	545	16,416 R	72.7%	24.3%	75.0%	25.0%
24,230	SEMINOLE	5,864	3,979	1,730	78	77	2,249 R	67.9%	29.5%	69.7%	30.3%
41,449	SEQUOYAH	10,256	7,671	2,288	192	105	5,383 R	74.8%	22.3%	77.0%	23.0%
43,180	STEPHENS	13,092	10,107	2,542	211	232	7,565 R	77.2%	19.4%	79.9%	20.1%
19,803	TEXAS	3,651	3,002	505	79	65	2,497 R	82.2%	13.8%	85.6%	14.4%
7,232	TILLMAN	1,840	1,388	393	25	34	995 R	75.4%	21.4%	77.9%	22.1%
652,649	TULSA	193,425	103,578	84,017	2,637	3,193	19,561 R	53.5%	43.4%	55.2%	44.8%
81,685	WAGONER	26,841	18,977	7,084	376	404	11,893 R	70.7%	26.4%	72.8%	27.2%
51,566	WASHINGTON	17,086	12,132	4,452	234	268	7,680 R	71.0%	26.1%	73.2%	26.8%
10,928	WASHITA	3,567	2,829	643	43	52	2,186 R	79.3%	18.0%	81.5%	18.5%
8,763	WOODS	2,699	2,040	575	40	44	1,465 R	75.6%	21.3%	78.0%	22.0%
20,102	WOODWARD	5,374	4,342	897	73	62	3,445 R	80.8%	16.7%	82.9%	17.1%
3,964,443	TOTAL	1,150,481					305,254 R	61.8%	35.2%	63.7%	36.3%

OKLAHOMA
HOUSE OF REPRESENTATIVES

CD	Year	Total Vote	Republican Vote	Candidate	Democratic Vote	Candidate	Other Vote	Rep.-Dem. Plurality	Total Vote Rep.	Dem.	Major Vote Rep.	Dem.
1	2022	233,495	142,800	HERN, KEVIN*	80,974	MARTIN, ADAM	9,721	61,826 R	61.2%	34.7%	63.8%	36.2%
1	2020	335,471	213,700	HERN, KEVIN*	109,641	ASAMOA-CAESAR, KOJO	12,130	104,059 R	63.7%	32.7%	66.1%	33.9%
1	2018	253,171	150,129	HERN, KEVIN	103,042	GILPIN, TIM		47,087 R	59.3%	40.7%	59.3%	40.7%
1	2016		Unopposed	BRIDENSTINE, JIM*								
1	2014		Unopposed	BRIDENSTINE, JIM*								
1	2012	285,312	181,084	BRIDENSTINE, JIM	91,421	OLSON, JOHN	12,807	89,663 R	63.5%	32.0%	66.5%	33.5%

OKLAHOMA

HOUSE OF REPRESENTATIVES

			Republican		Democratic		Other Vote	Rep.-Dem. Plurality	Percentage			
									Total Vote		Major Vote	
CD	Year	Total Vote	Vote	Candidate	Vote	Candidate			Rep.	Dem.	Rep.	Dem.
2	2022	231,672	167,843	BRECHEEN, JOSH	54,194	ANDREWS, NAOMI	9,635	113,649 R	72.4%	23.4%	75.6%	24.4%
2	2020	288,527	216,511	MULLIN, MARKWAYNE*	63,472	LANIER, DANYELL	8,544	153,039 R	75.0%	22.0%	77.3%	22.7%
2	2018	216,002	140,451	MULLIN, MARKWAYNE*	65,021	NICHOLS, JASON	10,530	75,430 R	65.0%	30.1%	68.4%	31.6%
2	2016	268,870	189,839	MULLIN, MARKWAYNE*	62,387	HARRIS-TILL, JOSHUA	16,644	127,452 R	70.6%	23.2%	75.3%	24.7%
2	2014	158,407	110,925	MULLIN, MARKWAYNE*	38,964	EVERETT, EARL E.	8,518	71,961 R	70.0%	24.6%	74.0%	26.0%
2	2012	250,612	143,701	MULLIN, MARKWAYNE	96,081	WALLACE, ROB	10,830	47,620 R	57.3%	38.3%	59.9%	40.1%
3	2022	197,772	147,418	LUCAS, FRANK D.*	50,354	ROSS, JEREMIAH A		97,064 R	74.5%	25.5%	74.5%	25.5%
3	2020	309,178	242,677	LUCAS, FRANK D.*	66,501	MIDYETT, ZOE ANN		176,176 R	78.5%	21.5%	78.5%	21.5%
3	2018	234,065	172,913	LUCAS, FRANK D.*	61,152	ROBBINS, FRANKIE		111,761 R	73.9%	26.1%	73.9%	26.1%
3	2016	290,615	227,525	LUCAS, FRANK D.*	63,090	ROBBINS, FRANKIE		164,435 R	78.3%	21.7%	78.3%	21.7%
3	2014	169,605	133,335	LUCAS, FRANK D.*	36,270	ROBBINS, FRANKIE		97,065 R	78.6%	21.4%	78.6%	21.4%
3	2012	268,003	201,744	LUCAS, FRANK D.*	53,472	MURRAY, TIMOTHY RAY	12,787	148,272 R	75.3%	20.0%	79.0%	21.0%
4	2022	224,546	149,879	COLE, TOM*	74,667	BRANNON, MARY		75,212 R	66.7%	33.3%	66.7%	33.3%
4	2020	314,358	213,096	COLE, TOM*	90,459	BRANNON, MARY	10,803	122,637 R	67.8%	28.8%	70.2%	29.8%
4	2018	236,638	149,227	COLE, TOM*	78,088	BRANNON, MARY	9,323	71,139 R	63.1%	33.0%	65.6%	34.4%
4	2016	293,189	204,143	COLE, TOM*	76,472	OWEN, CHRISTINA	12,574	127,671 R	69.6%	26.1%	72.7%	27.3%
4	2014	166,268	117,721	COLE, TOM*	40,998	SMITH, BERT	7,549	76,723 R	70.8%	24.7%	74.2%	25.8%
4	2012	260,331	176,740	COLE, THOMAS J.*	71,846	BEBO, DONNA MARIE	11,745	104,894 R	67.9%	27.6%	71.1%	28.9%
5	2022	258,826	152,699	BICE, STEPHANIE*	96,799	HARRIS-TILL, JOSHUA	9,328	55,900 R	59.0%	37.4%	61.2%	38.8%
5	2020	303,849	158,191	BICE, STEPHANIE	145,658	HORN, KENDRA*		12,533 R	52.1%	47.9%	52.1%	47.9%
5	2018	238,960	117,811	RUSSELL, STEVE D.*	121,149	HORN, KENDRA		3,338 D	49.3%	50.7%	49.3%	50.7%
5	2016	280,570	160,184	RUSSELL, STEVE D.*	103,273	MCAFFREY, AL	17,113	56,911 R	57.1%	36.8%	60.8%	39.2%
5	2014	159,133	95,632	RUSSELL, STEVE D.	57,790	MCAFFREY, AL	5,711	37,842 R	60.1%	36.3%	62.3%	37.7%
5	2012	261,677	153,603	LANKFORD, JAMES*	97,504	GUILD, TOM	10,570	56,099 R	58.7%	37.3%	61.2%	38.8%
TOTAL	2022	1,146,311	760,639		356,988		28,684	403,651 R	66.4%	31.1%	68.1%	31.9%
TOTAL	2020	1,551,383	1,044,175		475,731		31,477	568,444 R	67.3%	30.7%	68.7%	31.3%
TOTAL	2018	1,178,836	730,531		428,452		19,853	302,079 R	62.0%	36.3%	63.0%	37.0%
TOTAL	2016	1,133,244	781,691		305,222		46,331	476,469 R	69.0%	26.9%	71.9%	28.1%
TOTAL	2014	653,413	457,613		174,022		21,778	283,591 R	70.0%	26.6%	72.4%	27.6%
TOTAL	2012	1,325,935	856,872		410,324		58,739	446,548 R	64.6%	30.9%	67.6%	32.4%

Note: An asterisk (*) denotes incumbent.

OKLAHOMA

GENERAL AND PRIMARY ELECTIONS

GENERAL ELECTIONS: OTHER VOTES

Governor Other vote was 16,243 Libertarian (Natalie Bruno), 15,653 Independent (Ervin Yen)

Senate Other vote was 20,907 Independent (Michael Delaney), 20,495 Libertarian (Kenneth Blevins)

House Other vote was:

CD 1 9,721 Independent (Evelyn Rogers)
CD 2 9,635 Independent (Bulldog Ben Robinson)
CD 4 9,328 Independent (David Frosch)

2022 PRIMARY ELECTIONS: SUPPLEMENTARY INFORMATION

Primary	June 28, 2022	**Registration** (as of January 15, 2022)	2,218,374	Republican	1,122,582
				Democratic	696,723
Primary Runoff	August 23, 2022			Libertarian	17,981
				Independent	381,088

Primary Type Semi-Open—Only registered Democrats and Republicans could vote in their party's primary. Independent voters could vote in the Democratic primary.

OKLAHOMA

GENERAL AND PRIMARY ELECTIONS

	REPUBLICAN PRIMARIES			DEMOCRATIC PRIMARIES		
Senator	Lankford, James*	243,132	67.8%	Horn, Madison	60,691	37.2%
	Lahmeyer, Jackson	94,572	26.4%	Bollinger, Jason	27,374	16.8%
	Farr, Joan	20,761	5.8%	Baker, Dennis	22,467	13.8%
				Glenn, Jo	21,198	13.0%
				Wade, Brandon	19,986	12.2%
				Azma, Arya	11,478	7.0%
	TOTAL	358,465		TOTAL	163,194	
				PRIMARY RUNOFF		
				Horn, Madison	60,929	65.5%
				Bollinger, Jason	32,121	34.5%
				TOTAL	93,050	
Governor	Stitt, Kevin*	248,525	69.1%	Hofmeister, Joy	101,913	60.7%
	Kintsel, Joel	51,587	14.3%	Johnson, Constance "Connie"	65,894	39.3%
	Sherwood, Mark	47,713	13.3%			
	McCabe, Moira	12,046	3.3%			
	TOTAL	359,871		TOTAL	167,807	
Congressional District 1	Hern, Kevin*	Unopposed				
Congressional District 2	Frix, Avery	11,336	14.7%			
	Brecheen, Josh	10,579	13.8%			
	Teehee, Johnny	9,963	13.0%			
	Bennett, John	8,713	11.3%			
	Barker, Guy	8,444	11.0%			
	Quinn, Marty	5,612	7.3%			
	Nofire, Wes	4,859	6.3%			
	Derby, David	4,204	5.5%			
	Schiller, Chris	4,108	5.3%			
	Roberts, Dustin	3,746	4.9%			
	Gordon, Pamela	2,344	3.0%			
	Hopkins, Rhonda	1,281	1.7%			
	Johnson, Clint	1,128	1.5%			
	Wyatt, Erick Paul	615	0.8%			
	TOTAL	76,932				
	PRIMARY RUNOFF					
	Brecheen, Josh	33,517	52.2%			
	Frix, Avery	30,686	47.8%			
	TOTAL	64,203				
Congressional District 3	Lucas, Frank D.*	44,442	61.1%			
	Burleson, Wade	22,258	30.6%			
	Butler, Stephen	5,997	8.2%			
	TOTAL	72,697				
Congressional District 4	Cole, Tom*	43,894	69.8%			
	Taylor, James	16,980	27.0%			
	Blacke, Frank	2,038	3.2%			
	TOTAL	62,912				
Congressional District 5	Bice, Stephanie*	51,612	68.4%			
	Banks, Subrina	23,891	31.6%			
	TOTAL	75,503				

Note: An asterisk (*) denotes incumbent.

OREGON

Statewide Races

Oregon's most visible 2022 contest, its open-seat gubernatorial race, was unique in that it was a statewide race between opposing legislative leaders. Before they each resigned from the legislature to focus on running for governor, Democrat Tina Kotek was the speaker of the Oregon House while Republican Christine Drazan was the minority leader.

Though Kotek faced a credible opponent in state Treasurer Tobias Read, she won the May primary 56%–33%. The Republican primary was less clear. In a field where seven candidates took at least 5% of the vote, Drazan won with about 23%.

While the parties were settling on nominees, a third candidate was making headlines. Betsy Johnson, a Democratic state senator from the northwest, ran as an independent. In summer polls, she registered at as much as 30%. But as the general election approached, partisans seemed to "come home" to the major-party nominees. Drazan linked Kotek to the outgoing (and unpopular) Democratic incumbent, Kate Brown. With homelessness as a top issue, Kotek warned voters not to throw the baby out with the bathwater, "We certainly don't need a red state takeover to clean up the damn trash."

Kotek seemed to peak at the right time – she won with 47% to Drazan's 44%. In statewide races, Republicans have struggled to find the votes needed to cancel out Portland's Multnomah County, which casts about one in five of the state's votes. Kotek carried Multnomah by 52 points. Kotek's win represented the eleventh straight Democratic gubernatorial win in Oregon, the Democrats' longest such streak in the country – amazingly, all but one of those victories (1998) were decided by single-digit margins.

In a lower profile race, Democratic Sen. Ron Wyden won a fifth full term against conspiracy theorist Jo Rae Perkins, who was also the GOP nominee for the other seat, in 2020. Wyden's 56%–41% margin was comfortable, but it marked a decline from the 57%–33% he scored in 2016.

House Races

Oregon, which added a sixth seat for 2022, was among the first states to pass a new map. In one of her last acts as Speaker, Kotek helped pass a gerrymander intended to up the Democratic advantage in the delegation from 4-1 to 5-1. After the elections, Democrats held only a 4-2 edge.

The new 6th District appeared south of the Portland area and included the state capital, Salem. Democrats held it, but by just a 50%–48% margin. Democrats also held the open 4th District, which is a mix of college towns and working-class coastal counties.

But in the 5th District, which was redrawn to include the city of Bend, moderate Democrat Kurt Schrader lost his primary to a more progressive candidate, Jamie McLeod-Skinner. Republicans nominated Lori Chavez-DeRemer, a former mayor of the Portland suburb of Happy Valley. The 5th District, which would have gone 53%–44% for Biden in 2020, was the state's most expensive House race. Chavez-DeRemer won 51%–49%, marking the first time since the 1994 elections that Oregon sent two Republicans to the House (District 2, in the east, has long been in GOP hands).

OREGON
Congressional districts first established for elections held in 2022
6 members

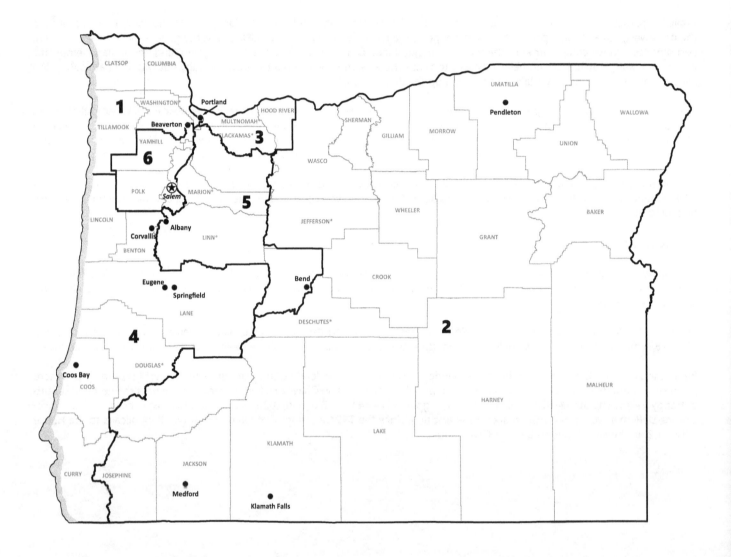

* Asterisk indicates a county whose boundaries include parts of two or more congressional districts.

OREGON

GOVERNOR
Tina Kotek (D). Elected 2022 to a four-year term.

SENATORS (2 Democrats)
Jeff Merkley (D). Reelected 2020 to a six-year term. Previously elected 2014, 2008.

Ron Wyden (D). Reelected 2022 to a six-year term. Previously elected 2016, 2010, 2004, 1998, and in a special election January 30, 1996, to serve the remaining three years of the term vacated when Senator Robert W. Packwood (R) resigned in October 1995.

REPRESENTATIVES (2 Republicans, 4 Democrats)
1. Suzanne Bonamici (D)
2. Cliff Bentz (R)
3. Earl Blumenauer (D)
4. Val T. Hoyle (D)
5. Lori Chavez-DeRemer (R)
6. Andrea Salinas (D)

POSTWAR VOTE FOR PRESIDENT

Year	Total Vote	Republican Vote	Republican Candidate	Democratic Vote	Democratic Candidate	Other Vote	Rep.-Dem. Plurality	Total Vote Rep.	Total Vote Dem.	Major Vote Rep.	Major Vote Dem.
2020	2,374,321	958,448	Trump, Donald J.*	1,340,383	Biden, Joseph R. Jr.	75,490	381,935 D	40.4%	56.5%	41.7%	58.3%
2016**	2,001,336	782,403	Trump, Donald J.	1,002,106	Clinton, Hillary Rodham	216,827	219,703 D	39.1%	50.1%	43.8%	56.2%
2012	1,789,270	754,175	Romney, W. Mitt	970,488	Obama, Barack H.*	64,607	216,313 D	42.1%	54.2%	43.7%	56.3%
2008	1,827,864	738,475	McCain, John S. III	1,037,291	Obama, Barack H.	52,098	298,816 D	40.4%	56.7%	41.6%	58.4%
2004	1,836,782	866,831	Bush, George W.*	943,163	Kerry, John F.	26,788	76,332 D	47.2%	51.3%	47.9%	52.1%
2000**	1,533,968	713,577	Bush, George W.	720,342	Gore, Albert Jr.	100,049	6,765 D	46.5%	47.0%	49.8%	50.2%
1996**	1,377,760	538,152	Dole, Robert "Bob"	649,641	Clinton, Bill*	189,967	111,489 D	39.1%	47.2%	45.3%	54.7%
1992**	1,462,643	475,757	Bush, George H.*	621,314	Clinton, Bill	365,572	145,557 D	32.5%	42.5%	43.4%	56.6%
1988	1,201,694	560,126	Bush, George H.	616,206	Dukakis, Michael S.	25,362	56,080 D	46.6%	51.3%	47.6%	52.4%
1984	1,226,527	685,700	Reagan, Ronald*	536,479	Mondale, Walter F.	4,348	149,221 R	55.9%	43.7%	56.1%	43.9%
1980**	1,181,516	571,044	Reagan, Ronald	456,890	Carter, Jimmy*	153,582	114,154 R	48.3%	38.7%	55.6%	44.4%
1976	1,029,876	492,120	Ford, Gerald R.*	490,407	Carter, Jimmy	47,349	1,713 R	47.8%	47.6%	50.1%	49.9%
1972	927,946	486,686	Nixon, Richard M.*	392,760	McGovern, George S.	48,500	93,926 R	52.4%	42.3%	55.3%	44.7%
1968**	819,622	408,433	Nixon, Richard M.	358,866	Humphrey, Hubert Horatio Jr.	52,323	49,567 R	49.8%	43.8%	53.2%	46.8%
1964	786,305	282,779	Goldwater, Barry M. Sr.	501,017	Johnson, Lyndon B.*	2,509	218,238 D	36.0%	63.7%	36.1%	63.9%
1960	776,421	408,060	Nixon, Richard M.	367,402	Kennedy, John F.	959	40,658 R	52.6%	47.3%	52.6%	47.4%
1956	736,132	406,393	Eisenhower, Dwight D.*	329,204	Stevenson, Adlai E. II	535	77,189 R	55.2%	44.7%	55.2%	44.8%
1952	695,059	420,815	Eisenhower, Dwight D.	270,579	Stevenson, Adlai E. II	3,665	150,236 R	60.5%	38.9%	60.9%	39.1%
1948	524,080	260,904	Dewey, Thomas E.	243,147	Truman, Harry S.*	20,029	17,757 R	49.8%	46.4%	51.8%	48.2%

Note: An asterisk (*) denotes incumbent. **In past elections, the other vote included: 2016 - 94,231 Libertarian (Gary Johnson); 2000 - 77,357 Green (Ralph Nader); 1996 - 121,221 Reform (Ross Perot); 1992 - 354,091 Independent (Perot); 1980 - 112,389 Independent (John Anderson); 1968 - 49,683 American Independent (George Wallace).

OREGON

POSTWAR VOTE FOR GOVERNOR

Year	Total Vote	Republican Vote	Republican Candidate	Democratic Vote	Democratic Candidate	Other Vote	Rep.-Dem. Plurality	Total Vote Rep.	Total Vote Dem.	Major Vote Rep.	Major Vote Dem.
2022	1,952,883	850,347	Drazan, Christine	917,074	Kotek, Tina	185,462	66,727 D	43.5%	47.0%	48.1%	51.9%
2018	1,866,997	814,988	Buehler, Knute	934,498	Brown, Kate*	117,511	119,510 D	43.7%	50.1%	46.6%	53.4%
2016S**	1,944,807	844,372	Pierce, Bud	985,022	Brown, Kate*	115,413	140,650 D	43.4%	50.6%	46.2%	53.8%
2014	1,469,717	648,542	Richardson, Dennis	733,230	Kitzhaber, John*	87,945	84,688 D	44.1%	49.9%	46.9%	53.1%
2010	1,453,548	694,287	Dudley, Chris	716,525	Kitzhaber, John	42,736	22,238 D	47.8%	49.3%	49.2%	50.8%
2006	1,379,475	589,748	Saxton, Ron	699,786	Kulongoski, Ted*	89,941	110,038 D	42.8%	50.7%	45.7%	54.3%
2002	1,260,497	581,785	Mannix, Kevin L.	618,004	Kulongoski, Ted	60,708	36,219 D	46.2%	49.0%	48.5%	51.5%
1998	1,113,098	334,001	Sizemore, Bill	717,061	Kitzhaber, John*	62,036	383,060 D	30.0%	64.4%	31.8%	68.2%
1994	1,221,010	517,874	Smith, Denny	622,083	Kitzhaber, John	81,053	104,209 D	42.4%	50.9%	45.4%	54.6%
1990**	1,112,847	444,646	Frohnmayer, Dave	508,749	Roberts, Barbara	159,452	64,103 D	40.0%	45.7%	46.6%	53.4%
1986	1,059,630	506,986	Paulus, Norma	549,456	Goldschmidt, Neil	3,188	42,470 D	47.8%	51.9%	48.0%	52.0%
1982	1,042,009	639,841	Atiyeh, Victor*	374,316	Kulongoski, Ted	27,852	265,525 R	61.4%	35.9%	63.1%	36.9%
1978	911,143	498,452	Atiyeh, Victor	409,411	Straub, Robert W.*	3,280	89,041 R	54.7%	44.9%	54.9%	45.1%
1974	770,574	324,751	Atiyeh, Victor	444,812	Straub, Robert W.	1,011	120,061 D	42.1%	57.7%	42.2%	57.8%
1970	666,394	369,964	McCall, Tom*	293,892	Straub, Robert W.	2,538	76,072 R	55.5%	44.1%	55.7%	44.3%
1966	682,862	377,346	McCall, Tom	305,008	Straub, Robert W.	508	72,338 R	55.3%	44.7%	55.3%	44.7%
1962	637,407	345,497	Hatfield, Mark O.*	265,359	Thornton, Robert Y.	26,551	80,138 R	54.2%	41.6%	56.6%	43.4%
1958	599,994	331,900	Hatfield, Mark O.	267,934	Holmes, Robert D.*	160	63,966 R	55.3%	44.7%	55.3%	44.7%
1956S**	731,279	361,840	Smith, Elmo E.	369,439	Holmes, Robert D.		7,599 D	49.5%	50.5%	49.5%	50.5%
1954	566,701	322,522	Patterson, Paul	244,179	Carson, Joseph K. Jr.		78,343 R	56.9%	43.1%	56.9%	43.1%
1950	505,910	334,160	McKay, Douglas*	171,750	Flegal, Austin F.		162,410 R	66.1%	33.9%	66.1%	33.9%
1948S**	509,624	271,295	McKay, Douglas	226,949	Wallace, Lew	11,380	44,346 R	53.2%	44.5%	54.5%	45.5%
1946	344,155	237,681	Snell, Earl*	106,474	Donaugh, Carl C.		131,207 R	69.1%	30.9%	69.1%	30.9%

Note: An asterisk (*) denotes incumbent. **In past elections, the other vote included: 1990 - 144,062 Independent (Al Mobley). The 1948, 1956, and 2016 elections were for short terms to fill a vacancy.

POSTWAR VOTE FOR SENATOR

Year	Total Vote	Republican Vote	Republican Candidate	Democratic Vote	Democratic Candidate	Other Vote	Rep.-Dem. Plurality	Total Vote Rep.	Total Vote Dem.	Major Vote Rep.	Major Vote Dem.
2022	1,927,949	788,991	Perkins, Jo Rae	1,076,424	Wyden, Ron*	62,534	287,433 D	40.9%	55.8%	42.3%	57.7%
2020	2,321,249	912,814	Perkins, Jo Rae	1,321,047	Merkley, Jeff*	87,388	408,233 D	39.3%	56.9%	40.9%	59.1%
2016	1,952,478	651,106	Callahan, Mark	1,105,119	Wyden, Ron*	196,253	454,013 D	33.3%	56.6%	37.1%	62.9%
2014	1,461,618	538,847	Wehby, Monica	814,537	Merkley, Jeff*	108,234	275,690 D	36.9%	55.7%	39.8%	60.2%
2010	1,442,588	566,199	Huffman, Jim	825,507	Wyden, Ron*	50,882	259,308 D	39.2%	57.2%	40.7%	59.3%
2008	1,767,504	805,159	Smith, Gordon H.*	864,392	Merkley, Jeff	97,953	59,233 D	45.6%	48.9%	48.2%	51.8%
2004	1,780,550	565,254	King, Al	1,128,728	Wyden, Ron*	86,568	563,474 D	31.7%	63.4%	33.4%	66.6%
2002	1,267,221	712,287	Smith, Gordon H.*	501,898	Bradbury, Bill	53,036	210,389 R	56.2%	39.6%	58.7%	41.3%
1998	1,117,747	377,739	Lim, John	682,425	Wyden, Ron*	57,583	304,686 D	33.8%	61.1%	35.6%	64.4%
1996	1,360,230	677,336	Smith, Gordon H.*	624,370	Bruggere, Tom	58,324	52,966 R	49.8%	45.9%	52.0%	48.0%
1996S**	1,196,608	553,519	Smith, Gordon H.	571,739	Wyden, Ron	71,350	18,220 D	46.3%	47.8%	49.2%	50.8%
1992	1,376,033	717,455	Packwood, Robert W.*	639,851	Aucoin, Les	18,727	77,604 R	52.1%	46.5%	52.9%	47.1%
1990	1,099,255	590,095	Hatfield, Mark O.*	507,743	Lonsdale, Harry	1,417	82,352 R	53.7%	46.2%	53.8%	46.2%
1986	1,042,555	656,317	Packwood, Robert W.*	375,735	Bauman, Rick	10,503	280,582 R	63.0%	36.0%	63.6%	36.4%
1984	1,214,735	808,152	Hatfield, Mark O.*	406,122	Hendriksen, Margie	461	402,030 R	66.5%	33.4%	66.6%	33.4%
1980	1,140,494	594,290	Packwood, Robert W.*	501,963	Kulongoski, Ted	44,241	92,327 R	52.1%	44.0%	54.2%	45.8%
1978	892,518	550,165	Hatfield, Mark O.*	341,616	Cook, Vernon	737	208,549 R	61.6%	38.3%	61.7%	38.3%
1974	766,414	420,984	Packwood, Robert W.*	338,591	Roberts, Betty	6,839	82,393 R	54.9%	44.2%	55.4%	44.6%
1972	920,833	494,671	Hatfield, Mark O.*	425,036	Morse, Wayne L.	1,126	69,635 R	53.7%	46.2%	53.8%	46.2%
1968	814,176	408,646	Packwood, Robert W.	405,353	Morse, Wayne L.*	177	3,293 R	50.2%	49.8%	50.2%	49.8%
1966	685,067	354,391	Hatfield, Mark O.	330,374	Duncan, Robert B.	302	24,017 R	51.7%	48.2%	51.8%	48.2%
1962	636,558	291,587	Unander, Sig	344,716	Morse, Wayne L.*	255	53,129 D	45.8%	54.2%	45.8%	54.2%
1960	755,875	343,009	Smith, Elmo E.	412,757	Neuberger, Maurine B.*	109	69,748 D	45.4%	54.6%	45.4%	54.6%
1956	732,254	335,405	McKay, Douglas	396,849	Morse, Wayne L.*		61,444 D	45.8%	54.2%	45.8%	54.2%
1954	569,088	283,313	Cordon, Guy*	285,775	Neuberger, Richard L.		2,462 D	49.8%	50.2%	49.8%	50.2%
1950	503,455	376,510	Morse, Wayne L.*	116,780	Latourette, Howard	10,165	259,730 R	74.8%	23.2%	76.3%	23.7%
1948	498,570	299,295	Cordon, Guy*	199,275	Wilson, Manley J.		100,020 R	60.0%	40.0%	60.0%	40.0%

Note: An asterisk (*) denotes incumbent. **The January 1996 election was for a short term to fill a vacancy.

OREGON
GOVERNOR 2022

2020 Census Population	County	Total Vote	Republican (Drazan)	Democratic (Kotek)	Other	Rep.-Dem. Plurality		Total Vote Rep.	Total Vote Dem.	Major Vote Rep.	Major Vote Dem.
16,165	BAKER	8,751	6,328	1,483	940	4,845	R	72.3%	16.9%	81.0%	19.0%
93,142	BENTON	45,319	14,658	27,128	3,533	12,470	D	32.3%	59.9%	35.1%	64.9%
420,373	CLACKAMAS	214,889	102,111	92,274	20,504	9,837	R	47.5%	42.9%	52.5%	47.5%
40,507	CLATSOP	20,201	7,375	8,051	4,775	676	D	36.5%	39.9%	47.8%	52.2%
52,605	COLUMBIA	27,384	13,420	8,036	5,928	5,384	R	49.0%	29.3%	62.5%	37.5%
64,908	COOS	31,429	18,611	9,437	3,381	9,174	R	59.2%	30.0%	66.4%	33.6%
24,708	CROOK	14,065	10,362	2,209	1,494	8,153	R	73.7%	15.7%	82.4%	17.6%
23,084	CURRY	12,679	7,272	4,143	1,264	3,129	R	57.4%	32.7%	63.7%	36.3%
199,817	DESCHUTES	109,678	50,513	46,879	12,286	3,634	R	46.1%	42.7%	51.9%	48.1%
111,731	DOUGLAS	54,553	37,245	12,013	5,295	25,232	R	68.3%	22.0%	75.6%	24.4%
1,927	GILLIAM	999	636	147	216	489	R	63.7%	14.7%	81.2%	18.8%
7,215	GRANT	4,170	3,145	576	449	2,569	R	75.4%	13.8%	84.5%	15.5%
7,438	HARNEY	3,834	2,973	485	376	2,488	R	77.5%	12.6%	86.0%	14.0%
23,451	HOOD RIVER	10,805	3,633	6,040	1,132	2,407	D	33.6%	55.9%	37.6%	62.4%
222,304	JACKSON	104,385	56,362	39,611	8,412	16,751	R	54.0%	37.9%	58.7%	41.3%
24,820	JEFFERSON	9,977	6,251	2,376	1,350	3,875	R	62.7%	23.8%	72.5%	27.5%
88,059	JOSEPHINE	42,962	27,578	11,610	3,774	15,968	R	64.2%	27.0%	70.4%	29.6%
68,578	KLAMATH	30,217	21,962	5,968	2,287	15,994	R	72.7%	19.8%	78.6%	21.4%
7,906	LAKE	4,008	3,282	430	296	2,852	R	81.9%	10.7%	88.4%	11.6%
384,378	LANE	183,669	72,087	95,847	15,735	23,760	D	39.2%	52.2%	42.9%	57.1%
50,373	LINCOLN	26,270	10,366	12,947	2,957	2,581	D	39.5%	49.3%	44.5%	55.5%
130,633	LINN	61,495	38,505	16,959	6,031	21,546	R	62.6%	27.6%	69.4%	30.6%
30,680	MALHEUR	9,187	6,921	1,656	610	5,265	R	75.3%	18.0%	80.7%	19.3%
349,860	MARION	134,850	70,741	51,238	12,871	19,503	R	52.5%	38.0%	58.0%	42.0%
11,642	MORROW	4,089	3,016	607	466	2,409	R	73.8%	14.8%	83.2%	16.8%
813,794	MULTNOMAH	366,043	72,158	265,805	28,080	193,647	D	19.7%	72.6%	21.4%	78.6%
86,735	POLK	41,510	21,898	15,570	4,042	6,328	R	52.8%	37.5%	58.4%	41.6%
1,789	SHERMAN	1,034	795	122	117	673	R	76.9%	11.8%	86.7%	13.3%
27,224	TILLAMOOK	14,611	6,631	5,266	2,714	1,365	R	45.4%	36.0%	55.7%	44.3%
78,120	UMATILLA	25,132	17,672	5,403	2,057	12,269	R	70.3%	21.5%	76.6%	23.4%
26,857	UNION	12,544	8,695	2,580	1,269	6,115	R	69.3%	20.6%	77.1%	22.9%
7,261	WALLOWA	4,597	3,138	1,116	343	2,022	R	68.3%	24.3%	73.8%	26.2%
26,839	WASCO	11,407	5,978	4,077	1,352	1,901	R	52.4%	35.7%	59.5%	40.5%
602,808	WASHINGTON	255,882	91,068	140,946	23,868	49,878	D	35.6%	55.1%	39.3%	60.7%
1,341	WHEELER	830	576	140	114	436	R	69.4%	16.9%	80.4%	19.6%
107,859	YAMHILL	49,428	26,385	17,899	5,144	8,486	R	53.4%	36.2%	59.6%	40.4%
4,236,931	TOTAL	1,952,883	850,347	917,074	185,462	66,727	D	43.5%	47.0%	48.1%	51.9%

OREGON
SENATOR 2022

2020 Census Population	County	Total Vote	Republican (Perkins)	Democratic (Wyden)	Other	Rep.-Dem. Plurality		Total Vote Rep.	Total Vote Dem.	Major Vote Rep.	Major Vote Dem.
16,165	BAKER	8,626	5,902	2,531	193	3,371	R	68.4%	29.3%	70.0%	30.0%
93,142	BENTON	45,126	13,407	29,953	1,766	16,546	D	29.7%	66.4%	30.9%	69.1%
420,373	CLACKAMAS	212,448	94,232	112,387	5,829	18,155	D	44.4%	52.9%	45.6%	54.4%
40,507	CLATSOP	19,889	8,135	11,149	605	3,014	D	40.9%	56.1%	42.2%	57.8%
52,605	COLUMBIA	26,996	14,221	11,810	965	2,411	R	52.7%	43.7%	54.6%	45.4%
64,908	COOS	31,110	17,595	12,560	955	5,035	R	56.6%	40.4%	58.3%	41.7%
24,708	CROOK	13,902	9,899	3,730	273	6,169	R	71.2%	26.8%	72.6%	27.4%
23,084	CURRY	12,606	7,049	5,220	337	1,829	R	55.9%	41.4%	57.5%	42.5%
199,817	DESCHUTES	107,893	46,886	57,865	3,142	10,979	D	43.5%	53.6%	44.8%	55.2%
111,731	DOUGLAS	52,840	34,523	16,935	1,382	17,588	R	65.3%	32.0%	67.1%	32.9%

OREGON
SENATOR 2022

2020 Census Population	County	Total Vote	Republican (Perkins)	Democratic (Wyden)	Other	Rep.-Dem. Plurality	Total Vote Rep.	Total Vote Dem.	Major Vote Rep.	Major Vote Dem.
1,927	GILLIAM	980	626	339	15	287 R	63.9%	34.6%	64.9%	35.1%
7,215	GRANT	4,114	2,935	1,066	113	1,869 R	71.3%	25.9%	73.4%	26.6%
7,438	HARNEY	3,744	2,683	972	89	1,711 R	71.7%	26.0%	73.4%	26.6%
23,451	HOOD RIVER	10,727	3,377	7,002	348	3,625 D	31.5%	65.3%	32.5%	67.5%
222,304	JACKSON	103,664	52,714	48,071	2,879	4,643 R	50.9%	46.4%	52.3%	47.7%
24,820	JEFFERSON	9,900	6,083	3,597	220	2,486 R	61.4%	36.3%	62.8%	37.2%
88,059	JOSEPHINE	42,482	25,948	15,396	1,138	10,552 R	61.1%	36.2%	62.8%	37.2%
68,578	KLAMATH	29,761	20,088	8,918	755	11,170 R	67.5%	30.0%	69.3%	30.7%
7,906	LAKE	3,948	2,999	858	91	2,141 R	76.0%	21.7%	77.8%	22.2%
384,378	LANE	182,053	65,606	110,577	5,870	44,971 D	36.0%	60.7%	37.2%	62.8%
50,373	LINCOLN	26,120	10,011	15,283	826	5,272 D	38.3%	58.5%	39.6%	60.4%
130,633	LINN	60,752	36,740	22,041	1,971	14,699 R	60.5%	36.3%	62.5%	37.5%
30,680	MALHEUR	9,063	6,469	2,336	258	4,133 R	71.4%	25.8%	73.5%	26.5%
349,860	MARION	130,496	65,606	60,614	4,276	4,992 R	50.3%	46.4%	52.0%	48.0%
11,642	MORROW	4,041	2,786	1,159	96	1,627 R	68.9%	28.7%	70.6%	29.4%
813,794	MULTNOMAH	362,953	62,324	286,167	14,462	223,843 D	17.2%	78.8%	17.9%	82.1%
86,735	POLK	40,956	20,746	18,920	1,290	1,826 R	50.7%	46.2%	52.3%	47.7%
1,789	SHERMAN	1,018	754	253	11	501 R	74.1%	24.9%	74.9%	25.1%
27,224	TILLAMOOK	14,457	6,909	7,176	372	267 D	47.8%	49.6%	49.1%	50.9%
78,120	UMATILLA	24,838	16,502	7,718	618	8,784 R	66.4%	31.1%	68.1%	31.9%
26,857	UNION	12,388	8,216	3,902	270	4,314 R	66.3%	31.5%	67.8%	32.2%
7,261	WALLOWA	4,537	2,917	1,521	99	1,396 R	64.3%	33.5%	65.7%	34.3%
26,839	WASCO	11,295	5,562	5,382	351	180 R	49.2%	47.6%	50.8%	49.2%
602,808	WASHINGTON	253,059	83,146	160,858	9,055	77,712 D	32.9%	63.6%	34.1%	65.9%
1,341	WHEELER	807	546	237	24	309 R	67.7%	29.4%	69.7%	30.3%
107,859	YAMHILL	48,360	24,849	21,921	1,590	2,928 R	51.4%	45.3%	53.1%	46.9%
4,236,931	TOTAL	1,927,949	788,991	1,076,424	62,534	287,433 D	40.9%	55.8%	42.3%	57.7%

OREGON
HOUSE OF REPRESENTATIVES

CD	Year	Total Vote	Republican Vote	Republican Candidate	Democratic Vote	Democratic Candidate	Other Vote	Rep.-Dem. Plurality	Total Vote Rep.	Total Vote Dem.	Major Vote Rep.	Major Vote Dem.
1	2022	310,243	99,042	MANN, CHRISTOPHER ALLAN	210,682	BONAMICI, SUZANNE*	519	111,640 D	31.9%	67.9%	32.0%	68.0%
1	2020	459,899	161,928	CHRISTENSEN, CHRISTOPHER C.	297,071	BONAMICI, SUZANNE*	900	135,143 D	35.2%	64.6%	35.3%	64.7%
1	2018	363,249	116,446	VERDECK, JOHN	231,198	BONAMICI, SUZANNE*	15,605	114,752 D	32.1%	63.6%	33.5%	66.5%
1	2016	378,095	139,756	HEINRICH, BRIAN J.	225,391	BONAMICI, SUZANNE*	12,948	85,635 D	37.0%	59.6%	38.3%	61.7%
1	2014	279,253	96,245	YATES, JASON	160,038	BONAMICI, SUZANNE*	22,970	63,793 D	34.5%	57.3%	37.6%	62.4%
1	2012	331,980	109,699	MORGAN, DELINDA	197,845	BONAMICI, SUZANNE*	24,436	88,146 D	33.0%	59.6%	35.7%	64.3%
2	2022	308,676	208,369	BENTZ, CLIFF*	99,882	YETTER, JOSEPH "JOE"	425	108,487 R	67.5%	32.4%	67.6%	32.4%
2	2020	457,433	273,835	BENTZ, CLIFF	168,881	SPENSER, ALEX	14,717	104,954 R	59.9%	36.9%	61.9%	38.1%
2	2018	368,709	207,597	WALDEN, GREG*	145,298	MCLEOD-SKINNER, JAMIE	15,814	62,299 R	56.3%	39.4%	58.8%	41.2%
2	2016	380,739	272,952	WALDEN, GREG*	106,640	CRARY, JAMES "JIM"	1,147	166,312 R	71.7%	28.0%	71.9%	28.1%
2	2014	287,425	202,374	WALDEN, GREG*	73,785	CHRISTOFFERSON, AELEA	11,266	128,589 R	70.4%	25.7%	73.3%	26.7%
2	2012	332,255	228,043	WALDEN, GREG*	96,741	SEGERS, JOYCE B.	7,471	131,302 R	68.6%	29.1%	70.2%	29.8%
3	2022	303,334	79,766	HARBOUR, JOANNA	212,119	BLUMENAUER, EARL*	11,449	132,353 D	26.3%	69.9%	27.3%	72.7%
3	2020	470,506	110,570	HARBOUR, JOANNA	343,574	BLUMENAUER, EARL*	16,362	233,004 D	23.5%	73.0%	24.3%	75.7%
3	2018	384,326	76,187	HARRISON, THOMAS S. IV	279,019	BLUMENAUER, EARL*	29,120	202,832 D	19.8%	72.6%	21.4%	78.6%
3	2016	382,355			274,687	BLUMENAUER, EARL*	107,668	274,687 D		71.8%		100.0%
3	2014	292,757	57,424	BUCHAL, JAMES	211,748	BLUMENAUER, EARL*	23,585	154,324 D	19.6%	72.3%	21.3%	78.7%
3	2012	355,875	70,325	GREEN, RONALD	264,979	BLUMENAUER, EARL*	20,571	194,654 D	19.8%	74.5%	21.0%	79.0%

OREGON

HOUSE OF REPRESENTATIVES

CD	Year	Total Vote	Republican Vote	Republican Candidate	Democratic Vote	Democratic Candidate	Other Vote	Rep.-Dem. Plurality	Total Vote Rep.	Total Vote Dem.	Major Vote Rep.	Major Vote Dem.
4	2022	339,077	146,055	SKARLATOS, ALEK	171,372	HOYLE, VAL	21,650	25,317 D	43.1%	50.5%	46.0%	54.0%
4	2020	467,705	216,081	SKARLATOS, ALEK	240,950	DEFAZIO, PETER A.*	10,674	24,869 D	46.2%	51.5%	47.3%	52.7%
4	2018	372,893	152,414	ROBINSON, ART	208,710	DEFAZIO, PETER A.*	11,769	56,296 D	40.9%	56.0%	42.2%	57.8%
4	2016	397,568	157,743	ROBINSON, ART	220,628	DEFAZIO, PETER A.*	19,197	62,885 D	39.7%	55.5%	41.7%	58.3%
4	2014	310,179	116,534	ROBINSON, ART	181,624	DEFAZIO, PETER A.*	12,021	65,090 D	37.6%	58.6%	39.1%	60.9%
4	2012	360,088	140,549	ROBINSON, ART	212,866	DEFAZIO, PETER A.*	6,673	72,317 D	39.0%	59.1%	39.8%	60.2%
5	2022	351,233	178,813	CHAVEZ-DEREMER, LORI	171,514	MCLEOD-SKINNER, JAMIE	906	7,299 R	50.9%	48.8%	51.0%	49.0%
5	2020	452,646	204,372	COURSER, AMY RYAN	234,863	SCHRADER, KURT*	13,411	30,491 D	45.2%	51.9%	46.5%	53.5%
5	2018	358,469	149,887	CALLAHAN, MARK	197,187	SCHRADER, KURT*	11,395	47,300 D	41.8%	55.0%	43.2%	56.8%
5	2016	373,108	160,443	WILLIS, COLM	199,505	SCHRADER, KURT*	13,160	39,062 D	43.0%	53.5%	44.6%	55.4%
5	2014	281,088	110,332	SMITH, TOOTIE	150,944	SCHRADER, KURT*	19,812	40,612 D	39.3%	53.7%	42.2%	57.8%
5	2012	327,970	139,223	THOMPSON, FRED	177,229	SCHRADER, KURT*	11,518	38,006 D	42.4%	54.0%	44.0%	56.0%
6	2022	294,377	139,946	ERICKSON, MIKE	147,156	SALINAS, ANDREA	7,275	7,210 D	47.5%	50.0%	48.7%	51.3%
TOTAL	2022	1,906,940	851,991		1,012,725		42,224	160,734 D	44.7%	53.1%	45.7%	54.3%
TOTAL	2020	2,308,189	966,786		1,285,339		56,064	318,553 D	41.9%	55.7%	42.9%	57.1%
TOTAL	2018	1,847,646	702,531		1,061,412		83,703	358,881 D	38.0%	57.4%	39.8%	60.2%
TOTAL	2016	1,911,865	730,894		1,026,851		154,120	295,957 D	38.2%	53.7%	41.6%	58.4%
TOTAL	2014	1,450,702	582,909		778,139		89,654	195,230 D	40.2%	53.6%	42.8%	57.2%
TOTAL	2012	1,708,168	687,839		949,660		70,669	261,821 D	40.3%	55.6%	42.0%	58.0%

Note: An asterisk (*) denotes incumbent.

OREGON

GENERAL AND PRIMARY ELECTIONS

GENERAL ELECTIONS: OTHER VOTES

Governor Other vote was 168,431 Non Affiliated (Betsy Johnson), 8,051 Constitution (Donice Smith), 6,867 Libertarian (R. Leon Noble), 2,113 Write-In (Write-In)

Senate Other vote was 36,883 Progressive (Chris Henry), 23,454 Pacific Green (Dan Pulju), 2,197 Write-In (Scattered Write-Ins)

House Other vote was:

- CD 1: 519 Write-In (Scattered Write-Ins)
- CD 2: 425 Write-In (Scattered Write-Ins)
- CD 3: 10, 982 Progressive (David Delk), 467 Write-In (Scattered Write-Ins)
- CD 4: 9,052 Independent (Levi Leatherberry), 490 Write-In (Scattered Write-Ins)
- CD 5: 906 Write-In (Scattered Write-Ins)
- CD 6: 6,762 Constitution (Larry McFarland), 513 Write-In (Scattered Write-Ins)

2022 PRIMARY ELECTIONS: SUPPLEMENTARY INFORMATION

Primary May 17, 2022

Registration (as of May 1, 2022) 2,962,892

Democratic	1,016,714
Republican	729,491
Independent	138,377
Libertarian	21,161
Working Families	8,455
Pacific Green	7,856
Constitution	3,902
Progressive	3,117
Other	16,161
Non-Affiliated	1,017,658

Primary Type Closed—Only registered Democrats and Republicans could vote in their party's primary.

OREGON

GENERAL AND PRIMARY ELECTIONS

	REPUBLICAN PRIMARIES			**DEMOCRATIC PRIMARIES**		
Senator	Perkins, Jo Rae	115,701	33.0%	Wyden, Ron	439,665	88.8%
	Harbick, Darin	107,506	30.7%	Barlow, William E III	35,025	7.1%
	Palmer, Sam	42,703	12.2%	Thompson, Brent	17,197	3.5%
	Beebe, Jason	39,456	11.3%	Scattered Write-Ins	3,279	0.7%
	Christensen, Christopher C.	28,433	8.1%			
	Fleming, Robert M	6,821	1.9%			
	Taher, Ibrahim A.	6,659	1.9%			
	Scattered Write-Ins	3,024	0.9%			
	TOTAL	350,303		TOTAL	495,166	
Governor	Drazan, Christine	85,255	22.5%	Kotek, Tina	275,301	56.0%
	Tiernan, Bob	66,089	17.5%	Read, Tobias	156,017	31.7%
	Pulliam, Stan	41,123	10.9%	Write-In	13,746	2.8%
	Barton, Bridget	40,886	10.8%	Starnes, Patrick	10,524	2.1%
	Pierce, Bud	32,965	8.7%	Carrillo, George L.	9,365	1.9%
	Thielman, Marc	30,076	7.9%	Trimble, Michael	5,000	1.0%
	McQuisten, Kerry	28,727	7.6%	Sweeney, John	4,193	0.9%
	Sizemore, Bill	13,261	3.5%	Bell, Julian	3,926	0.8%
	Gomez, Jessica	9,970	2.6%	Bright, Wilson R.	2,316	0.5%
	Write-In	7,407	2.0%	Stauffer, Dave	2,302	0.5%
	McCloud, Tim	4,400	1.2%	Diru, Ifeanyichukwu C.	1,780	0.4%
	Hess, Nick	4,287	1.1%	Merchant, Keisha Lanell	1,755	0.4%
	Boice, Court	4,040	1.1%	Wilson H, Genevieve	1,588	0.3%
	Merritt, Brandon C.	3,615	1.0%	Cross, Michael	1,342	0.3%
	Christensen, Reed	3,082	0.8%	Beem, David W.	1,308	0.3%
	Richardson, Amber R.	1,924	0.5%	Hall, Peter W.	982	0.2%
	Baldwin, Raymond	459	0.1%			
	Burch, David A.	406	0.1%			
	Presco, John G.	174				
	Strek, Stefan	171				
	TOTAL	378,317		TOTAL	491,445	
Congressional District 1	Mann, Christopher Allan	19,605	66.9%	Bonamici, Suzanne	80,317	88.2%
	Murray, Armidia "Army"	9,047	30.9%	Phillips, Scott	7,832	8.6%
	Scattered Write-Ins	671	2.3%	Robertson, Christian	2,625	2.9%
				Scattered Write-Ins	287	0.3%
	TOTAL	29,323		TOTAL	91,061	
Congressional District 2	Bentz, Cliff	67,051	75.0%	Yetter, Joseph "Joe"	27,814	69.1%
	Cavener, Mark	17,372	19.4%	Prine, Adam	11,669	29.0%
	Gallant, Katherine M.	4,598	5.1%	Scattered Write-Ins	788	2.0%
	Scattered Write-Ins	386	0.4%			
	TOTAL	89,407		TOTAL	40,271	
Congressional District 3	Harbour, Joanna	18,031	97.7%	Blumenauer, Earl	96,386	94.3%
	Scattered Write-Ins	429	2.3%	Polhemus, Jonathan	5,392	5.3%
				Scattered Write-Ins	428	0.4%
	TOTAL	18,460		TOTAL	102,206	
Congressional District 4	Skarlatos, Alek	58,655	98.3%	Hoyle, Val	56,153	63.5%
	Scattered Write-Ins	1,021	1.7%	Canning, Doyle Elizabeth	14,245	16.1%
				Al-Abdrabbuh, Sami	6,080	6.9%
				Selker, John	4,738	5.4%
				Kalloch, Andrew	4,322	4.9%
				Smith, G. Tommy	1,278	1.4%
				Scattered Write-Ins	663	0.8%
				Matthews, Jake	607	0.7%
				Laible, Steve William	292	0.3%
	TOTAL	59,676		TOTAL	88,378	

OREGON

GENERAL AND PRIMARY ELECTIONS

		REPUBLICAN PRIMARIES		DEMOCRATIC PRIMARIES		
Congressional District 5	Chavez-Deremer, Lori	30,438	42.8%	McLeod-Skinner, Jamie	47,148	54.6%
	Crumpacker, Jimmy	20,631	29.0%	Schrader, Kurt	38,726	44.8%
	Di Paola, John	11,486	16.1%	Scattered Write-Ins	537	0.6%
	Roses, Laurel	6,321	8.9%			
	Oatman, Madison	1,863	2.6%			
	Scattered Write-Ins	429	0.6%			
	TOTAL	71,168		TOTAL	86,411	
Congressional District 6	Erickson, Mike	21,675	34.7%	Salinas, Andrea	26,101	36.8%
	Noble, Ron	10,980	17.6%	Flynn, Carrick	13,052	18.4%
	Courser, Amy Ryan	10,176	16.3%	Reynolds, Steven Cody	7,951	11.2%
	Plowhead, Angela	8,271	13.2%	Smith, Loretta	7,064	10.0%
	Bunn, Jim	6,340	10.1%	West, Matt	5,658	8.0%
	Russ, David	2,398	3.8%	Harder, Kathleen	5,510	7.8%
	Sandvig, Nathan	2,222	3.6%	Alonso Leon, Teresa	4,626	6.5%
	Scattered Write-Ins	432	0.7%	Scattered Write-Ins	508	0.7%
				Barajas, Ricky	292	0.4%
				Goodwin, Greg	217	0.3%
	TOTAL	62,494		TOTAL	70,979	

Note: An asterisk (*) denotes incumbent.

PENNSYLVANIA

Statewide Races

Pennsylvania, Joe Biden's native state that he only narrowly carried when he was on the ballot himself in 2020, hosted two of 2022's blockbuster contests. Both contests for its Senate seat and governor's office were high-stakes races for open seats.

In the May primaries, state Attorney General Josh Shapiro and Lt. Gov. John Fetterman easily claimed the Democratic nominations for governor and senator, respectively. Shapiro was unopposed while Fetterman, a towering bald man who typically wore hoodies, had a stroke shortly before his primary. Though Republicans would make an issue of his health in the general election, it was not a liability with Democrats – he won the nomination with close to 60% of the vote. On the GOP side, Trump-aligned candidates emerged from contested primaries. For governor, Republicans nominated Doug Mastriano, an election-denying state senator. In the Senate race, television doctor Mehmet Oz secured the GOP nomination by a margin of 950 votes in a seven-way race. Oz ran especially well in the northeast, where his Trump endorsement likely carried weight.

Shapiro defeated Mastriano, who struggled to raise money, by a wide 56%–42% vote, the biggest margin in state history for a non-incumbent Democrat. Shapiro carried the suburban Philadelphia Collar Counties (Bucks, Chester, Delaware, and Montgomery) with a collective 65% and won Pittsburgh's Allegheny County with close to 70%. Just west of the collar counties, Mastriano carried Lancaster County, among the most historically Republican counties in the nation, with less than 50%.

In the Senate race, Oz proved to be an awkward campaigner and Democrats pointed to his tenuous connections to the state (he was a longtime resident of neighboring New Jersey and used his in-laws' address to register in Pennsylvania). Fetterman soldiered through the general election's only debate but, still recovering, struggled to articulate his thoughts. Oz, though, may have actually "lost" the debate, as he handed Democratic opposition researchers a viral clip: when asked about abortion, Oz said the decision should be left up to women, doctors, and "local political leaders." Fetterman won by five points.

House Races

When outgoing Democratic Gov. Tom Wolf and his GOP-controlled legislature couldn't agree on a redistricting map, the process got kicked to the state Supreme Court. As the state downsized from 18 seats to 17, Democrats emerged from the election with a 9–8 edge in the delegation.

In the state's most evenly-divided District, the Lehigh Valley-centric 7th District, Democrat Susan Wild won a rematch with Republican Lisa Scheller. Just to the north, Democrat Matt Cartwright was reelected in the Scranton-based 8th District – though this was Biden's native district, PA-8 would have supported Trump by a few points in 2020. Democrats also held the open 17th District, in the Pittsburgh suburbs.

In the gubernatorial race, Shapiro carried districts 1 and 10 by healthy margins – the former is roughly coterminous with Bucks County while the latter is the Harrisburg area. But their GOP incumbents, despite differing styles, were each reelected. The 1st District's Brian Fitzpatrick is one of the House's leading moderates, while Scott Perry, in the 10th District, is among the most conservative members.

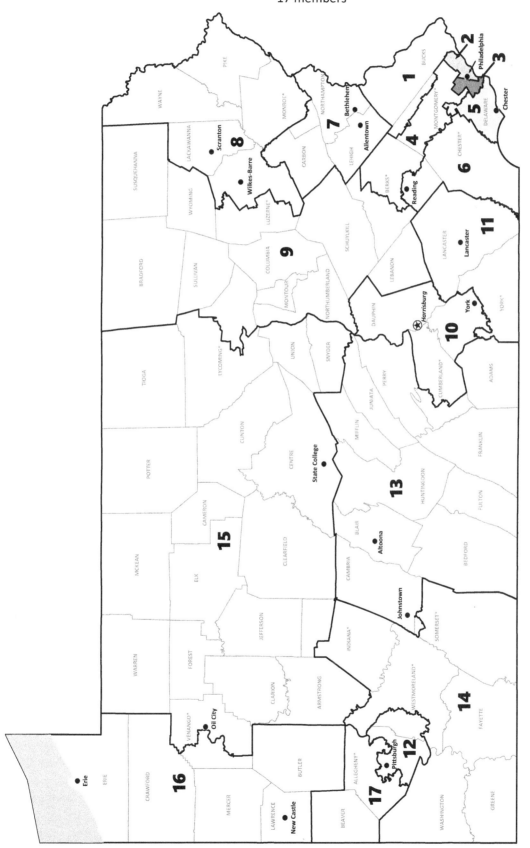

PENNSYLVANIA

GOVERNOR
Thomas W. Wolf (D). Reelected 2022 to a four-year term. Previously elected 2018, 2014.

SENATORS (2 Democrats)
Bob Casey Jr. (D). Reelected 2018 to a six-year term. Previously elected 2012, 2006.

John Fetterman (D). Elected 2022 to a six-year term.

REPRESENTATIVES (8 Republicans, 9 Democrats)
1. Brian K. Fitzpatrick (R)
2. Brendan F. Boyle (D)
3. Dwight Evans (D)
4. Madeleine Dean (D)
5. Mary Gay Scanlon (D)
6. Chrissy Houlahan (D)
7. Susan Wild (D)
8. Matt Cartwright (D)
9. Dan Meuser (R)
10. Scott Perry (R)
11. Lloyd K. Smucker (R)
12. Summer Lee (D)
13. John Joyce (R)
14. Guy Reschenthaler (R)
15. Glenn Thompson (R)
16. Mike Kelly (R)
17. Christopher Deluzio (D)

POSTWAR VOTE FOR PRESIDENT

		Republican		Democratic		Other Vote	Rep.-Dem. Plurality	Percentage			
								Total Vote		Major Vote	
Year	Total Vote	Vote	Candidate	Vote	Candidate			Rep.	Dem.	Rep.	Dem.
2020	6,915,283	3,377,674	Trump, Donald J.*	3,458,229	Biden, Joseph R. Jr.	79,380	80,555 D	48.8%	50.0%	49.4%	50.6%
2016**	6,165,478	2,970,733	Trump, Donald J.	2,926,441	Clinton, Hillary Rodham	268,304	44,292 R	48.2%	47.5%	50.4%	49.6%
2012	5,753,670	2,680,434	Romney, W. Mitt	2,990,274	Obama, Barack H.*	82,962	309,840 D	46.6%	52.0%	47.3%	52.7%
2008	6,013,272	2,655,885	McCain, John S. III	3,276,363	Obama, Barack H.	81,024	620,478 D	44.2%	54.5%	44.8%	55.2%
2004	5,769,590	2,793,847	Bush, George W.*	2,938,095	Kerry, John F.	37,648	144,248 D	48.4%	50.9%	48.7%	51.3%
2000**	4,913,119	2,281,127	Bush, George W.	2,485,967	Gore, Albert Jr.	146,025	204,840 D	46.4%	50.6%	47.9%	52.1%
1996**	4,506,118	1,801,169	Dole, Robert "Bob"	2,215,819	Clinton, Bill*	489,130	414,650 D	40.0%	49.2%	44.8%	55.2%
1992**	4,959,810	1,791,841	Bush, George H.*	2,239,164	Clinton, Bill	928,805	447,323 D	36.1%	45.1%	44.5%	55.5%
1988	4,536,251	2,300,087	Bush, George H.	2,194,944	Dukakis, Michael S.	41,220	105,143 R	50.7%	48.4%	51.2%	48.8%
1984	4,844,903	2,584,323	Reagan, Ronald*	2,228,131	Mondale, Walter F.	32,449	356,192 R	53.3%	46.0%	53.7%	46.3%
1980**	4,561,501	2,261,872	Reagan, Ronald	1,937,540	Carter, Jimmy*	362,089	324,332 R	49.6%	42.5%	53.9%	46.1%
1976	4,620,787	2,205,604	Ford, Gerald R.*	2,328,677	Carter, Jimmy	86,506	123,073 D	47.7%	50.4%	48.6%	51.4%
1972	4,592,106	2,714,521	Nixon, Richard M.*	1,796,951	McGovern, George S.	80,634	917,570 R	59.1%	39.1%	60.2%	39.8%
1968**	4,747,928	2,090,017	Nixon, Richard M.	2,259,405	Humphrey, Hubert Horatio Jr.	398,506	169,388 D	44.0%	47.6%	48.1%	51.9%
1964	4,822,690	1,673,657	Goldwater, Barry M. Sr.	3,130,954	Johnson, Lyndon B.*	18,079	1,457,297 D	34.7%	64.9%	34.8%	65.2%
1960	5,006,541	2,439,956	Nixon, Richard M.	2,556,282	Kennedy, John F.	10,303	116,326 D	48.7%	51.1%	48.8%	51.2%
1956	4,576,503	2,585,252	Eisenhower, Dwight D.*	1,981,769	Stevenson, Adlai E. II	9,482	603,483 R	56.5%	43.3%	56.6%	43.4%
1952	4,580,969	2,415,789	Eisenhower, Dwight D.	2,146,269	Stevenson, Adlai E. II	18,911	269,520 R	52.7%	46.9%	53.0%	47.0%
1948	3,735,348	1,902,197	Dewey, Thomas E.	1,752,426	Truman, Harry S.*	80,725	149,771 R	50.9%	46.9%	52.0%	48.0%

Note: An asterisk (*) denotes incumbent. **In past elections, the other vote included: 2016 - 146,715 Libertarian (Gary Johnson); 2000 - 103,392 Green (Ralph Nader); 1996 - 430,984 Reform (Ross Perot); 1992 - 902,667 Independent (Perot); 1980 - 292,921 Independent (John Anderson); 1968 - 378,582 American Independent (George Wallace).

PENNSYLVANIA

POSTWAR VOTE FOR GOVERNOR

		Republican		Democratic		Other Vote	Rep.-Dem. Plurality	Percentage			
								Total Vote		Major Vote	
Year	Total Vote	Vote	Candidate	Vote	Candidate			Rep.	Dem.	Rep.	Dem.
2022	5,366,179	2,238,477	Mastriano, Douglas	3,031,137	Shapiro, Joshua	96,565	792,660 D	41.7%	56.5%	42.5%	57.5%
2018	5,012,555	2,039,882	Wagner, Scott	2,895,652	Wolf, Thomas W.*	77,021	855,770 D	40.7%	57.8%	41.3%	58.7%
2014	3,495,866	1,575,511	Corbett, Tom*	1,920,355	Wolf, Thomas W.		344,844 D	45.1%	54.9%	45.1%	54.9%
2010	3,989,102	2,172,763	Corbett, Tom	1,814,788	Onorato, Dan	1,551	357,975 R	54.5%	45.5%	54.5%	45.5%
2006	4,096,077	1,622,135	Swann, Lynn	2,470,517	Rendell, Edward G.*	3,425	848,382 D	39.6%	60.3%	39.6%	60.4%
2002	3,583,179	1,589,408	Fisher, Mike	1,913,235	Rendell, Edward G.	80,536	323,827 D	44.4%	53.4%	45.4%	54.6%
1998**	3,025,152	1,736,844	Ridge, Thomas J.*	938,745	Itkin, Ivan	349,563	798,099 R	57.4%	31.0%	64.9%	35.1%
1994**	3,588,526	1,627,976	Ridge, Thomas J.	1,433,099	Singel, Mark S.	527,451	194,877 R	45.4%	39.9%	53.2%	46.8%
1990	3,052,760	987,516	Hafer, Barbara	2,065,244	Casey, Robert*		1,077,728 D	32.3%	67.7%	32.3%	67.7%
1986	3,388,275	1,638,268	Scranton, William III	1,717,484	Casey, Robert	32,523	79,216 D	48.4%	50.7%	48.8%	51.2%
1982	3,683,985	1,872,784	Thornburgh, Richard*	1,772,353	Ertel, Allen E.	38,848	100,431 R	50.8%	48.1%	51.4%	48.6%
1978	3,741,969	1,966,042	Thornburgh, Richard	1,737,888	Flaherty, Peter	38,039	228,154 R	52.5%	46.4%	53.1%	46.9%
1974	3,491,234	1,578,917	Lewis, Andrew L.	1,878,252	Shapp, Milton J.*	34,065	299,335 D	45.2%	53.8%	45.7%	54.3%
1970	3,700,060	1,542,854	Broderick, Raymond	2,043,029	Shapp, Milton J.	114,177	500,175 D	41.7%	55.2%	43.0%	57.0%
1966	4,050,668	2,110,349	Shafer, Raymond P.	1,868,719	Shapp, Milton J.	71,600	241,630 R	52.1%	46.1%	53.0%	47.0%
1962	4,378,042	2,424,918	Scranton, William W.	1,938,627	Dilworth, Richardson	14,497	486,291 R	55.4%	44.3%	55.6%	44.4%
1958	3,986,918	1,948,769	McGonigle, Arthur T.	2,024,852	Lawrence, David L.	13,297	76,083 D	48.9%	50.8%	49.0%	51.0%
1954	3,720,457	1,717,070	Wood, Lloyd H.	1,996,266	Leader, George M.	7,121	279,196 D	46.2%	53.7%	46.2%	53.8%
1950	3,540,059	1,796,119	Fine, John S.	1,710,355	Dilworth, Richardson	33,585	85,764 R	50.7%	48.3%	51.2%	48.8%
1946	3,123,994	1,828,462	Duff, James H.	1,270,947	Rice, John S.	24,585	557,515 R	58.5%	40.7%	59.0%	41.0%

Note: An asterisk (*) denotes incumbent. **In past elections, the other vote included: 1998 - 315,761 Constitutional (Peg Luksik); 1994 - 460,269 Constitutional (Luksik).

POSTWAR VOTE FOR SENATOR

		Republican		Democratic		Other Vote	Rep.-Dem. Plurality	Percentage			
								Total Vote		Major Vote	
Year	Total Vote	Vote	Candidate	Vote	Candidate			Rep.	Dem.	Rep.	Dem.
2022	5,368,021	2,487,260	Oz, Mehmet	2,751,012	Fetterman, John K.	129,749	263,752 D	46.3%	51.2%	47.5%	52.5%
2018	5,009,400	2,134,848	Barletta, Lou	2,792,437	Casey, Bob Jr.*	82,115	657,589 D	42.6%	55.7%	43.3%	56.7%
2016	6,051,856	2,951,702	Toomey, Pat*	2,865,012	McGinty, Katie A.	235,142	86,690 R	48.8%	47.3%	50.7%	49.3%
2012	5,629,491	2,509,132	Smith, Tom	3,021,364	Casey, Bob Jr.*	98,995	512,232 D	44.6%	53.7%	45.4%	54.6%
2010	3,977,661	2,028,945	Toomey, Pat	1,948,716	Sestak, Joe		80,229 R	51.0%	49.0%	51.0%	49.0%
2006	4,081,043	1,684,778	Santorum, Rick*	2,392,984	Casey, Bob Jr.	3,281	708,206 D	41.3%	58.6%	41.3%	58.7%
2004	5,559,105	2,925,080	Specter, Arlen*	2,334,126	Hoeffel, Joseph M.	299,899	590,954 R	52.6%	42.0%	55.6%	44.4%
2000	4,735,504	2,481,962	Santorum, Rick*	2,154,908	Klink, Ron	98,634	327,054 R	52.4%	45.5%	53.5%	46.5%
1998	2,957,772	1,814,180	Specter, Arlen*	1,028,839	Lloyd, Bill	114,753	785,341 R	61.3%	34.8%	63.8%	36.2%
1994	3,513,361	1,735,691	Santorum, Rick	1,648,481	Wofford, Harris*	129,189	87,210 R	49.4%	46.9%	51.3%	48.7%
1992	4,802,410	2,358,125	Specter, Arlen*	2,224,966	Yeakel, Lynn	219,319	133,159 R	49.1%	46.3%	51.5%	48.5%
1991S**	3,382,746	1,521,986	Thornburgh, Richard	1,860,760	Wofford, Harris*		338,774 D	45.0%	55.0%	45.0%	55.0%
1988	4,366,598	2,901,715	Heinz, Henry John III*	1,416,764	Vignola, Joseph C.	48,119	1,484,951 R	66.5%	32.4%	67.2%	32.8%
1986	3,378,226	1,906,537	Specter, Arlen*	1,448,219	Edgar, Robert W.	23,470	458,318 R	56.4%	42.9%	56.8%	43.2%
1982	3,604,108	2,136,418	Heinz, Henry John III*	1,412,965	Wecht, Cyril H.	54,725	723,453 R	59.3%	39.2%	60.2%	39.8%
1980	4,418,042	2,230,404	Specter, Arlen	2,122,391	Flaherty, Peter	65,247	108,013 R	50.5%	48.0%	51.2%	48.8%
1976	4,546,353	2,381,891	Heinz, Henry John III	2,126,977	Green, William J. III	37,485	254,914 R	52.4%	46.8%	52.8%	47.2%
1974	3,477,812	1,843,317	Schweiker, Richard S.*	1,596,121	Flaherty, Peter	38,374	247,196 R	53.0%	45.9%	53.6%	46.4%
1970	3,644,305	1,874,106	Scott, Hugh*	1,653,774	Sesler, William G.	116,425	220,332 R	51.4%	45.4%	53.1%	46.9%
1968	4,624,218	2,399,762	Schweiker, Richard S.	2,117,662	Clark, Joseph S.*	106,794	282,100 R	51.9%	45.8%	53.1%	46.9%
1964	4,803,835	2,429,858	Scott, Hugh*	2,359,223	Blatt, Genevieve	14,754	70,635 R	50.6%	49.1%	50.7%	49.3%
1962	4,383,475	2,134,649	Van Zandt, James E.	2,238,383	Clark, Joseph S.*	10,443	103,734 D	48.7%	51.1%	48.8%	51.2%
1958	3,988,622	2,042,586	Scott, Hugh	1,929,821	Leader, George M.	16,215	112,765 R	51.2%	48.4%	51.4%	48.6%
1956	4,529,874	2,250,671	Duff, James H.*	2,268,641	Clark, Joseph S.	10,562	17,970 D	49.7%	50.1%	49.8%	50.2%
1952	4,519,761	2,331,034	Martin, Edward*	2,168,546	Bard, Guy Kurtz	20,181	162,488 R	51.6%	48.0%	51.8%	48.2%
1950	3,548,703	1,820,400	Duff, James H.	1,694,076	Myers, Francis J.*	34,227	126,324 R	51.3%	47.7%	51.8%	48.2%
1946	3,127,860	1,853,458	Martin, Edward	1,245,338	Guffey, Joseph F.*	29,064	608,120 R	59.3%	39.8%	59.8%	40.2%

Note: An asterisk (*) denotes incumbent. **The 1991 election was for a short term to fill a vacancy.

PENNSYLVANIA
GOVERNOR 2022

2020 Census Population	County	Total Vote	Republican (Mastriano)	Democratic (Shapiro)	Other	Rep.-Dem. Plurality		Percentage Total Vote Rep.	Dem.	Major Vote Rep.	Dem.
103,207	ADAMS	46,459	26,819	18,821	819	7,998	R	57.7%	40.5%	58.8%	41.2%
1,217,156	ALLEGHENY	572,813	169,913	393,386	9,514	223,473	D	29.7%	68.7%	30.2%	69.8%
64,671	ARMSTRONG	28,457	18,419	9,523	515	8,896	R	64.7%	33.5%	65.9%	34.1%
164,155	BEAVER	73,262	34,777	36,917	1,568	2,140	D	47.5%	50.4%	48.5%	51.5%
47,927	BEDFORD	22,220	17,198	4,721	301	12,477	R	77.4%	21.2%	78.5%	21.5%
421,652	BERKS	154,818	72,185	78,757	3,876	6,572	D	46.6%	50.9%	47.8%	52.2%
121,996	BLAIR	50,334	31,823	17,716	795	14,107	R	63.2%	35.2%	64.2%	35.8%
60,314	BRADFORD	23,479	15,529	7,389	561	8,140	R	66.1%	31.5%	67.8%	32.2%
629,744	BUCKS	314,041	122,982	185,339	5,720	62,357	D	39.2%	59.0%	39.9%	60.1%
188,610	BUTLER	93,461	51,546	40,065	1,850	11,481	R	55.2%	42.9%	56.3%	43.7%
130,245	CAMBRIA	56,281	32,381	22,885	1,015	9,496	R	57.5%	40.7%	58.6%	41.4%
4,429	CAMERON	1,890	1,200	639	51	561	R	63.5%	33.8%	65.3%	34.7%
64,450	CARBON	26,264	14,943	10,743	578	4,200	R	56.9%	40.9%	58.2%	41.8%
162,483	CENTRE	62,017	25,201	35,653	1,163	10,452	D	40.6%	57.5%	41.4%	58.6%
526,101	CHESTER	258,025	92,585	160,796	4,644	68,211	D	35.9%	62.3%	36.5%	63.5%
38,447	CLARION	15,407	10,019	5,114	274	4,905	R	65.0%	33.2%	66.2%	33.8%
79,290	CLEARFIELD	31,411	20,525	10,326	560	10,199	R	65.3%	32.9%	66.5%	33.5%
38,697	CLINTON	14,073	8,512	5,293	268	3,219	R	60.5%	37.6%	61.7%	38.3%
65,158	COLUMBIA	24,703	13,959	10,148	596	3,811	R	56.5%	41.1%	57.9%	42.1%
84,595	CRAWFORD	32,829	19,541	12,609	679	6,932	R	59.5%	38.4%	60.8%	39.2%
254,512	CUMBERLAND	116,002	52,280	61,319	2,403	9,039	D	45.1%	52.9%	46.0%	54.0%
278,648	DAUPHIN	114,398	43,580	68,585	2,233	25,005	D	38.1%	60.0%	38.9%	61.1%
567,194	DELAWARE	250,855	76,880	170,162	3,813	93,282	D	30.6%	67.8%	31.1%	68.9%
29,940	ELK	13,678	8,597	4,843	238	3,754	R	62.9%	35.4%	64.0%	36.0%
269,522	ERIE	105,599	40,433	63,081	2,085	22,648	D	38.3%	59.7%	39.1%	60.9%
129,389	FAYETTE	46,877	26,165	20,120	592	6,045	R	55.8%	42.9%	56.5%	43.5%
7,267	FOREST	2,192	1,340	825	27	515	R	61.1%	37.6%	61.9%	38.1%
155,441	FRANKLIN	65,350	42,731	21,612	1,007	21,119	R	65.4%	33.1%	66.4%	33.6%
14,581	FULTON	6,287	5,092	1,128	67	3,964	R	81.0%	17.9%	81.9%	18.1%
36,139	GREENE	13,139	7,706	5,142	291	2,564	R	58.6%	39.1%	60.0%	40.0%
45,164	HUNTINGDON	18,448	12,579	5,597	272	6,982	R	68.2%	30.3%	69.2%	30.8%
84,134	INDIANA	32,742	19,179	13,032	531	6,147	R	58.6%	39.8%	59.5%	40.5%
43,459	JEFFERSON	17,820	12,433	5,038	349	7,395	R	69.8%	28.3%	71.2%	28.8%
24,821	JUNIATA	9,768	6,851	2,761	156	4,090	R	70.1%	28.3%	71.3%	28.7%
210,085	LACKAWANNA	88,843	32,697	54,442	1,704	21,745	D	36.8%	61.3%	37.5%	62.5%
546,497	LANCASTER	224,268	112,040	108,233	3,995	3,807	R	50.0%	48.3%	50.9%	49.1%
85,588	LAWRENCE	36,294	19,611	16,023	660	3,588	R	54.0%	44.1%	55.0%	45.0%
142,311	LEBANON	56,466	31,731	23,646	1,089	8,085	R	56.2%	41.9%	57.3%	42.7%
369,869	LEHIGH	136,334	53,468	79,991	2,875	26,523	D	39.2%	58.7%	40.1%	59.9%
317,760	LUZERNE	116,064	56,326	57,598	2,140	1,272	D	48.5%	49.6%	49.4%	50.6%
113,354	LYCOMING	46,285	29,755	15,643	887	14,112	R	64.3%	33.8%	65.5%	34.5%
40,628	MCKEAN	14,712	10,082	4,392	238	5,690	R	68.5%	29.9%	69.7%	30.3%
109,424	MERCER	45,331	26,273	18,282	776	7,991	R	58.0%	40.3%	59.0%	41.0%
46,166	MIFFLIN	16,847	11,460	5,119	268	6,341	R	68.0%	30.4%	69.1%	30.9%
170,974	MONROE	58,827	25,604	32,009	1,214	6,405	D	43.5%	54.4%	44.4%	55.6%
833,434	MONTGOMERY	413,016	121,289	285,712	6,015	164,423	D	29.4%	69.2%	29.8%	70.2%
18,230	MONTOUR	7,857	4,037	3,640	180	397	R	51.4%	46.3%	52.6%	47.4%
306,422	NORTHAMPTON	129,901	54,928	72,269	2,704	17,341	D	42.3%	55.6%	43.2%	56.8%
90,920	NORTHUMBERLAND	32,951	19,094	12,052	1,805	7,042	R	57.9%	36.6%	61.3%	38.7%
46,379	PERRY	20,240	12,928	6,912	400	6,016	R	63.9%	34.2%	65.2%	34.8%
1,583,217	PHILADELPHIA	498,260	65,293	426,885	6,082	361,592	D	13.1%	85.7%	13.3%	86.7%
56,097	PIKE	25,133	14,371	10,339	423	4,032	R	57.2%	41.1%	58.2%	41.8%
16,510	POTTER	7,105	5,235	1,513	357	3,722	R	73.7%	21.3%	77.6%	22.4%
141,622	SCHUYLKILL	55,435	33,008	21,203	1,224	11,805	R	59.5%	38.2%	60.9%	39.1%
40,432	SNYDER	15,360	10,215	4,867	278	5,348	R	66.5%	31.7%	67.7%	32.3%
73,548	SOMERSET	32,576	22,559	9,473	544	13,086	R	69.3%	29.1%	70.4%	29.6%
6,073	SULLIVAN	3,023	1,923	1,024	76	899	R	63.6%	33.9%	65.3%	34.7%
40,307	SUSQUEHANNA	17,316	11,153	5,768	395	5,385	R	64.4%	33.3%	65.9%	34.1%
40,686	TIOGA	16,658	11,840	4,494	324	7,346	R	71.1%	27.0%	72.5%	27.5%
44,894	UNION	16,113	8,897	6,898	318	1,999	R	55.2%	42.8%	56.3%	43.7%

PENNSYLVANIA
GOVERNOR 2022

2020 Census Population	County	Total Vote	Republican (Mastriano)	Democratic (Shapiro)	Other	Rep.-Dem. Plurality		Percentage			
								Total Vote		Major Vote	
								Rep.	Dem.	Rep.	Dem.
50,654	VENANGO	20,919	12,741	7,777	401	4,964	R	60.9%	37.2%	62.1%	37.9%
39,181	WARREN	16,065	9,704	6,032	329	3,672	R	60.4%	37.5%	61.7%	38.3%
207,454	WASHINGTON	93,617	47,052	45,030	1,535	2,022	R	50.3%	48.1%	51.1%	48.9%
51,472	WAYNE	22,743	13,868	8,466	409	5,402	R	61.0%	37.2%	62.1%	37.9%
349,632	WESTMORELAND	167,968	87,804	77,152	3,012	10,652	R	52.3%	45.9%	53.2%	46.8%
26,753	WYOMING	11,777	6,966	4,519	292	2,447	R	59.1%	38.4%	60.7%	39.3%
450,277	YORK	186,476	98,622	83,649	4,205	14,973	R	52.9%	44.9%	54.1%	45.9%
12,820,438	TOTAL	5,366,179	2,238,477	3,031,137	96,565	792,660	D	41.7%	56.5%	42.5%	57.5%

PENNSYLVANIA
SENATOR 2022

2020 Census Population	County	Total Vote	Republican (Oz)	Democratic (Fetterman)	Other	Rep.-Dem. Plurality		Percentage			
								Total Vote		Major Vote	
								Rep.	Dem.	Rep.	Dem.
103,207	ADAMS	46,419	29,039	16,096	1,284	12,943	R	62.6%	34.7%	64.3%	35.7%
1,217,156	ALLEGHENY	573,709	200,632	363,873	9,204	163,241	D	35.0%	63.4%	35.5%	64.5%
64,671	ARMSTRONG	28,413	19,575	8,065	773	11,510	R	68.9%	28.4%	70.8%	29.2%
164,155	BEAVER	73,443	38,772	32,692	1,979	6,080	R	52.8%	44.5%	54.3%	45.7%
47,927	BEDFORD	22,241	17,954	3,796	491	14,158	R	80.7%	17.1%	82.5%	17.5%
421,652	BERKS	154,824	78,019	71,349	5,456	6,670	R	50.4%	46.1%	52.2%	47.8%
121,996	BLAIR	50,220	34,214	14,763	1,243	19,451	R	68.1%	29.4%	69.9%	30.1%
60,314	BRADFORD	23,481	16,033	6,632	816	9,401	R	68.3%	28.2%	70.7%	29.3%
629,744	BUCKS	314,311	141,340	164,536	8,435	23,196	D	45.0%	52.3%	46.2%	53.8%
188,610	BUTLER	93,335	57,168	33,921	2,246	23,247	R	61.3%	36.3%	62.8%	37.2%
130,245	CAMBRIA	56,348	35,847	18,849	1,652	16,998	R	63.6%	33.5%	65.5%	34.5%
4,429	CAMERON	1,886	1,247	547	92	700	R	66.1%	29.0%	69.5%	30.5%
64,450	CARBON	26,232	15,659	9,682	891	5,977	R	59.7%	36.9%	61.8%	38.2%
162,483	CENTRE	62,061	27,902	32,597	1,562	4,695	D	45.0%	52.5%	46.1%	53.9%
526,101	CHESTER	257,963	104,020	147,559	6,384	43,539	D	40.3%	57.2%	41.3%	58.7%
38,447	CLARION	15,371	10,620	4,327	424	6,293	R	69.1%	28.2%	71.1%	28.9%
79,290	CLEARFIELD	31,399	21,948	8,533	918	13,415	R	69.9%	27.2%	72.0%	28.0%
38,697	CLINTON	14,017	8,791	4,750	476	4,041	R	62.7%	33.9%	64.9%	35.1%
65,158	COLUMBIA	24,745	14,830	9,023	892	5,807	R	59.9%	36.5%	62.2%	37.8%
84,595	CRAWFORD	33,033	20,992	11,081	960	9,911	R	63.5%	33.5%	65.5%	34.5%
254,512	CUMBERLAND	115,927	59,663	53,278	2,986	6,385	R	51.5%	46.0%	52.8%	47.2%
278,648	DAUPHIN	114,446	50,141	61,599	2,706	11,458	D	43.8%	53.8%	44.9%	55.1%
567,194	DELAWARE	250,667	87,322	157,599	5,746	70,277	D	34.8%	62.9%	35.7%	64.3%
29,940	ELK	13,619	9,128	4,066	425	5,062	R	67.0%	29.9%	69.2%	30.8%
269,522	ERIE	105,734	46,507	56,404	2,823	9,897	D	44.0%	53.3%	45.2%	54.8%
129,389	FAYETTE	46,824	28,234	17,731	859	10,503	R	60.3%	37.9%	61.4%	38.6%
7,267	FOREST	2,182	1,434	694	54	740	R	65.7%	31.8%	67.4%	32.6%
155,441	FRANKLIN	65,220	44,819	18,718	1,683	26,101	R	68.7%	28.7%	70.5%	29.5%
14,581	FULTON	6,246	5,171	953	122	4,218	R	82.8%	15.3%	84.4%	15.6%
36,139	GREENE	13,091	8,348	4,394	349	3,954	R	63.8%	33.6%	65.5%	34.5%
45,164	HUNTINGDON	18,264	13,035	4,665	564	8,370	R	71.4%	25.5%	73.6%	26.4%
84,134	INDIANA	32,755	20,769	11,218	768	9,551	R	63.4%	34.2%	64.9%	35.1%
43,459	JEFFERSON	17,786	13,139	4,135	512	9,004	R	73.9%	23.2%	76.1%	23.9%
24,821	JUNIATA	9,728	7,265	2,111	352	5,154	R	74.7%	21.7%	77.5%	22.5%
210,085	LACKAWANNA	88,943	36,534	50,489	1,920	13,955	D	41.1%	56.8%	42.0%	58.0%

PENNSYLVANIA
SENATOR 2022

2020 Census Population	County	Total Vote	Republican (Oz)	Democratic (Fetterman)	Other	Rep.-Dem. Plurality	Total Vote Rep.	Total Vote Dem.	Major Vote Rep.	Major Vote Dem.
546,497	LANCASTER	224,548	124,798	94,632	5,118	30,166 R	55.6%	42.1%	56.9%	43.1%
85,588	LAWRENCE	36,206	21,531	13,758	917	7,773 R	59.5%	38.0%	61.0%	39.0%
142,311	LEBANON	56,491	35,023	19,695	1,773	15,328 R	62.0%	34.9%	64.0%	36.0%
369,869	LEHIGH	136,301	59,219	73,096	3,986	13,877 D	43.4%	53.6%	44.8%	55.2%
317,760	LUZERNE	116,323	61,978	51,504	2,841	10,474 R	53.3%	44.3%	54.6%	45.4%
113,354	LYCOMING	46,233	31,171	13,573	1,489	17,598 R	67.4%	29.4%	69.7%	30.3%
40,628	MCKEAN	14,651	10,076	4,135	440	5,941 R	68.8%	28.2%	70.9%	29.1%
109,474	MERCER	45,352	27,049	17,080	1,223	9,969 R	59.6%	37.7%	61.3%	38.7%
46,166	MIFFLIN	16,785	12,263	3,965	557	8,298 R	73.1%	23.6%	75.6%	24.4%
170,974	MONROE	58,730	26,746	30,251	1,733	3,505 D	45.5%	51.5%	46.9%	53.1%
833,434	MONTGOMERY	412,954	143,077	260,207	9,670	117,130 D	34.6%	63.0%	35.5%	64.5%
18,230	MONTOUR	7,833	4,328	3,213	292	1,115 R	55.3%	41.0%	57.4%	42.6%
306,422	NORTHAMPTON	129,987	59,860	66,565	3,562	6,705 D	46.1%	51.2%	47.3%	52.7%
90,920	NORTHUMBERLAND	32,895	20,992	10,812	1,091	10,180 R	63.8%	32.9%	66.0%	34.0%
46,379	PERRY	20,231	13,956	5,646	629	8,310 R	69.0%	27.9%	71.2%	28.8%
1,583,217	PHILADELPHIA	499,151	78,408	412,841	7,902	334,433 D	15.7%	82.7%	16.0%	84.0%
56,097	PIKE	25,196	14,792	9,821	583	4,971 R	58.7%	39.0%	60.1%	39.9%
16,510	POTTER	7,108	5,486	1,415	207	4,071 R	77.2%	19.9%	79.5%	20.5%
141,622	SCHUYLKILL	55,413	35,293	17,954	2,166	17,339 R	63.7%	32.4%	66.3%	33.7%
40,432	SNYDER	15,336	10,657	4,220	459	6,437 R	69.5%	27.5%	71.6%	28.4%
73,548	SOMERSET	32,528	23,964	7,660	904	16,304 R	73.7%	23.5%	75.8%	24.2%
6,073	SULLIVAN	3,016	2,023	869	124	1,154 R	67.1%	28.8%	70.0%	30.0%
40,307	SUSQUEHANNA	17,311	11,520	5,245	546	6,275 R	66.5%	30.3%	68.7%	31.3%
40,686	TIOGA	16,632	11,988	4,103	541	7,885 R	72.1%	24.7%	74.5%	25.5%
44,894	UNION	16,094	9,401	6,249	444	3,152 R	58.4%	38.8%	60.1%	39.9%
50,654	VENANGO	20,854	13,406	6,777	671	6,629 R	64.3%	32.5%	66.4%	33.6%
39,181	WARREN	16,092	10,175	5,420	497	4,755 R	63.2%	33.7%	65.2%	34.8%
207,454	WASHINGTON	93,836	52,337	39,684	1,815	12,653 R	55.8%	42.3%	56.9%	43.1%
51,472	WAYNE	22,712	14,425	7,669	618	6,756 R	63.5%	33.8%	65.3%	34.7%
349,632	WESTMORELAND	168,009	98,238	66,240	3,531	31,998 R	58.5%	39.4%	59.7%	40.3%
26,753	WYOMING	11,779	7,338	4,059	382	3,279 R	62.3%	34.5%	64.4%	35.6%
450,277	YORK	186,551	109,631	71,929	4,991	37,702 R	58.8%	38.6%	60.4%	39.6%
12,820,438	TOTAL	5,368,021	2,487,260	2,751,012	129,749	263,752 D	46.3%	51.2%	47.5%	52.5%

PENNSYLVANIA
HOUSE OF REPRESENTATIVES

CD	Year	Total Vote	Republican Vote	Republican Candidate	Democratic Vote	Democratic Candidate	Other Vote	Rep.-Dem. Plurality	Total Vote Rep.	Total Vote Dem.	Major Vote Rep.	Major Vote Dem.
1	2022	367,380	201,571	FITZPATRICK, BRIAN K.*	165,809	EHASZ, ASHLEY		35,762 R	54.9%	45.1%	54.9%	45.1%
1**	2020	441,679	249,804	FITZPATRICK, BRIAN K.*	191,875	FINELLO, CHRISTINA		57,929 R	56.6%	43.4%	56.6%	43.4%
1**	2018	329,798	169,053	FITZPATRICK, BRIAN K.*	160,745	WALLACE, SCOTT		8,308 R	51.3%	48.7%	51.3%	48.7%
1	2016	299,010	53,219	WILLIAMS, DEBORAH L.	245,791	BRADY, ROBERT A.*		192,572 D	17.8%	82.2%	17.8%	82.2%
1	2014	158,441	27,193	RATH, MEGAN ANN	131,248	BRADY, ROBERT A.*		104,055 D	17.2%	82.8%	17.2%	82.8%
1	2012	277,102	41,708	FEATHERMAN, JOHN J.	235,394	BRADY, ROBERT A.*		193,686 D	15.1%	84.9%	15.1%	84.9%
2	2022	186,683	45,454	BASHIR, HAROON	141,229	BOYLE, BRENDAN F.*		95,775 D	24.3%	75.7%	24.3%	75.7%
2**	2020	273,162	75,022	TORRES, DAVID	198,140	BOYLE, BRENDAN F.*		123,118 D	27.5%	72.5%	27.5%	72.5%
2**	2018	201,982	42,382	TORRES, DAVID	159,600	BOYLE, BRENDAN F.*		117,218 D	21.0%	79.0%	21.0%	79.0%
2	2016	357,645	35,131	JONES, JAMES A.	322,514	EVANS, DWIGHT*		287,383 D	9.8%	90.2%	9.8%	90.2%
2	2014	206,538	25,397	JAMES, ARMOND	181,141	FATTAH, CHAKA*		155,744 D	12.3%	87.7%	12.3%	87.7%
2	2012	356,386	33,381	MANSFIELD, ROBERT	318,176	FATTAH, CHAKA*	4,829	284,795 D	9.4%	89.3%	9.5%	90.5%

PENNSYLVANIA

HOUSE OF REPRESENTATIVES

CD	Year	Total Vote	Republican Vote	Republican Candidate	Democratic Vote	Democratic Candidate	Other Vote	Rep.-Dem. Plurality	Total Vote Rep.	Total Vote Dem.	Major Vote Rep.	Major Vote Dem.
3	2022	263,935			251,115	EVANS, DWIGHT*	12,820	251,115 D		95.1%		100.0%
3**	2020	375,379	33,671	HARVEY, MICHAEL	341,708	EVANS, DWIGHT*		308,037 D	9.0%	91.0%	9.0%	91.0%
3**	2018	307,997	20,387	LEIB, BRYAN	287,610	EVANS, DWIGHT*		267,223 D	6.6%	93.4%	6.6%	93.4%
3	2016	244,893	244,893	KELLY, MIKE*				244,893 R	100.0%		100.0%	
3	2014	187,790	113,859	KELLY, MIKE*	73,931	LAVALLEE, DANIEL		39,928 R	60.6%	39.4%	60.6%	39.4%
3	2012	302,514	165,826	KELLY, MIKE*	123,933	EATON, MISSA	12,755	41,893 R	54.8%	41.0%	57.2%	42.8%
4	2022	366,785	141,986	NASCIMENTO, SERGIO CHRISTIAN	224,799	DEAN, MADELEINE*		82,813 D	38.7%	61.3%	38.7%	61.3%
4**	2020	444,563	179,926	BARNETTE, KATHY	264,637	DEAN, MADELEINE*		84,711 D	40.5%	59.5%	40.5%	59.5%
4**	2018	332,991	121,467	DAVID, DANIEL "DAN"	211,524	DEAN, MADELEINE		90,057 D	36.5%	63.5%	36.5%	63.5%
4	2016	334,000	220,628	PERRY, SCOTT*	113,372	BURKHOLDER, JOSHUA T.		107,256 R	66.1%	33.9%	66.1%	33.9%
4	2014	197,340	147,090	PERRY, SCOTT*	50,250	THOMPSON, LINDA DELIAH		96,840 R	74.5%	25.5%	74.5%	25.5%
4	2012	303,980	181,603	PERRY, SCOTT	104,643	PERKINSON, HARRY	17,734	76,960 R	59.7%	34.4%	63.4%	36.6%
5	2022	315,186	110,058	GALLUCH, DAVID LEWCZYK	205,128	SCANLON, MARY GAY*		95,070 D	34.9%	65.1%	34.9%	65.1%
5**	2020	395,295	139,552	PRUETT, DASHA	255,743	SCANLON, MARY GAY*		116,191 D	35.3%	64.7%	35.3%	64.7%
5**	2018	304,714	106,075	KIM, PEARL	198,639	SCANLON, MARY GAY		92,564 D	34.8%	65.2%	34.8%	65.2%
5	2016	307,843	206,761	THOMPSON, GLENN JR.*	101,082	TAYLOR, KERITH STRANO		105,679 R	67.2%	32.8%	67.2%	32.8%
5	2014	180,857	115,018	THOMPSON, GLENN JR.*	65,839	TAYLOR, KERITH STRANO		49,179 R	63.6%	36.4%	63.6%	36.4%
5	2012	282,465	177,740	THOMPSON, GLENN JR.*	104,725	DUMAS, CHARLES		73,015 R	62.9%	37.1%	62.9%	37.1%
6	2022	326,483	136,097	CIARROCCHI, GUY LOUIS	190,386	HOULAHAN, CHRISSY*		54,289 D	41.7%	58.3%	41.7%	58.3%
6**	2020	403,966	177,526	EMMONS, JOHN	226,440	HOULAHAN, CHRISSY*		48,914 D	43.9%	56.1%	43.9%	56.1%
6**	2018	301,828	124,124	MCCAULEY, GREG	177,704	HOULAHAN, CHRISSY		53,580 D	41.1%	58.9%	41.1%	58.9%
6	2016	362,469	207,469	COSTELLO, RYAN A.*	155,000	PARRISH, MICHAEL D.		52,469 R	57.2%	42.8%	57.2%	42.8%
6	2014	212,544	119,643	COSTELLO, RYAN A.	92,901	TRIVEDI, MANAN		26,742 R	56.3%	43.7%	56.3%	43.7%
6	2012	335,528	191,725	GERLACH, JAMES W.*	143,803	TRIVEDI, MANAN		47,922 R	57.1%	42.9%	57.1%	42.9%
7	2022	296,891	145,527	SCHELLER, LISA	151,364	WILD, SUSAN*		5,837 D	49.0%	51.0%	49.0%	51.0%
7**	2020	376,882	181,407	SCHELLER, LISA	195,475	WILD, SUSAN*		14,068 D	48.1%	51.9%	48.1%	51.9%
7**	2018	263,261	114,437	NOTHSTEIN, MARTY	140,813	WILD, SUSAN	8,011	26,376 D	43.5%	53.5%	44.8%	55.2%
7	2016	379,502	225,678	MEEHAN, PATRICK*	153,824	BALCHUNIS, MARY ELLEN		71,854 R	59.5%	40.5%	59.5%	40.5%
7	2014	235,125	145,869	MEEHAN, PATRICK*	89,256	BALCHUNIS, MARY ELLEN		56,613 R	62.0%	38.0%	62.0%	38.0%
7	2012	353,451	209,942	MEEHAN, PATRICK*	143,509	BADEY, GEORGE		66,433 R	59.4%	40.6%	59.4%	40.6%
8	2022	286,886	139,930	BOGNET, JIM	146,956	CARTWRIGHT, MATT*		7,026 D	48.8%	51.2%	48.8%	51.2%
8**	2020	343,787	165,783	BOGNET, JIM	178,004	CARTWRIGHT, MATT*		12,221 D	48.2%	51.8%	48.2%	51.8%
8**	2018	248,166	112,563	CHRIN, JOHN	135,603	CARTWRIGHT, MATT*		23,040 D	45.4%	54.6%	45.4%	54.6%
8	2016	380,818	207,263	FITZPATRICK, BRIAN K.	173,555	SANTARSIERO, STEVEN J.		33,708 R	54.4%	45.6%	54.4%	45.6%
8	2014	222,498	137,731	FITZPATRICK, MICHAEL G.*	84,767	STROUSE, KEVIN		52,964 R	61.9%	38.1%	61.9%	38.1%
8	2012	352,238	199,379	FITZPATRICK, MICHAEL G.*	152,859	BOOCKVAR, KATHY		46,520 R	56.6%	43.4%	56.6%	43.4%
9	2022	301,807	209,185	MEUSER, DAN*	92,622	WALDMAN, AMANDA		116,563 R	69.3%	30.7%	69.3%	30.7%
9**	2020	351,254	232,988	MEUSER, DAN*	118,266	WEGMAN, GARY		114,722 R	66.3%	33.7%	66.3%	33.7%
9**	2018	248,927	148,723	MEUSER, DAN	100,204	WOLFF, DENNY		48,519 R	59.7%	40.3%	59.7%	40.3%
9	2016	294,565	186,580	SHUSTER, BILL*	107,985	HALVORSON, ARTHUR		78,595 R	63.3%	36.7%	63.3%	36.7%
9	2014	173,317	110,094	SHUSTER, BILL*	63,223	HARTZOK, ALANNA K.		46,871 R	63.5%	36.5%	63.5%	36.5%
9	2012	274,305	169,177	SHUSTER, BILL*	105,128	RAMSBURG, KAREN		64,049 R	61.7%	38.3%	61.7%	38.3%
10	2022	314,546	169,331	PERRY, SCOTT*	145,215	DANIELS, SHAMAINE ANDREA		24,116 R	53.8%	46.2%	53.8%	46.2%
10**	2020	391,834	208,896	PERRY, SCOTT*	182,938	DEPASQUALE, EUGENE		25,958 R	53.3%	46.7%	53.3%	46.7%
10**	2018	291,033	149,365	PERRY, SCOTT*	141,668	SCOTT, GEORGE		7,697 R	51.3%	48.7%	51.3%	48.7%
10	2016	301,105	211,282	MARINO, THOMAS A.*	89,823	MOLESEVICH, MICHAEL M.		121,459 R	70.2%	29.8%	70.2%	29.8%
10	2014	180,322	112,851	MARINO, THOMAS A.*	44,737	BRION, SCOTT F.	22,734	68,114 R	62.6%	24.8%	71.6%	28.4%
10	2012	273,790	179,563	MARINO, THOMAS A.*	94,227	SCOLLO, PHILLIP		85,336 R	65.6%	34.4%	65.6%	34.4%
11	2022	316,826	194,991	SMUCKER, LLOYD K.*	121,835	HOLLISTER, ROBERT M.		73,156 R	61.5%	38.5%	61.5%	38.5%
11**	2020	383,240	241,915	SMUCKER, LLOYD K.*	141,325	HAMMOND, SARAH		100,590 R	63.1%	36.9%	63.1%	36.9%
11**	2018	277,584	163,708	SMUCKER, LLOYD K.*	113,876	KING, JESSICA		49,832 R	59.0%	41.0%	59.0%	41.0%
11	2016	313,221	199,421	BARLETTA, LOU*	113,800	MARSICANO, MICHAEL PAUL		85,621 R	63.7%	36.3%	63.7%	36.3%
11	2014	184,692	122,464	BARLETTA, LOU*	62,228	OSTROWSKI, ANDY J.		60,236 R	66.3%	33.7%	66.3%	33.7%
11	2012	285,198	166,967	BARLETTA, LOU*	118,231	STILP, GENE		48,736 R	58.5%	41.5%	58.5%	41.5%
12	2022	328,620	143,946	DOYLE, MICHAEL	184,674	LEE, SUMMER		40,728 D	43.8%	56.2%	43.8%	56.2%
12**	2020	340,234	241,035	KELLER, FRED*	99,199	GRIFFIN, LEE		141,836 R	70.8%	29.2%	70.8%	29.2%
12**	2018	243,872	161,047	MARINO, THOMAS A.*	82,825	FRIEDENBERG, MARC		78,222 R	66.0%	34.0%	66.0%	34.0%
12	2016	359,204	221,851	ROTHFUS, KEITH*	137,353	MCCLELLAND, ERIN		84,498 R	61.8%	38.2%	61.8%	38.2%
12	2014	215,921	127,993	ROTHFUS, KEITH*	87,928	MCCLELLAND, ERIN		40,065 R	59.3%	40.7%	59.3%	40.7%
12	2012	338,941	175,352	ROTHFUS, KEITH	163,589	CRITZ, MARK S.*		11,763 R	51.7%	48.3%	51.7%	48.3%

PENNSYLVANIA
HOUSE OF REPRESENTATIVES

CD	Year	Total Vote	Republican Vote	Republican Candidate	Democratic Vote	Democratic Candidate	Other Vote	Rep.-Dem. Plurality	Total Vote Rep.	Total Vote Dem.	Major Vote Rep.	Major Vote Dem.
13	2022	260,345	260,345	JOYCE, JOHN*				260,345 R	100.0%		100.0%	
13**	2020	364,401	267,789	JOYCE, JOHN*	96,612	ROWLEY, TODD		171,177 R	73.5%	26.5%	73.5%	26.5%
13**	2018	253,266	178,533	JOYCE, JOHN	74,733	OTTAWAY, BRENT		103,800 R	70.5%	29.5%	70.5%	29.5%
13	2016	239,316			239,316	BOYLE, BRENDAN F.*		239,316 D		100.0%		100.0%
13	2014	184,150	60,549	ADCOCK, CARSON DEE	123,601	BOYLE, BRENDAN F.		63,052 D	32.9%	67.1%	32.9%	67.1%
13	2012	303,819	93,918	ROONEY, JOE	209,901	SCHWARTZ, ALLYSON Y.*		115,983 D	30.9%	69.1%	30.9%	69.1%
14	2022	230,865	230,865	RESCHENTHALER, GUY*				230,865 R	100.0%		100.0%	
14**	2020	373,583	241,688	RESCHENTHALER, GUY*	131,895	MARX, WILLIAM A.		109,793 R	64.7%	35.3%	64.7%	35.3%
14**	2018	261,437	151,386	RESCHENTHALER, GUY	110,051	BOERIO, BIBIANA		41,335 R	57.9%	42.1%	57.9%	42.1%
14	2016	343,292	87,999	MCALLISTER, LEONARD FRANCIS JR.	255,293	DOYLE, MIKE*		167,294 D	25.6%	74.4%	25.6%	74.4%
14	2014	148,351			148,351	DOYLE, MIKE*		148,351 D		100.0%		100.0%
14	2012	327,634	75,702	LESSMANN, HANS	251,932	DOYLE, MIKE*		176,230 D	23.1%	76.9%	23.1%	76.9%
15	2022	305,146	213,417	THOMPSON, GLENN JR.*	91,729	MOLESEVICH, MICHAEL M.		121,688 R	69.9%	30.1%	69.9%	30.1%
15**	2020	347,214	255,058	THOMPSON, GLENN JR.*	92,156	WILLIAMS, ROBERT		162,902 R	73.5%	26.5%	73.5%	26.5%
15**	2018	243,572	165,245	THOMPSON, GLENN JR.*	78,327	BOSER, SUSAN		86,918 R	67.8%	32.2%	67.8%	32.2%
15	2016	326,474	190,618	DENT, CHARLIE W.*	124,129	DAUGHERTY, RICK	11,727	66,489 R	58.4%	38.0%	60.6%	39.4%
15	2014	128,285	128,285	DENT, CHARLIE W.*				128,285 R	100.0%		100.0%	
15	2012	297,724	168,960	DENT, CHARLIE W.*	128,764	DAUGHERTY, RICK		40,196 R	56.8%	43.2%	56.8%	43.2%
16	2022	320,989	190,546	KELLY, MIKE*	130,443	PASTORE, DANIEL		60,103 R	59.4%	40.6%	59.4%	40.6%
16**	2020	354,050	210,088	KELLY, MIKE*	143,962	GNIBUS, KRISTY		66,126 R	59.3%	40.7%	59.3%	40.7%
16**	2018	262,396	135,348	KELLY, MIKE*	124,109	DINICOLA, RONALD	2,939	11,239 R	51.6%	47.3%	52.2%	47.8%
16	2016	313,773	168,669	SMUCKER, LLOYD K.	134,586	HARTMAN, CHRISTINA M.	10,518	34,083 R	53.8%	42.9%	55.6%	44.4%
16	2014	176,235	101,722	PITTS, JOSEPH R.*	74,513	HOUGHTON, THOMAS D.		27,209 R	57.7%	42.3%	57.7%	42.3%
16	2012	284,781	156,192	PITTS, JOSEPH R.*	111,185	STRADER, ARYANNA	17,404	45,007 R	54.8%	39.0%	58.4%	41.6%
17	2022	362,628	169,013	SHAFFER, JEREMY KEVIN	193,615	DELUZIO, CHRISTOPHER		24,602 D	46.6%	53.4%	46.6%	53.4%
17**	2020	434,537	212,284	PARNELL, SEAN RICHARD	222,253	LAMB, CONOR*		9,969 D	48.9%	51.1%	48.9%	51.1%
17**	2018	325,579	142,417	ROTHFUS, KEITH*	183,162	LAMB, CONOR*		40,745 D	43.7%	56.3%	43.7%	56.3%
17	2016	293,164	135,430	CONNOLLY, MATTHEW DONALD "MATT"	157,734	CARTWRIGHT, MATT*		22,304 D	46.2%	53.8%	46.2%	53.8%
17	2014	165,051	71,371	MOYLAN III, DAVID J.	93,680	CARTWRIGHT, MATT*		22,309 D	43.2%	56.8%	43.2%	56.8%
17	2012	267,601	106,208	CUMMINGS, LAUREEN	161,393	CARTWRIGHT, MATT		55,185 D	39.7%	60.3%	39.7%	60.3%
18	2020	384,247	118,163	NEGRON, LUKE	266,084	DOYLE, MIKE*		147,921 D	30.8%	69.2%	30.8%	69.2%
18	2018	231,472			231,472	DOYLE, MIKE*		231,472 D		100.0%		100.0%
18	2016	293,684	293,684	MURPHY, TIMOTHY*				293,684 R	100.0%		100.0%	
18	2014	166,076	166,076	MURPHY, TIMOTHY*				166,076 R	100.0%		100.0%	
18	2012	338,873	216,727	MURPHY, TIMOTHY*	122,146	MAGGI, LARRY		94,581 R	64.0%	36.0%	64.0%	36.0%
TOTAL	2022	5,152,001	2,702,262		2,436,919		12,820	265,343 R	52.5%	47.3%	52.6%	47.4%
TOTAL	2020	6,779,307	3,432,595		3,346,712			85,883 R	50.6%	49.4%	50.6%	49.4%
TOTAL	2018	4,929,875	2,206,260		2,712,665		10,950	506,405 D	44.8%	55.0%	44.9%	55.1%
TOTAL	2016	5,743,978	3,096,576		2,625,157		22,245	471,419 R	53.9%	45.7%	54.1%	45.9%
TOTAL	2014	3,323,533	1,833,205		1,467,594		22,734	365,611 R	55.2%	44.2%	55.5%	44.5%
TOTAL	2012	5,556,330	2,710,070		2,793,538		52,722	83,468 D	48.8%	50.3%	49.2%	50.8%

Note: An asterisk (*) denotes incumbent.

PENNSYLVANIA

GENERAL AND PRIMARY ELECTIONS

GENERAL ELECTIONS: OTHER VOTES

Governor	Other vote was 51,611 Libertarian (Jonathan Hackenburg), 24,436 Green (Christina DiGiulio), 20,518 Keystone (Joseph Soloski)
Senate	Other vote was 72,887 Libertarian (Erik Gerhardt), 30,434 Green (Richard Weiss), 26,428 Keystone (Daniel Wassmer)
House	Other vote was:
CD 3	12,820 Socialist Workers Party (Christopher Hoeppner)

2022 PRIMARY ELECTIONS: SUPPLEMENTARY INFORMATION

Primary	May 17, 2022	Registration (as of May 17, 2022)	8,738,433	Democratic Republican Libertarian Green Other	4,000,436 3,450,289 44,150 9,863 1,233,695

Primary Type   Closed—Only registered Democrats and Republicans could vote in their party's primary.

	REPUBLICAN PRIMARIES			DEMOCRATIC PRIMARIES		
Senator	Oz, Mehmet McCormick, David Barnette, Kathy Sands, Carla Bartos, Jeffrey A. Gale, Sean Peter Bochetto, George TOTAL	420,168 419,218 331,903 73,360 66,684 20,266 14,492 1,346,091	31.2% 31.1% 24.7% 5.4% 5.0% 1.5% 1.1%	Fetterman, John K. Lamb, Conor Kenyatta, Malcolm Khalil, Alexandria Gloria TOTAL	753,557 337,498 139,393 54,460 1,284,908	58.6% 26.3% 10.8% 4.2%
Governor	Mastriano, Douglas Barletta, Lou McSwain, William "Bill" White, David J Hart, Melissa A. Gale, Joseph Charles "Joe" Corman, Jacob Doyle "Jake" III Gerow, Charles R. Zama, Nche TOTAL	591,240 273,252 212,886 129,058 54,752 27,920 26,091 17,922 16,238 1,349,359	43.8% 20.3% 15.8% 9.6% 4.1% 2.1% 1.9% 1.3% 1.2%	Shapiro, Joshua TOTAL	1,227,151 1,227,151	100.0%
Congressional District 1	Fitzpatrick, Brian K.* Entin, Alex TOTAL	60,502 31,772 92,274	65.6% 34.4%	Ehasz, Ashley TOTAL	79,546 79,546	100.0%
Congressional District 2	Bashir, Haroon TOTAL	11,796 11,796	100.0%	Boyle, Brendan F.* TOTAL	53,825 53,825	100.0%
Congressional District 3				Evans, Dwight* Hunt, Alexandra Marguerite Cogbill, Michael S. TOTAL	97,709 25,712 5,728 129,149	75.7% 19.9% 4.4%
Congressional District 4	Nascimento, Sergio Christian Burton, Daniel L. Jr. TOTAL	47,192 21,378 68,570	68.8% 31.2%	Dean, Madeleine* TOTAL	96,876 96,876	100.0%

PENNSYLVANIA

GENERAL AND PRIMARY ELECTIONS

	REPUBLICAN PRIMARIES			DEMOCRATIC PRIMARIES		
Congressional District 5	Galluch, David Lewczyk TOTAL	55,770 55,770	100.0%	Scanlon, Mary Gay* TOTAL	79,816 79,816	100.0%
Congressional District 6	Ciarrocchi, Guy Louis Fanelli, Stephen A. Vogel, Ronald Christopher Mauro, Regina TOTAL	23,369 21,146 15,628 10,565 70,708	33.1% 29.9% 22.1% 14.9%	Houlahan, Chrissy* TOTAL	71,950 71,950	100.0%
Congressional District 7	Scheller, Lisa Dellicker, Kevin Willard TOTAL	34,504 32,713 67,217	51.3% 48.7%	Wild, Susan* TOTAL	63,817 63,817	100.0%
Congressional District 8	Bognet, Jim Marsicano, Michael Paul TOTAL	47,097 21,436 68,533	68.7% 31.3%	Cartwright, Matt* TOTAL	68,696 68,696	100.0%
Congressional District 9	Meuser, Dan* TOTAL	102,180 102,180	100.0%	Waldman, Amanda TOTAL	41,622 41,622	100.0%
Congressional District 10	Perry, Scott* TOTAL	84,646 84,646	100.0%	Daniels, Shamaine Andrea Coplen, Richard Chase TOTAL	32,260 29,128 61,388	52.6% 47.4%
Congressional District 11	Smucker, Lloyd K.* TOTAL	96,886 96,886	100.0%	Hollister, Robert M. TOTAL	46,080 46,080	100.0%
Congressional District 12	Doyle, Michael TOTAL	39,531 39,531	100.0%	Lee, Summer Irwin, Steven Dane Dickinson, Gerald Woodard, Jeffrey D. Parker, William TOTAL	48,002 47,014 12,440 5,454 1,670 114,580	41.9% 41.0% 10.9% 4.8% 1.5%
Congressional District 13	Joyce, John* TOTAL	114,160 114,160	100.0%			
Congressional District 14	Reschenthaler, Guy* TOTAL	81,243 81,243	100.0%			
Congressional District 15	Thompson, Glenn Jr.* TOTAL	99,270 99,270	100.0%			
Congressional District 16	Kelly, Mike* TOTAL	87,028 87,028	100.0%	Pastore, Daniel Telesz, Richard E. TOTAL	44,262 19,788 64,050	69.1% 30.9%
Congressional District 17	Shaffer, Jeremy Kevin Killmeyer, Jason Coder, Kathleen Ann "Kathy" TOTAL	40,965 16,801 12,079 69,845	58.7% 24.1% 17.3%	Deluzio, Christopher Meloy, Sean Michael TOTAL	62,389 35,638 98,027	63.6% 36.4%

Note: An asterisk (*) denotes incumbent.

RHODE ISLAND

Statewide Races

With neither of its Senate seats up in 2022, Rhode Island's gubernatorial race was its highest statewide office. After two-term Democratic Gov. Gina Raimondo was tapped to lead Joe Biden's Department of Commerce, her lieutenant governor, Dan McKee, ascended to the state's top job in early 2021. In a state home to many ambitious Democrats, McKee, who arguably did not have the full benefits of incumbency, seemed potentially more vulnerable in a primary than in a general election.

That indeed turned out to be the case. In 2022, none of the 28 sitting governors who ran in primaries were denied their party's nod, but McKee came the closest to losing his. For much of the campaign, Rhode Island Secretary of State Nellie Gorbea seemed to be the most formidable not-McKee option. But businesswoman Helena Foulkes, whose resume included leading the CVS drug store chain, seemed to close strong, catching some late momentum. Foulkes was able to do some considerable self-funding and got an endorsement from then-House Speaker Nancy Pelosi. Gorbea carried the city of Providence while Foulkes ran well in some monied coastal towns. But McKee had the broadest coalition – he won the Democratic nomination with 33% of the vote. The general election was less eventful. McKee won the governorship in his own right by a 58%–39% margin over Republican Ashley Kalus.

House Races

One of the biggest surprises of the 2020 census was that Rhode Island, which was expected to become an At-Large district, retained both its districts. With that, its map saw minimal changes.

District 1, which includes most of Providence proper and the area of the state east of the Narragansett Bay, is safely Democratic. Rep. David Cicilline, a Democrat running for an eighth term in 2022, won with 64%.

District 2 includes the western, and more inland, part of the state – in 2020, it would have gone to Biden by 13 points. After serving since the 2000 election, veteran Rep. Jim Langevin retired. In the September primary, State Treasurer Seth Magaziner beat out several other Democrats and won the nomination with 54%. Meanwhile, Republicans were excited about their nominee, former Cranston Mayor Allan Fung. Though Fung had lost the 2014 and 2018 gubernatorial races to Raimondo, he was well-known throughout the state, and carried the 2nd District in his first run. The race attracted the attention of the national parties, and outside groups spent there. But the district's partisanship seemed to prevail: though Fung ran better than Donald Trump, he lost by four points.

RHODE ISLAND

Congressional districts first established for elections held in 2022

2 members

The city of Providence contains portions of CDs 1 and 2.

* Asterisk indicates a county whose boundaries include parts of two or more congressional districts.

RHODE ISLAND

GOVERNOR
Dan McKee (D). Reelected 2022 to a four-year term. Assumed office to complete the term of Gina Raimondo (D), following her resignation to become secretary of Commerce on March 2, 2021.

SENATORS (2 Democrats)
Jack F. Reed (D). Reelected 2020 to a six-year term. Previously elected 2014, 2008, 2002, 1996.

Sheldon Whitehouse (D). Reelected 2018 to a six-year term. Previously elected 2012, 2006.

REPRESENTATIVES (2 Democrats)
1. David N. Cicilline (D)
2. Seth Magaziner (D)

POSTWAR VOTE FOR PRESIDENT

Year	Total Vote	Republican Vote	Republican Candidate	Democratic Vote	Democratic Candidate	Other Vote	Rep.-Dem. Plurality	Total Vote Rep.	Total Vote Dem.	Major Vote Rep.	Major Vote Dem.
2020	517,757	199,922	Trump, Donald J.*	307,486	Biden, Joseph R. Jr.	10,349	107,564 D	38.6%	59.4%	39.4%	60.6%
2016**	464,144	180,543	Trump, Donald J.	252,525	Clinton, Hillary Rodham	31,076	71,982 D	38.9%	54.4%	41.7%	58.3%
2012	446,049	157,204	Romney, W. Mitt	279,677	Obama, Barack H.*	9,168	122,473 D	35.2%	62.7%	36.0%	64.0%
2008	471,766	165,391	McCain, John S. III	296,571	Obama, Barack H.	9,804	131,180 D	35.1%	62.9%	35.8%	64.2%
2004	437,134	169,046	Bush, George W.*	259,760	Kerry, John F.	8,328	90,714 D	38.7%	59.4%	39.4%	60.6%
2000**	409,047	130,555	Bush, George W.	249,508	Gore, Albert Jr.	28,984	118,953 D	31.9%	61.0%	34.4%	65.6%
1996**	390,284	104,683	Dole, Robert "Bob"	233,050	Clinton, Bill*	52,551	128,367 D	26.8%	59.7%	31.0%	69.0%
1992**	453,477	131,601	Bush, George H.*	213,299	Clinton, Bill	108,577	81,698 D	29.0%	47.0%	38.2%	61.8%
1988	404,620	177,761	Bush, George H.	225,123	Dukakis, Michael S.	1,736	47,362 D	43.9%	55.6%	44.1%	55.9%
1984	410,492	212,080	Reagan, Ronald*	197,106	Mondale, Walter F.	1,306	14,974 R	51.7%	48.0%	51.8%	48.2%
1980**	416,072	154,793	Reagan, Ronald	198,342	Carter, Jimmy*	62,937	43,549 D	37.2%	47.7%	43.8%	56.2%
1976	411,170	181,249	Ford, Gerald R.*	227,636	Carter, Jimmy	2,285	46,387 D	44.1%	55.4%	44.3%	55.7%
1972	415,808	220,383	Nixon, Richard M.*	194,645	McGovern, George S.	780	25,738 R	53.0%	46.8%	53.1%	46.9%
1968**	385,000	122,359	Nixon, Richard M.	246,518	Humphrey, Hubert Horatio Jr.	16,123	124,159 D	31.8%	64.0%	33.2%	66.8%
1964	390,091	74,615	Goldwater, Barry M. Sr.	315,463	Johnson, Lyndon B.*	13	240,848 D	19.1%	80.9%	19.1%	80.9%
1960	405,535	147,502	Nixon, Richard M.	258,032	Kennedy, John F.	1	110,530 D	36.4%	63.6%	36.4%	63.6%
1956	387,609	225,819	Eisenhower, Dwight D.*	161,790	Stevenson, Adlai E. II		64,029 R	58.3%	41.7%	58.3%	41.7%
1952	414,498	210,935	Eisenhower, Dwight D.	203,293	Stevenson, Adlai E. II	270	7,642 R	50.9%	49.0%	50.9%	49.1%
1948	327,702	135,787	Dewey, Thomas E.	188,736	Truman, Harry S.*	3,179	52,949 D	41.4%	57.6%	41.8%	58.2%

Note: An asterisk (*) denotes incumbent. **In past elections, the other vote included: 2016 - 14,746 Libertarian (Gary Johnson); 2000 - 25,052 Green (Ralph Nader); 1996 - 43,723 Reform (Ross Perot); 1992 - 105,045 Independent (Perot); 1980 - 59,819 Independent (John Anderson); 1968 - 15,678 American Independent (George Wallace).

RHODE ISLAND

POSTWAR VOTE FOR GOVERNOR

		Republican		Democratic		Other Vote	Rep.-Dem. Plurality	Percentage			
								Total Vote		Major Vote	
Year	Total Vote	Vote	Candidate	Vote	Candidate			Rep.	Dem.	Rep.	Dem.
2022	357,670	139,001	Kalus, Ashley Marie	207,166	McKee, Daniel*	11,503	68,165 D	38.9%	57.9%	40.2%	59.8%
2018	376,401	139,932	Fung, Allan	198,122	Raimondo, Gina*	38,347	58,190 D	37.2%	52.6%	41.4%	58.6%
2014**	324,055	117,428	Fung, Allan	131,899	Raimondo, Gina	74,728	14,471 D	36.2%	40.7%	47.1%	52.9%
2010**	342,545	114,911	Robitaille, John F.	78,896	Caprio, Frank T.	148,738	36,015 R#	33.5%	23.0%	59.3%	40.7%
2006	387,010	197,366	Carcieri, Donald L.*	189,562	Fogarty, Charles J.	82	7,804 R	51.0%	49.0%	51.0%	49.0%
2002	332,655	181,827	Carcieri, Donald L.	150,229	York, Myrth	599	31,598 R	54.7%	45.2%	54.8%	45.2%
1998	306,383	156,180	Almond, Lincoln C.*	129,105	York, Myrth	21,098	27,075 R	51.0%	42.1%	54.7%	45.3%
1994**	361,377	171,194	Almond, Lincoln C.	157,361	York, Myrth	32,822	13,833 R	47.4%	43.5%	52.1%	47.9%
1992	424,818	145,590	Leonard, Elizabeth Ann	261,484	Sundlun, Bruce G.*	17,744	115,894 D	34.3%	61.6%	35.8%	64.2%
1990	356,672	92,177	Diprete, Edward*	264,411	Sundlun, Bruce G.	84	172,234 D	25.8%	74.1%	25.8%	74.2%
1988	400,516	203,550	Diprete, Edward*	196,936	Sundlun, Bruce G.	30	6,614 R	50.8%	49.2%	50.8%	49.2%
1986	322,724	208,822	Diprete, Edward*	104,508	Sundlun, Bruce G.	9,394	104,314 R	64.7%	32.4%	66.6%	33.4%
1984	408,375	245,059	Diprete, Edward	163,311	Solomon, Anthony	5	81,748 R	60.0%	40.0%	60.0%	40.0%
1982	337,259	79,602	Marzullo, Vincent	247,208	Garrahy, J. Joseph*	10,449	167,606 D	23.6%	73.3%	24.4%	75.6%
1980	405,916	106,729	Cianci, Vincent A.	299,174	Garrahy, J. Joseph*	13	192,445 D	26.3%	73.7%	26.3%	73.7%
1978	314,363	96,596	Almond, Lincoln C.	197,386	Garrahy, J. Joseph*	20,381	100,790 D	30.7%	62.8%	32.9%	67.1%
1976	398,683	178,254	Taft, James L.	218,561	Garrahy, J. Joseph	1,868	40,307 D	44.7%	54.8%	44.9%	55.1%
1974	321,660	69,224	Nugent, James W.	252,436	Noel, Philip W.*		183,212 D	21.5%	78.5%	21.5%	78.5%
1972	412,866	194,315	DeSimone, Herbert F.	216,953	Noel, Philip W.	1,598	22,638 D	47.1%	52.5%	47.2%	52.8%
1970	346,342	171,549	DeSimone, Herbert F.	173,420	Licht, Frank*	1,373	1,871 D	49.5%	50.1%	49.7%	50.3%
1968	383,725	187,958	Chafee, John H.*	195,766	Licht, Frank	1	7,808 D	49.0%	51.0%	49.0%	51.0%
1966	332,064	210,202	Chafee, John H.*	121,862	Hobbs, Horace E.		88,340 R	63.3%	36.7%	63.3%	36.7%
1964	391,668	239,501	Chafee, John H.*	152,165	Gallogly, Edward P.	2	87,336 R	61.1%	38.9%	61.1%	38.9%
1962	327,506	163,952	Chafee, John H.	163,554	Notte, John A. Jr.*		398 R	50.1%	49.9%	50.1%	49.9%
1960	401,362	174,044	Del Sesto, Christopher*	227,318	Notte, John A. Jr.		53,274 D	43.4%	56.6%	43.4%	56.6%
1958	346,780	176,505	Del Sesto, Christopher	170,275	Roberts, Dennis J.*		6,230 R	50.9%	49.1%	50.9%	49.1%
1956	383,919	191,604	Del Sesto, Christopher	192,315	Roberts, Dennis J.*		711 D	49.9%	50.1%	49.9%	50.1%
1954	328,670	137,131	Lewis, Dean J.	189,595	Roberts, Dennis J.*	1,944	52,464 D	41.7%	57.7%	42.0%	58.0%
1952	409,689	194,102	Archambault, Raoul	215,587	Roberts, Dennis J.*		21,485 D	47.4%	52.6%	47.4%	52.6%
1950	296,808	120,683	Lachapelle, Eugene J.	176,125	Roberts, Dennis J.		55,442 D	40.7%	59.3%	40.7%	59.3%
1948	323,863	124,441	Ruerat, Albert P.	198,056	Pastore, John O.*	1,366	73,615 D	38.4%	61.2%	38.6%	61.4%
1946	275,341	126,456	Murphy, John G.	148,885	Pastore, John O.*		22,429 D	45.9%	54.1%	45.9%	54.1%

Note: An asterisk (*) denotes incumbent. A pound sign (#) in the plurality column indicates that the winner in 2010 did not run under the banner of either major party. **In past elections, the other vote included: 2014 - 69,278 Moderate (Robert J. Healey Jr.); 2010 - 123,571 Independent (Lincoln Chafee), who was elected with 36.1% of the total vote and a plurality of 8,660 votes. The term of office of Rhode Island's Governor was increased from two to four years effective with the 1994 election.

RHODE ISLAND

POSTWAR VOTE FOR SENATOR

Year	Total Vote	Republican		Democratic		Other Vote	Rep.-Dem. Plurality		Percentage			
									Total Vote		Major Vote	
		Vote	Candidate	Vote	Candidate				Rep.	Dem.	Rep.	Dem.
2020	493,429	164,855	Waters, Allen	328,574	Reed, Jack F.*	840	163,719	D	33.4%	66.5%	33.4%	66.6%
2018	376,738	144,421	Flanders, Robert Jr.	231,477	Whitehouse, Sheldon*	840	87,056	D	38.3%	61.4%	38.4%	61.6%
2014	316,898	92,684	Zaccaria, Mark S.	223,675	Reed, Jack F.*	539	130,991	D	29.2%	70.6%	29.3%	70.7%
2012	418,189	146,222	Hinckley, Barry	271,034	Whitehouse, Sheldon*	933	124,812	D	35.0%	64.8%	35.0%	65.0%
2008	438,812	116,174	Tingle, Robert G.	320,644	Reed, Jack F.*	1,994	204,470	D	26.5%	73.1%	26.6%	73.4%
2006	385,451	179,001	Chafee, Lincoln D.*	206,110	Whitehouse, Sheldon	340	27,109	D	46.4%	53.5%	46.5%	53.5%
2002	323,912	69,881	Tingle, Robert G.	253,922	Reed, Jack F.*	109	184,041	D	21.6%	78.4%	21.6%	78.4%
2000	391,537	222,588	Chafee, Lincoln D.*	161,023	Weygand, Robert A.	7,926	61,565	R	56.8%	41.1%	58.0%	42.0%
1996	363,371	127,368	Mayer, NancyJ.	230,676	Reed, Jack F.	5,327	103,308	D	35.1%	63.5%	35.6%	64.4%
1994	345,388	222,856	Chafee, John H.*	122,532	Kushner, Linda J.		100,324	R	64.5%	35.5%	64.5%	35.5%
1990	364,062	138,947	Schneider, Claudine	225,105	Pell, Claiborne*	10	86,158	D	38.2%	61.8%	38.2%	61.8%
1988	397,996	217,273	Chafee, John H.*	180,717	Licht, Richard A.	6	36,556	R	54.6%	45.4%	54.6%	45.4%
1984	395,285	108,492	Leonard, Barbara	286,780	Pell, Claiborne*	13	178,288	D	27.4%	72.6%	27.4%	72.6%
1982	342,779	175,495	Chafee, John H.*	167,283	Michaelson, Julius C.	1	8,212	R	51.2%	48.8%	51.2%	48.8%
1978	305,618	76,061	Reynolds, James G.	229,557	Pell, Claiborne*		153,496	D	24.9%	75.1%	24.9%	75.1%
1976	398,906	230,329	Chafee, John H.	167,665	Lorber, Richard P.	912	62,664	R	57.7%	42.0%	57.9%	42.1%
1972	413,432	188,990	Chafee, John H.	221,942	Pell, Claiborne*	2,500	32,952	D	45.7%	53.7%	46.0%	54.0%
1970	341,222	107,351	McLaughlin, John	230,469	Pastore, John O.*	3,402	123,118	D	31.5%	67.5%	31.8%	68.2%
1966	324,173	104,838	Briggs, Ruth M.	219,331	Pell, Claiborne*	4	114,493	D	32.3%	67.7%	32.3%	67.7%
1964	386,322	66,715	Lagueux, Ronald R.	319,607	Pastore, John O.*		252,892	D	17.3%	82.7%	17.3%	82.7%
1960	399,983	124,408	Archambault, Raoul	275,575	Pell, Claiborne		151,167	D	31.1%	68.9%	31.1%	68.9%
1958	344,519	122,353	Ewing, Bayard	222,166	Pastore, John O.*		99,813	D	35.5%	64.5%	35.5%	64.5%
1954	326,624	132,970	Sundlun, WalterI.	193,654	Green, Theodore Francis*		60,684	D	40.7%	59.3%	40.7%	59.3%
1952	410,978	185,850	Ewing, Bayard	225,128	Pastore, John O.*		39,278	D	45.2%	54.8%	45.2%	54.8%
1950S**	299,410	114,890	Levy, Austin T.	184,520	Pastore, John O.		69,630	D	38.4%	61.6%	38.4%	61.6%
1948	320,952	130,668	Hazard, Thomas P.	190,284	Green, Theodore Francis*		59,616	D	40.7%	59.3%	40.7%	59.3%
1946	273,528	122,780	Dyer, W. Gurnee	150,748	McGrath, J. Howard		27,968	D	44.9%	55.1%	44.9%	55.1%

Note: An asterisk (*) denotes incumbent. **The 1950 election was for a short term to fill a vacancy.

RHODE ISLAND

GOVERNOR 2022

2020 Census Population	County	Total Vote	Republican (Kalus)	Democratic (McKee)	Other	Rep.-Dem. Plurality		Percentage			
								Total Vote		Major Vote	
								Rep.	Dem.	Rep.	Dem.
48,535	BRISTOL	20,575	7,134	12,724	717	5,590	D	34.7%	61.8%	35.9%	64.1%
164,578	KENT	68,445	30,204	36,122	2,119	5,918	D	44.1%	52.8%	45.5%	54.5%
82,060	NEWPORT	32,398	11,397	19,964	1,037	8,567	D	35.2%	61.6%	36.3%	63.7%
639,097	PROVIDENCE	177,306	67,439	104,196	5,671	36,757	D	38.0%	58.8%	39.3%	60.7%
125,801	WASHINGTON	58,946	22,827	34,160	1,959	11,333	D	38.7%	58.0%	40.1%	59.9%
1,060,071	TOTAL	357,670	139,001	207,166	11,503	68,165	D	38.9%	57.9%	40.2%	59.8%

RHODE ISLAND

HOUSE OF REPRESENTATIVES

			Republican		Democratic		Other Vote	Rep.-Dem. Plurality	Percentage			
									Total Vote		Major Vote	
CD	Year	Total Vote	Vote	Candidate	Vote	Candidate			Rep.	Dem.	Rep.	Dem.
1	2022	156,734	100,318	CICILLINE, DAVID N.*	56,055	WATERS, ALLEN RODNEY	361	44,263 R	64.0%	35.8%	64.2%	35.8%
1	2020	223,860			158,550	CICILLINE, DAVID N.*	65,310	158,550 D		70.8%		100.0%
1	2018	174,083	57,567	DONOVAN, PATRICK J.	116,099	CICILLINE, DAVID N.*	417	58,532 D	33.1%	66.7%	33.1%	66.9%
1	2016	202,371	71,023	TAUB, H. RUSSELL	130,534	CICILLINE, DAVID N.*	814	59,511 D	35.1%	64.5%	35.2%	64.8%
1	2014	146,353	58,877	LYNCH, CORMICK	87,060	CICILLINE, DAVID N.*	416	28,183 D	40.2%	59.5%	40.3%	59.7%
1	2012	205,115	83,737	DOHERTY, BRENDAN P.	108,612	CICILLINE, DAVID N.*	12,766	24,875 D	40.8%	53.0%	43.5%	56.5%
2	2022	201,089	93,969	FUNG, ALLAN	101,432	MAGAZINER, SETH M.	5,688	7,463 D	46.7%	50.4%	48.1%	51.9%
2	2020	264,557	109,894	LANCIA, BOB	154,086	LANGEVIN, JAMES R.*	577	44,192 D	41.5%	58.2%	41.6%	58.4%
2	2018	199,197	72,271	CAIOZZO, SALVATORE	126,476	LANGEVIN, JAMES R.*	450	54,205 D	36.3%	63.5%	36.4%	63.6%
2	2016	229,148	70,301	REIS, RHUE	133,108	LANGEVIN, JAMES R.*	25,739	62,807 D	30.7%	58.1%	34.6%	65.4%
2	2014	169,904	63,844	REIS, RHUE	105,716	LANGEVIN, JAMES R.*	344	41,872 D	37.6%	62.2%	37.7%	62.3%
2	2012	222,660	78,189	RILEY, MICHAEL G.	124,067	LANGEVIN, JAMES R.*	20,404	45,878 D	35.1%	55.7%	38.7%	61.3%
TOTAL	2022	357,823	194,287		157,487		6,049	36,800 R	54.3%	44.0%	55.2%	44.8%
TOTAL	2020	488,417	109,894		312,636		65,887	202,742 D	22.5%	64.0%	26.0%	74.0%
TOTAL	2018	373,280	129,838		242,575		867	112,737 D	34.8%	65.0%	34.9%	65.1%
TOTAL	2016	431,519	141,324		263,642		26,553	122,318 D	32.8%	61.1%	34.9%	65.1%
TOTAL	2014	316,257	122,721		192,776		760	70,055 D	38.8%	61.0%	38.9%	61.1%
TOTAL	2012	427,775	161,926		232,679		33,170	70,753 D	37.9%	54.4%	41.0%	59.0%

Note: An asterisk (*) denotes incumbent.

RHODE ISLAND

GENERAL AND PRIMARY ELECTIONS

GENERAL ELECTIONS: OTHER VOTES

Governor — Other vote was 4,512 Independent (Zachary Hurwitz), 3,123 Independent (Paul Rianna), 2,811 Libertarian (Elijah Gizzarelli), 1,057 Write-In (Write-Ins)

House — Other vote was:
- CD 1: 361 Write-In (Write-Ins)
- CD 2: 199 Write-In (Write-Ins)

2022 PRIMARY ELECTIONS: SUPPLEMENTARY INFORMATION

Primary September 13, 2022

Registration (as of September 1, 2022) 712,945

- Democratic 290,805
- Republican 97,879
- Unaffiliated 324,261

Primary Type Semi-open—Registered Democrats and Republicans could vote only in their party's primary. Unaffiliated voters could participate in either party's primary.

RHODE ISLAND

GENERAL AND PRIMARY ELECTIONS

	REPUBLICAN PRIMARIES			DEMOCRATIC PRIMARIES		
Governor	Kalus, Ashley Marie	17,188	83.7%	McKee, Daniel*	37,288	32.8%
	Riccitelli, Jonathan	3,351	16.3%	Foulkes, Helena Buonanno	33,931	29.9%
				Gorbea, Nellie	29,811	26.2%
				Brown, Matthew "Matt"	9,021	7.9%
				Munoz, Luis Daniel	3,547	3.1%
	TOTAL	*20,539*		*TOTAL*	*113,598*	
Congressional District 1	Cicilline, David N.*	1,764	100.0%	Waters, Allen Rodney	389	100.0%
	TOTAL	*1,764*		*TOTAL*	*389*	
Congressional District 2						

Note: An asterisk (*) denotes incumbent.

SOUTH CAROLINA

Statewide Races

After South Carolina proved to be fool's gold for Democrats in 2020 – Republican Sen. Lindsey Graham was outraised by Democratic challenger Jamie Harrison and seemed locked in what some pundits called a toss-up race, only to win reelection by ten points – the Palmetto State's contests received much less attention in 2022.

Sen. Tim Scott (R) won a second full term by a 63%–37% vote, a margin almost identical to his 2016 showing. Scott flipped three counties since his last time on the ballot: Hampton and Jasper, which are adjacent and sit in the southern corner of the state, and Marlboro, which is on the North Carolina border. Hampton and Marlboro counties are majority-Black by composition, suggesting poor minority turnout. But Jasper was a more interesting case: in 2010, Black residents accounted for 47% of its population – by the 2020 census, that number was down to 35%. Jasper County sits next to Beaufort County, a fast-growing county on the coast, so it is likely seeing an influx of voters who are not loyal Democrats.

Though some urban counties have seen pro-Democratic trends, Republican margins have been buoyed by Horry County, which contains Myrtle Beach, a retiree magnet that often gives Republicans over 70%. In the state's 2010 Senate race, Horry County cast the sixth most votes of any county – in 2022, it was third, only behind Greenville and Charleston counties.

In the gubernatorial race, Republican Henry McMaster, a Trump ally, won a second full term over former 1st District Democratic Rep. Joe Cunningham. Cunningham, along with Iowa's Abby Finkenauer and Oklahoma's Kendra Horn, all were one-term members from red districts who were ousted in 2020 – each ran in, and lost, statewide races in 2022. McMaster ran behind Scott but still won comfortably, 58%–41%. Scott carried Charleston County by five points, but McMaster, facing a Charleston-based Democrat, lost it 56%–43%.

House Races

South Carolina Republicans passed a map that did not make comprehensive changes to the existing seven-district plan. After losing the Charleston-area SC-1 to Cunningham in 2018, Republicans narrowly regained it in 2020. Republican Nancy Mace, who ousted Cunningham by less than two points, was likely helped by Trump's 52%–46% margin in the district. Mappers increased Trump's margin in the district to nearly nine points. Mace had an easier general election: she defeated pediatrician Annie Andrews, who fundraised decently, by a 56%–42% margin.

But Mace had a more competitive primary. Early in her term, Mace was vaguely critical of Trump – which was enough to draw his ire. He endorsed Katie Arrington, the 2018 GOP nominee who lost to Cunningham, in the primary. Mace won by six points.

In the Myrtle Beach area, though, 7th District Republican Tim Rice did not have as much staying power. Rice was among the ten House Republicans who voted to impeach Trump. The former president endorsed state Rep. Russell Fry. In a field of seven candidates, Fry won the primary outright, taking 51% to Rice's 25%.

SOUTH CAROLINA

Congressional districts first established for elections held in 2022

7 members

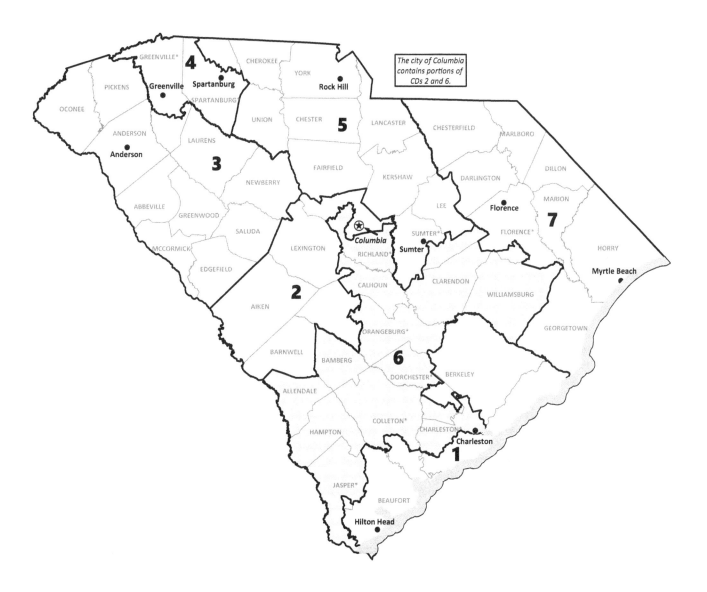

* Asterisk indicates a county whose boundaries include parts of two or more congressional districts.

CD 6 is highlighted for visibility.

SOUTH CAROLINA

GOVERNOR
Henry D. McMaster (R). Reelected 2022 to a four-year term. Assumed office January 25, 2017, to complete the remainder of the term vacated by the January 24, 2017, resignation of Nikki R. Haley to become U.S. ambassador to the United Nations. McMaster won a full four-year term in 2018.

SENATORS (2 Republicans)
Lindsey Graham (R). Reelected 2020 to a six-year term. Previously elected 2014, 2008, 2002.

Tim Scott (R). Elected 2022 to a six-year term. Previously elected 2016, and 2014 to fill out a short term. Initially sworn in on January 3, 2013, to fill the vacancy created by the resignation of Jim DeMint (R), who resigned two days earlier to become president of the Heritage Foundation.

REPRESENTATIVES (6 Republicans, 1 Democrat)
1. Nancy Mace (R)
2. Joe Wilson (R)
3. Jeff Duncan (R)
4. William Timmons (R)
5. Ralph Norman (R)
6. James E. Clyburn (D)
7. Russell Fry (R)

POSTWAR VOTE FOR PRESIDENT

Year	Total Vote	Republican Vote	Republican Candidate	Democratic Vote	Democratic Candidate	Other Vote	Rep.-Dem. Plurality	Total Vote Rep.	Total Vote Dem.	Major Vote Rep.	Major Vote Dem.
2020	2,513,329	1,385,103	Trump, Donald J.*	1,091,541	Biden, Joseph R. Jr.	36,685	293,562 R	55.1%	43.4%	55.9%	44.1%
2016**	2,103,027	1,155,389	Trump, Donald J.	855,373	Clinton, Hillary Rodham	92,265	300,016 R	54.9%	40.7%	57.5%	42.5%
2012	1,964,118	1,071,645	Romney, W. Mitt	865,941	Obama, Barack H.*	26,532	205,704 R	54.6%	44.1%	55.3%	44.7%
2008	1,920,969	1,034,896	McCain, John S. III	862,449	Obama, Barack H.	23,624	172,447 R	53.9%	44.9%	54.5%	45.5%
2004	1,617,730	937,974	Bush, George W.*	661,699	Kerry, John F.	18,057	276,275 R	58.0%	40.9%	58.6%	41.4%
2000**	1,382,717	785,937	Bush, George W.	565,561	Gore, Albert Jr.	31,219	220,376 R	56.8%	40.9%	58.2%	41.8%
1996**	1,151,689	573,458	Dole, Robert "Bob"	506,283	Clinton, Bill*	71,948	67,175 R	49.8%	44.0%	53.1%	46.9%
1992**	1,202,527	577,507	Bush, George H.*	479,514	Clinton, Bill	145,506	97,993 R	48.0%	39.9%	54.6%	45.4%
1988	986,009	606,443	Bush, George H.	370,554	Dukakis, Michael S.	9,012	235,889 R	61.5%	37.6%	62.1%	37.9%
1984	968,529	615,539	Reagan, Ronald*	344,459	Mondale, Walter F.	8,531	271,080 R	63.6%	35.6%	64.1%	35.9%
1980**	894,071	441,841	Reagan, Ronald	430,385	Carter, Jimmy*	21,845	11,456 R	49.4%	48.1%	50.7%	49.3%
1976	802,583	346,149	Ford, Gerald R.*	450,807	Carter, Jimmy	5,627	104,658 D	43.1%	56.2%	43.4%	56.6%
1972	673,960	477,044	Nixon, Richard M.*	186,824	McGovern, George S.	10,092	290,220 R	70.8%	27.7%	71.9%	28.1%
1968**	666,978	254,062	Nixon, Richard M.	197,486	Humphrey, Hubert Horatio Jr.	215,430	56,576 R	38.1%	29.6%	56.3%	43.7%
1964	524,779	309,048	Goldwater, Barry M. Sr.	215,723	Johnson, Lyndon B.*	8	93,325 R	58.9%	41.1%	58.9%	41.1%
1960	386,688	188,558	Nixon, Richard M.	198,129	Kennedy, John F.	1	9,571 D	48.8%	51.2%	48.8%	51.2%
1956**	300,583	75,700	Eisenhower, Dwight D.*	136,372	Stevenson, Adlai E. II	88,511	60,672 D	25.2%	45.4%	35.7%	64.3%
1952	341,087	168,082	Eisenhower, Dwight D.	173,004	Stevenson, Adlai E. II	1	4,922 D	49.3%	50.7%	49.3%	50.7%
1948**	142,571	5,386	Dewey, Thomas E.	34,423	Truman, Harry S.*	102,762	29,037 D#	3.8%	24.1%	13.5%	86.5%

Note: An asterisk (*) denotes incumbent. A pound sign (#) in the plurality column indicates that the winner in 1948 did not run under the banner of either major party. **In past elections, the other vote included: 2016 - 49,204 Libertarian (Gary Johnson); 2000 - 20,200 Green (Ralph Nader); 1996 - 64,386 Reform (Ross Perot); 1992 - 138,872 Independent (Perot); 1980 - 14,153 Independent (John Anderson); 1968 - 215,430 American Independent (George Wallace), who finished second; 1956 - 88,509 Uncommitted States' Rights electors, which placed second; 1948 - 102,607 States' Rights (Strom Thurmond), who won South Carolina with 72.0% of the total vote and a plurality of 68,184 votes.

SOUTH CAROLINA

POSTWAR VOTE FOR GOVERNOR

Year	Total Vote	Republican Vote	Republican Candidate	Democratic Vote	Democratic Candidate	Other Vote	Rep.-Dem. Plurality	Total Vote Rep.	Total Vote Dem.	Major Vote Rep.	Major Vote Dem.
2022	1,703,192	988,501	McMaster, Henry D.*	692,691	Cunningham, Joe	22,000	295,810 R	58.0%	40.7%	58.8%	41.2%
2018	1,707,569	921,342	McMaster, Henry D.*	784,182	Smith, James	2,045	137,160 R	54.0%	45.9%	54.0%	46.0%
2014	1,246,301	696,645	Haley, Nikki R.*	516,166	Sheheen, Vincent A.	33,490	180,479 R	55.9%	41.4%	57.4%	42.6%
2010	1,344,198	690,525	Haley, Nikki R.	630,534	Sheheen, Vincent A.	23,139	59,991 R	51.4%	46.9%	52.3%	47.7%
2006	1,091,952	601,868	Sanford, Marshall Clement "Mark" Jr.*	489,076	Moore, Tommy	1,008	112,792 R	55.1%	44.8%	55.2%	44.8%
2002	1,107,725	585,422	Sanford, Marshall Clement "Mark" Jr.	521,140	Hodges, James H.*	1,163	64,282 R	52.8%	47.0%	52.9%	47.1%
1998	1,070,869	484,088	Beasley, David*	570,070	Hodges, James H.	16,711	85,982 D	45.2%	53.2%	45.9%	54.1%
1994	933,850	470,756	Beasley, David	447,002	Theodore, Nick A.	16,092	23,754 R	50.4%	47.9%	51.3%	48.7%
1990	760,965	528,831	Campbell, Carroll*	212,034	Mitchell, Theo	20,100	316,797 R	69.5%	27.9%	71.4%	28.6%
1986	753,751	384,565	Campbell, Carroll	361,325	Daniel, Mike	7,861	23,240 R	51.0%	47.9%	51.6%	48.4%
1982	671,625	202,806	Workman, W. D. III	468,819	Riley, Richard W.*		266,013 D	30.2%	69.8%	30.2%	69.8%
1978	627,182	236,946	Young, Edward L.	384,898	Riley, Richard W.	5,338	147,952 D	37.8%	61.4%	38.1%	61.9%
1974	523,199	266,109	Edwards, James B.	248,938	Dorn, W.J. Bryan	8,152	17,171 R	50.9%	47.6%	51.7%	48.3%
1970	484,257	221,233	Watson, Albert W.	249,951	West, John C.	13,073	28,718 D	45.7%	51.6%	47.0%	53.0%
1966	439,942	184,088	Rogers, Joseph O. Jr.	255,854	McNair, Robert E.*		71,766 D	41.8%	58.2%	41.8%	58.2%
1962	253,721			253,704	Russell, Donald S.	17	253,704 D		100.0%		100.0%
1958	77,740			77,714	Hollings, Ernest F.	26	77,714 D		100.0%		100.0%
1954	214,212			214,204	Timmerman, George Bell	8	214,204 D		100.0%		100.0%
1950	50,642			50,633	Byrnes, James F.	9	50,633 D		100.0%		100.0%
1946	26,520			26,520	Thurmond, James Strom		26,520 D		100.0%		100.0%

Note: An asterisk (*) denotes incumbent. The Republican Party did not run a candidate in the gubernatorial elections of 1946, 1950, 1954, 1958, and 1962.

POSTWAR VOTE FOR SENATOR

Year	Total Vote	Republican Vote	Republican Candidate	Democratic Vote	Democratic Candidate	Other Vote	Rep.-Dem. Plurality	Total Vote Rep.	Total Vote Dem.	Major Vote Rep.	Major Vote Dem.
2022	1,695,702	1,066,274	Scott, Tim*	627,616	Matthews, Krystle	1,812	438,658 R	62.9%	37.0%	62.9%	37.1%
2020	2,515,104	1,369,137	Graham, Lindsey*	1,110,828	Harrison, Jaime	35,139	258,309 R	54.4%	44.2%	55.2%	44.8%
2016	2,049,893	1,241,609	Scott, Tim*	757,022	Dixon, Thomas	51,262	484,587 R	60.6%	36.9%	62.1%	37.9%
2014	1,240,075	672,941	Graham, Lindsey*	480,933	Hutto, C. Bradley "Brad"	86,201	192,008 R	54.3%	38.8%	58.3%	41.7%
2014S**	1,238,982	757,215	Scott, Tim*	459,583	Dickerson, Joyce	22,184	297,632 R	61.1%	37.1%	62.2%	37.8%
2010	1,318,794	810,771	DeMint, James W. "Jim"*	364,598	Greene, Alvin M.	143,425	446,173 R	61.5%	27.6%	69.0%	31.0%
2008	1,871,431	1,076,534	Graham, Lindsey*	790,621	Conley, Bob	4,276	285,913 R	57.5%	42.2%	57.7%	42.3%
2004	1,597,221	857,167	DeMint, James W. "Jim"	704,384	Tenenbaum, Inez M.	35,670	152,783 R	53.7%	44.1%	54.9%	45.1%
2002	1,102,948	600,010	Graham, Lindsey	487,359	Sanders, Alex	15,579	112,651 R	54.4%	44.2%	55.2%	44.8%
1998	1,068,367	488,132	Inglis, Robert D.	562,791	Hollings, Ernest F.*	17,444	74,659 D	45.7%	52.7%	46.4%	53.6%
1996	1,161,372	619,859	Thurmond, James Strom*	510,951	Close, Elliott	30,562	108,908 R	53.4%	44.0%	54.8%	45.2%
1992	1,180,438	554,175	Hartnett, Thomas F.	591,030	Hollings, Ernest F.*	35,233	36,855 D	46.9%	50.1%	48.4%	51.6%
1990	750,716	482,032	Thurmond, James Strom*	244,112	Cunningham, Bob	24,572	237,920 R	64.2%	32.5%	66.4%	33.6%
1986	737,962	262,886	McMaster, Henry D.	465,500	Hollings, Ernest F.*	9,576	202,614 D	35.6%	63.1%	36.1%	63.9%
1984	965,130	644,815	Thurmond, James Strom*	306,982	Purvis, Melvin	13,333	337,833 R	66.8%	31.8%	67.7%	32.3%
1980	870,594	257,946	Mays, Marshall T.	612,554	Hollings, Ernest F.*	94	354,608 D	29.6%	70.4%	29.6%	70.4%
1978	632,852	351,733	Thurmond, James Strom*	281,119	Ravenel, Charles D.		70,614 R	55.6%	44.4%	55.6%	44.4%
1974	512,397	146,645	Bush, Gwenfred	356,126	Hollings, Ernest F.*	9,626	209,481 D	28.6%	69.5%	29.2%	70.8%
1972	672,246	426,601	Thurmond, James Strom*	245,457	Zeigler, Eugene N.	188	181,144 R	63.5%	36.5%	63.5%	36.5%
1968	652,855	248,780	Parker, Marshall	404,060	Hollings, Ernest F.*	15	155,280 D	38.1%	61.9%	38.1%	61.9%
1966	436,252	271,297	Thurmond, James Strom*	164,955	Morrah, Bradley		106,342 R	62.2%	37.8%	62.2%	37.8%
1966S**		212,032	Parker, Marshall	223,790	Hollings, Ernest F.		11,758 D			48.7%	51.3%
1962	312,647	133,930	Workman, W. D. III	178,712	Johnston, Olin D.*	5	44,782 D	42.8%	57.2%	42.8%	57.2%
1960	330,266			330,164	Thurmond, James Strom*	102	330,164 D		100.0%		100.0%
1956	279,845	49,695	Crawford, L. P.	230,150	Johnston, Olin D.*		180,455 D	17.8%	82.2%	17.8%	82.2%
1956S**				245,371	Thurmond, James Strom*		245,371 D				100.0%
1954**	226,967			83,525	Brown, Edgar A.	143,442	83,525 D#		36.8%		100.0%
1950	50,277			50,240	Johnston, Olin D.*	37	50,240 D		99.9%		100.0%
1948	135,998			135,998	Maybank, Burnet R.*		135,998 D		100.0%		100.0%

Note: An asterisk (*) denotes incumbent. A pound sign (#) in the plurality column indicates that the winner in 1954 was an Independent Democrat. **In past elections, the other vote included: 1954 - 143,442 Independent Democratic (Strom Thurmond). Thurmond ran as a write-in candidate and won with 63.1 percent of the total vote and a plurality of 59,917 votes. One each of the 1956, 1966, and 2014 elections was for a short term to fill a vacancy. The Republican Party did not run a Senate candidate in 1948, 1950, 1954, 1956 (for the short term), and 1960.

SOUTH CAROLINA
GOVERNOR 2022

2020 Census Population	County	Total Vote	Republican (McMaster)	Democratic (Cunningham)	Other	Rep.-Dem. Plurality		Percentage Total Vote Rep.	Dem.	Major Vote Rep.	Dem.
24,585	ABBEVILLE	8,601	6,010	2,498	93	3,512	R	69.9%	29.0%	70.6%	29.4%
171,518	AIKEN	54,860	35,948	18,014	898	17,934	R	65.5%	32.8%	66.6%	33.4%
8,610	ALLENDALE	1,820	562	1,234	24	672	D	30.9%	67.8%	31.3%	68.7%
203,822	ANDERSON	63,419	46,144	16,541	734	29,603	R	72.8%	26.1%	73.6%	26.4%
14,055	BAMBERG	3,983	1,736	2,192	55	456	D	43.6%	55.0%	44.2%	55.8%
20,833	BARNWELL	6,257	3,643	2,543	71	1,100	R	58.2%	40.6%	58.9%	41.1%
193,403	BEAUFORT	71,706	41,839	29,265	602	12,574	R	58.3%	40.8%	58.8%	41.2%
230,499	BERKELEY	71,400	39,829	30,592	979	9,237	R	55.8%	42.8%	56.6%	43.4%
14,560	CALHOUN	5,622	3,238	2,301	83	937	R	57.6%	40.9%	58.5%	41.5%
413,253	CHARLESTON	153,488	66,475	85,433	1,580	18,958	D	43.3%	55.7%	43.8%	56.2%
57,479	CHEROKEE	16,142	12,300	3,685	157	8,615	R	76.2%	22.8%	76.9%	23.1%
32,294	CHESTER	9,583	5,762	3,695	126	2,067	R	60.1%	38.6%	60.9%	39.1%
45,666	CHESTERFIELD	12,557	7,983	4,435	139	3,548	R	63.6%	35.3%	64.3%	35.7%
33,784	CLARENDON	11,457	6,374	4,983	100	1,391	R	55.6%	43.5%	56.1%	43.9%
37,805	COLLETON	12,545	7,159	5,239	147	1,920	R	57.1%	41.8%	57.7%	42.3%
66,725	DARLINGTON	20,038	11,535	8,334	169	3,201	R	57.6%	41.6%	58.1%	41.9%
30,510	DILLON	7,915	4,341	3,508	66	833	R	54.8%	44.3%	55.3%	44.7%
163,262	DORCHESTER	49,794	27,358	21,741	695	5,617	R	54.9%	43.7%	55.7%	44.3%
27,356	EDGEFIELD	8,806	5,907	2,790	109	3,117	R	67.1%	31.7%	67.9%	32.1%
22,368	FAIRFIELD	8,413	3,658	4,619	136	961	D	43.5%	54.9%	44.2%	55.8%
138,348	FLORENCE	41,439	22,741	18,189	509	4,552	R	54.9%	43.9%	55.6%	44.4%
62,903	GEORGETOWN	27,501	16,373	10,889	239	5,484	R	59.5%	39.6%	60.1%	39.9%
526,317	GREENVILLE	178,134	108,222	66,943	2,969	41,279	R	60.8%	37.6%	61.8%	38.2%
70,953	GREENWOOD	21,801	14,196	7,330	275	6,866	R	65.1%	33.6%	65.9%	34.1%
19,216	HAMPTON	5,630	2,665	2,907	58	242	D	47.3%	51.6%	47.8%	52.2%
358,413	HORRY	133,661	92,708	39,813	1,140	52,895	R	69.4%	29.8%	70.0%	30.0%
30,255	JASPER	11,128	6,259	4,749	120	1,510	R	56.2%	42.7%	56.9%	43.1%
66,839	KERSHAW	22,402	14,024	8,072	306	5,952	R	62.6%	36.0%	63.5%	36.5%
99,144	LANCASTER	34,551	22,399	11,653	499	10,746	R	64.8%	33.7%	65.8%	34.2%
67,753	LAURENS	19,821	13,766	5,771	284	7,995	R	69.5%	29.1%	70.5%	29.5%
16,711	LEE	5,255	2,116	3,082	57	966	D	40.3%	58.6%	40.7%	59.3%
300,653	LEXINGTON	99,656	64,328	33,745	1,583	30,583	R	64.6%	33.9%	65.6%	34.4%
30,622	MARION	8,416	3,846	4,484	86	638	D	45.7%	53.3%	46.2%	53.8%
26,059	MARLBORO	6,537	3,209	3,247	81	38	D	49.1%	49.7%	49.7%	50.3%
9,488	MCCORMICK	4,567	2,757	1,759	51	998	R	60.4%	38.5%	61.0%	39.0%
38,569	NEWBERRY	12,835	8,413	4,248	174	4,165	R	65.5%	33.1%	66.4%	33.6%
80,021	OCONEE	28,965	21,622	6,988	355	14,634	R	74.6%	24.1%	75.6%	24.4%
86,045	ORANGEBURG	26,191	9,501	16,481	209	6,980	D	36.3%	62.9%	36.6%	63.4%
127,596	PICKENS	40,205	30,020	9,546	639	20,474	R	74.7%	23.7%	75.9%	24.1%
416,579	RICHLAND	127,368	41,008	84,541	1,819	43,533	D	32.2%	66.4%	32.7%	67.3%
20,567	SALUDA	6,560	4,695	1,783	82	2,912	R	71.6%	27.2%	72.5%	27.5%
322,177	SPARTANBURG	97,051	63,806	31,939	1,306	31,867	R	65.7%	32.9%	66.6%	33.4%
106,840	SUMTER	30,677	14,292	16,051	334	1,759	D	46.6%	52.3%	47.1%	52.9%
27,393	UNION	8,665	5,722	2,859	84	2,863	R	66.0%	33.0%	66.7%	33.3%
30,265	WILLIAMSBURG	9,792	3,858	5,839	95	1,981	D	39.4%	59.6%	39.8%	60.2%
283,935	YORK	95,978	58,154	36,141	1,683	22,013	R	60.6%	37.7%	61.7%	38.3%
5,176,048	TOTAL	1,703,192	988,501	692,691	22,000	295,810	R	58.0%	40.7%	58.8%	41.2%

SOUTH CAROLINA
SENATOR 2022

2020 Census Population	County	Total Vote	Republican (Scott)	Democratic (Matthews)	Other	Rep.-Dem. Plurality	Percentage Total Vote Rep.	Percentage Total Vote Dem.	Percentage Major Vote Rep.	Percentage Major Vote Dem.
24,585	ABBEVILLE	8,573	6,259	2,310	4	3,949 R	73.0%	26.9%	73.0%	27.0%
171,518	AIKEN	54,779	37,549	17,180	50	20,369 R	68.5%	31.4%	68.6%	31.4%
8,610	ALLENDALE	1,809	585	1,224		639 D	32.3%	67.7%	32.3%	67.7%
203,822	ANDERSON	63,264	48,801	14,391	72	34,410 R	77.1%	22.7%	77.2%	22.8%
14,055	BAMBERG	3,969	1,820	2,149		329 D	45.9%	54.1%	45.9%	54.1%
20,833	BARNWELL	6,265	3,808	2,453	4	1,355 R	60.8%	39.2%	60.8%	39.2%
193,403	BEAUFORT	71,405	45,023	26,337	45	18,686 R	63.1%	36.9%	63.1%	36.9%
230,499	BERKELEY	71,104	44,407	26,622	75	17,785 R	62.5%	37.4%	62.5%	37.5%
14,560	CALHOUN	5,599	3,430	2,159	10	1,271 R	61.3%	38.6%	61.4%	38.6%
413,253	CHARLESTON	151,799	79,586	71,983	230	7,603 R	52.4%	47.4%	52.5%	47.5%
57,479	CHEROKEE	16,120	12,753	3,355	12	9,398 R	79.1%	20.8%	79.2%	20.8%
32,294	CHESTER	9,579	5,954	3,621	4	2,333 R	62.2%	37.8%	62.2%	37.8%
45,666	CHESTERFIELD	12,538	8,298	4,234	6	4,064 R	66.2%	33.8%	66.2%	33.8%
33,784	CLARENDON	11,410	6,612	4,792	6	1,820 R	57.9%	42.0%	58.0%	42.0%
37,805	COLLETON	12,507	7,747	4,750	10	2,997 R	61.9%	38.0%	62.0%	38.0%
66,725	DARLINGTON	20,026	12,116	7,898	12	4,218 R	60.5%	39.4%	60.5%	39.5%
30,510	DILLON	7,882	4,456	3,420	6	1,036 R	56.5%	43.4%	56.6%	43.4%
163,262	DORCHESTER	49,512	30,814	18,643	55	12,171 R	62.2%	37.7%	62.3%	37.7%
27,356	EDGEFIELD	8,807	6,108	2,686	13	3,422 R	69.4%	30.5%	69.5%	30.5%
22,368	FAIRFIELD	8,334	3,883	4,444	7	561 D	46.6%	53.3%	46.6%	53.4%
138,348	FLORENCE	41,323	24,117	17,171	35	6,946 R	58.4%	41.6%	58.4%	41.6%
62,903	GEORGETOWN	27,357	17,457	9,885	15	7,572 R	63.8%	36.1%	63.8%	36.2%
526,317	GREENVILLE	177,399	117,974	59,109	316	58,865 R	66.5%	33.3%	66.6%	33.4%
70,953	GREENWOOD	21,765	15,033	6,720	12	8,313 R	69.1%	30.9%	69.1%	30.9%
19,216	HAMPTON	5,626	2,825	2,799	2	26 R	50.2%	49.8%	50.2%	49.8%
358,413	HORRY	133,205	96,941	36,198	66	60,743 R	72.8%	27.2%	72.8%	27.2%
30,255	JASPER	11,090	6,554	4,532	4	2,022 R	59.1%	40.9%	59.1%	40.9%
66,839	KERSHAW	22,308	14,935	7,359	14	7,576 R	66.9%	33.0%	67.0%	33.0%
99,144	LANCASTER	34,488	23,159	11,306	23	11,853 R	67.2%	32.8%	67.2%	32.8%
67,753	LAURENS	19,756	14,504	5,214	38	9,290 R	73.4%	26.4%	73.6%	26.4%
16,711	LEE	5,240	2,209	3,028	3	819 D	42.2%	57.8%	42.2%	57.8%
300,653	LEXINGTON	99,109	70,113	28,884	112	41,229 R	70.7%	29.1%	70.8%	29.2%
30,622	MARION	8,377	3,952	4,421	4	469 D	47.2%	52.8%	47.2%	52.8%
26,059	MARLBORO	6,486	3,308	3,169	9	139 R	51.0%	48.9%	51.1%	48.9%
9,488	MCCORMICK	4,566	2,818	1,748		1,070 R	61.7%	38.3%	61.7%	38.3%
38,569	NEWBERRY	12,752	8,967	3,775	10	5,192 R	70.3%	29.6%	70.4%	29.6%
80,021	OCONEE	28,919	22,923	5,975	21	16,948 R	79.3%	20.7%	79.3%	20.7%
86,045	ORANGEBURG	26,136	10,024	16,096	16	6,072 D	38.4%	61.6%	38.4%	61.6%
127,596	PICKENS	40,083	32,028	8,012	43	24,016 R	79.9%	20.0%	80.0%	20.0%
416,579	RICHLAND	126,355	46,989	79,130	236	32,141 D	37.2%	62.6%	37.3%	62.7%
20,567	SALUDA	6,545	4,938	1,605	2	3,333 R	75.4%	24.5%	75.5%	24.5%
322,177	SPARTANBURG	96,822	68,030	28,681	111	39,349 R	70.3%	29.6%	70.3%	29.7%
106,840	SUMTER	30,566	15,100	15,442	24	342 D	49.4%	50.5%	49.4%	50.6%
27,393	UNION	8,639	5,991	2,646	2	3,345 R	69.3%	30.6%	69.4%	30.6%
30,265	WILLIAMSBURG	9,744	4,047	5,695	2	1,648 D	41.5%	58.4%	41.5%	58.5%
283,935	YORK	95,765	61,329	34,365	71	26,964 R	64.0%	35.9%	64.1%	35.9%
5,176,048	TOTAL	1,695,702	1,066,274	627,616	1,812	438,658 R	62.9%	37.0%	62.9%	37.1%

SOUTH CAROLINA
HOUSE OF REPRESENTATIVES

			Republican		Democratic		Other Vote	Rep.-Dem. Plurality	Percentage			
									Total Vote		Major Vote	
CD	Year	Total Vote	Vote	Candidate	Vote	Candidate			Rep.	Dem.	Rep.	Dem.
1	2022	272,681	153,757	MACE, NANCY*	115,796	ANDREWS, ANNIE	3,128	37,961 R	56.4%	42.5%	57.0%	43.0%
1	2020	427,111	216,042	MACE, NANCY	210,627	CUNNINGHAM, JOE*	442	5,415 R	50.6%	49.3%	50.6%	49.4%
1	2018	287,433	141,473	ARRINGTON, KATIE	145,455	CUNNINGHAM, JOE	505	3,982 D	49.2%	50.6%	49.3%	50.7%
1	2016	325,170	190,410	SANFORD, MARSHALL CLEMENT "MARK" JR.*	119,779	CHERNY, DIMITRI	14,981	70,631 R	58.6%	36.8%	61.4%	38.6%
1	2014	127,815	119,392	SANFORD, MARSHALL CLEMENT "MARK" JR.*			8,423	119,392 R	93.4%		100.0%	
1	2012	290,013	179,908	SCOTT, TIM*	103,557	ROSE, BOBBIE G.	6,548	76,351 R	62.0%	35.7%	63.5%	36.5%
2	2022	246,126	147,699	WILSON, JOE*	98,081	LARKINS, JUDD	346	49,618 R	60.0%	39.8%	60.1%	39.9%
2	2020	364,215	202,715	WILSON, JOE*	155,118	BOROUGHS, ADAIR FORD	6,382	47,597 R	55.7%	42.6%	56.7%	43.3%
2	2018	257,139	144,642	WILSON, JOE*	109,199	CARRIGAN, SEAN	3,298	35,443 R	56.3%	42.5%	57.0%	43.0%
2	2016	304,996	183,746	WILSON, JOE*	109,452	BJORN, ARIK	11,798	74,294 R	60.2%	35.9%	62.7%	37.3%
2	2014	194,808	121,649	WILSON, JOE*	68,719	BLACK, PHIL	4,440	52,930 R	62.4%	35.3%	63.9%	36.1%
2	2012	203,718	196,116	WILSON, JOE*			7,602	196,116 R	96.3%		100.0%	
3	2022	194,569			189,971	DUNCAN, JEFF*	4,598	189,971 D		97.6%		100.0%
3	2020	333,564	237,544	DUNCAN, JEFF*	95,712	CLEVELAND, HOSEA	308	141,832 R	71.2%	28.7%	71.3%	28.7%
3	2018	226,204	153,338	DUNCAN, JEFF*	70,046	GEREN, MARY	2,820	83,292 R	67.8%	31.0%	68.6%	31.4%
3	2016	272,481	198,431	DUNCAN, JEFF*	73,766	CLEVELAND, HOSEA	284	124,665 R	72.8%	27.1%	72.9%	27.1%
3	2014	164,009	116,741	DUNCAN, JEFF*	47,181	MULLIS, BARBARA JO	87	69,560 R	71.2%	28.8%	71.2%	28.8%
3	2012	254,763	169,512	DUNCAN, JEFF*	84,735	DOYLE, BRIAN RYAN B.	516	84,777 R	66.5%	33.3%	66.7%	33.3%
4	2022	182,365	165,607	TIMMONS, WILLIAM*			16,758	165,607 R	90.8%		100.0%	
4	2020	360,550	222,126	TIMMONS, WILLIAM*	133,023	NELSON, KIMBERLY	5,401	89,103 R	61.6%	36.9%	62.5%	37.5%
4	2018	243,950	145,321	TIMMONS, WILLIAM	89,182	BROWN, BRANDON P.	9,447	56,139 R	59.6%	36.6%	62.0%	38.0%
4	2016	295,670	198,648	GOWDY, TREY	91,676	FEDALEI, CHRISTOPHER	5,346	106,972 R	67.2%	31.0%	68.4%	31.6%
4	2014	149,049	126,452	GOWDY, TREY*			22,597	126,452 R	84.8%		100.0%	
4	2012	266,884	173,201	GOWDY, TREY*	89,964	MORROW, DEB	3,719	83,237 R	64.9%	33.7%	65.8%	34.2%
5	2022	241,707	154,725	NORMAN, RALPH*	83,299	HUNDLEY, EVANGELINE	3,683	71,426 R	64.0%	34.5%	65.0%	35.0%
5	2020	366,258	220,006	NORMAN, RALPH*	145,979	BROWN, MOE	273	74,027 R	60.1%	39.9%	60.1%	39.9%
5	2018	248,579	141,757	NORMAN, RALPH*	103,129	PARNELL, ARCHIE	3,693	38,628 R	57.0%	41.5%	57.9%	42.1%
5	2016	297,781	175,909	MULVANEY, MICK*	115,437	PERSON, FRANCIS "FRAN"	6,435	60,472 R	59.1%	38.8%	60.4%	39.6%
5	2014	175,145	103,078	MULVANEY, MICK*	71,985	ADAMS, TOM A.	82	31,093 R	58.9%	41.1%	58.9%	41.1%
5	2012	278,003	154,324	MULVANEY, MICK*	123,443	KNOTT, JOYCE	236	30,881 R	55.5%	44.4%	55.6%	44.4%
6	2022	211,028	79,879	BUCKNER, DUKE	130,923	CLYBURN, JAMES E.*	226	51,044 D	37.9%	62.0%	37.9%	62.1%
6	2020	289,653	89,258	MCCOLLUM, JOHN	197,477	CLYBURN, JAMES E.*	2,918	108,219 D	30.8%	68.2%	31.1%	68.9%
6	2018	206,433	58,282	GRESSMANN, GERHARD	144,765	CLYBURN, JAMES E.*	3,386	86,483 D	28.2%	70.1%	28.7%	71.3%
6	2016	253,901	70,099	STERLING, LAURA	177,947	CLYBURN, JAMES E.*	5,855	107,848 D	27.6%	70.1%	28.3%	71.7%
6	2014	173,432	44,311	CULLER, ANTHONY	125,747	CLYBURN, JAMES E.*	3,374	81,436 D	25.5%	72.5%	26.1%	73.9%
6	2012	233,615			218,717	CLYBURN, JAMES E.*	14,898	218,717 D		93.6%		100.0%
7	2022	253,865	164,440	FRY, RUSSELL	89,030	SCOTT, DARYL	395	75,410 R	64.8%	35.1%	64.9%	35.1%
7	2020	364,091	224,993	RICE, TOM*	138,863	WATSON, MELISSA WARD	235	86,130 R	61.8%	38.1%	61.8%	38.2%
7	2018	239,554	142,681	RICE, TOM*	96,564	WILLIAMS, ROBERT	309	46,117 R	59.6%	40.3%	59.6%	40.4%
7	2016	289,463	176,468	RICE, TOM*	112,744	HYMAN, MAL	251	63,724 R	61.0%	38.9%	61.0%	39.0%
7	2014	171,524	102,833	RICE, TOM*	68,576	TINUBU, GLORIA BROMELL	115	34,257 R	60.0%	40.0%	60.0%	40.0%
7	2012	275,738	153,068	RICE, TOM	122,389	TINUBU, GLORIA BROMELL	281	30,679 R	55.5%	44.4%	55.6%	44.4%
TOTAL	2022	1,602,341	866,107		707,100		29,134	159,007 R	54.1%	44.1%	55.1%	44.9%
TOTAL	2020	2,505,442	1,412,684		1,076,799		15,959	335,885 R	56.4%	43.0%	56.7%	43.3%
TOTAL	2018	1,709,292	927,494		758,340		23,458	169,154 R	54.3%	44.4%	55.0%	45.0%
TOTAL	2016	2,039,462	1,193,711		800,801		44,950	392,910 R	58.5%	39.3%	59.8%	40.2%
TOTAL	2014	1,155,782	734,456		382,208		39,118	352,248 R	63.5%	33.1%	65.8%	34.2%
TOTAL	2012	1,802,734	1,026,129		742,805		33,800	283,324 R	56.9%	41.2%	58.0%	42.0%

Note: An asterisk (*) denotes incumbent.

SOUTH CAROLINA

GENERAL AND PRIMARY ELECTIONS

GENERAL ELECTIONS: OTHER VOTES

Governor	Other vote was 20,826 Libertarian (Morgan Reeves), 1,174 Write-In (Scattered Write-In)
Senate	1,812 Write-In (Scattered Write-In)
House	Other vote was:
CD 1	494 Write-In (Scattered Write-In)
CD 2	346 Write-In (Scattered Write-In)
CD 3	4,598 Write-In (Scattered Write-In)
CD 4	16,758 Write-In (Scattered Write-In)
CD 5	136 Write-In (Scattered Write-In)
CD 6	226 Write-In (Scattered Write-In)
CD 7	395 Write-In (Scattered Write-In)

2022 PRIMARY ELECTIONS: SUPPLEMENTARY INFORMATION

Primary	June 14, 2022	Registration (as of May 31, 2022)		3,317,279	No Party Registration
Primary Runoff	June 28, 2022				
Primary Type	Open—Any registered voter could participate in either the Democratic or Republican primary, although any voter who participated in one party's primary could not vote in a runoff of the other party.				

	REPUBLICAN PRIMARIES			DEMOCRATIC PRIMARIES		
Senator				Bruce, Catherine Fleming	20,064	44.2%
				Matthews, Krystle	57,278	33.2%
				Geter, Angela	55,281	32.1%
				TOTAL	172,336	
				PRIMARY RUNOFF		
				Matthews, Krystle	25,300	55.8%
				Bruce, Catherine Fleming	59,777	34.7%
				TOTAL	45,364	
Governor	McMaster, Henry D.*	306,543	83.3%	Cunningham, Joe	102,473	56.4%
	Musselwhite, Harrison	61,462	16.7%	Mcleod, Mia S.	56,406	31.1%
				Boyd, Carlton	9,579	5.3%
				Williams, William	6,829	3.8%
				Mcmillan, Calvin "CJ Mack"	6,303	3.5%
	TOTAL	368,005		TOTAL	181,590	
Congressional District 1	Mace, Nancy*	39,470	53.1%	Andrews, Annie	Unopposed	
	Arrington, Katie	33,589	45.2%			
	Piper-Loomis, Lynz	1,221	1.6%			
	TOTAL	74,280				
Congressional District 2	Wilson, Joe*	Unopposed		Larkins, Judd	Unopposed	
Congressional District 3	Duncan, Jeff*	Unopposed		Duncan, Jeff*	Unopposed	

SOUTH CAROLINA

GENERAL AND PRIMARY ELECTIONS

	REPUBLICAN PRIMARIES			DEMOCRATIC PRIMARIES		
Congressional District 4	Timmons, William*	24,800	52.7%	Hill, Ken	Unopposed	
	Burns, Mark	11,214	23.8%			
	LaPierre, Michael James	8,029	17.1%			
	Abuzeid, George	3,024	6.4%			
	TOTAL	47,067				
Congressional District 5	Norman, Ralph*	Unopposed		Hundley, Evangeline	11,257	57.6%
				Eckert, Kevin	8,274	42.4%
				TOTAL	19,531	
Congressional District 6	Buckner, Duke	15,638	74.4%	Clyburn, James E.*	48,729	87.9%
	Morris, A. Sonia	5,374	25.6%	Addison, Michael	4,203	7.6%
				Dixon, Greg Marcel	2,503	4.5%
	TOTAL	21,012		TOTAL	55,435	
Congressional District 7	Fry, Russell	43,509	51.1%	Scott, Daryl	Unopposed	
	Rice, Tom*	20,927	24.6%			
	Arthur, Barbara	10,481	12.3%			
	Richardson, Ken	6,021	7.1%			
	Barton, Garrett	2,154	2.5%			
	McBride, Mark	1,676	2.0%			
	Morris, Spencer	444	0.5%			
	TOTAL	85,212				

Note: An asterisk (*) denotes incumbent.

SOUTH DAKOTA

Statewide and House Races

Compared to the 2018 cycle, when the state hosted an unusually competitive contest for governor, South Dakota saw a quiet 2022.

Sen. John Thune, who was elevated to serve as the Republican Whip after the 2020 elections, got to the Senate in 2004. That year, in what was the most high-stakes non-presidential contest, he ousted then-Senate Minority Leader Tom Daschle (D) in a close race. But, because of the state's lean and his own strength as an incumbent, he has never been seriously challenged since. In 2010, his first reelection race, Thune was completely unopposed. Six years later, as Donald Trump carried South Dakota by nearly 30 points, Thune won by 44 points, carrying all but three counties. After he announced his reelection plans for 2022, Trump, who perceived Thune to be too close with Senate Minority Leader Mitch McConnell, called for a primary challenger. But no strong, Trump-aligned challenger emerged. Thune won a fourth term by the same 44 points that he did in 2016, and lost the same three counties: Buffalo, Oglala Dakota, and Todd, all of which contain Native American Reservations.

The gubernatorial race was somewhat more competitive, as Gov. Kristi Noem, a Republican who was on better terms with Trump, sought reelection. At a controversial Fourth of July celebration at Mount Rushmore in 2020, she presented Trump with a replica of the monument – it added his likeness to that of the other four presidents. Democrats nominated Jamie Smith, who led their caucus in the state House and accused the governor of neglecting the state in pursuit of building a national profile. Though the few public polls that were available showed a closer race, Noem won 62%–35%, a showing identical to Trump's 2020 margin in South Dakota. Noem lost the same three counties as Thune did, but also came up short in two Thune-won counties, Clay and Dewey. In her more competitive 2018 race, she lost the state's largest county, Minnehaha (Sioux Falls), by a 53%–45% spread – she carried it by the same margin in 2022.

As with neighboring North Dakota, Democrats in South Dakota did not field a candidate for the state's At-Large seat in the House. Against Libertarian Collin Duprel, Republican Rep. Dusty Johnson won a third term by a 77%–23% vote. Johnson carried everything but Oglala Lakota and Todd counties – the former includes the Pine Ridge Reservation while the latter overlaps with the Rosebud Reservation. They are the state's two most Democratic counties, and as the 2022 results show, will easily vote third-party before supporting a GOP candidate. The 2020 race also lacked a Democrat, and Johnson lost the same counties to another Libertarian.

SOUTH DAKOTA

One member At Large

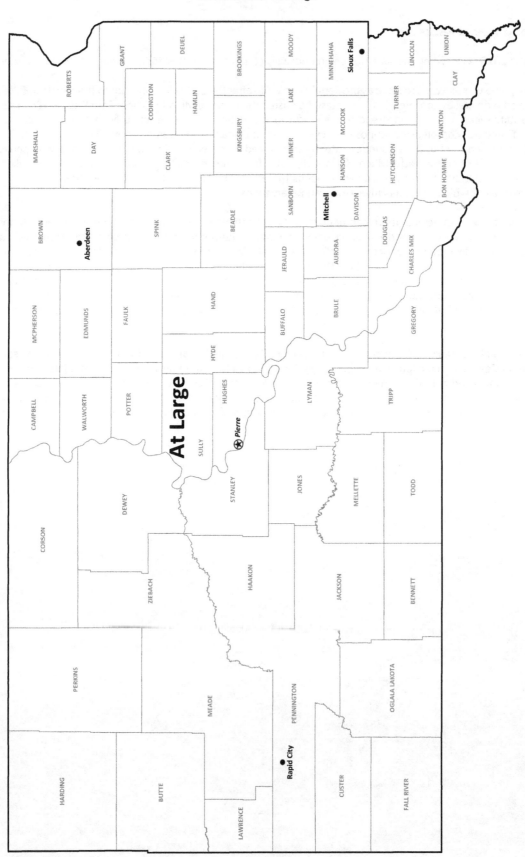

SOUTH DAKOTA

GOVERNOR
Kristi Noem (R). Reelected 2022 to a four-year term. Previously elected 2018.

SENATORS (2 Republicans)
Mike Rounds (R). Reelected 2020 to a six-year term. Previously elected 2014.

John Thune (R). Reelected 2022 to a six-year term. Previously elected 2016, 2010, 2004.

REPRESENTATIVE (1 Republican)
At Large. Dusty Johnson (R)

POSTWAR VOTE FOR PRESIDENT

		Republican		Democratic		Other Vote	Rep.-Dem. Plurality	Percentage			
								Total Vote		Major Vote	
Year	Total Vote	Vote	Candidate	Vote	Candidate			Rep.	Dem.	Rep.	Dem.
2020	422,609	261,043	Trump, Donald J.*	150,471	Biden, Joseph R. Jr.	11,095	110,572 R	61.8%	35.6%	63.4%	36.6%
2016**	370,093	227,721	Trump, Donald J.	117,458	Clinton, Hillary Rodham	24,914	110,263 R	61.5%	31.7%	66.0%	34.0%
2012	363,815	210,610	Romney, W. Mitt	145,039	Obama, Barack H.*	8,166	65,571 R	57.9%	39.9%	59.2%	40.8%
2008	381,975	203,054	McCain, John S. III	170,924	Obama, Barack H.	7,997	32,130 R	53.2%	44.7%	54.3%	45.7%
2004	388,215	232,584	Bush, George W.*	149,244	Kerry, John F.	6,387	83,340 R	59.9%	38.4%	60.9%	39.1%
2000	316,269	190,700	Bush, George W.	118,804	Gore, Albert Jr.	6,765	71,896 R	60.3%	37.6%	61.6%	38.4%
1996**	323,826	150,543	Dole, Robert "Bob"	139,333	Clinton, Bill*	33,950	11,210 R	46.5%	43.0%	51.9%	48.1%
1992**	336,254	136,718	Bush, George H.*	124,888	Clinton, Bill	74,648	11,830 R	40.7%	37.1%	52.3%	47.7%
1988	312,991	165,415	Bush, George H.	145,560	Dukakis, Michael S.	2,016	19,855 R	52.8%	46.5%	53.2%	46.8%
1984	317,867	200,267	Reagan, Ronald*	116,113	Mondale, Walter F.	1,487	84,154 R	63.0%	36.5%	63.3%	36.7%
1980**	327,703	198,343	Reagan, Ronald	103,855	Carter, Jimmy*	25,505	94,488 R	60.5%	31.7%	65.6%	34.4%
1976	300,678	151,505	Ford, Gerald R.*	147,068	Carter, Jimmy	2,105	4,437 R	50.4%	48.9%	50.7%	49.3%
1972	307,415	166,476	Nixon, Richard M.*	139,945	McGovern, George S.	994	26,531 R	54.2%	45.5%	54.3%	45.7%
1968**	281,264	149,841	Nixon, Richard M.	118,023	Humphrey, Hubert Horatio Jr.	13,400	31,818 R	53.3%	42.0%	55.9%	44.1%
1964	293,118	130,108	Goldwater, Barry M. Sr.	163,010	Johnson, Lyndon B.*		32,902 D	44.4%	55.6%	44.4%	55.6%
1960	306,487	178,417	Nixon, Richard M.	128,070	Kennedy, John F.		50,347 R	58.2%	41.8%	58.2%	41.8%
1956	293,857	171,569	Eisenhower, Dwight D.*	122,288	Stevenson, Adlai E. II		49,281 R	58.4%	41.6%	58.4%	41.6%
1952	294,283	203,857	Eisenhower, Dwight D.	90,426	Stevenson, Adlai E. II		113,431 R	69.3%	30.7%	69.3%	30.7%
1948	250,105	129,651	Dewey, Thomas E.	117,653	Truman, Harry S.*	2,801	11,998 R	51.8%	47.0%	52.4%	47.6%

Note: An asterisk (*) denotes incumbent. **In past elections, the other vote included: 2016 - 20,850 Libertarian (Gary Johnson); 1996 - 31,250 Reform (Ross Perot); 1992 - 73,295 Independent (Perot); 1980 - 21,431 Independent (John Anderson); 1968 - 13,400 American Independent (George Wallace).

SOUTH DAKOTA

POSTWAR VOTE FOR GOVERNOR

Year	Total Vote	Republican Vote	Republican Candidate	Democratic Vote	Democratic Candidate	Other Vote	Rep.-Dem. Plurality	Total Vote Rep.	Total Vote Dem.	Major Vote Rep.	Major Vote Dem.
2022	350,166	217,035	Noem, Kristi*	123,148	Smith, Jamie	9,983	93,887 R	62.0%	35.2%	63.8%	36.2%
2018	339,214	172,912	Noem, Kristi	161,454	Sutton, Billie	4,848	11,458 R	51.0%	47.6%	51.7%	48.3%
2014	277,403	195,477	Daugaard, Dennis*	70,549	Wismer, Susan	11,377	124,928 R	70.5%	25.4%	73.5%	26.5%
2010	317,083	195,046	Daugaard, Dennis	122,037	Heidepriem, Scott		73,009 R	61.5%	38.5%	61.5%	38.5%
2006	335,508	206,990	Rounds, Mike*	121,226	Billion, Jack	7,292	85,764 R	61.7%	36.1%	63.1%	36.9%
2002	334,559	189,920	Rounds, Mike	140,263	Abbott, Jim	4,376	49,657 R	56.8%	41.9%	57.5%	42.5%
1998	260,187	166,621	Janklow, William J.*	85,473	Hunhoff, Bernie	8,093	81,148 R	64.0%	32.9%	66.1%	33.9%
1994	311,613	172,515	Janklow, William J.	126,273	Beddow, Jim	12,825	46,242 R	55.4%	40.5%	57.7%	42.3%
1990	256,723	151,198	Mickelson, George S.*	105,525	Samuelson, Bob L.		45,673 R	58.9%	41.1%	58.9%	41.1%
1986	294,441	152,543	Mickelson, George S.	141,898	Herseth, R. Lars		10,645 R	51.8%	48.2%	51.8%	48.2%
1982	278,565	197,429	Janklow, William J.*	81,136	O'Connor, Michael J.		116,293 R	70.9%	29.1%	70.9%	29.1%
1978	259,795	147,116	Janklow, William J.	112,679	McKellips, Roger		34,437 R	56.6%	43.4%	56.6%	43.4%
1974	278,228	129,077	Olson, John E.	149,151	Kneip, Richard F.*		20,074 D	46.4%	53.6%	46.4%	53.6%
1972	308,177	123,165	Thompson, Carveth	185,012	Kneip, Richard F.*		61,847 D	40.0%	60.0%	40.0%	60.0%
1970	239,963	108,347	Farrar, Frank*	131,616	Kneip, Richard F.		23,269 D	45.2%	54.8%	45.2%	54.8%
1968	276,906	159,646	Farrar, Frank	117,260	Chamerlin, Robert		42,386 R	57.7%	42.3%	57.7%	42.3%
1966	228,214	131,710	Boe, Nils A.*	96,504	Chamerlin, Robert		35,206 R	57.7%	42.3%	57.7%	42.3%
1964	290,570	150,151	Boe, Nils A.	140,419	Lindley, John F.		9,732 R	51.7%	48.3%	51.7%	48.3%
1962	256,120	143,682	Gubbrud, Archie M.*	112,438	Herseth, Ralph		31,244 R	56.1%	43.9%	56.1%	43.9%
1960	304,625	154,530	Gubbrud, Archie M.	150,095	Herseth, Ralph*		4,435 R	50.7%	49.3%	50.7%	49.3%
1958	258,281	125,520	Saunders, Phil	132,761	Herseth, Ralph		7,241 D	48.6%	51.4%	48.6%	51.4%
1956	292,017	158,819	Foss, Joe*	133,198	Herseth, Ralph		25,621 R	54.4%	45.6%	54.4%	45.6%
1954	236,255	133,878	Foss, Joe	102,377	Martin, Ed C.		31,501 R	56.7%	43.3%	56.7%	43.3%
1952	289,514	203,102	Anderson, Sigurd*	86,412	Iverson, Sherman A.		116,690 R	70.2%	29.8%	70.2%	29.8%
1950	253,316	154,254	Anderson, Sigurd	99,062	Robbie, Joe		55,192 R	60.9%	39.1%	60.9%	39.1%
1948	245,372	149,883	Mickelson, George T.*	95,489	Volz, Harold J.		54,394 R	61.1%	38.9%	61.1%	38.9%
1946	162,292	108,998	Mickelson, George T.	53,294	Haeder, Richard		55,704 R	67.2%	32.8%	67.2%	32.8%

Note: An asterisk (*) denotes incumbent. The term of office of South Dakota's governor was increased from two to four years effective with the 1974 election.

POSTWAR VOTE FOR SENATOR

Year	Total Vote	Republican Vote	Republican Candidate	Democratic Vote	Democratic Candidate	Other Vote	Rep.-Dem. Plurality	Total Vote Rep.	Total Vote Dem.	Major Vote Rep.	Major Vote Dem.
2022	348,020	242,316	Thune, John*	91,007	Bengs, Brian L.	14,697	151,309 R	69.6%	26.1%	72.7%	27.3%
2020	420,219	276,232	Rounds, Mike*	143,987	Ahlers, Dan		132,245 R	65.7%	34.3%	65.7%	34.3%
2016	369,656	265,516	Thune, John*	104,140	Williams, Jay		161,376 R	71.8%	28.2%	71.8%	28.2%
2014**	279,412	140,741	Rounds, Mike	82,456	Weiland, Rick	56,215	58,285 R	50.4%	29.5%	63.1%	36.9%
2010	227,947	227,947	Thune, John*				227,947 R	100.0%		100.0%	
2008	380,673	142,784	Dykstra, Joel	237,889	Johnson, Timothy P.*		95,105 D	37.5%	62.5%	37.5%	62.5%
2004	391,188	197,848	Thune, John	193,340	Daschle, Thomas A.*		4,508 R	50.6%	49.4%	50.6%	49.4%
2002	337,508	166,957	Thune, John	167,481	Johnson, Timothy P.*	3,070	524 D	49.5%	49.6%	49.9%	50.1%
1998	262,111	95,431	Schmidt, Ron	162,884	Daschle, Thomas A.*	3,796	67,453 D	36.4%	62.1%	36.9%	63.1%
1996	324,487	157,954	Pressler, Larry*	166,533	Johnson, Timothy P.		8,579 D	48.7%	51.3%	48.7%	51.3%
1992	334,495	108,733	Haar, Charlene	217,095	Daschle, Thomas A.*	8,667	108,362 D	32.5%	64.9%	33.4%	66.6%
1990	258,976	135,682	Pressler, Larry*	116,727	Muenster, Ted	6,567	18,955 R	52.4%	45.1%	53.8%	46.2%
1986	295,830	143,257	Abdnor, James*	152,667	Daschle, Thomas A.		9,484 D	48.4%	51.6%	48.4%	51.6%
1984	315,713	235,176	Pressler, Larry*	80,537	Cunningham, George V.		154,639 R	74.5%	25.5%	74.5%	25.5%
1980	327,478	190,594	Abdnor, James	129,018	McGovern, George S.*	7,866	61,576 R	58.2%	39.4%	59.6%	40.4%
1978	255,599	170,832	Pressler, Larry	84,767	Barnett, Don		86,065 R	66.8%	33.2%	66.8%	33.2%
1974	278,884	130,955	Thorsness, Leo K.	147,929	McGovern, George S.*		16,974 D	47.0%	53.0%	47.0%	53.0%
1972	306,386	131,613	Hirsch, Robert W.	174,773	Abourezk, James George*		43,160 D	43.0%	57.0%	43.0%	57.0%
1968	279,912	120,951	Gubbrud, Archie M.	158,961	McGovern, George S.*		38,010 D	43.2%	56.8%	43.2%	56.8%
1966	227,080	150,517	Mundt, Karl E.*	76,563	Wright, Donn H.		73,954 R	66.3%	33.7%	66.3%	33.7%
1962	254,319	126,861	Bottum, Joe*	127,458	McGovern, George S.		597 D	49.9%	50.1%	49.9%	50.1%
1960	305,442	160,181	Mundt, Karl E.*	145,261	McGovern, George S.		14,920 R	52.4%	47.6%	52.4%	47.6%
1956	290,622	147,621	Case, Francis*	143,001	Holum, Kenneth		4,620 R	50.8%	49.2%	50.8%	49.2%
1954	235,745	135,071	Mundt, Karl E.*	100,674	Holum, Kenneth		34,397 R	57.3%	42.7%	57.3%	42.7%
1950	251,362	160,670	Case, Francis	90,692	Engel, John A.		69,978 R	63.9%	36.1%	63.9%	36.1%
1948	242,833	144,084	Mundt, Karl E.	98,749	Engel, John A.		45,335 R	59.3%	40.7%	59.3%	40.7%

Note: An asterisk (*) denotes incumbent. ** In past elections, the other vote included: 2014 - 47,741 Independent (Larry Pressler). The Democratic Party did not run a Senate candidate in the 2010 election.

SOUTH DAKOTA
GOVERNOR 2022

2020 Census Population	County	Total Vote	Republican (Noem)	Democratic (Smith)	Other	Rep.-Dem. Plurality		Percentage			
								Total Vote		Major Vote	
								Rep.	Dem.	Rep.	Dem.
2,749	AURORA	1,214	894	284	36	610	R	73.6%	23.4%	75.9%	24.1%
18,514	BEADLE	5,836	3,901	1,716	219	2,185	R	66.8%	29.4%	69.4%	30.6%
3,355	BENNETT	1,025	619	368	38	251	R	60.4%	35.9%	62.7%	37.3%
6,931	BON HOMME	2,562	1,858	650	54	1,208	R	72.5%	25.4%	74.1%	25.9%
35,117	BROOKINGS	12,427	6,974	5,096	357	1,878	R	56.1%	41.0%	57.8%	42.2%
38,874	BROWN	13,964	8,456	5,167	341	3,289	R	60.6%	37.0%	62.1%	37.9%
5,304	BRULE	2,109	1,463	589	57	874	R	69.4%	27.9%	71.3%	28.7%
1,955	BUFFALO	397	144	234	19	90	D	36.3%	58.9%	38.1%	61.9%
10,470	BUTTE	4,186	3,211	823	152	2,388	R	76.7%	19.7%	79.6%	20.4%
1,379	CAMPBELL	667	561	93	13	468	R	84.1%	13.9%	85.8%	14.2%
9,280	CHARLES MIX	3,091	2,187	849	55	1,338	R	70.8%	27.5%	72.0%	28.0%
3,742	CLARK	1,600	1,223	341	36	882	R	76.4%	21.3%	78.2%	21.8%
14,113	CLAY	4,745	2,054	2,581	110	527	D	43.3%	54.4%	44.3%	55.7%
27,993	CODINGTON	11,080	7,520	3,253	307	4,267	R	67.9%	29.4%	69.8%	30.2%
4,069	CORSON	928	522	379	27	143	R	56.2%	40.8%	57.9%	42.1%
9,000	CUSTER	5,077	3,633	1,293	151	2,340	R	71.6%	25.5%	73.8%	26.2%
19,760	DAVISON	7,239	4,887	2,179	173	2,708	R	67.5%	30.1%	69.2%	30.8%
5,437	DAY	2,521	1,599	876	46	723	R	63.4%	34.7%	64.6%	35.4%
4,353	DEUEL	1,991	1,479	458	54	1,021	R	74.3%	23.0%	76.4%	23.6%
5,882	DEWEY	1,574	662	862	50	200	D	42.1%	54.8%	43.4%	56.6%
2,926	DOUGLAS	1,484	1,272	188	24	1,084	R	85.7%	12.7%	87.1%	12.9%
3,825	EDMUNDS	1,701	1,321	346	34	975	R	77.7%	20.3%	79.2%	20.8%
6,750	FALL RIVER	3,668	2,679	859	130	1,820	R	73.0%	23.4%	75.7%	24.3%
2,301	FAULK	955	771	167	17	604	R	80.7%	17.5%	82.2%	17.8%
7,047	GRANT	3,215	2,328	830	57	1,498	R	72.4%	25.8%	73.7%	26.3%
4,198	GREGORY	2,054	1,618	393	43	1,225	R	78.8%	19.1%	80.5%	19.5%
1,903	HAAKON	987	892	82	13	810	R	90.4%	8.3%	91.6%	8.4%
6,185	HAMLIN	2,730	2,118	548	64	1,570	R	77.6%	20.1%	79.4%	20.6%
3,193	HAND	1,502	1,177	290	35	887	R	78.4%	19.3%	80.2%	19.8%
3,459	HANSON	1,632	1,267	336	29	931	R	77.6%	20.6%	79.0%	21.0%
1,301	HARDING	677	632	33	12	599	R	93.4%	4.9%	95.0%	5.0%
17,530	HUGHES	7,447	4,571	2,652	224	1,919	R	61.4%	35.6%	63.3%	36.7%
7,318	HUTCHINSON	3,174	2,507	604	63	1,903	R	79.0%	19.0%	80.6%	19.4%
1,304	HYDE	575	460	106	9	354	R	80.0%	18.4%	81.3%	18.7%
3,348	JACKSON	919	623	280	16	343	R	67.8%	30.5%	69.0%	31.0%
	JACKSON/WASHABAUGH	0	0	0	0	0		0.0%	0.0%	0.0%	0.0%
2,022	JERAULD	866	604	238	24	366	R	69.7%	27.5%	71.7%	28.3%
903	JONES	472	395	64	13	331	R	83.7%	13.6%	86.1%	13.9%
	KINGSBURG	0	0	0	0	0		0.0%	0.0%	0.0%	0.0%
4,939	KINGSBURY	2,551	1,792	692	67	1,100	R	70.2%	27.1%	72.1%	27.9%
12,843	LAKE	4,966	3,131	1,720	115	1,411	R	63.0%	34.6%	64.5%	35.5%
25,895	LAWRENCE	12,246	7,749	4,041	456	3,708	R	63.3%	33.0%	65.7%	34.3%
61,748	LINCOLN	28,161	16,828	10,727	606	6,101	R	59.8%	38.1%	61.1%	38.9%
3,752	LYMAN	1,318	879	405	34	474	R	66.7%	30.7%	68.5%	31.5%
4,974	MARSHALL	1,890	1,123	737	30	386	R	59.4%	39.0%	60.4%	39.6%
5,578	MCCOOK	2,547	1,851	625	71	1,226	R	72.7%	24.5%	74.8%	25.2%
2,387	MCPHERSON	1,100	911	167	22	744	R	82.8%	15.2%	84.5%	15.5%
28,509	MEADE	11,870	8,482	2,887	501	5,595	R	71.5%	24.3%	74.6%	25.4%
2,064	MELLETTE	630	386	214	30	172	R	61.3%	34.0%	64.3%	35.7%
2,225	MINER	1,007	732	248	27	484	R	72.7%	24.6%	74.7%	25.3%
194,180	MINNEHAHA	74,682	39,234	33,376	2,072	5,858	R	52.5%	44.7%	54.0%	46.0%
6,617	MOODY	2,649	1,668	910	71	758	R	63.0%	34.4%	64.7%	35.3%
14,118	OGLALA LAKOTA	2,480	221	2,172	87	1,951	D	8.9%	87.6%	9.2%	90.8%
114,285	PENNINGTON	45,388	27,586	16,215	1,587	11,371	R	60.8%	35.7%	63.0%	37.0%
2,858	PERKINS	1,372	1,142	177	53	965	R	83.2%	12.9%	86.6%	13.4%
2,153	POTTER	1,099	892	187	20	705	R	81.2%	17.0%	82.7%	17.3%
10,415	ROBERTS	3,565	2,164	1,315	86	849	R	60.7%	36.9%	62.2%	37.8%

SOUTH DAKOTA
GOVERNOR 2022

2020 Census Population	County	Total Vote	Republican (Noem)	Democratic (Smith)	Other	Rep.-Dem. Plurality	Total Vote Rep.	Total Vote Dem.	Major Vote Rep.	Major Vote Dem.
2,345	SANBORN	1,004	757	226	21	531 R	75.4%	22.5%	77.0%	23.0%
6,358	SPINK	2,670	1,832	765	73	1,067 R	68.6%	28.7%	70.5%	29.5%
3,110	STANLEY	1,447	999	407	41	592 R	69.0%	28.1%	71.1%	28.9%
1,392	SULLY	788	597	169	22	428 R	75.8%	21.4%	77.9%	22.1%
10,138	TODD	1,926	402	1,444	80	1,042 D	20.9%	75.0%	21.8%	78.2%
5,438	TRIPP	2,268	1,873	364	31	1,509 R	82.6%	16.0%	83.7%	16.3%
8,415	TURNER	3,865	2,834	919	112	1,915 R	73.3%	23.8%	75.5%	24.5%
16,018	UNION	6,740	4,723	1,848	169	2,875 R	70.1%	27.4%	71.9%	28.1%
5,470	WALWORTH	2,053	1,573	430	50	1,143 R	76.6%	20.9%	78.5%	21.5%
	WASHABAUGH	0	0	0	0	0	0.0%	0.0%	0.0%	0.0%
	WASHINGTON	0	0	0	0	0	0.0%	0.0%	0.0%	0.0%
22,885	YANKTON	8,910	5,247	3,350	313	1,897 R	58.9%	37.6%	61.0%	39.0%
2,755	ZIEBACH	683	345	304	34	41 R	50.5%	44.5%	53.2%	46.8%
887,654	TOTAL	350,166	217,035	123,148	9,983	93,887 R	62.0%	35.2%	63.8%	36.2%

SOUTH DAKOTA
SENATOR 2022

2020 Census Population	County	Total Vote	Republican (Thune)	Democratic (Bengs)	Other	Rep.-Dem. Plurality	Total Vote Rep.	Total Vote Dem.	Major Vote Rep.	Major Vote Dem.
2,749	AURORA	1,214	978	170	66	808 R	80.6%	14.0%	85.2%	14.8%
18,514	BEADLE	5,837	4,441	1,214	182	3,227 R	76.1%	20.8%	78.5%	21.5%
3,355	BENNETT	1,020	684	295	41	389 R	67.1%	28.9%	69.9%	30.1%
6,931	BON HOMME	2,554	2,010	453	91	1,557 R	78.7%	17.7%	81.6%	18.4%
35,117	BROOKINGS	12,351	7,990	3,816	545	4,174 R	64.7%	30.9%	67.7%	32.3%
38,874	BROWN	13,921	9,577	3,893	451	5,684 R	68.8%	28.0%	71.1%	28.9%
5,304	BRULE	2,098	1,573	428	97	1,145 R	75.0%	20.4%	78.6%	21.4%
1,955	BUFFALO	390	173	202	15	29 D	44.4%	51.8%	46.1%	53.9%
10,470	BUTTE	4,158	3,269	597	292	2,672 R	78.6%	14.4%	84.6%	15.4%
1,379	CAMPBELL	663	571	66	26	505 R	86.1%	10.0%	89.6%	10.4%
9,280	CHARLES MIX	3,089	2,323	666	100	1,657 R	75.2%	21.6%	77.7%	22.3%
3,742	CLARK	1,593	1,307	230	56	1,077 R	82.0%	14.4%	85.0%	15.0%
14,113	CLAY	4,713	2,522	2,042	149	480 R	53.5%	43.3%	55.3%	44.7%
27,993	CODINGTON	11,004	8,279	2,265	460	6,014 R	75.2%	20.6%	78.5%	21.5%
4,069	CORSON	925	534	334	57	200 R	57.7%	36.1%	61.5%	38.5%
9,000	CUSTER	5,040	3,756	1,017	267	2,739 R	74.5%	20.2%	78.7%	21.3%
19,760	DAVISON	7,210	5,420	1,524	266	3,896 R	75.2%	21.1%	78.1%	21.9%
5,437	DAY	2,514	1,796	602	116	1,194 R	71.4%	23.9%	74.9%	25.1%
4,353	DEUEL	1,986	1,548	346	92	1,202 R	77.9%	17.4%	81.7%	18.3%
5,882	DEWEY	1,560	770	720	70	50 R	49.4%	46.2%	51.7%	48.3%
2,926	DOUGLAS	1,467	1,308	117	42	1,191 R	89.2%	8.0%	91.8%	8.2%
3,825	EDMUNDS	1,687	1,385	253	49	1,132 R	82.1%	15.0%	84.6%	15.4%
6,750	FALL RIVER	3,641	2,754	665	222	2,089 R	75.6%	18.3%	80.5%	19.5%
2,301	FAULK	947	780	120	47	660 R	82.4%	12.7%	86.7%	13.3%
7,047	GRANT	3,198	2,492	601	105	1,891 R	77.9%	18.8%	80.6%	19.4%
4,198	GREGORY	2,024	1,663	279	82	1,384 R	82.2%	13.8%	85.6%	14.4%
1,903	HAAKON	970	864	56	50	808 R	89.1%	5.8%	93.9%	6.1%
6,185	HAMLIN	2,703	2,214	366	123	1,848 R	81.9%	13.5%	85.8%	14.2%
3,193	HAND	1,510	1,242	198	70	1,044 R	82.3%	13.1%	86.2%	13.8%
3,459	HANSON	1,629	1,323	254	52	1,069 R	81.2%	15.6%	83.9%	16.1%

SOUTH DAKOTA
SENATOR 2022

2020 Census Population	County	Total Vote	Republican (Thune)	Democratic (Bengs)	Other	Rep.-Dem. Plurality	Percentage Total Vote		Percentage Major Vote	
							Rep.	Dem.	Rep.	Dem.
1,301	HARDING	668	605	22	41	583 R	90.6%	3.3%	96.5%	3.5%
17,530	HUGHES	7,451	5,467	1,683	301	3,784 R	73.4%	22.6%	76.5%	23.5%
7,318	HUTCHINSON	3,142	2,619	417	106	2,202 R	83.4%	13.3%	86.3%	13.7%
1,304	HYDE	580	484	78	18	406 R	83.4%	13.4%	86.1%	13.9%
3,348	JACKSON	899	617	215	67	402 R	68.6%	23.9%	74.2%	25.8%
	JACKSON/WASHABAUGH	0	0	0	0	0	0.0%	0.0%	0.0%	0.0%
2,022	JERAULD	864	676	154	34	522 R	78.2%	17.8%	81.4%	18.6%
903	JONES	465	383	46	36	337 R	82.4%	9.9%	89.3%	10.7%
	KINGSBURG	0	0	0	0	0	0.0%	0.0%	0.0%	0.0%
4,939	KINGSBURY	2,530	2,000	441	89	1,559 R	79.1%	17.4%	81.9%	18.1%
12,843	LAKE	4,918	3,615	1,139	164	2,476 R	73.5%	23.2%	76.0%	24.0%
25,895	LAWRENCE	12,146	8,439	3,061	646	5,378 R	69.5%	25.2%	73.4%	26.6%
61,748	LINCOLN	27,980	19,703	7,365	912	12,338 R	70.4%	26.3%	72.8%	27.2%
3,752	LYMAN	1,299	944	290	65	654 R	72.7%	22.3%	76.5%	23.5%
4,974	MARSHALL	1,879	1,272	545	62	727 R	67.7%	29.0%	70.0%	30.0%
5,578	MCCOOK	2,533	2,033	408	92	1,625 R	80.3%	16.1%	83.3%	16.7%
2,387	MCPHERSON	1,102	954	108	40	846 R	86.6%	9.8%	89.8%	10.2%
28,509	MEADE	11,770	8,934	2,134	702	6,800 R	75.9%	18.1%	80.7%	19.3%
2,064	MELLETTE	624	415	165	44	250 R	66.5%	26.4%	71.6%	28.4%
2,225	MINER	1,004	813	161	30	652 R	81.0%	16.0%	83.5%	16.5%
194,180	MINNEHAHA	74,144	46,551	24,772	2,821	21,779 R	62.8%	33.4%	65.3%	34.7%
6,617	MOODY	2,642	1,839	694	109	1,145 R	69.6%	26.3%	72.6%	27.4%
14,118	OGLALA LAKOTA	2,440	422	1,889	129	1,467 D	17.3%	77.4%	18.3%	81.7%
114,285	PENNINGTON	45,153	30,398	12,441	2,314	17,957 R	67.3%	27.6%	71.0%	29.0%
2,858	PERKINS	1,369	1,141	133	95	1,008 R	83.3%	9.7%	89.6%	10.4%
2,153	POTTER	1,093	937	123	33	814 R	85.7%	11.3%	88.4%	11.6%
10,415	ROBERTS	3,531	2,384	1,000	147	1,384 R	67.5%	28.3%	70.4%	29.6%
2,345	SANBORN	1,002	821	154	27	667 R	81.9%	15.4%	84.2%	15.8%
6,358	SPINK	2,664	2,027	546	91	1,481 R	76.1%	20.5%	78.8%	21.2%
3,110	STANLEY	1,447	1,138	245	64	893 R	78.6%	16.9%	82.3%	17.7%
1,392	SULLY	783	622	114	47	508 R	79.4%	14.6%	84.5%	15.5%
10,138	TODD	1,911	502	1,308	101	806 D	26.3%	68.4%	27.7%	72.3%
5,438	TRIPP	2,237	1,861	263	113	1,598 R	83.2%	11.8%	87.6%	12.4%
8,415	TURNER	3,848	3,078	602	168	2,476 R	80.0%	15.6%	83.6%	16.4%
16,018	UNION	6,717	4,991	1,497	229	3,494 R	74.3%	22.3%	76.9%	23.1%
5,470	WALWORTH	2,038	1,645	301	92	1,344 R	80.7%	14.8%	84.5%	15.5%
	WASHABAUGH	0	0	0	0	0	0.0%	0.0%	0.0%	0.0%
	WASHINGTON	0	0	0	0	0	0.0%	0.0%	0.0%	0.0%
22,885	YANKTON	8,853	6,051	2,462	340	3,589 R	68.3%	27.8%	71.1%	28.9%
2,755	ZIEBACH	678	389	242	47	147 R	57.4%	35.7%	61.6%	38.4%
887,654	TOTAL	348,020	242,316	91,007	14,697	151,309 R	69.6%	26.1%	72.7%	27.3%

SOUTH DAKOTA

HOUSE OF REPRESENTATIVES

			Republican		Democratic		Other Vote	Rep.-Dem. Plurality	Total Vote %		Major Vote %	
CD	Year	Total Vote	Vote	Candidate	Vote	Candidate			Rep.	Dem.	Rep.	Dem.
At Large	2022	327,841	253,821	JOHNSON, DUSTY*			74,020	253,821 R	77.4%		100.0%	
At Large	2020	397,732	321,984	JOHNSON, DUSTY*			75,748	321,984 R	81.0%		100.0%	
At Large	2018	335,965	202,695	JOHNSON, DUSTY	121,033	BJORKMAN, TIMOTHY	12,237	81,662 R	60.3%	36.0%	62.6%	37.4%
At Large	2016	369,973	237,163	NOEM, KRISTI*	132,810	HAWKS, PAULA		104,353 R	64.1%	35.9%	64.1%	35.9%
At Large	2014	276,319	183,834	NOEM, KRISTI*	92,485	ROBINSON, CORINNA		91,349 R	66.5%	33.5%	66.5%	33.5%
At Large	2012	361,429	207,640	NOEM, KRISTI*	153,789	VARILEK, MATT		53,851 R	57.4%	42.6%	57.4%	42.6%
At Large	2010	319,426	153,703	NOEM, KRISTI	146,589	SANDLIN, STEPHANIE HERSETH*	19,134	7,114 R	48.1%	45.9%	51.2%	48.8%
At Large	2008	379,007	122,966	LIEN, CHRIS	256,041	SANDLIN, STEPHANIE HERSETH*		133,075 D	32.4%	67.6%	32.4%	67.6%
At Large	2006	333,562	97,864	WHALEN, BRUCE W.	230,468	SANDLIN, STEPHANIE HERSETH*	5,230	132,604 D	29.3%	69.1%	29.8%	70.2%
At Large	2004	389,468	178,823	DIEDRICH, LARRY W.	207,837	SANDLIN, STEPHANIE HERSETH*	2,808	29,014 D	45.9%	53.4%	46.2%	53.8%
At Large	2002	336,807	180,023	JANKLOW, WILLIAM J.	153,656	SANDLIN, STEPHANIE HERSETH	3,128	26,367 R	53.4%	45.6%	54.0%	46.0%
At Large	2000	314,761	231,083	THUNE, JOHN*	78,321	HOHN, CURT	5,357	152,762 R	73.4%	24.9%	74.7%	25.3%
At Large	1998	258,590	194,157	THUNE, JOHN*	64,433	MOSER, JEFF		129,724 R	75.1%	24.9%	75.1%	24.9%
At Large	1996	323,203	186,393	THUNE, JOHN	119,547	WEILAND, RICK	17,263	66,846 R	57.7%	37.0%	60.9%	39.1%
At Large	1994	305,922	112,054	BERKHOUT, JAN	183,036	JOHNSON, TIMOTHY P.*	10,832	70,982 D	36.6%	59.8%	38.0%	62.0%
At Large	1992	332,902	89,375	TIMMER, JOHN	230,070	JOHNSON, TIMOTHY P.*	13,457	140,695 D	26.8%	69.1%	28.0%	72.0%
At Large	1990	257,298	83,484	FRANKENFELD, DON	173,814	JOHNSON, TIMOTHY P.*		90,330 D	32.4%	67.6%	32.4%	67.6%
At Large	1988	311,916	88,157	VOLK, DAVID	223,759	JOHNSON, TIMOTHY P.*		135,602 D	28.3%	71.7%	28.3%	71.7%
At Large	1986	289,723	118,261	BELL, DALE	171,462	JOHNSON, TIMOTHY P.		53,201 D	40.8%	59.2%	40.8%	59.2%
At Large	1984	316,222	134,821	BELL, DALE	181,401	DASCHLE, THOMAS A.*		46,580 D	42.6%	57.4%	42.6%	57.4%
At Large	1982	275,652	133,530	ROBERTS, CLINT*	142,122	DASCHLE, THOMAS A.*		8,592 D	48.4%	51.6%	48.4%	51.6%

Note: An asterisk (*) denotes incumbent.

SOUTH DAKOTA

GENERAL AND PRIMARY ELECTIONS

GENERAL ELECTIONS: OTHER VOTES

Governor Other vote was 9,983 Libertarian (Tracey Quint)

Senate Other vote was 14,697 Libertarian (Tamara Lesnar)

House Other vote was:
  At Large 74,020 Libertarian (Collin Duprel)

2022 PRIMARY ELECTIONS: SUPPLEMENTARY INFORMATION

Primary	June 7, 2022	**Registration** (as of June 2, 2020 – includes 62,959 inactive registrants)	582,371	Republican	286,331
				Democratic	150,933
				Libertarian	2,651
				Other	1,380
				No Party Affiliation or Independent	141,076

Primary Type Republicans held a "closed" primary, with only registered Republicans allowed to vote in it. Democrats held a "semi-open" primary, with registered Democrats, Independents, and other voters not affiliated with a recognized political party eligible to cast a Democratic primary ballot.

SOUTH DAKOTA

GENERAL AND PRIMARY ELECTIONS

	REPUBLICAN PRIMARIES			DEMOCRATIC PRIMARIES	
Senator	Thune, John*	85,613	72.2%		
	Whalen, Bruce W.	24,071	20.3%		
	Mowry, Mark	8,827	7.4%		
	TOTAL	118,511			
Governor	Noem, Kristi*	91,661	76.4%	Smith, Jamie	Unopposed
	Haugaard, Steven	28,315	23.6%		
	TOTAL	119,976			
Congressional At Large	Johnson, Dusty*	70,728	59.2%		
	Howard, Taffy	48,645	40.8%		
	TOTAL	119,373			

Note: An asterisk (*) denotes incumbent.

TENNESSEE

Statewide Races

With neither of its Senate seats up in 2022, Tennessee's gubernatorial race was the foremost statewide contest on the ballot – and it was a boring one.

Republican Gov. Bill Lee first won his office in 2018, in a 60%–39% blowout. Four years later, as turnout dropped by over 20 percentage points, he expanded his margin to 65%–33%. Lee lost only the two most Democratic counties in the state, Nashville's Davidson and Memphis's Shelby, although there were some notable trends. As Lee upped his statewide margin by more than ten points, he lost Davidson County by roughly the same 30-point margin as he did in 2018, an indication of the county's increasing Democratic lean. In Shelby County, as turnout was better in the suburbs than in Memphis proper, Lee's share crept up from 37% to 43%. In 2018, Lee lost rural Haywood County, which is majority Black by composition, but carried it 51%–47% his second time around.

Though it is still heavily Republican, Williamson County, which is just south of Davidson and is the wealthiest county in the state, has seen some long-term pro-Democratic trends. In 2010, Republican Bill Haslam won the governorship by the same 32-point statewide margin as Lee did in 2022. Williamson County gave Haslam a crushing 80%–18% margin – a dozen years later, Lee carried it "only" 68%–31%.

House Races

Republicans have had a 7-2 advantage in Tennessee's nine-member delegation since the 2010 elections. After losing three traditionally blue rural districts in Obama's first midterm, Democrats were limited to Nashville's 5th District and Memphis's Black-majority 9th District. Though GOP legislators, who were drawing the maps after 2010, kicked around the idea of "cracking" the 5th District between the adjacent, Republican-held districts, they ultimately opted to keep the 7-2 arrangement.

But in 2022, Republicans were in a more aggressive mood. Davidson County, which was entirely confined to the 5th District under the old map, was split three ways. The numerical successor to the 5th District retained southern Davidson County, but also took in large swaths of several nearby counties. As Biden's share in the new 5th would have dropped from 62% to 43%, longtime Democratic Rep. Jim Cooper retired. Andy Ogles, a local official in exurban Maury County, won a crowded GOP primary and defeated Democratic state Sen. Heidi Campbell in the general election. Campbell got the same 43% that Biden would have earned in the district, carrying only its Davidson County portion.

The remainder of Davidson County was partitioned between Districts 6 and 7, which reelected their Republican incumbents in landslide margins. In the Memphis area, Republicans left District 9 largely intact – Democratic Rep. Steve Cohen, a white man who has represented this heavily Black seat since the 2006 elections, was reelected 70%–26%.

TENNESSEE
Congressional districts first established for elections held in 2022
9 members

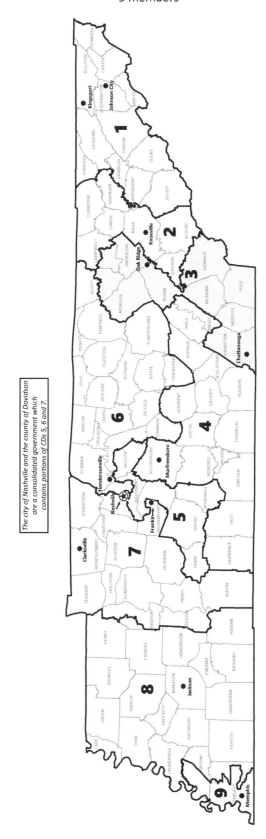

* Asterisk indicates a county whose boundaries include parts of two or more congressional districts.

TENNESSEE

GOVERNOR
Bill Lee (R). Reelected 2022 to a four-year term. Previously elected 2018.

SENATORS (2 Republicans)
Bill Hagerty (R). Elected 2020 to a six-year term.

Marsha Blackburn (R). Elected 2018 to a six-year term.

REPRESENTATIVES (8 Republicans, 1 Democrat)
1. Diana Harshbarger (R)
2. Tim Burchett (R)
3. Chuck Fleischmann (R)
4. Scott DesJarlais (R)
5. Andy Ogles (R)
6. John Rose (R)
7. Mark Green (R)
8. David Kustoff (R)
9. Steven I. Cohen (D)

POSTWAR VOTE FOR PRESIDENT

Year	Total Vote	Republican Vote	Republican Candidate	Democratic Vote	Democratic Candidate	Other Vote	Rep.-Dem. Plurality	Total Vote Rep.	Total Vote Dem.	Major Vote Rep.	Major Vote Dem.
2020	3,053,851	1,852,475	Trump, Donald J.*	1,143,711	Biden, Joseph R. Jr.	57,665	708,764 R	60.7%	37.5%	61.8%	38.2%
2016**	2,508,027	1,522,925	Trump, Donald J.	870,695	Clinton, Hillary Rodham	114,407	652,230 R	60.7%	34.7%	63.6%	36.4%
2012	2,458,577	1,462,330	Romney, W. Mitt	960,709	Obama, Barack H.*	35,538	501,621 R	59.5%	39.1%	60.4%	39.6%
2008	2,599,749	1,479,178	McCain, John S. III	1,087,437	Obama, Barack H.	33,134	391,741 R	56.9%	41.8%	57.6%	42.4%
2004	2,437,319	1,384,375	Bush, George W.*	1,036,477	Kerry, John F.	16,467	347,898 R	56.8%	42.5%	57.2%	42.8%
2000**	2,076,181	1,061,949	Bush, George W.	981,720	Gore, Albert Jr.	32,512	80,229 R	51.1%	47.3%	52.0%	48.0%
1996**	1,894,105	863,530	Dole, Robert "Bob"	909,146	Clinton, Bill*	121,429	45,616 D	45.6%	48.0%	48.7%	51.3%
1992**	1,982,638	841,300	Bush, George H.*	933,521	Clinton, Bill	207,817	92,221 D	42.4%	47.1%	47.4%	52.6%
1988	1,636,250	947,233	Bush, George H.	679,794	Dukakis, Michael S.	9,223	267,439 R	57.9%	41.5%	58.2%	41.8%
1984	1,711,994	990,212	Reagan, Ronald*	711,714	Mondale, Walter F.	10,068	278,498 R	57.8%	41.6%	58.2%	41.8%
1980**	1,617,616	787,761	Reagan, Ronald	783,051	Carter, Jimmy*	46,804	4,710 R	48.7%	48.4%	50.1%	49.9%
1976	1,476,345	633,969	Ford, Gerald R.*	825,879	Carter, Jimmy	16,497	191,910 D	42.9%	55.9%	43.4%	56.6%
1972	1,201,182	813,147	Nixon, Richard M.*	357,293	McGovern, George S.	30,742	455,854 R	67.7%	29.7%	69.5%	30.5%
1968**	1,248,617	472,592	Nixon, Richard M.	351,233	Humphrey, Hubert Horatio Jr.	424,792	121,359 R	37.8%	28.1%	57.4%	42.6%
1964	1,143,946	508,965	Goldwater, Barry M. Sr.	634,947	Johnson, Lyndon B.*	34	125,982 D	44.5%	55.5%	44.5%	55.5%
1960	1,051,792	556,577	Nixon, Richard M.	481,453	Kennedy, John F.	13,762	75,124 R	52.9%	45.8%	53.6%	46.4%
1956	939,404	462,288	Eisenhower, Dwight D.*	456,507	Stevenson, Adlai E. II	20,609	5,781 R	49.2%	48.6%	50.3%	49.7%
1952	892,553	446,147	Eisenhower, Dwight D.	443,710	Stevenson, Adlai E. II	2,696	2,437 R	50.0%	49.7%	50.1%	49.9%
1948**	550,283	202,914	Dewey, Thomas E.	270,402	Truman, Harry S.*	76,967	67,488 D	36.9%	49.1%	42.9%	57.1%

Note: An asterisk (*) denotes incumbent. **In past elections, the other vote included: 2016 - 70,397 Libertarian (Gary Johnson); 2000 - 19,781 Green (Ralph Nader); 1996 - 105,918 Reform (Ross Perot); 1992 - 199,968 Independent (Perot); 1980 - 35,991 Independent (John Anderson); 1968 - 424,792 American Independent (George Wallace), who finished second; 1948 - 73,815 States' Rights (Strom Thurmond).

TENNESSEE

POSTWAR VOTE FOR GOVERNOR

		Republican		Democratic		Other Vote	Rep.-Dem. Plurality	Total Vote		Major Vote	
Year	Total Vote	Vote	Candidate	Vote	Candidate			Rep.	Dem.	Rep.	Dem.
2022	1,739,882	1,129,390	Lee, Bill*	572,818	Martin, Jason Brantley	37,674	556,572 R	64.9%	32.9%	66.3%	33.7%
2018	2,243,294	1,336,106	Lee, Bill	864,863	Dean, Karl	42,325	471,243 R	59.6%	38.6%	60.7%	39.3%
2014	1,353,728	951,796	Haslam, Bill*	309,237	Brown, Charles V. "Charlie"	92,695	642,559 R	70.3%	22.8%	75.5%	24.5%
2010	1,601,549	1,041,545	Haslam, Bill	529,851	McWherter, Mike	30,153	511,694 R	65.0%	33.1%	66.3%	33.7%
2006	1,818,549	540,853	Bryson, Jim	1,247,491	Bredesen, Phil*	30,205	706,638 D	29.7%	68.6%	30.2%	69.8%
2002	1,653,167	786,803	Hilleary, Van	837,284	Bredesen, Phil	29,080	50,481 D	47.6%	50.6%	48.4%	51.6%
1998	976,236	669,973	Sundquist, Don*	287,750	Hooker, John Jay Jr.	18,513	382,223 R	68.6%	29.5%	70.0%	30.0%
1994	1,487,124	807,107	Sundquist, Don	664,243	Bredesen, Phil	15,774	142,864 R	54.3%	44.7%	54.9%	45.1%
1990	790,441	289,348	Henry, Dwight	480,885	McWherter, Ned*	20,208	191,537 D	36.6%	60.8%	37.6%	62.4%
1986	1,210,339	553,449	Dunn, Winfield	656,602	McWherter, Ned	288	103,153 D	45.7%	54.2%	45.7%	54.3%
1982	1,238,927	737,963	Alexander, Lamar*	500,937	Tyree, Randy	27	237,026 R	59.6%	40.4%	59.6%	40.4%
1978	1,189,695	661,959	Alexander, Lamar	523,495	Butcher, Jake	4,241	138,464 R	55.6%	44.0%	55.8%	44.2%
1974	1,040,714	455,467	Alexander, Lamar	576,833	Blanton, L. Ray	8,414	121,366 R	43.8%	55.4%	44.1%	55.9%
1970	1,108,247	575,777	Dunn, Winfield	509,521	Hooker, John Jay Jr.	22,949	66,256 R	52.0%	46.0%	53.1%	46.9%
1966	656,566			532,998	Ellington, Buford	123,568	532,998 D		81.2%		100.0%
1962**	620,758	99,884	Patty, Hubert D.	315,648	Clement, Frank G.	205,226	215,764 D	16.1%	50.8%	24.0%	76.0%
1958**	432,545	35,938	Wall, Thomas P.	248,874	Ellington, Buford	147,733	212,936 D	8.3%	57.5%	12.6%	87.4%
1954**	322,586			281,291	Clement, Frank G.*	41,295	281,291 D		87.2%		100.0%
1952	806,771	166,377	Witt, R. Beecher	640,290	Clement, Frank G.	104	473,913 D	20.6%	79.4%	20.6%	79.4%
1950**	236,194			184,437	Browning, Gordon*	51,757	184,437 D		78.1%		100.0%
1948	543,881	179,957	Acuff, Roy	363,903	Browning, Gordon	21	183,946 D	33.1%	66.9%	33.1%	66.9%
1946	229,456	73,222	Lowe, W. O.	149,937	McCord, James N.*	6,297	76,715 D	31.9%	65.3%	32.8%	67.2%

Note: An asterisk (*) denotes incumbent. **In past elections, the other vote included: 1962 - 203,765 Independent (William R. Anderson), who finished second; 1958 - 136,399 Independent (Jim Nance McCord), who finished second; 1954 - 39,574 Independent (John R. Neal), who finished second; 1950 - 51,757 Independent (Neal), who finished second. The Republican Party did not run a gubernatorial candidate in 1950, 1954, and 1966. The term of office of Tennessee's governor was increased from two to four years effective with the 1954 election.

POSTWAR VOTE FOR SENATOR

		Republican		Democratic		Other Vote	Rep.-Dem. Plurality	Total Vote		Major Vote	
Year	Total Vote	Vote	Candidate	Vote	Candidate			Rep.	Dem.	Rep.	Dem.
2020	2,959,761	1,840,926	Hagerty, Bill	1,040,691	Bradshaw, Marquita	78,144	800,235 R	62.2%	35.2%	63.9%	36.1%
2018	2,243,740	1,227,483	Blackburn, Marsha	985,450	Bredesen, Phil	30,807	242,033 R	54.7%	43.9%	55.5%	44.5%
2014	1,366,628	850,087	Alexander, Lamar*	437,848	Ball, Gordon	78,693	412,239 R	62.2%	32.0%	66.0%	34.0%
2012	2,321,477	1,506,443	Corker, Bob*	705,882	Clayton, Mark E.	109,152	800,561 R	64.9%	30.4%	68.1%	31.9%
2008	2,424,585	1,579,477	Alexander, Lamar*	767,236	Tuke, Robert D.	77,872	812,241 R	65.1%	31.6%	67.3%	32.7%
2006	1,833,695	929,911	Corker, Bob	879,976	Ford, Harold E. Jr.	23,808	49,935 R	50.7%	48.0%	51.4%	48.6%
2002	1,642,421	891,420	Alexander, Lamar	728,295	Clement, Robert Nelson	22,706	163,125 R	54.3%	44.3%	55.0%	45.0%
2000	1,928,613	1,255,444	Frist, William H.*	621,152	Clark, Jeff	52,017	634,292 R	65.1%	32.2%	66.9%	33.1%
1996	1,778,664	1,091,554	Thompson, Fred*	654,937	Houston, Gordon J.	32,173	436,617 R	61.4%	36.8%	62.5%	37.5%
1994	1,480,391	834,226	Frist, William H.	623,164	Sasser, James R.*	23,001	211,062 R	56.4%	42.1%	57.2%	42.8%
1994S**	1,465,862	885,998	Thompson, Fred	565,930	Cooper, Jim	13,934	320,068 R	60.4%	38.6%	61.0%	39.0%
1990	783,922	233,703	Hawkins, William R.	530,898	Gore, Albert Jr.*	19,321	297,195 D	29.8%	67.7%	30.6%	69.4%
1988	1,567,181	541,033	Anderson, Bill	1,020,061	Sasser, James R.*	6,087	479,028 D	34.5%	65.1%	34.7%	65.3%
1984	1,648,036	557,016	Ashe, Victor	1,000,607	Gore, Albert Jr.	90,413	443,591 D	33.8%	60.7%	35.8%	64.2%
1982	1,259,785	479,642	Beard, Robin L.	780,113	Sasser, James R.*	30	300,471 D	38.1%	61.9%	38.1%	61.9%
1978	1,157,094	642,644	Baker, Howard H. Jr.*	466,228	Eskind, Jane	48,222	176,416 R	55.5%	40.3%	58.0%	42.0%
1976	1,432,046	673,231	Brock, William E.*	751,180	Sasser, James R.	7,635	77,949 D	47.0%	52.5%	47.3%	52.7%
1972	1,164,195	716,539	Baker, Howard H. Jr.*	440,599	Blanton, L. Ray	7,057	275,940 R	61.5%	37.8%	61.9%	38.1%
1970	1,097,041	562,645	Brock, William E.	519,858	Gore, Albert Sr.*	14,538	42,787 R	51.3%	47.4%	52.0%	48.0%
1966	866,961	483,063	Baker, Howard H. Jr.	383,843	Clement, Frank G.	55	99,220 R	55.7%	44.3%	55.7%	44.3%
1964	1,064,018	493,475	Kuykendall, Daniel H.	570,542	Gore, Albert Sr.*	1	77,067 D	46.4%	53.6%	46.4%	53.6%
1964S**	1,091,093	517,330	Baker, Howard H. Jr.	568,905	Bass, Ross	4,858	51,575 D	47.4%	52.1%	47.6%	52.4%
1960	828,519	234,053	Frazier, A. Bradley	594,460	Kefauver, Estes*	6	360,407 D	28.2%	71.7%	28.2%	71.8%
1958	401,666	76,371	Atkins, Hobart F.	317,324	Gore, Albert Sr.*	7,971	240,953 D	19.0%	79.0%	19.4%	80.6%
1954	356,094	106,971	Wall, Tom	249,121	Kefauver, Estes*	2	142,150 D	30.0%	70.0%	30.0%	70.0%
1952	735,219	153,479	Atkins, Hobart F.	545,432	Gore, Albert Sr.	36,308	391,953 D	20.9%	74.2%	22.0%	78.0%
1948	499,138	166,947	Reece, B. Carroll	326,062	Kefauver, Estes	6,129	159,115 D	33.4%	65.3%	33.9%	66.1%
1946	218,713	57,237	Ladd, W. B.	145,654	McKellar, Kenneth D.*	15,822	88,417 D	26.2%	66.6%	28.2%	71.8%

Note: An asterisk (*) denotes incumbent. **One each of the 1964 and 1994 elections was for a short term to fill a vacancy.

TENNESSEE
GOVERNOR 2022

2020 Census Population	County	Total Vote	Republican (Lee)	Democratic (Martin)	Other	Rep.-Dem. Plurality	Percentage Total Vote Rep.	Dem.	Major Vote Rep.	Dem.
77,414	ANDERSON	21,280	14,003	6,832	445	7,171 R	65.8%	32.1%	67.2%	32.8%
49,949	BEDFORD	10,594	8,401	1,936	257	6,465 R	79.3%	18.3%	81.3%	18.7%
16,232	BENTON	4,103	3,247	756	100	2,491 R	79.1%	18.4%	81.1%	18.9%
15,092	BLEDSOE	3,408	2,933	418	57	2,515 R	86.1%	12.3%	87.5%	12.5%
133,854	BLOUNT	39,606	29,470	9,316	820	20,154 R	74.4%	23.5%	76.0%	24.0%
108,478	BRADLEY	25,198	20,655	4,096	447	16,559 R	82.0%	16.3%	83.5%	16.5%
39,864	CAMPBELL	7,550	6,188	1,197	165	4,991 R	82.0%	15.9%	83.8%	16.2%
14,792	CANNON	3,817	3,082	668	67	2,414 R	80.7%	17.5%	82.2%	17.8%
27,830	CARROLL	7,146	5,733	1,268	145	4,465 R	80.2%	17.7%	81.9%	18.1%
56,547	CARTER	14,484	11,602	2,575	307	9,027 R	80.1%	17.8%	81.8%	18.2%
40,761	CHEATHAM	11,658	8,309	3,138	211	5,171 R	71.3%	26.9%	72.6%	27.4%
17,376	CHESTER	4,496	3,756	622	118	3,134 R	83.5%	13.8%	85.8%	14.2%
32,064	CLAIBORNE	6,729	5,652	954	123	4,698 R	84.0%	14.2%	85.6%	14.4%
7,651	CLAY	1,813	1,451	307	55	1,144 R	80.0%	16.9%	82.5%	17.5%
36,168	COCKE	8,153	6,618	1,300	235	5,318 R	81.2%	15.9%	83.6%	16.4%
56,783	COFFEE	13,651	10,529	2,811	311	7,718 R	77.1%	20.6%	78.9%	21.1%
14,241	CROCKETT	3,322	2,734	539	49	2,195 R	82.3%	16.2%	83.5%	16.5%
60,916	CUMBERLAND	21,684	17,864	3,505	315	14,359 R	82.4%	16.2%	83.6%	16.4%
694,617	DAVIDSON	177,837	60,900	112,708	4,229	51,808 D	34.2%	63.4%	35.1%	64.9%
11,698	DECATUR	3,364	2,713	596	55	2,117 R	80.6%	17.7%	82.0%	18.0%
20,614	DEKALB	5,143	4,118	911	114	3,207 R	80.1%	17.7%	81.9%	18.1%
54,267	DICKSON	13,522	9,970	3,255	297	6,715 R	73.7%	24.1%	75.4%	24.6%
37,192	DYER	8,424	6,791	1,416	217	5,375 R	80.6%	16.8%	82.7%	17.3%
41,325	FAYETTE	14,314	10,868	3,212	234	7,656 R	75.9%	22.4%	77.2%	22.8%
18,613	FENTRESS	5,259	4,559	585	115	3,974 R	86.7%	11.1%	88.6%	11.4%
42,385	FRANKLIN	11,516	8,643	2,641	232	6,002 R	75.1%	22.9%	76.6%	23.4%
49,209	GIBSON	12,583	9,640	2,669	274	6,971 R	76.6%	21.2%	78.3%	21.7%
29,581	GILES	7,651	5,832	1,582	237	4,250 R	76.2%	20.7%	78.7%	21.3%
23,406	GRAINGER	5,380	4,588	706	86	3,882 R	85.3%	13.1%	86.7%	13.3%
69,253	GREENE	17,126	13,574	3,054	498	10,520 R	79.3%	17.8%	81.6%	18.4%
13,481	GRUNDY	3,384	2,735	538	111	2,197 R	80.8%	15.9%	83.6%	16.4%
65,103	HAMBLEN	13,106	10,335	2,492	279	7,843 R	78.9%	19.0%	80.6%	19.4%
369,150	HAMILTON	101,051	60,647	38,862	1,542	21,785 R	60.0%	38.5%	60.9%	39.1%
6,636	HANCOCK	1,312	1,110	165	37	945 R	84.6%	12.6%	87.1%	12.9%
25,022	HARDEMAN	5,586	3,486	1,983	117	1,503 R	62.4%	35.5%	63.7%	36.3%
25,752	HARDIN	6,524	5,606	812	106	4,794 R	85.9%	12.4%	87.3%	12.7%
56,894	HAWKINS	14,158	11,669	2,203	286	9,466 R	82.4%	15.6%	84.1%	15.9%
17,288	HAYWOOD	3,932	2,011	1,860	61	151 R	51.1%	47.3%	52.0%	48.0%
28,158	HENDERSON	6,484	5,551	822	111	4,729 R	85.6%	12.7%	87.1%	12.9%
32,457	HENRY	8,500	6,674	1,604	222	5,070 R	78.5%	18.9%	80.6%	19.4%
25,297	HICKMAN	5,811	4,577	1,128	106	3,449 R	78.8%	19.4%	80.2%	19.8%
8,246	HOUSTON	2,474	1,837	569	68	1,268 R	74.3%	23.0%	76.4%	23.6%
18,623	HUMPHREYS	4,481	3,344	1,024	113	2,320 R	74.6%	22.9%	76.6%	23.4%
11,826	JACKSON	3,186	2,415	637	134	1,778 R	75.8%	20.0%	79.1%	20.9%
54,772	JEFFERSON	13,255	10,806	2,107	342	8,699 R	81.5%	15.9%	83.7%	16.3%
17,837	JOHNSON	5,191	4,415	688	88	3,727 R	85.1%	13.3%	86.5%	13.5%
471,965	KNOX	128,242	76,880	49,140	2,222	27,740 R	59.9%	38.3%	61.0%	39.0%
7,147	LAKE	1,159	912	205	42	707 R	78.7%	17.7%	81.6%	18.4%
25,499	LAUDERDALE	4,793	3,346	1,321	126	2,025 R	69.8%	27.6%	71.7%	28.3%
44,353	LAWRENCE	10,097	8,276	1,549	272	6,727 R	82.0%	15.3%	84.2%	15.8%
12,332	LEWIS	3,400	2,723	613	64	2,110 R	80.1%	18.0%	81.6%	18.4%
34,465	LINCOLN	9,100	7,452	1,406	242	6,046 R	81.9%	15.5%	84.1%	15.9%
54,412	LOUDON	19,559	15,285	3,801	473	11,484 R	78.1%	19.4%	80.1%	19.9%
24,780	MACON	4,863	4,140	585	138	3,555 R	85.1%	12.0%	87.6%	12.4%
98,153	MADISON	24,082	15,357	8,246	479	7,111 R	63.8%	34.2%	65.1%	34.9%
29,043	MARION	7,700	5,947	1,610	143	4,337 R	77.2%	20.9%	78.7%	21.3%
34,599	MARSHALL	8,862	6,734	1,861	267	4,873 R	76.0%	21.0%	78.3%	21.7%
97,197	MAURY	30,718	22,198	7,910	610	14,288 R	72.3%	25.8%	73.7%	26.3%
53,988	MCMINN	12,908	10,371	1,858	679	8,513 R	80.3%	14.4%	84.8%	15.2%
25,740	MCNAIRY	7,060	5,864	1,036	160	4,828 R	83.1%	14.7%	85.0%	15.0%

TENNESSEE
GOVERNOR 2022

2020 Census Population	County	Total Vote	Republican (Lee)	Democratic (Martin)	Other	Rep.-Dem. Plurality	Total Vote Rep.	Total Vote Dem.	Major Vote Rep.	Major Vote Dem.
12,517	MEIGS	3,288	2,703	491	94	2,212 R	82.2%	14.9%	84.6%	15.4%
46,760	MONROE	11,853	9,830	1,748	275	8,082 R	82.9%	14.7%	84.9%	15.1%
210,495	MONTGOMERY	41,201	24,813	14,988	1,400	9,825 R	60.2%	36.4%	62.3%	37.7%
6,497	MOORE	2,070	1,725	302	43	1,423 R	83.3%	14.6%	85.1%	14.9%
21,456	MORGAN	4,578	3,844	624	110	3,220 R	84.0%	13.6%	86.0%	14.0%
30,090	OBION	7,767	6,418	1,173	176	5,245 R	82.6%	15.1%	84.5%	15.5%
22,347	OVERTON	6,125	4,805	1,147	173	3,658 R	78.4%	18.7%	80.7%	19.3%
8,120	PERRY	1,931	1,549	339	43	1,210 R	80.2%	17.6%	82.0%	18.0%
5,075	PICKETT	1,926	1,542	311	73	1,231 R	80.1%	16.1%	83.2%	16.8%
16,885	POLK	4,801	4,000	712	89	3,288 R	83.3%	14.8%	84.9%	15.1%
80,766	PUTNAM	19,628	14,217	4,875	536	9,342 R	72.4%	24.8%	74.5%	25.5%
33,353	RHEA	7,697	6,551	1,033	113	5,518 R	85.1%	13.4%	86.4%	13.6%
53,591	ROANE	15,780	11,871	3,337	572	8,534 R	75.2%	21.1%	78.1%	21.9%
72,075	ROBERTSON	18,514	14,066	4,048	400	10,018 R	76.0%	21.9%	77.7%	22.3%
335,013	RUTHERFORD	75,127	46,575	26,948	1,604	19,627 R	62.0%	35.9%	63.3%	36.7%
22,142	SCOTT	3,876	3,394	395	87	2,999 R	87.6%	10.2%	89.6%	10.4%
15,090	SEQUATCHIE	4,341	3,643	602	96	3,041 R	83.9%	13.9%	85.8%	14.2%
98,658	SEVIER	22,792	18,314	3,818	660	14,496 R	80.4%	16.8%	82.7%	17.3%
936,255	SHELBY	199,962	86,384	108,995	4,583	22,611 D	43.2%	54.5%	44.2%	55.8%
20,248	SMITH	5,288	4,205	927	156	3,278 R	79.5%	17.5%	81.9%	18.1%
13,769	STEWART	3,981	3,167	707	107	2,460 R	79.6%	17.8%	81.8%	18.2%
159,132	SULLIVAN	42,230	32,897	8,777	556	24,120 R	77.9%	20.8%	78.9%	21.1%
192,664	SUMNER	52,347	37,466	13,672	1,209	23,794 R	71.6%	26.1%	73.3%	26.7%
61,769	TIPTON	14,979	11,487	3,083	409	8,404 R	76.7%	20.6%	78.8%	21.2%
11,243	TROUSDALE	2,145	1,660	449	36	1,211 R	77.4%	20.9%	78.7%	21.3%
17,944	UNICOI	5,254	4,238	910	106	3,328 R	80.7%	17.3%	82.3%	17.7%
20,089	UNION	4,169	3,456	625	88	2,831 R	82.9%	15.0%	84.7%	15.3%
5,900	VAN BUREN	1,898	1,563	279	56	1,284 R	82.3%	14.7%	84.9%	15.1%
41,430	WARREN	8,857	6,668	1,963	226	4,705 R	75.3%	22.2%	77.3%	22.7%
129,815	WASHINGTON	35,047	24,330	10,046	671	14,284 R	69.4%	28.7%	70.8%	29.2%
16,711	WAYNE	3,573	3,094	398	81	2,696 R	86.6%	11.1%	88.6%	11.4%
33,341	WEAKLEY	8,129	6,417	1,489	223	4,928 R	78.9%	18.3%	81.2%	18.8%
27,519	WHITE	6,970	5,744	1,075	151	4,669 R	82.4%	15.4%	84.2%	15.8%
240,431	WILLIAMSON	85,417	58,132	26,116	1,169	32,016 R	68.1%	30.6%	69.0%	31.0%
145,878	WILSON	44,552	31,496	12,208	848	19,288 R	70.7%	27.4%	72.1%	27.9%
6,853,455	TOTAL	1,739,882	1,129,390	572,818	37,674	556,572 R	64.9%	32.9%	66.3%	33.7%

TENNESSEE
HOUSE OF REPRESENTATIVES

CD	Year	Total Vote	Republican Vote	Republican Candidate	Democratic Vote	Democratic Candidate	Other Vote	Rep.-Dem. Plurality	Total Vote Rep.	Total Vote Dem.	Major Vote Rep.	Major Vote Dem.
1	2022	188,003	147,241	HARSHBARGER, DIANA*	37,049	PARSONS, CAMERON	3,713	110,192 R	78.3%	19.7%	79.9%	20.1%
1	2020	305,423	228,181	HARSHBARGER, DIANA	68,617	WALSINGHAM, BLAIR NICOLE	8,625	159,564 R	74.7%	22.5%	76.9%	23.1%
1	2018	224,282	172,835	ROE, PHIL*	47,138	OLSEN, MARTIN	4,309	125,697 R	77.1%	21.0%	78.6%	21.4%
1	2016	253,025	198,293	ROE, PHIL*	39,024	BOHMS, ALAN	15,708	159,269 R	78.4%	15.4%	83.6%	16.4%
1	2014	139,470	115,533	ROE, PHIL*			23,937	115,533 R	82.8%		100.0%	
1	2012	239,672	182,252	ROE, PHIL*	47,663	WOODRUFF, ALAN	9,757	134,589 R	76.0%	19.9%	79.3%	20.7%
2	2022	207,762	141,089	BURCHETT, TIM*	66,673	HARMON, MARK		74,416 R	67.9%	32.1%	67.9%	32.1%
2	2020	353,197	238,907	BURCHETT, TIM*	109,684	HOYOS, RENEE	4,606	129,223 R	67.6%	31.1%	68.5%	31.5%
2	2018	262,134	172,856	BURCHETT, TIM	86,668	HOYOS, RENEE	2,610	86,188 R	65.9%	33.1%	66.6%	33.4%
2	2016	280,856	212,455	DUNCAN, JOHN J. JR.*	68,401	STARR, STUART		144,054 R	75.6%	24.4%	75.6%	24.4%
2	2014	166,751	120,883	DUNCAN, JOHN J. JR.*	37,612	SCOTT, BOB	8,256	83,271 R	72.5%	22.6%	76.3%	23.7%
2	2012	264,505	196,894	DUNCAN, JOHN J. JR.*	54,522	GOODALE, TROY	13,089	142,372 R	74.4%	20.6%	78.3%	21.7%

TENNESSEE

HOUSE OF REPRESENTATIVES

			Republican		Democratic		Other Vote	Rep.-Dem. Plurality	Percentage			
									Total Vote		Major Vote	
CD	Year	Total Vote	Vote	Candidate	Vote	Candidate			Rep.	Dem.	Rep.	Dem.
3	2022	199,830	136,639	FLEISCHMANN, CHUCK*	60,334	GORMAN, MEG	2,857	76,305 R	68.4%	30.2%	69.4%	30.6%
3	2020	320,299	215,571	FLEISCHMANN, CHUCK*	97,687	GORMAN, MEG	7,041	117,884 R	67.3%	30.5%	68.8%	31.2%
3	2018	245,765	156,512	FLEISCHMANN, CHUCK*	84,731	MITCHELL, DANIELLE	4,522	71,781 R	63.7%	34.5%	64.9%	35.1%
3	2016	266,006	176,613	FLEISCHMANN, CHUCK*	76,727	SHEKARI, MELODY	12,666	99,886 R	66.4%	28.8%	69.7%	30.3%
3	2014	156,097	97,344	FLEISCHMANN, CHUCK*	53,983	HEADRICK, MARY M.	4,770	43,361 R	62.4%	34.6%	64.3%	35.7%
3	2012	256,909	157,830	FLEISCHMANN, CHUCK*	91,094	HEADRICK, MARY M.	7,985	66,736 R	61.4%	35.5%	63.4%	36.6%
4	2022	173,437	122,401	DESJARLAIS, SCOTT*	44,648	STEELE, WAYNE	6,388	77,753 R	70.6%	25.7%	73.3%	26.7%
4	2020	335,710	223,802	DESJARLAIS, SCOTT*	111,908	HALE, CHRISTOPHER J.		111,894 R	66.7%	33.3%	66.7%	33.3%
4	2018	232,451	147,323	DESJARLAIS, SCOTT*	78,065	PHILLIPS, MARIAH	7,063	69,258 R	63.4%	33.6%	65.4%	34.6%
4	2016	254,937	165,796	DESJARLAIS, SCOTT*	89,141	REYNOLDS, STEVEN		76,655 R	65.0%	35.0%	65.0%	35.0%
4	2014	145,418	84,815	DESJARLAIS, SCOTT*	51,357	SHERRELL, LENDA	9,246	33,458 R	58.3%	35.3%	62.3%	37.7%
4	2012	230,590	128,568	DESJARLAIS, SCOTT*	102,022	STEWART, ERIC		26,546 R	55.8%	44.2%	55.8%	44.2%
5	2022	221,275	123,558	OGLES, ANDY	93,648	CAMPBELL, HEIDI	4,069	29,910 R	55.8%	42.3%	56.9%	43.1%
5	2020	252,169			252,155	COOPER, JIM*	14	252,155 D		100.0%		100.0%
5	2018	262,248	84,317	BALL, JODY	177,923	COOPER, JIM*	8	93,606 D	32.2%	67.8%	32.2%	67.8%
5	2016	273,544	102,433	SNYDER, STACY RIES	171,111	COOPER, JIM*		68,678 D	37.4%	62.6%	37.4%	62.6%
5	2014	154,276	55,078	RIES, BOB	96,148	COOPER, JIM*	3,050	41,070 D	35.7%	62.3%	36.4%	63.6%
5	2012	263,095	86,240	STAATS, BRAD	171,621	COOPER, JIM*	5,234	85,381 D	32.8%	65.2%	33.4%	66.6%
6	2022	195,063	129,388	ROSE, JOHN*	65,675	COOPER, RANDAL		63,713 R	66.3%	33.7%	66.3%	33.7%
6	2020	349,578	257,572	ROSE, JOHN*	83,852	FINLEY, CHRISTOPHER MARTIN	8,154	173,720 R	73.7%	24.0%	75.4%	24.6%
6	2018	248,740	172,810	ROSE, JOHN	70,370	BARLOW, DAWN	5,560	102,440 R	69.5%	28.3%	71.1%	28.9%
6	2016	284,490	202,234	BLACK, DIANE*	61,995	KENT, DAVID W.	20,261	140,239 R	71.1%	21.8%	76.5%	23.5%
6	2014	162,097	115,231	BLACK, DIANE*	37,232	POWERS, AMOS SCOTT	9,634	77,999 R	71.1%	23.0%	75.6%	24.4%
6	2012	241,241	184,383	BLACK, DIANE*			56,858	184,383 R	76.4%		100.0%	
7	2022	180,822	108,421	GREEN, MARK*	68,973	KELLY, ODESSA	3,428	39,448 R	60.0%	38.1%	61.1%	38.9%
7	2020	350,635	245,188	GREEN, MARK*	95,839	SREEPADA, KIRAN	9,608	149,349 R	69.9%	27.3%	71.9%	28.1%
7	2018	254,384	170,071	GREEN, MARK	81,661	KANEW, JUSTIN	2,652	88,410 R	66.9%	32.1%	67.6%	32.4%
7	2016	277,513	200,407	BLACKBURN, MARSHA*	65,226	CHANDLER, THARON	11,880	135,181 R	72.2%	23.5%	75.4%	24.6%
7	2014	157,907	110,534	BLACKBURN, MARSHA*	42,280	CRAMER, DANIEL N.	5,093	68,254 R	70.0%	26.8%	72.3%	27.7%
7	2012	257,306	182,730	BLACKBURN, MARSHA*	61,679	AMOUZOUVIK, CREDO	12,897	121,051 R	71.0%	24.0%	74.8%	25.2%
8	2022	210,315	155,602	KUSTOFF, DAVID*	51,102	WILLIAMS, LYNNETTE P.	3,611	104,500 R	74.0%	24.3%	75.3%	24.7%
8	2020	331,853	227,216	KUSTOFF, DAVID*	97,890	PEARSON, ERIKA STOTTS	6,747	129,326 R	68.5%	29.5%	69.9%	30.1%
8	2018	248,345	168,030	KUSTOFF, DAVID*	74,755	PEARSON, ERIKA STOTTS	5,560	93,275 R	67.7%	30.1%	69.2%	30.8%
8	2016	282,733	194,386	KUSTOFF, DAVID	70,925	HOBSON, RICKEY	17,422	123,461 R	68.8%	25.1%	73.3%	26.7%
8	2014	172,595	122,255	FINCHER, STEPHEN LEE*	42,433	BRADLEY, WES	7,907	79,822 R	70.8%	24.6%	74.2%	25.8%
8	2012	279,422	190,923	FINCHER, STEPHEN LEE*	79,490	DIXON, TIMOTHY	9,009	111,433 R	68.3%	28.4%	70.6%	29.4%
9	2022	133,918	35,123	BERGMANN, CHARLOTTE	93,800	COHEN, STEPHEN I.*	4,995	58,677 D	26.2%	70.0%	27.2%	72.8%
9	2020	242,880	48,818	BERGMANN, CHARLOTTE	187,905	COHEN, STEPHEN I.*	6,157	139,087 D	20.1%	77.4%	20.6%	79.4%
9	2018	181,476	34,901	BERGMANN, CHARLOTTE	145,139	COHEN, STEPHEN I.*	1,436	110,238 D	19.2%	80.0%	19.4%	80.6%
9	2016	217,957	41,123	ALBERSON, FLOYD WAYNE	171,631	COHEN, STEPHEN I.*	5,203	130,508 D	18.9%	78.7%	19.3%	80.7%
9	2014	116,550	27,173	BERGMANN, CHARLOTTE	87,376	COHEN, STEPHEN I.*	2,001	60,203 D	23.3%	75.0%	23.7%	76.3%
9	2012	250,987	59,742	FLINN, GEORGE S. JR.	188,422	COHEN, STEPHEN I.*	2,823	128,680 D	23.8%	75.1%	24.1%	75.9%
TOTAL	2022	1,710,425	1,099,462		581,902		29,061	517,560 R	64.3%	34.0%	65.4%	34.6%
TOTAL	2020	2,841,744	1,685,255		1,105,537		50,952	579,718 R	59.3%	38.9%	60.4%	39.6%
TOTAL	2018	2,159,825	1,279,655		846,450		33,720	433,205 R	59.2%	39.2%	60.2%	39.8%
TOTAL	2016	2,391,061	1,493,740		814,181		83,140	679,559 R	62.5%	34.1%	64.7%	35.3%
TOTAL	2014	1,371,161	848,846		448,421		73,894	400,425 R	61.9%	32.7%	65.4%	34.6%
TOTAL	2012	2,283,727	1,369,562		796,513		117,652	573,049 R	60.0%	34.9%	63.2%	36.8%

Note: An asterisk (*) denotes incumbent.

TENNESSEE

GENERAL AND PRIMARY ELECTIONS

GENERAL ELECTIONS: OTHER VOTES

Governor	Other vote was 15,395 Independent (John Gentry), 10,277 Independent (Constance Every), 3,772 Independent (Deborah Rouse), 2,380 Independent (Rick Tyler), 1,862 Independent (Charles Morgan), 1,568 Independent (Basil Marceaux), 1,216 Independent (Alfred O'Neil), 815 Independent (Michael Scantland), 389 Write-In (Write-Ins)
House	Other vote was:
CD 1	2,466 Republic (Richard Baker), 1,247 Independent (Matt Makrom)
CD 3	1,736 Independent (Rick Tyler), 1,121 Independent (Thomas Rumba)
CD 4	2,834 Independent (Mike Winton), 1,806 Independent (Clyde Benson), 708 Independent (David Jones), 585 Independent (Tharon Chandler), 455 Independent (Joseph Magyer)
CD 5	2,090 Independent (Derrick Brantley), 1,132 Independent (Daniel Cooper), 847 Independent (Rick Shannon)
CD 7	3,428 Independent (Steven Hooper)
CD 8	2,541 Independent (James Hart), 1,070 Independent (Ronnie Henley)
CD 9	3,349 Independent (George Flinn), 1,160 Independent (Dennis Clark), 485 Independent (Paul Cook)

2022 PRIMARY ELECTIONS: SUPPLEMENTARY INFORMATION

Primary	August 4, 2022	Registration (as of June 1, 2022 – includes 258,144 inactive registrants)	4,470,575	No Party Registration
Primary Type	Open—Any registered voter could participate in either the Democratic or the Republican primary but must declare affiliation with that party at the polls.			

	REPUBLICAN PRIMARIES			DEMOCRATIC PRIMARIES		
Governor	Lee, Bill*	494,362	100.0%	Martin, Jason Brantley	101,552	39.4%
				Smiley, JB Jr.	100,062	38.8%
				Atwater, Carnita Faye	56,227	21.8%
	TOTAL	494,362		TOTAL	257,841	
Congressional District 1	Harshbarger, Diana*	43,761	100.0%	Parsons, Cameron	6,099	100.0%
	TOTAL	43,761		TOTAL	6,099	
Congressional District 2	Burchett, Tim*	56,880	100.0%	Harmon, Mark	24,879	100.0%
	TOTAL	56,880		TOTAL	24,879	
Congressional District 3	Fleischmann, Chuck*	52,073	79.3%	Gorman, Meg	22,208	100.0%
	Casey, Sandy	13,609	20.7%			
	TOTAL	65,682		TOTAL	22,208	
Congressional District 4	DesJarlais, Scott*	60,699	100.0%	Steele, Wayne	11,168	65.1%
				White, Arnold J.	5,994	34.9%
	TOTAL	60,699		TOTAL	17,162	

TENNESSEE

GENERAL AND PRIMARY ELECTIONS

	REPUBLICAN PRIMARIES			DEMOCRATIC PRIMARIES		
Congressional District 5	Ogles, Andy	21,325	35.4%	Campbell, Heidi	30,830	100.0%
	Harwell, Beth	15,021	24.9%			
	Winstead, Kurt	12,721	21.1%			
	Beierlein, Jeff	4,093	6.8%			
	Newsom, Robert Starbuck (Write-In)	2,492	4.1%			
	Brooks, Natisha	1,747	2.9%			
	Batchelor, Geni	1,017	1.7%			
	Lee, Timothy Bruce	845	1.4%			
	Parks, Stewart Thomas	586	1.0%			
	Wittum, Tres	398	0.7%			
	TOTAL	*60,245*		*TOTAL*	*30,830*	
Congressional District 6	Rose, John*	57,162	100.0%	Cooper, Randal	17,332	74.7%
				Faircloth, Clay	5,870	25.3%
	TOTAL	*57,162*		*TOTAL*	*23,202*	
Congressional District 7	Green, Mark*	48,968	100.0%	Kelly, Odessa	24,854	100.0%
	TOTAL	*48,968*		*TOTAL*	*24,854*	
Congressional District 8	Kustoff, David*	69,538	83.7%	Williams, Lynnette P.	15,819	63.3%
	Hendry, Bob	6,990	8.4%	McDonald, Tim	9,187	36.7%
	Bridger, Danny Ray Jr.	4,233	5.1%			
	Clouse, Gary Dean	2,291	2.8%			
	TOTAL	*83,052*		*TOTAL*	*25,006*	
Congressional District 9	Bergmann, Charlotte	10,380	51.5%	Cohen, Stephen I.*	62,055	88.0%
	Dudley, Brown	8,760	43.5%	Williams, M. LaTroy	8,449	12.0%
	AwGoWhat, Leo	1,000	5.0%	Nelson, Ollie Oneal (Write-In)	2	
	TOTAL	*20,140*		*TOTAL*	*70,506*	

Note: An asterisk (*) denotes incumbent.

TEXAS

Statewide Races

The highest-profile statewide race in Texas during the 2022 cycle was its contest for governor – but it featured a candidate who built a national profile during a run for Senate. In 2018, then-Rep. Beto O'Rourke, an El Paso Democrat, gave Republican Sen. Ted Cruz, who was elected as an anti-establishment conservative, a serious challenge. Though O'Rourke lost, the 48% he took against Cruz represented the Democrats' most recent high-water mark in a state that has only elected Republicans to statewide office since 1998. O'Rourke went on to launch a short-lived presidential bid but then turned his efforts back to the Lone Star State, launching a 2022 bid for governor.

O'Rourke's problem, though, was that Republican Gov. Greg Abbott, who was seeking a third term, was not as polarizing as Cruz. In 2018, as O'Rourke held Cruz to a small win, Abbott won a second term by more than 13 points. O'Rourke blamed Abbott for the "Great Texas Freeze" – in February 2021, the state power grid failed amidst a winter storm – and criticized him on gun safety. But Abbott kept positive approval ratings and won 55%–44%.

Compared to his 2018 race with Cruz, O'Rourke lost ground in 252 of 254 counties, performing only a few ticks better in Ellis and Kaufman counties, two growing, red counties south of Dallas. Though heavily Hispanic South Texas leans Democratic, it continued to drift red. In 2018, O'Rourke's two best counties were Zavala and Starr, a pair of rural South Texas counties. Four years later, his best county was voter-rich Travis County (containing Austin, it was his third-best in 2018). Abbott carried Williamson (Round Rock) and Tarrant (Fort Worth) counties, which went for O'Rourke in 2018 and Joe Biden in 2020. The Houston area's GOP bastion, Montgomery County, performed for Abbott, giving him a margin of just over 100,000 votes.

House Races

With the state adding two seats in the 2020 census, Texas Republicans were mostly playing defense when they drew the new map. After the 2020 elections, Republicans had a 23–13 edge in the delegation – after the 2022 cycle, they held a slightly firmer 25–13 advantage.

With 36 existing seats, District 37 appeared as a deep blue seat in the Austin area while the inaugural version of the 38th District was a Republican-leaning Houston seat. Longtime Democrat Lloyd Doggett, who previously held the Austin-to-San Antonio 35th District, preferred to run in the Austin-only 37th. The 38th was tailor-made for Wesley Hunt, a Black Republican who ran against 7th District Rep. Lizzie Fletcher, a moderate Democrat, in 2020 but came up a few points short.

South Texas saw quite a bit of action in 2022. To start, Republicans picked up 15th District, which had been represented by a Democrat since its establishment, in 1902. In a member-on-member matchup, veteran Democrat Vicente Gonzalez beat Republican Mayra Flores, who won a summer 2022 special election, to represent the new 34th District. Finally, in TX-28, a Laredo-to-San Antonio seat, pro-life Blue Dog Henry Cuellar was forced into a primary runoff against a progressive but made it to the general election – he won by 14 points in a Biden +7 seat.

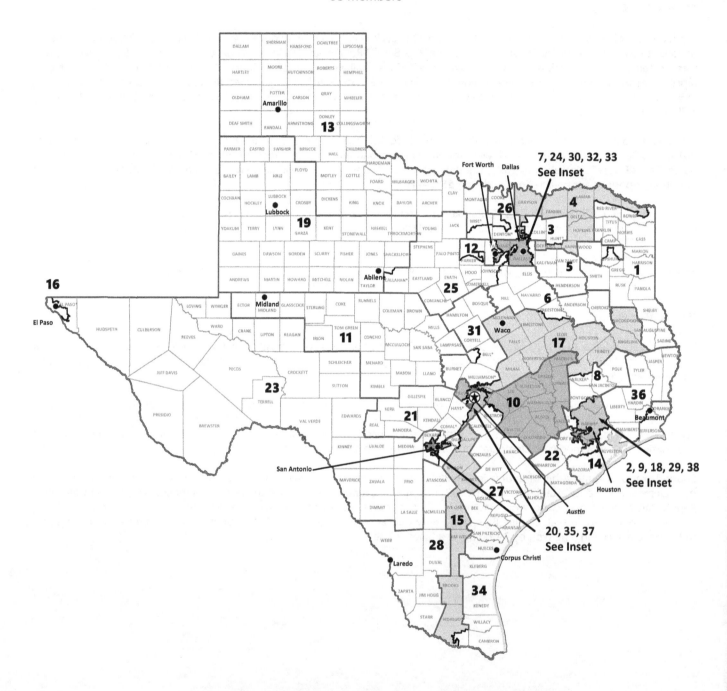

TEXAS
Congressional districts first established for elections held in 2022
38 members

* Asterisk indicates a county whose boundaries include parts of two or more congressional districts.

CDs 4, 10, 15, 17, 20, 35, and 37 are highlighted for visibility. See Insets for Dallas, Houston, Austin-San Antonio areas.

TEXAS

Greater Dallas-Fort Worth Area

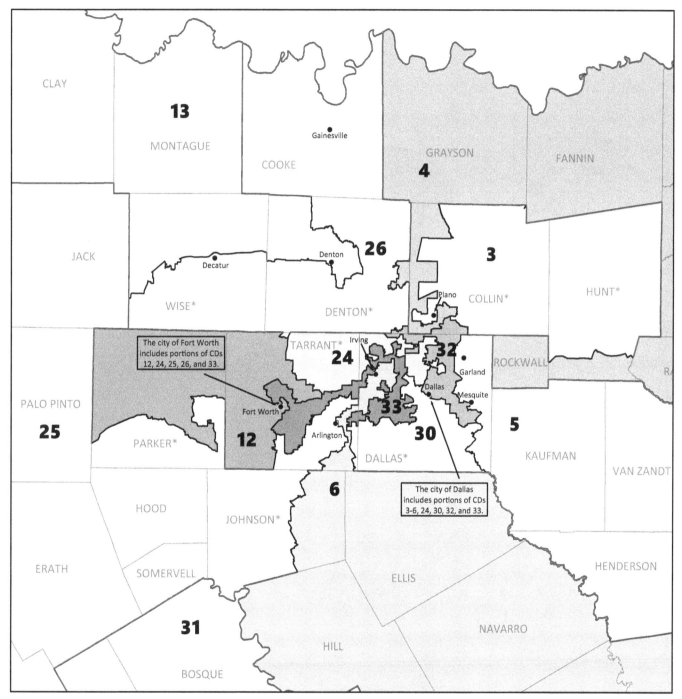

* Asterisk indicates a county whose boundaries include parts of two or more congressional districts.
CDs 4, 6, 12, 24, 32, and 33 are highlighted for visibility.

TEXAS
Greater Houston Area

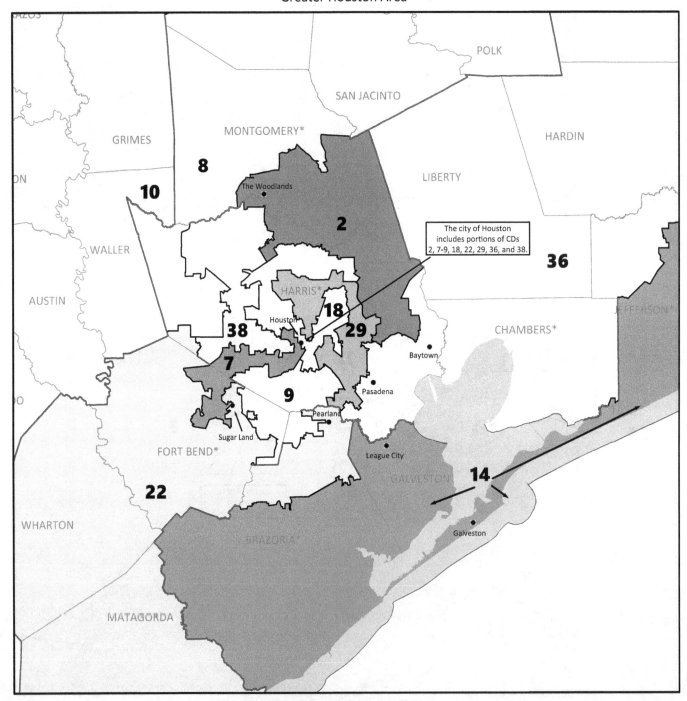

* Asterisk indicates a county whose boundaries include parts of two or more congressional districts.
CDs 2, 7, 14, and 29 are highlighted for visibility.

TEXAS
Greater San Antonio and Austin Areas

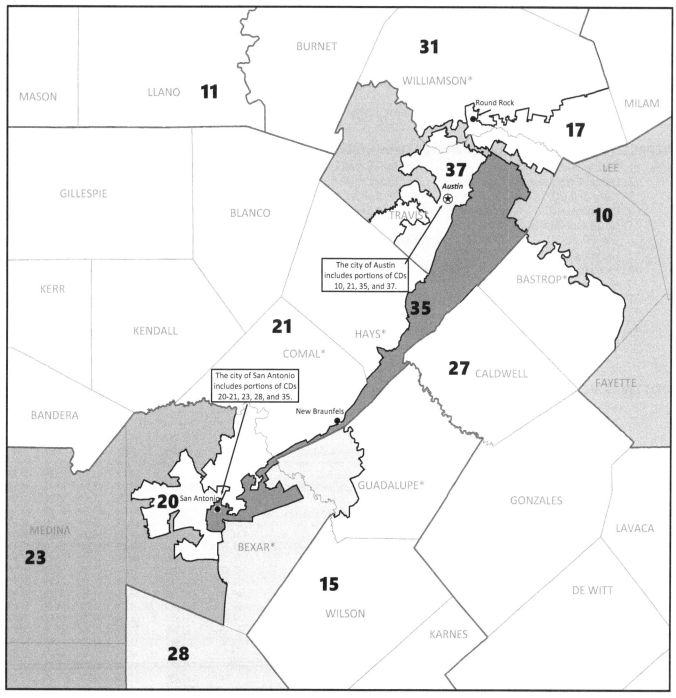

* Asterisk indicates a county whose boundaries include parts of two or more congressional districts.
CDs 10, 20, 23, 28, 35, and 37 are highlighted for visibility.

TEXAS

GOVERNOR
Greg Abbott (R). Reelected 2022 to a four-year term. Previously elected 2018, 2014.

SENATORS (2 Republicans)
John Cornyn (R). Reelected 2020 to a six-year term. Previously elected 2014, 2008, 2002.

Ted Cruz (R). Reelected 2018 to a six-year term. Previously elected 2012.

REPRESENTATIVES (25 Republicans, 13 Democrats)
1. Nathaniel Moran (R)
2. Daniel Crenshaw (R)
3. Keith Self (R)
4. Pat Fallon (R)
5. Lance Gooden (R)
6. Jake Ellzey (R)
7. Lizzie Pannill Fletcher (D)
8. Morgan Luttrell (R)
9. Al Green (D)
10. Michael McCaul (R)
11. August Pfluger (R)
12. Kay Granger (R)
13. Ronny Jackson (R)
14. Randy Weber (R)
15. Monica De La Cruz (R)
16. Veronica Escobar (D)
17. Pete Sessions (R)
18. Sheila Jackson Lee (D)
19. Jodey Arrington (R)
20. Joaquin Castro (D)
21. Chip Roy (R)
22. Troy Nehls (R)
23. Tony Gonzales (R)
24. Beth Van Duyne (R)
25. Roger Williams (R)
26. Michael C. Burgess (R)
27. Michael Cloud (R)
28. Henry Cuellar (D)
29. Sylvia R. Garcia (D)
30. Jasmine Crockett (D)
31. John Carter (R)
32. Colin Allred (D)
33. Marc Veasey (D)
34. Vicente Gonzalez Jr. (D)
35. Greg Casar (D)
36. Brian Babin (R)
37. Lloyd Doggett (D)
38. Wesley Hunt (R)

POSTWAR VOTE FOR PRESIDENT

Year	Total Vote	Republican Vote	Republican Candidate	Democratic Vote	Democratic Candidate	Other Vote	Rep.-Dem. Plurality		Total Vote Rep.	Total Vote Dem.	Major Vote Rep.	Major Vote Dem.
2020**	11,315,056	5,890,347	Trump, Donald J.*	5,259,126	Biden, Joseph R. Jr.	165,583	631,221	R	52.1%	46.5%	52.8%	47.2%
2016**	8,969,226	4,685,047	Trump, Donald J.	3,877,868	Clinton, Hillary Rodham	406,311	807,179	R	52.2%	43.2%	54.7%	45.3%
2012	7,993,851	4,569,843	Romney, W. Mitt	3,308,124	Obama, Barack H.*	115,884	1,261,719	R	57.2%	41.4%	58.0%	42.0%
2008	8,077,795	4,479,328	McCain, John S. III	3,528,633	Obama, Barack H.	69,834	950,695	R	55.5%	43.7%	55.9%	44.1%
2004	7,410,765	4,526,917	Bush, George W.*	2,832,704	Kerry, John F.	51,144	1,694,213	R	61.1%	38.2%	61.5%	38.5%
2000**	6,407,637	3,799,639	Bush, George W.	2,433,746	Gore, Albert Jr.	174,252	1,365,893	R	59.3%	38.0%	61.0%	39.0%
1996**	5,611,644	2,736,167	Dole, Robert "Bob"	2,459,683	Clinton, Bill*	415,794	276,484	R	48.8%	43.8%	52.7%	47.3%
1992**	6,154,018	2,496,071	Bush, George H.*	2,281,815	Clinton, Bill	1,376,132	214,256	R	40.6%	37.1%	52.2%	47.8%
1988	5,427,410	3,036,829	Bush, George H.	2,352,748	Dukakis, Michael S.	37,833	684,081	R	56.0%	43.3%	56.3%	43.7%
1984	5,397,571	3,433,428	Reagan, Ronald*	1,949,276	Mondale, Walter F.	14,867	1,484,152	R	63.6%	36.1%	63.8%	36.2%
1980**	4,541,636	2,510,705	Reagan, Ronald	1,881,147	Carter, Jimmy*	149,784	629,558	R	55.3%	41.4%	57.2%	42.8%
1976	4,071,884	1,953,300	Ford, Gerald R.*	2,082,319	Carter, Jimmy	36,265	129,019	D	48.0%	51.1%	48.4%	51.6%
1972	3,471,285	2,298,896	Nixon, Richard M.*	1,154,293	McGovern, George S.	18,096	1,144,603	R	66.2%	33.3%	66.6%	33.4%
1968**	3,079,216	1,227,844	Nixon, Richard M.	1,266,804	Humphrey, Hubert Horatio Jr.	584,568	38,960	D	39.9%	41.1%	49.2%	50.8%
1964	2,626,811	958,566	Goldwater, Barry M. Sr.	1,663,185	Johnson, Lyndon B.*	5,060	704,619	D	36.5%	63.3%	36.6%	63.4%
1960	2,311,084	1,121,310	Nixon, Richard M.	1,167,567	Kennedy, John F.	22,207	46,257	D	48.5%	50.5%	49.0%	51.0%
1956	1,955,168	1,080,619	Eisenhower, Dwight D.*	859,958	Stevenson, Adlai E. II	14,591	220,661	R	55.3%	44.0%	55.7%	44.3%
1952	2,075,946	1,102,878	Eisenhower, Dwight D.	969,228	Stevenson, Adlai E. II	3,840	133,650	R	53.1%	46.7%	53.2%	46.8%
1948**	1,249,577	303,467	Dewey, Thomas E.	824,235	Truman, Harry S.*	121,875	520,768	D	24.3%	66.0%	26.9%	73.1%

Note: An asterisk (*) denotes incumbent. **In past elections, the other vote included: 2020 - 126,423 Libertarian (Jo Jorgensen); 2016 - 283,492 Libertarian (Gary Johnson); 2000 - 137,994 Green (Ralph Nader); 1996 - 378,537 Reform (Ross Perot); 1992 -1,354,781 Independent (Perot); 1980 -111,613 Independent (John Anderson); 1968 - 584,269 American Independent (George Wallace); 1948 - 113,920 States' Rights (Strom Thurmond).

TEXAS

POSTWAR VOTE FOR GOVERNOR

Year	Total Vote	Republican Vote	Republican Candidate	Democratic Vote	Democratic Candidate	Other Vote	Rep.-Dem. Plurality	Total Vote % Rep.	Total Vote % Dem.	Major Vote % Rep.	Major Vote % Dem.
2022	8,102,908	4,437,099	Abbott, Greg*	3,553,656	O'Rourke, Beto	112,153	883,443 R	54.8%	43.9%	55.5%	44.5%
2018	8,343,443	4,656,196	Abbott, Greg*	3,546,615	Valdez, Lupe	140,632	1,109,581 R	55.8%	42.5%	56.8%	43.2%
2014	4,718,268	2,796,547	Abbott, Greg	1,835,596	Davis, Wendy R.	86,125	960,951 R	59.3%	38.9%	60.4%	39.6%
2010	4,979,870	2,737,481	Perry, Rick*	2,106,395	White, Bill	135,994	631,086 R	55.0%	42.3%	56.5%	43.5%
2006**	4,399,116	1,716,792	Perry, Rick*	1,310,337	Bell, Chris	1,371,987	406,455 R	39.0%	29.8%	56.7%	43.3%
2002	4,553,987	2,632,591	Perry, Rick*	1,819,798	Sanchez, Tony	101,598	812,793 R	57.8%	40.0%	59.1%	40.9%
1998	3,738,483	2,551,454	Bush, George W.*	1,165,444	Mauro, Garry	21,585	1,386,010 R	68.2%	31.2%	68.6%	31.4%
1994	4,396,242	2,350,994	Bush, George W.	2,016,928	Richards, Ann*	28,320	334,066 R	53.5%	45.9%	53.8%	46.2%
1990	3,892,487	1,826,231	Williams, Clayton	1,925,670	Richards, Ann	140,586	99,439 D	46.9%	49.5%	48.7%	51.3%
1986	3,441,460	1,813,779	Clements, William P.	1,584,515	White, Mark*	43,166	229,264 R	52.7%	46.0%	53.4%	46.6%
1982	3,191,091	1,465,937	Clements, William P.*	1,697,870	White, Mark	27,284	231,933 D	45.9%	53.2%	46.3%	53.7%
1978	2,369,764	1,183,839	Clements, William P.	1,166,979	Hill, John	18,946	16,860 R	50.0%	49.2%	50.4%	49.6%
1974**	1,654,957	514,725	Granberry, Jim	1,016,334	Briscoe, Dolph*	123,898	501,609 D	31.1%	61.4%	33.6%	66.4%
1972	3,410,071	1,534,060	Grover, Henry C.	1,633,913	Briscoe, Dolph	242,098	99,853 D	45.0%	47.9%	48.4%	51.6%
1970	2,235,855	1,037,723	Eggers, Paul W.	1,197,736	Smith, Preston*	396	160,013 D	46.4%	53.6%	46.4%	53.6%
1968	2,916,508	1,254,331	Eggers, Paul W.	1,662,019	Smith, Preston	158	407,688 D	43.0%	57.0%	43.0%	57.0%
1966	1,425,861	368,025	Kennerly, T. E.	1,037,517	Connally, John B.*	20,319	669,492 D	25.8%	72.8%	26.2%	73.8%
1964	2,544,753	661,675	Crichton, Jack	1,877,793	Connally, John B.*	5,285	1,216,118 D	26.0%	73.8%	26.1%	73.9%
1962	1,569,181	715,025	Cox, Jack	847,036	Connally, John B.	7,120	132,011 D	45.6%	54.0%	45.8%	54.2%
1960	2,250,718	612,963	Steger, William	1,637,755	Daniel, Price*		1,024,792 D	27.2%	72.8%	27.2%	72.8%
1958	789,133	94,098	Mayer, Edwin S.	695,035	Daniel, Price*		600,937 D	11.9%	88.1%	11.9%	88.1%
1956	1,826,242	271,088	Bryant, William R.	1,433,051	Daniel, Price	122,103	1,161,963 D	14.8%	78.5%	15.9%	84.1%
1954	636,892	66,154	Adams, Tod R.	569,533	Shivers, Allan*	1,205	503,379 D	10.4%	89.4%	10.4%	89.6%
1952	1,890,535			1,853,863	Shivers, Allan*	36,672	1,853,863 D		98.1%		100.0%
1950	407,138	39,793	Currie, Ralph W.	367,345	Shivers, Allan*		327,552 D	9.8%	90.2%	9.8%	90.2%
1948	1,208,860	177,399	Lane, Alvin H.	1,024,160	Jester, Beauford H.*	7,301	846,761 D	14.7%	84.7%	14.8%	85.2%
1946	378,784	33,277	Nolte, Eugene Jr.	345,507	Jester, Beauford H.		312,230 D	8.8%	91.2%	8.8%	91.2%

Note: An asterisk (*) denotes incumbent. **In past elections, the other vote included: 2006 - 796,851 Independent (Carole Keeton Strayhorn); 547,674 Independent (Richard "Kinky" Friedman). The term of office of Texas's governor was increased from two to four years effective with the 1974 election. The Republican Party did not run a candidate in the 1952 gubernatorial election.

TEXAS

POSTWAR VOTE FOR SENATOR

Year	Total Vote	Republican Vote	Republican Candidate	Democratic Vote	Democratic Candidate	Other Vote	Rep.-Dem. Plurality	Total Vote Rep. %	Total Vote Dem. %	Major Vote Rep. %	Major Vote Dem. %
2020	11,144,040	5,962,983	Cornyn, John*	4,888,764	Hegar, Mary "MJ"	292,293	1,074,219 R	53.5%	43.9%	54.9%	45.1%
2018	8,371,655	4,260,553	Cruz, Ted*	4,045,632	O'Rourke, Beto	65,470	214,921 R	50.9%	48.3%	51.3%	48.7%
2014	4,648,358	2,861,531	Cornyn, John*	1,597,387	Alameel, David	189,440	1,264,144 R	61.6%	34.4%	64.2%	35.8%
2012	7,864,822	4,440,137	Cruz, Ted	3,194,927	Sadler, Paul	229,758	1,245,210 R	56.5%	40.6%	58.2%	41.8%
2008	7,912,075	4,337,469	Cornyn, John*	3,389,365	Noriega, Richard J. "Rick"	185,241	948,104 R	54.8%	42.8%	56.1%	43.9%
2006	4,314,663	2,661,789	Hutchison, Kay Bailey*	1,555,202	Radnofsky, Barbara Ann	97,672	1,106,587 R	61.7%	36.0%	63.1%	36.9%
2002	4,514,012	2,496,243	Cornyn, John	1,955,758	Kirk, Ron	62,011	540,485 R	55.3%	43.3%	56.1%	43.9%
2000	6,276,652	4,082,091	Hutchison, Kay Bailey*	2,030,315	Kelly, Gene	164,246	2,051,776 R	65.0%	32.3%	66.8%	33.2%
1996	5,527,441	3,027,680	Gramm, W. Phil*	2,428,776	Morales, Victor M.	70,985	598,904 R	54.8%	43.9%	55.5%	44.5%
1994	4,279,940	2,604,218	Hutchison, Kay Bailey*	1,639,615	Mattox, Jim	36,107	964,603 R	60.8%	38.3%	61.4%	38.6%
1993S**	1,765,254	1,188,716	Hutchison, Kay Bailey	576,538	Krueger, Robert*		612,178 R	67.3%	32.7%	67.3%	32.7%
1990	3,822,157	2,302,357	Gramm, W. Phil*	1,429,986	Parmer, Hugh	89,814	872,371 R	60.2%	37.4%	61.7%	38.3%
1988	5,323,606	2,129,228	Boulter, E. Beau	3,149,806	Bentsen, Lloyd M. Jr.*	44,572	1,020,578 D	40.0%	59.2%	40.3%	59.7%
1984	5,319,178	3,116,348	Gramm, W. Phil	2,202,557	Doggett, Lloyd	273	913,791 R	58.6%	41.4%	58.6%	41.4%
1982	3,103,167	1,256,759	Collins, James M.	1,818,223	Bentsen, Lloyd M. Jr.*	28,185	561,464 D	40.5%	58.6%	40.9%	59.1%
1978	2,312,540	1,151,376	Tower, John G.*	1,139,149	Krueger, Robert	22,015	12,227 R	49.8%	49.3%	50.3%	49.7%
1976	3,874,516	1,636,370	Steelman, Alan	2,199,956	Bentsen, Lloyd M. Jr.*	38,190	563,586 D	42.2%	56.8%	42.7%	57.3%
1972	3,413,918	1,822,877	Tower, John G.*	1,511,985	Sanders, Barefoot	79,056	310,892 R	53.4%	44.3%	54.7%	45.3%
1970	2,231,671	1,035,794	Bush, George H.	1,194,069	Bentsen, Lloyd M. Jr.	1,808	158,275 D	46.4%	53.5%	46.5%	53.5%
1966	1,493,182	842,501	Tower, John G.*	643,855	Carr, Waggoner	6,826	198,646 R	56.4%	43.1%	56.7%	43.3%
1964	2,603,856	1,134,337	Bush, George H.	1,463,958	Yarborough, Ralph*	5,561	329,621 D	43.6%	56.2%	43.7%	56.3%
1961S**		448,217	Tower, John G.	437,874	Blakley, William A.*	886,091	10,343 R			50.6%	49.4%
1960	2,253,764	926,653	Tower, John G.	1,306,605	Johnson, Lyndon B.*	20,506	379,952 D	41.1%	58.0%	41.5%	58.5%
1958	787,128	185,926	Whittenburg, Roy	587,030	Yarborough, Ralph*	14,172	401,104 D	23.6%	74.6%	24.1%	75.9%
1957S**	874,899	219,591	Hutcheson, Thad	364,605	Yarborough, Ralph	290,803	655,408 R	25.1%	74.9%	25.1%	74.9%
1954	636,475	94,131	Watson, Carlos G.	539,319	Johnson, Lyndon B.*	3,025	445,188 D	14.8%	84.7%	14.9%	85.1%
1952**	1,894,671			1,894,671	Daniel, Price		1,894,671 D		100.0%		100.0%
1948	1,061,363	349,665	Porter, Jack	702,785	Johnson, Lyndon B.	8,913	353,120 D	32.9%	66.2%	33.2%	66.8%
1946	380,550	43,619	Sells, Murray C.	336,931	Connally, Tom T.*		293,312 D	11.5%	88.5%	11.5%	88.5%

Note: An asterisk (*) denotes incumbent. **The June 1993 election was for a short term to fill a vacancy; the vote above was for the special election runoff. The April 1957 and May 1961 elections were also for short terms to fill vacancies. Although neither vote was held with official party designations, the 1961 vote above reflected the result of a runoff between unofficial party candidates. In 1957 there was a single ballot without a runoff and Democrat Ralph Yarborough polled 364,605 votes (38.1% of the total vote) and won the election with a 73,802-vote plurality over Democrat Martin Dies, and the plurality listed takes into account the Democratic votes for both Yarborough and Dies. The Republican Party did not run a candidate in the 1952 Senate election.

TEXAS
GOVERNOR 2022

2020 Census Population	County	Total Vote	Republican (Abbott)	Democratic (O'Rourke)	Other	Rep.-Dem. Plurality	Percentage Total Vote Rep.	Dem.	Major Vote Rep.	Dem.
57,813	ANDERSON	14,445	11,762	2,545	138	9,217 R	81.4%	17.6%	82.2%	17.8%
18,868	ANDREWS	3,829	3,302	479	48	2,823 R	86.2%	12.5%	87.3%	12.7%
86,763	ANGELINA	24,595	19,142	5,174	279	13,968 R	77.8%	21.0%	78.7%	21.3%
23,511	ARANSAS	9,641	7,581	1,924	136	5,657 R	78.6%	20.0%	79.8%	20.2%
8,584	ARCHER	3,848	3,498	315	35	3,183 R	90.9%	8.2%	91.7%	8.3%
1,897	ARMSTRONG	903	833	60	10	773 R	92.2%	6.6%	93.3%	6.7%
51,470	ATASCOSA	12,699	8,801	3,709	189	5,092 R	69.3%	29.2%	70.4%	29.6%
30,128	AUSTIN	11,205	9,209	1,873	123	7,336 R	82.2%	16.7%	83.1%	16.9%
6,967	BAILEY	1,333	1,105	213	15	892 R	82.9%	16.0%	83.8%	16.2%
23,322	BANDERA	10,480	8,527	1,816	137	6,711 R	81.4%	17.3%	82.4%	17.6%
89,551	BASTROP	29,232	16,707	12,007	518	4,700 R	57.2%	41.1%	58.2%	41.8%
3,517	BAYLOR	1,307	1,183	105	19	1,078 R	90.5%	8.0%	91.8%	8.2%
32,602	BEE	6,408	4,347	1,976	85	2,371 R	67.8%	30.8%	68.7%	31.3%
364,726	BELL	87,936	51,888	34,785	1,263	17,103 R	59.0%	39.6%	59.9%	40.1%
2,012,291	BEXAR	540,768	221,993	311,023	7,752	89,030 D	41.1%	57.5%	41.6%	58.4%
12,068	BLANCO	6,774	5,142	1,522	110	3,620 R	75.9%	22.5%	77.2%	22.8%
652	BORDEN	317	306	9	2	297 R	96.5%	2.8%	97.1%	2.9%
18,834	BOSQUE	7,468	6,278	1,099	91	5,179 R	84.1%	14.7%	85.1%	14.9%
93,553	BOWIE	26,576	20,206	6,060	310	14,146 R	76.0%	22.8%	76.9%	23.1%
376,908	BRAZORIA	109,936	64,938	43,364	1,634	21,574 R	59.1%	39.4%	60.0%	40.0%
230,102	BRAZOS	59,954	35,768	23,103	1,083	12,665 R	59.7%	38.5%	60.8%	39.2%
9,198	BREWSTER	3,763	2,014	1,678	71	336 R	53.5%	44.6%	54.6%	45.4%
1,554	BRISCOE	592	539	49	4	490 R	91.0%	8.3%	91.7%	8.3%
7,088	BROOKS	2,008	785	1,204	19	419 D	39.1%	60.0%	39.5%	60.5%
38,006	BROWN	12,285	10,853	1,308	124	9,545 R	88.3%	10.6%	89.2%	10.8%
18,543	BURLESON	6,712	5,506	1,142	64	4,364 R	82.0%	17.0%	82.8%	17.2%
48,600	BURNET	21,111	16,505	4,337	269	12,168 R	78.2%	20.5%	79.2%	20.8%
43,937	CALDWELL	11,358	6,351	4,790	217	1,561 R	55.9%	42.2%	57.0%	43.0%
21,234	CALHOUN	5,592	4,228	1,292	72	2,936 R	75.6%	23.1%	76.6%	23.4%
13,986	CALLAHAN	5,266	4,770	444	52	4,326 R	90.6%	8.4%	91.5%	8.5%
423,584	CAMERON	77,095	34,290	41,667	1,138	7,377 D	44.5%	54.0%	45.1%	54.9%
13,143	CAMP	3,983	3,082	863	38	2,219 R	77.4%	21.7%	78.1%	21.9%
5,931	CARSON	2,394	2,177	183	34	1,994 R	90.9%	7.6%	92.2%	7.8%
30,125	CASS	9,969	8,415	1,460	94	6,955 R	84.4%	14.6%	85.2%	14.8%
7,517	CASTRO	1,493	1,226	239	28	987 R	82.1%	16.0%	83.7%	16.3%
44,310	CHAMBERS	15,736	12,964	2,559	213	10,405 R	82.4%	16.3%	83.5%	16.5%
52,835	CHEROKEE	14,483	12,023	2,323	137	9,700 R	83.0%	16.0%	83.8%	16.2%
7,283	CHILDRESS	1,751	1,562	162	27	1,400 R	89.2%	9.3%	90.6%	9.4%
10,498	CLAY	4,487	4,052	393	42	3,659 R	90.3%	8.8%	91.2%	8.8%
2,837	COCHRAN	616	506	95	15	411 R	82.1%	15.4%	84.2%	15.8%
3,412	COKE	1,389	1,260	114	15	1,146 R	90.7%	8.2%	91.7%	8.3%
8,179	COLEMAN	3,239	2,942	269	28	2,673 R	90.8%	8.3%	91.6%	8.4%
1,043,748	COLLIN	364,779	198,236	161,737	4,806	36,499 R	54.3%	44.3%	55.1%	44.9%
2,922	COLLINGSWORTH	925	845	75	5	770 R	91.4%	8.1%	91.8%	8.2%
21,499	COLORADO	7,546	6,084	1,395	67	4,689 R	80.6%	18.5%	81.3%	18.7%
158,871	COMAL	74,763	54,503	19,195	1,065	35,308 R	72.9%	25.7%	74.0%	26.0%
13,682	COMANCHE	4,826	4,203	567	56	3,636 R	87.1%	11.7%	88.1%	11.9%
3,004	CONCHO	943	818	109	16	709 R	86.7%	11.6%	88.2%	11.8%
41,487	COOKE	15,325	12,815	2,308	202	10,507 R	83.6%	15.1%	84.7%	15.3%
76,090	CORYELL	16,368	11,652	4,450	266	7,202 R	71.2%	27.2%	72.4%	27.6%
1,403	COTTLE	514	453	54	7	399 R	88.1%	10.5%	89.3%	10.7%
4,809	CRANE	1,147	983	150	14	833 R	85.7%	13.1%	86.8%	13.2%
3,468	CROCKETT	1,273	964	276	33	688 R	75.7%	21.7%	77.7%	22.3%
5,746	CROSBY	1,254	990	255	9	735 R	78.9%	20.3%	79.5%	20.5%
2,162	CULBERSON	736	391	328	17	63 R	53.1%	44.6%	54.4%	45.6%
7,197	DALLAM	1,050	958	78	14	880 R	91.2%	7.4%	92.5%	7.5%
2,634,796	DALLAS	625,391	224,684	392,634	8,073	167,950 D	35.9%	62.8%	36.4%	63.6%
12,720	DAWSON	2,516	2,088	402	26	1,686 R	83.0%	16.0%	83.9%	16.1%
20,212	DE WITT	6,061	5,151	878	32	4,273 R	85.0%	14.5%	85.4%	14.6%
18,503	DEAF SMITH	2,947	2,281	635	31	1,646 R	77.4%	21.5%	78.2%	21.8%

TEXAS
GOVERNOR 2022

2020 Census Population	County	Total Vote	Republican (Abbott)	Democratic (O'Rourke)	Other	Rep.-Dem. Plurality		Percentage			
								Total Vote		Major Vote	
								Rep.	Dem.	Rep.	Dem.
5,361	DELTA	2,027	1,711	295	21	1,416	R	84.4%	14.6%	85.3%	14.7%
896,053	DENTON	317,781	177,017	136,389	4,375	40,628	R	55.7%	42.9%	56.5%	43.5%
2,228	DICKENS	791	684	98	9	586	R	86.5%	12.4%	87.5%	12.5%
10,128	DIMMIT	2,876	1,080	1,757	39	677	D	37.6%	61.1%	38.1%	61.9%
3,272	DONLEY	1,192	1,084	97	11	987	R	90.9%	8.1%	91.8%	8.2%
11,169	DUVAL	3,676	1,600	2,018	58	418	D	43.5%	54.9%	44.2%	55.8%
18,418	EASTLAND	6,150	5,468	634	48	4,834	R	88.9%	10.3%	89.6%	10.4%
167,194	ECTOR	25,449	19,212	5,950	287	13,262	R	75.5%	23.4%	76.4%	23.6%
1,946	EDWARDS	814	712	99	3	613	R	87.5%	12.2%	87.8%	12.2%
840,417	EL PASO	165,446	57,573	105,156	2,717	47,583	D	34.8%	63.6%	35.4%	64.6%
186,805	ELLIS	67,770	45,564	21,338	868	24,226	R	67.2%	31.5%	68.1%	31.9%
43,006	ERATH	13,115	10,956	1,976	183	8,980	R	83.5%	15.1%	84.7%	15.3%
17,351	FALLS	4,703	3,480	1,168	55	2,312	R	74.0%	24.8%	74.9%	25.1%
35,799	FANNIN	11,665	9,694	1,831	140	7,863	R	83.1%	15.7%	84.1%	15.9%
25,471	FAYETTE	10,500	8,649	1,748	103	6,901	R	82.4%	16.6%	83.2%	16.8%
3,831	FISHER	1,401	1,172	210	19	962	R	83.7%	15.0%	84.8%	15.2%
5,712	FLOYD	1,467	1,250	201	16	1,049	R	85.2%	13.7%	86.1%	13.9%
1,157	FOARD	529	452	69	8	383	R	85.4%	13.0%	86.8%	13.2%
817,103	FORT BEND	250,066	117,249	129,116	3,701	11,867	D	46.9%	51.6%	47.6%	52.4%
10,734	FRANKLIN	3,917	3,369	512	36	2,857	R	86.0%	13.1%	86.8%	13.2%
19,763	FREESTONE	6,661	5,600	991	70	4,609	R	84.1%	14.9%	85.0%	15.0%
20,144	FRIO	3,728	1,872	1,791	65	81	R	50.2%	48.0%	51.1%	48.9%
21,555	GAINES	4,113	3,761	311	41	3,450	R	91.4%	7.6%	92.4%	7.6%
343,773	GALVESTON	110,734	68,822	40,229	1,683	28,593	R	62.2%	36.3%	63.1%	36.9%
6,304	GARZA	1,200	1,056	135	9	921	R	88.0%	11.2%	88.7%	11.3%
27,214	GILLESPIE	13,389	10,801	2,421	167	8,380	R	80.7%	18.1%	81.7%	18.3%
1,407	GLASSCOCK	572	542	27	3	515	R	94.8%	4.7%	95.3%	4.7%
7,685	GOLIAD	3,366	2,664	663	39	2,001	R	79.1%	19.7%	80.1%	19.9%
20,902	GONZALES	5,566	4,369	1,129	68	3,240	R	78.5%	20.3%	79.5%	20.5%
21,802	GRAY	5,558	5,013	478	67	4,535	R	90.2%	8.6%	91.3%	8.7%
137,247	GRAYSON	44,991	34,903	9,563	525	25,340	R	77.6%	21.3%	78.5%	21.5%
124,356	GREGG	33,215	24,223	8,662	330	15,561	R	72.9%	26.1%	73.7%	26.3%
29,086	GRIMES	9,432	7,607	1,732	93	5,875	R	80.7%	18.4%	81.5%	18.5%
168,350	GUADALUPE	57,202	36,882	19,356	964	17,526	R	64.5%	33.8%	65.6%	34.4%
33,419	HALE	6,329	5,094	1,165	70	3,929	R	80.5%	18.4%	81.4%	18.6%
2,963	HALL	877	772	94	11	678	R	88.0%	10.7%	89.1%	10.9%
8,508	HAMILTON	3,476	3,006	433	37	2,573	R	86.5%	12.5%	87.4%	12.6%
5,365	HANSFORD	1,522	1,419	91	12	1,328	R	93.2%	6.0%	94.0%	6.0%
3,931	HARDEMAN	985	866	114	5	752	R	87.9%	11.6%	88.4%	11.6%
57,817	HARDIN	19,629	17,447	2,035	147	15,412	R	88.9%	10.4%	89.6%	10.4%
4,713,171	HARRIS	1,102,418	490,261	595,653	16,504	105,392	D	44.5%	54.0%	45.1%	54.9%
66,694	HARRISON	21,356	16,472	4,688	196	11,784	R	77.1%	22.0%	77.8%	22.2%
5,552	HARTLEY	1,574	1,463	96	15	1,367	R	92.9%	6.1%	93.8%	6.2%
5,685	HASKELL	1,670	1,465	191	14	1,274	R	87.7%	11.4%	88.5%	11.5%
232,894	HAYS	89,683	39,085	48,970	1,628	9,885	D	43.6%	54.6%	44.4%	55.6%
3,790	HEMPHILL	1,361	1,198	138	25	1,060	R	88.0%	10.1%	89.7%	10.3%
83,294	HENDERSON	28,002	22,909	4,798	295	18,111	R	81.8%	17.1%	82.7%	17.3%
871,085	HIDALGO	141,196	56,783	82,671	1,742	25,888	D	40.2%	58.6%	40.7%	59.3%
36,944	HILL	11,385	9,418	1,830	137	7,588	R	82.7%	16.1%	83.7%	16.3%
23,041	HOCKLEY	5,531	4,690	786	55	3,904	R	84.8%	14.2%	85.6%	14.4%
62,512	HOOD	27,228	22,596	4,301	331	18,295	R	83.0%	15.8%	84.0%	16.0%
37,263	HOPKINS	12,351	10,223	1,999	129	8,224	R	82.8%	16.2%	83.6%	16.4%
23,045	HOUSTON	7,184	5,726	1,399	59	4,327	R	79.7%	19.5%	80.4%	19.6%
36,898	HOWARD	6,568	5,367	1,077	124	4,290	R	81.7%	16.4%	83.3%	16.7%
4,924	HUDSPETH	906	606	270	30	336	R	66.9%	29.8%	69.2%	30.8%
99,424	HUNT	30,540	23,744	6,422	374	17,322	R	77.7%	21.0%	78.7%	21.3%
20,908	HUTCHINSON	6,062	5,437	540	85	4,897	R	89.7%	8.9%	91.0%	9.0%
1,540	IRION	695	618	70	7	548	R	88.9%	10.1%	89.8%	10.2%
8,969	JACK	2,993	2,744	227	22	2,517	R	91.7%	7.6%	92.4%	7.6%
14,764	JACKSON	4,597	4,013	550	34	3,463	R	87.3%	12.0%	87.9%	12.1%

TEXAS
GOVERNOR 2022

2020 Census Population	County	Total Vote	Republican (Abbott)	Democratic (O'Rourke)	Other	Rep.-Dem. Plurality	Percentage Total Vote		Major Vote	
							Rep.	Dem.	Rep.	Dem.
35,651	JASPER	11,379	9,701	1,601	77	8,100 R	85.3%	14.1%	85.8%	14.2%
2,286	JEFF DAVIS	1,050	641	374	35	267 R	61.0%	35.6%	63.2%	36.8%
251,379	JEFFERSON	62,451	34,988	26,641	822	8,347 R	56.0%	42.7%	56.8%	43.2%
5,205	JIM HOGG	1,542	650	876	16	226 D	42.2%	56.8%	42.6%	57.4%
40,429	JIM WELLS	9,543	5,063	4,375	105	688 R	53.1%	45.8%	53.6%	46.4%
177,419	JOHNSON	55,864	42,954	12,266	644	30,688 R	76.9%	22.0%	77.8%	22.2%
20,144	JONES	4,992	4,349	581	62	3,768 R	87.1%	11.6%	88.2%	11.8%
15,560	KARNES	3,818	3,007	776	35	2,231 R	78.8%	20.3%	79.5%	20.5%
138,350	KAUFMAN	42,831	28,306	14,024	501	14,282 R	66.1%	32.7%	66.9%	33.1%
48,115	KENDALL	22,557	17,719	4,506	332	13,213 R	78.6%	20.0%	79.7%	20.3%
398	KENEDY	153	109	42	2	67 R	71.2%	27.5%	72.2%	27.8%
765	KENT	350	312	34	4	278 R	89.1%	9.7%	90.2%	9.8%
52,872	KERR	22,480	17,524	4,648	308	12,876 R	78.0%	20.7%	79.0%	21.0%
4,347	KIMBLE	1,876	1,666	188	22	1,478 R	88.8%	10.0%	89.9%	10.1%
270	KING	103	100	3		97 R	97.1%	2.9%	97.1%	2.9%
3,682	KINNEY	1,194	907	258	29	649 R	76.0%	21.6%	77.9%	22.1%
30,790	KLEBERG	7,629	4,074	3,463	92	611 R	53.4%	45.4%	54.1%	45.9%
3,664	KNOX	1,040	889	140	11	749 R	85.5%	13.5%	86.4%	13.6%
7,522	LA SALLE	1,437	761	662	14	99 R	53.0%	46.1%	53.5%	46.5%
49,972	LAMAR	15,342	12,521	2,657	164	9,864 R	81.6%	17.3%	82.5%	17.5%
12,890	LAMB	3,080	2,628	419	33	2,209 R	85.3%	13.6%	86.2%	13.8%
21,604	LAMPASAS	8,251	6,625	1,502	124	5,123 R	80.3%	18.2%	81.5%	18.5%
20,209	LAVACA	8,209	7,380	759	70	6,621 R	89.9%	9.2%	90.7%	9.3%
17,289	LEE	6,282	5,108	1,095	79	4,013 R	81.3%	17.4%	82.3%	17.7%
17,467	LEON	6,863	6,082	698	83	5,384 R	88.6%	10.2%	89.7%	10.3%
89,195	LIBERTY	19,791	16,080	3,488	223	12,592 R	81.2%	17.6%	82.2%	17.8%
23,516	LIMESTONE	6,851	5,390	1,366	95	4,024 R	78.7%	19.9%	79.8%	20.2%
3,215	LIPSCOMB	977	894	69	14	825 R	91.5%	7.1%	92.8%	7.2%
12,226	LIVE OAK	4,000	3,424	545	31	2,879 R	85.6%	13.6%	86.3%	13.7%
22,001	LLANO	11,029	8,977	1,920	132	7,057 R	81.4%	17.4%	82.4%	17.6%
175	LOVING	79	70	6	3	64 R	88.6%	7.6%	92.1%	7.9%
311,645	LUBBOCK	83,768	58,163	24,497	1,108	33,666 R	69.4%	29.2%	70.4%	29.6%
5,978	LYNN	1,727	1,502	196	29	1,306 R	87.0%	11.3%	88.5%	11.5%
14,328	MADISON	3,907	3,272	595	40	2,677 R	83.7%	15.2%	84.6%	15.4%
9,867	MARION	3,302	2,557	700	45	1,857 R	77.4%	21.2%	78.5%	21.5%
5,835	MARTIN	1,508	1,341	149	18	1,192 R	88.9%	9.9%	90.0%	10.0%
4,304	MASON	1,991	1,703	268	20	1,435 R	85.5%	13.5%	86.4%	13.6%
36,607	MATAGORDA	9,721	7,350	2,273	98	5,077 R	75.6%	23.4%	76.4%	23.6%
58,732	MAVERICK	9,583	3,862	5,555	166	1,693 D	40.3%	58.0%	41.0%	59.0%
7,999	MCCULLOCH	2,563	2,221	314	28	1,907 R	86.7%	12.3%	87.6%	12.4%
257,693	MCLENNAN	72,590	47,875	23,765	950	24,110 R	66.0%	32.7%	66.8%	33.2%
743	MCMULLEN	372	343	28	1	315 R	92.2%	7.5%	92.5%	7.5%
51,848	MEDINA	17,366	12,601	4,591	174	8,010 R	72.6%	26.4%	73.3%	26.7%
2,154	MENARD	775	659	110	6	549 R	85.0%	14.2%	85.7%	14.3%
178,043	MIDLAND	40,053	32,389	7,154	510	25,235 R	80.9%	17.9%	81.9%	18.1%
24,933	MILAM	8,358	6,717	1,559	82	5,158 R	80.4%	18.7%	81.2%	18.8%
4,898	MILLS	2,121	1,894	198	29	1,696 R	89.3%	9.3%	90.5%	9.5%
8,476	MITCHELL	1,781	1,576	185	20	1,391 R	88.5%	10.4%	89.5%	10.5%
19,934	MONTAGUE	7,852	7,004	765	83	6,239 R	89.2%	9.7%	90.2%	9.8%
613,316	MONTGOMERY	208,055	152,694	52,654	2,707	100,040 R	73.4%	25.3%	74.4%	25.6%
20,973	MOORE	3,603	3,081	479	43	2,602 R	85.5%	13.3%	86.5%	13.5%
12,438	MORRIS	3,996	3,041	921	34	2,120 R	76.1%	23.0%	76.8%	23.2%
1,203	MOTLEY	504	482	18	4	464 R	95.6%	3.6%	96.4%	3.6%
65,356	NACOGDOCHES	18,950	13,248	5,480	222	7,768 R	69.9%	28.9%	70.7%	29.3%
50,352	NAVARRO	14,133	10,830	3,157	146	7,673 R	76.6%	22.3%	77.4%	22.6%
13,577	NEWTON	4,373	3,660	689	24	2,971 R	83.7%	15.8%	84.2%	15.8%
14,671	NOLAN	3,803	3,093	647	63	2,446 R	81.3%	17.0%	82.7%	17.3%
362,464	NUECES	89,301	47,567	40,474	1,260	7,093 R	53.3%	45.3%	54.0%	46.0%
9,806	OCHILTREE	2,126	1,975	135	16	1,840 R	92.9%	6.3%	93.6%	6.4%
2,120	OLDHAM	770	710	50	10	660 R	92.2%	6.5%	93.4%	6.6%

TEXAS
GOVERNOR 2022

2020 Census Population	County	Total Vote	Republican (Abbott)	Democratic (O'Rourke)	Other	Rep.-Dem. Plurality	Percentage Total Vote Rep.	Dem.	Major Vote Rep.	Dem.
83,406	ORANGE	25,099	21,153	3,722	224	17,431 R	84.3%	14.8%	85.0%	15.0%
29,306	PALO PINTO	9,489	7,896	1,486	107	6,410 R	83.2%	15.7%	84.2%	15.8%
23,217	PANOLA	8,313	7,039	1,213	61	5,826 R	84.7%	14.6%	85.3%	14.7%
144,637	PARKER	63,437	52,523	10,123	791	42,400 R	82.8%	16.0%	83.8%	16.2%
9,610	PARMER	1,768	1,546	202	20	1,344 R	87.4%	11.4%	88.4%	11.6%
15,827	PECOS	3,682	2,548	1,043	91	1,505 R	69.2%	28.3%	71.0%	29.0%
51,850	POLK	16,776	13,377	3,229	170	10,148 R	79.7%	19.2%	80.6%	19.4%
117,197	POTTER	21,806	16,082	5,361	363	10,721 R	73.8%	24.6%	75.0%	25.0%
6,653	PRESIDIO	1,724	561	1,133	30	572 D	32.5%	65.7%	33.1%	66.9%
12,665	RAINS	4,987	4,339	596	52	3,743 R	87.0%	12.0%	87.9%	12.1%
138,607	RANDALL	48,019	39,243	8,228	548	31,015 R	81.7%	17.1%	82.7%	17.3%
3,838	REAGAN	716	616	90	10	526 R	86.0%	12.6%	87.3%	12.7%
3,470	REAL	1,569	1,337	218	14	1,119 R	85.2%	13.9%	86.0%	14.0%
12,053	RED RIVER	4,274	3,482	764	28	2,718 R	81.5%	17.9%	82.0%	18.0%
16,112	REEVES	2,177	1,341	801	35	540 R	61.6%	36.8%	62.6%	37.4%
6,925	REFUGIO	2,316	1,658	639	19	1,019 R	71.6%	27.6%	72.2%	27.8%
847	ROBERTS	444	430	7	7	423 R	96.8%	1.6%	98.4%	1.6%
17,123	ROBERTSON	6,017	4,643	1,293	81	3,350 R	77.2%	21.5%	78.2%	21.8%
106,387	ROCKWALL	42,871	30,211	12,132	528	18,079 R	70.5%	28.3%	71.3%	28.7%
10,303	RUNNELS	3,234	2,924	277	33	2,647 R	90.4%	8.6%	91.3%	8.7%
54,440	RUSK	15,628	12,762	2,697	169	10,065 R	81.7%	17.3%	82.6%	17.4%
10,602	SABINE	4,165	3,755	385	25	3,370 R	90.2%	9.2%	90.7%	9.3%
8,241	SAN AUGUSTINE	2,865	2,288	546	31	1,742 R	79.9%	19.1%	80.7%	19.3%
29,047	SAN JACINTO	9,549	7,882	1,540	127	6,342 R	82.5%	16.1%	83.7%	16.3%
66,732	SAN PATRICIO	17,898	12,028	5,643	227	6,385 R	67.2%	31.5%	68.1%	31.9%
6,072	SAN SABA	2,165	1,947	200	18	1,747 R	89.9%	9.2%	90.7%	9.3%
2,769	SCHLEICHER	1,008	834	159	15	675 R	82.7%	15.8%	84.0%	16.0%
16,670	SCURRY	4,128	3,607	480	41	3,127 R	87.4%	11.6%	88.3%	11.7%
3,264	SHACKELFORD	1,239	1,148	81	10	1,067 R	92.7%	6.5%	93.4%	6.6%
25,351	SHELBY	6,932	5,846	1,045	41	4,801 R	84.3%	15.1%	84.8%	15.2%
3,013	SHERMAN	708	665	35	8	630 R	93.9%	4.9%	95.0%	5.0%
233,917	SMITH	76,220	56,608	18,763	849	37,845 R	74.3%	24.6%	75.1%	24.9%
9,190	SOMERVELL	4,040	3,430	553	57	2,877 R	84.9%	13.7%	86.1%	13.9%
64,703	STARR	11,117	4,460	6,455	202	1,995 D	40.1%	58.1%	40.9%	59.1%
9,405	STEPHENS	2,745	2,511	217	17	2,294 R	91.5%	7.9%	92.0%	8.0%
1,296	STERLING	448	423	20	5	403 R	94.4%	4.5%	95.5%	4.5%
1,352	STONEWALL	565	492	70	3	422 R	87.1%	12.4%	87.5%	12.5%
3,759	SUTTON	1,162	970	178	14	792 R	83.5%	15.3%	84.5%	15.5%
7,418	SWISHER	1,666	1,399	238	29	1,161 R	84.0%	14.3%	85.5%	14.5%
2,108,659	TARRANT	591,368	303,600	279,423	8,345	24,177 R	51.3%	47.3%	52.1%	47.9%
138,325	TAYLOR	39,453	30,030	8,888	535	21,142 R	76.1%	22.5%	77.2%	22.8%
776	TERRELL	426	326	94	6	232 R	76.5%	22.1%	77.6%	22.4%
12,315	TERRY	2,590	2,167	377	46	1,790 R	83.7%	14.6%	85.2%	14.8%
1,503	THROCKMORTON	667	612	51	4	561 R	91.8%	7.6%	92.3%	7.7%
32,872	TITUS	7,322	5,701	1,535	86	4,166 R	77.9%	21.0%	78.8%	21.2%
119,536	TOM GREEN	31,847	23,873	7,516	458	16,357 R	75.0%	23.6%	76.1%	23.9%
1,281,160	TRAVIS	460,899	119,321	334,667	6,911	215,346 D	25.9%	72.6%	26.3%	73.7%
14,709	TRINITY	5,341	4,465	825	51	3,640 R	83.6%	15.4%	84.4%	15.6%
21,790	TYLER	7,246	6,343	816	87	5,527 R	87.5%	11.3%	88.6%	11.4%
41,979	UPSHUR	14,268	12,270	1,856	142	10,414 R	86.0%	13.0%	86.9%	13.1%
3,662	UPTON	1,058	908	124	26	784 R	85.8%	11.7%	88.0%	12.0%
26,722	UVALDE	7,946	4,779	3,048	119	1,731 R	60.1%	38.4%	61.1%	38.9%
49,032	VAL VERDE	9,509	5,530	3,814	165	1,716 R	58.2%	40.1%	59.2%	40.8%
56,946	VAN ZANDT	20,379	17,773	2,414	192	15,359 R	87.2%	11.8%	88.0%	12.0%
92,153	VICTORIA	25,288	18,519	6,452	317	12,067 R	73.2%	25.5%	74.2%	25.8%
72,886	WALKER	17,390	12,309	4,861	220	7,448 R	70.8%	28.0%	71.7%	28.3%
55,642	WALLER	16,704	11,381	5,100	223	6,281 R	68.1%	30.5%	69.1%	30.9%
12,063	WARD	2,518	2,065	418	35	1,647 R	82.0%	16.6%	83.2%	16.8%
35,975	WASHINGTON	13,972	10,965	2,824	183	8,141 R	78.5%	20.2%	79.5%	20.5%
276,781	WEBB	44,716	16,409	27,156	1,151	10,747 D	36.7%	60.7%	37.7%	62.3%

TEXAS
GOVERNOR 2022

2020 Census Population	County	Total Vote	Republican (Abbott)	Democratic (O'Rourke)	Other	Rep.-Dem. Plurality		Percentage Total Vote		Major Vote	
								Rep.	Dem.	Rep.	Dem.
41,620	WHARTON	12,154	9,354	2,697	103	6,657	R	77.0%	22.2%	77.6%	22.4%
5,036	WHEELER	1,686	1,569	103	14	1,466	R	93.1%	6.1%	93.8%	6.2%
132,532	WICHITA	31,631	23,328	7,824	479	15,504	R	73.8%	24.7%	74.9%	25.1%
12,800	WILBARGER	3,152	2,606	517	29	2,089	R	82.7%	16.4%	83.4%	16.6%
21,361	WILLACY	3,840	1,656	2,138	46	482	D	43.1%	55.7%	43.6%	56.4%
596,980	WILLIAMSON	225,553	111,488	110,242	3,823	1,246	R	49.4%	48.9%	50.3%	49.7%
51,470	WILSON	19,466	14,952	4,317	197	10,635	R	76.8%	22.2%	77.6%	22.4%
8,007	WINKLER	1,321	1,130	177	14	953	R	85.5%	13.4%	86.5%	13.5%
70,753	WISE	25,821	21,979	3,538	304	18,441	R	85.1%	13.7%	86.1%	13.9%
45,916	WOOD	18,173	15,678	2,331	164	13,347	R	86.3%	12.8%	87.1%	12.9%
8,689	YOAKUM	1,636	1,427	190	19	1,237	R	87.2%	11.6%	88.2%	11.8%
18,069	YOUNG	6,194	5,498	630	66	4,868	R	88.8%	10.2%	89.7%	10.3%
14,136	ZAPATA	3,443	1,817	1,585	41	232	R	52.8%	46.0%	53.4%	46.6%
11,813	ZAVALA	2,450	780	1,642	28	862	D	31.8%	67.0%	32.2%	67.8%
29,106,231	TOTAL	8,102,908	4,437,099	3,553,656	112,153	883,443	R	54.8%	43.9%	55.5%	44.5%

TEXAS
HOUSE OF REPRESENTATIVES

CD	Year	Total Vote	Republican Vote	Republican Candidate	Democratic Vote	Democratic Candidate	Other Vote	Rep.-Dem. Plurality		Total Vote Rep.	Total Vote Dem.	Major Vote Rep.	Major Vote Dem.
1	2022	234,662	183,224	MORAN, NATHANIEL	51,438	JEFFERSON, JRMAR		131,786	R	78.1%	21.9%	78.1%	21.9%
1	2020	302,742	219,726	GOHMERT, LOUIE*	83,016	GILBERT, HANK		136,710	R	72.6%	27.4%	72.6%	27.4%
1	2018	232,720	168,165	GOHMERT, LOUIE*	61,263	MCKELLAR, SHIRLEY J.	3,292	106,902	R	72.3%	26.3%	73.3%	26.7%
1	2016	260,409	192,434	GOHMERT, LOUIE*	62,847	MCKELLAR, SHIRLEY J.	5,128	129,587	R	73.9%	24.1%	75.4%	24.6%
1	2014	148,560	115,084	GOHMERT, LOUIE*	33,476	MCKELLAR, SHIRLEY J.		81,608	R	77.5%	22.5%	77.5%	22.5%
1	2012	249,658	178,322	GOHMERT, LOUIE*	67,222	MCKELLAR, SHIRLEY J.	4,114	111,100	R	71.4%	26.9%	72.6%	27.4%
2	2022	230,287	151,791	CRENSHAW, DANIEL*	78,496	FULFORD, ROBIN		73,295	R	65.9%	34.1%	65.9%	34.1%
2	2020	346,726	192,828	CRENSHAW, DANIEL*	148,374	LADJEVARDIAN, SIMA	5,524	44,454	R	55.6%	42.8%	56.5%	43.5%
2	2018	263,392	139,188	CRENSHAW, DANIEL	119,992	LITTON, TODD	4,212	19,196	R	52.8%	45.6%	53.7%	46.3%
2	2016	278,236	168,692	POE, TED*	100,231	BRYAN, PAT	9,313	68,461	R	60.6%	36.0%	62.7%	37.3%
2	2014	150,026	101,936	POE, TED*	44,462	LETSOS, NIKO	3,628	57,474	R	67.9%	29.6%	69.6%	30.4%
2	2012	246,328	159,664	POE, TED*	80,512	DOUGHERTY, JIM	6,152	79,152	R	64.8%	32.7%	66.5%	33.5%
3	2022	271,256	164,240	SELF, KEITH A.	100,121	SRIVASTAVA, SANDEEP	6,895	64,119	R	60.5%	36.9%	62.1%	37.9%
3	2020	418,591	230,512	TAYLOR, VAN*	179,458	SEIKALY, LULU	8,621	51,054	R	55.1%	42.9%	56.2%	43.8%
3	2018	312,511	169,520	TAYLOR, VAN	138,234	BURCH, LORIE	4,757	31,286	R	54.2%	44.2%	55.1%	44.9%
3	2016	316,467	193,684	JOHNSON, SAM*	109,420	BELL, ADAM P.	13,363	84,264	R	61.2%	34.6%	63.9%	36.1%
3	2014	138,280	113,404	JOHNSON, SAM*			24,876	113,404	R	82.0%		100.0%	
3	2012	187,180	187,180	JOHNSON, SAM*				187,180	R	100.0%		100.0%	
4	2022	256,009	170,781	FALLON, PAT*	79,179	OMERE, IRO	6,049	91,602	R	66.7%	30.9%	68.3%	31.7%
4	2020	337,803	253,837	FALLON, PAT	76,326	FOSTER, RUSSELL	7,640	177,511	R	75.1%	22.6%	76.9%	23.1%
4	2018	249,245	188,667	RATCLIFFE, JOHN*	57,400	KRANTZ, CATHERINE	3,178	131,267	R	75.7%	23.0%	76.7%	23.3%
4	2016	246,220	216,643	RATCLIFFE, JOHN*			29,577	216,643	R	88.0%		100.0%	
4	2014	115,085	115,085	RATCLIFFE, JOHN				115,085	R	100.0%		100.0%	
4	2012	250,343	182,679	HALL, RALPH M.*	60,214	HATHCOX, VALINDA	7,450	122,465	R	73.0%	24.1%	75.2%	24.8%
5	2022	211,965	135,595	GOODEN, LANCE*	71,930	HILL, TARTISHA	4,440	63,665	R	64.0%	33.9%	65.3%	34.7%
5	2020	280,413	173,836	GOODEN, LANCE*	100,743	SALTER, CAROLYN	5,834	73,093	R	62.0%	35.9%	63.3%	36.7%
5	2018	209,507	130,617	GOODEN, LANCE	78,666	WOOD, DAN	224	51,951	R	62.3%	37.5%	62.4%	37.6%
5	2016	192,875	155,469	HENSARLING, JEB*			37,406	155,469	R	80.6%		100.0%	
5	2014	104,262	88,998	HENSARLING, JEB*			15,264	88,998	R	85.4%		100.0%	
5	2012	208,230	134,091	HENSARLING, JEB*	69,178	MROSKO, LINDA S.	4,961	64,913	R	64.4%	33.2%	66.0%	34.0%

TEXAS
HOUSE OF REPRESENTATIVES

			Republican		Democratic		Other Vote	Rep.-Dem. Plurality	Percentage			
									Total Vote		Major Vote	
CD	Year	Total Vote	Vote	Candidate	Vote	Candidate			Rep.	Dem.	Rep.	Dem.
6	2022		Unopposed	ELLZEY, J.K. "JAKE"*								
6	2020	339,992	179,507	WRIGHT, RONALD*	149,530	DANIEL, STEPHEN	10,955	29,977 R	52.8%	44.0%	54.6%	45.4%
6	2018	256,042	135,961	WRIGHT, RONALD	116,350	SANCHEZ, JANA LYNNE	3,731	19,611 R	53.1%	45.4%	53.9%	46.1%
6	2016	273,296	159,444	BARTON, JOE L.*	106,667	WOOLRIDGE, RUBY FAYE	7,185	52,777 R	58.3%	39.0%	59.9%	40.1%
6	2014	150,996	92,334	BARTON, JOE L.*	55,027	COZAD, DAVID E.	3,635	37,307 R	61.1%	36.4%	62.7%	37.3%
6	2012	249,936	145,019	BARTON, JOE L.*	98,053	SANDERS, KENNETH	6,864	46,966 R	58.0%	39.2%	59.7%	40.3%
7	2022	181,829	65,835	TEAGUE, JOHNNY	115,994	FLETCHER, LIZZIE PANNILL*		50,159 D	36.2%	63.8%	36.2%	63.8%
7	2020	314,125	149,054	HUNT, WESLEY	159,529	FLETCHER, LIZZIE PANNILL*	5,542	10,475 D	47.5%	50.8%	48.3%	51.7%
7	2018	243,601	115,642	CULBERSON, JOHN*	127,959	FLETCHER, LIZZIE PANNILL		12,317 D	47.5%	52.5%	47.5%	52.5%
7	2016	255,533	143,542	CULBERSON, JOHN*	111,991	CARGAS, JAMES		31,551 R	56.2%	43.8%	56.2%	43.8%
7	2014	143,219	90,606	CULBERSON, JOHN*	49,478	CARGAS, JAMES	3,135	41,128 R	63.3%	34.5%	64.7%	35.3%
7	2012	234,837	142,793	CULBERSON, JOHN*	85,553	CARGAS, JAMES	6,491	57,240 R	60.8%	36.4%	62.5%	37.5%
8	2022	224,968	153,127	LUTTRELL, MORGAN	68,715	JONES, LAURA	3,126	84,412 R	68.1%	30.5%	69.0%	31.0%
8	2020	382,471	277,327	BRADY, KEVIN*	97,409	HERNANDEZ, ELIZABETH	7,735	179,918 R	72.5%	25.5%	74.0%	26.0%
8	2018	273,170	200,619	BRADY, KEVIN*	67,930	DAVID, STEVEN	4,621	132,689 R	73.4%	24.9%	74.7%	25.3%
8	2016	236,379	236,379	BRADY, KEVIN*				236,379 R	100.0%		100.0%	
8	2014	140,013	125,066	BRADY, KEVIN*			14,947	125,066 R	89.3%		100.0%	
8	2012	251,052	194,043	BRADY, KEVIN*	51,051	BURNS, NEIL	5,958	142,992 R	77.3%	20.3%	79.2%	20.8%
9	2022	163,607	38,161	LEON, JIMMY I.	125,446	GREEN, AL*		87,285 D	23.3%	76.7%	23.3%	76.7%
9	2020	229,107	49,575	TEAGUE, JOHNNY	172,938	GREEN, AL*	6,594	123,363 D	21.6%	75.5%	22.3%	77.7%
9	2018	153,001			136,256	GREEN, AL*	16,745	136,256 D		89.1%		100.0%
9	2016	188,523	36,491	MARTIN, JEFF	152,032	GREEN, AL*		115,541 D	19.4%	80.6%	19.4%	80.6%
9	2014	86,003			78,109	GREEN, AL*	7,894	78,109 D		90.8%		100.0%
9	2012	183,566	36,139	MUELLER, STEVE	144,075	GREEN, AL*	3,352	107,936 D	19.7%	78.5%	20.1%	79.9%
10	2022	251,937	159,469	MCCAUL, MICHAEL T.*	86,404	NUNO, LINDA	6,064	73,065 R	63.3%	34.3%	64.9%	35.1%
10	2020	413,894	217,216	MCCAUL, MICHAEL T.*	187,686	SIEGEL, MIKE	8,992	29,530 R	52.5%	45.3%	53.6%	46.4%
10	2018	307,827	157,166	MCCAUL, MICHAEL T.*	144,034	SIEGEL, MIKE	6,627	13,132 R	51.1%	46.8%	52.2%	47.8%
10	2016	312,600	179,221	MCCAUL, MICHAEL T.*	120,170	WALTER-CADIEN, TAWANA	13,209	59,051 R	57.3%	38.4%	59.9%	40.1%
10	2014	176,460	109,726	MCCAUL, MICHAEL T.*	60,243	WALTER-CADIEN, TAWANA	6,491	49,483 R	62.2%	34.1%	64.6%	35.4%
10	2012	264,019	159,783	MCCAUL, MICHAEL T.*	95,710	WALTER-CADIEN, TAWANA	8,526	64,073 R	60.5%	36.3%	62.5%	37.5%
11	2022		Unopposed	PFLUGER, AUGUST*								
11	2020	291,773	232,568	PFLUGER, AUGUST	53,394	HOGG, JON MARK	5,811	179,174 R	79.7%	18.3%	81.3%	18.7%
11	2018	220,377	176,603	CONAWAY, MIKE*	40,631	LEEDER, JENNIE LOU	3,143	135,972 R	80.1%	18.4%	81.3%	18.7%
11	2016	225,548	201,871	CONAWAY, MIKE*			23,677	201,871 R	89.5%		100.0%	
11	2014	119,574	107,939	CONAWAY, MIKE*			11,635	107,939 R	90.3%		100.0%	
11	2012	226,023	177,742	CONAWAY, MIKE*	41,970	RILEY, JIM	6,311	135,772 R	78.6%	18.6%	80.9%	19.1%
12	2022	237,979	152,953	GRANGER, KAY*	85,026	HUNT, TREY J		67,927 R	64.3%	35.7%	64.3%	35.7%
12	2020	367,021	233,853	GRANGER, KAY*	121,250	WELCH, LISA	11,918	112,603 R	63.7%	33.0%	65.9%	34.1%
12	2018	268,491	172,557	GRANGER, KAY*	90,994	ADIA, VANESSA	4,940	81,563 R	64.3%	33.9%	65.5%	34.5%
12	2016	283,115	196,482	GRANGER, KAY*	76,029	BRADSHAW, BILL	10,604	120,453 R	69.4%	26.9%	72.1%	27.9%
12	2014	158,730	113,186	GRANGER, KAY*	41,757	GREENE, MARK	3,787	71,429 R	71.3%	26.3%	73.1%	26.9%
12	2012	247,712	175,649	GRANGER, KAY*	66,080	ROBINSON, DAVE	5,983	109,569 R	70.9%	26.7%	72.7%	27.3%
13	2022	214,677	161,767	JACKSON, RONNY*	52,910	BROWN, KATHLEEN		108,857 R	75.4%	24.6%	75.4%	24.6%
13	2020	273,500	217,124	JACKSON, RONNY	50,477	TRUJILLO, GUS	5,907	166,647 R	79.4%	18.5%	81.1%	18.9%
13	2018	207,285	169,027	THORNBERRY, MAC*	35,083	SAGAN, GREG	3,175	133,944 R	81.5%	16.9%	82.8%	17.2%
13	2016	221,242	199,050	THORNBERRY, MAC*			22,192	199,050 R	90.0%		100.0%	
13	2014	131,451	110,842	THORNBERRY, MAC*	16,822	MINTER, MIKE G.	3,787	94,020 R	84.3%	12.8%	86.8%	13.2%
13	2012	206,388	187,775	THORNBERRY, MAC*			18,613	187,775 R	91.0%		100.0%	
14	2022	213,149	149,543	WEBER, RANDY*	63,606	WILLIAMS, MIKAL		85,937 R	70.2%	29.8%	70.2%	29.8%
14	2020	309,115	190,541	WEBER, RANDY*	118,574	BELL, ADRIENNE		71,967 R	61.6%	38.4%	61.6%	38.4%
14	2018	234,528	138,942	WEBER, RANDY*	92,212	BELL, ADRIENNE	3,374	46,730 R	59.2%	39.3%	60.1%	39.9%
14	2016	259,685	160,631	WEBER, RANDY*	99,054	COLE, MICHAEL K.		61,577 R	61.9%	38.1%	61.9%	38.1%
14	2014	145,698	90,116	WEBER, RANDY*	52,545	BROWN, DONALD G.	3,037	37,571 R	61.9%	36.1%	63.2%	36.8%
14	2012	245,839	131,460	WEBER, RANDY	109,697	LAMPSON, NICK	4,682	21,763 R	53.5%	44.6%	54.5%	45.5%
15	2022	151,889	80,978	DE LA CRUZ-HERNANDEZ, MONICA	68,097	VALLEJO, MICHELLE	2,814	12,881 R	53.3%	44.8%	54.3%	45.7%
15	2020	228,917	109,017	DE LA CRUZ-HERNANDEZ, MONICA	115,605	GONZALEZ, VICENTE*	4,295	6,588 D	47.6%	50.5%	48.5%	51.5%
15	2018	164,802	63,862	WESTLEY, TIM	98,333	GONZALEZ, VICENTE*	2,607	34,471 D	38.8%	59.7%	39.4%	60.6%
15	2016	177,479	66,877	WESTLEY, TIM	101,712	GONZALEZ, VICENTE	8,890	34,835 D	37.7%	57.3%	39.7%	60.3%
15	2014	90,184	39,016	ZAMORA, EDDIE	48,708	HINOJOSA, RUBEN*	2,460	9,692 D	43.3%	54.0%	44.5%	55.5%
15	2012	146,661	54,056	BRUEGGEMANN, DALE A.	89,296	HINOJOSA, RUBEN*	3,309	35,240 D	36.9%	60.9%	37.7%	62.3%

TEXAS
HOUSE OF REPRESENTATIVES

			Republican		Democratic		Other Vote	Rep.-Dem. Plurality	Percentage			
									Total Vote		Major Vote	
CD	Year	Total Vote	Vote	Candidate	Vote	Candidate			Rep.	Dem.	Rep.	Dem.
16	2022	150,496	54,986	ARMENDARIZ-JACKSON, IRENE	95,510	ESCOBAR, VERONICA*		40,524 D	36.5%	63.5%	36.5%	63.5%
16	2020	238,114	84,006	ARMENDARIZ-JACKSON, IRENE	154,108	ESCOBAR, VERONICA*		70,102 D	35.3%	64.7%	35.3%	64.7%
16	2018	181,754	49,127	SEEBERGER, RICK	124,437	ESCOBAR, VERONICA	8,190	75,310 D	27.0%	68.5%	28.3%	71.7%
16	2016	175,229			150,228	O'ROURKE, BETO*	25,001	150,228 D		85.7%		100.0%
16	2014	73,105	21,324	ROEN, COREY DEAN	49,338	O'ROURKE, BETO*	2,443	28,014 D	29.2%	67.5%	30.2%	69.8%
16	2012	155,005	51,043	CARRASCO, BARBARA	101,403	O'ROURKE, BETO	2,559	50,360 D	32.9%	65.4%	33.5%	66.5%
17	2022	217,209	144,408	SESSIONS, PETE*	72,801	WOODS, MARY JO		71,607 R	66.5%	33.5%	66.5%	33.5%
17	2020	306,873	171,390	SESSIONS, PETE	125,565	KENNEDY, RICK	9,918	45,825 R	55.9%	40.9%	57.7%	42.3%
17	2018	237,351	134,841	FLORES, BILL*	98,070	KENNEDY, RICK	4,440	36,771 R	56.8%	41.3%	57.9%	42.1%
17	2016	245,728	149,417	FLORES, BILL*	86,603	MATTA, WILLIAM	9,708	62,814 R	60.8%	35.2%	63.3%	36.7%
17	2014	132,865	85,807	FLORES, BILL*	43,049	HAYNES, NICK	4,009	42,758 R	64.6%	32.4%	66.6%	33.4%
17	2012	179,262	143,284	FLORES, BILL*			35,978	143,284 R	79.9%		100.0%	
18	2022	156,268	40,941	MONTIEL, CARMEN MARIA	110,511	JACKSON LEE, SHEILA*	4,816	69,570 D	26.2%	70.7%	27.0%	73.0%
18	2020	246,895	58,033	CHAMPION, WENDELL	180,952	JACKSON LEE, SHEILA*	7,910	122,919 D	23.5%	73.3%	24.3%	75.7%
18	2018	184,332	38,368	PATE, AVA REYNERO	138,704	JACKSON LEE, SHEILA*	7,260	100,336 D	20.8%	75.2%	21.7%	78.3%
18	2016	204,308	48,306	BARTLEY, LORI	150,157	JACKSON LEE, SHEILA*	5,845	101,851 D	23.6%	73.5%	24.3%	75.7%
18	2014	106,010	26,249	SEIBERT, SEAN	76,097	JACKSON LEE, SHEILA*	3,664	49,848 D	24.8%	71.8%	25.6%	74.4%
18	2012	194,932	44,015	SEIBERT, SEAN	146,223	JACKSON LEE, SHEILA*	4,694	102,208 D	22.6%	75.0%	23.1%	76.9%
19	2022	189,681	152,321	ARRINGTON, JODEY*			37,360	152,321 R	80.3%		100.0%	
19	2020	265,052	198,198	ARRINGTON, JODEY*	60,583	WATSON, THOMAS	6,271	137,615 R	74.8%	22.9%	76.6%	23.4%
19	2018	201,985	151,946	ARRINGTON, JODEY*	50,039	LEVARIO, MIGUEL		101,907 R	75.2%	24.8%	75.2%	24.8%
19	2016	203,475	176,314	ARRINGTON, JODEY			27,161	176,314 R	86.7%		100.0%	
19	2014	116,818	90,160	NEUGEBAUER, RANDY*	21,458	MARCHBANKS, JAMES NEAL "NEAL"	5,200	68,702 R	77.2%	18.4%	80.8%	19.2%
19	2012	192,063	163,239	NEUGEBAUER, RANDY*			28,824	163,239 R	85.0%		100.0%	
20	2022	168,599	53,226	SINCLAIR, KYLE	115,352	CASTRO, JOAQUIN*	21	62,126 D	31.6%	68.4%	31.6%	68.4%
20	2020	270,723	89,628	GARZA, MAURO	175,078	CASTRO, JOAQUIN*	6,017	85,450 D	33.1%	64.7%	33.9%	66.1%
20	2018	171,963			139,038	CASTRO, JOAQUIN*	32,925	139,038 D		80.9%		100.0%
20	2016	187,669			149,640	CASTRO, JOAQUIN*	38,029	149,640 D		79.7%		100.0%
20	2014	87,964			66,554	CASTRO, JOAQUIN*	21,410	66,554 D		75.7%		100.0%
20	2012	186,177	62,376	ROSA, DAVID	119,032	CASTRO, JOAQUIN	4,769	56,656 D	33.5%	63.9%	34.4%	65.6%
21	2022	330,081	207,426	ROY, CHIP*	122,655	ZAPATA, CLAUDIA ANDREANA		84,771 R	62.8%	37.2%	62.8%	37.2%
21	2020	453,750	235,740	ROY, CHIP*	205,780	DAVIS, WENDY R.	12,230	29,960 R	52.0%	45.4%	53.4%	46.6%
21	2018	353,617	177,654	ROY, CHIP	168,421	KOPSER, JOSEPH	7,542	9,233 R	50.2%	47.6%	51.3%	48.7%
21	2016	356,031	202,967	SMITH, LAMAR*	129,765	WAKELY, TOM	23,299	73,202 R	57.0%	36.4%	61.0%	39.0%
21	2014	188,996	135,660	SMITH, LAMAR*			53,336	135,660 R	71.8%		100.0%	
21	2012	308,865	187,015	SMITH, LAMAR*	109,326	DUVAL, CANDACE E.	12,524	77,689 R	60.5%	35.4%	63.1%	36.9%
22	2022	241,215	150,014	NEHLS, TROY*	85,653	JORDAN, JAMIE KAYE	5,548	64,361 R	62.2%	35.5%	63.7%	36.3%
22	2020	408,048	210,259	NEHLS, TROY	181,998	KULKARNI, SRI PRESTON	15,791	28,261 R	51.5%	44.6%	53.6%	46.4%
22	2018	297,405	152,750	OLSON, PETE*	138,153	KULKARNI, SRI PRESTON	6,502	14,597 R	51.4%	46.5%	52.5%	47.5%
22	2016	305,543	181,864	OLSON, PETE*	123,679	GIBSON, MARK		58,185 R	59.5%	40.5%	59.5%	40.5%
22	2014	151,566	100,861	OLSON, PETE*	47,844	BRISCOE, FRANK	2,861	53,017 R	66.5%	31.6%	67.8%	32.2%
22	2012	250,911	160,668	OLSON, PETE*	80,203	ROGERS, KESHA	10,040	80,465 R	64.0%	32.0%	66.7%	33.3%
23	2022	208,776	116,649	GONZALES, ERNEST ANTHONY "TONY" II*	80,947	LIRA, JOHN	11,180	35,702 R	55.9%	38.8%	59.0%	41.0%
23	2020	295,457	149,395	GONZALES, ERNEST ANTHONY II	137,693	JONES, GINA ORTIZ	8,369	11,702 R	50.6%	46.6%	52.0%	48.0%
23	2018	210,069	103,285	HURD, WILL*	102,359	JONES, GINA ORTIZ	4,425	926 R	49.2%	48.7%	50.2%	49.8%
23	2016	228,965	110,577	HURD, WILL*	107,526	GALLEGO, PETE P.	10,862	3,051 R	48.3%	47.0%	50.7%	49.3%
23	2014	115,429	57,459	HURD, WILL	55,037	GALLEGO, PETE P.*	2,933	2,422 R	49.8%	47.7%	51.1%	48.9%
23	2012	192,169	87,547	CANSECO, FRANCISCO "QUICO"*	96,676	GALLEGO, PETE P.	7,946	9,129 D	45.6%	50.3%	47.5%	52.5%
24	2022	297,825	177,947	VAN DUYNE, ELIZABETH ANN "BETH"*	119,878	MCDOWELL, JAN		58,069 R	59.7%	40.3%	59.7%	40.3%
24	2020	344,021	167,910	VAN DUYNE, ELIZABETH ANN "BETH"	163,326	VALENZUELA, CANDACE	12,785	4,584 R	48.8%	47.5%	50.7%	49.3%
24	2018	263,418	133,317	MARCHANT, KENNY E.*	125,231	MCDOWELL, JAN	4,870	8,086 R	50.6%	47.5%	51.6%	48.4%
24	2016	275,635	154,845	MARCHANT, KENNY E.*	108,389	MCDOWELL, JAN	12,401	46,456 R	56.2%	39.3%	58.8%	41.2%
24	2014	144,073	93,712	MARCHANT, KENNY E.*	46,548	MCGEHEARTY, PATRICK F.	3,813	47,164 R	65.0%	32.3%	66.8%	33.2%
24	2012	243,489	148,586	MARCHANT, KENNY E.*	87,645	RUSK, TIM	7,258	60,941 R	61.0%	36.0%	62.9%	37.1%
25	2022		Unopposed	WILLIAMS, ROGER*								
25	2020	393,523	220,088	WILLIAMS, ROGER*	165,697	OLIVER, JULIE	7,738	54,391 R	55.9%	42.1%	57.0%	43.0%
25	2018	304,553	163,023	WILLIAMS, ROGER*	136,385	OLIVER, JULIE	5,145	26,638 R	53.5%	44.8%	54.4%	45.6%
25	2016	310,196	180,988	WILLIAMS, ROGER*	117,073	THOMAS, KATHI	12,135	63,915 R	58.3%	37.7%	60.7%	39.3%
25	2014	177,883	107,120	WILLIAMS, ROGER*	64,463	MONTOYA, MARCO	6,300	42,657 R	60.2%	36.2%	62.4%	37.6%
25	2012	263,932	154,245	WILLIAMS, ROGER	98,827	HENDERSON, ELAINE M.	10,860	55,418 R	58.4%	37.4%	60.9%	39.1%

TEXAS
HOUSE OF REPRESENTATIVES

			Republican		Democratic				Percentage			
									Total Vote		Major Vote	
CD	Year	Total Vote	Vote	Candidate	Vote	Candidate	Other Vote	Rep.-Dem. Plurality	Rep.	Dem.	Rep.	Dem.
26	2022	265,023	183,639	BURGESS, MICHAEL C.*			81,384	183,639 R	69.3%		100.0%	
26	2020	432,215	261,963	BURGESS, MICHAEL C.*	161,009	IANNUZZI, CAROL HIGBEE	9,243	100,954 R	60.6%	37.3%	61.9%	38.1%
26	2018	312,505	185,551	BURGESS, MICHAEL C.*	121,938	FAGAN, LINSEY	5,016	63,613 R	59.4%	39.0%	60.3%	39.7%
26	2016	319,080	211,730	BURGESS, MICHAEL C.*	94,507	MAUCK, ERIC	12,843	117,223 R	66.4%	29.6%	69.1%	30.9%
26	2014	141,470	116,944	BURGESS, MICHAEL C.*			24,526	116,944 R	82.7%		100.0%	
26	2012	258,723	176,642	BURGESS, MICHAEL C.*	74,237	SANCHEZ, DAVID	7,844	102,405 R	68.3%	28.7%	70.4%	29.6%
27	2022	207,027	133,416	CLOUD, MICHAEL*	73,611	PEREZ, MACLOVIO JR.		59,805 R	64.4%	35.6%	64.4%	35.6%
27	2020	273,253	172,305	CLOUD, MICHAEL*	95,466	DE LA FUENTE, RICARDO	5,482	76,839 R	63.1%	34.9%	64.3%	35.7%
27	2018	207,421	125,118	CLOUD, MICHAEL*	75,929	HOLGUIN, ERIC	6,374	49,189 R	60.3%	36.6%	62.2%	37.8%
27	2016	230,580	142,251	FARENTHOLD, R. BLAKE*	88,329	BARRERA, RAUL "ROY"		53,922 R	61.7%	38.3%	61.7%	38.3%
27	2014	131,047	83,342	FARENTHOLD, R. BLAKE*	44,152	REED, WESLEY C.	3,553	39,190 R	63.6%	33.7%	65.4%	34.6%
27	2012	212,651	120,684	FARENTHOLD, R. BLAKE*	83,395	HARRISON, ROSE MEZA	8,572	37,289 R	56.8%	39.2%	59.1%	40.9%
28	2022	165,581	71,778	GARCIA, CASANDRA "CASSY"	93,803	CUELLAR, HENRY*		22,025 D	43.3%	56.7%	43.3%	56.7%
28	2020	235,844	91,925	WHITTEN, SANDRA	137,494	CUELLAR, HENRY*	6,425	45,569 D	39.0%	58.3%	40.1%	59.9%
28	2018	139,226			117,494	CUELLAR, HENRY*	21,732	117,494 D		84.4%		100.0%
28	2016	184,442	57,740	HARDIN, ZEFFEN	122,086	CUELLAR, HENRY*	4,616	64,346 D	31.3%	66.2%	32.1%	67.9%
28	2014	76,136			62,508	CUELLAR, HENRY*	13,628	62,508 D		82.1%		100.0%
28	2012	165,645	49,309	HAYWARD, WILLIAM R. "GUILLERMO"	112,456	CUELLAR, HENRY*	3,880	63,147 D	29.8%	67.9%	30.5%	69.5%
29	2022	100,602	28,765	SCHAFRANEK, ROBERT	71,837	GARCIA, SYLVIA R.*		43,072 D	28.6%	71.4%	28.6%	71.4%
29	2020	156,473	42,840	BLANCO, JAIMY Z.	111,305	GARCIA, SYLVIA R.*	2,328	68,465 D	27.4%	71.1%	27.8%	72.2%
29	2018	117,494	28,098	ARONOFF, PHILLIP	88,188	GARCIA, SYLVIA R.	1,208	60,090 D	23.9%	75.1%	24.2%	75.8%
29	2016	131,982	31,646	GARZA, JULIO	95,649	GREEN, GENE*	4,687	64,003 D	24.0%	72.5%	24.9%	75.1%
29	2014	46,143			41,321	GREEN, GENE*	4,822	41,321 D		89.5%		100.0%
29	2012	95,611			86,053	GREEN, GENE*	9,558	86,053 D		90.0%		100.0%
30	2022	180,513	39,209	RODGERS, JAMES	134,876	CROCKETT, JASMINE	6,428	95,667 D	21.7%	74.7%	22.5%	77.5%
30	2020	264,464	48,685	PENNIE, TRE	204,928	JOHNSON, EDDIE BERNICE*	10,851	156,243 D	18.4%	77.5%	19.2%	80.8%
30	2018	183,174			166,784	JOHNSON, EDDIE BERNICE*	16,390	166,784 D		91.1%		100.0%
30	2016	218,826	41,518	LINGERFELT, CHARLES	170,502	JOHNSON, EDDIE BERNICE*	6,806	128,984 D	19.0%	77.9%	19.6%	80.4%
30	2014	105,793			93,041	JOHNSON, EDDIE BERNICE*	12,752	93,041 D		87.9%		100.0%
30	2012	217,014	41,222	WASHINGTON, TRAVIS	171,059	JOHNSON, EDDIE BERNICE*	4,733	129,837 D	19.0%	78.8%	19.4%	80.6%
31	2022		Unopposed	CARTER, JOHN*								
31	2020	398,057	212,695	CARTER, JOHN*	176,293	IMAM, DONNA	9,069	36,402 R	53.4%	44.3%	54.7%	45.3%
31	2018	286,007	144,680	CARTER, JOHN*	136,362	HEGAR, MARY JENNINGS "MJ"	4,965	8,318 R	50.6%	47.7%	51.5%	48.5%
31	2016	284,588	166,060	CARTER, JOHN*	103,852	CLARK, MIKE	14,676	62,208 R	58.4%	36.5%	61.5%	38.5%
31	2014	143,028	91,607	CARTER, JOHN*	45,715	MINOR, LOUIE	5,706	45,892 R	64.0%	32.0%	66.7%	33.3%
31	2012	237,187	145,348	CARTER, JOHN*	82,977	WYMAN, STEPHEN M.	8,862	62,371 R	61.3%	35.0%	63.7%	36.3%
32	2022	177,499	61,494	SWAD, ANTONIO	116,005	ALLRED, COLIN*		54,511 D	34.6%	65.4%	34.6%	65.4%
32	2020	343,687	157,867	COLLINS, GENEVIEVE	178,542	ALLRED, COLIN*	7,278	20,675 D	45.9%	51.9%	46.9%	53.1%
32	2018	275,620	126,101	SESSIONS, PETE*	144,067	ALLRED, COLIN	5,452	17,966 D	45.8%	52.3%	46.7%	53.3%
32	2016	229,171	162,868	SESSIONS, PETE*			66,303	162,868 R	71.1%		100.0%	
32	2014	156,096	96,495	SESSIONS, PETE*	55,325	PEREZ, FRANK	4,276	41,170 R	61.8%	35.4%	63.6%	36.4%
32	2012	251,636	146,653	SESSIONS, PETE*	99,288	MCGOVERN, KATHERINE SAVERS	5,695	47,365 R	58.3%	39.5%	59.6%	40.4%
33	2022	114,030	29,203	GILLESPIE, PATRICK DAVID	82,081	VEASEY, MARC*	2,746	52,878 D	25.6%	72.0%	26.2%	73.8%
33	2020	157,606	39,638	VASQUEZ, FABIAN CORDOVA	105,317	VEASEY, MARC*	12,651	65,679 D	25.2%	66.8%	27.3%	72.7%
33	2018	119,224	26,120	BILLUPS, WILLIE	90,805	VEASEY, MARC*	2,299	64,685 D	21.9%	76.2%	22.3%	77.7%
33	2016	126,369	33,222	MITCHELL, M. MARK	93,147	VEASEY, MARC*		59,925 D	26.3%	73.7%	26.3%	73.7%
33	2014	50,592			43,769	VEASEY, MARC*	6,823	43,769 D		86.5%		100.0%
33	2012	117,375	30,252	BRADLEY, CHUCK	85,114	VEASEY, MARC	2,009	54,862 D	25.8%	72.5%	26.2%	73.8%
34	2022	134,439	59,464	FLORES, MAYRA	70,896	GONZALEZ, VICENTE*	4,079	11,432 D	44.2%	52.7%	45.6%	54.4%
34	2020	201,027	84,119	GONZALEZ, REY JR.	111,439	VELA, FILEMON*	5,469	27,320 D	41.8%	55.4%	43.0%	57.0%
34	2018	143,068	57,243	GONZALEZ, REY JR.	85,825	VELA, FILEMON*		28,582 D	40.0%	60.0%	40.0%	60.0%
34	2016	166,961	62,323	GONZALEZ, REY JR.	104,638	VELA, FILEMON*		42,315 D	37.3%	62.7%	37.3%	62.7%
34	2014	79,877	30,811	SMITH, LARRY S.	47,503	VELA, FILEMON*	1,563	16,692 D	38.6%	59.5%	39.3%	60.7%
34	2012	144,778	52,448	BRADSHAW, JESSICA PUENTE	89,606	VELA, FILEMON	2,724	37,158 D	36.2%	61.9%	36.9%	63.1%
35	2022	178,568	48,969	MCQUEEN, DAN	129,599	CASAR, GREG		80,630 D	27.4%	72.6%	27.4%	72.6%
35	2020	269,797	80,795	SHARON, JENNIFER "JENNY"	176,373	DOGGETT, LLOYD*	12,629	95,578 D	29.9%	65.4%	31.4%	68.6%
35	2018	194,067	50,553	SMALLING, DAVID	138,278	DOGGETT, LLOYD*	5,236	87,725 D	26.0%	71.3%	26.8%	73.2%
35	2016	197,576	62,384	NARVAIZ, SUSAN	124,612	DOGGETT, LLOYD*	10,580	62,228 D	31.6%	63.1%	33.4%	66.6%
35	2014	96,225	32,040	NARVAIZ, SUSAN	60,124	DOGGETT, LLOYD*	4,061	28,084 D	33.3%	62.5%	34.8%	65.2%
35	2012	165,179	52,894	NARVAIZ, SUSAN	105,626	DOGGETT, LLOYD*	6,659	52,732 D	32.0%	63.9%	33.4%	66.6%
36	2022	209,615	145,599	BABIN, BRIAN*	64,016	HAIRE, JONATHAN "JON"		81,583 R	69.5%	30.5%	69.5%	30.5%
36	2020	302,549	222,712	BABIN, BRIAN*	73,418	LEWIS, RASHAD	6,419	149,294 R	73.6%	24.3%	75.2%	24.8%
36	2018	221,956	161,048	BABIN, BRIAN*	60,908	STEELE, DAYNA		100,140 R	72.6%	27.4%	72.6%	27.4%
36	2016	218,565	193,675	BABIN, BRIAN*			24,890	193,675 R	88.6%		100.0%	
36	2014	133,842	101,663	BABIN, BRIAN	29,543	COLE, MICHAEL K.	2,636	72,120 R	76.0%	22.1%	77.5%	22.5%
36	2012	233,832	165,405	STOCKMAN, STEVE	62,143	MARTIN, MAX	6,284	103,262 R	70.7%	26.6%	72.7%	27.3%

TEXAS

HOUSE OF REPRESENTATIVES

CD	Year	Total Vote	Republican Vote	Republican Candidate	Democratic Vote	Democratic Candidate	Other Vote	Rep.-Dem. Plurality	Total Vote Rep.	Total Vote Dem.	Major Vote Rep.	Major Vote Dem.
37	2022	285,789	59,923	GARCIA SHARON, JENNY	219,358	DOGGETT, LLOYD*	6,508	159,435 D	21.0%	76.8%	21.5%	78.5%
38	2022	259,869	163,597	HUNT, WESLEY	92,302	KLUSSMANN, DUNCAN FOSTER	3,970	71,295 R	63.0%	35.5%	63.9%	36.1%
TOTAL	2022	7,082,919	3,890,438		2,999,053		193,428	891,385 R	54.9%	42.3%	56.5%	43.5%
TOTAL	2020	11,093,626	5,926,712		4,896,673		270,241	1,030,039 R	53.4%	44.1%	54.8%	45.2%
TOTAL	2018	8,202,708	4,135,359		3,852,752		214,597	282,607 R	50.4%	47.0%	51.8%	48.2%
TOTAL	2016	8,528,526	4,877,605		3,160,535		490,386	1,717,070 R	57.2%	37.1%	60.7%	39.3%
TOTAL	2014	4,453,499	2,684,592		1,474,016		294,891	1,210,576 R	60.3%	33.1%	64.6%	35.4%
TOTAL	2012	7,664,208	4,429,270		2,949,900		285,038	1,479,370 R	57.8%	38.5%	60.0%	40.0%

Note: An asterisk (*) denotes incumbent.

TEXAS
GENERAL AND PRIMARY ELECTIONS

GENERAL ELECTIONS: OTHER VOTES

Governor	Other vote was 81,932 Libertarian (Mark Tippetts), 28,584 Green (Delilah Barrios), 1,243 Write-In (Jacqueline Abernathy), 394 Write-In (Mark Goloby)
House	Other vote was:
CD 3	6,895 Libertarian (Christopher Claytor)
CD 4	6,049 Libertarian (John Simmons)
CD 5	4,293 Libertarian (Kevin Hale), 147 Write-In (Ruth Torres)
CD 8	3,126 Libertarian (Roy Eriksen)
CD 10	6,064 Libertarian (Bill Kelsey)
CD 15	2,814 Libertarian (Ross Leone)
CD 18	2,766 Independent (Vince Duncan), 2,050 Libertarian (Phil Kurtz)
CD 19	37,360 Independent (Nathan Lewis)
CD 20	21 Write-In (Adam Jonasz)
CD 22	5,378 Libertarian (Joseph LeBlanc), 170 Write-In (Jim Squires)
CD 23	11,180 Independent (Francisco Lopez)
CD 26	81,384 Libertarian (Mike Kolls)
CD 30	3,820 Independent (Zachariah Manning), 1,870 Libertarian (Phil Gray), 738 Write-In (Deborah Walker)
CD 33	2,746 Libertarian (Ken Ashby)
CD 34	4,079 Independent (Chris Royal)
CD 37	6,332 Libertarian (Clark Patterson), 176 Write-In (Sherri Taylor)
CD 38	3,970 Independent (Joel Dejean)

2022 PRIMARY ELECTIONS: SUPPLEMENTARY INFORMATION

Primary	March 1, 2022	**Registration** (as of March 1, 2020)	17,183,996	No Party Registration
Primary Runoff	May 24, 2022			
Primary Type	Open—Any registered voter could participate in the Democratic or Republican primary, although if he or she voted in the primary of one party, he or she could not vote in the runoff of the other party.			

TEXAS

GENERAL AND PRIMARY ELECTIONS

	REPUBLICAN PRIMARIES			DEMOCRATIC PRIMARIES		
Governor	Abbott, Greg*	1,299,059	66.5%	O'Rourke, Beto	983,182	91.4%
	West, Allen	239,557	12.3%	Diaz, Joy	33,622	3.1%
	Huffines, Donald Blaine "Don"	234,138	12.0%	Cooper, Michael	32,673	3.0%
	Prather, Chad	74,173	3.8%	Wakeland, Rich	13,237	1.2%
	Perry, James Richard "Rick"	61,424	3.1%	Barrientez, Inocencio "Inno"	12,887	1.2%
	Horn, Kandy Kaye	23,605	1.2%			
	Belew, Paul	11,387	0.6%			
	Harrison, Danny	10,829	0.6%			
	TOTAL	1,954,172		TOTAL	1,075,601	
Congressional District 1	Moran, Nathaniel	51,312	63.0%	Jefferson, Jrmar	7,411	45.5%
	McDaniel, Joseph "Joe"	19,708	24.2%	Dunn, Victor D.	4,554	27.9%
	Atholi, Aditya	6,186	7.6%	Kocen, Stephen Martin	2,457	15.1%
	Porro, John	4,238	5.2%	Dass, Gavin	1,881	11.5%
	TOTAL	81,444		TOTAL	16,303	
				PRIMARY RUNOFF		
				Jefferson, Jrmar	5,607	75.9%
				Dunn, Victor D.	1,783	24.1%
				TOTAL	7,390	
Congressional District 2	Crenshaw, Daniel*	45,863	74.5%	Fulford, Robin	17,160	100.0%
	Ellis, Jameson	10,195	16.6%			
	Etwop, Martin	2,785	4.5%			
	Langella, Milam	2,741	4.5%			
	TOTAL	61,584		TOTAL	17,160	
Congressional District 3	Taylor, Van*	31,489	48.8%	Srivastava, Sandeep	13,865	61.9%
	Self, Keith A.	17,058	26.5%	Shelby, Doc	8,531	38.1%
	Harp, Suzanne	13,375	20.7%			
	Williams, Rickey	1,731	2.7%			
	Ivanovskis, Jeremy Daniel	818	1.3%			
	TOTAL	64,471		TOTAL	22,396	
Congressional District 4	Fallon, Pat*	41,297	59.0%	Omere, Iro	16,404	100.0%
	Thomas, Daniel M. "Dan"	21,168	30.2%			
	Harper, John Edward	7,576	10.8%			
	TOTAL	70,041		TOTAL	16,404	
Congressional District 5	Gooden, Lance*	47,692	100.0%	Hill, Tartisha	10,689	52.7%
				Bailey, Kathleen Cordelia	9,605	47.3%
	TOTAL	47,692		TOTAL	20,294	
Congressional District 6	Ellzey, J.K. "Jake"*	38,683	71.2%			
	Buford, James R.	8,636	15.9%			
	Payne, Bill	7,008	12.9%			
	TOTAL	54,327				
Congressional District 7	Teague, Johnny	9,293	43.0%	Fletcher, Lizzie Pannill*	29,579	100.0%
	Stroud, Tim	6,346	29.4%			
	Cohen, Tina Blum	1,792	8.3%			
	Stewart, Lance	1,764	8.2%			
	Atencio, Rudy	1,024	4.7%			
	Rehman, Laique	977	4.5%			
	Gitau, Benson	422	2.0%			
	TOTAL	21,618		TOTAL	29,579	
	PRIMARY RUNOFF					
	Teague, Johnny	9,152	63.6%			
	Stroud, Tim	5,239	36.4%			
	TOTAL	14,391				

TEXAS

GENERAL AND PRIMARY ELECTIONS

	REPUBLICAN PRIMARIES			DEMOCRATIC PRIMARIES		
Congressional District 8	Luttrell, Morgan	34,271	52.1%	Jones, Laura	14,496	100.0%
	Collins, Christian	14,659	22.3%			
	Hullihan, Jonathan	8,296	12.6%			
	McKaughan, Dan	1,585	2.4%			
	Wellington, Jessica	1,550	2.4%			
	Burrows, Candice C.	1,519	2.3%			
	Montgomery, Chuck	1,169	1.8%			
	Philips, Michael	871	1.3%			
	Mitchell, Jonathan Andrew	791	1.2%			
	Bates, Betsy	712	1.1%			
	Whichard, Taylor Marshall IV	295	0.4%			
	TOTAL	65,718		TOTAL	14,496	
Congressional District 9	Leon, Jimmy I.	10,503	100.0%	Green, Al*	42,782	100.0%
	TOTAL	10,503		TOTAL	42,782	
Congressional District 10	McCaul, Michael T.*	63,920	100.0%	Nuno, Linda	20,537	100.0%
	TOTAL	63,920		TOTAL	20,537	
Congressional District 11	Pfluger, August*	61,479	100.0%			
	TOTAL	61,479				
Congressional District 12	Granger, Kay*	46,779	75.2%	Hunt, Trey J	20,561	100.0%
	Catala, Ryan J.	8,759	14.1%			
	Rieg, Alysia	6,662	10.7%			
	TOTAL	62,200		TOTAL	20,561	
Congressional District 13	Jackson, Ronny*	71,554	100.0%	Brown, Kathleen	10,807	100.0%
	TOTAL	71,554		TOTAL	10,807	
Congressional District 14	Weber, Randy*	58,439	89.3%	Williams, Mikal	10,691	50.2%
	Casey, Keith	5,178	7.9%	Howard, Eugene	10,619	49.8%
	Dante, Ruben Landon	1,854	2.8%			
	TOTAL	65,471		TOTAL	21,310	
Congressional District 15	De La Cruz-Hernandez, Monica	16,835	56.5%	Ramirez, Ruben Ramon	9,221	28.3%
	Garza, Mauro	4,544	15.3%	Vallejo, Michelle	6,570	20.1%
	Canady, Sara	2,741	9.2%	Villarreal Rigney, John	6,268	19.2%
	Krause, Ryan	2,728	9.2%	Alvarado, Eliza	5,398	16.5%
	Schmuker, Steve Jr.	1,064	3.6%	Tijerina, Vanessa S.	3,470	10.6%
	Lerma, John C,	658	2.2%	Garza, Julio	1,693	5.2%
	Cavazos, Aizar	504	1.7%			
	Juarez, Angela	416	1.4%			
	Churchill, Vangela	298	1.0%			
	TOTAL	29,788		TOTAL	32,620	
				PRIMARY RUNOFF		
				Vallejo, Michelle	6,079	50.1%
				Ramirez, Ruben Ramon	6,049	49.9%
				TOTAL	12,128	
Congressional District 16	Armendariz-Jackson, Irene	12,623	100.0%	Escobar, Veronica*	30,954	88.0%
				Montanez Berrios, Deliris	4,235	12.0%
	TOTAL	12,623		TOTAL	35,189	
Congressional District 17	Sessions, Pete*	48,222	69.9%	Woods, Mary Jo	17,085	100.0%
	Nelson, Jason "Stormchaser"	8,371	12.1%			
	Carson, Paulette	7,246	10.5%			
	Rosenberger, Rob	5,100	7.4%			
	TOTAL	68,939		TOTAL	17,085	
Congressional District 18	Montiel, Carmen Maria	11,087	100.0%	Jackson Lee, Sheila*	35,194	100.0%
	TOTAL	11,087		TOTAL	35,194	

TEXAS

GENERAL AND PRIMARY ELECTIONS

	REPUBLICAN PRIMARIES			DEMOCRATIC PRIMARIES		
Congressional District 19	Arrington, Jodey* TOTAL	68,503 68,503	100.0%			
Congressional District 20	Sinclair, Kyle TOTAL	15,938 15,938	100.0%	Castro, Joaquin* TOTAL	33,214 33,214	100.0%
Congressional District 21	Roy, Chip* Lowry, Robert Zavorka, Dana French, Michael Alexander TOTAL	78,087 7,642 4,206 3,886 93,821	83.2% 8.1% 4.5% 4.1%	Zapata, Claudia Andreana Villarreal, Ricardo Branscum, Coy Gee II Anderson, David Lee Jr. Sturm, Scott William Gacis, Cherif TOTAL **PRIMARY RUNOFF** Zapata, Claudia Andreana Villarreal, Ricardo TOTAL	16,604 9,590 3,157 3,038 1,865 902 35,156 13,886 7,996 21,882	47.2% 27.3% 9.0% 8.6% 5.3% 2.6% 63.5% 36.5%
Congressional District 22	Nehls, Troy* Thorne, Gregory Jonathan TOTAL	50,281 7,378 57,659	87.2% 12.8%	Jordan, Jamie Kaye TOTAL	20,818 20,818	100.0%
Congressional District 23	Gonzales, Ernest Anthony "Tony" II* Arredondo-Lynch, Alma Garcia-Ureste, Alia TOTAL	37,212 7,261 3,235 47,708	78.0% 15.2% 6.8%	Lira, John Golden, Priscilla TOTAL	19,816 15,664 35,480	55.9% 44.1%
Congressional District 24	Van Duyne, Elizabeth Ann "Beth"* Weymouth, Nathaniel "Nate" TOTAL	61,768 10,868 72,636	85.0% 15.0%	McDowell, Jan Gay, Derrik Fragnoli, Kathy TOTAL **PRIMARY RUNOFF** McDowell, Jan Gay, Derrik TOTAL	11,467 9,571 8,139 29,177 7,118 6,788 13,906	39.3% 32.8% 27.9% 51.2% 48.8%
Congressional District 25	Williams, Roger* TOTAL	69,418 69,418	100.0%			
Congressional District 26	Burgess, Michael C.* Gallo, Vincent Brazeal, Brian Smith, Issac Harrison, Raven TOTAL	42,006 6,437 5,892 5,085 3,427 62,847	66.8% 10.2% 9.4% 8.1% 5.5%			
Congressional District 27	Cloud, Michael* Louderback, Andrew John "AJ" Mapp, Christopher K. Alvarez, Andrew Mireles, Eric TOTAL	45,741 7,704 4,542 2,648 2,478 63,113	72.5% 12.2% 7.2% 4.2% 3.9%	Perez, Maclovio Jr. Tristan, Anthony James Melgoza, Victor TOTAL	13,044 5,733 3,289 22,066	59.1% 26.0% 14.9%

TEXAS

GENERAL AND PRIMARY ELECTIONS

		REPUBLICAN PRIMARIES		DEMOCRATIC PRIMARIES		
Congressional District 28	Garcia, Casandra "Cassy"	5,923	23.5%	Cuellar, Henry*	23,988	48.7%
	Whitten, Sandra	4,534	18.0%	Cisneros, Jessica	22,983	46.6%
	Fowler, Steven	3,388	13.5%	Benavides, Tannya	2,324	4.7%
	Ng, Willie Vasquez	3,358	13.3%			
	Cabrera, Ed	3,343	13.3%			
	Hohman, Eric	2,988	11.9%			
	Rodriguez, Rolando	1,622	6.4%			
	TOTAL	25,156		TOTAL	49,295	
	PRIMARY RUNOFF			**PRIMARY RUNOFF**		
	Garcia, Casandra "Cassy"	8,485	57.0%	Cuellar, Henry*	22,895	50.3%
	Whitten, Sandra	6,413	43.0%	Cisneros, Jessica	22,614	49.7%
	TOTAL	14,898		TOTAL	45,509	
Congressional District 29	Schafranek, Robert	3,299	39.3%	Garcia, Sylvia R.	19,402	100.0%
	Garza, Julio	2,629	31.4%			
	Blanco, Jaimy Z.	2,212	26.4%			
	Ejigu, Lulite	244	2.9%			
	TOTAL	8,384		TOTAL	19,402	
	PRIMARY RUNOFF					
	Schafranek, Robert	2,875	60.7%			
	Garza, Julio	1,859	39.3%			
	TOTAL	4,734				
Congressional District 30	Harris, James Frank	3,952	32.9%	Crockett, Jasmine	26,798	48.5%
	Rodgers, James	3,754	31.3%	Hamilton, Jane Hope	9,436	17.1%
	Goodwin-Castillo, Kelvin	2,023	16.8%	Williams Lankford, Keisha	4,323	7.8%
	Diaz, Lizbeth	1,416	11.8%	Caraway, Barbara Mallory	4,277	7.7%
	Jefferson, Dakinya "Kinya"	703	5.9%	Mulugheta, Abel	3,284	5.9%
	Roc'ellerpitts, Angeigh	160	1.3%	Williams, Roy Jr.	2,746	5.0%
				Jones Hill, Vonciel	1,886	3.4%
				Mason, Jessica	1,858	3.4%
				Dixon, Arthur	677	1.2%
	TOTAL	12,008		TOTAL	55,285	
	PRIMARY RUNOFF			**PRIMARY RUNOFF**		
	Rodgers, James	3,090	56.9%	Crockett, Jasmine	17,462	60.6%
	Harris, James Frank	2,339	43.1%	Hamilton, Jane Hope	11,369	39.4%
	TOTAL	5,429		TOTAL	28,831	
Congressional District 31	Carter, John*	50,887	71.1%			
	Williams, Mike	14,115	19.7%			
	Garapati, Abhiram	6,590	9.2%			
	TOTAL	71,592				
Congressional District 32	Swad, Antonio	8,962	40.3%	Allred, Colin*	31,805	100.0%
	Webb, Justin	4,007	18.0%			
	Davis, Nathan	3,549	16.0%			
	Day, Darrell	2,321	10.4%			
	Namdar, Brad	2,270	10.2%			
	Okpa, Edward "EE"	1,128	5.1%			
	TOTAL	22,237		TOTAL	31,805	
	PRIMARY RUNOFF					
	Swad, Antonio	6,929	57.0%			
	Webb, Justin	5,226	43.0%			
	TOTAL	12,155				
Congressional District 33	Gillespie, Patrick David	5,709	63.5%	Veasey, Marc*	16,806	69.5%
	MacGlaflin, Robert	3,284	36.5%	Quintanilla, Carlos	7,373	30.5%
	TOTAL	8,993		TOTAL	24,179	

TEXAS

GENERAL AND PRIMARY ELECTIONS

	REPUBLICAN PRIMARIES			DEMOCRATIC PRIMARIES		
Congressional District 34	Flores, Mayra	9,490	60.3%	Gonzalez, Vicente	23,531	64.8%
	McCaffrey, Frank	3,444	21.9%	Cisneros, Laura	8,456	23.3%
	Kunkle, Gregory Scott Jr.	1,677	10.7%	Reynoso, Beatriz	1,287	3.5%
	Cantu-Cabrera, Juana "Janie"	1,115	7.1%	Thompson, William	1,085	3.0%
				Meza, Filemon	920	2.5%
				Zavala, Diego	718	2.0%
				Rodriguez Haro, Osbert	331	0.9%
	TOTAL	15,726		TOTAL	36,328	
Congressional District 35	McQueen, Dan	2,900	21.3%	Casar, Greg	25,505	61.1%
	Rodriguez, Michael	2,034	14.9%	Rodriguez, Eduardo R. "Eddie"	6,526	15.6%
	Condict, Bill	1,529	11.2%	Viagran, Rebecca	6,511	15.6%
	Jackson, Marilyn	1,473	10.8%	Sisco, Carla Joy	3,190	7.6%
	Sawatzky, Dan	1,414	10.4%			
	Sundt, Jennifer	1,299	9.5%			
	Montoya, Sam	1,227	9.0%			
	Ledezma, Alejandro	833	6.1%			
	Aragona, Jenai	589	4.3%			
	Palagi, Asa George Kent	327	2.4%			
	TOTAL	13,625		TOTAL	41,732	
	PRIMARY RUNOFF					
	McQueen, Dan	4,161	61.3%			
	Rodriguez, Michael	2,632	38.7%			
	TOTAL	6,793				
Congressional District 36	Babin, Brian*	59,381	100.0%	Haire, Jonathan "Jon"	16,589	100.0%
	TOTAL	59,381		TOTAL	16,589	
Congressional District 37	Garcia Sharon, Jenny	9,087	46.8%	Doggett, Lloyd	60,007	79.3%
	Lingsch, Rod	5,403	27.8%	Imam, Donna	13,385	17.7%
	Diacogiannis, Jeremiah	4,938	25.4%	Jones, Chris	1,503	2.0%
				Beaubouef, Richard Quinton "Q"	804	1.1%
	TOTAL	19,428		TOTAL	75,699	
	PRIMARY RUNOFF					
	Garcia Sharon, Jenny	6,923	59.1%			
	Lingsch, Rod	4,791	40.9%			
	TOTAL	11,714				
Congressional District 38	Hunt, Wesley	35,291	55.3%	Martinez Alexander, Diana	9,861	44.6%
	Ramsey, Mark	19,352	30.3%	Klussmann, Duncan Foster	8,698	39.3%
	Hogan, David	3,125	4.9%	Reed, Centrell	3,550	16.1%
	Lopez, Roland	2,048	3.2%			
	Guillory, Brett	1,416	2.2%			
	Ford, Jerry Sr.	997	1.6%			
	Welch, Richard	633	1.0%			
	Cross, Alex	460	0.7%			
	Mockus, Damien Matthew Peter	249	0.4%			
	Covarrubias, Phil	228	0.4%			
	TOTAL	63,799		TOTAL	22,109	
				PRIMARY RUNOFF		
				Klussmann, Duncan Foster	6,449	61.1%
				Martinez Alexander, Diana	4,111	38.9%
				TOTAL	10,560	

Note: An asterisk (*) denotes incumbent.

UTAH

Statewide Races

Utah saw its most competitive race in nearly five decades in 2022, but it was not a contest between a Democrat and a Republican.

In late 2021, Evan McMullin, a 2016 candidate for president, launched a campaign for Senate as an independent. A former CIA agent who was a Republican before 2016, McMullin launched a third-party presidential effort once it was clear that Donald Trump would be the GOP nominee. Nationally, he took less than 1% of the vote, but he ran best in his native Utah, pulling 21%. Sounding a centrist tone, one of McMullin's complaints in 2022 was that Republican Sen. Mike Lee had aligned himself too closely with Trump. In 2016, for example, Lee was critical of his party's then-nominee – as McMullin was quick to point out, he got Lee's vote in the 2016 election. But by 2020, the senator was campaigning with the then-president.

McMullin got a break in spring 2022, when state Democrats opted not to run their own candidate and threw their support to him. In late April, Lee overwhelmingly won the state Republican party's endorsement at a convention. A few months later, in a late June primary, he beat out his main Republican rival, state Rep. Rebecca Edwards, two-to-one to become the GOP nominee.

In the general election, Lee garnered endorsements from 48 of his 49 fellow Republican senators – the sole exception was his home state colleague, Mitt Romney. Still, Lee had a financial advantage and in Utah, his partisan label seemed to be enough – he was reelected to a third term 53%–43% over McMullin. McMullin carried the same three counties that went for Joe Biden in 2020: Grand, Summit, and Salt Lake. Salt Lake County (named for the city it contains) is the state's most populous and went for McMullin by 19 points, up from Biden's 11-point margin. Though he still lost it, McMullin ran almost 15 points better than Biden in Provo's Utah County, the state's second-most populous county and the home of Brigham Young University. McMullin's crossover support diminished as one moved further south of the Provo area – in Washington County (St. George), making up Utah's southwestern corner, Lee's 71%–26% margin was only a few points weaker than Trump's.

House Races

In 2018, Utah voters narrowly passed a ballot measure aimed at establishing an independent redistricting commission. In response, the heavily Republican legislature enacted a law in 2020 that enabled them to bypass the commission's recommendations. With that, Republicans had a free hand at preserving their 4-0 advantage in the state's House delegation.

Republicans' most pressing goal was to strengthen their hold on the 4th District, held by first-term Rep. Burgess Owens. Over the past decade, the usually red-leaning district had seen some competitive races, even electing Democrats in 2012 and 2018. Republican mappers sliced up Salt Lake County as if it were a pizza, giving every district part of the blue-leaning county. The gerrymander worked as intended: all four Republicans in the delegation were reelected by margins of more than 25 points.

UTAH

Congressional districts first established for elections held in 2022

4 members

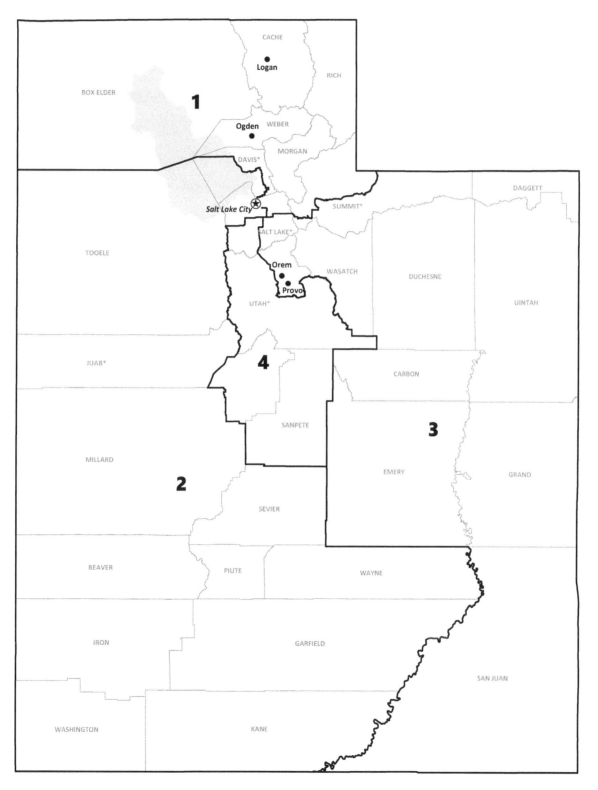

* Asterisk indicates a county whose boundaries include parts of two or more congressional districts.

UTAH

GOVERNOR
Spencer Cox (R). Elected 2020 to a four-year term.

SENATORS (2 Republicans)
Mitt Romney (R). Elected 2018 to a six-year term.

Mike Lee (R). Reelected 2022 to a six-year term. Previously elected 2016, 2010.

REPRESENTATIVES (4 Republicans)
1. Blake Moore (R)
2. Chris Stewart (R)
3. John Curtis (R)
4. Burgess Owens (R)

POSTWAR VOTE FOR PRESIDENT

Year	Total Vote	Republican Vote	Republican Candidate	Democratic Vote	Democratic Candidate	Other Vote	Rep.-Dem. Plurality	Total Vote Rep.	Total Vote Dem.	Major Vote Rep.	Major Vote Dem.
2020	1,488,289	865,140	Trump, Donald J.*	560,282	Biden, Joseph R. Jr.	62,867	304,858 R	58.1%	37.6%	60.7%	39.3%
2016**	1,131,430	515,231	Trump, Donald J.	310,676	Clinton, Hillary Rodham	305,523	204,555 R	45.5%	27.5%	62.4%	37.6%
2012	1,017,440	740,600	Romney, W. Mitt	251,813	Obama, Barack H.*	25,027	488,787 R	72.8%	24.7%	74.6%	25.4%
2008	952,370	596,030	McCain, John S. III	327,670	Obama, Barack H.	28,670	268,360 R	62.6%	34.4%	64.5%	35.5%
2004	927,844	663,742	Bush, George W.*	241,199	Kerry, John F.	22,903	422,543 R	71.5%	26.0%	73.3%	26.7%
2000**	770,754	515,096	Bush, George W.	203,053	Gore, Albert Jr.	52,605	312,043 R	66.8%	26.3%	71.7%	28.3%
1996**	665,629	361,911	Dole, Robert "Bob"	221,633	Clinton, Bill*	82,085	140,278 R	54.4%	33.3%	62.0%	38.0%
1992**	743,999	322,632	Bush, George H.*	183,429	Clinton, Bill	237,938	139,203 R	43.4%	24.7%	63.8%	36.2%
1988	647,008	428,442	Bush, George H.	207,343	Dukakis, Michael S.	11,223	221,099 R	66.2%	32.0%	67.4%	32.6%
1984	629,656	469,105	Reagan, Ronald*	155,369	Mondale, Walter F.	5,182	313,736 R	74.5%	24.7%	75.1%	24.9%
1980**	604,222	439,687	Reagan, Ronald	124,266	Carter, Jimmy*	40,269	315,421 R	72.8%	20.6%	78.0%	22.0%
1976	541,198	337,908	Ford, Gerald R.*	182,110	Carter, Jimmy	21,180	155,798 R	62.4%	33.6%	65.0%	35.0%
1972	478,476	323,643	Nixon, Richard M.*	126,284	McGovern, George S.	28,549	197,359 R	67.6%	26.4%	71.9%	28.1%
1968**	422,568	238,728	Nixon, Richard M.	156,665	Humphrey, Hubert Horatio Jr.	27,175	82,063 R	56.5%	37.1%	60.4%	39.6%
1964	401,413	181,785	Goldwater, Barry M. Sr.	219,628	Johnson, Lyndon B.*		37,843 D	45.3%	54.7%	45.3%	54.7%
1960	374,709	205,361	Nixon, Richard M.	169,248	Kennedy, John F.	100	36,113 R	54.8%	45.2%	54.8%	45.2%
1956	333,995	215,631	Eisenhower, Dwight D.*	118,364	Stevenson, Adlai E. II		97,267 R	64.6%	35.4%	64.6%	35.4%
1952	329,554	194,190	Eisenhower, Dwight D.	135,364	Stevenson, Adlai E. II		58,826 R	58.9%	41.1%	58.9%	41.1%
1948	276,306	124,402	Dewey, Thomas E.	149,151	Truman, Harry S.*	2,753	24,749 D	45.0%	54.0%	45.5%	54.5%

Note: An asterisk (*) denotes incumbent. **In past elections, the other vote included: 2016 - 243,690 Unaffiliated (Evan McMullin), 39,608 Libertarian (Gary Johnson); 2000 - 35,850 Green (Ralph Nader); 1996 - 66,461 Reform (Ross Perot); 1992 - 203,400 Independent (Perot), who finished second; 1980 - 30,284 Independent (John Anderson); 1968 - 26,906 American Independent (George Wallace).

UTAH

POSTWAR VOTE FOR GOVERNOR

Year	Total Vote	Republican Vote	Republican Candidate	Democratic Vote	Democratic Candidate	Other Vote	Rep.-Dem. Plurality	Total Vote Rep.	Total Vote Dem.	Major Vote Rep.	Major Vote Dem.
2020	1,438,711	918,754	Cox, Spencer	442,754	Peterson, Christopher	77,203	476,000 R	63.9%	30.8%	67.5%	32.5%
2016	1,125,035	750,850	Herbert, Gary R.*	323,349	Weinholtz, Mike	50,836	427,501 R	66.7%	28.7%	69.9%	30.1%
2012	1,006,524	688,592	Herbert, Gary R.*	277,622	Cooke, Peter S.	40,310	410,970 R	68.4%	27.6%	71.3%	28.7%
2010S**	643,307	412,151	Herbert, Gary R.*	205,246	Corroon, Peter	25,910	206,905 R	64.1%	31.9%	66.8%	33.2%
2008	945,525	734,049	Huntsman, Jon Jr.*	186,503	Springmeyer, Bob	24,973	547,546 R	77.6%	19.7%	79.7%	20.3%
2004	919,960	531,190	Huntsman, Jon Jr.	380,359	Matheson, Scot Jr.	8,411	150,831 R	57.7%	41.3%	58.3%	41.7%
2000	761,806	424,837	Leavitt, Mike O.*	321,979	Orton, Bill	14,990	102,858 R	55.8%	42.3%	56.9%	43.1%
1996	671,879	503,693	Leavitt, Mike O.*	156,616	Bradley, Jim	11,570	347,077 R	75.0%	23.3%	76.3%	23.7%
1992**	762,549	321,713	Leavitt, Mike O.	177,181	Hanson, Stewart	263,655	144,532 R	42.2%	23.2%	64.5%	35.5%
1988**	649,114	260,462	Bangerter, Norman H.*	249,321	Wilson, Ted	139,331	11,141 R	40.1%	38.4%	51.1%	48.9%
1984	629,619	351,792	Bangerter, Norman H.	275,669	Owens, Wayne	2,158	76,123 R	55.9%	43.8%	56.1%	43.9%
1980	600,019	266,578	Wright, Bob	330,974	Matheson, Scott M.*	2,467	64,396 D	44.4%	55.2%	44.6%	55.4%
1976	539,649	248,027	Romney, Vernon B.	280,706	Matheson, Scott M.	10,916	32,679 D	46.0%	52.0%	46.9%	53.1%
1972	476,447	144,449	Strike, Nicholas L.	331,998	Rampton, Calvin L.*		187,549 D	30.3%	69.7%	30.3%	69.7%
1968	421,012	131,729	Buehner, Carl W.	289,283	Rampton, Calvin L.*		157,554 D	31.3%	68.7%	31.3%	68.7%
1964	398,256	171,300	Melich, Mitchell	226,956	Rampton, Calvin L.		55,656 D	43.0%	57.0%	43.0%	57.0%
1960	371,489	195,634	Clyde, George Dewey*	175,855	Barlocker, William A.		19,779 R	52.7%	47.3%	52.7%	47.3%
1956**	332,889	127,164	Clyde, George Dewey	111,297	Romney, L. C.	94,428	15,867 R	38.2%	33.4%	53.3%	46.7%
1952	327,704	180,516	Lee, J. Bracken*	147,188	Glade, Earl J.		33,328 R	55.1%	44.9%	55.1%	44.9%
1948	275,067	151,253	Lee, J. Bracken	123,814	Maw, Herbert B.*		27,439 R	55.0%	45.0%	55.0%	45.0%

Note: An asterisk (*) denotes incumbent. **In past elections, the other vote included: 1992 - 255,753 Independent (Merrill Cook), who finished second; 1988 - 136,651 Independent (Cook); 1956 - 94,428 Independent (J. Bracken Lee). The 2010 election was for a short term to fill a vacancy.

POSTWAR VOTE FOR SENATOR

Year	Total Vote	Republican Vote	Republican Candidate	Democratic Vote	Democratic Candidate	Other Vote	Rep.-Dem. Plurality	Total Vote Rep.	Total Vote Dem.	Major Vote Rep.	Major Vote Dem.
2022	1,076,061	571,974	Lee, Mike*			504,087	571,974 R	53.2%		100.0%	
2018	1,062,897	665,215	Romney, W. Mitt	328,541	Wilson, Jenny	69,141	336,674 R	62.6%	30.9%	66.9%	33.1%
2016	1,115,608	760,241	Lee, Mike*	301,860	Snow, Misty K.	53,507	458,381 R	68.1%	27.1%	71.6%	28.4%
2012	1,006,901	657,608	Hatch, Orrin G.*	301,873	Howell, Scott N.	47,420	355,735 R	65.3%	30.0%	68.5%	31.5%
2010	633,829	390,179	Lee, Mike	207,685	Granato, Sam	35,965	182,494 R	61.6%	32.8%	65.3%	34.7%
2006	571,252	356,238	Hatch, Orrin G.*	177,459	Ashdown, Pete	37,555	178,779 R	62.4%	31.1%	66.7%	33.3%
2004	911,726	626,640	Bennett, Robert F.*	258,955	Van Dam, R. Paul	26,131	367,685 R	68.7%	28.4%	70.8%	29.2%
2000	769,704	504,803	Hatch, Orrin G.*	242,569	Howell, Scott N.	22,332	262,234 R	65.6%	31.5%	67.5%	32.5%
1998	494,909	316,652	Bennett, Robert F.*	163,172	Leckman, Scott	15,085	153,480 R	64.0%	33.0%	66.0%	34.0%
1994	519,323	357,297	Hatch, Orrin G.*	146,938	Shea, Patrick A.	15,088	210,359 R	68.8%	28.3%	70.9%	29.1%
1992	758,479	420,069	Bennett, Robert F.	301,228	Owens, Wayne	37,182	118,841 R	55.4%	39.7%	58.2%	41.8%
1988	640,702	430,089	Hatch, Orrin G.*	203,364	Moss, Brian	7,249	226,725 R	67.1%	31.7%	67.9%	32.1%
1986	435,111	314,608	Garn, E. J.*	115,523	Oliver, Craig	4,980	199,085 R	72.3%	26.6%	73.1%	26.9%
1982	530,802	309,332	Hatch, Orrin G.*	219,482	Wilson, Ted	1,988	89,850 R	58.3%	41.3%	58.5%	41.5%
1980	594,298	437,675	Garn, E. J.*	151,454	Berman, Dan	5,169	286,221 R	73.6%	25.5%	74.3%	25.7%
1976	540,108	290,221	Hatch, Orrin G.	241,948	Moss, Frank E.*	7,939	48,273 R	53.7%	44.8%	54.5%	45.5%
1974	420,642	210,299	Garn, E. J.	185,377	Owens, Wayne	24,966	24,922 R	50.0%	44.1%	53.1%	46.9%
1970	374,303	159,004	Burton, Laurence J.	210,207	Moss, Frank E.*	5,092	51,203 D	42.5%	56.2%	43.1%	56.9%
1968	419,262	225,075	Bennett, Wallace F.*	192,168	Weilenmann, Milton	2,019	32,907 R	53.7%	45.8%	53.9%	46.1%
1964	397,384	169,562	Wilkinson, Ernest L.	227,822	Moss, Frank E.*		58,260 D	42.7%	57.3%	42.7%	57.3%
1962	318,411	166,755	Bennett, Wallace F.*	151,656	King, David S.		15,099 R	52.4%	47.6%	52.4%	47.6%
1958**	291,311	101,471	Watkins, Arthur V.*	112,827	Moss, Frank E.	77,013	11,356 D	34.8%	38.7%	47.4%	52.6%
1956	330,381	178,261	Bennett, Wallace F.*	152,120	Hopkin, Alonzo F.		26,141 R	54.0%	46.0%	54.0%	46.0%
1952	327,033	177,435	Watkins, Arthur V.*	149,598	Granger, Walter K.		27,837 R	54.3%	45.7%	54.3%	45.7%
1950	264,440	142,427	Bennett, Wallace F.	121,198	Thomas, Elbert D.*	815	21,229 R	53.9%	45.8%	54.0%	46.0%
1946	197,399	101,142	Watkins, Arthur V.	96,257	Murdock, Abe*		4,885 R	51.2%	48.8%	51.2%	48.8%

Note: An asterisk (*) denotes incumbent. **In past elections, the other vote included: 1958 - 77,013 Independent (J. Bracken Lee).

UTAH

SENATOR 2022

2020 Census Population	County	Total Vote	Republican (Lee)	Democratic	Other	Rep.-Dem. Plurality	Total Vote Rep.	Total Vote Dem.	Major Vote Rep.	Major Vote Dem.
6,725	BEAVER	2,447	1,971		476	1,971 R	80.5%		100.0%	
56,345	BOX ELDER	19,903	14,434		5,469	14,434 R	72.5%		100.0%	
128,849	CACHE	41,990	24,588		17,402	24,588 R	58.6%		100.0%	
20,560	CARBON	6,729	4,265		2,464	4,265 R	63.4%		100.0%	
1,030	DAGGETT	498	377		121	377 R	75.7%		100.0%	
356,803	DAVIS	123,778	66,385		57,393	66,385 R	53.6%		100.0%	
19,882	DUCHESNE	6,283	5,170		1,113	5,170 R	82.3%		100.0%	
10,017	EMERY	4,107	3,269		838	3,269 R	79.6%		100.0%	
5,087	GARFIELD	2,385	1,795		590	1,795 R	75.3%		100.0%	
9,803	GRAND	4,643	1,901		2,742	1,901 R	40.9%		100.0%	
55,582	IRON	17,309	12,923		4,386	12,923 R	74.7%		100.0%	
12,092	JUAB	4,731	3,886		845	3,886 R	82.1%		100.0%	
7,964	KANE	3,659	2,553		1,106	2,553 R	69.8%		100.0%	
13,240	MILLARD	5,130	4,279		851	4,279 R	83.4%		100.0%	
12,208	MORGAN	5,157	3,665		1,492	3,665 R	71.1%		100.0%	
1,490	PIUTE	783	692		91	692 R	88.4%		100.0%	
2,497	RICH	1,073	844		229	844 R	78.7%		100.0%	
1,164,021	SALT LAKE	381,195	144,931		236,264	144,931 R	38.0%		100.0%	
15,416	SAN JUAN	5,562	3,118		2,444	3,118 R	56.1%		100.0%	
31,151	SANPETE	10,004	7,829		2,175	7,829 R	78.3%		100.0%	
21,688	SEVIER	7,775	6,411		1,364	6,411 R	82.5%		100.0%	
42,247	SUMMIT	20,358	7,305		13,053	7,305 R	35.9%		100.0%	
72,942	TOOELE	22,074	13,371		8,703	13,371 R	60.6%		100.0%	
35,688	UINTAH	10,834	8,905		1,929	8,905 R	82.2%		100.0%	
639,599	UTAH	206,100	127,096		79,004	127,096 R	61.7%		100.0%	
34,547	WASATCH	13,464	7,528		5,936	7,528 R	55.9%		100.0%	
179,541	WASHINGTON	69,501	49,420		20,081	49,420 R	71.1%		100.0%	
2,711	WAYNE	1,514	1,056		458	1,056 R	69.7%		100.0%	
261,558	WEBER	77,075	42,007		35,068	42,007 R	54.5%		100.0%	
3,221,283	TOTAL	1,076,061	571,974		504,087	571,974 R	53.2%		100.0%	

UTAH

HOUSE OF REPRESENTATIVES

CD	Year	Total Vote	Republican Vote	Republican Candidate	Democratic Vote	Democratic Candidate	Other Vote	Rep.-Dem. Plurality	Total Vote Rep.	Total Vote Dem.	Major Vote Rep.	Major Vote Dem.
1	2022	266,420	178,434	MOORE, BLAKE DAVID*	87,986	JONES, RICK EDWIN		90,448 R	67.0%	33.0%	67.0%	33.0%
1	2020	342,182	237,988	MOORE, BLAKE DAVID	104,194	PARRY, DARREN BRUCE		133,794 R	69.6%	30.4%	69.6%	30.4%
1	2018	254,333	156,692	BISHOP, ROBERT "ROB"*	63,308	CASTILLO, LEE	34,333	93,384 R	61.6%	24.9%	71.2%	28.8%
1	2016	277,455	182,928	BISHOP, ROBERT "ROB"*	73,381	CLEMENS, PETER C.	21,146	109,547 R	65.9%	26.4%	71.4%	28.6%
1	2014	130,034	84,231	BISHOP, ROBERT "ROB"*	36,422	MCALEER, DONNA M.	9,381	47,809 R	64.8%	28.0%	69.8%	30.2%
1	2012	245,528	175,487	BISHOP, ROBERT "ROB"*	60,611	MCALEER, DONNA M.	9,430	114,876 R	71.5%	24.7%	74.3%	25.7%
2	2022	259,399	154,883	STEWART, CHRIS*	88,224	MITCHELL, NICHOLAS	16,292	66,659 R	59.7%	34.0%	63.7%	36.3%
2	2020	354,224	208,997	STEWART, CHRIS*	129,762	WESTON, KAEL	15,465	79,235 R	59.0%	36.6%	61.7%	38.3%
2	2018	270,044	151,489	STEWART, CHRIS*	105,051	GHORBANI, SHIREEN	13,504	46,438 R	56.1%	38.9%	59.1%	40.9%
2	2016	276,841	170,542	STEWART, CHRIS*	93,780	ALBARRAN, CHARLENE	12,519	76,762 R	61.6%	33.9%	64.5%	35.5%
2	2014	146,188	88,915	STEWART, CHRIS*	47,585	ROBLES, LUZ	9,688	41,330 R	60.8%	32.6%	65.1%	34.9%
2	2012	248,545	154,523	STEWART, CHRIS	83,176	SEEGMILLER, JAY	10,846	71,347 R	62.2%	33.5%	65.0%	35.0%
3	2022	283,380	182,497	CURTIS, JOHN*	83,687	WRIGHT, GLENN	17,196	98,810 R	64.4%	29.5%	68.6%	31.4%
3	2020	358,670	246,674	CURTIS, JOHN*	96,067	THORPE, DEVIN	15,929	150,607 R	68.8%	26.8%	72.0%	28.0%
3	2018	258,858	174,856	CURTIS, JOHN*	70,686	SINGER, JAMES	13,316	104,170 R	67.5%	27.3%	71.2%	28.8%
3	2016	285,305	209,589	CHAFFETZ, JASON*	75,716	TRYON, STEPHEN		133,873 R	73.5%	26.5%	73.5%	26.5%
3	2014	142,580	102,952	CHAFFETZ, JASON*	32,059	WONNACOTT, BRIAN	7,569	70,893 R	72.2%	22.5%	76.3%	23.7%
3	2012	259,547	198,828	CHAFFETZ, JASON*	60,719	SIMONSEN, SOREN D.		138,109 R	76.6%	23.4%	76.6%	23.4%

UTAH

HOUSE OF REPRESENTATIVES

			Republican		Democratic		Other Vote	Rep.-Dem. Plurality	Percentage			
									Total Vote		Major Vote	
CD	Year	Total Vote	Vote	Candidate	Vote	Candidate			Rep.	Dem.	Rep.	Dem.
4	2022	254,056	155,110	OWENS, BURGESS*	82,181	MCDONALD, DARLENE	16,765	72,929 R	61.1%	32.3%	65.4%	34.6%
4	2020	376,701	179,688	OWENS, BURGESS	175,923	MCADAMS, BEN*	21,090	3,765 R	47.7%	46.7%	50.5%	49.5%
4	2018	269,271	134,270	LOVE, MIA B.*	134,964	MCADAMS, BEN	37	694 D	49.9%	50.1%	49.9%	50.1%
4	2016	274,569	147,597	LOVE, MIA B.*	113,413	OWENS, DOUG	13,559	34,184 R	53.8%	41.3%	56.5%	43.5%
4	2014	147,168	74,936	LOVE, MIA B.	67,425	OWENS, DOUG	4,807	7,511 R	50.9%	45.8%	52.6%	47.4%
4	2012	245,277	119,035	LOVE, MIA B.	119,803	MATHESON, JIM*	6,439	768 D	48.5%	48.8%	49.8%	50.2%
TOTAL	2022	1,063,255	670,924		342,078		50,253	328,846 R	63.1%	32.2%	66.2%	33.8%
TOTAL	2020	1,431,777	873,347		505,946		52,484	367,401 R	61.0%	35.3%	63.3%	36.7%
TOTAL	2018	1,052,506	617,307		374,009		61,190	243,298 R	58.7%	35.5%	62.3%	37.7%
TOTAL	2016	1,114,170	710,656		356,290		47,224	354,366 R	63.8%	32.0%	66.6%	33.4%
TOTAL	2014	565,970	351,034		183,491		31,445	167,543 R	62.0%	32.4%	65.7%	34.3%
TOTAL	2012	998,897	647,873		324,309		26,715	323,564 R	64.9%	32.5%	66.6%	33.4%

Note: An asterisk (*) denotes incumbent.

UTAH

GENERAL AND PRIMARY ELECTIONS

GENERAL ELECTIONS: OTHER VOTES

Senate	Other vote was 459,958 Independent (Evan McMullin), 31,784 Libertarian (James Hansen), 12,103 Independent American (Tommy Williams), 242 Write-In (Write-Ins)
House	Other vote was:
CD 2	8,622 United Utah Party (Jay McFarland), 7,670 Constitution (Cassie Easley)
CD 3	8,287 Libertarian (Michael Stoddard), 4,874 Constitution (Daniel Cummings), 4,035 Independent American (Aaron Heineman)
CD 4	16,740 United Utah Party (January Walker), 25 Write-In (Jonathan Peterson)

2022 PRIMARY ELECTIONS: SUPPLEMENTARY INFORMATION

Primary	June 28, 2022	Registration (as of June 2, 2022 – includes 211,093 inactive registrants)	1,885,103	Republican	954,666
				Democratic	269,374
				Independent American	71,727
				Libertarian	23,967
				Constitution	7,651
				Green	2,208
				United Utah	2,680
				Unaffiliated	555,038
Primary Type	Semi-Open—Registered Democrats and unaffiliated voters could participate in the Democratic primary. Only registered Republicans could vote in the Republican primary.				

UTAH

GENERAL AND PRIMARY ELECTIONS

	REPUBLICAN PRIMARIES			DEMOCRATIC PRIMARIES	
Senator	Lee, Mike*	258,089	61.9%		
	Edwards, Becky	123,617	29.7%		
	Isom, Ally	34,997	8.4%		
	TOTAL	416,703			
Congressional District 1	Moore, Blake David*	58,408	57.6%		
	Badger, Andrew	28,437	28.0%		
	Cannon, Tina	14,577	14.4%		
	TOTAL	101,422			
Congressional District 2	Stewart, Chris*	75,586	72.6%	Mitchell, Nicholas	Unopposed
	Rider, Erin	28,480	27.4%		
	TOTAL	104,066			
Congressional District 3	Curtis, John*	78,341	69.6%	Wright, Glenn	Unopposed
	Herrod, Christopher	34,204	30.4%		
	TOTAL	112,545			
Congressional District 4	Owens, Burgess*	56,397	61.9%	McDonald, Darlene	Unopposed
	Hunsaker, Jake	34,728	38.1%		
	TOTAL	91,125			

Note: An asterisk (*) denotes incumbent.

VERMONT

Statewide and House Races

Though five of the six Senatorial retirements of the 2022 cycle came on the Republican side of the aisle, the sole Democratic retirement was a significant one: After seven terms in office, Vermont's Patrick Leahy did not seek reelection. Leahy was initially elected in 1974 and was the last remaining senator to be sworn into office by the late Vice President Nelson Rockefeller. After the 2020 elections, when Democrats took control of the chamber, he become President Pro Tempore, as the most senior member of the majority party.

In the primary to replace Leahy, state Democrats largely deferred to Rep. Peter Welch, who had held the state's At-Large seat since 2006. At age 76, Welch won the Democratic primary with 87% against two minor candidates. Three candidates ran in the Republican primary. Christina Nolan, a former U. S. Attorney who tried to keep her distance from her party's national leadership, seemed like the Republican best-positioned for the general election (although it would have been an uphill race for any Republican). But Gerald Malloy, a pro-Trump candidate, won the August primary 42%–38% over Nolan. In November, Welch won by 40 points, running ahead of the 35-point margin that Joe Biden carried the state by in 2020. Welch carried every county but Essex County, up in the Northeast Kingdom, which he missed by 6 votes.

The early favorite to replace Welch in the House was Democratic Lt. Gov. Molly Gray, who had won the state's second-highest office in 2020. Leahy endorsed Gray, but Bernie Sanders, the state's other senator (who had much more of a national profile), backed state Senate President pro tempore Becca Balint. Fairly or not, the primary became seen as a race between an establishment candidate and a progressive – the latter won out. Balint took 60% to Gray's 37%. In the general election, Balint ran a few points behind Welch, but won by a landslide 63%–28% – she also took everything but Essex County.

While Welch and Balint scored huge wins, the statewide candidate who won by the largest margin was actually a Republican. Gov. Phil Scott, who is probably in the running for the most liberal Republican officeholder in the nation, won by a fourth term by a 71%–24% margin. In 2016, Scott declined to endorse then-candidate Trump for president, and, in 2020, supported Biden. In national surveys, he was typically ranked among the most popular governors. Scott's 2022 landslide was so large that, for the first time in his career, he carried every municipality in the state.

VERMONT

One member At Large

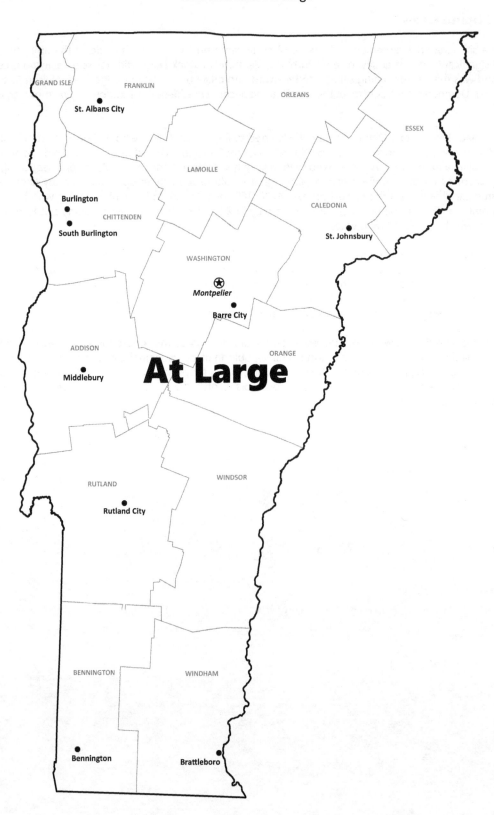

VERMONT

GOVERNOR
Phil Scott (R). Reelected 2022 to a two-year term. Previously elected 2020, 2018, 2016.

SENATORS (1 Democrat, 1 Independent)
Peter Welch (D). Elected 2022 to a six-year term.

Bernard Sanders (I). Reelected 2018 to a six-year term. Previously elected 2012, 2006.

REPRESENTATIVE (1 Democrat)
At Large. Becca Balint (D)

POSTWAR VOTE FOR PRESIDENT

Year	Total Vote	Republican Vote	Republican Candidate	Democratic Vote	Democratic Candidate	Other Vote	Rep.-Dem. Plurality	Total Vote Rep.	Total Vote Dem.	Major Vote Rep.	Major Vote Dem.
2020	367,428	112,704	Trump, Donald J.*	242,820	Biden, Joseph R. Jr.	11,904	130,116 D	30.7%	66.1%	31.7%	68.3%
2016**	315,067	95,369	Trump, Donald J.	178,573	Clinton, Hillary Rodham	41,125	83,204 D	30.3%	56.7%	34.8%	65.2%
2012	299,290	92,698	Romney, W. Mitt	199,239	Obama, Barack H.*	7,353	106,541 D	31.0%	66.6%	31.8%	68.2%
2008	325,046	98,974	McCain, John S. III	219,262	Obama, Barack H.	6,810	120,288 D	30.4%	67.5%	31.1%	68.9%
2004	312,309	121,180	Bush, George W.*	184,067	Kerry, John F.	7,062	62,887 D	38.8%	58.9%	39.7%	60.3%
2000**	294,308	119,775	Bush, George W.	149,022	Gore, Albert Jr.	25,511	29,247 D	40.7%	50.6%	44.6%	55.4%
1996**	258,449	80,352	Dole, Robert "Bob"	137,894	Clinton, Bill*	40,203	57,542 D	31.1%	53.4%	36.8%	63.2%
1992**	289,701	88,122	Bush, George H.*	133,592	Clinton, Bill	67,987	45,470 D	30.4%	46.1%	39.7%	60.3%
1988	243,328	124,331	Bush, George H.	115,776	Dukakis, Michael S.	3,221	8,555 R	51.1%	47.6%	51.8%	48.2%
1984	234,561	135,865	Reagan, Ronald*	95,730	Mondale, Walter F.	2,966	40,135 R	57.9%	40.8%	58.7%	41.3%
1980**	213,299	94,628	Reagan, Ronald	81,952	Carter, Jimmy*	36,719	12,676 R	44.4%	38.4%	53.6%	46.4%
1976	187,765	102,085	Ford, Gerald R.*	80,954	Carter, Jimmy	4,726	21,131 R	54.4%	43.1%	55.8%	44.2%
1972	186,947	117,149	Nixon, Richard M.*	68,174	McGovern, George S.	1,624	48,975 R	62.7%	36.5%	63.2%	36.8%
1968**	161,404	85,142	Nixon, Richard M.	70,255	Humphrey, Hubert Horatio Jr.	6,007	14,887 R	52.8%	43.5%	54.8%	45.2%
1964	163,089	54,942	Goldwater, Barry M. Sr.	108,127	Johnson, Lyndon B.*	20	53,185 D	33.7%	66.3%	33.7%	66.3%
1960	167,324	98,131	Nixon, Richard M.	69,186	Kennedy, John F.	7	28,945 R	58.6%	41.3%	58.6%	41.4%
1956	152,978	110,390	Eisenhower, Dwight D.*	42,549	Stevenson, Adlai E. II	39	67,841 R	72.2%	27.8%	72.2%	27.8%
1952	153,557	109,717	Eisenhower, Dwight D.	43,355	Stevenson, Adlai E. II	485	66,362 R	71.5%	28.2%	71.7%	28.3%
1948	123,382	75,926	Dewey, Thomas E.	45,557	Truman, Harry S.*	1,899	30,369 R	61.5%	36.9%	62.5%	37.5%

Note: An asterisk (*) denotes incumbent. **In past elections, the other vote included: 2016 - 10,078 Libertarian (Gary Johnson); 2000 - 20,374 Green (Ralph Nader); 1996 - 31,024 Reform (Ross Perot); 1992 - 65,991 Independent (Perot); 1980 - 31,761 Independent (John Anderson); 1968 - 5,104 American Independent (George Wallace).

VERMONT

POSTWAR VOTE FOR GOVERNOR

Year	Total Vote	Republican Vote	Republican Candidate	Democratic Vote	Democratic Candidate	Other Vote	Rep.-Dem. Plurality	Total Vote Rep.	Total Vote Dem.	Major Vote Rep.	Major Vote Dem.
2022	284,801	202,147	Scott, Phil*	68,248	Siegel, Brenda	14,406	133,899 R	71.0%	24.0%	74.8%	25.2%
2020	362,711	248,412	Scott, Phil*	99,214	Zuckerman, David	15,085	149,198 R	68.5%	27.4%	71.5%	28.5%
2018	274,087	151,261	Scott, Phil*	110,335	Hallquist, Christine	12,491	40,926 R	55.2%	40.3%	57.8%	42.2%
2016	315,295	166,817	Scott, Phil	139,253	Minter, Sue	9,225	27,564 R	52.9%	44.2%	54.5%	45.5%
2014**	193,087	87,075	Milne, Scott	89,509	Shumlin, Peter*	16,503	2,434 D	45.1%	46.4%	49.3%	50.7%
2012	295,261	110,940	Brock, Randy	170,598	Shumlin, Peter*	13,723	59,658 D	37.6%	57.8%	39.4%	60.6%
2010**	241,605	115,212	Dubie, Brian E.	119,543	Shumlin, Peter	6,850	4,331 D	47.7%	49.5%	49.1%	50.9%
2008**	319,085	170,492	Douglas, Jim*	69,534	Symington, Gaye	79,059	100,958 R	53.4%	21.8%	71.0%	29.0%
2006	262,524	148,014	Douglas, Jim*	108,090	Parker, Scudder	6,420	39,924 R	56.4%	41.2%	57.8%	42.2%
2004	309,285	181,540	Douglas, Jim*	117,327	Clavell, Peter	10,418	64,213 R	58.7%	37.9%	60.7%	39.3%
2002**	230,161	103,436	Douglas, Jim	97,565	Racine, Doug	29,160	5,871 R	44.9%	42.4%	51.5%	48.5%
2000	293,473	111,359	Dwyer, Ruth	148,059	Dean, Howard B.*	34,055	36,700 D	37.9%	50.5%	42.9%	57.1%
1998	218,120	89,726	Dwyer, Ruth	121,425	Dean, Howard B.*	6,969	31,699 D	41.1%	55.7%	42.5%	57.5%
1996	254,648	57,161	Gropper, John L.	179,544	Dean, Howard B.*	17,943	122,383 D	22.4%	70.5%	24.1%	75.9%
1994	212,046	40,292	Kelley, David F.	145,661	Dean, Howard B.*	26,093	105,369 D	19.0%	68.7%	21.7%	78.3%
1992	285,728	65,837	McClaughry, John	213,523	Dean, Howard B.*	6,368	147,686 D	23.0%	74.7%	23.6%	76.4%
1990	211,422	109,540	Snelling, Richard A.	97,321	Welch, Peter	4,561	12,219 R	51.8%	46.0%	53.0%	47.0%
1988	242,879	105,191	Bernhardt, Michael	134,438	Kunin, Madeline*	3,250	29,247 D	43.3%	55.4%	43.9%	56.1%
1986**	196,716	75,162	Smith, Peter	92,379	Kunin, Madeline*	29,175	17,217 D	38.2%	47.0%	44.9%	55.1%
1984	233,753	113,264	Easton, John J.	116,938	Kunin, Madeline	3,551	3,674 D	48.5%	50.0%	49.2%	50.8%
1982	169,251	93,111	Snelling, Richard A.*	74,394	Kunin, Madeline	1,746	18,717 R	55.0%	44.0%	55.6%	44.4%
1980	210,381	123,229	Snelling, Richard A.*	77,363	Diamond, M. Jerome	9,789	45,866 R	58.6%	36.8%	61.4%	38.6%
1978	124,482	78,181	Snelling, Richard A.*	42,482	Granai, Edwin C.	3,819	35,699 R	62.8%	34.1%	64.8%	35.2%
1976	185,929	99,268	Snelling, Richard A.	75,262	Hackel, Stella B.	11,399	24,006 R	53.4%	40.5%	56.9%	43.1%
1974	141,156	53,672	Kennedy, Walter L.	79,842	Salmon, Thomas P.*	7,642	26,170 D	38.0%	56.6%	40.2%	59.8%
1972	189,237	82,491	Hackett, Luther F.	104,533	Salmon, Thomas P.	2,213	22,042 D	43.6%	55.2%	44.1%	55.9%
1970	153,528	87,458	Davis, Deane C.*	66,028	O'Brien, Leo	42	21,430 R	57.0%	43.0%	57.0%	43.0%
1968	161,089	89,387	Davis, Deane C.	71,656	Daley, John J.	46	17,731 R	55.5%	44.5%	55.5%	44.5%
1966	136,262	57,577	Snelling, Richard A.	78,669	Hoff, Philip H.*	16	21,092 D	42.3%	57.7%	42.3%	57.7%
1964	164,199	57,576	Foote, Ralph A.	106,611	Hoff, Philip H.*	12	49,035 D	35.1%	64.9%	35.1%	64.9%
1962	121,422	60,035	Keyser, F. Ray Jr.*	61,383	Hoff, Philip H.	4	1,348 D	49.4%	50.6%	49.4%	50.6%
1960	164,632	92,861	Keyser, F. Ray Jr.	71,755	Niquette, Russell F.	16	21,106 R	56.4%	43.6%	56.4%	43.6%
1958	123,728	62,222	Stafford, Robert T.	61,503	Leddy, Bernard J.	3	719 R	50.3%	49.7%	50.3%	49.7%
1956	153,809	88,379	Johnson, Joseph B.*	65,420	Branon, E. Frank	10	22,959 R	57.5%	42.5%	57.5%	42.5%
1954	114,360	59,778	Johnson, Joseph B.	54,554	Branon, E. Frank	28	5,224 R	52.3%	47.7%	52.3%	47.7%
1952	150,836	78,338	Emerson, Lee Earl*	60,051	Larrow, Robert W.	12,447	18,287 R	51.9%	39.8%	56.6%	43.4%
1950	87,155	64,915	Emerson, Lee Earl	22,227	Moran, J. Edward	13	42,688 R	74.5%	25.5%	74.5%	25.5%
1948	120,183	86,394	Gibson, Ernest Willard Jr.*	33,588	Ryan, Charles F.	201	52,806 R	71.9%	27.9%	72.0%	28.0%
1946	72,044	57,849	Gibson, Ernest Willard Jr.	14,096	Coburn, Berthold C.	99	43,753 R	80.3%	19.6%	80.4%	19.6%

Note: An asterisk (*) denotes incumbent. **In past elections, the other vote included: 2008 - 69,791 Independent (Anthony Pollina), who finished second; 1986 - 28,430 Independent (Bernard Sanders). In 1986, 2002, 2010, and 2014, in the absence of a majority of the total vote for any candidate, the State Legislature elected the governor—Democrat Madeleine M. Kunin in January 1987, Republican Jim Douglas in January 2003, and Democrat Peter Shumlin in January 2011 and January 2015.

VERMONT

POSTWAR VOTE FOR SENATOR

Year	Total Vote	Republican Vote	Republican Candidate	Democratic Vote	Democratic Candidate	Other Vote	Rep.-Dem. Plurality	Total Vote Rep.	Total Vote Dem.	Major Vote Rep.	Major Vote Dem.
2022	287,100	80,468	Malloy, Gerald	196,575	Welch, Peter	10,057	116,107 D	28.0%	68.5%	29.0%	71.0%
2018**	272,624	74,815	Zupan, Lawrence			197,809	74,815 R#	27.4%		100.0%	
2016	313,809	103,637	Milne, Scott	192,243	Leahy, Patrick J.*	17,929	88,606 D	33.0%	61.3%	35.0%	65.0%
2012**	294,267	73,198	MacGovern, John			221,069	73,798 R#	24.9%		100.0%	
2010	235,178	72,699	Britton, Len	151,281	Leahy, Patrick J.*	11,198	78,582 D	30.9%	64.3%	32.5%	67.5%
2006**	262,419	84,924	Tarrant, Richard			177,495	84,924 R#	32.4%		100.0%	
2004	307,208	75,398	McMullen, Jack	216,972	Leahy, Patrick J.*	14,838	141,574 D	24.5%	70.6%	25.8%	74.2%
2000	288,500	189,133	Jeffords, James M.*	73,352	Flanagan, Ed	26,015	115,781 R	65.6%	25.4%	72.1%	27.9%
1998	214,036	48,051	Tuttle, Fred	154,567	Leahy, Patrick J.*	11,418	106,516 D	22.4%	72.2%	23.7%	76.3%
1994	211,672	106,505	Jeffords, James M.*	85,868	Backus, Jan	19,299	20,637 R	50.3%	40.6%	55.4%	44.6%
1992	285,739	123,854	Douglas, Jim	154,762	Leahy, Patrick J.*	7,123	30,908 D	43.3%	54.2%	44.5%	55.5%
1988	240,108	163,183	Jeffords, James M.	71,460	Gray, William	5,465	91,723 R	68.0%	29.8%	69.5%	30.5%
1986	196,532	67,798	Snelling, Richard A.	124,123	Leahy, Patrick J.*	4,611	56,325 D	34.5%	63.2%	35.3%	64.7%
1982	168,003	84,450	Stafford, Robert T.*	79,340	Guest, James A.	4,213	5,110 R	50.3%	47.2%	51.6%	48.4%
1980	209,124	101,421	Ledbetter, Stewart M.	104,176	Leahy, Patrick J.*	3,527	2,755 D	48.5%	49.8%	49.3%	50.7%
1976	189,046	94,481	Stafford, Robert T.*	85,682	Salmon, Thomas P.	8,883	8,799 R	50.0%	45.3%	52.4%	47.6%
1974	142,772	66,223	Mallary, Richard W.	70,629	Leahy, Patrick J.	5,920	4,406 D	46.4%	49.5%	48.4%	51.6%
1972S**	71,348	45,888	Stafford, Robert T.*	23,842	Major, Randolph T.	1,618	22,046 R	64.3%	33.4%	65.8%	34.2%
1970	154,899	91,198	Prouty, Winston L.*	62,271	Hoff, Philip H.	1,430	28,927 R	58.9%	40.2%	59.4%	40.6%
1968**	157,375	157,154	Aiken, George David*			221	157,154 R	99.9%		100.0%	
1964	164,350	87,879	Prouty, Winston L.*	76,457	Fayette, Frederick J.	14	11,422 R	53.5%	46.5%	53.5%	46.5%
1962	121,571	81,241	Aiken, George David*	40,134	Johnson, W. Robert	196	41,107 R	66.8%	33.0%	66.9%	33.1%
1958	124,442	64,900	Prouty, Winston L.	59,536	Fayette, Frederick J.	6	5,364 R	52.2%	47.8%	52.2%	47.8%
1956	155,289	103,101	Aiken, George David*	52,184	O'Shea, Bernard G.	4	50,917 R	66.4%	33.6%	66.4%	33.6%
1952	154,052	111,468	Flanders, Ralph E.*	42,630	Johnston, Allan R.	16	68,776 R	72.3%	27.7%	72.3%	27.7%
1950	89,171	69,543	Aiken, George David*	19,608	Bigelow, James E.	20	49,935 R	78.0%	22.0%	78.0%	22.0%
1946	73,340	54,729	Flanders, Ralph E.	18,594	McDevitt, Charles P.	17	36,135 R	74.6%	25.4%	74.6%	25.4%

Note: An asterisk (*) denotes incumbent. A pound sign (#) indicates that the winner was an independent. **In past elections, the other vote included: 2018 - 183,649 Independent (Bernard Sanders), who received 67.4% of the total vote and was re-elected with a plurality of 108,834 votes; 2012 - 209,053 Independent (Bernard Sanders), who received 71.0% of the total vote and was re-elected with a plurality of 135,855 votes; 2006 - 171,638 Independent (Bernard Sanders), who received 65.4% of the total vote and was elected with a plurality of 86,714 votes. Sanders also won the Democratic primary in 2006, 2012, and 2018, but declined the nomination each time in order to run as an Independent. The Democratic Party did not run a candidate in the 2006, 2012, and 2018 Senate elections. The January 1972 election was for a short term to fill a vacancy. In 1968, the Republican candidate (George D. Aiken) won both major party nominations.

VERMONT

GOVERNOR 2022

2020 Census Population	County	Total Vote	Republican (Scott)	Democratic (Siegel)	Other	Rep.-Dem. Plurality	Total Vote Rep.	Total Vote Dem.	Major Vote Rep.	Major Vote Dem.
36,876	ADDISON	17,993	12,856	4,447	690	8,409 R	71.5%	24.7%	74.3%	25.7%
35,555	BENNINGTON	15,827	10,642	3,741	1,444	6,901 R	67.2%	23.6%	74.0%	26.0%
30,002	CALEDONIA	12,760	9,507	2,425	828	7,082 R	74.5%	19.0%	79.7%	20.3%
164,350	CHITTENDEN	75,809	52,215	21,193	2,401	31,022 R	68.9%	28.0%	71.1%	28.9%
6,177	ESSEX	2,375	1,880	314	181	1,566 R	79.2%	13.2%	85.7%	14.3%
49,536	FRANKLIN	19,699	15,667	2,741	1,291	12,926 R	79.5%	13.9%	85.1%	14.9%
7,276	GRAND ISLE	3,954	3,115	654	185	2,461 R	78.8%	16.5%	82.6%	17.4%
25,401	LAMOILLE	11,468	8,625	2,317	526	6,308 R	75.2%	20.2%	78.8%	21.2%
28,951	ORANGE	13,837	10,013	3,137	687	6,876 R	72.4%	22.7%	76.1%	23.9%
27,133	ORLEANS	10,649	7,840	1,755	1,054	6,085 R	73.6%	16.5%	81.7%	18.3%
58,210	RUTLAND	26,137	20,134	4,307	1,696	15,827 R	77.0%	16.5%	82.4%	17.6%
58,698	WASHINGTON	27,823	18,938	7,799	1,086	11,139 R	68.1%	28.0%	70.8%	29.2%
42,164	WINDHAM	19,659	11,737	6,887	1,035	4,850 R	59.7%	35.0%	63.0%	37.0%
55,114	WINDSOR	26,811	18,978	6,531	1,302	12,447 R	70.8%	24.4%	74.4%	25.6%
625,443	TOTAL	284,801	202,147	68,248	14,406	133,899 R	71.0%	24.0%	74.8%	25.2%

VERMONT
SENATOR 2022

2020 Census Population	County	Total Vote	Republican (Malloy)	Democratic (Welch)	Other	Rep.-Dem. Plurality	Total Vote Rep.	Total Vote Dem.	Major Vote Rep.	Major Vote Dem.
36,876	ADDISON	18,085	4,843	12,720	522	7,877 D	26.8%	70.3%	27.6%	72.4%
35,555	BENNINGTON	15,908	4,937	10,075	896	5,138 D	31.0%	63.3%	32.9%	67.1%
30,002	CALEDONIA	12,781	4,544	7,789	448	3,245 D	35.6%	60.9%	36.8%	63.2%
164,350	CHITTENDEN	76,361	15,589	58,534	2,238	42,945 D	20.4%	76.7%	21.0%	79.0%
6,177	ESSEX	2,410	1,156	1,150	104	6 R	48.0%	47.7%	50.1%	49.9%
49,536	FRANKLIN	19,796	7,712	11,478	606	3,766 D	39.0%	58.0%	40.2%	59.8%
7,276	GRAND ISLE	3,967	1,341	2,533	93	1,192 D	33.8%	63.9%	34.6%	65.4%
25,401	LAMOILLE	11,551	2,953	8,259	339	5,306 D	25.6%	71.5%	26.3%	73.7%
28,951	ORANGE	13,943	4,501	8,947	495	4,446 D	32.3%	64.2%	33.5%	66.5%
27,133	ORLEANS	10,720	4,293	6,041	386	1,748 D	40.0%	56.4%	41.5%	58.5%
58,210	RUTLAND	26,370	10,718	14,848	804	4,130 D	40.6%	56.3%	41.9%	58.1%
58,698	WASHINGTON	28,114	6,371	20,676	1,067	14,305 D	22.7%	73.5%	23.6%	76.4%
42,164	WINDHAM	20,039	4,248	14,581	1,210	10,333 D	21.2%	72.8%	22.6%	77.4%
55,114	WINDSOR	27,055	7,262	18,944	849	11,682 D	26.8%	70.0%	27.7%	72.3%
625,443	TOTAL	287,100	80,468	196,575	10,057	116,107 D	28.0%	68.5%	29.0%	71.0%

VERMONT
HOUSE OF REPRESENTATIVES

CD	Year	Total Vote	Republican Vote	Republican Candidate	Democratic Vote	Democratic Candidate	Other Vote	Rep.-Dem. Plurality	Total Vote Rep.	Total Vote Dem.	Major Vote Rep.	Major Vote Dem.
At Large	2022	282,026	78,397	MADDEN, LIAM	176,494	BALINT, BECCA	27,135	98,097 D	27.8%	62.6%	30.8%	69.2%
At Large	2020	354,837	95,830	BERRY, MIRIAM	238,827	WELCH, PETER*	20,180	142,997 D	27.0%	67.3%	28.6%	71.4%
At Large	2018	272,451	70,705	TYNIO, ANYA	188,547	WELCH, PETER*	13,199	117,842 D	26.0%	69.2%	27.3%	72.7%
At Large	2016	295,334			264,414	WELCH, PETER*	30,920	264,414 D		89.5%		100.0%
At Large	2014	191,504	59,432	DONKA, MARK	123,349	WELCH, PETER*	8,723	63,917 D	31.0%	64.4%	32.5%	67.5%
At Large	2012	289,931	67,543	DONKA, MARK	208,600	WELCH, PETER*	13,788	141,057 D	23.3%	71.9%	24.5%	75.5%
At Large	2010	238,521	76,403	BEAUDRY, PAUL D.	154,006	WELCH, PETER*	8,112	77,603 D	32.0%	64.6%	33.2%	66.8%
At Large	2008	298,151			248,203	WELCH, PETER*	49,948	248,203 D		83.2%		100.0%
At Large	2006	262,726	117,023	RAINVILLE, MARTHA	139,815	WELCH, PETER	5,888	22,792 D	44.5%	53.2%	45.6%	54.4%
At Large	2004	305,008	74,271	PARKE, GREG	21,684	DROWN, LARRY	209,053	52,587 R	24.4%	7.1%	77.4%	22.6%
At Large	2002	225,476	72,813	MEUB, WILLIAM			152,663	72,813 R	32.3%		100.0%	
At Large	2000	283,366	51,977	KERIN, KAREN ANN	14,918	DIAMONDSTONE, PETE	216,471	37,059 R	18.3%	5.3%	77.7%	22.3%
At Large	1998	215,133	70,740	CANDON, MARK			144,393	70,740 R	32.9%		100.0%	
At Large	1996	254,706	83,021	SWEETSER, SUSAN W.	23,830	LONG, JACK	147,855	59,191 R	32.6%	9.4%	77.7%	22.3%
At Large	1994	211,449	98,523	CARROLL, JOHN			112,926	98,523 R	46.6%		100.0%	
At Large	1992	281,626	86,901	PHILBIN, TIMOTHY	22,279	YOUNG, LEWIS E.	172,446	64,622 R	30.9%	7.9%	79.6%	20.4%
At Large	1990	209,856	82,938	SMITH, PETER*	6,315	SANDOVAL, DOLORES	120,603	76,623 R	39.5%	3.0%	92.9%	7.1%
At Large	1988	240,131	98,937	SMITH, PETER	45,330	POIRIER, PAUL N.	95,864	53,607 R	41.2%	18.9%	68.6%	31.4%
At Large	1986	188,954	168,403	JEFFORDS, JAMES M.*			20,551	168,403 R	89.1%		100.0%	
At Large	1984	226,297	148,025	JEFFORDS, JAMES M.*	60,360	POLLINA, ANTHONY	17,912	87,665 R	65.4%	26.7%	71.0%	29.0%
At Large	1982	164,951	114,191	JEFFORDS, JAMES M.*	38,296	KAPLAN, MARK A.	12,464	75,895 R	69.2%	23.2%	74.9%	25.1%
At Large	1980	194,697	154,274	JEFFORDS, JAMES M.*			40,423	154,274 R	79.2%		100.0%	
At Large	1978	120,502	90,688	JEFFORDS, JAMES M.*	23,228	DIETZ, S. MARIE	6,586	67,460 R	75.3%	19.3%	79.6%	20.4%
At Large	1976	184,783	124,458	JEFFORDS, JAMES M.*	60,202	BURGESS, JOHN A.	123	64,256 R	67.4%	32.6%	67.4%	32.6%
At Large	1974	140,899	74,561	JEFFORDS, JAMES M.	56,342	CAIN, FRANCIS J.	9,996	18,219 R	52.9%	40.0%	57.0%	43.0%
At Large	1972	186,028	120,924	MALLARY, RICHARD W.	65,062	MEYER, WILLIAM H.	42	55,862 R	65.0%	35.0%	65.0%	35.0%
At Large	1970	152,557	103,806	STAFFORD, ROBERT T.*	44,415	O'SHEA, BERNARD G.	4,336	59,391 R	68.0%	29.1%	70.0%	30.0%
At Large	1968	157,133	156,956	STAFFORD, ROBERT T.*			177	156,956 R	99.9%		100.0%	
At Large	1966	135,748	89,097	STAFFORD, ROBERT T.*	46,643	RYAN, WILLIAM J.	8	42,454 R	65.6%	34.4%	65.6%	34.4%
At Large	1964	163,452	92,252	STAFFORD, ROBERT T.*	71,193	O'SHEA, BERNARD G.	7	21,059 R	56.4%	43.6%	56.4%	43.6%
At Large	1962	121,381	68,822	STAFFORD, ROBERT T.*	52,535	REYNOLDS, HAROLD	24	16,287 R	56.7%	43.3%	56.7%	43.3%
At Large	1960	166,035	94,905	STAFFORD, ROBERT T.	71,111	MEYER, WILLIAM H.*	19	23,794 R	57.2%	42.8%	57.2%	42.8%
At Large	1958	122,702	59,536	ARTHUR, HAROLD J.	63,131	MEYER, WILLIAM H.	35	3,595 D	48.5%	51.5%	48.5%	51.5%
At Large	1956	154,536	103,736	PROUTY, WINSTON L.*	50,797	ST. AMOUR, CAMILLE	3	52,939 R	67.1%	32.9%	67.1%	32.9%
At Large	1954	114,289	70,143	PROUTY, WINSTON L.*	44,141	BOYLAN, JOHN J.	5	26,002 R	61.4%	38.6%	61.4%	38.6%
At Large	1952	153,060	109,871	PROUTY, WINSTON L.*	43,187	COMINGS, HERBERT B.	2	66,684 R	71.8%	28.2%	71.8%	28.2%
At Large	1950	88,851	65,248	PROUTY, WINSTON L.	22,709	COMINGS, HERBERT B.	894	42,539 R	73.4%	25.6%	74.2%	25.8%
At Large	1948	121,968	74,076	PLUMLEY, CHARLES A.*	47,767	READY, ROBERT W.	125	26,309 R	60.7%	39.2%	60.8%	39.2%
At Large	1946	73,066	46,985	PLUMLEY, CHARLES A.*	26,056	CALDBECK, MATTHEW J.	25	20,929 R	64.3%	35.7%	64.3%	35.7%

Note: An asterisk (*) denotes incumbent.

VERMONT

GENERAL AND PRIMARY ELECTIONS

GENERAL ELECTIONS: OTHER VOTES

Governor Other vote was 6,022 Independent (Kevin Hoyt), 4,723 Independent (Peter Duval), 2,315 Independent (Bernard Peters), 1,346 Write-In (Write-Ins)

Senate Other vote was 2,752 Independent (Dawn Ellis), 1,574 Green Mountain (Natasha Diamondstone-Kohout), 1,532 Independent (Kerry Raheb), 1,273 Independent (Mark Coester), 1,209 Independent (Stephen Duke), 1,105 Independent (Ericson Cris), 612 Write-In (Write-Ins)

House Other vote was:

  At Large 12,590 Libertarian (Ericka Redic), 5,737 Independent (Matt Druzba), 4,428 Independent (Luke Talbot), 3,376 Independent (Adam Ortiz), 1,004 Write-In (Write-Ins)

2022 PRIMARY ELECTIONS: SUPPLEMENTARY INFORMATION

Primary August 9, 2022 **Registration** (as of August 2022) 500,148 No Party Registration

Primary Type Open—Any registered voter could participate in the primary of any recognized party.

	REPUBLICAN PRIMARIES			**DEMOCRATIC PRIMARIES**		
Senator	Malloy, Gerald	12,169	42.4%	Welch, Peter	86,603	87.0%
	Nolan, Christina	10,825	37.7%	Evans-Frantz, Isaac	7,230	7.3%
	Mermel, Myers	5,227	18.2%	Thran, Alexandra Nicole "Niki"	5,104	5.1%
	Write-In	489	1.7%	Write-In	599	0.6%
	TOTAL	28,710		TOTAL	99,536	
Governor	Scott, Phil*	20,319	68.6%	Siegel, Brenda	56,287	85.9%
	Bellows, Stephen C.	5,402	18.2%	Write-In (Write-In)	9,235	14.1%
	Duval, Peter	3,627	12.2%			
	Write-In	290	1.0%			
	TOTAL	29,638		TOTAL	65,522	
Congressional At Large	Madden, Liam	10,701	40.0%	Balint, Becca	61,025	60.5%
	Redic, Ericka Bundy	8,255	30.8%	Gray, Molly	37,266	36.9%
	Tynio, Anya	6,908	25.8%	Meyers, Louis	1,593	1.6%
	Write-In	914	3.4%	Clifford, Sianay Chase	885	0.9%
				Write-In	145	0.1%
	TOTAL	26,778		TOTAL	100,914	

Note: An asterisk (*) denotes incumbent.

VIRGINIA

Statewide Races

Without a Senate race on the ballot, Virginia's House races took center stage in 2022. But a year earlier, it's 2021 gubernatorial race became a nationally watched contest – Republicans hoped the result of that race would offer a preview of 2022's results. As it turned out, though, not everything from 2021 carried over to 2022.

In May, Virginia Republicans opted to hold a nominating convention, in lieu of a primary. Businessman Glenn Youngkin emerged after several rounds of balloting. The next month, Democrats nominated former Gov. Terry McAuliffe, who was seeking a comeback after four years out of office. Initially a favorite, McAuliffe's position suffered as Joe Biden's approval ratings slumped – and it was hard to pigeonhole Youngkin, who crafted a fatherly image and wore a distinctive sweater vest, as a Donald Trump clone.

Virginia, which had gone to Biden by ten points in 2020, gave Youngkin a two-point win a year later. Part of Youngkin's formula was that he made already-red areas of the state appear even redder. He carried the Appalachian 9th District, for instance, by 50 points, up from Trump's 40-point margin. As turnout increased by 25 percentage points statewide from 2017 (the previous gubernatorial contest), it shot up by closer to 35 points in pockets of the Appalachian southwest. Conversely, turnout was relatively weak in minority precincts and in college towns. Still, in some worse news for Republicans, 2021 confirmed the longer term, pro-Democratic trend of many suburban localities: Youngkin ran behind Mitt Romney's 2012 showing in large suburban counties like Henrico, Loudoun, and Stafford.

House Races

In 2020, Virginia voters opted to establish a nonpartisan redistricting commission. But once in session, the commission was marred by disfunction. The Supreme Court of Virginia stepped in to redraw the commonwealth's 11-seat map. On the new map, the three most vulnerable members were all Democratic women who were first elected in the anti-Trump 2018 wave.

In the Virginia Beach area's 2nd District, Democrat Elaine Luria got a more marginal seat. Republicans recruited state Sen. Jen Kiggans, who, like Luria, had a background in the Navy. Though Luria outraised Kiggans and narrowly carried Virginia Beach, it was not enough to offset her losses in the rest of the district. Kiggans won by just over three points.

Though 7th District Democrat Abigail Spanberger was given a bluer seat, much of the redrawn district was new to her. Previously, the 7th District was a Richmond-area seat – the new district's center of gravity included the southern suburbs of Washington, D.C. In this very expensive race, Youngkin campaigned for Yesli Vega, the Republican nominee who stressed her background as a Salvadorian American and her experience in law enforcement. But Spanberger, a deft campaigner and serious legislator, won with 52% of the vote – the same share that the district would have given Biden in 2020 and Youngkin in 2022.

Finally, in Northern Virginia, Republicans made a serious attempt at the 10th District, which included Loudoun County. Hung Cao, a Vietnamese American Navy veteran, lost to Democratic Rep. Jennifer Wexton, but his 47% was more respectable than the 40% that the seat would have given Trump in 2020.

VIRGINIA
Congressional districts first established for elections held in 2022
11 members

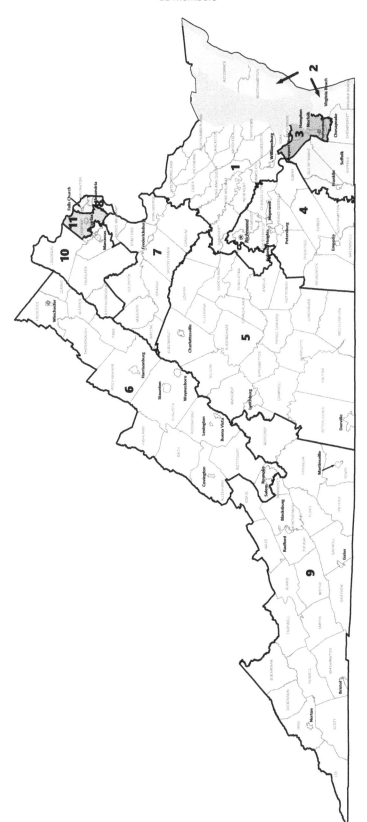

Independent cities are treated as county equivalents; some city boundaries are coextensive with the former county boundaries.

* Asterisk indicates a county whose boundaries include parts of two or more congressional districts.
Districts 2, 3, 8, and 11 are highlighted for visibility.

VIRGINIA

GOVERNOR
Glenn Youngkin (R). Elected 2021 to a four-year term.

SENATORS (2 Democrats)
Tim Kaine (D). Reelected 2018 to a six-year term. Previously elected 2012.

Mark R. Warner (D). Reelected 2020 to a six-year term. Previously elected 2014, 2008.

REPRESENTATIVES (5 Republicans, 6 Democrats)
1. Robert J. "Rob" Wittman (R)
2. Jennifer Kiggans (R)
3. Robert C. "Bobby" Scott (D)
4. Jennifer McClellan (D)
5. Bob Good (R)
6. Benjamin Cline (R)
7. Abigail Spanberger (D)
8. Donald S. Beyer Jr. (D)
9. H. Morgan Griffith (R)
10. Jennifer Wexton (D)
11. Gerald E. "Gerry" Connolly (D)

Note: A. Donald McEachin (D) of the Virginia 4th District left office on November 8, 2022 and died on November 28, 2022. Jennifer McClellan won a special election on February 21, 2023, to succeed McEachin and was sworn in on March 7, 2023.

POSTWAR VOTE FOR PRESIDENT

Year	Total Vote	Republican Vote	Republican Candidate	Democratic Vote	Democratic Candidate	Other Vote	Rep.-Dem. Plurality		Total Vote Rep.	Total Vote Dem.	Major Vote Rep.	Major Vote Dem.
2020	4,460,524	1,962,430	Trump, Donald J.*	2,413,568	Biden, Joseph R. Jr.	84,526	451,138	D	44.0%	54.1%	44.8%	55.2%
2016**	3,982,752	1,769,443	Trump, Donald J.	1,981,473	Clinton, Hillary Rodham	231,836	212,030	D	44.4%	49.8%	47.2%	52.8%
2012	3,854,489	1,822,522	Romney, W. Mitt	1,971,820	Obama, Barack H.*	60,147	149,298	D	47.3%	51.2%	48.0%	52.0%
2008	3,723,260	1,725,005	McCain, John S. III	1,959,532	Obama, Barack H.	38,723	234,527	D	46.3%	52.6%	46.8%	53.2%
2004	3,198,367	1,716,959	Bush, George W.*	1,454,742	Kerry, John F.	26,666	262,217	R	53.7%	45.5%	54.1%	45.9%
2000**	2,739,447	1,437,490	Bush, George W.	1,217,290	Gore, Albert Jr.	84,667	220,200	R	52.5%	44.4%	54.1%	45.9%
1996**	2,416,642	1,138,350	Dole, Robert "Bob"	1,091,060	Clinton, Bill*	187,232	47,290	R	47.1%	45.1%	51.1%	48.9%
1992**	2,558,665	1,150,517	Bush, George H.*	1,038,650	Clinton, Bill	369,498	111,867	R	45.0%	40.6%	52.6%	47.4%
1988	2,191,609	1,309,162	Bush, George H.	859,799	Dukakis, Michael S.	22,648	449,363	R	59.7%	39.2%	60.4%	39.6%
1984	2,146,635	1,337,078	Reagan, Ronald*	796,250	Mondale, Walter F.	13,307	540,828	R	62.3%	37.1%	62.7%	37.3%
1980**	1,866,032	989,609	Reagan, Ronald	752,174	Carter, Jimmy*	124,249	237,435	R	53.0%	40.3%	56.8%	43.2%
1976	1,697,094	836,554	Ford, Gerald R.*	813,896	Carter, Jimmy	46,644	22,658	R	49.3%	48.0%	50.7%	49.3%
1972	1,457,019	988,493	Nixon, Richard M.*	438,887	McGovern, George S.	29,639	549,606	R	67.8%	30.1%	69.3%	30.7%
1968**	1,361,491	590,319	Nixon, Richard M.	442,387	Humphrey, Hubert Horatio Jr.	328,785	147,932	R	43.4%	32.5%	57.2%	42.8%
1964	1,042,267	481,334	Goldwater, Barry M. Sr.	558,038	Johnson, Lyndon B.*	2,895	76,704	D	46.2%	53.5%	46.3%	53.7%
1960	771,449	404,521	Nixon, Richard M.	362,327	Kennedy, John F.	4,601	42,194	R	52.4%	47.0%	52.8%	47.2%
1956	697,978	386,459	Eisenhower, Dwight D.*	267,760	Stevenson, Adlai E. II	43,759	118,699	R	55.4%	38.4%	59.1%	40.9%
1952	619,689	349,037	Eisenhower, Dwight D.	268,677	Stevenson, Adlai E. II	1,975	80,360	R	56.3%	43.4%	56.5%	43.5%
1948**	419,256	172,070	Dewey, Thomas E.	200,786	Truman, Harry S.*	46,400	28,716	D	41.0%	47.9%	46.1%	53.9%

Note: An asterisk (*) denotes incumbent. **In past elections, the other vote included: 2016 - 118,274 Libertarian (Gary Johnson); 2000 - 59,398 Green (Ralph Nader); 1996 - 159,861 Reform (Ross Perot); 1992 - 348,639 Independent (Perot); 1980 - 95,418 Independent (John Anderson); 1968 - 321,833 American Independent (George Wallace); 1948 - 43,393 States' Rights (Strom Thurmond).

VIRGINIA

POSTWAR VOTE FOR GOVERNOR

		Republican		Democratic		Other Vote	Rep.-Dem. Plurality		Percentage			
									Total Vote		Major Vote	
Year	Total Vote	Vote	Candidate	Vote	Candidate				Rep.	Dem.	Rep.	Dem.
2021	3,288,318	1,663,158	Youngkin, Glenn Allen	1,599,470	McAuliffe, Terry R.	25,690	63,688	R	50.6%	48.6%	51.0%	49.0%
2017	2,614,282	1,175,731	Gillespie, Edward W. "Ed"	1,409,175	Northam, Ralph S.	29,376	233,444	D	45.0%	53.9%	45.5%	54.5%
2013	2,241,071	1,013,354	Cuccinelli, Ken	1,069,789	McAuliffe, Terry R.	157,928	56,435	D	45.2%	47.7%	48.6%	51.4%
2009	1,985,103	1,163,651	McDonnell, Robert F.	818,950	Deeds, R. Creigh	2,502	344,701	R	58.6%	41.3%	58.7%	41.3%
2005	1,983,778	912,327	Kilgore, Jerry W.	1,025,942	Kaine, Tim	45,509	113,615	D	46.0%	51.7%	47.1%	52.9%
2001	1,886,721	887,234	Earley, Mark	984,177	Warner, Mark R.	15,310	96,943	D	47.0%	52.2%	47.4%	52.6%
1997	1,736,314	969,062	Gilmore, James S. III	738,971	Beyer, Donald S. Jr.	28,281	230,091	R	55.8%	42.6%	56.7%	43.3%
1993	1,793,916	1,045,319	Allen, George F.	733,527	Terry, Mary Sue	15,070	311,792	R	58.3%	40.9%	58.8%	41.2%
1989	1,789,078	890,195	Coleman, J. Marshall	896,936	Wilder, L. Douglas	1,947	6,741	D	49.8%	50.1%	49.8%	50.2%
1985	1,343,240	601,649	Durrette, Wyatt B.	741,438	Baliles, Gerald L.	153	139,789	D	44.8%	55.2%	44.8%	55.2%
1981	1,420,638	659,398	Coleman, J. Marshall	760,384	Robb, Charles S.	856	100,986	D	46.4%	53.5%	46.4%	53.6%
1977	1,250,940	699,302	Dalton, John N.	541,319	Howell, Henry	10,319	157,983	R	55.9%	43.3%	56.4%	43.6%
1973**	1,035,495	525,075	Godwin, Mills E. Jr.			510,420	525,075	R	50.7%		100.0%	
1969	915,764	480,869	Holton, Linwood	415,695	Battle, William C.	19,200	65,174	R	52.5%	45.4%	53.6%	46.4%
1965**	562,789	212,207	Holton, Linwood	269,526	Godwin, Mills E. Jr.	81,056	57,319	D	37.7%	47.9%	44.1%	55.9%
1961	394,490	142,567	Pearson, H. Clyde	251,861	Harrison, Albertis S. Jr.	62	109,294	D	36.1%	63.8%	36.1%	63.9%
1957	517,655	188,628	Dalton, Ted	326,921	Almond, J. Lindsay Jr.	2,106	138,293	D	36.4%	63.2%	36.6%	63.4%
1953	414,025	183,328	Dalton, Ted	226,998	Stanley, Thomas B.	3,699	43,670	D	44.3%	54.8%	44.7%	55.3%
1949	262,350	71,991	Johnson, Walter	184,772	Battle, John S.	5,587	112,781	D	27.4%	70.4%	28.0%	72.0%
1945	164,741	52,386	Landreth, S. Lloyd	112,355	Tuck, William M.		59,969	D	31.8%	68.2%	31.8%	68.2%

Note: An asterisk (*) denotes incumbent. **In past elections, the other vote included: 1973 - 510,103 Independent (Henry Howell); 1965 - 75,307 Conservative (William J. Story Jr.). The plurality is the difference between the Republican and Democratic vote. The Democratic Party did not run a candidate in the 1973 gubernatorial election.

POSTWAR VOTE FOR SENATOR

		Republican		Democratic		Other Vote	Rep.-Dem. Plurality		Percentage			
									Total Vote		Major Vote	
Year	Total Vote	Vote	Candidate	Vote	Candidate				Rep.	Dem.	Rep.	Dem.
2020	4,405,087	1,934,199	Gade, Daniel	2,466,500	Warner, Mark R.*	4,388	532,301	D	43.9%	56.0%	44.0%	56.0%
2018	3,351,373	1,374,313	Stewart, Corey A.	1,910,370	Kaine, Tim*	66,690	536,057	D	41.0%	57.0%	41.8%	58.2%
2014	2,184,473	1,055,940	Gillespie, Edward W. "Ed"	1,073,667	Warner, Mark R.*	54,866	17,727	D	48.3%	49.1%	49.6%	50.4%
2012	3,802,196	1,785,542	Allen, George F.	2,010,067	Kaine, Tim	6,587	224,525	D	47.0%	52.9%	47.0%	53.0%
2008	3,643,294	1,228,830	Gilmore, James S. III	2,369,327	Warner, Mark R.	45,137	1,140,497	D	33.7%	65.0%	34.2%	65.8%
2006	2,370,445	1,166,277	Allen, George F.*	1,175,606	Webb, Jim H. Jr.	28,562	9,329	D	49.2%	49.6%	49.8%	50.2%
2002	1,489,422	1,229,894	Warner, John W.*			259,528	1,229,894	R	82.6%		100.0%	
2000	2,718,301	1,420,460	Allen, George F.	1,296,093	Robb, Charles S.*	1,748	124,367	R	52.3%	47.7%	52.3%	47.7%
1996	2,354,715	1,235,744	Warner, John W.*	1,115,982	Warner, Mark R.	2,989	119,762	R	52.5%	47.4%	52.5%	47.5%
1994**	2,057,463	882,213	North, Oliver L.	938,376	Robb, Charles S.*	236,874	56,163	D	42.9%	45.6%	48.5%	51.5%
1990**	1,083,660	876,782	Warner, John W.*			206,878	876,782	R	80.9%		100.0%	
1988	2,068,897	593,652	Dawkins, Maurice A.	1,474,086	Robb, Charles S.	1,159	880,434	D	28.7%	71.2%	28.7%	71.3%
1984	2,007,487	1,406,194	Warner, John W.*	601,142	Harrison, Edythe C.	151	805,052	R	70.0%	29.9%	70.1%	29.9%
1982	1,415,622	724,571	Trible, Paul	690,839	Davis, Richard	212	33,732	R	51.2%	48.8%	51.2%	48.8%
1978	1,222,256	613,232	Warner, John W.	608,511	Miller, Andrew P.	513	4,721	R	50.2%	49.8%	50.2%	49.8%
1976**	1,557,500			596,009	Zumwalt, Elmo R.	961,491	596,009	D#		38.3%		100.0%
1972	1,396,268	718,337	Scott, William L.	643,963	Spong, William B.*	33,968	74,374	R	51.4%	46.1%	52.7%	47.3%
1970**	946,751	145,031	Garland, Ray L.	295,057	Rawlings, George C.	506,663	150,026	D#	15.3%	31.2%	33.0%	67.0%
1966	733,879	245,681	Ould, James P. Jr.	429,855	Spong, William B.	58,343	184,174	D	33.5%	58.6%	36.4%	63.6%
1966S**	729,839	272,804	Traylor, Lawrence M.	389,028	Byrd, Harry Flood Jr.*	68,007	116,224	D	37.4%	53.3%	41.2%	58.8%
1964**	928,363	176,624	May, Richard A.	592,260	Byrd, Harry F.*	159,479	415,636	D	19.0%	63.8%	23.0%	77.0%
1960**	622,820			506,169	Robertson, A. Willis*	116,651	506,169	D		81.3%		100.0%
1958**	457,640			317,221	Byrd, Harry F.*	140,419	317,221	D		69.3%		100.0%
1954**	306,447			244,844	Robertson, A. Willis*	61,603	244,844	D		79.9%		100.0%
1952**	543,516			398,677	Byrd, Harry F.*	144,839	398,677	D		73.4%		100.0%
1948	386,998	119,366	Woods, Robert H.	253,865	Robertson, A. Willis*	13,767	134,499	D	30.8%	65.6%	32.0%	68.0%
1946	252,863	77,005	Parsons, Lester S.	163,960	Byrd, Harry F.*	11,898	86,955	D	30.5%	64.8%	32.0%	68.0%
1946S**	248,962	72,253	Woods, Robert H.	169,680	Robertson, A. Willis	7,029	97,427	D	29.0%	68.2%	29.9%	70.1%

Note: An asterisk (*) denotes incumbent. A pound sign (#) indicates that winner was an independent. **In past elections, the other vote included: 1994 - 235,324 Independent (J. Marshall Coleman); 1990 - 196,755 Independent (Nancy Spannaus), who finished second; 1976 - 890,778 Independent (Harry Flood Byrd Jr.), who won the election with 57.2% of the total vote and a plurality of 294,769 votes; 1970 - 506,633 Independent (Harry Flood Byrd Jr.), who won the election with 53.5% of the total vote and a plurality of 211,576 votes; 1964 - 95,526 Independent (James W. Respess); 1960 - 88,718 Independent Democrat (Stuart D. Baker), who finished second; 1958 - 120,224 Independent (Louis Wensel), who finished second; 1954 - 32,681 Independent Democrat (Charles William Lewis Jr.), who finished second; 1952 - 69,133 Independent Democrat (H. M. Vise Sr.), who finished second; 67,281 Social Democrat (Clarke T. Robb). One each of the 1946 and 1966 elections was for a short term to fill a vacancy. The Democratic Party did not run a candidate in the Senate elections of 1990 and 2002. The Republican Party did not run a candidate in the Senate elections of 1952, 1954, 1958, 1960, and 1976.

VIRGINIA

2021 VIRGINIA GUBERNATORIAL GENERAL

2020 Census Population	County	Total Vote	(W) Republican (Glenn Youngkin)	Democrat (Terry McAuliffe)	Write-In Scattered (Write-Ins)	Other (Princess Blanding)	Rep.-Dem. Plurality		Percentage Total Vote Rep.	Dem.	Major Vote Rep.	Dem.
32,256	ACCOMACK	12,897	7,878	4,948	4	67	2,930	R	61.1%	38.4%	61.4%	38.6%
109,785	ALBEMARLE	51,443	19,141	31,919	36	347	12,778	D	37.2%	62.0%	37.5%	62.5%
159,299	ALEXANDRIA	58,330	14,013	43,866	66	385	29,853	D	24.0%	75.2%	24.2%	75.8%
14,848	ALLEGHANY	6,079	4,530	1,518	5	26	3,012	R	74.5%	25.0%	74.9%	25.1%
13,195	AMELIA	6,362	4,720	1,617	2	23	3,103	R	74.2%	25.4%	74.5%	25.5%
31,605	AMHERST	13,706	9,731	3,897	6	72	5,834	R	71.0%	28.4%	71.4%	28.6%
15,957	APPOMATTOX	7,440	5,971	1,438	5	26	4,533	R	80.3%	19.3%	80.6%	19.4%
237,016	ARLINGTON	95,231	21,548	73,013	116	554	51,465	D	22.6%	76.7%	22.8%	77.2%
75,832	AUGUSTA	33,613	26,196	7,231	16	170	18,965	R	77.9%	21.5%	78.4%	21.6%
4,161	BATH	1,947	1,539	396	1	11	1,143	R	79.0%	20.3%	79.5%	20.5%
79,279	BEDFORD	39,079	30,912	8,001	21	145	22,911	R	79.1%	20.5%	79.4%	20.6%
6,222	BEDFORD CITY	0	0	0	0	0	0		0.0%	0.0%	0.0%	0.0%
6,284	BLAND	2,651	2,274	364	1	12	1,910	R	85.8%	13.7%	86.2%	13.8%
33,520	BOTETOURT	17,125	13,066	3,990	8	61	9,076	R	76.3%	23.3%	76.6%	23.4%
16,734	BRISTOL	5,147	3,773	1,342	2	30	2,431	R	73.3%	26.1%	73.8%	26.2%
16,206	BRUNSWICK	6,084	2,880	3,165	5	34	285	D	47.3%	52.0%	47.6%	52.4%
20,908	BUCHANAN	6,000	5,083	903	6	8	4,180	R	84.7%	15.0%	84.9%	15.1%
17,191	BUCKINGHAM	6,153	3,894	2,222	2	35	1,672	R	63.3%	36.1%	63.7%	36.3%
6,408	BUENA VISTA	1,963	1,459	481	1	22	978	R	74.3%	24.5%	75.2%	24.8%
54,854	CAMPBELL	23,235	18,213	4,930	15	77	13,283	R	78.4%	21.2%	78.7%	21.3%
30,846	CAROLINE	12,061	6,917	5,045	8	91	1,872	R	57.4%	41.8%	57.8%	42.2%
29,837	CARROLL	11,825	9,868	1,910	4	43	7,958	R	83.5%	16.2%	83.8%	16.2%
6,960	CHARLES CITY	3,387	1,550	1,822	0	15	272	D	45.8%	53.8%	46.0%	54.0%
11,876	CHARLOTTE	4,774	3,354	1,396	3	21	1,958	R	70.3%	29.2%	70.6%	29.4%
47,416	CHARLOTTESVILLE	17,347	2,774	14,378	22	173	11,604	D	16.0%	82.9%	16.2%	83.8%
245,878	CHESAPEAKE	91,699	48,079	42,907	59	654	5,172	R	52.4%	46.8%	52.8%	47.2%
354,707	CHESTERFIELD	156,277	80,889	74,085	109	1,194	6,804	R	51.8%	47.4%	52.2%	47.8%
14,685	CLARKE	7,422	4,642	2,739	7	34	1,903	R	62.5%	36.9%	62.9%	37.1%
17,513	COLONIAL HEIGHTS	6,705	4,913	1,729	10	53	3,184	R	73.3%	25.8%	74.0%	26.0%
5,507	COVINGTON	1,793	1,198	579	0	16	619	R	66.8%	32.3%	67.4%	32.6%
5,141	CRAIG	2,500	2,079	400	4	17	1,679	R	83.2%	16.0%	83.9%	16.1%
52,816	CULPEPER	20,214	13,436	6,661	10	107	6,775	R	66.5%	33.0%	66.9%	33.1%
9,950	CUMBERLAND	4,225	2,678	1,515	5	27	1,163	R	63.4%	35.9%	63.9%	36.1%
40,024	DANVILLE	12,864	5,907	6,872	5	80	965	D	45.9%	53.4%	46.2%	53.8%
14,294	DICKENSON	4,815	3,867	934	3	11	2,933	R	80.3%	19.4%	80.5%	19.5%
28,539	DINWIDDIE	11,582	7,335	4,181	7	59	3,154	R	63.3%	36.1%	63.7%	36.3%
5,256	EMPORIA	1,832	723	1,087	2	20	364	D	39.5%	59.3%	39.9%	60.1%
10,983	ESSEX	4,709	2,684	1,980	6	39	704	R	57.0%	42.0%	57.5%	42.5%
1,145,312	FAIRFAX	440,786	152,110	286,316	12	2,348	134,206	D	34.5%	65.0%	34.7%	65.3%
22,565	FAIRFAX CITY	10,618	3,606	6,465	488	59	2,859	D	34.0%	60.9%	35.8%	64.2%
14,786	FALLS CHURCH	7,026	1,590	5,388	6	42	3,798	D	22.6%	76.7%	22.8%	77.2%
71,619	FAUQUIER	33,992	22,252	11,570	14	156	10,682	R	65.5%	34.0%	65.8%	34.2%
15,799	FLOYD	7,498	5,230	2,203	6	59	3,027	R	69.8%	29.4%	70.4%	29.6%
27,395	FLUVANNA	12,454	7,068	5,312	9	65	1,756	R	56.8%	42.7%	57.1%	42.9%
56,175	FRANKLIN	23,760	17,842	5,894	10	14	11,948	R	75.1%	24.8%	75.2%	24.8%
8,582	FRANKLIN CITY	3,053	1,270	1,680	1	102	410	D	41.6%	55.0%	43.1%	56.9%
89,939	FREDERICK	36,376	25,063	11,164	19	130	13,899	R	68.9%	30.7%	69.2%	30.8%
29,069	FREDERICKSBURG	9,035	3,503	5,402	17	113	1,899	D	38.8%	59.8%	39.3%	60.7%
6,394	GALAX	1,926	1,424	492	1	9	932	R	73.9%	25.5%	74.3%	25.7%
16,778	GILES	7,389	5,788	1,535	5	61	4,253	R	78.3%	20.8%	79.0%	21.0%
37,442	GLOUCESTER	17,391	12,585	4,712	6	88	7,873	R	72.4%	27.1%	72.8%	27.2%
23,980	GOOCHLAND	14,552	9,585	4,910	5	52	4,675	R	65.9%	33.7%	66.1%	33.9%

VIRGINIA

2021 VIRGINIA GUBERNATORIAL GENERAL

2020 Census Population	County	Total Vote	(W) Republican (Glenn Youngkin)	Democrat (Terry McAuliffe)	Write-In Scattered (Write-Ins)	Other (Princess Blanding)	Rep.-Dem. Plurality		Percentage Total Vote		Major Vote	
									Rep.	Dem.	Rep.	Dem.
15,536	GRAYSON	6,237	5,144	1,062	4	27	4,082	R	82.5%	17.0%	82.9%	17.1%
19,897	GREENE	8,842	5,961	2,806	7	68	3,155	R	67.4%	31.7%	68.0%	32.0%
11,399	GREENSVILLE	3,638	1,709	1,915	2	12	206	D	47.0%	52.6%	47.2%	52.8%
33,891	HALIFAX	13,522	8,641	4,804	2	75	3,837	R	63.9%	35.5%	64.3%	35.7%
134,502	HAMPTON	45,104	14,651	29,971	33	449	15,320	D	32.5%	66.4%	32.8%	67.2%
108,403	HANOVER	57,960	39,515	18,107	34	304	21,408	R	68.2%	31.2%	68.6%	31.4%
53,070	HARRISONBURG	11,337	4,382	6,812	12	131	2,430	D	38.7%	60.1%	39.1%	60.9%
331,469	HENRICO	138,667	55,796	81,409	120	1,342	25,613	D	40.2%	58.7%	40.7%	59.3%
50,586	HENRY	18,536	12,902	5,547	13	74	7,355	R	69.6%	29.9%	69.9%	30.1%
2,195	HIGHLAND	1,303	969	325	1	8	644	R	74.4%	24.9%	74.9%	25.1%
22,599	HOPEWELL	6,276	3,095	3,085	9	87	10	R	49.3%	49.2%	50.1%	49.9%
37,270	ISLE OF WIGHT	18,672	12,000	6,565	16	91	5,435	R	64.3%	35.2%	64.6%	35.4%
77,062	JAMES CITY	40,091	21,048	18,836	21	186	2,212	R	52.5%	47.0%	52.8%	47.2%
7,053	KING AND QUEEN	3,261	2,112	1,130	1	18	982	R	64.8%	34.7%	65.1%	34.9%
26,931	KING GEORGE	10,701	7,286	3,317	7	91	3,969	R	68.1%	31.0%	68.7%	31.3%
17,242	KING WILLIAM	8,572	6,286	2,247	6	33	4,039	R	73.3%	26.2%	73.7%	26.3%
10,685	LANCASTER	5,873	3,448	2,406	3	16	1,042	R	58.7%	41.0%	58.9%	41.1%
23,367	LEE	7,274	6,372	882	2	18	5,490	R	87.6%	12.1%	87.8%	12.2%
7,435	LEXINGTON	2,078	775	1,289	4	10	514	D	37.3%	62.0%	37.5%	62.5%
416,080	LOUDOUN	161,793	71,467	89,390	133	803	17,923	D	44.2%	55.2%	44.4%	55.6%
37,902	LOUISA	17,639	11,649	5,896	7	87	5,753	R	66.0%	33.4%	66.4%	33.6%
12,163	LUNENBURG	4,597	3,019	1,567	0	11	1,452	R	65.7%	34.1%	65.8%	34.2%
82,661	LYNCHBURG	24,901	13,668	11,000	35	198	2,668	R	54.9%	44.2%	55.4%	44.6%
13,318	MADISON	6,728	4,721	1,973	5	29	2,748	R	70.2%	29.3%	70.5%	29.5%
41,182	MANASSAS	11,306	5,050	6,155	14	87	1,105	D	44.7%	54.4%	45.1%	54.9%
17,426	MANASSAS PARK	3,597	1,379	2,158	14	46	779	D	38.3%	60.0%	39.0%	61.0%
12,670	MARTINSVILLE	3,945	1,676	2,224	5	40	548	D	42.5%	56.4%	43.0%	57.0%
8,891	MATHEWS	4,881	3,493	1,363	7	18	2,130	R	71.6%	27.9%	71.9%	28.1%
30,670	MECKLENBURG	12,037	7,922	4,075	3	37	3,847	R	65.8%	33.9%	66.0%	34.0%
10,626	MIDDLESEX	5,613	3,703	1,860	3	47	1,843	R	66.0%	33.1%	66.6%	33.4%
	MILTON	0	0	0	0	0	0		0.0%	0.0%	0.0%	0.0%
98,852	MONTGOMERY	32,794	17,041	15,355	21	377	1,686	R	52.0%	46.8%	52.6%	47.4%
14,980	NELSON	7,680	4,259	3,346	11	64	913	R	55.5%	43.6%	56.0%	44.0%
23,370	NEW KENT	12,066	8,569	3,439	6	52	5,130	R	71.0%	28.5%	71.4%	28.6%
178,968	NEWPORT NEWS	54,276	21,241	32,399	48	588	11,158	D	39.1%	59.7%	39.6%	60.4%
242,393	NORFOLK	0	0	0	0	0	0		0.0%	0.0%	0.0%	0.0%
242,803	NORFOLK CITY	60,061	18,888	40,324	60	789	21,436	D	31.4%	67.1%	31.9%	68.1%
11,705	NORTHAMPTON	5,264	2,650	2,584	3	27	66	R	50.3%	49.1%	50.6%	49.4%
12,119	NORTHUMBERLAND	6,516	4,167	2,312	0	37	1,855	R	64.0%	35.5%	64.3%	35.7%
3,993	NORTON	1,203	866	320	4	13	546	R	72.0%	26.6%	73.0%	27.0%
15,250	NOTTOWAY	5,416	3,497	1,892	3	24	1,605	R	64.6%	34.9%	64.9%	35.1%
37,319	ORANGE	16,110	10,670	5,351	9	80	5,319	R	66.2%	33.2%	66.6%	33.4%
23,971	PAGE	9,622	7,594	1,995	5	28	5,599	R	78.9%	20.7%	79.2%	20.8%
17,650	PATRICK	7,239	5,946	1,255	6	32	4,691	R	82.1%	17.3%	82.6%	17.4%
31,520	PETERSBURG	8,944	1,207	7,591	5	141	6,384	D	13.5%	84.9%	13.7%	86.3%
60,415	PITTSYLVANIA	25,950	19,543	6,319	12	76	13,224	R	75.3%	24.4%	75.6%	24.4%
12,333	POQUOSON	6,298	4,897	1,364	5	32	3,533	R	77.8%	21.7%	78.2%	21.8%
94,161	PORTSMOUTH	29,833	9,946	19,513	19	355	9,567	D	33.3%	65.4%	33.8%	66.2%
29,810	POWHATAN	16,371	12,582	3,721	10	58	8,861	R	76.9%	22.7%	77.2%	22.8%
22,858	PRINCE EDWARD	7,125	3,876	3,210	3	36	666	R	54.4%	45.1%	54.7%	45.3%
38,389	PRINCE GEORGE	13,222	8,548	4,577	13	84	3,971	R	64.6%	34.6%	65.1%	34.9%
470,928	PRINCE WILLIAM	153,218	64,658	87,352	97	1,111	22,694	D	42.2%	57.0%	42.5%	57.5%

VIRGINIA

2021 VIRGINIA GUBERNATORIAL GENERAL

2020 Census Population	County	Total Vote	(W) Republican (Glenn Youngkin)	Democrat (Terry McAuliffe)	Write-In Scattered (Write-Ins)	Other (Princess Blanding)	Rep.-Dem. Plurality		Percentage Total Vote Rep.	Dem.	Major Vote Rep.	Dem.
34,083	PULASKI	13,005	9,631	3,277	9	88	6,354	R	74.1%	25.2%	74.6%	25.4%
18,512	RADFORD	4,194	2,266	1,879	5	44	387	R	54.0%	44.8%	54.7%	45.3%
7,352	RAPPAHANNOCK	4,217	2,507	1,686	5	19	821	R	59.4%	40.0%	59.8%	40.2%
9,098	RICHMOND	3,271	2,225	936	90	20	1,289	R	68.0%	28.6%	70.4%	29.6%
204,214	RICHMOND CITY	80,053	15,713	61,929	2	2,409	46,216	D	19.6%	77.4%	20.2%	79.8%
99,499	ROANOKE	42,859	28,157	14,445	37	220	13,712	R	65.7%	33.7%	66.1%	33.9%
97,032	ROANOKE CITY	29,147	12,024	16,817	34	272	4,793	D	41.3%	57.7%	41.7%	58.3%
22,665	ROCKBRIDGE	10,024	6,906	3,071	7	40	3,835	R	68.9%	30.6%	69.2%	30.8%
82,301	ROCKINGHAM	35,539	26,765	8,569	23	182	18,196	R	75.3%	24.1%	75.7%	24.3%
26,556	RUSSELL	9,701	8,229	1,452	3	17	6,777	R	84.8%	15.0%	85.0%	15.0%
25,485	SALEM	9,556	6,144	3,344	8	60	2,800	R	64.3%	35.0%	64.8%	35.2%
21,544	SCOTT	8,131	7,065	1,034	4	28	6,031	R	86.9%	12.7%	87.2%	12.8%
43,767	SHENANDOAH	18,346	13,693	4,535	11	107	9,158	R	74.6%	24.7%	75.1%	24.9%
30,113	SMYTH	10,269	8,477	1,751	6	35	6,726	R	82.5%	17.1%	82.9%	17.1%
17,600	SOUTHAMPTON	7,834	5,084	2,717	4	29	2,367	R	64.9%	34.7%	65.2%	34.8%
136,944	SPOTSYLVANIA	54,279	32,478	21,426	29	346	11,052	R	59.8%	39.5%	60.3%	39.7%
153,837	STAFFORD	57,603	31,680	25,463	35	425	6,217	R	55.0%	44.2%	55.4%	44.6%
25,159	STAUNTON	9,771	4,640	5,004	8	119	364	D	47.5%	51.2%	48.1%	51.9%
92,505	SUFFOLK	36,716	17,351	19,079	34	252	1,728	D	47.3%	52.0%	47.6%	52.4%
6,423	SURRY	3,536	1,768	1,756	3	9	12	R	50.0%	49.7%	50.2%	49.8%
11,154	SUSSEX	4,025	1,973	2,028	0	24	55	D	49.0%	50.4%	49.3%	50.7%
40,542	TAZEWELL	13,910	12,045	1,821	4	40	10,224	R	86.6%	13.1%	86.9%	13.1%
449,825	VIRGINIA BEACH	162,197	86,973	73,965	99	1,160	13,008	R	53.6%	45.6%	54.0%	46.0%
40,343	WARREN	15,718	11,294	4,328	7	89	6,966	R	71.9%	27.5%	72.3%	27.7%
53,985	WASHINGTON	21,996	17,395	4,505	18	78	12,890	R	79.1%	20.5%	79.4%	20.6%
22,747	WAYNESBORO	7,856	4,473	3,275	9	99	1,198	R	56.9%	41.7%	57.7%	42.3%
18,111	WESTMORELAND	7,620	4,614	2,971	5	30	1,643	R	60.6%	39.0%	60.8%	39.2%
14,933	WILLIAMSBURG	4,931	1,703	3,185	3	40	1,482	D	34.5%	64.6%	34.8%	65.2%
28,072	WINCHESTER	8,496	4,137	4,294	5	60	157	D	48.7%	50.5%	49.1%	50.9%
37,343	WISE	11,551	9,691	1,796	11	53	7,895	R	83.9%	15.5%	84.4%	15.6%
28,761	WYTHE	11,565	9,458	2,043	5	59	7,415	R	81.8%	17.7%	82.2%	17.8%
68,329	YORK	29,841	17,485	12,190	16	150	5,295	R	58.6%	40.8%	58.9%	41.1%
	Votes Not Reported by County	0	0	0	0	0	0		0.0%	0.0%	0.0%	0.0%
8,776,425	TOTAL	3,288,318					63,688	R	50.6%	48.6%	51.0%	49.0%

VIRGINIA

HOUSE OF REPRESENTATIVES

CD	Year	Total Vote	Republican Vote	Candidate	Democratic Vote	Candidate	Other Vote	Rep.-Dem. Plurality		Percentage Total Vote Rep.	Dem.	Major Vote Rep.	Dem.
1	2022	342,742	191,828	WITTMAN, ROBERT J. "ROB"*	147,229	JONES, HERB	3,685	44,599	R	56.0%	43.0%	56.6%	43.4%
1	2020	448,178	260,614	WITTMAN, ROBERT J. "ROB"*	186,923	RASHID, QASIM	641	73,691	R	58.1%	41.7%	58.2%	41.8%
1	2018	332,101	183,250	WITTMAN, ROBERT J. "ROB"*	148,464	WILLIAMS, VANGIE	387	34,786	R	55.2%	44.7%	55.2%	44.8%
1	2016	384,655	230,213	WITTMAN, ROBERT J. "ROB"*	140,785	ROWE, MATT	13,657	89,428	R	59.8%	36.6%	62.1%	37.9%
1	2014	209,621	131,861	WITTMAN, ROBERT J. "ROB"*	72,059	MOSHER, NORMAN "NORM"	5,701	59,802	R	62.9%	34.4%	64.7%	35.3%
1	2012	356,806	200,845	WITTMAN, ROBERT J. "ROB"*	147,036	COOK, ADAM M.	8,925	53,809	R	56.3%	41.2%	57.7%	42.3%

VIRGINIA

HOUSE OF REPRESENTATIVES

			Republican		Democratic		Other Vote	Rep.-Dem. Plurality	Percentage			
									Total Vote		Major Vote	
CD	Year	Total Vote	Vote	Candidate	Vote	Candidate			Rep.	Dem.	Rep.	Dem.
2	2022	296,996	153,328	KIGGANS, JEN A.	143,219	LURIA, ELAINE*	449	10,109 R	51.6%	48.2%	51.7%	48.3%
2	2020	360,277	165,031	TAYLOR, SCOTT W.	185,733	LURIA, ELAINE*	9,513	20,702 D	45.8%	51.6%	47.0%	53.0%
2	2018	273,400	133,458	TAYLOR, SCOTT W.*	139,571	LURIA, ELAINE	371	6,113 D	48.8%	51.1%	48.9%	51.1%
2	2016	310,640	190,475	TAYLOR, SCOTT W.	119,440	BROWN, SHAUN DENISE	725	71,035 R	61.3%	38.4%	61.5%	38.5%
2	2014	173,060	101,558	RIGELL, E. SCOTT*	71,178	PATRICK, SUZANNE	324	30,380 R	58.7%	41.1%	58.8%	41.2%
2	2012	309,222	166,231	RIGELL, E. SCOTT*	142,548	HIRSCHBIEL, PAUL O. JR.	443	23,683 R	53.8%	46.1%	53.8%	46.2%
3	2022	207,850	67,668	NAMKUNG, TERRY T.	139,659	SCOTT, ROBERT C. "BOBBY"*	523	71,991 D	32.6%	67.2%	32.6%	67.4%
3	2020	341,361	107,299	COLLICK, JOHN WILLIAM JR.	233,326	SCOTT, ROBERT C. "BOBBY"*	736	126,027 D	31.4%	68.4%	31.5%	68.5%
3	2018	217,722			198,615	SCOTT, ROBERT C. "BOBBY"*	19,107	198,615 D		91.2%		100.0%
3	2016	312,371	103,289	WILLIAMS, MARTIN "MARTY"	208,337	SCOTT, ROBERT C. "BOBBY"*	745	105,048 D	33.1%	66.7%	33.1%	66.9%
3	2014	147,402			139,197	SCOTT, ROBERT C. "BOBBY"*	8,205	139,197 D		94.4%		100.0%
3	2012	318,936	58,931	LONGO, DEAN J.	259,199	SCOTT, ROBERT C. "BOBBY"*	806	200,268 D	18.5%	81.3%	18.5%	81.5%
4	2022	244,978	85,503	BENJAMIN, LEON	159,044	MCEACHIN, A. DONALD*	431	73,541 D	34.9%	64.9%	35.0%	65.0%
4	2020	391,345	149,625	BENJAMIN, LEON	241,142	MCEACHIN, A. DONALD*	578	91,517 D	38.2%	61.6%	38.3%	61.7%
4	2018	299,854	107,706	MCADAMS, RYAN	187,642	MCEACHIN, A. DONALD*	4,506	79,936 D	35.9%	62.6%	36.5%	63.5%
4	2016	346,699	145,731	WADE, MIKE	200,136	MCEACHIN, A. DONALD	832	54,405 D	42.0%	57.7%	42.1%	57.9%
4	2014	200,638	120,684	FORBES, J. RANDY*	75,270	FAUSZ, ELLIOTT	4,684	45,414 R	60.2%	37.5%	61.6%	38.4%
4	2012	350,046	199,292	FORBES, J. RANDY*	150,190	WARD, ELLA P.	564	49,102 R	56.9%	42.9%	57.0%	43.0%
5	2022	307,790	177,191	GOOD, ROBERT*	129,996	THRONEBURG, JOSHUA	603	47,195 R	57.6%	42.2%	57.7%	42.3%
5	2020	402,317	210,988	GOOD, ROBERT	190,315	WEBB, CAMERON BRYANT	1,014	20,673 R	52.4%	47.3%	52.6%	47.4%
5	2018	310,926	165,339	RIGGLEMAN, DENVER III	145,040	COCKBURN, LESLIE	547	20,299 R	53.2%	46.6%	53.3%	46.7%
5	2016	356,765	207,758	GARRETT, TOM	148,339	DITTMAR, JANE	668	59,419 R	58.2%	41.6%	58.3%	41.7%
5	2014	204,945	124,735	HURT, ROBERT*	73,482	GAUGHAN, WALTER LAWRENCE "LAWRENCE"	6,728	51,253 R	60.9%	35.9%	62.9%	37.1%
5	2012	348,111	193,009	HURT, ROBERT*	149,214	DOUGLASS, JOHN WADE	5,888	43,795 R	55.4%	42.9%	56.4%	43.6%
6	2022	269,234	173,352	CLINE, BENJAMIN*	95,410	LEWIS, JENNIFER	472	77,942 R	64.4%	35.4%	64.5%	35.5%
6	2020	381,813	246,606	CLINE, BENJAMIN*	134,729	BETTS, NICHOLAS	478	111,877 R	64.6%	35.3%	64.7%	35.3%
6	2018	281,377	167,957	CLINE, BENJAMIN	113,133	LEWIS, JENNIFER	287	54,824 R	59.7%	40.2%	59.8%	40.2%
6	2016	338,456	225,471	GOODLATTE, ROBERT W. "BOB"*	112,170	DEGNER, KAI	815	113,301 R	66.6%	33.1%	66.8%	33.2%
6	2014	179,708	133,898	GOODLATTE, ROBERT W. "BOB"*			45,810	133,898 R	74.5%		100.0%	
6	2012	323,893	211,278	GOODLATTE, ROBERT W. "BOB"*	111,949	SCHMOOKLER, ANDY	666	99,329 R	65.2%	34.6%	65.4%	34.6%
7	2022	274,590	130,586	VEGA, YESLI	143,357	SPANBERGER, ABIGAIL*	647	12,771 D	47.6%	52.2%	47.7%	52.3%
7	2020	454,339	222,623	FREITAS, NICK	230,893	SPANBERGER, ABIGAIL*	823	8,270 D	49.0%	50.8%	49.1%	50.9%
7	2018	349,803	169,295	BRAT, DAVID*	176,079	SPANBERGER, ABIGAIL	4,429	6,784 D	48.4%	50.3%	49.0%	51.0%
7	2016	379,209	218,057	BRAT, DAVID*	160,159	BEDELL, EILEEN	993	57,898 R	57.5%	42.2%	57.7%	42.3%
7	2014	243,351	148,026	BRAT, DAVID	89,914	TRAMMELL, JOHN K. "JACK"	5,411	58,112 R	60.8%	36.9%	62.2%	37.8%
7	2012	381,909	222,983	CANTOR, ERIC I.*	158,012	POWELL, E. WAYNE	914	64,971 R	58.4%	41.4%	58.5%	41.5%
8	2022	268,936	66,589	LIPSMAN, KARINA	197,760	BEYER, DONALD S. JR.*	4,587	131,171 D	24.8%	73.5%	25.2%	74.8%
8	2020	397,745	95,365	JORDAN, JEFF	301,454	BEYER, DONALD S. JR.*	926	206,089 D	24.0%	75.8%	24.0%	76.0%
8	2018	324,748	76,899	OH, THOMAS	247,137	BEYER, DONALD S. JR.*	712	170,238 D	23.7%	76.1%	23.7%	76.3%
8	2016	360,687	98,387	HERNICK, CHARLES ALAN	246,653	BEYER, DONALD S. JR.*	15,647	148,266 D	27.3%	68.4%	28.5%	71.5%
8	2014	203,076	63,810	EDMOND, MICAH	128,102	BEYER, DONALD S. JR.	11,164	64,292 D	31.4%	63.1%	33.2%	66.8%
8	2012	351,187	107,370	MURRAY, J. PATRICK	226,847	MORAN, JAMES P. JR.*	16,970	119,477 D	30.6%	64.6%	32.1%	67.9%
9	2022	248,792	182,207	GRIFFITH, H. MORGAN*	66,027	DEVAUGHAN, TAYSHA	558	116,180 R	73.2%	26.5%	73.4%	26.6%
9	2020	289,274	271,851	GRIFFITH, H. MORGAN*			17,423	271,851 R	94.0%		100.0%	
9	2018	246,980	160,933	GRIFFITH, H. MORGAN*	85,833	FLACCAVENTO, ANTHONY J.	214	75,100 R	65.2%	34.8%	65.2%	34.8%
9	2016	310,327	212,838	GRIFFITH, H. MORGAN*	87,877	KITTS, DEREK	9,612	124,961 R	68.6%	28.3%	70.8%	29.2%
9	2014	162,815	117,465	GRIFFITH, H. MORGAN*			45,350	117,465 R	72.1%		100.0%	
9	2012	301,658	184,882	GRIFFITH, H. MORGAN*	116,400	FLACCAVENTO, ANTHONY J.	376	68,482 R	61.3%	38.6%	61.4%	38.6%
10	2022	296,145	138,163	CAO, HUNG	157,405	WEXTON, JENNIFER*	577	19,242 D	46.7%	53.2%	46.7%	53.3%
10	2020	475,546	206,253	ANDREWS, ALISCIA	268,734	WEXTON, JENNIFER*	559	62,481 D	43.4%	56.5%	43.4%	56.6%
10	2018	367,795	160,841	COMSTOCK, BARBARA*	206,356	WEXTON, JENNIFER	598	45,515 D	43.7%	56.1%	43.8%	56.2%
10	2016	400,117	210,791	COMSTOCK, BARBARA*	187,712	BENNETT, LUANN	1,614	23,079 R	52.7%	46.9%	52.9%	47.1%
10	2014	222,910	125,914	COMSTOCK, BARBARA	89,957	FOUST, JOHN	7,039	35,957 R	56.5%	40.4%	58.3%	41.7%
10	2012	366,444	214,038	WOLF, FRANK R.*	142,024	CABRAL, KRISTIN A.	10,382	72,014 R	58.4%	38.8%	60.1%	39.9%
11	2022	289,676	95,634	MYLES, JAMES	193,190	CONNOLLY, GERALD E. "GERRY"*	852	97,556 D	33.0%	66.7%	33.1%	66.9%
11	2020	393,241	111,380	ANANTATMULA, MANGA	280,725	CONNOLLY, GERALD E. "GERRY"*	1,136	169,345 D	28.3%	71.4%	28.4%	71.6%
11	2018	308,250	83,023	DOVE, JEFFREY	219,191	CONNOLLY, GERALD E. "GERRY"*	6,036	136,168 D	26.9%	71.1%	27.5%	72.5%
11	2016	282,322			247,818	CONNOLLY, GERALD E. "GERRY"*	34,504	247,818 D		87.8%		100.0%
11	2014	187,787	75,796	SCHOLTE, SUZANNE	106,780	CONNOLLY, GERALD E. "GERRY"*	5,211	30,984 D	40.4%	56.9%	41.5%	58.5%
11	2012	332,243	117,902	PERKINS, CHRIS S.	202,606	CONNOLLY, GERALD E. "GERRY"*	11,735	84,704 D	35.5%	61.0%	36.8%	63.2%

VIRGINIA

HOUSE OF REPRESENTATIVES

CD	Year	Total Vote	Republican Vote	Republican Candidate	Democratic Vote	Democratic Candidate	Other Vote	Rep.-Dem. Plurality	Total Vote Rep.	Total Vote Dem.	Major Vote Rep.	Major Vote Dem.
TOTAL	2022	3,047,729	1,462,049		1,572,296		13,384	110,247 D	48.0%	51.6%	48.2%	51.8%
TOTAL	2020	4,335,436	2,047,635		2,253,974		33,827	206,339 D	47.2%	52.0%	47.6%	52.4%
TOTAL	2018	3,312,956	1,408,701		1,867,061		37,194	458,360 D	42.5%	56.4%	43.0%	57.0%
TOTAL	2016	3,782,248	1,843,010		1,859,426		79,812	16,416 D	48.7%	49.2%	49.8%	50.2%
TOTAL	2014	2,135,313	1,143,747		845,939		145,627	297,808 R	53.6%	39.6%	57.5%	42.5%
TOTAL	2012	3,740,455	1,876,761		1,806,025		57,669	70,736 R	50.2%	48.3%	51.0%	49.0%

Note: An asterisk (*) denotes incumbent.

VIRGINIA

GENERAL AND PRIMARY ELECTIONS

GENERAL ELECTIONS: OTHER VOTES

Governor (2021)   Other vote was 23,107 Other (Princess Blanding), 2,583 Write-In (Scattered Write-Ins)

House   Other vote was:

CD 1	3,388 Independent (David Foster), 297 Write-In (Write-Ins)
CD 2	449 Write-In (Write-Ins)
CD 3	523 Write-In (Write-Ins)
CD 4	431 Write-In (Write-Ins)
CD 5	603 Write-In (Write-Ins)
CD 6	472 Write-In (Write-Ins)
CD 7	647 Write-In (Write-Ins)
CD 8	4,078 Independent (Theodore Fikre), 509 Write-In (Write-Ins)
CD 9	558 Write-In (Write-Ins)
CD 10	557 Write-In (Write-Ins)
CD 11	852 Write-In (Write-Ins)

2022 PRIMARY ELECTIONS: SUPPLEMENTARY INFORMATION

Primary   June 21, 2022   **Registration** (as of May 31, 2022)   662,157   No Party Registration

Primary Type   Open—Any registered voter could participate in the primary of either party.

	REPUBLICAN PRIMARIES			DEMOCRATIC PRIMARIES	
Congressional District 1	Wittman, Robert J. "Rob"*	Unopposed		Jones, Herb	Unopposed
Congressional District 2	Kiggans, Jen A. Bell, Jarome Altman, L. Thomas "Tommy" III Baan, Andrew G. "Andy" TOTAL	23,300 11,330 5,972 1,237 41,839	55.7% 27.1% 14.3% 3.0%	Luria, Elaine*	Unopposed
Congressional District 3	Namkung, Terry T. Engquist, Ted TOTAL	6,293 4,116 10,409	60.5% 39.5%	Scott, Robert C. "Bobby"*	Unopposed

VIRGINIA

GENERAL AND PRIMARY ELECTIONS

	REPUBLICAN PRIMARIES			DEMOCRATIC PRIMARIES		
Congressional District 4	Benjamin, Leon	Unopposed		McEachin, A. Donald*		
Congressional District 5	Good, Bob*			Throneburg, Joshua	Unopposed	
Congressional District 6	Cline, Benjamin Hale, Merritt TOTAL	19,620 4,264 23,884	82.1% 17.9%			
Congressional District 7	Vega, Yesli Anderson, Derrick Reeves, Bryce E. Vanuch, Crystal L. Ross, David L. Ciarcia, Gina R. TOTAL	10,913 8,966 7,580 6,400 2,284 1,565 37,708	28.9% 23.8% 20.1% 17.0% 6.1% 4.2%	Spanberger, Abigail*	Unopposed	
Congressional District 8	Lipsman, Karina			Beyer, Donald S. Jr.* Virasingh, Victoria TOTAL	39,062 11,583 50,645	77.1% 22.9%
Congressional District 9	Griffith, H. Morgan*			DeVaughan, Taysha	Unopposed	
Congressional District 10	Cao, Hung			Wexton, Jennifer*	Unopposed	
Congressional District 11	Myles, James			Connolly, Gerald E. "Gerry"*	Unopposed	

Note: An asterisk (*) denotes incumbent.

WASHINGTON

Statewide Races

The 2022 election gave political forecasters several conflicting, and outright confounding, signals. One of the best electoral indicators, though, turned out to be Washington state, specifically its early August primary.

Early in the cycle, National Republican Senate Committee Chair Rick Scott was bullish on his party's chances in the Evergreen State. With five-term Democratic Sen. Patty Murray seeking another term, Republicans found a first-time candidate with an appealing background: Tiffany Smiley, a nurse and veteran's advocate.

Washington uses a blanket primary system: all candidates run on a primary ballot and the top two advance to a second round. Despite polling showing Smiley within striking distance of Murray, primary balloting showed that the incumbent was on solid ground with voters. In a primary field that featured close to twenty candidates, Murray took 52% to Smiley's 34%. More tellingly, Democratic candidates combined for 57% of the aggregate two-party vote. King County, which houses Seattle and casts close to one-third of the statewide vote, gave Democratic candidates close to three-fourths of the vote.

Post-primary Washington polls varied widely, with polling aggregators settling on a single-digit advantage for Murray. Instead, the November result was a near carbon copy of the August primary: Murray defeated Smiley 57%–43%. Though realignment was catching up with Murray, as she lost a few Obama-to-Trump counties along the Pacific Coast for the first time in her career, her King County "firewall" held: she took 75% of the vote there. One bright spot for Smiley was Whitman County – in the state's southeastern corner, it contains Washington State University, in Pullman. As Pullman punched under its weight in terms of turnout, Smiley carried it by 24 votes after it went 53%–43% for Biden in 2020.

House Races

With Washington state remaining at ten districts after the 2020 census, the state's redistricting commission passed a map that only made minor changes to the outgoing plan.

Going into the 2022 elections, Democrats held a 7-3 edge in the state's delegation. The most vulnerable Democratic incumbent was Kim Schrier, who represented the suburban-Seattle 8th District and did not get much help in redistricting – she retained a seat that Biden carried with only 52%. But the August primary again proved prescient. Schrier, together with a few minor Democrats, combined for more votes than the Republican field, which featured three serious candidates. Schrier went on to win by seven points.

In the southwestern 3rd District, Rep. Jaime Herrera Beutler, a center-right Republican who voted to impeach Trump, was squeezed out of the top two. In a major upset, Democrat Marie Gluesenkamp Perez, a 34-year-old auto repair shop owner, beat out Republican Joe Kent, a populist conservative who questioned America's support for Ukraine.

Finally, of the ten House Republicans who voted to support Trump's impeachment in early 2021, Rep. Dan Newhouse was one of just two who secured reelection (the other was California's David Valadao). With six Republicans seemingly splitting the anti-Newhouse vote in the primary, the incumbent made the general election with a Democrat. In the state's reddest district, Newhouse won easily.

WASHINGTON
Congressional districts first established for elections held in 2022
10 members

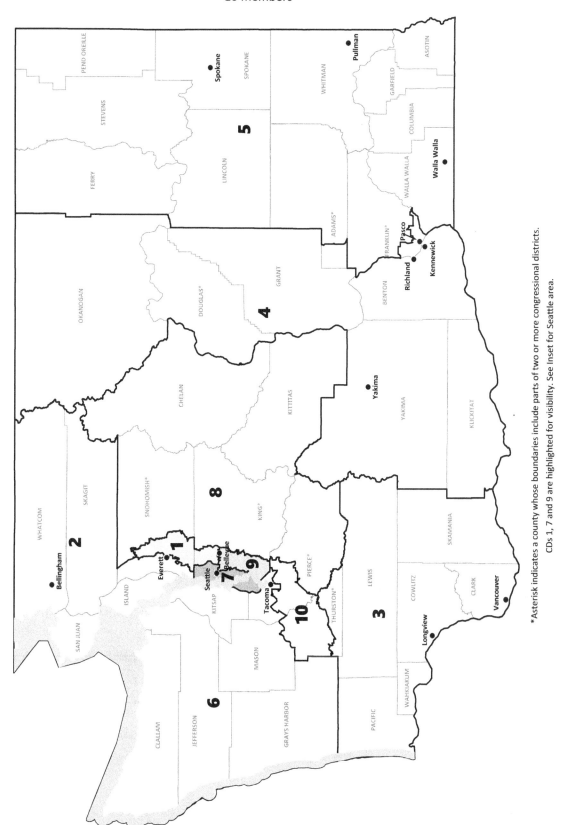

*Asterisk indicates a county whose boundaries include parts of two or more congressional districts. CDs 1, 7 and 9 are highlighted for visibility. See Inset for Seattle area.

WASHINGTON
Greater Seattle Area

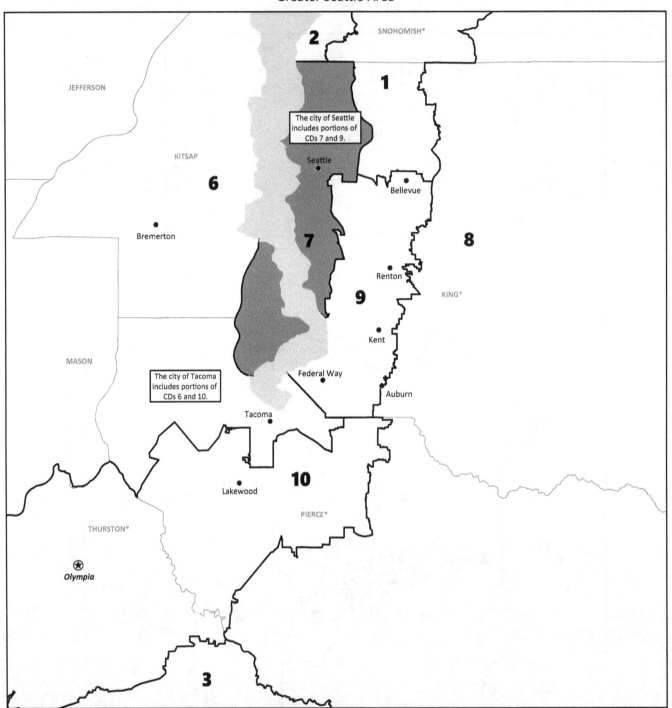

* Asterisk indicates a county whose boundaries include parts of two or more congressional districts.
CD 7 is highlighted for visibility.

WASHINGTON

GOVERNOR
Jay Inslee (D). Reelected 2020 to a four-year term. Previously elected 2016, 2012.

SENATORS (2 Democrats)
Maria Cantwell (D). Reelected 2018 to a six-year term. Previously elected 2012, 2006, 2000.

Patty Murray (D). Reelected 2022 to a six-year term. Previously elected 2016, 2010, 2004, 1998, 1992.

REPRESENTATIVES (2 Republicans, 8 Democrats)
1. Suzan DelBene (D)
2. Rick Larsen (D)
3. Marie Gluesenkamp Pérez (D)
4. Dan Newhouse (R)
5. Cathy McMorris Rodgers (R)
6. Derek Kilmer (D)
7. Pramila Jayapal (D)
8. Kim Schrier (D)
9. Adam Smith (D)
10. Marilyn Strickland (D)

POSTWAR VOTE FOR PRESIDENT

Year	Total Vote	Republican Vote	Republican Candidate	Democratic Vote	Democratic Candidate	Other Vote	Rep.-Dem. Plurality	Total Vote Rep.	Total Vote Dem.	Major Vote Rep.	Major Vote Dem.
2020**	4,087,631	1,584,651	Trump, Donald J.*	2,369,612	Biden, Joseph R. Jr.	133,368	784,961 D	38.8%	58.0%	40.1%	59.9%
2016**	3,317,019	1,221,747	Trump, Donald J.	1,742,718	Clinton, Hillary Rodham	352,554	520,971 D	36.8%	52.5%	41.2%	58.8%
2012	3,125,516	1,290,670	Romney, W. Mitt	1,755,396	Obama, Barack H.*	79,450	464,726 D	41.3%	56.2%	42.4%	57.6%
2008	3,036,878	1,229,216	McCain, John S. III	1,750,848	Obama, Barack H.	56,814	521,632 D	40.5%	57.7%	41.2%	58.8%
2004	2,859,084	1,304,894	Bush, George W.*	1,510,201	Kerry, John F.	43,989	205,307 D	45.6%	52.8%	46.4%	53.6%
2000**	2,487,433	1,108,864	Bush, George W.	1,247,652	Gore, Albert Jr.	130,917	138,788 D	44.6%	50.2%	47.1%	52.9%
1996**	2,253,837	840,712	Dole, Robert "Bob"	1,123,323	Clinton, Bill*	289,802	282,611 D	37.3%	49.8%	42.8%	57.2%
1992**	2,288,230	731,234	Bush, George H.*	993,037	Clinton, Bill	563,959	261,803 D	32.0%	43.4%	42.4%	57.6%
1988	1,865,253	903,835	Bush, George H.	933,516	Dukakis, Michael S.	27,902	29,681 D	48.5%	50.0%	49.2%	50.8%
1984	1,883,910	1,051,670	Reagan, Ronald*	807,352	Mondale, Walter F.	24,888	244,318 R	55.8%	42.9%	56.6%	43.4%
1980**	1,742,394	865,244	Reagan, Ronald	650,193	Carter, Jimmy*	226,957	215,051 R	49.7%	37.3%	57.1%	42.9%
1976	1,555,534	777,732	Ford, Gerald R.*	717,323	Carter, Jimmy	60,479	60,409 R	50.0%	46.1%	52.0%	48.0%
1972	1,470,847	837,135	Nixon, Richard M.*	568,334	McGovern, George S.	65,378	268,801 R	56.9%	38.6%	59.6%	40.4%
1968**	1,304,281	588,510	Nixon, Richard M.	616,037	Humphrey, Hubert Horatio Jr.	99,734	27,527 D	45.1%	47.2%	48.9%	51.1%
1964	1,258,556	470,366	Goldwater, Barry M. Sr.	779,881	Johnson, Lyndon B.*	8,309	309,515 D	37.4%	62.0%	37.6%	62.4%
1960	1,241,572	629,273	Nixon, Richard M.	599,298	Kennedy, John F.	13,001	29,975 R	50.7%	48.3%	51.2%	48.8%
1956	1,150,889	620,430	Eisenhower, Dwight D.*	523,002	Stevenson, Adlai E. II	7,457	97,428 R	53.9%	45.4%	54.3%	45.7%
1952	1,102,708	599,107	Eisenhower, Dwight D.	492,845	Stevenson, Adlai E. II	10,756	106,262 R	54.3%	44.7%	54.9%	45.1%
1948	905,058	386,314	Dewey, Thomas E.	476,165	Truman, Harry S.*	42,579	89,851 D	42.7%	52.6%	44.8%	55.2%

Note: An asterisk (*) denotes incumbent. **In past elections, the other vote included: 2020 - 80,500 Libertarian (Jo Jorgenson); 2016 - 160,879 Libertarian (Gary Johnson); 2000 - 103,002 Green (Ralph Nader); 1996 - 201,003 Reform (Ross Perot); 1992 - 541,780 Independent (Perot); 1980 - 185,073 Independent (John Anderson); 1968 - 96,990 American Independent (George Wallace).

WASHINGTON

POSTWAR VOTE FOR GOVERNOR

Year	Total Vote	Republican Vote	Republican Candidate	Democratic Vote	Democratic Candidate	Other Vote	Rep.-Dem. Plurality	Total Vote Rep.	Total Vote Dem.	Major Vote Rep.	Major Vote Dem.
2020	4,056,454	1,749,066	Culp, Loren	2,294,243	Inslee, Jay*	13,145	545,177 D	43.1%	56.6%	43.3%	56.7%
2016	3,245,282	1,476,346	Bryant, Bill	1,760,520	Inslee, Jay*	8,416	284,174 D	45.5%	54.2%	45.6%	54.4%
2012	3,071,047	1,488,245	McKenna, Rob	1,582,802	Inslee, Jay		94,557 D	48.5%	51.5%	48.5%	51.5%
2008	3,002,862	1,404,124	Rossi, Dino	1,598,738	Gregoire, Christine*		194,614 D	46.8%	53.2%	46.8%	53.2%
2004**	2,810,058	1,373,232	Rossi, Dino	1,373,361	Gregoire, Christine	63,465	129 D	48.9%	48.9%	50.0%	50.0%
2000	2,469,852	980,060	Carlson, John	1,441,973	Locke, Gary*	47,819	461,913 D	39.7%	58.4%	40.5%	59.5%
1996	2,237,030	940,538	Craswell, Ellen	1,296,492	Locke, Gary		355,954 D	42.0%	58.0%	42.0%	58.0%
1992	2,270,826	1,086,216	Eikenberry, Ken	1,184,315	Lowry, Mike	295	98,099 D	47.8%	52.2%	47.8%	52.2%
1988	1,874,929	708,481	Williams, Bob	1,166,448	Gardner, Booth*		457,967 D	37.8%	62.2%	37.8%	62.2%
1984	1,888,987	881,994	Spellman, John D.*	1,006,993	Gardner, Booth		124,999 D	46.7%	53.3%	46.7%	53.3%
1980	1,730,896	981,083	Spellman, John D.	749,813	McDermott, James A.		231,270 R	56.7%	43.3%	56.7%	43.3%
1976	1,546,380	687,039	Spellman, John D.	821,797	Ray, Dixy Lee	37,544	134,758 D	44.4%	53.1%	45.5%	54.5%
1972	1,472,542	747,825	Evans, Daniel J.*	630,613	Rosellini, Albert D.	94,104	117,212 R	50.8%	42.8%	54.3%	45.7%
1968	1,265,354	692,377	Evans, Daniel J.*	560,262	O'Connell, John J.	12,715	132,115 R	54.7%	44.3%	55.3%	44.7%
1964	1,250,274	697,256	Evans, Daniel J.	548,692	Rosellini, Albert D.*	4,326	148,564 R	55.8%	43.9%	56.0%	44.0%
1960	1,215,748	594,122	Andrews, Lloyd J.	611,987	Rosellini, Albert D.*	9,639	17,865 D	48.9%	50.3%	49.3%	50.7%
1956	1,128,977	508,041	Anderson, Emmett T.	616,773	Rosellini, Albert D.	4,163	108,732 D	45.0%	54.6%	45.2%	54.8%
1952	1,078,497	567,822	Langlie, Arthur B.*	510,675	Mitchell, Hugh B.		57,147 R	52.6%	47.4%	52.6%	47.4%
1948	883,141	445,958	Langlie, Arthur B.	417,035	Wallgren, Monrad C.*	20,148	28,923 R	50.5%	47.2%	51.7%	48.3%

Note: An asterisk (*) denotes incumbent. **In 2004, the initial official vote count put Republican Dino Rossi ahead by 261 votes. A machine recount reduced Rossi's margin to 42 votes. A subsequent manual recount gave Democrat Christine Gregoire the election by a margin of 129 votes (see above), and she was inaugurated governor.

POSTWAR VOTE FOR SENATOR

Year	Total Vote	Republican Vote	Republican Candidate	Democratic Vote	Democratic Candidate	Other Vote	Rep.-Dem. Plurality	Total Vote Rep.	Total Vote Dem.	Major Vote Rep.	Major Vote Dem.
2022	3,047,900	1,299,322	Smiley, Tiffany	1,741,827	Murray, Patty*	6,751	442,505 D	42.6%	57.1%	42.7%	57.3%
2018	3,086,168	1,282,804	Hutchison, Susan	1,803,364	Cantwell, Maria*		520,560 D	41.6%	58.4%	41.6%	58.4%
2016	3,243,317	1,329,338	Vance, Chris	1,913,979	Murray, Patty*		584,641 D	41.0%	59.0%	41.0%	59.0%
2012	3,069,417	1,213,924	Baumgartner, Michael	1,855,493	Cantwell, Maria*		641,569 D	39.5%	60.5%	39.5%	60.5%
2010	2,511,094	1,196,164	Rossi, Dino	1,314,930	Murray, Patty*		118,766 D	47.6%	52.4%	47.6%	52.4%
2006	2,083,734	832,106	McGavick, Mike	1,184,659	Cantwell, Maria*	66,969	352,553 D	39.9%	56.9%	41.3%	58.7%
2004	2,818,651	1,204,584	Nethercutt, George R.	1,549,708	Murray, Patty*	64,359	345,124 D	42.7%	55.0%	43.7%	56.3%
2000	2,461,379	1,197,208	Gorton, Slade*	1,199,437	Cantwell, Maria	64,734	2,229 D	48.6%	48.7%	50.0%	50.0%
1998	1,888,561	785,377	Smith, Linda	1,103,184	Murray, Patty*		317,807 D	41.6%	58.4%	41.6%	58.4%
1994	1,700,173	947,821	Gorton, Slade*	752,352	Sims, Ron		195,469 R	55.7%	44.3%	55.7%	44.3%
1992	2,219,162	1,020,829	Chandler, Rod	1,197,973	Murray, Patty	360	177,144 D	46.0%	54.0%	46.0%	54.0%
1988	1,848,542	944,359	Gorton, Slade	904,183	Lowry, Mike		40,176 R	51.1%	48.9%	51.1%	48.9%
1986	1,337,367	650,931	Gorton, Slade*	677,471	Adams, Brock	8,965	26,540 D	48.7%	50.7%	49.0%	51.0%
1983S**	1,213,307	672,326	Evans, Daniel J.*	540,981	Lowry, Mike		131,345 R	55.4%	44.6%	55.4%	44.6%
1982	1,368,476	332,273	Jewett, Doug	943,655	Jackson, Henry M.*	92,548	611,382 D	24.3%	69.0%	26.0%	74.0%
1980	1,728,369	936,317	Gorton, Slade	792,052	Magnuson, Warren G.*		144,265 R	54.2%	45.8%	54.2%	45.8%
1976	1,491,111	361,546	Brown, George M.	1,071,219	Jackson, Henry M.*	58,346	709,673 D	24.2%	71.8%	25.2%	74.8%
1974	1,007,847	363,626	Metcalf, Jack	611,811	Magnuson, Warren G.*	32,410	248,185 D	36.1%	60.7%	37.3%	62.7%
1970	1,066,807	170,790	Elicker, Charles W.	879,385	Jackson, Henry M.*	16,632	708,595 D	16.0%	82.4%	16.3%	83.7%
1968	1,236,063	435,894	Metcalf, Jack	796,183	Magnuson, Warren G.*	3,986	360,289 D	35.3%	64.4%	35.4%	64.6%
1964	1,213,088	337,138	Andrews, Lloyd J.	875,950	Jackson, Henry M.*		538,812 D	27.8%	72.2%	27.8%	72.2%
1962	943,229	446,204	Christensen, Richard G.	491,365	Magnuson, Warren G.*	5,660	45,161 D	47.3%	52.1%	47.6%	52.4%
1958	886,822	278,271	Bantz, William B.	597,040	Jackson, Henry M.*	11,511	318,769 D	31.4%	67.3%	31.8%	68.2%
1956	1,122,217	436,652	Langlie, Arthur B.	685,565	Magnuson, Warren G.*		248,913 D	38.9%	61.1%	38.9%	61.1%
1952	1,058,735	460,884	Cain, Harry P.*	595,288	Jackson, Henry M.	2,563	134,404 D	43.5%	56.2%	43.6%	56.4%
1950	744,783	342,464	Williams, Walter	397,719	Magnuson, Warren G.*	4,600	55,255 D	46.0%	53.4%	46.3%	53.7%
1946	660,342	358,847	Cain, Harry P.	298,683	Mitchell, Hugh B.	2,812	60,164 R	54.3%	45.2%	54.6%	45.4%

Note: An asterisk (*) denotes incumbent. **The 1983 election was for a short term to fill a vacancy.

WASHINGTON

SENATOR 2022

2020 Census Population	County	Total Vote	Republican (Smiley)	Democratic (Murray)	Other	Rep.-Dem. Plurality		Percentage			
								Total Vote		Major Vote	
								Rep.	Dem.	Rep.	Dem.
19,951	ADAMS	4,131	3,150	969	12	2,181	R	76.3%	23.5%	76.5%	23.5%
22,661	ASOTIN	9,018	5,824	3,181	13	2,643	R	64.6%	35.3%	64.7%	35.3%
205,544	BENTON	75,749	50,108	25,513	128	24,595	R	66.2%	33.7%	66.3%	33.7%
77,560	CHELAN	34,273	19,833	14,373	67	5,460	R	57.9%	41.9%	58.0%	42.0%
77,895	CLALLAM	40,279	19,401	20,784	94	1,383	D	48.2%	51.6%	48.3%	51.7%
491,178	CLARK	205,616	100,260	105,058	298	4,798	D	48.8%	51.1%	48.8%	51.2%
3,994	COLUMBIA	2,179	1,575	592	12	983	R	72.3%	27.2%	72.7%	27.3%
111,506	COWLITZ	44,942	27,446	17,439	57	10,007	R	61.1%	38.8%	61.1%	38.9%
43,661	DOUGLAS	16,117	10,806	5,275	36	5,531	R	67.0%	32.7%	67.2%	32.8%
7,654	FERRY	3,415	2,348	1,060	7	1,288	R	68.8%	31.0%	68.9%	31.1%
95,621	FRANKLIN	22,214	15,174	7,022	18	8,152	R	68.3%	31.6%	68.4%	31.6%
2,230	GARFIELD	1,287	977	307	3	670	R	75.9%	23.9%	76.1%	23.9%
97,947	GRANT	26,912	19,655	7,221	36	12,434	R	73.0%	26.8%	73.1%	26.9%
75,631	GRAYS HARBOR	29,399	15,718	13,600	81	2,118	R	53.5%	46.3%	53.6%	46.4%
85,674	ISLAND	43,057	19,275	23,680	102	4,405	D	44.8%	55.0%	44.9%	55.1%
32,497	JEFFERSON	21,199	6,185	14,970	44	8,785	D	29.2%	70.6%	29.2%	70.8%
2,253,103	KING	890,942	220,307	668,692	1,943	448,385	D	24.7%	75.1%	24.8%	75.2%
272,826	KITSAP	123,351	52,134	70,939	278	18,805	D	42.3%	57.5%	42.4%	57.6%
48,272	KITTITAS	20,798	12,446	8,318	34	4,128	R	59.8%	40.0%	59.9%	40.1%
22,577	KLICKITAT	11,455	6,639	4,798	18	1,841	R	58.0%	41.9%	58.0%	42.0%
81,237	LEWIS	35,992	24,654	11,263	75	13,391	R	68.5%	31.3%	68.6%	31.4%
11,025	LINCOLN	6,154	4,716	1,423	15	3,293	R	76.6%	23.1%	76.8%	23.2%
67,320	MASON	29,475	15,612	13,777	86	1,835	R	53.0%	46.7%	53.1%	46.9%
42,267	OKANOGAN	16,604	9,926	6,644	34	3,282	R	59.8%	40.0%	59.9%	40.1%
22,618	PACIFIC	11,943	6,137	5,771	35	366	R	51.4%	48.3%	51.5%	48.5%
13,832	PEND OREILLE	6,787	4,739	2,032	16	2,707	R	69.8%	29.9%	70.0%	30.0%
908,629	PIERCE	332,454	156,331	175,164	959	18,833	D	47.0%	52.7%	47.2%	52.8%
17,750	SAN JUAN	11,326	3,055	8,254	17	5,199	D	27.0%	72.9%	27.0%	73.0%
129,990	SKAGIT	56,849	27,394	29,316	139	1,922	D	48.2%	51.6%	48.3%	51.7%
12,148	SKAMANIA	6,227	3,599	2,620	8	979	R	57.8%	42.1%	57.9%	42.1%
825,706	SNOHOMISH	320,633	135,339	184,430	864	49,091	D	42.2%	57.5%	42.3%	57.7%
526,261	SPOKANE	221,531	120,369	100,719	443	19,650	R	54.3%	45.5%	54.4%	45.6%
46,019	STEVENS	22,919	16,803	6,073	43	10,730	R	73.3%	26.5%	73.5%	26.5%
292,672	THURSTON	126,106	52,570	73,189	347	20,619	D	41.7%	58.0%	41.8%	58.2%
4,537	WAHKIAKUM	2,565	1,551	1,007	7	544	R	60.5%	39.3%	60.6%	39.4%
61,044	WALLA WALLA	24,260	14,192	10,039	29	4,153	R	58.5%	41.4%	58.6%	41.4%
230,843	WHATCOM	111,170	45,038	65,950	182	20,912	D	40.5%	59.3%	40.6%	59.4%
50,295	WHITMAN	15,707	7,848	7,824	35	24	R	50.0%	49.8%	50.1%	49.9%
251,228	YAKIMA	62,865	40,188	22,541	136	17,647	R	63.9%	35.9%	64.1%	35.9%
7,643,403	TOTAL	3,047,900	1,299,322	1,741,827	6,751	442,505	D	42.6%	57.1%	42.7%	57.3%

WASHINGTON

HOUSE OF REPRESENTATIVES

CD	Year	Total Vote	Republican		Democratic		Other Vote	Rep.-Dem. Plurality		Percentage			
			Vote	Candidate	Vote	Candidate				Total Vote		Major Vote	
										Rep.	Dem.	Rep.	Dem.
1	2022	286,684	104,329	CAVALERI, VINCENT J.	181,992	DELBENE, SUZAN*	363	77,663	D	36.4%	63.5%	36.4%	63.6%
1	2020	426,862	176,407	BEELER, JEFFREY SR.	249,944	DELBENE, SUZAN*	511	73,537	D	41.3%	58.6%	41.4%	58.6%
1	2018	332,743	135,534	BEELER, JEFFREY SR.	197,209	DELBENE, SUZAN*		61,675	D	40.7%	59.3%	40.7%	59.3%
1	2016	349,398	155,779	SUTHERLAND, ROBERT	193,619	DELBENE, SUZAN*		37,840	D	44.6%	55.4%	44.6%	55.4%
1	2014	225,579	101,428	CELIS, PEDRO	124,151	DELBENE, SUZAN*		22,723	D	45.0%	55.0%	45.0%	55.0%
1	2012	328,212	151,187	KOSTER, JOHN	177,025	DELBENE, SUZAN*		25,838	D	46.1%	53.9%	46.1%	53.9%

WASHINGTON

HOUSE OF REPRESENTATIVES

			Republican		Democratic		Other Vote	Rep.-Dem. Plurality		Percentage			
										Total Vote		Major Vote	
CD	Year	Total Vote	Vote	Candidate	Vote	Candidate				Rep.	Dem.	Rep.	Dem.
2	2022	337,923	134,335	MATTHEWS, DAN	202,980	LARSEN, RICK*	608	68,645 D		39.8%	60.1%	39.8%	60.2%
2	2020	404,598	148,384	HAZELO, TIMOTHY S.	255,252	LARSEN, RICK*	962	106,868 D		36.7%	63.1%	36.8%	63.2%
2	2018	294,833			210,187	LARSEN, RICK*	84,646	210,187 D			71.3%		100.0%
2	2016	325,408	117,094	HENNEMANN, MARC	208,314	LARSEN, RICK*		91,220 D		36.0%	64.0%	36.0%	64.0%
2	2014	201,691	79,518	GUILLOT, B.J.	122,173	LARSEN, RICK*		42,655 D		39.4%	60.6%	39.4%	60.6%
2	2012	302,291	117,465	MATTHEWS, DAN	184,826	LARSEN, RICK*		67,361 D		38.9%	61.1%	38.9%	61.1%
3	2022	319,759	157,685	KENT, JOE	160,314	GLUESENKAMP PEREZ, MARIE	1,760	2,629 D		49.3%	50.1%	49.6%	50.4%
3	2020	417,903	235,579	BEUTLER, JAIME HERRERA*	181,347	LONG, CAROLYN	977	54,232 R		56.4%	43.4%	56.5%	43.5%
3	2018	307,226	161,819	BEUTLER, JAIME HERRERA*	145,407	LONG, CAROLYN		16,412 R		52.7%	47.3%	52.7%	47.3%
3	2016	313,277	193,457	BEUTLER, JAIME HERRERA*	119,820	MOELLER, JIM		73,637 R		61.8%	38.2%	61.8%	38.2%
3	2014	202,814	124,796	BEUTLER, JAIME HERRERA*	78,018	DINGETHAL, BOB		46,778 R		61.5%	38.5%	61.5%	38.5%
3	2012	293,884	177,446	BEUTLER, JAIME HERRERA*	116,438	HAUGEN, JON T.		61,008 R		60.4%	39.6%	60.4%	39.6%
4	2022	226,647	150,619	NEWHOUSE, DAN M.*	70,710	WHITE, DOUG	5,318	79,909 R		66.5%	31.2%	68.1%	31.9%
4	2020	305,263	202,108	NEWHOUSE, DAN M.*	102,667	MCKINLEY, DOUG	488	99,441 R		66.2%	33.6%	66.3%	33.7%
4	2018	225,336	141,551	NEWHOUSE, DAN M.*	83,785	BROWN, CHRISTINE		57,766 R		62.8%	37.2%	62.8%	37.2%
4	2016	229,919	132,517	NEWHOUSE, DAN M.*			97,402	132,517 R		57.6%		100.0%	
4	2014	153,079	77,772	NEWHOUSE, DAN M.			75,307	77,772 R		50.8%		100.0%	
4	2012	233,689	154,749	HASTINGS, DOC*	78,940	BAECHLER, MARY		75,809 R		66.2%	33.8%	66.2%	33.8%
5	2022	317,006	188,648	RODGERS, CATHY MCMORRIS*	127,585	HILL, NATASHA	773	61,063 R		59.5%	40.2%	59.7%	40.3%
5	2020	404,360	247,815	RODGERS, CATHY MCMORRIS*	155,737	WILSON, DAVE	808	92,078 R		61.3%	38.5%	61.4%	38.6%
5	2018	320,347	175,422	RODGERS, CATHY MCMORRIS*	144,925	BROWN, LISA		30,497 R		54.8%	45.2%	54.8%	45.2%
5	2016	323,534	192,959	RODGERS, CATHY MCMORRIS*	130,575	PAKOOTAS, JOSEPH "JOE"		62,384 R		59.6%	40.4%	59.6%	40.4%
5	2014	223,242	135,470	RODGERS, CATHY MCMORRIS*	87,772	PAKOOTAS, JOSEPH "JOE"		47,698 R		60.7%	39.3%	60.7%	39.3%
5	2012	308,578	191,066	RODGERS, CATHY MCMORRIS*	117,512	COWAN, RICH		73,554 R		61.9%	38.1%	61.9%	38.1%
6	2022	347,873	138,754	KREISELMAIER, ELIZABETH	208,710	KILMER, DEREK*	409	69,956 D		39.9%	60.0%	39.9%	60.1%
6	2020	417,216	168,783	KREISELMAIER, ELIZABETH	247,429	KILMER, DEREK*	1,004	78,646 D		40.5%	59.3%	40.6%	59.4%
6	2018	323,086	116,677	DIGHTMAN, DOUGLAS	206,409	KILMER, DEREK*		89,732 D		36.1%	63.9%	36.1%	63.9%
6	2016	327,834	126,116	BLOOM, TODD	201,718	KILMER, DEREK*		75,602 D		38.5%	61.5%	38.5%	61.5%
6	2014	224,290	83,025	MCCLENDON, MARTIN "MARTY"	141,265	KILMER, DEREK*		58,240 D		37.0%	63.0%	37.0%	63.0%
6	2012	316,386	129,725	DRISCOLL, BILL	186,661	KILMER, DEREK		56,936 D		41.0%	59.0%	41.0%	59.0%
7	2022	346,647	49,207	MOON, CLIFF	295,998	JAYAPAL, PRAMILA*	1,442	246,791 D		14.2%	85.4%	14.3%	85.7%
7	2020	466,462	78,240	KELLER, CRAIG	387,109	JAYAPAL, PRAMILA*	1,113	308,869 D		16.8%	83.0%	16.8%	83.2%
7	2018	394,681	64,881	KELLER, CRAIG	329,800	JAYAPAL, PRAMILA*		264,919 D		16.4%	83.6%	16.4%	83.6%
7	2016	378,754			212,010	JAYAPAL, PRAMILA	166,744	212,010 D			56.0%		100.0%
7	2014	251,875	47,921	KELLER, CRAIG	203,954	MCDERMOTT, JAMES A.*		156,033 D		19.0%	81.0%	19.0%	81.0%
7	2012	374,580	76,212	BEMIS, RON	298,368	MCDERMOTT, JAMES A.*		222,156 D		20.3%	79.7%	20.3%	79.7%
8	2022	336,038	155,976	LARKIN, MATT	179,003	SCHRIER, KIM*	1,059	23,027 D		46.4%	53.3%	46.6%	53.4%
8	2020	412,112	198,423	JENSEN, JESSE	213,123	SCHRIER, KIM*	566	14,700 D		48.1%	51.7%	48.2%	51.8%
8	2018	313,057	148,968	ROSSI, DINO	164,089	SCHRIER, KIM		15,121 D		47.6%	52.4%	47.6%	52.4%
8	2016	320,865	193,145	REICHERT, DAVID GEORGE "DAVE"*	127,720	VENTRELLA, TONY		65,425 R		60.2%	39.8%	60.2%	39.8%
8	2014	198,744	125,741	REICHERT, DAVID GEORGE "DAVE"*	73,003	RITCHIE, JASON		52,738 R		63.3%	36.7%	63.3%	36.7%
8	2012	302,090	180,204	REICHERT, DAVID GEORGE "DAVE"*	121,886	PORTERFIELD, KAREN		58,318 R		59.7%	40.3%	59.7%	40.3%
9	2022	239,848	67,631	BASLER, DOUG	171,746	SMITH, ADAM*	471	104,115 D		28.2%	71.6%	28.3%	71.7%
9	2020	349,050	89,697	BASLER, DOUG	258,771	SMITH, ADAM*	582	169,074 D		25.7%	74.1%	25.7%	74.3%
9	2018	240,567			163,345	SMITH, ADAM*	77,222	163,345 D			67.9%		100.0%
9	2016	281,482	76,317	BASLER, DOUG	205,165	SMITH, ADAM*		128,848 D		27.1%	72.9%	27.1%	72.9%
9	2014	166,794	48,662	BASLER, DOUG	118,132	SMITH, ADAM*		69,470 D		29.2%	70.8%	29.2%	70.8%
9	2012	268,139	76,105	POSTMA, JAMES	192,034	SMITH, ADAM*		115,929 D		28.4%	71.6%	28.4%	71.6%
10	2022	267,748	114,777	SWANK, KEITH	152,544	STRICKLAND, MARILYN*	427	37,767 D		42.9%	57.0%	42.9%	57.1%
10	2020	340,407			167,937	STRICKLAND, MARILYN	172,470	167,937 D			49.3%		100.0%
10	2018	270,075	103,860	BRUMBLES, JOSEPH	166,215	HECK, DENNY*		62,355 D		38.5%	61.5%	38.5%	61.5%
10	2016	290,564	120,104	POSTMA, JAMES	170,460	HECK, DENNY*		50,356 D		41.3%	58.7%	41.3%	58.7%
10	2014	181,492	82,213	MCDONALD, JOYCE	99,279	HECK, DENNY*		17,066 D		45.3%	54.7%	45.3%	54.7%
10	2012	278,417	115,381	MURI, RICHARD	163,036	HECK, DENNY		47,655 D		41.4%	58.6%	41.4%	58.6%
TOTAL	2022	3,026,173	1,261,961		1,751,582		12,630	489,621 D		41.7%	57.9%	41.9%	58.1%
TOTAL	2020	3,944,233	1,545,436		2,219,316		179,481	673,880 D		39.2%	56.3%	41.1%	58.9%
TOTAL	2018	3,021,951	1,048,712		1,811,371		161,868	762,659 D		34.7%	59.9%	36.7%	63.3%
TOTAL	2016	3,141,035	1,307,488		1,569,401		264,146	261,913 D		41.6%	50.0%	45.4%	54.6%
TOTAL	2014	2,029,600	906,546		1,047,747		75,307	141,201 D		44.7%	51.6%	46.4%	53.6%
TOTAL	2012	3,006,266	1,369,540		1,636,726			267,186 D		45.6%	54.4%	45.6%	54.4%

Note: An asterisk (*) denotes incumbent.

WASHINGTON

GENERAL AND PRIMARY ELECTIONS

GENERAL ELECTIONS: OTHER VOTES

Senate	Other vote was 6,751 Write-In (Write-Ins)
House	Other vote was:
CD 1	363 Write-In (Write-Ins)
CD 2	608 Write-In (Write-Ins)
CD 3	1,760 Write-In (Write-Ins)
CD 4	5,318 Write-In (Write-Ins)
CD 5	773 Write-In (Write-Ins)
CD 6	409 Write-In (Write-Ins)
CD 7	1,442 Write-In (Write-Ins)
CD 8	1,059 Write-In (Write-Ins)
CD 9	471 Write-In (Write-Ins)
CD 10	427 Write-In (Write-Ins)

2022 PRIMARY ELECTIONS: SUPPLEMENTARY INFORMATION

Primary	August 2, 2022	**Registration** (as of August 2, 2022)	4,806,852		No Party Registration
Primary Type	Open—Any registered voter could participate in the primary, in which candidates of all parties ran together on the same ballot. The top two vote-getters advanced to the November general election.				

ALL-PARTY PRIMARIES

Senator	Murray, Patty* (Democrat)	1,002,811	52.2%
	Smiley, Tiffany (Republican)	646,917	33.7%
	Lawson, Leon Aaron (Trump Republican)	59,134	3.1%
	Guenther, John (Republican)	55,426	2.9%
	Pierre, Ravin (Democrat)	22,172	1.2%
	Saulibio, Dave (Trump Republican)	19,341	1.0%
	Paul, Naz (Independent)	18,858	1.0%
	Hirt, Bill (Republican)	15,276	0.8%
	Said, Mohammad (Democrat)	13,995	0.7%
	Dennison, Henry Clay (Socialist Workers Party)	13,901	0.7%
	Churchill, Pano (Democrat)	11,859	0.6%
	Solstin, Bryan (Democrat)	9,627	0.5%
	Jackson, Charlie R. (Independent)	8,604	0.4%
	Butler, Jon (Independent)	5,413	0.3%
	Amundson, Thor (Independent)	5,133	0.3%
	Hash, Martin (No Party Preference)	4,725	0.2%
	Doan, Dan Phan (No Party Preference)	3,049	0.2%
	Cusmir, Sam (Democrat)	2,688	0.1%
	Write-In (Write-Ins)	1,511	0.1%
	TOTAL	1,920,440	
Congressional District 1	DelBene, Suzan* (Democrat)	102,857	61.9%
	Cavaleri, Vincent J. (Republican)	32,998	19.9%
	Heines, Matthew D. (Republican)	13,634	8.2%
	Chartrand, Derek (Republican)	11,536	6.9%
	Spears, Tom (No Party Preference)	4,840	2.9%
	Write-In (Write-Ins)	168	0.1%
	TOTAL	166,033	

WASHINGTON

GENERAL AND PRIMARY ELECTIONS

ALL-PARTY PRIMARIES

Congressional District 2	Larsen, Rick* (Democrat)	100,631	45.8%
	Matthews, Dan (Republican)	37,393	17.0%
	Call, Jason (Democrat)	31,991	14.6%
	Hart, Cody (Republican)	22,176	10.1%
	Wheeler, Bill (Republican)	9,124	4.2%
	Kennedy, Carrie R. (Republican)	8,802	4.0%
	Johnson, Leif (Republican)	5,582	2.5%
	Welch, Jon (Conservative)	1,699	0.8%
	Stalnaker, Brandon Lee (Republican)	1,366	0.6%
	Revelle, Doug "Yoshe" (No Party Preference)	927	0.4%
	Write-In (Write-Ins)	161	0.1%
	TOTAL	219,852	
Congressional District 3	Gluesenkamp Perez, Marie (Democrat)	68,190	31.0%
	Kent, Joe (Republican)	50,097	22.8%
	Beutler, Jaime Herrera* (Republican)	49,001	22.3%
	St. John, Heidi (Republican)	35,219	16.0%
	Kraft, Vicki (Republican)	7,033	3.2%
	Ray, Davy (Democrat)	4,870	2.2%
	Byrd, Chris (Independent)	3,817	1.7%
	French, Leslie Leigh (Republican)	1,100	0.5%
	Black, Oliver (American Solidarity Party)	456	0.2%
	Write-In (Write-Ins)	142	0.1%
	TOTAL	219,925	
Congressional District 4	Newhouse, Dan M.* (Republican)	38,331	25.5%
	White, Doug (Democrat)	37,760	25.1%
	Culp, Loren (Republican)	32,497	21.6%
	Sessler, Jerrod (Republican)	18,495	12.3%
	Klippert, Brad (Republican)	15,430	10.3%
	Gibson, Corey (Republican)	5,080	3.4%
	Garcia, Benancio "Benny" III (Republican)	2,148	1.4%
	Kobiesa, Jacek (Republican)	490	0.3%
	Write-In (Write-Ins)	149	0.1%
	TOTAL	150,380	
Congressional District 5	McMorris Rodgers, Cathy* (Republican)	106,072	51.5%
	Hill, Natasha (Democrat)	61,851	30.0%
	Danimus, Ann Marie (Democrat)	21,123	10.2%
	Clynch, Sean (Republican)	16,831	8.2%
	Write-In (Write-Ins)	247	0.1%
	TOTAL	206,124	
Congressional District 6	Kilmer, Derek* (Democrat)	115,725	50.4%
	Kreiselmaier, Elizabeth (Republican)	54,621	23.8%
	Bloom, Todd (Republican)	24,036	10.5%
	Parson, Rebecca (Democrat)	21,523	9.4%
	Binns, Chris (Republican)	11,074	4.8%
	Triggs, Tom (Independent)	2,674	1.2%
	Write-In (Write-Ins)	125	0.1%
	TOTAL	229,778	
Congressional District 7	Jayapal, Pramila* (Democrat)	177,665	84.6%
	Moon, Cliff (Republican)	15,834	7.5%
	Glumaz, Paul (Republican)	10,982	5.2%
	James, Jesse A. (Independent)	4,859	2.3%
	Write-In (Write-Ins)	551	0.3%
	TOTAL	209,891	

WASHINGTON

GENERAL AND PRIMARY ELECTIONS

ALL-PARTY PRIMARIES

Congressional District 8	Schrier, Kim* (Democrat)	97,700	47.9%
	Larkin, Matt (Republican)	34,684	17.0%
	Dunn, Reagan (Republican)	29,494	14.4%
	Jensen, Jesse (Republican)	26,350	12.9%
	Stephenson, Scott (Republican)	7,954	3.9%
	Ward, Emet (Democrat)	1,832	0.9%
	Chapman, Dave (Republican)	1,811	0.9%
	Arnold, Keith (Democrat)	1,669	0.8%
	Greywolf, Justin (Libertarian)	1,518	0.7%
	Burkett, Ryan Dean (No Party Preference)	701	0.3%
	Dillon, Patrick (Independent)	296	0.1%
	Write-In (Write-Ins)	122	0.1%
	TOTAL	*204,131*	
Congressional District 9	Smith, Adam* (Democrat)	78,272	55.2%
	Basler, Doug (Republican)	29,144	20.6%
	Gallardo, Stephanie (Democrat)	22,531	15.9%
	Chan, Sea M. (Republican)	5,338	3.8%
	Pedersen, Seth D. (Republican)	4,781	3.4%
	Anderson, David Michael (Independent)	1,541	1.1%
	Write-In (Write-Ins)	153	0.1%
	TOTAL	*141,760*	
Congressional District 10	Strickland, Marilyn* (Democrat)	90,093	55.3%
	Swank, Keith (Republican)	55,231	33.9%
	Gordon, Dan Earnest (Republican)	10,315	6.3%
	Mahaffy, Eric (Democrat)	3,710	2.3%
	Boyce, Richard (Congress Sucks)	3,250	2.0%
	Write-In (Write-Ins)	189	0.1%
	TOTAL	*162,788*	

Note: An asterisk (*) denotes incumbent.

WEST VIRGINIA

Statewide Races

Neither of West Virginia's Senate seats were up in 2022, and it elects governors in presidential years.

House Races

After barely keeping its third seat in the 2010 census, West Virginia dropped down to two seats when the Census Bureau released its 2020 count. To some degree, West Virginia Republicans fell victim to their own success: they had held all three of the state's seats since the 2014 elections – so one Republican would have to go.

On the state's outgoing three-seat map, Republican Rep. Alex Mooney's district, in the middle of the state, was the most contorted district. It ran the span of the state, going from the eastern panhandle west to the Charleston metro. Mooney's district was essentially split in half. The state capital of Charleston was put with the southern coalfields in Rep. Carroll Miller's 1st District. Meanwhile, the eastern panhandle, which bumps up against the Washington, D.C. suburbs of northern Virginia, was placed with Morgantown and Wheeling, in the northern 2nd District. Importantly, both Reps. Mooney and David McKinley lived in the district, forcing a primary.

On paper, McKinley would have been a favorite: more of the new district came from his old seat, and he pointed to Mooney's short history in the state – until moving to the state ahead of the 2014, he was involved in Maryland politics. But McKinley, who was first elected in 2010, was not a fire-breathing partisan. In late 2021, he voted for the legislation that became known as the Bipartisan Infrastructure Act, which President Biden signed into law. This prompted Trump to endorse Mooney, who was already a brash conservative. McKinley got support from popular Republican Gov. Jim Justice, as well as a cross-party endorsement from Democratic Sen. Joe Manchin. But Trump's support was critical to Mooney: he won 54%–36%. McKinley carried his home county, Wheeling's Ohio County, but little else, while Mooney carried the eastern panhandle with over 70%.

In the general election, both Miller and Mooney won with about two-thirds of the vote.

WEST VIRGINIA

Congressional districts first established for elections held in 2022

2 members

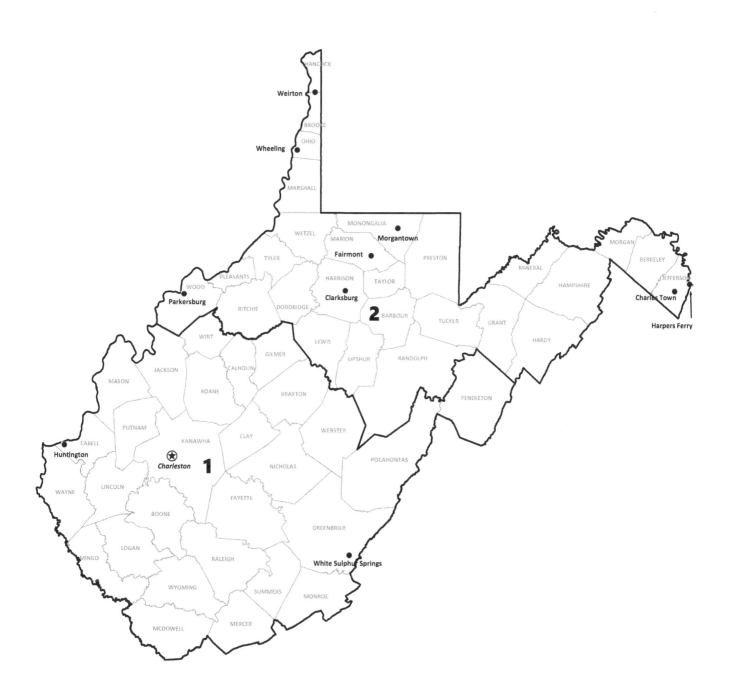

WEST VIRGINIA

GOVERNOR

Jim Justice (R). Reelected 2020 to a four-year term. Previously elected 2016. (Justice was elected as a Democrat in 2016 but became a Republican on August 3, 2017.)

SENATORS (1 Republican, 1 Democrat)

Shelley Moore Capito (R). Reelected 2020 to a six-year term. Previously elected 2014.

Joe Manchin III (D). Reelected 2018 to a six-year term. Previously elected 2012, and 2010 to fill the remaining two years of the term vacated by the death of Robert C. Byrd (D) in June 2010. Carte Goodwin (D) was appointed to fill the vacancy until the special election could be held in November 2010.

REPRESENTATIVES (2 Republicans)

1. Alex X. Mooney (R)
2. Carol Miller (R)

POSTWAR VOTE FOR PRESIDENT

Year	Total Vote	Republican Vote	Republican Candidate	Democratic Vote	Democratic Candidate	Other Vote	Rep.-Dem. Plurality	Total Vote Rep.	Total Vote Dem.	Major Vote Rep.	Major Vote Dem.
2020	794,731	545,382	Trump, Donald J.*	235,984	Biden, Joseph R. Jr.	13,365	309,398 R	68.6%	29.7%	69.8%	30.2%
2016**	714,423	489,371	Trump, Donald J.	188,794	Clinton, Hillary Rodham	36,258	300,577 R	68.5%	26.4%	72.2%	27.8%
2012	670,438	417,655	Romney, W. Mitt	238,269	Obama, Barack H.*	14,514	179,386 R	62.3%	35.5%	63.7%	36.3%
2008	713,451	397,466	McCain, John S. III	303,857	Obama, Barack H.	12,128	93,609 R	55.7%	42.6%	56.7%	43.3%
2004	755,887	423,778	Bush, George W.*	326,541	Kerry, John F.	5,568	97,237 R	56.1%	43.2%	56.5%	43.5%
2000**	648,124	336,475	Bush, George W.	295,497	Gore, Albert Jr.	16,152	40,978 R	51.9%	45.6%	53.2%	46.8%
1996**	636,459	233,946	Dole, Robert "Bob"	327,812	Clinton, Bill*	74,701	93,866 D	36.8%	51.5%	41.6%	58.4%
1992**	683,762	241,974	Bush, George H.*	331,001	Clinton, Bill	110,787	89,027 D	35.4%	48.4%	42.2%	57.8%
1988	653,311	310,065	Bush, George H.	341,016	Dukakis, Michael S.	2,230	30,951 D	47.5%	52.2%	47.6%	52.4%
1984	735,742	405,483	Reagan, Ronald*	328,125	Mondale, Walter F.	2,134	77,358 R	55.1%	44.6%	55.3%	44.7%
1980**	737,715	334,206	Reagan, Ronald	367,462	Carter, Jimmy*	36,047	33,256 D	45.3%	49.8%	47.6%	52.4%
1976	750,964	314,760	Ford, Gerald R.*	435,914	Carter, Jimmy	290	121,154 D	41.9%	58.0%	41.9%	58.1%
1972	762,399	484,964	Nixon, Richard M.*	277,435	McGovern, George S.		207,529 R	63.6%	36.4%	63.6%	36.4%
1968**	754,206	307,555	Nixon, Richard M.	374,091	Humphrey, Hubert Horatio Jr.	72,560	66,536 D	40.8%	49.6%	45.1%	54.9%
1964	792,040	253,953	Goldwater, Barry M. Sr.	538,087	Johnson, Lyndon B.*		284,134 D	32.1%	67.9%	32.1%	67.9%
1960	837,781	395,995	Nixon, Richard M.	441,786	Kennedy, John F.		45,791 D	47.3%	52.7%	47.3%	52.7%
1956	830,831	449,297	Eisenhower, Dwight D.*	381,534	Stevenson, Adlai E. II		67,763 R	54.1%	45.9%	54.1%	45.9%
1952	873,548	419,970	Eisenhower, Dwight D.	453,578	Stevenson, Adlai E. II		33,608 D	48.1%	51.9%	48.1%	51.9%
1948	748,750	316,251	Dewey, Thomas E.	429,188	Truman, Harry S.*	3,311	112,937 D	42.2%	57.3%	42.4%	57.6%

Note: An asterisk (*) denotes incumbent. **In past elections, the other vote included: 2016 - 23,004 Libertarian (Gary Johnson); 2000 - 10,680 Green (Ralph Nader); 1996 - 71,639 Reform (Ross Perot); 1992 - 108,829 Independent (Perot); 1980 - 31,691 Independent (John Anderson); 1968 - 72,560 American Independent (George Wallace).

WEST VIRGINIA

POSTWAR VOTE FOR GOVERNOR

Year	Total Vote	Republican Vote	Republican Candidate	Democratic Vote	Democratic Candidate	Other Vote	Rep.-Dem. Plurality	Total Vote Rep.	Total Vote Dem.	Major Vote Rep.	Major Vote Dem.
2020	768,804	497,944	Justice, Jim*	237,024	Salango, Ben	33,836	260,920 R	64.8%	30.8%	67.8%	32.2%
2016	713,879	301,987	Cole, Bill	350,408	Justice, Jim	61,484	48,421 D	42.3%	49.1%	46.3%	53.7%
2012	664,455	303,291	Maloney, Bill	335,468	Tomblin, Earl Ray*	25,696	32,177 D	45.6%	50.5%	47.5%	52.5%
2011S**	301,084	141,656	Maloney, Bill	149,202	Tomblin, Earl Ray*	10,226	7,546 D	47.0%	49.6%	48.7%	51.3%
2008	706,046	181,612	Weeks, Russ	492,697	Manchin, Joe III*	31,737	311,085 D	25.7%	69.8%	26.9%	73.1%
2004	744,433	253,131	Warner, Monty	472,758	Manchin, Joe III	18,544	219,627 D	34.0%	63.5%	34.9%	65.1%
2000	648,047	305,926	Underwood, Cecil H.*	324,822	Wise, Robert Ellsworth	17,299	18,896 D	47.2%	50.1%	48.5%	51.5%
1996	628,559	324,518	Underwood, Cecil H.	287,870	Pritt, Charlotte	16,171	36,648 R	51.6%	45.8%	53.0%	47.0%
1992	657,193	240,390	Benedict, Cleveland K.	368,302	Caperton, Gaston*	48,501	127,912 D	36.6%	56.0%	39.5%	60.5%
1988	649,593	267,172	Moore, Arch A. Jr.*	382,421	Caperton, Gaston		115,249 D	41.1%	58.9%	41.1%	58.9%
1984	741,502	394,937	Moore, Arch A. Jr.	346,565	See, Clyde M.		48,372 R	53.3%	46.7%	53.3%	46.7%
1980	742,150	337,240	Moore, Arch A. Jr.	401,863	Rockefeller, John D. IV	3,047	64,623 D	45.4%	54.1%	45.6%	54.4%
1976	749,270	253,420	Underwood, Cecil H.	495,661	Rockefeller, John D. IV	189	242,241 D	33.8%	66.2%	33.8%	66.2%
1972	774,279	423,817	Moore, Arch A. Jr.*	350,462	Rockefeller, John D. IV		73,355 R	54.7%	45.3%	54.7%	45.3%
1968	743,845	378,315	Moore, Arch A. Jr.	365,530	Sprouse, James M.		12,785 R	50.9%	49.1%	50.9%	49.1%
1964	788,582	355,559	Underwood, Cecil H.	433,023	Smith, Hulett		77,464 D	45.1%	54.9%	45.1%	54.9%
1960	827,420	380,665	Neely, Harold E.	446,755	Barron, W. W.		66,090 D	46.0%	54.0%	46.0%	54.0%
1956	817,623	440,502	Underwood, Cecil H.	377,121	Mollohan, Robert H.		63,381 R	53.9%	46.1%	53.9%	46.1%
1952	882,527	427,629	Holt, Rush D.	454,898	Marland, William C.		27,269 D	48.5%	51.5%	48.5%	51.5%
1948	768,061	329,309	Boreman, Herbert S.	438,752	Patteson, Okey L.		109,443 D	42.9%	57.1%	42.9%	57.1%

Note: An asterisk (*) denotes incumbent. **The 2011 election was for a short term to fill a vacancy.

POSTWAR VOTE FOR SENATOR

Year	Total Vote	Republican Vote	Republican Candidate	Democratic Vote	Democratic Candidate	Other Vote	Rep.-Dem. Plurality	Total Vote Rep.	Total Vote Dem.	Major Vote Rep.	Major Vote Dem.
2020	778,918	547,454	Capito, Shelley Moore*	210,309	Swearengin, Paula	21,155	337,145 R	70.3%	27.0%	72.2%	27.8%
2018	586,034	271,113	Morrisey, Patrick	290,510	Manchin, Joe III*	24,411	19,397 D	46.3%	49.6%	48.3%	51.7%
2014	453,659	281,820	Capito, Shelley Moore	156,360	Tennant, Natalie E.	15,479	125,460 R	62.1%	34.5%	64.3%	35.7%
2012	660,212	240,787	Raese, John R.	399,908	Manchin, Joe III*	19,517	159,121 D	36.5%	60.6%	37.6%	62.4%
2010S**	529,948	230,013	Raese, John R.	283,358	Manchin, Joe III	16,577	53,345 D	43.4%	53.5%	44.8%	55.2%
2008	702,308	254,629	Wolfe, Jay	447,560	Rockefeller, John D. IV*	119	192,931 D	36.3%	63.7%	36.3%	63.7%
2006	459,884	155,043	Raese, John R.	296,276	Byrd, Robert C.*	8,565	141,233 D	33.7%	64.4%	34.4%	65.6%
2002	436,183	160,902	Wolfe, M. Jay	275,281	Rockefeller, John D. IV*		114,379 D	36.9%	63.1%	36.9%	63.1%
2000	603,477	121,635	Gallaher, David T.	469,215	Byrd, Robert C.*	12,627	347,580 D	20.2%	77.8%	20.6%	79.4%
1996	595,614	139,088	Burks, Betty A.	456,526	Rockefeller, John D. IV*		317,438 D	23.4%	76.6%	23.4%	76.6%
1994	420,936	130,441	Klos, Stan	290,495	Byrd, Robert C.*		160,054 D	31.0%	69.0%	31.0%	69.0%
1990	404,305	128,071	Yoder, John	276,234	Rockefeller, John D. IV*		148,163 D	31.7%	68.3%	31.7%	68.3%
1988	634,547	223,564	Wolfe, M. Jay	410,983	Byrd, Robert C.*		187,419 D	35.2%	64.8%	35.2%	64.8%
1984	722,212	344,680	Raese, John R.	374,233	Rockefeller, John D. IV	3,299	29,553 D	47.7%	51.8%	47.9%	52.1%
1982	565,314	173,910	Benedict, Cleveland K.	387,170	Byrd, Robert C.*	4,234	213,260 D	30.8%	68.5%	31.0%	69.0%
1978	493,351	244,317	Moore, Arch A. Jr.	249,034	Randolph, Jennings*		4,717 D	49.5%	50.5%	49.5%	50.5%
1976	566,790			566,423	Byrd, Robert C.*	367	566,423 D		99.9%		100.0%
1972	731,841	245,531	Leonard, Louise	486,310	Randolph, Jennings*		240,779 D	33.5%	66.5%	33.5%	66.5%
1970	445,623	99,658	Dodson, Elmer H.	345,965	Byrd, Robert C.*		246,307 D	22.4%	77.6%	22.4%	77.6%
1966	491,216	198,891	Love, Francis J.	292,325	Randolph, Jennings*		93,434 D	40.5%	59.5%	40.5%	59.5%
1964	761,087	246,072	Benedict, Cooper P.	515,015	Byrd, Robert C.*		268,943 D	32.3%	67.7%	32.3%	67.7%
1960	828,292	369,935	Underwood, Cecil H.	458,355	Randolph, Jennings*	2	88,420 D	44.7%	55.3%	44.7%	55.3%
1958	644,917	263,172	Revercomb, Chapman*	381,745	Byrd, Robert C.		118,573 D	40.8%	59.2%	40.8%	59.2%
1958S**	630,677	256,510	Hoblitzell, John D. Jr.*	374,167	Randolph, Jennings		117,657 D	40.7%	59.3%	40.7%	59.3%
1956S**	805,174	432,123	Revercomb, Chapman	373,051	Marland, William C.		59,072 R	53.7%	46.3%	53.7%	46.3%
1954	593,329	268,066	Sweeney, Thomas	325,263	Neely, Matthew M.*		57,197 D	45.2%	54.8%	45.2%	54.8%
1952	876,573	406,554	Revercomb, Chapman	470,019	Kilgore, Harley M.*		63,465 D	46.4%	53.6%	46.4%	53.6%
1948	763,888	328,534	Revercomb, Chapman*	435,354	Neely, Matthew M.		106,820 D	43.0%	57.0%	43.0%	57.0%
1946	542,768	269,617	Sweeney, Thomas	273,151	Kilgore, Harley M.*		3,534 D	49.7%	50.3%	49.7%	50.3%

Note: An asterisk (*) denotes incumbent. **The 1956 election, one of the 1958 elections, and the 2010 election were for short terms to fill a vacancy. The Republican Party did not run a candidate in the 1976 Senate election.

WEST VIRGINIA

HOUSE OF REPRESENTATIVES

			Republican		Democratic		Other Vote	Rep.-Dem. Plurality	Percentage			
									Total Vote		Major Vote	
CD	Year	Total Vote	Vote	Candidate	Vote	Candidate			Rep.	Dem.	Rep.	Dem.
1	2022	227,196	151,511	MILLER, CAROL*	65,428	WATSON, EUGENE LACY	10,257	86,083 R	66.7%	28.8%	69.8%	30.2%
1	2020	261,723	180,488	MCKINLEY, DAVID*	81,177	CLINE, NATALIE	58	99,311 R	69.0%	31.0%	69.0%	31.0%
1	2018	198,214	127,997	MCKINLEY, DAVID*	70,217	FERSHEE, KENDRA		57,780 R	64.6%	35.4%	64.6%	35.4%
1	2016	237,003	163,469	MCKINLEY, DAVID*	73,534	MANYPENNY, MIKE		89,935 R	69.0%	31.0%	69.0%	31.0%
1	2014	144,600	92,491	MCKINLEY, DAVID*	52,109	GAINER, GLEN B. III		40,382 R	64.0%	36.0%	64.0%	36.0%
1	2012	214,151	133,809	MCKINLEY, DAVID*	80,342	THORN, SUE		53,467 R	62.5%	37.5%	62.5%	37.5%
2	2022	244,771	160,493	MOONEY, ALEX X.*	84,278	WENDELL, BARRY LEE		76,215 R	65.6%	34.4%	65.6%	34.4%
2	2020	272,994	172,195	MOONEY, ALEX X.*	100,799	KUNKEL, CATHERINE		71,396 R	63.1%	36.9%	63.1%	36.9%
2	2018	204,792	110,504	MOONEY, ALEX X.*	88,011	SERGENT, TALLEY	6,277	22,493 R	54.0%	43.0%	55.7%	44.3%
2	2016	242,014	140,807	MOONEY, ALEX X.*	101,207	HUNT, MARK		39,600 R	58.2%	41.8%	58.2%	41.8%
2	2014	154,238	72,619	MOONEY, ALEX X.	67,687	CASEY, NICK	13,932	4,932 R	47.1%	43.9%	51.8%	48.2%
2	2012	226,766	158,206	CAPITO, SHELLEY MOORE*	68,560	SWINT, HOWARD		89,646 R	69.8%	30.2%	69.8%	30.2%
3	2020	226,668	161,585	MILLER, CAROL*	64,927	TURNER, HILARY	156	96,658 R	71.3%	28.6%	71.3%	28.7%
3	2018	174,985	98,645	MILLER, CAROL	76,340	OJEDA, RICHARD II		22,305 R	56.4%	43.6%	56.4%	43.6%
3	2016	207,332	140,741	JENKINS, EVAN*	49,708	DETCH, MATT	16,883	91,033 R	67.9%	24.0%	73.9%	26.1%
3	2014	140,401	77,713	JENKINS, EVAN	62,688	RAHALL, NICK J. II*		15,025 R	55.4%	44.6%	55.4%	44.6%
3	2012	200,437	92,238	SNUFFER, RICK	108,199	RAHALL, NICK J. II*		15,961 D	46.0%	54.0%	46.0%	54.0%
TOTAL	2022	471,967	312,004		149,706		10,257	162,298 R	66.1%	31.7%	67.6%	32.4%
TOTAL	2020	761,385	514,268		246,903		214	267,365 R	67.5%	32.4%	67.6%	32.4%
TOTAL	2018	577,991	337,146		234,568		6,277	102,578 R	58.3%	40.6%	59.0%	41.0%
TOTAL	2016	686,349	445,017		224,449		16,883	220,568 R	64.8%	32.7%	66.5%	33.5%
TOTAL	2014	439,239	242,823		182,484		13,932	60,339 R	55.3%	41.5%	57.1%	42.9%
TOTAL	2012	641,354	384,253		257,101			127,152 R	59.9%	40.1%	59.9%	40.1%

Note: An asterisk (*) denotes incumbent.

WEST VIRGINIA

GENERAL AND PRIMARY ELECTIONS

GENERAL ELECTIONS: OTHER VOTES

House   Other vote was:

CD 1   10,257 Independent (Belinda Fox-Spencer)

2022 PRIMARY ELECTIONS: SUPPLEMENTARY INFORMATION

Primary	May 10, 2022	**Registration** (as of April 19, 2022)	1,135,437	Democratic	384,537
				Republican	440,631
				Libertarian	9,563
				Mountain	2,305
				Other	37,317
				No Party	261,084

Primary Type   Semi-Open—Registered Democrats and registered Republicans could vote only in their party's primary. Those voters registered with no party could participate in either the Democratic or the Republican primary.

WEST

GENERAL AND PRIMARY ELECTIONS

	REPUBLICAN PRIMARIES			DEMOCRATIC PRIMARIES		
Congressional District 1	Miller, Carol	41,852	66.3%	Watson, Eugene Lacy	32,686	100.0%
	Fuller, Scott	6,197	9.8%			
	Lawhorn, Zane	5,530	8.8%			
	Houser, James Edwin	4,877	7.7%			
	Stevens, Kent	4,658	7.4%			
	TOTAL	63,114		TOTAL	32,686	
Congressional District 2	Mooney, Alex X.	45,164	54.2%	Wendell, Barry Lee	22,139	57.1%
	McKinley, David	29,619	35.6%	Dwyer, Angela Joyce	16,653	42.9%
	Buchser-Lochocki, Susan	3,329	4.0%			
	Seckman, Mike	3,076	3.7%			
	Hercules, Rhonda A.	2,083	2.5%			
	TOTAL	83,271		TOTAL	38,792	

Note: An asterisk (*) denotes incumbent.

WISCONSIN

Statewide Races

In Wisconsin, which was among the closest states in the 2016 and 2020 presidential elections, a pair of incumbents, representing opposite parties, ran for reelection in the state's top two contests. The result was something of a rarity in Badger State elections: a split-ticket outcome. 2022 became the first midterm election cycle since 1998 where the state elected a senator and governor of different parties.

In 2018, then-state Superintendent of Public Instruction Tony Evers, a Democrat with a soft-spoken, grandfatherly image narrowly ousted GOP Gov. Scott Walker, a polarizing, but battle-tested, incumbent. Evers spent much of his term battling with a hostile legislature – despite Wisconsin's swingy image, Republicans have heavy majorities in both legislative chambers. Still, Evers kept generally positive approval ratings. In the primary, GOP voters turned down Rebecca Kleefisch, who served as Walker's lieutenant governor and was aligned with his wing of the party, in favor of Trump-endorsed businessman Tim Michels, who ran as more of a populist. Though polling showed a close race, Evers won reelection by more than three percentage points (a landslide, by Wisconsin standards). Compared to 2018, Evers's margins slid in rural Wisconsin, but he improved most in the traditionally GOP suburbs around Milwaukee. Ozaukee County, for example, which used to routinely give Walker about 70% of the vote, went to Michels by only a 55-to-44 margin.

In the Senate race, Democrats nominated Lt. Gov. Mandela Barnes against two-term Republican Sen. Ron Johnson. Johnson, who was elected in 2010 as a Tea Party candidate, ousted veteran Democrat Russ Feingold and, impressively, held on in a rematch in 2016. Ahead of the August primary, Barnes got a boost as most of his rivals dropped out and endorsed him, although their names remained on the ballot. Johnson, painted Barnes as soft on crime while Democrats pointed to Johnson's numerous outlandish statements. Johnson prevailed but his margin, one point, was closer than what polling suggested. Door County, which juts out into Lake Michigan, retained its generally good record as a state bellwether, as one of three Evers/Johnson counties (the others were Columbia and Vernon, which each backed Donald Trump in 2020).

House Races

After Evers vetoed a map passed by the legislature, redistricting in Wisconsin fell to the state Supreme Court. The court, which at the time had a conservative majority, surprised Democrats by going with a minimal change plan that Evers favored. Still, Republicans picked up a seat, expanding their advantage in the state delegation from 5-to-3 to 6-to-2.

In 2020, Republican Brad Van Orden held longtime Democratic Rep. Ron Kind to just a four-point win in the western Wisconsin 3rd District as Trump carried the seat by a similar margin. Kind retired and Van Orden flipped the seat, although state Sen. Brad Pfaff, the Democratic nominee, put up a respectable effort. In southeastern Wisconsin, the remap weakened three-term Republican Bryan Steil's hand in the First District – Trump's 2020 margin in the district would have dropped from nine points to just two. But national Democrats did not see Steil as a top target, and he was reelected by eight points.

WISCONSIN

Congressional districts first established for elections held in 2022

8 members

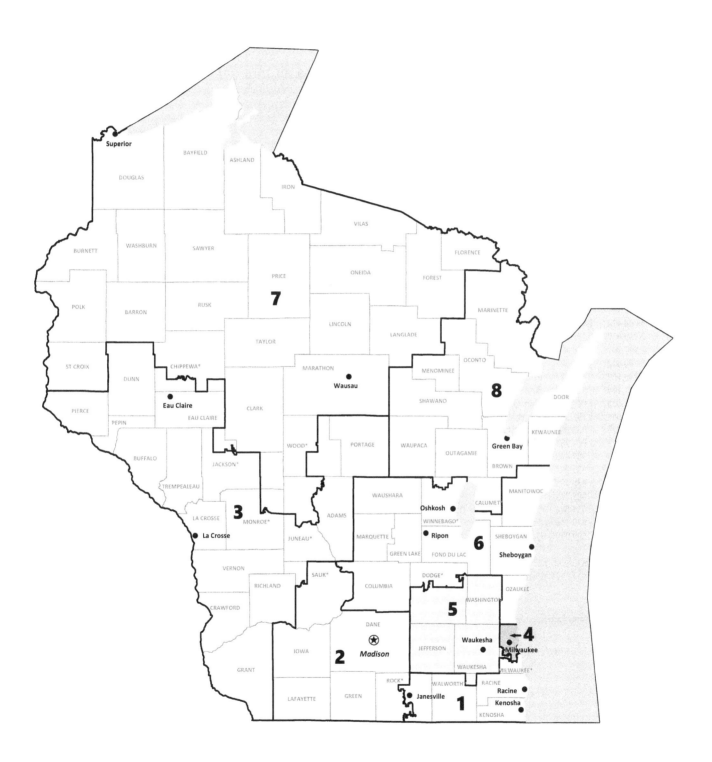

* Asterisk indicates a county whose boundaries include parts of two or more congressional districts.

CDs 4 and 5 are highlighted for visibility.

WISCONSIN

GOVERNOR
Tony Evers (D). Elected 2022 to a four-year term. Previously elected 2018.

SENATORS (1 Republican, 1 Democrat)
Tammy Baldwin (D). Reelected 2018 to a six-year term. Previously elected 2012.

Ron Johnson (R). Reelected 2022 to a six-year term. Previously elected 2016, 2010.

REPRESENTATIVES (6 Republicans, 2 Democrats)
1. Bryan Steil (R)
2. Mark Pocan (D)
3. Derrick Van Orden (R)
4. Gwen Moore (D)
5. Scott Fitzgerald (R)
6. Glenn S. Grothman (R)
7. Tom Tiffany (R)
8. Mike Gallagher (R)

POSTWAR VOTE FOR PRESIDENT

Year	Total Vote	Republican Vote	Republican Candidate	Democratic Vote	Democratic Candidate	Other Vote	Rep.-Dem. Plurality	Total Vote Rep.	Total Vote Dem.	Major Vote Rep.	Major Vote Dem.
2020	3,298,041	1,610,184	Trump, Donald J.*	1,630,866	Biden, Joseph R. Jr.	56,991	20,682 D	48.8%	49.4%	49.7%	50.3%
2016**	2,976,150	1,405,284	Trump, Donald J.	1,382,536	Clinton, Hillary Rodham	188,330	22,748 R	47.2%	16.5%	50.4%	49.6%
2012	3,068,434	1,407,966	Romney, W. Mitt	1,620,985	Obama, Barack H.*	39,483	213,019 D	45.9%	2.8%	46.5%	53.5%
2008	2,983,417	1,262,393	McCain, John S. III	1,677,211	Obama, Barack H.	43,813	414,818 D	42.3%	6.2%	42.9%	57.1%
2004	2,997,007	1,478,120	Bush, George W.*	1,489,504	Kerry, John F.	29,383	11,384 D	49.3%	19.7%	49.8%	50.2%
2000**	2,598,607	1,237,279	Bush, George W.	1,242,987	Gore, Albert Jr.	118,341	5,708 D	47.6%	7.8%	49.9%	50.1%
1996**	2,196,169	845,029	Dole, Robert "Bob"	1,071,971	Clinton, Bill*	279,169	226,942 D	38.5%	8.8%	44.1%	55.9%
1992**	2,531,114	930,855	Bush, George H.*	1,041,066	Clinton, Bill	559,193	110,211 D	36.8%	1.1%	47.2%	52.8%
1988	2,191,608	1,047,499	Bush, George H.	1,126,794	Dukakis, Michael S.	17,315	79,295 D	47.8%	1.4%	48.2%	51.8%
1984	2,211,689	1,198,584	Reagan, Ronald*	995,740	Mondale, Walter F.	17,365	202,844 R	54.2%	5.0%	54.6%	45.4%
1980**	2,273,221	1,088,845	Reagan, Ronald	981,584	Carter, Jimmy*	202,792	107,261 R	47.9%	3.2%	52.6%	47.4%
1976	2,104,175	1,004,987	Ford, Gerald R.*	1,040,232	Carter, Jimmy	58,956	35,245 D	47.8%	9.4%	49.1%	50.9%
1972	1,852,890	989,430	Nixon, Richard M.*	810,174	McGovern, George S.	53,286	179,256 R	53.4%	3.7%	55.0%	45.0%
1968**	1,691,538	809,997	Nixon, Richard M.	748,804	Humphrey, Hubert Horatio Jr.	132,737	61,193 R	47.9%	4.3%	52.0%	48.0%
1964	1,691,815	638,495	Goldwater, Barry M. Sr.	1,050,424	Johnson, Lyndon B.*	2,896	411,929 D	37.7%	2.1%	37.8%	62.2%
1960	1,729,082	895,175	Nixon, Richard M.	830,805	Kennedy, John F.	3,102	64,370 R	51.8%	8.0%	51.9%	48.1%
1956	1,550,558	954,844	Eisenhower, Dwight D.*	586,768	Stevenson, Adlai E. II	8,946	368,076 R	61.6%	7.8%	61.9%	38.1%
1952	1,607,370	979,744	Eisenhower, Dwight D.	622,175	Stevenson, Adlai E. II	5,451	357,569 R	61.0%	8.7%	61.2%	38.8%
1948	1,276,800	590,959	Dewey, Thomas E.	647,310	Truman, Harry S.*	38,531	56,351 D	46.3%	0.7%	47.7%	52.3%

Note: An asterisk (*) denotes incumbent. **In past elections, the other vote included: 2016 - 106,674 Libertarian (Gary Johnson); 2000 - 94,070 Green (Ralph Nader); 1996 - 227,339 Reform (Ross Perot); 1992 - 544,479 Independent (Perot); 1980 - 160,657 Independent (John Anderson); 1968 - 127,835 American Independent (George Wallace).

WISCONSIN

POSTWAR VOTE FOR GOVERNOR

Year	Total Vote	Republican Vote	Republican Candidate	Democratic Vote	Democratic Candidate	Other Vote	Rep.-Dem. Plurality	Total Vote Rep.	Total Vote Dem.	Major Vote Rep.	Major Vote Dem.
2022	2,656,490	1,268,535	Michels, Tim	1,358,774	Evers, Tony*	29,181	90,239 D	47.8%	51.1%	48.3%	51.7%
2018	2,673,308	1,295,080	Walker, Scott*	1,324,307	Evers, Tony	53,921	29,227 D	48.4%	49.5%	49.4%	50.6%
2014	2,410,314	1,259,706	Walker, Scott*	1,122,913	Burke, Mary	27,695	136,793 R	52.3%	46.6%	52.9%	47.1%
2012S**	2,516,065	1,335,585	Walker, Scott*	1,164,480	Barrett, Thomas M.	16,000	171,105 R	53.1%	46.3%	53.4%	46.6%
2010	2,160,832	1,128,941	Walker, Scott	1,004,303	Barrett, Thomas M.	27,588	124,638 R	52.2%	46.5%	52.9%	47.1%
2006	2,161,700	979,427	Green, Mark	1,139,115	Doyle, James E.*	43,158	159,688 D	45.3%	52.7%	46.2%	53.8%
2002**	1,775,349	734,779	McCallum, Scott*	800,515	Doyle, James E.	240,055	65,736 D	41.4%	45.1%	47.9%	52.1%
1998	1,756,014	1,047,716	Thompson, TommyG.*	679,553	Garvey, Ed	28,745	368,163 R	59.7%	38.7%	60.7%	39.3%
1994	1,563,835	1,051,326	Thompson, TommyG.*	482,850	Chvala, Chuck	29,659	568,476 R	67.2%	30.9%	68.5%	31.5%
1990	1,379,727	802,321	Thompson, TommyG.*	576,280	Loftus, Thomas	1,126	226,041 R	58.2%	41.8%	58.2%	41.8%
1986	1,526,960	805,090	Thompson, Tommy G.	705,578	Earl, Anthony S.*	16,292	99,512 R	52.7%	46.2%	53.3%	46.7%
1982	1,580,344	662,838	Kohler, Terry J.	896,812	Earl, Anthony S.	20,694	233,974 D	41.9%	56.7%	42.5%	57.5%
1978	1,500,996	816,056	Dreyfus, Lee S.	673,813	Schreiber, Martin J.*	11,127	142,243 R	54.4%	44.9%	54.8%	45.2%
1974	1,181,976	497,195	Dyke, William D.	628,639	Lucey, Patrick J.*	56,142	131,444 D	42.1%	53.2%	44.2%	55.8%
1970**	1,343,160	602,617	Olson, Jack B.	728,403	Lucey, Patrick J.	12,140	125,786 D	44.9%	54.2%	45.3%	54.7%
1968	1,689,738	893,463	Knowles, Warren P.*	791,100	Lafollette, Bronson C.	5,175	102,363 R	52.9%	46.8%	53.0%	47.0%
1966	1,170,173	626,041	Knowles, Warren P.*	539,258	Lucey, Patrick J.	4,874	86,783 R	53.5%	46.1%	53.7%	46.3%
1964	1,694,887	856,779	Knowles, Warren P.	837,901	Reynolds, John W.*	207	18,878 R	50.6%	49.4%	50.6%	49.4%
1962	1,265,900	625,536	Kuehn, Philip G.	637,491	Reynolds, John W.	2,873	11,955 D	49.4%	50.4%	49.5%	50.5%
1960	1,728,009	837,123	Kuehn, Philip G.	890,868	Nelson, Gaylord Anton*	18	53,745 D	48.4%	51.6%	48.4%	51.6%
1958	1,202,219	556,391	Thomson, Vernon W.*	644,296	Nelson, Gaylord Anton	1,532	87,905 D	46.3%	53.6%	46.3%	53.7%
1956	1,557,788	808,273	Thomson, Vernon W.	749,421	Proxmire, William	94	58,852 R	51.9%	48.1%	51.9%	48.1%
1954	1,158,666	596,158	Kohler, Walter J. Jr.*	560,747	Proxmire, William	1,761	35,411 R	51.5%	48.4%	51.5%	48.5%
1952	1,615,214	1,009,171	Kohler, Walter J. Jr.*	601,844	Proxmire, William	4,199	407,327 R	62.5%	37.3%	62.6%	37.4%
1950	1,138,148	605,649	Kohler, Walter J. Jr.	525,319	Thompson, Carl W.	7,180	80,330 R	53.2%	46.2%	53.6%	46.4%
1948	1,266,139	684,839	Rennebohm, Oscar*	558,497	Thompson, Carl W.	22,803	126,342 R	54.1%	44.1%	55.1%	44.9%
1946	1,040,444	621,970	Goodland, Walter S.*	406,499	Hoan, Daniel W.	11,975	215,471 R	59.8%	39.1%	60.5%	39.5%

Note: An asterisk (*) denotes incumbent. **The 2012 Wisconsin gubernatorial contest was a special recall election held in June 2012. Governor Scott Walker retained his office. In past elections, the other vote included: 2002 -185,455 Libertarian (Ed Thompson). The term of office of Wisconsin's Governor was increased from two to four years effective with the 1970 election.

WISCONSIN

POSTWAR VOTE FOR SENATOR

		Republican		Democratic		Other Vote	Rep.-Dem. Plurality	Percentage			
								Total Vote		Major Vote	
Year	Total Vote	Vote	Candidate	Vote	Candidate			Rep.	Dem.	Rep.	Dem.
2022	2,652,477	1,337,185	Johnson, Ron*	1,310,467	Barnes, Mandela	4,825	26,718 R	50.4%	49.4%	50.5%	49.5%
2018	2,660,763	1,184,885	Vukmir, Leah	1,472,914	Baldwin, Tammy*	2,964	288,029 D	44.5%	55.4%	44.6%	55.4%
2016	2,948,741	1,479,471	Johnson, Ron*	1,380,335	Feingold, Russell D.	88,935	99,136 R	50.2%	46.8%	51.7%	48.3%
2012	3,009,411	1,380,126	Thompson, Tommy G.	1,547,104	Baldwin, Tammy	82,181	166,978 D	45.9%	51.4%	47.1%	52.9%
2010	2,171,331	1,125,999	Johnson, Ron	1,020,958	Feingold, Russell D.*	24,374	105,041 R	51.9%	47.0%	52.4%	47.6%
2006	2,138,297	630,299	Lorge, Robert Gerald	1,439,214	Kohl, Herbert H.*	68,784	808,915 D	29.5%	67.3%	30.5%	69.5%
2004	2,949,743	1,301,183	Michels, Tim	1,632,697	Feingold, Russell D.*	15,863	331,514 D	44.1%	55.4%	44.4%	55.6%
2000	2,540,083	940,744	Gillespie, John	1,563,238	Kohl, Herbert H.*	36,101	622,494 D	37.0%	61.5%	37.6%	62.4%
1998	1,760,836	852,272	Neumann, Mark W.	890,059	Feingold, Russell D.*	18,505	37,787 D	48.4%	50.5%	48.9%	51.1%
1994	1,565,628	636,989	Welch, Robert T.	912,662	Kohl, Herbert H.*	15,977	275,673 D	40.7%	58.3%	41.1%	58.9%
1992	2,455,124	1,129,599	Kasten, Robert W.*	1,290,662	Feingold, Russell D.	34,863	161,063 D	46.0%	52.6%	46.7%	53.3%
1988	2,168,190	1,030,440	Engeleiter, Susan	1,128,625	Kohl, Herbert H.	9,125	98,185 D	47.5%	52.1%	47.7%	52.3%
1986	1,483,174	754,573	Kasten, Robert W.*	702,963	Garvey, Ed	25,638	51,610 R	50.9%	47.4%	51.8%	48.2%
1982	1,544,981	527,355	McCallum, Scott	983,311	Proxmire, William*	34,315	455,956 D	34.1%	63.6%	34.9%	65.1%
1980	2,204,202	1,106,311	Kasten, Robert W.	1,065,487	Nelson, Gaylord Anton*	32,404	40,824 R	50.2%	48.3%	50.9%	49.1%
1976	1,935,183	521,902	York, Stanley	1,396,970	Proxmire, William*	16,311	875,068 D	27.0%	72.2%	27.2%	72.8%
1974	1,199,495	429,327	Petri, Thomas E.	740,700	Nelson, Gaylord Anton*	29,468	311,373 D	35.8%	61.8%	36.7%	63.3%
1970	1,338,967	381,297	Erickson, John E.	948,445	Proxmire, William*	9,225	567,148 D	28.5%	70.8%	28.7%	71.3%
1968	1,654,861	633,910	Leonard, Jerris	1,020,931	Nelson, Gaylord Anton*	20	387,021 D	38.3%	61.7%	38.3%	61.7%
1964	1,673,776	780,116	Renk, Wilbur N.	892,013	Proxmire, William*	1,647	111,897 D	46.6%	53.3%	46.7%	53.3%
1962	1,260,168	594,846	Wiley, Alexander*	662,342	Nelson, Gaylord Anton	2,980	67,496 D	47.2%	52.6%	47.3%	52.7%
1958	1,194,678	510,398	Steinle, Roland J.	682,440	Proxmire, William*	1,840	172,042 D	42.7%	57.1%	42.8%	57.2%
1957S**	772,620	312,931	Kohler, Walter J. Jr.	435,985	Proxmire, William	23,704	123,054 D	40.5%	56.4%	41.8%	58.2%
1956	1,523,356	892,473	Wiley, Alexander*	627,903	Maier, Henry W.	2,980	264,570 R	58.6%	41.2%	58.7%	41.3%
1952	1,605,228	870,444	McCarthy, Joseph R.*	731,402	Fairchild, Thomas E.	3,382	139,042 R	54.2%	45.6%	54.3%	45.7%
1950	1,116,135	595,283	Wiley, Alexander*	515,539	Fairchild, Thomas E.	5,313	79,744 R	53.3%	46.2%	53.6%	46.4%
1946	1,014,594	620,430	McCarthy, Joseph R.	378,772	McMurray, Howard J.	15,392	241,658 R	61.2%	37.3%	62.1%	37.9%

Note: An asterisk (*) denotes incumbent. **The August 1957 election was for a short term to fill a vacancy.

WISCONSIN

GOVERNOR 2022

2020 Census Population	County	Total Vote	Republican (Michels)	Democratic (Evers)	Other	Rep.-Dem. Plurality	Percentage			
							Total Vote		Major Vote	
							Rep.	Dem.	Rep.	Dem.
20,295	ADAMS	9,908	5,856	3,860	192	1,996 R	59.1%	39.0%	60.3%	39.7%
15,570	ASHLAND	7,015	2,905	4,034	76	1,129 D	41.4%	57.5%	41.9%	58.1%
45,356	BARRON	20,133	12,246	7,552	335	4,694 R	60.8%	37.5%	61.9%	38.1%
15,102	BAYFIELD	9,291	3,843	5,367	81	1,524 D	41.4%	57.8%	41.7%	58.3%
265,223	BROWN	114,205	58,986	53,887	1,332	5,099 R	51.6%	47.2%	52.3%	47.7%
13,029	BUFFALO	6,138	3,638	2,391	109	1,247 R	59.3%	39.0%	60.3%	39.7%
15,479	BURNETT	8,142	5,061	2,964	117	2,097 R	62.2%	36.4%	63.1%	36.9%
50,171	CALUMET	25,025	14,828	9,935	262	4,893 R	59.3%	39.7%	59.9%	40.1%
64,853	CHIPPEWA	29,201	16,792	11,994	415	4,798 R	57.5%	41.1%	58.3%	41.7%
34,805	CLARK	11,692	7,690	3,797	205	3,893 R	65.8%	32.5%	66.9%	33.1%
57,659	COLUMBIA	27,476	13,008	14,168	300	1,160 D	47.3%	51.6%	47.9%	52.1%
16,160	CRAWFORD	7,006	3,486	3,429	91	57 R	49.8%	48.9%	50.4%	49.6%
548,462	DANE	301,033	62,300	236,577	2,156	174,277 D	20.7%	78.6%	20.8%	79.2%
88,047	DODGE	39,082	25,428	13,240	414	12,188 R	65.1%	33.9%	65.8%	34.2%
27,789	DOOR	17,305	8,145	8,984	176	839 D	47.1%	51.9%	47.6%	52.4%

WISCONSIN
GOVERNOR 2022

							Percentage				
							Total Vote			Major Vote	
2020 Census Population	County	Total Vote	Republican (Michels)	Democratic (Evers)	Other	Rep.-Dem. Plurality	Rep.	Dem.	Rep.	Dem.
43,204	DOUGLAS	18,639	7,823	10,606	210	2,783 D	42.0%	56.9%	42.4%	57.6%
45,521	DUNN	18,435	9,899	8,299	237	1,600 R	53.7%	45.0%	54.4%	45.6%
104,836	EAU CLAIRE	48,461	19,856	28,063	542	8,207 D	41.0%	57.9%	41.4%	58.6%
4,319	FLORENCE	2,517	1,838	655	24	1,183 R	73.0%	26.0%	73.7%	26.3%
103,698	FOND DU LAC	46,718	29,642	16,598	478	13,044 R	63.4%	35.5%	64.1%	35.9%
9,011	FOREST	4,190	2,670	1,452	68	1,218 R	63.7%	34.7%	64.8%	35.2%
51,522	GRANT	20,094	10,594	9,234	266	1,360 R	52.7%	46.0%	53.4%	46.6%
37,039	GREEN	17,532	7,681	9,603	248	1,922 D	43.8%	54.8%	44.4%	55.6%
19,009	GREEN LAKE	8,714	5,864	2,746	104	3,118 R	67.3%	31.5%	68.1%	31.9%
23,734	IOWA	11,678	4,717	6,837	124	2,120 D	40.4%	58.5%	40.8%	59.2%
5,709	IRON	3,260	1,964	1,259	37	705 R	60.2%	38.6%	60.9%	39.1%
20,678	JACKSON	7,999	4,375	3,505	119	870 R	54.7%	43.8%	55.5%	44.5%
84,882	JEFFERSON	38,732	21,488	16,765	479	4,723 R	55.5%	43.3%	56.2%	43.8%
26,786	JUNEAU	10,738	6,516	4,048	174	2,468 R	60.7%	37.7%	61.7%	38.3%
170,000	KENOSHA	66,073	33,068	32,176	829	892 R	50.0%	48.7%	50.7%	49.3%
20,462	KEWAUNEE	9,893	6,229	3,529	135	2,700 R	63.0%	35.7%	63.8%	36.2%
118,274	LA CROSSE	55,169	22,325	32,119	725	9,794 D	40.5%	58.2%	41.0%	59.0%
16,671	LAFAYETTE	6,569	3,498	3,005	66	493 R	53.3%	45.7%	53.8%	46.2%
19,245	LANGLADE	9,035	5,966	2,958	111	3,008 R	66.0%	32.7%	66.9%	33.1%
27,628	LINCOLN	13,552	8,084	5,226	242	2,858 R	59.7%	38.6%	60.7%	39.3%
79,127	MANITOWOC	36,038	21,573	13,937	528	7,636 R	59.9%	38.7%	60.8%	39.2%
135,735	MARATHON	61,770	35,860	25,163	747	10,697 R	58.1%	40.7%	58.8%	41.2%
40,466	MARINETTE	18,541	12,164	6,110	267	6,054 R	65.6%	33.0%	66.6%	33.4%
15,654	MARQUETTE	7,338	4,549	2,697	92	1,852 R	62.0%	36.8%	62.8%	37.2%
4,573	MENOMINEE	1,245	254	979	12	725 D	20.4%	78.6%	20.6%	79.4%
944,245	MILWAUKEE	346,889	97,471	246,073	3,345	148,602 D	28.1%	70.9%	28.4%	71.6%
46,373	MONROE	17,341	10,153	6,931	257	3,222 R	58.5%	40.0%	59.4%	40.6%
38,100	OCONTO	19,537	13,363	5,910	264	7,453 R	68.4%	30.3%	69.3%	30.7%
35,754	ONEIDA	20,230	11,297	8,667	266	2,630 R	55.8%	42.8%	56.6%	43.4%
188,401	OUTAGAMIE	86,102	45,601	39,572	929	6,029 R	53.0%	46.0%	53.5%	46.5%
89,524	OZAUKEE	52,367	28,827	23,104	436	5,723 R	55.0%	44.1%	55.5%	44.5%
7,309	PEPIN	3,311	1,990	1,280	41	710 R	60.1%	38.7%	60.9%	39.1%
42,935	PIERCE	18,029	9,779	7,967	283	1,812 R	54.2%	44.2%	55.1%	44.9%
43,940	POLK	20,445	12,548	7,587	310	4,961 R	61.4%	37.1%	62.3%	37.7%
70,776	PORTAGE	33,681	15,361	17,947	373	2,586 D	45.6%	53.3%	46.1%	53.9%
13,389	PRICE	7,062	4,369	2,596	97	1,773 R	61.9%	36.8%	62.7%	37.3%
196,612	RACINE	81,528	42,359	38,241	928	4,118 R	52.0%	46.9%	52.6%	47.4%
17,240	RICHLAND	7,008	3,562	3,354	92	208 R	50.8%	47.9%	51.5%	48.5%
163,774	ROCK	65,276	26,722	37,755	799	11,033 D	40.9%	57.8%	41.4%	58.6%
14,222	RUSK	6,387	4,120	2,180	87	1,940 R	64.5%	34.1%	65.4%	34.6%
64,622	SAUK	28,960	13,348	15,285	327	1,937 D	46.1%	52.8%	46.6%	53.4%
16,615	SAWYER	8,566	4,735	3,734	97	1,001 R	55.3%	43.6%	55.9%	44.1%
40,974	SHAWANO	17,937	11,875	5,853	209	6,022 R	66.2%	32.6%	67.0%	33.0%
115,651	SHEBOYGAN	53,661	30,679	22,325	657	8,354 R	57.2%	41.6%	57.9%	42.1%
91,057	ST. CROIX	44,039	24,968	18,516	555	6,452 R	56.7%	42.0%	57.4%	42.6%
20,373	TAYLOR	8,702	6,296	2,262	144	4,034 R	72.4%	26.0%	73.6%	26.4%
29,655	TREMPEALEAU	12,249	6,813	5,281	155	1,532 R	55.6%	43.1%	56.3%	43.7%
30,885	VERNON	13,201	6,409	6,597	195	188 D	48.5%	50.0%	49.3%	50.7%
22,335	VILAS	13,220	7,983	5,088	149	2,895 R	60.4%	38.5%	61.1%	38.9%
104,293	WALWORTH	45,926	26,700	18,569	657	8,131 R	58.1%	40.4%	59.0%	41.0%
15,790	WASHBURN	8,351	5,032	3,198	121	1,834 R	60.3%	38.3%	61.1%	38.9%
136,505	WASHINGTON	74,029	50,749	22,698	582	28,051 R	68.6%	30.7%	69.1%	30.9%
405,395	WAUKESHA	224,603	134,212	88,564	1,827	45,648 R	59.8%	39.4%	60.2%	39.8%
51,100	WAUPACA	23,227	14,939	7,990	298	6,949 R	64.3%	34.4%	65.2%	34.8%
24,553	WAUSHARA	11,340	7,459	3,766	115	3,693 R	65.8%	33.2%	66.4%	33.6%
172,363	WINNEBAGO	74,712	37,242	36,512	958	730 R	49.8%	48.9%	50.5%	49.5%
73,064	WOOD	32,992	18,865	13,624	503	5,241 R	57.2%	41.3%	58.1%	41.9%
5,833,607	TOTAL	2,656,490	1,268,535	1,358,774	29,181	90,239 D	47.8%	51.1%	48.3%	51.7%

WISCONSIN
SENATOR 2022

2020 Census Population	County	Total Vote	Republican (Johnson)	Democratic (Barnes)	Other	Rep.-Dem. Plurality		Percentage			
								Total Vote		Major Vote	
								Rep.	Dem.	Rep.	Dem.
20,295	ADAMS	9,884	6,202	3,644	38	2,558	R	62.7%	36.9%	63.0%	37.0%
15,570	ASHLAND	6,986	3,074	3,903	9	829	D	44.0%	55.9%	44.1%	55.9%
45,356	BARRON	20,079	12,928	7,121	30	5,807	R	64.4%	35.5%	64.5%	35.5%
15,102	BAYFIELD	9,280	4,082	5,183	15	1,101	D	44.0%	55.9%	44.1%	55.9%
265,223	BROWN	113,879	62,221	51,421	237	10,800	R	54.6%	45.2%	54.8%	45.2%
13,029	BUFFALO	6,118	3,907	2,201	10	1,706	R	63.9%	36.0%	64.0%	36.0%
15,479	BURNETT	8,196	5,362	2,834		2,528	R	65.4%	34.6%	65.4%	34.6%
50,171	CALUMET	24,951	15,466	9,444	41	6,022	R	62.0%	37.9%	62.1%	37.9%
64,853	CHIPPEWA	28,823	17,694	11,069	60	6,625	R	61.4%	38.4%	61.5%	38.5%
34,805	CLARK	11,654	8,181	3,451	22	4,730	R	70.2%	29.6%	70.3%	29.7%
57,659	COLUMBIA	27,373	13,899	13,410	64	489	R	50.8%	49.0%	50.9%	49.1%
16,160	CRAWFORD	6,989	3,797	3,179	13	618	R	54.3%	45.5%	54.4%	45.6%
548,462	DANE	300,728	68,228	231,818	682	163,590	D	22.7%	77.1%	22.7%	77.3%
88,047	DODGE	38,744	25,914	12,830		13,084	R	66.9%	33.1%	66.9%	33.1%
27,789	DOOR	17,322	8,685	8,611	26	74	R	50.1%	49.7%	50.2%	49.8%
43,204	DOUGLAS	18,665	8,373	10,270	22	1,897	D	44.9%	55.0%	44.9%	55.1%
45,521	DUNN	18,420	10,544	7,876		2,668	R	57.2%	42.8%	57.2%	42.8%
104,836	EAU CLAIRE	47,852	21,208	26,529	115	5,321	D	44.3%	55.4%	44.4%	55.6%
4,319	FLORENCE	2,518	1,898	620		1,278	R	75.4%	24.6%	75.4%	24.6%
103,698	FOND DU LAC	46,604	30,584	15,982	38	14,602	R	65.6%	34.3%	65.7%	34.3%
9,011	FOREST	4,163	2,785	1,371	7	1,414	R	66.9%	32.9%	67.0%	33.0%
51,522	GRANT	20,109	11,397	8,671	41	2,726	R	56.7%	43.1%	56.8%	43.2%
37,039	GREEN	17,480	8,350	9,097	33	747	D	47.8%	52.0%	47.9%	52.1%
19,009	GREEN LAKE	8,692	6,061	2,626	5	3,435	R	69.7%	30.2%	69.8%	30.2%
23,734	IOWA	11,621	5,082	6,514	25	1,432	D	43.7%	56.1%	43.8%	56.2%
5,709	IRON	3,265	2,064	1,197	4	867	R	63.2%	36.7%	63.3%	36.7%
20,678	JACKSON	7,988	4,700	3,288		1,412	R	58.8%	41.2%	58.8%	41.2%
84,882	JEFFERSON	38,607	22,402	16,141	64	6,261	R	58.0%	41.8%	58.1%	41.9%
26,786	JUNEAU	10,746	6,944	3,782	20	3,162	R	64.6%	35.2%	64.7%	35.3%
170,000	KENOSHA	65,923	34,393	31,371	159	3,022	R	52.2%	47.6%	52.3%	47.7%
20,462	KEWAUNEE	9,920	6,627	3,273	20	3,354	R	66.8%	33.0%	66.9%	33.1%
118,274	LA CROSSE	55,223	24,413	30,695	115	6,282	D	44.2%	55.6%	44.3%	55.7%
16,671	LAFAYETTE	6,566	3,779	2,787		992	R	57.6%	42.4%	57.6%	42.4%
19,245	LANGLADE	9,008	6,190	2,818		3,372	R	68.7%	31.3%	68.7%	31.3%
27,628	LINCOLN	13,490	8,541	4,920	29	3,621	R	63.3%	36.5%	63.4%	36.6%
79,127	MANITOWOC	35,918	22,561	13,288	69	9,273	R	62.8%	37.0%	62.9%	37.1%
135,735	MARATHON	61,542	37,527	23,912	103	13,615	R	61.0%	38.9%	61.1%	38.9%
40,466	MARINETTE	18,535	12,677	5,816	42	6,861	R	68.4%	31.4%	68.6%	31.4%
15,654	MARQUETTE	7,353	4,753	2,589	11	2,164	R	64.6%	35.2%	64.7%	35.3%
4,573	MENOMINEE	1,226	264	962		698	D	21.5%	78.5%	21.5%	78.5%
944,245	MILWAUKEE	348,059	103,666	243,638	755	139,972	D	29.8%	70.0%	29.8%	70.2%
46,373	MONROE	17,311	10,001	6,461	49	4,340	R	62.4%	37.3%	62.6%	37.4%
38,100	OCONTO	19,535	13,961	5,527	47	8,434	R	71.5%	28.3%	71.6%	28.4%
35,754	ONEIDA	20,186	11,866	8,279	41	3,587	R	58.8%	41.0%	58.9%	41.1%
188,401	OUTAGAMIE	85,727	47,805	37,922		9,883	R	55.8%	44.2%	55.8%	44.2%
89,524	OZAUKEE	52,293	30,209	21,954	130	8,255	R	57.8%	42.0%	57.9%	42.1%
7,309	PEPIN	3,300	2,122	1,177	1	945	R	64.3%	35.7%	64.3%	35.7%
42,935	PIERCE	18,037	10,313	7,709	15	2,604	R	57.2%	42.7%	57.2%	42.8%
43,940	POLK	20,447	13,132	7,313	2	5,819	R	64.2%	35.8%	64.2%	35.8%
70,776	PORTAGE	33,575	16,339	17,186	50	847	D	48.7%	51.2%	48.7%	51.3%
13,389	PRICE	7,047	4,584	2,459	4	2,125	R	65.0%	34.9%	65.1%	34.9%
196,612	RACINE	81,691	44,221	37,252	218	6,969	R	54.1%	45.6%	54.3%	45.7%
17,240	RICHLAND	7,012	3,827	3,173	12	654	R	54.6%	45.3%	54.7%	45.3%
163,774	ROCK	64,942	28,758	36,024	160	7,266	D	44.3%	55.5%	44.4%	55.6%
14,222	RUSK	6,384	4,326	2,056	2	2,270	R	67.8%	32.2%	67.8%	32.2%
64,622	SAUK	28,907	14,289	14,618		329	D	49.4%	50.6%	49.4%	50.6%
16,615	SAWYER	8,559	4,949	3,597	13	1,352	R	57.8%	42.0%	57.9%	42.1%
40,974	SHAWANO	17,912	12,415	5,495	2	6,920	R	69.3%	30.7%	69.3%	30.7%
115,651	SHEBOYGAN	53,537	32,058	21,350	129	10,708	R	59.9%	39.9%	60.0%	40.0%
91,057	ST. CROIX	44,022	26,143	17,827	52	8,316	R	59.4%	40.5%	59.5%	40.5%

WISCONSIN
SENATOR 2022

2020 Census Population	County	Total Vote	Republican (Johnson)	Democratic (Barnes)	Other	Rep.-Dem. Plurality		Total Vote		Major Vote	
								Rep.	Dem.	Rep.	Dem.
20,373	TAYLOR	8,657	6,527	2,130		4,397	R	75.4%	24.6%	75.4%	24.6%
29,655	TREMPEALEAU	12,255	7,322	4,920	13	2,402	R	59.7%	40.1%	59.8%	40.2%
30,885	VERNON	13,174	6,950	6,206	18	744	R	52.8%	47.1%	52.8%	47.2%
22,335	VILAS	13,177	8,350	4,803	24	3,547	R	63.4%	36.4%	63.5%	36.5%
104,293	WALWORTH	45,931	27,995	17,824	112	10,171	R	61.0%	38.8%	61.1%	38.9%
15,790	WASHBURN	8,355	5,277	3,074	4	2,203	R	63.2%	36.8%	63.2%	36.8%
136,505	WASHINGTON	73,967	52,401	21,566		30,835	R	70.8%	29.2%	70.8%	29.2%
405,395	WAUKESHA	224,073	140,156	83,408	509	56,748	R	62.5%	37.2%	62.7%	37.3%
51,100	WAUPACA	23,220	15,525	7,653	42	7,872	R	66.9%	33.0%	67.0%	33.0%
24,553	WAUSHARA	11,335	7,765	3,567	3	4,198	R	68.5%	31.5%	68.5%	31.5%
172,363	WINNEBAGO	74,417	39,372	34,860	185	4,512	R	52.9%	46.8%	53.0%	47.0%
73,064	WOOD	32,993	20,004	12,925	64	7,079	R	60.6%	39.2%	60.7%	39.3%
5,833,607	TOTAL	2,652,477	1,337,185	1,310,467	4,825	26,718	R	50.4%	49.4%	50.5%	49.5%

WISCONSIN
HOUSE OF REPRESENTATIVES

CD	Year	Total Vote	Republican Vote	Candidate	Democratic Vote	Candidate	Other Vote	Rep.-Dem. Plurality		Total Vote Rep.	Total Vote Dem.	Major Vote Rep.	Major Vote Dem.
1	2022	300,867	162,610	STEIL, BRYAN*	135,825	ROE, ANN	2,432	26,785	R	54.0%	45.1%	54.5%	45.5%
1	2020	401,754	238,271	STEIL, BRYAN*	163,170	POLACK, ROGER	313	75,101	R	59.3%	40.6%	59.4%	40.6%
1	2018	325,317	177,492	STEIL, BRYAN	137,508	BRYCE, RANDY	10,317	39,984	R	54.6%	42.3%	56.3%	43.7%
1	2016	354,245	230,072	RYAN, PAUL D.*	107,003	SOLEN, RYAN	17,170	123,069	R	64.9%	30.2%	68.3%	31.7%
1	2014	288,170	182,316	RYAN, PAUL D.*	105,552	ZERBAN, ROB	302	76,764	R	63.3%	36.6%	63.3%	36.7%
1	2012	365,058	200,423	RYAN, PAUL D.*	158,414	ZEBRAN, ROB	6,221	42,009	R	54.9%	43.4%	55.9%	44.1%
2	2022	378,537	101,890	OLSEN, ERIK	268,740	POCAN, MARK*	7,907	166,850	D	26.9%	71.0%	27.5%	72.5%
2	2020	457,205	138,306	THERON, PETER	318,523	POCAN, MARK*	376	180,217	D	30.3%	69.7%	30.3%	69.7%
2	2018	317,295			309,116	POCAN, MARK*	8,179	309,116	D		97.4%		100.0%
2	2016	398,060	124,044	THERON, PETER	273,537	POCAN, MARK*	479	149,493	D	31.2%	68.7%	31.2%	68.8%
2	2014	328,847	103,619	THERON, PETER	224,920	POCAN, MARK*	308	121,301	D	31.5%	68.4%	31.5%	68.5%
2	2012	390,898	124,683	LEE, CHAD	265,422	POCAN, MARK	793	140,739	D	31.9%	67.9%	32.0%	68.0%
3	2022	317,922	164,743	VAN ORDEN, DERRICK F.	152,977	PFAFF, BRAD	202	11,766	R	51.8%	48.1%	51.9%	48.1%
3	2020	389,618	189,524	VAN ORDEN, DERRICK F.	199,870	KIND, RON*	224	10,346	D	48.6%	51.3%	48.7%	51.3%
3	2018	314,989	126,980	TOFT, STEVE	187,888	KIND, RON*	121	60,908	D	40.3%	59.6%	40.3%	59.7%
3	2016	260,370			257,401	KIND, RON*	2,969	257,401	D		98.9%		100.0%
3	2014	275,161	119,540	KURTZ, TONY	155,368	KIND, RON*	253	35,828	D	43.4%	56.5%	43.5%	56.5%
3	2012	339,764	121,713	BOLAND, RAY	217,712	KIND, RON*	339	95,999	D	35.8%	64.1%	35.9%	64.1%
4	2022	255,012	57,660	ROGERS, TIM	191,955	MOORE, GWEN*	5,397	134,295	D	22.6%	75.3%	23.1%	76.9%
4	2020	311,697	70,769	ROGERS, TIM	232,668	MOORE, GWEN*	8,260	161,899	D	22.7%	74.6%	23.3%	76.7%
4	2018	273,087	59,091	ROGERS, TIM	206,487	MOORE, GWEN*	7,509	147,396	D	21.6%	75.6%	22.2%	77.8%
4	2016	286,909			220,181	MOORE, GWEN*	66,728	220,181	D		76.7%		100.0%
4	2014	254,892	68,490	SEBRING, DAN	179,045	MOORE, GWEN*	7,357	110,555	D	26.9%	70.2%	27.7%	72.3%
4	2012	325,788	80,787	SEBRING, DAN	235,257	MOORE, GWEN*	9,744	154,470	D	24.8%	72.2%	25.6%	74.4%
5	2022	378,523	243,741	FITZGERALD, SCOTT*	134,581	VAN SOMEREN, MIKE	201	109,160	R	64.4%	35.6%	64.4%	35.6%
5	2020	441,599	265,434	FITZGERALD, SCOTT	175,902	PALZEWICZ, TOM	263	89,532	R	60.1%	39.8%	60.1%	39.9%
5	2018	364,288	225,619	SENSENBRENNER, F. JAMES JR.*	138,385	PALZEWICZ, TOM	284	87,234	R	61.9%	38.0%	62.0%	38.0%
5	2016	390,844	260,706	SENSENBRENNER, F. JAMES JR.*	114,477	PENEBAKER, KHARY	15,661	146,229	R	66.7%	29.3%	69.5%	30.5%
5	2014	332,826	231,160	SENSENBRENNER, F. JAMES JR.*	101,190	ROCKWOOD, CHRIS B.	476	129,970	R	69.5%	30.4%	69.6%	30.4%
5	2012	369,664	250,335	SENSENBRENNER, F. JAMES JR.*	118,478	HEASTER, DAVE	851	131,857	R	67.7%	32.1%	67.9%	32.1%

WISCONSIN

HOUSE OF REPRESENTATIVES

CD	Year	Total Vote	Republican Vote	Republican Candidate	Democratic Vote	Democratic Candidate	Other Vote	Rep.-Dem. Plurality	Total Vote Rep. %	Total Vote Dem. %	Major Vote Rep. %	Major Vote Dem. %
6	2022	251,999	239,231	GROTHMAN, GLENN S.*			12,768	239,231 R	94.9%		100.0%	
6	2020	403,333	238,874	GROTHMAN, GLENN S.*	164,239	KING, JESSICA JEANE	220	74,635 R	59.2%	40.7%	59.3%	40.7%
6	2018	325,065	180,311	GROTHMAN, GLENN S.*	144,536	KOHL, DAN	218	35,775 R	55.5%	44.5%	55.5%	44.5%
6	2016	357,183	204,147	GROTHMAN, GLENN S.*	133,072	LLOYD, SARAH	19,964	71,075 R	57.2%	37.3%	60.5%	39.5%
6	2014	299,033	169,767	GROTHMAN, GLENN S.	122,212	HARRIS, MARK L.	7,054	47,555 R	56.8%	40.9%	58.1%	41.9%
6	2012	359,745	223,460	PETRI, THOMAS E.*	135,921	KALLAS, JOSEPH C.	364	87,539 R	62.1%	37.8%	62.2%	37.8%
7	2022	338,268	209,224	TIFFANY, TOM*	128,877	AUSMAN, RICHARD "DICK"	167	80,347 R	61.9%	38.1%	61.9%	38.1%
7	2020	415,007	252,048	TIFFANY, TOM*	162,741	ZUNKER, TRICIA	218	89,307 R	60.7%	39.2%	60.8%	39.2%
7	2018	322,840	194,061	DUFFY, SEAN*	124,307	ENGEBRETSON, MARGARET	4,472	69,754 R	60.1%	38.5%	61.0%	39.0%
7	2016	362,271	223,418	DUFFY, SEAN*	138,643	HOEFT, MARY	210	84,775 R	61.7%	38.3%	61.7%	38.3%
7	2014	286,603	169,891	DUFFY, SEAN*	112,949	WESTLUND, KELLY	3,763	56,942 R	59.3%	39.4%	60.1%	39.9%
7	2012	359,669	201,720	DUFFY, SEAN*	157,524	KREITLOW, PAT	425	44,196 R	56.1%	43.8%	56.2%	43.8%
8	2022	310,196	223,981	GALLAGHER, MIKE*			86,215	223,981 R	72.2%		100.0%	
8	2020	417,838	268,173	GALLAGHER, MIKE*	149,558	STUCK, AMANDA	107	118,615 R	64.2%	35.8%	64.2%	35.8%
8	2018	328,774	209,410	GALLAGHER, MIKE*	119,265	LIEGEOIS, BEAU	99	90,145 R	63.7%	36.3%	63.7%	36.3%
8	2016	363,780	227,892	GALLAGHER, MIKE	135,682	NELSON, TOM	206	92,210 R	62.6%	37.3%	62.7%	37.3%
8	2014	290,048	188,553	RIBBLE, REID J.*	101,345	GRUETT, RON	150	87,208 R	65.0%	34.9%	65.0%	35.0%
8	2012	355,464	198,874	RIBBLE, REID J.*	156,287	WALL, JAMIE	303	42,587 R	55.9%	44.0%	56.0%	44.0%
TOTAL	2022	2,531,324	1,403,080		1,012,955		115,289	390,125 R	55.4%	40.0%	58.1%	41.9%
TOTAL	2020	3,238,051	1,661,399		1,566,671		9,981	94,728 R	51.3%	48.4%	51.5%	48.5%
TOTAL	2018	2,571,655	1,172,964		1,367,492		31,199	194,528 D	45.6%	53.2%	46.2%	53.8%
TOTAL	2016	2,773,662	1,270,279		1,379,996		123,387	109,717 D	45.8%	49.8%	47.9%	52.1%
TOTAL	2014	2,355,580	1,233,336		1,102,581		19,663	130,755 R	52.4%	46.8%	52.8%	47.2%
TOTAL	2012	2,866,050	1,401,995		1,445,015		19,040	43,020 D	48.9%	50.4%	49.2%	50.8%

Note: An asterisk (*) denotes incumbent.

WISCONSIN

GENERAL AND PRIMARY ELECTIONS

GENERAL ELECTIONS: OTHER VOTES

Governor Other vote was 27,198 Independent (Joan Beglinger), 1,983 Write-In (Scattered Write-Ins)

Senate Other vote was 4,825 Write-In (Scattered Write-Ins)

House Other vote was:

- CD 1 2,247 Other (Charles Barman), 185 Write-In (Scattered Write-Ins)
- CD 2 7,689 Independent (Douglas Alexander), 218 Write-In (Scattered Write-Ins)
- CD 3 202 Write-In (Write-Ins)
- CD 4 5,164 Independent (Robert Raymond), 233 Write-In (Scattered Write-Ins)
- CD 5 201 Write-In (Scattered Write-Ins)
- CD 6 12,428 Write-In (Scattered Write-Ins), 340 Write-In (Tom Powell)
- CD 7 167 Write-In (Scattered Write-Ins)
- CD 8 48,896 Independent (Paul Boucher), 3,160 Write-In (Julie Hancock), 135 Write-In (Scattered Write-Ins)

2022 PRIMARY ELECTIONS: SUPPLEMENTARY INFORMATION

Primary August 9, 2022 **Registration** (as of August 1, 2022) 3,468,390 No Party Registration

Primary Type Open—Any registered voter could participate in the party primary of his or her choice.

WISCONSIN

GENERAL AND PRIMARY ELECTIONS

	REPUBLICAN PRIMARIES			DEMOCRATIC PRIMARIES		
Senator	Johnson, Ron*	563,871	83.6%	Barnes, Mandela	390,279	77.8%
	Schroeder, David	109,917	16.3%	Lasry, Alex	44,609	8.9%
	Scattered Write-Ins	693	0.1%	Godlewski, Sarah	40,555	8.1%
				Nelson, Tom	10,995	2.2%
				Olikara, Steven	5,619	1.1%
				Williams, Darrell	3,646	0.7%
				Lee, Kou C.	3,434	0.7%
				Peckarsky, Peter	2,446	0.5%
				Scattered Write-Ins	177	
	TOTAL	674,481		TOTAL	501,760	
Governor	Michels, Tim	326,969	47.1%	Evers, Tony*	491,656	99.8%
	Kleefisch, Rebecca	291,384	42.0%	Scattered Write-Ins	975	0.2%
	Ramthun, Timothy	41,639	6.0%			
	Nicholson, Kevin	24,884	3.6%			
	Fischer, Adam	8,139	1.2%			
	Scattered Write-Ins	504	0.1%			
	TOTAL	693,519		TOTAL	492,631	
Congressional District 1	Steil, Bryan*	73,191	99.2%	Roe, Ann	48,148	99.8%
	Scattered Write-Ins	571	0.8%	Scattered Write-Ins	112	0.2%
	TOTAL	73,762		TOTAL	48,260	
Congressional District 2	Olsen, Erik	21,774	49.8%	Pocan, Mark*	106,595	99.8%
	Barry, Charity	21,711	49.7%	Scattered Write-Ins	198	0.2%
	Scattered Write-Ins	225	0.5%			
	TOTAL	43,710		TOTAL	106,793	
Congressional District 3	Van Orden, Derrick F.	65,164	99.3%	Pfaff, Brad	24,041	38.9%
	Scattered Write-Ins	471	0.7%	Cooke, Rebecca	19,221	31.1%
				McGrath, Deb	11,770	19.1%
				Neumann, Mark A.	6,672	10.8%
				Scattered Write-Ins	25	
	TOTAL	65,635		TOTAL	61,729	
Congressional District 4	Rogers, Tim	16,528	74.3%	Moore, Gwen*	72,845	99.6%
	Clark, Travis	5,583	25.1%	Scattered Write-Ins	325	0.4%
	Scattered Write-Ins	135	0.6%			
	TOTAL	22,246		TOTAL	73,170	
Congressional District 5	Fitzgerald, Scott*	118,411	99.4%	Van Someren, Mike	44,305	99.9%
	Scattered Write-Ins	769	0.6%	Scattered Write-Ins	62	0.1%
	TOTAL	119,180		TOTAL	44,367	
Congressional District 6	Grothman, Glenn S.*	84,056	82.5%	Scattered Write-Ins	1,343	100.0%
	Mullenix, Douglas H.	17,773	17.4%			
	Scattered Write-Ins	82	0.1%			
	TOTAL	101,911		TOTAL	1,343	
Congressional District 7	Tiffany, Tom*	80,675	86.6%	Ausman, Richard "Dick"	43,265	99.8%
	Kunelius, David W. II	12,456	13.4%	Scattered Write-Ins	67	0.2%
	Scattered Write-Ins	52	0.1%			
	TOTAL	93,183		TOTAL	43,332	
Congressional District 8	Gallagher, Mike*	79,096	84.6%	Hancock, Julie(Write-In)	4,120	73.3%
	Clarmont, Shaun	14,377	15.4%	Scattered Write-Ins	1,504	26.7%
	Scattered Write-Ins	76	0.1%			
	TOTAL	93,549		TOTAL	5,624	

Note: An asterisk (*) denotes incumbent.

WYOMING

Statewide and House Races

In 2022, Wyoming, which was Donald Trump's best state in both the 2016 and 2020 general elections, saw a contest that involved Trump's biggest intraparty critic.

On January 6, 2021, Liz Cheney, daughter of the former Vice President Dick Cheney, was the chair of the House Republican Conference, the House GOP's third-highest position. After the attempted insurrection by pro-Trump forces, the Wyoming Republican was among ten House Republicans who voted to impeach the president, and, in the following months, repeatedly criticized him. Though Cheney was able to hold onto her leadership position for a time, by May 2021, she was removed from her post. The next year, Cheney would become a household name, as vice chair of the select committee investigating January 6th.

Though Cheney's principled stances seemed admirable in a time when politicians often equivocate, siding against Trump did not play well in Wyoming. Harriet Hageman, an environmental lawyer, got into the race and consolidated much of the anti-Cheney vote. As Trump, and most of the House GOP conference endorsed Hageman, Cheney received support from a mix of older-school Republicans – such as former President George W. Bush and Sen. Mitt Romney – and Democrats. Cheney outraised Hageman, but much of the electorate's mind was made up. Hageman led in every public poll and won by a 66%–29% margin. Cheney carried Albany County (Laramie) by a few points and Teton County (containing the Jackson Hole ski area) by three-to-one but failed to break 40% in any of the other 21 counties. In January 2022, Republicans made up just under 70% of registered voters in Wyoming, but, speaking to the interest in the primary, that number ticked up to 75% by the time of the August contest.

With the primary over, there was little question that Hageman would win the general election easily, which she did. She defeated Democrat Lynnette Grey Bull in a 68%–24% vote, losing the same two counties that she did in the primary. After her defeat, Cheney campaigned for and endorsed several Democratic candidates for Congress and governor, and compiled a strong win record – examples of her endorsees included Arizona's Katie Hobbs and Virginia's Abigail Spanberger.

Neither of Wyoming's Senate seats were up in 2022, but Gov. Mark Gordon was on the ballot for reelection. Often one of the nation's most popular, if low-key, state executives, he won by close to 60 points and swept every county.

WYOMING

One member At Large

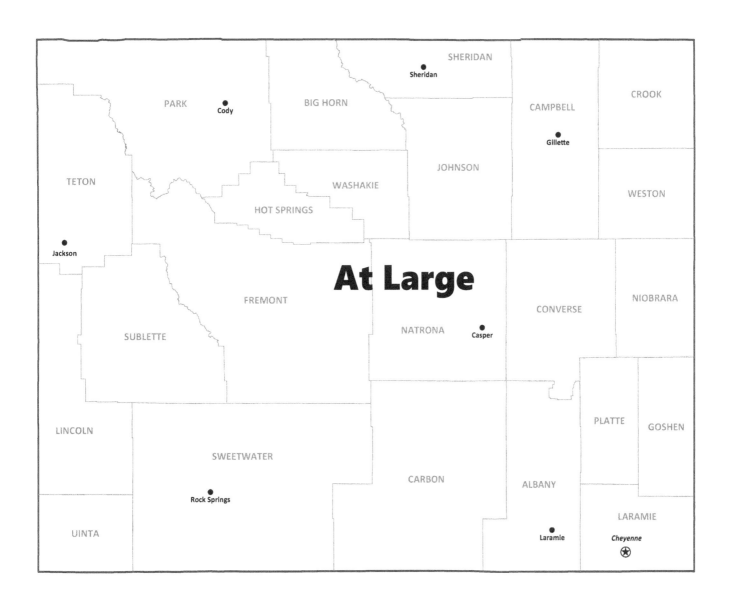

WYOMING

GOVERNOR
Mark Gordon (R). Reelected 2022 to a four-year term. Previously elected 2018.

SENATORS (2 Republicans)
John Barrasso (R). Reelected 2018 to a six-year term. Previously elected 2012, and 2008 to complete the remaining four years of the term vacated by the June 2007 death of Senator Craig Thomas (R); sworn in as Thomas's successor June 25, 2007.

Cynthia Lummis (R). Elected 2020 to a six-year term.

REPRESENTATIVE (1 Republican)
At Large. Harriet M. Hageman (R)

POSTWAR VOTE FOR PRESIDENT

Year	Total Vote	Republican Vote	Republican Candidate	Democratic Vote	Democratic Candidate	Other Vote	Rep.-Dem. Plurality	Total Vote Rep.	Total Vote Dem.	Major Vote Rep.	Major Vote Dem.
2020	276,765	193,559	Trump, Donald J.*	73,491	Biden, Joseph R. Jr.	9,715	120,068 R	69.9%	26.6%	72.5%	27.5%
2016**	255,849	174,419	Trump, Donald J.	55,973	Clinton, Hillary Rodham	25,457	118,446 R	68.2%	21.9%	75.7%	24.3%
2012	249,061	170,962	Romney, W. Mitt	69,286	Obama, Barack H.*	8,813	101,676 R	68.6%	27.8%	71.2%	28.8%
2008	254,658	164,958	McCain, John S. III	82,868	Obama, Barack H.	6,832	82,090 R	64.8%	32.5%	66.6%	33.4%
2004	243,428	167,629	Bush, George W.*	70,776	Kerry, John F.	5,023	96,853 R	68.9%	29.1%	70.3%	29.7%
2000**	218,351	147,947	Bush, George W.	60,481	Gore, Albert Jr.	9,923	87,466 R	67.8%	27.7%	71.0%	29.0%
1996**	211,571	105,388	Dole, Robert "Bob"	77,934	Clinton, Bill*	28,249	27,454 R	49.8%	36.8%	57.5%	42.5%
1992**	200,598	79,347	Bush, George H.*	68,160	Clinton, Bill	53,091	11,187 R	39.6%	34.0%	53.8%	46.2%
1988	176,551	106,867	Bush, George H.	67,113	Dukakis, Michael S.	2,571	39,754 R	60.5%	38.0%	61.4%	38.6%
1984	188,968	133,241	Reagan, Ronald*	53,370	Mondale, Walter F.	2,357	79,871 R	70.5%	28.2%	71.4%	28.6%
1980**	176,713	110,700	Reagan, Ronald	49,427	Carter, Jimmy*	16,586	61,273 R	62.6%	28.0%	69.1%	30.9%
1976	156,343	92,717	Ford, Gerald R.*	62,239	Carter, Jimmy	1,387	30,478 R	59.3%	39.8%	59.8%	40.2%
1972	145,570	100,464	Nixon, Richard M.*	44,358	McGovern, George S.	748	56,106 R	69.0%	30.5%	69.4%	30.6%
1968**	127,205	70,927	Nixon, Richard M.	45,173	Humphrey, Hubert Horatio Jr.	11,105	25,754 R	55.8%	35.5%	61.1%	38.9%
1964	142,716	61,998	Goldwater, Barry M. Sr.	80,718	Johnson, Lyndon B.*		18,720 D	43.4%	56.6%	43.4%	56.6%
1960	140,782	77,451	Nixon, Richard M.	63,331	Kennedy, John F.		14,120 R	55.0%	45.0%	55.0%	45.0%
1956	124,127	74,573	Eisenhower, Dwight D.*	49,554	Stevenson, Adlai E. II		25,019 R	60.1%	39.9%	60.1%	39.9%
1952	129,253	81,049	Eisenhower, Dwight D.	47,934	Stevenson, Adlai E. II	270	33,115 R	62.7%	37.1%	62.8%	37.2%
1948	101,425	47,947	Dewey, Thomas E.	52,354	Truman, Harry S.*	1,124	4,407 D	47.3%	51.6%	47.8%	52.2%

Note: An asterisk (*) denotes incumbent. **In past elections, the other vote included: 2016 - 13,287 Libertarian (Gary Johnson); 2000 - 4,625 Green (Ralph Nader); 1996 - 25,928 Reform (Ross Perot); 1992 - 51,263 Independent (Perot); 1980 - 12,072 Independent (John Anderson), 1968 - 11,105 American Independent (George Wallace)

WYOMING

POSTWAR VOTE FOR GOVERNOR

		Republican		Democratic		Other Vote	Rep.-Dem. Plurality	Percentage			
								Total Vote		Major Vote	
Year	Total Vote	Vote	Candidate	Vote	Candidate			Rep.	Dem.	Rep.	Dem.
2022	194,000	143,696	Gordon, Mark*	30,686	Livingston, Theresa	19,618	113,010 R	74.1%	15.8%	82.4%	17.6%
2018	203,238	136,412	Gordon, Mark	55,965	Throne, Mary A.	10,861	80,447 R	67.1%	27.5%	70.9%	29.1%
2014	167,877	99,700	Mead, Matt*	45,752	Gosar, Peter	22,425	53,948 R	59.4%	27.3%	68.5%	31.5%
2010	188,463	123,780	Mead, Matt	43,240	Petersen, Leslie	21,443	80,540 R	65.7%	22.9%	74.1%	25.9%
2006	193,892	58,100	Hunkins, Ray	135,516	Freudenthal, Dave*	276	77,416 D	30.0%	69.9%	30.0%	70.0%
2002	185,459	88,873	Bebout, Eli	92,662	Freudenthal, Dave	3,924	3,789 D	47.9%	50.0%	49.0%	51.0%
1998	174,888	97,235	Geringer, Jim*	70,754	Vinich, John P.	6,899	26,481 R	55.6%	40.5%	57.9%	42.1%
1994	200,990	118,016	Geringer, Jim	80,747	Karpan, Kathy	2,227	37,269 R	58.7%	40.2%	59.4%	40.6%
1990	160,109	55,471	Mead, Mary	104,638	Sullivan, Mike*		49,167 D	34.6%	65.4%	34.6%	65.4%
1986	164,720	75,841	Simpson, Peter	88,879	Sullivan, Mike		13,038 D	46.0%	54.0%	46.0%	54.0%
1982	168,555	62,128	Morton, Warren A.	106,427	Herschler, Ed*		44,299 D	36.9%	63.1%	36.9%	63.1%
1978	137,567	67,595	Ostlund, John C.	69,972	Herschler, Ed*		2,377 D	49.1%	50.9%	49.1%	50.9%
1974	128,386	56,645	Jones, Dick	71,741	Herschler, Ed		15,096 D	44.1%	55.9%	44.1%	55.9%
1970	118,257	74,249	Hathaway, Stanley K.*	44,008	Rooney, John J.		30,241 R	62.8%	37.2%	62.8%	37.2%
1966	120,873	65,624	Hathaway, Stanley K.	55,249	Wilkerson, Ernest		10,375 R	54.3%	45.7%	54.3%	45.7%
1962	119,268	64,970	Hansen, Clifford P.	54,298	Gage, Jack R.*		10,672 R	54.5%	45.5%	54.5%	45.5%
1958	112,537	52,488	Simpson, Milward L.*	55,070	Hickey, John J.	4,979	2,582 D	46.6%	48.9%	48.8%	51.2%
1954	111,438	56,275	Simpson, Milward L.	55,163	Jack, William		1,112 R	50.5%	49.5%	50.5%	49.5%
1950	96,959	54,441	Barrett, Frank A.	42,518	McIntyre, John J.		11,923 R	56.1%	43.9%	56.1%	43.9%
1946	81,353	38,333	Wright, Earl	43,020	Hunt, Lester C.*		4,687 D	47.1%	52.9%	47.1%	52.9%

Note: An asterisk (*) denotes incumbent.

POSTWAR VOTE FOR SENATOR

		Republican		Democratic		Other Vote	Rep.-Dem. Plurality	Percentage			
								Total Vote		Major Vote	
Year	Total Vote	Vote	Candidate	Vote	Candidate			Rep.	Dem.	Rep.	Dem.
2020	271,937	198,100	Lummis, Cynthia	72,766	Ben-David, Merav	1,071	125,334 R	72.8%	26.8%	73.1%	26.9%
2018	203,420	136,210	Barrasso, John*	61,227	Trauner, Gary	5,983	74,983 R	67.0%	30.1%	69.0%	31.0%
2014	168,390	121,554	Enzi, Michael B.*	29,377	Hardy, Charles E. "Charlie"	17,459	92,177 R	72.2%	17.4%	80.5%	19.5%
2012	244,862	185,250	Barrasso, John*	53,019	Chestnut, Tim	6,593	132,231 R	75.7%	21.7%	77.7%	22.3%
2008	249,946	189,046	Enzi, Michael B.*	60,631	Rothfuss, Chris	269	128,415 R	75.6%	24.3%	75.7%	24.3%
2008S**	249,558	183,063	Barrasso, John*	66,202	Carter, Nick	293	116,861 R	73.4%	26.5%	73.4%	26.6%
2006	193,136	135,174	Thomas, Craig*	57,671	Groutage, Dale	291	77,503 R	70.0%	29.9%	70.1%	29.9%
2002	183,280	133,710	Enzi, Michael B.*	49,570	Corcoran, Joyce Jansa		84,140 R	73.0%	27.0%	73.0%	27.0%
2000	213,659	157,622	Thomas, Craig*	47,087	Logan, Mel	8,950	110,535 R	73.8%	22.0%	77.0%	23.0%
1996	211,077	114,116	Enzi, Michael B.	89,103	Karpan, Kathy	7,858	25,013 R	54.1%	42.2%	56.2%	43.8%
1994	201,710	118,754	Thomas, Craig	79,287	Sullivan, Mike	3,669	39,467 R	58.9%	39.3%	60.0%	40.0%
1990	157,632	100,784	Simpson, Alan K.*	56,848	Helling, Kathy		43,936 R	63.9%	36.1%	63.9%	36.1%
1988	180,964	91,143	Wallop, Malcolm*	89,821	Vinich, John P.		1,322 R	50.4%	49.6%	50.4%	49.6%
1984	186,898	146,373	Simpson, Alan K.*	40,525	Ryan, Victor A.		105,848 R	78.3%	21.7%	78.3%	21.7%
1982	167,191	94,725	Wallop, Malcolm*	72,466	McDaniel, Rodger		22,259 R	56.7%	43.3%	56.7%	43.3%
1978	133,364	82,908	Simpson, Alan K.	50,456	Whitaker, Raymond B.		32,452 R	62.2%	37.8%	62.2%	37.8%
1976	155,368	84,810	Wallop, Malcolm	70,558	McGee, Gale*		14,252 R	54.6%	45.4%	54.6%	45.4%
1972	142,067	101,314	Hansen, Clifford P.*	40,753	Vinich, Mike		60,561 R	71.3%	28.7%	71.3%	28.7%
1970	120,486	53,279	Wold, John S.	67,207	McGee, Gale*		13,928 D	44.2%	55.8%	44.2%	55.8%
1966	122,689	63,548	Hansen, Clifford P.	59,141	Roncalio, Teno		4,407 R	51.8%	48.2%	51.8%	48.2%
1964	141,670	65,185	Wold, John S.	76,485	McGee, Gale*		11,300 D	46.0%	54.0%	46.0%	54.0%
1962S**	119,372	69,043	Simpson, Milward L.	50,329	Hickey, John J.*		18,714 R	57.8%	42.2%	57.8%	42.2%
1960	138,550	78,103	Thomson, E. Keith	60,447	Whitaker, Raymond B.		17,656 R	56.4%	43.6%	56.4%	43.6%
1958	114,157	56,122	Barrett, Frank A.*	58,035	McGee, Gale		1,913 D	49.2%	50.8%	49.2%	50.8%
1954	112,252	54,407	Harrison, William Henry	57,845	O' Mahoney, Joseph C.*		3,438 D	48.5%	51.5%	48.5%	51.5%
1952	130,097	67,176	Barrett, Frank A.	62,921	O' Mahoney, Joseph C.*		4,255 R	51.6%	48.4%	51.6%	48.4%
1948	101,480	43,527	Robertson, Edward V.*	57,953	Hunt, Lester C.		14,426 D	42.9%	57.1%	42.9%	57.1%
1946	81,557	35,714	Henderson, Harry B.	45,843	O' Mahoney, Joseph C.*		10,129 D	43.8%	56.2%	43.8%	56.2%

Note: An asterisk (*) denotes incumbent. **The 1962 election and one of the 2008 elections were for short terms to fill a vacancy.

WYOMING

GOVERNOR 2022

2020 Census Population	County	Total Vote	Republican (Gordon)	Democratic (Livingston)	Other	Rep.-Dem. Plurality	Total Vote Rep.	Total Vote Dem.	Major Vote Rep.	Major Vote Dem.
38,807	ALBANY	12,600	7,462	4,143	995	3,319 R	59.2%	32.9%	64.3%	35.7%
11,811	BIG HORN	4,239	3,529	305	405	3,224 R	83.3%	7.2%	92.0%	8.0%
46,121	CAMPBELL	12,262	9,787	757	1,718	9,030 R	79.8%	6.2%	92.8%	7.2%
14,741	CARBON	4,703	3,681	598	424	3,083 R	78.3%	12.7%	86.0%	14.0%
13,816	CONVERSE	4,977	3,796	355	826	3,441 R	76.3%	7.1%	91.4%	8.6%
7,602	CROOK	3,248	2,516	200	532	2,316 R	77.5%	6.2%	92.6%	7.4%
39,197	FREMONT	13,398	9,866	1,939	1,593	7,927 R	73.6%	14.5%	83.6%	16.4%
13,231	GOSHEN	4,813	3,972	440	401	3,532 R	82.5%	9.1%	90.0%	10.0%
4,392	HOT SPRINGS	2,171	1,525	218	428	1,307 R	70.2%	10.0%	87.5%	12.5%
8,468	JOHNSON	3,865	3,182	268	415	2,914 R	82.3%	6.9%	92.2%	7.8%
99,801	LARAMIE	29,911	22,067	5,765	2,079	16,302 R	73.8%	19.3%	79.3%	20.7%
19,914	LINCOLN	7,482	6,021	699	762	5,322 R	80.5%	9.3%	89.6%	10.4%
79,808	NATRONA	22,491	17,246	3,303	1,942	13,943 R	76.7%	14.7%	83.9%	16.1%
2,344	NIOBRARA	1,047	704	46	297	658 R	67.2%	4.4%	93.9%	6.1%
29,348	PARK	12,698	9,700	1,286	1,712	8,414 R	76.4%	10.1%	88.3%	11.7%
8,409	PLATTE	3,921	2,915	411	595	2,504 R	74.3%	10.5%	87.6%	12.4%
30,632	SHERIDAN	12,191	9,335	1,616	1,240	7,719 R	76.6%	13.3%	85.2%	14.8%
9,845	SUBLETTE	3,544	2,899	341	304	2,558 R	81.8%	9.6%	89.5%	10.5%
42,226	SWEETWATER	11,917	8,827	1,871	1,219	6,956 R	74.1%	15.7%	82.5%	17.5%
23,376	TETON	10,146	4,943	4,926	277	17 R	48.7%	48.6%	50.1%	49.9%
20,194	UINTA	6,596	5,224	754	618	4,470 R	79.2%	11.4%	87.4%	12.6%
7,793	WASHAKIE	3,045	2,466	267	312	2,199 R	81.0%	8.8%	90.2%	9.8%
6,916	WESTON	2,735	2,033	178	524	1,855 R	74.3%	6.5%	91.9%	8.1%
578,792	TOTAL	194,000	143,696	30,686	19,618	113,010 R	74.1%	15.8%	82.4%	17.6%

WYOMING

HOUSE OF REPRESENTATIVES

CD	Year	Total Vote	Republican Vote	Republican Candidate	Democratic Vote	Democratic Candidate	Other Vote	Rep.-Dem. Plurality	Total Vote Rep.	Total Vote Dem.	Major Vote Rep.	Major Vote Dem.
At Large	2022	193,902	132,206	HAGEMAN, HARRIET M.	47,250	GREY BULL, LYNNETTE	14,446	84,956 R	68.2%	24.4%	73.7%	26.3%
At Large	2020	270,892	185,732	CHENEY, ELIZABETH "LIZ"*	66,576	GREY BULL, LYNNETTE	18,584	119,156 R	68.6%	24.6%	73.6%	26.4%
At Large	2018	201,245	127,963	CHENEY, ELIZABETH "LIZ"*	59,903	HUNTER, GREG	13,379	68,060 R	63.6%	29.8%	68.1%	31.9%
At Large	2016	251,776	156,176	CHENEY, ELIZABETH "LIZ"	75,466	GREENE, RYAN	20,134	80,710 R	62.0%	30.0%	67.4%	32.6%
At Large	2014	165,100	113,038	LUMMIS, CYNTHIA M.*	37,803	GRAYSON, RICHARD	14,259	75,235 R	68.5%	22.9%	74.9%	25.1%
At Large	2012	241,621	166,452	LUMMIS, CYNTHIA M.*	57,573	HENRICHSEN, CHRIS	17,596	108,879 R	68.9%	23.8%	74.3%	25.7%
At Large	2010	186,969	131,661	LUMMIS, CYNTHIA M.*	45,768	WENDT, DAVID	9,540	85,893 R	70.4%	24.5%	74.2%	25.8%
At Large	2008	249,395	131,244	LUMMIS, CYNTHIA M.	106,758	TRAUNER, GARY	11,393	24,486 R	52.6%	42.8%	55.1%	44.9%
At Large	2006	193,369	93,336	CUBIN, BARBARA*	92,324	TRAUNER, GARY	7,709	1,012 R	48.3%	47.7%	50.3%	49.7%
At Large	2004	239,034	132,107	CUBIN, BARBARA*	99,989	LADD, TED	6,938	32,118 R	55.3%	41.8%	56.9%	43.1%
At Large	2002	182,152	110,229	CUBIN, BARBARA*	65,961	AKIN, RON	5,962	44,268 R	60.5%	36.2%	62.6%	37.4%
At Large	2000	212,312	141,848	CUBIN, BARBARA*	60,638	GREEN, MICHAEL ALLEN	9,826	81,210 R	66.8%	28.6%	70.1%	29.9%
At Large	1998	174,219	100,687	CUBIN, BARBARA*	67,399	FARRIS, SCOTT	6,133	33,288 R	57.8%	38.7%	59.9%	40.1%
At Large	1996	209,983	116,004	CUBIN, BARBARA*	85,724	MAXFIELD, PETE	8,255	30,280 R	55.2%	40.8%	57.5%	42.5%
At Large	1994	196,197	104,426	CUBIN, BARBARA	81,022	SCHUSTER, BOB	10,749	23,404 R	53.2%	41.3%	56.3%	43.7%
At Large	1992	196,977	113,882	THOMAS, CRAIG*	77,418	HERSCHLER, JON	5,677	36,464 R	57.8%	39.3%	59.5%	40.5%
At Large	1990	158,055	87,078	THOMAS, CRAIG	70,977	MAXFIELD, PETE		16,101 R	55.1%	44.9%	55.1%	44.9%
At Large	1988	177,651	118,350	CHENEY, RICHARD*	56,527	SHARRATT, BRYAN	2,774	61,823 R	66.6%	31.8%	67.7%	32.3%
At Large	1986	159,787	111,007	CHENEY, RICHARD*	48,780	GILMORE, RICK		62,227 R	69.5%	30.5%	69.5%	30.5%
At Large	1984	187,904	138,234	CHENEY, RICHARD*	45,857	MCFADDEN, HUGH B.	3,813	92,377 R	73.6%	24.4%	75.1%	24.9%
At Large	1982	159,277	113,236	CHENEY, RICHARD*	46,041	HOMMEL, THEODORE H.		67,195 R	71.1%	28.9%	71.1%	28.9%
At Large	1980	169,699	116,361	CHENEY, RICHARD*	53,338	ROGERS, JIM		63,023 R	68.6%	31.4%	68.6%	31.4%
At Large	1978	129,377	75,855	CHENEY, RICHARD	53,522	BAGLEY, BILL		22,333 R	58.6%	41.4%	58.6%	41.4%
At Large	1976	151,868	66,147	HART, LARRY	85,721	RONCALIO, TENO*		19,574 D	43.6%	56.4%	43.6%	56.4%
At Large	1974	126,933	57,499	STROOCK, TOM	69,434	RONCALIO, TENO*		11,935 D	45.3%	54.7%	45.3%	54.7%
At Large	1972	146,299	70,667	KIDD, WILLIAM	75,632	RONCALIO, TENO*		4,965 D	48.3%	51.7%	48.3%	51.7%
At Large	1970	116,304	57,848	ROBERTS, HARRY	58,456	RONCALIO, TENO*		608 D	49.7%	50.3%	49.7%	50.3%

WYOMING
HOUSE OF REPRESENTATIVES

			Republican		Democratic		Other Vote	Rep.-Dem. Plurality	Percentage			
									Total Vote		Major Vote	
CD	Year	Total Vote	Vote	Candidate	Vote	Candidate			Rep.	Dem.	Rep.	Dem.
At Large	1968	123,313	77,363	WOLD, JOHN S.	45,950	LINFORD, VELMA		31,413 R	62.7%	37.3%	62.7%	37.3%
At Large	1966	120,426	62,984	HARRISON, WILLIAM HENRY	57,442	CHRISTIAN, AL		5,542 R	52.3%	47.7%	52.3%	47.7%
At Large	1964	139,175	68,482	HARRISON, WILLIAM HENRY	70,693	RONCALIO, TENO*		2,211 D	49.2%	50.8%	49.2%	50.8%
At Large	1962	116,474	71,489	HARRISON, WILLIAM HENRY*	44,985	MANKUS, LOUIS A.		26,504 R	61.4%	38.6%	61.4%	38.6%
At Large	1960	134,331	70,241	HARRISON, WILLIAM HENRY	64,090	ARMSTRONG, HEPBURN T.		6,151 R	52.3%	47.7%	52.3%	47.7%
At Large	1958	111,780	59,894	THOMSON, E. KEITH*	51,886	WHITAKER, RAYMOND B.		8,008 R	53.6%	46.4%	53.6%	46.4%
At Large	1956	120,128	69,903	THOMSON, E. KEITH*	50,225	O'CALLAGHAN, JERRY A.		19,678 R	58.2%	41.8%	58.2%	41.8%
At Large	1954	108,771	61,111	THOMSON, E. KEITH	47,660	TULLY, SAM		13,451 R	56.2%	43.8%	56.2%	43.8%
At Large	1952	126,720	76,161	HARRISON, WILLIAM HENRY*	50,559	ROSS, ROBERT R. JR.		25,602 R	60.1%	39.9%	60.1%	39.9%
At Large	1950	93,348	50,865	HARRISON, WILLIAM HENRY	42,483	CLARK, JOHN B.		8,382 R	54.5%	45.5%	54.5%	45.5%
At Large	1948	97,464	50,218	BARRETT, FRANK A.*	47,246	FLANNERY, L. G.		2,972 R	51.5%	48.5%	51.5%	48.5%
At Large	1946	79,438	44,482	BARRETT, FRANK A.*	34,956	MCINTYRE, JOHN J.		9,526 R	56.0%	44.0%	56.0%	44.0%

Note: An asterisk (*) denotes incumbent.

WYOMING
GENERAL AND PRIMARY ELECTIONS

GENERAL ELECTIONS: OTHER VOTES

Governor	Other vote was 11,461 Write-In (Write-Ins), 8,157 Libertarian (Jared Baldes)
House	Other vote was:
At Large	5,420 Libertarian (Richard Brubaker), 4,521 Write-In (Write-Ins), 4,505 Constitution (Marissa Selvig)

2022 PRIMARY ELECTIONS: SUPPLEMENTARY INFORMATION

Primary	August 16, 2022	**Registration** (as of August 1, 2022)	284,557	Republican	207,674
				Democratic	39,753
				Libertarian	2,595
				Constitution	738
				Other	28
				Unaffiliated	33,769

Primary Type — Open—Only registered Democrats and Republicans could vote in their party's primary, although on primary day, any voter, regardless of previous affiliation, could register with the party of his or her choice and any previously registered voter could participate in another party's primary by changing his or her registration to that party.

WYOMING

GENERAL AND PRIMARY ELECTIONS

		REPUBLICAN PRIMARIES			DEMOCRATIC PRIMARIES	
Governor	Gordon, Mark*	101,140	61.5%	Livingston, Theresa	4,993	69.1%
	Bien, Brent	48,572	29.6%	Wilde, Rex	2,016	27.9%
	Rammell, Rex	9,378	5.7%	Write-In	214	3.0%
	Quick, James Scott	4,728	2.9%			
	Write-In	533	0.3%			
	TOTAL	*164,351*		*TOTAL*	*7,223*	
Congressional At Large	Hageman, Harriet M.	113,079	66.3%	Grey Bull, Lynnette	4,507	59.7%
	Cheney, Elizabeth "Liz"	49,339	28.9%	Jensen, Meghan R.	1,833	24.3%
	Bouchard, Anthony	4,508	2.6%	Helling, Steve	897	11.9%
	Knapp, Denton	2,258	1.3%	Write-In	309	4.1%
	Belinskey, Robyn M.	1,306	0.8%			
	Write-In	175	0.1%			
	TOTAL	*170,665*		*TOTAL*	*7,546*	

Note: An asterisk (*) denotes incumbent.

DISTRICT OF COLUMBIA

One member At Large

City Council Wards, established for the 2022 elections, are the main political subdivisions of the District of Columbia. Areas highlighted are (R to L) the Capitol Complex, National Mall, the Ellipse, and the White House.

DISTRICT OF COLUMBIA

DELEGATE

Eleanor Holmes Norton (D). Reelected 2022 to a two-year term. Previously elected 2020, 2018, 2016, 2014, 2012, 2010, 2008, 2006, 2004, 2002, 2000, 1998, 1996, 1994, 1992, 1990.

POSTWAR VOTE FOR PRESIDENT

		Republican		Democratic		Other Vote	Rep.-Dem. Plurality	Total Vote		Major Vote	
Year	Total Vote	Vote	Candidate	Vote	Candidate			Rep.	Dem.	Rep.	Dem.
2020	344,356	18,586	Trump, Donald J.*	317,323	Biden, Joseph R. Jr.	8,447	298,737 D	5.4%	92.1%	5.5%	94.5%
2016**	311,268	12,723	Trump, Donald J.	282,830	Clinton, Hillary Rodham	15,715	270,107 D	4.1%	90.9%	4.3%	95.7%
2012	293,764	21,381	Romney, W. Mitt	267,070	Obama, Barack H.*	5,313	245,689 D	7.3%	90.9%	7.4%	92.6%
2008	265,853	17,367	McCain, John S. III	245,800	Obama, Barack H.	2,686	228,433 D	6.5%	92.5%	6.6%	93.4%
2004	227,586	21,256	Bush, George W.*	202,970	Kerry, John F.	3,360	181,714 D	9.3%	89.2%	9.5%	90.5%
2000**	201,894	18,073	Bush, George W.	171,923	Gore, Albert Jr.	11,898	153,850 D	9.0%	85.2%	9.5%	90.5%
1996**	185,726	17,339	Dole, Robert "Bob"	158,220	Clinton, Bill*	10,167	140,881 D	9.3%	85.2%	9.9%	90.1%
1992**	227,572	20,698	Bush, George H.*	192,619	Clinton, Bill	14,255	171,921 D	9.1%	84.6%	9.7%	90.3%
1988	192,877	27,590	Bush, George H.	159,407	Dukakis, Michael S.	5,880	131,817 D	14.3%	82.6%	14.8%	85.2%
1984	211,288	29,009	Reagan, Ronald*	180,408	Mondale, Walter F.	1,871	151,399 D	13.7%	85.4%	13.9%	86.1%
1980**	175,237	23,545	Reagan, Ronald	131,113	Carter, Jimmy*	20,579	107,568 D	13.4%	74.8%	15.2%	84.8%
1976	168,830	27,873	Ford, Gerald R.*	137,818	Carter, Jimmy	3,139	109,945 D	16.5%	81.6%	16.8%	83.2%
1972	163,421	35,226	Nixon, Richard M.*	127,627	McGovern, George S.	568	92,401 D	21.6%	78.1%	21.6%	78.4%
1968	170,578	31,012	Nixon, Richard M.	139,566	Humphrey, Hubert Horatio Jr.		108,554 D	18.2%	81.8%	18.2%	81.8%
1964**	198,597	28,801	Goldwater, Barry M. Sr.	169,796	Johnson, Lyndon B.*		140,995 D	14.5%	85.5%	14.5%	85.5%

Note: An asterisk (*) denotes incumbent. **In past elections, the other vote included: 2016 - 4,906 Libertarian (Gary Johnson); 2000 - 10,576 Green (Ralph Nader); 1996 - 3,611 Reform (Ross Perot); 1992 - 9,681 Independent (Perot); 1980 - 16,337 Independent (John Anderson). Under the Twenty-third Amendment to the Constitution, the District of Columbia could choose presidential electors beginning with the 1964 election.

POSTWAR VOTE FOR DELEGATE

		Republican		Democratic		Other Vote	Rep.-Dem. Plurality	Total Vote		Major Vote	
Year	Total Vote	Vote	Candidate	Vote	Candidate			Rep.	Dem.	Rep.	Dem.
2022	201,330	11,701	Rimensnyder, Nelson F.	174,238	Norton, Eleanor Holmes*	15,391	162,537 D	5.8%	86.5%	6.3%	93.7%
2020	326,587			281,831	Norton, Eleanor Holmes*	44,756	281,831 D		86.3%		100.0%
2018	228,769	9,700	Rimensnyder, Nelson F.	199,124	Norton, Eleanor Holmes*	19,945	189,424 D	4.2%	87.0%	4.6%	95.4%
2016	300,906			265,178	Norton, Eleanor Holmes*	35,728	265,178 D		88.1%		100.0%
2014	171,893	11,673	Rimensnyder, Nelson F.	143,923	Norton, Eleanor Holmes*	16,297	132,250 D	6.8%	83.7%	7.5%	92.5%
2012	278,563			246,664	Norton, Eleanor Holmes*	31,899	246,664 D		88.5%		100.0%
2010	132,656	8,109	Smith, Missy Reilly	117,990	Norton, Eleanor Holmes*	6,557	109,881 D	6.1%	88.9%	6.4%	93.6%
2008	247,741			228,376	Norton, Eleanor Holmes*	19,095	228,376 D		92.3%		100.0%
2006	114,777			111,726	Norton, Eleanor Holmes*	3,051	111,726 D		97.3%		100.0%
2004	221,213	18,296	Monroe, Michael Andrew	202,027	Norton, Eleanor Holmes*	890	183,731 D	8.3%	91.3%	8.3%	91.7%
2002	128,233			119,268	Norton, Eleanor Holmes*	8,965	119,628 D		93.0%		100.0%
2000	175,631	10,258	Wolterbeek, Edward	158,824	Norton, Eleanor Holmes*	6,549	148,566 D	5.8%	90.4%	6.1%	93.9%
1998	136,359	8,610	Wolterbeek, Edward	122,228	Norton, Eleanor Holmes*	5,221	113,618 D	6.3%	89.6%	6.6%	93.4%
1996	149,998	11,306	Simonds, Sprague	134,996	Norton, Eleanor Holmes*	3,696	123,690 D	7.5%	90.0%	7.7%	92.3%
1994	173,664	13,828	Saltz, Donald	154,988	Norton, Eleanor Holmes*	4,848	141,160 D	8.0%	89.2%	8.2%	91.8%
1992	196,574	20,108	Emerson, Susan	166,808	Norton, Eleanor Holmes*	9,838	146,700 D	10.2%	84.8%	10.8%	89.2%
1990	159,627	41,999	Singleton, Harry M.	98,442	Norton, Eleanor Holmes	19,186	56,443 D	26.3%	61.7%	29.9%	70.1%
1988	170,933	22,936	Reed, William	121,817	Fauntroy, Walter E.*	26180	98,881 D	13.4%	71.3%	15.8%	84.2%
1986	126,855	17,643	King, Mary L.H.	101,604	Fauntroy, Walter E.*	7,608	83,961 D	13.9%	80.1%	14.8%	85.2%
1984	161,771			154,583	Fauntroy, Walter E.*	7,188	154,583 D		95.6%		100.0%
1982	112,543	17,242	West, John	93,422	Fauntroy, Walter E.*	1,879	76,180 D	15.3%	83.0%	15.6%	84.4%
1980	151,046	21,245	Roehr, Robert J.	112,339	Fauntroy, Walter E.*	17,462	91,094 D	14.1%	74.4%	15.9%	84.1%
1978	96,306	11,677	Champion, Jackson R.	76,557	Fauntroy, Walter E.*	8,072	64,880 D	12.1%	79.5%	13.2%	86.8%
1976	159,790	21,699	Hall, Daniel L.	123,464	Fauntroy, Walter E.*	14,627	101,765 D	13.6%	77.3%	14.9%	85.1%
1974	104,014	9,166	Phillips, William R.	66,337	Fauntroy, Walter E.*	28,511	57,171 D	8.8%	63.8%	12.1%	87.9%
1972	159,612	39,487	Chin-Lee, William	95,300	Fauntroy, Walter E.*	24,825	55,813 D	24.7%	59.7%	29.3%	70.7%
1971S**	116,635	29,249	Nevius, John A.	68,166	Fauntroy, Walter E.	19,220	38,917 D	25.1%	58.4%	30.0%	70.0%

Note: An asterisk (*) denotes incumbent, who is a non-voting member of the House of Representatives. **The 1971 election was held in March for a short term until the end of the 92nd Congress.

DISTRICT OF COLUMBIA

GENERAL AND PRIMARY ELECTIONS

GENERAL ELECTIONS: OTHER VOTES

Delegate Other vote was 9,867 Statehood Green (Natale Stracuzzi), 4,003 Libertarian (Bruce Majors), 6,702 Socialist Workers (Omari Musa), 1,521 Write-In (Write-In)

2022 PRIMARY ELECTIONS: SUPPLEMENTARY INFORMATION

Primary	June 21, 2022	**Registration** (as of May 31, 2022)	489,109	Democratic	374,510
				Republican	26,412
				Statehood Green	3,806
				Libertarian	2,257
				Other	1,340
				No Party Affiliation	80,784

Primary Type Closed—Only registered Democrats and Republicans could vote in their party's primary.